Big Java
Early Objects

7/e

Cay Horstmann

San Jose State University

WILEY

VICE PRESIDENT AND EXECUTIVE PUBLISHER	Laurie Rosatone
EXECUTIVE EDITOR	Joanna Dingle
PROJECT MANAGER/DEVELOPMENT EDITOR	Cindy Johnson
EDITORIAL ASSISTANT	Crystal Franks
LEAD PRODUCT DESIGNER	Tom Kulesa
MARKETING MANAGER	Michael MacDougald
PRODUCTION MANAGER	Nichole Urban
PRODUCTION MANAGER	Nicole Repasky
PRODUCTION MANAGEMENT SERVICES	Cindy Johnson, Publishing Services
PHOTO EDITOR	Anindita Adiyal
COVER DESIGNER	Joanna Vieira
COVER PHOTOS	(tiger) © ArtMediaFactory/Shutterstock; (rhino) © GUDKOV ANDREY/Shutterstock; (bird) © Jeremy Woodhouse/Holly Wilmeth/ Getty Images; (tree frog) © kuritafsheen/Getty Images.

This book was set in 10.5/12 Stempel Garamond LT Std by Publishing Services, and printed and bound by Quad Graphics/Versailles. The cover was printed by Quad Graphics/Versailles.

Founded in 1807, John Wiley & Sons, Inc. has been a valued source of knowledge and understanding for more than 200 years, helping people around the world meet their needs and fulfill their aspirations. Our company is built on a foundation of principles that include responsibility to the communities we serve and where we live and work. In 2008, we launched a Corporate Citizenship Initiative, a global effort to address the environmental, social, economic, and ethical challenges we face in our business. Among the issues we are addressing are carbon impact, paper specifications and procurement, ethical conduct within our business and among our vendors, and community and charitable support. For more information, please visit our website: www.wiley.com/go/citizenship.

This book is printed on acid-free paper. ∞

ePUB ISBN 978-1-119-49909-1

Printed in the United States of America.

The inside back cover will contain printing identification and country of origin if omitted from this page. In addition, if the ISBN on the back cover differs from the ISBN on this page, the one on the back cover is correct.

SKY10034954_062322

PREFACE

This book is an introduction to Java and computer programming that focuses on the essentials—and on effective learning. The book is designed to serve a wide range of student interests and abilities and is suitable for a first course in programming for computer scientists, engineers, and students in other disciplines. No prior programming experience is required, and only a modest amount of high school algebra is needed.

Here are the key features of this book:

Start objects early, teach object orientation gradually.

In Chapter 2, students learn how to use objects and classes from the standard library. Chapter 3 shows the mechanics of implementing classes from a given specification. Students then use simple objects as they master branches, loops, and arrays. Object-oriented design starts in Chapter 8. This gradual approach allows students to use objects throughout their study of the core algorithmic topics, without teaching bad habits that must be un-learned later.

Guidance and worked examples help students succeed.

Beginning programmers often ask "How do I start? Now what do I do?" Of course, an activity as complex as programming cannot be reduced to cookbook-style instructions. However, step-by-step guidance is immensely helpful for building confidence and providing an outline for the task at hand. "How To" guides help students with common programming tasks. Numerous Worked Examples demonstrate how to apply chapter concepts to interesting problems.

Problem solving strategies are made explicit.

Practical, step-by-step illustrations of techniques help students devise and evaluate solutions to programming problems. Introduced where they are most relevant, these strategies address barriers to success for many students. Strategies included are:

- Algorithm Design (with pseudocode)
- Tracing Objects
- First Do It By Hand (doing sample calculations by hand)
- Flowcharts
- Selecting Test Cases
- Hand-Tracing
- Storyboards
- Solve a Simpler Problem First
- Adapting Algorithms
- Discovering Algorithms by Manipulating Physical Objects
- Patterns for Object Data
- Thinking Recursively
- Estimating the Running Time of an Algorithm

Practice makes perfect.

Of course, programming students need to be able to implement nontrivial programs, but they first need to have the confidence that they can succeed. Each section contains numerous exercises that ask students to carry out progressively more complex tasks: trace code and understand its effects, produce program snippets from prepared parts, and complete simple programs. Additional review and programming problems are provided at the end of each chapter.

A visual approach motivates the reader and eases navigation.

Photographs present visual analogies that explain the nature and behavior of computer concepts. Step-by-step figures illustrate complex program operations. Syntax boxes and example tables present a variety of typical and special cases in a compact format. It is easy to get the "lay of the land" by browsing the visuals, before focusing on the textual material.

Visual features help the reader with navigation.

Focus on the essentials while being technically accurate.

An encyclopedic coverage is not helpful for a beginning programmer, but neither is the opposite—reducing the material to a list of simplistic bullet points. In this book, the essentials are presented in digestible chunks, with separate notes that go deeper into good practices or language features when the reader is ready for the additional information. You will not find artificial over-simplifications that give an illusion of knowledge.

Reinforce sound engineering practices.

A multitude of useful tips on software quality and common errors encourage the development of good programming habits. The optional testing track focuses on test-driven development, encouraging students to test their programs systematically.

Provide an optional graphics track.

Graphical shapes are splendid examples of objects. Many students enjoy writing programs that create drawings or use graphical user interfaces. If desired, these topics can be integrated into the course by using the materials at the end of Chapters 2, 3, and 10.

Engage with optional science and business exercises.

Review exercises are enhanced with problems from scientific and business domains. Designed to engage students, the exercises illustrate the value of programming in applied fields.

New to This Edition

Adapted to Java Versions 8 Through 11

This edition takes advantage of modern Java features when they are pedagogically sensible. I continue to use "pure" interfaces with only abstract methods. Default, static, and private interface methods are introduced in a Special Topic. Lambda expressions are optional for user interface callback, but they are used in the chapter on the stream library and its applications for "big data" processing.

The "diamond" syntax for generic classes is introduced as a Special Topic in Chapter 7 and used systematically starting with Chapter 15. Local type inference with the var keyword is described in a Special Topic.

Useful features such as the try-with-resources statement are integrated into the text. Chapter 21 covers the utilities provided by the Paths and Files classes.

Interactive Learning

With this edition, interactive content is front and center. Immersive activities integrate with this text and engage students in activities designed to foster in-depth learning.

Students don't just watch animations and code traces, they work on generating them. Live code samples invite the reader to experiment and to learn programming constructs first hand. The activities provide instant feedback to show students what they did right and where they need to study more.

A Tour of the Book

The book can be naturally grouped into four parts, as illustrated by Figure 1 on page vi. The organization of chapters offers the same flexibility as the previous edition; dependencies among the chapters are also shown in the figure.

Part A: Fundamentals (Chapters 1–7)

Chapter 1 contains a brief introduction to computer science and Java programming. Chapter 2 shows how to manipulate objects of predefined classes. In Chapter 3, you will build your own simple classes from given specifications. Fundamental data types, branches, loops, and arrays are covered in Chapters 4–7.

Part B: Object-Oriented Design (Chapters 8–12)

Chapter 8 takes up the subject of class design in a systematic fashion, and it introduces a very simple subset of the UML notation. Chapter 9 covers inheritance and polymorphism, whereas Chapter 10 covers interfaces. Exception handling and basic file input/output are covered in Chapter 11. The exception hierarchy gives a useful example for inheritance. Chapter 12 contains an introduction to object-oriented design, including two significant case studies.

Part C: Data Structures and Algorithms (Chapters 13–19)

Chapters 13 through 19 contain an introduction to algorithms and data structures, covering recursion, sorting and searching, linked lists, binary trees, and hash tables. These topics may be outside the scope of a one-semester course, but can be covered as desired after Chapter 7 (see Figure 1). Recursion, in Chapter 13, starts with simple examples and progresses to meaningful applications that would be difficult to implement iteratively. Chapter 14 covers quadratic sorting algorithms as well as merge sort, with an informal introduction to big-Oh notation. Each data structure is presented in the context of the standard Java collections library. You will learn the essential abstractions of the standard library (such as iterators, sets, and maps) as well as the performance characteristics of the various collections. Chapter 18 introduces Java generics. This chapter is suitable for advanced students who want to implement their own generic classes and methods. Finally, Chapter 19 introduces the Java 8 streams library and shows how it can be used to analyze complex real-world data.

Part D: Applied Topics (Chapters 20–25)

Chapters 20 through 25 cover Java programming techniques that definitely go beyond a first course in Java (21–25 are in the eText). Although, as already mentioned, a comprehensive coverage of the Java library would span many volumes, many instructors prefer that a textbook should give students additional reference material valuable beyond their first course. Some institutions also teach a second-semester course that covers more practical programming aspects such as database and network programming, rather than the more traditional in-depth material on data structures and algorithms. This book can be used in a two-semester course to give students an introduction to programming fundamentals and broad coverage of applications. Alternatively, the material in the final chapters can be useful for student projects. The applied topics include graphical user-interface design, advanced file handling, multi-threading, and those technologies that are of particular interest to server-side programming: networking, databases, and XML. The Internet has made it possible to

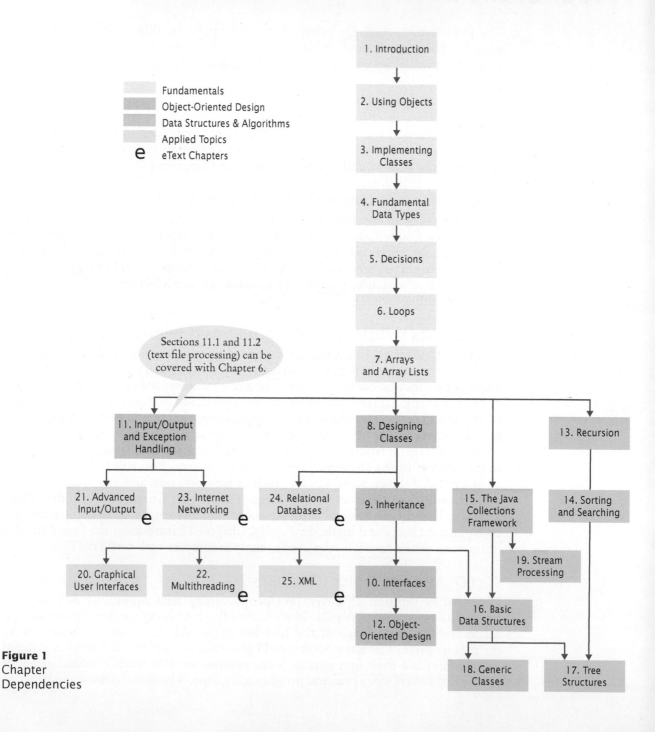

Figure 1
Chapter Dependencies

deploy many useful applications on servers, often accessed by nothing more than a browser. This server-centric approach to application development was in part made possible by the Java language and libraries, and today, much of the industrial use of Java is in server-side programming.

Appendices

Many instructors find it highly beneficial to require a consistent style for all assignments. If the style guide in Appendix E conflicts with instructor sentiment or local customs, however, it is available in electronic form so that it can be modified. Appendices F–J are available in the eText.

A. The Basic Latin and Latin-1 Subsets of Unicode	F. Tool Summary
	G. Number Systems
B. Java Operator Summary	H. UML Summary
C. Java Reserved Word Summary	I. Java Syntax Summary
D. The Java Library	J. HTML Summary
E. Java Language Coding Guidelines	

Interactive eText Designed for Programming Students

Available online through wiley.com, vitalsource.com, or at your local bookstore, the enhanced eText features integrated student coding activities that foster in-depth learning. Designed by Cay Horstmann, these activities provide instant feedback to show students what they did right and where they need to study more. Students do more than just watch animations and code traces; they work on generating them right in the eText environment. For a preview of these activities, check out www.wiley.com/college/Horstmann.

Customized formats are also available in both print and digital formats and provide your students with curated content based on your unique syllabus.

Please contact your Wiley sales rep for more information about any of these options.

Web Resources

This book is complemented by a complete suite of online resources. Visit the online companion sites at www.Wiley.com. The online resources include

- Source code for all example programs in the book and its Worked Examples, plus additional example programs.
- Worked Examples that apply the problem-solving steps in the book to other realistic examples.
- Lecture presentation slides (for instructors only).
- Solutions to all review and programming exercises (for instructors only).
- A test bank that focuses on skills, not just terminology (for instructors only). This extensive set of multiple-choice questions can be used with a word processor or imported into a course management system.
- CodeCheck®, an innovative online service that allows instructors to design their own automatically graded programming exercises.

Walkthrough of the Learning Aids

The pedagogical elements in this book work together to focus on and reinforce key concepts and fundamental principles of programming, with additional tips and detail organized to support and deepen these fundamentals. In addition to traditional features, such as chapter objectives and a wealth of exercises, each chapter contains elements geared to today's visual learner.

Throughout each chapter, **margin notes** show where new concepts are introduced and provide an outline of key ideas.

Annotated **syntax boxes** provide a quick, visual overview of new language constructs.

Annotations explain required components and point to more information on common errors or best practices associated with the syntax.

Analogies to everyday objects are used to explain the nature and behavior of concepts such as variables, data types, loops, and more.

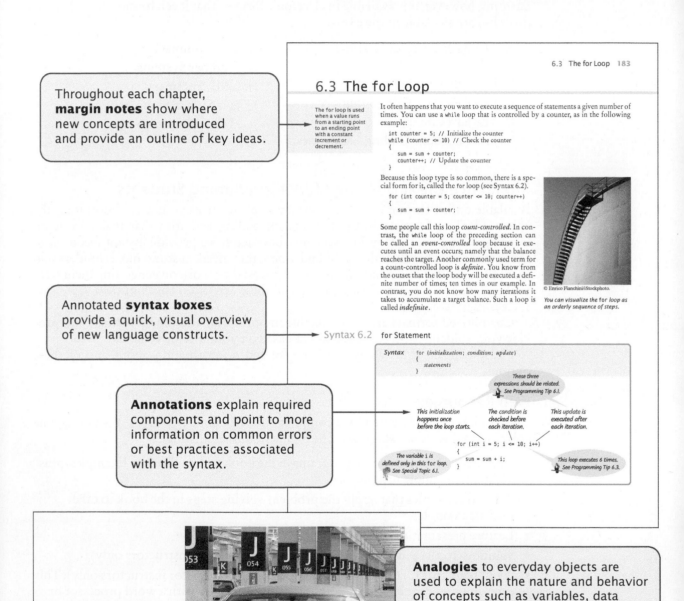

6.3   The for Loop   183

6.3 The for Loop

The for loop is used when a value runs from a starting point to an ending point with a constant increment or decrement.

It often happens that you want to execute a sequence of statements a given number of times. You can use a while loop that is controlled by a counter, as in the following example:

```
int counter = 5; // Initialize the counter
while (counter <= 10) // Check the counter
{
    sum = sum + counter;
    counter++; // Update the counter
}
```

Because this loop type is so common, there is a special form for it, called the for loop (see Syntax 6.2).

```
for (int counter = 5; counter <= 10; counter++)
{
    sum = sum + counter;
}
```

Some people call this loop *count-controlled*. In contrast, the while loop of the preceding section can be called an *event-controlled* loop because it executes until an event occurs; namely that the balance reaches the target. Another commonly used term for a count-controlled loop is *definite*. You know from the outset that the loop body will be executed a definite number of times; ten times in our example. In contrast, you do not know how many iterations it takes to accumulate a target balance. Such a loop is called *indefinite*.

© Enrico Fianchini/iStockphoto.

You can visualize the for loop as an orderly sequence of steps.

Syntax 6.2   for Statement

```
Syntax    for (initialization; condition; update)
          {
              statements
          }
```

These three expressions should be related. *See Programming Tip 6.1.*

This initialization happens once before the loop starts.

The condition is checked before each iteration.

This update is executed after each iteration.

```
for (int i = 5; i <= 10; i++)
{
    sum = sum + i;
}
```

The variable i is defined only in this for loop. *See Special Topic 6.1.*

This loop executes 6 times. *See Programming Tip 6.3.*

Like a variable in a computer program, a parking space has an identifier and a contents.

Memorable photos reinforce analogies and help students remember the concepts.

In the same way that there can be a street named "Main Street" in different cities, a Java program can have multiple variables with the same name.

Problem Solving sections teach techniques for generating ideas and evaluating proposed solutions, often using pencil and paper or other artifacts. These sections emphasize that most of the planning and problem solving that makes students successful happens away from the computer.

7.5   Problem Solving: Discovering Algorithms by Manipulating Physical Objects   333

Now how does that help us with our problem, switching the first and the second half of the array?

Let's put the first coin into place, by swapping it with the fifth coin. However, as Java programmers, we will say that we swap the coins in positions 0 and 4:

Next, we swap the coins in positions 1 and 5:

HOW TO 6.1
Writing a Loop

This How To walks you through the process of implementing a loop statement. We will illustrate the steps with the following example problem.

Problem Statement Read twelve temperature values (one for each month) and display the number of the month with the highest temperature. For example, according to http://worldclimate.com, the average maximum temperatures for Death Valley are (in order by month, in degrees Celsius):

18.2 22.6 26.4 31.1 36.6 42.2
45.7 44.5 40.2 33.1 24.2 17.6

In this case, the month with the highest temperature (45.7 degrees Celsius) is July, and the program should display 7.

© Stevegeer/iStockphoto.

How To guides give step-by-step guidance for common programming tasks, emphasizing planning and testing. They answer the beginner's question, "Now what do I do?" and integrate key concepts into a problem-solving sequence.

Step 1   Decide what work must be done *inside* the loop.

Every loop needs to do some kind of repetitive work, such as

WORKED EXAMPLE 6.1
Credit Card Processing

Learn how to use a loop to remove spaces from a credit card number. See your eText or visit wiley.com/go/bjeo7.

© MorePixels/iStockphoto.

Worked Examples apply the steps in the How To to a different example, showing how they can be used to plan, implement, and test a solution to another programming problem.

Table 1 Variable Declarations in Java	
Variable Name	Comment
`int width = 20;`	Declares an integer variable and initializes it with 20.
`int perimeter = 4 * width;`	The initial value need not be a fixed value. (Of course, width must have been previously declared.)
`String greeting = "Hi!";`	This variable has the type String and is initialized with the string "Hi".
🚫 `height = 30;`	**Error:** The type is missing. This statement is not a declaration but an assignment of a new value to an existing variable—see Section 2.2.5.
🚫 `int width = "20";`	**Error:** You cannot initialize a number with the string "20". (Note the quotation marks.)
`int width;`	Declares an integer variable without initializing it. This can be a cause for errors—see Common Error 2.1.
`int width, height;`	Declares two integer variables in a single statement. In this book, we will declare each variable in a separate statement.

Example tables support beginners with multiple, concrete examples. These tables point out common errors and present another quick reference to the section's topic.

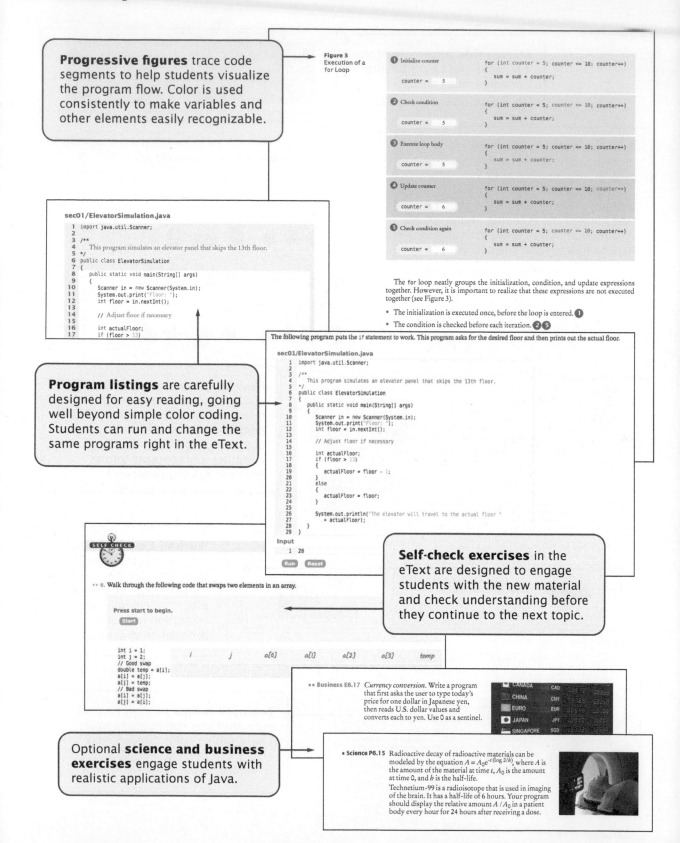

Progressive figures trace code segments to help students visualize the program flow. Color is used consistently to make variables and other elements easily recognizable.

Figure 3
Execution of a for Loop

1 Initialize counter
```
for (int counter = 5; counter <= 10; counter++)
{
    sum = sum + counter;
}
```
counter =   5

2 Check condition
```
for (int counter = 5; counter <= 10; counter++)
{
    sum = sum + counter;
}
```
counter =   5

3 Execute loop body
```
for (int counter = 5; counter <= 10; counter++)
{
    sum = sum + counter;
}
```
counter =   5

4 Update counter
```
for (int counter = 5; counter <= 10; counter++)
{
    sum = sum + counter;
}
```
counter =   6

5 Check condition again
```
for (int counter = 5; counter <= 10; counter++)
{
    sum = sum + counter;
}
```
counter =   6

sec01/ElevatorSimulation.java
```
 1  import java.util.Scanner;
 2
 3  /**
 4     This program simulates an elevator panel that skips the 13th floor.
 5  */
 6  public class ElevatorSimulation
 7  {
 8     public static void main(String[] args)
 9     {
10        Scanner in = new Scanner(System.in);
11        System.out.print("Floor: ");
12        int floor = in.nextInt();
13
14        // Adjust floor if necessary
15
16        int actualFloor;
17        if (floor > 13)
```

The for loop neatly groups the initialization, condition, and update expressions together. However, it is important to realize that these expressions are not executed together (see Figure 3).

• The initialization is executed once, before the loop is entered. 1
• The condition is checked before each iteration. 2 5

The following program puts the if statement to work. This program asks for the desired floor and then prints out the actual floor.

sec01/ElevatorSimulation.java
```
 1  import java.util.Scanner;
 2
 3  /**
 4     This program simulates an elevator panel that skips the 13th floor.
 5  */
 6  public class ElevatorSimulation
 7  {
 8     public static void main(String[] args)
 9     {
10        Scanner in = new Scanner(System.in);
11        System.out.print("Floor: ");
12        int floor = in.nextInt();
13
14        // Adjust floor if necessary
15
16        int actualFloor;
17        if (floor > 13)
18        {
19           actualFloor = floor - 1;
20        }
21        else
22        {
23           actualFloor = floor;
24        }
25
26        System.out.println("The elevator will travel to the actual floor "
27           + actualFloor);
28     }
29  }
```
Input
```
 1   20
```
Run   Reset

Program listings are carefully designed for easy reading, going well beyond simple color coding. Students can run and change the same programs right in the eText.

SELF CHECK

•• 8. Walk through the following code that swaps two elements in an array.

Press start to begin.
Start

```
int i = 1;
int j = 2;
// Good swap
double temp = a[i];
a[i] = a[j];
a[j] = temp;
// Bad swap
a[i] = a[j];
a[j] = a[i];
```

	i	*j*	*a[0]*	*a[1]*	*a[2]*	*a[3]*	*temp*

Self-check exercises in the eText are designed to engage students with the new material and check understanding before they continue to the next topic.

== Business E6.17 *Currency conversion.* Write a program that first asks the user to type today's price for one dollar in Japanese yen, then reads U.S. dollar values and converts each to yen. Use 0 as a sentinel.

CANADA	CAD		
CHINA	CNY		
EURO	EUR		
JAPAN	JPY		
SINGAPORE	SGD		

Optional **science and business exercises** engage students with realistic applications of Java.

■ Science P6.15 Radioactive decay of radioactive materials can be modeled by the equation $A = A_0 e^{-t(\log 2/h)}$, where A is the amount of the material at time t, A_0 is the amount at time 0, and h is the half-life.

Technetium-99 is a radioisotope that is used in imaging of the brain. It has a half-life of 6 hours. Your program should display the relative amount A / A_0 in a patient body every hour for 24 hours after receiving a dose.

Common Errors describe the kinds of errors that students often make, with an explanation of why the errors occur, and what to do about them.

Common Error 7.4

Length and Size

Unfortunately, the Java syntax for determining the number of elements in an array, an array list, and a string is not at all consistent. It is a common error to confuse these. You just have to remember the correct syntax for every data type.

Data Type	Number of Elements
Array	a.length
Array list	a.size()
String	a.length()

Programming Tips explain good programming practices, and encourage students to be more productive with tips and techniques such as hand-tracing.

Programming Tip 5.5

Hand-Tracing

A very useful technique for understanding whether a program works correctly is called *hand-tracing*. You simulate the program's activity on a sheet of paper. You can use this method with pseudocode or Java code.

Get an index card, a cocktail napkin, or whatever sheet of paper is within reach. Make a column for each variable. Have the program code ready. Use a marker, such as a paper clip, to mark the current statement. In your mind, execute statements one at a time. Every time the value of a variable changes, cross out the old value and write the new value below the old one.

© thomasd007/iStockphoto.

Hand-tracing helps you understand whether a program works correctly.

For example, let's trace the getTax method with the data from the program run above. When the TaxReturn object is constructed, the income instance variable is set to 80,000 and status is set to MARRIED. Then the getTax method is called. In lines 31 and 32 of Tax-Return.java, tax1 and tax2 are initialized to 0.

```
29  public double getTax()
30  {
31      double tax1 = 0;
32      double tax2 = 0;
33
```

income	status	tax1	tax2
80000	MARRIED	0	0

Because status is not SINGLE, we move to the else branch of the outer if statement (line 46).

```
34      if (status == SINGLE)
35      {
36          if (income <= RATE1_SINGLE_LIMIT)
37          {
38              tax1 = RATE1 * income;
39          }
40          else
41          {
```

Special Topics present optional topics and provide additional explanation of others.

Special Topic 11.2

File Dialog Boxes

In a program with a graphical user interface, you will want to use a file dialog box (such as the one shown in the figure below) whenever your program need to pick a file. The JFileChooser class implements a file dialog box for the Swing user-interface toolkit.

The JFileChooser class has many options to fine-tune the display of the dialog box, but in its most basic form it is quite simple: Construct a file chooser object; then call the showOpenDialog or showSaveDialog method. Both methods show the same dialog box, but the button for selecting a file is labeled "Open" or "Save", depending on which method you call.

For better placement of the dialog box on the screen, you can specify the user-interface component over which to pop up the dialog box. If you don't care where the dialog box pops up, you can simply pass null. The showOpenDialog and showSaveDialog methods return either JFileChooser.APPROVE_OPTION, if the user has chosen a file, or JFileChooser.CANCEL_OPTION, if the user canceled the selection. If a file was chosen, then you call the getSelectedFile method to obtain a File object that describes the file.

Here is a complete example:

```
JFileChooser chooser = new JFileChooser();
Scanner in = null;
if (chooser.showOpenDialog(null) == JFileChooser.APPROVE_OPTION)
{
    File selectedFile = chooser.getSelectedFile();
    in = new Scanner(selectedFile);
    . . .
}
```

Additional **full code examples** throughout the text provide complete programs for students to run and modify.

EXAMPLE CODE See special_topic_2 of your eText or companion code for a program that demonstrates how to use a file chooser.

Computing & Society presents social and historical topics on computing—for interest and to fulfill the "historical and social context" requirements of the ACM/IEEE curriculum guidelines.

Computing & Society 1.1 Computers Are Everywhere

When computers were first invented in the 1940s, a computer filled an entire room. The photo below shows the ENIAC (electronic *numerical integrator and computer*), completed in 1946 at the University of Pennsylvania. The ENIAC was used by the military to compute the trajectories of projectiles. Nowadays, computing facilities of search engines, Internet shops, and social networks fill huge buildings called data centers. At the other end of the spectrum, computers are all around us. Your cell phone has a computer inside, as do many credit cards and fare cards for public transit. A modern car has several computers—to control the engine, brakes, lights, and the radio.

The advent of ubiquitous computing changed many aspects of our lives. Factories used to employ people to do repetitive assembly tasks that are today carried out by computer-controlled robots, operated by a few people who know how to work with those computers. Books, music, and movies are nowadays often consumed on computers, and computers are almost always involved in their production. The book that you are reading right now

This transit card contains a computer.

could not have been written without computers.

Interactive activities in the eText
engage students in active reading as they...

Trace through a code segment

Complete a program and get immediate feedback

5. Write a program that reads a num[...]

- it is zero.
- it is even.
- it has a single digit (positive or negative).

Numbers.java

```
1
2    import java.util.Scanner;
3
4    public class Numbers
5    {
6       public static void main(String[] args)
7       {
8          System.out.print("Enter an integer: ");
9          Scanner in = new Scanner(System.in);
10         int n = in.nextInt();
11         if (. . .)
12         {
13            System.out.println("The input is zero.");
14         }
15         if (. . .)
16         {
17            System.out.println("The input is even.");
18         }
19         if (. . .)
20         {
21            System.out.println("The input has a single digit.");
22         }
23      }
24   }
```

CodeCheck   Reset

1. In this activity, trace through the code by clicking on the line that will be executed next. Observe the inp[...]
table below. They denote hours in "military time" between 0 and 23. For each input, click on the line ins[...]
will be executed when the hour variable has that value.

Select the next line to be executed.

```
   int hour = in.nextInt();
=> if (hour < 12)
   {
      greeting = "Good morning";
   }
   else
   {
      greeting = "Good afternoon";
   }
   System.out.println(greeting);
```

hour	greeting
11	Good morning
13	Good afternoon
12	

4 correct, 0 errors

Start over

Arrange code to fulfill a task

1. Assume that weekdays are coded as 0 = Monday, 1 = Tuesday, ..., 4 = Friday, 5 = Saturday, 6 = Sunday. Rearrange the lines of code so
that weekday is set to the next working day (Monday through Friday). Not all lines are useful.

Order the statements by moving them into the left window. Use the guidelines for proper indenting.

Done

```
if (weekday < 4)
{
   weekday++;
}
else
{
}
```

```
if (weekday < 5)
weekday = 5;
if (weekday <= 5)
weekday = 1;
weekday = 0;
```

Build an example table

```
if (hour < 21)
{
   response = "Goodbye";
}
else
{
   response = "Goodnight";
}
```

Determine the value of response when hour has the values given in the table

Complete the second column. Press Enter to submit each entry.

hour	response	Explanation
20	"Goodbye"	20 < 21, and the first branch of the statement executes.
22	"Goodnight"	It is not true that 22 < 21, so the else clause executes.
21		

Create a memory diagram

2. Step through this activity of array operations when two variables refer to the same array object.

```
int[] a = { 3, 1, 4, 1, 5, 9 };  ①
int[] b = a;  ②
a[0] = 1;  ③
b[1] = 0;  ④
```

③ Update a[0]

Enter the new value.

2. Try out the following activity to learn how to count how many array elements match a criterion. For example[...]
counts how many elements are negative.

```
count = 0;
for (i = 0; i < a.length; i++)
{
   if (a[i] < 0)
   {
      count++;
   }
}
```

Press the buttons below in the order in which the loop actions are executed for a given array. Press Start to se[...]

Select the next action.

```
                  i
a:  -79   65   -42   -40   50   62
```

count: 2

Explore common algorithms

errors   Start over

Acknowledgments

Many thanks to Joanna Dingle, Crystal Franks, Graig Donini, and Michael Mac-Dougald at John Wiley & Sons, and Vickie Piercey at Publishing Services for their help with this project. An especially deep acknowledgment and thanks goes to Cindy Johnson for her hard work, sound judgment, and amazing attention to detail.

Special thanks to Stephen Gilbert, *Orange Coast College*, for his excellent help with the interactive exercises.

Many thanks to the individuals who worked through the many new activities in this edition, reviewed the manuscript, made valuable suggestions, and brought errors and omissions to my attention. They include:

Radhouane Chouchane, *Columbus State University*

Sussan Einakian, *California Polytechnic State University*

Jon Hanrath, *Illinois Institute of Technology*

Brian King, *Bucknell University*

Kathleen O'Brien, *San Jose State University*

Eman Saleh, *University of Georgia*

William Wei, *New York Institute of Technology*

Each new edition builds on the suggestions and experiences of prior reviewers, contributors, and users. I am grateful for the invaluable contributions these individuals have made:

Eric Aaron, *Wesleyan University*

James Agnew, *Anne Arundel Community College*

Tim Andersen, *Boise State University*

Ivan Bajic, *San Diego State University*

Greg Ballinger, *Miami Dade College*

Ted Bangay, *Sheridan Institute of Technology*

Ian Barland, *Radford University*

George Basham, *Franklin University*

Jon Beck, *Truman State University*

Sambit Bhattacharya, *Fayetteville State University*

Rick Birney, *Arizona State University*

Paul Bladek, *Edmonds Community College*

Matt Boutell, *Rose-Hulman Institute of Technology*

Joseph Bowbeer, *Vizrea Corporation*

Timothy A. Budd, *Oregon State University*

John Bundy, *DeVry University Chicago*

Robert P. Burton, *Brigham Young University*

Frank Butt, *IBM*

Jerry Cain, *Stanford University*

Adam Cannon, *Columbia University*

Michael Carney, *Finger Lakes Community College*

Robin Carr, *Drexel University*

Christopher Cassa, *Massachusetts Institute of Technology*

Nancy Chase, *Gonzaga University*

Dr. Suchindran S. Chatterjee, *Arizona State University*

Archana Chidanandan, *Rose-Hulman Institute of Technology*

Vincent Cicirello, *The Richard Stockton College of New Jersey*

Gerald Cohen, *The Richard Stockton College of New Jersey*

Teresa Cole, *Boise State University*

Deborah Coleman, *Rochester Institute of Technology*

Tina Comston, *Franklin University*

Lennie Cooper, *Miami Dade College*

Jose Cordova, *University of Louisiana, Monroe*

Valentino Crespi, *California State University, Los Angeles*

Jim Cross, *Auburn University*

Russell Deaton, *University of Arkansas*

Geoffrey Decker, *Northern Illinois University*

Suzanne Dietrich, *Arizona State University, West Campus*

Mike Domaratzki, *University of Manitoba*

H. E. Dunsmore, *Purdue University*

Robert Duvall, *Duke University*

Sherif Elfayoumy, *University of North Florida*

Eman El-Sheikh, *University of West Florida*

Henry A. Etlinger, *Rochester Institute of Technology*

John Fendrich, *Bradley University*

David Freer, *Miami Dade College*

John Fulton, *Franklin University*

David Geary, *Sabreware, Inc.*

Margaret Geroch, *Wheeling Jesuit University*

Ahmad Ghafarian, *North Georgia College & State University*

Rick Giles, *Acadia University*

Stacey Grasso, *College of San Mateo*

Jianchao Han, *California State University, Dominguez Hills*

Lisa Hansen, *Western New England College*

Elliotte Harold

Eileen Head, *Binghamton University*

Cecily Heiner, *University of Utah*

Guy Helmer, *Iowa State University*

Ed Holden, *Rochester Institute of Technology*

Brian Howard, *Depauw University*

Lubomir Ivanov, *Iona College*

Norman Jacobson, *University of California, Irvine*

Steven Janke, *Colorado College*

Curt Jones, *Bloomsburg University*

Mark Jones, *Lock Haven University of Pennsylvania*

Dr. Mustafa Kamal, *University of Central Missouri*

Aaron Keen, *California Polytechnic State University, San Luis Obispo*

Mugdha Khaladkar, *New Jersey Institute of Technology*

Gary J. Koehler, *University of Florida*

Elliot Koffman, *Temple University*

Ronald Krawitz, *DeVry University*

Norm Krumpe, *Miami University Ohio*

Jim Leone, *Rochester Institute of Technology*

Kevin Lillis, *St. Ambrose University*

Darren Lim, *Siena College*

Hong Lin, *DeVry University*

Kathy Liszka, *University of Akron*

Hunter Lloyd, *Montana State University*

Youmin Lu, *Bloomsburg University*

Peter Lutz, *Rochester Institute of Technology*

Kuber Maharjan, *Purdue University College of Technology at Columbus*

John S. Mallozzi, *Iona College*

John Martin, *North Dakota State University*

Jeanna Matthews, *Clarkson University*

Patricia McDermott-Wells, *Florida International University*

Scott McElfresh, *Carnegie Mellon University*

Joan McGrory, *Christian Brothers University*

Carolyn Miller, *North Carolina State University*

Sandeep R. Mitra, *State University of New York, Brockport*

Teng Moh, *San Jose State University*

Bill Mongan, *Drexel University*

John Moore, *The Citadel*

Jose-Arturo Mora-Soto, Jesica Rivero-Espinosa, and Julio-Angel Cano-Romero, *University of Madrid*

Faye Navabi, *Arizona State University*

Parviz Partow-Navid, *California State University, Los Angeles*

George Novacky, *University of Pittsburgh*

Kevin O'Gorman, *California Polytechnic State University, San Luis Obispo*

Michael Olan, *Richard Stockton College*

Mimi Opkins, *California State University Long Beach*

Derek Pao, *City University of Hong Kong*

Kevin Parker, *Idaho State University*

Jim Perry, *Ulster County Community College*

Cornel Pokorny, *California Polytechnic State University, San Luis Obispo*

Roger Priebe, *University of Texas, Austin*

C. Robert Putnam, *California State University, Northridge*

Kai Qian, *Southern Polytechnic State University*

Cyndi Rader, *Colorado School of Mines*

Neil Rankin, *Worcester Polytechnic Institute*

Brad Rippe, *Fullerton College*

Pedro I. Rivera Vega, *University of Puerto Rico, Mayaguez*

Daniel Rogers, *SUNY Brockport*

Chaman Lal Sabharwal, *Missouri University of Science and Technology*

Katherine Salch, *Illinois Central College*

John Santore, *Bridgewater State College*

Javad Shakib, *DeVry University*

Carolyn Schauble, *Colorado State University*

Brent Seales, *University of Kentucky*

Christian Shin, *SUNY Geneseo*

Charlie Shu, *Franklin University*

Jeffrey Six, *University of Delaware*

Don Slater, *Carnegie Mellon University*

Ken Slonneger, *University of Iowa*

Aurelia Smith, *Columbus State University*

Donald Smith, *Columbia College*

Joslyn A. Smith, *Florida International University*

Stephanie Smullen, *University of Tennessee, Chattanooga*

Robert Strader, *Stephen F. Austin State University*

Monica Sweat, *Georgia Institute of Technology*

Peter Stanchev, *Kettering University*

Aakash Taneja, *The Richard Stockton College of New Jersey*

Craig Tanis, *University of Tennessee at Chattanooga*

Shannon Tauro, *University of California, Irvine*

Ron Taylor, *Wright State University*

Russell Tessier, *University of Massachusetts, Amherst*

Jonathan L. Tolstedt, *North Dakota State University*

David Vineyard, *Kettering University*

Joseph Vybihal, *McGill University*

Xiaoming Wei, *Iona College*

Jonathan S. Weissman, *Finger Lakes Community College*

Todd Whittaker, *Franklin University*

Robert Willhoft, *Roberts Wesleyan College*

Brent Wilson, *George Fox University*

Katherine Winters, *University of Tennessee at Chattanooga*

Lea Wittie, *Bucknell University*

David Womack, *University of Texas at San Antonio*

David Woolbright, *Columbus State University*

Tom Wulf, *University of Cincinnati*

Catherine Wyman, *DeVry University*

Arthur Yanushka, *Christian Brothers University*

Qi Yu, *Rochester Institute of Technology*

Salih Yurttas, *Texas A&M University*

CONTENTS

*See your eText or visit www.wiley.com/go/bjeo7.

ALPHABETICAL LIST OF   SYNTAX BOXES

CHAPTER	Common Errors	How Tos and Worked Examples

Programming Tips

Special Topics

Computing & Society

CHAPTER	Common Errors		How Tos and Worked Examples	
7 Arrays and Array Lists	Bounds Errors	227	Working with Arrays	242
	Uninitialized and Unfilled Arrays	227	Rolling the Dice	245
			A World Population Table	253
	Underestimating the Size of a Data Set	240		
	Length and Size	264		
8 Designing Classes	Trying to Access Instance Variables in Static Methods	288	Programming with Packages	299
	Confusing Dots	298		
9 Inheritance	Replicating Instance Variables from the Superclass	313	Developing an Inheritance Hierarchy	325
	Confusing Super- and Subclasses	313	Implementing an Employee Hierarchy for Payroll Processing	330
	Accidental Overloading	317		
	Forgetting to Use super When Invoking a Superclass Method	318		
	Don't Use Type Tests	335		
10 Interfaces	Forgetting to Declare Implementing Methods as Public	346	Investigating Number Sequences	350
	Trying to Instantiate an Interface	346		
	Modifying Parameter Types in the Implementing Method	367		
	Trying to Call Listener Methods	368		
	Forgetting to Attach a Listener	371		
	Forgetting to Repaint	373		
11 Input/Output and Exception Handling	Backslashes in File Names	386	Processing Text Files	399
	Constructing a Scanner with a String	386	Analyzing Baby Names	403

Programming Tips		Special Topics		Computing & Society	
Use Arrays for Sequences of Related Items	228	Methods with a Variable Number of Arguments	229	Computer Viruses	229
Make Parallel Arrays into Arrays of Objects	228	Sorting with the Java Library	240	Liability for Software Malfunction	267
Batch Files and Shell Scripts	266	Two-Dimensional Arrays with Variable Row Lengths	254		
		Multidimensional Arrays	255		
		The Diamond Syntax	264		
Consistency	277	Call by Value and Call by Reference	278	Personal Computing	302
Minimize the Use of Static Methods	289	Alternative Forms of Instance and Static Variable Initialization	289		
		Static Imports	290		
		Package Access	298		
Use a Single Class for Variation in Values, Inheritance for Variation in Behavior	309	Calling the Superclass Constructor	318	Who Controls the Internet?	337
		Dynamic Method Lookup and the Implicit Parameter	322		
		Abstract Classes	323		
		Final Methods and Classes	324		
		Protected Access	324		
		Inheritance and the toString Method	335		
		Inheritance and the equals Method	336		
Comparing Integers and Floating-Point Numbers	351	Constants in Interfaces	346	Open Source and Free Software	379
		Nonabstract Interface Methods	347		
		The clone Method and the Cloneable Interface	352		
		Lambda Expressions	358		
		Generic Interface Types	360		
		Keyboard Events	377		
		Event Adapters	378		
Throw Early, Catch Late	411	Reading Web Pages	387	Encryption Algorithms	402
Do Not Squelch Exceptions	411	File Dialog Boxes	387	The Ariane Rocket Incident	417
Do Throw Specific Exceptions	411	Character Encodings	388		
		Regular Expressions	395		
		Reading an Entire File	396		
		Assertions	411		
		The try/finally Statement	412		

Programming Tips		Special Topics		Computing & Society	
		Attributes and Methods in UML Diagrams	426	Electronic Privacy	439
		Multiplicities	427		
		Aggregation, Association, and Composition	427		
				The Limits of Computation	461
		Oh, Omega, and Theta	486	The First Programmer	499
		Insertion Sort	487		
		The Quicksort Algorithm	493		
		The Comparator Interface	506		
		Comparators with Lambda Expressions	507		
Use Interface References to Manipulate Data Structures	524	Updating Map Entries	527	Standardization	519
		Hash Functions	529		
		Reverse Polish Notation	542		
		Static Classes	560		
		Open Addressing	578		
		Wildcard Types	638		
		Reflection	642		
One Stream Operation Per Line	651	Infinite Streams	651		
Keep Lambda Expressions Short	656	Method and Constructor References	656		
		Higher-Order Functions	657		
		Higher-Order Functions and Comparators	658		
Use a GUI Builder	694	Adding the main Method to the Frame Class	679		

CHAPTER	Common Errors		How Tos and Worked Examples	
21 Advanced Input/Output* (eTEXT ONLY)	Negative byte Values	W714	Choosing a File Format	W723
22 Multithreading* (eTEXT ONLY)	Calling await Without Calling signalAll	W755		
	Calling signalAll Without Locking the Object	W755		
23 Internet Networking* (eTEXT ONLY)			Designing Client/Server Programs	W786
24 Relational Databases* (eTEXT ONLY)	Joining Tables Without Specifying a Link Condition	W809	Programming a Bank Database	W831
	Constructing Queries from Arbitrary Strings	W820		
25 XML* (eTEXT ONLY)	XML Elements Describe Objects, Not Classes	W853	Designing an XML Document Format	W845
			Writing an XML Document	W859
			Writing a DTD	W869

*See your eText or visit www.wiley.com/go/bjeo7.

Programming Tips

Special Topics

Computing & Society

INTRODUCTION

© JanPietruszka/iStockphoto.

Just as you gather tools, study a project, and make a plan for tackling it, in this chapter you will gather up the basics you need to start learning to program. After a brief introduction to computer hardware, software, and programming in general, you will learn how to write and run your first Java program. You will also learn how to diagnose and fix programming errors, and how to use pseudocode to describe an algorithm—a step-by-step description of how to solve a problem—as you plan your computer programs.

1.1 Computer Programs

Computers execute very basic instructions in rapid succession.

You have probably used a computer for work or fun. Many people use computers for everyday tasks such as electronic banking or writing a term paper. Computers are good for such tasks. They can handle repetitive chores, such as totaling up numbers or placing words on a page, without getting bored or exhausted.

The flexibility of a computer is quite an amazing phenomenon. The same machine can balance your checkbook, lay out your term paper, and play a game. In contrast, other machines carry out a much narrower range of tasks; a car drives and a toaster toasts. Computers can carry out a wide range of tasks because they execute different programs, each of which directs the computer to work on a specific task.

A computer program is a sequence of instructions and decisions.

The computer itself is a machine that stores data (numbers, words, pictures), interacts with devices (the monitor, the sound system, the printer), and executes programs. A **computer program** tells a computer, in minute detail, the sequence of steps that are needed to fulfill a task. The physical computer and peripheral devices are collectively called the **hardware**. The programs the computer executes are called the **software**.

Today's computer programs are so sophisticated that it is hard to believe that they are composed of extremely primitive instructions. A typical instruction may be one of the following:

- Put a red dot at a given screen position.
- Add up two numbers.
- If this value is negative, continue the program at a certain instruction.

The computer user has the illusion of smooth interaction because a program contains a huge number of such instructions, and because the computer can execute them at great speed.

Programming is the act of designing and implementing computer programs.

The act of designing and implementing computer programs is called **programming**. In this book, you will learn how to program a computer—that is, how to direct the computer to execute tasks.

To write a computer game with motion and sound effects or a word processor that supports fancy fonts and pictures is a complex task that requires a team of many highly-skilled programmers. Your first programming efforts will be more mundane. The concepts and skills you learn in this book form an important foundation, and you should not be disappointed if your first programs do not rival the sophisticated software that is familiar to you. Actually, you will find that there is an immense thrill even in simple programming tasks. It is an amazing experience to see the computer precisely and quickly carry out a task that would take you hours of drudgery, to make small changes in a program that lead to immediate improvements, and to see the computer become an extension of your mental powers.

1.2 The Anatomy of a Computer

To understand the programming process, you need to have a rudimentary understanding of the building blocks that make up a computer. We will look at a personal computer. Larger computers have faster, larger, or more powerful components, but they have fundamentally the same design.

At the heart of the computer lies the **central processing unit (CPU)** (see Figure 1). The inside wiring of the CPU is enormously complicated. For example, the Intel Core processor (a popular CPU for personal computers at the time of this writing) is composed of several hundred million structural elements, called *transistors*.

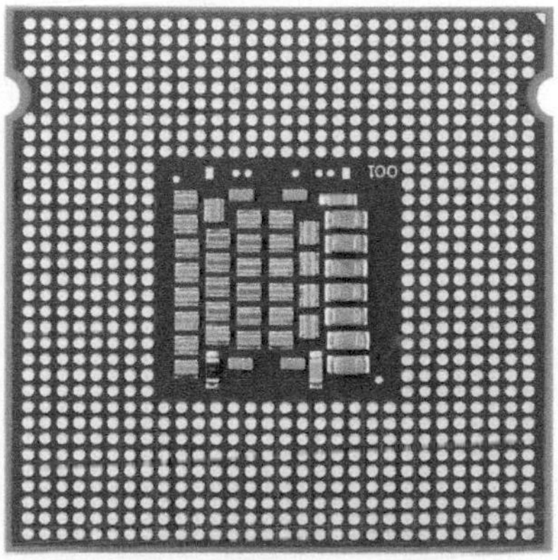

The central processing unit (CPU) performs program control and data processing.

The CPU performs program control and data processing. That is, the CPU locates and executes the program instructions; it carries out arithmetic operations such as addition, subtraction, multiplication, and division; it fetches data from external memory or devices and places processed data into storage.

© Amorphis/iStockphoto.

Figure 1 Central Processing Unit

Storage devices include memory and secondary storage.

There are two kinds of storage. Primary storage, or memory, is made from electronic circuits that can store data, provided they are supplied with electric power. **Secondary storage**, usually a **hard disk** (see Figure 2) or a solid-state drive, provides slower and less expensive storage that persists without electricity. A hard disk consists of rotating platters, which are coated with a magnetic

© PhotoDisc, Inc./Getty Images, Inc.

Figure 2 A Hard Disk

material. A solid-state drive uses electronic components that can retain information without power, and without moving parts.

To interact with a human user, a computer requires peripheral devices. The computer transmits information (called *output*) to the user through a display screen, speakers, and printers. The user can enter information (called *input*) for the computer by using a keyboard or a pointing device such as a mouse.

Some computers are self-contained units, whereas others are interconnected through **networks**. Through the network cabling, the computer can read data and programs from central storage locations or send data to other computers. To the user of a networked computer, it may not even be obvious which data reside on the computer itself and which are transmitted through the network.

Figure 3 gives a schematic overview of the architecture of a personal computer. Program instructions and data (such as text, numbers, audio, or video) reside in secondary storage or elsewhere on the network. When a program is started, its instructions are brought into memory, where the CPU can read them. The CPU reads and executes one instruction at a time. As directed by these instructions, the CPU reads data, modifies it, and writes it back to memory or secondary storage. Some program instructions will cause the CPU to place dots on the display screen or printer or to vibrate the speaker. As these actions happen many times over and at great speed, the human user will perceive images and sound. Some program instructions read user input from the keyboard, mouse, touch sensor, or microphone. The program analyzes the nature of these inputs and then executes the next appropriate instruction.

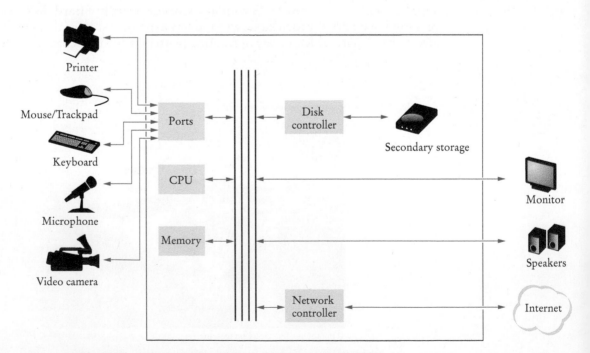

Figure 3 Schematic Design of a Personal Computer

Computing & Society 1.1 Computers Are Everywhere

When computers were first invented in the 1940s, a computer filled an entire room. The photo below shows the ENIAC (*electronic numerical integrator and computer*), completed in 1946 at the University of Pennsylvania. The ENIAC was used by the military to compute the trajectories of projectiles. Nowadays, computing facilities of search engines, Internet shops, and social networks fill huge buildings called data centers. At the other end of the spectrum, computers are all around us. Your cell phone has a computer inside, as do many credit cards and fare cards for public transit. A modern car has several computers—to control the engine, brakes, lights, and the radio.

The advent of ubiquitous computing changed many aspects of our lives. Factories used to employ people to do repetitive assembly tasks that are today carried out by computer-controlled robots, operated by a few people who know how to work with those computers. Books, music, and movies nowadays are often consumed on computers, and computers are almost always involved in their production. The book that you are reading right now could not have been written without computers.

© Maurice Savage/Alamy Limited.

This transit card contains a computer.

Knowing about computers and how to program them has become an essential skill in many careers. Engineers design computer-controlled cars and medical equipment that preserve lives. Computer scientists develop programs that help people come together to support social causes. For example, activists used social networks to share videos showing abuse by repressive regimes, and this information was instrumental in changing public opinion.

As computers, large and small, become ever more embedded in our everyday lives, it is increasingly important for everyone to understand how they work, and how to work with them. As you use this book to learn how to program a computer, you will develop a good understanding of computing fundamentals that will make you a more informed citizen and, perhaps, a computing professional.

© UPPA/Photoshot.

The ENIAC

1.3 The Java Programming Language

In order to write a computer program, you need to provide a sequence of instructions that the CPU can execute. A computer program consists of a large number of simple CPU instructions, and it is tedious and error-prone to specify them one by one. For that reason, **high-level programming languages** have been created. In a high-level language, you specify the actions that your program should carry out. A **compiler** translates the high-level instructions into the more detailed instructions (called **machine code**) required by the CPU. Many different programming languages have been designed for different purposes.

In 1991, a group led by James Gosling and Patrick Naughton at Sun Microsystems designed a programming language, code-named "Green", for use in consumer devices, such as intelligent television "set-top" boxes. The language was designed to be simple, secure, and usable for many different processor types. No customer was ever found for this technology.

© James Sullivan/Getty Images.

James Gosling

> Java was originally designed for programming consumer devices, but it was first successfully used to write Internet applets.

Gosling recounts that in 1994 the team realized, "We could write a really cool browser. It was one of the few things in the client/server mainstream that needed some of the weird things we'd done: architecture neutral, real-time, reliable, secure." Java was introduced to an enthusiastic crowd at the SunWorld exhibition in 1995, together with a browser that ran **applets**—Java code that can be located anywhere on the Internet. The figure at right shows a typical example of an applet.

Since then, Java has grown at a phenomenal rate. Programmers have embraced the language because it is easier to use than its closest rival, C++. In addition, Java has a rich **library** that makes it possible to write portable programs that can bypass proprietary operating systems—a feature that was eagerly sought by those who wanted to be independent of those proprietary systems and was bitterly fought by their vendors. A "micro edition" and an "enterprise edition" of the Java library allow Java programmers to target hardware ranging from smart cards to the largest Internet servers.

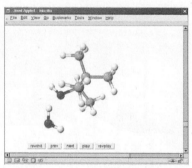

An Applet for Visualizing Molecules

Table 1   Java Versions (since Version 1.0 in 1996)

Version	Year	Important New Features	Version	Year	Important New Features
1.1	1997	Inner classes	6	2006	Library improvements
1.2	1998	Swing, Collections framework	7	2011	Small language changes and library improvements
1.3	2000	Performance enhancements	8	2014	Function expressions, streams, new date/time library
1.4	2002	Assertions, XML support	9	2017	Modules
5	2004	Generic classes, enhanced for loop, auto-boxing, enumerations, annotations	10, 11	2018	Versions with incremental improvements are released every six months

Java was designed to be safe and portable, benefiting both Internet users and students.

Because Java was designed for the Internet, it has two attributes that make it very suitable for beginners: safety and portability.

Java was designed so that anyone can execute programs in their browser without fear. The safety features of the Java language ensure that a program is terminated if it tries to do something unsafe. Having a safe environment is also helpful for anyone learning Java. When you make an error that results in unsafe behavior, your program is terminated and you receive an accurate error report.

Java programs are distributed as instructions for a virtual machine, making them platform-independent.

The other benefit of Java is portability. The same Java program will run, without change, on Windows, UNIX, Linux, or Macintosh. In order to achieve portability, the Java compiler does not translate Java programs directly into CPU instructions. Instead, compiled Java programs contain instructions for the Java **virtual machine**, a program that simulates a real CPU. Portability is another benefit for the beginning student. You do not have to learn how to write programs for different platforms.

At this time, Java is firmly established as one of the most important languages for general-purpose programming as well as for computer science instruction. However, although Java is a good language for beginners, it is not perfect, for three reasons.

Because Java was not specifically designed for students, no thought was given to making it really simple to write basic programs. A certain amount of technical machinery is necessary to write even the simplest programs. This is not a problem for professional programmers, but it can be a nuisance for beginning students. As you learn how to program in Java, there will be times when you will be asked to be satisfied with a preliminary explanation and wait for more complete detail in a later chapter.

Java has been extended many times during its life—see Table 1. In this book, we assume that you have Java version 8 or later.

Java has a very large library. Focus on learning those parts of the library that you need for your programming projects.

Finally, you cannot hope to learn all of Java in one course. The Java language itself is relatively simple, but Java contains a vast set of *library packages* that are required to write useful programs. There are packages for graphics, user-interface design, cryptography, networking, sound, database storage, and many other purposes. Even expert Java programmers cannot hope to know the contents of all of the packages—they just use those that they need for particular projects.

Using this book, you should expect to learn a good deal about the Java language and about the most important packages. Keep in mind that the central goal of this book is not to make you memorize Java minutiae, but to teach you how to think about programming.

1.4 Becoming Familiar with Your Programming Environment

Set aside time to become familiar with the programming environment that you will use for your class work.

Many students find that the tools they need as programmers are very different from the software with which they are familiar. You should spend some time making yourself familiar with your programming environment. Because computer systems vary widely, this book can only give an outline of the steps you need to follow. It is a good idea to participate in a hands-on lab, or to ask a knowledgeable friend to give you a tour.

Step 1 Start the Java development environment.

Computer systems differ greatly in this regard. On many computers there is an **integrated development environment** in which you can write and test your programs.

Figure 4
Running the
HelloPrinter
Program in an
Integrated
Development
Environment

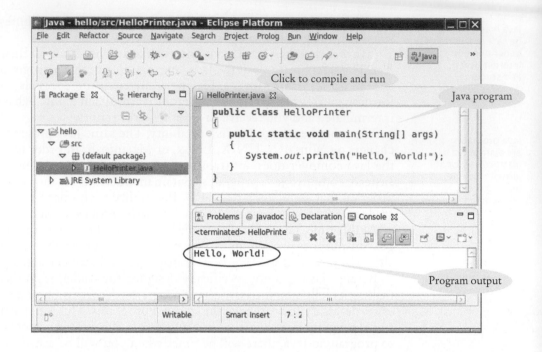

An editor is a
program for entering
and modifying
text, such as a Java
program.

On other computers you first launch an **editor**, a program that functions like a word processor, in which you can enter your Java instructions; you then open a *console window* and type commands to execute your program. You need to find out how to get started with your environment.

Step 2   Write a simple program.

The traditional choice for the very first program in a new programming language is a program that displays a simple greeting: "Hello, World!". Let us follow that tradition. Here is the "Hello, World!" program in Java:

```java
public class HelloPrinter
{
   public static void main(String[] args)
   {
      System.out.println("Hello, World!");
   }
}
```

We will examine this program in the next section.

No matter which programming environment you use, you begin your activity by typing the program statements into an editor window.

Create a new file and call it HelloPrinter.java, using the steps that are appropriate for your environment. (If your environment requires that you supply a project name in addition to the file name, use the name hello for the project.) Enter the program instructions *exactly* as they are given above. Alternatively, locate the electronic copy in this book's companion code and paste it into your editor.

Java is case sensitive.
You must be careful
about distinguishing
between upper- and
lowercase letters.

As you write this program, pay careful attention to the various symbols, and keep in mind that Java is **case sensitive**. You must enter upper- and lowercase letters exactly as they appear in the program listing. You cannot type MAIN or PrintLn. If you are not careful, you will run into problems—see Common Error 1.2.

Figure 5 Running the HelloPrinter Program in a Console Window

Step 3 Run the program.

The process for running a program depends greatly on your programming environment. You may have to click a button or enter some commands. When you run the test program, the message

    Hello, World!

will appear somewhere on the screen (see Figure 4 and Figure 5).

In order to run your program, the Java compiler translates your **source files** (that is, the statements that you wrote) into *class files*. (A class file contains instructions for the Java virtual machine.) After the compiler has translated your **source code** into virtual machine instructions, the virtual machine executes them. During execution, the virtual machine accesses a library of pre-written code, including the implementations of the System and PrintStream classes that are necessary for displaying the program's output. Figure 6 summarizes the process of creating and running a Java program. In some programming environments, the compiler and virtual machine are essentially invisible to the programmer—they are automatically executed whenever you ask to run a Java program. In other environments, you need to launch the compiler and virtual machine explicitly.

> The Java compiler translates source code into class files that contain instructions for the Java virtual machine.

Step 4 Organize your work.

As a programmer, you write programs, try them out, and improve them. You store your programs in **files**. Files are stored in **folders** or **directories**. A folder can contain

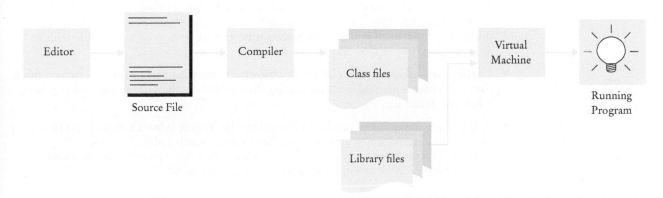

Figure 6 From Source Code to Running Program

files as well as other folders, which themselves can contain more files and folders (see Figure 7). This hierarchy can be quite large, and you need not be concerned with all of its branches. However, you should create folders for organizing your work. It is a good idea to make a separate folder for your programming coursework. Inside that folder, make a separate folder for each program.

Some programming environments place your programs into a default location if you don't specify a folder yourself. In that case, you need to find out where those files are located.

Be sure that you understand where your files are located in the folder hierarchy. This information is essential when you submit files for grading, and for making *backup copies* (see Programming Tip 1.1).

Figure 7   A Folder Hierarchy

Programming Tip 1.1

Backup Copies

Develop a strategy for keeping backup copies of your work before disaster strikes.

You will spend many hours creating and improving Java programs. It is easy to delete a file by accident, and occasionally files are lost because of a computer malfunction. Retyping the contents of lost files is frustrating and time-consuming. It is therefore crucially important that you learn how to safeguard files and get in the habit of doing so *before* disaster strikes. Backing up files on a memory stick is an easy and convenient storage method for many people. Another increasingly popular form of backup is Internet file storage.

© Tatiana Popova/iStockphoto.

Here are a few pointers to keep in mind:

- *Back up often.* Backing up a file takes only a few seconds, and you will hate yourself if you have to spend many hours recreating work that you could have saved easily. I recommend that you back up your work once every thirty minutes.

- *Rotate backups.* Use more than one directory for backups, and rotate them. That is, first back up onto the first directory. Then back up onto the second directory. Then use the third, and then go back to the first. That way you always have three recent backups. If your recent changes made matters worse, you can then go back to the older version.

- *Pay attention to the backup direction.* Backing up involves copying files from one place to another. It is important that you do this right—that is, copy from your work location to the backup location. If you do it the wrong way, you will overwrite a newer file with an older version.

- *Check your backups once in a while.* Double-check that your backups are where you think they are. There is nothing more frustrating than to find out that the backups are not there when you need them.

- *Relax, then restore.* When you lose a file and need to restore it from a backup, you are likely to be in an unhappy, nervous state. Take a deep breath and think through the recovery process before you start. It is not uncommon for an agitated computer user to wipe out the last backup when trying to restore a damaged file.

1.5 Analyzing Your First Program

© Amanda Rohde/iStockphoto.

In this section, we will analyze the first Java program in detail. Here again is the source code.

sec04/HelloPrinter.java

```java
1  public class HelloPrinter
2  {
3     public static void main(String[] args)
4     {
5        // Display a greeting in the console window
6
7        System.out.println("Hello, World!");
8     }
9  }
```

The line

```java
public class HelloPrinter
```

indicates the declaration of a **class** called HelloPrinter.

Every Java program consists of one or more classes. We will discuss classes in more detail in Chapters 2 and 3.

> Classes are the fundamental building blocks of Java programs.

The word public denotes that the class is usable by the "public". You will later encounter private features.

In Java, every source file can contain at most one public class, and the name of the public class must match the name of the file containing the class. For example, the class HelloPrinter must be contained in a file named HelloPrinter.java.

The construction

```java
public static void main(String[] args)
{
   . . .
}
```

declares a **method** called main. A method contains a collection of programming instructions that describe how to carry out a particular task.

Every Java application must have a **main method**. Most Java programs contain other methods besides main, and you will see in Chapter 3 how to write other methods.

> Every Java application contains a class with a main method. When the application starts, the instructions in the main method are executed.

The term static is explained in more detail in Chapter 8, and the meaning of String[] args is covered in Chapter 11. At this time, simply consider

```java
public class ClassName
{
   public static void main(String[] args)
   {
      . . .
   }
}
```

> Each class contains declarations of methods. Each method contains a sequence of instructions.

as a part of the "plumbing" that is required to create a Java program. Our first program has all instructions inside the main method of the class.

The main method contains one or more instructions called **statements**. Each statement ends in a semicolon (;). When a program runs, the statements in the main method are executed one by one.

In our example program, the main method has a single statement:

```
System.out.println("Hello, World!");
```

This statement prints a line of text, namely "Hello, World!". In this statement, we *call* a method which, for reasons that we will not explain here, is specified by the rather long name System.out.println.

We do not have to implement this method—the programmers who wrote the Java library already did that for us. We simply want the method to perform its intended task, namely to print a value.

Whenever you call a method in Java, you need to specify

> **A method is called by specifying the method and its arguments.**

1. The method you want to use (in this case, System.out.println).
2. Any values the method needs to carry out its task (in this case, "Hello, World!"). The technical term for such a value is an **argument**. Arguments are enclosed in parentheses. Multiple arguments are separated by commas.

A sequence of characters enclosed in quotation marks

```
"Hello, World!"
```

> **A string is a sequence of characters enclosed in quotation marks.**

is called a **string**. You must enclose the contents of the string inside quotation marks so that the compiler knows you literally mean "Hello, World!". There is a reason for this requirement. Suppose you need to print the word *main*. By enclosing it in quotation marks, "main", the compiler knows you mean the sequence of characters m a i n, not the method named main. The rule is simply that you must enclose all text strings in quotation marks, so that the compiler considers them plain text and does not try to interpret them as program instructions.

You can also print numerical values. For example, the statement

```
System.out.println(3 + 4);
```

evaluates the expression 3 + 4 and displays the number 7.

Syntax 1.1   Java Program

Every program contains at least one class. Choose a class name that describes the program action.

Every Java program contains a main *method with this header.*

```
public class HelloPrinter
{
   public static void main(String[] args)
   {
      System.out.println("Hello, World!");
   }
}
```

The statements inside the main *method are executed when the program runs.*

Replace this statement when you write your own programs.

Each statement ends in a semicolon. See Common Error 1.1.

Be sure to match the opening and closing braces.

The System.out.println method prints a string or a number and then starts a new line. For example, the sequence of statements

```
System.out.println("Hello");
System.out.println("World!");
```

prints two lines of text:

```
Hello
World!
```

There is a second method, System.out.print, that you can use to print an item without starting a new line. For example, the output of the two statements

```
System.out.print("00");
System.out.println(3 + 4);
```

is the single line

```
007
```

EXAMPLE CODE   See sec05 of your eText or companion code for a program that demonstrates print commands.

Common Error 1.1

Omitting Semicolons

In Java every statement must end in a semicolon. Forgetting to type a semicolon is a common error. It confuses the compiler, because the compiler uses the semicolon to find where one statement ends and the next one starts. The compiler does not use line breaks or closing braces to recognize the end of statements. For example, the compiler considers

```
System.out.println("Hello")
System.out.println("World!");
```

a single statement, as if you had written

```
System.out.println("Hello") System.out.println("World!");
```

Then it doesn't understand that statement, because it does not expect the word System following the closing parenthesis after "Hello".

The remedy is simple. Scan every statement for a terminating semicolon, just as you would check that every English sentence ends in a period. However, do not add a semicolon at the end of public class Hello or public static void main. These lines are not statements.

1.6 Errors

Experiment a little with the HelloPrinter program. What happens if you make a typing error such as

```
System.ou.println("Hello, World!");
System.out.println("Hello, Word!");
```

In the first case, the compiler will complain. It will say that it has no clue what you mean by ou. The exact wording of the error message is dependent on your development environment, but it might be something like "Cannot find symbol ou". This is a **compile-time error**. Something is wrong according to the rules of the language and the compiler finds it. For this reason, compile-time errors are often called **syntax errors**. When the compiler finds one or more errors, it refuses to translate the program into Java virtual machine instructions, and as a consequence you have no program that you can run. You must fix the error and compile again. In fact, the compiler is quite picky, and it is common to go through several rounds of fixing compile-time errors before compilation succeeds for the first time.

> A compile-time error is a violation of the programming language rules that is detected by the compiler.

If the compiler finds an error, it will not simply stop and give up. It will try to report as many errors as it can find, so you can fix them all at once.

Sometimes, an error throws the compiler off track. Suppose, for example, you forget the quotation marks around a string: `System.out.println(Hello, World!)`. The compiler will not complain about the missing quotation marks. Instead, it will report "Cannot find symbol Hello". Unfortunately, the compiler is not very smart and it does not realize that you meant to use a string. It is up to you to realize that you need to enclose strings in quotation marks.

© Martin Carlsson/iStockphoto.

Programmers spend a fair amount of time fixing compile-time and run-time errors.

The error in the second line above is of a different kind. The program will compile and run, but its output will be wrong. It will print

```
Hello, Word!
```

> A run-time error causes a program to take an action that the programmer did not intend.

This is a **run-time error**. The program is syntactically correct and does something, but it doesn't do what it is supposed to do. Because run-time errors are caused by logical flaws in the program, they are often called **logic errors**.

This particular run-time error did not include an error message. It simply produced the wrong output. Some kinds of run-time errors are so severe that they generate an **exception**: an error message from the Java virtual machine. For example, if your program includes the statement

```
System.out.println(1 / 0);
```

you will get a run-time error message "Division by zero".

During program development, errors are unavoidable. Once a program is longer than a few lines, it would require superhuman concentration to enter it correctly without slipping up once. You will find yourself omitting semicolons or quotation marks more often than you would like, but the compiler will track down these problems for you.

Run-time errors are more troublesome. The compiler will not find them—in fact, the compiler will cheerfully translate any program as long as its syntax is correct—but the resulting program will do something wrong. It is the responsibility of the program author to test the program and find any run-time errors.

EXAMPLE CODE   See sec06 of your eText or companion code for three programs that illustrate errors.

Common Error 1.2
Misspelling Words

If you accidentally misspell a word, then strange things may happen, and it may not always be completely obvious from the error messages what went wrong. Here is a good example of how simple spelling errors can cause trouble:

```
public class HelloPrinter
{
   public static void Main(String[] args)
   {
      System.out.println("Hello, World!");
   }
}
```

This class declares a method called Main. The compiler will not consider this to be the same as the main method, because Main starts with an uppercase letter and the Java language is case sensitive. Upper- and lowercase letters are considered to be completely different from each other, and to the compiler Main is no better match for main than rain. The compiler will cheerfully compile your Main method, but when the Java virtual machine reads the compiled file, it will complain about the missing main method and refuse to run the program. Of course, the message "missing main method" should give you a clue where to look for the error.

If you get an error message that seems to indicate that the compiler or virtual machine is on the wrong track, check for spelling and capitalization. If you misspell the name of a symbol (for example, ou instead of out), the compiler will produce a message such as "cannot find symbol ou". That error message is usually a good clue that you made a spelling error.

1.7 Problem Solving: Algorithm Design

You will soon learn how to program calculations and decision making in Java. But before we look at the mechanics of implementing computations in the next chapter, let's consider how you can describe the steps that are necessary for finding the solution to a problem.

1.7.1 The Algorithm Concept

You may have run across advertisements that encourage you to pay for a computerized service that matches you up with a love partner. Think how this might work. You fill out a form and send it in. Others do the same. The data are processed by a computer program. Is it reasonable to assume that the computer can perform the task of finding the best match for you? Suppose your younger brother, not the computer, had all the forms on his desk. What instructions could you give him? You can't say, "Find the best-looking person who likes inline skating and browsing the Internet". There is no objective standard for good looks, and your brother's opinion (or that of a computer program analyzing the photos of prospective partners) will likely be different from yours. If you can't give written instructions for someone to solve the problem, there is no way the computer can magically find the right solution. The computer can only do what you tell it to do. It just does it faster, without getting bored or exhausted.

© mammamaart/iStockphoto.

Finding the perfect partner is not a problem that a computer can solve.

For that reason, a computerized match-making service cannot guarantee to find the optimal match for you. Instead, you may be presented with a set of potential partners who share common interests with you. That is a task that a computer program can solve.

In order for a computer program to provide an answer to a problem that computes an answer, it must follow a sequence of steps that is

- Unambiguous
- Executable
- Terminating

> An algorithm for solving a problem is a sequence of steps that is unambiguous, executable, and terminating.

The step sequence is *unambiguous* when there are precise instructions for what to do at each step and where to go next. There is no room for guesswork or personal opinion. A step is *executable* when it can be carried out in practice. For example, a computer can list all people that share your hobbies, but it can't predict who will be your life-long partner. Finally, a sequence of steps is *terminating* if it will eventually come to an end. A program that keeps working without delivering an answer is clearly not useful.

A sequence of steps that is unambiguous, executable, and terminating is called an **algorithm**. Although there is no algorithm for finding a partner, many problems do have algorithms for solving them. The next section gives an example.

© Claudiad/iStockphoto.

An algorithm is a recipe for finding a solution.

1.7.2 An Algorithm for Solving an Investment Problem

Consider the following investment problem:

> You put $10,000 into a bank account that earns 5 percent interest per year. How many years does it take for the account balance to be double the original?

Could you solve this problem by hand? Sure, you could. You figure out the balance as follows:

year	interest	balance
0		10000
1	10000.00 x 0.05 = 500.00	10000.00 + 500.00 = 10500.00
2	10500.00 x 0.05 = 525.00	10500.00 + 525.00 = 11025.00
3	11025.00 x 0.05 = 551.25	11025.00 + 551.25 = 11576.25
4	11576.25 x 0.05 = 578.81	11576.25 + 578.81 = 12155.06

You keep going until the balance is at least $20,000. Then the last number in the year column is the answer.

Of course, carrying out this computation is intensely boring to you or your younger brother. But computers are very good at carrying out repetitive calculations quickly and flawlessly. What is important to the computer is a description of the steps for finding the solution. Each step must be clear and unambiguous, requiring no guesswork. Here is such a description:

Set year to 0, balance to 10000.

year	interest	balance
0		10000

While the balance is less than $20,000
  Add 1 to the year.
  Set the interest to balance x 0.05 (i.e., 5 percent interest).
  Add the interest to the balance.

year	interest	balance
0		10000
1	500.00	10500.00
14	942.82	19799.32
(15)	989.96	20789.28

Report year as the answer.

These steps are not yet in a language that a computer can understand, but you will soon learn how to formulate them in Java. This informal description is called **pseudocode**. We examine the rules for writing pseudocode in the next section.

1.7.3 Pseudocode

There are no strict requirements for pseudocode because it is read by human readers, not a computer program. Here are the kinds of pseudocode statements and how we will use them in this book:

Pseudocode is an informal description of a sequence of steps for solving a problem.

- Use statements such as the following to describe how a value is set or changed:

  total cost = purchase price + operating cost
  Multiply the balance value by 1.05.
  Remove the first and last character from the word.

- Describe decisions and repetitions as follows:

  If total cost 1 < total cost 2
  While the balance is less than $20,000
  For each picture in the sequence

  Use indentation to indicate which statements should be selected or repeated:

  For each car
    operating cost = 10 x annual fuel cost
    total cost = purchase price + operating cost

  Here, the indentation indicates that both statements should be executed for each car.

- Indicate results with statements such as:

Choose carl.
Report year as the answer.

1.7.4 From Algorithms to Programs

Understand the problem

Develop and describe an algorithm

Test the algorithm with simple inputs

Translate the algorithm into Java

Compile and test your program

In Section 1.7.2, we developed pseudocode for finding how long it takes to double an investment. Let's double-check that the pseudocode represents an algorithm; that is, that it is unambiguous, executable, and terminating.

Our pseudocode is unambiguous. It simply tells how to update values in each step. The pseudocode is executable because we use a fixed interest rate. Had we said to use the actual interest rate that will be charged in years to come, and not a fixed rate of 5 percent per year, the instructions would not have been executable. There is no way for anyone to know what the interest rate will be in the future. It requires a bit of thought to see that the steps are terminating: With every step, the balance goes up by at least $500, so eventually it must reach $20,000.

Therefore, we have found an algorithm to solve our investment problem, and we know we can find the solution by programming a computer. The existence of an algorithm is an essential prerequisite for programming a task. You need to first discover and describe an algorithm for the task before you start programming (see Figure 8). In the chapters that follow, you will learn how to express algorithms in the Java language.

Figure 8 The Software Development Process

HOW TO 1.1

Describing an Algorithm with Pseudocode

This is the first of many "How To" sections in this book that give you step-by-step procedures for carrying out important tasks in developing computer programs.

Before you are ready to write a program in Java, you need to develop an algorithm—a method for arriving at a solution for a particular problem. Describe the algorithm in pseudocode—a sequence of precise steps formulated in English. To illustrate, we'll devise an algorithm for this problem:

Problem Statement You have the choice of buying one of two cars. One is more fuel efficient than the other, but also more expensive. You know the price and fuel efficiency (in miles per gallon, mpg) of both cars. You plan to keep the car for ten years. Assume a price of $4 per gallon of gas and usage of 15,000 miles per year. You will pay cash for the car and not worry about financing costs. Which car is the better deal?

© David H. Lewis/Getty Images.

Step 1   Determine the inputs and outputs.

In our sample problem, we have these inputs:

- *purchase price1* and *fuel efficiency1*, the price and fuel efficiency (in mpg) of the first car
- *purchase price2* and *fuel efficiency2*, the price and fuel efficiency of the second car

We simply want to know which car is the better buy. That is the desired output.

Step 2   Break down the problem into smaller tasks.

For each car, we need to know the total cost of driving it. Let's do this computation separately for each car. Once we have the total cost for each car, we can decide which car is the better deal.

The total cost for each car is *purchase price + operating cost.*

We assume a constant usage and gas price for ten years, so the operating cost depends on the cost of driving the car for one year.

The operating cost is *10 x annual fuel cost.*

The annual fuel cost is *price per gallon x annual fuel consumed.*

The annual fuel consumed is *annual miles driven / fuel efficiency.* For example, if you drive the car for 15,000 miles and the fuel efficiency is 15 miles/gallon, the car consumes 1,000 gallons.

Step 3   Describe each subtask in pseudocode.

In your description, arrange the steps so that any intermediate values are computed before they are needed in other computations. For example, list the step

    total cost = purchase price + operating cost

after you have computed *operating cost.*

Here is the algorithm for deciding which car to buy:

    For each car, compute the total cost as follows:
        annual fuel consumed = annual miles driven / fuel efficiency
        annual fuel cost = price per gallon x annual fuel consumed
        operating cost = 10 x annual fuel cost
        total cost = purchase price + operating cost
    If total cost of car1 < total cost of car2
        Choose car1.
    Else
        Choose car2.

Step 4   Test your pseudocode by working a problem.

We will use these sample values:

    Car 1: $25,000, 50 miles/gallon
    Car 2: $20,000, 30 miles/gallon

Here is the calculation for the cost of the first car:

    annual fuel consumed = annual miles driven / fuel efficiency = 15000 / 50 = 300
    annual fuel cost = price per gallon x annual fuel consumed = 4 x 300 = 1200
    operating cost = 10 x annual fuel cost = 10 x 1200 = 12000
    total cost = purchase price + operating cost = 25000 + 12000 = 37000

Similarly, the total cost for the second car is $40,000. Therefore, the output of the algorithm is to choose car 1.

The following Worked Example demonstrates how to use the concepts in this chapter and the steps in the How To to solve another problem. In this case, you will see how to develop an algorithm for laying tile in an alternating pattern of colors. You should read the Worked Examples to review what you have learned, and for help in tackling another problem.

In future chapters, Worked Examples are indicated by a brief description of the problem tackled in the example, plus a reminder to view it in your eText or download it from the book's companion web site at www.wiley.com/go/bjeo7. You will find any code related to the Worked Example included with the book's companion code for the chapter. When you see the Worked Example description, go to the example and view and run the code to learn how the problem was solved.

WORKED EXAMPLE 1.1

Writing an Algorithm for Tiling a Floor

Problem Statement   Write an algorithm for tiling a rectangular bathroom floor with alternating black and white tiles measuring 4 × 4 inches. The floor dimensions, measured in inches, are multiples of 4.

Step 1   Determine the inputs and outputs.

The inputs are the floor dimensions (length × width), measured in inches. The output is a tiled floor.

Step 2   Break down the problem into smaller tasks.

A natural subtask is to lay one row of tiles. If you can solve that task, then you can solve the problem by laying one row next to the other, starting from a wall, until you reach the opposite wall.

How do you lay a row? Start with a tile at one wall. If it is white, put a black one next to it. If it is black, put a white one next to it. Keep going until you reach the opposite wall. The row will contain *width* / 4 tiles.

© rban/iStockphoto.

Step 3   Describe each subtask in pseudocode.

In the pseudocode, you want to be more precise about exactly where the tiles are placed.

> *Place a black tile in the northwest corner.*
> *While the floor is not yet filled*
>   *Repeat width / 4 – 1 times*
>   *Place a tile east of the previously placed tile. If the previously placed tile was white, pick a black one; otherwise, a white one.*
>   *Locate the tile at the beginning of the row that you just placed. If there is space to the south, place a tile of the opposite color below it.*

Step 4   Test your pseudocode by working a problem.

Suppose you want to tile an area measuring 20 × 12 inches. The first step is to place a black tile in the northwest corner.

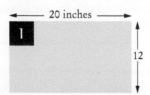

Next, alternate four tiles until reaching the east wall. (*width* / 4 − 1 = 20 / 4 − 1 = 4)

There is room to the south. Locate the tile at the beginning of the completed row. It is black. Place a white tile south of it.

Complete the row.

1 2 3 4 5
6 7 8 9 10

There is still room to the south. Locate the tile at the beginning of the completed row. It is white. Place a black tile south of it.

1 2 3 4 5
6 7 8 9 10
11

Complete the row.

1 2 3 4 5
6 7 8 9 10
11 12 13 14 15

Now the entire floor is filled, and you are done.

CHAPTER SUMMARY

Define "computer program" and programming.

- Computers execute very basic instructions in rapid succession.
- A computer program is a sequence of instructions and decisions.
- Programming is the act of designing and implementing computer programs.

Describe the components of a computer.

- The central processing unit (CPU) performs program control and data processing.
- Storage devices include memory and secondary storage.

Describe the process of translating high-level languages to machine code.

- Java was originally designed for programming consumer devices, but it was first successfully used to write Internet applets.
- Java was designed to be safe and portable, benefiting both Internet users and students.
- Java programs are distributed as instructions for a virtual machine, making them platform-independent.
- Java has a very large library. Focus on learning those parts of the library that you need for your programming projects.

Become familiar with your Java programming environment.

- Set aside time to become familiar with the programming environment that you will use for your class work.
- An editor is a program for entering and modifying text, such as a Java program.
- Java is case sensitive. You must be careful about distinguishing between upper- and lowercase letters.
- The Java compiler translates source code into class files that contain instructions for the Java virtual machine.
- Develop a strategy for keeping backup copies of your work before disaster strikes.

Describe the building blocks of a simple program.

- Classes are the fundamental building blocks of Java programs.
- Every Java application contains a class with a main method. When the application starts, the instructions in the main method are executed.
- Each class contains declarations of methods. Each method contains a sequence of instructions.
- A method is called by specifying the method and its arguments.
- A string is a sequence of characters enclosed in quotation marks.

Classify program errors as compile-time and run-time errors.

- A compile-time error is a violation of the programming language rules that is detected by the compiler.
- A run-time error causes a program to take an action that the programmer did not intend.

Write pseudocode for simple algorithms.

- An algorithm for solving a problem is a sequence of steps that is unambiguous, executable, and terminating.
- Pseudocode is an informal description of a sequence of steps for solving a problem.

STANDARD LIBRARY ITEMS INTRODUCED IN THIS CHAPTER

```
java.io.PrintStream          java.lang.System
  print                        out
  println
```

- **R1.1** Explain the difference between using a computer program and programming a computer.

- **R1.2** Which parts of a computer can store program code? Which can store user data?

- **R1.3** Which parts of a computer serve to give information to the user? Which parts take user input?

- **R1.4** A toaster is a single-function device, but a computer can be programmed to carry out different tasks. Is your cell phone a single-function device, or is it a programmable computer? (Your answer will depend on your cell phone model.)

- **R1.5** Explain two benefits of using Java over machine code.

- **R1.6** On your own computer or on a lab computer, find the exact location (folder or directory name) of
    - **a.** The sample file `HelloPrinter.java`, which you wrote with the editor.
    - **b.** The Java program launcher `java.exe` or `java`.
    - **c.** The library file `rt.jar` that contains the run-time library.

- **R1.7** What does this program print?

```java
public class Test
{
    public static void main(String[] args)
    {
        System.out.println("39 + 3");
        System.out.println(39 + 3);
    }
}
```

- **R1.8** What does this program print? Pay close attention to spaces.

```java
public class Test
{
    public static void main(String[] args)
    {
        System.out.print("Hello");
        System.out.println("World");
    }
}
```

- **R1.9** What is the compile-time error in this program?

```java
public class Test
{
    public static void main(String[] args)
    {
        System.out.println("Hello", "World!");
    }
}
```

- **R1.10** Write three versions of the `HelloPrinter.java` program that have different compile-time errors. Write a version that has a run-time error.

- **R1.11** How do you discover syntax errors? How do you discover logic errors?

■■■ **R1.12** The cafeteria offers a discount card for sale that entitles you, during a certain period, to a free meal whenever you have bought a given number of meals at the regular price. The exact details of the offer change from time to time. Describe an algorithm that lets you determine whether a particular offer is a good buy. What other inputs do you need?

■■ **R1.13** Write an algorithm to settle the following question: A bank account starts out with $10,000. Interest is compounded monthly at 6 percent per year (0.5 percent per month). Every month, $500 is withdrawn to meet college expenses. After how many years is the account depleted?

■■■ **R1.14** Consider the question in Exercise ●● R1.13. Suppose the numbers ($10,000, 6 percent, $500) were user selectable. Are there values for which the algorithm you developed would not terminate? If so, change the algorithm to make sure it always terminates.

■■■ **R1.15** In order to estimate the cost of painting a house, a painter needs to know the surface area of the exterior. Develop an algorithm for computing that value. Your inputs are the width, length, and height of the house, the number of windows and doors, and their dimensions. (Assume the windows and doors have a uniform size.)

■■ **R1.16** In How To 1.1, you made assumptions about the price of gas and annual usage to compare cars. Ideally, you would like to know which car is the better deal without making these assumptions. Why can't a computer program solve that problem?

■■ **R1.17** Suppose you put your younger brother in charge of backing up your work. Write a set of detailed instructions for carrying out his task. Explain how often he should do it, and what files he needs to copy from which folder to which location. Explain how he should verify that the backup was carried out correctly.

■ **R1.18** Write pseudocode for an algorithm that describes how to prepare Sunday breakfast in your household.

■■ **R1.19** The ancient Babylonians had an algorithm for determining the square root of a number a. Start with an initial guess of $a/2$. Then find the average of your guess g and a/g. That's your next guess. Repeat until two consecutive guesses are close enough. Write pseudocode for this algorithm.

PRACTICE EXERCISES

■ **E1.1** Write a program that prints a greeting of your choice, perhaps in a language other than English.

■■ **E1.2** Write a program that prints the sum of the first ten positive integers, $1 + 2 + \cdots + 10$.

■■ **E1.3** Write a program that prints the product of the first ten positive integers, $1 \times 2 \times \cdots \times 10$. (Use * to indicate multiplication in Java.)

■■ **E1.4** Write a program that prints the balance of an account after the first, second, and third year. The account has an initial balance of $1,000 and earns 5 percent interest per year.

■ **E1.5** Write a program that displays your name inside a box on the screen, like this: `Dave` Do your best to approximate lines with characters such as | - +.

■■■ **E1.6** Write a program that prints your name in large letters, such as

```
*   *   **   ****   ****   *   *
*   *  *  *  *      *      *   *
*****  *  *  ****   ****    * *
*   * ****** *      *      *   *
*   *  *  *  *      *      *   *
```

■■ **E1.7** Write a program that prints your name in Morse code, like this:

```
.... .- .-. .-. -.--
```

Use a separate call to System.out.print for each letter.

■■ **E1.8** Write a program that prints a face similar to (but different from) the following:

```
 /////
+"""""+
(| o o |)
|   ^   |
|  '-'  |
+-----+
```

■■ **E1.9** Write a program that prints an imitation of a Piet Mondrian painting. (Search the Internet if you are not familiar with his paintings.) Use character sequences such as @@@ or ::: to indicate different colors, and use - and | to form lines.

■■ **E1.10** Write a program that prints a house that looks exactly like the following:

```
    +
   + +
  +   +
 +-----+
 | .-. |
 | | | |
 +-+-+-+
```

■■■ **E1.11** Write a program that prints an animal speaking a greeting, similar to (but different from) the following:

```
 /\_/\      -----
( ' ' )   / Hello \
(  -  )  <  Junior |
 | | |    \ Coder!/
(_|_)       -----
```

■ **E1.12** Write a program that prints three items, such as the names of your three best friends or favorite movies, on three separate lines.

■ **E1.13** Write a program that prints a poem of your choice. If you don't have a favorite poem, search the Internet for "Emily Dickinson" or "e e cummings".

■■ **E1.14** Write a program that prints the United States flag, using * and = characters.

■■ **E1.15** Type in and run the following program. Then modify it to show the message "Hello, *your name*!".

```java
import javax.swing.JOptionPane;

public class DialogViewer
{
   public static void main(String[] args)
   {
      JOptionPane.showMessageDialog(null, "Hello, World!");
```

```
      }
   }
```

■■ **E1.16** Type in and run the following program. Then modify it to print "Hello, *name*!", displaying the name that the user typed in.

```
import javax.swing.JOptionPane;

public class DialogViewer
{
   public static void main(String[] args)
   {
      String name = JOptionPane.showInputDialog("What is your name?");
      System.out.println(name);
   }
}
```

■■■ **E1.17** Modify the program from Exercise ●● E1.16 so that the dialog continues with the message "My name is Hal! What would you like me to do?" Discard the user's input and display a message such as

```
I'm sorry, Dave. I'm afraid I can't do that.
```

Replace Dave with the name that was provided by the user.

■■ **E1.18** Type in and run the following program. Then modify it to show a different greeting and image.

```
import java.net.URL;
import javax.swing.ImageIcon;
import javax.swing.JOptionPane;

public class Test
{
   public static void main(String[] args) throws Exception
   {
      URL imageLocation = new URL(
            "http://horstmann.com/java4everyone/duke.gif");
      JOptionPane.showMessageDialog(null, "Hello", "Title",
            JOptionPane.PLAIN_MESSAGE, new ImageIcon(imageLocation));
   }
}
```

■ **Business E1.19** Write a program that prints a two-column list of your friends' birthdays. In the first column, print the names of your best friends; in the second, print their birthdays.

■ **Business E1.20** In the United States there is no federal sales tax, so every state may impose its own sales taxes. Look on the Internet for the sales tax charged in five U.S. states, then write a program that prints the tax rate for five states of your choice.

```
Sales Tax Rates
- - - - - - - - - - - - - - -
Alaska:      0%
Hawaii:      4%
   . . .
```

■ **Business E1.21** To speak more than one language is a valuable skill in the labor market today. One of the basic skills is learning to greet people. Write a program that prints a two-column list with the greeting phrases shown in the table. In the first column, print the phrase in English, in the second column, print the phrase in a language of your choice. If you don't speak a language other than English, use an online translator or ask a friend.

List of Phrases to Translate
Good morning.
It is a pleasure to meet you.
Please call me tomorrow.
Have a nice day!

PROGRAMMING PROJECTS

■■ P1.1 You want to decide whether you should drive your car to work or take the train. You know the one-way distance from your home to your place of work, and the fuel efficiency of your car (in miles per gallon). You also know the one-way price of a train ticket. You assume the cost of gas at $4 per gallon, and car maintenance at 5 cents per mile. Write an algorithm to decide which commute is cheaper.

■■ P1.2 You want to find out which fraction of your car's use is for commuting to work, and which is for personal use. You know the one-way distance from your home to work. For a particular period, you recorded the beginning and ending mileage on the odometer and the number of work days. Write an algorithm to settle this question.

■■■ P1.3 The value of π can be computed according to the following formula:

$$\frac{\pi}{4} = 1 - \frac{1}{3} + \frac{1}{5} - \frac{1}{7} + \frac{1}{9} - \cdots$$

Write an algorithm to compute π. Because the formula is an infinite series and an algorithm must stop after a finite number of steps, you should stop when you have the result determined to six significant digits.

■ Business P1.4 Imagine that you and a number of friends go to a luxury restaurant, and when you ask for the bill you want to split the amount and the tip (15 percent) between all. Write pseudocode for calculating the amount of money that everyone has to pay. Your program should print the amount of the bill, the tip, the total cost, and the amount each person has to pay. It should also print how much of what each person pays is for the bill and for the tip.

■■ P1.5 Write an algorithm to create a tile pattern composed of black and white tiles, with a fringe of black tiles all around and two or three black tiles in the center, equally spaced from the boundary. The inputs to your algorithm are the total number of rows and columns in the pattern.

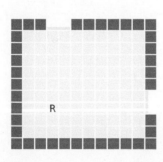

■■■ P1.6 Write an algorithm that allows a robot to mow a rectangular lawn, provided it has been placed in a corner, like this:

The robot (marked as R) can:
- Move forward by one unit.
- Turn left or right.
- Sense the color of the ground one unit in front of it.

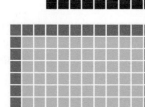

■■■ P1.7 Consider a robot that is placed in a room. The robot can:
- Move forward by one unit.
- Turn left or right.
- Sense what is in front of it: a wall, a window, or neither.

Write an algorithm that enables the robot, placed anywhere in the room, to count the number of windows. For example, in the room at right, the robot (marked as R) should find that it has two windows.

••• P1.8 Consider a robot that has been placed in a maze. The right-hand rule tells you how to escape from a maze: Always have the right hand next to a wall, and eventually you will find an exit. The robot can:

- Move forward by one unit.
- Turn left or right.
- Sense what is in front of it: a wall, an exit, or neither.

Write an algorithm that lets the robot escape the maze. You may assume that there is an exit that is reachable by the right-hand rule. Your challenge is to deal with situations in which the path turns. The robot can't see turns. It can only see what is directly in front of it.

© Skip ODonnell/iStockphoto.

••• Business P1.9 Suppose you received a loyalty promotion that lets you purchase one item, valued up to $100, from an online catalog. You want to make the best of the offer. You have a list of all items for sale, some of which are less than $100, some more. Write an algorithm to produce the item that is closest to $100. If there is more than one such item, list them all. Remember that a computer will inspect one item at a time—it can't just glance at a list and find the best one.

•• Science P1.10 A television manufacturer advertises that a television set has a certain size, measured diagonally. You wonder how the set will fit into your living room. Write an algorithm that yields the horizontal and vertical size of the television. Your inputs are the diagonal size and the aspect ratio (the ratio of width to height, usually 16 : 9 for television sets).

© Don Bayley/iStockPhoto.

••• Science P1.11 Cameras today can correct "red eye" problems caused when the photo flash makes eyes look red. Write pseudocode for an algorithm that can detect red eyes. Your input is a pattern of colors, such as that at right.

You are given the number of rows and columns. For any row or column number, you can query the color, which will be red, black, or something else. If you find that the center of the black pixels coincides with the center of the red pixels, you have found a red eye, and your output should be "yes". Otherwise, your output is "no".

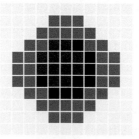

CHAPTER **2**

USING OBJECTS

© Lisa F. Young/iStockphoto.

CHAPTER GOALS

To learn about variables

To understand the concepts of classes and objects

To be able to call methods

To learn about arguments and return values

To be able to browse the API documentation

To implement test programs

To understand the difference between objects and object references

To write programs that display simple shapes

CHAPTER CONTENTS

Most useful programs don't just manipulate numbers and strings. Instead, they deal with data items that are more complex and that more closely represent entities in the real world. Examples of these data items include bank accounts, employee records, and graphical shapes.

The Java language is ideally suited for designing and manipulating such data items, or *objects*. In Java, you implement *classes* that describe the behavior of these objects. In this chapter, you will learn how to manipulate objects that belong to classes that have already been implemented. This will prepare you for the next chapter, in which you will learn how to implement your own classes.

2.1 Objects and Classes

When you write a computer program, you put it together from certain "building blocks". In Java, you build programs from objects. Each object has a particular behavior, and you can manipulate it to achieve certain effects.

As an analogy, think of a home builder who constructs a house from certain parts: doors, windows, walls, pipes, a furnace, a water heater, and so on. Each of these elements has a particular function, and they work together to fulfill a common purpose. Note that the home builder is not concerned with how to build a window or a water heater. These elements are readily available, and the builder's job is to integrate them into the house.

Of course, computer programs are more abstract than houses, and the objects that make up a computer program aren't as tangible as a window or a water heater. But the analogy holds well: A programmer produces a working program from elements with the desired functionality—the objects. In this chapter, you will learn the basics about using objects written by other programmers.

© Luc Meaille/iStockphoto.

Each part that a home builder uses, such as a furnace or a water heater, fulfills a particular function. Similarly, you build programs from objects, each of which has a particular behavior.

2.1.1 Using Objects

Objects are entities in your program that you manipulate by calling methods.

An **object** is an entity that you can manipulate by calling one or more of its **methods**. A method consists of a sequence of instructions that can access the internal data of an object. When you call the method, you do not know exactly what those instructions are, or even how the object is organized internally. However, the behavior of the method is well defined, and that is what matters to us when we use it.

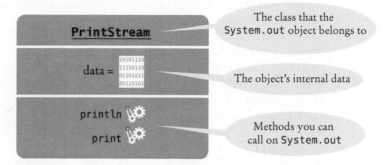

Figure 1   Representation of the System.out Object

> A method is a sequence of instructions that accesses the data of an object.

For example, you saw in Chapter 1 that System.out refers to an object. You manipulate it by calling the println method. When the println method is called, some activities occur inside the object, and the ultimate effect is that text appears in the console window. You don't know how that happens, and that's OK. What matters is that the method carries out the work that you requested.

Figure 1 shows a representation of the System.out object. The internal data is symbolized by a sequence of zeroes and ones. Think of each method (symbolized by the gears) as a piece of machinery that carries out its assigned task.

In general, think of an object as an entity that can do work for you when you call its methods. How the work is done is not important to the programmer using the object.

In the remainder of this chapter, you will see other objects and the methods that they can carry out.

You can think of a water heater as an object that can carry out the "get hot water" method. When you call that method to enjoy a hot shower, you don't care whether the water heater uses gas or solar power.

© Steven Frame/iStockphoto.

2.1.2 Classes

In Chapter 1, you encountered two objects:

- System.out
- "Hello, World!"

Each of these objects belongs to a different **class**. The System.out object belongs to the PrintStream class. The "Hello, World!" object belongs to the String class. Of course, there are many more String objects, such as "Goodbye" or "Mississippi". They all have something in common—you can invoke the same methods on all strings. You will see some of these methods in Section 2.3.

> A class describes a set of objects with the same behavior.

As you will see in Chapter 11, you can construct objects of the PrintStream class other than System.out. Those objects write data to files or other destinations instead of the console. Still, all PrintStream objects share common behavior. You can invoke the println and print methods on any PrintStream object, and the printed values are sent to their destination.

Of course, the objects of the Print-Stream class have a completely different behavior than the objects of the String class. You could not call println on a String object. A string wouldn't know how to send itself to a console window or file.

© Arcaid Images/Alamy Inc.

As you can see, different classes have different responsibilities. A string knows about the letters that it contains, but it does not know how to display them to a human or to save them to a file.

All objects of a Window *class share the same behavior.*

2.2 Variables

Before we continue with the main topic of this chapter—the behavior of objects—we need to go over some basic programming terminology. In the following sections, you will learn about the concepts of variables, types, and assignment.

2.2.1 Variable Declarations

When your program manipulates objects, you will want to store the objects and the values that their methods return, so that you can use them later. In a Java program, you use variables to store values. The following statement declares a variable named width:

```
int width = 20;
```

A variable is a storage location with a name.

A **variable** is a storage location in a computer program. Each variable has a name and holds a value.

A variable is similar to a parking space in a parking garage. The parking space has an identifier (such as "J 053"), and it can hold a vehicle. A variable has a name (such as width), and it can hold a value (such as 20).

Like a variable in a computer program, a parking space has an identifier and contents.

Javier Larrea/Age Fotostock.

Syntax 2.1 Variable Declaration

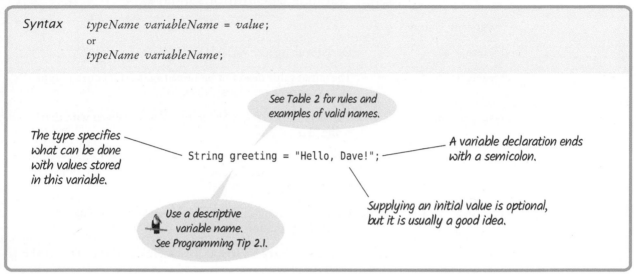

Syntax   *typeName* *variableName* = *value*;
           or
           typeName *variableName*;

The type specifies what can be done with values stored in this variable.

See Table 2 for rules and examples of valid names.

`String greeting = "Hello, Dave!";`

A variable declaration ends with a semicolon.

Use a descriptive variable name. See Programming Tip 2.1.

Supplying an initial value is optional, but it is usually a good idea.

When declaring a variable, you usually specify an initial value.

When declaring a variable, you usually want to **initialize** it. That is, you specify the value that should be stored in the variable. Consider again this variable declaration:

```
int width = 20;
```

The variable width is initialized with the value 20.

When declaring a variable, you also specify the type of its values.

Like a parking space that is restricted to a certain type of vehicle (such as a compact car, motorcycle, or electric vehicle), a variable in Java stores data of a specific type. Java supports quite a few data types: numbers, text strings, files, dates, and many others. You must specify the type whenever you declare a variable (see Syntax 2.1).

The width variable is an **integer**, a whole number without a fractional part. In Java, this type is called int.

Note that the type comes before the variable name:

```
int width = 20;
```

After you have declared and initialized a variable, you can use it. For example,

```
int width = 20;
System.out.println(width);
int area = width * width;
```

Table 1 shows several examples of variable declarations.

Each parking space is suitable for a particular type of vehicle, just as each variable holds a value of a particular type.   © Ingenui/iStockphoto.

Table 1   Variable Declarations in Java

Variable Name	Comment
`int width = 20;`	Declares an integer variable and initializes it with 20.
`int perimeter = 4 * width;`	The initial value need not be a fixed value. (Of course, `width` must have been previously declared.)
`String greeting = "Hi!";`	This variable has the type `String` and is initialized with the string "Hi".
🚫 `height = 30;`	**Error:** The type is missing. This statement is not a declaration but an assignment of a new value to an existing variable—see Section 2.2.5.
🚫 `int width = "20";`	**Error:** You cannot initialize a number with the string "20". (Note the quotation marks.)
`int width;`	Declares an integer variable without initializing it. This can be a cause for errors—see Common Error 2.1.
`int width, height;`	Declares two integer variables in a single statement. In this book, we will declare each variable in a separate statement.

2.2.2 Types

Use the int type for numbers that cannot have a fractional part.

In Java, there are several different types of numbers. You use the `int` type to denote a whole number without a fractional part. For example, suppose you count the number of cars in a parking lot. The counter must be an integer number—you cannot have a fraction of a car.

When a fractional part is required (such as in the number 22.5), we use **floating-point numbers**. The most commonly used type for floating-point numbers in Java is called `double`. Here is the declaration of a floating-point variable:

```
double milesPerGallon = 22.5;
```

Use the double type for floating-point numbers.

You can combine numbers with the + and - operators, as in `width + 10` or `width - 1`. To multiply two numbers, use the * operator. For example, 2 × *width* is written as `2 * width`. Use the / operator for division, such as `width / 2`.

Numbers can be combined by arithmetic operators such as +, -, and *.

As in mathematics, the * and / operator bind more strongly than the + and - operators. That is, `width + height * 2` means the sum of `width` and the product `height * 2`. If you want to multiply the sum by 2, use parentheses: `(width + height) * 2`.

Not all types are number types. For example, the value `"Hello"` has the type `String`. You need to specify that type when you define a variable that holds a string:

```
String greeting = "Hello";
```

A type specifies the operations that can be carried out with its values.

Types are important because they indicate what you can do with a variable. For example, consider the variable `width`. It's type is `int`. Therefore, you can multiply the value that it holds with another number. But the type of `greeting` is `String`. You can't multiply a string with another number. (You will see in Section 2.3.1 what you can do with strings.)

2.2.3 Names

When you declare a variable, you should pick a name that explains its purpose. For example, it is better to use a descriptive name, such as milesPerGallon, than a terse name, such as mpg.

In Java, there are a few simple rules for the names of variables, methods, and classes:

1. Names must start with a letter or the underscore (_) character, and the remaining characters must be letters, numbers, or underscores. (Technically, the $ symbol is allowed as well, but you should not use it—it is intended for names that are automatically generated by tools.)

2. You cannot use other symbols such as ? or %. Spaces are not permitted inside names either. You can use uppercase letters to denote word boundaries, as in milesPerGallon. This naming convention is called *camel case* because the uppercase letters in the middle of the name look like the humps of a camel.)

© GlobalP/iStockphoto.

3. Names are **case sensitive**, that is, milesPerGallon and milespergallon are different names.

4. You cannot use **reserved words** such as double or class as names; these words are reserved exclusively for their special Java meanings. (See Appendix C for a listing of all reserved words in Java.)

> By convention, variable names should start with a lowercase letter.

It is a convention among Java programmers that names of variables and methods start with a lowercase letter (such as milesPerGallon). Class names should start with an uppercase letter (such as HelloPrinter). That way, it is easy to tell them apart.

Table 2 shows examples of legal and illegal variable names in Java.

Table 2 Variable Names in Java

Variable Name	Comment
distance_1	Names consist of letters, numbers, and the underscore character.
x	In mathematics, you use short variable names such as *x* or *y*. This is legal in Java, but not very common, because it can make programs harder to understand (see Programming Tip 2.1).
⚠ CanVolume	**Caution:** Names are case sensitive. This variable name is different from canVolume, and it violates the convention that variable names should start with a lowercase letter.
🚫 6pack	**Error:** Names cannot start with a number.
🚫 can volume	**Error:** Names cannot contain spaces.
🚫 double	**Error:** You cannot use a reserved word as a name.
🚫 miles/gal	**Error:** You cannot use symbols such as / in names.

2.2.4 Comments

As your programs get more complex, you should add **comments**, explanations for human readers of your code. For example, here is a comment that explains the value used to initialize a variable:

```
double milesPerGallon = 35.5; // The average fuel efficiency of new U.S. cars in 2013
```

This comment explains the significance of the value **35.5** to a human reader. The compiler does not process comments at all. It ignores everything from a // delimiter to the end of the line.

> Use comments to add explanations for humans who read your code. The compiler ignores comments.

It is a good practice to provide comments. This helps programmers who read your code understand your intent. In addition, you will find comments helpful when you review your own programs.

You use the // delimiter for short comments. If you have a longer comment, enclose it between /* and */ delimiters. The compiler ignores these delimiters and everything in between. For example,

```
/*
    In most countries, fuel efficiency is measured in liters per hundred
    kilometer. Perhaps that is more useful—it tells you how much gas you need
    to purchase to drive a given distance. Here is the conversion formula.
*/
double fuelEfficiency = 235.214583 / milesPerGallon;
```

2.2.5 Assignment

> Use the assignment operator (=) to change the value of a variable.

You can change the value of a variable with the assignment operator (=). For example, consider the variable declaration

```
int width = 10; ❶
```

If you want to change the value of the variable, simply assign the new value:

```
width = 20; ❷
```

The assignment replaces the original value of the variable (see Figure 2).

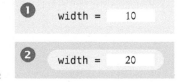

Figure 2
Assigning a New Value to a Variable

It is an error to use a variable that has never had a value assigned to it. For example, the following assignment statement has an error:

```
int height;
int width = height;   // ERROR—uninitialized variable height
```

The compiler will complain about an **"uninitialized variable"** when you use a variable that has never been assigned a value. (See Figure 3.)

Figure 3
An Uninitialized Variable

height = [   ]   No value has been assigned.

Syntax 2.2 Assignment

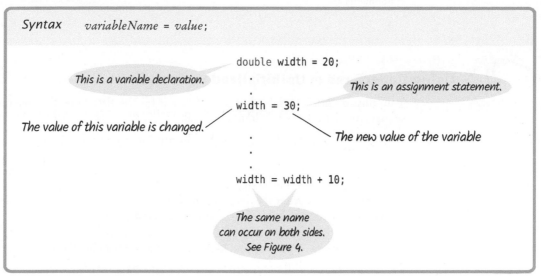

Syntax	*variableName = value;*

This is a variable declaration. → `double width = 20;` ← This is an assignment statement.

The value of this variable is changed. → `width = 30;` ← The new value of the variable

`width = width + 10;`

The same name can occur on both sides. See Figure 4.

All variables must be initialized before you access them.

The remedy is to assign a value to the variable before you use it:

```
int height = 20;
int width = height; // OK
```

The right-hand side of the = symbol can be a mathematical expression. For example,

```
width = height + 10;
```

This means "compute the value of `height + 10` and store that value in the variable `width`".

The assignment operator = does *not* denote mathematical equality.

In the Java programming language, the = operator denotes an *action*, namely to replace the value of a variable. This usage differs from the mathematical usage of the = symbol as a statement about equality. For example, in Java, the following statement is entirely legal:

```
width = width + 10;
```

This means "compute the value of `width + 10` ❶ and store that value in the variable `width` ❷" (see Figure 4).

In Java, it is not a problem that the variable width is used on both sides of the = symbol. Of course, in mathematics, the equation *width = width* + 10 has no solution.

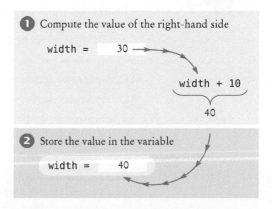

❶ Compute the value of the right-hand side

width =   30 →

width + 10

40

❷ Store the value in the variable

width =   40

Figure 4
Executing the Statement
`width = width + 10`

EXAMPLE CODE See sec02 of your eText or companion code for a program that demonstrates variables and assignments.

Common Error 2.1

Using Undeclared or Uninitialized Variables

You must declare a variable before you use it for the first time. For example, the following sequence of statements would not be legal:

```
int perimeter = 4 * width; // ERROR: width not yet declared
int width = 20;
```

In your program, the statements are compiled in order. When the compiler reaches the first statement, it does not know that width will be declared in the next line, and it reports an error. The remedy is to reorder the declarations so that each variable is declared before it is used.

A related error is to leave a variable uninitialized:

```
int width;
int perimeter = 4 * width; // ERROR: width not yet initialized
```

The Java compiler will complain that you are using a variable that has not yet been given a value. The remedy is to assign a value to the variable before it is used.

Common Error 2.2

Confusing Variable Declarations and Assignment Statements

Suppose your program declares a variable as follows:

```
int width = 20;
```

If you want to change the value of the variable, you use an assignment statement:

```
width = 30;
```

It is a common error to accidentally use another variable declaration:

```
int width = 30; // ERROR—starts with int and is therefore a declaration
```

But there is already a variable named width. The compiler will complain that you are trying to declare another variable with the same name.

Programming Tip 2.1

Choose Descriptive Variable Names

In algebra, variable names are usually just one letter long, such as p or A, maybe with a subscript such as p_1. You might be tempted to save yourself a lot of typing by using short variable names in your Java programs:

```
int a = w * h;
```

Compare that statement with the following one:

```
int area = width * height;
```

The advantage is obvious. Reading width is much easier than reading w and then figuring out that it must mean "width".

In practical programming, descriptive variable names are particularly important when programs are written by more than one person. It may be obvious to you that w stands for width, but is it obvious to the person who needs to update your code years later? For that matter, will you yourself remember what w means when you look at the code a month from now?

Special Topic 2.1

Variable Type Inference

As of Java 10, you need not specify the type of a variable that you initialize. For example, instead of

```
double milesPerGallon = 22.5;
String greeting = "Hello";
```

you can write:

```
var milesPerGallon = 22.5;
var greeting = "Hello";
```

The Java compiler infers the type of the variable from the type of the initial value. This is a convenient shortcut for longer type names. However, the explicit types provide useful information, and we will not use the var syntax in this book.

2.3 Calling Methods

A program performs useful work by calling methods on its objects. In this section, we examine how to supply values in a method, and how to obtain the result of the method.

2.3.1 The Public Interface of a Class

You use an object by calling its methods. All objects of a given class share a common set of methods. For example, the PrintStream class provides methods for its objects (such as println and print). Similarly, the String class provides methods that you can apply to String objects. One of them is the length method. The length method counts the number of characters in a string. You can apply that method to any object of type String. For example, the sequence of statements:

```
String greeting = "Hello, World!";
int numberOfCharacters = greeting.length();
```

sets numberOfCharacters to the length of the String object "Hello, World!". After the instructions in the length method are executed, numberOfCharacters is set to 13. (The quotation marks are not part of the string, and the length method does not count them.)

When calling the length method, you do not supply any values inside the parentheses. Also note that the length method does not produce any visible output. It returns a value that is subsequently used in the program.

Let's look at another method of the String class. When you apply the toUpperCase method to a String object, the method creates another String object that contains the characters of the original string, with lowercase letters converted to uppercase. For example, the sequence of statements

```
String river = "Mississippi";
String bigRiver = river.toUpperCase();
```

sets bigRiver to the String object "MISSISSIPPI".

© Damir Cudic/iStockphoto.

The controls of a car form its public interface. The private implementation is under the hood.

> The public interface of a class specifies what you can do with its objects. The hidden implementation describes how these actions are carried out.

The String class declares many other methods besides the length and toUpper-Case methods—you will learn about many of them in Chapter 4. Collectively, the methods form the **public interface** of the class, telling you what you can do with the objects of the class. A class also declares a *private implementation*, describing the data inside its objects and the instructions for its methods. Those details are hidden from the programmers who use objects and call methods.

Figure 5 shows two objects of the String class. Each object stores its own data (drawn as boxes that contain characters). Both objects support the same set of methods—the public interface that is specified by the String class.

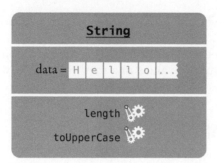
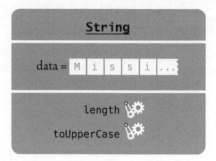

Figure 5 A Representation of Two String Objects

2.3.2 Method Arguments

> An argument is a value that is supplied in a method call.

Most methods require values that give details about the work that the method needs to do. For example, when you call the println method, you must supply the string that should be printed. Computer scientists use the technical term **argument** for method inputs.

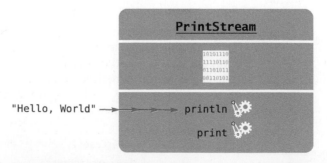

Figure 6 Passing an Argument to the println Method

We say that the string `greeting` is an argument of the method call

```
System.out.println(greeting);
```

Figure 6 illustrates passing the argument to the method.

Some methods require multiple arguments; others don't require any arguments at all. An example of the latter is the `length` method of the `String` class (see Figure 7). All the information that the `length` method requires to do its job—namely, the character sequence of the string—is stored in the object that carries out the method.

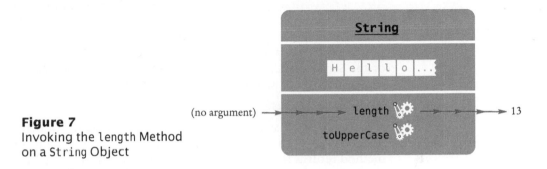

Figure 7
Invoking the `length` Method
on a `String` Object

2.3.3 Return Values

The return value of a method is a result that the method has computed.

Some methods, such as the `println` method, carry out an action for you. Other methods compute and return a value. For example, the `length` method *returns a value*, namely the number of characters in the string. You can store the return value in a variable:

```
int numberOfCharacters = greeting.length();
```

You can also use the return value of one method as an argument of another method:

```
System.out.println(greeting.length());
```

The method call `greeting.length()` returns a value—the integer 13. The return value becomes an argument of the `println` method. Figure 8 shows the process.

Not all methods return values. One example is the `println` method. The `println` method interacts with the operating system, causing characters to appear in a window. But it does not return a value to the code that calls it.

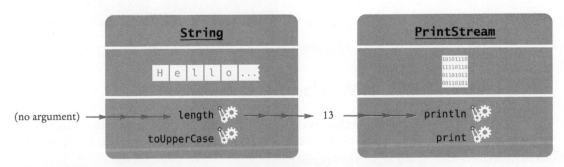

Figure 8   Passing the Result of a Method Call to Another Method

At this tailor shop, the customer's measurements and the fabric are the arguments of the sew method. The return value is the finished garment.

© Loentura/iStockphoto.

Let us analyze a more complex method call. Here, we will call the `replace` method of the `String` class. The `replace` method carries out a search-and-replace operation, similar to that of a word processor. For example, the call

```
river.replace("issipp", "our")
```

constructs a new string that is obtained by replacing all occurrences of `"issipp"` in `"Mississippi"` with `"our"`. (In this situation, there was only one replacement.) The method returns the `String` object `"Missouri"`. You can save that string in a variable:

```
river = river.replace("issipp", "our");
```

Or you can pass it to another method:

```
System.out.println(river.replace("issipp", "our"));
```

As Figure 9 shows, this method call

- Is invoked on a `String` object: `"Mississippi"`
- Has two arguments: the strings `"issipp"` and `"our"`
- Returns a value: the string `"Missouri"`

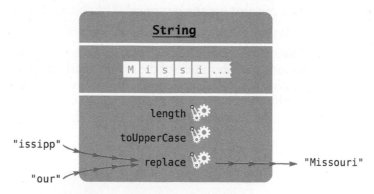

Figure 9 Calling the replace Method

2.3.4 Method Declarations

When a method is declared in a class, the declaration specifies the types of the arguments and the return value. For example, the `String` class declares the `length` method as

```
public int length()
```

Table 3   Method Arguments and Return Values

Example	Comments
`System.out.println(greeting)`	`greeting` is an argument of the `println` method.
`greeting.replace("e","3")`	The `replace` method has two arguments, in this case `"e"` and `"3"`.
`greeting.length()`	The `length` method has no arguments.
`int n = greeting.length();`	The `length` method returns an integer value.
`System.out.println(n);`	The `println` method returns no value. In the API documentation, its return type is `void`.
`System.out.println(greeting.length());`	The return value of one method can become the argument of another.

That is, there are no arguments, and the return value has the type `int`. (For now, all the methods that we consider will be "public" methods—see Chapter 9 for more restricted methods.)

The `replace` method is declared as

```
public String replace(String target, String replacement)
```

To call the `replace` method, you supply two arguments, `target` and `replacement`, which both have type `String`. The returned value is another string.

When a method returns no value, the return type is declared with the reserved word **void**. For example, the `PrintStream` class declares the `println` method as

```
public void println(String output)
```

Occasionally, a class declares two methods with the same name and different argument types. For example, the `PrintStream` class declares a second method, also called `println`, as

```
public void println(int output)
```

That method is used to print an integer value. We say that the `println` name is **overloaded** because it refers to more than one method.

EXAMPLE CODE   See sec03 of your eText or companion code for a program that demonstrates method calls.

Programming Tip 2.2
Learn By Trying

When you learn about a new method, write a small program to try it out. For example, you can go right now to your Java development environment and run this program:

```
public class ReplaceDemo
{
   public static void main(String[] args)
   {
      String river = "Mississippi";
      System.out.println(river.replace("issipp", "our"));
   }
}
```

Then you can see with your own eyes what the `replace` method does. Also, you can run experiments. Does `replace` change every match, or only the first one? Try it out:

```
System.out.println(river.replace("i", "x"));
```

Set up your work environment to make this kind of experimentation easy and natural. Keep a file with the blank outline of a Java program around, so you can copy and paste it when needed. Some development environments let you type commands into a window and show you the result right away, without having to make a `main` method, and without calling `System.out.println` (see Figure 10).

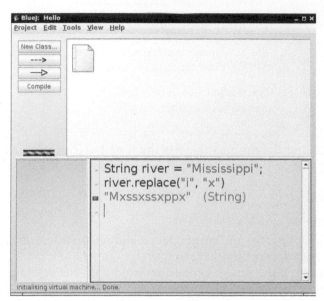

Figure 10 The BlueJ Code Pad and JShell

2.4 Constructing Objects

Generally, when you want to use objects in your program, you need to specify their initial properties by *constructing* them.

To learn about object construction, we need to go beyond `String` objects and the `System.out` object. Let us turn to another class in the Java library: the `Rectangle` class. Objects of type `Rectangle` describe rectangular shapes. These objects are useful for a variety of purposes. You can assemble rectangles into bar charts, and you can program simple games by moving rectangles inside a window.

Note that a `Rectangle` object isn't a rectangular shape—it's an object that contains a set of numbers. The numbers *describe* the rectangle (see Figure 11). Each rectangle is described by the *x*- and *y*-coordinates of its top-left corner, its width, and its height.

© sinankocasian/iStockphoto.

Objects of the `Rectangle` *class describe rectangular shapes.*

Rectangle			Rectangle			Rectangle	
x =	5		x =	35		x =	45
y =	10		y =	30		y =	0
width =	20		width =	20		width =	30
height =	30		height =	20		height =	20

Figure 11 Rectangle Objects

It is very important that you understand this distinction. In the computer, a Rectangle object is a block of memory that holds four numbers, for example $x = 5$, $y = 10$, $width = 20$, $height = 30$. In the imagination of the programmer who uses a Rectangle object, the object describes a geometric figure.

> Use the new operator, followed by a class name and arguments, to construct new objects.

To make a new rectangle, you need to specify the x, y, *width*, and *height* values. Then *invoke the* new *operator*, specifying the name of the class and the argument(s) required for constructing a new object. For example, you can make a new rectangle with its top-left corner at (5, 10), width 20, and height 30 as follows:

```
new Rectangle(5, 10, 20, 30)
```

Here is what happens in detail:

1. The new operator makes a Rectangle object.
2. It uses the arguments (in this case, 5, 10, 20, and 30) to initialize the object's data.
3. It returns the object.

The process of creating a new object is called **construction**. The four values 5, 10, 20, and 30 are called the *construction arguments*.

The new expression yields an object, and you need to store the object if you want to use it later. Usually you assign the output of the new operator to a variable. For example,

```
Rectangle box = new Rectangle(5, 10, 20, 30);
```

Syntax 2.3 Object Construction

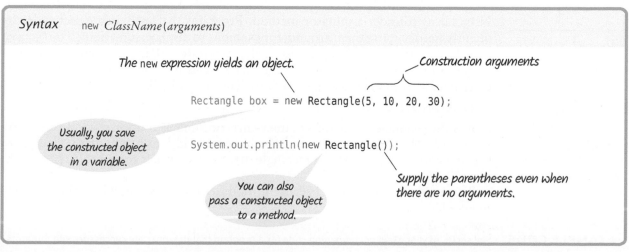

Syntax   new *ClassName(arguments)*

The new *expression yields an object.*   *Construction arguments*

```
Rectangle box = new Rectangle(5, 10, 20, 30);
```

Usually, you save the constructed object in a variable.

```
System.out.println(new Rectangle());
```

You can also pass a constructed object to a method.

Supply the parentheses even when there are no arguments.

Some classes let you construct objects in multiple ways. For example, you can also obtain a Rectangle object by supplying no construction arguments at all (but you must still supply the parentheses):

```
new Rectangle()
```

This expression constructs a (rather useless) rectangle with its top-left corner at the origin (0, 0), width 0, and height 0.

EXAMPLE CODE   See sec04 of your eText or companion code for a program that demonstrates constructors.

Common Error 2.3

Trying to Invoke a Constructor Like a Method

Constructors are not methods. You can only use a constructor with the new operator, not to reinitialize an existing object:

```
box.Rectangle(20, 35, 20, 30); // Error—can't reinitialize object
```

The remedy is simple: Make a new object and overwrite the current one stored by box.

```
box = new Rectangle(20, 35, 20, 30); // OK
```

2.5 Accessor and Mutator Methods

An accessor method does not change the internal data of the object on which it is invoked. A mutator method changes the data.

In this section we introduce a useful terminology for the methods of a class. A method that accesses an object and returns some information about it, without changing the object, is called an **accessor method**. In contrast, a method whose purpose is to modify the internal data of an object is called a **mutator method**.

For example, the length method of the String class is an accessor method. It returns information about a string, namely its length. But it doesn't modify the string at all when counting the characters.

The Rectangle class has a number of accessor methods. The getX, getY, getWidth, and getHeight methods return the x- and y-coordinates of the top-left corner, the width, and the height values. For example,

```
double width = box.getWidth();
```

Now let us consider a mutator method. Programs that manipulate rectangles frequently need to move them around, for example, to display animations. The Rectangle class has a method for that purpose, called translate. (Mathematicians use the term "translation" for a rigid motion of the plane.) This method moves a rectangle by a certain distance in the x- and y-directions. The method call,

```
box.translate(15, 25);
```

moves the rectangle by 15 units in the x-direction and 25 units in the y-direction (see Figure 12). Moving a rectangle doesn't change its width or height, but it changes the top-left corner. Afterward, the rectangle that had its top-left corner at (5, 10) now has it at (20, 35).

This method is a mutator because it modifies the object on which the method is invoked.

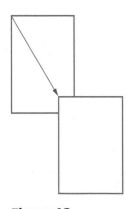

Figure 12
Using the translate Method to Move a Rectangle

EXAMPLE CODE   See sec05 of your eText or companion code for a program that demonstrates accessors and mutators.

2.6 The API Documentation

The API (Application Programming Interface) documentation lists the classes and methods of the Java library.

The classes and methods of the Java library are listed in the **API documentation**. The API is the "application programming interface". A programmer who uses the Java classes to put together a computer program (or *application*) is an *application programmer*. That's you. In contrast, the programmers who designed and implemented the library classes such as PrintStream and Rectangle are *system programmers*.

You can find the API documentation on the Web. Point your web browser to http://docs.oracle.com/javase/10/docs/api/index.html. An abbreviated version of the API documentation is provided in Appendix D that may be easier to use at first, but you should eventually move on to the real thing.

2.6.1 Browsing the API Documentation

The API documentation documents all classes in the Java library—there are thousands of them (see Figure 13, top). Most of the classes are rather specialized, and only a few are of interest to the beginning programmer.

Locate the Rectangle link in the left pane, preferably by using the search function of your browser. Click on the link, and the right pane shows all the features of the Rectangle class (see Figure 13, bottom).

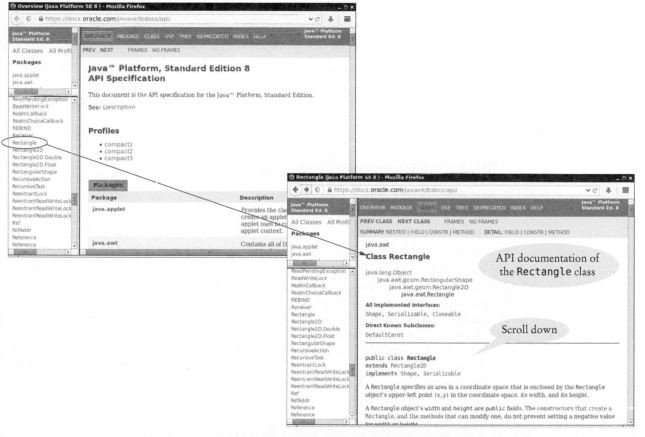

Figure 13 The API Documentation of the Standard Java Library

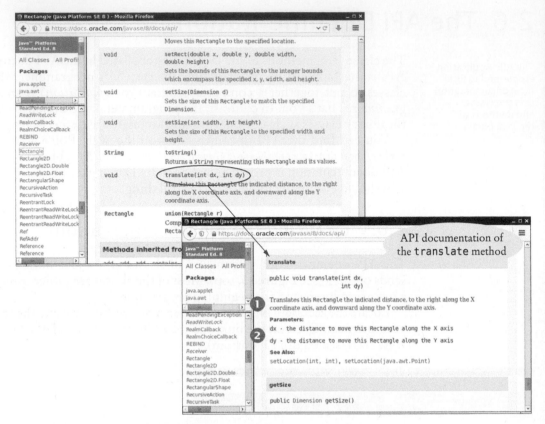

Figure 14 The Method Summary for the Rectangle Class

The API documentation for each class starts out with a section that describes the purpose of the class. Then come summary tables for the constructors and methods (see Figure 14, top). Click on a method's link to get a detailed description (see Figure 14, bottom).

The detailed description of a method shows

- The action that the method carries out. ❶
- The types and names of the parameter variables that receive the arguments when the method is called. ❷
- The value that it returns (or the reserved word void if the method doesn't return any value).

As you can see, the Rectangle class has quite a few methods. While occasionally intimidating for the beginning programmer, this is a strength of the standard library. If you ever need to do a computation involving rectangles, chances are that there is a method that does all the work for you.

For example, suppose you want to change the width or height of a rectangle. If you browse through the API documentation, you will find a setSize method with the description "Sets the size of this Rectangle to the specified width and height." The method has two arguments, described as

- width - the new width for this Rectangle
- height - the new height for this Rectangle

We can use this information to change the box object so that it is a square of side length 40. The name of the method is setSize, and we supply two arguments: the new width and height:

```
box.setSize(40, 40);
```

2.6.2 Packages

The API documentation contains another important piece of information about each class. The classes in the standard library are organized into **packages**. A package is a collection of classes with a related purpose. The Rectangle class belongs to the package java.awt (where awt is an abbreviation for "Abstract Windowing Toolkit"), which contains many classes for drawing windows and graphical shapes. You can see the package name java.awt in Figure 13, just above the class name.

To use the Rectangle class from the java.awt package, you must *import* the package. Simply place the following line at the top of your program:

```
import java.awt.Rectangle;
```

> Java classes are grouped into packages. Use the import statement to use classes that are declared in other packages.

Why don't you have to import the System and String classes? Because the System and String classes are in the java.lang package, and all classes from this package are automatically imported, so you never need to import them yourself.

Syntax 2.4   Importing a Class from a Package

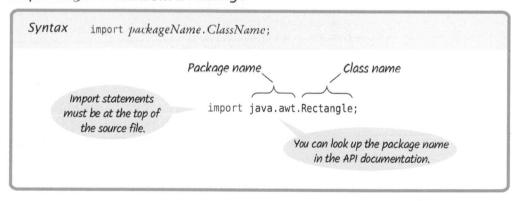

![toucan]

Programming Tip 2.3

Don't Memorize—Use Online Help

The Java library has thousands of classes and methods. It is neither necessary nor useful trying to memorize them. Instead, you should become familiar with using the API documentation. Because you will need to use the API documentation all the time, it is best to download and install it onto your computer, particularly if your computer is not always connected to the Internet. You can download the documentation from http://www.oracle.com/technetwork/java/javase/downloads/index.html.

2.7 Implementing a Test Program

A test program
verifies that methods
behave as expected.

In this section, we discuss the steps that are necessary to implement a test program. The purpose of a test program is to verify that one or more methods have been implemented correctly. A test program calls methods and checks that they return the expected results. Writing test programs is a very important skill.

In this section, we will develop a simple program that tests a method in the Rectangle class using these steps:

1. Provide a tester class.
2. Supply a main method.
3. Inside the main method, construct one or more objects.
4. Apply methods to the objects.
5. Display the results of the method calls.
6. Display the values that you expect to get.

Our sample test program tests the behavior of the translate method. Here are the key steps (which have been placed inside the main method of the MoveTester class).

```java
Rectangle box = new Rectangle(5, 10, 20, 30);

// Move the rectangle
box.translate(15, 25);

// Print information about the moved rectangle
System.out.print("x: ");
System.out.println(box.getX());
System.out.println("Expected: 20");
```

We print the value that is returned by the getX method, and then we print a message that describes the value we expect to see.

Determining the
expected result
in advance is an
important part
of testing.

This is a very important step. You want to spend some time thinking about the expected result before you run a test program. This thought process will help you understand how your program should behave, and it can help you track down errors at an early stage. Finding and fixing errors early is a very effective strategy that can save you a great deal of time.

In our case, the rectangle has been constructed with the top-left corner at (5, 10). The x-direction is moved by 15, so we expect an x-value of 5 + 15 = 20 after the move.

Here is the program that tests the moving of a rectangle.

sec07/MoveTester.java

```java
1  import java.awt.Rectangle;
2
3  public class MoveTester
4  {
5     public static void main(String[] args)
6     {
7        Rectangle box = new Rectangle(5, 10, 20, 30);
8
9        // Move the rectangle
10       box.translate(15, 25);
11
```

```
12         // Print information about the moved rectangle
13         System.out.print("x: ");
14         System.out.println(box.getX());
15         System.out.println("Expected: 20");
16
17         System.out.print("y: ");
18         System.out.println(box.getY());
19         System.out.println("Expected: 35");
20      }
21  }
```

Program Run

```
x: 20
Expected: 20
y: 35
Expected: 35
```

Special Topic 2.2

Testing Classes in an Interactive Environment

Some development environments are specifically designed to help students explore objects without having to provide tester classes. These environments can be very helpful for gaining insight into the behavior of objects, and for promoting object-oriented thinking. The BlueJ environment (shown in the figure) displays objects as blobs on a workbench.

You can construct new objects, put them on the workbench, invoke methods, and see the return values, all without writing a line of code. You can download BlueJ at no charge from http://www.bluej.org. Another excellent environment for interactively exploring objects is Dr. Java at http://drjava.sourceforge.net.

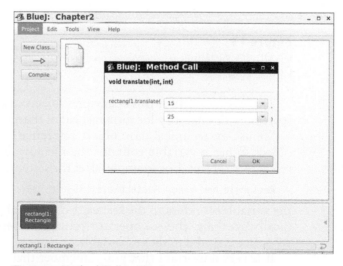

Testing a Method Call in BlueJ

WORKED EXAMPLE 2.1

How Many Days Have You Been Alive?

Explore the API of a class Day that represents a calendar day. Using that class, learn to write a program that computes how many days have elapsed since the day you were born. See your eText or visit wiley.com/go/bjeo7.

WORKED EXAMPLE 2.2

Working with Pictures

Learn how to use the API of a Picture class to edit photos. See your eText or visit wiley.com/go/bjeo7.

Cay Horstmann.

2.8 Object References

In Java, an object variable (that is, a variable whose type is a class) does not actually hold an object. It merely holds the *memory location* of an object. The object itself is stored elsewhere—see Figure 15.

box =

Rectangle

x =	5
y =	10
width =	20
height =	30

Figure 15
An Object Variable
Containing an Object Reference

There is a reason for this behavior. Objects can be very large. It is more efficient to store only the memory location instead of the entire object.

We use the technical term **object reference** to denote the memory location of an object. When a variable contains the memory location of an object, we say that it *refers* to an object. For example, after the statement

> An object reference describes the location of an object.

```java
Rectangle box = new Rectangle(5, 10, 20, 30);
```

the variable box refers to the Rectangle object that the new operator constructed. Technically speaking, the new operator returned a reference to the new object, and that reference is stored in the box variable.

It is very important that you remember that the box variable *does not contain* the object. It *refers* to the object. Two object variables can refer to the same object:

> Multiple object variables can contain references to the same object.

```java
Rectangle box2 = box;
```

Now you can access the same Rectangle object as box and as box2, as shown in Figure 16.

© Jacob Wackerhausen/iStockphoto.

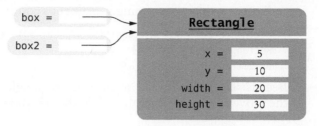

Figure 16 Two Object Variables Referring to the Same Object

In Java, numbers are not objects. Number variables actually store numbers. When you declare

```
int luckyNumber = 13;
```

then the luckyNumber variable holds the number 13, not a reference to the number (see Figure 17). The reason is again efficiency. Because numbers require little storage, it is more efficient to store them directly in a variable.

> luckyNumber = 13

Figure 17 A Number Variable Stores a Number

Number variables store numbers. Object variables store references.

You can see the difference between number variables and object variables when you make a copy of a variable. When you copy a number, the original and the copy of the number are independent values. But when you copy an object reference, both the original and the copy are references to the same object.

Consider the following code, which copies a number and then changes the copy (see Figure 18):

```
int luckyNumber = 13; ❶
int luckyNumber2 = luckyNumber; ❷
luckyNumber2 = 12; ❸
```

Now the variable luckyNumber contains the value 13, and luckyNumber2 contains 12.

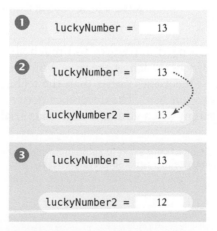

Figure 18 Copying Numbers

Now consider the seemingly analogous code with Rectangle objects (see Figure 19).

```
Rectangle box = new Rectangle(5, 10, 20, 30); ❶
Rectangle box2 = box; ❷
box2.translate(15, 25);   ❸
```

Because box and box2 refer to the same rectangle after step ❷, both variables refer to the moved rectangle after the call to the translate method.

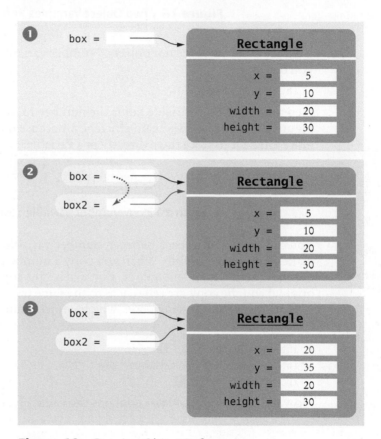

Figure 19   Copying Object References

You need not worry too much about the difference between objects and object references. Much of the time, you will have the correct intuition when you think of the "object box" rather than the technically more accurate "object reference stored in variable box". The difference between objects and object references only becomes apparent when you have multiple variables that refer to the same object.

EXAMPLE CODE   See sec08 of your eText or companion code for a program that demonstrates the difference between copying numbers and object references.

Computing & Society 2.1   Computer Monopoly

When International Business Machines Corporation (IBM), a successful manufacturer of punched-card equipment for tabulating data, first turned its attention to designing computers in the early 1950s, its planners assumed that there was a market for perhaps 50 such devices, for installation by the government, the military, and a few of the country's largest corporations. Instead, they sold about 1,500 machines of their System 650 model and went on to build and sell more powerful computers.

These computers, called mainframes, were huge. They filled rooms, which had to be climate-controlled to protect the delicate equipment. IBM was not the first company to build mainframe computers; that honor belongs to the Univac Corporation. However, IBM soon became the major player, partially because of its technical excellence and attention to customer needs and partially because it exploited its strengths and structured its products and services in a way that made it difficult for customers to mix them with those of other vendors.

As all of IBM's competitors fell on hard times, the U.S. government brought an antitrust suit against IBM in 1969. In the United States, it is legal to be a monopoly supplier, but it is not legal to use one's monopoly in one market to gain supremacy in another. IBM was accused of forcing customers to buy bundles of computers, software, and peripherals, making it impossible for other vendors of software and peripherals to compete.

The suit went to trial in 1975 and dragged on until 1982, when it was abandoned, largely because new

© Timofeev Vladimir/Shutterstock.

A Mainframe Computer

waves of smaller computers had made it irrelevant.

In fact, when IBM offered its first personal computers, its operating system was supplied by an outside vendor, Microsoft, which became so dominant that it too was sued by the U.S. government for abusing its monopoly position in 1998. Microsoft was accused of bundling its web browser with its operating system. At the time, Microsoft allegedly threatened hardware makers that they would not receive a Windows license if they distributed the competing Netscape browser. In 2000, the company was found guilty of antitrust violations, and the judge ordered it broken up into an operating systems unit and an

applications unit. The breakup was reversed on appeal, and a settlement in 2001 was largely unsuccessful in establishing alternatives for desktop software.

Now the computing landscape is shifting once again, toward mobile devices and cloud computing. As you observe that change, you may well see new monopolies in the making. For example, you may observe that you have little choice for a provider of social networks, e-book readers, or Internet search services. If a provider uses the lack of alternatives to coerce consumers, publishers, or advertisers, the question arises whether such conduct is illegal exploitation of a monopoly position.

2.9 Graphical Applications

The following optional sections teach you how to write *graphical applications:* applications that display drawings inside a window. The drawings are made up of shape objects: rectangles, ellipses, and lines. The shape objects provide another source of examples, and many students enjoy the visual feedback.

2.9.1 Frame Windows

To show a frame, construct a JFrame object, set its size, and make it visible.

A graphical application shows information inside a **frame**: a window with a title bar, as shown in Figure 20. In this section, you will learn how to display a frame. In Section 2.9.2, you will learn how to create a drawing inside the frame.

To show a frame, carry out the following steps:

1. Construct an object of the JFrame class:

   ```
   JFrame frame = new JFrame();
   ```

2. Set the size of the frame:

   ```
   frame.setSize(300, 400);
   ```

   This frame will be 300 pixels wide and 400 pixels tall. If you omit this step the frame will be 0 by 0 pixels, and you won't be able to see it. (Pixels are the tiny dots from which digital images are composed.)

A graphical application shows information inside a frame.

3. If you'd like, set the title of the frame:

   ```
   frame.setTitle("An empty frame");
   ```

   If you omit this step, the title bar is simply left blank.

4. Set the "default close operation":

   ```
   frame.setDefaultCloseOperation(JFrame.EXIT_ON_CLOSE);
   ```

   When the user closes the frame, the program automatically exits. Don't omit this step. If you do, the program keeps running even after the frame is closed.

5. Make the frame visible:

   ```
   frame.setVisible(true);
   ```

The simple program below shows all of these steps. It produces the empty frame shown in Figure 20.

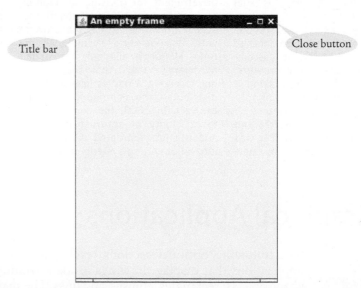

Figure 20 A Frame Window

The JFrame class is a part of the javax.swing package. Swing is the nickname for the graphical user interface library in Java. The "x" in javax denotes the fact that Swing started out as a Java *extension* before it was added to the standard library.

We will go into much greater detail about Swing programming in Chapters 3, 10, and 20. For now, consider this program to be the essential plumbing that is required to show a frame.

sec09_01/EmptyFrameViewer.java

```java
 1  import javax.swing.JFrame;
 2
 3  public class EmptyFrameViewer
 4  {
 5     public static void main(String[] args)
 6     {
 7        JFrame frame = new JFrame();
 8        frame.setSize(300, 400);
 9        frame.setTitle("An empty frame");
10        frame.setDefaultCloseOperation(JFrame.EXIT_ON_CLOSE);
11        frame.setVisible(true);
12     }
13  }
```

2.9.2 Drawing on a Component

In this section, you will learn how to make shapes appear inside a frame window. The first drawing will be exceedingly modest: just two rectangles (see Figure 21). You'll soon see how to produce more interesting drawings. The purpose of this example is to show you the basic outline of a program that creates a drawing.

You cannot draw directly onto a frame. Instead, drawing happens in a **component** object. In the Swing toolkit, the JComponent class represents a blank component.

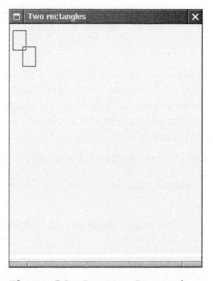

Figure 21   Drawing Rectangles

In order to display a
drawing in a frame,
declare a class
that extends the
JComponent class.

Because we don't want to add a blank component, we have to modify the JComponent class and specify how the component should be painted. The solution is to
declare a new class that extends the JComponent class. You will learn about the process
of extending classes in Chapter 9.

For now, simply use the following code as a template:

```java
public class RectangleComponent extends JComponent
{
    public void paintComponent(Graphics g)
    {
        Drawing instructions.
    }
}
```

Place drawing
instructions inside
the paintComponent
method. That
method is called
whenever the
component needs to
be repainted.

The extends reserved word indicates that our component class, RectangleComponent, can
be used like a JComponent. However, the RectangleComponent class will be different from
the plain JComponent class in one respect: Its paintComponent method will contain instructions to draw the rectangles.

When the component is shown for the first time, the paintComponent method is
called automatically. The method is also called when the window is resized, or when
it is shown again after it was hidden.

Use a cast to recover
the Graphics2D object
from the Graphics
argument of the
paintComponent
method.

The paintComponent method receives an object of type Graphics as its argument. The
Graphics object stores the graphics state—the current color, font, and so on—that are
used for drawing operations. However, the Graphics class is not very useful. When
programmers clamored for a more object-oriented approach to drawing graphics, the
designers of Java created the Graphics2D class, which extends the Graphics class. Whenever the Swing toolkit calls the paintComponent method, it actually passes an object of
type Graphics2D as the argument. Because we want to use the more sophisticated methods to draw two-dimensional graphics objects, we need to use the Graphics2D class.
This is accomplished by using a **cast**:

```java
public class RectangleComponent extends JComponent
{
    public void paintComponent(Graphics g)
    {
        // Recover Graphics2D
        Graphics2D g2 = (Graphics2D) g;
        . . .
    }
}
```

Chapter 9 has more information about casting. For now, you should simply include
the cast at the top of your paintComponent methods.

Now you are ready to draw shapes. The draw method of the Graphics2D class can
draw shapes, such as rectangles, ellipses, line segments, polygons, and arcs. Here we
draw a rectangle:

```java
public class RectangleComponent extends JComponent
{
    public void paintComponent(Graphics g)
    {
        . . .
        Rectangle box = new Rectangle(5, 10, 20, 30);
        g2.draw(box);
        . . .
    }
}
```

When positioning the shapes, you need to pay attention to the coordinate system. It is different from the one used in mathematics. The origin (0, 0) is at the upper-left corner of the component, and the *y*-coordinate grows downward.

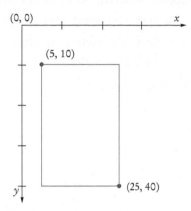

Following is the source code for the RectangleComponent class. Note that the paint-Component method of the RectangleComponent class draws two rectangles. As you can see from the import statements, the Graphics and Graphics2D classes are part of the java.awt package.

sec09_02/RectangleComponent.java

```java
1  import java.awt.Graphics;
2  import java.awt.Graphics2D;
3  import java.awt.Rectangle;
4  import javax.swing.JComponent;
5
6  /**
7     A component that draws two rectangles.
8  */
9  public class RectangleComponent extends JComponent
10 {
11    public void paintComponent(Graphics g)
12    {
13       // Recover Graphics2D
14       Graphics2D g2 = (Graphics2D) g;
15
16       // Construct a rectangle and draw it
17       Rectangle box = new Rectangle(5, 10, 20, 30);
18       g2.draw(box);
19
20       // Move rectangle 15 units to the right and 25 units down
21       box.translate(15, 25);
22
23       // Draw moved rectangle
24       g2.draw(box);
25    }
26 }
```

2.9.3 Displaying a Component in a Frame

In a graphical application, you need a frame to show the application, and you need a component for the drawing. In this section, you will see how to combine the two.

Follow these steps:

1. Construct a frame object and configure it.
2. Construct an object of your component class:

   ```
   RectangleComponent component = new RectangleComponent();
   ```

3. Add the component to the frame:

   ```
   frame.add(component);
   ```

4. Make the frame visible.

The following listing shows the complete process.

sec09_03/RectangleViewer.java

```
 1  import javax.swing.JFrame;
 2
 3  public class RectangleViewer
 4  {
 5     public static void main(String[] args)
 6     {
 7        JFrame frame = new JFrame();
 8
 9        frame.setSize(300, 400);
10        frame.setTitle("Two rectangles");
11        frame.setDefaultCloseOperation(JFrame.EXIT_ON_CLOSE);
12
13        RectangleComponent component = new RectangleComponent();
14        frame.add(component);
15
16        frame.setVisible(true);
17     }
18  }
```

Note that the rectangle drawing program consists of two classes:

- The RectangleComponent class, whose paintComponent method produces the drawing.
- The RectangleViewer class, whose main method constructs a frame and a Rectangle-Component, adds the component to the frame, and makes the frame visible.

2.10 Ellipses, Lines, Text, and Color

In Section 2.9 you learned how to write a program that draws rectangles. In the following sections, you will learn how to draw other shapes: ellipses and lines. With these graphical elements, you can draw quite a few interesting pictures.

2.10.1 Ellipses and Circles

To draw an ellipse, you specify its bounding box (see Figure 22) in the same way that you would specify a rectangle,

You can make simple drawings out of lines, rectangles, and circles.   © Alexey Avdeev/iStockphoto.

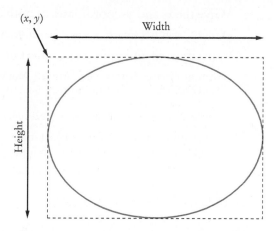

Figure 22   An Ellipse and Its Bounding Box

namely by the *x*- and *y*-coordinates of the top-left corner and the width and height of the box.

However, there is no simple `Ellipse` class that you can use. Instead, you must use one of the two classes `Ellipse2D.Float` and `Ellipse2D.Double`, depending on whether you want to store the ellipse coordinates as single- or double-precision floating-point values. Because the latter are more convenient to use in Java, we will always use the `Ellipse2D.Double` class.

Here is how you construct an ellipse:

```
Ellipse2D.Double ellipse = new Ellipse2D.Double(x, y, width, height);
```

The `Ellipse2D.Double` and `Line2D.Double` classes describe graphical shapes.

The class name `Ellipse2D.Double` looks different from the class names that you have encountered up to now. It consists of two class names `Ellipse2D` and `Double` separated by a period (.). This indicates that `Ellipse2D.Double` is a so-called **inner class** inside `Ellipse2D`. When constructing and using ellipses, you don't actually need to worry about the fact that `Ellipse2D.Double` is an inner class—just think of it as a class with a long name. However, in the `import` statement at the top of your program, you must be careful that you import only the outer class:

```
import java.awt.geom.Ellipse2D;
```

Drawing an ellipse is easy: Use exactly the same `draw` method of the `Graphics2D` class that you used for drawing rectangles.

```
g2.draw(ellipse);
```

To draw a circle, simply set the width and height to the same values:

```
Ellipse2D.Double circle = new Ellipse2D.Double(x, y, diameter, diameter);
g2.draw(circle);
```

Notice that (*x*, *y*) is the top-left corner of the bounding box, not the center of the circle.

2.10.2 Lines

To draw a line, use an object of the `Line2D.Double` class. A line is constructed by specifying its two end points. You can do this in two ways.

Give the x- and y-coordinates of both end points:

```
Line2D.Double segment = new Line2D.Double(x1, y1, x2, y2);
```

Or specify each end point as an object of the `Point2D.Double` class:

```
Point2D.Double from = new Point2D.Double(x1, y1);
Point2D.Double to = new Point2D.Double(x2, y2);

Line2D.Double segment = new Line2D.Double(from, to);
```

The second option is more object-oriented and is often more useful, particularly if the point objects can be reused elsewhere in the same drawing.

2.10.3 Drawing Text

> The drawString method draws a string, starting at its basepoint.

You often want to put text inside a drawing, for example, to label some of the parts. Use the `drawString` method of the `Graphics2D` class to draw a string anywhere in a window. You must specify the string and the x- and y-coordinates of the basepoint of the first character in the string (see Figure 23). For example,

```
g2.drawString("Message", 50, 100);
```

Figure 23   Basepoint and Baseline

2.10.4 Colors

When you first start drawing, all shapes and strings are drawn with a black pen. To change the color, you need to supply an object of type `Color`. Java uses the RGB color model. That is, you specify a color by the amounts of the primary colors—red, green, and blue—that make up the color. The amounts are given as integers between 0 (primary color not present) and 255 (maximum amount present). For example,

```
Color magenta = new Color(255, 0, 255);
```

constructs a `Color` object with maximum red, no green, and maximum blue, yielding a bright purple color called magenta.

For your convenience, a variety of colors have been declared in the `Color` class. Table 4 shows those colors and their RGB values. For example, `Color.PINK` has been declared to be the same color as `new Color(255, 175, 175)`.

> When you set a new color in the graphics context, it is used for subsequent drawing operations.

To draw a shape in a different color, first set the color of the `Graphics2D` object, then call the `draw` method:

```
g2.setColor(Color.RED);
g2.draw(circle); // Draws the shape in red
```

If you want to color the inside of the shape, use the `fill` method instead of the `draw` method. For example,

```
g2.fill(circle);
```

fills the inside of the circle with the current color.

Table 4 Predefined Colors		
Color		RGB Values
Color.BLACK		0, 0, 0
Color.BLUE		0, 0, 255
Color.CYAN		0, 255, 255
Color.GRAY		128, 128, 128
Color.DARK_GRAY		64, 64, 64
Color.LIGHT_GRAY		192, 192, 192
Color.GREEN		0, 255, 0
Color.MAGENTA		255, 0, 255
Color.ORANGE		255, 200, 0
Color.PINK		255, 175, 175
Color.RED		255, 0, 0
Color.WHITE		255, 255, 255
Color.YELLOW		255, 255, 0

The following program puts all these shapes to work, creating a simple drawing (see Figure 24).

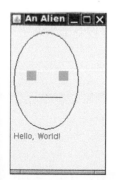

Figure 24
An Alien Face

sec10/FaceViewer.java

```java
1  import javax.swing.JFrame;
2
3  public class FaceViewer
4  {
5     public static void main(String[] args)
6     {
7        JFrame frame = new JFrame();
8        frame.setSize(150, 250);
9        frame.setTitle("An Alien Face");
10       frame.setDefaultCloseOperation(JFrame.EXIT_ON_CLOSE);
11
12       FaceComponent component = new FaceComponent();
13       frame.add(component);
14
15       frame.setVisible(true);
16    }
17 }
```

sec10/FaceComponent.java

```java
1  import java.awt.Color;
2  import java.awt.Graphics;
```

```
 3  import java.awt.Graphics2D;
 4  import java.awt.Rectangle;
 5  import java.awt.geom.Ellipse2D;
 6  import java.awt.geom.Line2D;
 7  import javax.swing.JComponent;
 8
 9  /**
10     A component that draws an alien face.
11  */
12  public class FaceComponent extends JComponent
13  {
14     public void paintComponent(Graphics g)
15     {
16        // Recover Graphics2D
17        Graphics2D g2 = (Graphics2D) g;
18
19        // Draw the head
20        Ellipse2D.Double head = new Ellipse2D.Double(5, 10, 100, 150);
21        g2.draw(head);
22
23        // Draw the eyes
24        g2.setColor(Color.GREEN);
25        Rectangle eye = new Rectangle(25, 70, 15, 15);
26        g2.fill(eye);
27        eye.translate(50, 0);
28        g2.fill(eye);
29
30        // Draw the mouth
31        Line2D.Double mouth = new Line2D.Double(30, 110, 80, 110);
32        g2.setColor(Color.RED);
33        g2.draw(mouth);
34
35        // Draw the greeting
36        g2.setColor(Color.BLUE);
37        g2.drawString("Hello, World!", 5, 175);
38     }
39  }
```

CHAPTER SUMMARY

Identify objects, methods, and classes.

- Objects are entities in your program that you manipulate by calling methods.
- A method is a sequence of instructions that accesses the data of an object.
- A class describes a set of objects with the same behavior.

Write variable declarations and assignments.

- A variable is a storage location with a name.
- When declaring a variable, you usually specify an initial value.
- When declaring a variable, you also specify the type of its values.
- Use the int type for numbers that cannot have a fractional part.

- Use the double type for floating-point numbers.
- Numbers can be combined by arithmetic operators such as +, -, and *.
- By convention, variable names should start with a lowercase letter.
- Use comments to add explanations for humans who read your code. The compiler ignores comments.

- Use the assignment operator (=) to change the value of a variable.
- All variables must be initialized before you access them.
- The assignment operator = does *not* denote mathematical equality.

Recognize arguments and return values of methods.

- The public interface of a class specifies what you can do with its objects. The hidden implementation describes how these actions are carried out.
- An argument is a value that is supplied in a method call.
- The return value of a method is a result that the method has computed.

Use constructors to construct new objects.

- Use the new operator, followed by a class name and arguments, to construct new objects.

Classify methods as accessor and mutator methods.

- An accessor method does not change the internal data of the object on which it is invoked. A mutator method changes the data.

Use the API documentation for finding method descriptions and packages.

- The API (Application Programming Interface) documentation lists the classes and methods of the Java library.
- Java classes are grouped into packages. Use the import statement to use classes that are declared in other packages.

Write programs that test the behavior of methods.

- A test program verifies that methods behave as expected.
- Determining the expected result in advance is an important part of testing.

Describe how multiple object references can refer to the same object.

- An object reference describes the location of an object.
- Multiple object variables can contain references to the same object.
- Number variables store numbers. Object variables store references.

Write programs that display frame windows.

- To show a frame, construct a JFrame object, set its size, and make it visible.
- In order to display a drawing in a frame, declare a class that extends the JComponent class.
- Place drawing instructions inside the paintComponent method. That method is called whenever the component needs to be repainted.
- Use a cast to recover the Graphics2D object from the Graphics argument of the paintComponent method.

Use the Java API for drawing simple figures.

- The Ellipse2D.Double and Line2D.Double classes describe graphical shapes.
- The drawString method draws a string, starting at its basepoint.
- When you set a new color in the graphics context, it is used for subsequent drawing operations.

STANDARD LIBRARY ITEMS INTRODUCED IN THIS CHAPTER

java.awt.Color
java.awt.Component
  getHeight
  getWidth
  setSize
  setVisible
java.awt.Frame
  setTitle
java.awt.geom.Ellipse2D.Double
java.awt.geom.Line2D.Double
java.awt.geom.Point2D.Double
java.awt.Graphics
  setColor
java.awt.Graphics2D
  draw
  drawString
  fill

java.awt.Rectangle
  getX
  getY
  getHeight
  getWidth
  setSize
  translate
java.lang.String
  length
  replace
  toLowerCase
  toUpperCase
javax.swing.JComponent
  paintComponent
javax.swing.JFrame
  setDefaultCloseOperation

REVIEW EXERCISES

- **R2.1** In Java, objects are grouped into classes according to their behavior. Would a window object and a water heater object belong to the same class or to different classes? Why?

- **R2.2** Some light bulbs use a glowing filament, others use a fluorescent gas. If you consider a light bulb a Java object with an "illuminate" method, would you need to know which kind of bulb it is?

- **R2.3** Explain the difference between an object and a class.

- **R2.4** Give three examples of objects that belong to the String class. Give an example of an object that belongs to the PrintStream class. Name two methods that belong to the String class but not the PrintStream class. Name a method of the PrintStream class that does not belong to the String class.

- **R2.5** What is the *public interface* of a class? How does it differ from the *implementation* of a class?

- **R2.6** Declare and initialize variables for holding the price and the description of an article that is available for sale.

- **R2.7** What is the value of mystery after this sequence of statements?

    ```
    int mystery = 1;
    mystery = 1 - 2 * mystery;
    mystery = mystery + 1;
    ```

- **R2.8** What is wrong with the following sequence of statements?

    ```
    int mystery = 1;
    mystery = mystery + 1;
    int mystery = 1 - 2 * mystery;
    ```

- ■■ **R2.9** Explain the difference between the = symbol in Java and in mathematics.

- ■■ **R2.10** Give an example of a method that has an argument of type int. Give an example of a method that has a return value of type int. Repeat for the type String.

- ■■ **R2.11** Write Java statements that initialize a string message with "Hello" and then change it to "HELLO". Use the toUpperCase method.

- ■■ **R2.12** Write Java statements that initialize a string message with "Hello" and then change it to "hello". Use the replace method.

- ■■ **R2.13** Write Java statements that initialize a string message with a message such as "Hello, World" and then remove punctuation characters from the message, using repeated calls to the replace method.

- ■ **R2.14** Explain the difference between an object and an object variable.

- ■■ **R2.15** Give the Java code for constructing an *object* of class Rectangle, and for declaring an *object variable* of class Rectangle.

- ■■ **R2.16** Give Java code for objects with the following descriptions:

    a. A rectangle with center (100, 100) and all side lengths equal to 50

    b. A string with the contents "Hello, Dave"

    Create objects, not object variables.

■■ **R2.17** Repeat Exercise •• R2.16, but now declare object variables that are initialized with the required objects.

■■ **R2.18** Write a Java statement to initialize a variable square with a rectangle object whose top-left corner is (10, 20) and whose sides all have length 40. Then write a statement that replaces square with a rectangle of the same size and top-left corner (20, 20).

■■ **R2.19** Write Java statements that initialize two variables square1 and square2 to refer to the same square with center (20, 20) and side length 40.

■■ **R2.20** Find the errors in the following statements:

```
a. Rectangle r = (5, 10, 15, 20);
b. double width = Rectangle(5, 10, 15, 20).getWidth();
c. Rectangle r;
   r.translate(15, 25);
d. r = new Rectangle();
   r.translate("far, far away!");
```

■ **R2.21** Name two accessor methods and two mutator methods of the Rectangle class.

■■ **R2.22** Consult the API documentation to find methods for

- Concatenating two strings, that is, making a string consisting of the first string, followed by the second string.
- Removing leading and trailing white space of a string.
- Converting a rectangle to a string.
- Computing the smallest rectangle that contains two given rectangles.
- Returning a random floating-point number.

For each method, list the class in which it is defined, the return type, the method name, and the types of the arguments.

■ **R2.23** Explain the difference between an object and an object reference.

■ **Graphics R2.24** What is the difference between a console application and a graphical application?

■■ **Graphics R2.25** Who calls the paintComponent method of a component? When does the call to the paintComponent method occur?

■■ **Graphics R2.26** Why does the argument of the paintComponent method have type Graphics and not Graphics2D?

■■ **Graphics R2.27** What is the purpose of a graphics context?

■■ **Graphics R2.28** Why are separate viewer and component classes used for graphical programs?

■ **Graphics R2.29** How do you specify a text color?

PRACTICE EXERCISES

■■ **E2.1** Write a program that initializes a string with "Mississippi". Then replace all "i" with "ii" and print the length of the resulting string. In that string, replace all "ss" with "s" and print the length of the resulting string.

■ **E2.2** Look into the API documentation of the String class and locate the trim method. Write a program demonstrating what it does. Then show how you can use the replace method to remove all spaces from a string.

■ **Testing E2.3** Write an AreaTester program that constructs a Rectangle object and then computes and prints its area. Use the getWidth and getHeight methods. Also print the expected answer.

■ **Testing E2.4** Write a PerimeterTester program that constructs a Rectangle object and then computes and prints its perimeter. Use the getWidth and getHeight methods. Also print the expected answer.

■ **E2.5** Write a program that constructs a rectangle with area 42 and a rectangle with perimeter 42. Print the widths and heights of both rectangles.

■■ **Testing E2.6** Look into the API documentation of the Rectangle class and locate the method

```
void add(int newx, int newy)
```

Read through the method documentation. Then determine the result of the following statements:

```
Rectangle box = new Rectangle(5, 10, 20, 30);
box.add(0, 0);
```

Write a program AddTester that prints the expected and actual location, width, and height of box after the call to add.

■■ **Testing E2.7** Write a program ReplaceTester that encodes a string by replacing all letters "i" with "!" and all letters "s" with "$". Use the replace method. Demonstrate that you can correctly encode the string "Mississippi". Print both the actual and expected result.

■■■ **E2.8** Write a program HollePrinter that switches the letters "e" and "o" in a string. Use the replace method repeatedly. Demonstrate that the string "Hello, World!" turns into "Holle, Werld!"

■ **Testing E2.9** The StringBuilder class has a method for reversing a string. In a ReverseTester class, construct a StringBuilder from a given string (such as "desserts"), call the reverse method followed by the toString method, and print the result. Also print the expected value.

© PeskyMonkey/iStockphoto.

■■ **E2.10** In the Java library, a color is specified by its red, green, and blue components between 0 and 255 (see Table 4 on page 57). Write a program BrighterDemo that constructs a Color object with red, green, and blue values of 50, 100, and 150. Then apply the brighter method of the Color class and print the red, green, and blue values of the resulting color. (You won't actually see the color—see Exercise ●● Graphics E2.11 on how to display the color.)

■■ **Graphics E2.11** Repeat Exercise ●● E2.10, but place your code into the following class. Then the color will be displayed.

```
import java.awt.Color;
import javax.swing.JFrame;

public class BrighterDemo
{
   public static void main(String[] args)
   {
```

```
                        JFrame frame = new JFrame();
                        frame.setSize(200, 200);
                        Color myColor = . . .;
                        frame.getContentPane().setBackground(myColor);
                        frame.setDefaultCloseOperation(JFrame.EXIT_ON_CLOSE);
                        frame.setVisible(true);
                    }
                }
```

■■ E2.12   Repeat Exercise ●● E2.10, but apply the darker method of the Color class twice to the object Color.RED. Call your class DarkerDemo.

■■ E2.13   The Random class implements a *random number generator*, which produces sequences of numbers that appear to be random. To generate random integers, you construct an object of the Random class, and then apply the nextInt method. For example, the call generator.nextInt(6) gives you a random number between 0 and 5.

Write a program DieSimulator that uses the Random class to simulate the cast of a die, printing a random number between 1 and 6 every time that the program is run.

■■ E2.14   Write a program RandomPrice that prints a random price between $10.00 and $19.95 every time the program is run.

■■ Testing E2.15   Look at the API of the Point class and find out how to construct a Point object. In a PointTester program, construct two points with coordinates (3, 4) and (–3, –4). Find the distance between them, using the distance method. Print the distance, as well as the expected value. (Draw a sketch on graph paper to find the value you will expect.)

■ E2.16   Using the Day class of Worked Example 2.1, write a DayTester program that constructs a Day object representing today, adds ten days to it, and then computes the difference between that day and today. Print the difference and the expected value.

■■ E2.17   Using the Picture class of Worked Example 2.2, write a HalfSizePicture program that loads a picture and shows it at half the original size, centered in the window.

■■ E2.18   Using the Picture class of Worked Example 2.2, write a DoubleSizePicture program that loads a picture, doubles its size, and shows the center of the picture in the window.

■■ Graphics E2.19   Write a graphics program that draws two squares, both with the same center. Provide a class TwoSquareViewer and a class TwoSquareComponent.

■■ Graphics E2.20   Write a program that draws two solid squares: one in pink and one in purple. Use a standard color for one of them and a custom color for the other. Provide a class TwoSquareViewer and a class TwoSquareComponent.

■■ Graphics E2.21   Write a graphics program that draws your name in red, contained inside a blue rectangle. Provide a class NameViewer and a class NameComponent.

PROGRAMMING PROJECTS

■■ P2.1   Write a program called FourRectanglePrinter that constructs a Rectangle object, prints its location by calling System.out.println(box), and then translates and prints it three more times, so that, if the rectangles were drawn, they would form one large rectangle, as shown at right.

Your program will not produce a drawing. It will simply print the locations of the four rectangles.

■■ **P2.2** Write a GrowSquarePrinter program that constructs a Rectangle object square representing a square with top-left corner (100, 100) and side length 50, prints its location by calling System.out. println(square), applies the translate and grow methods, and calls System.out.println(square) again. The calls to translate and grow should modify the square so that it has twice the size and the same top-left corner as the original. If the squares were drawn, they would look like the figure at right.

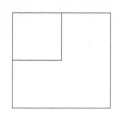

Your program will not produce a drawing. It will simply print the locations of square before and after calling the mutator methods.

Look up the description of the grow method in the API documentation.

■■■ **P2.3** Write a CenteredSquaresPrinter program that constructs a Rectangle object square representing a square with top-left corner (100, 100) and side length 200, prints its location by calling System.out. println(square), applies the grow and translate methods, and calls System.out.println(square) again. The calls to grow and translate should modify the square so that it has half the width and is centered in the original square. If the squares were drawn, they

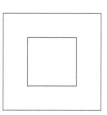

would look like the figure at right. Your program will not produce a drawing. It will simply print the locations of square before and after calling the mutator methods. Look up the description of the grow method in the API documentation.

■■■ **P2.4** The intersection method computes the *intersection* of two rectangles—that is, the rectangle that would be formed by two overlapping rectangles if they were drawn, as shown at right.

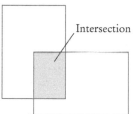

You call this method as follows:

```
Rectangle r3 = r1.intersection(r2);
```

Write a program IntersectionPrinter that constructs two rectangle objects, prints them as described in Exercise ●● P2.1, and then prints the rectangle object that describes the intersection. Then the program should print the result of the intersection method when the rectangles do not overlap. Add a comment to your program that explains how you can tell whether the resulting rectangle is empty.

■■■ **Graphics P2.5** In this exercise, you will explore a simple way of visualizing a Rectangle object. The setBounds method of the JFrame class moves a frame window to a given rectangle. Complete the following program to visually show the translate method of the Rectangle class:

```
import java.awt.Rectangle;
import javax.swing.JFrame;
import javax.swing.JOptionPane;

public class TranslateDemo
{
    public static void main(String[] args)
    {
        // Construct a frame and show it
        JFrame frame = new JFrame();
        frame.setDefaultCloseOperation(JFrame.EXIT_ON_CLOSE);
        frame.setVisible(true);
```

```
                    // Your work goes here: Construct a rectangle and set the frame bounds

                    JOptionPane.showMessageDialog(frame, "Click OK to continue");

                    // Your work goes here: Move the rectangle and set the frame bounds again
               }
         }
```

■■ P2.6 The BigInteger class represents integer numbers with an arbitrary number of digits. (As you will see in Chapter 4, the int type cannot express very large integers.) You can construct a BigInteger object by providing a string of its digits, such as

```
BigInteger a = new BigInteger("12345678987654321");
```

Write a program that prints the square, fourth power, and eighth power of a, using one of the methods of the BigInteger class.

■■■ P2.7 Write a program LotteryPrinter that picks a combination in a lottery. In this lottery, players can choose 6 numbers (possibly repeated) between 1 and 49. Construct an object of the Random class (see Exercise ●● E2.13) and invoke an appropriate method to generate each number. (In a real lottery, repetitions aren't allowed, but we haven't yet discussed the programming constructs that would be required to deal with that problem.) Your

© Feng Yu/iStockphoto.

program should print out a sentence such as "Play this combination—it'll make you rich!", followed by a lottery combination.

■■ P2.8 Using the Day class of Worked Example 2.1, write a program that generates a Day object representing February 28 of this year, and three more such objects that represent February 28 of the next three years. Advance each object by one day, and print each object. Also print the expected values:

```
2019-02-29
Expected: 2019-02-29
2020-03-01
Expected: 2020-03-01
. . .
```

■■■ P2.9 The GregorianCalendar class describes a point in time, as measured by the Gregorian calendar, the standard calendar that is commonly used throughout the world today. You construct a GregorianCalendar object from a year, month, and day of the month, like this:

```
GregorianCalendar cal = new GregorianCalendar(); // Today's date
GregorianCalendar eckertsBirthday = new GregorianCalendar(1919,
      Calendar.APRIL, 9);
```

Use the values Calendar.JANUARY . . . Calendar.DECEMBER to specify the month.

The add method can be used to add a number of days to a GregorianCalendar object:

```
cal.add(Calendar.DAY_OF_MONTH, 10); // Now cal is ten days from today
```

This is a mutator method—it changes the cal object.

The get method can be used to query a given GregorianCalendar object:

```
int dayOfMonth = cal.get(Calendar.DAY_OF_MONTH);
int month = cal.get(Calendar.MONTH);
```

```
int year = cal.get(Calendar.YEAR);
int weekday = cal.get(Calendar.DAY_OF_WEEK);
    // 1 is Sunday, 2 is Monday, ... , 7 is Saturday
```

Your task is to write a program that prints:

- The date and weekday that is 100 days from today.
- The weekday of your birthday.
- The date that is 10,000 days from your birthday.

Use the birthday of a computer scientist if you don't want to reveal your own.

Hint: The GregorianCalendar class is complex, and it is a really good idea to write a few test programs to explore the API before tackling the whole problem. Start with a program that constructs today's date, adds ten days, and prints out the day of the month and the weekday.

■■ **P2.10** The LocalDate class describes a calendar date that does not depend on a location or time zone. You construct a date like this:

```
LocalDate today = LocalDate.now(); // Today's date
LocalDate eckertsBirthday = LocalDate.of(1919, 4, 9);
```

The plusDays method can be used to add a number of days to a LocalDate object:

```
LocalDate later = today.plusDays(10); // Ten days from today
```

This method does not mutate the today object, but it returns a new object that is a given number of days away from today.

To get the year of a day, call

```
int year = today.getYear();
```

To get the weekday of a LocalDate, call

```
String weekday = today.getDayOfWeek().toString();
```

Your task is to write a program that prints

- The weekday of "Pi day", that is, March 14, of the current year.
- The date and weekday of "Programmer's day" in the current year; that is, the 256th day of the year. (The number 256, or 2^8, is useful for some programming tasks.)
- The date and weekday of the date that is 10,000 days earlier than today.

■■■ **Testing P2.11** Write a program LineDistanceTester that constructs a line joining the points (100, 100) and (200, 200), then constructs points (100, 200), (150, 150), and (250, 50). Print the distance from the line to each of the three points, using the ptSegDist method of the Line2D class. Also print the expected values. (Draw a sketch on graph paper to find what values you expect.)

■■ **Graphics P2.12** Repeat Exercise ●●● Testing P2.11, but now write a graphical application that shows the line and the points. Draw each point as a tiny circle. Use the drawString method to draw each distance next to the point, using calls

```
g2.drawString("Distance: " + distance, p.getX(), p.getY());
```

■■ **Graphics P2.13** Write a graphics program that draws 12 strings, one each for the 12 standard colors (except Color.WHITE), each in its own color. Provide a class ColorNameViewer and a class ColorNameComponent.

•• **Graphics P2.14** Write a program to plot the face at right. Provide a class FaceViewer and a class FaceComponent.

•• **Graphics P2.15** Write a graphical program that draws a traffic light.

•• **Graphics P2.16** Run the following program:

```java
import java.awt.Color;
import javax.swing.JFrame;
import javax.swing.JLabel;

public class FrameViewer
{
   public static void main(String[] args)
   {
      JFrame frame = new JFrame();
      frame.setSize(200, 200);
      JLabel label = new JLabel("Hello, World!");
      label.setOpaque(true);
      label.setBackground(Color.PINK);
      frame.add(label);
      frame.setDefaultCloseOperation(JFrame.EXIT_ON_CLOSE);
      frame.setVisible(true);
   }
}
```

Modify the program as follows:

- Double the frame size.
- Change the greeting to "Hello, *your name!*".
- Change the background color to pale green (see Exercise •• Graphics E2.11).
- For extra credit, add an image of yourself. (*Hint:* Construct an ImageIcon.)

© Kris Hanke/iStockphoto.

CHAPTER 3

IMPLEMENTING CLASSES

CHAPTER GOALS

To become familiar with the process of implementing classes

To be able to implement and test simple methods

To understand the purpose and use of constructors

To understand how to access instance variables and local variables

To be able to write javadoc comments

To implement classes for drawing graphical shapes

CHAPTER CONTENTS

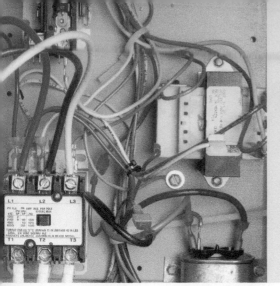

In this chapter, you will learn how to implement your own classes. You will start with a given design that specifies the public interface of the class—that is, the methods through which programmers can manipulate the objects of the class. Then you will learn the steps to completing the class—creating the internal "workings" like the inside of an air conditioner shown here. You need to implement the methods, which entails finding a data representation for the objects and supplying the instructions for each method. You need to document your efforts so that other programmers can understand and use your creation. And you need to provide a tester to validate that your class works correctly.

3.1 Instance Variables and Encapsulation

In Chapter 1, you learned how to use objects from existing classes. In this chapter, you will start implementing your own classes. We begin with a very simple example that shows you how objects store their data, and how methods access the data of an object. Our first example is a class that models a *tally counter*, a mechanical device that is used to count people—for example, to find out how many people attend a concert or board a bus (see Figure 1).

© Jasmin Awad/iStockphoto.

Figure 1   A Tally Counter

3.1.1 Instance Variables

Whenever the operator clicks the button of a tally counter, the counter value advances by one. We model this operation with a click method of a Counter class. A physical counter has a display to show the current value. In our simulation, we use a getValue method to get the current value. For example,

```
Counter tally = new Counter();
tally.click();
tally.click();
int result = tally.getValue(); // Sets result to 2
```

When implementing the Counter class, you need to determine the data that each counter object contains. In this simple example, that is very straightforward. Each counter needs a variable that keeps track of the number of simulated button clicks.

An object stores its data in **instance variables**. An *instance* of a class is an object of the class. Thus, an instance variable is a storage location that is present in each object of the class.

You specify instance variables in the class declaration:

```
public class Counter
{
   private int value;
   . . .
}
```

> An object's instance variables store the data required for executing its methods.

Syntax 3.1   Instance Variable Declaration

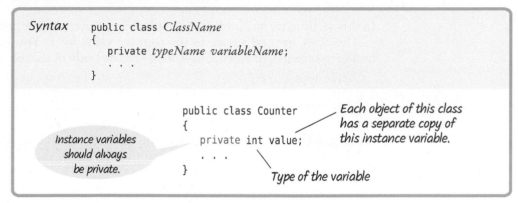

An instance variable declaration consists of the following parts:

- An **access specifier** (private)
- The **type** of the instance variable (such as int)
- The name of the instance variable (such as value)

Each object of a class has its own set of instance variables.

Each object of a class has its own set of instance variables. For example, if concert-Counter and boardingCounter are two objects of the Counter class, then each object has its own value variable (see Figure 2).

As you will see in Section 3.3, the instance variable value is set to 0 when a Counter object is constructed.

Figure 2
Instance Variables

These clocks have common behavior, but each of them has a different state. Similarly, objects of a class can have their instance variables set to different values.

© Mark Evans/iStockphoto.

3.1.2 The Methods of the Counter Class

In this section, we will look at the implementation of the methods of the Counter class.

The click method advances the counter value by 1. You have seen the method header syntax in Chapter 2. Now, focus on the body of the method inside the braces.

```java
public void click()
{
    value = value + 1;
}
```

Note how the click method accesses the instance variable value. *Which* instance variable? The one belonging to the object on which the method is invoked. For example, consider the call

```java
concertCounter.click();
```

This call advances the value variable of the concertCounter object.

The getValue method returns the current value:

```java
public int getValue()
{
    return value;
}
```

The return statement is a special statement that terminates the method call and returns a result (the **return value**) to the method's caller.

Instance variables are generally declared with the access specifier private. That specifier means that they can be accessed only by the methods of the *same class*, not by any other method. For example, the value variable can be accessed by the click and getValue methods of the Counter class but not by a method of another class. Those other methods need to use the Counter class methods if they want to manipulate a counter's internal data.

Private instance variables can only be accessed by methods of the same class.

3.1.3 Encapsulation

In the preceding section, you learned that you should hide instance variables by making them private. Why would a programmer want to hide something?

The strategy of information hiding is not unique to computer programming—it is used in many engineering disciplines. Consider the thermostat that you find in your home. It is a device that allows a user to set temperature preferences and that controls the furnace and the air conditioner. If you ask your contractor what is inside the thermostat, you will likely get a shrug.

The thermostat is a *black box*, something that magically does its thing. A contractor would never open the control module—it contains electronic parts that can only be serviced at the factory. In general, engineers use the term "black box" to describe any device whose inner workings are hidden. Note that a black box is not totally mysterious. Its interface with the outside world is well-defined. For example, the contractor understands how the thermostat must be connected with the furnace and air conditioner.

Encapsulation is the process of hiding implementation details and providing methods for data access.

The process of hiding implementation details while publishing an interface is called **encapsulation**. In Java, the class construct provides encapsulation. The public methods of a class are the interface through which the private implementation is manipulated.

A thermostat functions as a "black box" whose inner workings are hidden.

© yenwen/iStockphoto.

Why do contractors use prefabricated components such as thermostats and furnaces? These "black boxes" greatly simplify the work of the contractor. In ancient times, builders had to know how to construct furnaces from brick and mortar, and how to produce some rudimentary temperature controls. Nowadays, a contractor just makes a trip to the hardware store, without needing to know what goes on inside the components.

Similarly, a programmer using a class is not burdened by unnecessary detail, as you know from your own experience. In Chapter 2, you used classes for strings, streams, and windows without worrying how these classes are implemented.

Encapsulation also helps with diagnosing errors. A large program may consist of hundreds of classes and thousands of methods, but if there is an error with the internal data of an object, you only need to look at the methods of one class. Finally, encapsulation makes it possible to change the implementation of a class without having to tell the programmers who use the class.

In Chapter 2, you learned to be an object user. You saw how to obtain objects, how to manipulate them, and how to assemble them into a program. In that chapter, you treated objects as black boxes. Your role was roughly analogous to the contractor who installs a new thermostat.

In this chapter, you will move on to implementing classes. In these sections, your role is analogous to the hardware manufacturer who puts together a thermostat from buttons, sensors, and other electronic parts. You will learn the necessary Java programming techniques that enable your objects to carry out the desired behavior.

> Encapsulation allows a programmer to use a class without having to know its implementation.

> Information hiding makes it simpler for the implementor of a class to locate errors and change implementations.

sec01/Counter.java

```java
1  /**
2      This class models a tally counter.
3  */
4  public class Counter
5  {
6      private int value;
7
8      /**
9          Gets the current value of this counter.
10         @return the current value
11     */
12     public int getValue()
13     {
14         return value;
15     }
16
```

```
17    /**
18        Advances the value of this counter by 1.
19    */
20    public void click()
21    {
22        value = value + 1;
23    }
24
25    /**
26        Resets the value of this counter to 0.
27    */
28    public void reset()
29    {
30        value = 0;
31    }
32 }
```

EXAMPLE CODE   See sec01 of your eText or companion code for a demonstration program for the Counter class.

3.2 Specifying the Public Interface of a Class

In the following sections, we will discuss the process of specifying the public interface of a class. Imagine that you are a member of a team that works on banking software. A fundamental concept in banking is a *bank account*. Your task is to design a BankAccount class that can be used by other programmers to manipulate bank accounts. What methods should you provide? What information should you give the programmers who use this class? You will want to settle these questions before you implement the class.

3.2.1 Specifying Methods

In order to implement a class, you first need to know which methods are required.

You need to know exactly what operations of a bank account need to be implemented. Some operations are essential (such as taking deposits), whereas others are not important (such as giving a gift to a customer who opens a bank account). Deciding which operations are essential is not always an easy task. We will revisit that issue in Chapters 8 and 12. For now, we will assume that a competent designer has decided that the following are considered the essential operations of a bank account:

- Deposit money
- Withdraw money
- Get the current balance

In Java, you call a method when you want to apply an operation to an object. To figure out the exact specification of the method calls, imagine how a programmer would carry out the bank account operations. We'll assume that the variable harrysChecking contains a reference to an object of type BankAccount. We want to support method calls such as the following:

```
harrysChecking.deposit(2240.59);
harrysChecking.withdraw(500);
double currentBalance = harrysChecking.getBalance();
```

The first two methods are mutators. They modify the balance of the bank account and don't return a value. The third method is an accessor. It returns a value that you store in a variable or pass to a method.

From the sample calls, we decide the BankAccount class should declare three methods:

- `public void deposit(double amount)`
- `public void withdraw(double amount)`
- `public double getBalance()`

Recall from Chapter 2 that double denotes the double-precision floating-point type, and void indicates that a method does not return a value.

Here we only give the method *headers*. When you declare a method, you also need to provide the method **body**, which consists of statements that are executed when the method is called.

```
public void deposit(double amount)
{
    method body—implementation filled in later
}
```

We will supply the method bodies in Section 3.3.

Note that the methods have been declared as public, indicating that all other methods in a program can call them. Occasionally, it can be useful to have private methods. They can only be called from other methods of the same class.

Some people like to fill in the bodies so that they compile, like this:

```
public double getBalance()
{
    // TODO: fill in implementation
    return 0;
}
```

That is a good idea if you compose your method specification in your development environment—you won't get warnings about incorrect code.

3.2.2 Specifying Constructors

Constructors set the initial data for objects.

As you know from Chapter 2, constructors are used to initialize objects. In Java, a **constructor** is very similar to a method, with two important differences:

- The name of the constructor is always the same as the name of the class (e.g., BankAccount).
- Constructors have no return type (not even void).

We want to be able to construct bank accounts that initially have a zero balance, as well as accounts that have a given initial balance.
For this purpose, we specify two constructors:

- `public BankAccount()`
- `public BankAccount(double initialBalance)`

They are used as follows:

```
BankAccount harrysChecking = new BankAccount();
BankAccount momsSavings = new BankAccount(5000);
```

Syntax 3.2 Class Declaration

Syntax   *accessSpecifier* class *ClassName*
```
{
    instance variables
    constructors
    methods
}
```

```
                    public class Counter
                    {
                        private int value;  ──────────────────────────┐
                                                                        │
                        public Counter(int initialValue) { value = initialValue; }  ──┐   Private
Public interface  ─<                                                                    >  implementation
                        public void click() { value = value + 1; }  ──────────┘
                        public int getValue() { return value; }  ──────────────┘
                    }
```

The constructor
name is always
the same as the
class name.

Don't worry about the fact that there are two constructors with the same name—*all* constructors of a class have the same name, that is, the name of the class. The compiler can tell them apart because they take different arguments. The first constructor takes no arguments at all. Such a constructor is called a **no-argument constructor**. The second constructor takes an argument of type double.

Just like a method, a constructor also has a body—a sequence of statements that is executed when a new object is constructed.

```
public BankAccount()
{
    constructor body—implementation filled in later
}
```

The statements in the constructor body will set the instance variables of the object that is being constructed—see Section 3.3.

When declaring a class, you place all constructor and method declarations inside, like this:

```
public class BankAccount
{
    private instance variables—filled in later

    // Constructors
    public BankAccount()
    {
        implementation—filled in later
    }

    public BankAccount(double initialBalance)
    {
        implementation—filled in later
    }

    // Methods
    public void deposit(double amount)
    {
        implementation—filled in later
```

```
    }

    public void withdraw(double amount)
    {
        implementation—filled in later
    }

    public double getBalance()
    {
        implementation—filled in later
    }
}
```

The public constructors and methods of a class form the **public interface** of the class. These are the operations that any programmer can use to create and manipulate BankAccount objects.

3.2.3   Using the Public Interface

Our BankAccount class is simple, but it allows programmers to carry out all of the important operations that commonly occur with bank accounts. For example, consider this program segment, authored by a programmer who uses the BankAccount class. These statements transfer an amount of money from one bank account to another:

```
// Transfer from one account to another
double transferAmount = 500;
momsSavings.withdraw(transferAmount);
harrysChecking.deposit(transferAmount);
```

And here is a program segment that adds interest to a savings account:

```
double interestRate = 5; // 5 percent interest
double interestAmount = momsSavings.getBalance() * interestRate / 100;
momsSavings.deposit(interestAmount);
```

As you can see, programmers can use objects of the BankAccount class to carry out meaningful tasks, without knowing how the BankAccount objects store their data or how the BankAccount methods do their work.

Of course, as implementors of the BankAccount class, we will need to supply the private implementation. We will do so in Section 3.3. First, however, an important step remains: *documenting* the public interface. That is the topic of the next section.

3.2.4   Commenting the Public Interface

When you implement classes and methods, you should get into the habit of thoroughly *commenting* their behaviors. In Java there is a very useful standard form for **documentation comments**. If you use this form in your classes, a program called **javadoc** can automatically generate a neat set of HTML pages that describe them. (See Programming Tip 3.1 for a description of this utility.)

A documentation comment is placed before the class or method declaration that is being documented. It starts with a /**, a special comment delimiter used by the javadoc utility. Then you describe the method's *purpose*. Then, for each argument, you supply a line that starts with @param, followed by the name of the variable that holds the argument (which is called a **parameter variable**). Supply a short explanation for

Use documentation comments to describe the classes and public methods of your programs.

each argument after the variable name. Finally, you supply a line that starts with @ return, describing the return value. You omit the @param tag for methods that have no arguments, and you omit the @return tag for methods whose return type is void.

The javadoc utility copies the *first* sentence of each comment to a summary table in the HTML documentation. Therefore, it is best to write that first sentence with some care. It should start with an uppercase letter and end with a period. It does not have to be a grammatically complete sentence, but it should be meaningful when it is pulled out of the comment and displayed in a summary.

Here are two typical examples:

```
/**
    Withdraws money from the bank account.
    @param amount the amount to withdraw
*/
public void withdraw(double amount)
{
    implementation—filled in later
}


/**
    Gets the current balance of the bank account.
    @return the current balance
*/
public double getBalance()
{
    implementation—filled in later
}
```

The comments you have just seen explain individual *methods*. Supply a brief comment for each *class*, too, explaining its purpose. Place the documentation comment above the class declaration:

```
/**
    A bank account has a balance that can be changed by
    deposits and withdrawals.
*/
public class BankAccount
{
    . . .
}
```

Your first reaction may well be "Whoa! Am I supposed to write all this stuff?" Sometimes, documentation comments seem pretty repetitive, but in most cases, they are informative. Even with seemingly repetitive comments, you should take the time to write them.

It is always a good idea to write the method comment *first*, before writing the code in the method body. This is an excellent test to see that you firmly understand what you need to program. If you can't explain what a class or method does, you aren't ready to implement it.

What about very simple methods? You can easily spend more time pondering whether a comment is too trivial to write than it takes to write it. In practical programming, very simple methods are rare. It is harmless to have a trivial method over-commented, whereas a complicated method without any comment can cause real grief to future maintenance programmers. According to the standard Java documentation style, *every* class, *every* method, *every* parameter variable, and *every* return value should have a comment.

Provide documentation comments for every class, every method, every parameter variable, and every return value.

The javadoc utility formats your comments into a neat set of documents that you can view in a web browser. It makes good use of the seemingly repetitive phrases. The first sentence of the comment is used for a *summary table* of all methods of your class (see Figure 3).

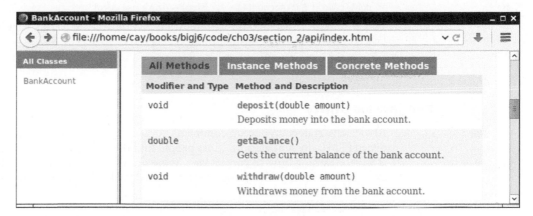

Figure 3   A Method Summary Generated by javadoc

The @param and @return comments are neatly formatted in the detail description of each method (see Figure 4). If you omit any of the comments, then javadoc generates documents that look strangely empty.

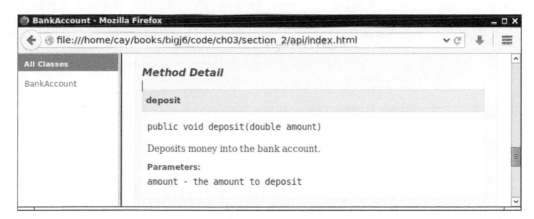

Figure 4   Method Detail Generated by javadoc

This documentation format should look familiar. The programmers who implement the Java library use javadoc themselves. They too document every class, every method, every parameter variable, and every return value, and then use javadoc to extract the documentation in HTML format.

EXAMPLE CODE   See sec02 of your eText or companion code for the BankAccount class with documentation but without implementation.

Common Error 3.1
Declaring a Constructor as void

Do not use the void reserved word when you declare a constructor:

```
public void BankAccount()  // Error—don't use void!
```

This would declare a method with return type void and *not* a constructor. Unfortunately, the Java compiler does not consider this a syntax error.

Programming Tip 3.1
The javadoc Utility

Always insert documentation comments in your code, whether or not you use javadoc to produce HTML documentation. Most people find the HTML documentation convenient, so it is worth learning how to run javadoc. Some programming environments (such as BlueJ) can execute javadoc for you. Alternatively, you can invoke the javadoc utility from a shell window, by issuing the command

```
javadoc MyClass.java
```

or, if you want to document multiple Java files,

```
javadoc *.java
```

The javadoc utility produces files such as MyClass.html in HTML format, which you can inspect in a browser. If you know HTML (see Appendix J), you can embed HTML tags into the comments to specify fonts or add images. Perhaps most importantly, javadoc automatically provides *hyperlinks* to other classes and methods.

You can run javadoc before implementing any methods. Just leave all the method bodies empty. Don't run the compiler—it would complain about missing return values. Simply run javadoc on your file to generate the documentation for the public interface that you are about to implement.

The javadoc tool is wonderful because it does one thing right: It allows you to put the documentation *together with your code*. That way, when you update your programs, you can see right away which documentation needs to be updated. Hopefully, you will update it right then and there. Afterward, run javadoc again and get updated information that is timely and nicely formatted.

3.3 Providing the Class Implementation

Now that you understand the specification of the public interface of the BankAccount class, let's provide the implementation.

3.3.1 Providing Instance Variables

First, we need to determine the data that each bank account object contains. In the case of our simple bank account class, each object needs to store a single value, the current balance. (A more complex bank account class might store additional data—perhaps an account number, the interest rate paid, the date for mailing out the next statement, and so on.)

The private implementation of a class consists of instance variables, and the bodies of constructors and methods.

```
public class BankAccount
{
    private double balance;
    // Methods and constructors below
    . . .
}
```

In general, it can be challenging to find a good set of instance variables. Ask yourself what an object needs to remember so that it can carry out any of its methods.

Like a wilderness explorer who needs to carry all items that may be needed, an object needs to store the data required for its method calls.   © iStockphoto.com/migin.

3.3.2 Providing Constructors

A **constructor** has a simple job: to initialize the instance variables of an object.

Recall that we designed the BankAccount class to have two constructors. The first constructor simply sets the balance to zero:

```
public BankAccount()
{
    balance = 0;
}
```

The second constructor sets the balance to the value supplied as the construction argument:

```
public BankAccount(double initialBalance)
{
    balance = initialBalance;
}
```

© Ann Marie Kurtz/iStockphoto.

A constructor is like a set of assembly instructions for an object.

To see how these constructors work, let us trace the statement

```
BankAccount harrysChecking = new BankAccount(1000);
```

one step at a time.

Here are the steps that are carried out when the statement executes (see Figure 5):

- Create a new object of type BankAccount. ❶
- Call the second constructor (because an argument is supplied in the constructor call).
- Set the parameter variable initialBalance to 1000. ❷
- Set the balance instance variable of the newly created object to initialBalance. ❸
- Return an object reference, that is, the memory location of the object, as the value of the new expression.
- Store that object reference in the harrysChecking variable. ❹

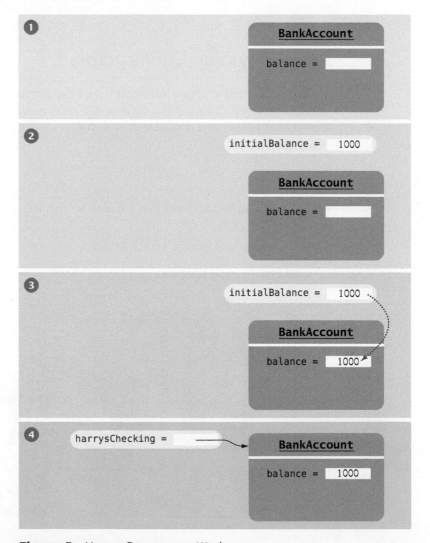

Figure 5   How a Constructor Works

In general, when you implement constructors, be sure that each constructor initializes all instance variables, and that you make use of all parameter variables (see Common Error 3.2).

3.3.3 Providing Methods

In this section, we finish implementing the methods of the BankAccount class.

When you implement a method, ask yourself whether it is an accessor or mutator method. A mutator method needs to update the instance variables in some way. An accessor method retrieves or computes a result.

Here is the deposit method. It is a mutator method, updating the balance:

```java
public void deposit(double amount)
{
    balance = balance + amount;
}
```

The withdraw method is very similar to the deposit method:

```java
public void withdraw(double amount)
{
    balance = balance - amount;
}
```

Table 1 Implementing Classes

Example	Comments
`public class BankAccount { . . . }`	This is the start of a class declaration. Instance variables, methods, and constructors are placed inside the braces.
`private double balance;`	This is an instance variable of type double. Instance variables should be declared as private.
`public double getBalance() { . . . }`	This is a method declaration. The body of the method must be placed inside the braces.
`. . . { return balance; }`	This is the body of the getBalance method. The return statement returns a value to the caller of the method.
`public void deposit(double amount) { . . . }`	This is a method with a parameter variable (amount). Because the method is declared as void, it has no return value.
`. . . { balance = balance + amount; }`	This is the body of the deposit method. It does not have a return statement.
`public BankAccount() { . . . }`	This is a constructor declaration. A constructor has the same name as the class and no return type.
`. . . { balance = 0; }`	This is the body of the constructor. A constructor should initialize the instance variables.

There is one method left, getBalance. Unlike the deposit and withdraw methods, which modify the instance variable of the object on which they are invoked, the getBalance method returns a value:

```java
public double getBalance()
{
   return balance;
}
```

We have now completed the implementation of the BankAccount class—see the code listing below. There is only one step remaining: testing that the class works correctly. That is the topic of the next section.

sec03/BankAccount.java

```java
1  /**
2      A bank account has a balance that can be changed by
3      deposits and withdrawals.
4  */
5  public class BankAccount
6  {
7     private double balance;
8
9     /**
10        Constructs a bank account with a zero balance.
11     */
12     public BankAccount()
13     {
14        balance = 0;
15     }
16
17     /**
18        Constructs a bank account with a given balance.
19        @param initialBalance the initial balance
20     */
21     public BankAccount(double initialBalance)
22     {
23        balance = initialBalance;
24     }
25
26     /**
27        Deposits money into the bank account.
28        @param amount the amount to deposit
29     */
30     public void deposit(double amount)
31     {
32        balance = balance + amount;
33     }
34
35     /**
36        Withdraws money from the bank account.
37        @param amount the amount to withdraw
38     */
39     public void withdraw(double amount)
40     {
41        balance = balance - amount;
42     }
43
```

```
44    /**
45        Gets the current balance of the bank account.
46        @return  the current balance
47    */
48    public double getBalance()
49    {
50        return balance;
51    }
52 }
```

Common Error 3.2

Ignoring Parameter Variables

A surprisingly common beginner's error is to ignore parameter variables of methods or constructors. This usually happens when an assignment gives an example with specific values. For example, suppose you are asked to provide a class Letter with a recipient and a sender, and you are given a sample letter like this:

```
Dear John:

I am sorry we must part.
I wish you all the best.

Sincerely,

Mary
```

Now look at this incorrect attempt:

```
public class Letter
{
    private String recipient;
    private String sender;

    public Letter(String aRecipient, String aSender)
    {
        recipient = "John"; // Error—should use parameter variable
        sender = "Mary"; // Same error
    }
    . . .
}
```

The constructor ignores the names of the recipient and sender arguments that were provided to the constructor. If a user constructs a

```
new Letter("John", "Yoko")
```

the sender is still set to "Mary", which is bound to be embarrassing.

The constructor should use the parameter variables, like this:

```
public Letter(String aRecipient, String aSender)
{
    recipient = aRecipient;
    sender = aSender;
}
```

HOW TO 3.1

Implementing a Class

This "How To" section tells you how you implement a class from a given specification.

Problem Statement Implement a class that models a self-service cash register. The customer scans the price tags and deposits money in the machine. The machine dispenses the change.

Step 1   Find out which methods you are asked to supply.

In a simulation, you won't have to provide every feature that occurs in the real world—there are too many. In the cash register example, we don't deal with sales tax or credit card payments. The assignment tells you *which aspects* of the self-service cash register your class should simulate. Make a list of them:

- *Process the price of each purchased item.*
- *Receive payment.*
- *Calculate the amount of change due to the customer.*

Step 2   Specify the public interface.

Turn the list in Step 1 into a set of methods, with specific types for the parameter variables and the return values. Many programmers find this step simpler if they write out method calls that are applied to a sample object, like this:

```
CashRegister register = new CashRegister();
register.recordPurchase(29.95);
register.recordPurchase(9.95);
register.receivePayment(50);
double change = register.giveChange();
```

Now we have a specific list of methods:

- `public void recordPurchase(double amount)`
- `public void receivePayment(double amount)`
- `public double giveChange()`

To complete the public interface, you need to specify the constructors. Ask yourself what information you need in order to construct an object of your class. Sometimes you will want two constructors: one that sets all instance variables to a default and one that sets them to user-supplied values.

In the case of the cash register example, we can get by with a single constructor that creates an empty register. A more realistic cash register might start out with some coins and bills so that we can give exact change, but that is well beyond the scope of our assignment.

Thus, we add a single constructor:

- `public CashRegister()`

Step 3   Document the public interface.

Here is the documentation, with comments, that describes the class and its methods:

```
/**
    A cash register totals up sales and computes change due.
*/
public class CashRegister
{
```

```java
/**
   Constructs a cash register with no money in it.
*/
public CashRegister()
{
}

/**
   Records the sale of an item.
   @param amount the price of the item
*/
public void recordPurchase(double amount)
{
}

/**
   Processes a payment received from the customer.
   @param amount the amount of the payment
*/
public void receivePayment(double amount)
{
}

/**
   Computes the change due and resets the machine for the next customer.
   @return the change due to the customer
*/
public double giveChange()
{
}
}
```

Step 4 Determine instance variables.

Ask yourself what information an object needs to store to do its job. Remember, the methods can be called in any order. The object needs to have enough internal memory to be able to process every method using just its instance variables and the parameter variables. Go through each method, perhaps starting with a simple one or an interesting one, and ask yourself what you need to carry out the method's task. Make instance variables to store the information that the method needs.

Just as importantly, don't introduce unnecessary instance variables (see Common Error 3.4). If a value can be computed from other instance variables, it is generally better to compute it on demand than to store it.

In the cash register example, you need to keep track of the total purchase amount and the payment. You can compute the change due from these two amounts.

```java
public class CashRegister
{
    private double purchase;
    private double payment;
    . . .
}
```

Step 5 Implement constructors and methods.

Implement the constructors and methods in your class, one at a time, starting with the easiest ones. Here is the implementation of the recordPurchase method:

```java
public void recordPurchase(double amount)
{
    purchase = purchase + amount;
}
```

The receivePayment method looks almost the same,

```java
public void receivePayment(double amount)
{
    payment = payment + amount;
}
```

but why does the method add the amount, instead of simply setting payment = amount? A customer might provide two separate payments, such as two $10 bills, and the machine must process them both. Remember, methods can be called more than once, and they can be called in any order.

Finally, here is the giveChange method. This method is a bit more sophisticated—it computes the change due, and it also resets the cash register for the next sale.

```java
public double giveChange()
{
    double change = payment - purchase;
    purchase = 0;
    payment = 0;
    return change;
}
```

If you find that you have trouble with the implementation, you may need to rethink your choice of instance variables. It is common for a beginner to start out with a set of instance variables that cannot accurately reflect the state of an object. Don't hesitate to go back and add or modify instance variables.

Step 6   Test your class.

Write a short tester program and execute it. The tester program should carry out the method calls that you found in Step 2.

how_to_1/CashRegisterTester.java

```java
 1  /**
 2      A class to test the CashRegister class.
 3  */
 4  public class CashRegisterTester
 5  {
 6     public static void main(String[] args)
 7     {
 8        CashRegister register = new CashRegister();
 9
10        register.recordPurchase(29.50);
11        register.recordPurchase(9.25);
12        register.receivePayment(50);
13
14        double change = register.giveChange();
15
16        System.out.println(change);
17        System.out.println("Expected: 11.25");
18     }
19  }
```

Program Run

```
11.25
Expected: 11.25
```

EXAMPLE CODE   You can find the complete implementation in your eText or in the how_to_1 directory of your companion code.

3.4 Unit Testing **81**

WORKED EXAMPLE 3.1
Making a Simple Menu

Learn how to implement a class that constructs simple text-based menus. See your eText or visit wiley.com/go/bjeo7.

© Mark Evans/iStockphoto.

3.4 Unit Testing

In the preceding section, we completed the implementation of the BankAccount class. What can you do with it? Of course, you can compile the file BankAccount.java. However, you can't *execute* the resulting BankAccount.class file. It doesn't contain a main method. That is normal—most classes don't contain a main method.

In the long run, your class may become a part of a larger program that interacts with users, stores data in files, and so on. However, before integrating a class into a program, it is always a good idea to test it in isolation. Testing in isolation, outside a complete program, is called **unit testing**.

> A unit test verifies that a class works correctly in isolation, outside a complete program.

© Chris Fertnig/iStockphoto.

An engineer tests a part in isolation. This is an example of unit testing.

To test your class, you have two choices. Some interactive development environments have commands for constructing objects and invoking methods (see Special Topic 2.2). Then you can test a class simply by constructing an object, calling methods, and verifying that you get the expected return values. Figure 6 shows the result of calling the getBalance method on a BankAccount object in BlueJ.

Figure 6
The Return Value of the getBalance Method in BlueJ

Alternatively, you can write a *tester class*. A tester class is a class with a main method that contains statements to run methods of another class. As discussed in Section 2.7, a tester class typically carries out the following steps:

1. Construct one or more objects of the class that is being tested.
2. Invoke one or more methods.
3. Print out one or more results.
4. Print the expected results.

The MoveTester class in Section 2.7 is a good example of a tester class. That class runs methods of the Rectangle class—a class in the Java library.

Following is a class to run methods of the BankAccount class. The main method constructs an object of type BankAccount, invokes the deposit and withdraw methods, and then displays the remaining balance on the console.

We also print the value that we expect to see. In our sample program, we deposit $2,000 and withdraw $500. We therefore expect a balance of $1,500.

sec04/BankAccountTester.java

```java
 1  /**
 2      A class to test the BankAccount class.
 3  */
 4  public class BankAccountTester
 5  {
 6     /**
 7         Tests the methods of the BankAccount class.
 8         @param args not used
 9     */
10     public static void main(String[] args)
11     {
12        BankAccount harrysChecking = new BankAccount();
13        harrysChecking.deposit(2000);
14        harrysChecking.withdraw(500);
15        System.out.println(harrysChecking.getBalance());
16        System.out.println("Expected: 1500");
17     }
18  }
```

Program Run

```
1500
Expected: 1500
```

To produce a program, you need to combine the BankAccount and the BankAccountTester classes. The details for building the program depend on your compiler and development environment. In most environments, you need to carry out these steps:

1. Make a new subfolder for your program.
2. Make two files, one for each class.
3. Compile both files.
4. Run the test program.

Many students are surprised that such a simple program contains two classes. However, this is normal. The two classes have entirely different purposes. The BankAccount class describes objects that compute bank balances. The `BankAccountTester` class runs a test that puts a `BankAccount` object through its paces.

Computing & Society 3.1   Electronic Voting

In the 2000 presidential elections in the United States, votes were tallied by a variety of machines. Some machines processed cardboard ballots into which voters punched holes to indicate their choices (see below).

When voters were not careful, remains of paper—the now infamous "chads"—were partially stuck in the punch cards, causing votes to be miscounted. A manual recount was necessary, but it was not carried out everywhere due to time constraints and procedural wrangling. The election was very close, and there remain doubts in the minds of many people whether the election outcome would have been different if the voting machines had accurately counted the intent of the voters.

Subsequently, voting machine manufacturers have argued that electronic voting machines would avoid the problems caused by punch cards or optically scanned forms. In an electronic voting machine, voters indicate their preferences by pressing buttons or touching icons on a computer screen. Typically, each voter is presented with a summary screen for review before casting the ballot. The process is very similar to using a bank's automated teller machine.

It seems plausible that these machines make it more likely that a

vote is counted in the same way that the voter intends. However, there has been significant controversy surrounding some types of electronic voting machines. If a machine simply records the votes and reports the totals after the election has been completed, then how do you know that the machine worked correctly? Inside the machine is a computer that executes a program, and, as you may know from your own experience, programs can have bugs.

In fact, some electronic voting machines do have bugs. There is also increasing fear that the machines can be attacked remotely. When a machine reports far more or far fewer votes than voters, then it is clear that it malfunctioned. Unfortunately, it is then impossible to find out the actual votes. More insidiously, if the results are plausible, nobody may ever investigate.

Many computer scientists have spoken out on this issue and confirmed that it is impossible, with today's technology, to tell that software is error free and has not been tampered with. Many of them recommend that electronic voting machines should employ a *voter-verifiable audit trail*. (A good source of information is http://verifiedvoting.org.) Typically, a voter-verifiable machine prints out a ballot. Each voter has a chance to review the printout, and then deposits it in an old-fashioned ballot box. If there is a problem with the electronic equipment, the printouts can be scanned or counted by hand.

Some states require random manual audits in which a small percentage of the votes is hand-tallied and compared with the electronic results. Naturally, this process, recommended as a best practice by security experts, is only meaningful when paper ballots are available. Elections that take place over the Internet have so many

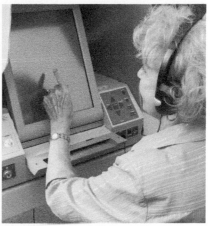

© Lisa F. Young/iStockphoto.

Touch Screen Voting Machine

security concerns that most experts strongly advise against them.

What do you think? You probably use an automated bank teller machine to get cash from your bank account. Do you review the paper record that the machine issues? Do you check your bank statement? Even if you don't, do you put your faith in other people who double-check their balances, so that the bank won't get away with widespread cheating?

Is the integrity of banking equipment more important or less important than that of voting machines? Won't every voting process have some room for error and fraud anyway? Is the added cost for equipment, paper, and staff time reasonable to combat a potentially slight risk of malfunction and fraud? Computer scientists cannot answer these questions—an informed society must make these tradeoffs. But, like all professionals, they have an obligation to speak out and give accurate testimony about the capabilities and limitations of computing equipment.

© Peter Nguyen/iStockphoto.

Punch Card Ballot

3.5 Problem Solving: Tracing Objects

Researchers have studied why some students have an easier time learning how to program than others. One important skill of successful programmers is the ability to simulate the actions of a program with pencil and paper. In this section, you will see how to develop this skill by tracing method calls on objects.

> Write the methods on the front of a card and the instance variables on the back.

Use an index card or a sticky note for each object. On the front, write the methods that the object can execute. On the back, make a table for the values of the instance variables.

Here is a card for a CashRegister object:

CashRegister reg1	*reg1.purchase*	*reg1.payment*
recordPurchase *receivePayment* *giveChange*		

front   *back*

In a small way, this gives you a feel for encapsulation. An object is manipulated through its public interface (on the front of the card), and the instance variables are hidden on the back.

When an object is constructed, fill in the initial values of the instance variables:

reg1.purchase	*reg1.payment*
0	*0*

> Update the values of the instance variables when a mutator method is called.

Whenever a mutator method is executed, cross out the old values and write the new ones below. Here is what happens after a call to the recordPurchase method:

reg1.purchase	*reg1.payment*
~~*0*~~ *19.95*	*0*

If you have more than one object in your program, you will have multiple cards, one for each object:

reg1.purchase	reg1.payment
~~0~~ 19.95	~~0~~ 19.95

reg2.purchase	reg2.payment
~~0~~ ~~29.50~~ 9.25	~~0~~ 50.00

These diagrams are also useful when you design a class. Suppose you are asked to enhance the CashRegister class to compute the sales tax. Add methods recordTaxable-Purchase and getSalesTax to the front of the card. Now turn the card over, look over the instance variables, and ask yourself whether the object has sufficient information to compute the answer. Remember that each object is an autonomous unit. Any value that can be used in a computation must be

- An instance variable.
- A method argument.
- A static variable (uncommon; see Section 8.4).

To compute the sales tax, we need to know the tax rate and the total of the taxable items. (Food items are usually not subject to sales tax.) We don't have that information available. Let us introduce additional instance variables for the tax rate and the taxable total. The tax rate can be set in the constructor (assuming it stays fixed for the lifetime of the object). When adding an item, we need to be told whether the item is taxable. If so, we add its price to the taxable total.

For example, consider the following statements.

```
CashRegister reg3 = new CashRegister(7.5); // 7.5 percent sales tax
reg3.recordPurchase(3.95); // Not taxable
reg3.recordTaxablePurchase(19.95); // Taxable
```

When you record the effect on a card, it looks like this:

reg3.purchase	reg3.taxablePurchase	reg3.payment	reg3.taxRate
~~0~~ 3.95	~~0~~ 19.95	0	7.5

With this information, we can compute the tax. It is *taxablePurchase × taxRate / 100*. Tracing the object helped us understand the need for additional instance variables.

EXAMPLE CODE   See sec05 of your eText or companion code for an enhanced CashRegister class that computes the sales tax.

3.6 Local Variables

Local variables are declared in the body of a method.

In this section, we discuss the behavior of *local* variables. A **local variable** is a variable that is declared in the body of a method. For example, the giveChange method in How To 3.1 declares a local variable change:

```java
public double giveChange()
{
   double change = payment - purchase;
   purchase = 0;
   payment = 0;
   return change;
}
```

Parameter variables are similar to local variables, but they are declared in method headers. For example, the following method declares a parameter variable amount:

```java
public void receivePayment(double amount)
```

When a method exits, its local variables are removed.

Local and parameter variables belong to methods. When a method runs, its local and parameter variables come to life. When the method exits, they are removed immediately. For example, if you call register.giveChange(), then a variable change is created. When the method exits, that variable is removed.

In contrast, instance variables belong to objects, not methods. When an object is constructed, its instance variables are created. The instance variables stay alive until no method uses the object any longer. (The Java virtual machine contains an agent called a **garbage collector** that periodically reclaims objects when they are no longer used.)

Instance variables are initialized to a default value, but you must initialize local variables.

An important difference between instance variables and local variables is initialization. You must **initialize** all local variables. If you don't initialize a local variable, the compiler complains when you try to use it. (Note that parameter variables are initialized when the method is called.)

Instance variables are initialized with a default value before a constructor is invoked. Instance variables that are numbers are initialized to 0. Object references are set to a special value called null. If an object reference is null, then it refers to no object at all. We will discuss the null value in greater detail in Section 5.2.5.

EXAMPLE CODE   See sec06 of your eText or companion code for a demonstration of local variables.

Common Error 3.3

Duplicating Instance Variables in Local Variables

Beginning programmers commonly add types to assignment statements, thereby changing them into local variable declarations. For example,

```java
public double giveChange()
{
   double change = payment - purchase;
   double purchase = 0; // ERROR! This declares a local variable.
   double payment = 0;  // ERROR! The instance variable is not updated.
   return change;
}
```

Another common error is to declare a parameter variable with the same name as an instance variable. For example, consider this BankAccount constructor:

```
public BankAccount(double balance)
{
    balance = balance; // ERROR! Does not set the instance variable
}
```

This constructor simply sets the parameter variable to itself, leaving it unchanged. A simple remedy is to come up with a different name for the parameter variable:

```
public BankAccount(double initialBalance)
{
    balance = initialBalance; // OK
}
```

Common Error 3.4

Providing Unnecessary Instance Variables

A common beginner's mistake is to use instance variables when local variables would be more appropriate. For example, consider the change variable of the giveChange method. It is not needed anywhere else—that's why it is local to the method. But what if it had been declared as an instance variable?

```
public class CashRegister
{
    private double purchase;
    private double payment;
    private double change; // Not appropriate

    public double giveChange()
    {
        change = payment - purchase;
        purchase = 0;
        payment = 0;
        return change;
    }
    . . .
}
```

This class will work, but there is a hidden danger. Other methods can read and write to the change instance variable, which can be a source of confusion.

Use instance variables for values that an object needs to remember between method calls. Use local variables for values that don't need to be retained when a method has completed.

Common Error 3.5

Forgetting to Initialize Object References in a Constructor

Just as it is a common error to forget to initialize a local variable, it is easy to forget about instance variables. Every constructor needs to ensure that all instance variables are set to appropriate values.

If you do not initialize an instance variable, the Java compiler will initialize it for you. Numbers are initialized with 0, but object references—such as string variables—are set to the null reference.

Of course, 0 is often a convenient default for numbers. However, null is hardly ever a convenient default for objects. Consider this "lazy" constructor for a modified version of the BankAccount class:

```
public class BankAccount
{
```

```
        private double balance;
        private String owner;
        . . .
        public BankAccount(double initialBalance)
        {
            balance = initialBalance;
        }
    }
```

Then `balance` is initialized, but the `owner` variable is set to a `null` reference. This can be a problem—it is illegal to call methods on the `null` reference.

To avoid this problem, it is a good idea to initialize every instance variable:

```
    public BankAccount(double initialBalance)
    {
        balance = initialBalance;
        owner = "None";
    }
```

3.7 The this Reference

When you call a method, you pass two kinds of inputs to the method:

- The object on which you invoke the method
- The method arguments

For example, when you call

```
    momsSavings.deposit(500);
```

the `deposit` method needs to know the account object (`momsSavings`) as well as the amount that is being deposited (500).

When you implement the method, you provide a parameter variable for each argument. But you don't need to provide a parameter variable for the object on which the method is being invoked. That object is called the **implicit parameter**. All other parameter variables (such as the amount to be deposited in our example) are called **explicit parameters**.

Look again at the code of the `deposit` method:

```
    public void deposit(double amount)
    {
        balance = balance + amount;
    }
```

Here, `amount` is an explicit parameter. You don't see the implicit parameter—that is why it is called "implicit". But consider what `balance` means exactly. After all, our program may have multiple `BankAccount` objects, and *each of them* has its own balance.

Because we are depositing the money into `momsSavings`, `balance` must mean `moms-Savings.balance`. In general, when you refer to an instance variable inside a method, it means the instance variable of the implicit parameter.

In any method, you can access the implicit parameter—the object on which the method is called—with the reserved word `this`. For example, in the preceding method invocation, `this` refers to the same object as `momsSavings` (see Figure 7).

The statement

```
    balance = balance + amount;
```

> Use of an instance variable name in a method denotes the instance variable of the implicit parameter.

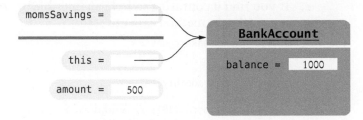

Figure 7 The Implicit Parameter of a Method Call

actually means

```
this.balance = this.balance + amount;
```

When you refer to an instance variable in a method, the compiler automatically applies it to the this reference. Some programmers actually prefer to manually insert the this reference before every instance variable because they find it makes the code clearer. Here is an example:

```
public BankAccount(double initialBalance)
{
    this.balance = initialBalance;
}
```

You may want to try it out and see if you like that style.

The this reference can also be used to distinguish between instance variables and local or parameter variables. Consider the constructor

```
public BankAccount(double balance)
{
    this.balance = balance;
}
```

The expression this.balance clearly refers to the balance instance variable. However, the expression balance by itself seems ambiguous. It could denote either the parameter variable or the instance variable. The Java language specifies that in this situation the local variable wins out. It "shadows" the instance variable. Therefore,

```
this.balance = balance;
```

means: "Set the instance variable balance to the parameter variable balance".

There is another situation in which it is important to understand implicit parameters. Consider the following modification to the BankAccount class. We add a method to apply the monthly account fee:

```
public class BankAccount
{
    . . .
    public void monthlyFee()
    {
        withdraw(10); // Withdraw $10 from this account
    }
}
```

That means to withdraw from the *same* bank account object that is carrying out the monthlyFee operation. In other words, the implicit parameter of the withdraw method is the (invisible) implicit parameter of the monthlyFee method.

If you find it confusing to have an invisible parameter, you can use the this refer-ence to make the method easier to read:

```java
public class BankAccount
{
    . . .
    public void monthlyFee()
    {
        this.withdraw(10); // Withdraw $10 from this account
    }
}
```

You have now seen how to use objects and implement classes, and you have learned some important technical details about variables and method parameters. The remainder of this chapter continues the optional graphics track. In the next chapter, you will learn more about the most fundamental data types of the Java language.

EXAMPLE CODE   See sec07 of your eText or companion code for a Counter class that uses the this reference.

Special Topic 3.1
Calling One Constructor from Another

Consider the BankAccount class. It has two constructors: a no-argument constructor to initialize the balance with zero, and another constructor to supply an initial balance. Rather than explic-itly setting the balance to zero, one constructor can call another constructor of the same class instead. There is a shorthand notation to achieve this result:

```java
public class BankAccount
{
    public BankAccount(double initialBalance)
    {
        balance = initialBalance;
    }

    public BankAccount()
    {
        this(0);
    }
    . . .
}
```

The command this(0); means "Call another constructor of this class and supply the value 0". Such a call to another constructor can occur only as the *first line in a constructor*.

This syntax is a minor convenience. We will not use it in this book. Actually, the use of the reserved word this is a little confusing. Normally, this denotes a reference to the implicit parameter, but if this is followed by parentheses, it denotes a call to another constructor of the same class.

3.8 Shape Classes

In this section, we continue the optional graphics track by discussing how to orga-nize complex drawings in a more object-oriented fashion.

When you produce a drawing that has multiple shapes, or parts made of multi-ple shapes, such as the car in Figure 8, it is a good idea to make a separate class for

It is a good idea to make a class for any part of a drawing that can occur more than once.

each part. The class should have a draw method that draws the shape, and a constructor to set the position of the shape.

For example, here is the outline of the Car class:

```
public class Car
{
    public Car(int x, int y)
    {
        Remember position.
        . . .
    }

    public void draw(Graphics2D g2)
    {
        Drawing instructions.
        . . .
    }
}
```

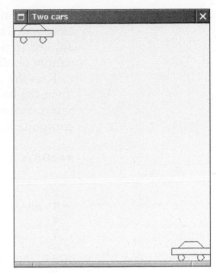

Figure 8
The Car Component Draws
Two Car Shapes

You will find the complete class declaration at the end of this section. The draw method contains a rather long sequence of instructions for drawing the body, roof, and tires.

The coordinates of the car parts seem a bit arbitrary. To come up with suitable values, draw the image on graph paper and read off the coordinates (Figure 9).

The program that produces Figure 8 is composed of three classes.

To figure out how to draw a complex shape, make a sketch on graph paper.

- The Car class is responsible for drawing a single car. Two objects of this class are constructed, one for each car.
- The CarComponent class displays the drawing.
- The CarViewer class shows a frame that contains a CarComponent.

Let us look more closely at the CarComponent class. The paintComponent method draws two cars. We place one car in the top-left corner of the window, and the other car in the bottom-right corner. To compute the bottom-right position, we call the getWidth and getHeight methods of the JComponent class. These methods return the dimensions of the component. We subtract the dimensions of the car to determine the position of car2:

```
Car car1 = new Car(0, 0);
int x = getWidth() - 60;
int y = getHeight() - 30;
Car car2 = new Car(x, y);
```

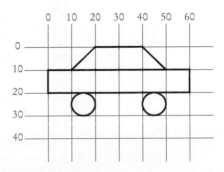

Figure 9
Using Graph Paper to Find Shape Coordinates

Pay close attention to the call to getWidth inside the paintComponent method of Car-Component. The method call has no implicit parameter, which means that the method is applied to the same object that executes the paintComponent method. The component simply obtains *its own* width.

Run the program and resize the window. Note that the second car always ends up at the bottom-right corner of the window. Whenever the window is resized, the paintComponent method is called and the car position is recomputed, taking the current component dimensions into account.

sec08/CarViewer.java

```java
1   import javax.swing.JFrame;
2
3   public class CarViewer
4   {
5      public static void main(String[] args)
6      {
7         JFrame frame = new JFrame();
8
9         frame.setSize(300, 400);
10        frame.setTitle("Two cars");
11        frame.setDefaultCloseOperation(JFrame.EXIT_ON_CLOSE);
12
13        CarComponent component = new CarComponent();
14        frame.add(component);
15
16        frame.setVisible(true);
17     }
18  }
```

sec08/CarComponent.java

```java
1   import java.awt.Graphics;
2   import java.awt.Graphics2D;
3   import javax.swing.JComponent;
4
5   /**
6      This component draws two car shapes.
7   */
8   public class CarComponent extends JComponent
9   {
10     public void paintComponent(Graphics g)
11     {
12        Graphics2D g2 = (Graphics2D) g;
13
14        Car car1 = new Car(0, 0);
15
16        int x = getWidth() - 60;
17        int y = getHeight() - 30;
18
19        Car car2 = new Car(x, y);
20
21        car1.draw(g2);
22        car2.draw(g2);
23     }
24  }
```

sec08/Car.java

```java
1  import java.awt.Graphics2D;
2  import java.awt.Rectangle;
3  import java.awt.geom.Ellipse2D;
4  import java.awt.geom.Line2D;
5  import java.awt.geom.Point2D;
6
7  /**
8     A car shape that can be positioned anywhere on the screen.
9  */
10 public class Car
11 {
12    private int xLeft;
13    private int yTop;
14
15    /**
16       Constructs a car with a given top left corner.
17       @param x the x-coordinate of the top-left corner
18       @param y the y-coordinate of the top-left corner
19    */
20    public Car(int x, int y)
21    {
22       xLeft = x;
23       yTop = y;
24    }
25
26    /**
27       Draws the car.
28       @param g2 the graphics context
29    */
30    public void draw(Graphics2D g2)
31    {
32       Rectangle body = new Rectangle(xLeft, yTop + 10, 60, 10);
33       Ellipse2D.Double frontTire
34             = new Ellipse2D.Double(xLeft + 10, yTop + 20, 10, 10);
35       Ellipse2D.Double rearTire
36             = new Ellipse2D.Double(xLeft + 40, yTop + 20, 10, 10);
37
38       // The bottom of the front windshield
39       Point2D.Double r1 = new Point2D.Double(xLeft + 10, yTop + 10);
40       // The front of the roof
41       Point2D.Double r2 = new Point2D.Double(xLeft + 20, yTop);
42       // The rear of the roof
43       Point2D.Double r3 = new Point2D.Double(xLeft + 40, yTop);
44       // The bottom of the rear windshield
45       Point2D.Double r4 = new Point2D.Double(xLeft + 50, yTop + 10);
46
47       Line2D.Double frontWindshield = new Line2D.Double(r1, r2);
48       Line2D.Double roofTop = new Line2D.Double(r2, r3);
49       Line2D.Double rearWindshield = new Line2D.Double(r3, r4);
50
51       g2.draw(body);
52       g2.draw(frontTire);
53       g2.draw(rearTire);
54       g2.draw(frontWindshield);
55       g2.draw(roofTop);
56       g2.draw(rearWindshield);
57    }
58 }
```

HOW TO 3.2

Drawing Graphical Shapes

Suppose you want to write a program that displays graphical shapes such as cars, aliens, charts, or any other images that can be obtained from rectangles, lines, and ellipses. These instructions give you a step-by-step procedure for decomposing a drawing into parts and implementing a program that produces the drawing.

Problem Statement   Create a program that draws a national flag.

Step 1   Determine the shapes that you need for the drawing.

You can use the following shapes:
- Squares and rectangles
- Circles and ellipses
- Lines

The outlines of these shapes can be drawn in any color, and you can fill the insides of these shapes with any color. You can also use text to label parts of your drawing.

Some national flags consist of three equally wide sections of different colors, side by side.

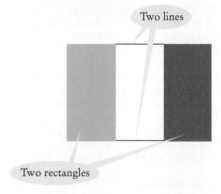

Punchstock.

You could draw such a flag using three rectangles. But if the middle rectangle is white, as it is, for example, in the flag of Italy (green, white, red), it is easier and looks better to draw a line on the top and bottom of the middle portion:

Step 2   Find the coordinates for the shapes.

You now need to find the exact positions for the geometric shapes.
- For rectangles, you need the x- and y-position of the top-left corner, the width, and the height.
- For ellipses, you need the top-left corner, width, and height of the bounding rectangle.

- For lines, you need the *x*- and *y*-positions of the start and end points.
- For text, you need the *x*- and *y*-position of the basepoint.

A commonly-used size for a window is 300 by 300 pixels. You may not want the flag crammed all the way to the top, so perhaps the upper-left corner of the flag should be at point (100, 100).

Many flags, such as the flag of Italy, have a width : height ratio of 3 : 2. (You can often find exact proportions for a particular flag by doing a bit of Internet research on one of several Flags of the World sites.) For example, if you make the flag 90 pixels wide, then it should be 60 pixels tall. (Why not make it 100 pixels wide? Then the height would be $100 \cdot 2 / 3 \approx 67$, which seems more awkward.)

Now you can compute the coordinates of all the important points of the shape:

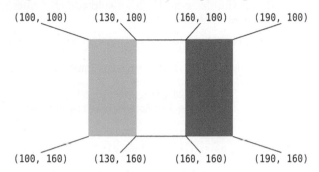

Step 3   Write Java statements to draw the shapes.

In our example, there are two rectangles and two lines:

```
Rectangle leftRectangle = new Rectangle(100, 100, 30, 60);
Rectangle rightRectangle = new Rectangle(160, 100, 30, 60);
Line2D.Double topLine = new Line2D.Double(130, 100, 160, 100);
Line2D.Double bottomLine = new Line2D.Double(130, 160, 160, 160);
```

If you are more ambitious, then you can express the coordinates in terms of a few variables. In the case of the flag, we have arbitrarily chosen the top-left corner and the width. All other coordinates follow from those choices. If you decide to follow the ambitious approach, then the rectangles and lines are determined as follows:

```
Rectangle leftRectangle = new Rectangle(
      xLeft, yTop,
      width / 3, width * 2 / 3);
Rectangle rightRectangle = new Rectangle(
      xLeft + 2 * width / 3, yTop,
      width / 3, width * 2 / 3);
Line2D.Double topLine = new Line2D.Double(
      xLeft + width / 3, yTop,
      xLeft + width * 2 / 3, yTop);
Line2D.Double bottomLine = new Line2D.Double(
      xLeft + width / 3, yTop + width * 2 / 3,
      xLeft + width * 2 / 3, yTop + width * 2 / 3);
```

Now you need to fill the rectangles and draw the lines. For the flag of Italy, the left rectangle is green and the right rectangle is red. Remember to switch colors before the filling and drawing operations:

```
g2.setColor(Color.GREEN);
g2.fill(leftRectangle);
g2.setColor(Color.RED);
g2.fill(rightRectangle);
g2.setColor(Color.BLACK);
g2.draw(topLine);
g2.draw(bottomLine);
```

Step 4   Combine the drawing statements with the component "plumbing".

```java
public class MyComponent extends JComponent
{
    public void paintComponent(Graphics g)
    {
        Graphics2D g2 = (Graphics2D) g;
        Drawing instructions.
        . . .
    }
}
```

In our simple example, you could add all shapes and drawing instructions inside the paint-Component method:

```java
public class ItalianFlagComponent extends JComponent
{
    public void paintComponent(Graphics g)
    {
        Graphics2D g2 = (Graphics2D) g;
        Rectangle leftRectangle = new Rectangle(100, 100, 30, 60);
        . . .
        g2.setColor(Color.GREEN);
        g2.fill(leftRectangle);
        . . .
    }
}
```

That approach is acceptable for simple drawings, but it is not very object-oriented. After all, a flag is an object. It is better to make a separate class for the flag. Then you can draw different flags at different positions. Specify the sizes in a constructor and supply a draw method:

```java
public class ItalianFlag
{
    private int xLeft;
    private int yTop;
    private int width;

    public ItalianFlag(int x, int y, int aWidth)
    {
        xLeft = x;
        yTop = y;
        width = aWidth;
    }

    public void draw(Graphics2D g2)
    {
        Rectangle leftRectangle = new Rectangle(
            xLeft, yTop,
            width / 3, width * 2 / 3);
        . . .
        g2.setColor(Color.GREEN);
        g2.fill(leftRectangle);
        . . .
    }
}
```

You still need a separate class for the component, but it is very simple:

```java
public class ItalianFlagComponent extends JComponent
{
    public void paintComponent(Graphics g)
    {
```

```
            Graphics2D g2 = (Graphics2D) g;
            ItalianFlag flag = new ItalianFlag(100, 100, 90);
            flag.draw(g2);
        }
    }
```

Step 5   Write the viewer class.

Provide a viewer class, with a main method in which you construct a frame, add your component, and make your frame visible. The viewer class is completely routine; you only need to change a single line to show a different component.

```
public class ItalianFlagViewer
{
    public static void main(String[] args)
    {
        JFrame frame = new JFrame();

        frame.setSize(300, 400);
        frame.setDefaultCloseOperation(JFrame.EXIT_ON_CLOSE);

        ItalianFlagComponent component = new ItalianFlagComponent();
        frame.add(component);

        frame.setVisible(true);
    }
}
```

EXAMPLE CODE   See how_to_2 of your eText or companion code for the complete flag drawing program.

CHAPTER SUMMARY

Understand instance variables and the methods that access them.

- An object's instance variables store the data required for executing its methods.
- Each object of a class has its own set of instance variables.
- Private instance variables can only be accessed by methods of the same class.
- Encapsulation is the process of hiding implementation details and providing methods for data access.

- Encapsulation allows a programmer to use a class without having to know its implementation.
- Information hiding makes it simpler for the implementor of a class to locate errors and change implementations.

Write method and constructor headers that describe the public interface of a class.

- In order to implement a class, you first need to know which methods are required.
- Constructors set the initial data for objects.
- The constructor name is always the same as the class name.

- Use documentation comments to describe the classes and public methods of your programs.
- Provide documentation comments for every class, every method, every parameter variable, and every return value.

Implement a class.

- The private implementation of a class consists of instance variables, and the bodies of constructors and methods.

Write tests that verify that a class works correctly.

- A unit test verifies that a class works correctly in isolation, outside a complete program.
- To test a class, use an environment for interactive testing, or write a tester class to execute test instructions.

Use the technique of object tracing for visualizing object behavior.

- Write the methods on the front of a card and the instance variables on the back.
- Update the values of the instance variables when a mutator method is called.

Compare initialization and lifetime of instance, local, and parameter variables.

- Local variables are declared in the body of a method.
- When a method exits, its local variables are removed.
- Instance variables are initialized to a default value, but you must initialize local variables.

Recognize the use of the implicit parameter in method declarations.

- Use of an instance variable name in a method denotes the instance variable of the implicit parameter.
- The this reference denotes the implicit parameter.
- A local variable shadows an instance variable with the same name. You can access the instance variable name through the this reference.
- A method call without an implicit parameter is applied to the same object.

Implement classes that draw graphical shapes.

- It is a good idea to make a class for any part of a drawing that can occur more than once.
- To figure out how to draw a complex shape, make a sketch on graph paper.

REVIEW EXERCISES

- **R3.1** It is possible to replace an old-fashioned thermostat with a device that can be controlled through a smart phone, without making any other changes to the heating system. Explain this by using the terms "interface", "encapsulation", and "implementation".

- **R3.2** What is the public interface of the Counter class in Section 3.1? How does it differ from the implementation of the class?

- **R3.3** What is encapsulation? Why is it useful?

- **R3.4** Instance variables are a part of the hidden implementation of a class, but they aren't actually hidden from programmers who have the source code of the class. Explain to what extent the private reserved word provides information hiding.

- **R3.5** Consider a class Grade that represents a letter grade, such as A+ or B. Give two choices of instance variables that can be used for implementing the Grade class.

- **R3.6** Consider a class Time that represents a point in time, such as 9 a.m. or 3:30 p.m. Give two different sets of instance variables that can be used for implementing the Time class.

- **R3.7** Suppose the implementor of the Time class of Exercise •• R3.6 changes from one implementation strategy to another, keeping the public interface unchanged. What do the programmers who use the Time class need to do?

- **R3.8** You can read the value instance variable of the Counter class with the getValue accessor method. Should there be a setValue mutator method to change it? Explain why or why not.

- **R3.9** Show that the BankAccount(double initialBalance) constructor is not strictly necessary. That is, if we removed that constructor from the public interface, how could a programmer still obtain BankAccount objects with an arbitrary balance?

    Conversely, could we keep only the BankAccount(double initialBalance) constructor and remove the BankAccount() constructor?

- **R3.10** Why does the BankAccount class not have a reset method?

- **R3.11** What happens in our implementation of the BankAccount class when more money is withdrawn from the account than the current balance?

- **R3.12** What is the this reference? Why would you use it?

- **R3.13** Which of the methods in the CashRegister class of How To 3.1 are accessor methods? Which are mutator methods?

- **R3.14** What does the following method do? Give an example of how you can call the method.

```java
public class BankAccount
{
    public void mystery(BankAccount that, double amount)
    {
        this.balance = this.balance - amount;
        that.balance = that.balance + amount;
```

```
        }
        . . . // Other bank account methods
    }
```

■■ R3.15 Suppose you want to implement a class TimeDepositAccount. A time deposit account has a fixed interest rate that should be set in the constructor, together with the initial balance. Provide a method to get the current balance. Provide a method to add the earned interest to the account. This method should have no arguments because the interest rate is already known. It should have no return value because you already provided a method for obtaining the current balance. It is not possible to deposit additional funds into this account. Provide a withdraw method that removes the entire balance. Partial withdrawals are not allowed.

■ R3.16 Consider the following implementation of a class Square:

```java
public class Square
{
    private int sideLength;
    private int area; // Not a good idea

    public Square(int length)
    {
        sideLength = length;
    }

    public int getArea()
    {
        area = sideLength * sideLength;
        return area;
    }
}
```

Why is it not a good idea to introduce an instance variable for the area? Rewrite the class so that area is a local variable.

■■ R3.17 Consider the following implementation of a class Square:

```java
public class Square
{
    private int sideLength;
    private int area;

    public Square(int initialLength)
    {
        sideLength = initialLength;
        area = sideLength * sideLength;
    }

    public int getArea() { return area; }
    public void grow() { sideLength = 2 * sideLength; }
}
```

What error does this class have? How would you fix it?

■■ Testing R3.18 Provide a unit test class for the Counter class in Section 3.1.

■■ Testing R3.19 Read Exercise ●● E3.13, but do not implement the Car class yet. Write a tester class that tests a scenario in which gas is added to the car, the car is driven, more gas is added, and the car is driven again. Print the actual and expected amount of gas in the tank.

- **R3.20** Using the object tracing technique described in Section 3.5, trace the program at the end of Section 3.4.

- **R3.21** Using the object tracing technique described in Section 3.5, trace the program in How To 3.1.

- **R3.22** Using the object tracing technique described in Section 3.5, trace the program in Worked Example 3.1.

- **R3.23** Design a modification of the BankAccount class in which the first five transactions per month are free and a $1 fee is charged for every additional transaction. Provide a method that deducts the fee at the end of a month. What additional instance variables do you need? Using the object tracing technique described in Section 3.5, trace a scenario that shows how the fees are computed over two months.

- **Graphics R3.24** Suppose you want to extend the car viewer program in Section 3.8 to show a suburban scene, with several cars and houses. Which classes do you need?

- **Graphics R3.25** Explain why the calls to the getWidth and getHeight methods in the CarComponent class have no explicit parameter.

- **Graphics R3.26** How would you modify the Car class in order to show cars of varying sizes?

PRACTICE EXERCISES

- **E3.1** We want to add a button to the tally counter in Section 3.1 that allows an operator to undo an accidental button click. Provide a method

  ```
  public void undo()
  ```

  that simulates such a button. As an added precaution, make sure that clicking the undo button more often than the click button has no effect. (*Hint:* The call Math.max(n, 0) returns n if n is greater than zero, zero otherwise.)

- **E3.2** Simulate a tally counter that can be used to admit a limited number of people. First, the limit is set with a call

  ```
  public void setLimit(int maximum)
  ```

  If the click button is clicked more often than the limit, it has no effect. (*Hint:* The call Math.min(n, limit) returns n if n is less than limit, and limit otherwise.)

- **E3.3** Write a class RangeInput that allows users to enter a value within a range of values that is provided in the constructor. An example would be a temperature control switch in a car that allows inputs between 60 and 80 degrees Fahrenheit. The input control has "up" and "down" buttons. Provide up and down methods to change the current value. The initial value is the midpoint between the limits. As with the preceding exercises, use Math.min and Math.max to limit the value. Write a sample program that simulates clicks on controls for the passenger and driver seats.

- **E3.4** Simulate a circuit for controlling a hallway light that has switches at both ends of the hallway. Each switch can be up or down, and the light can be on or off. Toggling either switch turns the lamp on or off.

Provide methods

```
public int getFirstSwitchState() // 0 for down, 1 for up
public int getSecondSwitchState()
public int getLampState() // 0 for off, 1 for on
public void toggleFirstSwitch()
public void toggleSecondSwitch()
```

- **Testing E3.5** Write a `CircuitTester` class that tests all switch combinations in Exercise •• E3.4, printing out actual and expected states for the switches and lamps.

- **■■■ E3.6** Change the public interface of the circuit class of Exercise •• E3.4 so that it has the following methods:

```
public int getSwitchState(int switchNum)
public int getLampState()
public void toggleSwitch(int switchNum)
```

Provide an implementation using only language features that have been introduced. The challenge is to find a data representation from which to recover the switch states.

- **Testing E3.7** Write a `BankAccountTester` class whose `main` method constructs a bank account, deposits $1,000, withdraws $500, withdraws another $400, and then prints the remaining balance. Also print the expected result.

- **■ E3.8** Add a method

```
public void addInterest(double rate)
```

to the `BankAccount` class that adds interest at the given rate. For example, after the statements

```
BankAccount momsSavings = new BankAccount(1000);
momsSavings.addInterest(10); // 10 percent interest
```

the balance in `momsSavings` is $1,100. Also supply a `BankAccountTester` class that prints the actual and expected balance.

- **■ E3.9** Write a class `SavingsAccount` that is similar to the `BankAccount` class, except that it has an added instance variable `interest`. Supply a constructor that sets both the initial balance and the interest rate. Supply a method `addInterest` (with no explicit parameter) that adds interest to the account. Write a `SavingsAccountTester` class that constructs a savings account with an initial balance of $1,000 and an interest rate of 10 percent. Then apply the `addInterest` method and print the resulting balance. Also compute the expected result by hand and print it.

- **■■■ E3.10** Add a method `printReceipt` to the `CashRegister` class. The method should print the prices of all purchased items and the total amount due. *Hint:* You will need to form a string of all prices. Use the `concat` method of the `String` class to add additional items to that string. To turn a price into a string, use the call `String.valueOf(price)`.

- **■ E3.11** After closing time, the store manager would like to know how much business was transacted during the day. Modify the `CashRegister` class to enable this functionality. Supply methods `getSalesTotal` and `getSalesCount` to get the total amount of all sales and the number of sales. Supply a method `reset` that resets any counters and totals so that the next day's sales start from zero.

- **■■ E3.12** Implement a class `Employee`. An employee has a name (a string) and a salary (a double). Provide a constructor with two arguments

```
public Employee(String employeeName, double currentSalary)
```

and methods

```
public String getName()
public double getSalary()
public void raiseSalary(double byPercent)
```

These methods return the name and salary, and raise the employee's salary by a certain percentage. Sample usage:

```
Employee harry = new Employee("Hacker, Harry", 50000);
harry.raiseSalary(10); // Harry gets a 10 percent raise
```

Supply an `EmployeeTester` class that tests all methods.

■■ **E3.13** Implement a class `Car` with the following properties. A car has a certain fuel efficiency (measured in miles/gallon or liters/km—pick one) and a certain amount of fuel in the gas tank. The efficiency is specified in the constructor, and the initial fuel level is 0. Supply a method `drive` that simulates driving the car for a certain distance, reducing the amount of gasoline in the fuel tank. Also supply methods `getGasInTank`, returning the current amount of gasoline in the fuel tank, and `addGas`, to add gasoline to the fuel tank. Sample usage:

```
Car myHybrid = new Car(50); // 50 miles per gallon
myHybrid.addGas(20); // Tank 20 gallons
myHybrid.drive(100); // Drive 100 miles
double gasLeft = myHybrid.getGasInTank(); // Get gas remaining in tank
```

You may assume that the `drive` method is never called with a distance that consumes more than the available gas. Supply a `CarTester` class that tests all methods.

■ **E3.14** Implement a class `Product`. A product has a name and a price, for example new `Product("Toaster", 29.95)`. Supply methods `getName`, `getPrice`, and `reducePrice`. Supply a program `ProductPrinter` that makes two products, prints each name and price, reduces their prices by $5.00, and then prints the prices again.

■■ **E3.15** Provide a class for authoring a simple letter. In the constructor, supply the names of the sender and the recipient:

```
public Letter(String from, String to)
```

Supply a method

```
public void addLine(String line)
```

to add a line of text to the body of the letter.

Supply a method

```
public String getText()
```

that returns the entire text of the letter. The text has the form:

```
Dear recipient name:
blank line
first line of the body
second line of the body
. . .
last line of the body
blank line
Sincerely,
blank line
sender name
```

Also supply a class LetterPrinter that prints this letter.

```
Dear John:

I am sorry we must part.
I wish you all the best.

Sincerely,

Mary
```

Construct an object of the Letter class and call addLine twice.

Hints: (1) Use the concat method to form a longer string from two shorter strings. (2) The special string "\n" represents a new line. For example, the statement

```
body = body.concat("Sincerely,").concat("\n");
```

adds a line containing the string "Sincerely," to the body.

■■ **E3.16** Write a class Bug that models a bug moving along a horizontal line. The bug moves either to the right or left. Initially, the bug moves to the right, but it can turn to change its direction. In each move, its position changes by one unit in the current direction. Provide a constructor

```
public Bug(int initialPosition)
```

and methods

```
public void turn()
public void move()
public int getPosition()
```

Sample usage:

```
Bug bugsy = new Bug(10);
bugsy.move(); // Now the position is 11
bugsy.turn();
bugsy.move(); // Now the position is 10
```

Your BugTester should construct a bug, make it move and turn a few times, and print the actual and expected position.

■■ **E3.17** Implement a class Moth that models a moth flying along a straight line. The moth has a position, which is the distance from a fixed origin. When the moth moves toward a point of light, its new position is halfway between its old position and the position of the light source. Supply a constructor

```
public Moth(double initialPosition)
```

and methods

```
public void moveToLight(double lightPosition)
public double getPosition()
```

Your MothTester should construct a moth, move it toward a couple of light sources, and check that the moth's position is as expected.

■■■ **Graphics E3.18** Write a program that fills the window with a large ellipse, with a black outline and filled with your favorite color. The ellipse should touch the window boundaries, even if the window is resized. Call the getWidth and getHeight methods of the JComponent class in the paintComponent method.

■■ **Graphics E3.19** Draw a shooting target—a set of concentric rings in alternating black and white colors. *Hint:* Fill a black circle, then fill a smaller white circle on top, and so on. Your program should be composed of classes `Target`, `TargetComponent`, and `TargetViewer`.

■■ **Graphics E3.20** Write a program that draws a picture of a house. It could be as simple as the accompanying figure, or if you like, more elaborate (3-D, skyscraper, marble columns in the entryway, whatever). Implement a class `House` and supply a method `draw(Graphics2D g2)` that draws the house.

■■ **Graphics E3.21** Extend Exercise ●● Graphics E3.20 by supplying a `House` constructor for specifying the position and size. Then populate your screen with a few houses of different sizes.

■■ **Graphics E3.22** Change the car viewer program in Section 3.8 to make the cars appear in different colors. Each `Car` object should store its own color. Supply modified `Car` and `CarComponent` classes.

■■ **Graphics E3.23** Change the `Car` class so that the size of a car can be specified in the constructor. Change the `CarComponent` class to make one of the cars appear twice the size of the original example.

■■ **Graphics E3.24** Write a program to plot the string "HELLO", using only lines and circles. Do not call `drawString`, and do not use `System.out`. Make classes `LetterH`, `LetterE`, `LetterL`, and `LetterO`.

■■ **Graphics E3.25** Write a program that displays the Olympic rings. Color the rings in the Olympic colors. Provide classes `OlympicRing`, `OlympicRingViewer`, and `OlympicRingComponent`.

■■ **Graphics E3.26** Make a bar chart to plot the following data set. Label each bar. Make the bars horizontal for easier labeling. Provide a class `BarChartViewer` and a class `BarChartComponent`.

Bridge Name	Longest Span (ft)
Golden Gate	4,200
Brooklyn	1,595
Delaware Memorial	2,150
Mackinac	3,800

PROGRAMMING PROJECTS

■ **P3.1** Enhance the CashRegister class so that it counts the purchased items. Provide a get-ItemCount method that returns the count.

■■■ **P3.2** Support computing sales tax in the CashRegister class. The tax rate should be supplied when constructing a CashRegister object. Add recordTaxablePurchase and getTotal-Tax methods. (Amounts added with recordPurchase are not taxable.) The giveChange method should correctly reflect the sales tax that is charged on taxable items.

■■ **P3.3** Implement a class Balloon. A balloon starts out with radius 0. Supply a method

```
public void inflate(double amount)
```

that increases the radius by the given amount. Supply a method

```
public double getVolume()
```

that returns the current volume of the balloon. Use Math.PI for the value of π. To compute the cube of a value r, just use r * r * r.

■■ **P3.4** Most countries (with the exception of Canada, Colombia, the Dominican Republic, Mexico, and the United States) follow the ISO 216 standard for paper sizes. An A0 sheet has dimensions 841 × 1189 millimeters. An A1 sheet is obtained by cutting an A0 sheet in half along the larger dimension, yielding a 594 × 841 sheet. An A2 sheet is obtained by cutting it in half again, yielding a 420 × 594 sheet, and so on. Implement a class Sheet whose constructor makes an A0 sheet. Provide a method cutInHalf that yields a Sheet object of half the size. Also provide methods width, height, and name, returning the width and height in millimeters, as well as the name (such as "A2").

■■ **P3.5** A microwave control panel has four buttons: one for increasing the time by 30 seconds, one for switching between power levels 1 and 2, a reset button, and a start button. Implement a class that simulates the microwave, with a method for each button. The method for the start button should print a message "Cooking for ... seconds at level ...".

■■ **P3.6** A Person has a name (just a first name for simplicity) and friends. Store the names of the friends in a string, separated by spaces. Provide a constructor that constructs a person with a given name and no friends. Provide methods

```
public void befriend(Person p)
public void unfriend(Person p)
public String getFriendNames()
```

■ **P3.7** Add a method

```
public int getFriendCount()
```

to the Person class of Exercise ●● P3.6.

■■■ **P3.8** Implement a class Student. For the purpose of this exercise, a student has a name and a total quiz score. Supply an appropriate constructor and methods getName(), addQuiz(int score), getTotalScore(), and getAverageScore(). To compute the average, you also need to store the *number of quizzes* that the student took.

Supply a StudentTester class that tests all methods.

■ **P3.9** Write a class Battery that models a rechargeable battery. A battery has a constructor

```
public Battery(double capacity)
```

where capacity is a value measured in milliampere hours. A typical AA battery has a capacity of 2000 to 3000 mAh. The method

```
public void drain(double amount)
```

drains the capacity of the battery by the given amount. The method

```
public void charge()
```

charges the battery to its original capacity.

The method

```
public double getRemainingCapacity()
```

gets the remaining capacity of the battery.

■■ **Graphics P3.10** Write a program that draws three stars like the one at right. Use classes Star, StarComponent, and StarViewer.

■■ **P3.11** Implement a class RoachPopulation that simulates the growth of a roach population. The constructor takes the size of the initial roach population. The breed method simulates a period in which the roaches breed, which doubles their population. The spray(double percent) method simulates spraying with insecticide, which reduces the population by the given percentage. The getRoaches method returns the current number of roaches. A program called RoachSimulation simulates a population that starts out with 10 roaches. Breed, spray to reduce the population by 10 percent, and print the roach count. Repeat three more times.

■■ **P3.12** Implement a VotingMachine class that can be used for a simple election. Have methods to clear the machine state, to vote for a Democrat, to vote for a Republican, and to get the tallies for both parties.

■■■ **P3.13** In this project, you will enhance the BankAccount class and see how abstraction and encapsulation enable evolutionary changes to software.

Begin with a simple enhancement: charging a fee for every deposit and withdrawal. Supply a mechanism for setting the fee and modify the deposit and withdraw methods so that the fee is levied. Test your class and check that the fee is computed correctly.

Now make a more complex change. The bank will allow a fixed number of free transactions (deposits or withdrawals) every month, and charge for transactions exceeding the free allotment. The charge is not levied immediately but at the end of the month.

Supply a new method deductMonthlyCharge to the BankAccount class that deducts the monthly charge and resets the transaction count. (*Hint:* Use Math.max(actual transaction count, free transaction count) in your computation.)

Produce a test program that verifies that the fees are calculated correctly over several months.

■■■ **P3.14** In this project, you will explore an object-oriented alternative to the "Hello, World" program in Chapter 1.

Begin with a simple Greeter class that has a single method, sayHello. That method should *return* a string, not print it. Create two objects of this class and invoke their sayHello methods. Of course, both objects return the same answer.

Enhance the Greeter class so that each object produces a customized greeting. For example, the object constructed as new Greeter("Dave") should say "Hello, Dave". (Use the concat method to combine strings to form a longer string, or peek ahead at Section 4.5 to see how you can use the + operator for the same purpose.)

Add a method sayGoodbye to the Greeter class.

Finally, add a method refuseHelp to the Greeter class. It should return a string such as "I am sorry, Dave. I am afraid I can't do that."

If you use BlueJ, place two Greeter objects on the workbench (one that greets the world and one that greets Dave) and invoke methods on them. Otherwise, write a tester program that constructs these objects, invokes methods, and prints the results.

CHAPTER 4

FUNDAMENTAL DATA TYPES

© samxmeg/iStockphoto.

CHAPTER GOALS

To understand integer and floating-point numbers

To recognize the limitations of the numeric types

To become aware of causes for overflow and roundoff errors

To understand the proper use of constants

To write arithmetic expressions in Java

To use the String type to manipulate character strings

To write programs that read input and produce formatted output

CHAPTER CONTENTS

Numbers and character strings (such as the ones on this display board) are important data types in any Java program. In this chapter, you will learn how to work with numbers and text, and how to write simple programs that perform useful tasks with them. We also cover the important topic of input and output, which enables you to implement interactive programs.

4.1 Numbers

We start this chapter with information about numbers. The following sections tell you how to choose the most appropriate number types for your numeric values, and how to work with constants—numeric values that do not change.

4.1.1 Number Types

Java has eight primitive types, including four integer types and two floating-point types.

In Java, every value is either a reference to an object, or it belongs to one of the eight **primitive types** shown in Table 1.

Six of the primitive types are number types; four of them for integers and two for floating-point numbers.

Each of the number types has a different range. Appendix G explains why the range limits are related to powers of two. The largest number that can be represented in an int is denoted by Integer.MAX_VALUE. Its value is about 2.14 billion. Similarly, the smallest integer is Integer.MIN_VALUE, about −2.14 billion.

Table 1 Primitive Types		
Type	Description	Size
int	The integer type, with range −2,147,483,648 (Integer.MIN_VALUE) . . . 2,147,483,647 (Integer.MAX_VALUE, about 2.14 billion)	4 bytes
byte	The type describing a single byte, with range −128 . . . 127	1 byte
short	The short integer type, with range −32,768 . . . 32,767	2 bytes
long	The long integer type, with range −9,223,372,036,854,775,808 . . . 9,223,372,036,854,775,807	8 bytes
double	The double-precision floating-point type, with a range of about $\pm10^{308}$ and about 15 significant decimal digits	8 bytes
float	The single-precision floating-point type, with a range of about $\pm10^{38}$ and about 7 significant decimal digits	4 bytes
char	The character type, representing code units in the Unicode encoding scheme (see Computing & Society 4.2)	2 bytes
boolean	The type with the two truth values false and true (see Chapter 5)	1 bit

Table 2 Number Literals in Java

Number	Type	Comment
6	int	An integer has no fractional part.
–6	int	Integers can be negative.
0	int	Zero is an integer.
0.5	double	A number with a fractional part has type double.
1.0	double	An integer with a fractional part .0 has type double.
1E6	double	A number in exponential notation: 1×10^6 or 1000000. Numbers in exponential notation always have type double.
2.96E-2	double	Negative exponent: $2.96 \times 10^{-2} = 2.96 / 100 = 0.0296$
100000L	long	The L suffix indicates a long literal.
⃠ 100,000		**Error:** Do not use a comma as a decimal separator.
100_000	int	You can use underscores in number literals.
⃠ 3 1/2		**Error:** Do not use fractions; use decimal notation: 3.5

When a value such as 6 or 0.335 occurs in a Java program, it is called a **number literal**. If a number literal has a decimal point, it is a floating-point number; otherwise, it is an integer. Table 2 shows how to write integer and floating-point literals in Java.

Generally, you will use the int type for integer quantities. Occasionally, however, calculations involving integers can *overflow*. This happens if the result of a computation exceeds the range for the number type. For example,

```java
int n = 1000000;
System.out.println(n * n);  // Prints –727379968, which is clearly wrong
```

The product n * n is 10^{12}, which is larger than the largest integer (about $2 \cdot 10^9$). The result is truncated to fit into an int, yielding a value that is completely wrong. Unfortunately, there is no warning when an integer overflow occurs.

If you run into this problem, the simplest remedy is to use the long type. Special Topic 4.1 shows you how to use the BigInteger type in the unlikely event that even the long type overflows.

Overflow is not usually a problem for double-precision floating-point numbers. The double type has a range of about $\pm 10^{308}$. Floating-point numbers have a different problem—limited precision. The double type has about 15 significant digits, and there are many numbers that cannot be accurately represented as double values.

When a value cannot be represented exactly, it is rounded to the nearest match. Consider this example:

```java
double f = 4.35;
System.out.println(100 * f); // Prints 434.99999999999994
```

A numeric computation overflows if the result falls outside the range for the number type.

If a computation yields an integer that is larger than the largest int value (about 2.14 billion), it overflows.

© Douglas Allen/iStockphoto.

Floating-point numbers have limited precision. Not every value can be represented precisely, and roundoff errors can occur.

© caracterdesign/iStockphoto.

Rounding errors occur when an exact representation of a floating-point number is not possible.

The problem arises because computers represent numbers in the binary number system. In the binary number system, there is no exact representation of the fraction 1/10, just as there is no exact representation of the fraction 1/3 = 0.33333 in the decimal number system. (See Appendix G for more information.)

For this reason, the `double` type is not appropriate for financial calculations. In this book, we will continue to use `double` values for bank balances and other financial quantities so that we keep our programs as simple as possible. However, professional programs need to use the `BigDecimal` type for this purpose—see Special Topic 4.1.

In Java, it is legal to assign an integer value to a floating-point variable:

```
int dollars = 100;
double balance = dollars; // OK
```

But the opposite assignment is an error: You cannot assign a floating-point expression to an integer variable.

```
double balance = 13.75;
int dollars = balance; // Error
```

You will see in Section 4.2.5 how to convert a value of type `double` into an integer.

In this book, we do not use the `float` type. It has less than 7 significant digits, which greatly increases the risk of **roundoff errors**. Some programmers use `float` to save on memory if they need to store a huge set of numbers that do not require much precision.

4.1.2 Constants

In many programs, you need to use numerical **constants**—values that do not change and that have a special significance for a computation.

A typical example for the use of constants is a computation that involves coin values, such as the following:

```
payment = dollars + quarters * 0.25 + dimes * 0.1
    + nickels * 0.05 + pennies * 0.01;
```

Most of the code is self-documenting. However, the four numeric quantities, 0.25, 0.1, 0.05, and 0.01 are included in the arithmetic expression without any explanation. Of course, in this case, you know that the value of a nickel is five cents, which explains the 0.05, and so on. However, the next person who needs to maintain this code may live in another country and may not know that a nickel is worth five cents.

Thus, it is a good idea to use symbolic names for all values, even those that appear obvious. Here is a clearer version of the computation of the total:

```
double quarterValue = 0.25;
double dimeValue = 0.1;
double nickelValue = 0.05;
double pennyValue = 0.01;
```

```
payment = dollars + quarters * quarterValue + dimes * dimeValue
        + nickels * nickelValue + pennies * pennyValue;
```

There is another improvement we can make. There is a difference between the `nickels` and `nickelValue` variables. The `nickels` variable can truly vary over the life of the program, as we calculate different payments. But `nickelValue` is always 0.05.

In Java, constants are identified with the reserved word `final`. A variable tagged as `final` can never change after it has been set. If you try to change the value of a `final` variable, the compiler will report an error and your program will not compile.

A final variable is a constant. Once its value has been set, it cannot be changed.

Many programmers use all-uppercase names for constants (`final` variables), such as `NICKEL_VALUE`. That way, it is easy to distinguish between variables (with mostly lowercase letters) and constants. We will follow this convention in this book. However, this rule is a matter of good style, not a requirement of the Java language. The compiler will not complain if you give a `final` variable a name with lowercase letters.

Here is an improved version of the code that computes the value of a payment.

Use named constants to make your programs easier to read and maintain.

```
final double QUARTER_VALUE = 0.25;
final double DIME_VALUE = 0.1;
final double NICKEL_VALUE = 0.05;
final double PENNY_VALUE = 0.01;
payment = dollars + quarters * QUARTER_VALUE + dimes * DIME_VALUE
        + nickels * NICKEL_VALUE + pennies * PENNY_VALUE;
```

Frequently, constant values are needed in several methods. Then you should declare them together with the instance variables of a class and tag them as `static` and `final`. As before, `final` indicates that the value is a constant. The `static` reserved word means that the constant belongs to the class—this is explained in greater detail in Chapter 8.)

```
public class CashRegister
{
    // Constants
    public static final double QUARTER_VALUE = 0.25;
    public static final double DIME_VALUE = 0.1;
    public static final double NICKEL_VALUE = 0.05;
    public static final double PENNY_VALUE = 0.01;

    // Instance variables
    private double purchase;
    private double payment;

    // Methods
    . . .
}
```

We declared the constants as `public`. There is no danger in doing this because constants cannot be modified. Methods of other classes can access a public constant by first specifying the name of the class in which it is declared, then a period, then the name of the constant, such as `CashRegister.NICKEL_VALUE`.

The `Math` class from the standard library declares a couple of useful constants:

```
public class Math
{
    . . .
    public static final double E = 2.7182818284590452354;
    public static final double PI = 3.14159265358979323846;
}
```

You can refer to these constants as `Math.PI` and `Math.E` in any method. For example,

```
double circumference = Math.PI * diameter;
```

Syntax 4.1   Constant Declaration

Syntax   Declared in a method: final *typeName variableName* = *expression*;

Declared in a class: *accessSpecifier* static final *typeName variableName* = *expression*;

Declared in a method

```
final double NICKEL_VALUE = 0.05;
```

The final *reserved word indicates that this value cannot be modified.*

Use uppercase letters for constants.

```
public static final double LITERS_PER_GALLON = 3.785;
```

Declared in a class

The sample program below puts constants to work. The program shows a refinement of the CashRegister class of How To 3.1. The public interface of that class has been modified in order to solve a common business problem.

Busy cashiers sometimes make mistakes totaling up coin values. Our CashRegister class features a method whose inputs are the *coin counts.* For example, the call

```
register.receivePayment(1, 2, 1, 1, 4);
```

processes a payment consisting of one dollar, two quarters, one dime, one nickel, and four pennies. The receivePayment method figures out the total value of the payment, $1.69. As you can see from the code listing, the method uses named constants for the coin values.

sec01/CashRegisterTester.java

```
1  /**
2      This class tests the CashRegister class.
3  */
4  public class CashRegisterTester
5  {
6     public static void main(String[] args)
7     {
8        CashRegister register = new CashRegister();
9
10       register.recordPurchase(0.75);
11       register.recordPurchase(1.50);
12       register.receivePayment(2, 0, 5, 0, 0);
13       System.out.print("Change: ");
14       System.out.println(register.giveChange());
15       System.out.println("Expected: 0.25");
16
17       register.recordPurchase(2.25);
18       register.recordPurchase(19.25);
19       register.receivePayment(23, 2, 0, 0, 0);
20       System.out.print("Change: ");
21       System.out.println(register.giveChange());
```

```
22        System.out.println("Expected: 2.0");
23      }
24 }
```

sec01/CashRegister.java

```
 1 /**
 2      A cash register totals up sales and computes change due.
 3 */
 4 public class CashRegister
 5 {
 6     public static final double QUARTER_VALUE = 0.25;
 7     public static final double DIME_VALUE = 0.1;
 8     public static final double NICKEL_VALUE = 0.05;
 9     public static final double PENNY_VALUE = 0.01;
10
11     private double purchase;
12     private double payment;
13
14     /**
15         Constructs a cash register with no money in it.
16     */
17     public CashRegister()
18     {
19         purchase = 0;
20         payment = 0;
21     }
22
23     /**
24         Records the purchase price of an item.
25         @param amount the price of the purchased item
26     */
27     public void recordPurchase(double amount)
28     {
29         purchase = purchase + amount;
30     }
31
32     /**
33         Processes the payment received from the customer.
34         @param dollars the number of dollars in the payment
35         @param quarters the number of quarters in the payment
36         @param dimes the number of dimes in the payment
37         @param nickels the number of nickels in the payment
38         @param pennies the number of pennies in the payment
39     */
40     public void receivePayment(int dollars, int quarters,
41             int dimes, int nickels, int pennies)
42     {
43         payment = dollars + quarters * QUARTER_VALUE + dimes * DIME_VALUE
44                 + nickels * NICKEL_VALUE + pennies * PENNY_VALUE;
45     }
46
47     /**
48         Computes the change due and resets the machine for the next customer.
49         @return the change due to the customer
50     */
51     public double giveChange()
52     {
53         double change = payment - purchase;
54         purchase = 0;
```

```
55        payment = 0;
56        return change;
57    }
58 }
```

Program Run

```
Change: 0.25
Expected: 0.25
Change: 2.0
Expected: 2.0
```

Programming Tip 4.1

Do Not Use Magic Numbers

A **magic number** is a numeric constant that appears in your code without explanation. For example, consider the following scary example that actually occurs in the Java library source:

```
h = 31 * h + ch;
```

Why 31? The number of days in January? One less than the number of bits in an integer? Actually, this code computes a "hash code" from a string—a number that is derived from the characters in such a way that different strings are likely to yield different hash codes. The value 31 turns out to scramble the character values nicely.

A better solution is to use a named constant:

```
final int HASH_MULTIPLIER = 31;
h = HASH_MULTIPLIER * h + ch;
```

© FinnBrandt/iStockphoto.

We prefer programs that are easy to understand over those that appear to work by magic.

You should never use magic numbers in your code. Any number that is not completely self-explanatory should be declared as a named constant. Even the most reasonable cosmic constant is going to change one day. You think there are 365 days in a year? Your customers on Mars are going to be pretty unhappy about your silly prejudice. Make a constant

```
final int DAYS_PER_YEAR = 365;
```

Special Topic 4.1

Big Numbers

If you want to compute with really large numbers, you can use big number objects. Big number objects are objects of the BigInteger and BigDecimal classes in the java.math package. Unlike the number types such as int or double, big number objects have essentially no limits on their size and precision. However, computations with big number objects are much slower than those that involve number types. Perhaps more importantly, you can't use the familiar arithmetic operators such as (+ - *) with them. Instead, you have to use methods called add, subtract, and multiply. Here is an example of how to create a BigInteger object and how to call the multiply method:

```
BigInteger n = new BigInteger("1000000");
BigInteger r = n.multiply(n);
System.out.println(r); // Prints 1000000000000
```

The BigDecimal type carries out floating-point computations without roundoff errors. For example,

```
BigDecimal d = new BigDecimal("4.35");
BigDecimal e = new BigDecimal("100");
```

```
BigDecimal f = d.multiply(e);
System.out.println(f); // Prints 435.00
```

4.2 Arithmetic

In this section, you will learn how to carry out arithmetic calculations in Java.

4.2.1 Arithmetic Operators

Java supports the same four basic arithmetic operations as a calculator—addition, subtraction, multiplication, and division—but it uses different symbols for the multiplication and division **operators**.

You must write a * b to denote multiplication. Unlike in mathematics, you cannot write a b, a · b, or a × b. Similarly, division is always indicated with the / operator, never a ÷ or a fraction bar. For example, $\frac{a+b}{2}$ becomes (a + b) / 2.

The combination of variables, literals, operators, and/or method calls is called an **expression**. For example, (a + b) / 2 is an expression.

Parentheses are used just as in algebra: to indicate in which order the parts of the expression should be computed. For example, in the expression (a + b) / 2, the sum a + b is computed first, and then the sum is divided by 2. In contrast, in the expression

```
a + b / 2
```

only b is divided by 2, and then the sum of a and b / 2 is formed. As in regular algebraic notation, multiplication and division have a *higher precedence* than addition and subtraction. For example, in the expression a + b / 2, the / is carried out first, even though the + operation occurs further to the left (see Appendix B).

> Mixing integers and floating-point values in an arithmetic expression yields a floating-point value.

If you mix integer and floating-point values in an arithmetic expression, the result is a floating-point value. For example, 7 + 4.0 is the floating-point value 11.0.

4.2.2 Increment and Decrement

> The ++ operator adds 1 to a variable; the -- operator subtracts 1.

Changing a variable by adding or subtracting 1 is so common that there is a special shorthand for it. The ++ operator increments a variable (see Figure 1):

```
counter++; // Adds 1 to the variable counter
```

Similarly, the -- operator decrements a variable:

```
counter--; // Subtracts 1 from counter
```

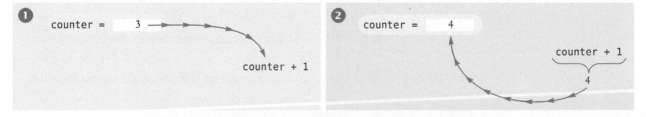

Figure 1 Incrementing a Variable

4.2.3 Integer Division and Remainder

If both arguments of / are integers, the remainder is discarded.

Division works as you would expect, as long as at least one of the numbers involved is a floating-point number. That is,

```
7.0 / 4.0
7 / 4.0
7.0 / 4
```

all yield 1.75. However, if *both* numbers are integers, then the result of the **integer division** is always an integer, with the remainder discarded. That is,

```
7 / 4
```

evaluates to 1 because 7 divided by 4 is 1 with a remainder of 3 (which is discarded). This can be a source of subtle programming errors—see Common Error 4.1.

If you are interested in the remainder only, use the % operator:

The % operator computes the remainder of an integer division.

```
7 % 4
```

is 3, the remainder of the integer division of 7 by 4. The % symbol has no analog in algebra. It was chosen because it looks similar to /, and the remainder operation is related to division. The operator is called **modulus**. (Some people call it *modulo* or *mod.*) It has no relationship with the percent operation that you find on some calculators.

Here is a typical use for the integer / and % operations. Suppose you have an amount of pennies in a piggybank:

```
int pennies = 1729;
```

You want to determine the value in dollars and cents. You obtain the dollars through an integer division by 100:

```
int dollars = pennies / 100;   // Sets dollars to 17
```

The integer division discards the remainder. To obtain the remainder, use the % operator:

```
int cents = pennies % 100;   // Sets cents to 29
```

See Table 3 for additional examples.

© Michael Flippo/iStockphoto.

Integer division and the % operator yield the dollar and cent values of a piggybank full of pennies.

Table 3 Integer Division and Remainder

Expression (where n = 1729)	Value	Comment
n % 10	9	n % 10 is always the last digit of n.
n / 10	172	This is always n without the last digit.
n % 100	29	The last two digits of n.
n / 10.0	172.9	Because 10.0 is a floating-point number, the fractional part is not discarded.
−n % 10	-9	Because the first argument is negative, the remainder is also negative.
n % 2	1	n % 2 is 0 if n is even, 1 or −1 if n is odd.

4.2.4 Powers and Roots

The Java library declares many mathematical functions, such as Math.sqrt (square root) and Math.pow (raising to a power).

In Java, there are no symbols for powers and roots. To compute them, you must call methods. To take the square root of a number, you use the Math.sqrt method. For example, $\sqrt{x}$ is written as Math.sqrt(x). To compute x^n, you write Math.pow(x, n).

In algebra, you use fractions, exponents, and roots to arrange expressions in a compact two-dimensional form. In Java, you have to write all expressions in a linear arrangement. For example, the mathematical expression

$$b \times \left(1 + \frac{r}{100}\right)^n$$

becomes

```
b * Math.pow(1 + r / 100, n)
```

Figure 2 shows how to analyze such an expression. Table 4 shows additional mathematical methods.

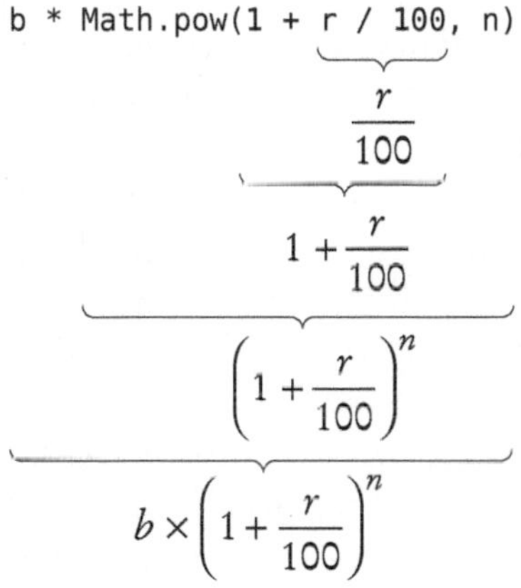

Figure 2
Analyzing an Expression

Table 4 Mathematical Methods

Method	Returns	Method	Returns
Math.sqrt(x)	Square root of x (≥ 0)	Math.abs(x)	Absolute value $\lvert x \rvert$
Math.pow(x, y)	x^y ($x > 0$, or $x = 0$ and $y > 0$, or $x < 0$ and y is an integer)	Math.max(x, y)	The larger of x and y
Math.sin(x)	Sine of x (x in radians)	Math.min(x, y)	The smaller of x and y
Math.cos(x)	Cosine of x	Math.exp(x)	e^x
Math.tan(x)	Tangent of x	Math.log(x)	Natural log ($\ln(x)$, $x > 0$)
Math.round(x)	Closest integer to x (as a long)	Math.log10(x)	Decimal log ($\log_{10}(x)$, $x > 0$)
Math.ceil(x)	Smallest integer $\geq x$ (as a double)	Math.floor(x)	Largest integer $\leq x$ (as a double)
Math.toRadians(x)	Convert x degrees to radians (i.e., returns $x \cdot \pi / 180$)	Math.toDegrees(x)	Convert x radians to degrees (i.e., returns $x \cdot 180 / \pi$)

4.2.5 Converting Floating-Point Numbers to Integers

Occasionally, you have a value of type double that you need to convert to the type int. It is an error to assign a floating-point value to an integer:

```
double balance = total + tax;
int dollars = balance; // Error: Cannot assign double to int
```

The compiler disallows this assignment because it is potentially dangerous:

- The fractional part is lost.
- The magnitude may be too large. (The largest integer is about 2 billion, but a floating-point number can be much larger.)

You use a cast (*typeName*) to convert a value to a different type.

You must use the **cast** operator (int) to convert a convert floating-point value to an integer. Write the cast operator before the expression that you want to convert:

```
double balance = total + tax;
int dollars = (int) balance;
```

The cast (int) converts the floating-point value balance to an integer by discarding the fractional part. For example, if balance is 13.75, then dollars is set to 13.

When applying the cast operator to an arithmetic expression, you need to place the expression inside parentheses:

```
int dollars = (int) (total + tax);
```

Discarding the fractional part is not always appropriate. If you want to round a floating-point number to the nearest whole number, use the Math.round method. This method returns a long integer, because large floating-point numbers cannot be stored in an int.

```
long rounded = Math.round(balance);
```

If balance is 13.75, then rounded is set to 14.

If you know that the result can be stored in an int and does not require a long, you can use a cast:

```
int rounded = (int) Math.round(balance);
```

Syntax 4.2   Cast

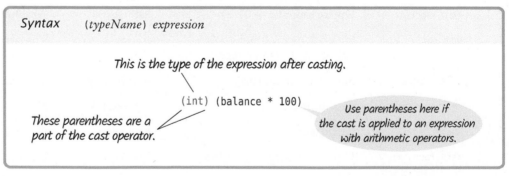

Syntax   (*typeName*) *expression*

This is the type of the expression after casting.

(int) (balance * 100)

These parentheses are a part of the cast operator.

Use parentheses here if the cast is applied to an expression with arithmetic operators.

EXAMPLE CODE   See sec02 of your eText or companion code to see a program that demonstrates casts, rounding, and the % operator.

Table 5 Arithmetic Expressions

Mathematical Expression	Java Expression	Comments
$\dfrac{x + y}{2}$	`(x + y) / 2`	The parentheses are required; x + y / 2 computes $x + \frac{y}{2}$.
$\dfrac{xy}{2}$	`x * y / 2`	Parentheses are not required; operators with the same precedence are evaluated left to right.
$\left(1 + \dfrac{r}{100}\right)^n$	`Math.pow(1 + r / 100, n)`	Use `Math.pow(x, n)` to compute x^n.
$\sqrt{a^2 + b^2}$	`Math.sqrt(a * a + b * b)`	`a * a` is simpler than `Math.pow(a, 2)`.
$\dfrac{i + j + k}{3}$	`(i + j + k) / 3.0`	If i, j, and k are integers, using a denominator of 3.0 forces floating-point division.
π	`Math.PI`	`Math.PI` is a constant declared in the `Math` class.

Common Error 4.1

Unintended Integer Division

It is unfortunate that Java uses the same symbol, namely /, for both integer and floating-point division. These are really quite different operations. It is a common error to use **integer division** by accident. Consider this segment that computes the average of three integers:

```
int score1 = 10;
int score2 = 4;
int score3 = 9;
double average = (score1 + score2 + score3) / 3; // Error
System.out.println("Average score: " + average); // Prints 7.0, not 7.666666666666667
```

What could be wrong with that? Of course, the average of score1, score2, and score3 is

$$\frac{\text{score1} + \text{score2} + \text{score3}}{3}$$

Here, however, the / does not mean division in the mathematical sense. It denotes integer division because both 3 and the sum of score1 + score2 + score3 are integers. Because the scores add up to 23, the average is computed to be 7, the result of the integer division of 23 by 3. That integer 7 is then moved into the floating-point variable average. The remedy is to make the numerator or denominator into a floating-point number:

```
double total = score1 + score2 + score3;
double average = total / 3;
```

or

```
double average = (score1 + score2 + score3) / 3.0;
```

Common Error 4.2
Unbalanced Parentheses

Consider the expression

```
((a + b) * t / 2 * (1 - t)
```

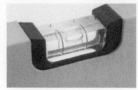

What is wrong with it? Count the parentheses. There are three (
and two). The parentheses are *unbalanced*. This kind of typing
error is very common with complicated expressions. Now consider this expression.

© Croko/iStockphoto.

```
(a + b) * t) / (2 * (1 - t)
```

This expression has three (and three), but it still is not correct. In the middle,

```
(a + b) * t) / (2 * (1 - t)
         ↑
```

there is only one (but two), which is an error. In the middle of an expression, the count of (
must be greater than or equal to the count of), and at the end of the expression the two counts
must be the same.

Here is a simple trick to make the counting easier without using pencil and paper. It is difficult for the brain to keep two counts simultaneously. Keep only one count when scanning the
expression. Start with 1 at the first opening parenthesis, add 1 whenever you see an opening
parenthesis, and subtract one whenever you see a closing parenthesis. Say the numbers aloud
as you scan the expression. If the count ever drops below zero, or is not zero at the end, the
parentheses are unbalanced. For example, when scanning the previous expression, you would
mutter

```
(a + b) * t) / (2 * (1 - t)
1       0   -1
```

and you would find the error.

Programming Tip 4.2
Spaces in Expressions

It is easier to read

```
x1 = (-b + Math.sqrt(b * b - 4 * a * c)) / (2 * a);
```

than

```
x1=(-b+Math.sqrt(b*b-4*a*c))/(2*a);
```

Simply put spaces around all operators + - * / % =. However, don't put a space after a *unary*
minus: a – used to negate a single quantity, such as -b. That way, it can be easily distinguished
from a *binary* minus, as in a - b.

It is customary not to put a space after a method name. That is, write `Math.sqrt(x)` and not
`Math.sqrt (x)`.

Special Topic 4.2
Avoiding Negative Remainders

The % operator yields negative values when the first operand is negative. This can be an annoyance. For example, suppose a robot keeps track of directions in degrees between 0 and 359.
Now the robot turns by some number of degrees. You can't simply compute the new direction

as (direction + turn) % 360 because you might get a negative result (see Exercise •• R4.7). You can instead call

    Math.floorMod(direction + turn, 360)

to compute the correct remainder. The result of Math.floorMod(m, n) is always positive when n is positive.

EXAMPLE CODE See special_topic_2 of your eText or companion code to see a program that demonstrates the floorMod method.

Special Topic 4.3
Combining Assignment and Arithmetic

In Java, you can combine arithmetic and assignment. For example, the instruction

    balance += amount;

is a shortcut for balance = balance + amount;
Similarly,

    total *= 2;

is another way of writing total = total * 2;
  Many programmers find this a convenient shortcut. If you like it, go ahead and use it in your own code. For simplicity, we won't use it in this book, though.

Special Topic 4.4
Instance Methods and Static Methods

In the preceding section, you encountered the Math class, which contains a collection of helpful methods for carrying out mathematical computations. These methods do not operate on an object. That is, you don't call

    double root = 2.sqrt(); // Error

In Java, numbers are not objects, so you can never invoke a method on a number. Instead, you pass a number as an argument (explicit parameter) to a method, enclosing the number in parentheses after the method name:

    double root = Math.sqrt(2);

Such methods are called **static methods**. (The term "static" is a historical holdover from the C and C++ programming languages. It has nothing to do with the usual meaning of the word.)
  Static methods do not operate on objects, but they are still declared inside classes. When calling the method, you specify the class to which the sqrt method belongs:

The name of the class \ / *The name of the static method*

    Math.sqrt(2)

In contrast, a method that is invoked on an object is called an **instance method**. As a rule of thumb, you use static methods when you manipulate numbers. You will learn more about the distinction between static and instance methods in Chapter 8.

Computing & Society 4.1   **Bugs in Silicon**

In the summer of 1994, Dr. Thomas Nicely of Lynchburg College in Virginia ran an extensive set of computations to analyze the sums of reciprocals of certain sequences of prime numbers, using a newly released Intel Pentium processor. The results were not always what his theory predicted, even after he took into account the inevitable roundoff errors. Then Dr. Nicely noted that the same program did produce the correct results when running on the slower 486 processor that preceded the Pentium in Intel's lineup. This should not have happened. The optimal roundoff behavior of floating-point calculations has been standardized by the Institute for Electrical and Electronics Engineers (IEEE) and Intel claimed to adhere to the IEEE standard in both the 486 and the Pentium processors. Upon further checking, Dr. Nicely discovered that indeed there was a very small set of numbers for which the product of two numbers was computed differently on the two processors. For example,

$$4,195,835 - ((4,195,835/3,145,727) \times 3,145,727)$$

is mathematically equal to 0, and it did compute as 0 on a 486 processor. On his Pentium processor the result was 256.

As it turned out, Intel had independently discovered the bug in its testing and had started to produce chips that fixed it. The bug was caused by an error in a table that was used to speed up the floating-point multiplication algorithm of the processor. Intel determined that the problem was exceedingly rare. They claimed that under normal use, a typical consumer would only notice the problem once every 27,000 years. Unfortunately for Intel, Dr. Nicely had not been a normal user.

Intel had to replaced the defective chips, at a cost of about 475 million dollars.

In 2018, security researchers found flaws that are present in nearly every computer chip manufactured in the previous twenty years. These chips exploit an optimization called "speculative execution"—computing results ahead of time and discarding those that are not needed. Normally, a program cannot read data belonging to another program. But an adversary can make the processor read the data speculatively, and then use it in a way that has a measurable effect. The details are complex and require chip manufacturers to make fundamental changes in processor designs.

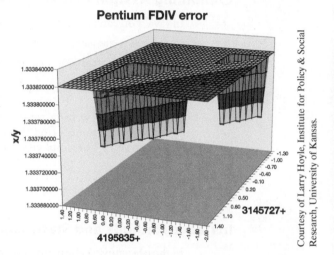

This graph shows a set of numbers for which the original Pentium processor obtained the wrong quotient.

4.3 Input and Output

In the following sections, you will see how to read user input and how to control the appearance of the output that your programs produce.

4.3.1 Reading Input

You can make your programs more flexible if you ask the program user for inputs rather than using fixed values. Consider, for example, a program that processes prices and quantities of soda containers. Prices and quantities are likely to fluctuate. The program user should provide them as inputs.

When a program asks for user input, it should first print a message that tells the user which input is expected. Such a message is called a **prompt**.

```
System.out.print("Please enter the number of bottles: "); // Display prompt
```

Syntax 4.3 Input Statement

Include this line so you can use the Scanner class. ────
```
import java.util.Scanner;
    .
```

Create a Scanner object to read keyboard input. ────
```
Scanner in = new Scanner(System.in);
    .
```
Don't use println *here.*

Display a prompt in the console window. ────
```
System.out.print("Please enter the number of bottles: ");
```
Define a variable to hold the input value. ────
```
int bottles = in.nextInt();
```
The program waits for user input, then places the input into the variable.

Use the print method, not println, to display the prompt. You want the input to appear after the colon, not on the following line. Also remember to leave a space after the colon.

Because output is sent to System.out, you might think that you use System.in for input. Unfortunately, it isn't quite that simple. When Java was first designed, not much attention was given to reading keyboard input. It was assumed that all programmers would produce graphical user interfaces with text fields and menus. System.in was given a minimal set of features and must be combined with other classes to be useful.

© Media Bakery.

A supermarket scanner reads bar codes. The Java Scanner reads numbers and text.

Use the Scanner class to read keyboard input in a console window.

To read keyboard input, you use a class called Scanner. You obtain a Scanner object by using the following statement:

```
Scanner in = new Scanner(System.in);
```

Once you have a scanner, you use its nextInt method to read an integer value:

```
System.out.print("Please enter the number of bottles: ");
int bottles = in.nextInt();
```

When the nextInt method is called, the program waits until the user types a number and presses the Enter key. After the user supplies the input, the number is placed into the bottles variable, and the program continues.

To read a floating-point number, use the nextDouble method instead:

```
System.out.print("Enter price: ");
double price = in.nextDouble();
```

The Scanner class belongs to the package java.util. When using the Scanner class, import it by placing the following declaration at the top of your program file:

```
import java.util.Scanner;
```

4.3.2 Formatted Output

When you print the result of a computation, you often want to control its appearance. For example, when you print an amount in dollars and cents, you usually want it to be rounded to two significant digits.

You use the `printf` *method to line up your output in neat columns.*

© Koele/iStockphoto.

That is, you want the output to look like

```
Price per liter: 1.22
```

instead of

```
Price per liter: 1.215962441314554
```

Use the `printf` method to specify how values should be formatted.

The following command displays the price with two digits after the decimal point:

```
System.out.printf("%.2f", price);
```

You can also specify a *field width*:

```
System.out.printf("%10.2f", price);
```

The price is printed using ten characters: six spaces followed by the four characters 1.22.

```
      1 . 2 2
```

The construct `%10.2f` is called a *format specifier:* it describes how a value should be formatted. The letter `f` at the end of the format specifier indicates that we are displaying a floating-point number. Use `d` for an integer and `s` for a string; see Table 6 for examples.

A format string contains format specifiers and literal characters. Any characters that are not format specifiers are printed verbatim. For example, the command

```
System.out.printf("Price per liter:%10.2f", price);
```

prints

```
Price per liter:      1.22
```

You can print multiple values with a single call to the `printf` method. Here is a typical example:

```
System.out.printf("Quantity: %d Total: %10.2f", quantity, total);
```

These spaces are spaces in the format string.

width 10

The `printf` *method does not start a new line here.*

```
Q u a n t i t y :   2 4   T o t a l :                 1 7 . 2 9
```

No field width was specified, so no padding added

Two digits after the decimal point

Table 6 Format Specifier Examples

Format String	Sample Output	Comments
"%d"	24	Use d with an integer.
"%5d"	24	Spaces are added so that the field width is 5.
"Quantity:%5d"	Quantity: 24	Characters inside a format string but outside a format specifier appear in the output.
"%f"	1.21997	Use f with a floating-point number.
"%.2f"	1.22	Prints two digits after the decimal point.
"%7.2f"	1.22	Spaces are added so that the field width is 7.
"%s"	Hello	Use s with a string.
"%d %.2f"	24 1.22	You can format multiple values at once.
"Hello%nWorld%n"	Hello World	Each %n causes subsequent output to continue on a new line.

The printf method, like the print method, does not start a new line after the output. If you want output to continue on a new line, add the %n format specifier. For example,

```
System.out.printf("Quantity: %7d%nTotal: %10.2f%n", quantity, total);
```

yields a printout

```
Quantity:      24
Total:      17.29
```

Our next example program will prompt for the price of a six-pack of soda and a two-liter bottle, and then print out the price per liter for both. The program puts to work what you just learned about reading input and formatting output.

cans: © blackred/iStockphoto.
bottle: © travismanley/iStockphoto.

What is the better deal? A six-pack of 12-ounce cans or a two-liter bottle?

sec03/Volume.java

```
1   import java.util.Scanner;
2
3   /**
4      This program prints the price per liter for a six-pack of cans and
5      a two-liter bottle.
6   */
7   public class Volume
8   {
9      public static void main(String[] args)
10     {
11        // Read price per pack
12
13        Scanner in = new Scanner(System.in);
14
15        System.out.print("Please enter the price for a six-pack: ");
16        double packPrice = in.nextDouble();
17
```

```
18        // Read price per bottle
19
20        System.out.print("Please enter the price for a two-liter bottle: ");
21        double bottlePrice = in.nextDouble();
22
23        final double CANS_PER_PACK = 6;
24        final double CAN_VOLUME = 0.355; // 12 oz. = 0.355 l
25        final double BOTTLE_VOLUME = 2;
26
27        // Compute and print price per liter
28
29        double packPricePerLiter = packPrice / (CANS_PER_PACK * CAN_VOLUME);
30        double bottlePricePerLiter = bottlePrice / BOTTLE_VOLUME;
31
32        System.out.printf("Pack price per liter:   %8.2f", packPricePerLiter);
33        System.out.println();
34
35        System.out.printf("Bottle price per liter: %8.2f", bottlePricePerLiter);
36        System.out.println();
37    }
38 }
```

Program Run

```
Please enter the price for a six-pack: 2.95
Please enter the price for a two-liter bottle: 2.85
Pack price per liter:     1.38
Bottle price per liter:   1.43
```

HOW TO 4.1

Carrying Out Computations

Many programming problems require arithmetic computations. This How To shows you how to turn a problem statement into pseudocode and, ultimately, a Java program.

Problem Statement　Suppose you are asked to write a program that simulates a vending machine. A customer selects an item for purchase and inserts a bill into the vending machine. The vending machine dispenses the purchased item and gives change. We will assume that all item prices are multiples of 25 cents, and the machine gives all change in dollar coins and quarters. Your task is to compute how many coins of each type to return.

Step 1　Understand the problem: What are the inputs? What are the desired outputs?

In this problem, there are two inputs:

- The denomination of the bill that the customer inserts
- The price of the purchased item

There are two desired outputs:

- The number of dollar coins that the machine returns
- The number of quarters that the machine returns

Step 2　Work out examples by hand.

This is a very important step. If you can't compute a couple of solutions by hand, it's unlikely that you'll be able to write a program that automates the computation.

Let's assume that a customer purchased an item that cost $2.25 and inserted a $5 bill. The customer is due $2.75, or two dollar coins and three quarters, in change.

That is easy for you to see, but how can a Java program come to the same conclusion? The key is to work in pennies, not dollars. The change due the customer is 275 pennies. Dividing by 100 yields 2, the number of dollars. Dividing the remainder (75) by 25 yields 3, the number of quarters.

Step 3 Write pseudocode for computing the answers.

In the previous step, you worked out a specific instance of the problem. You now need to come up with a method that works in general.

Given an arbitrary item price and payment, how can you compute the coins due? First, compute the change due in pennies:

change due = 100 x bill value - item price in pennies

To get the dollars, divide by 100 and discard the remainder:

dollar coins = change due / 100 (without remainder)

The remaining change due can be computed in two ways. If you are familiar with the modulus operator, you can simply compute

change due = change due % 100

Alternatively, subtract the penny value of the dollar coins from the change due:

change due = change due - 100 x dollar coins

To get the quarters due, divide by 25:

quarters = change due / 25

Step 4 Declare the variables and constants that you need, and specify their types.

Here, we have five variables:

- billValue
- itemPrice
- changeDue
- dollarCoins
- quarters

Should we introduce constants to explain 100 and 25 as PENNIES_PER_DOLLAR and PENNIES_PER_QUARTER? Doing so will make it easier to convert the program to international markets, so we will take this step.

It is very important that changeDue and PENNIES_PER_DOLLAR are of type int because the computation of dollarCoins uses integer division. Similarly, the other variables are integers.

A vending machine takes bills and gives change in coins.

Step 5   Turn the pseudocode into Java statements.

If you did a thorough job with the pseudocode, this step should be easy. Of course, you have to know how to express mathematical operations (such as powers or integer division) in Java.

```
changeDue = PENNIES_PER_DOLLAR * billValue - itemPrice;
dollarCoins = changeDue / PENNIES_PER_DOLLAR;
changeDue = changeDue % PENNIES_PER_DOLLAR;
quarters = changeDue / PENNIES_PER_QUARTER;
```

Step 6   Provide input and output.

Before starting the computation, we prompt the user for the bill value and item price:

```
System.out.print("Enter bill value (1 = $1 bill, 5 = $5 bill, etc.): ");
billValue = in.nextInt();
System.out.print("Enter item price in pennies: ");
itemPrice = in.nextInt();
```

When the computation is finished, we display the result. For extra credit, we use the `printf` method to make sure that the output lines up neatly.

```
System.out.printf("Dollar coins: %6d", dollarCoins);
System.out.printf("Quarters:     %6d", quarters);
```

Step 7   Provide a class with a `main` method.

Your computation needs to be placed into a class. Find an appropriate name for the class that describes the purpose of the computation. In our example, we will choose the name `Vending-Machine`.

Inside the class, supply a `main` method.

In the `main` method, you need to declare constants and variables (Step 4), carry out computations (Step 5), and provide input and output (Step 6). Clearly, you will want to first get the input, then do the computations, and finally show the output. Declare the constants at the beginning of the method, and declare each variable just before it is needed.

Here is the complete program.

how_to_1/VendingMachine.java

```java
1  import java.util.Scanner;
2
3  /**
4      This program simulates a vending machine that gives change.
5  */
6  public class VendingMachine
7  {
8     public static void main(String[] args)
9     {
10        Scanner in = new Scanner(System.in);
11
12        final int PENNIES_PER_DOLLAR = 100;
13        final int PENNIES_PER_QUARTER = 25;
14
15        System.out.print("Enter bill value (1 = $1 bill, 5 = $5 bill, etc.): ");
16        int billValue = in.nextInt();
17        System.out.print("Enter item price in pennies: ");
18        int itemPrice = in.nextInt();
19
20        // Compute change due
21
22        int changeDue = PENNIES_PER_DOLLAR * billValue - itemPrice;
23        int dollarCoins = changeDue / PENNIES_PER_DOLLAR;
24        changeDue = changeDue % PENNIES_PER_DOLLAR;
```

```
25        int quarters = changeDue / PENNIES_PER_QUARTER;
26
27        // Print change due
28
29        System.out.printf("Dollar coins: %6d", dollarCoins);
30        System.out.println();
31        System.out.printf("Quarters:     %6d", quarters);
32        System.out.println();
33    }
34 }
```

Program Run

```
Enter bill value (1 = $1 bill, 5 = $5 bill, etc.): 5
Enter item price in pennies: 225
Dollar coins:    2
Quarters:        3
```

WORKED EXAMPLE 4.1

Computing the Volume and Surface Area of a Pyramid

Learn how to design a class for computing the volume and surface area of a pyramid. See your eText or visit wiley.com/go/bjeo7.

© Holger Mette/iStockphoto.

4.4 Problem Solving: First Do It By Hand

A very important step for developing an algorithm is to first carry out the computations *by hand*. If you can't compute a solution yourself, it's unlikely that you'll be able to write a program that automates the computation.

To illustrate the use of hand calculations, consider the following problem.

A row of black and white tiles needs to be placed along a wall. For aesthetic reasons, the architect has specified that the first and last tile shall be black.

Your task is to compute the number of tiles needed and the gap at each end, given the space available and the width of each tile.

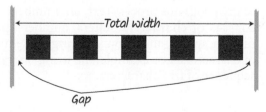

To make the problem more concrete, let's assume the following dimensions:

Pick concrete values for a typical situation to use in a hand calculation.

- Total width: 100 inches
- Tile width: 5 inches

The obvious solution would be to fill the space with 20 tiles, but that would not work—the last tile would be white.

Instead, look at the problem this way: The first tile must always be black, and then we add some number of white/black pairs:

The first tile takes up 5 inches, leaving 95 inches to be covered by pairs. Each pair is 10 inches wide. Therefore the number of pairs is 95/10 = 9.5. However, we need to discard the fractional part because we can't have fractions of tile pairs.

Therefore, we will use 9 tile pairs or 18 tiles, plus the initial black tile. Altogether, we require 19 tiles.

The tiles span 19 × 5 = 95 inches, leaving a total gap of 100 − 19 × 5 = 5 inches.

The gap should be evenly distributed at both ends. At each end, the gap is (100 − 19 × 5) / 2 = 2.5 inches.

This computation gives us enough information to devise an algorithm with arbitrary values for the total width and tile width.

number of pairs = integer part of (total width - tile width) / (2 x tile width)
number of tiles = 1 + 2 x number of pairs
gap at each end = (total width - number of tiles x tile width) / 2

As you can see, doing a hand calculation gives enough insight into the problem that it becomes easy to develop an algorithm.

EXAMPLE CODE   See sec04 of your eText or companion code for a program that implements this algorithm.

WORKED EXAMPLE 4.2
Computing Travel Time

Learn how to develop a hand calculation to compute the time that a robot requires to retrieve an item from rocky terrain. See your eText or visit wiley.com/go/bjeo7.

Courtesy NASA.

4.5 Strings

Strings are sequences of characters.

Many programs process text, not numbers. Text consists of **characters**: letters, numbers, punctuation, spaces, and so on. A **string** is a sequence of characters. For example, the string "Harry" is a sequence of five characters.

© essxboy/iStockphoto.

4.5.1 The String Type

You can declare variables that hold strings.

```
String name = "Harry";
```

We distinguish between string variables (such as the variable `name` declared above) and string **literals** (character sequences enclosed in quotes, such as `"Harry"`). A string variable is simply a variable that can hold a string, just as an integer variable can hold an integer. A string literal denotes a particular string, just as a number literal (such as 2) denotes a particular number.

The length method yields the number of characters in a string.

The number of characters in a string is called the *length* of the string. For example, the length of `"Harry"` is 5. As you saw in Section 2.3, you can compute the length of a string with the `length` method.

```
int n = name.length();
```

A string of length 0 is called the *empty string*. It contains no characters and is written as `""`.

4.5.2 Concatenation

Use the + operator to *concatenate* strings; that is, to put them together to yield a longer string.

Given two strings, such as `"Harry"` and `"Morgan"`, you can **concatenate** them to one long string. The result consists of all characters in the first string, followed by all characters in the second string. In Java, you use the + operator to concatenate two strings.

For example,

```
String fName = "Harry";
String lName = "Morgan";
String name = fName + lName;
```

results in the string

```
"HarryMorgan"
```

What if you'd like the first and last name separated by a space? No problem:

```
String name = fName + " " + lName;
```

This statement concatenates three strings: `fName`, the string literal `" "`, and `lName`. The result is

```
"Harry Morgan"
```

When the expression to the left or the right of a + operator is a string, the other one is automatically forced to become a string as well, and both strings are concatenated.

For example, consider this code:

```
String jobTitle = "Agent";
int employeeId = 7;
String bond = jobTitle + employeeId;
```

Whenever one of the arguments of the + operator is a string, the other argument is converted to a string.

Because `jobTitle` is a string, `employeeId` is converted from the integer 7 to the string `"7"`. Then the two strings `"Agent"` and `"7"` are concatenated to form the string `"Agent7"`.

This concatenation is very useful for reducing the number of `System.out.print` instructions. For example, you can combine

```
System.out.print("The total is ");
System.out.println(total);
```

to the single call

```
System.out.println("The total is " + total);
```

The concatenation `"The total is " + total` computes a single string that consists of the string `"The total is "`, followed by the string equivalent of the number `total`.

4.5.3 String Input

You can read a string from the console:

```
System.out.print("Please enter your name: ");
String name = in.next();
```

When a string is read with the next method, only one word is read. For example, suppose the user types

```
Harry Morgan
```

> Use the next method of the Scanner class to read a string containing a single word.

as the response to the prompt. This input consists of two words. The call in.next() yields the string "Harry". You can use another call to in.next() to read the second word.

4.5.4 Escape Sequences

To include a quotation mark in a literal string, precede it with a backslash (\), like this:

```
"He said \"Hello\""
```

The backslash is not included in the string. It indicates that the quotation mark that follows should be a part of the string and not mark the end of the string. The sequence \" is called an **escape sequence**.

To include a backslash in a string, use the escape sequence \\, like this:

```
"C:\\Temp\\Secret.txt"
```

Another common escape sequence is \n, which denotes a **newline** character. Printing a newline character causes the start of a new line on the display. For example, the statement

```
System.out.print("*\n**\n***\n");
```

prints the characters

```
*
**
***
```

on three separate lines.

However, in Windows, you need to add a "return" character \r before each \n. If you use the %n format specifier in a call to System.out.printf, it is automatically translated into \n or \r\n:

```
System.out.printf("Price: %10.2f%n", price);
```

4.5.5 Strings and Characters

Strings are sequences of **Unicode** characters (see Computing & Society 4.2). In Java, a **character** is a value of the type char. Characters have numeric values. You can find the values of the characters that are used in Western European languages in Appendix A. For example, if you look up the value for the character 'H', you can see that it is actually encoded as the number 72.

© slpix/iStockphoto.

A string is a sequence of characters.

Character literals are delimited by single quotes, and you should not confuse them with strings.

- 'H' is a character, a value of type char.
- "H" is a string containing a single character, a value of type String.

The charAt method returns a char value from a string. The first string position is labeled 0, the second one 1, and so on.

String positions are counted starting with 0.

```
H   a   r   r   y
0   1   2   3   4
```

The position number of the last character (4 for the string "Harry") is always one less than the length of the string. For example, the statement

```
String name = "Harry";
char start = name.charAt(0);
char last = name.charAt(4);
```

sets start to the value 'H' and last to the value 'y'.

4.5.6 Substrings

Use the substring method to extract a part of a string.

Once you have a string, you can extract substrings by using the substring method. The method call

```
str.substring(start, pastEnd)
```

returns a string that is made up of the characters in the string str, starting at position start, and containing all characters up to, but not including, the position pastEnd. Here is an example:

```
String greeting = "Hello, World!";
String sub = greeting.substring(0, 5); // sub is "Hello"
```

Here the substring operation makes a string that consists of the first five characters taken from the string greeting.

```
H   e   l   l   o   ,       W   o   r   l   d   !
0   1   2   3   4   5   6   7   8   9   10  11  12
```

Let's figure out how to extract the substring "World". Count characters starting at 0, not 1. You find that W has position number 7. The first character that you don't want, !, is the character at position 12. Therefore, the appropriate substring command is

```
String sub2 = greeting.substring(7, 12);
```

It is curious that you must specify the position of the first character that you do want and then the first character that you don't want. There is one advantage to this setup. You can easily compute the length of the substring: It is pastEnd - start. For example, the string "World" has length 12 − 7 = 5.

If you omit the end position when calling the substring method, then all characters from the starting position to the end of the string are copied. For example,

```
String tail = greeting.substring(7); // Copies all characters from position 7 on
```

sets tail to the string "World!".

Table 7 String Operations

Statement	Result	Comment
`string str = "Ja";` `str = str + "va";`	str is set to "Java"	When applied to strings, + denotes concatenation.
`System.out.println("Please"` `   + " enter your name: ");`	Prints `Please enter your name:`	Use concatenation to break up strings that don't fit into one line.
`team = 49 + "ers"`	team is set to "49ers"	Because "ers" is a string, 49 is converted to a string.

`String first = in.next();`
`String last = in.next();`
`(User input: Harry Morgan)`
	first contains "Harry"
	last contains "Morgan"
		The next method places the next word into the string variable.

`String greeting = "H & S";` `int n = greeting.length();`	n is set to 5	Each space counts as one character.
`String str = "Sally";` `char ch = str.charAt(1);`	ch is set to 'a'	This is a char value, not a String. Note that the initial position is 0.
`String str = "Sally";` `String str2 = str.substring(1, 4);`	str2 is set to "all"	Extracts the substring starting at position 1 and ending before position 4.
`String str = "Sally";` `String str2 = str.substring(1);`	str2 is set to "ally"	If you omit the end position, all characters from the position until the end of the string are included.
`String str = "Sally";` `String str2 = str.substring(1, 2);`	str2 is set to "a"	Extracts a String of length 1; contrast with str.charAt(1).
`String last = str.substring(` `   str.length() - 1);`	last is set to the string containing the last character in str	The last character has position str.length() - 1.

Following is a simple program that puts these concepts to work. The program asks for your name and that of your significant other. It then prints out your initials.

The operation `first.substring(0, 1)` makes a string consisting of one character, taken from the start of `first`. The program does the same for the `second`. Then it concatenates the resulting one-character strings with the string literal `"&"` to get a string of length 3, the `initials` string. (See Figure 3.)

© Rich Legg/iStockphoto.

Initials are formed from the first letter of each name.

```
first =  R  o  d  o  l  f  o
         0  1  2  3  4  5  6

second = S  a  l  l  y
         0  1  2  3  4

initials = R  &  S
           0  1  2
```

Figure 3 Building the initials String

sec05/Initials.java

```java
1  import java.util.Scanner;
2
3  /**
4     This program prints a pair of initials.
5  */
6  public class Initials
7  {
8     public static void main(String[] args)
9     {
10        Scanner in = new Scanner(System.in);
11
12        // Get the names of the couple
13
14        System.out.print("Enter your first name: ");
15        String first = in.next();
16        System.out.print("Enter your significant other's first name: ");
17        String second = in.next();
18
19        // Compute and display the inscription
20
21        String initials = first.substring(0, 1)
22           + "&" + second.substring(0, 1);
23        System.out.println(initials);
24     }
25  }
```

Program Run

```
Enter your first name: Rodolfo
Enter your significant other's first name: Sally
R&S
```

Programming Tip 4.3

Reading Exception Reports

You will often have programs that terminate and display an error message, such as

```
Exception in thread "main" java.lang.StringIndexOutOfBoundsException:
    String index out of range: -4
  at java.lang.String.substring(String.java:1444)
  at Homework1.main(Homework1.java:16)
```

If this happens to you, don't say "it didn't work" or "my program died". Instead, read the error message. Admittedly, the format of the exception report is not very friendly. But it is actually easy to decipher it.

When you have a close look at the error message, you will notice two pieces of useful information:

1. The name of the exception, such as StringIndexOutOfBoundsException
2. The line number of the code that contained the statement that caused the exception, such as Homework1.java:16

The name of the exception is always in the first line of the report, and it ends in Exception. If you get a StringIndexOutOfBoundsException, then there was a problem with accessing an invalid position in a string. That is useful information.

The line number of the offending code is a little harder to determine. The exception report contains the entire **stack trace**—that is, the names of all methods that were pending when the exception hit. The first line of the stack trace is the method that actually generated the exception. The last line of the stack trace is a line in main. Often, the exception was thrown by a method that is in the standard library. Look for the first line in your code that appears in the exception report. For example, skip the line that refers to

```
java.lang.String.substring(String.java:1444)
```

The next line in our example mentions a line number in your code, Homework1.java. Once you have the line number in your code, open up the file, go to that line, and look at it! Also look at the name of the exception. In most cases, these two pieces of information will make it completely obvious what went wrong, and you can easily fix your error.

Special Topic 4.5
Using Dialog Boxes for Input and Output

Most program users find the console window rather old-fashioned. The easiest alternative is to create a separate pop-up window for each input.

Call the static showInputDialog method of the JOptionPane class, and supply the string that prompts the input from the user.

For example,

An Input Dialog Box

```
String input = JOptionPane.showInputDialog("Enter price:");
```

That method returns a String object. Of course, often you need the input as a number. Use the Integer.parseInt and Double.parseDouble methods to convert the string to a number:

```
double price = Double.parseDouble(input);
```

You can also display output in a dialog box:

```
JOptionPane.showMessageDialog(null, "Price: " + price);
```

EXAMPLE CODE   See special_topic_5 of your eText or companion code for a program that uses option panes for input and output.

Computing & Society 4.2   International Alphabets and Unicode

The English alphabet is pretty simple: upper- and lowercase *a* to *z*. Other European languages have accent marks and special characters.

© pvachier/iStockphoto.

The German Keyboard Layout

For example, German has three so-called *umlaut* characters, ä, ö, ü, and a *double-s* character ß. These are not optional frills; you couldn't write a page of German text without using these characters a few times. German keyboards have keys for these characters.

Many countries don't use the Roman script at all. Russian, Greek, Hebrew, Arabic, and Thai letters, to name just a few, have completely different shapes. To complicate matters, Hebrew and Arabic are typed from right to left. Each of these alphabets has about as many characters as the English alphabet.

The Chinese languages as well as Japanese and Korean use Chinese characters. Each character represents

© Joel Carillet/iStockphoto.

Hebrew, Arabic, and English

an idea or thing. Words are made up of one or more of these ideographic characters. Over 70,000 ideographs are known.

Starting in 1987, a consortium of hardware and software manufacturers developed a uniform encoding scheme called **Unicode** that is capable of encoding text in essentially all written languages of the world. An early version of Unicode used 16 bits for each character. The Java char type corresponds to that encoding.

© Saipg/iStockphoto.

The Chinese Script

Today Unicode has grown to a 21-bit code, with definitions for over 100,000 characters (http://www.unicode.org). There are even plans to add codes for extinct languages, such as Egyptian hieroglyphics. Unfortunately, that means that a Java char value does not always correspond to a Unicode character. Some characters in languages such as Chinese or ancient Egyptian, as well as the ubiquitous emoticons, occupy two char values.

CHAPTER SUMMARY

Choose appropriate types for representing numeric data.

- Java has eight primitive types, including four integer types and two floating-point types.
- A numeric computation overflows if the result falls outside the range for the number type.
- Rounding errors occur when an exact conversion between numbers is not possible.
- A final variable is a constant. Once its value has been set, it cannot be changed.
- Use named constants to make your programs easier to read and maintain.

Write arithmetic expressions in Java.

- Mixing integers and floating-point values in an arithmetic expression yields a floating-point value.
- The ++ operator adds 1 to a variable; the -- operator subtracts 1.
- If both arguments of / are integers, the remainder is discarded.
- The % operator computes the remainder of an integer division.
- The Java library declares many mathematical functions, such as Math.sqrt (square root) and Math.pow (raising to a power).
- You use a cast (*typeName*) to convert a value to a different type.

Write programs that read user input and print formatted output.

- Use the Scanner class to read keyboard input in a console window.
- Use the printf method to specify how values should be formatted.

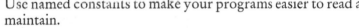

Carry out hand calculations when developing an algorithm.

- Pick concrete values for a typical situation to use in a hand calculation.

Write programs that process strings.

- Strings are sequences of characters.
- The length method yields the number of characters in a string.

- Use the + operator to *concatenate* strings; that is, to put them together to yield a longer string.
- Whenever one of the arguments of the + operator is a string, the other argument is converted to a string.
- Use the next method of the Scanner class to read a string containing a single word.

- String positions are counted starting with 0.
- Use the substring method to extract a part of a string.

STANDARD LIBRARY ITEMS INTRODUCED IN THIS CHAPTER

```
java.io.PrintStream
  printf
java.lang.Double
  parseDouble
java.lang.Integer
  MAX_VALUE
  MIN_VALUE
  parseInt
java.lang.Math
  PI
  abs
  ceil
  cos
  exp
  floor
  floorMod
  log
  log10
  max
  min
  pow
  round
  sin
  sqrt
  tan
  toDegrees
  toRadians
```

```
java.lang.String
  charAt
  length
  substring
java.lang.System
  in
java.math.BigDecimal
  add
  multiply
  subtract
java.math.BigInteger
  add
  multiply
  subtract
java.util.Scanner
  next
  nextDouble
  nextInt
javax.swing.JOptionPane
  showInputDialog
  showMessageDialog
```

REVIEW EXERCISES

■ **R4.1** Write declarations for storing the following quantities. Choose between integers and floating-point numbers. Declare constants when appropriate.

    a. The number of days per week

    b. The number of days until the end of the semester

    c. The number of centimeters in an inch

    d. The height of the tallest person in your class, in centimeters

■ **R4.2** What is the value of mystery after this sequence of statements?

```
int mystery = 1;
mystery = 1 - 2 * mystery;
mystery = mystery + 1;
```

■ **R4.3** What is wrong with the following sequence of statements?

```
int mystery = 1;
mystery = mystery + 1;
int mystery = 1 - 2 * mystery;
```

■■ **R4.4** Write the following Java expressions in mathematical notation.

    a. `dm = m * (Math.sqrt(1 + v / c) / Math.sqrt(1 - v / c) - 1);`

    b. `volume = Math.PI * r * r * h;`

    c. `volume = 4 * Math.PI * Math.pow(r, 3) / 3;`

    d. `z = Math.sqrt(x * x + y * y);`

■■ **R4.5** Write the following mathematical expressions in Java.

$$s = s_0 + v_0 t + \frac{1}{2} g t^2 \qquad\qquad FV = PV \cdot \left(1 + \frac{INT}{100}\right)^{YRS}$$

$$G = 4\pi^2 \frac{a^3}{p^2(m_1 + m_2)} \qquad\qquad c = \sqrt{a^2 + b^2 - 2ab\cos\gamma}$$

■■ **R4.6** Assuming that a and b are variables of type int, fill in the following table:

a	b	Math.pow(a, b)	Math.max(a, b)	a / b	a % b	Math.floorMod(a, b)
2	3					
3	2					
2	−3					
3	−2					
−3	2					
−3	−2					

■■ **R4.7** Suppose `direction` is an integer angle between 0 and 359 degrees. You turn by a given angle and update the direction as

```
direction = (direction + turn) % 360;
```

In which situation do you get the wrong result? How can you fix that without using the `Math.floorMod` method described in Special Topic 4.2?

■■ **R4.8** What are the values of the following expressions? In each line, assume that

```
double x = 2.5;
double y = -1.5;
int m = 18;
int n = 4;
```

a. x + n * y - (x + n) * y

b. m / n + m % n

c. 5 * x - n / 5

d. 1 - (1 - (1 - (1 - (1 - n))))

e. Math.sqrt(Math.sqrt(n))

■ **R4.9** What are the values of the following expressions, assuming that n is 17 and m is 18?

a. n / 10 + n % 10

b. n % 2 + m % 2

c. (m + n) / 2

d. (m + n) / 2.0

e. (int) (0.5 * (m + n))

f. (int) Math.round(0.5 * (m + n))

■■ **R4.10** What are the values of the following expressions? In each line, assume that

```
String s = "Hello";
String t = "World";
```

a. s.length() + t.length()

b. s.substring(1, 2)

c. s.substring(s.length() / 2, s.length())

d. s + t

e. t + s

■ **R4.11** Given a string s, write expressions for:

- The string consisting of the first letter
- The string consisting of the first and last letter
- The string consisting of all but the first and last letter
- The first half of the string (discarding the middle letter if the string has odd length)
- The second half of the string (discarding the middle letter if the string has odd length)
- The string consisting of the middle letter if the string has odd length, or the middle two letters otherwise

■ **R4.12** Find at least five *compile-time* errors in the following program.

```
public class HasErrors
{
```

```
        public static void main();
        {
            System.out.print(Please enter two numbers:)
            x = in.readDouble;
            y = in.readDouble;
            System.out.printline("The sum is " + x + y);
        }
    }
```

■■ R4.13 Find three *run-time* errors in the following program.

```
public class HasErrors
{
    public static void main(String[] args)
    {
        int x = 0;
        int y = 0;
        Scanner in = new Scanner("System.in");
        System.out.print("Please enter an integer:");
        x = in.readInt();
        System.out.print("Please enter another integer: ");
        x = in.readInt();
        System.out.println("The sum is " + x + y);
    }
}
```

■■ R4.14 Consider the following code:

```
CashRegister register = new CashRegister();
register.recordPurchase(19.93);
register.receivePayment(20, 0, 0, 0, 0);
System.out.print("Change: ");
System.out.println(register.giveChange());
```

The code segment prints the total as 0.070000000000000028. Explain why. Give a recommendation to improve the code so that users will not be confused.

■ R4.15 Explain the differences between 2, 2.0, '2', "2", and "2.0".

■ R4.16 Explain what each of the following program segments computes.

    a. x = 2;
       y = x + x;
    b. s = "2";
       t = s + s;

■■ R4.17 Write pseudocode for a program that reads a word and then prints the first character, the last character, and the characters in the middle. For example, if the input is Harry, the program prints H y arr.

■■ R4.18 Write pseudocode for a program that reads a name (such as Harold James Morgan) and then prints a monogram consisting of the initial letters of the first, middle, and last name (such as HJM).

■■■ R4.19 Write pseudocode for a program that computes the first and last digit of a number. For example, if the input is 23456, the program should print 2 and 6. *Hint:* Use % and Math.log10.

■ R4.20 Modify the pseudocode for the program in How To 4.1 so that the program gives change in quarters, dimes, and nickels. You can assume that the price is a multiple of 5 cents. To develop your pseudocode, first work with a couple of specific values.

••• R4.21 In Worked Example 4.1, it is easy enough to measure the width of a pyramid. To measure the height without climbing to the top, you can use a theodolite and determine the angle between the ground and the line joining the theodolite's position and the top of the pyramid. What other information do you need in order to compute the surface area?

••• R4.22 Suppose an ancient civilization had constructed circular pyramids. Write pseudocode for a program that determines the surface area from measurements that you can determine from the ground.

•• R4.23 A cocktail shaker is composed of three cone sections.

The volume of a cone section with height h and top and bottom radius r_1 and r_2 is

$$V = \pi \frac{\left(r_1^2 + r_1 r_2 + r_2^2\right)h}{3}$$

Compute the total volume by hand for one set of realistic values for the radii and heights. Then develop an algorithm that works for arbitrary dimensions.

••• R4.24 You are cutting off a piece of pie like this, where c is the length of the straight part (called the chord length) and h is the height of the piece.

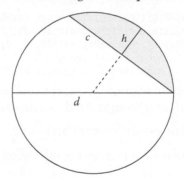

There is an approximate formula for the area:

$$A \approx \frac{2}{3} ch + \frac{h^3}{2c}$$

However, h is not so easy to measure, whereas the diameter d of a pie is usually well-known. Calculate the area where the diameter of the pie is 12 inches and the chord length of the segment is 10 inches. Generalize to an algorithm that yields the area for any diameter and chord length.

•• R4.25 The following pseudocode describes how to obtain the name of a day, given the day number (0 = Sunday, 1 = Monday, and so on.)

> *Declare a string called names containing "SunMonTueWedThuFriSat".*
> *Compute the starting position as 3 x the day number.*
> *Extract the substring of names at the starting position with length 3.*

Check this pseudocode, using the day number 4. Draw a diagram of the string that is being computed, similar to Figure 3.

© Media Bakery.

■■■ R4.26 Suppose you are given a string *str* and two positions *i* and *j*, where *i* comes before *j*. The following pseudocode describes how to swap two letters in a word.

Set first to the substring from the start of the string to the last position before i.
Set middle to the substring from positions i + 1 to j - 1.
Set last to the substring from position j + 1 to the end of the string.
Concatenate the following five strings: first, the string containing just the character at position j,
   middle, the string containing just the character at position i, and last.

Check this pseudocode, using the string "Gateway" and positions 2 and 4. Draw a diagram of the string that is being computed, similar to Figure 3.

■■ R4.27 How do you get the first character of a string? The last character? How do you remove the first character? The last character?

■■ R4.28 For each of the following computations in Java, determine whether the result is exact, an overflow, or a roundoff error.

   a. `2.0 - 1.1`
   b. `1.0E6 * 1.0E6`
   c. `65536 * 65536`
   d. `1_000_000L * 1_000_000L`

■■■ R4.29 Write a program that prints the values

```
3 * 1000 * 1000 * 1000
3.0 * 1000 * 1000 * 1000
```

Explain the results.

PRACTICE EXERCISES

■ E4.1 Write a program that displays the properties of a letter-size (8.5 × 11 inches) sheet of paper in millimeters. There are 25.4 millimeters per inch. The program should print:
   - The width and height
   - The perimeter
   - The length of the diagonal

Use constants and comments in your program.

■ E4.2 Write a program that reads a number and displays the square, cube, and fourth power. Use the `Math.pow` method only for the fourth power.

■■ E4.3 Write a program that prompts the user for two integers and then prints
   - The sum
   - The difference
   - The product
   - The average
   - The distance (absolute value of the difference)
   - The maximum (the larger of the two)
   - The minimum (the smaller of the two)

Hint: The `max` and `min` functions are declared in the `Math` class.

■■ **E4.4**   Enhance the output of Exercise ●● E4.3 so that the numbers are properly aligned:

```
Sum:           45
Difference:    -5
Product:       500
Average:       22.50
Distance:      5
Maximum:       25
Minimum:       20
```

■■ **E4.5**   Write a program that prompts the user for a measurement in meters and then converts it to miles, feet, and inches.

■ **E4.6**   Write a program that prompts the user for a radius and then prints
   • The area and circumference of a circle with that radius
   • The volume and surface area of a sphere with that radius

■■ **E4.7**   Write a program that asks the user for the lengths of a rectangle's sides. Then print
   • The area and perimeter of the rectangle
   • The length of the diagonal (use the Pythagorean theorem)

■ **E4.8**   Improve the program discussed in How To 4.1 to allow input of quarters in addition to bills.

■■ **E4.9**   Write a program that asks the user to input
   • The number of gallons of gas in the tank
   • The fuel efficiency in miles per gallon
   • The price of gas per gallon
   Then print the cost per 100 miles and how far the car can go with the gas in the tank.

■■ **E4.10**   Change the Menu class in Worked Example 3.1 so that the menu options are labeled A, B, C, and so on. *Hint:* Make a string of the labels.

■ **E4.11**   *File names and extensions.* Write a program that prompts the user for the drive letter (C), the path (\Windows\System), the file name (Readme), and the extension (txt). Then print the complete file name C:\Windows\System\Readme.txt. (If you use UNIX or a Macintosh, skip the drive name and use / instead of \ to separate directories.)

■■■ **E4.12**   Write a program that reads a number between 1,000 and 999,999 from the user, where the user enters a comma in the input. Then print the number without a comma.

   Here is a sample dialog; the user input is in color:

```
Please enter an integer between 1,000 and 999,999: 23,456
23456
```

   Hint: Read the input as a string. Measure the length of the string. Suppose it contains n characters. Then extract substrings consisting of the first $n - 4$ characters and the last three characters.

■■ **E4.13**   Write a program that reads a number between 1,000 and 999,999 from the user and prints it with a comma separating the thousands. Here is a sample dialog; the user input is in color:

```
Please enter an integer between 1000 and 999999: 23456
23,456
```

■ **E4.14** *Printing a grid.* Write a program that prints the following grid to play tic-tac-toe.

```
+--+--+--+
|  |  |  |
+--+--+--+
|  |  |  |
+--+--+--+
|  |  |  |
+--+--+--+
```

Of course, you could simply write seven statements of the form

```
System.out.println("+--+--+--+");
```

You should do it the smart way, though. Declare string variables to hold two kinds of patterns: a comb-shaped pattern and the bottom line. Print the comb three times and the bottom line once.

■■ **E4.15** Write a program that reads in an integer and breaks it into a sequence of individual digits. For example, the input 16384 is displayed as

```
1 6 3 8 4
```

You may assume that the input has no more than five digits and is not negative.

■■ **E4.16** Write a program that reads two times in military format (0900, 1730) and prints the number of hours and minutes between the two times. Here is a sample run. User input is in color.

```
Please enter the first time: 0900
Please enter the second time: 1730
8 hours 30 minutes
```

Extra credit if you can deal with the case where the first time is later than the second:

```
Please enter the first time: 1730
Please enter the second time: 0900
15 hours 30 minutes
```

■■■ **E4.17** *Writing large letters.* A large letter H can be produced like this:

```
*   *
*   *
*****
*   *
*   *
```

It can be declared as a string literal like this:

```
final string LETTER_H = "*   *%n*   *%n*****%n*   *%n*   *";
```

Print the string with System.out.printf. The %n format specifiers cause line breaks in the output. Do the same for the letters E, L, and O. Then write the message

```
H
E
L
L
O
```

in large letters.

■■ **E4.18** Write a program that transforms numbers 1, 2, 3, ..., 12 into the corresponding month names January, February, March, ..., December. *Hint:* Make a very long string "January February March ...", in which you add spaces such that each month name has *the same length*. Then use substring to extract the month you want.

© José Luis Gutiérrez/iStockphoto.

■■ **E4.19** Write a program that prints a Christmas tree:

```
      /\
     /  \
    /    \
   /      \
   --------
    "    "
    "    "
    "    "
```

Remember to use escape sequences.

■■ **E4.20** Enhance the CashRegister class by adding separate methods enterDollars, enterQuarters, enterDimes, enterNickels, and enterPennies.

Use this tester class:

```java
public class CashRegisterTester
{
    public static void main (String[] args)
    {
        CashRegister register = new CashRegister();
        register.recordPurchase(20.37);
        register.enterDollars(20);
        register.enterQuarters(2);
        System.out.println("Change: " + register.giveChange());
        System.out.println("Expected: 0.13");
    }
}
```

■■ **E4.21** Implement a class IceCreamCone with methods getSurfaceArea() and getVolume(). In the constructor, supply the height and radius of the cone. Be careful when looking up the formula for the surface area—you should only include the outside area along the side of the cone because the cone has an opening on the top to hold the ice cream.

■■ **E4.22** Implement a class SodaCan whose constructor receives the height and diameter of the soda can. Supply methods getVolume and getSurfaceArea. Supply a SodaCanTester class that tests your class.

■■■ **E4.23** Implement a class Balloon that models a spherical balloon that is being filled with air. The constructor constructs an empty balloon. Supply these methods:
- void addAir(double amount) adds the given amount of air
- double getVolume() gets the current volume
- double getSurfaceArea() gets the current surface area
- double getRadius() gets the current radius

Supply a BalloonTester class that constructs a balloon, adds 100 cm³ of air, tests the three accessor methods, adds another 100 cm³ of air, and tests the accessor methods again.

PROGRAMMING PROJECTS

■■■ **P4.1** Write a program that helps a person decide whether to buy a hybrid car. Your program's inputs should be:

- The cost of a new car
- The estimated miles driven per year
- The estimated gas price
- The efficiency in miles per gallon
- The estimated resale value after 5 years

Compute the total cost of owning the car for five years. (For simplicity, we will not take the cost of financing into account.) Obtain realistic prices for a new and used hybrid and a comparable car from the Web. Run your program twice, using today's gas price and 15,000 miles per year. Include pseudocode and the program runs with your assignment.

© asiseeit/iStockphoto.

■■ **P4.2** Easter Sunday is the first Sunday after the first full moon of spring. To compute the date, you can use this algorithm, invented by the mathematician Carl Friedrich Gauss in 1800:

1. Let y be the year (such as 1800 or 2001).

2. Divide y by 19 and call the remainder a. Ignore the quotient.

3. Divide y by 100 to get a quotient b and a remainder c.

4. Divide b by 4 to get a quotient d and a remainder e.

5. Divide 8 * b + 13 by 25 to get a quotient g. Ignore the remainder.

6. Divide 19 * a + b - d - g + 15 by 30 to get a remainder h. Ignore the quotient.

7. Divide c by 4 to get a quotient j and a remainder k.

8. Divide a + 11 * h by 319 to get a quotient m. Ignore the remainder.

9. Divide 2 * e + 2 * j - k - h + m + 32 by 7 to get a remainder r. Ignore the quotient.

10. Divide h - m + r + 90 by 25 to get a quotient n. Ignore the remainder.

11. Divide h - m + r + n + 19 by 32 to get a remainder p. Ignore the quotient.

Then Easter falls on day p of month n. For example, if y is 2001:

```
a = 6           g = 6           m = 0       n = 4
b = 20, c = 1   h = 18          r = 6       p = 15
d = 5, e = 0    j = 0, k = 1
```

Therefore, in 2001, Easter Sunday fell on April 15. Write a program that prompts the user for a year and prints out the month and day of Easter Sunday.

■■ **P4.3** Write a program that reads a number from the user and does the following: Discard all but the last three digits. Reverse the digits, subtract the original from the reversed (discarding any minus sign), reverse the digits of the difference, and add the difference and the reversed difference. Then print the sum. For example:

Input: 371

Reversed: 173

Difference: 198

Reversed: 891

Sum: 1089

This procedure is sometimes called the "1089 puzzle" because the final result is 1089 in most cases.

■■■ **P4.4** In this project, you will perform calculations with triangles. A triangle is defined by the x- and y-coordinates of its three corner points.

Your job is to compute the following properties of a given triangle:

- the lengths of all sides
- the angles at all corners
- the perimeter
- the area

Implement a Triangle class with appropriate methods. Supply a program that prompts a user for the corner point coordinates and produces a nicely formatted table of the triangle properties.

■■ **P4.5** A boat floats in a two-dimensional ocean. It has a position and a direction. It can move by a given distance in its current direction, and it can turn by a given angle. Provide methods

```
public double getX()
public double getY()
public double getDirection()
public void turn(double degrees)
public void move(double distance)
```

■■■ **P4.6** The CashRegister class has an unfortunate limitation: It is closely tied to the coin system in the United States and Canada. Research the system used in most of Europe. Your goal is to produce a cash register that works with euros and cents. Rather than designing another limited CashRegister implementation for the European market, you should design a separate Coin class and a cash register that can work with coins of all types.

■■ **Business P4.7** The following pseudocode describes how a bookstore computes the price of an order from the total price and the number of the books that were ordered.

Read the total book price and the number of books.
Compute the tax (7.5 percent of the total book price).
Compute the shipping charge ($2 per book).
The price of the order is the sum of the total book price, the tax, and the shipping charge.
Print the price of the order.

Translate this pseudocode into a Java program.

■■ Business P4.8 The following pseudocode describes how to turn a string containing a ten-digit phone number (such as `"4155551212"`) into a more readable string with parentheses and dashes, like this: `"(415) 555-1212"`.

> *Take the substring consisting of the first three characters and surround it with "(" and ")".*
> *This is the area code.*
> *Concatenate the area code, the substring consisting of the next three characters, a hyphen, and the substring consisting of the last four characters. This is the formatted number.*

Translate this pseudocode into a Java program that reads a telephone number into a string variable, computes the formatted number, and prints it.

■■ Business P4.9 The following pseudocode describes how to extract the dollars and cents from a price given as a floating-point value. For example, a price 2.95 yields values 2 and 95 for the dollars and cents.

> *Assign the price to an integer variable dollars.*
> *Multiply the difference price – dollars by 100 and add 0.5.*
> *Assign the result to an integer variable cents.*

Translate this pseudocode into a Java program. Read a price and print the dollars and cents. Test your program with inputs 2.95 and 4.35.

■■ Business P4.10 *Giving change.* Implement a program that directs a cashier how to give change. The program has two inputs: the amount due and the amount received from the customer. Display the dollars, quarters, dimes, nickels, and pennies that the customer should receive in return. In order to avoid roundoff errors, the program user should supply both amounts in pennies, for example 274 instead of 2.74.

© Captainflash/iStockphoto.

■ Business P4.11 An online bank wants you to create a program that shows prospective customers how their deposits will grow. Your program should read the initial balance and the annual interest rate. Interest is compounded monthly. Print out the balances after the first three months. Here is a sample run:

```
Initial balance: 1000
Annual interest rate in percent: 6.0
After first month:     1005.00
After second month:    1010.03
After third month:     1015.08
```

■■ Business P4.12 A video club wants to reward its best members with a discount based on the member's number of movie rentals and the number of new members referred by the member. The discount is in percent and is equal to the sum of the rentals and the referrals, but it cannot exceed 75 percent. (*Hint:* `Math.min.`) Write a program `Discount-Calculator` to calculate the value of the discount.

Here is a sample run:

```
Enter the number of movie rentals: 56
Enter the number of members referred to the video club: 3
The discount is equal to:    59.00 percent.
```

■ Science P4.13 Consider the following circuit.

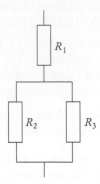

Write a program that reads the resistances of the three resistors and computes the total resistance, using Ohm's law.

■■ Science P4.14 The dew point temperature T_d can be calculated (approximately) from the relative humidity RH and the actual temperature T by

$$T_d = \frac{b \cdot f(T,RH)}{a - f(T,RH)}$$

$$f(T,RH) = \frac{a \cdot T}{b + T} + \ln(RH)$$

where $a = 17.27$ and $b = 237.7°$ C.

Write a program that reads the relative humidity (between 0 and 1) and the temperature (in degrees C) and prints the dew point value. Use the Java function log to compute the natural logarithm.

■■■ Science P4.15 The pipe clip temperature sensors shown here are robust sensors that can be clipped directly onto copper pipes to measure the temperature of the liquids in the pipes.

Each sensor contains a device called a *thermistor*. Thermistors are semiconductor devices that exhibit a temperature-dependent resistance described by:

$$R = R_0 \, e^{\beta\left(\frac{1}{T} - \frac{1}{T_0}\right)}$$

where R is the resistance (in Ω) at the temperature T (in °K), and R_0 is the resistance (in Ω) at the temperature T_0 (in °K). β is a constant that depends on the material used to make the thermistor. Thermistors are specified by providing values for R_0, T_0, and β.

The thermistors used to make the pipe clip temperature sensors have $R_0 = 1075 \, \Omega$ at $T_0 = 85 \, °C$, and $\beta = 3969 \, °K$. (Notice that β has units of °K. Recall that the temperature in °K is obtained by adding 273 to the temperature in °C.) The liquid temperature, in °C, is determined from the resistance R, in Ω, using

$$T = \frac{\beta T_0}{T_0 \ln\left(\dfrac{R}{R_0}\right) + \beta} - 273$$

Write a Java program that prompts the user for the thermistor resistance R and prints a message giving the liquid temperature in °C.

■■■ **Science P4.16** The circuit shown below illustrates some important aspects of the connection between a power company and one of its customers. The customer is represented by three parameters, V_t, P, and pf. V_t is the voltage accessed by plugging into a wall outlet. Customers depend on having a dependable value of V_t in order for their appliances to work properly. Accordingly, the power company regulates the value of V_t carefully.

© TebNad/iStockphoto.

P describes the amount of power used by the customer and is the primary factor in determining the customer's electric bill. The power factor, pf, is less familiar. (The power factor is calculated as the cosine of an angle so that its value will always be between zero and one.) In this problem you will be asked to write a Java program to investigate the significance of the power factor.

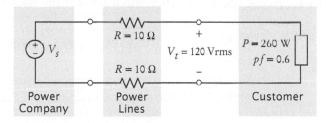

In the figure, the power lines are represented, somewhat simplistically, as resistances in Ohms. The power company is represented as an AC voltage source. The source voltage, V_s, required to provide the customer with power P at voltage V_t can be determined using the formula

$$V_s = \sqrt{\left(V_t + \frac{2RP}{V_t}\right)^2 + \left(\frac{2RP}{pf V_t}\right)^2 \left(1 - pf^2\right)}$$

(V_s has units of Vrms.) This formula indicates that the value of V_s depends on the value of pf. Write a Java program that prompts the user for a power factor value and then prints a message giving the corresponding value of V_s, using the values for P, R, and V_t shown in the figure above.

■■■ **Science P4.17** Consider the following tuning circuit connected to an antenna, where C is a variable capacitor whose capacitance ranges from $C_{\min}$ to $C_{\max}$.

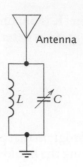

The tuning circuit selects the frequency $f = \dfrac{1}{2\pi\sqrt{LC}}$. To design this circuit for a given frequency, take $C = \sqrt{C_{min}C_{max}}$ and calculate the required inductance L from f and C. Now the circuit can be tuned to any frequency in the range

$$f_{min} = \frac{1}{2\pi\sqrt{LC_{max}}} \text{ to } f_{max} = \frac{1}{2\pi\sqrt{LC_{min}}}.$$

Write a Java program to design a tuning circuit for a given frequency, using a variable capacitor with given values for C_{min} and C_{max}. (A typical input is $f = 16.7$ MHz, $C_{min} = 14$ pF, and $C_{max} = 365$ pF.) The program should read in f (in Hz), C_{min} and C_{max} (in F), and print the required inductance value and the range of frequencies to which the circuit can be tuned by varying the capacitance.

- **Science P4.18** According to the Coulomb force law, the electric force between two charged particles of charge Q_1 and Q_2 Coulombs, that are a distance r meters apart, is

$$F = \frac{Q_1 Q_2}{4\pi\varepsilon r^2}$$ Newtons, where $\varepsilon = 8.854 \times 10^{-12}$ Farads/meter. Write a program that calculates the force on a pair of charged particles, based on the user input of Q_1 Coulombs, Q_2 Coulombs, and r meters, and then computes and displays the electric force.

CHAPTER **5**

DECISIONS

CHAPTER GOALS

To implement decisions using
if statements

To compare integers, floating-point numbers, and strings

To write statements using the Boolean data type

To develop strategies for testing your programs

To validate user input

CHAPTER CONTENTS

One of the essential features of computer programs is their ability to make decisions. Like a train that changes tracks depending on how the switches are set, a program can take different actions depending on inputs and other circumstances. In this chapter, you will learn how to program simple and complex decisions. You will apply what you learn to the task of checking user input.

5.1 The if Statement

The if statement is used to implement a decision (see Syntax 5.1). When a condition is fulfilled, one set of statements is executed. Otherwise, another set of statements is executed.

> The if statement allows a program to carry out different actions depending on the nature of the data to be processed.

Here is an example using the if statement: In many countries, the number 13 is considered unlucky. Rather than offending superstitious tenants, building owners sometimes skip the thirteenth floor; floor 12 is immediately followed by floor 14. Of course, floor 13 is not usually left empty. It is simply called floor 14. The computer that controls the building elevators needs to compensate for this foible and adjust all floor numbers above 13.

Let's simulate this process in Java. We will ask the user to type in the desired floor number and then compute the actual floor. When the input is above 13, then we need to decrement the input to obtain the actual floor. For example, if the user provides an input of 20, the program determines the actual floor to be 19. Otherwise, it simply uses the supplied floor number.

© DrGrounds/iStockphoto.

This elevator panel "skips" the thirteenth floor. The floor is not actually missing—the computer that controls the elevator adjusts the floor numbers above 13.

```java
int actualFloor;

if (floor > 13)
{
   actualFloor = floor - 1;
}
else
{
   actualFloor = floor;
}
```

An if statement is like a fork in the road. Depending upon a decision, different parts of the program are executed.

© Media Bakery.

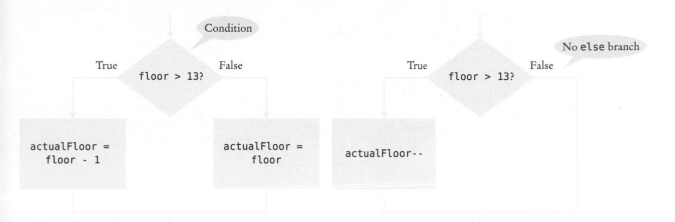

Figure 1
Flowchart for if Statement

Figure 2
Flowchart for if Statement with No else Branch

The flowchart in Figure 1 shows the branching behavior.

In our example, each branch of the if statement contains a single statement. You can include as many statements in each branch as you like. Sometimes, it happens that there is nothing to do in the else branch of the statement. In that case, you can omit it entirely, as in this example:

```java
int actualFloor = floor;

if (floor > 13)
{
    actualFloor--;
}
// No else needed
```

See Figure 2 for the flowchart.

The following program puts the if statement to work. This program asks for the desired floor and then prints out the actual floor.

sec01/ElevatorSimulation.java

```java
1  import java.util.Scanner;
2
3  /**
4      This program simulates an elevator panel that skips the 13th floor.
5  */
6  public class ElevatorSimulation
7  {
8     public static void main(String[] args)
9     {
10        Scanner in = new Scanner(System.in);
11        System.out.print("Floor: ");
12        int floor = in.nextInt();
13
14        // Adjust floor if necessary
15
16        int actualFloor;
17        if (floor > 13)
```

```
18      {
19          actualFloor = floor - 1;
20      }
21      else
22      {
23          actualFloor = floor;
24      }
25
26      System.out.println("The elevator will travel to the actual floor "
27          + actualFloor);
28   }
29 }
```

Program Run

```
Floor: 20
The elevator will travel to the actual floor 19
```

Syntax 5.1   if Statement

Syntax

```
if (condition)            if (condition) { statements₁ }
{                         else { statements₂ }
    statements
}
```

A condition that is true or false. Often uses relational operators: == != < <= > >= *(See Table 1.)*

Braces are not required if the branch contains a single statement, but it's good to always use them. See Programming Tip 5.2.

Don't put a semicolon here! See Common Error 5.1.

```
if (floor > 13)
{
    actualFloor = floor - 1;
}
else
{
    actualFloor = floor;
}
```

If the condition is true, the statement(s) in this branch are executed in sequence; if the condition is false, they are skipped.

Omit the else branch if there is nothing to do.

If the condition is false, the statement(s) in this branch are executed in sequence; if the condition is true, they are skipped.

Lining up braces is a good idea. See Programming Tip 5.1.

Common Error 5.1

A Semicolon After the if Condition

The following code fragment has an unfortunate error:

```
if (floor > 13) ; // Error
{
    floor--;
```

```
}
```

There should be no semicolon after the `if` condition. The compiler interprets this statement as follows: If `floor` is greater than 13, execute the statement that is denoted by a single semicolon, that is, the do-nothing statement. The statement in braces is no longer a part of the `if` statement. It is always executed. In other words, even if the value of `floor` is not above 13, it is decremented.

Programming Tip 5.1

Brace Layout

The compiler doesn't care where you place braces. In this book, we follow the simple rule of making { and } line up.

```
if (floor > 13)
{
    floor--;
}
```

This style makes it easy to spot matching braces. Some programmers put the opening brace on the same line as the `if`:

```
if (floor > 13) {
    floor--;
}
```

This style makes it harder to match the braces, but it saves a line of code, allowing you to view more code on the screen without scrolling. There are passionate advocates of both styles.

It is important that you pick a layout style and stick with it consistently within a given programming project. Which style you choose may depend on your personal preference or a coding style guide that you need to follow.

© Timothy Large/iStockphoto.

Properly lining up your code makes your programs easier to read.

Programming Tip 5.2

Always Use Braces

When the body of an `if` statement consists of a single statement, you need not use braces. For example, the following is legal:

```
if (floor > 13)
    floor--;
```

However, it is a good idea to always include the braces:

```
if (floor > 13)
{
    floor--;
}
```

The braces make your code easier to read. They also make it easier for you to maintain the code because you won't have to worry about adding braces when you add statements inside an `if` statement.

Programming Tip 5.3
Tabs

Block-structured code has the property that nested statements are indented by one or more levels:

```
public class ElevatorSimulation
{
   public static void main(String[] args)
   {
      int floor;
      . . .
      if (floor > 13)
      {
         floor--;
      }
      . . .
   }
}
0  1  2  3    Indentation level
```

How do you move the cursor from the leftmost column to the appropriate indentation level? A perfectly reasonable strategy is to hit the space bar a sufficient number of times. With most editors, you can use the Tab key instead. A tab moves the cursor to the next indentation level. Some editors even have an option to fill in the tabs automatically.

While the Tab *key* is nice, some editors use **tab characters** for alignment, which is not so nice. Tab characters can lead to problems when you send your file to another person or a printer. There is no universal agreement on the width of a tab character, and some software will ignore tab characters altogether. It is therefore best to save your files with spaces instead of tabs. Most editors have a setting to automatically convert all tabs to spaces. Look at the documentation of your development environment to find out how to activate this useful setting.

© Vincent LaRussa/John Wiley & Sons, Inc.

You use the Tab key to move the cursor to the next indentation level.

Programming Tip 5.4
Avoid Duplication in Branches

Look to see whether you *duplicate code* in each branch. If so, move it out of the if statement. Here is an example of such duplication:

```
if (floor > 13)
{
   actualFloor = floor - 1;
   System.out.println("Actual floor: " + actualFloor);
}
else
{
   actualFloor = floor;
   System.out.println("Actual floor: " + actualFloor);
}
```

The output statement is exactly the same in both branches. This is not an error—the program will run correctly. But you can simplify the program by moving the duplicated statement:

```java
if (floor > 13)
{
    actualFloor = floor - 1;
}
else
{
    actualFloor = floor;
}
System.out.println("Actual floor: " + actualFloor);
```

Removing duplication is particularly important when programs are maintained for a long time. When there are two sets of statements with the same effect, it can easily happen that a programmer modifies one set but not the other.

Special Topic 5.1

The Conditional Operator

Java has a *conditional operator* of the form

$$condition\ ?\ value_1\ :\ value_2$$

The value of that expression is either $value_1$ if the test passes or $value_2$ if it fails. For example, we can compute the actual floor number as

```java
actualFloor = floor > 13 ? floor - 1 : floor;
```

which is equivalent to

```java
if (floor > 13) { actualFloor = floor - 1; } else { actualFloor = floor; }
```

You can use the conditional operator anywhere that a value is expected, for example:

```java
System.out.println("Actual floor: " + (floor > 13 ? floor - 1 : floor));
```

We don't use the conditional operator in this book, but it is a convenient construct that you will find in many Java programs.

5.2 Comparing Values

Every if statement contains a condition. In many cases, the condition involves comparing two values. In the following sections, you will learn how to implement comparisons in Java.

In Java, you use a relational operator to check whether one value is greater than another. © arturbo/iStockphoto.

5.2.1 Relational Operators

Use relational
operators
(< <= > >= == !=)
to compare numbers.

A **relational operator** tests the relationship between two values. An example is the >
operator that we used in the test floor > 13. Java has six relational operators (see
Table 1).

Table 1 Relational Operators		
Java	Math Notation	Description
>	>	Greater than
>=	≥	Greater than or equal
<	<	Less than
<=	≤	Less than or equal
==	=	Equal
!=	≠	Not equal

As you can see, only two Java relational operators (> and <) look as you would expect
from the mathematical notation. Computer keyboards do not have keys for ≥, ≤, or
≠, but the >=, <=, and != operators are easy to remember because they look similar. The
== operator is initially confusing to most newcomers to Java.

Syntax 5.2   Comparisons

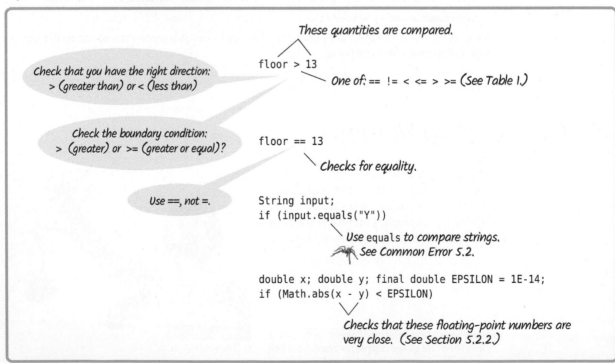

In Java, = already has a meaning, namely assignment. The == operator denotes equality testing:

```
floor = 13; // Assign 13 to floor

if (floor == 13)   // Test whether floor equals 13
```

You must remember to use == inside tests and to use = outside tests.

The relational operators in Table 1 have a lower precedence than the arithmetic operators. That means you can write arithmetic expressions on either side of the relational operator without using parentheses. For example, in the expression

```
floor - 1 < 13
```

both sides (floor - 1 and 13) of the < operator are evaluated, and the results are compared. Appendix B shows a table of the Java operators and their precedence.

> Relational operators compare values. The == operator tests for equality.

5.2.2 Comparing Floating-Point Numbers

You have to be careful when comparing floating-point numbers in order to cope with roundoff errors. For example, the following code multiplies the square root of 2 by itself and then subtracts 2.

```
double r = Math.sqrt(2);
double d = r * r - 2;
if (d == 0)
{
    System.out.println("sqrt(2) squared minus 2 is 0");
}
else
{
    System.out.println("sqrt(2) squared minus 2 is not 0 but " + d);
}
```

Even though the laws of mathematics tell us that $\left(\sqrt{2}\right)^2 - 2$ equals 0, this program fragment prints

```
sqrt(2) squared minus 2 is not 0 but 4.440892098500626E-16
```

Unfortunately, such roundoff errors are unavoidable. It plainly does not make sense in most circumstances to compare floating-point numbers exactly. Instead, test whether they are *close enough*.

To test whether a number x is close to zero, you can test whether the absolute value $|x|$ (that is, the number with its sign removed) is less than a very small threshold number. That threshold value is often called ε (the Greek letter epsilon). It is common to set ε to 10^{-14} when testing double numbers.

Similarly, you can test whether two numbers are approximately equal by checking whether their difference is close to 0.

> When comparing floating-point numbers, don't test for equality. Instead, check whether they are close enough.

$$|x - y| < \varepsilon$$

In Java, we program the test as follows:

```
final double EPSILON = 1E-14;
if (Math.abs(x - y) <= EPSILON)
{
    // x is approximately equal to y
}
```

5.2.3 Comparing Strings

To test whether two strings are equal to each other, you must use the method called equals:

```
if (string1.equals(string2)) . . .
```

Do not use the == operator to compare strings. The comparison

```
if (string1 == string2) // Not useful
```

has an unrelated meaning. It tests whether the two strings are stored in the same memory location. You can have strings with identical contents stored in different locations, so this test never makes sense in actual programming; see Common Error 5.2.

If two strings are not identical, you still may want to know the relationship between them. The compareTo method compares strings in **lexicographic order**. This ordering is very similar to the way in which words are sorted in a dictionary. If

```
string1.compareTo(string2) < 0
```

then the string string1 comes before the string string2 in the dictionary. For example, this is the case if string1 is "Harry" and string2 is "Hello".

Conversely, if

```
string1.compareTo(string2) > 0
```

then string1 comes after string2 in dictionary order.

Finally, if

```
string1.compareTo(string2) == 0
```

then string1 and string2 are equal.

There are a few technical differences between the ordering in a dictionary and the lexicographic ordering in Java. In Java:

- All uppercase letters come before the lowercase letters. For example, "Z" comes before "a".
- The space character comes before all printable characters.
- Numbers come before letters.
- For the ordering of punctuation marks, see Appendix A.

When comparing two strings, you compare the first letters of each word, then the second letters, and so on, until one of the strings ends or you find the first letter pair that doesn't match.

If one of the strings ends, the longer string is considered the "larger" one. For example, compare "car" with "cart". The first three letters match, and we reach the end of the first string. Therefore "car" comes before "cart" in lexicographic ordering.

When you reach a mismatch, the string containing the "larger" character is considered "larger". For example, compare "cat" with "cart". The first two letters match. Because t comes after r, the string "cat" comes after "cart" in the lexicographic ordering.

Do not use the == operator to compare strings. Use the equals method instead.

The compareTo method compares strings in lexicographic order.

| c | a | r |

| c | a | r | t |

| c | a | t |

Letters   r comes
match   before t

*Lexicographic
Ordering*

*To see which of two terms comes first in the dictionary,
consider the first letter in which they differ.*   Fuse/Getty Images.

5.2.4 Comparing Objects

If you compare two object references with the == operator, you test whether the references refer to the same object. Here is an example:

```
Rectangle box1 = new Rectangle(5, 10, 20, 30);
Rectangle box2 = box1;
Rectangle box3 = new Rectangle(5, 10, 20, 30);
```

The comparison

```
box1 == box2
```

is true. Both object variables refer to the same object. But the comparison

```
box1 == box3
```

is false. The two object variables refer to different objects (see Figure 3). It does not matter that the objects have identical contents.

> The == operator tests whether two object references are identical. To compare the contents of objects, you need to use the equals method.

You can use the equals method to test whether two rectangles have the same contents, that is, whether they have the same upper-left corner and the same width and height. For example, the test

```
box1.equals(box3)
```

is true.

However, you must be careful when using the equals method. It works correctly only if the implementors of the class have supplied it. The Rectangle class has an equals method that is suitable for comparing rectangles.

For your own classes, you need to supply an appropriate equals method. You will learn how to do that in Chapter 9. Until that point, you should not use the equals method to compare objects of your own classes.

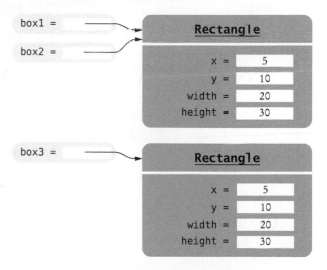

Figure 3
Comparing Object References

5.2.5 Testing for null

> The null reference refers to no object.

An object reference can have the special value null if it refers to no object at all. It is common to use the null value to indicate that a value has never been set. For example,

```
String middleInitial = null; // Not set
if ( . . . )
{
   middleInitial = middleName.substring(0, 1);
}
```

You use the == operator (and not equals) to test whether an object reference is a null reference:

```
if (middleInitial == null)
{
    System.out.println(firstName + " " + lastName);
}
else
{
    System.out.println(firstName + " " + middleInitial + ". " + lastName);
}
```

Note that the **null reference** is not the same as the empty string "". The empty string is a valid string of length 0, whereas a null indicates that a string variable refers to no string at all.

Table 2 summarizes how to compare values in Java.

Table 2 Relational Operator Examples

Expression	Value	Comment
3 <= 4	true	3 is less than 4; <= tests for "less than or equal".
🚫 3 =< 4	**Error**	The "less than or equal" operator is <=, not =<. The "less than" symbol comes first.
3 > 4	false	> is the opposite of <=.
4 < 4	false	The left-hand side must be strictly smaller than the right-hand side.
4 <= 4	true	Both sides are equal; <= tests for "less than or equal".
3 == 5 - 2	true	== tests for equality.
3 != 5 - 1	true	!= tests for inequality. It is true that 3 is not 5 − 1.
🚫 3 = 6 / 2	**Error**	Use == to test for equality.
1.0 / 3.0 == 0.333333333	false	Although the values are very close to one another, they are not exactly equal. See Section 5.2.2.
🚫 "10" > 5	**Error**	You cannot compare a string to a number.
"Tomato".substring(0, 3).equals("Tom")	true	Always use the equals method to check whether two strings have the same contents.
"Tomato".substring(0, 3) == ("Tom")	false	Never use == to compare strings; it only checks whether the strings are stored in the same location. See Common Error 5.2.

EXAMPLE CODE   See sec02 of your eText or companion code for program that demonstrates comparisons of numbers and strings.

Common Error 5.2

Using == to Compare Strings

If you write

```
if (nickname == "Rob")
```

then the test succeeds only if the variable nickname refers to the exact same location as the string literal "Rob".

The test will pass if a string variable was initialized with the same string literal:

```
String nickname = "Rob";
. . .
if (nickname == "Rob") // Test is true
```

However, if the string with the letters R o b has been assembled in some other way, then the test will fail:

```
String name = "Robert";
String nickname = name.substring(0, 3);
. . .
if (nickname == "Rob") // Test is false
```

In this case, the substring method produces a string in a different memory location. Even though both strings have the same contents, the comparison fails.

You must remember never to use == to compare strings. Always use equals to check whether two strings have the same contents.

HOW TO 5.1

Implementing an if Statement

This How To walks you through the process of implementing an if statement. We will illustrate the steps with the following example problem.

Problem Statement The university bookstore has a Kilobyte Day sale every October 24, giving an 8 percent discount on all computer accessory purchases if the price is less than $128, and a 16 percent discount if the price is at least $128. Write a program that asks the cashier for the original price and then prints the discounted price.

Step 1 Decide upon the branching condition.

In our sample problem, the obvious choice for the condition is:

original price < 128?

That is just fine, and we will use that condition in our solution.

But you could equally well come up with a correct solution if you choose the opposite condition: Is the original price at least $128? You might choose this condition if you put yourself into the position of a shopper who wants to know when the bigger discount applies.

© MikePanic/iStockphoto.

Sales discounts are often higher for expensive products. Use the if statement to implement such a decision.

Step 2   Give pseudocode for the work that needs to be done when the condition is true.

In this step, you list the action or actions that are taken in the "positive" branch. The details depend on your problem. You may want to print a message, compute values, or even exit the program.

In our example, we need to apply an 8 percent discount:

discounted price = 0.92 x original price

Step 3   Give pseudocode for the work (if any) that needs to be done when the condition is *not* true.

What do you want to do in the case that the condition of Step 1 is not satisfied? Sometimes, you want to do nothing at all. In that case, use an if statement without an else branch.

In our example, the condition tested whether the price was less than $128. If that condition is *not* true, the price is at least $128, so the higher discount of 16 percent applies to the sale:

discounted price = 0.84 x original price

Step 4   Double-check relational operators.

First, be sure that the test goes in the right *direction*. It is a common error to confuse > and <. Next, consider whether you should use the < operator or its close cousin, the <= operator.

What should happen if the original price is exactly $128? Reading the problem carefully, we find that the lower discount applies if the original price is *less than* $128, and the higher discount applies when it is *at least* $128. A price of $128 should therefore *not* fulfill our condition, and we must use <, not <=.

Step 5   Remove duplication.

Check which actions are common to both branches, and move them outside. (See Programming Tip 5.4.)

In our example, we have two statements of the form

discounted price = ___ x original price

They only differ in the discount rate. It is best to just set the rate in the branches, and to do the computation afterwards:

If original price < 128
    discount rate = 0.92
Else
    discount rate = 0.84
discounted price = discount rate x original price

Step 6   Test both branches.

Formulate two test cases, one that fulfills the condition of the if statement, and one that does not. Ask yourself what should happen in each case. Then follow the pseudocode and act each of them out.

In our example, let us consider two scenarios for the original price: $100 and $200. We expect that the first price is discounted by $8, the second by $32.

When the original price is 100, then the condition 100 < 128 is true, and we get

discount rate = 0.92
discounted price = 0.92 x 100 = 92

When the original price is 200, then the condition 200 < 128 is false, and

discount rate = 0.84
discounted price = 0.84 x 200 = 168

In both cases, we get the expected answer.

Step 7   Assemble the `if` statement in Java.

Type the skeleton

```
if ()
{
}
else
{
}
```

and fill it in, as shown in Syntax 5.1. Omit the `else` branch if it is not needed.
In our example, the completed statement is

```
if (originalPrice < 128)
{
   discountRate = 0.92;
}
else
{
   discountRate = 0.84;
}

discountedPrice = discountRate * originalPrice;
```

EXAMPLE CODE   See how_to_1 of your eText or companion code to run the program for calculating a discounted price.

Computing & Society 5.1   **Dysfunctional Computerized Systems**

Making decisions is an essential part of any computer program. Nowhere is this more obvious than in a computer system that helps sort luggage at an airport. After scanning the luggage identification codes, the system sorts the items and routes them to different conveyor belts. Human operators then place the items onto trucks. When the city of Denver built a huge airport to replace an outdated and congested facility, the luggage system contractor went a step further. The new system was designed to replace the human operators with robotic carts. Unfortunately, the system plainly did not work. It was plagued by mechanical problems, such as luggage falling onto the tracks and jamming carts. Equally frustrating were the software glitches. Carts would uselessly accumulate at some locations when they were needed elsewhere.

The airport had been scheduled to open in 1993, but without a functioning luggage system, the opening was delayed for over a year while the contractor tried to fix the problems. The contractor never succeeded, and ultimately a manual system was installed. The delay cost the city and airlines close to a billion dollars, and the contractor, once the leading luggage systems vendor in the United States, went bankrupt.

Clearly, it is very risky to build a large system based on a technology that has never been tried on a smaller scale. In 2013, the rollout of universal healthcare in the United States was put in jeopardy by a dysfunctional web site for selecting insurance plans. The system promised an insurance shopping experience similar to booking airline flights. But, the `HealthCare.gov` site didn't simply present the available insurance plans. It also had to check the income level of each applicant and use that information to determine the subsidy level. That task turned out to be quite a bit harder than checking whether a credit card had sufficient credit to pay for an airline ticket. The Obama administration would have been well advised to design a signup process that did not rely on an untested computer program.

The Denver airport originally had a fully automatic system for moving luggage, replacing human operators with robotic carts. Unfortunately, the system never worked and was dismantled before the airport was opened.

Lyn Alweis/The Denver Post via/Getty Images, Inc.

WORKED EXAMPLE 5.1
Extracting the Middle

Learn how to extract the middle character from a string, or the two middle characters if the length of the string is even. See your eText or visit wiley. com/go/bjeo7.

c	r	a	t	e
0	1	2	3	4

5.3 Multiple Alternatives

Multiple if statements can be combined to evaluate complex decisions.

In Section 5.1, you saw how to program a two-way branch with an if statement. In many situations, there are more than two cases. In this section, you will see how to implement a decision with multiple alternatives.

For example, consider a program that displays the effect of an earthquake, as measured by the Richter scale (see Table 3).

The 1989 Loma Prieta earthquake that damaged the Bay Bridge in San Francisco and destroyed many buildings measured 7.1 on the Richter scale.

© kevinruss/iStockphoto.

Table 3 Richter Scale	
Value	Effect
8	Most structures fall
7	Many buildings destroyed
6	Many buildings considerably damaged, some collapse
4.5	Damage to poorly constructed buildings

The Richter scale is a measurement of the strength of an earthquake. Every step in the scale, for example from 6.0 to 7.0, signifies a tenfold increase in the strength of the quake.

In this case, there are five branches: one each for the four descriptions of damage, and one for no destruction. Figure 4 shows the flowchart for this multiple-branch statement.

You use multiple if statements to implement multiple alternatives, like this:

```
if (richter >= 8.0)
{
    description = "Most structures fall";
}
else if (richter >= 7.0)
{
    description = "Many buildings destroyed";
}
else if (richter >= 6.0)
{
```

```
      description = "Many buildings considerably damaged, some collapse";
   }
   else if (richter >= 4.5)
   {
      description = "Damage to poorly constructed buildings";
   }
   else
   {
      description = "No destruction of buildings";
   }
```

As soon as one of the four tests succeeds, the effect is displayed, and no further tests are attempted. If none of the four cases applies, the final `else` clause applies, and a default message is printed.

Here you must sort the conditions and test against the largest cutoff first.

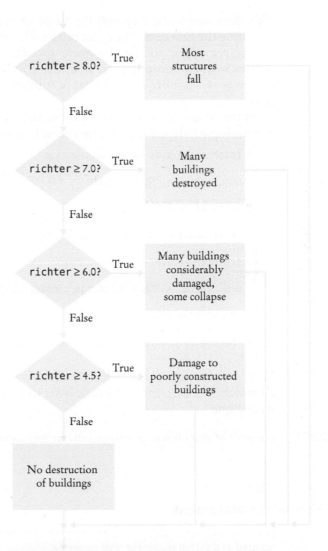

Figure 4 Multiple Alternatives

Suppose we reverse the order of tests:

```
if (richter >= 4.5) // Tests in wrong order
{
   description = "Damage to poorly constructed buildings";
}
else if (richter >= 6.0)
{
   description = "Many buildings considerably damaged, some collapse";
}
else if (richter >= 7.0)
{
   description = "Many buildings destroyed";
}
else if (richter >= 8.0)
{
   description = "Most structures fall";
}
```

This does not work. Suppose the value of `richter` is 7.1. That value is at least 4.5, matching the first case. The other tests will never be attempted.

> When using multiple if statements, test general conditions after more specific conditions.

The remedy is to test the more specific conditions first. Here, the condition `richter >= 8.0` is more specific than the condition `richter >= 7.0`, and the condition `richter >= 4.5` is more general (that is, fulfilled by more values) than either of the first two.

In this example, it is also important that we use an `if/else if/else` sequence, not just multiple independent `if` statements. Consider this sequence of independent tests.

```
if (richter >= 8.0) // Didn't use else
{
   description = "Most structures fall";
}
if (richter >= 7.0)
{
   description = "Many buildings destroyed";
}
if (richter >= 6.0)
{
   description = "Many buildings considerably damaged, some collapse";
}
if (richter >= 4.5)
{
   "Damage to poorly constructed buildings";
}
```

Now the alternatives are no longer exclusive. If `richter` is 7.1, then the last *three* tests all match. The `description` variable is set to three different strings, ending up with the wrong one.

EXAMPLE CODE   See sec03 of your eText or companion code for the program for printing earthquake descriptions.

Special Topic 5.2

The switch Statement

An `if/else if/else` sequence that compares a *value* against several alternatives can be implemented as a switch statement. For example,

```
int digit = . . .;
```

```
switch (digit)
{
   case 1: digitName = "one"; break;
   case 2: digitName = "two"; break;
   case 3: digitName = "three"; break;
   case 4: digitName = "four"; break;
   case 5: digitName = "five"; break;
   case 6: digitName = "six"; break;
   case 7: digitName = "seven"; break;
   case 8: digitName = "eight"; break;
   case 9: digitName = "nine"; break;
   default: digitName = ""; break;
}
```

This is a shortcut for

```
int digit = . . .;
if (digit == 1) { digitName = "one"; }
else if (digit == 2) { digitName = "two"; }
else if (digit == 3) { digitName = "three"; }
else if (digit == 4) { digitName = "four"; }
else if (digit == 5) { digitName = "five"; }
else if (digit == 6) { digitName = "six"; }
else if (digit == 7) { digitName = "seven"; }
else if (digit == 8) { digitName = "eight"; }
else if (digit == 9) { digitName = "nine"; }
else { digitName = ""; }
```

© travelpixpro/iStockphoto.

The switch *statement lets you choose from a fixed set of alternatives.*

It isn't much of a shortcut, but it has one advantage—it is obvious that all branches test the *same* value, namely digit.

The switch statement can be applied only in narrow circumstances. The values in the case clauses must be constants. They can be integers, characters, or string literals. You cannot use a switch statement to branch on floating-point values.

Every branch of the switch should be terminated by a break instruction. If the break is missing, execution *falls through* to the next branch, and so on, until a break or the end of the switch is reached. In practice, this fall-through behavior is rarely useful, but it is a common cause of errors. If you accidentally forget a break statement, your program compiles but executes unwanted code. Many programmers consider the switch statement somewhat dangerous and prefer the if statement.

We leave it to you to use the switch statement for your own code or not. At any rate, you need to have a reading knowledge of switch in case you find it in other programmers' code.

5.4 Nested Branches

When a decision statement is contained inside the branch of another decision statement, the statements are *nested*.

It is often necessary to include an if statement inside another. Such an arrangement is called a *nested* set of statements.

Here is a typical example: In the United States, different tax rates are used depending on the taxpayer's marital status. There are different tax schedules for single and for married taxpayers. Married taxpayers add their income together and pay taxes on the total. Table 4 gives the tax rate computations, using a simplification of the schedules that were in effect for the 2008 tax year. A different tax rate applies to each "bracket". In this schedule, the income in the first bracket is taxed at 10 percent, and

Computing income taxes requires multiple levels of decisions.

the income in the second bracket is taxed at 25 percent. The income limits for each bracket depend on the marital status.

Table 4 Federal Tax Rate Schedule		
If your status is Single and if the taxable income is	the tax is	of the amount over
at most $32,000	10%	$0
over $32,000	$3,200 + 25%	$32,000
If your status is Married and if the taxable income is	the tax is	of the amount over
at most $64,000	10%	$0
over $64,000	$6,400 + 25%	$64,000

Nested decisions are required for problems that have two levels of decision making.

Now compute the taxes due, given a marital status and an income figure. The key point is that there are two *levels* of decision making. First, you must branch on the marital status. Then, for each marital status, you must have another branch on income level.

The two-level decision process is reflected in two levels of if statements in the program at the end of this section. (See Figure 5 for a flowchart.) In theory, nesting can go deeper than two levels. A three-level decision process (first by state, then by marital status, then by income level) requires three nesting levels.

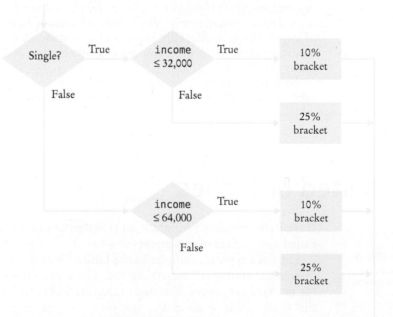

Figure 5 Income Tax Computation

sec04/TaxReturn.java

```java
1   /**
2       A tax return of a taxpayer in 2008.
3   */
4   public class TaxReturn
5   {
6       public static final int SINGLE = 1;
7       public static final int MARRIED = 2;
8
9       private static final double RATE1 = 0.10;
10      private static final double RATE2 = 0.25;
11      private static final double RATE1_SINGLE_LIMIT = 32000;
12      private static final double RATE1_MARRIED_LIMIT = 64000;
13
14      private double income;
15      private int status;
16
17      /**
18          Constructs a TaxReturn object for a given income and
19          marital status.
20          @param anIncome the taxpayer income
21          @param aStatus either SINGLE or MARRIED
22      */
23      public TaxReturn(double anIncome, int aStatus)
24      {
25          income = anIncome;
26          status = aStatus;
27      }
28
29      public double getTax()
30      {
31          double tax1 = 0;
32          double tax2 = 0;
33
34          if (status == SINGLE)
35          {
36              if (income <= RATE1_SINGLE_LIMIT)
37              {
38                  tax1 = RATE1 * income;
39              }
40              else
41              {
42                  tax1 = RATE1 * RATE1_SINGLE_LIMIT;
43                  tax2 = RATE2 * (income - RATE1_SINGLE_LIMIT);
44              }
45          }
46          else
47          {
48              if (income <= RATE1_MARRIED_LIMIT)
49              {
50                  tax1 = RATE1 * income;
51              }
52              else
53              {
54                  tax1 = RATE1 * RATE1_MARRIED_LIMIT;
55                  tax2 = RATE2 * (income - RATE1_MARRIED_LIMIT);
56              }
57          }
58
```

```
59        return tax1 + tax2;
60    }
61 }
```

sec04/TaxCalculator.java

```java
1  import java.util.Scanner;
2
3  /**
4     This program calculates a simple tax return.
5  */
6  public class TaxCalculator
7  {
8     public static void main(String[] args)
9     {
10        Scanner in = new Scanner(System.in);
11
12        System.out.print("Please enter your income: ");
13        double income = in.nextDouble();
14
15        System.out.print("Are you married? (Y/N) ");
16        String input = in.next();
17        int status;
18        if (input.equals("Y"))
19        {
20           status = TaxReturn.MARRIED;
21        }
22        else
23        {
24           status = TaxReturn.SINGLE;
25        }
26        TaxReturn aTaxReturn = new TaxReturn(income, status);
27        System.out.println("Tax: "
28              + aTaxReturn.getTax());
29     }
30 }
```

Program Run

```
Please enter your income: 80000
Are you married? (Y/N) Y
Tax: 10400.0
```

Common Error 5.3

The Dangling else Problem

When an if statement is nested inside another if statement, the following error may occur.

```java
double shippingCharge = 5.00; // $5 inside continental U.S.
if (country.equals("USA"))
   if (state.equals("HI"))
      shippingCharge = 10.00; // Hawaii is more expensive
else // Pitfall!
   shippingCharge = 20.00; // As are foreign shipments
```

The indentation level seems to suggest that the else is grouped with the test country. equals("USA"). Unfortunately, that is not the case. The compiler ignores all indentation and matches the else with the preceding if. That is, the code is actually

```
       double shippingCharge = 5.00; // $5 inside continental U.S.
       if (country.equals("USA"))
          if (state.equals("HI"))
             shippingCharge = 10.00; // Hawaii is more expensive
          else // Pitfall!
             shippingCharge = 20.00; // As are foreign shipments
```

That isn't what you want. You want to group the else with the first if.

The ambiguous else is called a *dangling else*. You can avoid this pitfall if you always use braces, as recommended in Programming Tip 5.2:

```
       double shippingCharge = 5.00; // $5 inside continental U.S.
       if (country.equals("USA"))
       {
          if (state.equals("HI"))
          {
             shippingCharge = 10.00; // Hawaii is more expensive
          }
       }
       else
       {
          shippingCharge = 20.00; // As are foreign shipments
       }
```

Programming Tip 5.5

Hand-Tracing

A very useful technique for understanding whether a program works correctly is called *hand-tracing*. You simulate the program's activity on a sheet of paper. You can use this method with pseudocode or Java code.

Get an index card, a cocktail napkin, or whatever sheet of paper is within reach. Make a column for each variable. Have the program code ready. Use a marker, such as a paper clip, to mark the current statement. In your mind, execute statements one at a time. Every time the value of a variable changes, cross out the old value and write the new value below the old one.

For example, let's trace the getTax method with the data from the program run above. When the TaxReturn object is constructed, the income instance variable is set to 80,000 and status is set to MARRIED. Then the getTax method is called. In lines 31 and 32 of TaxReturn.java, tax1 and tax2 are initialized to 0.

© thomasd007/iStockphoto.

Hand-tracing helps you understand whether a program works correctly.

```
29 public double getTax()
30 {
31    double tax1 = 0;
32    double tax2 = 0;
33
```

income	status	tax1	tax2
80000	MARRIED	0	0

Because status is not SINGLE, we move to the else branch of the outer if statement (line 46).

```
34    if (status == SINGLE)
35    {
36       if (income <= RATE1_SINGLE_LIMIT)
37       {
38          tax1 = RATE1 * income;
39       }
40       else
41       {
42          tax1 = RATE1 * RATE1_SINGLE_LIMIT;
43          tax2 = RATE2 * (income - RATE1_SINGLE_LIMIT);
```

```
44        }
45    }
46    else
47    {
```

Because income is not <= 64000, we move to the else branch of the inner if statement (line 52).

```
48        if (income <= RATE1_MARRIED_LIMIT)
49        {
50            tax1 = RATE1 * income;
51        }
52        else
53        {
54            tax1 = RATE1 * RATE1_MARRIED_LIMIT;
55            tax2 = RATE2 * (income - RATE1_MARRIED_LIMIT);
56        }
```

The values of tax1 and tax2 are updated.

```
53        {
54            tax1 = RATE1 * RATE1_MARRIED_LIMIT;
55            tax2 = RATE2 * (income - RATE1_MARRIED_LIMIT);
56        }
57    }
```

income	status	tax1	tax2
80000	MARRIED	ø̸	ø̸
		6400	4000

Their sum is returned and the method ends.

```
58
59    return tax1 + tax2;
60 }
```

income	status	tax1	tax2	return value
80000	MARRIED	ø̸	ø̸	
		6400	4000	10400

Because the program trace shows the expected return value ($10,400), it successfully demonstrates that this test case works correctly.

Special Topic 5.3
Block Scope

A **block** is a sequence of statements that is enclosed in braces. For example, consider this statement:

```
if (status == TAXABLE)
{
    double tax = price * TAX_RATE;
    price = price + tax;
}
```

The highlighted part is a block. You can declare a variable in a block, such as the tax variable in this example. Such a variable is only visible inside the block.

```
{
    double tax = price * TAX_RATE; // Variable declared inside a block
    price = price + tax;
}
// You can no longer access the tax variable here
```

In fact, the variable is only created after the program enters the block, and it is removed as soon as the program exits the block. Such a variable is said to have *block scope*. In general, the **scope** of a variable is the part of the program in which the variable can be accessed. A variable with block scope is visible only inside a block.

It is considered good design to minimize the scope of a variable. This reduces the possibility of accidental modification and name conflicts. For example, as long as the tax variable is not needed outside the block, it is a good idea to declare it inside the block. However, if you need the variable outside the block, you must define it outside. For example,

```
double tax = 0;
if (status == TAXABLE)
{
```

```
      tax = price * TAX_RATE;
   }
   price = price + tax;
```

Here, the tax variable is used outside the block of the if statement, and you must declare it outside.

In Java, the scope of a local variable can never contain the declaration of another local variable with the same name. For example, the following is an error:

```
double tax = 0;
if (status == TAXABLE)
{
   double tax = price * TAX_RATE;
   // Error: Cannot declare another variable with the same name
   price = price + tax;
}
```

However, you can have local variables with identical names if their scopes do not overlap, such as

```
if (Math.random() > 0.5)
{
   Rectangle r = new Rectangle(5, 10, 20, 30);
   . . .
} // Scope of r ends here
else
{
   int r = 5;
   // OK—it is legal to declare another r here
   . . .
}
```

These variables are independent from each other. You can have local variables with the same name, as long as their scopes don't overlap.

© jchamp/iStockphoto (Railway and Main); © StevenCarrieJohnson/iStockphoto (Main and N. Putnam); © jsmith/iStockphoto (Main and South St.).

In the same way that there can be a street named "Main Street" in different cities, a Java program can have multiple variables with the same name.

Special Topic 5.4

Enumeration Types

In many programs, you use variables that can hold one of a finite number of values. For example, in the tax return class, the status instance variable holds one of the values SINGLE or MARRIED. We arbitrarily declared SINGLE as the number 1 and MARRIED as 2. If, due to some programming error, the status variable is set to another integer value (such as -1, 0, or 3), then the programming logic may produce invalid results.

In a simple program, this is not really a problem. But as programs grow over time, and more cases are added (such as the "married filing separately" status), errors can slip in. **Enumeration types** provide a remedy. An enumeration type has a finite set of values, for example

```
public enum FilingStatus { SINGLE, MARRIED, MARRIED_FILING_SEPARATELY }
```

You can have any number of values, but you must include them all in the enum declaration.

You can declare variables of the enumeration type:

```
FilingStatus status = FilingStatus.SINGLE;
```

If you try to assign a value that isn't a FilingStatus, such as 2 or "S", then the compiler reports an error.

Use the == operator to compare enumeration values, for example:

```
if (status == FilingStatus.SINGLE) . . .
```

Place the enum declaration inside the class that implements your program, such as

```
public class TaxReturn
{
    public enum FilingStatus { SINGLE, MARRIED, MARRIED_FILING_SEPARATELY }
    . . .
}
```

5.5 Problem Solving: Flowcharts

Flow charts are made up of elements for tasks, input/output, and decisions.

You have seen examples of flowcharts earlier in this chapter. A flowchart shows the structure of decisions and tasks that are required to solve a problem. When you have to solve a complex problem, it can help to draw a flowchart to visualize the flow of control.

The basic flowchart elements are shown in Figure 6.

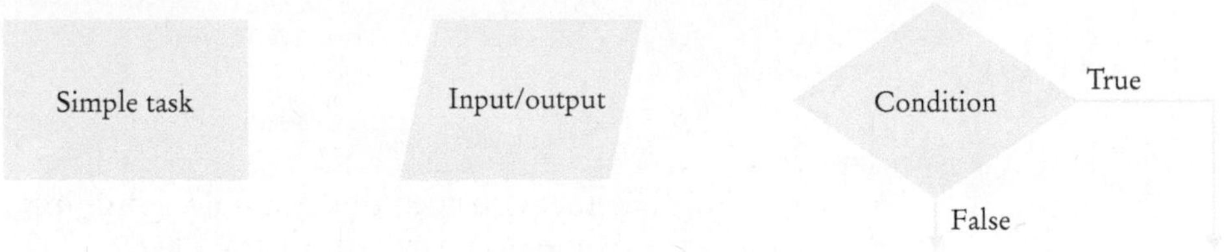

Figure 6
Flowchart Elements

The basic idea is simple enough. Link tasks and input/output boxes in the sequence in which they should be executed. Whenever you need to make a decision, draw a diamond with two outcomes (see Figure 7).

Each branch of a decision can contain tasks and further decisions.

Each branch can contain a sequence of tasks and even additional decisions. If there are multiple choices for a value, lay them out as in Figure 8.

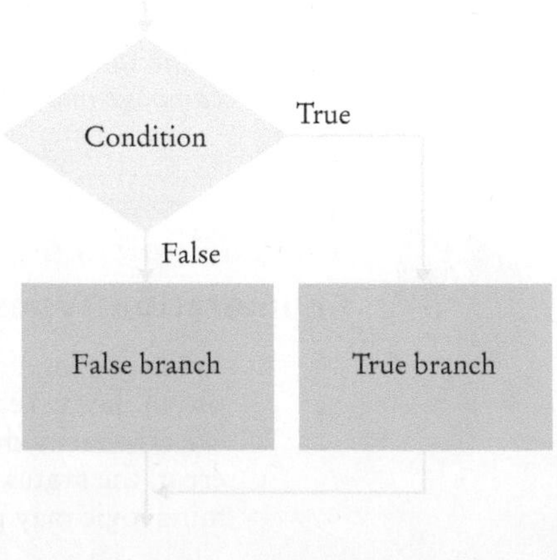

Figure 7
Flowchart with Two Outcomes

Figure 8
Flowchart with Multiple Choices

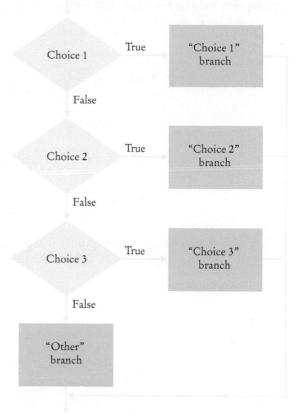

There is one issue that you need to be aware of when drawing flowcharts. Unconstrained branching and merging can lead to "spaghetti code", a messy network of possible pathways through a program.

There is a simple rule for avoiding spaghetti code: Never point an arrow *inside another branch*.

Never point an arrow inside another branch.

To understand the rule, consider this example: Shipping costs are $5 inside the United States, except that to Hawaii and Alaska they are $10. International shipping costs are also $10. You might start out with a flowchart like the following:

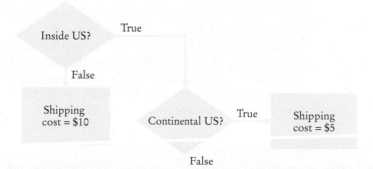

Now you may be tempted to reuse the "shipping cost = $10" task:

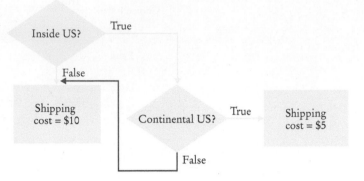

Don't do that! The red arrow points inside a different branch. Instead, add another task that sets the shipping cost to $10, like this:

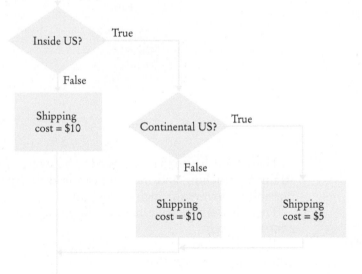

Not only do you avoid spaghetti code, but it is also a better design. In the future it may well happen that the cost for international shipments is different from that to Alaska and Hawaii.

Flowcharts can be very useful for getting an intuitive understanding of the flow of an algorithm. However, they get large rather quickly when you add more details. At that point, it makes sense to switch from flowcharts to pseudocode.

© Ekspansio/iStockphoto.

Spaghetti code has so many pathways that it becomes impossible to understand.

EXAMPLE CODE   See sec05 of your eText or companion code for a program that computes shipping costs.

5.6 Problem Solving: Selecting Test Cases

Black-box testing describes a testing method that does not take the structure of the implementation into account.

Testing the functionality of a program without consideration of its internal structure is called **black-box testing**. This is an important part of testing, because, after all, the users of a program do not know its internal structure. If a program works perfectly on all inputs, then it surely does its job.

However, it is impossible to ensure absolutely that a program will work correctly on all inputs just by supplying a finite number of test cases. As the famous computer scientist Edsger Dijkstra pointed out, testing can show only the presence of bugs — not their absence. To gain more confidence in the correctness of a program, it is useful to consider its internal structure. Testing strategies that look inside a program are called **white-box testing**. Performing unit tests of each method is a part of white-box testing.

White-box testing uses information about the structure of a program.

You want to make sure that each part of your program is exercised at least once by one of your test cases. This is called **code coverage**. If some code is never executed by any of your test cases, you have no way of knowing whether that code would perform correctly if it ever were executed by user input. That means that you need to look at every if/else branch to see that each of them is reached by some test case. Many conditional branches are in the code only to take care of strange and abnormal inputs, but they still do something. It is a common phenomenon that they end up doing something incorrectly, but those faults are never discovered during testing, because nobody supplied the strange and abnormal inputs. The remedy is to ensure that each part of the code is covered by some test case.

Code coverage is a measure of how many parts of a program have been tested.

For example, in testing the getTax method of the TaxReturn class, you want to make sure that every if statement is entered for at least one test case. You should test both single and married taxpayers, with incomes in each of the three tax brackets.

When you select test cases, you should make it a habit to include **boundary test cases**: legal values that lie at the boundary of the set of acceptable inputs.

Boundary test cases are test cases that are at the boundary of acceptable inputs.

Here is a plan for obtaining a comprehensive set of test cases for the tax program:

- There are two possibilities for the marital status and two tax brackets for each status, yielding four test cases.

- Test a handful of *boundary* conditions, such as an income that is at the boundary between two brackets, and a zero income.

- If you are responsible for error checking (which is discussed in Section 5.8), also test an invalid input, such as a negative income.

Make a list of the test cases and the expected outputs:

Test Case	Married	Expected Output	Comment
30,000	N	3,000	10% bracket
72,000	N	13,200	3,200 + 25% of 40,000
50,000	Y	5,000	10% bracket
104,000	Y	16,400	6,400 + 25% of 40,000
32,000	N	3,200	boundary case
0		0	boundary case

It is a good idea to design test cases before implementing a program.

When you develop a set of test cases, it is helpful to have a flowchart of your program (see Section 5.5). Check off each branch that has a test case. Include test cases for the boundary cases of each decision. For example, if a decision checks whether an input is less than 100, test with an input of 100.

It is always a good idea to design test cases *before* starting to code. Working through the test cases gives you a better understanding of the algorithm that you are about to implement.

Programming Tip 5.6

Make a Schedule and Make Time for Unexpected Problems

Commercial software is notorious for being delivered later than promised. For example, Microsoft originally promised that its Windows Vista operating system would be available late in 2003, then in 2005, then in March 2006; it finally was released in January 2007. Some of the early promises might not have been realistic. It was in Microsoft's interest to let prospective customers expect the imminent availability of the product. Had customers known the actual delivery date, they might have switched to a different product in the meantime. Undeniably, though, Microsoft had not anticipated the full complexity of the tasks it had set itself to solve.

Microsoft can delay the delivery of its product, but it is likely that you cannot. As a student or a programmer, you are expected to manage your time wisely and to finish your assignments on time. You can probably do simple programming exercises the night before the due date, but an assignment that looks twice as hard may well take four times as long, because more things can go wrong. You should therefore make a schedule whenever you start a programming project.

Bananastock/Media Bakery.

Make a schedule for your programming work and build in time for problems.

First, estimate realistically how much time it will take you to:

- Design the program logic.
- Develop test cases.
- Type the program in and fix syntax errors.
- Test and debug the program.

For example, for the income tax program I might estimate an hour for the design; 30 minutes for developing test cases; an hour for data entry and fixing syntax errors; and an hour for testing and debugging. That is a total of 3.5 hours. If I work two hours a day on this project, it will take me almost two days.

Then think of things that can go wrong. Your computer might break down. You might be stumped by a problem with the computer system. (That is a particularly important concern for beginners. It is *very* common to lose a day over a trivial problem just because it takes time to track down a person who knows the magic command to overcome it.) As a rule of thumb, *double* the time of your estimate. That is, you should start four days, not two days, before the due date. If nothing went wrong, great; you have the program done two days early. When the inevitable problem occurs, you have a cushion of time that protects you from embarrassment and failure.

Special Topic 5.5

Logging

Sometimes you run a program and you are not sure where it spends its time. To get a printout of the program flow, you can insert **trace messages** into the program, such as this one:

```
if (status == SINGLE)
{
   System.out.println("status is SINGLE");
   . . .
}
```

However, there is a problem with using `System.out.println` for trace messages. When you are done testing the program, you need to remove all print statements that produce trace messages. If you find another error, however, you need to stick the print statements back in.

To overcome this problem, you should use the `Logger` class, which allows you to turn off the trace messages without removing them from the program.

> Logging messages can be deactivated when testing is complete.

Instead of printing directly to `System.out`, use the global logger object that is returned by the call `Logger.getGlobal()`. Then call the `info` method:

```
Logger.getGlobal().info("status is SINGLE");
```

By default, the message is printed. But if you call

```
Logger.getGlobal().setLevel(Level.OFF);
```

at the beginning of the main method of your program, all log message printing is suppressed. Set the level to `Level.INFO` to turn logging of `info` messages on again. Thus, you can turn off the log messages when your program works fine, and you can turn them back on if you find another error. In other words, using `Logger.getGlobal().info` is just like `System.out.println`, except that you can easily activate and deactivate the logging.

The `Logger` class has many other options for industrial-strength logging. Check out the API documentation if you want to have more control over logging.

5.7 Boolean Variables and Operators

> The Boolean type `boolean` has two values, `false` and `true`.

Sometimes, you need to evaluate a logical condition in one part of a program and use it elsewhere. To store a condition that can be true or false, you use a *Boolean variable*. Boolean variables are named after the mathematician George Boole (1815–1864), a pioneer in the study of logic.

In Java, the `boolean` data type has exactly two values, denoted `false` and `true`. These values are not strings or integers; they are special values, just for Boolean variables. Here is a declaration of a Boolean variable:

```
boolean failed = true;
```

You can use the value later in your program to make a decision:

```
if (failed) // Only executed if failed has been set to true
{
   . . .
}
```

A Boolean variable is also called a flag because it can be either up (true) or down (false).

When you make complex decisions, you often need to combine Boolean values. An operator that combines Boolean conditions is called a **Boolean operator**. In Java, the `&&` operator (called *and*) yields `true` only when both conditions are true. The `||` operator (called *or*) yields the result `true` if at least one of the conditions is true.

At this geyser in Iceland, you can see ice, liquid water, and steam.

© toos/iStockphoto.

Java has two Boolean operators that combine conditions: && (*and*) and || (*or*).

Suppose you write a program that processes temperature values, and you want to test whether a given temperature corresponds to liquid water. (At sea level, water freezes at 0 degrees Celsius and boils at 100 degrees.) Water is liquid if the temperature is greater than zero *and* less than 100:

```
if (temp > 0 && temp < 100) { System.out.println("Liquid"); }
```

The condition of the test has two parts, joined by the && operator. Each part is a Boolean value that can be true or false. The combined expression is true if both individual expressions are true. If either one of the expressions is false, then the result is also false (see Figure 9).

The Boolean operators && and || have a lower precedence than the relational operators. For that reason, you can write relational expressions on either side of the Boolean operators without using parentheses. For example, in the expression

```
temp > 0 && temp < 100
```

the expressions temp > 0 and temp < 100 are evaluated first. Then the && operator combines the results. Appendix B shows a table of the Java operators and their precedence.

Conversely, let's test whether water is *not* liquid at a given temperature. That is the case when the temperature is at most 0 *or* at least 100.

Use the || (*or*) operator to combine the expressions:

```
if (temp <= 0 || temp >= 100) { System.out.println("Not liquid"); }
```

Figure 10 shows flowcharts for these examples.

A	B	A && B
true	true	true
true	false	false
false	true	false
false	false	false

A	B	A || B
true	true	true
true	false	true
false	true	true
false	false	false

A	!A
true	false
false	true

Figure 9   Boolean Truth Tables

Figure 10
Flowcharts
for *and* and *or*
Combinations

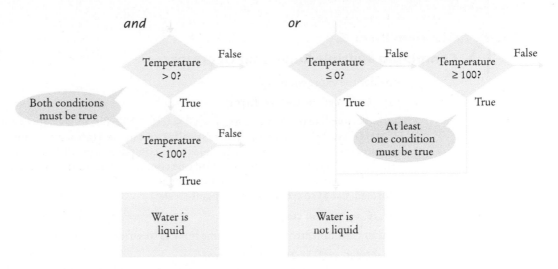

Sometimes you need to *invert* a condition with the *not* Boolean operator. The !
operator takes a single condition and evaluates to true if that condition is false and to
false if the condition is true. In this example, output occurs if the value of the Boolean
variable frozen is false: .

To invert a condition,
use the ! (*not*)
operator.

```
if (!frozen) { System.out.println("Not frozen"); }
```

Table 5 illustrates additional examples of evaluating Boolean operators.

Table 5 Boolean Operator Examples

Expression	Value	Comment
0 < 200 && 200 < 100	false	Only the first condition is true.
0 < 200 || 200 < 100	true	The first condition is true.
0 < 200 || 100 < 200	true	The || is not a test for "either-or". If both conditions are true, the result is true.
0 < x && x < 100 || x == -1	(0 < x && x < 100) || x == -1	The && operator has a higher precedence than the || operator (see Appendix B).
🚫 0 < x < 100	**Error**	**Error:** This expression does not test whether x is between 0 and 100. The expression 0 < x is a Boolean value. You cannot compare a Boolean value with the integer 100.
🚫 x && y > 0	**Error**	**Error:** This expression does not test whether x and y are positive. The left-hand side of && is an integer, x, and the right-hand side, y > 0, is a Boolean value. You cannot use && with an integer argument.
!(0 < 200)	false	0 < 200 is true, therefore its negation is false.
frozen == true	frozen	There is no need to compare a Boolean variable with true.
frozen == false	!frozen	It is clearer to use ! than to compare with false.

EXAMPLE CODE See your eText or companion code for a program that compares numbers using Boolean expressions.

Common Error 5.4

Combining Multiple Relational Operators

Consider the expression

```
if (0 <= temp <= 100) // Error
```

This looks just like the mathematical test $0 \leq \text{temp} \leq 100$. But in Java, it is a compile-time error.

Let us dissect the condition. The first half, `0 <= temp`, is a test with an outcome `true` or `false`. The outcome of that test (`true` or `false`) is then compared against 100. This seems to make no sense. Is `true` larger than 100 or not? Can one compare truth values and numbers? In Java, you cannot. The Java compiler rejects this statement.

Instead, use && to combine two separate tests:

```
if (0 <= temp && temp <= 100) . . .
```

Another common error, along the same lines, is to write

```
if (input == 1 || 2) . . . // Error
```

to test whether `input` is 1 or 2. Again, the Java compiler flags this construct as an error. You cannot apply the || operator to numbers. You need to write two Boolean expressions and join them with the || operator:

```
if (input == 1 || input == 2) . . .
```

Common Error 5.5

Confusing && and || Conditions

It is a surprisingly common error to confuse *and* and *or* conditions. A value lies between 0 and 100 if it is at least 0 *and* at most 100. It lies outside that range if it is less than 0 *or* greater than 100. There is no golden rule; you just have to think carefully.

Often the *and* or *or* is clearly stated, and then it isn't too hard to implement it. But sometimes the wording isn't as explicit. It is quite common that the individual conditions are nicely set apart in a bulleted list, but with little indication of how they should be combined.

Consider these instructions for filing a tax return. You can claim single filing status if any one of the following is true:

- You were never married.
- You were legally separated or divorced on the last day of the tax year.
- You were widowed, and did not remarry.

Because the test passes if *any one* of the conditions is true, you must combine the conditions with *or*.

Elsewhere, the same instructions state that you may use the more advantageous status of married filing jointly if all five of the following conditions are true:

- Your spouse died less than two years ago and you did not remarry.
- You have a child whom you can claim as dependent.
- That child lived in your home for all of the tax year.
- You paid over half the cost of keeping up your home for this child.
- You filed a joint return with your spouse the year he or she died.

Because *all* of the conditions must be true for the test to pass, you must combine them with an *and*.

Special Topic 5.6

Short-Circuit Evaluation of Boolean Operators

The && and || operators are computed using short-circuit evaluation. In other words, logical expressions are evaluated from left to right, and evaluation stops as soon as the truth value is determined. When an && is evaluated and the first condition is false, the second condition is not evaluated, because it does not matter what the outcome of the second test is.

For example, consider the expression

The && and || operators are computed using *short-circuit evaluation:* As soon as the truth value is determined, no further conditions are evaluated.

```
quantity > 0 && price / quantity < 10
```

Suppose the value of quantity is zero. Then the test quantity > 0 fails, and the second test is not attempted. That is just as well, because it is illegal to divide by zero.

Similarly, when the first condition of an || expression is true, then the remainder is not evaluated because the result must be true.

This process is called **short-circuit evaluation**.

In a short circuit, electricity travels along the path of least resistance. Similarly, short-circuit evaluation takes the fastest path for computing the result of a Boolean expression.

© YouraPechkin/iStockphoto.

Special Topic 5.7

De Morgan's Law

Humans generally have a hard time comprehending logical conditions with *not* operators applied to *and/or* expressions. **De Morgan's Law**, named after the logician Augustus De Morgan (1806–1871), can be used to simplify these Boolean expressions.

Suppose we want to charge a higher shipping rate if we don't ship within the continental United States:

```
if (!(country.equals("USA") && !state.equals("AK") && !state.equals("HI")))
{
   shippingCharge = 20.00;
}
```

This test is a little bit complicated, and you have to think carefully through the logic. When it is *not* true that the country is USA *and* the state is not Alaska *and* the state is not Hawaii, then charge $20.00. Huh? It is not true that some people won't be confused by this code.

The computer doesn't care, but it takes human programmers to write and maintain the code. Therefore, it is useful to know how to simplify such a condition.

De Morgan's Law has two forms: one for the negation of an *and* expression and one for the negation of an *or* expression:

```
!(A && B)    is the same as    !A || !B
!(A || B)    is the same as    !A && !B
```

De Morgan's Law tells you how to negate && and || conditions.

Pay particular attention to the fact that the *and* and *or* operators are *reversed* by moving the *not* inward. For example, the negation of "the state is Alaska *or* it is Hawaii",

```
!(state.equals("AK") || state.equals("HI"))
```

is "the state is not Alaska *and* it is not Hawaii":

```
!state.equals("AK") && !state.equals("HI")
```

Now apply the law to our shipping charge computation:

```
!(country.equals("USA")
    && !state.equals("AK")
    && !state.equals("HI"))
```

is equivalent to

```
!country.equals("USA")
    || !!state.equals("AK")
    || !!state.equals("HI"))
```

Because two ! cancel each other out, the result is the simpler test

```
!country.equals("USA")
    || state.equals("AK")
    || state.equals("HI"))
```

In other words, higher shipping charges apply when the destination is outside the United States or in Alaska or Hawaii.

To simplify conditions with negations of *and* or *or* expressions, it is usually a good idea to apply De Morgan's Law to move the negations to the innermost level.

5.8 Application: Input Validation

etra Images/Media Bakery.

Like a quality control worker, you want to make sure that user input is correct before processing it.

An important application for the if statement is *input validation*. Whenever your program accepts user input, you need to make sure that the user-supplied values are valid before you use them in your computations.

Consider our elevator simulation program. Assume that the elevator panel has buttons labeled 1 through 20 (but not 13). The following are illegal inputs:

- The number 13
- Zero or a negative number
- A number larger than 20
- An input that is not a sequence of digits, such as five

In each of these cases, we want to give an error message and exit the program.

It is simple to guard against an input of 13:

```
if (floor == 13)
{
    System.out.println("Error: There is no thirteenth floor.");
}
```

Here is how you ensure that the user doesn't enter a number outside the valid range:

```
if (floor <= 0 || floor > 20)
{
    System.out.println("Error: The floor must be between 1 and 20.");
}
```

Call the hasNextInt
or hasNextDouble
method to ensure
that the next input is
a number.

However, dealing with an input that is not a valid integer is a more serious problem.
When the statement

```
floor = in.nextInt();
```

is executed, and the user types in an input that is not an integer (such as five), then
the integer variable floor is not set. Instead, a run-time exception occurs and the program is terminated. To avoid this problem, you should first call the hasNextInt method
which checks whether the next input is an integer. If that method returns true, you
can safely call nextInt. Otherwise, print an error message and exit the program:

```
if (in.hasNextInt())
{
    int floor = in.nextInt();
    Process the input value.
}
else
{
    System.out.println("Error: Not an integer.");
}
```

Here is the complete elevator simulation program with input validation.

sec08/ElevatorSimulation2.java

```java
1   import java.util.Scanner;
2
3   /**
4      This program simulates an elevator panel that skips the 13th floor, checking for
5      input errors.
6   */
7   public class ElevatorSimulation2
8   {
9       public static void main(String[] args)
10      {
11          Scanner in = new Scanner(System.in);
12          System.out.print("Floor: ");
13          if (in.hasNextInt())
14          {
15              // Now we know that the user entered an integer
16
17              int floor = in.nextInt();
18
19              if (floor == 13)
20              {
21                  System.out.println("Error: There is no thirteenth floor.");
22              }
23              else if (floor <= 0 || floor > 20)
24              {
25                  System.out.println("Error: The floor must be between 1 and 20.");
26              }
27              else
28              {
29                  // Now we know that the input is valid
30
31                  int actualFloor = floor;
32                  if (floor > 13)
33                  {
34                      actualFloor = floor - 1;
35                  }
36
```

```
37              System.out.println("The elevator will travel to the actual floor "
38                 + actualFloor);
39           }
40        }
41        else
42        {
43           System.out.println("Error: Not an integer.");
44        }
45     }
46 }
```

Program Run

```
Floor: 13
Error: There is no thirteenth floor.
```

Computing & Society 5.2   Artificial Intelligence

When one uses a sophisticated computer program such as a tax preparation package, one is bound to attribute some intelligence to the computer. The computer asks sensible questions and makes computations that we find a mental challenge. After all, if doing one's taxes were easy, we wouldn't need a computer to do it for us.

As programmers, however, we know that all this apparent intelligence is an illusion. Human programmers have carefully "coached" the software in all possible scenarios, and it simply replays the actions and decisions that were programmed into it.

Would it be possible to write computer programs that are genuinely intelligent in some sense? From the earliest days of computing, there was a sense that the human brain might be nothing but an immense computer, and that it might well be feasible to program computers to imitate some processes of human thought. Serious research into *artificial intelligence* began in the mid-1950s, and the first twenty years brought some impressive successes. Programs that play chess—surely an activity that appears to require remarkable intellectual powers—have become so good that they now routinely beat all but the best human players. As far back as 1975, an *expert-system* program called Mycin gained fame for being better in diagnosing meningitis in patients than the average physician.

From the very outset, one of the stated goals of the AI community was to produce software that could translate text from one language to another, for example from English to Russian. That undertaking proved to be enormously complicated. Human language appears to be much more subtle and interwoven with the human experience than had originally been thought. Systems such as Apple's Siri can answer common questions about the weather, appointments, and traffic. However, beyond a narrow range, they are more entertaining than useful.

In some areas, artificial intelligence technology has seen substantial advances. One of the most astounding examples is the advent of self-driving cars. In 2004, the Defense Advanced Research Projects Agency (DARPA) invited competitors to submit a computer-controlled vehicle that had to complete an obstacle course without a human driver or remote control. The event was a disappointment, with none of the entrants finishing the route. However, by 2007, a competition in an "urban" environment—an abandoned air force base—had vehicles successfully interact with each other and follow California traffic laws. Within the next decade, technologies for partially or fully autonomous driving became commercially viable. We can now envision a future where self-driving vehicles become ubiquitous.

When a system with artificial intelligence replaces a human in an activity such as giving medical advice or driving a vehicle, an important question arises. Who is responsible for mistakes? We accept that human doctors and drivers occasionally make mistakes with lethal consequences. Will we do the same for medical expert systems and self-driving cars?

Vaughn Youtz/Zuma Press.

Winner of the 2007 DARPA Urban Challenge

CHAPTER SUMMARY

Use the `if` statement to implement a decision.

- The `if` statement allows a program to carry out different actions depending on the nature of the data to be processed.

Implement comparisons of numbers and objects.

- Use relational operators (`< <= > >= == !=`) to compare numbers.
- Relational operators compare values. The `==` operator tests for equality.
- When comparing floating-point numbers, don't test for equality. Instead, check whether they are close enough.
- Do not use the `==` operator to compare strings. Use the `equals` method instead.
- The `compareTo` method compares strings in lexicographic order.
- The `==` operator tests whether two object references are identical. To compare the contents of objects, you need to use the `equals` method.
- The `null` reference refers to no object.

Implement complex decisions that require multiple `if` statements.

- Multiple `if` statements can be combined to evaluate complex decisions.
- When using multiple `if` statements, test general conditions after more specific conditions.

Implement decisions whose branches require further decisions.

- When a decision statement is contained inside the branch of another decision statement, the statements are *nested*.
- Nested decisions are required for problems that have two levels of decision making.

Draw flowcharts for visualizing the control flow of a program.

- Flow charts are made up of elements for tasks, input/output, and decisions.
- Each branch of a decision can contain tasks and further decisions.
- Never point an arrow inside another branch.

Design test cases for your programs.

- Black-box testing describes a testing method that does not take the structure of the implementation into account.
- White-box testing uses information about the structure of a program.
- Code coverage is a measure of how many parts of a program have been tested.
- Boundary test cases are test cases that are at the boundary of acceptable inputs.
- It is a good idea to design test cases before implementing a program.
- Logging messages can be deactivated when testing is complete.

Use the Boolean data type to store and combine conditions that can be true or false.

- The Boolean type `boolean` has two values, `false` and `true`.
- Java has two Boolean operators that combine conditions: `&&` (*and*) and `||` (*or*).
- To invert a condition, use the `!` (*not*) operator.
- The `&&` and `||` operators are computed using short-circuit evaluation: As soon as the truth value is determined, no further conditions are evaluated.
- De Morgan's Law tells you how to negate `&&` and `||` conditions.

Apply `if` statements to detect whether user input is valid.

- Call the `hasNextInt` or `hasNextDouble` method to ensure that the next input is a number.

STANDARD LIBRARY ITEMS INTRODUCED IN THIS CHAPTER

```
java.awt.Rectangle              java.util.logging.Level
   equals                          INFO
java.lang.String                   OFF
   equals                       java.util.logging.Logger
   compareTo                       getGlobal
java.util.Scanner                  info
   hasNextDouble                   setLevel
   hasNextInt
```

REVIEW EXERCISES

- **R5.1** What is the value of each variable after the if statement?

   a. `int n = 1; int k = 2; int r = n;`
   `if (k < n) { r = k; }`

   b. `int n = 1; int k = 2; int r;`
   `if (n < k) { r = k; }`
   `else { r = k + n; }`

   c. `int n = 1; int k = 2; int r = k;`
   `if (r < k) { n = r; }`
   `else { k = n; }`

   d. `int n = 1; int k = 2; int r = 3;`
   `if (r < n + k) { r = 2 * n; }`
   `else { k = 2 * r; }`

- **R5.2** Assume that n is 1. For each of the combinations of a, b, and c given at right, what is the value of n after each compound if statement?

a	b	c
1	2	3
2	1	3
2	3	1

   a. `if (a < b) { if (b < c) { n = 2; } else { n = 3; } }`
   b. `if (a < b) { if (b < c) { n = 2; } } else { n = 3; }`
   c. `if (a < b) if (b < c) { n = 2; } else { n = 3;}`
   d. `if (a < b) n = 2; else if (b < c) n = 3;`

- **R5.3** Explain the difference between

   ```
   s = 0;
   if (x > 0) { s++; }
   if (y > 0) { s++; }
   ```

   and

   ```
   s = 0;
   if (x > 0) { s++; }
   else if (y > 0) { s++; }
   ```

- **R5.4** Find the errors in the following if statements.

   a. `if x > 0 then System.out.print(x);`
   b. `if (1 + x > Math.pow(x, Math.sqrt(2))) { y = y + x; }`
   c. `if (x = 1) { y++; }`
   d.
   ```
   x = in.nextInt();
   if (in.hasNextInt())
   {
      sum = sum + x;
   }
   else
   {
      System.out.println("Bad input for x");
   }
   ```
   e.
   ```
   String letterGrade = "F";
   if (grade >= 90) { letterGrade = "A"; }
   if (grade >= 80) { letterGrade = "B"; }
   if (grade >= 70) { letterGrade = "C"; }
   if (grade >= 60) { letterGrade = "D"; }
   ```

▪ **R5.5** What do these code fragments print?

a.
```
int n = 1;
int m = -1;
if (n < -m) { System.out.print(n); }
else { System.out.print(m); }
```

b.
```
int n = 1;
int m = -1;
if (-n >= m) { System.out.print(n); }
else { System.out.print(m); }
```

c.
```
double x = 0;
double y = 1;
if (Math.abs(x - y) < 1) { System.out.print(x); }
else { System.out.print(y); }
```

d.
```
double x = Math.sqrt(2);
double y = 2;
if (x * x == y) { System.out.print(x); }
else { System.out.print(y); }
```

▪▪ **R5.6** Suppose x and y are variables of type double. Write a code fragment that sets y to x if x is positive and to 0 otherwise.

▪▪ **R5.7** Suppose x and y are variables of type double. Write a code fragment that sets y to the absolute value of x without calling the Math.abs function. Use an if statement.

▪▪ **R5.8** Explain why it is more difficult to compare floating-point numbers than integers. Write Java code to test whether an integer n equals 10 and whether a floating-point number x is approximately equal to 10.

▪▪ **R5.9** Given two pixels on a computer screen with integer coordinates (x_1, y_1) and (x_2, y_2), write conditions to test whether they are

a. The same pixel.

b. Very close together (with distance < 5).

▪ **R5.10** It is easy to confuse the = and == operators. Write a test program with the statement

```
if (floor = 13)
```

What error message do you get? Write another test program with the statement

```
count == 0;
```

What does your compiler do when you compile the program?

▪▪ **R5.11** Each square on a chess board can be described by a letter and number, such as g5 in the example at right. The following pseudocode describes an algorithm that determines whether a square with a given letter and number is dark (black) or light (white).

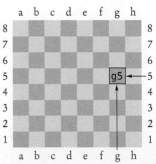

> *If the letter is an a, c, e, or g*
>   *If the number is odd* -
>   *color = "black"*
>   *Else*
>   *color = "white"*
> *Else*
>   *If the number is even*
>   *color = "black"*
>   *Else*
>   *color = "white"*

Using the procedure in Programming Tip 5.5, trace this pseudocode with input g5.

Testing R5.12 Give a set of four test cases for the algorithm of Exercise •• R5.11 that covers all branches.

R5.13 In a scheduling program, we want to check whether two appointments overlap. For simplicity, appointments start at a full hour, and we use military time (with hours 0–23). The following pseudocode describes an algorithm that determines whether the appointment with start time *start1* and end time *end1* overlaps with the appointment with start time *start2* and end time *end2*.

> *If start1 > start2*
>   *s = start1*
> *Else*
>   *s = start2*
> *If end1 < end2*
>   *e = end1*
> *Else*
>   *e = end2*
> *If s < e*
>   *The appointments overlap.*
> *Else*
>   *The appointments don't overlap.*

Trace this algorithm with an appointment from 10–12 and one from 11–13, then with an appointment from 10–11 and one from 12–13.

R5.14 Draw a flow chart for the algorithm in Exercise •• R5.13.

R5.15 Draw a flow chart for the algorithm in Exercise •• E5.12.

R5.16 Draw a flow chart for the algorithm in Exercise •• P5.1.

Testing R5.17 Develop a set of test cases for the algorithm in Exercise •• R5.13.

Testing R5.18 Develop a set of test cases for the algorithm in Exercise •• P5.1.

R5.19 Write pseudocode for a program that prompts the user for a month and day and prints out whether it is one of the following four holidays:
- New Year's Day (January 1)
- Independence Day (July 4)
- Veterans Day (November 11)
- Christmas Day (December 25)

R5.20 Write pseudocode for a program that assigns letter grades for a quiz, according to the following table:

```
Score  Grade
90-100 A
80-89  B
70-79  C
60-69  D
 < 60  F
```

R5.21 Explain how the lexicographic ordering of strings in Java differs from the ordering of words in a dictionary or telephone book. *Hint:* Consider strings such as IBM, wiley. com, Century 21, and While-U-Wait.

■■ **R5.22** Of the following pairs of strings, which comes first in lexicographic order?

    a. "Tom", "Jerry"

    b. "Tom", "Tomato"

    c. "church", "Churchill"

    d. "car manufacturer", "carburetor"

    e. "Harry", "hairy"

    f. "Java", " Car"

    g. "Tom", "Tom"

    h. "Car", "Carl"

    i. "car", "bar"

■ **R5.23** Explain the difference between an `if/else if/else` sequence and nested `if` statements. Give an example of each.

■■ **R5.24** Give an example of an `if/else if/else` sequence where the order of the tests does not matter. Give an example where the order of the tests matters.

■ **R5.25** Rewrite the condition in Section 5.3 to use < operators instead of >= operators. What is the impact on the order of the comparisons?

■■ **Testing R5.26** Give a set of test cases for the tax program in Exercise •• P5.3. Manually compute the expected results.

■ **R5.27** Make up a Java code example that shows the dangling `else` problem using the following statement: A student with a GPA of at least 1.5, but less than 2, is on probation. With less than 1.5, the student is failing.

■■■ **R5.28** Complete the following truth table by finding the truth values of the Boolean expressions for all combinations of the Boolean inputs p, q, and r.

p	q	r	(p && q) || !r	!(p && (q || !r))
false	false	false		
false	false	true		
false	true	false		
. . .				
5 more combinations				
. . .				

■■■ **R5.29** True or false? A && B is the same as B && A for any Boolean conditions A and B.

■ **R5.30** The "advanced search" feature of many search engines allows you to use Boolean operators for complex queries, such as "(cats OR dogs) AND NOT pets". Contrast these search operators with the Boolean operators in Java.

■■ **R5.31** Suppose the value of b is false and the value of x is 0. What is the value of each of the following expressions?

    a. b && x == 0

    b. b || x == 0

    c. !b && x == 0

    d. !b || x == 0

    e. b && x != 0

    f. b || x != 0

    g. !b && x != 0

    h. !b || x != 0

■■ **R5.32** Simplify the following expressions. Here, b is a variable of type boolean.

    a. b == true

    b. b == false

    c. b != true

    d. b != false

■■■ **R5.33** Simplify the following statements. Here, b is a variable of type boolean and n is a variable of type int.

    a. if (n == 0) { b = true; } else { b = false; }

    (Hint: What is the value of n == 0?)

    b. if (n == 0) { b = false; } else { b = true; }

    c. b = false; if (n > 1) { if (n < 2) { b = true; } }

    d. if (n < 1) { b = true; } else { b = n > 2; }

■ **R5.34** What is wrong with the following program?

```
System.out.print("Enter the number of quarters: ");
int quarters = in.nextInt();
if (in.hasNextInt())
{
    total = total + quarters * 0.25;
    System.out.println("Total: " + total);
}
else
{
    System.out.println("Input error.");
}
```

PRACTICE EXERCISES

■ **E5.1** Write a program that reads an integer and prints whether it is negative, zero, or positive.

■■ **E5.2** Write a program that reads a floating-point number and prints "zero" if the number is zero. Otherwise, print "positive" or "negative". Add "small" if the absolute value of the number is less than 1, or "large" if it exceeds 1,000,000.

■■ **E5.3** Write a program that reads an integer and prints how many digits the number has, by checking whether the number is ≥ 10, ≥ 100, and so on. (Assume that all integers are less than ten billion.) If the number is negative, first multiply it with –1.

■■ **E5.4** Write a program that reads a string, compares the first and last letter, and and prints "first and last letter same" or "first and last letter different".

■■ **E5.5** Write a program that reads a word, compares the first and second half of the word, and prints "first and second half same" or "first and second half different". If the length of the word is odd, ignore the middle letter.

■■ **E5.6** Write a program that reads three numbers and prints "all the same" if they are all the same, "all different" if they are all different, and "neither" otherwise.

■■ **E5.7** Write a program that reads three numbers and prints "increasing" if they are in increasing order, "decreasing" if they are in decreasing order, and "neither" otherwise. Here, "increasing" means "strictly increasing", with each value larger than its predecessor. The sequence 3 4 4 would not be considered increasing.

■■ **E5.8** Repeat Exercise ●● E5.7, but before reading the numbers, ask the user whether increasing/decreasing should be "strict" or "lenient". In lenient mode, the sequence 3 4 4 is increasing and the sequence 4 4 4 is both increasing and decreasing.

■■ **E5.9** Write a program that reads in three integers and prints "in order" if they are sorted in ascending *or* descending order, or "not in order" otherwise. For example,

```
1 2 5    in order
1 5 2    not in order
5 2 1    in order
1 2 2    in order
```

■■ **E5.10** Write a program that reads four integers and prints "two pairs" if the input consists of two matching pairs (in some order) and "not two pairs" otherwise. For example,

```
1 2 2 1    two pairs
1 2 2 3    not two pairs
2 2 2 2    two pairs
```

■■ **E5.11** A compass needle points a given number of degrees away from North, measured clockwise. Write a program that reads the angle and prints out the nearest compass direction; one of N, NE, E, SE, S, SW, W, NW. In the case of a tie, prefer the nearest principal direction (N, E, S, or W).

■■ **E5.12** When two points in time are compared, each given as hours (in military time, ranging from 0 and 23) and minutes, the following pseudocode determines which comes first.

> If hour1 < hour2
>   time1 comes first.
> Else if hour1 and hour2 are the same
>   If minute1 < minute2
>   time1 comes first.
>   Else if minute1 and minute2 are the same
>   time1 and time2 are the same.
>   Else
>   time2 comes first.
> Else
>   time2 comes first.

Write a program that prompts the user for two points in time and prints the time that comes first, then the other time. In your program, supply a class `Time` and a method

```
public int compareTo(Time other)
```

that returns −1 if the time comes before the other, 0 if both are the same, and 1 otherwise.

•• E5.13 Write a program that translates a letter grade into a number grade. Letter grades are A, B, C, D, and F, possibly followed by + or −. Their numeric values are 4, 3, 2, 1, and 0. There is no F+ or F−. A + increases the numeric value by 0.3, a − decreases it by 0.3. However, an A+ has value 4.0.

```
Enter a letter grade: B-
The numeric value is 2.7.
```

Use a class `Grade` with a method `getNumericGrade`.

•• E5.14 Write a program that translates a number between 0 and 4 into the closest letter grade. For example, the number 2.8 (which might have been the average of several grades) would be converted to B−. Break ties in favor of the better grade; for example 2.85 should be a B.

Use a class `Grade` with a method `getLetterGrade`.

•• E5.15 The original U.S. income tax of 1913 was quite simple. The tax was

- 1 percent on the first $50,000.
- 2 percent on the amount over $50,000 up to $75,000.
- 3 percent on the amount over $75,000 up to $100,000.
- 4 percent on the amount over $100,000 up to $250,000.
- 5 percent on the amount over $250,000 up to $500,000.
- 6 percent on the amount over $500,000.

There was no separate schedule for single or married taxpayers. Write a program that computes the income tax according to this schedule.

•• E5.16 Write a program that takes user input describing a playing card in the following shorthand notation:

A	Ace
2 ... 10	Card values
J	Jack
Q	Queen
K	King
D	Diamonds
H	Hearts
S	Spades
C	Clubs

Your program should print the full description of the card. For example,

```
Enter the card notation: QS
Queen of Spades
```

Implement a class `Card` whose constructor takes the card notation string and whose `getDescription` method returns a description of the card. If the notation string is not in the correct format, the `getDescription` method should return the string `"Unknown"`.

■■ E5.17 Write a program that reads in three floating-point numbers and prints the largest of the three inputs. For example:

```
Please enter three numbers: 4 9 2.5
The largest number is 9.
```

■■ E5.18 Write a program that reads in three strings and sorts them lexicographically.

```
Enter three strings: Charlie Able Baker
Able
Baker
Charlie
```

■■ E5.19 Write a program that reads in two floating-point numbers and tests whether they are the same up to two decimal places. Here are two sample runs.

```
Enter two floating-point numbers: 2.0 1.99998
They are the same up to two decimal places.
Enter two floating-point numbers: 2.0 1.98999
They are different.
```

■ E5.20 Write a program that prompts the user to provide a single character from the alphabet. Print Vowel or Consonant, depending on the user input. If the user input is not a letter (between a and z or A and Z), or is a string of length > 1, print an error message.

■■ E5.21 Write a program that asks the user to enter a month (1 for January, 2 for February, etc.) and then prints the number of days in the month. For February, print "28 days".

```
Enter a month: 5
30 days
```

Use a class Month with a method

```
public int getLength()
```

Do not use a separate if/else branch for each month. Use Boolean operators.

■■ Business E5.22 Write a program that reads in the name and salary of an employee. Here the salary will denote an *hourly* wage, such as $9.25. Then ask how many hours the employee worked in the past week. Be sure to accept fractional hours. Compute the pay. Any overtime work (over 40 hours per week) is paid at 150 percent of the regular wage. Print a paycheck for the employee. In your solution, implement a class Paycheck.

■ Business E5.23 A supermarket awards coupons depending on how much a customer spends on groceries. For example, if you spend $50, you will get a coupon worth eight percent of that amount. The following table shows the percent used to calculate the coupon awarded for different amounts spent.

Money Spent	Coupon Percentage
Less than $10	No coupon
From $10 to $60	8%
More than $60 to $150	10%
More than $150 to $210	12%
More than $210	14%

Write a program that calculates and prints the value of the coupon a person can receive based on groceries purchased.

Here is a sample run:

```
Please enter the cost of your groceries: 14
You win a discount coupon of $ 1.12. (8% of your purchase)
```

■ **Science E5.24** Write a program that reads a temperature value and the letter C for Celsius or F for Fahrenheit. Print whether water is liquid, solid, or gaseous at the given temperature at sea level.

■ **Science E5.25** The boiling point of water drops by about one degree centigrade for every 300 meters (or 1,000 feet) of altitude. Improve the program of Exercise ● Science E5.24 to allow the user to supply the altitude in meters or feet.

■ **Science E5.26** Add error handling to Exercise ● Science E5.25. If the user does not enter a number when expected, or provides an invalid unit for the altitude, print an error message and end the program.

PROGRAMMING PROJECTS

■■ **P5.1** The following algorithm yields the season (Spring, Summer, Fall, or Winter) for a given month and day.

> *If month is 1, 2, or 3, season = "Winter"*
> *Else if month is 4, 5, or 6, season = "Spring"*
> *Else if month is 7, 8, or 9, season = "Summer"*
> *Else if month is 10, 11, or 12, season = "Fall"*
> *If month is divisible by 3 and day >= 21*
>   *If season is "Winter", season = "Spring"*
>   *Else if season is "Spring", season = "Summer"*
>   *Else if season is "Summer", season = "Fall"*
>   *Else season = "Winter"*

© rotofrank/iStockphoto.

Write a program that prompts the user for a month and day and then prints the season, as determined by this algorithm. Use a class Date with a method getSeason.

■■ **P5.2** Write a program that prompts for the day and month of the user's birthday and then prints a horoscope. Make up fortunes for programmers, like this:

```
Please enter your birthday (month and day): 6 16
Gemini are experts at figuring out the behavior of complicated programs.
You feel where bugs are coming from and then stay one step ahead. Tonight,
your style wins approval from a tough critic.
```

Each fortune should contain the name of the astrological sign. (You will find the names and date ranges of the signs at a distressingly large number of sites on the Internet.) Use a class Date with a method getFortune.

© lillisphotography/iStockphoto.

■■ **P5.3** Write a program that computes taxes for the following schedule.

If your status is Single and if the taxable income is over	but not over	the tax is	of the amount over
$0	$8,000	10%	$0
$8,000	$32,000	$800 + 15%	$8,000
$32,000		$4,400 + 25%	$32,000
If your status is Married and if the taxable income is over	but not over	the tax is	of the amount over
$0	$16,000	10%	$0
$16,000	$64,000	$1,600 + 15%	$16,000
$64,000		$8,800 + 25%	$64,000

■■■ **P5.4** The TaxReturn.java program in Section 5.4 uses a simplified version of the 2008 U.S. income tax schedule. Look up the tax brackets and rates for the current year, for both single and married filers, and implement a program that computes the actual income tax.

■■■ **P5.5** *Unit conversion.* Write a unit conversion program that asks the users from which unit they want to convert (fl. oz, gal, oz, lb, in, ft, mi) and to which unit they want to convert (ml, l, g, kg, mm, cm, m, km). Reject incompatible conversions (such as gal → km). Ask for the value to be converted, then display the result:

```
Convert from? gal
Convert to? ml
Value? 2.5
2.5 gal = 9462.5 ml
```

■ **P5.6** Write a program that reads in the *x*- and *y*-coordinates of two corner points of a rectangle and then prints out whether the rectangle is a square, or is in "portrait" or "landscape" orientation.

■■ **P5.7** Write a program that reads in the *x*- and *y*-coordinates of three corner points of a triangle and prints out whether it has an obtuse angle, a right angle, or only acute angles.

■■■ **P5.8** Write a program that reads in the *x*- and *y*-coordinates of four corner points of a quadrilateral and prints out whether it is a square, a rectangle, a trapezoid, a rhombus, or none of those shapes.

■■■ **P5.9** A year with 366 days is called a leap year. Leap years are necessary to keep the calendar synchronized with the sun because the earth revolves around the sun once every 365.25 days. Actually, that figure is not entirely precise, and for all dates after 1582 the *Gregorian correction* applies. Usually years that are divisible by 4 are leap years, for example 1996. However, years that are divisible by 100 (for example, 1900) are not leap years, but years that are divisible by 400 are leap years (for example, 2000). Write a program that asks the user for a year and computes whether that year is a leap year. Provide a class Year with a method isLeapYear. Use a single if statement and Boolean operators.

• • • **P5.10** *Roman numbers.* Write a program that converts a positive integer into the Roman number system. The Roman number system has digits

I	1
V	5
X	10
L	50
C	100
D	500
M	1,000

© Charles Schultz/iStockphoto.

Numbers are formed according to the following rules:

a. Only numbers up to 3,999 are represented.

b. As in the decimal system, the thousands, hundreds, tens, and ones are expressed separately.

c. The numbers 1 to 9 are expressed as

I	1
II	2
III	3
IV	4
V	5
VI	6
VII	7
VIII	8
IX	9

As you can see, an I preceding a V or X is subtracted from the value, and you can never have more than three I's in a row.

d. Tens and hundreds are done the same way, except that the letters X, L, C and C, D, M are used instead of I, V, X, respectively.

Your program should take an input, such as 1978, and convert it to Roman numerals, MCMLXXVIII.

• • • **P5.11** French country names are feminine when they end with the letter e, masculine otherwise, except for the following which are masculine even though they end with e:

• le Belize
• le Cambodge
• le Mexique
• le Mozambique
• le Zaïre
• le Zimbabwe

Write a program that reads the French name of a country and adds the article: le for masculine or la for feminine, such as le Canada or la Belgique.

However, if the country name starts with a vowel, use l'; for example, l'Afghanistan. For the following plural country names, use les:

- les Etats-Unis
- les Pays-Bas

■■■ Business P5.12 Write a program to simulate a bank transaction. There are two bank accounts: checking and savings. First, ask for the initial balances of the bank accounts; reject negative balances. Then ask for the transactions; options are deposit, withdrawal, and transfer. Then ask for the account; options are checking and savings. Reject transactions that overdraw an account. At the end, print the balances of both accounts.

■■ Business P5.13 When you use an automated teller machine (ATM) with your bank card, you need to use a personal identification number (PIN) to access your account. If a user fails more than three times when entering the PIN, the machine will block the card. Assume that the user's PIN is "1234" and write a program that asks the user for the PIN no more than three times, and does the following:

- If the user enters the right number, print a message saying, "Your PIN is correct", and end the program.
- If the user enters a wrong number, print a message saying, "Your PIN is incorrect" and, if you have asked for the PIN less than three times, ask for it again.
- If the user enters a wrong number three times, print a message saying "Your bank card is blocked" and end the program.

© Mark Evans/iStockphoto.

■ Business P5.14 Calculating the tip when you go to a restaurant is not difficult, but your restaurant wants to suggest a tip according to the service diners receive. Write a program that calculates a tip according to the diner's satisfaction as follows:

- Ask for the diners' satisfaction level using these ratings: 1 = Totally satisfied, 2 = Satisfied, 3 = Dissatisfied.
- If the diner is totally satisfied, calculate a 20 percent tip.
- If the diner is satisfied, calculate a 15 percent tip.
- If the diner is dissatisfied, calculate a 10 percent tip.
- Report the satisfaction level and tip in dollars and cents.

■ Science P5.15 Write a program that prompts the user for a wavelength value and prints a description of the corresponding part of the electromagnetic spectrum, as given in the following table.

© drxy/iStockphoto.

Electromagnetic Spectrum		
Type	Wavelength (m)	Frequency (Hz)
Radio Waves	$> 10^{-1}$	$< 3 \times 10^9$
Microwaves	10^{-3} to 10^{-1}	3×10^9 to 3×10^{11}
Infrared	7×10^{-7} to 10^{-3}	3×10^{11} to 4×10^{14}
Visible light	4×10^{-7} to 7×10^{-7}	4×10^{14} to 7.5×10^{14}

Electromagnetic Spectrum		
Type	Wavelength (m)	Frequency (Hz)
Ultraviolet	10^{-8} to 4×10^{-7}	7.5×10^{14} to 3×10^{16}
X-rays	10^{-11} to 10^{-8}	3×10^{16} to 3×10^{19}
Gamma rays	$< 10^{-11}$	$> 3 \times 10^{19}$

■ **Science P5.16** Repeat Exercise • Science P5.15, modifying the program so that it prompts for the frequency instead.

■■ **Science P5.17** Repeat Exercise • Science P5.15, modifying the program so that it first asks the user whether the input will be a wavelength or a frequency.

■■■ **Science P5.18** A minivan has two sliding doors. Each door can be opened by either a dashboard switch, its inside handle, or its outside handle. However, the inside handles do not work if a child lock switch is activated. In order for the sliding doors to open, the gear shift must be in park, *and* the master unlock switch must be activated. (This book's author is the long-suffering owner of just such a vehicle.)

Your task is to simulate a portion of the control software for the vehicle. The input is a sequence of values for the switches and the gear shift, in the following order:

- Dashboard switches for left and right sliding door, child lock, and master unlock (0 for off or 1 for activated)
- Inside and outside handles on the left and right sliding doors (0 or 1)
- The gear shift setting (one of P N D 1 2 3 R).

A typical input would be 0 0 0 1 0 1 0 0 P.

Print "left door opens" and/or "right door opens" as appropriate. If neither door opens, print "both doors stay closed".

© nano/iStockphoto.

■ **Science P5.19** Sound level L in units of decibel (dB) is determined by

$$L = 20 \log_{10}(p/p_0)$$

where p is the sound pressure of the sound (in Pascals, abbreviated Pa), and p_0 is a reference sound pressure equal to 20×10^{-6} Pa (where L is 0 dB). The following table gives descriptions for certain sound levels.

Threshold of pain	130 dB
Possible hearing damage	120 dB
Jack hammer at 1 m	100 dB
Traffic on a busy roadway at 10 m	90 dB
Normal conversation	60 dB
Calm library	30 dB
Light leaf rustling	0 dB

© Photobuff/iStockphoto.

Write a program that reads a value and a unit, either dB or Pa, and then prints the closest description from the list above.

■■ Science P5.20 The electric circuit shown below is designed to measure the temperature of the gas in a chamber.

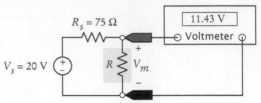

The resistor R represents a temperature sensor enclosed in the chamber. The resistance R, in Ω, is related to the temperature T, in °C, by the equation

$$R = R_0 + kT$$

In this device, assume $R_0 = 100\ \Omega$ and $k = 0.5$. The voltmeter displays the value of the voltage, V_m, across the sensor. This voltage V_m indicates the temperature, T, of the gas according to the equation

$$T = \frac{R}{k} - \frac{R_0}{k} = \frac{R_s}{k} \frac{V_m}{V_s - V_m} - \frac{R_0}{k}$$

Suppose the voltmeter voltage is constrained to the range $V_{min} = 12$ volts $\leq V_m \leq V_{max} = 18$ volts. Write a program that accepts a value of V_m and checks that it is between 12 and 18. The program should return the gas temperature in degrees Celsius when V_m is between 12 and 18 and an error message when it isn't.

■■■ Science P5.21 Crop damage due to frost is one of the many risks confronting farmers. The figure below shows a simple alarm circuit designed to warn of frost. The alarm circuit uses a device called a thermistor to sound a buzzer when the temperature drops below freezing. Thermistors are semiconductor devices that exhibit a temperature dependent resistance described by the equation

© rotofrank/iStockphoto.

$$R = R_0 e^{\beta\left(\frac{1}{T} - \frac{1}{T_0}\right)}$$

where R is the resistance, in Ω, at the temperature T in °K, and R_0 is the resistance, in Ω, at the temperature T_0 in °K. β is a constant that depends on the material used to make the thermistor.

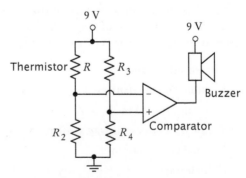

The circuit is designed so that the alarm will sound when

$$\frac{R_2}{R + R_2} < \frac{R_4}{R_3 + R_4}$$

The thermistor used in the alarm circuit has $R_0 = 33{,}192\ \Omega$ at $T_0 = 40\ °C$, and $\beta = 3{,}310\ °K$. (Notice that β has units of $°K$. The temperature in $°K$ is obtained by adding $273°$ to the temperature in $°C$.) The resistors R_2, R_3, and R_4 have a resistance of $156.3\ k\Omega = 156{,}300\ \Omega$.

Write a Java program that prompts the user for a temperature in $°F$ and prints a message indicating whether or not the alarm will sound at that temperature.

■ **Science P5.22** A mass $m = 2$ kilograms is attached to the end of a rope of length $r = 3$ meters. The mass is whirled around at high speed. The rope can withstand a maximum tension of $T = 60$ Newtons. Write a program that accepts a rotation speed v and determines whether such a speed will cause the rope to break. *Hint:* $T = mv^2/r$.

■ **Science P5.23** A mass m is attached to the end of a rope of length $r = 3$ meters. The rope can only be whirled around at speeds of 1, 10, 20, or 40 meters per second. The rope can withstand a maximum tension of $T = 60$ Newtons. Write a program where the user enters the value of the mass m, and the program determines the greatest speed at which it can be whirled without breaking the rope. *Hint:* $T = mv^2/r$.

■■ **Science P5.24** The average person can jump off the ground with a velocity of 7 mph without fear of leaving the planet. However, if an astronaut jumps with this velocity while standing on Halley's Comet, will the astronaut ever come back down? Create a program that allows the user to input a launch velocity (in mph) from the surface of Halley's Comet and determine whether a jumper will return to the surface. If not, the program should calculate how much more massive the comet must be in order to return the jumper to the surface.

Courtesy NASA/JPL-Caltech.

Hint: Escape velocity is $v_{escape} = \sqrt{2\dfrac{GM}{R}}$, where $G = 6.67 \times 10^{-11}\ N\,m^2/kg^2$ is the gravitational constant, $M = 1.3 \times 10^{22}$ kg is the mass of Halley's comet, and

$R = 1.153 \times 10^6$ m is its radius.

CHAPTER **6**

LOOPS

CHAPTER GOALS

To implement while, for, and do loops

To hand-trace the execution of a program

To learn to use common loop algorithms

To understand nested loops

To implement programs that read and process data sets

To use a computer for simulations

To learn about the debugger

CHAPTER CONTENTS

In a loop, a part of a program is repeated over and over, until a specific goal is reached. Loops are important for calculations that require repeated steps and for processing input consisting of many data items. In this chapter, you will learn about loop statements in Java, as well as techniques for writing programs that process input and simulate activities in the real world.

6.1 The while Loop

In this section, you will learn about *loop statements* that repeatedly execute instructions until a goal has been reached.

Recall the investment problem from Chapter 1. You put $10,000 into a bank account that earns 5 percent interest per year. How many years does it take for the account balance to be double the original investment?

In Chapter 1 we developed the following algorithm for this problem:

© AlterYourReality/iStockphoto.

Because the interest earned also earns interest, a bank balance grows exponentially.

Set year to 0, balance to 10000.

year	interest	balance
0		$10,000

While the balance is less than $20,000
    Add 1 to the year.
    Set interest to balance x 0.05 (i.e., 5 percent interest).
    Add the interest to the balance.
Report year as the answer.

You now know how to declare and update the variables in Java. What you don't yet know is how to carry out "Repeat steps while the balance is less than $20,000".

In a particle accelerator, subatomic particles traverse a loop-shaped tunnel multiple times, gaining the speed required for physical experiments. Similarly, in computer science, statements in a loop are executed while a condition is true.

© mmac72/iStockphoto.

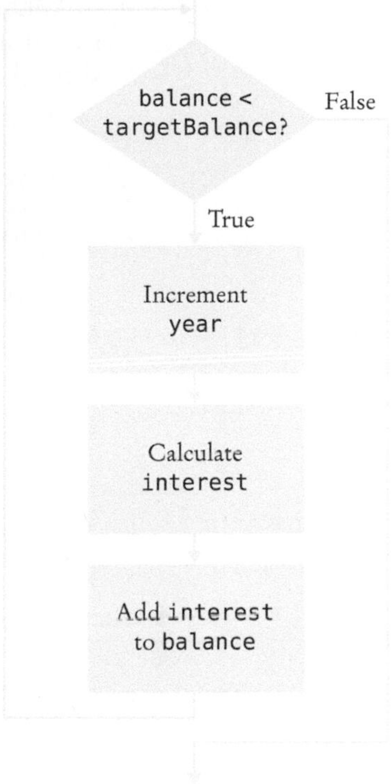

Figure 1   Flowchart of a while Loop

In Java, the while statement implements such a repetition (see Syntax 6.1). It has the form

```
while (condition)
{
    statements
}
```

A loop executes instructions repeatedly while a condition is true.

As long as the condition remains true, the statements inside the while statement are executed. These statements are called the **body** of the while statement.

In our case, we want to increment the year counter and add interest while the balance is less than the target balance of $20,000:

```
while (balance < targetBalance)
{
    year++;
    double interest = balance * RATE / 100;
    balance = balance + interest;
}
```

A while statement is an example of a **loop**. If you draw a flowchart, the flow of execution loops again to the point where the condition is tested (see Figure 1).

balance < targetBalance?   False

True

Increment year

Calculate interest

Add interest to balance

Syntax 6.1   while Statement

Syntax
```
while (condition)
{
    statements
}
```

This variable is declared outside the loop and updated in the loop.

Beware of "off-by-one" errors in the loop condition.
See Common Error 6.3.

```
double balance = 0;
.
.
.
```

If the condition never becomes false, an infinite loop occurs.
See Common Error 6.2.

Don't put a semicolon here!
See Common Error 5.1.

```
while (balance < targetBalance)
{
    double interest = balance * RATE / 100;
    balance = balance + interest;
}
```

This variable is created in each loop iteration.

These statements are executed while the condition is true.

Lining up braces is a good idea.
See Programming Tip 5.1.

Braces are not required if the body contains a single statement, but it's good to always use them.
See Programming Tip 5.2.

When you declare a variable *inside* the loop body, the variable is created for each iteration of the loop and removed after the end of each iteration. For example, consider the interest variable in this loop:

```
while (balance < targetBalance)
{
    year++;
    double interest = balance * RATE / 100;
    balance = balance + interest;
}
// interest no longer declared here
```

A new interest variable is created in each iteration.

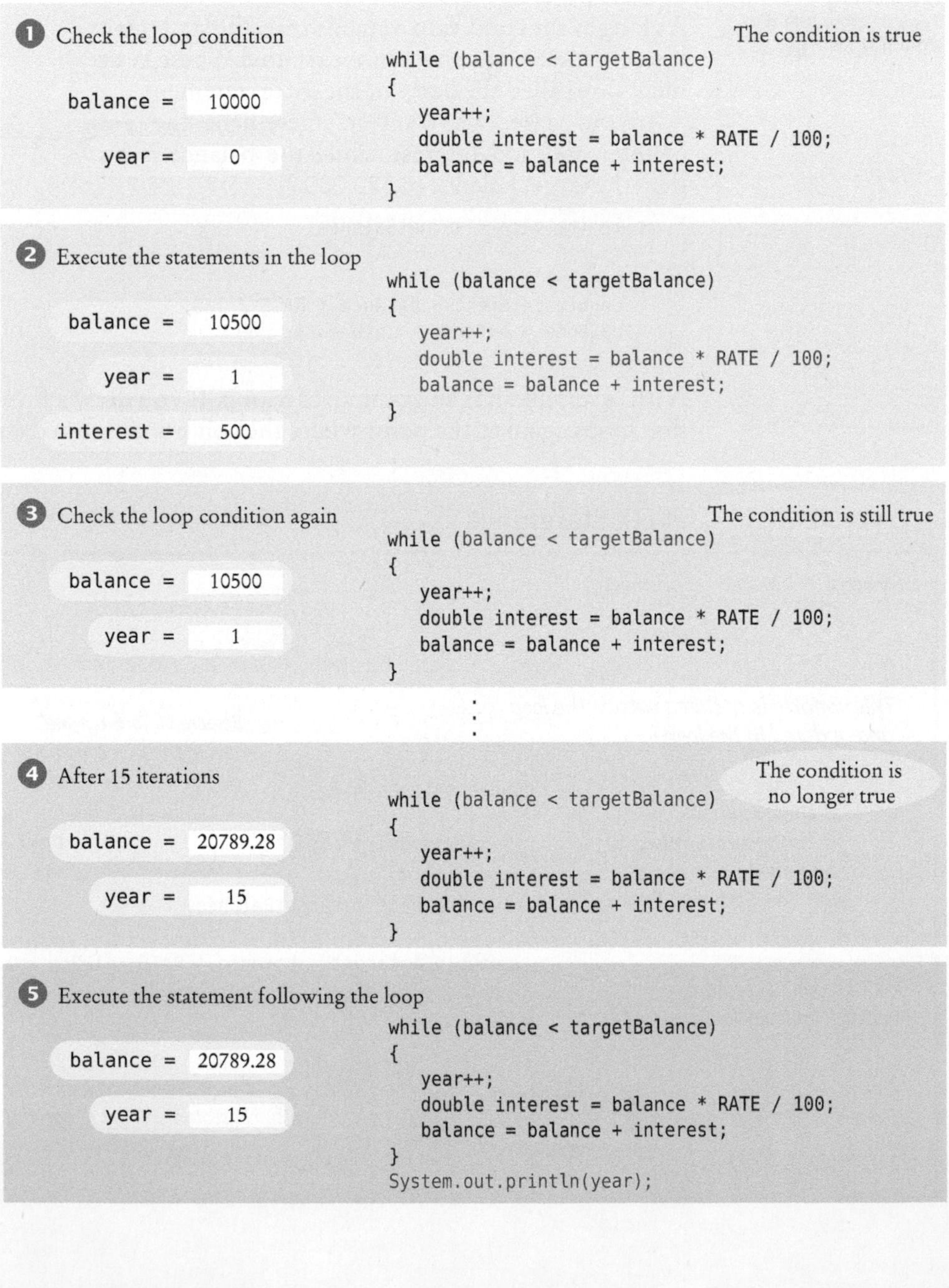

① Check the loop condition
The condition is true

```
balance =    10000

year =       0
```

```
while (balance < targetBalance)
{
    year++;
    double interest = balance * RATE / 100;
    balance = balance + interest;
}
```

② Execute the statements in the loop

```
balance =    10500

year =       1

interest =   500
```

```
while (balance < targetBalance)
{
    year++;
    double interest = balance * RATE / 100;
    balance = balance + interest;
}
```

③ Check the loop condition again
The condition is still true

```
balance =    10500

year =       1
```

```
while (balance < targetBalance)
{
    year++;
    double interest = balance * RATE / 100;
    balance = balance + interest;
}
```

⋮

④ After 15 iterations
The condition is no longer true

```
balance =    20789.28

year =       15
```

```
while (balance < targetBalance)
{
    year++;
    double interest = balance * RATE / 100;
    balance = balance + interest;
}
```

⑤ Execute the statement following the loop

```
balance =    20789.28

year =       15
```

```
while (balance < targetBalance)
{
    year++;
    double interest = balance * RATE / 100;
    balance = balance + interest;
}
System.out.println(year);
```

Figure 2
Execution of the
Investment Loop

In contrast, the balance and year variables were declared outside the loop body. That way, the same variable is used for all iterations of the loop.

Following is the program that solves the investment problem. Figure 2 illustrates the loop's execution.

sec01/InvestmentRunner.java

```java
1  /**
2      This program computes how long it takes for an investment
3      to double.
4  */
5  public class InvestmentRunner
6  {
7      public static void main(String[] args)
8      {
9          final double INITIAL_BALANCE = 10000;
10         final double RATE = 5;
11         Investment invest = new Investment(INITIAL_BALANCE, RATE);
12         invest.waitForBalance(2 * INITIAL_BALANCE);
13         int years = invest.getYears();
14         System.out.println("The investment doubled after "
15             + years + " years");
16     }
17 }
```

sec01/Investment.java

```java
1  /**
2      A class to monitor the growth of an investment that
3      accumulates interest at a fixed annual rate.
4  */
5  public class Investment
6  {
7      private double balance;
8      private double rate;
9      private int year;
10
11     /**
12         Constructs an Investment object from a starting balance and
13         interest rate.
14         @param aBalance the starting balance
15         @param aRate the interest rate in percent
16     */
17     public Investment(double aBalance, double aRate)
18     {
19         balance = aBalance;
20         rate = aRate;
21         year = 0;
22     }
23
24     /**
25         Keeps accumulating interest until a target balance has
26         been reached.
27         @param targetBalance the desired balance
28     */
29     public void waitForBalance(double targetBalance)
30     {
31         while (balance < targetBalance)
32         {
```

```
33              year++;
34              double interest = balance * rate / 100;
35              balance = balance + interest;
36          }
37      }
38
39      /**
40          Gets the current investment balance.
41          @return the current balance
42      */
43      public double getBalance()
44      {
45          return balance;
46      }
47
48      /**
49          Gets the number of years this investment has accumulated
50          interest.
51          @return the number of years since the start of the investment
52      */
53      public int getYears()
54      {
55          return year;
56      }
57 }
```

Program Run

```
The investment doubled after 15 years.
```

Table 1 shows examples of simple loops.

Table 1 while Loop Examples

Loop	Output	Explanation

`i = 0; sum = 0;`
`while (sum < 10)`
`{`
`   i++; sum = sum + i;`
`   Print i and sum;`
`}`
	1 1
	2 3
	3 6
	4 10
		When sum is 10, the loop condition is false, and the loop ends.

`i = 0; sum = 0;`
`while (sum < 10)`
`{`
`   i++; sum = sum - i;`
`   Print i and sum;`
`}`
	1 -1
	2 -3
	3 -6
	4 -10
	. . .
		Because sum never reaches 10, this is an "infinite loop" (see Common Error 6.2).

`i = 0; sum = 0;`
`while (sum < 0)`
`{`
`   i++; sum = sum - i;`
`   Print i and sum;`
`}`
	(No output)	The statement sum < 0 is false when the condition is first checked, and the loop is never executed.

Table 1 while Loop Examples

Loop	Output	Explanation

```i = 0; sum = 0;```
```while (sum >= 10)```
```{```
   ```i++; sum = sum + i;```
   Print i *and* sum;
```}```
	(No output)	The programmer probably thought, "Stop when the sum is at least 10." However, the loop condition controls when the loop is executed, not when it ends (see Common Error 6.1).

```i = 0; sum = 0;```
```while (sum < 10) ;```
```{```
   ```i++; sum = sum + i;```
   Print i *and* sum;
```}```
	(No output, program does not terminate)	Note the semicolon before the {. This loop has an empty body. It runs forever, checking whether sum < 10 and doing nothing in the body.

Common Error 6.1

Don't Think "Are We There Yet?"

When doing something repetitive, most of us want to know when we are done. For example, you may think, "I want to get at least $20,000," and set the loop condition to

```
balance >= targetBalance
```

But the while loop thinks the opposite: How long am I allowed to keep going? The correct loop condition is

```
while (balance < targetBalance)
```

In other words: "Keep at it while the balance is less than the target."

When writing a loop condition, don't ask, "Are we there yet?" The condition determines how long the loop will keep going.

© MsSponge/iStockphoto.

Common Error 6.2

Infinite Loops

A very annoying loop error is an *infinite loop:* a loop that runs forever and can be stopped only by killing the program or restarting the computer. If there are output statements in the program, then reams and reams of output flash by on the screen. Otherwise, the program just sits there and *hangs*, seeming to do nothing. On some systems, you can kill a hanging program by hitting Ctrl + C. On others, you can close the window in which the program runs.

A common reason for infinite loops is forgetting to update the variable that controls the loop:

```
int year = 1;
while (year <= 20)
{
```

```
      double interest = balance * RATE / 100;
      balance = balance + interest;
   }
```

Here the programmer forgot to add a year++ command in the loop. As a result, the year always stays at 1, and the loop never comes to an end.

Another common reason for an infinite loop is accidentally incrementing a counter that should be decremented (or vice versa). Consider this example:

```
int year = 20;
while (year > 0)
{
   double interest = balance * RATE / 100;
   balance = balance + interest;
   year++;
}
```

© ohiophoto/iStockphoto.

Like this hamster who can't stop running in the treadmill, an infinite loop never ends.

The year variable really should have been decremented, not incremented. This is a common error because incrementing counters is so much more common than decrementing that your fingers may type the ++ on autopilot. As a consequence, year is always larger than 0, and the loop never ends. (Actually, year may eventually exceed the largest representable positive integer and *wrap around* to a negative number. Then the loop ends—of course, with a completely wrong result.)

Common Error 6.3

Off-by-One Errors

Consider our computation of the number of years that are required to double an investment:

```
int year = 0;
while (balance < targetBalance)
{
   year++;
   balance = balance * (1 + RATE / 100);
}
System.out.println("The investment doubled after " + year + " years.");
```

Should year start at 0 or at 1? Should you test for balance < targetBalance or for balance <= targetBalance? It is easy to be *off by one* in these expressions.

Some people try to solve **off-by-one errors** by randomly inserting +1 or -1 until the program seems to work—a terrible strategy. It can take a long time to compile and test all the various possibilities. Expending a small amount of mental effort is a real time saver.

An off-by-one error is a common error when programming loops. Think through simple test cases to avoid this type of error.

Fortunately, off-by-one errors are easy to avoid, simply by thinking through a couple of test cases and using the information from the test cases to come up with a rationale for your decisions.

Should year start at 0 or at 1? Look at a scenario with simple values: an initial balance of $100 and an interest rate of 50 percent. After year 1, the balance is $150, and after year 2 it is $225, or over $200. So the investment doubled after 2 years. The loop executed two times, incrementing year each time. Hence year must start at 0, not at 1.

year	balance
0	$100
1	$150
2	$225

In other words, the `balance` variable denotes the balance after the end of the year. At the outset, the `balance` variable contains the balance after year 0 and not after year 1.

Next, should you use a `<` or `<=` comparison in the test? This is harder to figure out, because it is rare for the balance to be exactly twice the initial balance. There is one case when this happens, namely when the interest is 100 percent. The loop executes once. Now year is 1, and `balance` is exactly equal to `2 * INITIAL_BALANCE`. Has the investment doubled after one year? It has. Therefore, the loop should not execute again. If the test condition is `balance < targetBalance`, the loop stops, as it should. If the test condition had been `balance <= targetBalance`, the loop would have executed once more.

In other words, you keep adding interest while the balance *has not yet doubled*.

6.2 Problem Solving: Hand-Tracing

Hand-tracing is a simulation of code execution in which you step through instructions and track the values of the variables.

In Programming Tip 5.5, you learned about the method of hand-tracing. When you hand-trace code or pseudocode, you write the names of the variables on a sheet of paper, mentally execute each step of the code, and update the variables.

It is best to have the code written or printed on a sheet of paper. Use a marker, such as a paper clip, to mark the current line. Whenever a variable changes, cross out the old value and write the new value below. When a program produces output, also write down the output in another column.

Consider this example. What value is displayed?

```java
int n = 1729;
int sum = 0;
while (n > 0)
{
   int digit = n % 10;
   sum = sum + digit;
   n = n / 10;
}
System.out.println(sum);
```

There are three variables: `n`, `sum`, and `digit`.

n	sum	digit

The first two variables are initialized with 1729 and 0 before the loop is entered.

```java
      int n = 1729;
⊂⊃    int sum = 0;
      while (n > 0)
      {
         int digit = n % 10;
         sum = sum + digit;
         n = n / 10;
      }
      System.out.println(sum);
```

n	sum	digit
1729	0	

Because n is greater than zero, enter the loop. The variable digit is set to 9 (the remainder of dividing 1729 by 10). The variable sum is set to 0 + 9 = 9.

```
int n = 1729;
int sum = 0;
while (n > 0)
{
    int digit = n % 10;
    sum = sum + digit;
    n = n / 10;
}
System.out.println(sum);
```

n	sum	digit
1729	0̸	
	9	9

Finally, n becomes 172. (Recall that the remainder in the division 1729/10 is discarded because both arguments are integers.)

Cross out the old values and write the new ones under the old ones.

```
int n = 1729;
int sum = 0;
while (n > 0)
{
    int digit = n % 10;
    sum = sum + digit;
    n = n / 10;
}
System.out.println(sum);
```

n	sum	digit
1̶7̶2̶9̶	0̸	
172	9	9

Now check the loop condition again.

```
int n = 1729;
int sum = 0;
while (n > 0)
{
    int digit = n % 10;
    sum = sum + digit;
    n = n / 10;
}
System.out.println(sum);
```

Because n is still greater than zero, repeat the loop. Now digit becomes 2, sum is set to 9 + 2 = 11, and n is set to 17.

n	sum	digit
1̶7̶2̶9̶	0̸	
1̶7̶2̶	9̸	9̸
17	11	2

Repeat the loop once again, setting digit to 7, sum to 11 + 7 = 18, and n to 1.

n	sum	digit
1729	0	
172	9	9
17	11	2
1	18	7

Enter the loop for one last time. Now digit is set to 1, sum to 19, and n becomes zero.

n	sum	digit
1729	0	
172	9	9
17	11	2
1	18	7
0	19	1

```
int n = 1729;
int sum = 0;
while (n > 0)
{
    int digit = n % 10;
    sum = sum + digit;
    n = n / 10;
}
System.out.println(sum);
```

Because n equals zero, this condition is not true.

The condition n > 0 is now false. Continue with the statement after the loop.

```
int n = 1729;
int sum = 0;
while (n > 0)
{
    int digit = n % 10;
    sum = sum + digit;
    n = n / 10;
}
System.out.println(sum);
```

n	sum	digit	output
1729	0		
172	9	9	
17	11	2	
1	18	7	
0	19	1	19

This statement is an output statement. The value that is output is the value of sum, which is 19.

Of course, you can get the same answer by just running the code. However, hand-tracing can give you an *insight* that you would not get if you simply ran the code. Consider again what happens in each iteration:

- We extract the last digit of n.
- We add that digit to sum.
- We strip the digit off n.

Hand-tracing can help you understand how an unfamiliar algorithm works.

In other words, the loop forms the sum of the digits in n. You now know what the loop does for any value of n, not just the one in the example. (Why would anyone want to form the sum of the digits? Operations of this kind are useful for checking the validity of credit card numbers and other forms of ID numbers.)

Hand-tracing can show errors in code or pseudocode.

Hand-tracing does not just help you understand code that works correctly. It is a powerful technique for finding errors in your code. When a program behaves in a way that you don't expect, get out a sheet of paper and track the values of the variables as you mentally step through the code.

You don't need a working program to do hand-tracing. You can hand-trace pseudocode. In fact, it is an excellent idea to hand-trace your pseudocode before you go to the trouble of translating it into actual code, to confirm that it works correctly.

Computing & Society 6.1   Digital Piracy

As you read this, you will have written a few computer programs and experienced firsthand how much effort it takes to write even the humblest of programs. Writing a real software product, such as a financial application or a computer game, takes a lot of time and money. Few people, and fewer companies, are going to spend that kind of time and money if they don't have a reasonable chance to make more money from their effort. Revenue comes from licensing fees or advertising.

When a mass market for personal computer software first appeared, it was an easy matter for an unscrupulous person to make copies of computer programs without paying for them. In most countries that is illegal. Most governments provide legal protection, such as copyright laws and patents, to encourage the development of new products. Countries that tolerate widespread piracy have found that they have an ample cheap supply of foreign software, but no local manufacturers willing to design good software for their own citizens, such as word processors in the local script or financial programs adapted to the local tax laws.

Because it is so easy and inexpensive to pirate software, and the chance of being found out is minimal, you have to make a moral choice for yourself. If a package that you would really like to have is too expensive for your budget, do you steal it, or do you stay honest and get by with a more affordable product?

Of course, piracy is not limited to software. The same issues arise for other digital products as well. You may have had the opportunity to obtain copies of songs or movies without payment. Or you may have been frustrated by a copy protection device on your music player that made it difficult for you to listen to songs that you paid for. Admittedly, it can be difficult to have a lot of sympathy for a musical ensemble whose publisher charges a lot of money for what seems to have been very little effort on their part, at least when compared to the effort that goes into designing and implementing a software package. Nevertheless, it seems only fair that artists and authors receive some compensation for their efforts.

How to pay artists, authors, and programmers fairly, without burdening honest customers, is an unsolved problem at the time of this writing, and many computer scientists are engaged in research in this area.

© RapidEye/iStockphoto.

6.3 The for Loop

The for loop is used when a value runs from a starting point to an ending point with a constant increment or decrement.

It often happens that you want to execute a sequence of statements a given number of times. You can use a while loop that is controlled by a counter, as in the following example:

```
int counter = 5; // Initialize the counter
while (counter <= 10) // Check the counter
{
    sum = sum + counter;
    counter++; // Update the counter
}
```

Because this loop type is so common, there is a special form for it, called the for loop (see Syntax 6.2).

```
for (int counter = 5; counter <= 10; counter++)
{
    sum = sum + counter;
}
```

Some people call this loop *count-controlled*. In contrast, the while loop of the preceding section can be called an *event-controlled* loop because it executes until an event occurs; namely that the balance reaches the target. Another commonly used term for a count-controlled loop is *definite*. You know from the outset that the loop body will be executed a definite number of times; ten times in our example. In contrast, you do not know how many iterations it takes to accumulate a target balance. Such a loop is called *indefinite*.

© Enrico Fianchini/iStockphoto.

You can visualize the for loop as an orderly sequence of steps.

Syntax 6.2   for Statement

Syntax
```
for (initialization; condition; update)
{
    statements
}
```

These three expressions should be related.
See Programming Tip 6.1.

This initialization happens once before the loop starts.

The condition is checked before each iteration.

This update is executed after each iteration.

```
for (int i = 5; i <= 10; i++)
{
    sum = sum + i;
}
```

The variable i is defined only in this for loop.
See Special Topic 6.1.

This loop executes 6 times.
See Programming Tip 6.3.

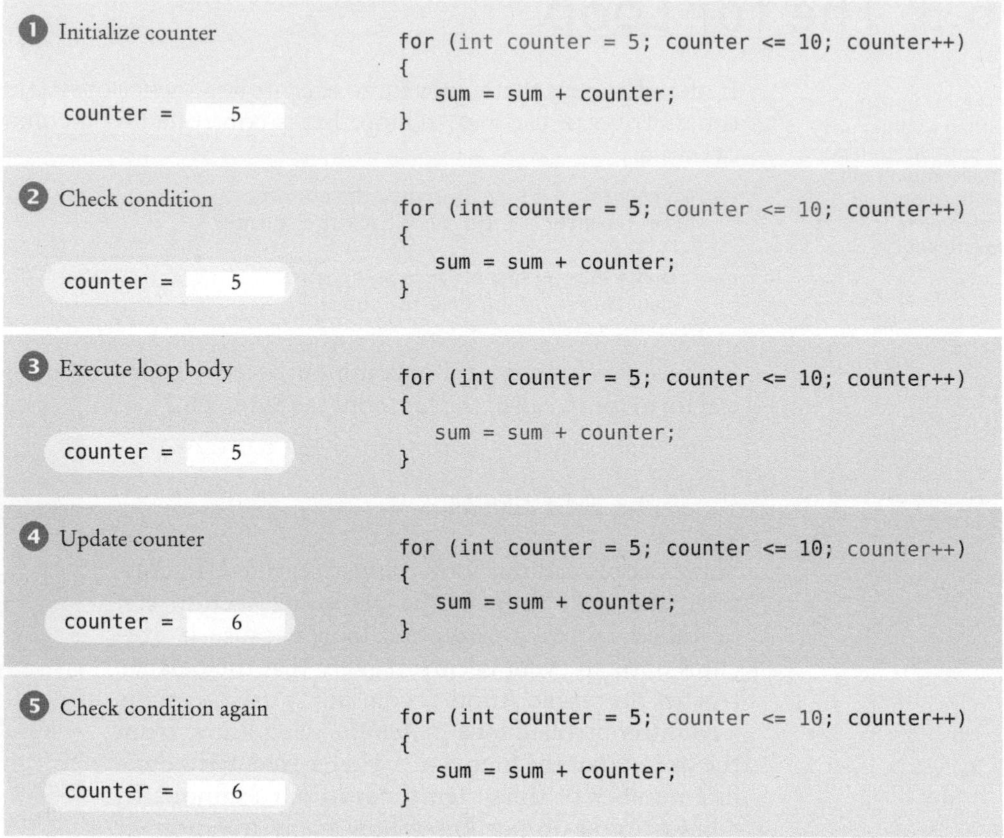

Figure 3 Execution of a for Loop

The for loop neatly groups the initialization, condition, and update expressions together. However, it is important to realize that these expressions are not executed together (see Figure 3).

- The initialization is executed once, before the loop is entered. ❶
- The condition is checked before each iteration. ❷ ❺
- The update is executed after each iteration. ❹

A for loop can count down instead of up:

```
for (int counter = 10; counter >= 5; counter--) . . .
```

The increment or decrement need not be in steps of 1:

```
for (int counter = 0; counter <= 10; counter = counter + 2) . . .
```

See Table 2 on page 187 for additional variations.

So far, we have always declared the counter variable in the loop initialization:

```
for (int counter = 5; counter <= 10; counter++)
{
    . . .
}
// counter no longer declared here
```

Such a variable is declared for all iterations of the loop, but you cannot use it after the loop. If you declare the counter variable before the loop, you can continue to use it after the loop:

```
int counter;
for (counter = 5; counter <= 10; counter++)
{
    . . .
}
// counter still declared here
```

A common use of the for loop is to traverse all characters of a string:

```
for (int i = 0; i < str.length(); i++)
{
    char ch = str.charAt(i);
    Process ch.
}
```

Note that the counter variable i starts at 0, and the loop is terminated when i reaches the length of the string. For example, if str has length 5, i takes on the values 0, 1, 2, 3, and 4. These are the valid positions in the string.

Here is another typical use of the for loop. We want to compute the growth of our savings account over a period of years, as shown in this table:

Year	Balance
1	10500.00
2	11025.00
3	11576.25
4	12155.06
5	12762.82

The for loop pattern applies because the variable year starts at 1 and then moves in constant increments until it reaches the target:

```
for (int year = 1; year <= numberOfYears; year++)
{
    Update balance.
}
```

Following is the complete program. Figure 4 shows the corresponding flowchart.

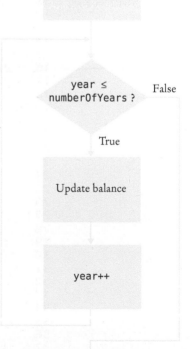

Figure 4 Flowchart of a for Loop

sec03/InvestmentRunner.java

```
1   /**
2       This program computes how much an investment grows in
3       a given number of years.
4   */
5   public class InvestmentRunner
6   {
7       public static void main(String[] args)
8       {
9           final double INITIAL_BALANCE = 10000;
10          final double RATE = 5;
11          final int YEARS = 20;
12          Investment invest = new Investment(INITIAL_BALANCE, RATE);
13          invest.waitYears(YEARS);
14          double balance = invest.getBalance();
15          System.out.printf("The balance after %d years is %.2f%n",
16              YEARS, balance);
17      }
18  }
```

sec03/Investment.java

```
1   /**
2       A class to monitor the growth of an investment that
3       accumulates interest at a fixed annual rate.
4   */
5   public class Investment
6   {
7       private double balance;
8       private double rate;
9       private int year;
10
11      /**
12          Constructs an Investment object from a starting balance and
13          interest rate.
14          @param aBalance the starting balance
15          @param aRate the interest rate in percent
16      */
17      public Investment(double aBalance, double aRate)
18      {
19          balance = aBalance;
20          rate = aRate;
21          year = 0;
22      }
23
24      /**
25          Keeps accumulating interest until a target balance has
26          been reached.
27          @param targetBalance the desired balance
28      */
29      public void waitForBalance(double targetBalance)
30      {
31          while (balance < targetBalance)
32          {
33              year++;
34              double interest = balance * rate / 100;
35              balance = balance + interest;
36          }
37      }
38
```

```
39    /**
40        Keeps accumulating interest for a given number of years.
41        @param numberOfYears the number of years to wait
42    */
43    public void waitYears(int numberOfYears)
44    {
45        for (int i = 1; i <= numberOfYears; i++)
46        {
47            double interest = balance * rate / 100;
48            balance = balance + interest;
49        }
50        year = year + numberOfYears;
51    }
52
53    /**
54        Gets the current investment balance.
55        @return the current balance
56    */
57    public double getBalance()
58    {
59        return balance;
60    }
61
62    /**
63        Gets the number of years this investment has accumulated
64        interest.
65        @return the number of years since the start of the investment
66    */
67    public int getYears()
68    {
69        return year;
70    }
71 }
```

Program Run

```
The balance after 20 years is 26532.98
```

Table 2 for Loop Examples

Loop	Values of i	Comment
for (i = 0; i <= 5; i++)	0 1 2 3 4 5	Note that the loop is executed 6 times. (See Programming Tip 6.3.)
for (i = 5; i >= 0; i--)	5 4 3 2 1 0	Use i-- for decreasing values.
for (i = 0; i < 9; i = i + 2)	0 2 4 6 8	Use i = i + 2 for a step size of 2.
for (i = 0; i != 9; i = i + 2)	0 2 4 6 8 10 12 14 ... (infinite loop)	You can use < or <= instead of != to avoid this problem.
for (i = 1; i <= 20; i = i * 2)	1 2 4 8 16	You can specify any rule for modifying i, such as doubling it in every step.
for (i = 0; i < str.length(); i++)	0 1 2 ... until the last valid index of the string str	In the loop body, use the expression str.charAt(i) to get the ith character.

Programming Tip 6.1

Use for Loops for Their Intended Purpose Only

A for loop is an *idiom* for a loop of a particular form. A value runs from the start to the end, with a constant increment or decrement.

The compiler won't check whether the initialization, condition, and update expressions are related. For example, the following loop is legal:

```
// Confusing—unrelated expressions
for (System.out.print("Inputs: "); in.hasNextDouble(); sum = sum + x)
{
   x = in.nextDouble();
}
```

However, programmers reading such a for loop will be confused because it does not match their expectations. Use a while loop for iterations that do not follow the for idiom.

You should also be careful not to update the loop counter in the body of a for loop. Consider the following example:

```
for (int counter = 1; counter <= 100; counter++)
{
   if (counter % 10 == 0) // Skip values that are divisible by 10
   {
      counter++; // Bad style—you should not update the counter in a for loop
   }
   System.out.println(counter);
}
```

Updating the counter inside a for loop is confusing because the counter is updated *again* at the end of the loop iteration. In some loop iterations, counter is incremented once, in others twice. This goes against the intuition of a programmer who sees a for loop.

If you find yourself in this situation, you can either change from a for loop to a while loop, or implement the "skipping" behavior in another way. For example:

```
for (int counter = 1; counter <= 100; counter++)
{
   if (counter % 10 != 0) // Skip values that are divisible by 10
   {
      System.out.println(counter);
   }
}
```

Programming Tip 6.2

Choose Loop Bounds That Match Your Task

Suppose you want to print line numbers that go from 1 to 10. Of course, you will use a loop:

```
for (int i = 1; i <= 10; i++)
```

The values for i are bounded by the relation $1 \leq i \leq 10$. Because there are $\leq$ on both bounds, the bounds are called **symmetric bounds**.

When traversing the characters in a string, it is more natural to use the bounds

```
for (int i = 0; i < str.length(); i++)
```

In this loop, i traverses all valid positions in the string. You can access the ith character as str.charAt(i). The values for i are bounded by $0 \leq i < str.length()$, with a $\leq$ to the left and a $<$ to the right. That is appropriate, because str.length() is not a valid position. Such bounds are called **asymmetric bounds**.

In this case, it is not a good idea to use symmetric bounds:

```
for (int i = 0; i <= str.length() - 1; i++) // Use < instead
```

The asymmetric form is easier to understand.

Programming Tip 6.3

Count Iterations

Finding the correct lower and upper bounds for an iteration can be confusing. Should you start at 0 or at 1? Should you use <= b or < b as a termination condition?

Counting the number of iterations is a very useful device for better understanding a loop. Counting is easier for loops with asymmetric bounds. The loop

```
for (int i = a; i < b; i++)
```

is executed b - a times. For example, the loop traversing the characters in a string,

```
for (int i = 0; i < str.length(); i++)
```

runs str.length() times. That makes perfect sense, because there are str.length() characters in a string.

The loop with symmetric bounds,

```
for (int i = a; i <= b; i++)
```

is executed b - a + 1 times. That "+1" is the source of many programming errors.

For example,

```
for (int i = 0; i <= 10; i++)
```

runs 11 times. Maybe that is what you want; if not, start at 1 or use < 10.

One way to visualize this "+1" error is by looking at a fence. Each section has one fence post to the left, and there is a final post on the right of the last section. Forgetting to count the last value is often called a "fence post error".

How many posts do you need for a fence with four sections? It is easy to be "off by one" with problems such as this one. © akaplummer/iStockphoto.

Special Topic 6.1

Variables Declared in a for Loop Header

As mentioned, it is legal in Java to declare a variable in the header of a for loop. Here is the most common form of this syntax:

```
for (int i = 1; i <= n; i++)
{
    . . .
}
// i no longer defined here
```

The scope of the variable extends to the end of the for loop. Therefore, i is no longer defined after the loop ends. If you need to use the value of the variable beyond the end of the loop, then you need to declare it outside the loop. In this loop, you don't need the value of i—you know it is n + 1 when the loop is finished. (Actually, that is not quite true—it is possible to break out of a loop before its end; see Special Topic 6.4). When you have two or more exit conditions, though, you may still need the variable. For example, consider the loop

```
for (i = 1; balance < targetBalance && i <= n; i++)
{
    . . .
}
```

You want the balance to reach the target but you are willing to wait only a certain number of years. If the balance doubles sooner, you may want to know the value of i. Therefore, in this case, it is not appropriate to declare the variable in the loop header.

Note that the variables named i in the following pair of for loops are independent:

```
for (int i = 1; i <= 10; i++)
{
    System.out.println(i * i);
}

for (int i = 1; i <= 10; i++) // Declares a new variable i
{
    System.out.println(i * i * i);
}
```

In the loop header, you can declare multiple variables, as long as they are of the same type, and you can include multiple update expressions, separated by commas:

```
for (int i = 0, j = 10; i <= 10; i++, j--)
{
    . . .
}
```

However, many people find it confusing if a for loop controls more than one variable. I recommend that you not use this form of the for statement (see Programming Tip 6.1). Instead, make the for loop control a single counter, and update the other variable explicitly:

```
int j = 10;
for (int i = 0; i <= 10; i++)
{
    . . .
    j--;
}
```

6.4 The do Loop

Sometimes you want to execute the body of a loop at least once and perform the loop test after the body is executed. The do loop serves that purpose:

```
do
{
    statements
}
while (condition);
```

The body of the do loop is executed first, then the condition is tested.

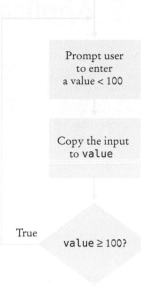

Some people call such a loop a *post-test loop* because the condition is tested after completing the loop body. In contrast, while and for loops are *pre-test loops*. In those loop types, the condition is tested before entering the loop body.

A typical example for a do loop is input validation. Suppose you ask a user to enter a value < 100. If the user doesn't pay attention and enters a larger value, you ask again, until the value is correct. Of course, you cannot test the value until the user has entered it. This is a perfect fit for the do loop (see Figure 5):

> The do loop is appropriate when the loop body must be executed at least once.

```java
int value;
do
{
   System.out.print("Enter an integer < 100: ");
   value = in.nextInt();
}
while (value >= 100);
```

Figure 5 Flowchart of a do Loop

EXAMPLE CODE See sec04 of your eText or companion code for a program that illustrates the use of the do loop for input validation.

Programming Tip 6.4

Flowcharts for Loops

In Section 5.5 you learned how to use flowcharts to visualize the flow of control in a program. There are two types of loops that you can include in a flowchart; they correspond to a while loop and a do loop in Java. They differ in the placement of the condition—either before or after the loop body.

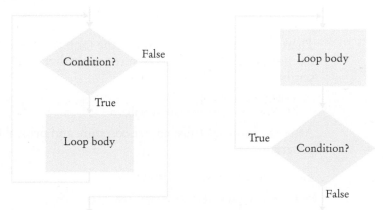

As described in Section 5.5, you want to avoid "spaghetti code" in your flowcharts. For loops, that means that you never want to have an arrow that points inside a loop body.

6.5 Application: Processing Sentinel Values

> A sentinel value denotes the end of a data set, but it is not part of the data.

In this section, you will learn how to write loops that read and process a sequence of input values.

Whenever you read a sequence of inputs, you need to have some method of indicating the end of the sequence. Sometimes you are lucky and no input value can be zero. Then you can prompt the user to keep entering numbers, or 0 to finish the sequence. If zero is allowed but negative numbers are not, you can use −1 to indicate termination.

Such a value, which is not an actual input, but serves as a signal for termination, is called a **sentinel**.

Let's put this technique to work in a program that computes the average of a set of salary values. In our sample program, we will use −1 as a sentinel. An employee would surely not work for a negative salary, but there may be volunteers who work for free.

Inside the loop, we read an input. If the input is not −1, we process it. In order to compute the average, we need the total sum of all salaries, and the number of inputs.

© Rhoberazzi/iStockphoto.

In the military, a sentinel guards a border or passage. In computer science, a sentinel value denotes the end of an input sequence or the border between input sequences.

```java
salary = in.nextDouble();
if (salary != -1)
{
   sum = sum + salary;
   count++;
}
```

We stay in the loop while the sentinel value is not detected.

```java
while (salary != -1)
{
   . . .
}
```

There is just one problem: When the loop is entered for the first time, no data value has been read. We must make sure to initialize salary with some value other than the sentinel:

```java
double salary = 0;
// Any value other than −1 will do
```

After the loop has finished, we compute and print the average. Here is the complete program.

sec05/SentinelDemo.java

```java
1  import java.util.Scanner;
2
3  /**
4     This program prints the average of salary values that are terminated with a sentinel.
5  */
```

```
 6  public class SentinelDemo
 7  {
 8     public static void main(String[] args)
 9     {
10        double sum = 0;
11        int count = 0;
12        double salary = 0;
13        System.out.print("Enter salaries, -1 to finish: ");
14        Scanner in = new Scanner(System.in);
15
16        // Process data until the sentinel is entered
17
18        while (salary != -1)
19        {
20           salary = in.nextDouble();
21           if (salary != -1)
22           {
23              sum = sum + salary;
24              count++;
25           }
26        }
27
28        // Compute and print the average
29
30        if (count > 0)
31        {
32           double average = sum / count;
33           System.out.println("Average salary: " + average);
34        }
35        else
36        {
37           System.out.println("No data");
38        }
39     }
40  }
```

Program Run

```
Enter salaries, -1 to finish: 10 10 40 -1
Average salary: 20
```

You can use a Boolean variable to control a loop. Set the variable before entering the loop, then set it to the opposite to leave the loop.

Some programmers don't like the "trick" of initializing the input variable with a value other than the sentinel. Another approach is to use a Boolean variable:

```
System.out.print("Enter salaries, -1 to finish: ");
boolean done = false;
while (!done)
{
   value = in.nextDouble();
   if (value == -1)
   {
      done = true;
   }
   else
   {
      Process value.
   }
}
```

Special Topic 6.4 shows an alternative mechanism for leaving such a loop.

Now consider the case in which any number (positive, negative, or zero) can be an acceptable input. In such a situation, you must use a sentinel that is not a number (such as the letter Q). As you have seen in Section 5.8, the condition

```
in.hasNextDouble()
```

is false if the next input is not a floating-point number. Therefore, you can read and process a set of inputs with the following loop:

```
System.out.print("Enter values, Q to quit: ");
while (in.hasNextDouble())
{
   value = in.nextDouble();
   Process value.
}
```

Special Topic 6.2

Redirection of Input and Output

Consider the SentinelDemo program that computes the average value of an input sequence. If you use such a program, then it is quite likely that you already have the values in a file, and it seems a shame that you have to type them all in again. The command line interface of your operating system provides a way to link a file to the input of a program, as if all the characters in the file had actually been typed by a user. If you type

```
java SentinelDemo < numbers.txt
```

the program is executed, but it no longer expects input from the keyboard. All input commands get their input from the file numbers.txt. This process is called input **redirection**.

Input redirection is an excellent tool for testing programs. When you develop a program and fix its bugs, it is boring to keep entering the same input every time you run the program. Spend a few minutes putting the inputs into a file, and use redirection.

You can also redirect output. In this program, that is not terribly useful. If you run

```
java SentinelDemo < numbers.txt > output.txt
```

the file output.txt contains the input prompts and the output, such as

```
Enter salaries, -1 to finish: Enter salaries, -1 to finish:
Enter salaries, -1 to finish: Enter salaries, -1 to finish:
Average salary: 15
```

However, redirecting output is obviously useful for programs that produce lots of output. You can format or print the file containing the output.

> Use input redirection to read input from a file. Use output redirection to capture program output in a file.

Special Topic 6.3

The "Loop and a Half" Problem

Reading input data sometimes requires a loop such as the following, which is somewhat unsightly:

```
boolean done = false;
while (!done)
{
   String input = in.next();
   if (input.equals("Q"))
   {
```

```
         done = true;
      }
      else
      {
         Process data.
      }
   }
```

The true test for loop termination is in the middle of the loop, not at the top. This is called a "loop and a half", because one must go halfway into the loop before knowing whether one needs to terminate.

Some programmers dislike the introduction of an additional Boolean variable for loop control. Two Java language features can be used to alleviate the "loop and a half" problem. I don't think either is a superior solution, but both approaches are fairly common, so it is worth knowing about them when reading other people's code.

You can combine an assignment and a test in the loop condition:

```
while (!(input = in.next()).equals("Q"))
{
   Process data.
}
```

The expression

```
(input = in.next()).equals("Q")
```

means, "First call in.next(), then assign the result to input, then test whether it equals "Q"". This is an expression with a side effect. The primary purpose of the expression is to serve as a test for the while loop, but it also does some work—namely, reading the input and storing it in the variable input. In general, it is a bad idea to use side effects, because they make a program hard to read and maintain. In this case, however, that practice is somewhat seductive, because it eliminates the control variable done, which also makes the code hard to read and maintain.

The other solution is to exit the loop from the middle, either by a return statement or by a break statement (see Special Topic 6.4).

```
public void processInput(Scanner in)
{
   while (true)
   {
      String input = in.next();
      if (input.equals("Q"))
      {
         return;
      }
      Process data.
   }
}
```

Special Topic 6.4
The break **and** continue **Statements**

You already encountered the break statement in Special Topic 5.2, where it was used to exit a switch statement. In addition to breaking out of a switch statement, a break statement can also be used to exit a while, for, or do loop.

For example, the break statement in the following loop terminates the loop when the end of input is reached.

```
while (true)
{
```

```
   String input = in.next();
   if (input.equals("Q"))
   {
      break;
   }
   double x = Double.parseDouble(input);
   data.add(x);
}
```

A loop with break statements can be difficult to understand because you have to look closely to find out how to exit the loop. However, when faced with the bother of introducing a separate loop control variable, some programmers find that break statements are beneficial in the "loop and a half" case. This issue is often the topic of heated (and quite unproductive) debate. In this book, we won't use the break statement, and we leave it to you to decide whether you like to use it in your own programs.

In Java, there is a second form of the break statement that is used to break out of a nested statement. The statement break *label*; immediately jumps to the *end* of the statement that is tagged with a label. Any statement (including if and block statements) can be tagged with a label—the syntax is

label: *statement*

The labeled break statement was invented to break out of a set of nested loops.

```
outerloop:
while (outer loop condition)
{  . . .
   while (inner loop condition)
   {  . . .
      if (something really bad happened)
      {
         break outerloop;
      }
   }
}
Jumps here if something really bad happened.
```

Naturally, this situation is quite rare. We recommend that you try to introduce additional methods instead of using complicated nested loops.

Finally, there is the continue statement, which jumps to the end of the *current iteration* of the loop. Here is a possible use for this statement:

```
while (!done)
{
   String input = in.next();
   if (input.equals("Q"))
   {
      done = true;
      continue; // Jump to the end of the loop body
   }
   double x = Double.parseDouble(input);
   data.add(x);
   // continue statement jumps here
}
```

By using the continue statement, you don't need to place the remainder of the loop code inside an else clause. This is a minor benefit. Few programmers use this statement.

6.6 Problem Solving: Storyboards

When you design a program that interacts with a user, you need to make a plan for that interaction. What information does the user provide, and in which order? What information will your program display, and in which format? What should happen when there is an error? When does the program quit?

> A storyboard consists of annotated sketches for each step in an action sequence.

This planning is similar to the development of a movie or a computer game, where *storyboards* are used to plan action sequences. A storyboard is made up of panels that show a sketch of each step. Annotations explain what is happening and note any special situations. Storyboards are also used to develop software—see Figure 6.

Making a storyboard is very helpful when you begin designing a program. You need to ask yourself which information you need in order to compute the answers that the program user wants. You need to decide how to present those answers. These are important considerations that you want to settle before you design an algorithm for computing the answers.

> Developing a storyboard helps you understand the inputs and outputs that are required for a program.

Let's look at a simple example. We want to write a program that helps users with questions such as "How many tablespoons are in a pint?" or "How many inches are 30 centimeters?"

What information does the user provide?

- The quantity and unit to convert from
- The unit to convert to

What if there is more than one quantity? A user may have a whole table of centimeter values that should be converted into inches.

What if the user enters units that our program doesn't know how to handle, such as ångström?

What if the user asks for impossible conversions, such as inches to gallons?

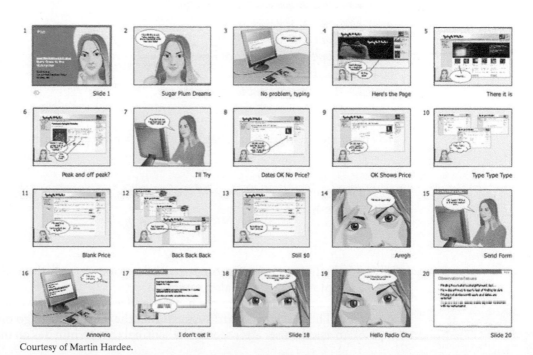

Figure 6
Storyboard for the Design of a Web Application

Courtesy of Martin Hardee.

Let's get started with a storyboard panel. It is a good idea to write the user inputs in a different color. (Underline them if you don't have a color pen handy.)

Converting a Sequence of Values

What unit do you want to convert from? *cm*
What unit do you want to convert to? *in*
Enter values, terminated by zero ——————— Allows conversion of multiple values
30
30 cm = 11.81 in ——
100   —— Format makes clear what got converted
100 cm = 39.37 in
0
What unit do you want to convert from?

The storyboard shows how we deal with a potential confusion. A user who wants to know how many inches are 30 centimeters may not read the first prompt carefully and specify inches. But then the output is "30 in = 76.2 cm", alerting the user to the problem.

The storyboard also raises an issue. How is the user supposed to know that "cm" and "in" are valid units? Would "centimeter" and "inches" also work? What happens when the user enters a wrong unit? Let's make another storyboard to demonstrate error handling.

Handling Unknown Units (needs improvement)

What unit do you want to convert from? *cm*
What unit do you want to convert to? *inches*
Sorry, unknown unit.
What unit do you want to convert to? *inch*
Sorry, unknown unit.
What unit do you want to convert to? *grr*

To eliminate frustration, it is better to list the units that the user can supply.

From unit (in, ft, mi, mm, cm, m, km, oz, lb, g, kg, tsp, tbsp, pint, gal): *cm*
To unit: *in* ——
            —— No need to list the units again

We switched to a shorter prompt to make room for all the unit names. Exercise • R6.24 explores a different alternative.

There is another issue that we haven't addressed yet. How does the user quit the program? The first storyboard suggests that the program will go on forever.

We can ask the user after seeing the sentinel that terminates an input sequence.

Exiting the Program

From unit (in, ft, mi, mm, cm, m, km, oz, lb, g, kg, tsp, tbsp, pint, gal): cm
To unit: in
Enter values, terminated by zero
30
30 cm = 11.81 in
0 ——————————————— *Sentinel triggers the prompt to exit*
More conversions (y, n)? n
(Program exits)

As you can see from this case study, a storyboard is essential for developing a working program. You need to know the flow of the user interaction in order to structure your program.

6.7 Common Loop Algorithms

In the following sections, we discuss some of the most common algorithms that are implemented as loops. You can use them as starting points for your loop designs.

6.7.1 Sum and Average Value

Computing the sum of a number of inputs is a very common task. Keep a *running total*, a variable to which you add each input value. Of course, the total should be initialized with 0.

```
double total = 0;
while (in.hasNextDouble())
{
   double input = in.nextDouble();
   total = total + input;
}
```

Note that the total variable is declared outside the loop. We want the loop to update a single variable. The input variable is declared inside the loop. A separate variable is created for each input and removed at the end of each loop iteration.

To compute an average, count how many values you have, and divide by the count. Be sure to check that the count is not zero.

To compute an average, keep a total and a count of all values.

```
double total = 0;
int count = 0;
while (in.hasNextDouble())
{
   double input = in.nextDouble();
   total = total + input;
   count++;
}
double average = 0;
if (count > 0)
{
   average = total / count;
}
```

6.7.2 Counting Matches

To count values that fulfill a condition, check all values and increment a counter for each match.

You often want to know how many values fulfill a particular condition. For example, you may want to count how many spaces are in a string. Keep a *counter*, a variable that is initialized with 0 and incremented whenever there is a match.

```java
int spaces = 0;
for (int i = 0; i < str.length(); i++)
{
   char ch = str.charAt(i);
   if (ch == ' ')
   {
      spaces++;
   }
}
```

For example, if str is "My Fair Lady", spaces is incremented twice (when i is 2 and 7).

Note that the spaces variable is declared outside the loop. We want the loop to update a single variable. The ch variable is declared inside the loop. A separate variable is created for each iteration and removed at the end of each loop iteration.

This loop can also be used for scanning inputs. The following loop reads text a word at a time and counts the number of words with at most three letters:

```java
int shortWords = 0;
while (in.hasNext())
{
   String input = in.next();
   if (input.length() <= 3)
   {
      shortWords++;
   }
}
```

In a loop that counts matches, a counter is incremented whenever a match is found.

© Hiob/iStockphoto.

6.7.3 Finding the First Match

If your goal is to find a match, exit the loop when the match is found.

When you count the values that fulfill a condition, you need to look at all values. However, if your task is to find a match, then you can stop as soon as the condition is fulfilled.

Here is a loop that finds the first letter A in a string. Because we do not visit all elements in the string, a while loop is a better choice than a for loop:

```java
boolean found = false;
char ch = '?';
int position = 0;
while (!found && position < str.length())
{
```

© drflet/iStockphoto.

When searching, you look at items until a match is found.

```
         ch = str.charAt(position);
         if (ch == 'A' || ch == 'a') { found = true; }
         else { position++; }
      }
```

If a match was found, then found is true, ch is the first matching character, and position is the index of the first match. If the loop did not find a match, then found remains false after the end of the loop.

Note that the variable ch is declared *outside* the while loop because you may want to use the input after the loop has finished. If it had been declared inside the loop body, you would not be able to use it outside the loop.

6.7.4 Prompting Until a Match is Found

In the preceding example, we searched a string for a character that matches a condition. You can apply the same process to user input. Suppose you are asking a user to enter a positive value < 100. Keep asking until the user provides a correct input:

```
boolean valid = false;
double input = 0;
while (!valid)
{
   System.out.print("Please enter a positive value < 100: ");
   input = in.nextDouble();
   if (0 < input && input < 100) { valid = true; }
   else { System.out.println("Invalid input."); }
}
```

Note that the variable input is declared *outside* the while loop because you will want to use the input after the loop has finished.

6.7.5 Maximum and Minimum

To find the largest value, update the largest value seen so far whenever you see a larger one.

To compute the largest value in a sequence, keep a variable that stores the largest element that you have encountered, and update it when you find a larger one.

```
double largest = in.nextDouble();
while (in.hasNextDouble())
{
   double input = in.nextDouble();
   if (input > largest)
   {
      largest = input;
   }
}
```

This algorithm requires that there is at least one input.

To find the height of the tallest bus rider, remember the largest value so far, and update it whenever you see a taller one. © CEFutcher/iStockphoto.

To compute the smallest value, simply reverse the comparison:

```java
double smallest = in.nextDouble();
while (in.hasNextDouble())
{
   double input = in.nextDouble();
   if (input < smallest)
   {
      smallest = input;
   }
}
```

6.7.6 Comparing Adjacent Values

To compare adjacent inputs, store the preceding input in a variable.

When processing a sequence of values in a loop, you sometimes need to compare a value with the value that just preceded it. For example, suppose you want to check whether a sequence of inputs, such as 1 7 2 9 9 4 9, contains adjacent duplicates.

Now you face a challenge. Consider the typical loop for reading a value:

```java
double input;
while (in.hasNextDouble())
{
   input = in.nextDouble();
   . . .
}
```

How can you compare the current input with the preceding one? At any time, input contains the current input, overwriting the previous one.

The answer is to store the previous input, like this:

```java
double input = 0;
while (in.hasNextDouble())
{
   double previous = input;
   input = in.nextDouble();
   if (input == previous)
   {
      System.out.println("Duplicate input");
   }
}
```

One problem remains. When the loop is entered for the first time, input has not yet been read. You can solve this problem with an initial input operation outside the loop:

```java
double input = in.nextDouble();
while (in.hasNextDouble())
{
   double previous = input;
   input = in.nextDouble();
   if (input == previous)
   {
      System.out.println("Duplicate input");
   }
}
```

© tingberg/iStockphoto.

When comparing adjacent values, store the previous value in a variable.

EXAMPLE CODE   See sec07 of your eText or companion code for a program that uses common loop algorithms.

HOW TO 6.1

Writing a Loop

This How To walks you through the process of implementing a loop statement. We will illustrate the steps with the following example problem.

Problem Statement Read twelve temperature values (one for each month) and display the number of the month with the highest temperature. For example, according to http://worldclimate.com, the average maximum temperatures for Death Valley are (in order by month, in degrees Celsius):

18.2 22.6 26.4 31.1 36.6 42.2
45.7 44.5 40.2 33.1 24.2 17.6

In this case, the month with the highest temperature (45.7 degrees Celsius) is July, and the program should display 7.

© Stevegeer/iStockphoto.

Step 1 Decide what work must be done *inside* the loop.

Every loop needs to do some kind of repetitive work, such as

- Reading another item.
- Updating a value (such as a bank balance or total).
- Incrementing a counter.

If you can't figure out what needs to go inside the loop, start by writing down the steps that you would take if you solved the problem by hand. For example, with the temperature reading problem, you might write

Read the first value.
Read the second value.
If the second value is higher than the first value
  Set highest temperature to the second value.
  Set highest month to 2.
Read the next value.
If the value is higher than the first and second values
  Set highest temperature to the value.
  Set highest month to 3.
Read the next value.
If the value is higher than the highest temperature seen so far
  Set highest temperature to the value.
  Set highest month to 4.
  . . .

Now look at these steps and reduce them to a set of *uniform* actions that can be placed into the loop body. The first action is easy:

Read the next value.

The next action is trickier. In our description, we used tests "higher than the first", "higher than the first and second", "higher than the highest temperature seen so far". We need to settle on one test that works for all iterations. The last formulation is the most general.

Similarly, we must find a general way of setting the highest month. We need a variable that stores the current month, running from 1 to 12. Then we can formulate the second loop action:

If the value is higher than the highest temperature
  Set highest temperature to the value.
  Set highest month to current month.

Altogether our loop is

While ...
  Read the next value.
  If the value is higher than the highest temperature
    Set the highest temperature to the value.
    Set highest month to current month.
  Increment current month.

Step 2   Specify the loop condition.

What goal do you want to reach in your loop? Typical examples are

- Has a counter reached its final value?
- Have you read the last input value?
- Has a value reached a given threshold?

In our example, we simply want the current month to reach 12.

Step 3   Determine the loop type.

We distinguish between two major loop types. A *count-controlled* loop is executed a definite number of times. In an *event-controlled* loop, the number of iterations is not known in advance—the loop is executed until some event happens.

Count-controlled loops can be implemented as `for` statements. For other loops, consider the loop condition. Do you need to complete one iteration of the loop body before you can tell when to terminate the loop? In that case, choose a `do` loop. Otherwise, use a `while` loop.

Sometimes, the condition for terminating a loop changes in the middle of the loop body. In that case, you can use a Boolean variable that specifies when you are ready to leave the loop. Follow this pattern:

```
boolean done = false;
while (!done)
{
    Do some work.
    If all work has been completed
    {
        done = true;
    }
    else
    {
        Do more work.
    }
}
```

Such a variable is called a **flag**. In summary,

- If you know in advance how many times a loop is repeated, use a `for` loop.
- If the loop body must be executed at least once, use a `do` loop.
- Otherwise, use a `while` loop.

In our example, we read 12 temperature values. Therefore, we choose a `for` loop.

Step 4   Set up variables for entering the loop for the first time.

List all variables that are used and updated in the loop, and determine how to initialize them. Commonly, counters are initialized with 0 or 1, totals with 0.

In our example, the variables are

current month
highest value
highest month

We need to be careful how we set up the highest temperature value. We can't simply set it to 0. After all, our program needs to work with temperature values from Antarctica, all of which may be negative.

A good option is to set the highest temperature value to the first input value. Of course, then we need to remember to read in only 11 more values, with the current month starting at 2.

We also need to initialize the highest month with 1. After all, in an Australian city, we may never find a month that is warmer than January.

Step 5   Process the result after the loop has finished.

In many cases, the desired result is simply a variable that was updated in the loop body. For example, in our temperature program, the result is the highest month. Sometimes, the loop computes values that contribute to the final result. For example, suppose you are asked to average the temperatures. Then the loop should compute the sum, not the average. After the loop has completed, you are ready to compute the average: divide the sum by the number of inputs.

Here is our complete loop.

> *Read value.*
> *highest temperature = value*
> *highest month = 1*
> *For current month from 2 to 12*
>   *Read next value.*
>   *If the value is higher than the highest temperature*
>   *Set highest temperature to the value.*
>   *Set highest month to current month.*

Step 6   Trace the loop with typical examples.

Hand-trace your loop code, as described in Section 6.2. Choose example values that are not too complex—executing the loop 3–5 times is enough to check for the most common errors. Pay special attention when entering the loop for the first and last time.

Sometimes, you want to make a slight modification to make tracing feasible. For example, when hand-tracing the investment doubling problem, use an interest rate of 20 percent rather than 5 percent. When hand-tracing the temperature loop, use 4 data values, not 12.

Let's say the data are 22.6 36.6 44.5 24.2. Here is the walkthrough:

current month	current value	highest month	highest value
		~~1~~	~~22.6~~
~~2~~	36.6	~~2~~	~~36.6~~
~~3~~	44.5	3	44.5
4	24.2		

The trace demonstrates that *highest month* and *highest value* are properly set.

Step 7   Implement the loop in Java.

Here's the loop for our example. Exercise •• E6.4 asks you to complete the program.

```java
double highestValue;
highestValue = in.nextDouble();
int highestMonth = 1;
```

```
for (int currentMonth = 2; currentMonth <= 12; currentMonth++)
{
   double nextValue = in.nextDouble();
   if (nextValue > highestValue)
   {
      highestValue = nextValue;
      highestMonth = currentMonth;
   }
}
System.out.println(highestMonth);
```

WORKED EXAMPLE 6.1
Credit Card Processing

Learn how to use a loop to remove spaces from a credit card number. See your eText or visit wiley.com/go/bjeo7.

© MorePixels/iStockphoto.

6.8 Nested Loops

When the body of a loop contains another loop, the loops are nested. A typical use of nested loops is printing a table with rows and columns.

In Section 5.4, you saw how to nest two `if` statements. Similarly, complex iterations sometimes require a **nested loop**: a loop inside another loop statement. When processing tables, nested loops occur naturally. An outer loop iterates over all rows of the table. An inner loop deals with the columns in the current row.

In this section you will see how to print a table. For simplicity, we will simply print the powers of x, x^n, as in the table at right.

Here is the pseudocode for printing the table:

Print table header.
For x from 1 to 10
  Print table row.
  Print new line.

x^1	x^2	x^3	x^4
1	1	1	1
2	4	8	16
3	9	27	81
...	...	...	...
10	100	1000	10000

How do you print a table row? You need to print a value for each exponent. This requires a second loop.

For n from 1 to 4
  Print x^n.

This loop must be placed inside the preceding loop. We say that the inner loop is *nested* inside the outer loop.

The hour and minute displays in a digital clock are an example of nested loops. The hours loop 12 times, and for each hour, the minutes loop 60 times.

© davejkahn/iStockphoto.

Figure 7
Flowchart of a Nested Loop

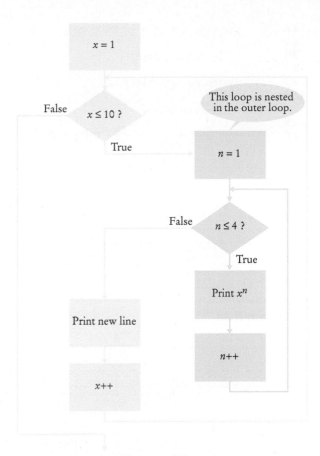

There are 10 rows in the outer loop. For each x, the program prints four columns in the inner loop (see Figure 7). Thus, a total of $10 \times 4 = 40$ values are printed.

Following is the complete program. Note that we also use two loops to print the table header. However, those loops are not nested.

sec08/PowerTable.java

```java
1  /**
2      This program prints a table of powers of x.
3  */
4  public class PowerTable
5  {
6     public static void main(String[] args)
7     {
8        final int NMAX = 4;
9        final double XMAX = 10;
10
11       // Print table header
12
13       for (int n = 1; n <= NMAX; n++)
14       {
15          System.out.printf("%10d", n);
16       }
17       System.out.println();
```

```
18        for (int n = 1; n <= NMAX; n++)
19        {
20           System.out.printf("%10s", "x ");
21        }
22        System.out.println();
23
24        // Print table body
25
26        for (double x = 1; x <= XMAX; x++)
27        {
28           // Print table row
29
30           for (int n = 1; n <= NMAX; n++)
31           {
32              System.out.printf("%10.0f", Math.pow(x, n));
33           }
34           System.out.println();
35        }
36     }
37  }
```

Program Run

```
         1         2         3         4
         x         x         x         x

         1         1         1         1
         2         4         8        16
         3         9        27        81
         4        16        64       256
         5        25       125       625
         6        36       216      1296
         7        49       343      2401
         8        64       512      4096
         9        81       729      6561
        10       100      1000     10000
```

See Table 3 for additional examples of nested loops.

Table 3 Nested Loop Examples

Nested Loops	Output	Explanation

`for (i = 1; i <= 3; i++)`
`{`
`   for (j = 1; j <= 4; j++) { Print "*" }`
`   System.out.println();`
`}`
	****
	****
	****
		Prints 3 rows of 4 asterisks each.

`for (i = 1; i <= 4; i++)`
`{`
`   for (j = 1; j <= 3; j++) { Print "*" }`
`   System.out.println();`
`}`
	***
	***
	***
	***
		Prints 4 rows of 3 asterisks each.

Table 3 Nested Loop Examples

Nested Loops	Output	Explanation
| ```
for (i = 1; i <= 4; i++)
{
    for (j = 1; j <= i; j++) { Print "*" }
    System.out.println();
}
``` | `*`<br>`**`<br>`***`<br>`****` | Prints 4 rows of lengths 1, 2, 3, and 4. |
| ```
for (i = 1; i <= 3; i++)
{
    for (j = 1; j <= 5; j++)
    {
        if (j % 2 == 0) { Print "*" }
        else { Print "-" }
    }
    System.out.println();
}
``` | `-*-*-`<br>`-*-*-`<br>`-*-*-` | Prints asterisks in even columns, dashes in odd columns. |
| ```
for (i = 1; i <= 3; i++)
{
    for (j = 1; j <= 5; j++)
    {
        if (i % 2 == j % 2) { Print "*" }
        else { Print " " }
    }
    System.out.println();
}
``` | `* * *`<br>` * * `<br>`* * *` | Prints a checkerboard pattern. |

WORKED EXAMPLE 6.2

Manipulating the Pixels in an Image

Learn how to use nested loops for manipulating the pixels in an image. The outer loop traverses the rows of the image, and the inner loop accesses each pixel of a row. See your eText or visit wiley.com/go/bjeo7.

Cay Horstmann.

6.9 Application: Random Numbers and Simulations

In a simulation, you use the computer to simulate an activity.

A *simulation program* uses the computer to simulate an activity in the real world (or an imaginary one). Simulations are commonly used for predicting climate change, analyzing traffic, picking stocks, and many other applications in science and business. In many simulations, one or more loops are used to modify the state of a system and observe the changes. You will see examples in the following sections.
```

6.9.1 Generating Random Numbers

Many events in the real world are difficult to predict with absolute precision, yet we can sometimes know the average behavior quite well. For example, a store may know from experience that a customer arrives every five minutes. Of course, that is an average—customers don't arrive in five minute intervals. To accurately model customer traffic, you want to take that random fluctuation into account. Now, how can you run such a simulation in the computer?

You can introduce randomness by calling the random number generator.

The Random class of the Java library implements a *random number generator* that produces numbers that appear to be completely random. To generate random numbers, you construct an object of the Random class, and then apply one of the following methods:

Method	Returns
nextInt(n)	A random integer between the integers 0 (inclusive) and n (exclusive)
nextDouble()	A random floating-point number between 0 (inclusive) and 1 (exclusive)

For example, you can simulate the cast of a die as follows:

```
Random generator = new Random();
int d = 1 + generator.nextInt(6);
```

The call generator.nextInt(6) gives you a random number between 0 and 5 (inclusive). Add 1 to obtain a number between 1 and 6.

To give you a feeling for the random numbers, run the following program a few times.

sec09_01/DieSimulator.java

```
1   /**
2       This program simulates casting a die ten times.
3   */
4   public class DieSimulator
5   {
6       public static void main(String[] args)
7       {
8           Die d = new Die(6);
9           final int TRIES = 10;
10          for (int i = 1; i <= TRIES; i++)
11          {
12              int n = d.cast();
13              System.out.print(n + " ");
14          }
15          System.out.println();
16      }
17  }
```

© ktsimage/iStockphoto.

sec09_01/Die.java

```
1   import java.util.Random;
2
3   /**
4       This class models a die that, when cast, lands on a
5       random face.
6   */
```

```
 7  public class Die
 8  {
 9     private Random generator;
10     private int sides;
11
12     /**
13         Constructs a die with a given number of sides.
14         @param s the number of sides, e.g., 6 for a normal die
15     */
16     public Die(int s)
17     {
18        sides = s;
19        generator = new Random();
20     }
21
22     /**
23         Simulates a throw of the die.
24         @return the face of the die
25     */
26     public int cast()
27     {
28        return 1 + generator.nextInt(sides);
29     }
30  }
```

Typical Program Run

```
6 5 6 3 2 6 3 4 4 1
```

Typical Program Run (Second Run)

```
3 2 2 1 6 5 3 4 1 2
```

As you can see, this program produces a different stream of simulated die casts every time it is run.

Actually, the numbers are not completely random. They are drawn from very long sequences of numbers that don't repeat for a long time. These sequences are computed from fairly simple formulas; they just behave like random numbers. For that reason, they are often called **pseudorandom numbers**. Generating good sequences of numbers that behave like truly random sequences is an important and well-studied problem in computer science. We won't investigate this issue further, though; we'll just use the random numbers produced by the Random class.

6.9.2 The Monte Carlo Method

The Monte Carlo method is an ingenious method for finding approximate solutions to problems that cannot be precisely solved. (The method is named after the famous casino in Monte Carlo.) Here is a typical example. It is difficult to compute the number π, but you can approximate it quite well with the following simulation.

© timstarkey/iStockphoto.

Simulate shooting a dart into a square surrounding a circle of radius 1. That is easy: generate random x- and y-coordinates between -1 and 1.

If the generated point lies inside the circle, we count it as a *hit*. That is the case when $x^2 + y^2 \leq 1$. Because our shots are entirely random, we expect that the ratio of *hits/tries* is approximately equal to the ratio of the areas of the circle and the square, that is, $\pi/4$. Therefore, our estimate for π is $4 \times$ *hits/tries*. This method yields an estimate for π, using nothing but simple arithmetic.

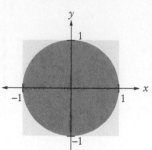

To generate a random floating-point value between -1 and 1, you compute:

```
double r = generator.nextDouble(); // 0 ≤ r < 1
double x = -1 + 2 * r; // -1 ≤ x < 1
```

As r ranges from 0 (inclusive) to 1 (exclusive), x ranges from $-1 + 2 \times 0 = -1$ (inclusive) to $-1 + 2 \times 1 = 1$ (exclusive). In our application, it does not matter that x never reaches 1. The points that fulfill the equation $x = 1$ lie on a line with area 0.

Here is the program that carries out the simulation.

sec09_02/MonteCarlo.java

```
1   import java.util.Random;
2
3   /**
4      This program computes an estimate of pi by simulating
5      dart throws onto a square.
6   */
7   public class MonteCarlo
8   {
9      public static void main(String[] args)
10     {
11        final int TRIES = 10000;
12        Random generator = new Random();
13
14        int hits = 0;
15        for (int i = 1; i <= TRIES; i++)
16        {
17           // Generate two random numbers between -1 and 1
18
19           double r = generator.nextDouble();
20           double x = -1 + 2 * r; // Between -1 and 1
21           r = generator.nextDouble();
22           double y = -1 + 2 * r;
23
24           // Check whether the point lies in the unit circle
25
26           if (x * x + y * y <= 1) { hits++; }
27        }
28
29        /*
30           The ratio hits / tries is approximately the same as the ratio
31           circle area / square area = pi / 4
32        */
33
34        double piEstimate = 4.0 * hits / TRIES;
35        System.out.println("Estimate for pi: " + piEstimate);
```

```
36    }
37 }
```

Program Run

```
Estimate for pi: 3.1504
```

6.10 Using a Debugger

As you have undoubtedly realized by now, computer programs rarely run perfectly the first time. At times, it can be quite frustrating to find the bugs. Of course, you can insert print commands, run the program, and try to analyze the printout. If the printout does not clearly point to the problem, you may need to add and remove print commands and run the program again. That can be a time-consuming process.

> A debugger is a program that you can use to execute another program and analyze its run-time behavior.

Modern development environments contain special programs, called **debuggers**, that help you locate bugs by letting you follow the execution of a program. You can stop and restart your program and see the contents of variables whenever your program is temporarily stopped. At each stop, you have the choice of what variables to inspect and how many program steps to run until the next stop.

Some people feel that debuggers are just a tool to make programmers lazy. Admittedly some people write sloppy programs and then fix them up with a debugger, but the majority of programmers make an honest effort to write the best program they can before trying to run it through a debugger. These programmers realize that a debugger, while more convenient than print commands, is not cost-free. It does take time to set up and carry out an effective debugging session.

In actual practice, you cannot avoid using a debugger. The larger your programs get, the harder it is to debug them simply by inserting print commands. The time invested in learning about a debugger will be amply repaid in your programming career.

Like compilers, debuggers vary widely from one system to another. Some are quite primitive and require you to memorize a small set of arcane commands; others have an intuitive window interface. Figure 8 shows the debugger in the Eclipse development environment, downloadable for free from the Eclipse Foundation (http://eclipse.org). Other development environments, such as BlueJ, Netbeans, and IntelliJ IDEA also include debuggers.

> You can make effective use of a debugger by mastering just three concepts: breakpoints, single-stepping, and inspecting variables.

You will have to find out how to prepare a program for debugging and how to start a debugger on your system. If you use an integrated development environment (with an editor, compiler, and debugger), this step is usually easy. You build the program in the usual way and pick a command to start debugging. On some systems, you must manually build a debug version of your program and invoke the debugger.

Once you have started the debugger, you can go a long way with just three debugging commands: "set breakpoint", "single step", and "inspect variable". The names and keystrokes or mouse clicks for these commands differ widely, but all debuggers support these basic commands. You can find out how, either from the documentation or a lab manual, or by asking someone who has used the debugger before.

When you start the debugger, it runs at full speed until it reaches a **breakpoint**. Then execution stops, and the breakpoint that causes the stop is displayed (Figure 8). You can now inspect variables and step through the program one line at a time, or

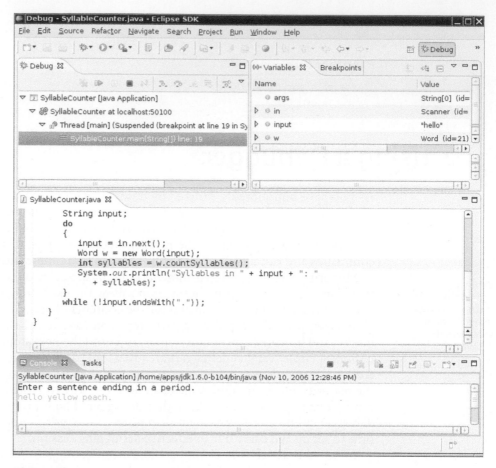

Figure 8   Stopping at a Breakpoint

continue running the program at full speed until it reaches the next breakpoint. When the program terminates, the debugger stops as well.

Breakpoints stay active until you remove them, so you should periodically clear the breakpoints that you no longer need.

Once the program has stopped, you can look at the current values of variables. Again, the method for selecting the variables differs among debuggers. Some debuggers always show you a window with the current local variables. On other debuggers you issue a command such as "inspect variable" and type in or click on the variable. The debugger then displays the contents of the variable. If all variables contain what you expected, you can run the program until the next point where you want to stop.

When inspecting objects, you often need to give a command to "open up" the object, for example by clicking on a tree node. Once the object is opened up, you see its instance variables (see Figure 9).

Running to a breakpoint gets you there speedily, but you don't know how the program got there. You can also step through the program one line at a time. Then you know how the program flows, but it can take a long time to step through it. The *single-step command* executes the current line and stops at the next program line. Most debuggers have two single-step commands, one called *step into*, which steps inside method calls, and one called *step over*, which skips over method calls.

When a debugger executes a program, the execution is suspended whenever a breakpoint is reached.

The single-step command executes the program one line at a time.

Figure 9
Inspecting Variables

For example, suppose the current line is

```
String input = in.next();
Word w = new Word(input);
int syllables = w.countSyllables();
System.out.println("Syllables in " + input + ": " + syllables);
```

When you step over method calls, you get to the next line:

```
String input = in.next();
Word w = new Word(input);
int syllables = w.countSyllables();
System.out.println("Syllables in " + input + ": " + syllables);
```

However, if you step into method calls, you enter the first line of the countSyllables method.

```
public int countSyllables()
{
   int count = 0;
   int end = text.length() - 1;
   . . .
}
```

You should step *into* a method to check whether it carries out its job correctly. You should step *over* a method if you know it works correctly.

Finally, when the program has finished running, the debug session is also finished. To debug the program again, you must restart it in the debugger.

A debugger can be an effective tool for finding and removing bugs in your program. However, it is no substitute for good design and careful programming. If the debugger does not find any errors, it does not mean that your program is bug-free. Testing and debugging can only show the presence of bugs, not their absence.

HOW TO 6.2

Debugging

Knowing all about the mechanics of debugging may still leave you helpless when you fire up a debugger to look at a sick program. This How To presents a number of strategies that you can use to recognize bugs and their causes.

Step 1   Reproduce the error.

As you test your program, you notice that it sometimes does something wrong. It gives the wrong output, it seems to print something random, it goes in an infinite loop, or it crashes. Find out exactly how to reproduce that behavior. What numbers did you enter? Where did you click with the mouse?

Run the program again; type in exactly the same numbers, and click with the mouse on the same spots (or as close as you can get). Does the program exhibit the same behavior? If so, then it makes sense to fire up a debugger to study this particular problem. Debuggers are good for analyzing particular failures. They aren't terribly useful for studying a program in general.

Step 2   Simplify the error.

Before you start up a debugger, it makes sense to spend a few minutes trying to come up with a simpler input that also produces an error. Can you use shorter words or simpler numbers and still have the program misbehave? If so, use those values during your debugging session.

Step 3   Divide and conquer.

Use the divide-and-conquer technique to locate the point of failure of a program.

Now that you have a particular failure, you want to get as close to the failure as possible. The key point of debugging is to locate the code that produces the failure. Just as with real insect pests, finding the bug can be hard, but once you find it, squashing it is usually the easy part. Suppose your program dies with a division by 0. Because there are many division operations in a typical program, it is often not feasible to set breakpoints to all of them. Instead, use a technique of *divide and conquer*. Step over the methods in main, but don't step inside them. Eventually, the failure will happen again. Now you know which method contains the bug: It is the last method that was called from main before the program died. Restart the debugger and go back to that line in main, then step inside that method. Repeat the process.

Eventually, you will have pinpointed the line that contains the bad division. Maybe it is obvious from the code why the denominator is not correct. If not, you need to find the location where it is computed. Unfortunately, you can't go back in the debugger. You need to restart the program and move to the point where the denominator computation happens.

Step 4   Know what your program should do.

During debugging, compare the actual contents of variables against the values you know they should have.

A debugger shows you what the program does. You must know what the program *should* do, or you will not be able to find bugs. Before you trace through a loop, ask yourself how many iterations you expect the program to make. Before you inspect a variable, ask yourself what you expect to see. If you have no clue, set aside some time and think first. Have a calculator handy to make independent computations. When you know what the value should be, inspect the variable. If the value is what you expected, you must look further for the bug. If the value is different, you may be on to something. Double-check your computation. If you are sure your value is correct, find out why your program comes up with a different value.

In many cases, program bugs are the result of simple errors such as loop termination conditions that are off by one. Quite often, however, programs make computational errors. Maybe they are supposed to add two numbers, but by accident the code was written to subtract them. Programs don't make a special effort to ensure that everything is a simple integer (and neither do real-world problems). You will need to make some calculations with large integers or nasty floating-point numbers. Sometimes these calculations can be avoided if you just ask yourself, "Should this quantity be positive? Should it be larger than that value?" Then inspect variables to verify those theories.

Step 5   Look at all details.

When you debug a program, you often have a theory about what the problem is. Nevertheless, keep an open mind and look at all details. What strange messages are displayed? Why does the program take another unexpected action? These details count. When you run a debugging session, you really are a detective who needs to look at every clue available.

If you notice another failure on the way to the problem that you are about to pin down, don't just say, "I'll come back to it later". That very failure may be the original cause for your current problem. It is better to make a note of the current problem, fix what you just found, and then return to the original mission.

Step 6 Make sure you understand each bug before you fix it.

Once you find that a loop makes too many iterations, it is very tempting to apply a "Band-Aid" solution and subtract 1 from a variable so that the particular problem doesn't appear again. Such a quick fix has an overwhelming probability of creating trouble elsewhere. You really need to have a thorough understanding of how the program should be written before you apply a fix.

It does occasionally happen that you find bug after bug and apply fix after fix, and the problem just moves around. That usually is a symptom of a larger problem with the program logic. There is little you can do with the debugger. You must rethink the program design and reorganize it.

WORKED EXAMPLE 6.3

A Sample Debugging Session

Learn how to find bugs in an algorithm for counting the syllables of a word. See your eText or visit wiley.com/go/bjeo7.

© Mark Poprocki/iStockphoto.

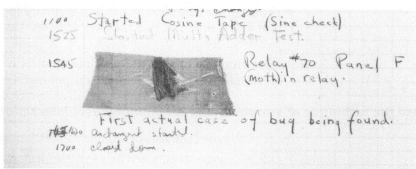

Computing & Society 6.2   **The First Bug**

According to legend, the first bug was found in the Mark II, a huge electromechanical computer at Harvard University. It really was caused by a bug—a moth was trapped in a relay switch.

Actually, from the note that the operator left in the log book next to the moth (see the photo), it appears as if the term "bug" had already been in active use at the time.

The pioneering computer scientist Maurice Wilkes wrote, "Somehow, at the Moore School and afterwards, one had always assumed there would be no particular difficulty in getting programs right. I can remember the exact instant in time at which it dawned on me that a great part of my future life would be spent finding mistakes in my own programs."

The First Bug   Courtesy of the Naval Surface Warfare Center, Dahlgren, VA, 1988. NHHC Collection.

CHAPTER SUMMARY

Explain the flow of execution in a loop.

- A loop executes instructions repeatedly while a condition is true.
- An off-by-one error is a common error when programming loops. Think through simple test cases to avoid this type of error.

Use the technique of hand-tracing to analyze the behavior of a program.

- Hand-tracing is a simulation of code execution in which you step through instructions and track the values of the variables.
- Hand-tracing can help you understand how an unfamiliar algorithm works.
- Hand-tracing can show errors in code or pseudocode.

Use for loops for implementing count-controlled loops.

- The for loop is used when a value runs from a starting point to an ending point with a constant increment or decrement.

Choose between the while loop and the do loop.

- The do loop is appropriate when the loop body must be executed at least once.

Implement loops that read sequences of input data.

- A sentinel value denotes the end of a data set, but it is not part of the data.
- You can use a Boolean variable to control a loop. Set the variable before entering the loop, then set it to the opposite to leave the loop.
- Use input redirection to read input from a file. Use output redirection to capture program output in a file.

Use the technique of storyboarding for planning user interactions.

- A storyboard consists of annotated sketches for each step in an action sequence.
- Developing a storyboard helps you understand the inputs and outputs that are required for a program.

Know the most common loop algorithms.

- To compute an average, keep a total and a count of all values.
- To count values that fulfill a condition, check all values and increment a counter for each match.
- If your goal is to find a match, exit the loop when the match is found.
- To find the largest value, update the largest value seen so far whenever you see a larger one.
- To compare adjacent inputs, store the preceding input in a variable.

Use nested loops to implement multiple levels of iteration.

- When the body of a loop contains another loop, the loops are nested. A typical use of nested loops is printing a table with rows and columns.

Apply loops to the implementation of simulations.

- In a simulation, you use the computer to simulate an activity.
- You can introduce randomness by calling the random number generator.

Use a debugger to analyze your programs.

- A debugger is a program that you can use to execute another program and analyze its run-time behavior.
- You can make effective use of a debugger by mastering just three concepts: breakpoints, single-stepping, and inspecting variables.
- When a debugger executes a program, the execution is suspended whenever a breakpoint is reached.
- The single-step command executes the program one line at a time.
- Use the divide-and-conquer technique to locate the point of failure of a program.
- During debugging, compare the actual contents of variables against the values you know they should have.

STANDARD LIBRARY ITEMS INTRODUCED IN THIS CHAPTER

```
java.util.Random
    nextDouble
    nextInt
```

▪ **R6.1** Given the variables

```
String stars = "*****";
String stripes = "=====";
```

what do these loops print?

a.
```
int i = 0;
while (i < 5)
{
   System.out.println(stars.substring(0, i));
   i++;
}
```

b.
```
int i = 0;
while (i < 5)
{
   System.out.print(stars.substring(0, i));
   System.out.println(stripes.substring(i, 5));
   i++;
}
```

c.
```
int i = 0;
while (i < 10)
{
   if (i % 2 == 0) { System.out.println(stars); }
   else { System.out.println(stripes); }
}
```

d.
```
int i = 0; int j = 9;
while (i < j) { System.out.println(i + stars + j); i++; j--; }
```

e.
```
int i = 0; int j = 9;
while (i < j) { System.out.println(i + stars + j); i++; j++; }
```

▪ **R6.2** What do these code snippets print?

a.
```
int result = 0;
for (int i = 1; i <= 10; i++) { result = result + i; }
System.out.println(result);
```

b.
```
int result = 1;
for (int i = 1; i <= 10; i++) { result = i - result; }
System.out.println(result);
```

c.
```
int result = 1;
for (int i = 5; i > 0; i--) { result = result * i; }
System.out.println(result);
```

d.
```
int result = 1;
for (int i = 1; i <= 10; i = i * 2) { result = result * i; }
System.out.println(result);
```

▪ **R6.3** Write a while loop that prints

a. All squares less than n. For example, if n is 100, print 0 1 4 9 16 25 36 49 64 81.

b. All positive numbers that are divisible by 10 and less than n. For example, if n is 100, print 10 20 30 40 50 60 70 80 90.

c. All powers of two less than n. For example, if n is 100, print 1 2 4 8 16 32 64.

■■ R6.4 Write a loop that computes

    a. The sum of all even numbers between 2 and 100 (inclusive).

    b. The sum of all squares between 1 and 100 (inclusive).

    c. The sum of all odd numbers between a and b (inclusive).

    d. The sum of all odd digits of n. (For example, if n is 32677, the sum would be $3 + 7 + 7 = 17$.)

■ R6.5 Provide trace tables for these loops.

    a. `int i = 0; int j = 10; int n = 0;`
       `while (i < j) { i++; j--; n++; }`

    b. `int i = 0; int j = 0; int n = 0;`
       `while (i < 10) { i++; n = n + i + j; j++; }`

    c. `int i = 10; int j = 0; int n = 0;`
       `while (i > 0) { i--; j++; n = n + i - j; }`

    d. `int i = 0; int j = 10; int n = 0;`
       `while (i != j) { i = i + 2; j = j - 2; n++; }`

■ R6.6 What do these loops print?

    a. `for (int i = 1; i < 10; i++) { System.out.print(i + " "); }`

    b. `for (int i = 1; i < 10; i += 2) { System.out.print(i + " "); }`

    c. `for (int i = 10; i > 1; i--) { System.out.print(i + " "); }`

    d. `for (int i = 0; i < 10; i++) { System.out.print(i + " "); }`

    e. `for (int i = 1; i < 10; i = i * 2) { System.out.print(i + " "); }`

    f. `for (int i = 1; i < 10; i++) { if (i % 2 == 0) { System.out.print(i + " "); } }`

■ R6.7 What is an infinite loop? On your computer, how can you terminate a program that executes an infinite loop?

■ R6.8 Write a program trace for the pseudocode in Exercise • E6.6, assuming the input values are 4 7 –2 –5 0.

■■ R6.9 What is an "off-by-one" error? Give an example from your own programming experience.

■ R6.10 What is a sentinel value? Give a simple rule when it is appropriate to use a numeric sentinel value.

■ R6.11 Which loop statements does Java support? Give simple rules for when to use each loop type.

■ R6.12 How many iterations do the following loops carry out? Assume that i is not changed in the loop body.

    a. `for (int i = 1; i <= 10; i++) . . .`

    b. `for (int i = 0; i < 10; i++) . . .`

    c. `for (int i = 10; i > 0; i--) . . .`

    d. `for (int i = -10; i <= 10; i++) . . .`

    e. `for (int i = 10; i >= 0; i++) . . .`

    f. `for (int i = -10; i <= 10; i = i + 2) . . .`

    g. `for (int i = -10; i <= 10; i = i + 3) . . .`

•• R6.13 Write pseudocode for a program that prints a calendar such as the following.

```
Su  M  T  W Th  F Sa
             1  2  3  4
 5  6  7  8  9 10 11
12 13 14 15 16 17 18
19 20 21 22 23 24 25
26 27 28 29 30 31
```

• R6.14 Write pseudocode for a program that prints a Celsius/Fahrenheit conversion table such as the following.

```
Celsius | Fahrenheit
--------+-----------
      0 |         32
     10 |         50
     20 |         68
    . . .        . . .
    100 |        212
```

• R6.15 Write pseudocode for a program that reads a student record, consisting of the student's first and last name, followed by a sequence of test scores and a sentinel of –1. The program should print the student's average score. Then provide a trace table for this sample input:

```
Harry Morgan 94 71 86 95 -1
```

•• R6.16 Write pseudocode for a program that reads a sequence of student records and prints the total score for each student. Each record has the student's first and last name, followed by a sequence of test scores and a sentinel of –1. The sequence is terminated by the word END. Here is a sample sequence:

```
Harry Morgan 94 71 86 95 -1
Sally Lin 99 98 100 95 90 -1
END
```

Provide a trace table for this sample input.

• R6.17 Rewrite the following for loop into a while loop.

```
int s = 0;
for (int i = 1; i <= 10; i++)
{
    s = s + i;
}
```

• R6.18 Rewrite the following do loop into a while loop.

```
int n = in.nextInt();
double x = 0;
double s;
do
{
    s = 1.0 / (1 + n * n);
    n++;
    x = x + s;
}
while (s > 0.01);
```

- **R6.19** Provide trace tables of the following loops.

  a.
  ```
  int s = 1;
  int n = 1;
  while (s < 10) { s = s + n; }
  n++;
  ```

  b.
  ```
  int s = 1;
  for (int n = 1; n < 5; n++) { s = s + n; }
  ```

  c.
  ```
  int s = 1;
  int n = 1;
  do
  {
     s = s + n;
     n++;
  }
  while (s < 10 * n);
  ```

- **R6.20** What do the following loops print? Work out the answer by tracing the code, not by using the computer.

  a.
  ```
  int s = 1;
  for (int n = 1; n <= 5; n++)
  {
     s = s + n;
     System.out.print(s + " ");
  }
  ```

  b.
  ```
  int s = 1;
  for (int n = 1; s <= 10; System.out.print(s + " "))
  {
     n = n + 2;
     s = s + n;
  }
  ```

  c.
  ```
  int s = 1;
  int n;
  for (n = 1; n <= 5; n++)
  {
     s = s + n;
     n++;
  }
  System.out.print(s + " " + n);
  ```

- **R6.21** What do the following program segments print? Find the answers by tracing the code, not by using the computer.

  a.
  ```
  int n = 1;
  for (int i = 2; i < 5; i++) { n = n + i; }
  System.out.print(n);
  ```

  b.
  ```
  int i;
  double n = 1 / 2;
  for (i = 2; i <= 5; i++) { n = n + 1.0 / i; }
  System.out.print(i);
  ```

  c.
  ```
  double x = 1;
  double y = 1;
  int i = 0;
  do
  {
     y = y / 2;
     x = x + y;
     i++;
  ```

```
    }
    while (x < 1.8);
    System.out.print(i);
 d. double x = 1;
    double y = 1;
    int i = 0;
    while (y >= 1.5)
    {
        x = x / 2;
        y = x + y;
        i++;
    }
    System.out.print(i);
```

■■ **R6.22** Give an example of a for loop where symmetric bounds are more natural. Give an example of a for loop where asymmetric bounds are more natural.

■ **R6.23** Add a storyboard panel for the conversion program in Section 6.6 that shows a scenario where a user enters incompatible units.

■ **R6.24** In Section 6.6, we decided to show users a list of all valid units in the prompt. If the program supports many more units, this approach is unworkable. Give a storyboard panel that illustrates an alternate approach: If the user enters an unknown unit, a list of all known units is shown.

■ **R6.25** Change the storyboards in Section 6.6 to support a menu that asks users whether they want to convert units, see program help, or quit the program. The menu should be displayed at the beginning of the program, when a sequence of values has been converted, and when an error is displayed.

■ **R6.26** Draw a flow chart for a program that carries out unit conversions as described in Section 6.6.

■■ **R6.27** In Section 6.7.5, the code for finding the largest and smallest input initializes the largest and smallest variables with an input value. Why can't you initialize them with zero?

■ **R6.28** What are nested loops? Give an example where a nested loop is typically used.

■■ **R6.29** The nested loops

```
for (int i = 1; i <= height; i++)
{
    for (int j = 1; j <= width; j++) { System.out.print("*"); }
    System.out.println();
}
```

display a rectangle of a given width and height, such as

```
****
****
****
```

Write a *single* for loop that displays the same rectangle.

■■ **R6.30** Suppose you design an educational game to teach children how to read a clock. How do you generate random values for the hours and minutes?

■■■ **R6.31** In a travel simulation, Harry will visit one of his friends that are located in three states. He has ten friends in California, three in Nevada, and two in Utah. How do you produce a random number between 1 and 3, denoting the destination state, with a probability that is proportional to the number of friends in each state?

■ **Testing R6.32** Explain the differences between these debugger operations:
- Stepping into a method
- Stepping over a method

■■ **Testing R6.33** Explain in detail how to inspect the string stored in a `String` object in your debugger.

■■ **Testing R6.34** Explain in detail how to inspect the information stored in a `Rectangle` object in your debugger.

■■ **Testing R6.35** Explain in detail how to use your debugger to inspect the balance stored in a `BankAccount` object.

■■ **Testing R6.36** Explain the divide-and-conquer strategy to get close to a bug in a debugger.

PRACTICE EXERCISES

■ **E6.1** Write programs with loops that compute
- **a.** The sum of all even numbers between 2 and 100 (inclusive).
- **b.** The sum of all squares between 1 and 100 (inclusive).
- **c.** All powers of 2 from 2^0 up to 2^{20}.
- **d.** The sum of all odd numbers between a and b (inclusive), where a and b are inputs.
- **e.** The sum of all odd digits of an input. (For example, if the input is 32677, the sum would be $3 + 7 + 7 = 17$.)

■■ **E6.2** Write programs that read a sequence of integer inputs and print
- **a.** The smallest and largest of the inputs.
- **b.** The number of even and odd inputs.
- **c.** Cumulative totals. For example, if the input is 1 7 2 9, the program should print 1 8 10 19.
- **d.** All adjacent duplicates. For example, if the input is 1 3 3 4 5 5 6 6 6 2, the program should print 3 5 6.

■■ **E6.3** Write programs that read a line of input as a string and print
- **a.** Only the uppercase letters in the string.
- **b.** Every second letter of the string.
- **c.** The string, with all vowels replaced by an underscore.
- **d.** The number of vowels in the string.
- **e.** The positions of all vowels in the string.

■■ **E6.4** Complete the program in How To 6.1. Your program should read twelve temperature values and print the month with the highest temperature.

■■ **E6.5** Write a program that reads a set of floating-point values. Ask the user to enter the values (prompting only a single time for the values), then print

- the average of the values.
- the smallest of the values.
- the largest of the values.
- the range, that is the difference between the smallest and largest.

Your program should use a class DataSet. That class should have a method

```
public void add(double value)
```

and methods getAverage, getSmallest, getLargest, and getRange.

■ **E6.6** Translate the following pseudocode for finding the minimum value from a set of inputs into a Java program.

> *Set a Boolean variable "first" to true.*
> *If the scanner has more numbers*
>   *Read the next value.*
>   *If first is true*
>   *Set the minimum to the value.*
>   *Set first to false.*
>   *Else if the value is less than the minimum*
>   *Set the minimum to the value.*
> *Print the minimum.*

■■■ **E6.7** Translate the following pseudocode for randomly permuting the characters in a string into a Java program.

> *Read a word.*
> *Repeat word.length() times*
>   *Pick a random position i in the word, but not the last position.*
>   *Pick a random position j > i in the word.*
>   *Swap the letters at positions j and i.*
> *Print the word.*

© Anthony Rosenberg/iStockphoto.

To swap the letters, construct substrings as follows:

first   i   middle   j   last

Then replace the string with

```
first + word.charAt(j) + middle + word.charAt(i) + last
```

■ **E6.8** Write a program that reads a word and prints each character of the word on a separate line. For example, if the user provides the input "Harry", the program prints

```
H
a
r
r
y
```

■■ **E6.9** Write a program that reads a word and prints the word in reverse. For example, if the user provides the input "Harry", the program prints

```
yrraH
```

E6.10 Write a program that reads a word and prints the number of vowels in the word. For this exercise, assume that a e i o u y are vowels. For example, if the user provides the input "Harry", the program prints 2 vowels.

E6.11 Write a program that reads a word and prints all substrings, sorted by length. For example, if the user provides the input "rum", the program prints

```
r
u
m
ru
um
rum
```

E6.12 Write a program that prints all powers of 2 from 2^0 up to 2^{20}.

E6.13 Write a program that reads a number and prints all of its *binary digits:* Print the remainder number % 2, then replace the number with number / 2. Keep going until the number is 0. For example, if the user provides the input 13, the output should be

```
1
0
1
1
```

E6.14 Using the Picture class from Worked Example 6.2, apply a sunset effect to a picture, increasing the red value of each pixel by 30 percent (up to a maximum of 255).

E6.15 Using the Picture class from Worked Example 6.2, apply a "telescope" effect, turning all pixels black that are outside a circle. The center of the circle should be the image center, and the radius should be 40 percent of the width or height, whichever is smaller.

© Cay Horstmann

E6.16 Write a program that prints a multiplication table, like this:

```
 1  2  3  4  5  6  7  8  9 10
 2  4  6  8 10 12 14 16 18 20
 3  6  9 12 15 18 21 24 27 30
   . . .
10 20 30 40 50 60 70 80 90 100
```

E6.17 Write a program that reads an integer and displays, using asterisks, a filled and hollow square, placed next to each other. For example, if the side length is 5, the program should display

```
***** *****
***** *   *
***** *   *
***** *   *
***** *****
```

■ ■ **E6.18** Write a program that reads an integer and displays, using asterisks, a filled diamond of the given side length. For example, if the side length is 4, the program should display

```
   *
  ***
 *****
*******
 *****
  ***
   *
```

■ ■ ■ **E6.19** Print a diamond shape, as in the preceding exercise, with the asterisks in the middle row and column omitted, like this:

```
  *   *
 **   **
***   ***

***   ***
 **   **
  *   *
```

Your program should read the side length of each part (3 in the example above).

■ ■ **E6.20** Print an X shape in a box of a given side length, like this:

```
********
**    **
* *  * *
*  **  *
*  **  *
* *  * *
**    **
********
```

■ ■ **Business E6.21** *Currency conversion.* Write a program that first asks the user to type today's price for one dollar in Japanese yen, then reads U.S. dollar values and converts each to yen. Use 0 as a sentinel.

© hatman12/iStockphoto.

■ ■ **Business E6.22** Write a program that first asks the user to type in today's price of one dollar in Japanese yen, then reads U.S. dollar values and converts each to Japanese yen. Use 0 as the sentinel value to denote the end of dollar inputs. Then the program reads a sequence of yen amounts and converts them to dollars. The second sequence is terminated by another zero value.

■ ■ **E6.23** *The Monty Hall Paradox.* Marilyn vos Savant described the following problem (loosely based on a game show hosted by Monty Hall) in a popular magazine: "Suppose you're on a game show, and you're given the choice of three doors: Behind one door is a car; behind the others, goats. You pick a door, say No. 1, and the host, who knows what's behind the doors, opens another door, say No. 3, which has a goat. He then says to you, "Do you want to pick door No. 2?" Is it to your advantage to switch your choice?"

Ms. vos Savant proved that it is to your advantage, but many of her readers, including some mathematics professors, disagreed, arguing that the probability would not change because another door was opened.

Your task is to simulate this game show. In each iteration, randomly pick a door number between 1 and 3 for placing the car. Randomly have the player pick a door. Randomly have the game show host pick a door having a goat (but not the door that the player picked). Increment a counter for strategy 1 if the player wins by switching to the third door, and increment a counter for strategy 2 if the player wins by sticking with the original choice. Run 1,000 iterations and print both counters.

PROGRAMMING PROJECTS

■■ **P6.1** Enhance Worked Example 6.1 to check that the credit card number is valid. A valid credit card number will yield a result divisible by 10 when you:

Form the sum of all digits. Add to that sum every second digit, starting with the second digit from the right. Then add the number of digits in the second step that are greater than four. The result should be divisible by 10.

For example, consider the number 4012 8888 8888 1881. The sum of all digits is 89. The sum of the colored digits is 46. There are five colored digits larger than four, so the result is 140. 140 is divisible by 10 so the card number is valid.

■■ **P6.2** The *Fibonacci numbers* are defined by the sequence

$$f_1 = 1$$
$$f_2 = 1$$
$$f_n = f_{n-1} + f_{n-2}$$

Reformulate that as

© GlobalP/iStockphoto.

```
fold1 = 1;
fold2 = 1;
fnew = fold1 + fold2;
```

Fibonacci numbers describe the growth of a rabbit population.

After that, discard `fold2`, which is no longer needed, and set `fold2` to `fold1` and `fold1` to `fnew`. Repeat an appropriate number of times.

Implement a program that prompts the user for an integer *n* and prints the *n*th Fibonacci number, using the above algorithm.

■■■ **P6.3** *Factoring of integers.* Write a program that asks the user for an integer and then prints out all its factors. For example, when the user enters 150, the program should print

```
2
3
5
5
```

Use a class `FactorGenerator` with a constructor `FactorGenerator(int numberToFactor)` and methods `nextFactor` and `hasMoreFactors`. Supply a class `FactorPrinter` whose `main` method reads a user input, constructs a `FactorGenerator` object, and prints the factors.

■■■ P6.4 *Prime numbers.* Write a program that prompts the user for an integer and then prints out all prime numbers up to that integer. For example, when the user enters 20, the program should print

```
2
3
5
7
11
13
17
19
```

Recall that a number is a prime number if it is not divisible by any number except 1 and itself.

Use a class PrimeGenerator with methods nextPrime and isPrime. Supply a class Prime-Printer whose main method reads a user input, constructs a PrimeGenerator object, and prints the primes.

■■■ P6.5 *The game of Nim.* This is a well-known game with a number of variants. The following variant has an interesting winning strategy. Two players alternately take marbles from a pile. In each move, a player chooses how many marbles to take. The player must take at least one but at most half of the marbles. Then the other player takes a turn. The player who takes the last marble loses.

Write a program in which the computer plays against a human opponent. Generate a random integer between 10 and 100 to denote the initial size of the pile. Generate a random integer between 0 and 1 to decide whether the computer or the human takes the first turn. Generate a random integer between 0 and 1 to decide whether the computer plays *smart* or *stupid*. In stupid mode the computer simply takes a random legal value (between 1 and $n/2$) from the pile whenever it has a turn. In smart mode the computer takes off enough marbles to make the size of the pile a power of two minus 1—that is, 3, 7, 15, 31, or 63. That is always a legal move, except when the size of the pile is currently one less than a power of two. In that case, the computer makes a random legal move.

You will note that the computer cannot be beaten in smart mode when it has the first move, unless the pile size happens to be 15, 31, or 63. Of course, a human player who has the first turn and knows the winning strategy can win against the computer.

■■ P6.6 *The Drunkard's Walk.* A drunkard in a grid of streets randomly picks one of four directions and stumbles to the next intersection, then again randomly picks one of four directions, and so on. You might think that on average the drunkard doesn't move very far because the choices cancel each other out, but that is not the case.

Represent locations as integer pairs (x, y). Implement the drunkard's walk over 100 intersections, starting at $(0, 0)$, and print the ending location.

■ P6.7 A simple random generator is obtained by the formula

$$r_{\text{new}} = (a \cdot r_{\text{old}} + b) \% m$$

and then setting r_{old} to r_{new}. If m is chosen as 2^{32}, then you can compute

$$r_{\text{new}} = a \cdot r_{\text{old}} + b$$

because the truncation of an overflowing result to the int type is equivalent to computing the remainder.

Write a program that asks the user to enter a value for r_{old}. (Such a value is often called a *seed*). Then print the first 100 random integers generated by this formula, using $a = 32310901$ and $b = 1729$.

P6.8   *The Buffon Needle Experiment.* The following experiment was devised by Comte Georges-Louis Leclerc de Buffon (1707–1788), a French naturalist. A needle of length 1 inch is dropped onto paper that is ruled with lines 2 inches apart. If the needle drops onto a line, we count it as a *hit*. (See Figure 13.) Buffon discovered that the quotient *tries/hits* approximates π.

For the Buffon needle experiment, you must generate two random numbers: one to describe the starting position and one to describe the angle of the needle with the x-axis. Then you need to test whether the needle touches a grid line.

Generate the *lower* point of the needle. Its x-coordinate is irrelevant, and you may assume its y-coordinate y_{low} to be any random number between 0 and 2. The angle α between the needle and the x-axis can be any value between 0 degrees and 180 degrees (π radians). The upper end of the needle has y-coordinate

$$y_{high} = y_{low} + \sin \alpha$$

The needle is a hit if y_{high} is at least 2, as shown in Figure 14. Stop after 10,000 tries and print the quotient *tries/hits*. (This program is not suitable for computing the value of π. You need π in the computation of the angle.)

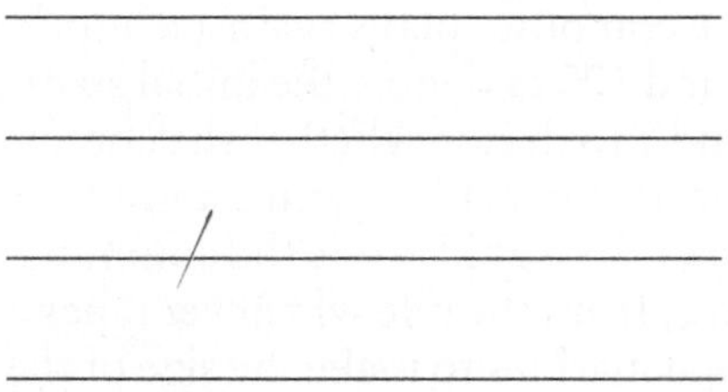

Figure 13
The Buffon Needle Experiment

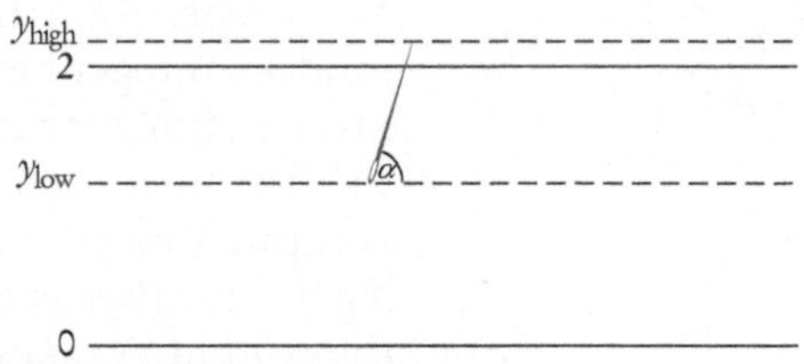

Figure 14
A Hit in the Buffon Needle Experiment

P6.9   In the 17th century, the discipline of probability theory got its start when a gambler asked a mathematician friend to explain some observations about dice games. Why did he, on average, win a bet that at least one six would appear when rolling a die four times? And why did he seem to lose a similar bet, getting at least one double-six when rolling a pair of dice 24 times?

Nowadays, it seems astounding that any person would roll a pair of dice 24 times in a row, and then repeat that many times over. Let's do that experiment on a computer instead. Simulate each game a million times and print out the wins and losses, assuming each bet was for $1.

P6.10   *Mean and standard deviation.* Write a program that reads a set of floating-point data values. Choose an appropriate mechanism for prompting for the end of the data set.

When all values have been read, print out the count of the values, the average, and the standard deviation. The average of a data set $\{x_1, \ldots, x_n\}$ is $\bar{x} = \sum x_i / n$, where $\sum x_i = x_1 + \cdots + x_n$ is the sum of the input values. The standard deviation is

$$s = \sqrt{\frac{\sum (x_i - \bar{x})^2}{n - 1}}$$

However, this formula is not suitable for the task. By the time the program has computed $\bar{x}$, the individual x_i are long gone. Until you know how to save these values, use the numerically less stable formula

$$s = \sqrt{\frac{\sum x_i^2 - \frac{1}{n}\left(\sum x_i\right)^2}{n-1}}$$

You can compute this quantity by keeping track of the count, the sum, and the sum of squares as you process the input values.

Your program should use a class DataSet. That class should have a method

```
public void add(double value)
```

and methods getAverage and getStandardDeviation.

••• P6.11 A bicycle combination lock has four rings with numbers 0 through 9. Given the actual numbers and the combination to unlock, print instructions to unlock the lock using the minimum number of twists. A "twist up" increases the number value of a ring, and a "twist down" decreases it. For example, if the actual number shown is 1729 and the desired combination is 5714, write your instructions like this:

```
Ring 1: Twist up 4 times
Ring 3: Twist down once
Ring 4: Twist up or down 5 times
```

•• Business P6.12 Your company has shares of stock it would like to sell when their value exceeds a certain target price. Write a program that reads the target price and then reads the current stock price until it is at least the target price. Your program should use a Scanner to read a sequence of double values from standard input. Once the minimum is reached, the program should report that the stock price exceeds the target price.

•• Business P6.13 Write an application to pre-sell a limited number of cinema tickets. Each buyer can buy as many as 4 tickets. No more than 100 tickets can be sold. Implement a program called TicketSeller that prompts the user for the desired number of tickets and then displays the number of remaining tickets. Repeat until all tickets have been sold, and then display the total number of buyers.

•• Business P6.14 You need to control the number of people who can be in an oyster bar at the same time. Groups of people can always leave the bar, but a group cannot enter the bar if they would make the number of people in the bar exceed the maximum of 100 occupants. Write a program that reads the sizes of the groups that arrive or depart. Use negative numbers for departures. After each input, display the current number of occupants. As soon as the bar holds the maximum number of people, report that the bar is full and exit the program.

•• Science P6.15 In a predator-prey simulation, you compute the populations of predators and prey, using the following equations:

$$prey_{n+1} = prey_n \times (1 + A - B \times pred_n)$$
$$pred_{n+1} = pred_n \times (1 - C + D \times prey_n)$$

Here, A is the rate at which prey birth exceeds natural death, B is the rate of predation, C is the rate at which predator deaths exceed births without food, and D represents predator increase in the presence of food.

© Charles Gibson/iStockphoto.

Write a program that prompts users for these rates, the initial population sizes, and the number of periods. Then print the populations for the given number of periods. As inputs, try $A = 0.1$, $B = C = 0.01$, and $D = 0.00002$ with initial prey and predator populations of 1,000 and 20.

■ ■ **Science P6.16** *Projectile flight.* Suppose a cannonball is propelled straight into the air with a starting velocity v_0. Any calculus book will state that the position of the ball after t seconds is $s(t) = -1/2gt^2 + v_0t$, where $g = 9.81$ m/s^2 is the gravitational force of the earth. No calculus textbook ever states why someone would want to carry out such an obviously dangerous experiment, so we will do it in the safety of the computer.

© MOF/iStockphoto.

In fact, we will confirm the theorem from calculus by a simulation. In our simulation, we will consider how the ball moves in very short time intervals Δt. In a short time interval the velocity v is nearly constant, and we can compute the distance the ball moves as $\Delta s = v\Delta t$. In our program, we will simply set

```
final double DELTA_T = 0.01;
```

and update the position by

```
s = s + v * DELTA_T;
```

The velocity changes constantly—in fact, it is reduced by the gravitational force of the earth. In a short time interval, $\Delta v = -g\Delta t$, we must keep the velocity updated as

```
v = v - g * DELTA_T;
```

In the next iteration the new velocity is used to update the distance.

Now run the simulation until the cannonball falls back to the earth. Get the initial velocity as an input (100 m/s is a good value). Update the position and velocity 100 times per second, but print out the position only every full second. Also printout the values from the exact formula $s(t) = -1/2gt^2 + v_0t$ for comparison.

Note: You may wonder whether there is a benefit to this simulation when an exact formula is available. Well, the formula from the calculus book is *not* exact. Actually, the gravitational force diminishes the farther the cannonball is away from the surface of the earth. This complicates the algebra sufficiently that it is not possible to give an exact formula for the actual motion, but the computer simulation can simply be extended to apply a variable gravitational force. For cannonballs, the calculus-book formula is actually good enough, but computers are necessary to compute accurate trajectories for higher-flying objects such as ballistic missiles.

■ ■ ■ **Science P6.17** A simple model for the hull of a ship is given by

$$|y| = \frac{B}{2}\left[1 - \left(\frac{2x}{L}\right)^2\right]\left[1 - \left(\frac{z}{T}\right)^2\right]$$

where B is the beam, L is the length, and T is the draft.

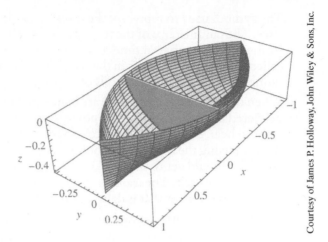

(*Note:* There are two values of y for each x and z because the hull is symmetric from starboard to port.)

The cross-sectional area at a point x is called the "section" in nautical parlance. To compute it, let z go from 0 to $-T$ in n increments, each of size T/n. For each value of z, compute the value for y. Then sum the areas of trapezoidal strips. At right are the strips where $n = 4$.

Write a program that reads in values for B, L, T, x, and n and then prints out the cross-sectional area at x.

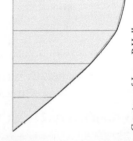

■ **Science P6.18** Radioactive decay of radioactive materials can be modeled by the equation $A = A_0 e^{-t(\log 2/h)}$, where A is the amount of the material at time t, A_0 is the amount at time 0, and h is the half-life.

Technetium-99 is a radioisotope that is used in imaging of the brain. It has a half-life of 6 hours. Your program should display the relative amount A/A_0 in a patient body every hour for 24 hours after receiving a dose.

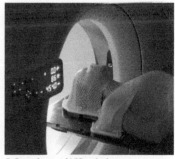

■■■ **Science P6.19** The photo at left shows an electric device called a "transformer". Transformers are often constructed by wrapping coils of wire around a ferrite core. The figure below illustrates a situation that occurs in various audio devices such as cell phones and music players. In this circuit, a transformer is used to connect a speaker to the output of an audio amplifier.

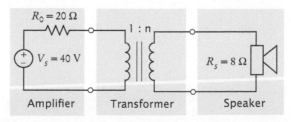

The symbol used to represent the transformer is intended to suggest two coils of wire. The parameter n of the transformer is called the "turns ratio" of the transformer. (The number of times that a wire is wrapped around the core to form a coil is called the number of turns in the coil. The turns ratio is literally the ratio of the number of turns in the two coils of wire.)

When designing the circuit, we are concerned primarily with the value of the power delivered to the speakers—that power causes the speakers to produce the sounds we want to hear. Suppose we were to connect the speakers directly to the amplifier without using the transformer. Some fraction of the power available from the amplifier would get to the speakers. The rest of the available power would be lost in the amplifier itself. The transformer is added to the circuit to increase the fraction of the amplifier power that is delivered to the speakers.

The power, P_s, delivered to the speakers is calculated using the formula

$$P_s = R_s \left(\frac{n V_s}{n^2 R_0 + R_s} \right)^2$$

Write a program that models the circuit shown and varies the turns ratio from 0.01 to 2 in 0.01 increments, then determines the value of the turns ratio that maximizes the power delivered to the speakers.

- **Graphics P6.20** Write a graphical application that displays a checkerboard with 64 squares, alternating white and black.

- - **Graphics P6.21** Write a graphical application that draws a spiral, such as the following:

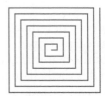

- - **Graphics P6.22** It is easy and fun to draw graphs of curves with the Java graphics library. Simply draw 100 line segments joining the points $(x, f(x))$ and $(x + d, f(x + d))$, where x ranges from x_{min} to x_{max} and $d = (x_{max} - x_{min}) / 100$.

  Draw the curve $f(x) = 0.00005x^3 - 0.03x^2 + 4x + 200$, where x ranges from 0 to 400 in this fashion.

- - **Graphics P6.23** Draw a picture of the "four-leaved rose" whose equation in polar coordinates is $r = \cos(2\theta)$. Let θ go from 0 to 2π in 100 steps. Each time, compute r and then compute the (x, y) coordinates from the polar coordinates by using the formula

$$x = r \cdot \cos(\theta), y = r \cdot \sin(\theta)$$

© traveler1116/iStockphoto.

CHAPTER 7

ARRAYS AND ARRAY LISTS

CHAPTER GOALS

To collect elements using arrays and array lists

To use the enhanced for loop for traversing arrays and array lists

To learn common algorithms for processing arrays and array lists

To work with two-dimensional arrays

To understand the concept of regression testing

CHAPTER CONTENTS

In many programs, you need to collect large numbers of values. In Java, you use the array and array list constructs for this purpose. Arrays have a more concise syntax, whereas array lists can automatically grow to any desired size. In this chapter, you will learn about arrays, array lists, and common algorithms for processing them.

7.1 Arrays

We start this chapter by introducing the array data type. Arrays are the fundamental mechanism in Java for collecting multiple values. In the following sections, you will learn how to declare arrays and how to access array elements.

7.1.1 Declaring and Using Arrays

Suppose you write a program that reads a sequence of values and prints out the sequence, marking the largest value, like this:

```
32
54
67.5
29
35
80
115 <= largest value
44.5
100
65
```

You do not know which value to mark as the largest one until you have seen them all. After all, the last value might be the largest one. Therefore, the program must first store all values before it can print them.

Could you simply store each value in a separate variable? If you know that there are ten values, then you could store the values in ten variables value1, value2, value3, ..., value10. However, such a sequence of variables is not very practical to use. You would have to write quite a bit of code ten times, once for each of the variables. In Java, an **array** is a much better choice for storing a sequence of values of the same type.

Here we create an array that can hold ten values of type double:

```
new double[10]
```

The number of elements (here, 10) is called the *length* of the array.

The new operator constructs the array. You will want to store the array in a variable so that you can access it later.

The type of an array variable is the type of the element to be stored, followed by []. In this example, the type is double[], because the element type is double.

Here is the declaration of an array variable of type double[] (see Figure 1):

```
double[] values; ❶
```

When you declare an array variable, it is not yet initialized. You need to initialize the variable with the array:

```
double[] values = new double[10]; ❷
```

> An array collects a sequence of values of the same type.

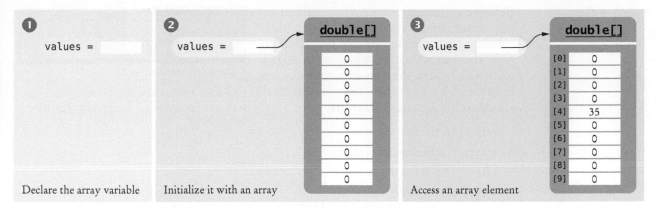

Figure 1 An Array of Size 10

Now values is initialized with an array of 10 numbers. By default, each number in the array is 0.

When you declare an array, you can specify the initial values. For example,

```
double[] moreValues = { 32, 54, 67.5, 29, 35, 80, 115, 44.5, 100, 65 };
```

When you supply initial values, you don't use the new operator. The compiler determines the length of the array by counting the initial values.

Individual elements in an array are accessed by an integer index i, using the notation *array*[i].

To access a value in an array, you specify which "slot" you want to use. That is done with the [] operator:

```
values[4] = 35; ❸
```

Now the number 4 slot of values is filled with 35 (see Figure 1). This "slot number" is called an *index*. Each slot in an array contains an *element*.

An array element can be used like any variable.

Because values is an array of double values, each element values[i] can be used like any variable of type double. For example, you can display the element with index 4 with the following command:

```
System.out.println(values[4]);
```

Syntax 7.1 Arrays

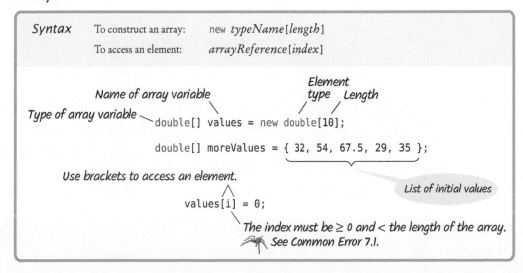

Syntax   To construct an array: new *typeName*[*length*]

To access an element: *arrayReference*[*index*]

Name of array variable

Element type   Length

Type of array variable

```
double[] values = new double[10];
```

```
double[] moreValues = { 32, 54, 67.5, 29, 35 };
```

List of initial values

Use brackets to access an element.

```
values[i] = 0;
```

The index must be ≥ 0 and < the length of the array.
See Common Error 7.1.

Before continuing, we must take care of an important detail of Java arrays. If you look carefully at Figure 1, you will find that the *fifth* element was filled when we changed `values[4]`. In Java, the elements of arrays are numbered *starting at 0*. That is, the legal elements for the `values` array are

© Luckie8/iStockphoto.

Like a post office box that is identified by a box number, an array element is identified by an index.

`values[0]`, the first element

`values[1]`, the second element

`values[2]`, the third element

`values[3]`, the fourth element

`values[4]`, the fifth element

. . .

`values[9]`, the tenth element

In other words, the declaration

```
double[] values = new double[10];
```

creates an array with ten elements. In this array, an index can be any integer ranging from 0 to 9.

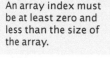

An array index must be at least zero and less than the size of the array.

You have to be careful that the index stays within the valid range. Trying to access an element that does not exist in the array is a serious error. For example, if `values` has ten elements, you are not allowed to access `values[20]`. Attempting to access an element whose index is not within the valid index range is called a **bounds error**. The compiler does not catch this type of error. When a bounds error occurs at run time, it causes a run-time exception.

Here is a very common bounds error:

A bounds error, which occurs if you supply an invalid array index, can cause your program to terminate.

```
double[] values = new double[10];
values[10] = value;
```

There is no `values[10]` in an array with ten elements—the index can range from 0 to 9.

To avoid bounds errors, you will want to know how many elements are in an array. The expression `values.length` yields the length of the `values` array. Note that there are no parentheses following `length`.

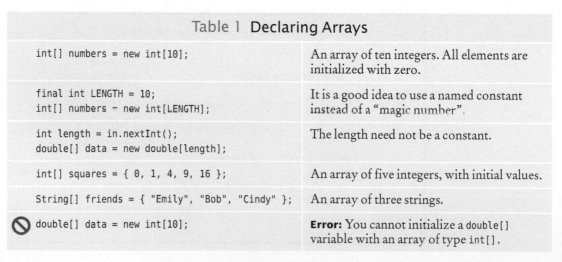

Table 1 Declaring Arrays

`int[] numbers = new int[10];`	An array of ten integers. All elements are initialized with zero.
`final int LENGTH = 10;` `int[] numbers - new int[LENGTH];`	It is a good idea to use a named constant instead of a "magic number".
`int length = in.nextInt();` `double[] data = new double[length];`	The length need not be a constant.
`int[] squares = { 0, 1, 4, 9, 16 };`	An array of five integers, with initial values.
`String[] friends = { "Emily", "Bob", "Cindy" };`	An array of three strings.
🚫 `double[] data = new int[10];`	**Error:** You cannot initialize a `double[]` variable with an array of type `int[]`.

Use the expression *array*.length to find the number of elements in an array.

The following code ensures that you only access the array when the index variable i is within the legal bounds:

```
if (0 <= i && i < values.length) { values[i] = value; }
```

Arrays suffer from a significant limitation: *their length is fixed*. If you start out with an array of 10 elements and later decide that you need to add additional elements, then you need to make a new array and copy all elements of the existing array into the new array. We will discuss this process in detail in Section 7.3.9.

To visit all elements of an array, use a variable for the index. Suppose values has ten elements and the integer variable i is set to 0, 1, 2, and so on, up to 9. Then the expression values[i] yields each element in turn. For example, this loop displays all elements in the values array:

```
for (int i = 0; i < 10; i++)
{
    System.out.println(values[i]);
}
```

Note that in the loop condition the index is *less than* 10 because there is no element corresponding to values[10].

7.1.2 Array References

An array reference specifies the location of an array. Copying the reference yields a second reference to the same array.

If you look closely at Figure 1, you will note that the variable values does not store any numbers. Instead, the array is stored elsewhere and the values variable holds a **reference** to the array. (The reference denotes the location of the array in memory.) You have already seen this behavior with objects in Section 2.8. When you access an object or array, you need not be concerned about the fact that Java uses references. This only becomes important when you copy a reference.

When you copy an array variable into another, both variables refer to the same array (see Figure 2).

```
int[] scores = { 10, 9, 7, 4, 5 };
int[] values = scores; // Copying array reference
```

You can modify the array through either of the variables:

```
scores[3] = 10;
System.out.println(values[3]); // Prints 10
```

Section 7.3.9 shows how you can make a copy of the *contents* of the array.

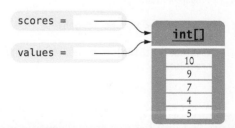

Figure 2
Two Array Variables Referencing the Same Array

7.1.3 Using Arrays with Methods

Arrays can be method arguments and return values, just like any other values.

When you define a method with an array argument, you provide a parameter variable for the array. For example, the following method adds scores to a Student object:

```java
public void addScores(int[] values)
{
   for (int i = 0; i < values.length; i++)
   {
      totalScore = totalScore + values[i];
   }
}
```

To call this method, you have to provide an array:

```java
int[] scores = { 10, 9, 7, 10 };
fred.addScores(scores);
```

Conversely, a method can return an array. For example, a Student class can have a method

```java
public int[] getScores()
```

that returns an array with all of the student's scores.

7.1.4 Partially Filled Arrays

With a partially filled array, you need to remember how many elements are filled.

An array cannot change size at run time. This is a problem when you don't know in advance how many elements you need. In that situation, you must come up with a good guess on the maximum number of elements that you need to store. For example, we may decide that we sometimes want to store more than ten elements, but never more than 100:

```java
final int LENGTH = 100;
double[] values = new double[LENGTH];
```

In a typical program run, only a part of the array will be occupied by actual elements. We call such an array a **partially filled array**. You must keep a *companion variable* that counts how many elements are actually used. In Figure 3 we call the companion variable currentSize.

The following loop collects inputs and fills up the values array:

```java
int currentSize = 0;
Scanner in = new Scanner(System.in);
while (in.hasNextDouble())
{
   if (currentSize < values.length)
   {
      values[currentSize] = in.nextDouble();
      currentSize++;
   }
}
```

At the end of this loop, currentSize contains the actual number of elements in the array. Note that you have to stop accepting inputs if the currentSize companion variable reaches the array length.

Figure 3
A Partially Filled Array

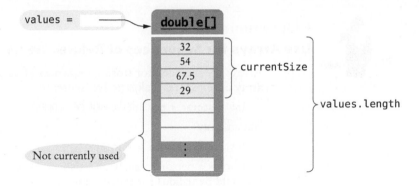

To process the gathered array elements, you again use the companion variable, not the array length. This loop prints the partially filled array:

```java
for (int i = 0; i < currentSize; i++)
{
    System.out.println(values[i]);
}
```

EXAMPLE CODE   See sec01 of your eText or companion code for a program that demonstrates array operations.

Common Error 7.1

Bounds Errors

Perhaps the most common error in using arrays is accessing a nonexistent element.

```java
double[] values = new double[10];
values[10] = 5.4;
    // Error—values has 10 elements, and the index can range from 0 to 9
```

If your program accesses an array through an out-of-bounds index, there is no compiler error message. Instead, the program will generate an exception at run time.

Common Error 7.2

Uninitialized and Unfilled Arrays

A common error is to allocate an array variable, but not an actual array.

```java
double[] values;
values[0] = 29.95; // Error—values not initialized
```

Array variables work exactly like object variables—they are only references to the actual array. To construct the actual array, you must use the new operator:

```java
double[] values = new double[10];
```

Another common error is to allocate an array of objects and expect it to be filled with objects.

```java
BankAccount[] accounts = new BankAccount[10]; // Contains ten null references
```

This array contains null references, not default bank accounts. You need to remember to fill the array, for example:

```java
for (int i = 0; i < 10; i++)
{
    accounts[i] = new BankAccount();
}
```

Programming Tip 7.1
Use Arrays for Sequences of Related Items

Arrays are intended for storing sequences of values with the same meaning. For example, an array of test scores makes perfect sense:

```
int[] scores = new int[NUMBER_OF_SCORES];
```

But an array

```
int[] personalData = new int[3];
```

that holds a person's age, bank balance, and shoe size in positions 0, 1, and 2 is bad design. It would be tedious for the programmer to remember which of these data values is stored in which array location. In this situation, it is far better to use three separate variables.

Programming Tip 7.2
Make Parallel Arrays into Arrays of Objects

Programmers who are familiar with arrays, but unfamiliar with object-oriented programming, sometimes distribute information across separate arrays. Here is a typical example: A program needs to manage bank data, consisting of account numbers and balances. Don't store the account numbers and balances in separate arrays.

```
// Don't do this
int[] accountNumbers;
double[] balances;
```

Arrays such as these are called **parallel arrays** (see Figure 4). The ith slice (accountNumbers[i] and balances[i]) contains data that need to be processed together.

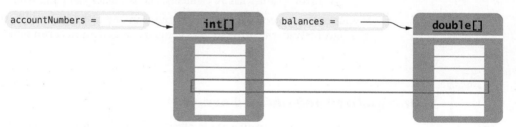

Figure 4   Avoid Parallel Arrays

Avoid parallel arrays by changing them into arrays of objects.

If you find yourself using two arrays that have the same length, ask yourself whether you couldn't replace them with a single array of a class type. Look at a slice and find the concept that it represents. Then make the concept into a class. In our example each slice contains an account number and a balance, describing a bank account. Therefore, it is an easy matter to use a single array of objects

```
BankAccount[] accounts;
```

(See Figure 5.)

Why is this beneficial? Think ahead. Maybe your program will change and you will need to store the owner of the bank account as well. It is a simple matter to update the BankAccount class. It may well be quite complicated to add a new array and make sure that all methods that accessed the original two arrays now also correctly access the third one.

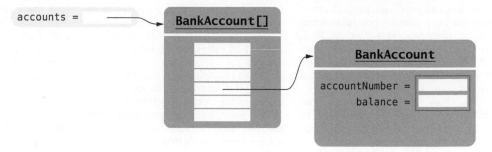

Figure 5 Reorganizing Parallel Arrays into an Array of Objects

Special Topic 7.1

Methods with a Variable Number of Arguments

It is possible to declare methods that receive a variable number of arguments. For example, we can write a method that can add an arbitrary number of scores to a student:

```
fred.addScores(10, 7); // This method call has two arguments
fred.addScores(1, 7, 2, 9); // Another call to the same method, now with four arguments
```

The method must be declared as

```
public void addScores(int... values)
```

The int... type indicates that the method can receive any number of int arguments. The values parameter variable is actually an int[] array that contains all arguments that were passed to the method.

The method implementation traverses the values array and processes the elements:

```
public void addScores(int... values)
{
    for (int i = 0; i < values.length; i++) // values is an int[]
    {
        totalScore = totalScore + values[i];
    }
}
```

Computing & Society 7.1 **Computer Viruses**

In November 1988, Robert Morris, a student at Cornell University, launched a so-called virus program that infected a significant fraction of computers connected to the Internet (which was much smaller then than it is now).

In order to attack a computer, a virus has to find a way to get its instructions executed. This particular program carried out a "buffer overrun" attack, providing an unexpectedly large input to a program on another machine. That program allocated an array of 512 characters, under the assumption that nobody would ever provide such a long input. Unfortunately, that program was written in the C programming language. C, unlike Java, does not check that an array index is less than the length of the array. If you write into an array using an index that is too large, you simply overwrite memory locations that belong to some other objects. C programmers are supposed to provide safety checks, but that had not happened in the program under attack. The virus program purposefully filled the 512-character array with 536 bytes. The excess 24 bytes overwrote a return address, which the attacker knew was stored just after the array. When the method that read the input was finished, it didn't return to its caller but to code supplied by the virus (see the figure). The virus was thus able to execute its code on a remote machine and infect it.

In Java, as in C, all programmers must be very careful not to overrun array boundaries. However, in Java, this error causes a run-time exception, and it never corrupts memory outside the array. This is one of the safety features of Java.

One may well speculate what would possess the virus author to spend weeks designing a program that disabled thousands of computers. It appears that the break-in was fully intended by the author, but the disabling of the computers was a bug caused by continuous reinfection. Morris was sentenced to three years probation, 400 hours of community service, and a $10,000 fine.

In recent years, computer attacks have intensified and the motives have become more sinister. Instead of disabling computers, viruses often take permanent residence in the attacked computers. Criminal enterprises rent out the processing power of millions of hijacked computers for sending spam e-mail or mining cryptocurrencies. Other viruses monitor every keystroke and send those that look like credit card numbers or banking passwords to their master.

Typically, a machine gets infected because a user executes code downloaded from the Internet, clicking on an icon or link that purports to be a game or video clip. Antivirus programs check all downloaded programs against an ever-growing list of known viruses.

When you use a computer for managing your finances, you need to be aware of the risk of infection. If a virus reads your banking password and empties your account, you will have a hard time convincing your financial institution that it wasn't your act, and you will most likely lose your money. Keep your operating system and antivirus program up to date, and don't click on suspicious links on a web page or in your e-mail inbox. Use banks that require "two-factor authentication" for major transactions, such as a callback on your cell phone.

Viruses are even used for military purposes. In 2010, a virus dubbed Stuxnet spread through Microsoft Windows and infected USB sticks. The virus looked for Siemens industrial computers and reprogrammed them in subtle ways. It appears that the virus was designed to damage the centrifuges of the Iranian nuclear enrichment operation. The computers controlling the centrifuges were not connected to the Internet, but they were configured with USB sticks, some of which were infected. Security researchers believe that the virus was developed by U.S. and Israeli intelligence agencies, and that it was successful in slowing down the Iranian nuclear program. Neither country has officially acknowledged or denied their role in the attacks.

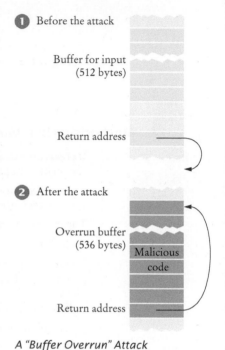

A "Buffer Overrun" Attack

7.2 The Enhanced for Loop

You can use the enhanced for loop to visit all elements of an array.

Often, you need to visit all elements of an array. The *enhanced* for *loop* makes this process particularly easy to program.

Here is how you use the enhanced for loop to total up all elements in an array named values:

```
double[] values = . . .;
double total = 0;
for (double element : values)
{
    total = total + element;
}
```

The loop body is executed for each element in the array values. At the beginning of each loop iteration, the next element is assigned to the variable element. Then the loop body is executed. You should read this loop as "for each element in values".

This loop is equivalent to the following for loop with an explicit index variable:

```java
for (int i = 0; i < values.length; i++)
{
   double element = values[i];
   total = total + element;
}
```

Note an important difference between the enhanced for loop and the basic for loop. In the enhanced for loop, the *element variable* is assigned values[0], values[1], and so on. In the basic for loop, the *index variable* i is assigned 0, 1, and so on.

© Steve Cole/iStockphoto.

The enhanced for loop is a convenient mechanism for traversing all elements in a collection.

> **Use the enhanced for loop if you do not need the index values in the loop body.**

Keep in mind that the enhanced for loop has a very specific purpose: getting the elements of a collection, from the beginning to the end. It is not suitable for all array algorithms. In particular, the enhanced for loop does not allow you to modify the contents of an array. The following loop does not fill an array with zeroes:

```java
for (double element : values)
{
   element = 0; // ERROR: this assignment does not modify array elements
}
```

When the loop is executed, the variable element is set to values[0]. Then element is set to 0, then to values[1], then to 0, and so on. The values array is not modified. The remedy is simple: Use a basic for loop.

```java
for (int i = 0; i < values.length; i++)
{
   values[i] = 0; // OK
}
```

Syntax 7.2   The Enhanced for Loop

Syntax   for (*typeName variable* : *collection*)
        {
           statements
        }

This variable is set in each loop iteration. It is only defined inside the loop.

An array

```java
for (double element : values)
{
   sum = sum + element;
}
```

These statements are executed for each element.

The variable contains an element, not an index.

EXAMPLE CODE   See sec02 of your eText or companion code for a program that demonstrates the enhanced for loop.

7.3 Common Array Algorithms

In the following sections, we discuss some of the most common algorithms for working with arrays. If you use a partially filled array, remember to replace values.length with the companion variable that represents the current size of the array.

7.3.1 Filling

This loop fills an array with squares (0, 1, 4, 9, 16, ...). Note that the element with index 0 contains 0^2, the element with index 1 contains 1^2, and so on.

```
for (int i = 0; i < values.length; i++)
{
    values[i] = i * i;
}
```

7.3.2 Sum and Average Value

You have already encountered this algorithm in Section 6.7.1. When the values are located in an array, the code looks much simpler:

```
double total = 0;
for (double element : values)
{
    total = total + element;
}
double average = 0;
if (values.length > 0) { average = total / values.length; }
```

7.3.3 Maximum and Minimum

© CEFutcher/iStockphoto.

Use the algorithm from Section 6.7.5 that keeps a variable for the largest element already encountered. Here is the implementation of that algorithm for an array:

```
double largest = values[0];
for (int i = 1; i < values.length; i++)
{
    if (values[i] > largest)
    {
        largest = values[i];
    }
}
```

Note that the loop starts at 1 because we initialize largest with values[0].

To compute the smallest element, reverse the comparison.

These algorithms require that the array contain at least one element.

7.3.4 Element Separators

When you display the elements of an array, you usually want to separate them, often with commas or vertical lines, like this:

32 | 54 | 67.5 | 29 | 35

Note that there is one fewer separator than there are numbers.
Print the separator before each element in the sequence *except
the initial one* (with index 0) like this:

```java
for (int i = 0; i < values.length; i++)
{
   if (i > 0)
   {
      System.out.print(" | ");
   }
   System.out.print(values[i]);
}
```

© trutenka/iStockphoto.

*To print five
elements, you need
four separators.*

If you want comma separators, you can use the `Arrays.toString`
method. (You'll need to import `java.util.Arrays`.) The expression

```java
Arrays.toString(values)
```

returns a string describing the contents of the array `values` in the form

```java
[32, 54, 67.5, 29, 35]
```

The elements are surrounded by a pair of brackets and separated by commas. This
method can be convenient for debugging:

```java
System.out.println("values=" + Arrays.toString(values));
```

7.3.5 Linear Search

You often need to search for the position of a specific element in an array so that you can replace or remove it. Visit
all elements until you have found a match or you have come
to the end of the array. Here we search for the position of the
first element in an array that is equal to 100:

© yekorzh/Getty Images.

*To search for a specific
element, visit the
elements and stop when
you encounter
the match.*

```java
int searchedValue = 100;
int pos = 0;
boolean found = false;
while (pos < values.length && !found)
{
   if (values[pos] == searchedValue)
   {
      found = true;
   }
   else
   {
      pos++;
   }
}
if (found) { System.out.println("Found at position: " + pos); }
else { System.out.println("Not found"); }
```

This algorithm is called **linear search** or *sequential search* because you inspect the
elements in sequence. If the array is sorted, you can use the more efficient **binary
search** algorithm. We discuss binary search in Chapter 14.

7.3.6 Removing an Element

Suppose you want to remove the element with index pos from the array values. As explained in Section 7.1.4, you need a companion variable for tracking the number of elements in the array. In this example, we use a companion variable called currentSize.

If the elements in the array are not in any particular order, simply overwrite the element to be removed with the *last* element of the array, then decrement the current-Size variable. (See Figure 6.)

```
values[pos] = values[currentSize - 1];
currentSize--;
```

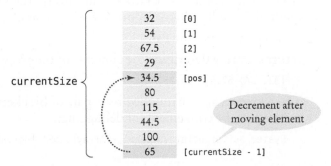

Figure 6   Removing an Element in an Unordered Array

The situation is more complex if the order of the elements matters. Then you must move all elements following the element to be removed to a lower index, and then decrement the variable holding the size of the array. (See Figure 7.)

```
for (int i = pos + 1; i < currentSize; i++)
{
   values[i - 1] = values[i];
}
currentSize--;
```

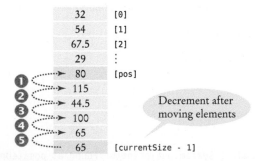

Figure 7   Removing an Element in an Ordered Array

7.3.7 Inserting an Element

In this section, you will see how to insert an element into an array. Note that you need a companion variable for tracking the array size, as explained in Section 7.1.4.

If the order of the elements does not matter, you can simply insert new elements at the end, incrementing the variable tracking the size.

```
if (currentSize < values.length)
{
    currentSize++;
    values[currentSize - 1] = newElement;
}
```

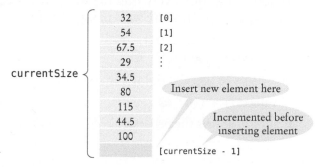

Figure 8 Inserting an Element in an Unordered Array

It is more work to insert an element at a particular position in the middle of an array. First, move all elements after the insertion location to a higher index. Then insert the new element (see Figure 9).

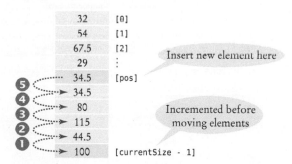

Figure 9 Inserting an Element in an Ordered Array

Note the order of the movement: When you remove an element, you first move the next element to a lower index, then the one after that, until you finally get to the end of the array. When you insert an element, you start at the end of the array, move that element to a higher index, then move the one before that, and so on until you finally get to the insertion location.

> Before inserting an element, move elements to the end of the array *starting with the last one.*

```
if (currentSize < values.length)
{
    currentSize++;
    for (int i = currentSize - 1; i > pos; i--)
    {
        values[i] = values[i - 1];
    }
    values[pos] = newElement;
}
```

7.3.8 Swapping Elements

You often need to swap elements of an array. For example, you can sort an array by repeatedly swapping elements that are not in order.

Consider the task of swapping the elements at positions i and j of an array values. We'd like to set values[i] to values[j]. But that overwrites the value that is currently stored in values[i], so we want to save that first:

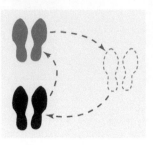

> Use a temporary variable when swapping two elements.

```
double temp = values[i]; ❷
values[i] = values[j]; ❸
```

Now we can set values[j] to the saved value.

```
values[j] = temp; ❹
```

Figure 10 shows the process.

To swap two elements, you need a temporary variable.

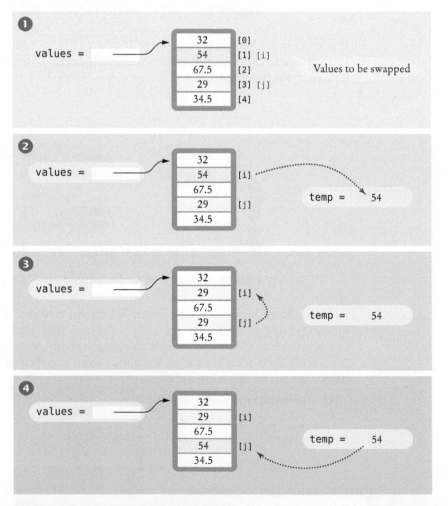

Figure 10 Swapping Array Elements

7.3.9 Copying Arrays

Array variables do not themselves hold array elements. They hold a reference to the actual array. If you copy the reference, you get another reference to the same array (see Figure 11):

```
double[] values = new double[6];
. . .  // Fill array
double[] prices = values; ❶
```

> Use the Arrays.
> copyOf method to
> copy the elements of
> an array into a
> new array.

If you want to make a true copy of an array, call the Arrays.copyOf method (as shown in Figure 11).

```
double[] prices = Arrays.copyOf(values, values.length); ❷
```

The call Arrays.copyOf(values, n) allocates an array of length n, copies the first n elements of values (or the entire values array if n > values.length) into it, and returns the new array.

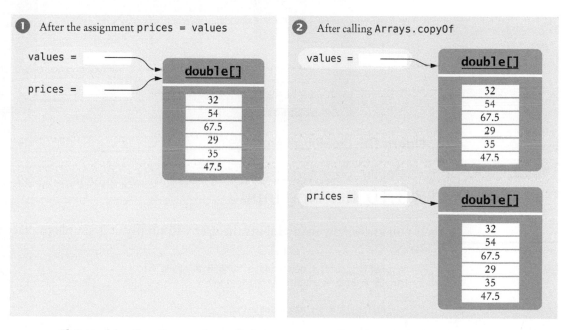

Figure 11   Copying an Array Reference versus Copying an Array

In order to use the Arrays class, you need to add the following statement to the top of your program:

```
import java.util.Arrays;
```

Another use for Arrays.copyOf is to grow an array that has run out of space. The following statements have the effect of doubling the length of an array (see Figure 12):

```
double[] newValues = Arrays.copyOf(values, 2 * values.length); ❶
values = newValues; ❷
```

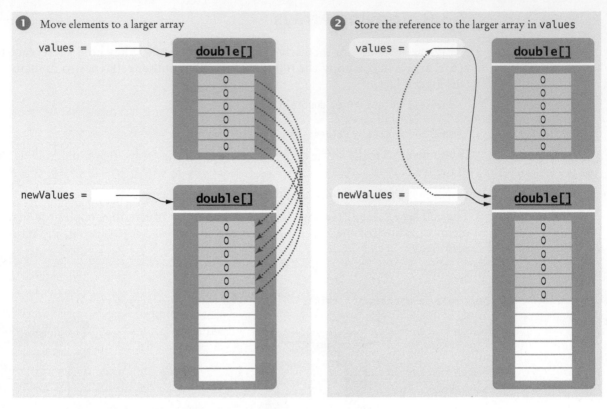

Figure 12 Growing an Array

7.3.10 Reading Input

If you know how many inputs the user will supply, it is simple to place them into an array:

```
double[] inputs = new double[NUMBER_OF_INPUTS];
for (i = 0; i < inputs.length; i++)
{
   inputs[i] = in.nextDouble();
}
```

However, this technique does not work if you need to read a sequence of arbitrary length. In that case, add the inputs to an array until the end of the input has been reached.

```
int currentSize = 0;
while (in.hasNextDouble() && currentSize < inputs.length)
{
   inputs[currentSize] = in.nextDouble();
   currentSize++;
}
```

Now `inputs` is a partially filled array, and the companion variable `currentSize` is set to the number of inputs.

However, this loop silently throws away inputs that don't fit into the array. A better approach is to grow the array to hold all inputs.

```
double[] inputs = new double[INITIAL_SIZE];
int currentSize = 0;
while (in.hasNextDouble())
{
   // Grow the array if it has been completely filled
   if (currentSize >= inputs.length)
   {
      inputs = Arrays.copyOf(inputs, 2 * inputs.length); // Grow the inputs array
   }

   inputs[currentSize] = in.nextDouble();
   currentSize++;
}
```

When you are done, you can discard any excess (unfilled) elements:

```
inputs = Arrays.copyOf(inputs, currentSize);
```

The following program puts these algorithms to work, solving the task that we set ourselves at the beginning of this chapter: to mark the largest value in an input sequence.

sec03/LargestInArray.java

```
1  import java.util.Scanner;
2
3  /**
4      This program reads a sequence of values and prints them,
5      marking the largest value.
6  */
7  public class LargestInArray
8  {
9     public static void main(String[] args)
10    {
11       final int LENGTH = 100;
12       double[] values = new double[LENGTH];
13       int currentSize = 0;
14
15       // Read inputs
16
17       System.out.println("Please enter values, Q to quit:");
18       Scanner in = new Scanner(System.in);
19       while (in.hasNextDouble() && currentSize < values.length)
20       {
21          values[currentSize] = in.nextDouble();
22          currentSize++;
23       }
24
25       // Find the largest value
26
27       double largest = values[0];
28       for (int i = 1; i < currentSize; i++)
29       {
30          if (values[i] > largest)
31          {
32             largest = values[i];
33          }
34       }
35
36       // Print all values, marking the largest
37
```

```
38          for (int i = 0; i < currentSize; i++)
39          {
40             System.out.print(values[i]);
41             if (values[i] == largest)
42             {
43                System.out.print(" <== largest value");
44             }
45             System.out.println();
46          }
47       }
48  }
```

Program Run

```
Please enter values, Q to quit:
34.5 80 115 44.5 Q
34.5
80
115 <== largest value
44.5
```

Common Error 7.3

Underestimating the Size of a Data Set

Programmers commonly underestimate the amount of input data that a user will pour into an unsuspecting program. Suppose you write a program to search for text in a file. You store each line in a string, and keep an array of strings. How big do you make the array? Surely nobody is going to challenge your program with an input that is more than 100 lines. Really? It is very easy to feed in the entire text of *Alice in Wonderland* or *War and Peace* (which are available on the Internet). All of a sudden, your program has to deal with tens or hundreds of thousands of lines. You either need to allow for large inputs or politely reject the excess input.

Special Topic 7.2

Sorting with the Java Library

Sorting an array efficiently is not an easy task. You will learn in Chapter 14 how to implement efficient sorting algorithms. Fortunately, the Java library provides an efficient sort method.

To sort an array values, call

```
Arrays.sort(values);
```

If the array is partially filled, call

```
Arrays.sort(values, 0, currentSize);
```

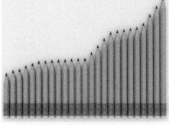

© ProstoVova/iStockphoto.

7.4 Problem Solving: Adapting Algorithms

In Section 7.3, you were introduced to a number of fundamental array algorithms. These algorithms form the building blocks for many programs that process arrays. In general, it is a good problem-solving strategy to have a repertoire of fundamental algorithms that you can combine and adapt.

By combining fundamental algorithms, you can solve complex programming tasks.

Consider this example problem: You are given the quiz scores of a student. You are to compute the final quiz score, which is the sum of all scores after dropping the lowest one. For example, if the scores are

```
8  7  8.5  9.5  7  4  10
```

then the final score is 50.

We do not have a ready-made algorithm for this situation. Instead, consider which algorithms may be related. These include:

- Calculating the sum (Section 7.3.2)
- Finding the minimum value (Section 7.3.3)
- Removing an element (Section 7.3.6)

We can formulate a plan of attack that combines these algorithms:

Find the minimum.
Remove the minimum from the array.
Calculate the sum.

Let's try it out with our example. The minimum of

```
[0]  [1]  [2]  [3]  [4]  [5]  [6]
 8    7   8.5  9.5   7    4   10
```

is 4. How do we remove it?

Now we have a problem. The removal algorithm in Section 7.3.6 locates the element to be removed by using the *position* of the element, not the value.

But we have another algorithm for that:

- Linear search (Section 7.3.5)

We need to fix our plan of attack:

Find the minimum value.
Find the position of the minimum.
Remove the element at the position.
Calculate the sum.

Will it work? Let's continue with our example.

We found a minimum value of 4. Linear search tells us that the value 4 occurs at position 5.

```
[0]  [1]  [2]  [3]  [4]  [5]  [6]
 8    7   8.5  9.5   7    4   10
```

We remove it:

```
[0]  [1]  [2]  [3]  [4]  [5]
 8    7   8.5  9.5   7   10
```

Finally, we compute the sum: $8 + 7 + 8.5 + 9.5 + 7 + 10 = 50$.

This walkthrough demonstrates that our strategy works.

Can we do better? It seems a bit inefficient to find the minimum and then make another pass through the array to obtain its position.

We can adapt the algorithm for finding the minimum to yield the position of the minimum.

You should be familiar with the implementation of fundamental algorithms so that you can adapt them.

Here is the original algorithm:

```
double smallest = values[0];
for (int i = 1; i < values.length; i++)
{
   if (values[i] < smallest)
   {
      smallest = values[i];
   }
}
```

When we find the smallest value, we also want to update the position:

```
if (values[i] < smallest)
{
   smallest = values[i];
   smallestPosition = i;
}
```

In fact, then there is no reason to keep track of the smallest value any longer. It is simply values[smallestPosition]. With this insight, we can adapt the algorithm as follows:

```
int smallestPosition = 0;
for (int i = 1; i < values.length; i++)
{
   if (values[i] < values[smallestPosition])
   {
      smallestPosition = i;
   }
}
```

With this adaptation, our problem is solved with the following strategy:

Find the position of the minimum.
Remove the element at the position.
Calculate the sum.

The next section shows you a technique for discovering a new algorithm when none of the fundamental algorithms can be adapted to a task.

EXAMPLE CODE   See sec04 of your eText or companion code for a program that uses the adapted algorithm for finding the minimum.

HOW TO 7.1

Working with Arrays

In many data processing situations, you need to process a sequence of values. This How To walks you through the steps for storing input values in an array and carrying out computations with the array elements.

Problem Statement Consider again the problem from Section 7.4: A final quiz score is computed by adding all the scores, except for the lowest one. For example, if the scores are

8 7 8.5 9.5 7 5 10

then the final score is 50.

Thierry Dosogne/The Image Bank/Getty Images, Inc.

Step 1   Decompose your task into steps.

You will usually want to break down your task into multiple steps, such as

- Reading the data into an array.
- Processing the data in one or more steps.
- Displaying the results.

When deciding how to process the data, you should be familiar with the array algorithms in Section 7.3. Most processing tasks can be solved by using one or more of these algorithms.

In our sample problem, we will want to read the data. Then we will remove the minimum and compute the total. For example, if the input is 8 7 8.5 9.5 7 5 10, we will remove the minimum of 5, yielding 8 7 8.5 9.5 7 10. The sum of those values is the final score of 50.

Thus, we have identified three steps:

Read inputs.
Remove the minimum.
Calculate the sum.

Step 2   Determine which algorithm(s) you need.

Sometimes, a step corresponds to exactly one of the basic array algorithms in Section 7.3. That is the case with calculating the sum (Section 7.3.2) and reading the inputs (Section 7.3.10). At other times, you need to combine several algorithms. To remove the minimum value, you can find the minimum value (Section 7.3.3), find its position (Section 7.3.5), and remove the element at that position (Section 7.3.6).

We have now refined our plan as follows:

Read inputs.
Find the minimum.
Find the position of the minimum.
Remove the element at the position.
Calculate the sum.

This plan will work—see Section 7.4. But here is an alternate approach. It is easy to compute the sum and subtract the minimum. Then we don't have to find its position. The revised plan is

Read inputs.
Find the minimum.
Calculate the sum.
Subtract the minimum from the sum.

Step 3   Use classes and methods to structure the program.

Even though it may be possible to put all steps into the main method, this is rarely a good idea. It is better to carry out each processing step in a separate method. It is also a good idea to come up with a class that is responsible for collecting and processing the data.

In our example, let's provide a class Student. A student has an array of scores.

```java
public class Student
{
    private double[] scores;
    private double scoresSize;

    . . .
    public Student(int capacity) { . . . }
    public boolean addScore(double score) { . . . }
    public double finalScore() { . . . }
}
```

A second class, ScoreAnalyzer, is responsible for reading the user input and displaying the result. Its main method simply calls the Student methods:

```
Student fred = new Student(100);
System.out.println("Please enter values, Q to quit:");
while (in.hasNextDouble())
{
   if (!fred.addScore(in.nextDouble()))
   {
      System.out.println("Too many scores.");
      return;
   }
}
System.out.println("Final score: " + fred.finalScore());
```

Now the finalScore method must do the heavy lifting. It too should not have to do all the work. Instead, we will supply helper methods

```
public double sum()
public double minimum()
```

These methods simply implement the algorithms in Sections 7.3.2 and 7.3.3.

Then the finalScore method becomes

```
public double finalScore()
{
   if (scoresSize == 0)
   {
      return 0;
   }
   else
   {
      return sum() - minimum();
   }
}
```

Step 4   Assemble and test the program.

Place your methods into a class. Review your code and check that you handle both normal and exceptional situations. What happens with an empty array? One that contains a single element? When no match is found? When there are multiple matches? Consider these boundary conditions and make sure that your program works correctly.

In our example, it is impossible to compute the minimum if the array is empty. In that case, we should terminate the program with an error message *before* attempting to call the minimum method.

What if the minimum value occurs more than once? That means that a student had more than one test with the same low score. We subtract only one of the occurrences of that low score, and that is the desired behavior.

The following table shows test cases and their expected output:

Test Case	Expected Output	Comment
8 7 8.5 9.5 7 5 10	50	See Step 1.
8 7 7 9	24	Only one instance of the low score should be removed.
8	0	After removing the low score, no score remains.
(no inputs)	**Error**	That is not a legal input.

EXAMPLE CODE   See your eText or the how_to_1 folder of your companion code for the complete program.

WORKED EXAMPLE 7.1
Rolling the Dice

Learn how to analyze a set of die tosses to see whether the die is "fair". See your eText or visit wiley.com/go/bjeo7.

© ktsimage/iStockphoto.

7.5 Problem Solving: Discovering Algorithms by Manipulating Physical Objects

In Section 7.4, you saw how to solve a problem by combining and adapting known algorithms. But what do you do when none of the standard algorithms is sufficient for your task? In this section, you will learn a technique for discovering algorithms by manipulating physical objects.

Consider the following task: You are given an array whose size is an even number, and you are to switch the first and the second half. For example, if the array contains the eight numbers

| 9 | 13 | 21 | 4 | 11 | 7 | 1 | 3 |

then you should change it to

| 11 | 7 | 1 | 3 | 9 | 13 | 21 | 4 |

Many students find it quite challenging to come up with an algorithm. They may know that a loop is required, and they may realize that elements should be inserted (Section 7.3.7) or swapped (Section 7.3.8), but they do not have sufficient intuition to draw diagrams, describe an algorithm, or write down pseudocode.

One useful technique for discovering an algorithm is to manipulate physical objects. Start by lining up some objects to denote an array. Coins, playing cards, or small toys are good choices.

Here we arrange eight coins:

> **Use a sequence of coins, playing cards, or toys to visualize an array of values.**

coins: © jamesbenet/iStockphoto; dollar coins: © JordiDelgado/iStockphoto.

Now let's step back and see what we can do to change the order of the coins.

Manipulating physical objects can give you ideas for discovering algorithms.

© JenCon/iStockphoto.

We can remove a coin (Section 7.3.6):

*Visualizing the
removal of an
array element*

We can insert a coin (Section 7.3.7):

*Visualizing the
insertion of an
array element*

Or we can swap two coins (Section 7.3.8).

*Visualizing the
swapping of two coins*

Go ahead—line up some coins and try out these three operations right now so that you get a feel for them.

Now how does that help us with our problem, switching the first and the second half of the array?

Let's put the first coin into place, by swapping it with the fifth coin. However, as Java programmers, we will say that we swap the coins in positions 0 and 4:

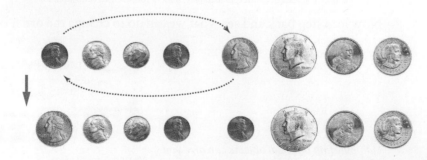

Next, we swap the coins in positions 1 and 5:

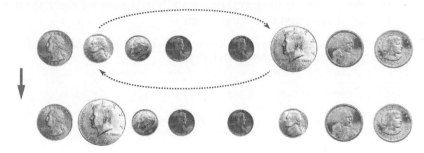

Two more swaps, and we are done:

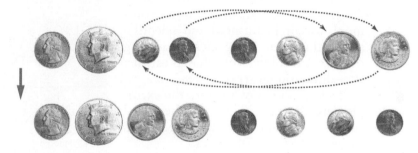

Now an algorithm is becoming apparent:

```
i = 0
j = ...  // We'll think about that in a minute
While   // Don't know yet
    Swap elements at positions i and j.
    i++
    j++
```

Where does the variable *j* start? When we have eight coins, the coin at position zero is moved to position 4. In general, it is moved to the middle of the array, or to position *size / 2*.

And how many iterations do we make? We need to swap all coins in the first half. That is, we need to swap *size / 2* coins.

The pseudocode is

```
i = 0
j = size / 2
While i < size / 2
    Swap elements at positions i and j.
    i++
    j++
```

You can use paper clips as position markers or counters.

It is a good idea to make a walkthrough of the pseudocode (see Section 6.2). You can use paper clips to denote the positions of the variables *i* and *j*. If the walkthrough is successful, then we know that there was no "off-by-one" error in the pseudocode. Exercise • E7.9 asks you to translate the pseudocode to Java. Exercise •• R7.25 suggests a different algorithm for switching the two halves of an array, by repeatedly removing and inserting coins.

Many people find that the manipulation of physical objects is less intimidating than drawing diagrams or mentally envisioning algorithms. Give it a try when you need to design a new algorithm!

EXAMPLE CODE See sec05 of your eText or companion code for a program that implements the algorithm that switches the first and second halves of an array.

7.6 Two-Dimensional Arrays

It often happens that you want to store collections of values that have a two-dimensional layout. Such data sets commonly occur in financial and scientific applications. An arrangement consisting of rows and columns of values is called a **two-dimensional array**, or a *matrix*.

Let's explore how to store the example data shown in Figure 13: the medal counts of the figure skating competitions at the 2014 Winter Olympics.

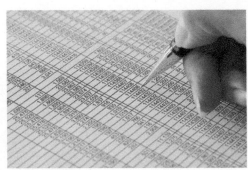

© Trub/iStockphoto.

© technotr/iStockphoto.

	Gold	Silver	Bronze
Canada	0	3	0
Italy	0	0	1
Germany	0	0	1
Japan	1	0	0
Kazakhstan	0	0	1
Russia	3	1	1
South Korea	0	1	0
United States	1	0	1

Figure 13 Figure Skating Medal Counts

7.6.1 Declaring Two-Dimensional Arrays

Use a two-dimensional array to store tabular data.

In Java, you obtain a two-dimensional array by supplying the number of rows and columns. For example, new int[7][3] is an array with seven rows and three columns. You store a reference to such an array in a variable of type int[][]. Here is a complete declaration of a two-dimensional array, suitable for holding our medal count data:

```
final int COUNTRIES = 8;
final int MEDALS = 3;
int[][] counts = new int[COUNTRIES][MEDALS];
```

Syntax 7.3   **Two-Dimensional Array Declaration**

Name   *Element type*   *Number of rows*
Number of columns

```
double[][] tableEntries = new double[7][3];
```

All values are initialized with 0.

Name

```
int[][] data = {
                 { 16, 3, 2, 13 },
                 { 5, 10, 11, 8 },
                 { 9, 6, 7, 12 },
                 { 4, 15, 14, 1 },
               };
```

List of initial values

Alternatively, you can declare and initialize the array by grouping each row:

```
int[][] counts =
  {
    { 0, 3, 0 },
    { 0, 0, 1 },
    { 0, 0, 1 },
    { 1, 0, 0 },
    { 0, 0, 1 },
    { 3, 1, 1 },
    { 0, 1, 0 }
    { 1, 0, 1 }
  };
```

As with one-dimensional arrays, you cannot change the size of a two-dimensional array once it has been declared.

7.6.2 Accessing Elements

> Individual elements in a two-dimensional array are accessed by using two index values, *array*[i][j].

To access a particular element in the two-dimensional array, you need to specify two index values in separate brackets to select the row and column, respectively (see Figure 14):

```
int medalCount = counts[3][1];
```

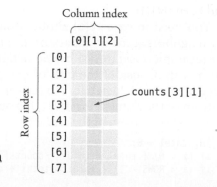

Figure 14
Accessing an Element in a
Two-Dimensional Array

To access all elements in a two-dimensional array, you use nested loops. For example, the following loop prints all elements of counts:

```
for (int i = 0; i < COUNTRIES; i++)
{
    // Process the ith row
    for (int j = 0; j < MEDALS; j++)
    {
        // Process the jth column in the ith row
        System.out.printf("%8d", counts[i][j]);
    }
    System.out.println(); // Start a new line at the end of the row
}
```

In these loops, the number of rows and columns were given as constants. Alternatively, you can use the following expressions:

- counts.length is the number of rows.
- counts[0].length is the number of columns. (See Special Topic 7.3 for an explanation of this expression.)

With these expressions, the nested loops become

```
for (int i = 0; i < counts.length; i++)
{
    for (int j = 0; j < counts[0].length; j++)
    {
        System.out.printf("%8d", counts[i][j]);
    }
    System.out.println();
}
```

7.6.3 Locating Neighboring Elements

Some programs that work with two-dimensional arrays need to locate the elements that are adjacent to an element. This task is particularly common in games. Figure 15 shows how to compute the index values of the neighbors of an element.

For example, the neighbors of counts[3][1] to the left and right are counts[3][0] and counts[3][2]. The neighbors to the top and bottom are counts[2][1] and counts[4][1].

You need to be careful about computing neighbors at the boundary of the array. For example, counts[0][1] has no neighbor to the top. Consider the task of computing the sum of the neighbors to the top and bottom of the element count[i][j]. You need to check whether the element is located at the top or bottom of the array:

[i - 1][j - 1]	[i - 1][j]	[i - 1][j + 1]
[i][j - 1]	[i][j]	[i][j + 1]
[i + 1][j - 1]	[i + 1][j]	[i + 1][j + 1]

Figure 15 Neighboring Locations in a Two-Dimensional Array

```
int total = 0;
if (i > 0) { total = total + counts[i - 1][j]; }
if (i < ROWS - 1) { total = total + counts[i + 1][j]; }
```

7.6.4 Accessing Rows and Columns

You often need to access all elements in a row or column, for example to compute the sum of the elements or the largest element in a row or column. In our sample array, the row totals give us the total number of medals won by a particular country.

Finding the correct index values is a bit tricky, and it is a good idea to make a quick sketch. To compute the total of row i, we need to visit the following elements:

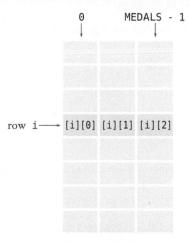

As you can see, we need to compute the sum of counts[i][j], where j ranges from 0 to MEDALS - 1. The following loop computes the total:

```
int total = 0;
for (int j = 0; j < MEDALS; j++)
{
    total = total + counts[i][j];
}
```

Computing column totals is similar. Form the sum of counts[i][j], where i ranges from 0 to COUNTRIES - 1.

```
int total = 0;
for (int i = 0; i < COUNTRIES; i++)
{
    total = total + counts[i][j];
}
```

column j

[0][j]   ← 0

[1][j]

[2][j]

[3][j]

[4][j]

[5][j]

[6][j]

[7][j]   ← COUNTRIES - 1

7.6.5 Two-Dimensional Array Parameters

When you use a two-dimensional array, you do not need to use separate variables for the dimensions of the array. If values is a two-dimensional array, then

- values.length is the number of rows.
- values[0].length is the number of columns. (See Special Topic 7.4 for an explanation of this expression.)

For example, the following method computes the sum of all elements in a two-dimensional array:

```java
public class Data
{
   private int[][] values;
   . . .

   public int sum()
   {
      int total = 0;
      for (int i = 0; i < values.length; i++)
      {
         for (int j = 0; j < values[0].length; j++)
         {
            total = total + values[i][j];
         }
      }
      return total;
   }
}
```

Working with two-dimensional arrays is illustrated in the following program. The program prints out the medal counts and the row totals.

sec06/Medals.java

```java
1  /**
2     This program prints a table of medal winner counts with row totals.
3  */
4  public class Medals
5  {
6     public static void main(String[] args)
7     {
8        final int COUNTRIES = 8;
9        final int MEDALS = 3;
10
11       String[] countries =
12          {
13             "Canada",
14             "Italy",
15             "Germany",
16             "Japan",
17             "Kazakhstan",
18             "Russia",
19             "South Korea",
20             "United States"
21          };
22
```

```
23        int[][] counts =
24           {
25              { 0, 3, 0 },
26              { 0, 0, 1 },
27              { 0, 0, 1 },
28              { 1, 0, 0 },
29              { 0, 0, 1 },
30              { 3, 1, 1 },
31              { 0, 1, 0 },
32              { 1, 0, 1 }
33           };
34
35        System.out.println("        Country   Gold  Silver  Bronze    Total");
36
37        // Print countries, counts, and row totals
38        for (int i = 0; i < COUNTRIES; i++)
39        {
40           // Process the ith row
41           System.out.printf("%15s", countries[i]);
42
43           int total = 0;
44
45           // Print each row element and update the row total
46           for (int j = 0; j < MEDALS; j++)
47           {
48              System.out.printf("%8d", counts[i][j]);
49              total = total + counts[i][j];
50           }
51
52           // Display the row total and print a new line
53           System.out.printf("%8d%n", total);
54        }
55     }
56 }
```

Program Run

Country	Gold	Silver	Bronze	Total
Canada	0	3	0	3
Italy	0	0	1	1
Germany	0	0	1	1
Japan	1	0	0	1
Kazakhstan	0	0	1	1
Russia	3	1	1	5
South Korea	0	1	0	1
United States	1	0	1	2

WORKED EXAMPLE 7.2
A World Population Table

Learn how to print world population data in a table with row and column headers, and with totals for each of the data columns. See your eText or visit wiley.com/go/bjeo7.

Special Topic 7.3

Two-Dimensional Arrays with Variable Row Lengths

When you declare a two-dimensional array with the command

```
int[][] a = new int[3][3];
```

you get a 3 × 3 matrix that can store 9 elements:

```
a[0][0] a[0][1] a[0][2]
a[1][0] a[1][1] a[1][2]
a[2][0] a[2][1] a[2][2]
```

In this matrix, all rows have the same length.

In Java it is possible to declare arrays in which the row length varies. For example, you can store an array that has a triangular shape, such as:

```
b[0][0]
b[1][0] b[1][1]
b[2][0] b[2][1] b[2][2]
```

To allocate such an array, you must work harder. First, you allocate space to hold three rows. Indicate that you will manually set each row by leaving the second array index empty:

```
double[][] b = new double[3][];
```

Then allocate each row separately (see Figure 16):

```
for (int i = 0; i < b.length; i++)
{
   b[i] = new double[i + 1];
}
```

You can access each array element as b[i][j]. The expression b[i] selects the ith row, and the [j] operator selects the jth element in that row.

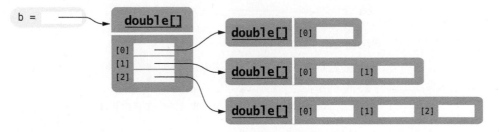

Figure 16   A Triangular Array

Note that the number of rows is b.length, and the length of the ith row is b[i].length. For example, the following pair of loops prints a ragged array:

```
for (int i = 0; i < b.length; i++)
{
   for (int j = 0; j < b[i].length; j++)
   {
      System.out.print(b[i][j]);
   }
   System.out.println();
}
```

Alternatively, you can use two enhanced for loops:

```
for (double[] row : b)
{
```

```
      for (double element : row)
      {
         System.out.print(element);
      }
      System.out.println();
   }
```

Naturally, such "ragged" arrays are not very common.

Java implements plain two-dimensional arrays in exactly the same way as ragged arrays: as arrays of one-dimensional arrays. The expression `new int[3][3]` automatically allocates an array of three rows, and three arrays for the rows' contents.

Special Topic 7.4

Multidimensional Arrays

You can declare arrays with more than two dimensions. For example, here is a three-dimensional array:

```
   int[][][] rubiksCube = new int[3][3][3];
```

Each array element is specified by three index values:

```
   rubiksCube[i][j][k]
```

7.7 Array Lists

An array list stores a sequence of values whose size can change.

When you write a program that collects inputs, you don't always know how many inputs you will have. In such a situation, an **array list** offers two significant advantages:

- Array lists can grow and shrink as needed.
- The `ArrayList` class supplies methods for common tasks, such as inserting and removing elements.

In the following sections, you will learn how to work with array lists.

An array list expands to hold as many elements as needed. © Michael Brake/iStockphoto.

7.7.1 Declaring and Using Array Lists

The following statement declares an array list of strings:

```
   ArrayList<String> names = new ArrayList<String>();
```

Syntax 7.4 Array Lists

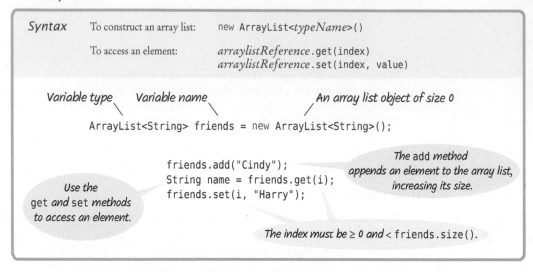

Syntax To construct an array list: new ArrayList<*typeName*>()

To access an element: *arraylistReference*.get(index)
arraylistReference.set(index, value)

Variable type *Variable name* *An array list object of size 0*

```
ArrayList<String> friends = new ArrayList<String>();
```

```
friends.add("Cindy");
String name = friends.get(i);
friends.set(i, "Harry");
```

The add *method appends an element to the array list, increasing its size.*

Use the get *and* set *methods to access an element.*

The index must be ≥ *0 and* < friends.size().

The ArrayList class is a generic class: ArrayList<*Type*> collects elements of the specified type.

The ArrayList class is contained in the java.util package. In order to use array lists in your program, you need to use the statement import java.util.ArrayList.

The type ArrayList<String> denotes an array list of String elements. The angle brackets around the String type tell you that String is a **type parameter**. You can replace String with any other class and get a different array list type. For that reason, ArrayList is called a **generic class**. However, you cannot use primitive types as type parameters—there is no ArrayList<int> or ArrayList<double>. Section 7.7.4 shows how you can collect numbers in an array list.

It is a common error to forget the initialization:

```
ArrayList<String> names;
names.add("Harry"); // Error—names not initialized
```

Here is the proper initialization:

```
ArrayList<String> names = new ArrayList<String>();
```

Note the () after new ArrayList<String> on the right-hand side of the initialization. It indicates that the **constructor** of the ArrayList<String> class is being called.

When the ArrayList<String> is first constructed, it has size 0. You use the add method to add an element to the end of the array list.

```
names.add("Emily"); // Now names has size 1 and element "Emily"
names.add("Bob"); // Now names has size 2 and elements "Emily", "Bob"
names.add("Cindy"); // names has size 3 and elements "Emily", "Bob", and "Cindy"
```

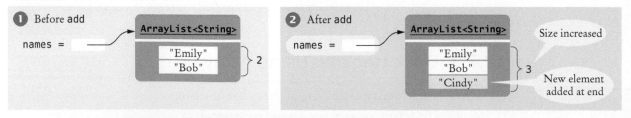

Figure 17 Adding an Array List Element with add

The size increases after each call to add (see Figure 17). The size method yields the current size of the array list.

To obtain an array list element, use the get method, not the [] operator. As with arrays, index values start at 0. For example, names.get(2) retrieves the name with index 2, the third element in the array list:

> Use the size method to obtain the current size of an array list.

```java
String name = names.get(2);
```

As with arrays, it is an error to access a nonexistent element. A very common bounds error is to use the following:

> Use the get and set methods to access an array list element at a given index.

```java
int i = names.size();
name = names.get(i);  // Error
```

The last valid index is names.size() - 1.

To set an array list element to a new value, use the set method:

```java
names.set(2, "Carolyn");
```

This call sets position 2 of the names array list to "Carolyn", overwriting whatever value was there before.

The set method overwrites existing values. It is different from the add method, which adds a new element to the array list.

You can insert an element in the middle of an array list. For example, the call names.add(1, "Ann") adds a new element at position 1 and moves all elements with index 1 or larger by one position. After each call to the add method, the size of the array list increases by 1 (see Figure 18).

> Use the add and remove methods to add and remove array list elements.

Conversely, the remove method removes the element at a given position, moves all elements after the removed element down by one position, and reduces the size of the array list by 1. Part 3 of Figure 18 illustrates the result of names.remove(1).

© Danijelm/iStockphoto.

An array list has methods for adding and removing elements in the middle.

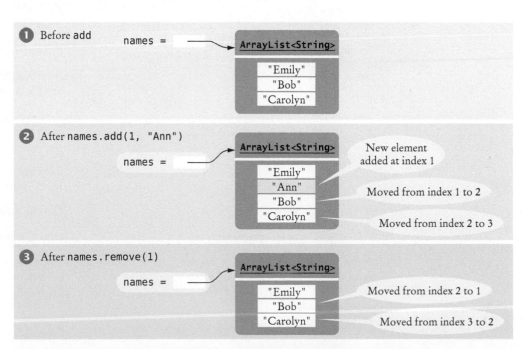

Figure 18 Adding and Removing Elements in the Middle of an Array List

With an array list, it is very easy to get a quick printout. Simply pass the array list to the `println` method:

```
System.out.println(names); // Prints [Emily, Bob, Carolyn]
```

7.7.2 Using the Enhanced for Loop with Array Lists

You can use the enhanced `for` loop to visit all elements of an array list. For example, the following loop prints all names:

```
ArrayList<String> names = . . . ;
for (String name : names)
{
    System.out.println(name);
}
```

This loop is equivalent to the following basic `for` loop:

```
for (int i = 0; i < names.size(); i++)
{
    String name = names.get(i);
    System.out.println(name);
}
```

Table 2 Working with Array Lists

`ArrayList<String> names = new ArrayList<String>();`	Constructs an empty array list that can hold strings.
`names.add("Ann");` `names.add("Cindy");`	Adds elements to the end of the array list.
`System.out.println(names);`	Prints `[Ann, Cindy]`.
`names.add(1, "Bob");`	Inserts an element at index 1. `names` is now `[Ann, Bob, Cindy]`.
`names.remove(0);`	Removes the element at index 0. `names` is now `[Bob, Cindy]`.
`names.set(0, "Bill");`	Replaces an element with a different value. `names` is now `[Bill, Cindy]`.
`String name = names.get(i);`	Gets an element.
`String last = names.get(names.size() - 1);`	Gets the last element.

`ArrayList<Integer> squares = new ArrayList<Integer>();`
`for (int i = 0; i < 10; i++)`
`{`
`    squares.add(i * i);`
`}`
	Constructs an array list holding the first ten squares.

7.7.3 Copying Array Lists

As with arrays, you need to remember that array list variables hold references. Copying the reference yields two references to the same array list (see Figure 19).

```
ArrayList<String> friends = names;
friends.add("Harry");
```

Now both `names` and `friends` reference the same array list to which the string `"Harry"` was added.

If you want to make a copy of an array list, construct the copy and pass the original list into the constructor:

```
ArrayList<String> newNames = new ArrayList<String>(names);
```

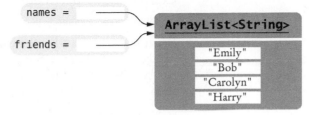

Figure 19
Copying an Array List Reference

7.7.4 Wrappers and Auto-boxing

In Java, you cannot directly insert primitive type values—numbers, characters, or `boolean` values—into array lists. For example, you cannot form an `ArrayList<double>`. Instead, you must use one of the **wrapper classes** shown in the following table.

Primitive Type	Wrapper Class
byte	Byte
boolean	Boolean
char	Character
double	Double
float	Float
int	Integer
long	Long
short	Short

For example, to collect `double` values in an array list, you use an `ArrayList<Double>`. Note that the wrapper class names start with uppercase letters, and that two of them differ from the names of the corresponding primitive type: `Integer` and `Character`.

Conversion between primitive types and the corresponding wrapper classes is automatic. This process is called **auto-boxing** (even though *auto-wrapping* would have been more consistent).

```
wrapper =
```

Double

```
value =    29.95
```

Figure 20   A Wrapper Class Variable

For example, if you assign a `double` value to a `Double` variable, the number is automatically "put into a box" (see Figure 20).

```
Double wrapper = 29.95;
```

Conversely, wrapper values are automatically "unboxed" to primitive types:

```
double x = wrapper;
```

Because boxing and unboxing is automatic, you don't need to think about it. Simply remember to use the wrapper type when you declare array lists of numbers. From then on, use the primitive type and rely on auto-boxing.

```
ArrayList<Double> values = new ArrayList<Double>();
values.add(29.95);
double x = values.get(0);
```

Like truffles that must be in a wrapper to be sold, a number must be placed in a wrapper to be stored in an array list.   © sandoclr/iStockphoto.

7.7.5 Using Array Algorithms with Array Lists

The array algorithms in Section 7.3 can be converted to array lists simply by using the array list methods instead of the array syntax (see Table 3 on page 262). For example, this code snippet finds the largest element in an array:

```
double largest = values[0];
for (int i = 1; i < values.length; i++)
{
   if (values[i] > largest)
   {
      largest = values[i];
   }
}
```

Here is the same algorithm, now using an array list:

```
double largest = values.get(0);
for (int i = 1; i < values.size(); i++)
{
   if (values.get(i) > largest)
   {
      largest = values.get(i);
   }
}
```

7.7.6 Storing Input Values in an Array List

When you collect an unknown number of inputs, array lists are *much* easier to use than arrays. Simply read inputs and add them to an array list:

```
ArrayList<Double> inputs = new ArrayList<Double>();
while (in.hasNextDouble())
{
    inputs.add(in.nextDouble());
}
```

7.7.7 Removing Matches

It is easy to remove elements from an array list, by calling the remove method. A common processing task is to remove all elements that match a particular condition. Suppose, for example, that we want to remove all strings of length < 4 from an array list.

Of course, you traverse the array list and look for matching elements:

```
ArrayList<String> words = . . .;
for (int i = 0; i < words.size(); i++)
{
    String word = words.get(i);
    if (word.length() < 4)
    {
        Remove the element at index i.
    }
}
```

But there is a subtle problem. After you remove the element, the for loop increments i, skipping past the *next* element.

Consider this concrete example, where words contains the strings "Welcome", "to", "the", "island!". When i is 1, we remove the word "to" at index 1. Then i is incremented to 2, and the word "the", which is now at position 1, is never examined.

i	words
~~0~~	~~"Welcome", "to", "the", "island"~~
~~1~~	"Welcome", "the", "island"
2	

We should not increment the index when removing a word. The appropriate pseudocode is

If the element at index i matches the condition
    Remove the element.
Else
    Increment i.

Because we don't always increment the index, a for loop is not appropriate for this algorithm. Instead, use a while loop:

```
int i = 0;
while (i < words.size())
{
```

```
String word = words.get(i);
if (word.length() < 4)
{
   words.remove(i);
}
else
{
   i++;
}
}
```

7.7.8 Choosing Between Array Lists and Arrays

For most programming tasks, array lists are easier to use than arrays. Array lists can grow and shrink. On the other hand, arrays have a nicer syntax for element access and initialization.

Which of the two should you choose? Here are some recommendations.

- If the size of a collection never changes, use an array.
- If you collect a long sequence of primitive type values and you are concerned about efficiency, use an array.
- Otherwise, use an array list.

Table 3 Comparing Array and Array List Operations		
Operation	Arrays	Array Lists
Get an element.	`x = values[4];`	`x = values.get(4);`
Replace an element.	`values[4] = 35;`	`values.set(4, 35);`
Number of elements.	`values.length`	`values.size()`
Number of filled elements.	`currentSize` (companion variable, see Section 7.1.4)	`values.size()`
Remove an element.	See Section 7.3.6.	`values.remove(4);`
Add an element, growing the collection.	See Section 7.3.7.	`values.add(35);`
Initializing a collection.	`int[] values = { 1, 4, 9 };`	No initializer list syntax; call add three times.

The following program shows how to mark the largest value in a sequence of values stored in an array list. Note how the program is an improvement over the array version in Section 7.3.10 on page 239. This program can process input sequences of arbitrary length.

sec07/LargestInArrayList.java

```java
 1  import java.util.ArrayList;
 2  import java.util.Scanner;
 3
 4  /**
 5     This program reads a sequence of values and prints them, marking the largest
     value.
 6  */
 7  public class LargestInArrayList
 8  {
 9     public static void main(String[] args)
10     {
11        ArrayList<Double> values = new ArrayList<Double>();
12
13        // Read inputs
14
15        System.out.println("Please enter values, Q to quit:");
16        Scanner in = new Scanner(System.in);
17        while (in.hasNextDouble())
18        {
19           values.add(in.nextDouble());
20        }
21
22        // Find the largest value
23
24        double largest = values.get(0);
25        for (int i = 1; i < values.size(); i++)
26        {
27           if (values.get(i) > largest)
28           {
29              largest = values.get(i);
30           }
31        }
32
33        // Print all values, marking the largest
34
35        for (double element : values)
36        {
37           System.out.print(element);
38           if (element == largest)
39           {
40              System.out.print(" <== largest value");
41           }
42           System.out.println();
43        }
44     }
45  }
```

Program Run

```
Please enter values, Q to quit:
35 80 115 44.5 Q
35
80
115 <== largest value
44.5
```

Common Error 7.4
Length and Size

Unfortunately, the Java syntax for determining the number of elements in an array, an array list, and a string is not at all consistent. It is a common error to confuse these. You just have to remember the correct syntax for every data type.

Data Type	Number of Elements
Array	`a.length`
Array list	`a.size()`
String	`a.length()`

Special Topic 7.5
The Diamond Syntax

There is a convenient syntax enhancement for declaring array lists and other generic classes. In a statement that declares and constructs an array list, you need not repeat the type parameter in the constructor. That is, you can write

```
ArrayList<String> names = new ArrayList<>();
```

instead of

```
ArrayList<String> names = new ArrayList<String>();
```

This shortcut is called the "diamond syntax" because the empty brackets <> look like a diamond shape.

For now, we will use the explicit syntax and include the type parameters with constructors. In later chapters, we will switch to the diamond syntax.

7.8 Regression Testing

A test suite is a set of tests for repeated testing.

Regression testing involves repeating previously run tests to ensure that known failures of prior versions do not appear in new versions of the software.

It is a common and useful practice to make a new test whenever you find a program bug. You can use that test to verify that your bug fix really works. Don't throw the test away; feed it to the next version after that and all subsequent versions. Such a collection of test cases is called a **test suite**.

You will be surprised how often a bug that you fixed will reappear in a future version. This is a phenomenon known as *cycling*. Sometimes you don't quite understand the reason for a bug and apply a quick fix that appears to work. Later, you apply a different quick fix that solves a second problem but makes the first problem appear again. Of course, it is always best to think through what really causes a bug and fix the root cause instead of doing a sequence of "Band-Aid" solutions. If you don't succeed in doing that, however, you at least want to have an honest appraisal of how well the program works. By keeping all old test cases around and testing them against every new version, you get that feedback. The process of checking each version of a program against a test suite is called **regression testing**.

How do you organize a suite of tests? An easy technique is to produce multiple tester classes, such as ScoreTester1, ScoreTester2, and so on, where each program runs with a separate set of test data. For example, here is a tester for the Student class.

```java
public class ScoreTester1
{
   public static void main(String[] args)
   {
      Student fred = new Student(100);
      fred.addScore(10);
      fred.addScore(20);
      fred.addScore(5);
      System.out.println("Final score: " + fred.finalScore());
      System.out.println("Expected: 30");
   }
}
```

Another useful approach is to provide a generic tester and feed it inputs from multiple files, as in the following.

sec08/ScoreTester2.java

```java
 1  import java.util.Scanner;
 2
 3  public class ScoreTester2
 4  {
 5     public static void main(String[] args)
 6     {
 7        Scanner in = new Scanner(System.in);
 8        double expected = in.nextDouble();
 9        Student fred = new Student(100);
10        while (in.hasNextDouble())
11        {
12           if (!fred.addScore(in.nextDouble()))
13           {
14              System.out.println("Too many scores.");
15              return;
16           }
17        }
18        System.out.println("Final score: " + fred.finalScore());
19        System.out.println("Expected: " + expected);
20     }
21  }
```

The program reads the expected result and the scores. By running the program with different inputs, we can test different scenarios.

Of course, it would be tedious to type in the input values by hand every time the test is executed. It is much better to save the inputs in a file, such as the following:

sec08/input1.txt

```
30
10
20
5
```

When running the program from a shell window, one can link the input file to the input of a program, as if all the characters in the file had actually been typed by a user. Type the following command into a shell window:

```
java ScoreTester < input1.txt
```

The program is executed, but it no longer reads input from the keyboard. Instead, the System.in object (and the Scanner that reads from System.in) gets the input from the file input1.txt. We discussed this process, called input **redirection**, in Special Topic 6.2.

The output is still displayed in the console window:

Program Run

```
Final score: 30
Expected: 30
```

You can also redirect output. To capture the program's output in a file, use the command

```
java ScoreTester < input1.txt > output1.txt
```

This is useful for archiving test cases.

Programming Tip 7.3

Batch Files and Shell Scripts

If you need to perform the same tasks repeatedly on the command line, then it is worth learning about the automation features offered by your operating system.

Under Windows, you use batch files to execute a number of commands automatically. For example, suppose you need to test a program by running three testers:

```
java ScoreTester1
java ScoreTester < input1.txt
java ScoreTester < input2.txt
```

Then you find a bug, fix it, and run the tests again. Now you need to type the three commands once more. There has to be a better way. Under Windows, put the commands in a text file and call it test.bat:

File test.bat

```
1   java ScoreTester1
2   java ScoreTester < input1.txt
3   java ScoreTester < input2.txt
```

Then you just type

```
test.bat
```

and the three commands in the batch file execute automatically.

Batch files are a feature of the operating system, not of Java. On Linux, Mac OS, and UNIX, shell scripts are used for the same purpose. In this simple example, you can execute the commands by typing

```
sh test.bat
```

There are many uses for batch files and shell scripts, and it is well worth it to learn more about their advanced features, such as parameters and loops.

Computing & Society 7.2   Liability for Software Malfunction

The Therac-25 is a computerized device to deliver radiation treatment to cancer patients (see the figure). Between June 1985 and January 1987, several of these machines delivered serious overdoses to at least six patients, killing some of them and seriously maiming the others.

The machines were controlled by a computer program. Bugs in the program were directly responsible for the overdoses. The program was written by a single programmer, who had since left the manufacturing company producing the device and could not be located. None of the company employees interviewed could say anything about the educational level or qualifications of the programmer.

The investigation by the federal Food and Drug Administration (FDA) found that the program was poorly documented and that there was neither a specification document nor a formal test plan. (This should make you think. Do you have a formal test plan for your programs?)

The overdoses were caused by the amateurish design of the software that had to control different devices concurrently, namely the keyboard, the display, the printer, and of course the radiation device itself. Synchronization and data sharing between the tasks were done in an ad hoc way, even though safe multitasking techniques were known at the time. Had the programmer enjoyed a formal education that involved these techniques, or taken the effort to study the literature, a safer machine could have been built.

The same flaws were present in the software controlling the predecessor model, the Therac-20, but that machine had hardware interlocks that mechanically prevented overdoses. The hardware safety devices were removed in the Therac-25 and replaced by checks in the software, presumably to save cost.

Frank Houston of the FDA wrote in 1985, "A significant amount of software for life-critical systems comes from small firms, especially in the medical device industry; firms that fit the profile of those resistant to or uninformed of the principles of either system safety or software engineering."

Who is to blame? The programmer? The manager who not only failed to ensure that the programmer was up to the task but also didn't insist on comprehensive testing? The hospitals that installed the device, or the FDA, for not reviewing the design process? Unfortunately, even today there are no firm standards for what constitutes a safe software design process.

Nowadays, we interact with vast numbers of computer-controlled machines that can endanger us. Self-driving vehicles are a good example. Overall, those machines may well make us safer, but the question remains: What risks are acceptable?

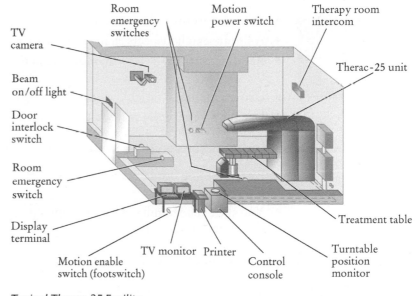

Typical Therac-25 Facility

CHAPTER SUMMARY

Use arrays for collecting values.

- An array collects a sequence of values of the same type.
- Individual elements in an array are accessed by an integer index i, using the notation *array*[i].
- An array element can be used like any variable.

- An array index must be at least zero and less than the size of the array.
- A bounds error, which occurs if you supply an invalid array index, can cause your program to terminate.
- Use the expression *array*.length to find the number of elements in an array.
- An array reference specifies the location of an array. Copying the reference yields a second reference to the same array.
- Arrays can occur as method arguments and return values.
- With a partially filled array, keep a companion variable for the current size.
- Avoid parallel arrays by changing them into arrays of objects.

Know when to use the enhanced for loop.

- You can use the enhanced for loop to visit all elements of an array.
- Use the enhanced for loop if you do not need the index values in the loop body.

Know and use common array algorithms.

- When separating elements, don't place a separator before the first element.
- A linear search inspects elements in sequence until a match is found.
- Before inserting an element, move elements to the end of the array *starting with the last one*.
- Use a temporary variable when swapping two elements.
- Use the Arrays.copyOf method to copy the elements of an array into a new array.

Combine and adapt algorithms for solving a programming problem.

- By combining fundamental algorithms, you can solve complex programming tasks.
- You should be familiar with the implementation of fundamental algorithms so that you can adapt them.

Discover algorithms by manipulating physical objects.

- Use a sequence of coins, playing cards, or toys to visualize an array of values.
- You can use paper clips as position markers or counters.

Use two-dimensional arrays for data that is arranged in rows and columns.

- Use a two-dimensional array to store tabular data.
- Individual elements in a two-dimensional array are accessed by using two index values, *array*[i][j].

Use array lists for managing collections whose size can change.

- An array list stores a sequence of values whose size can change.
- The `ArrayList` class is a generic class: `ArrayList<Type>` collects elements of the specified type.
- Use the `size` method to obtain the current size of an array list.
- Use the `get` and `set` methods to access an array list element at a given index.
- Use the `add` and `remove` methods to add and remove array list elements.
- To collect numbers in array lists, you must use wrapper classes.

Describe the process of regression testing.

- A test suite is a set of tests for repeated testing.
- Regression testing involves repeating previously run tests to ensure that known failures of prior versions do not appear in new versions of the software.

STANDARD LIBRARY ITEMS INTRODUCED IN THIS CHAPTER

```
java.lang.Boolean              java.util.ArrayList<E>
java.lang.Double                  add
java.lang.Integer                 get
java.util.Arrays                  remove
   copyOf                         set
   toString                       size
```

REVIEW EXERCISES

■■ R7.1 Carry out the following tasks with an array:
    a. Allocate an array a of ten integers.
    b. Put the number 17 as the initial element of the array.
    c. Put the number 29 as the last element of the array.
    d. Fill the remaining elements with –1.
    e. Add 1 to each element of the array.
    f. Print all elements of the array, one per line.
    g. Print all elements of the array in a single line, separated by commas.

■ R7.2 Write a program that contains a bounds error. Run the program. What happens on your computer?

■■ R7.3 Write code that fills an array values with each set of numbers below.
    a. 1 2 3 4 5 6 7 8 9 10
    b. 0 2 4 6 8 10 12 14 16 18 20
    c. 1 4 9 16 25 36 49 64 81 100
    d. 0 0 0 0 0 0 0 0 0 0
    e. 1 4 9 16 9 7 4 9 11
    f. 0 1 0 1 0 1 0 1 0 1
    g. 0 1 2 3 4 0 1 2 3 4

■■ R7.4 Consider the following array:

```
int[] a = { 1, 2, 3, 4, 5, 4, 3, 2, 1, 0 };
```

What is the value of total after the following loops complete?

```
a. int total = 0;
   for (int i = 0; i < 10; i++) { total = total + a[i]; }
b. int total = 0;
   for (int i = 0; i < 10; i = i + 2) { total = total + a[i]; }
c. int total = 0;
   for (int i = 1; i < 10; i = i + 2) { total = total + a[i]; }
d. int total = 0;
   for (int i = 2; i <= 10; i++) { total = total + a[i]; }
e. int total = 0;
   for (int i = 1; i < 10; i = 2 * i) { total = total + a[i]; }
f. int total = 0;
   for (int i = 9; i >= 0; i--) { total = total + a[i]; }
g. int total = 0;
   for (int i = 9; i >= 0; i = i - 2) { total = total + a[i]; }
h. int total = 0;
   for (int i = 0; i < 10; i++) { total = a[i] - total; }
```

■■ R7.5 Consider the following array:

```
int[] a = { 1, 2, 3, 4, 5, 4, 3, 2, 1, 0 };
```

What are the contents of the array a after the following loops complete?

```
a. for (int i = 1; i < 10; i++) { a[i] = a[i - 1]; }
```

b. `for (int i = 9; i > 0; i--) { a[i] = a[i - 1]; }`

c. `for (int i = 0; i < 9; i++) { a[i] = a[i + 1]; }`

d. `for (int i = 8; i >= 0; i--) { a[i] = a[i + 1]; }`

e. `for (int i = 1; i < 10; i++) { a[i] = a[i] + a[i - 1]; }`

f. `for (int i = 1; i < 10; i = i + 2) { a[i] = 0; }`

g. `for (int i = 0; i < 5; i++) { a[i + 5] = a[i]; }`

h. `for (int i = 1; i < 5; i++) { a[i] = a[9 - i]; }`

■■■ **R7.6** Write a loop that fills an array values with ten random numbers between 1 and 100. Write code for two nested loops that fill values with ten *different* random numbers between 1 and 100.

■■ **R7.7** Write Java code for a loop that simultaneously computes both the maximum and minimum of an array.

■ **R7.8** What is wrong with each of the following code segments?

a.
```
int[] values = new int[10];
for (int i = 1; i <= 10; i++)
{
    values[i] = i * i;
}
```

b.
```
int[] values;
for (int i = 0; i < values.length; i++)
{
    values[i] = i * i;
}
```

■■ **R7.9** Write enhanced for loops for the following tasks.

a. Printing all elements of an array in a single row, separated by spaces.

b. Computing the maximum of all elements in an array.

c. Counting how many elements in an array are negative.

■■ **R7.10** Rewrite the following loops without using the enhanced for loop construct. Here, values is an array of floating-point numbers.

a. `for (double x : values) { total = total + x; }`

b. `for (double x : values) { if (x == target) { return true; } }`

c.
```
int i = 0;
for (double x : values) { values[i] = 2 * x; i++; }
```

■■ **R7.11** Rewrite the following loops using the enhanced for loop construct. Here, values is an array of floating-point numbers.

a. `for (int i = 0; i < values.length; i++) { total = total + values[i]; }`

b. `for (int i = 1; i < values.length; i++) { total = total + values[i]; }`

c.
```
for (int i = 0; i < values.length; i++)
{
    if (values[i] == target) { return i; }
}
```

■ **R7.12** What is wrong with each of the following code segments?

a. `ArrayList<int> values = new ArrayList<int>();`

b. `ArrayList<Integer> values = new ArrayList();`

c. `ArrayList<Integer> values = new ArrayList<Integer>;`

```
        d. ArrayList<Integer> values = new ArrayList<Integer>();
           for (int i = 1; i <= 10; i++)
           {
              values.set(i - 1, i * i);
           }
        e. ArrayList<Integer> values;
           for (int i = 1; i <= 10; i++)
           {
              values.add(i * i);
           }
```

■ ■ **R7.13** For the operations on partially filled arrays below, provide the header of a method. Do not implement the methods.

   a. Sort the elements in decreasing order.

   b. Print all elements, separated by a given string.

   c. Count how many elements are less than a given value.

   d. Remove all elements that are less than a given value.

   e. Place all elements that are less than a given value in another array.

■ **R7.14** Trace the flow of the loop in Section 7.3.4 with the given example. Show two columns, one with the value of i and one with the output.

■ **R7.15** Consider the following loop for collecting all elements that match a condition; in this case, that the element is larger than 100.

```
        ArrayList<Double> matches = new ArrayList<Double>();
        for (double element : values)
        {
           if (element > 100)
           {
              matches.add(element);
           }
        }
```

Trace the flow of the loop, where values contains the elements 110 90 100 120 80. Show two columns, for element and matches.

■ **R7.16** Trace the flow of the loop in Section 7.3.5, where values contains the elements 80 90 100 120 110. Show two columns, for pos and found. Repeat the trace when values contains the elements 80 90 120 70.

■ ■ **R7.17** Trace the algorithm for removing an element described in Section 7.3.6. Use an array values with elements 110 90 100 120 80, and remove the element at index 2.

■ ■ **R7.18** Give pseudocode for an algorithm that rotates the elements of an array by one position, moving the initial element to the end of the array, like this:

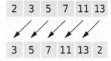

■ ■ **R7.19** Give pseudocode for an algorithm that removes all negative values from an array, preserving the order of the remaining elements.

■ ■ **R7.20** Suppose values is a *sorted* array of integers. Give pseudocode that describes how a new value can be inserted so that the resulting array stays sorted.

■■■ **R7.21** A *run* is a sequence of adjacent repeated values. Give pseudocode for computing the length of the longest run in an array. For example, the longest run in the array with elements

1 2 5 5 3 1 2 4 3 2 2 2 2 3 6 5 5 6 3 1

has length 4.

■■■ **R7.22** What is wrong with the following method that aims to fill an array with random numbers?

```java
public void makeCombination(int[] values, int n)
{
   Random generator = new Random();
   int[] numbers = new int[values.length];
   for (int i = 0; i < numbers.length; i++)
   {
      numbers[i] = generator.nextInt(n);
   }
   values = numbers;
}
```

■■ **R7.23** You are given two arrays denoting x- and y-coordinates of a set of points in a plane. For plotting the point set, we need to know the x- and y-coordinates of the smallest rectangle containing the points. How can you obtain these values from the fundamental algorithms in Section 7.3?

■ **R7.24** Solve the quiz score problem described in Section 7.4 by sorting the array first. How do you need to modify the algorithm for computing the total?

■■ **R7.25** Solve the task described in Section 7.5 using an algorithm that removes and inserts elements instead of switching them. Write the pseudocode for the algorithm, assuming that methods for removal and insertion exist. Act out the algorithm with a sequence of coins and explain why it is less efficient than the swapping algorithm developed in Section 7.5.

■■ **R7.26** Develop an algorithm for finding the most frequently occurring value in an array of numbers. Use a sequence of coins. Place paper clips below each coin that count how many other coins of the same value are in the sequence. Give the pseudocode for an algorithm that yields the correct answer, and describe how using the coins and paper clips helped you find the algorithm.

■■ **R7.27** Write Java statements for performing the following tasks with an array declared as

```java
int[][] values = new int[ROWS][COLUMNS];
```

- Fill all entries with 0.
- Fill elements alternately with 0s and 1s in a checkerboard pattern.
- Fill only the elements in the top and bottom rows with zeroes.
- Compute the sum of all elements.
- Print the array in tabular form.

■■ **R7.28** Write pseudocode for an algorithm that fills the first and last columns as well as the first and last rows of a two-dimensional array of integers with –1.

■ **R7.29** Section 7.7.7 shows that you must be careful about updating the index value when you remove elements from an array list. Show how you can avoid this problem by traversing the array list backwards.

■■ **R7.30** True or false?

   a. All elements of an array are of the same type.

   b. Arrays cannot contain strings as elements.

   c. Two-dimensional arrays always have the same number of rows and columns.

   d. Elements of different columns in a two-dimensional array can have different types.

   e. A method cannot return a two-dimensional array.

   f. A method cannot change the length of an array argument.

   g. A method cannot change the number of columns of an argument that is a two-dimensional array.

■■ **R7.31** How do you perform the following tasks with array lists in Java?

   a. Test that two array lists contain the same elements in the same order.

   b. Copy one array list to another.

   c. Fill an array list with zeroes, overwriting all elements in it.

   d. Remove all elements from an array list.

■ **R7.32** True or false?

   a. All elements of an array list are of the same type.

   b. Array list index values must be integers.

   c. Array lists cannot contain strings as elements.

   d. Array lists can change their size, getting larger or smaller.

   e. A method cannot return an array list.

   f. A method cannot change the size of an array list argument.

■ **Testing R7.33** Define the terms regression testing and test suite.

■■ **Testing R7.34** What is the debugging phenomenon known as *cycling*? What can you do to avoid it?

PRACTICE EXERCISES

■ **E7.1** Write a loop that reads ten numbers and a second loop that displays them in the opposite order from which they were entered.

■■ **E7.2** Write a program that initializes an array with ten random integers and then prints four lines of output, containing

   • Every element at an even index.

   • Every even element.

   • All elements in reverse order.

   • Only the first and last element.

■ **E7.3** Modify the LargestInArray.java program in Section 7.3.10 to mark both the smallest and the largest elements.

■■ **E7.4** Write a method sumWithoutSmallest that computes the sum of an array of values, except for the smallest one, in a single loop. In the loop, update the sum and the smallest value. After the loop, return the difference.

■ **E7.5** Add a method removeMin to the Student class of Section 7.4 that removes the minimum score without calling other methods.

■■ **E7.6** Compute the *alternating sum* of all elements in an array. For example, if your program reads the input

$$1 \quad 4 \quad 9 \quad 16 \quad 9 \quad 7 \quad 4 \quad 9 \quad 11$$

then it computes

$$1 - 4 + 9 - 16 + 9 - 7 + 4 - 9 + 11 = -2$$

■ **E7.7** Write a method that reverses the sequence of elements in an array. For example, if you call the method with the array

$$1 \quad 4 \quad 9 \quad 16 \quad 9 \quad 7 \quad 4 \quad 9 \quad 11$$

then the array is changed to

$$11 \quad 9 \quad 4 \quad 7 \quad 9 \quad 16 \quad 9 \quad 4 \quad 1$$

■■■ **E7.8** Write a program that produces ten random permutations of the numbers 1 to 10. To generate a random permutation, you need to fill an array with the numbers 1 to 10 so that no two entries of the array have the same contents. You could do it by brute force, generating random values until you have a value that is not yet in the array. But that is inefficient. Instead, follow this algorithm:

> Make a second array and fill it with the numbers 1 to 10.
> Repeat 10 times
>   Pick a random position in the second array.
>   Remove the element at the position from the second array.
>   Append the removed element to the permutation array.

■ **E7.9** Write a method that implements the algorithm developed in Section 7.5.

■■ **E7.10** Write a class DataSet that stores a number of values of type double. Provide a constructor

```
public DataSet(int maximumNumberOfValues)
```

and a method

```
public void add(double value)
```

that adds a value, provided there is still room.

Provide methods to compute the sum, average, maximum, and minimum value.

■■ **E7.11** Write array methods that carry out the following tasks for an array of integers by completing the ArrayMethods class below. For each method, provide a test program.

```
public class ArrayMethods
{
    private int[] values;
    public ArrayMethods(int[] initialValues) { values = initialValues; }
    public void swapFirstAndLast() { . . . }
    public void shiftRight() { . . . }
    . . .
}
```

a. Swap the first and last elements in the array.

b. Shift all elements to the right by one and move the last element into the first position. For example, 1 4 9 16 25 would be transformed into 25 1 4 9 16.

c. Replace all even elements with 0.

d. Replace each element except the first and last by the larger of its two neighbors.

e. Remove the middle element if the array length is odd, or the middle two elements if the length is even.

f. Move all even elements to the front, otherwise preserving the order of the elements.

g. Return the second-largest element in the array.

h. Return true if the array is currently sorted in increasing order.

i. Return true if the array contains two adjacent duplicate elements.

j. Return true if the array contains duplicate elements (which need not be adjacent).

■■ **E7.12** Consider the following class:

```
public class Sequence
{
    private int[] values;
    public Sequence(int size) { values = new int[size]; }
    public void set(int i, int n) { values[i] = n; }
    public int get(int i) { return values[i]; }
    public int size() { return values.length; }
}
```

Add a method

```
public boolean equals(Sequence other)
```

that checks whether two sequences have the same values in the same order.

■■ **E7.13** Add a method

```
public boolean sameValues(Sequence other)
```

to the Sequence class of Exercise ■■ E7.12 that checks whether two sequences have the same values in some order, ignoring duplicates. For example, the two sequences

$$1 \quad 4 \quad 9 \quad 16 \quad 9 \quad 7 \quad 4 \quad 9 \quad 11$$

and

$$11 \quad 11 \quad 7 \quad 9 \quad 16 \quad 4 \quad 1$$

would be considered identical. You will probably need one or more helper methods.

■■■ **E7.14** Add a method

```
public boolean isPermutationOf(Sequence other)
```

to the Sequence class of Exercise ■■ E7.12 that checks whether two sequences have the same values in some order, with the same multiplicities. For example,

$$1 \quad 4 \quad 9 \quad 16 \quad 9 \quad 7 \quad 4 \quad 9 \quad 11$$

is a permutation of

$$11 \quad 1 \quad 4 \quad 9 \quad 16 \quad 9 \quad 7 \quad 4 \quad 9$$

but

$$1 \quad 4 \quad 9 \quad 16 \quad 9 \quad 7 \quad 4 \quad 9 \quad 11$$

is not a permutation of

$$11 \quad 11 \quad 7 \quad 9 \quad 16 \quad 4 \quad 1 \quad 4 \quad 9$$

You will probably need one or more helper methods.

■■ **E7.15** Add a method

```
public Sequence sum(Sequence other)
```

to the Sequence class of Exercise ●● E7.12 that yields the sum of this sequence and another. If the sequences don't have the same length, assume that the missing elements are zero. For example, the sum of

$$1 \quad 4 \quad 9 \quad 16 \quad 9 \quad 7 \quad 4 \quad 9 \quad 11$$

and

$$11 \quad 11 \quad 7 \quad 9 \quad 16 \quad 4 \quad 1$$

is the sequence

$$12 \quad 15 \quad 16 \quad 25 \quad 25 \quad 11 \quad 5 \quad 9 \quad 11$$

■■ **E7.16** Write a program that generates a sequence of 20 random values between 0 and 99 in an array, prints the sequence, sorts it, and prints the sorted sequence. Use the sort method from the standard Java library.

■■ **E7.17** Add a method to the Table class below that computes the average of the neighbors of a table element in the eight directions shown in Figure 15:

```
public double neighborAverage(int row, int column)
```

However, if the element is located at the boundary of the array, include only the neighbors that are in the table. For example, if row and column are both 0, there are only three neighbors.

```
public class Table
{
    private int[][] values;
    public Table(int rows, int columns) { values = new int[rows][columns]; }
    public void set(int i, int j, int n) { values[i][j] = n; }
}
```

■■ **E7.18** Given the Table class of Exercise ●● E7.17 , add a method that returns the sum of the ith row (if horizontal is true) or column (if horizontal is false):

```
public double sum(int i, boolean horizontal)
```

■■ **E7.19** Write a program that reads a sequence of input values and displays a bar chart of the values, using asterisks, like this:

```
**********************
****************************************
***************************
*************************
**************
```

You may assume that all values are positive. First figure out the maximum value. That value's bar should be drawn with 40 asterisks. Shorter bars should use proportionally fewer asterisks.

■■■ **E7.20** Repeat Exercise •• E7.19, but make the bars vertical, with the tallest bar twenty asterisks high.

```
*
*
*
*
*
*
**
***
***
****
****
****
****
*****
*****
*****
*****
*****
*****
*****
```

■■■ **E7.21** Improve the program of Exercise •• E7.19 to work correctly when the data set contains negative values.

■■ **E7.22** Improve the program of Exercise •• E7.19 by adding captions for each bar. Prompt the user for the captions and data values. The output should look like this:

```
      Egypt *********************
     France *****************************************
      Japan ******************************
    Uruguay **************************
Switzerland **************
```

■ **E7.23** Consider the following class:

```java
public class Sequence
{
    private ArrayList<Integer> values;
    public Sequence() { values = new ArrayList<Integer>(); }
    public void add(int n) { values.add(n); }
    public String toString() { return values.toString(); }
}
```

Add a method

```java
public Sequence append(Sequence other)
```

that creates a new sequence, appending this and the other sequence, without modifying either sequence. For example, if a is

$$1 \quad 4 \quad 9 \quad 16$$

and b is the sequence

$$9 \quad 7 \quad 4 \quad 9 \quad 11$$

then the call a.append(b) returns the sequence

$$1 \quad 4 \quad 9 \quad 16 \quad 9 \quad 7 \quad 4 \quad 9 \quad 11$$

without modifying a or b.

▪▪ E7.24 Add a method

```
public Sequence merge(Sequence other)
```

to the Sequence class of Exercise • E7.23 that merges two sequences, alternating elements from both sequences. If one sequence is shorter than the other, then alternate as long as you can and then append the remaining elements from the longer sequence. For example, if a is

$$1 \quad 4 \quad 9 \quad 16$$

and b is

$$9 \quad 7 \quad 4 \quad 9 \quad 11$$

then a.merge(b) returns the sequence

$$1 \quad 9 \quad 4 \quad 7 \quad 9 \quad 4 \quad 16 \quad 9 \quad 11$$

without modifying a or b.

▪▪ E7.25 Add a method

```
public Sequence mergeSorted(Sequence other)
```

to the Sequence class of Exercise • E7.23 that merges two sorted sequences, producing a new sorted sequence. Keep an index into each sequence, indicating how much of it has been processed already. Each time, append the smallest unprocessed value from either sequence, then advance the index. For example, if a is

$$1 \quad 4 \quad 9 \quad 16$$

and b is

$$4 \quad 7 \quad 9 \quad 9 \quad 11$$

then a.mergeSorted(b) returns the sequence

$$1 \quad 4 \quad 4 \quad 7 \quad 9 \quad 9 \quad 9 \quad 11 \quad 16$$

If a or b is not sorted, merge the longest prefixes of a and b that are sorted.

PROGRAMMING PROJECTS

▪▪ P7.1 A smartphone keeps track of the x- and y-position of a person once per minute. Use this data to solve a vexing problem: Where did the person last park their car? Look for positions that indicate a stopped vehicle, then a person walking out of the car.

▪▪ P7.2 A *run* is a sequence of adjacent repeated values. Write a program that generates a sequence of 20 random die tosses in an array and that prints the die values, marking the runs by including them in parentheses, like this:

```
1 2 (5 5) 3 1 2 4 3 (2 2 2 2) 3 6 (5 5) 6 3 1
```

Use the following pseudocode:

inRun = false
For each valid index i in the array
    If inRun
        If values[i] is different from the preceding value
            Print).
            inRun = false

> *If not inRun*
>   *If values[i] is the same as the following value*
>   *Print (.*
>   *inRun = true*
>   *Print values[i].*
>   *If inRun, print).*

■■ P7.3 Write a program that generates a sequence of 20 random die tosses in an array and that prints the die values, marking only the longest run, like this:

    1 2 5 5 3 1 2 4 3 (2 2 2 2) 3 6 5 5 6 3 1

If there is more than one run of maximum length, mark the first one.

■■ P7.4 It is a well-researched fact that men in a restroom generally prefer to maximize their distance from already occupied stalls, by occupying the middle of the longest sequence of unoccupied places.

For example, consider the situation where ten stalls are empty.

    _ _ _ _ _ _ _ _ _ _

The first visitor will occupy a middle position:

    _ _ _ _ _ X _ _ _ _

The next visitor will be in the middle of the empty area at the left.

    _ _ X _ _ X _ _ _ _

Write a program that reads the number of stalls and then prints out diagrams in the format given above when the stalls become filled, one at a time. *Hint:* Use an array of `boolean` values to indicate whether a stall is occupied.

■■■ P7.5 In this assignment, you will model the game of *Bulgarian Solitaire*. The game starts with 45 cards. (They need not be playing cards. Unmarked index cards work just as well.) Randomly divide them into some number of piles of random size. For example, you might start with piles of size 20, 5, 1, 9, and 10. In each round, you take one card from each pile, forming a new pile with these cards. For example, the sample starting configuration would be transformed into piles of size 19, 4, 8, 9, and 5. The solitaire is over when the piles have size 1, 2, 3, 4, 5, 6, 7, 8, and 9, in some order. (It can be shown that you always end up with such a configuration.)

In your program, produce a random starting configuration and print it. Then keep applying the solitaire step and print the result. Stop when the solitaire final configuration is reached.

■■■ P7.6 *Magic squares.* An $n \times n$ matrix that is filled with the numbers $1, 2, 3, \ldots, n^2$ is a magic square if the sum of the elements in each row, in each column, and in the two diagonals is the same value.

16	3	2	13
5	10	11	8
9	6	7	12
4	15	14	1

Write a program that reads in 16 values from the keyboard and tests whether they form a magic square when put into a 4×4 array.

You need to test two features:

    1. Does each of the numbers 1, 2, ..., 16 occur in the user input?

    2. When the numbers are put into a square, are the sums of the rows, columns, and diagonals equal to each other?

P7.7 Implement the following algorithm to construct magic $n \times n$ squares; it works only if n is odd.

> Set row = n – 1, column = n / 2.
> For k = 1 ... n * n
>   Place k at [row][column].
>   Increment row and column.
>   If the row or column is n, replace it with 0.
>   If the element at [row][column] has already been filled
>   Set row and column to their previous values.
>   Decrement row.

Here is the 5×5 square that you get if you follow this method:

11	18	25	2	9
10	12	19	21	3
4	6	13	20	22
23	5	7	14	16
17	24	1	8	15

Write a program whose input is the number n and whose output is the magic square of order n if n is odd.

P7.8 A theater seating chart is implemented as a two-dimensional array of ticket prices, like this:

```
10 10 10 10 10 10 10 10 10 10
10 10 10 10 10 10 10 10 10 10
10 10 10 10 10 10 10 10 10 10
10 10 20 20 20 20 20 20 10 10
10 10 20 20 20 20 20 20 10 10
10 10 20 20 20 20 20 20 10 10
20 20 30 30 40 40 30 30 20 20
20 30 30 40 50 50 40 30 30 20
30 40 50 50 50 50 50 50 40 30
```

Write a program that prompts users to pick either a seat or a price. Mark sold seats by changing the price to 0. When a user specifies a seat, make sure it is available. When a user specifies a price, find any seat with that price.

© lepas2004/iStockphoto.

P7.9 Write a program that plays tic-tac-toe. The tic-tac-toe game is played on a 3×3 grid as in the photo at right.

The game is played by two players, who take turns. The first player marks moves with a circle, the second with a cross. The player who has formed a horizontal, vertical, or diagonal sequence of three marks wins. Your program should draw the game board, ask the user for the coordinates of the next mark, change the players after every successful move, and pronounce the winner.

© KathyMuller/iStockphoto.

P7.10 In this assignment, you will implement a simulation of a popular casino game usually called video poker. The card deck contains 52 cards, 13 of each suit. At the beginning of the game, the deck is shuffled. You need to devise a fair method for shuffling. (It does not have to be efficient.) The player pays a token for each game. Then the top five cards of the deck are presented to the player. The player can reject none, some, or all of the cards. The rejected cards are replaced from the top of the deck. Now the hand is scored. Your program should pronounce it to be one of the following:

- No pair—The lowest hand, containing five separate cards that do not match up to create any of the hands below.

- One pair—Two cards of the same value, for example two queens. Payout: 1

- Two pairs—Two pairs, for example two queens and two 5's. Payout: 2

- Three of a kind—Three cards of the same value, for example three queens. Payout: 3

- Straight—Five cards with consecutive values, not necessarily of the same suit, such as 4, 5, 6, 7, and 8. The ace can either precede a 2 or follow a king. Payout: 4

- Flush—Five cards, not necessarily in order, of the same suit. Payout: 5

- Full House—Three of a kind and a pair, for example three queens and two 5's. Payout: 6

- Four of a Kind—Four cards of the same value, such as four queens. Payout: 25

- Straight Flush—A straight and a flush: Five cards with consecutive values of the same suit. Payout: 50

- Royal Flush—The best possible hand in poker. A 10, jack, queen, king, and ace, all of the same suit. Payout: 250

■■■ **P7.11** *The Game of Life* is a well-known mathematical game that gives rise to amazingly complex behavior, although it can be specified by a few simple rules. (It is not actually a game in the traditional sense, with players competing for a win.) Here are the rules. The game is played on a rectangular board. Each square can be either empty or occupied. At the beginning, you can specify empty and occupied cells in some way; then the game runs automatically. In each *generation*, the next generation is computed. A new cell is born on an empty square if it is surrounded by exactly three occupied neighbor cells. A cell dies of overcrowding if it is surrounded by four or more neighbors, and it dies of loneliness if it is surrounded by zero or one neighbor. A neighbor is an occupant of an adjacent square to the left, right, top, or bottom or in a diagonal direction. Figure 21 shows a cell and its neighbor cells.

Many configurations show interesting behavior when subjected to these rules. Figure 22 shows a *glider*, observed over five generations. After four generations, it is transformed into the identical shape, but located one square to the right and below.

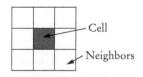

Figure 21
Neighborhood of a Cell

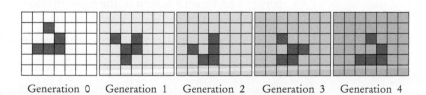

Generation 0   Generation 1   Generation 2   Generation 3   Generation 4

Figure 22   Glider

One of the more amazing configurations is the glider gun: a complex collection of cells that, after 30 moves, turns back into itself and a glider (see Figure 23).

Program the game to eliminate the drudgery of computing successive generations by hand. Use a two-dimensional array to store the rectangular configuration. Write a program that shows successive generations of the game. Ask the user to specify the original configuration, by typing in a configuration of spaces and o characters.

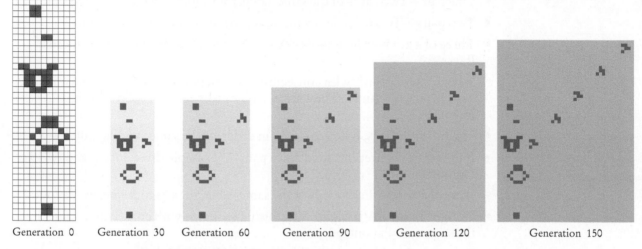

Generation 0   Generation 30   Generation 60   Generation 90   Generation 120   Generation 150

Figure 23   Glider Gun

■ ■ **Business P7.12**   A pet shop wants to give a discount to its clients if they buy one or more pets and at least five other items. The discount is equal to 20 percent of the cost of the other items, but not the pets.

Use a class Item to describe an item, with any needed methods and a constructor

```
public Item(double price, boolean isPet, int quantity)
```

An invoice holds a collection of Item objects; use an array or array list to store them. In the Invoice class, implement methods

```
public void add(Item anItem)
public double getDiscount()
```

Write a program that prompts a cashier to enter each price and quantity, and then a Y
© joshblake/iStockphoto.

for a pet or N for another item. Use a price of –1 as a sentinel. In the loop, call the add method; after the loop, call the getDiscount method and display the returned value.

■ ■ **Business P7.13**   A supermarket wants to reward its best customer of each day, showing the customer's name on a screen in the supermarket. For that purpose, the store keeps an ArrayList<Customer>. In the Store class, implement methods

```
public void addSale(String customerName, double amount)
public String nameOfBestCustomer()
```

to record the sale and return the name of the customer with the largest sale.

Write a program that prompts the cashier to enter all prices and names, adds them to a Store object, and displays the best customer's name. Use a price of 0 as a sentinel.

■■■ **Business P7.14** Improve the program of Exercise •• Business P7.13 so that it displays the top customers, that is, the topN customers with the largest sales, where topN is a value that the user of the program supplies. Implement a method

```
public ArrayList<String> nameOfBestCustomers(int topN)
```

If there were fewer than topN customers, include all of them.

■■ **Science P7.15** Sounds can be represented by an array of "sample values" that describe the intensity of the sound at a point in time. The program in ch07/sound of your companion code reads a sound file (in WAV format), processes the sample values, and shows the result. Your task is to process the sound by introducing an echo. For each sound value, add the value from 0.2 seconds ago. Scale the result so that no value is larger than 32767.

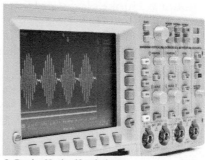

© GordonHeeley/iStockphoto.

■■■ **Science P7.16** You are given a two-dimensional array of values that give the height of a terrain at different points in a square. Write a constructor

```
public Terrain(double[][] heights)
```

and a method

```
public void printFloodMap(double waterLevel)
```

that prints out a flood map, showing which of the points in the terrain would be flooded if the water level was the given value.

In the flood map, print a * for each flooded point and a space for each point that is not flooded.

Here is a sample map:

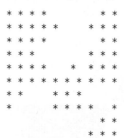

© nicolamargaret/iStockphoto.

Then write a program that reads one hundred terrain height values and shows how the terrain gets flooded when the water level increases in ten steps from the lowest point in the terrain to the highest.

■■ Science P7.17 Sample values from an experiment often need to be smoothed out. One simple approach is to replace each value in an array with the average of the value and its two neighboring values (or one neighboring value if it is at either end of the array). Given a class Data with instance fields

```
private double[] values;
private double valuesSize;
```

implement a method

```
public void smooth()
```

that carries out this operation. You should not create another array in your solution.

■■■ Science P7.18 Write a program that models the movement of an object with mass m that is attached to an oscillating spring. When a spring is displaced from its equilibrium position by an amount x, Hooke's law states that the restoring force is

$$F = -kx$$

where k is a constant that depends on the spring. (Use 10 N/m for this simulation.)

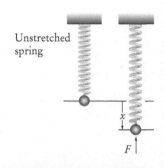

Start with a given displacement x (say, 0.5 meter). Set the initial velocity v to 0. Compute the acceleration a from Newton's law ($F = ma$) and Hooke's law, using a mass of 1 kg. Use a small time interval $\Delta t = 0.01$ second. Update the velocity—it changes by $a\Delta t$. Update the displacement—it changes by $v\Delta t$.

Every ten iterations, plot the spring displacement as a bar, where 1 pixel represents 1 cm, as shown here.

■■ Graphics P7.19 Generate the image of a checkerboard.

■ Graphics P7.20 Generate the image of a sine wave. Draw a line of pixels for every five degrees.

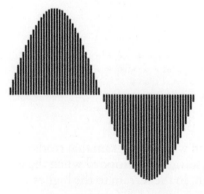

■ **Graphics P7.21**   Implement a class Cloud that contains an array list of Point2D.Double objects. Support methods

```
public void add(Point2D.Double aPoint)
public void draw(Graphics2D g2)
```

Draw each point as a tiny circle. Write a graphical application that draws a cloud of 100 random points.

■■ **Graphics P7.22**   Implement a class Polygon that contains an array list of Point2D.Double objects. Support methods

```
public void add(Point2D.Double aPoint)
public void draw(Graphics2D g2)
```

Draw the polygon by joining adjacent points with a line, and then closing it up by joining the end and start points. Write a graphical application that draws a square and a pentagon using two Polygon objects.

■ **Graphics P7.23**   Write a class Chart with methods

```
public void add(int value)
public void draw(Graphics2D g2)
```

that displays a stick chart of the added values, like this:

You may assume that the values are pixel positions.

■■ **Graphics P7.24**   Write a class BarChart with methods

```
public void add(double value)
public void draw(Graphics2D g2)
```

that displays a bar chart of the added values. You may assume that all added values are positive. Stretch the bars so that they fill the entire area of the screen. You must figure out the maximum of the values, then scale each bar.

■■■ **Graphics P7.25**   Improve the BarChart class of Exercise •• Graphics P7.24 to work correctly when the data contains negative values.

■■ **Graphics P7.26**   Write a class PieChart with methods

```
public void add(double value)
public void draw(Graphics2D g2)
```

that displays a pie chart of the added values. Assume that all data values are positive.

CHAPTER **8**

DESIGNING CLASSES

© Ivan Stevanovic/iStockphoto.

CHAPTER GOALS

To learn how to choose appropriate classes for a given problem

To understand the concept of cohesion

To minimize dependencies and side effects

To learn how to find a data representation for a class

To understand static methods and variables

To learn about packages

To learn about unit testing frameworks

CHAPTER CONTENTS

Good design should be both functional and attractive. When designing classes, each class should be dedicated to a particular purpose, and classes should work well together. In this chapter, you will learn how to discover classes, design good methods, and choose appropriate data representations. You will also learn how to design features that belong to the class as a whole, not individual objects, by using static methods and variables. You will see how to use packages to organize your classes. Finally, we introduce the JUnit testing framework that lets you verify the functionality of your classes.

8.1 Discovering Classes

You have used a good number of classes in the preceding chapters and probably designed a few classes yourself as part of your programming assignments. Designing a class can be a challenge—it is not always easy to tell how to start or whether the result is of good quality.

What makes a good class? Most importantly, a class should *represent a single concept* from a problem domain. Some of the classes that you have seen represent concepts from mathematics:

- Point
- Rectangle
- Ellipse

Other classes are abstractions of real-life entities:

- BankAccount
- CashRegister

> A class should represent a single concept from a problem domain, such as business, science, or mathematics.

For these classes, the properties of a typical object are easy to understand. A Rectangle object has a width and height. Given a BankAccount object, you can deposit and withdraw money. Generally, concepts from a domain related to the program's purpose, such as science, business, or gaming, make good classes. The name for such a class should be a noun that describes the concept. In fact, a simple rule of thumb for getting started with class design is to look for nouns in the problem description.

One useful category of classes can be described as *actors*. Objects of an actor class carry out certain tasks for you. Examples of actors are the Scanner class of Chapter 4 and the Random class in Chapter 6. A Scanner object scans a stream for numbers and strings. A Random object generates random numbers. It is a good idea to choose class names for actors that end in "-er" or "-or". (A better name for the Random class might be RandomNumberGenerator.)

Very occasionally, a class has no objects, but it contains a collection of related static methods and constants. The Math class is an example. Such a class is called a *utility class*.

Finally, you have seen classes with only a main method. Their sole purpose is to start a program. From a design perspective, these are somewhat degenerate examples of classes.

What might not be a good class? If you can't tell from the class name what an object of the class is supposed to do, then you are probably not on the right track. For example, your homework assignment might ask you to write a program that prints paychecks. Suppose you start by trying to design a class PaycheckProgram. What would an object of this class do? An object of this class would have to do everything that the homework needs to do. That doesn't simplify anything. A better class would be Paycheck. Then your program can manipulate one or more Paycheck objects.

Another common mistake is to turn a single operation into a class. For example, if your homework assignment is to compute a paycheck, you may consider writing a class ComputePaycheck. But can you visualize a "ComputePaycheck" object? The fact that "ComputePaycheck" isn't a noun tips you off that you are on the wrong track. On the other hand, a Paycheck class makes intuitive sense. The word "paycheck" is a noun. You can visualize a paycheck object. You can then think about useful methods of the Paycheck class, such as computeTaxes, that help you solve the assignment.

8.2 Designing Good Methods

In the following sections, you will learn several useful criteria for analyzing and improving the public interface of a class.

8.2.1 Providing a Cohesive Public Interface

The public interface of a class is cohesive if all of its features are related to the concept that the class represents.

A class should represent a single concept. All interface features should be closely related to the single concept that the class represents. Such a public interface is said to be **cohesive**.

If you find that the public interface of a class refers to multiple concepts, then that is a good sign that it may be time to use separate classes instead. Consider, for example, the public interface of the CashRegister class in Chapter 4:

```
public class CashRegister
{
    public static final double QUARTER_VALUE = 0.25;
    public static final double DIME_VALUE = 0.1;
    public static final double NICKEL_VALUE = 0.05;
    . . .
    public void receivePayment(int dollars, int quarters,
            int dimes, int nickels, int pennies)
    . . .
}
```

The members of a cohesive team have a common goal.

© Sergey Ivanov/iStockphoto.

There are really two concepts here: a cash register that holds coins and computes their total, and the values of individual coins. (For simplicity, we assume that the cash register only holds coins, not bills. Exercise • E8.3 discusses a more general solution.)

It makes sense to have a separate Coin class and have coins responsible for knowing their values.

```
public class Coin
{
   . . .
   public Coin(double aValue, String aName) { . . . }
   public double getValue() { . . . }
   . . .
}
```

Then the CashRegister class can be simplified:

```
public class CashRegister
{
   . . .
   public void receivePayment(int coinCount, Coin coinType) { . . . }
   {
      payment = payment + coinCount * coinType.getValue();
   }
   . . .
}
```

Now the CashRegister class no longer needs to know anything about coin values. The same class can equally well handle euros or zorkmids!

This is clearly a better solution, because it separates the responsibilities of the cash register and the coins. The only reason we didn't follow this approach in Chapter 4 was to keep the CashRegister example simple.

8.2.2 Minimizing Dependencies

A class depends on another class if its methods use that class in any way.

Many methods need other classes in order to do their jobs. For example, the receivePayment method of the restructured CashRegister class now uses the Coin class. We say that the CashRegister class depends on the Coin class.

To visualize relationships between classes, such as dependence, programmers draw class diagrams. In this book, we use the UML ("**Unified Modeling Language**") notation for objects and classes. UML is a notation for object-oriented analysis and design invented by Grady Booch, Ivar Jacobson, and James Rumbaugh, three leading researchers in object-oriented software development. (Appendix H has a summary of the UML notation used in this book.) The UML notation distinguishes between *object diagrams* and *class diagrams*. In an object diagram the class names are underlined; in a class diagram the class names are not underlined. In a class diagram, you denote dependency by a dashed line with a ⊁-shaped open arrow tip that points to the dependent class. Figure 1 shows a class diagram indicating that the CashRegister class depends on the Coin class.

Note that the Coin class does *not* depend on the CashRegister class. All Coin methods can carry out their work without ever calling any method in the CashRegister class. Conceptually, coins have no idea that they are being collected in cash registers.

Here is an example of minimizing dependencies. Consider how we have always printed a bank balance:

```
System.out.println("The balance is now $" + momsSavings.getBalance());
```

Figure 1
Dependency Relationship
Between the CashRegister
and Coin Classes

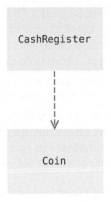

Why don't we simply have a `printBalance` method?

```
public void printBalance() // Not recommended
{
    System.out.println("The balance is now $" + balance);
}
```

The method depends on `System.out`. Not every computing environment has `System.out`. For example, an automatic teller machine doesn't display console messages. In other words, this design violates the rule of minimizing dependencies. The `printBalance` method couples the `BankAccount` class with the `System` and `PrintStream` classes.

It is best to place the code for producing output or consuming input in a separate class. That way, you decouple input/output from the actual work of your classes.

8.2.3 Separating Accessors and Mutators

A **mutator method** changes the state of an object. Conversely, an **accessor method** asks an object to compute a result, without changing the state.

Some classes have been designed to have only accessor methods and no mutator methods at all. Such classes are called **immutable**. An example is the `String` class. Once a string has been constructed, its content never changes. No method in the `String` class can modify the contents of a string. For example, the `toUpperCase` method does not change characters from the original string. Instead, it constructs a *new* string that contains the uppercase characters:

```
String name = "John Q. Public";
String uppercased = name.toUpperCase(); // name is not changed
```

An immutable class has a major advantage: It is safe to give out references to its objects freely. If no method can change the object's value, then no code can modify the object at an unexpected time.

Not every class should be immutable. Immutability makes most sense for classes that represent values, such as strings, dates, currency amounts, colors, and so on.

In mutable classes, it is still a good idea to cleanly separate accessors and mutators, in order to avoid accidental mutation. As a rule of thumb, a method that returns a value should not be a mutator. For example, one would not expect that calling `getBalance` on a `BankAccount` object would change the balance. (You would be pretty upset

An immutable
class has no
mutator methods.

References to
objects of an
immutable class can
be safely shared.

if your bank charged you a "balance inquiry fee".) If you follow this rule, then all mutators of your class have return type void.

Sometimes, this rule is bent a bit, and mutator methods return an informational value. For example, the ArrayList class has a remove method to remove an object.

```
ArrayList<String> names = . . .;
boolean success = names.remove("Romeo");
```

That method returns true if the removal was successful; that is, if the list contained the object. Returning this value might be bad design if there was no other way to check whether an object exists in the list. However, there is such a method—the contains method. It is acceptable for a mutator to return a value if there is also an accessor that computes it.

The situation is less happy with the Scanner class. The next method is a mutator that returns a value. (The next method really is a mutator. If you call next twice in a row, it can return different results, so it must have mutated something inside the Scanner object.) Unfortunately, there is no accessor that returns the same value. This sometimes makes it awkward to use a Scanner. You must carefully hang on to the value that the next method returns because you have no second chance to ask for it. It would have been better if there was another method, say peek, that yields the next input without consuming it.

To check the temperature of the water in the bottle, you could take a sip, but that would be the equivalent of a mutator method.   © manley099/iStockphoto.

8.2.4 Minimizing Side Effects

> A side effect of a method is any externally observable data modification.

A **side effect** of a method is any kind of modification of data that is observable outside the method. Mutator methods have a side effect, namely the modification of the implicit parameter.

There is another kind of side effect that you should avoid. A method should generally not modify its parameter variables. Consider this example:

```
/**
    Computes the total balance of the given accounts.
    @param accounts a list of bank accounts
*/
    public double getTotalBalance(ArrayList<BankAccount> accounts)
    {
        double sum = 0;
        while (accounts.size() > 0)
        {
            BankAccount account = accounts.remove(0); // Not recommended
            sum = sum + account.getBalance();
        }
        return sum;
    }
}
```

This method *removes* all names from the accounts parameter variable. After a call

```
double total = getTotalBalance(allAccounts);
```

allAccounts is empty! Such a side effect would not be what most programmers expect. It is better if the method visits the elements from the list without removing them.

Another example of a side effect is output. Consider again the printBalance method that we discussed in Section 8.2.2:

```
public void printBalance() // Not recommended
{
    System.out.println("The balance is now $" + balance);
}
```

This method mutates the System.out object, which is not a part of the BankAccount object. That is a side effect.

To avoid this side effect, keep most of your classes free from input and output operations, and concentrate input and output in one place, such as the main method of your program.

> When designing methods, minimize side effects.

This taxi has an undesirable side effect, spraying bystanders with muddy water. AP Photo/Frank Franklin II.

EXAMPLE CODE   See your eText or companion code for a cash register program that uses the Coin class.

Programming Tip 8.1

Consistency

In this section you learned of two criteria for analyzing the quality of the public interface of a class. You should maximize cohesion and remove unnecessary dependencies. There is another criterion that we would like you to pay attention to—*consistency*. When you have a set of methods, follow a consistent scheme for their names and parameter variables. This is simply a sign of good craftsmanship.

Sadly, you can find any number of inconsistencies in the standard library. Here is an example: To show an input dialog box, you call

```
JOptionPane.showInputDialog(promptString)
```

To show a message dialog box, you call

```
JOptionPane.showMessageDialog(null, messageString)
```

What's the null argument? It turns out that the showMessageDialog method needs an argument to specify the parent window, or null if no parent window is required. But the showInputDialog method requires no parent window. Why the inconsistency? There is no reason. It would have been an easy matter to supply a showMessageDialog method that exactly mirrors the showInput-Dialog method.

Inconsistencies such as these are not fatal flaws, but they are an annoyance, particularly because they can be so easily avoided.

While it is possible to eat with mismatched silverware, consistency is more pleasant.

Special Topic 8.1
Call by Value and Call by Reference

In Section 8.2.4, we recommended that you don't invoke a mutator method on a parameter variable. In this Special Topic, we discuss a related issue—what happens when you assign a new value to a parameter variable. Consider this method:

```java
public class BankAccount
{
    . . .
    /**
        Transfers money from this account and tries to add it to a balance.
        @param amount  the amount of money to transfer
        @param otherBalance balance to add the amount to
    */
    public void transfer(double amount, double otherBalance) ❷
    {
        balance = balance - amount;
        otherBalance = otherBalance + amount;
            // Won't update the argument
    } ❸
}
```

Now let's see what happens when we call the transfer method:

```java
double savingsBalance = 1000;
harrysChecking.transfer(500, savingsBalance); ❶
System.out.println(savingsBalance); ❹
```

You might expect that after the call, the savingsBalance variable has been incremented to 1500. However, that is not the case. As the method starts, the parameter variable otherBalance is set to the same value as savingsBalance (see Figure 2). Then the otherBalance variable is set to a different value. That modification has no effect on savingsBalance, because otherBalance is a separate variable. When the method terminates, the otherBalance variable is removed, and savingsBalance isn't increased.

In Java, parameter variables are initialized with the values of the argument expressions. When the method exits, the parameter variables are removed. Computer scientists refer to this call mechanism as "call by value".

For that reason, a Java method can never change the contents of a variable that is passed as an argument—the method manipulates a different variable.

Other programming languages such as C++ support a mechanism, called "call by reference", that can change the arguments of a method call. You will sometimes read in Java books that "numbers are passed by value, objects are passed by reference". That is technically not

> In Java, a method can never change the contents of a variable that is passed to a method.

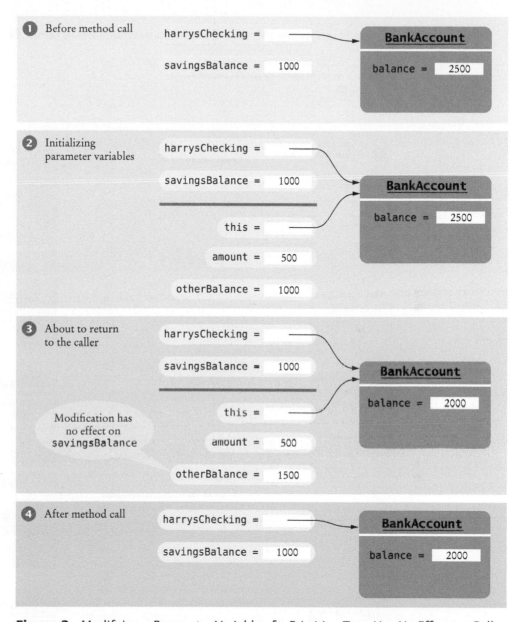

Figure 2 Modifying a Parameter Variable of a Primitive Type Has No Effect on Caller

quite correct. In Java, objects themselves are never passed as arguments; instead, both numbers and *object references* are passed by value.

The confusion arises because a Java method can mutate an object when it receives an object reference as an argument (see Figure 3).

```java
public class BankAccount
{
    . . .
    /**
        Transfers money from this account to another.
        @param amount the amount of money to transfer
        @param otherAccount account to add the amount to
```

```
    */
    public void transfer(double amount, BankAccount otherAccount)  ❷
    {
        balance = balance - amount;
        otherAccount.deposit(amount);
    }  ❸
}
```

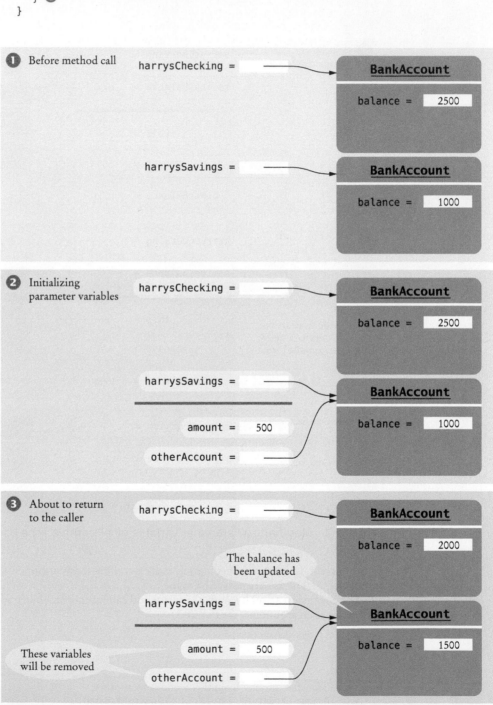

Figure 3 Methods Can Mutate Any Objects to Which They Hold References

Now we pass an object reference to the transfer method:

```
BankAccount harrysSavings = new BankAccount(1000);
harrysChecking.transfer(500, harrysSavings); ❶
System.out.println(harrysSavings.getBalance());
```

This example works as expected. The parameter variable otherAccount contains a *copy* of the object reference harrysSavings. You saw in Section 2.8 what is means to make a copy of an object reference—you get another reference to the same object. Through that reference, the method is able to modify the object.

However, a method cannot *replace* an object reference that is passed as an argument. To appreciate this subtle difference, consider this method that tries to set the otherAccount parameter variable to a new object:

```
public class BankAccount
{
   . . .
   public void transfer(double amount, BankAccount otherAccount)
   {
      balance = balance - amount;
      double newBalance = otherAccount.balance + amount;
      otherAccount = new BankAccount(newBalance); // Won't work
   }
}
```

In this situation, we are not trying to change the *state* of the object to which the parameter variable otherAccount refers; instead, we are trying to replace the object with a different one (see Figure 4). Now the reference stored in parameter variable otherAccount is replaced with a reference to a new account. But if you call the method with

```
harrysChecking.transfer(500, savingsAccount);
```

then that change does not affect the savingsAccount variable that is supplied in the call. This example demonstrates that objects are not passed by reference.

In Java, a method can change the state of an object reference argument, but it cannot replace the object reference with another.

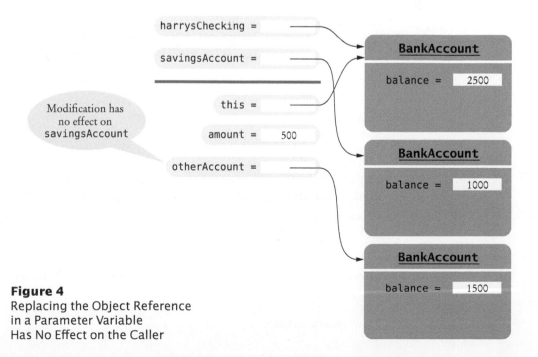

Figure 4
Replacing the Object Reference
in a Parameter Variable
Has No Effect on the Caller

To summarize:

- A Java method can't change the contents of any variable passed as an argument.
- A Java method can mutate an object when it receives a reference to it as an argument.

EXAMPLE CODE   See special_topic_1 of your eText or companion code for the program demonstrating call by value.

8.3 Problem Solving: Patterns for Object Data

When you design a class, you first consider the needs of the programmers who use the class. You provide the methods that the users of your class will call when they manipulate objects. When you implement the class, you need to come up with the instance variables for the class. It is not always obvious how to do this. Fortunately, there is a small set of recurring patterns that you can adapt when you design your own classes. We introduce these patterns in the following sections.

8.3.1 Keeping a Total

Many classes need to keep track of a quantity that can go up or down as certain methods are called. Examples:

- A bank account has a balance that is increased by a deposit, decreased by a withdrawal.
- A cash register has a total that is increased when an item is added to the sale, cleared after the end of the sale.
- A car has gas in the tank, which is increased when fuel is added and decreased when the car drives.

> An instance variable for the total is updated in methods that increase or decrease the total amount.

In all of these cases, the implementation strategy is similar. Keep an instance variable that represents the current total. For example, for the cash register:

```java
private double purchase;
```

Locate the methods that affect the total. There is usually a method to increase it by a given amount:

```java
public void recordPurchase(double amount)
{
    purchase = purchase + amount;
}
```

Depending on the nature of the class, there may be a method that reduces or clears the total. In the case of the cash register, one can provide a clear method:

```java
public void clear()
{
    purchase = 0;
}
```

There is usually a method that yields the current total. It is easy to implement:

```java
public double getAmountDue()
{
    return purchase;
}
```

All classes that manage a total follow the same basic pattern. Find the methods that affect the total and provide the appropriate code for increasing or decreasing it. Find the methods that report or use the total, and have those methods read the current total.

8.3.2 Counting Events

You often need to count how many times certain events occur in the life of an object. For example:

- In a cash register, you may want to know how many items have been added in a sale.
- A bank account charges a fee for each transaction; you need to count them.

Keep a counter, such as

```
private int itemCount;
```

> A counter that counts events is incremented in methods that correspond to the events.

Increment the counter in those methods that correspond to the events that you want to count:

```
public void recordPurchase(double amount)
{
    purchase = purchase + amount;
    itemCount++;
}
```

You may need to clear the counter, for example at the end of a sale or a statement period:

```
public void clear()
{
    purchase = 0;
    itemCount = 0;
}
```

There may or may not be a method that reports the count to the class user. The count may only be used to compute a fee or an average. Find out which methods in your class make use of the count, and read the current value in those methods.

8.3.3 Collecting Values

Some objects collect numbers, strings, or other objects. For example, each multiple-choice question has a number of choices. A cash register may need to store all prices of the current sale.

> An object can collect other objects in an array or array list.

Use an array list or an array to store the values. (An array list is usually simpler because you won't need to track the number of values.) For example,

```
public class Question
{
    private ArrayList<String> choices;
    . . .
}
```

A shopping cart object needs to manage a collection of items. © paul prescott/iStockphoto.

In the constructor, initialize the instance variable to an empty collection:

```
public Question()
{
    choices = new ArrayList<String>();
}
```

You need to supply some mechanism for adding values. It is common to provide a method for appending a value to the collection:

```
public void add(String option)
{
    choices.add(option);
}
```

The user of a Question object can call this method multiple times to add the choices.

8.3.4 Managing Properties of an Object

A property is a value of an object that an object user can set and retrieve. For example, a Student object may have a name and an ID. Provide an instance variable to store the property's value and methods to get and set it.

```
public class Student
{
    private String name;
    . . .
    public String getName() { return name; }
    public void setName(String newName) { name = newName; }
    . . .
}
```

It is common to add error checking to the setter method. For example, we may want to reject a blank name:

```
public void setName(String newName)
{
    if (newName.length() > 0) { name = newName; }
}
```

Some properties should not change after they have been set in the constructor. For example, a student's ID may be fixed (unlike the student's name, which may change). In that case, don't supply a setter method.

```
public class Student
{
    private int id;
    . . .
    public Student(int anId) { id = anId; }
    public String getId() { return id; }
    // No setId method
    . . .
}
```

EXAMPLE CODE   See sec03_04 of your eText or companion code for a class with getter and setter methods.

8.3.5 Modeling Objects with Distinct States

Some objects have behavior that varies depending on what has happened in the past. For example, a Fish object may look for food when it is hungry and ignore food after it has eaten. Such an object would need to remember whether it has recently eaten.

Supply an instance variable that models the state, together with some constants for the state values:

```java
public class Fish
{
   private int hungry;

   public static final int NOT_HUNGRY = 0;
   public static final int SOMEWHAT_HUNGRY = 1;
   public static final int VERY_HUNGRY = 2;
   . . .
}
```

(Alternatively, you can use an enumeration—see Special Topic 5.4.)

Determine which methods change the state. In this example, a fish that has just eaten won't be hungry. But as the fish moves, it will get hungrier:

```java
public void eat()
{
   hungry = NOT_HUNGRY;
   . . .
}

public void move()
{
   . . .
   if (hungry < VERY_HUNGRY) { hungry++; }
}
```

© John Alexander/iStockphoto.

If a fish is in a hungry state, its behavior changes.

Finally, determine where the state affects behavior. A fish that is very hungry will want to look for food first:

```java
public void move()
{
   if (hungry == VERY_HUNGRY)
   {
      Look for food.
   }
   . . .
}
```

EXAMPLE CODE   See sec03_05 of your eText or companion code for the Fish class.

8.3.6 Describing the Position of an Object

Some objects move around during their lifetime, and they remember their current position. For example,

- A train drives along a track and keeps track of the distance from the terminus.
- A simulated bug living on a grid crawls from one grid location to the next, or makes 90 degree turns to the left or right.
- A cannonball is shot into the air, then descends as it is pulled by the gravitational force.

Such objects need to store their position. Depending on the nature of their movement, they may also need to store their orientation or velocity.

If the object moves along a line, you can represent the position as a distance from a fixed point:

```
private double distanceFromTerminus;
```

If the object moves in a grid, remember its current location and direction in the grid:

```
private int row;
private int column;
private int direction; // 0 = North, 1 = East, 2 = South, 3 = West
```

When you model a physical object such as a cannonball, you need to track both the position and the velocity, possibly in two or three dimensions. Here we model a cannonball that is shot upward into the air:

```
private double zPosition;
private double zVelocity;
```

There will be methods that update the position. In the simplest case, you may be told by how much the object moves:

```
public void move(double distanceMoved)
{
    distanceFromTerminus = distanceFromTerminus + distanceMoved;
}
```

If the movement happens in a grid, you need to update the row or column, depending on the current orientation.

```
public void moveOneUnit()
{
    if (direction == NORTH) { row--; }
    else if (direction == EAST) { column++; }
    else if (direction == SOUTH) { row++; }
    else if (direction == WEST) { column--; }
}
```

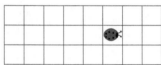

A bug in a grid needs to store its row, column, and direction.

Exercise ••• Science P8.11 shows you how to update the position of a physical object with known velocity.

Whenever you have a moving object, keep in mind that your program will simulate the actual movement in some way. Find out the rules of that simulation, such as movement along a line or in a grid with integer coordinates. Those rules determine how to represent the current position. Then locate the methods that move the object, and update the positions according to the rules of the simulation.

EXAMPLE CODE   See sec03_06 of your eText or companion code for two classes that update position data.

8.4 Static Variables and Methods

A static variable belongs to the class, not to any object of the class.

Sometimes, a value properly belongs to a class, not to any object of the class. You use a **static variable** for this purpose.

The reserved word static *is a holdover from the C++ language. Its use in Java has no relationship to the normal use of the term.*

© Diane Diederich/iStockphoto.

Here is a typical example: We want to assign bank account numbers sequentially. That is, we want the bank account constructor to construct the first account with number 1001, the next with number 1002, and so on. To solve this problem, we need to have a single value of lastAssignedNumber that is a property of the *class*, not any object of the class. Such a variable is called a static variable because you declare it using the static reserved word.

```
public class BankAccount
{
   private double balance;
   private int accountNumber;
   private static int lastAssignedNumber = 1000;

   public BankAccount()
   {
      lastAssignedNumber++;
      accountNumber = lastAssignedNumber;
   }
   . . .
}
```

Every BankAccount object has its own balance and accountNumber instance variables, but all objects share a single copy of the lastAssignedNumber variable (see Figure 5). That variable is stored in a separate location, outside any BankAccount objects.

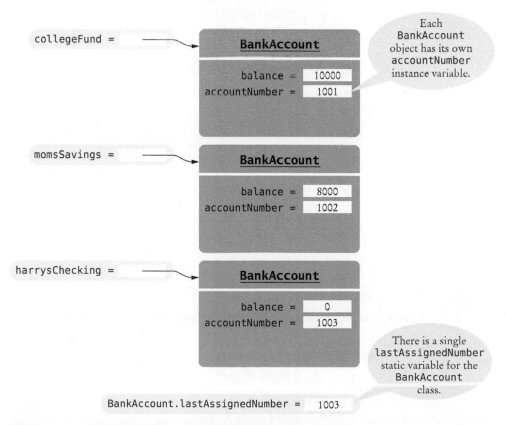

Figure 5 A Static Variable and Instance Variables

Like instance variables, static variables should always be declared as `private` to ensure that methods of other classes do not change their values. However, static *constants* may be either private or public.

For example, the `BankAccount` class can define a public constant value, such as

```java
public class BankAccount
{
    public static final double OVERDRAFT_FEE = 29.95;
    . . .
}
```

Methods from any class can refer to such a constant as `BankAccount.OVERDRAFT_FEE`.

> A static method is not invoked on an object.

Sometimes a class defines methods that are not invoked on an object. Such a method is called a **static method**. A typical example of a static method is the `sqrt` method in the `Math` class. Because numbers aren't objects, you can't invoke methods on them. For example, if `x` is a number, then the call `x.sqrt()` is not legal in Java. Therefore, the `Math` class provides a static method that is invoked as `Math.sqrt(x)`. No object of the `Math` class is constructed. The `Math` qualifier simply tells the compiler where to find the `sqrt` method.

You can define your own static methods for use in other classes. Here is an example:

```java
public class Financial
{
    /**
        Computes a percentage of an amount.
        @param percentage the percentage to apply
        @param amount the amount to which the percentage is applied
        @return the requested percentage of the amount
    */
    public static double percentOf(double percentage, double amount)
    {
        return (percentage / 100) * amount;
    }
}
```

When calling this method, supply the name of the class containing it:

```java
double tax = Financial.percentOf(taxRate, total);
```

In object-oriented programming, static methods are not very common. Nevertheless, the `main` method is always static. When the program starts, there aren't any objects. Therefore, the first method of a program must be a static method.

EXAMPLE CODE   See sec04 of your eText or companion code for a bank account class that includes static variables and uses a static method.

Common Error 8.1

Trying to Access Instance Variables in Static Methods

A static method does not operate on an object. In other words, it has no implicit parameter, and you cannot directly access any instance variables. For example, the following code is wrong:

```java
public class SavingsAccount
{
    private double balance;
    private double interestRate;
```

```java
public static double interest(double amount)
{
   return (interestRate / 100) * amount;
      // Error: Static method accesses instance variable
}
}
```

Because different savings accounts can have different interest rates, the interest method should not be a static method.

Programming Tip 8.2

Minimize the Use of Static Methods

It is possible to solve programming problems by using classes with only static methods. In fact, before object-oriented programming was invented, that approach was quite common. However, it usually leads to a design that is not object-oriented and makes it hard to evolve a program.

Consider the task of How To 7.1. A program reads scores for a student and prints the final score, which is obtained by dropping the lowest one. We solved the problem by implementing a Student class that stores student scores. Of course, we could have simply written a program with a few static methods:

```java
public class ScoreAnalyzer
{
   public static double[] readInputs() { . . . }
   public static double sum(double[] values) { . . . }
   public static double minimum(double[] values) { . . . }
   public static double finalScore(double[] values)
   {
      if (values.length == 0) { return 0; }
      else if (values.length == 1) { return values[0]; }
      else { return sum(values) - minimum(values); }
   }

   public static void main(String[] args)
   {
      System.out.println(finalScore(readInputs()));
   }
}
```

That solution is fine if one's sole objective is to solve a simple homework problem. But suppose you need to modify the program so that it deals with multiple students. An object-oriented program can evolve the Student class to store grades for many students. In contrast, adding more functionality to static methods gets messy quickly (see Exercise ••• E8.9).

Special Topic 8.2

Alternative Forms of Instance and Static Variable Initialization

As you have seen, instance variables are initialized with a default value (0, false, or null, depending on their type). You can then set them to any desired value in a constructor, and that is the style that we prefer in this book.

However, there are two other mechanisms to specify an initial value. Just as with local variables, you can specify initialization values for instance variables. For example,

```java
public class Coin
{
```

```
   private double value = 1;
   private String name = "Dollar";
   . . .
}
```

These default values are used for *every* object that is being constructed.

There is also another, much less common, syntax. You can place one or more *initialization blocks* inside the class declaration. All statements in that block are executed whenever an object is being constructed. Here is an example:

```
public class Coin
{
   private double value;
   private String name;
   {
      value = 1;
      name = "Dollar";
   }
   . . .
}
```

For static variables, you use a static initialization block:

```
public class BankAccount
{
   private static int lastAssignedNumber;
   static
   {
      lastAssignedNumber = 1000;
   }
   . . .
}
```

All statements in the static initialization block are executed once when the class is loaded. Initialization blocks are rarely used in practice.

When an object is constructed, the initializers and initialization blocks are executed in the order in which they appear. Then the code in the constructor is executed. Because the rules for the alternative initialization mechanisms are somewhat complex, we recommend that you simply use constructors to do the job of construction.

Special Topic 8.3

Static Imports

There is a variant of the import directive that lets you use static methods and variables without class prefixes. For example,

```
import static java.lang.System.*;
import static java.lang.Math.*;

public class RootTester
{
   public static void main(String[] args)
   {
      double r = sqrt(PI);   // Instead of Math.sqrt(Math.PI)
      out.println(r);        // Instead of System.out
   }
}
```

Static imports can make programs easier to read, particularly if they use many mathematical functions.

8.5 Problem Solving: Solve a Simpler Problem First

As you learn more about programming, the complexity of the tasks that you are asked to solve will increase. When you face a complex task, you should apply an important skill: simplifying the problem, and solving the simpler problem first.

This is a good strategy for several reasons. Usually, you learn something useful from solving the simpler task. Moreover, the complex problem can seem unsurmountable, and you may find it difficult to know where to get started. When you are successful with a simpler problem first, you will be much more motivated to try the harder one.

It takes practice and a certain amount of courage to break down a problem into a sequence of simpler ones. The best way to learn this strategy is to practice it. When you work on your next assignment, ask yourself what is the absolutely simplest part of the task that is helpful for the end result, and start from there. With some experience, you will be able to design a plan that builds up a complete solution as a manageable sequence of intermediate steps.

Let us look at an example. You are asked to arrange pictures, lining them up along the top edges, separating them with small gaps, and starting a new row whenever you run out of room in the current row.

National Gallery of Art (see Credits page for details.)

A Picture class is given to you. It has methods

```
public void load(String source)
public int getWidth()
public int getHeight()
public void move(int dx, int dy)
```

Instead of tackling the entire assignment at once, here is a plan that solves a series of simpler problems.

1. Draw one picture.

2. Draw two pictures next to each other.

3. Draw two pictures with a gap between them.

4. Draw all pictures in a long row.

5. Draw a row of pictures until you run out of room, then put one more picture in the next row.

Let's get started with this plan.

1. The purpose of the first step is to become familiar with the Picture class. As it turns out, the pictures are in files picture1.jpg ... picture20.jpg. Let's load the first one.

```
public class Gallery1
{
    public static void main(String[] args)
    {
        Picture pic = new Picture();
        pic.load("picture1.jpg");
    }
}
```

That's enough to show the picture.

2. Now let's put the next picture after the first. We need to move it to the right-most x-coordinate of the preceding picture.

pic.getWidth()

```
Picture pic = new Picture();
pic.load("picture1.jpg");
Picture pic2 = new Picture();
```

```
pic2.load("picture2.jpg");
pic2.move(pic.getWidth(), 0);
```

3. The next step is to separate the two by a small gap when the second is moved:

```
pic.getWidth()
```

GAP

```
final int GAP = 10;

Picture pic = new Picture();
pic.load("picture1.jpg");
Picture pic2 = new Picture();
pic2.load("picture2.jpg");
int x = pic.getWidth() + GAP;
pic2.move(x, 0);
```

4. Now let's put all pictures in a row. Read the pictures in a loop, and then put each picture to the right of the one that preceded it. In the loop, you need to track two pictures: the one that is being read in, and the one that preceded it (see Section 6.7.6).

previous   pic

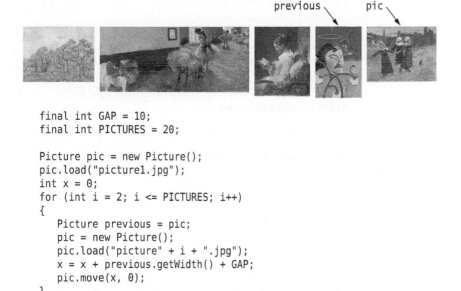

```
final int GAP = 10;
final int PICTURES = 20;

Picture pic = new Picture();
pic.load("picture1.jpg");
int x = 0;
for (int i = 2; i <= PICTURES; i++)
{
   Picture previous = pic;
   pic = new Picture();
   pic.load("picture" + i + ".jpg");
   x = x + previous.getWidth() + GAP;
   pic.move(x, 0);
}
```

5. Of course, we don't want to have all pictures in a row. The right margin of a picture should not extend past MAX_WIDTH.

```
x = x + previous.getWidth() + GAP;
if (x + pic.getWidth() < MAX_WIDTH)
{
   Place pic on current row.
}
else
{
   Place pic on next row.
}
```

If the image doesn't fit any more, then we need to put it on the next row, below all the pictures in the current row. We'll set a variable maxY to the maximum *y*-coordinate of all placed pictures, updating it whenever a new picture is placed:

```
maxY = Math.max(maxY, pic.getHeight());
```

The following statement places a picture on the next row:

```
pic.move(0, maxY + GAP);
```

Now we have written complete programs for all preliminary stages. We know how to line up the pictures, how to separate them with gaps, how to find out when to start a new row, and where to start it.

EXAMPLE CODE See your companion code for the listings of all preliminary stages of the gallery program.

With this knowledge, producing the final version is straightforward. Here is the program listing.

sec05/Gallery6.java

```
1   public class Gallery6
2   {
3      public static void main(String[] args)
4      {
5         final int MAX_WIDTH = 720;
6         final int GAP = 10;
7         final int PICTURES = 20;
8
9         Picture pic = new Picture();
10        pic.load("picture1.jpg");
11        int x = 0;
12        int y = 0;
13        int maxY = 0;
14
15        for (int i = 2; i <= PICTURES; i++)
16        {
17           maxY = Math.max(maxY, y + pic.getHeight());
18           Picture previous = pic;
19           pic = new Picture();
20           pic.load("picture" + i + ".jpg");
21           x = x + previous.getWidth() + GAP;
22           if (x + pic.getWidth() >= MAX_WIDTH)
23           {
24              x = 0;
25              y = maxY + GAP;
```

```
26        }
27        pic.move(x, y);
28      }
29    }
30 }
```

8.6 Packages

A Java program consists of a collection of classes. So far, most of your programs have consisted of a small number of classes. As programs get larger, however, simply distributing the classes over multiple files isn't enough. An additional structuring mechanism is needed.

In Java, packages provide this structuring mechanism. A Java **package** is a set of related classes. For example, the Java library consists of several hundred packages, some of which are listed in Table 1.

Table 1 Important Packages in the Java Library

Package	Purpose	Sample Class
java.lang	Language support	Math
java.util	Utilities	Random
java.io	Input and output	PrintStream
java.awt	Abstract Windowing Toolkit	Color
java.applet	Applets	Applet
java.net	Networking	Socket
java.sql	Database access through Structured Query Language	ResultSet
javax.swing	Swing user interface	JButton
org.w3c.dom	Document Object Model for XML documents	Document

8.6.1 Organizing Related Classes into Packages

To put one of your classes in a package, you must place a line

```
package packageName;
```

as the first instruction in the source file containing the class. A package name consists of one or more identifiers separated by periods. (See Section 8.6.3 for tips on constructing package names.)

For example, let's put the Financial class introduced in this chapter into a package named com.horstmann.bigjava.

The Financial.java file must start as follows:

```
package com.horstmann.bigjava;
public class Financial
{
```

```
        . . .
    }
```

In addition to the named packages (such as `java.util` or `com.horstmann.bigjava`), there is a special package, called the *default package*, which has no name. If you did not include any `package` statement at the top of your source file, its classes are placed in the default package.

In Java, related classes are grouped into packages.

© Don Wilkie/iStockphoto.

8.6.2 Importing Packages

If you want to use a class from a package, you can refer to it by its full name (package name plus class name). For example, `java.util.Scanner` refers to the `Scanner` class in the `java.util` package:

```
java.util.Scanner in = new java.util.Scanner(System.in);
```

The `import` directive lets you refer to a class of a package by its class name, without the package prefix.

Naturally, that is somewhat inconvenient. For that reason, you usually import a name with an `import` statement:

```
import java.util.Scanner;
```

Then you can refer to the class as `Scanner` without the package prefix.

You can import *all classes* of a package with an `import` statement that ends in `.*`. For example, you can use the statement

```
import java.util.*;
```

to import all classes from the `java.util` package. That statement lets you refer to classes like `Scanner` or `Random` without a `java.util` prefix.

However, you never need to import the classes in the `java.lang` package explicitly. That is the package containing the most basic Java classes, such as `Math` and `Object`.

Syntax 8.1   Package Specification

> *Syntax*   package *packageName*;
>
> package com.horstmann.bigjava;
>
> The classes in this file belong to this package.
>
> A good choice for a package name is a domain name in reverse.

These classes are always available to you. In effect, an automatic `import java.lang.*;` statement has been placed into every source file.

Finally, you don't need to import other classes in the same package. For example, when you implement the class `homework1.Tester`, you don't need to import the class `homework1.Bank`. The compiler will find the `Bank` class without an `import` statement because it is located in the same package, `homework1`.

8.6.3 Package Names

Placing related classes into a package is clearly a convenient mechanism to organize classes. However, there is a more important reason for packages: to avoid **name clashes**. In a large project, it is inevitable that two people will come up with the same name for the same concept. This even happens in the standard Java class library (which has now grown to thousands of classes). There is a class `Timer` in the `java.util` package and another class called `Timer` in the `javax.swing` package. You can still tell the Java compiler exactly which `Timer` class you need, simply by referring to them as `java.util.Timer` and `javax.swing.Timer`.

Of course, for the package-naming convention to work, there must be some way to ensure that package names are unique. It wouldn't be good if the car maker BMW placed all its Java code into the package `bmw`, and some other programmer (perhaps Britney M. Walters) had the same bright idea. To avoid this problem, the inventors of Java recommend that you use a package-naming scheme that takes advantage of the uniqueness of Internet domain names.

Use a domain name in reverse to construct an unambiguous package name.

For example, I have a domain name `horstmann.com`, and there is nobody else on the planet with the same domain name. (I was lucky that the domain name `horstmann.com` had not been taken by anyone else when I applied. If your name is Walters, you will sadly find that someone else beat you to `walters.com`.) To get a package name, turn the domain name around to produce a package name prefix, such as `com.horstmann`.

If you don't have your own domain name, you can still create a package name that has a high probability of being unique by writing your e-mail address backwards. For example, if Britney Walters has an e-mail address `walters@cs.sjsu.edu`, then she can use a package name `edu.sjsu.cs.walters` for her own classes.

Some instructors will want you to place each of your assignments into a separate package, such as `homework1`, `homework2`, and so on. The reason is again to avoid name collision. You can have two classes, `homework1.Bank` and `homework2.Bank`, with slightly different properties.

8.6.4 Packages and Source Files

The path of a class file must match its package name.

A source file must be located in a subdirectory that matches the package name. The parts of the name between periods represent successively nested directories. For example, the source files for classes in the package `com.horstmann.bigjava` would be placed in a subdirectory `com/horstmann/bigjava`. You place the subdirectory inside the *base directory* holding your program's files. For example, if you do your homework assignment in a directory `/home/britney/hw8/problem1`, then you can place the class files for the `com.horstmann.bigjava` package into the directory `/home/britney/hw8/problem1/com/horstmann/bigjava`, as shown in Figure 6. (Here, we are using UNIX-style file names. Under Windows, you might use c:\Users\Britney\hw8\problem1\com\horstmann\bigjava.)

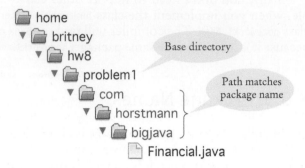

Figure 6   Base Directories and Subdirectories for Packages

Common Error 8.2

Confusing Dots

In Java, the dot symbol (.) is used as a separator in the following situations:

- Between package names (java.util)
- Between package and class names (homework1.Bank)
- Between class and inner class names (Ellipse2D.Double)
- Between class and instance variable names (Math.PI)
- Between objects and methods (account.getBalance())

When you see a long chain of dot-separated names, it can be a challenge to find out which part is the package name, which part is the class name, which part is an instance variable name, and which part is a method name. Consider

```
java.lang.System.out.println(x);
```

Because println is followed by an opening parenthesis, it must be a method name. Therefore, out must be either an object or a class with a static println method. (Of course, we know that out is an object reference of type PrintStream.) Again, it is not at all clear, without context, whether System is another object, with a public variable out, or a class with a static variable. Judging from the number of pages that the Java language specification devotes to this issue, even the compiler has trouble interpreting these dot-separated sequences of strings.

To avoid problems, it is helpful to adopt a strict coding style. If class names always start with an uppercase letter, and variable, method, and package names always start with a lower-case letter, then confusion can be avoided.

Special Topic 8.4

Package Access

If a class, instance variable, or method has no public or private modifier, then all methods of classes in the same package can access the feature. For example, if a class is declared as public, then all other classes in all packages can use it. But if a class is declared without an access modifier, then only the other classes in the *same* package can use it. Package access is a reasonable default for classes, but it is extremely unfortunate for instance variables.

It is a common error to *forget* the reserved word private, thereby opening up a potential security hole.

For example, at the time of this writing, the Window class in the java.awt package contained the following declaration:

```
public class Window extends Container
{
    String warningString;
    . . .
}
```

An instance variable or method that is not declared as public or private can be accessed by all classes in the same package, which is usually not desirable.

There actually was no good reason to grant package access to the warningString instance variable—no other class accesses it.

Package access for instance variables is rarely useful and always a potential security risk. Most instance variables are given package access by accident because the programmer simply forgot the private reserved word. It is a good idea to get into the habit of scanning your instance variable declarations for missing private modifiers.

HOW TO 8.1

Programming with Packages

This How To explains in detail how to place your programs into packages.

Problem Statement Place each homework assignment into a separate package. That way, you can have classes with the same name but different implementations in separate packages (such as homework1.problem1.Bank and homework1.problem2.Bank).

© Don Wilkie/iStockphoto.

Step 1 Come up with a package name.

Your instructor may give you a package name to use, such as homework1.problem2. Or, perhaps you want to use a package name that is unique to you. Start with your e-mail address, written backwards. For example, walters@cs.sjsu.edu becomes edu.sjsu.cs.walters. Then add a subpackage that describes your project, such as edu.sjsu.cs.walters.cs1project.

Step 2 Pick a *base directory*.

The base directory is the directory that contains the directories for your various packages, for example, /home/britney or c:\Users\Britney.

Step 3 Make a subdirectory from the base directory that matches your package name.

The subdirectory must be contained in your base directory. Each segment must match a segment of the package name. For example,

```
mkdir -p /home/britney/homework1/problem2 (in UNIX)
```
or
```
mkdir /s c:\Users\Britney\homework1\problem2 (in Windows)
```

Step 4 Place your source files into the package subdirectory.

For example, if your homework consists of the files Tester.java and Bank.java, then you place them into

```
/home/britney/homework1/problem2/Tester.java
/home/britney/homework1/problem2/Bank.java
```
or
```
c:\Users\Britney\homework1\problem2\Tester.java
c:\Users\Britney\homework1\problem2\Bank.java
```

Step 5   Use the package statement in each source file.

The first noncomment line of each file must be a package statement that lists the name of the package, such as

```
package homework1.problem2;
```

Step 6   Compile your source files from the *base directory*.

Change to the base directory (from Step 2) to compile your files. For example,

```
cd /home/britney
javac homework1/problem2/Tester.java
```

or

```
c:
cd \Users\Britney
javac homework1\problem2\Tester.java
```

Note that the Java compiler needs the *source file name and not the class name*. That is, you need to supply file separators (/ on UNIX, \ on Windows) and a file extension (.java).

Step 7   Run your program from the *base directory*.

Unlike the Java compiler, the Java interpreter needs the *class name (not a file name) of the class containing the* main *method*. That is, use periods as package separators, and don't use a file extension. For example,

```
cd /home/britney
java homework1.problem2.Tester
```

or

```
c:
cd \Users\Britney
java homework1.problem2.Tester
```

8.7 Unit Test Frameworks

Up to now, we have used a very simple approach to testing. We provided tester classes whose main method computes values and prints actual and expected values. However, that approach has limitations. The main method gets messy if it contains many tests. And if an exception occurs during one of the tests, the remaining tests are not executed.

> Unit test frameworks simplify the task of writing classes that contain many test cases.

Unit testing frameworks were designed to quickly execute and evaluate test suites and to make it easy to incrementally add test cases. One of the most popular testing frameworks is JUnit. It is freely available at http://junit.org, and it is also built into a number of development environments, including BlueJ and Eclipse. Here we describe JUnit 4, the most current version of the library as this book is written.

When you use JUnit, you design a companion test class for each class that you develop. You provide a method for each test case that you want to have executed. You use "annotations" to mark the test methods. An annotation is an advanced Java feature that places a marker into the code that is interpreted by another tool. In the case of JUnit, the @Test annotation is used to mark test methods.

In each test case, you make some computations and then compute some condition that you believe to be true. You then pass the result to a method that communicates a test result to the framework, most commonly the assertEquals method.

The `assertEquals` method takes as arguments the expected and actual values and, for floating-point numbers, a tolerance value.

It is also customary (but not required) that the name of the test class ends in `Test`, such as `CashRegisterTest`. Here is a typical example:

```
import org.junit.Test;
import org.junit.Assert;

public class CashRegisterTest
{
   @Test public void twoPurchases()
   {
      CashRegister register = new CashRegister();
      register.recordPurchase(0.75);
      register.recordPurchase(1.50);
      register.receivePayment(2, 0, 5, 0, 0);
      double expected = 0.25;
      Assert.assertEquals(expected, register.giveChange(), EPSILON);
   }
   // More test cases
   . . .
}
```

If all test cases pass, the JUnit tool shows a green bar (see Figure 7). If any of the test cases fail, the JUnit tool shows a red bar and an error message.

Your test class can also have other methods (whose names should not be annotated with `@Test`). These methods typically carry out steps that you want to share among test methods.

> The JUnit philosophy is to run all tests whenever you change your code.

The JUnit philosophy is simple. Whenever you implement a class, also make a companion test class. You design the tests as you design the program, one test method at a time. The test cases just keep accumulating in the test class. Whenever you have detected an actual failure, add a test case that flushes it out, so that you can be sure that you won't introduce that particular bug again. Whenever you modify your class, simply run the tests again.

If all tests pass, the user interface shows a green bar and you can relax. Otherwise, there is a red bar, but that's also good. It is much easier to fix a bug in isolation than inside a complex program.

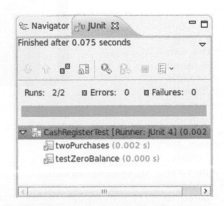

Figure 7   Unit Testing with JUnit

Computing & Society 8.1   Personal Computing

In 1971, Marcian E. "Ted" Hoff, an engineer at Intel Corporation, was working on a chip for a manufacturer of electronic calculators. He realized that it would be a better idea to develop a *general-purpose* chip that could be *programmed* to interface with the keys and display of a calculator, rather than to do yet another custom design. Thus, the *microprocessor* was born. At the time, its primary application was as a controller for calculators, washing machines, and the like. It took years for the computer industry to notice that a genuine central processing unit was now available as a single chip.

Hobbyists were the first to catch on. In 1974 the first computer *kit,* the Altair 8800, was available from MITS Electronics for about $350. The kit consisted of the microprocessor, a circuit board, a very small amount of memory, toggle switches, and a row of display lights. Purchasers had to solder and assemble it, then program it in machine language through the toggle switches. It was not a big hit.

The first big hit was the Apple II. It was a real computer with a keyboard, a monitor, and a floppy disk drive. When it was first released, users had a $3,000 machine that could play Space Invaders, run a primitive bookkeeping program, or let users program it in BASIC. The original Apple II did not even support lowercase letters, making it worthless for word processing. The breakthrough came in 1979 with a new spreadsheet program, VisiCalc. In a spreadsheet, you enter financial data and their relationships into a grid of rows and columns (see the figure). Then you modify some of the data and watch in real time how the others change. For example, you can see how changing the mix of widgets in a manufacturing plant might affect estimated costs and profits. Corporate managers snapped up VisiCalc and the computer that was needed to run it. For them, the computer was a spreadsheet machine.

More importantly, it was a personal device. The managers were free to do the calculations that they wanted to do, not just the ones that the "high priests" in the data center provided.

Personal computers have been with us ever since, and countless users have tinkered with their hardware and software. This "freedom to tinker" is an important part of personal computing. On a personal device, you should be able to install the software that you want to install to make you more productive or creative, even if that's not the same software that most people use. For the first thirty years of personal computing, this freedom was largely taken for granted.

We are now entering an era where smart phones, tablets, and smart TV sets are replacing functions that were traditionally fulfilled by personal computers. While it is amazing to carry more computing power in your cell phone than in the best personal computers of the 1990s, it is disturbing that we lose a degree of personal control. With some phone or tablet brands, you can install only those applications that the manufacturer publishes on the "app store". For example, Apple rejected MIT's iPad app for the educational language Scratch because it contained a virtual machine. You'd think it would be in Apple's interest to encourage the next generation to be enthusiastic about programming, but they have a general policy of denying programmability on "their" devices.

When you select a device for making phone calls or watching movies, it is worth asking who is in control. Are you purchasing a personal device that you can use in any way you choose, or are you being tethered to a flow of data that is controlled by somebody else?

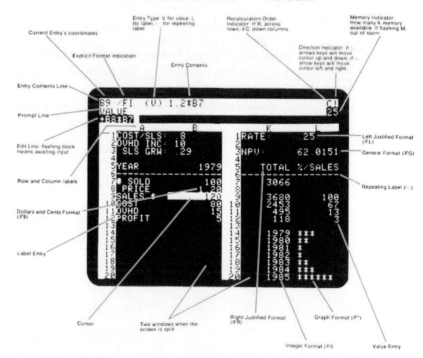

The VisiCalc Spreadsheet Running on an Apple II

CHAPTER SUMMARY

Find classes that are appropriate for solving a programming problem.

- A class should represent a single concept from a problem domain, such as business, science, or mathematics.

Design methods that are cohesive, consistent, and minimize side effects.

- The public interface of a class is cohesive if all of its features are related to the concept that the class represents.
- A class depends on another class if its methods use that class in any way.

- An immutable class has no mutator methods.
- References to objects of an immutable class can be safely shared.
- A side effect of a method is any externally observable data modification.
- When designing methods, minimize side effects.

- In Java, a method can never change the contents of a variable that is passed to a method.
- In Java, a method can change the state of an object reference argument, but it cannot replace the object reference with another.

Use patterns to design the data representation of an object.

- An instance variable for the total is updated in methods that increase or decrease the total amount.
- A counter that counts events is incremented in methods that correspond to the events.
- An object can collect other objects in an array or array list.
- An object property can be accessed with a getter method and changed with a setter method.
- If your object can have one of several states that affect the behavior, supply an instance variable for the current state.
- To model a moving object, you need to store and update its position.

Understand the behavior of static variables and static methods.

- A static variable belongs to the class, not to any object of the class.
- A static method is not invoked on an object.

Design programs that carry out complex tasks.

- When developing a solution to a complex problem, first solve a simpler task.
- Make a plan consisting of a series of tasks, each a simple extension of the previous one, and ending with the original problem.

Use packages to organize sets of related classes.

- A package is a set of related classes.
- The import directive lets you refer to a class of a package by its class name, without the package prefix.
- Use a domain name in reverse to construct an unambiguous package name.
- The path of a class file must match its package name.
- An instance variable or method that is not declared as public or private can be accessed by all classes in the same package, which is usually not desirable.

Use JUnit for writing unit tests.

- Unit test frameworks simplify the task of writing classes that contain many test cases.
- The JUnit philosophy is to run all tests whenever you change your code.

REVIEW EXERCISES

- **R8.1** Consider a car share system in which drivers pick up other riders, enabling them to make money during their commute while reducing traffic congestion. Riders wait at pickup points, are dropped off at their destinations, and pay for the distance traveled. Drivers get a monthly payment. An app lets drivers and riders enter their route and time. It notifies drivers and riders and handles billing. Find classes that would be useful for designing such a system.

- **R8.2** Suppose you want to design a social network for internship projects at your university. Students can register their skills and availability. Project sponsors describe projects, required skills, expected work effort, and desired completion date. A search facility lets students find matching projects. Find classes that would be useful for designing such a system.

- **R8.3** Your task is to write a program that simulates a vending machine. Users select a product and provide payment. If the payment is sufficient to cover the purchase price of the product, the product is dispensed and change is given. Otherwise, the payment is returned to the user. Name an appropriate class for implementing this program. Name two classes that would not be appropriate and explain why.

- **R8.4** Your task is to write a program that reads a customer's name and address, followed by a sequence of purchased items and their prices, and prints an invoice.

  Discuss which of the following would be good classes for implementing this program:

  - **a.** `Invoice`
  - **b.** `InvoicePrinter`
  - **c.** `PrintInvoice`
  - **d.** `InvoiceProgram`

- **R8.5** Your task is to write a program that computes paychecks. Employees are paid an hourly rate for each hour worked; however, if they worked more than 40 hours per week, they are paid at 150 percent of the regular rate for those overtime hours. Name an actor class that would be appropriate for implementing this program. Then name a class that isn't an actor class that would be an appropriate alternative. How does the choice between these alternatives affect the program structure?

- **R8.6** Look at the public interface of the `java.lang.System` class and discuss whether or not it is cohesive.

- **R8.7** Suppose an `Invoice` object contains descriptions of the products ordered, and the billing and shipping addresses of the customer. Draw a UML diagram showing the dependencies between the classes `Invoice`, `Address`, `Customer`, and `Product`.

- **R8.8** Suppose a vending machine contains products, and users insert coins into the vending machine to purchase products. Draw a UML diagram showing the dependencies between the classes `VendingMachine`, `Coin`, and `Product`.

- **R8.9** On which classes does the class `Integer` in the standard library depend?

- **R8.10** On which classes does the class `Rectangle` in the standard library depend?

- **R8.11** Classify the methods of the class `Scanner` that are used in this book as accessors and mutators.

■ **R8.12** Classify the methods of the class Rectangle as accessors and mutators.

■ **R8.13** Is the Resistor class in Exercise •• Science P8.13 a mutable or immutable class? Why?

■ **R8.14** Which of the following classes are immutable?
>   **a.** Rectangle
>   **b.** String
>   **c.** Random

■ **R8.15** Which of the following classes are immutable?
>   **a.** PrintStream
>   **b.** Date
>   **c.** Integer

■■■ **R8.16** Consider a method

```
public class DataSet
{
    /**
        Reads all numbers from a scanner and adds them to this data set.
        @param in a Scanner
    */
    public void read(Scanner in) { . . . }
    . . .
}
```

Describe the side effects of the read method. Which of them are not recommended, according to Section 8.2.4? Which redesign eliminates the unwanted side effect? What is the effect of the redesign on coupling?

■■ **R8.17** What side effect, if any, do the following three methods have?

```
public class Coin
{
    . . .
    public void print()
    {
        System.out.println(name + " " + value);
    }

    public void print(PrintStream stream)
    {
        stream.println(name + " " + value);
    }

    public String toString()
    {
        return name + " " + value;
    }
}
```

■■■ **R8.18** Ideally, a method should have no side effects. Can you write a program in which no method has a side effect? Would such a program be useful?

■■ **R8.19** Consider the following method that is intended to swap the values of two integers:

```
public static void falseSwap(int a, int b)
{
```

```
      int temp = a;
      a = b;
      b = temp;
   }

   public static void main(String[] args)
   {
      int x = 3;
      int y = 4;
      falseSwap(x, y);
      System.out.println(x + " " + y);
   }
```

Why doesn't the method swap the contents of x and y?

■■■ **R8.20** How can you write a method that swaps two floating-point numbers?
Hint: java.awt.Point.

■■ **R8.21** Draw a memory diagram that shows why the following method can't swap two
BankAccount objects:

```
   public static void falseSwap(BankAccount a, BankAccount b)
   {
      BankAccount temp = a;
      a = b;
      b = temp;
   }
```

■ **R8.22** Consider an enhancement of the Die class of Chapter 6 with a static variable

```
   public class Die
   {
      private int sides;
      private static Random generator = new Random();
      public Die(int s) { . . . }
      public int cast() { . . . }
   }
```

Draw a memory diagram that shows three dice:

```
   Die d4 = new Die(4);
   Die d6 = new Die(6);
   Die d8 = new Die(8);
```

Be sure to indicate the values of the sides and generator variables.

■ **R8.23** Try compiling the following program. Explain the error message that you get.

```
   public class Print13
   {
      public void print(int x)
      {
         System.out.println(x);
      }

      public static void main(String[] args)
      {
         int n = 13;
         print(n);
      }
   }
```

■ **R8.24** Look at the methods in the Integer class. Which are static? Why?

■■ **R8.25** Look at the methods in the String class (but ignore the ones that take an argument of type char[]). Which are static? Why?

■■ **R8.26** Suppose you are asked to find all words in which no letter is repeated from a list of words. What simpler problem could you try first?

■■ **R8.27** You need to write a program for DNA analysis that checks whether a substring of one string is contained in another string. What simpler problem can you solve first?

■■ **R8.28** Consider the task of finding numbers in a string. For example, the string "In 1987, a typical personal computer cost $3,000 and had 512 kilobytes of RAM." has three numbers. Break this task down into a sequence of simpler tasks.

■ **R8.29** Is a Java program without import statements limited to using the default and java.lang packages?

■ **R8.30** Suppose your homework assignments are located in the directory /home/me/cs101 (c:\Users\Me\cs101 on Windows). Your instructor tells you to place your homework into packages. In which directory do you place the class hw1.problem1.TicTacToeTester?

■■ **R8.31** Consider the task of *fully justifying* a paragraph of text to a target length, by putting as many words as possible on each line and evenly distributing extra spaces so that each line has the target length. Devise a plan for writing a program that reads a paragraph of text and prints it fully justified. Describe a sequence of progressively more complex intermediate programs, similar to the approach in Section 8.5.

■■ **R8.32** The in and out variables of the System class are public static variables of the System class. Is that good design? If not, how could you improve on it?

■■ **R8.33** Every Java program can be rewritten to avoid import statements. Explain how, and rewrite RectangleComponent.java from Section 2.9.3 to avoid import statements.

■ **R8.34** What is the default package? Have you used it before this chapter in your programming?

■■ **Testing R8.35** What does JUnit do when a test method throws an exception? Try it out and report your findings.

PRACTICE EXERCISES

■■ **E8.1** Implement the Coin class described in Section 8.2. Modify the CashRegister class so that coins can be added to the cash register, by supplying a method

```
void receivePayment(int coinCount, Coin coinType)
```

The caller needs to invoke this method multiple times, once for each type of coin that is present in the payment.

■■ **E8.2** Modify the giveChange method of the CashRegister class so that it returns the number of coins of a particular type to return:

```
int giveChange(Coin coinType)
```

The caller needs to invoke this method for each coin type, in decreasing value.

■ **E8.3** Real cash registers can handle both bills and coins. Design a single class that expresses the commonality of these concepts. Redesign the CashRegister class and provide a method for entering payments that are described by your class. Your primary challenge is to come up with a good name for this class.

■■ **E8.4** As pointed out in Section 8.2.3, the Scanner.next method is a mutator that returns a value. Implement a class Reader that reads from System.in and does not suffer from that shortcoming. Provide methods

```
public boolean hasMoreElements()   // Checks whether there is another element
public String getCurrent()   // Yields the current element without consuming it
public void next()   // Consumes the current element
```

■■ **E8.5** Reimplement the BankAccount class so that it is immutable. The deposit and withdraw methods need to return new BankAccount objects with the appropriate balance.

■ **E8.6** Reimplement the Day class of Worked Example 2.1 to be mutable. Change the methods addDays, nextDay, and previousDay to mutate the implicit parameter and to return void. Also change the demonstration program.

■■ **E8.7** Write static methods

- `public static double cubeVolume(double h)`
- `public static double cubeSurface(double h)`
- `public static double sphereVolume(double r)`
- `public static double sphereSurface(double r)`
- `public static double cylinderVolume(double r, double h)`
- `public static double cylinderSurface(double r, double h)`
- `public static double coneVolume(double r, double h)`
- `public static double coneSurface(double r, double h)`

© DNY59/iStockphoto.

that compute the volume and surface area of a cube with height h, sphere with radius r, a cylinder with circular base with radius r and height h, and a cone with circular base with radius r and height h. Place them into a class Geometry. Then write a program that prompts the user for the values of r and h, calls the six methods, and prints the results.

■■ **E8.8** Solve Exercise •• E8.7 by implementing classes Cube, Sphere, Cylinder, and Cone. Which approach is more object-oriented?

■■■ **E8.9** Modify the application of How To 7.1 so that it can deal with multiple students. First, ask the user for all student names. Then read in the scores for all quizzes, prompting for the score of each student. Finally, print the names of all students and their final scores. Use a single class and only static methods.

■■■ **E8.10** Repeat Exercise ••• E8.9, using multiple classes. Provide a GradeBook class that collects objects of type Student.

■■■ **E8.11** Write methods

```
public static double perimeter(Ellipse2D.Double e);
public static double area(Ellipse2D.Double e);
```

that compute the area and the perimeter of the ellipse e. Add these methods to a class Geometry. The challenging part of this assignment is to find and implement an accurate formula for the perimeter. Why does it make sense to use a static method in this case?

■■ **E8.12** Write methods

```
public static double angle(Point2D.Double p, Point2D.Double q)
public static double slope(Point2D.Double p, Point2D.Double q)
```

that compute the angle between the x-axis and the line joining two points, measured in degrees, and the slope of that line. Add the methods to the class Geometry. Supply suitable preconditions. Why does it make sense to use a static method in this case?

■■■ **E8.13** Write methods

```
public static boolean isInside(Point2D.Double p, Ellipse2D.Double e)
public static boolean isOnBoundary(Point2D.Double p, Ellipse2D.Double e)
```

that test whether a point is inside or on the boundary of an ellipse. Add the methods to the class Geometry.

■■ **E8.14** Using the Picture class from Worked Example 6.2, write a method

```
public static Picture superimpose(Picture pic1, Picture pic2)
```

that superimposes two pictures, yielding a picture whose width and height are the larger of the widths and heights of pic1 and pic2. In the area where both pictures have pixels, average the colors.

■■ **E8.15** Using the Picture class from Worked Example 6.2, write a method

```
public static Picture greenScreen(Picture pic1, Picture pic2)
```

that superimposes two pictures, yielding a picture whose width and height are the larger of the widths and heights of pic1 and pic2. In the area where both pictures have pixels, use pic1, except when its pixels are green, in which case, you use pic2.

■ **E8.16** Write a method

```
public static int readInt(
        Scanner in, String prompt, String error, int min, int max)
```

that displays the prompt string, reads an integer, and tests whether it is between the minimum and maximum. If not, print an error message and repeat reading the input. Add the method to a class Input.

■■ **E8.17** Consider the following algorithm for computing x^n for an integer n. If $n < 0$, x^n is $1/x^{-n}$. If n is positive and even, then $x^n = (x^{n/2})^2$. If n is positive and odd, then $x^n = x^{n-1} \times x$. Implement a static method double intPower(double x, int n) that uses this algorithm. Add it to a class called Numeric.

■■ **E8.18** Improve the Die class of Chapter 6. Turn the generator variable into a static variable so that all dice share a single random number generator.

■■ **E8.19** Implement Coin and CashRegister classes as described in Exercise ●● E8.1. Place the classes into a package called money. Keep the CashRegisterTester class in the default package.

■ **E8.20** Place a BankAccount class in a package whose name is derived from your e-mail address, as described in Section 8.6. Keep the BankAccountTester class in the default package.

■■ **Testing E8.21** Provide a JUnit test class StudentTest with three test methods, each of which tests a different method of the Student class in How To 7.1.

■■ **Testing E8.22** Provide JUnit test class TaxReturnTest with three test methods that test different tax situations for the TaxReturn class in Chapter 5.

■ **Graphics E8.23**   Write methods

- `public static void drawH(Graphics2D g2, Point2D.Double p);`
- `public static void drawE(Graphics2D g2, Point2D.Double p);`
- `public static void drawL(Graphics2D g2, Point2D.Double p);`
- `public static void drawO(Graphics2D g2, Point2D.Double p);`

that show the letters H, E, L, O in the graphics window, where the point p is the top-left corner of the letter. Then call the methods to draw the words "HELLO" and "HOLE" on the graphics display. Draw lines and ellipses. Do not use the `drawString` method. Do not use `System.out`.

■■ **Graphics E8.24**   Repeat Exercise • Graphics E8.23 by designing classes `LetterH`, `LetterE`, `LetterL`, and `LetterO`, each with a constructor that takes a `Point2D.Double` parameter (the top-left corner) and a method `draw(Graphics2D g2)`. Which solution is more object-oriented?

■■ **E8.25**   Add a method `ArrayList<Double> getStatement()` to the `BankAccount` class that returns a list of all deposits and withdrawals as positive or negative values. Also add a method `void clearStatement()` that resets the statement.

■■ **E8.26**   Implement a class `LoginForm` that simulates a login form that you find on many web pages. Supply methods

```
public void input(String text)
public void click(String button)
public boolean loggedIn()
```

The first input is the user name, the second input is the password. The `click` method can be called with arguments `"Submit"` and `"Reset"`. Once a user has been successfully logged in, by supplying the user name, password, and clicking on the submit button, the `loggedIn` method returns true and further input has no effect. When a user tries to log in with an invalid user name and password, the form is reset.

Supply a constructor with the expected user name and password.

■■ **E8.27**   Implement a class `Robot` that simulates a robot wandering on an infinite plane. The robot is located at a point with integer coordinates and faces north, east, south, or west. Supply methods

```
public void turnLeft()
public void turnRight()
public void move()
public Point getLocation()
public String getDirection()
```

The `turnLeft` and `turnRight` methods change the direction but not the location. The `move` method moves the robot by one unit in the direction it is facing. The `getDirection` method returns a string `"N"`, `"E"`, `"S"`, or `"W"`.

PROGRAMMING PROJECTS

■■■ **P8.1**   Declare a class `ComboLock` that works like the combination lock in a gym locker, as shown here. The lock is constructed with a combination—three numbers between 0 and 39. The `reset` method resets the dial so that it points to 0. The `turnLeft` and `turnRight` methods turn the dial by a given number of ticks to the left or right. The `open` method attempts to open the lock. The lock

opens if the user first turned it right to the first number in the combination, then left to the second, and then right to the third.

```
public class ComboLock
{
    . . .
    public ComboLock(int secret1, int secret2, int secret3) { . . . }
    public void reset() { . . . }
    public void turnLeft(int ticks) { . . . }
    public void turnRight(int ticks) { . . . }
    public boolean open() { . . . }
}
```

■■■ P8.2 Improve the picture gallery program in Section 8.5 to fill the space more efficiently. Instead of lining up all pictures along the top edge, find the first available space where you can insert a picture (still respecting the gaps).

National Gallery of Art (see page C-1).

Hint: Solve a simpler problem first, lining up the pictures without gaps.

National Gallery of Art (see page C-1).

That is still not easy. You need to test whether a new picture fits. Put the bounding rectangles of all placed pictures in an ArrayList and implement a method

```
public static boolean intersects(Rectangle r, ArrayList<Rectangle> rectangles)
```

that checks whether r intersects any of the given rectangles. Use the intersects method in the Rectangle class.

Then you need to figure out where you can try putting the new picture. Try something simple first, and check the corner points of all existing rectangles. Try points with smaller *y*-coordinates first.

For a better fit, check all points whose x- and y-coordinates are the x- and y-coordinates of corner points, but not necessarily the same point.

Once that works, add the gaps between images.

■■■ **P8.3** In a tile matching game, tiles are arranged on a grid with rows and columns. Two tiles are turned over at a time, and if they match, the player earns a point. If they are adjacent, the player earns an additional point. Implement such a game, using classes `Tile`, `Location` (encapsulating a row and column), `Grid`, and `MatchingGame`. You can implement the game using pictures, as in Section 8.5, or tiles with words. When designing your classes, pay attention to cohesion and coupling.

■■ **P8.4** Simulate a car sharing system in which car commuters pick up and drop off passengers at designated stations. Assume that there are 30 such stations, one at every mile along a route. At each station, randomly generate a number of cars and passengers, each of them with a desired target station.

Each driver picks up three random passengers whose destination is on the way to the car's destination, drops them off where requested, and picks up more if possible. A driver gets paid per passenger per mile. Run the simulation 1,000 times and report the average revenue per mile.

Use classes `Car`, `Passenger`, `Station`, and `Simulation` in your solution.

■■ **P8.5** In Exercise •• P8.4, drivers picked up passengers at random. Try improving that scheme. Are drivers better off picking passengers that want to go as far as possible along their route? Is it worth looking at stations along the route to optimize the loading plan? Come up with a solution that increases average revenue per mile.

■■ **P8.6** Tabular data are often saved in the CSV (comma-separated values) format. Each table row is stored in a line, and column entries are separated by commas. However, if an entry contains a comma or quotation marks, they enclosed in quotation marks, doubling any quotation marks of the entry. For example,

```
John Jacob Astor,1763,1848
"William Backhouse Astor, Jr.",1829,1892
"John Jacob ""Jakey"" Astor VI",1912,1992
```

Provide a class `Table` with methods

```
public void addLine(String line)
public String getEntry(int row, int column)
public int rows()
public int columns()
```

Solve this problem by producing progressively more complex intermediate versions of your class and a tester, similar to the approach in Section 8.5.

■■■ **P8.7** For faster sorting of letters, the U.S. Postal Service encourages companies that send large volumes of mail to use a bar code denoting the ZIP code (see Figure 8).

The encoding scheme for a five-digit ZIP code is shown in Figure 9. There are full-height frame bars on each side. The five encoded digits are followed by a check digit, which is computed as follows: Add up all digits, and choose the check digit to make the sum a multiple of 10. For example, the sum of the digits in the ZIP code 95014 is 19, so the check digit is 1 to make the sum equal to 20.

```
*************** ECRLOT ** CO57

CODE C671RTS2
JOHN DOE                          CO57
1009 FRANKLIN BLVD
SUNNYVALE      CA 95014 – 5143
```

Frame bars

Digit 1 Digit 2 Digit 3 Digit 4 Digit 5 Check Digit

```
||l..l.ll|....||.l.l.l.l....||.l.l..ll.l.l.l|
```

Figure 8 A Postal Bar Code

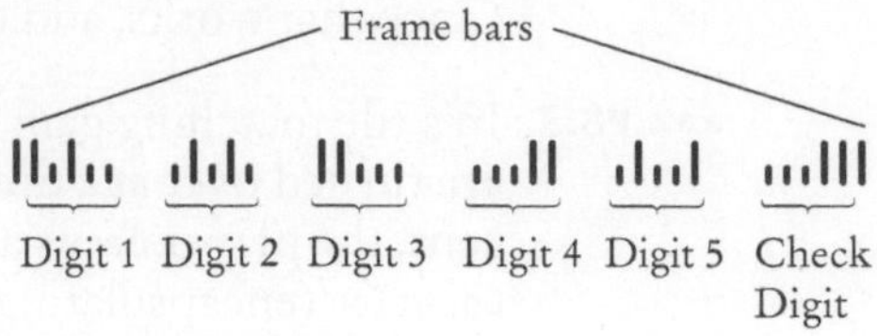

Figure 9 Encoding for Five-Digit Bar Codes

Each digit of the ZIP code, and the check digit, is encoded according to the table at right, where 0 denotes a half bar and 1 a full bar. Note that they represent all combinations of two full and three half bars. The digit can be computed easily from the bar code using the column weights 7, 4, 2, 1, 0. For example, 01100 is

$$0 \times 7 + 1 \times 4 + 1 \times 2 + 0 \times 1 + 0 \times 0 = 6$$

The only exception is 0, which would yield 11 according to the weight formula.

Digit	Weight				
	7	4	2	1	0
1	0	0	0	1	1
2	0	0	1	0	1
3	0	0	1	1	0
4	0	1	0	0	1
5	0	1	0	1	0
6	0	1	1	0	0
7	1	0	0	0	1
8	1	0	0	1	0
9	1	0	1	0	0
0	1	1	0	0	0

Write a program that asks the user for a ZIP code and prints the bar code. Use : for half bars, | for full bars. For example, 95014 becomes

```
||:|:::|:|:||::::::||:|::|:::|||
```

(Alternatively, write a graphical application that draws real bars.)

Your program should also be able to carry out the opposite conversion: Translate bars into their ZIP code, reporting any errors in the input format or a mismatch of the digits.

••• **Business P8.8** Implement a program that prints paychecks for a group of student assistants. Deduct federal and Social Security taxes. (You may want to use the tax computation used in Chapter 5. Find out about Social Security taxes on the Internet.) Your program should prompt for the names, hourly wages, and hours worked of each student.

■■ **Business P8.9** Design a `Customer` class to handle a customer loyalty marketing campaign. After accumulating $100 in purchases, the customer receives a $10 discount on the next purchase. Provide methods

```
void makePurchase(double amount)
boolean discountReached()
```

Provide a test program and test a scenario in which a customer has earned a discount and then made over $90, but less than $100 in purchases. This should not result in a second discount. Then add another purchase that results in the second discount.

■■■ **Business P8.10** The Downtown Marketing Association wants to promote downtown shopping with a loyalty program similar to the one in Exercise ●● Business P8.9. Shops are identi-fied by a number between 1 and 20. Add a new parameter variable to the `makePurchase` method that indicates the shop. The discount is awarded if a customer makes purchases in at least three different shops, spending a total of $100 or more.

© ThreeJays/iStockphoto.

■■■ **Science P8.11** Design a class `Cannonball` to model a cannon-ball that is fired into the air. A ball has

- An x- and a y-position.
- An x- and a y-velocity.

Supply the following methods:

- A constructor with an x-position (the y-position is initially 0).
- A method `move(double deltaSec)` that moves the ball to the next position. First compute the distance traveled in `deltaSec` seconds, using the current velocities, then update the x- and y-positions; then update the y-velocity by taking into account the gravitational acceleration of -9.81 m/s^2; the x-velocity is unchanged.
- A method `Point getLocation()` that gets the current location of the cannonball, rounded to integer coordinates.
- A method `ArrayList<Point> shoot(double alpha, double v, double deltaSec)` whose arguments are the angle α and initial velocity v. (Compute the x-velocity as $v \cos \alpha$ and the y-velocity as $v \sin \alpha$; then keep calling `move` with the given time interval until the y-position is 0; return an array list of locations after each call to `move`.)

Use this class in a program that prompts the user for the starting angle and the initial velocity. Then call `shoot` and print the locations.

■ **Graphics P8.12** Continue Exercise ●●● Science P8.11, and draw the trajectory of the cannonball.

■■ **Science P8.13** The colored bands on the top-most resistor shown in the photo below indicate a resistance of 6.2 kΩ ±5 percent. The resistor tolerance of ±5 percent indicates the acceptable variation in the resistance. A 6.2 kΩ ±5 percent resistor could have a resistance as small as 5.89 kΩ or as large as 6.51 kΩ. We say that 6.2 kΩ is the *nominal* *value* of the resistance and that the actual value of the resistance can be any value between 5.89 kΩ and 6.51 kΩ.

Write a program that represents a resistor as a class. Provide a single constructor that accepts values for the nominal resistance and tolerance and then determines the actual value randomly. The class should provide public methods to get the nominal resistance, tolerance, and the actual resistance.

© Maria Toutoudaki/iStockphoto.

Write a main method for the program that demonstrates that the class works properly by displaying actual resistances for ten 330 Ω ±10 percent resistors.

■■ **Science P8.14** In the Resistor class from Exercise ●● Science P8.13, supply a method that returns a description of the "color bands" for the resistance and tolerance. A resistor has four color bands:

- The first band is the first significant digit of the resistance value.
- The second band is the second significant digit of the resistance value.
- The third band is the decimal multiplier.
- The fourth band indicates the tolerance.

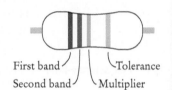

First band — Second band — Multiplier — Tolerance

Color	Digit	Multiplier	Tolerance
Black	0	$\times 10^0$	—
Brown	1	$\times 10^1$	±1%
Red	2	$\times 10^2$	±2%
Orange	3	$\times 10^3$	—
Yellow	4	$\times 10^4$	—
Green	5	$\times 10^5$	±0.5%
Blue	6	$\times 10^6$	±0.25%
Violet	7	$\times 10^7$	±0.1%
Gray	8	$\times 10^8$	±0.05%
White	9	$\times 10^9$	—
Gold	—	$\times 10^{-1}$	±5%
Silver	—	$\times 10^{-2}$	±10%
None	—	—	±20%

For example (using the values from the table as a key), a resistor with red, violet, green, and gold bands (left to right) will have 2 as the first digit, 7 as the second digit, a multiplier of 10^5, and a tolerance of ± 5 percent, for a resistance of 2,700 kΩ, plus or minus 5 percent.

■■ **Science P8.15** The figure below shows a frequently used electric circuit called a "voltage divider". The input to the circuit is the voltage v_i. The output is the voltage v_o. The output of a voltage divider is proportional to the input, and the constant of proportionality is called the "gain" of the circuit. The voltage divider is represented by the equation

$$G = \frac{v_o}{v_i} = \frac{R_2}{R_1 + R_2}$$

where G is the gain and R_1 and R_2 are the resistances of the two resistors that comprise the voltage divider.

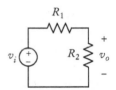

Manufacturing variations cause the actual resistance values to deviate from the nominal values, as described in Exercise ●● Science P8.13. In turn, variations in the resistance values cause variations in the values of the gain of the voltage divider. We calculate the *nominal value of the gain* using the nominal resistance values and the *actual value of the gain* using actual resistance values.

Write a program that contains two classes, VoltageDivider and Resistor. The Resistor class is described in Exercise ●● Science P8.13. The VoltageDivider class should have two instance variables that are objects of the Resistor class. Provide a single constructor that accepts two Resistor objects, nominal values for their resistances, and the resistor tolerance. The class should provide public methods to get the nominal and actual values of the voltage divider's gain.

Write a main method for the program that demonstrates that the class works properly by displaying nominal and actual gain for ten voltage dividers each consisting of 5 percent resistors having nominal values $R_1 = 250\ \Omega$ and $R_2 = 750\ \Omega$.

INHERITANCE

Jason Hosking/Getty Images, Inc.

CHAPTER GOALS

To learn about inheritance

To implement subclasses that inherit
and override superclass methods

To understand the concept of polymorphism

To be familiar with the common superclass Object and its methods

CHAPTER CONTENTS

Objects from related classes usually share common behavior. For example, cars, bicycles, and buses all provide transportation. In this chapter, you will learn how the notion of inheritance expresses the relationship between specialized and general classes. By using inheritance, you will be able to share code between classes and provide services that can be used by multiple classes.

9.1 Inheritance Hierarchies

A subclass inherits data and behavior from a superclass.

In object-oriented design, **inheritance** is a relationship between a more general class (called the **superclass**) and a more specialized class (called the **subclass**). The subclass inherits data and behavior from the superclass. For example, consider the relationships between different kinds of vehicles depicted in Figure 1.

Every car *is a* vehicle. Cars share the common traits of all vehicles, such as the ability to transport people from one place to another. We say that the class Car inherits from the class Vehicle. In this relationship, the Vehicle class is the superclass and the Car class is the subclass. In Figure 2, the superclass and subclass are joined with an arrow that points to the superclass.

When you use inheritance in your programs, you can reuse code instead of duplicating it. This reuse comes in two forms. First, a subclass inherits the methods of the superclass. For example, if the Vehicle class has a drive method, then a subclass Car automatically inherits the method. It need not be duplicated.

You can always use a subclass object in place of a superclass object.

The second form of reuse is more subtle. You can reuse algorithms that manipulate Vehicle objects. Because a car is a special kind of vehicle, we can use a Car object in such an algorithm, and it will work correctly. The **substitution principle** states that

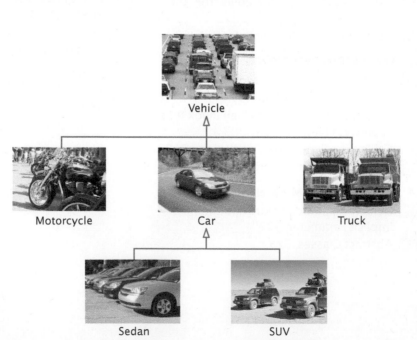

Figure 1
An Inheritance Hierarchy of Vehicle Classes

Figure 2
An Inheritance Diagram

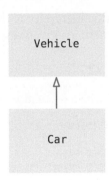

you can always use a subclass object when a superclass object is expected. For example, consider a method that takes an argument of type Vehicle:

```
void processVehicle(Vehicle v)
```

Because Car is a subclass of Vehicle, you can call that method with a Car object:

```
Car myCar = new Car(. . .);
processVehicle(myCar);
```

Why provide a method that processes Vehicle objects instead of Car objects? That method is more useful because it can handle *any* kind of vehicle (including Truck and Motorcycle objects).

In this chapter, we will consider a simple hierarchy of classes. Most likely, you have taken computer-graded quizzes. A quiz consists of questions, and there are different kinds of questions:

- Fill-in-the-blank
- Choice (single or multiple)
- Numeric (where an approximate answer is ok; e.g., 1.33 when the actual answer is 4/3)
- Free response

© paul kline/iStockphoto.

We will develop a simple but flexible quiz-taking program to illustrate inheritance.

Figure 3 shows an inheritance hierarchy for these question types.

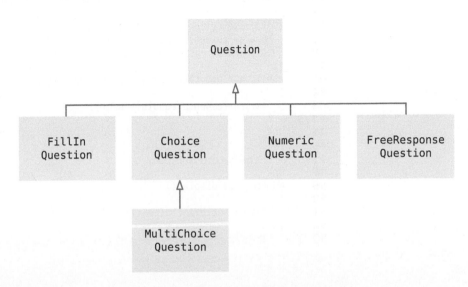

Figure 3
Inheritance Hierarchy
of Question Types

At the root of this hierarchy is the Question type. A question can display its text, and it can check whether a given response is a correct answer.

sec01/Question.java

```java
1  /**
2     A question with a text and an answer.
3  */
4  public class Question
5  {
6     private String text;
7     private String answer;
8
9     /**
10       Constructs a question with empty question and answer.
11    */
12    public Question()
13    {
14       text = "";
15       answer = "";
16    }
17
18    /**
19       Sets the question text.
20       @param questionText the text of this question
21    */
22    public void setText(String questionText)
23    {
24       text = questionText;
25    }
26
27    /**
28       Sets the answer for this question.
29       @param correctResponse the answer
30    */
31    public void setAnswer(String correctResponse)
32    {
33       answer = correctResponse;
34    }
35
36    /**
37       Checks a given response for correctness.
38       @param response the response to check
39       @return true if the response was correct, false otherwise
40    */
41    public boolean checkAnswer(String response)
42    {
43       return response.equals(answer);
44    }
45
46    /**
47       Displays this question.
48    */
49    public void display()
50    {
51       System.out.println(text);
52    }
53 }
```

This Question class is very basic. It does not handle multiple-choice questions, numeric questions, and so on. In the following sections, you will see how to form subclasses of the Question class.

Here is a simple test program for the Question class.

sec01/QuestionDemo1.java

```java
 1  import java.util.Scanner;
 2
 3  /**
 4     This program shows a simple quiz with one question.
 5  */
 6  public class QuestionDemo1
 7  {
 8     public static void main(String[] args)
 9     {
10        Scanner in = new Scanner(System.in);
11
12        Question q = new Question();
13        q.setText("Who was the inventor of Java?");
14        q.setAnswer("James Gosling");
15
16        q.display();
17        System.out.print("Your answer: ");
18        String response = in.nextLine();
19        System.out.println(q.checkAnswer(response));
20     }
21  }
```

Program Run

```
Who was the inventor of Java?
Your answer: James Gosling
true
```

Programming Tip 9.1

Use a Single Class for Variation in Values, Inheritance for Variation in Behavior

The purpose of inheritance is to model objects with different *behavior*. When students first learn about inheritance, they have a tendency to overuse it, by creating multiple classes even though the variation could be expressed with a simple instance variable.

Consider a program that tracks the fuel efficiency of a fleet of cars by logging the distance traveled and the refueling amounts. Some cars in the fleet are hybrids. Should you create a subclass HybridCar? Not in this application. Hybrids don't behave any differently than other cars when it comes to driving and refueling. They just have a better fuel efficiency. A single Car class with an instance variable

```java
double milesPerGallon;
```

is entirely sufficient.

However, if you write a program that shows how to repair different kinds of vehicles, then it makes sense to have a separate class HybridCar. When it comes to repairs, hybrid cars behave differently from other cars.

9.2 Implementing Subclasses

In this section, you will see how to form a subclass and how a subclass automatically inherits functionality from its superclass.

Suppose you want to write a program that handles questions such as the following:

```
In which country was the inventor of Java born?
1. Australia
2. Canada
3. Denmark
4. United States
```

You could write a ChoiceQuestion class from scratch, with methods to set up the question, display it, and check the answer. But you don't have to. Instead, use inheritance and implement ChoiceQuestion as a subclass of the Question class (see Figure 4).

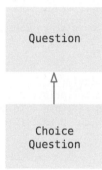

Figure 4
The ChoiceQuestion Class is a
Subclass of the Question Class

A subclass inherits all methods that it does not override.

In Java, you form a subclass by specifying what makes the subclass *different from* its superclass.

Subclass objects automatically have the instance variables that are declared in the superclass. You only declare instance variables that are not part of the superclass objects.

A subclass can override a superclass method by providing a new implementation.

The subclass inherits all public methods from the superclass. You declare any methods that are *new* to the subclass, and *change* the implementation of inherited methods if the inherited behavior is not appropriate. When you supply a new implementation for an inherited method, you **override** the method.

A ChoiceQuestion object differs from a Question object in three ways:

- Its objects store the various choices for the answer.
- There is a method for adding answer choices.
- The display method of the ChoiceQuestion class shows these choices so that the respondent can choose one of them.

*Like the manufacturer of a
stretch limo, who starts with a
regular car and modifies it, a
programmer makes a subclass by
modifying another class.*

Media Bakery.

Syntax 9.1   Subclass Declaration

Syntax   public class *SubclassName* extends *SuperclassName*
{
    instance variables
    methods
}

> The reserved word extends
> denotes inheritance.

Declare instance variables
that are *added* to
the subclass.

                                    Subclass   Superclass

    public class ChoiceQuestion extends Question
    {
Declare methods that are   private ArrayList<String> choices;
added to the subclass.

                             public void addChoice(String choice, boolean correct) { . . . }

Declare methods that   public void display() { . . . }
the subclass *overrides*.   }

When the ChoiceQuestion class inherits from the Question class, it needs to spell out these three differences:

```
public class ChoiceQuestion extends Question
{
    // This instance variable is added to the subclass
    private ArrayList<String> choices;

    // This method is added to the subclass
    public void addChoice(String choice, boolean correct) { . . . }

    // This method overrides a method from the superclass
    public void display() { . . . }
}
```

The *extends* reserved word indicates that a class inherits from a superclass.

The reserved word extends denotes inheritance. Figure 5 shows how the methods and instance variables are captured in a UML diagram.

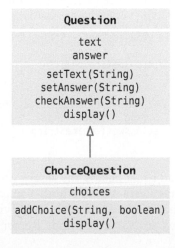

Figure 5
The ChoiceQuestion Class Adds an Instance Variable and a Method, and Overrides a Method

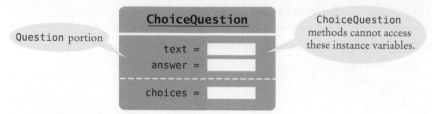

Figure 6   Data Layout of a Subclass Object

Figure 6 shows the layout of a ChoiceQuestion object. It has the text and answer instance variables that are declared in the Question superclass, and it adds an additional instance variable, choices.

The addChoice method is specific to the ChoiceQuestion class. You can only apply it to ChoiceQuestion objects, not general Question objects.

In contrast, the display method is a method that already exists in the superclass. The subclass overrides this method, so that the choices can be properly displayed.

All other methods of the Question class are automatically inherited by the Choice-Question class.

You can call the inherited methods on a subclass object:

```
choiceQuestion.setAnswer("2");
```

However, the private instance variables of the superclass are inaccessible. Because these variables are private data of the superclass, only the superclass has access to them. The subclass has no more access rights than any other class.

In particular, the ChoiceQuestion methods cannot directly access the instance variable answer. These methods must use the public interface of the Question class to access its private data, just like every other method.

To illustrate this point, let's implement the addChoice method. The method has two arguments: the choice to be added (which is appended to the list of choices), and a Boolean value to indicate whether this choice is correct.

For example,

```
choiceQuestion.addChoice("Canada", true);
```

The first argument is added to the choices variable. If the second argument is true, then the answer instance variable becomes the number of the current choice. For example, if choices.size() is 2, then answer is set to the string "2".

```
public void addChoice(String choice, boolean correct)
{
   choices.add(choice);
   if (correct)
   {
      // Convert choices.size() to string
      String choiceString = "" + choices.size();
      setAnswer(choiceString);
   }
}
```

You can't just access the answer variable in the superclass. Fortunately, the Question class has a setAnswer method. You can call that method. On which object? The question that you are currently modifying—that is, the implicit parameter of the Choice-Question.addChoice method. Remember, if you invoke a method on the implicit parameter, you don't have to specify the implicit parameter and can write just the method name:

```
setAnswer(choiceString);
```

If you prefer, you can make it clear that the method is executed on the implicit parameter:

```
this.setAnswer(choiceString);
```

EXAMPLE CODE   See sec02 of your eText or companion code for a program that shows a simple Car class extending a Vehicle class.

Common Error 9.1

Replicating Instance Variables from the Superclass

A subclass has no access to the private instance variables of the superclass.

```
public ChoiceQuestion(String questionText)
{
    text = questionText; // Error—tries to access private superclass variable
}
```

When faced with a compiler error, beginners commonly "solve" this issue by adding *another* instance variable with the same name to the subclass:

```
public class ChoiceQuestion extends Question
{
    private ArrayList<String> choices;
    private String text; // Don't!
    . . .
}
```

Sure, now the constructor compiles, but it doesn't set the correct text! Such a ChoiceQuestion object has two instance variables, both named text. The constructor sets one of them, and the display method displays the other. The correct solution is to access the instance variable of the superclass through the public interface of the superclass. In our example, the ChoiceQuestion constructor should call the setText method of the Question class.

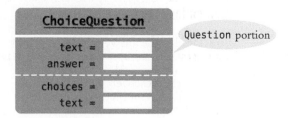

Common Error 9.2

Confusing Super- and Subclasses

If you compare an object of type ChoiceQuestion with an object of type Question, you find that

- The reserved word extends suggests that the ChoiceQuestion object is an extended version of a Question.
- The ChoiceQuestion object is larger; it has an added instance variable, choices.
- The ChoiceQuestion object is more capable; it has an addChoice method.

It seems a superior object in every way. So why is ChoiceQuestion called the *subclass* and Question the *superclass*?

The *super/sub* terminology comes from set theory. Look at the set of all questions. Not all of them are ChoiceQuestion objects; some of them are other kinds of questions. Therefore, the set of ChoiceQuestion objects is a *subset* of the set of all Question objects, and the set of Question objects is a *superset* of the set of ChoiceQuestion objects. The more specialized objects in the subset have a richer state and more capabilities.

9.3 Overriding Methods

An overriding method can extend or replace the functionality of the superclass method.

The subclass inherits the methods from the superclass. If you are not satisfied with the behavior of an inherited method, you **override** it by specifying a new implementation in the subclass.

Consider the display method of the ChoiceQuestion class. It overrides the superclass display method in order to show the choices for the answer. This method *extends* the functionality of the superclass version. This means that the subclass method carries out the action of the superclass method (in our case, displaying the question text), and it also does some additional work (in our case, displaying the choices). In other cases, a subclass method *replaces* the functionality of a superclass method, implementing an entirely different behavior.

Let us turn to the implementation of the display method of the ChoiceQuestion class. The method needs to

- *Display the question text.*
- *Display the answer choices.*

The second part is easy because the answer choices are an instance variable of the subclass.

```java
public class ChoiceQuestion
{
   . . .
   public void display()
   {
      // Display the question text
      . . .
      // Display the answer choices
      for (int i = 0; i < choices.size(); i++)
      {
         int choiceNumber = i + 1;
         System.out.println(choiceNumber + ": " + choices.get(i));
      }
   }
}
```

But how do you get the question text? You can't access the text variable of the super-class directly because it is private.

Use the reserved word super to call a superclass method.

Instead, you can call the display method of the superclass, by using the reserved word super:

```java
public void display()
{
   // Display the question text
   super.display(); // OK
   // Display the answer choices
   . . .
}
```

Syntax 9.2 Calling a Superclass Method

Syntax   super.*methodName*(*parameters*);

```
                              public void deposit(double amount)
                              {
Calls the method                  transactionCount++;
of the superclass                 super.deposit(amount);
instead of the method         }
of the current class.
                                        If you omit super, this method calls itself.
                                                See Common Error 9.4.
```

If you omit the reserved word super, then the method will not work as intended.

```
public void display()
{
    // Display the question text
    display(); // Error—invokes this.display()
    . . .
}
```

Because the implicit parameter this is of type ChoiceQuestion, and there is a method named display in the ChoiceQuestion class, that method will be called—but that is just the method you are currently writing! The method would call itself over and over.

Note that super, unlike this, is *not* a reference to an object. There is no separate superclass object—the subclass object contains the instance variables of the superclass. Instead, super is simply a reserved word that forces execution of the superclass method.

Here is the complete program that lets you take a quiz consisting of two ChoiceQuestion objects. We construct both objects and pass them to a method presentQuestion. That method displays the question to the user and checks whether the user response is correct.

sec03/QuestionDemo2.java

```java
1   import java.util.Scanner;
2
3   /**
4       This program shows a simple quiz with two choice questions.
5   */
6   public class QuestionDemo2
7   {
8       public static void main(String[] args)
9       {
10          ChoiceQuestion first = new ChoiceQuestion();
11          first.setText("What was the original name of the Java language?");
12          first.addChoice("*7", false);
13          first.addChoice("Duke", false);
14          first.addChoice("Oak", true);
15          first.addChoice("Gosling", false);
16
17          ChoiceQuestion second = new ChoiceQuestion();
18          second.setText("In which country was the inventor of Java born?");
19          second.addChoice("Australia", false);
20          second.addChoice("Canada", true);
```

```
21       second.addChoice("Denmark", false);
22       second.addChoice("United States", false);
23
24       presentQuestion(first);
25       presentQuestion(second);
26    }
27
28    /**
29       Presents a question to the user and checks the response.
30       @param q the question
31    */
32    public static void presentQuestion(ChoiceQuestion q)
33    {
34       q.display();
35       System.out.print("Your answer: ");
36       Scanner in = new Scanner(System.in);
37       String response = in.nextLine();
38       System.out.println(q.checkAnswer(response));
39    }
40 }
```

sec03/ChoiceQuestion.java

```
 1  import java.util.ArrayList;
 2
 3  /**
 4     A question with multiple choices.
 5  */
 6  public class ChoiceQuestion extends Question
 7  {
 8     private ArrayList<String> choices;
 9
10     /**
11        Constructs a choice question with no choices.
12     */
13     public ChoiceQuestion()
14     {
15        choices = new ArrayList<String>();
16     }
17
18     /**
19        Adds an answer choice to this question.
20        @param choice the choice to add
21        @param correct true if this is the correct choice, false otherwise
22     */
23     public void addChoice(String choice, boolean correct)
24     {
25        choices.add(choice);
26        if (correct)
27        {
28           // Convert choices.size() to string
29           String choiceString = "" + choices.size();
30           setAnswer(choiceString);
31        }
32     }
33
34     public void display()
35     {
36        // Display the question text
37        super.display();
```

```
38          // Display the answer choices
39          for (int i = 0; i < choices.size(); i++)
40          {
41              int choiceNumber = i + 1;
42              System.out.println(choiceNumber + ": " + choices.get(i));
43          }
44      }
45 }
```

Program Run

```
What was the original name of the Java language?
1: *7
2: Duke
3: Oak
4: Gosling
Your answer: *7
false
In which country was the inventor of Java born?
1: Australia
2: Canada
3: Denmark
4: United States
Your answer: 2
true
```

Common Error 9.3

Accidental Overloading

In Java, two methods can have the same name, provided they differ in their parameter types. For example, the PrintStream class has methods called println with headers

```
void println(int x)
```

and

```
void println(String x)
```

These are different methods, each with its own implementation. The Java compiler considers them to be completely unrelated. We say that the println name is **overloaded**. This is different from overriding, where a subclass method provides an implementation of a method whose parameter variables have the *same* types.

If you mean to override a method but use a parameter variable with a different type, then you accidentally introduce an overloaded method. For example,

```
public class ChoiceQuestion extends Question
{
    . . .
    public void display(PrintStream out)
    // Does not override void display()
    {
        . . .
    }
}
```

The compiler will not complain. It thinks that you want to provide a method just for Print-Stream arguments, while inheriting another method void display().

When overriding a method, be sure to check that the types of the parameter variables match exactly.

Common Error 9.4

Forgetting to Use super When Invoking a Superclass Method

A common error in extending the functionality of a superclass method is to forget the reserved word super. For example, to compute the salary of a manager, get the salary of the underlying Employee object and add a bonus:

```
public class Manager
{
   . . .
   public double getSalary()
   {
      double baseSalary = getSalary();
         // Error: should be super.getSalary()
      return baseSalary + bonus;
   }
}
```

Here getSalary() refers to the getSalary method applied to the implicit parameter of the method. The implicit parameter is of type Manager, and there is a getSalary method in the Manager class. Calling that method is a recursive call, which will never stop. Instead, you must tell the compiler to invoke the superclass method.

Whenever you call a superclass method from a subclass method with the same name, be sure to use the reserved word super.

Special Topic 9.1

Calling the Superclass Constructor

Consider the process of constructing a subclass object. A subclass constructor can only initialize the instance variables of the subclass. But the superclass instance variables also need to be initialized. Unless you specify otherwise, the superclass instance variables are initialized with the constructor of the superclass that has no arguments.

> Unless specified otherwise, the subclass constructor calls the superclass constructor with no arguments.

Syntax 9.3 Constructor with Superclass Initializer

Syntax
```
public ClassName(parameterType parameterName, . . .)
{
   super(arguments);
   . . .
}
```

The superclass constructor is called first.
```
public ChoiceQuestion(String questionText)
{
   super(questionText);
   choices = new ArrayList<String>();
}
```

The constructor body can contain additional statements.

If you omit the superclass constructor call, the superclass constructor with no arguments is invoked.

In order to specify another constructor, you use the super reserved word, together with the arguments of the superclass constructor, as the *first statement* of the subclass constructor.

For example, suppose the Question superclass had a constructor for setting the question text. Here is how a subclass constructor could call that superclass constructor:

> To call a superclass constructor, use the super reserved word in the first statement of the subclass constructor.

```
public ChoiceQuestion(String questionText)
{
    super(questionText);
    choices = new ArrayList<String>();
}
```

In our example program, we used the superclass constructor with no arguments. However, if all superclass constructors have arguments, you must use the super syntax and provide the arguments for a superclass constructor.

> The constructor of a subclass can pass arguments to a superclass constructor, using the reserved word super.

When the reserved word super is followed by a parenthesis, it indicates a call to the superclass constructor. When used in this way, the constructor call must be *the first statement of the subclass constructor*. If super is followed by a period and a method name, on the other hand, it indicates a call to a superclass method, as you saw in the preceding section. Such a call can be made anywhere in any subclass method.

9.4 Polymorphism

In this section, you will learn how to use inheritance for processing objects of different types in the same program.

Consider our first sample program. It presented two Question objects to the user. The second sample program presented two ChoiceQuestion objects. Can we write a program that shows a mixture of both question types?

With inheritance, this goal is very easy to realize. In order to present a question to the user, we need not know the exact type of the question. We just display the question and check whether the user supplied the correct answer. The Question superclass has methods for displaying and checking. Therefore, we can simply declare the parameter variable of the presentQuestion method to have the type Question:

```
public static void presentQuestion(Question q)
{
    q.display();
    System.out.print("Your answer: ");
    Scanner in = new Scanner(System.in);
    String response = in.nextLine();
    System.out.println(q.checkAnswer(response));
}
```

> A subclass reference can be used when a superclass reference is expected.

As discussed in Section 9.1, we can substitute a subclass object whenever a superclass object is expected:

```
ChoiceQuestion second = new ChoiceQuestion();
. . .
presentQuestion(second); // OK to pass a ChoiceQuestion
```

When the presentQuestion method executes, the object references stored in second and q refer to the same object of type ChoiceQuestion (see Figure 7).

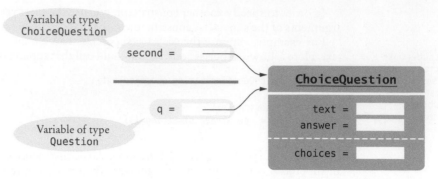

Figure 7   Variables of Different Types Referring to the Same Object

However, the *variable* q knows less than the full story about the object to which it refers (see Figure 8).

Because q is a variable of type Question, you can call the display and checkAnswer methods. You cannot call the addChoice method, though—it is not a method of the Question superclass.

This is as it should be. After all, it happens that in this method call, q refers to a ChoiceQuestion. In another method call, q might refer to a plain Question or an entirely different subclass of Question.

Now let's have a closer look inside the presentQuestion method. It starts with the call

```
q.display(); // Does it call Question.display or ChoiceQuestion.display?
```

> When the virtual machine calls an instance method, it locates the method of the implicit parameter's class. This is called dynamic method lookup.

Which display method is called? If you look at the program output on page 322, you will see that the method called depends on the contents of the parameter variable q. In the first case, q refers to a Question object, so the Question.display method is called. But in the second case, q refers to a ChoiceQuestion, so the ChoiceQuestion.display method is called, showing the list of choices.

In Java, method calls *are always determined by the type of the actual object*, not the type of the variable containing the object reference. This is called **dynamic method lookup**.

> Polymorphism ("having multiple forms") allows us to manipulate objects that share a set of tasks, even though the tasks are executed in different ways.

Dynamic method lookup allows us to treat objects of different classes in a uniform way. This feature is called **polymorphism**. We ask multiple objects to carry out a task, and each object does so in its own way.

Polymorphism makes programs *easily extensible*. Suppose we want to have a new kind of question for calculations, where we are willing to accept an approximate answer. All we need to do is to declare a new class NumericQuestion that extends Question, with its own checkAnswer method. Then we can call the presentQuestion method

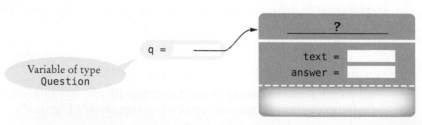

Figure 8   A Question Reference Can Refer to an Object of Any Subclass of Question

In the same way that vehicles can differ in their method of locomotion, polymorphic objects carry out tasks in different ways.

© Alpophoto/iStockphoto.

with a mixture of plain questions, choice questions, and numeric questions. The presentQuestion method need not be changed at all! Thanks to dynamic method lookup, method calls to the display and checkAnswer methods automatically select the correct method of the newly declared classes.

sec04/QuestionDemo3.java

```java
1   import java.util.Scanner;
2
3   /**
4      This program shows a simple quiz with two question types.
5   */
6   public class QuestionDemo3
7   {
8      public static void main(String[] args)
9      {
10        Question first = new Question();
11        first.setText("Who was the inventor of Java?");
12        first.setAnswer("James Gosling");
13
14        ChoiceQuestion second = new ChoiceQuestion();
15        second.setText("In which country was the inventor of Java born?");
16        second.addChoice("Australia", false);
17        second.addChoice("Canada", true);
18        second.addChoice("Denmark", false);
19        second.addChoice("United States", false);
20
21        presentQuestion(first);
22        presentQuestion(second);
23      }
24
25      /**
26         Presents a question to the user and checks the response.
27         @param q the question
28      */
29      public static void presentQuestion(Question q)
30      {
31        q.display();
32        System.out.print("Your answer: ");
33        Scanner in = new Scanner(System.in);
```

```
34        String response = in.nextLine();
35        System.out.println(q.checkAnswer(response));
36    }
37 }
```

Program Run

```
Who was the inventor of Java?
Your answer: Bjarne Stroustrup
false
In which country was the inventor of Java born?
1: Australia
2: Canada
3: Denmark
4: United States
Your answer: 2
true
```

Special Topic 9.2

Dynamic Method Lookup and the Implicit Parameter

Suppose we add the presentQuestion method to the Question class itself:

```java
void presentQuestion()
{
   display();
   System.out.print("Your answer: ");
   Scanner in = new Scanner(System.in);
   String response = in.nextLine();
   System.out.println(checkAnswer(response));
}
```

Now consider the call

```java
ChoiceQuestion cq = new ChoiceQuestion();
cq.setText("In which country was the inventor of Java born?");
. . .
cq.presentQuestion();
```

Which display and checkAnswer method will the presentQuestion method call? If you look inside the code of the presentQuestion method, you can see that these methods are executed on the implicit parameter:

```java
public class Question
{
   public void presentQuestion()
   {
      this.display();
      System.out.print("Your answer: ");
      Scanner in = new Scanner(System.in);
      String response = in.nextLine();
      System.out.println(this.checkAnswer(response));
   }
}
```

The implicit parameter this in our call is a reference to an object of type ChoiceQuestion. Because of dynamic method lookup, the ChoiceQuestion versions of the display and checkAnswer methods are called automatically. This happens even though the presentQuestion method is declared in the Question class, which has *no knowledge* of the ChoiceQuestion class.

As you can see, polymorphism is a very powerful mechanism. The Question class supplies a presentQuestion method that specifies the common nature of presenting a question, namely to display it and check the response. How the displaying and checking are carried out is left to the subclasses.

Special Topic 9.3

Abstract Classes

When you extend an existing class, you have the choice whether or not to override the methods of the superclass. Sometimes, it is desirable to *force* programmers to override a method. That happens when there is no good default for the superclass and only the subclass programmer can know how to implement the method properly.

Here is an example: Suppose the First National Bank of Java decides that every account type must have some monthly fees. Therefore, a deductFees method should be added to the Account class:

```
public class Account
{
    public void deductFees() { . . . }
    . . .
}
```

But what should this method do? Of course, we could have the method do nothing. But then a programmer implementing a new subclass might simply forget to implement the deductFees method, and the new account would inherit the do-nothing method of the superclass. There is a better way—declare the deductFees method as an **abstract method**:

```
public abstract void deductFees();
```

An abstract method has no implementation. This forces the implementors of subclasses to specify concrete implementations of this method. (Of course, some subclasses might decide to implement a do-nothing method, but then that is their choice—not a silently inherited default.)

You cannot construct objects of classes with abstract methods. For example, once the Account class has an abstract method, the compiler will flag an attempt to create a new Account() as an error.

A class for which you cannot create objects is called an **abstract class**. A class for which you can create objects is sometimes called a **concrete class**. In Java, you must declare all abstract classes with the reserved word abstract:

```
public abstract class Account
{
    public abstract void deductFees();
    . . .
}

public class SavingsAccount extends Account // Not abstract
{
    . . .
    public void deductFees() // Provides an implementation
    {
        . . .
    }
}
```

If a class extends an abstract class without providing an implementation of all abstract methods, it too is abstract.

```
public abstract class BusinessAccount
{
```

```
      // No implementation of deductFees
   }
```

Note that you cannot construct an *object* of an abstract class, but you can still have an *object reference* whose type is an abstract class. Of course, the actual object to which it refers must be an instance of a concrete subclass:

```
Account anAccount; // OK
anAccount = new Account(); // Error—Account is abstract
anAccount = new SavingsAccount(); // OK
anAccount = null; // OK
```

When you declare a method as abstract, you force programmers to provide implementations in subclasses. This is better than coming up with a default that might be inherited accidentally.

Special Topic 9.4
Final Methods and Classes

In Special Topic 9.3 you saw how you can force other programmers to create subclasses of abstract classes and override abstract methods. Occasionally, you may want to do the opposite and *prevent* other programmers from creating subclasses or from overriding certain methods. In these situations, you use the final reserved word. For example, the String class in the standard Java library has been declared as

```
public final class String { . . . }
```

That means that nobody can extend the String class. When you have a reference of type String, it must contain a String object, never an object of a subclass.

You can also declare individual methods as final:

```
public class SecureAccount extends BankAccount
{
   . . .
   public final boolean checkPassword(String password)
   {
      . . .
   }
}
```

This way, nobody can override the checkPassword method with another method that simply returns true.

Special Topic 9.5
Protected Access

We ran into a hurdle when trying to implement the display method of the ChoiceQuestion class. That method wanted to access the instance variable text of the superclass. Our remedy was to use the appropriate method of the superclass to display the text.

Java offers another solution to this problem. The superclass can declare an instance variable as *protected:*

```
public class Question
{
   protected String text;
   . . .
}
```

Protected data in an object can be accessed by the methods of the object's class and all its subclasses. For example, ChoiceQuestion inherits from Question, so its methods can access the protected instance variables of the Question superclass.

Some programmers like the protected access feature because it seems to strike a balance between absolute protection (making instance variables private) and no protection at all (making instance variables public). However, experience has shown that protected instance variables are subject to the same kinds of problems as public instance variables. The designer of the superclass has no control over the authors of subclasses. Any of the subclass methods can corrupt the superclass data. Furthermore, classes with protected variables are hard to modify. Even if the author of the superclass would like to change the data implementation, the protected variables cannot be changed, because someone somewhere out there might have written a subclass whose code depends on them.

In Java, protected variables have another drawback—they are accessible not just by subclasses, but also by other classes in the same package (see Special Topic 8.4).

It is best to leave all data private. If you want to grant access to the data to subclass methods only, consider making the *accessor* method protected.

HOW TO 9.1

Developing an Inheritance Hierarchy

When you work with a set of classes, some of which are more general and others more specialized, you want to organize them into an inheritance hierarchy. This enables you to process objects of different classes in a uniform way.

As an example, we will consider a bank that offers customers the following account types:

- A savings account that earns interest. The interest compounds monthly and is computed on the minimum monthly balance.

- A checking account that has no interest, gives you three free withdrawals per month, and charges a $1 transaction fee for each additional withdrawal.

Problem Statement Design and implement a program that will manage a set of accounts of both types. It should be structured so that other account types can be added without affecting the main processing loop. Supply a menu

```
D)eposit W)ithdraw M)onth end Q)uit
```

For deposits and withdrawals, query the account number and amount. Print the balance of the account after each transaction.

In the "Month end" command, accumulate interest or clear the transaction counter, depending on the type of the bank account. Then print the balance of all accounts.

Step 1 List the classes that are part of the hierarchy.

In our case, the problem description yields two classes: SavingsAccount and CheckingAccount. Of course, you could implement each of them separately. But that would not be a good idea because the classes would have to repeat common functionality, such as updating an account balance. We need another class that can be responsible for that common functionality. The problem statement does not explicitly mention such a class. Therefore, we need to discover it. Of course, in this case, the solution is simple. Savings accounts and checking accounts are special cases of a bank account. Therefore, we will introduce a common superclass BankAccount.

Step 2   Organize the classes into an inheritance hierarchy.

Draw an inheritance diagram that shows super- and subclasses. Here is one for our example:

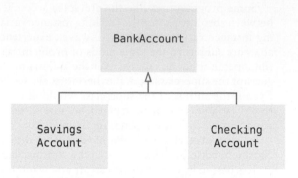

Step 3   Determine the common responsibilities.

In Step 2, you will have identified a class at the base of the hierarchy. That class needs to have sufficient responsibilities to carry out the tasks at hand. To find out what those tasks are, write pseudocode for processing the objects.

> *For each user command*
> *   If it is a deposit or withdrawal*
> *   Deposit or withdraw the amount from the specified account.*
> *   Print the balance.*
> *   If it is month end processing*
> *   For each account*
> *   Call month end processing.*
> *   Print the balance.*

From the pseudocode, we obtain the following list of common responsibilities that every bank account must carry out:

> *Deposit money.*
> *Withdraw money.*
> *Get the balance.*
> *Carry out month end processing.*

Step 4   Decide which methods are overridden in subclasses.

For each subclass and each of the common responsibilities, decide whether the behavior can be inherited or whether it needs to be overridden. Be sure to declare any methods that are inherited or overridden in the root of the hierarchy.

```
public class BankAccount
{
   . . .
   /**
      Makes a deposit into this account.
      @param amount the amount of the deposit
   */
   public void deposit(double amount) { . . . }

   /**
      Makes a withdrawal from this account, or charges a penalty if
      sufficient funds are not available.
      @param amount the amount of the withdrawal
   */
   public void withdraw(double amount) { . . . }
```

```
/**
    Carries out the end of month processing that is appropriate
    for this account.
*/
public void monthEnd() { . . . }

/**
    Gets the current balance of this bank account.
    @return the current balance
*/
public double getBalance() { . . . }
}
```

The SavingsAccount and CheckingAccount classes will both override the monthEnd method. The SavingsAccount class must also override the withdraw method to track the minimum balance. The CheckingAccount class must update a transaction count in the withdraw method.

Step 5 Declare the public interface of each subclass.

Typically, subclasses have responsibilities other than those of the superclass. List those, as well as the methods that need to be overridden. You also need to specify how the objects of the subclasses should be constructed.

In this example, we need a way of setting the interest rate for the savings account. In addition, we need to specify constructors and overridden methods.

```
public class SavingsAccount extends BankAccount
{
    . . .
    /**
        Constructs a savings account with a zero balance.
    */
    public SavingsAccount() { . . . }

    /**
        Sets the interest rate for this account.
        @param rate the monthly interest rate in percent
    */
    public void setInterestRate(double rate) { . . . }

    // These methods override superclass methods
    public void withdraw(double amount) { . . . }
    public void monthEnd() { . . . }
}

public class CheckingAccount extends BankAccount
{
    . . .
    /**
        Constructs a checking account with a zero balance.
    */
    public CheckingAccount() { . . . }

    // These methods override superclass methods
    public void withdraw(double amount) { . . . }
    public void monthEnd() { . . . }
}
```

Step 6 Identify instance variables.

List the instance variables for each class. If you find an instance variable that is common to all classes, be sure to place it in the base of the hierarchy.

All accounts have a balance. We store that value in the BankAccount superclass:

```
public class BankAccount
{
   private double balance;
   . . .
}
```

The SavingsAccount class needs to store the interest rate. It also needs to store the minimum monthly balance, which must be updated by all withdrawals.

```
public class SavingsAccount extends BankAccount
{
   private double interestRate;
   private double minBalance;
   . . .
}
```

The CheckingAccount class needs to count the withdrawals, so that the charge can be applied after the free withdrawal limit is reached.

```
public class CheckingAccount extends BankAccount
{
   private int withdrawals;
   . . .
}
```

Step 7 Implement constructors and methods.

The methods of the BankAccount class update or return the balance.

```
public void deposit(double amount)
{
   balance = balance + amount;
}

public void withdraw(double amount)
{
   balance = balance - amount;
}

public double getBalance()
{
   return balance;
}
```

At the level of the BankAccount superclass, we can say nothing about end of month processing. We choose to make that method do nothing:

```
public void monthEnd()
{
}
```

In the withdraw method of the SavingsAccount class, the minimum balance is updated. Note the call to the superclass method:

```
public void withdraw(double amount)
{
   super.withdraw(amount);
   double balance = getBalance();
   if (balance < minBalance)
   {
      minBalance = balance;
   }
}
```

In the monthEnd method of the SavingsAccount class, the interest is deposited into the account. We must call the deposit method because we have no direct access to the balance instance variable. The minimum balance is reset for the next month.

```
public void monthEnd()
{
    double interest = minBalance * interestRate / 100;
    deposit(interest);
    minBalance = getBalance();
}
```

The withdraw method of the CheckingAccount class needs to check the withdrawal count. If there have been too many withdrawals, a charge is applied. Again, note how the method invokes the superclass method:

```
public void withdraw(double amount)
{
    final int FREE_WITHDRAWALS = 3;
    final int WITHDRAWAL_FEE = 1;

    super.withdraw(amount);
    withdrawals++;
    if (withdrawals > FREE_WITHDRAWALS)
    {
        super.withdraw(WITHDRAWAL_FEE);
    }
}
```

End of month processing for a checking account simply resets the withdrawal count.

```
public void monthEnd()
{
    withdrawals = 0;
}
```

Step 8 Construct objects of different subclasses and process them.

In our sample program, we allocate five checking accounts and five savings accounts and store their addresses in an array of bank accounts. Then we accept user commands and execute deposits, withdrawals, and monthly processing.

```
BankAccount[] accounts = . . .;
. . .
Scanner in = new Scanner(System.in);
boolean done = false;
while (!done)
{
    System.out.print("D)eposit  W)ithdraw  M)onth end  Q)uit: ");
    String input = in.next();
    if (input.equals("D") || input.equals("W")) // Deposit or withdrawal
    {
        System.out.print("Enter account number and amount: ");
        int num = in.nextInt();
        double amount = in.nextDouble();

        if (input.equals("D")) { accounts[num].deposit(amount); }
        else { accounts[num].withdraw(amount); }

        System.out.println("Balance: " + accounts[num].getBalance());
    }
    else if (input.equals("M")) // Month end processing
    {
```

```
                 for (int n = 0; n < accounts.length; n++)
                 {
                    accounts[n].monthEnd();
                    System.out.println(n + " " + accounts[n].getBalance());
                 }
              }
              else if (input.equals("Q"))
              {
                 done = true;
              }
           }
```

EXAMPLE CODE   See how_to_1 of your companion code for the program with BankAccount, SavingsAccount, and CheckingAccount classes.

WORKED EXAMPLE 9.1
Implementing an Employee Hierarchy for Payroll Processing

Learn how to implement payroll processing that works for different kinds of employees. See your eText or visit wiley.com/go/bjeo7.

Jose Luis Pelaez Inc./Getty Images, Inc.

9.5 Object: The Cosmic Superclass

In Java, every class that is declared without an explicit extends clause automatically extends the class Object. That is, the class Object is the direct or indirect superclass of *every* class in Java (see Figure 9). The Object class defines several very general methods, including

- toString, which yields a string describing the object (Section 9.5.1).
- equals, which compares objects with each other (Section 9.5.2).
- hashCode, which yields a numerical code for storing the object in a set (see Special Topic 15.2).

9.5.1 Overriding the toString Method

The toString method returns a string representation for each object. It is often used for debugging.

For example, consider the Rectangle class in the standard Java library. Its toString method shows the state of a rectangle:

```
Rectangle box = new Rectangle(5, 10, 20, 30);
String s = box.toString();
   // Sets s to "java.awt.Rectangle[x=5,y=10,width=20,height=30]"
```

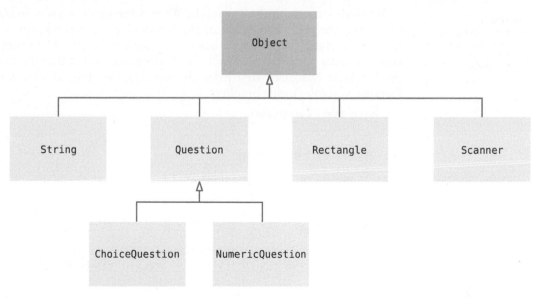

Figure 9 The Object Class Is the Superclass of Every Java Class

The toString method is called automatically whenever you concatenate a string with an object. Here is an example:

```
"box=" + box;
```

On one side of the + concatenation operator is a string, but on the other side is an object reference. The Java compiler automatically invokes the toString method to turn the object into a string. Then both strings are concatenated. In this case, the result is the string

```
"box=java.awt.Rectangle[x=5,y=10,width=20,height=30]"
```

The compiler can invoke the toString method, because it knows that *every* object has a toString method: Every class extends the Object class, and that class declares toString.

As you know, numbers are also converted to strings when they are concatenated with other strings. For example,

```
int age = 18;
String s = "Harry's age is " + age;
   // Sets s to "Harry's age is 18"
```

In this case, the toString method is *not* involved. Numbers are not objects, and there is no toString method for them. Fortunately, there is only a small set of primitive types, and the compiler knows how to convert them to strings.

Let's try the toString method for the BankAccount class:

```
BankAccount momsSavings = new BankAccount(5000);
String s = momsSavings.toString();
   // Sets s to something like "BankAccount@d24606bf"
```

That's disappointing—all that's printed is the name of the class, followed by the **hash code**, a seemingly random code. The hash code can be used to tell objects apart—different objects are likely to have different hash codes. (See Special Topic 15.2 for the details.)

Override the
toString method to
yield a string that
describes the
object's state.

We don't care about the hash code. We want to know what is *inside* the object. But, of course, the toString method of the Object class does not know what is inside the BankAccount class. Therefore, we have to override the method and supply our own version in the BankAccount class. We'll follow the same format that the toString method of the Rectangle class uses: first print the name of the class, and then the values of the instance variables inside brackets.

```java
public class BankAccount
{
   . . .
   public String toString()
   {
      return "BankAccount[balance=" + balance + "]";
   }
}
```

This works better:

```java
BankAccount momsSavings = new BankAccount(5000);
String s = momsSavings.toString(); // Sets s to "BankAccount[balance=5000]"
```

9.5.2 The equals Method

The equals method
checks whether two
objects have the
same contents.

In addition to the toString method, the Object class also provides an equals method, whose purpose is to check whether two objects have the same contents:

```java
if (stamp1.equals(stamp2)) . . .    // Contents are the same—see Figure 10
```

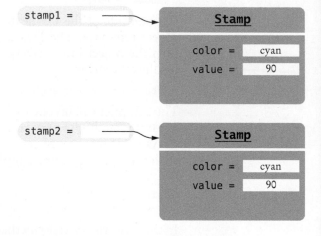

Figure 10
Two References to Equal Objects

This is different from the test with the == operator, which tests whether two references are identical, referring to the *same object:*

```java
if (stamp1 == stamp2) . . .    // Objects are the same—see Figure 11
```

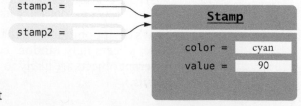

Figure 11
Two References to the Same Object

The equals *method checks whether two objects have the same contents.*

© Ken Brown/iStockphoto.

Let's implement the equals method for a Stamp class. You need to override the equals method of the Object class:

```
public class Stamp
{
   private String color;
   private int value;
   . . .
   public boolean equals(Object otherObject)
   {
      . . .
   }
   . . .
}
```

Now you have a slight problem. The Object class knows nothing about stamps, so it declares the otherObject parameter variable of the equals method to have the type Object. When overriding the method, you are not allowed to change the type of the parameter variable. Cast the parameter variable to the class Stamp:

```
Stamp other = (Stamp) otherObject;
```

Then you can compare the two stamps:

```
public boolean equals(Object otherObject)
{
   Stamp other = (Stamp) otherObject;
   return color.equals(other.color)
         && value == other.value;
}
```

Note that this equals method can access the instance variables of *any* Stamp object: the access other.color is perfectly legal.

9.5.3 The instanceof Operator

As you have seen, it is legal to store a subclass reference in a superclass variable:

```
ChoiceQuestion cq = new ChoiceQuestion();
Question q = cq; // OK
Object obj = cq; // OK
```

Very occasionally, you need to carry out the opposite conversion, from a superclass reference to a subclass reference.

For example, you may have a variable of type Object, and you happen to know that it actually holds a Question reference. In that case, you can use a cast to convert the type:

```
Question q = (Question) obj;
```

If you know that an object belongs to a given class, use a cast to convert the type.

However, this cast is somewhat dangerous. If you are wrong, and obj actually refers to an object of an unrelated type, then a "class cast" exception is thrown.

To protect against bad casts, you can use the instanceof operator. It tests whether an object belongs to a particular type. For example,

The instanceof operator tests whether an object belongs to a particular type.

```
obj instanceof Question
```

returns true if the type of obj is convertible to Question. This happens if obj refers to an actual Question or to a subclass such as ChoiceQuestion.

Using the instanceof operator, a safe cast can be programmed as follows:

```
if (obj instanceof Question)
{
    Question q = (Question) obj;
}
```

Note that instanceof is *not* a method. It is an operator, just like + or <. However, it does not operate on numbers. To the left is an object, and to the right a type name.

Do *not* use the instanceof operator to bypass polymorphism:

```
if (q instanceof ChoiceQuestion) // Don't do this—see Common Error 9.5
{
    // Do the task the ChoiceQuestion way
}
else if (q instanceof Question)
{
    // Do the task the Question way
}
```

In this case, you should implement a method doTheTask in the Question class, override it in ChoiceQuestion, and call

```
q.doTheTask();
```

Syntax 9.4   The instanceof Operator

Syntax   *object* instanceof *TypeName*

If anObject *is* null, instanceof *returns* false.

Returns true *if* anObject *can be cast to a* Question.

The object may belong to a subclass of Question.

```
if (anObject instanceof Question)
{
    Question q = (Question) anObject;
    . . .
}
```

You can invoke Question methods on this variable.

Two references to the same object.

EXAMPLE CODE   See sec05 of your eText or companion code for a program that demonstrates the toString method and the instanceof operator.

Common Error 9.5
Don't Use Type Tests

Some programmers use specific type tests in order to implement behavior that varies with each class:

```
if (q instanceof ChoiceQuestion) // Don't do this
{
    // Do the task the ChoiceQuestion way
}
else if (q instanceof Question)
{
    // Do the task the Question way
}
```

This is a poor strategy. If a new class such as NumericQuestion is added, then you need to revise all parts of your program that make a type test, adding another case:

```
else if (q instanceof NumericQuestion)
{
    // Do the task the NumericQuestion way
}
```

In contrast, consider the addition of a class NumericQuestion to our quiz program. *Nothing* needs to change in that program because it uses polymorphism, not type tests.

Whenever you find yourself trying to use type tests in a hierarchy of classes, reconsider and use polymorphism instead. Declare a method doTheTask in the superclass, override it in the subclasses, and call

```
q.doTheTask();
```

Special Topic 9.6
Inheritance and the toString Method

You just saw how to write a toString method: Form a string consisting of the class name and the names and values of the instance variables. However, if you want your toString method to be usable by subclasses of your class, you need to work a bit harder.

Instead of hardcoding the class name, call the getClass method (which every class inherits from the Object class) to obtain an object that describes a class and its properties. Then invoke the getName method to get the name of the class:

```
public String toString()
{
    return getClass().getName() + "[balance=" + balance + "]";
}
```

Then the toString method prints the correct class name when you apply it to a subclass, say a SavingsAccount.

```
SavingsAccount momsSavings = . . . ;
System.out.println(momsSavings);
    // Prints "SavingsAccount[balance=10000]"
```

Of course, in the subclass, you should override toString and add the values of the subclass instance variables. Note that you must call super.toString to get the instance variables of the superclass—the subclass can't access them directly.

```
public class SavingsAccount extends BankAccount
{
```

```
   . . .
   public String toString()
   {
      return super.toString() + "[interestRate=" + interestRate + "]";
   }
}
```

Now a savings account is converted to a string such as SavingsAccount[balance=10000][interest-Rate=5]. The brackets show which variables belong to the superclass.

Special Topic 9.7

Inheritance and the equals Method

You just saw how to write an equals method: Cast the otherObject parameter variable to the type of your class, and then compare the instance variables of the implicit parameter and the explicit parameter.

But what if someone called stamp1.equals(x) where x wasn't a Stamp object? Then the bad cast would generate an exception. It is a good idea to test whether otherObject really is an instance of the Stamp class. The easiest test would be with the instanceof operator. However, that test is not specific enough. It would be possible for otherObject to belong to some subclass of Stamp. To rule out that possibility, you should test whether the two objects belong to the same class. If not, return false.

```
if (getClass() != otherObject.getClass()) { return false; }
```

Moreover, the Java language specification demands that the equals method return false when otherObject is null.

Here is an improved version of the equals method that takes these two points into account:

```
public boolean equals(Object otherObject)
{
   if (otherObject == null) { return false; }
   if (getClass() != otherObject.getClass()) { return false; }
   Stamp other = (Stamp) otherObject;
   return color.equals(other.color) && value == other.value;
}
```

When you implement equals in a subclass, you should first call equals in the superclass to check whether the superclass instance variables match. Here is an example:

```
public CollectibleStamp extends Stamp
{
   private int year;
   . . .
   public boolean equals(Object otherObject)
   {
      if (!super.equals(otherObject)) { return false; }
      CollectibleStamp other = (CollectibleStamp) otherObject;
      return year == other.year;
   }
}
```

Computing & Society 9.1   Who Controls the Internet?

In 1962, J.C.R. Licklider was head of the first computer research program at DARPA, the Defense Advanced Research Projects Agency. He wrote a series of papers describing a "galactic network" through which computer users could access data and programs from other sites. This was well before computer networks were invented. By 1969, four computers—three in California and one in Utah—were connected to the ARPANET, the precursor of the Internet. The network grew quickly, linking computers at many universities and research organizations. It was originally thought that most network users wanted to run programs on remote computers. Using remote execution, a researcher at one institution would be able to access an under-utilized computer at a different site. It quickly became apparent that remote execution was not what the network was actually used for. Instead, the "killer application" was electronic mail: the transfer of messages between computer users at different locations.

In 1972, Bob Kahn proposed to extend ARPANET into the *Internet:* a collection of interoperable networks. All networks on the Internet share common *protocols* for data transmission. Kahn and Vinton Cerf developed a protocol, now called TCP/IP (Transmission Control Protocol/Internet Protocol). On January 1, 1983, all hosts on the Internet simultaneously switched to the TCP/IP protocol (which is used to this day).

Over time, researchers, computer scientists, and hobbyists published increasing amounts of information on the Internet. For example, Project Gutenberg makes available the text of important classical books, whose copyright has expired, in computer-readable form (http://www.gutenberg.org). In 1989, Tim Berners-Lee, a computer scientist at CERN (the European organization for nuclear research) started work on hyperlinked documents, allowing users to browse by following links to related documents.

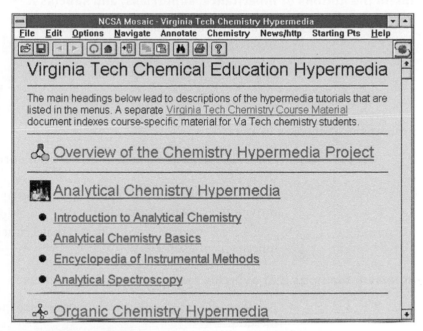

The NCSA Mosaic Browser

This infrastructure is now known as the World Wide Web.

The first interfaces to retrieve this information were, by today's standards, unbelievably clumsy and hard to use. In March 1993, WWW traffic was 0.1 percent of all Internet traffic. All that changed when Marc Andreesen, then a graduate student working for the National Center for Supercomputing Applications (NCSA), released Mosaic. Mosaic displayed web pages in graphical form, using images, fonts, and colors (see the figure). Andreesen went on to fame and fortune at Netscape, and Microsoft licensed the Mosaic code to create Internet Explorer. By 1996, WWW traffic accounted for more than half of the data transported on the Internet.

The Internet has a very democratic structure. Anyone can publish anything, and anyone can read whatever has been published. This does not always sit well with governments and corporations.

Many governments control the Internet infrastructure in their country.

For example, an Internet user in China, searching for the Tiananmen Square massacre or air pollution in their hometown, may find nothing. Vietnam blocks access to Facebook, perhaps fearing that anti-government protesters might use it to organize themselves. The U.S. government has required publicly funded libraries and schools to install filters that block sexually-explicit and hate speech, and its security organizations have spied on the Internet usage of citizens.

When the Internet is delivered by phone or TV cable companies, those companies sometimes slow down or block competing offerings. As this book is written, Americans discuss the merit of "net neutrality", the principle that carriers should give equal treatment to all data.

The Internet has become a powerful force for delivering information—both good and bad. It is our responsibility as citizens to demand of our government that we can control which information to access.

CHAPTER SUMMARY

Explain the notions of inheritance, superclass, and subclass.

- A subclass inherits data and behavior from a superclass.
- You can always use a subclass object in place of a superclass object.

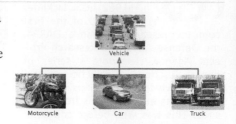

Implement subclasses in Java.

- A subclass inherits all methods that it does not override.
- A subclass can override a superclass method by providing a new implementation.
- The extends reserved word indicates that a class inherits from a superclass.

Implement methods that override methods from a superclass.

- An overriding method can extend or replace the functionality of the superclass method.
- Use the reserved word super to call a superclass method.
- Unless specified otherwise, the subclass constructor calls the superclass constructor with no arguments.
- To call a superclass constructor, use the super reserved word in the first statement of the subclass constructor.
- The constructor of a subclass can pass arguments to a superclass constructor, using the reserved word super.

Use polymorphism for processing objects of related types.

- A subclass reference can be used when a superclass reference is expected.
- When the virtual machine calls an instance method, it locates the method of the implicit parameter's class. This is called dynamic method lookup.
- Polymorphism ("having multiple forms") allows us to manipulate objects that share a set of tasks, even though the tasks are executed in different ways.

Work with the Object class and its methods.

- Override the toString method to yield a string that describes the object's state.
- The equals method checks whether two objects have the same contents.
- If you know that an object belongs to a given class, use a cast to convert the type.
- The instanceof operator tests whether an object belongs to a particular type.

REVIEW EXERCISES

- **R9.1** What are all the superclasses of the JFrame class? Consult the Java API documentation or Appendix D.

- **R9.2** In Worked Example 9.1,
  - **a.** What are the subclasses of Employee?
  - **b.** What are the superclasses of Manager?
  - **c.** What are the super- and subclasses of SalariedEmployee?
  - **d.** Which classes override the weeklyPay method of the Employee class?
  - **e.** Which classes override the setName method of the Employee class?
  - **f.** What are the instance variables of an HourlyEmployee object?

- **R9.3** Identify the superclass and subclass in each of the following pairs of classes.
  - **a.** Employee, Manager
  - **b.** GraduateStudent, Student
  - **c.** Person, Student
  - **d.** Employee, Professor
  - **e.** BankAccount, CheckingAccount
  - **f.** Vehicle, Car
  - **g.** Vehicle, Minivan
  - **h.** Car, Minivan
  - **i.** Truck, Vehicle

- **R9.4** Consider a program for managing inventory in a small appliance store. Why isn't it useful to have a superclass SmallAppliance and subclasses Toaster, CarVacuum, TravelIron, and so on?

- **R9.5** Which methods does the ChoiceQuestion class inherit from its superclass? Which methods does it override? Which methods does it add?

- **R9.6** Which methods does the SavingsAccount class in How To 9.1 inherit from its superclass? Which methods does it override? Which methods does it add?

- **R9.7** List the instance variables of a CheckingAccount object from How To 9.1.

- **R9.8** Suppose the class Sub extends the class Sandwich. Which of the following assignments are legal?
  ```
  Sandwich x = new Sandwich();
  Sub y = new Sub();
  ```
  - **a.** x = y;
  - **b.** y = x;
  - **c.** y = new Sandwich();
  - **d.** x = new Sub();

■ **R9.9** Draw an inheritance diagram that shows the inheritance relationships between these classes.

- Person
- Employee
- Student
- Instructor
- Classroom
- Object

■ **R9.10** In an object-oriented traffic simulation system, we have the classes listed below. Draw an inheritance diagram that shows the relationships between these classes.

- Vehicle
- Car
- Truck
- Sedan
- Coupe
- PickupTruck
- SportUtilityVehicle
- Minivan
- Bicycle
- Motorcycle

■ **R9.11** What inheritance relationships would you establish among the following classes?

- Student
- Professor
- TeachingAssistant
- Employee
- Secretary
- DepartmentChair
- Janitor
- SeminarSpeaker
- Person
- Course
- Seminar
- Lecture
- ComputerLab

■■ **R9.12** How does a cast such as (BankAccount) x differ from a cast of number values such as (int) x?

■■■ **R9.13** Which of these conditions returns true? Check the Java documentation for the inheritance patterns. Recall that System.out is an object of the PrintStream class.

a. System.out instanceof PrintStream
b. System.out instanceof OutputStream

    c. `System.out instanceof LogStream`

    d. `System.out instanceof Object`

    e. `System.out instanceof String`

    f. `System.out instanceof Writer`

PRACTICE EXERCISES

■■ E9.1 Suppose the class `Employee` is declared as follows:

```
public class Employee
{
    private String name;
    private double baseSalary;

    public void setName(String newName) { . . . }
    public void setBaseSalary(double newSalary) { . . . }
    public String getName() { . . . }
    public double getSalary() { . . . }
}
```

Declare a class `Manager` that inherits from the class `Employee` and adds an instance variable `bonus` for storing a salary bonus. Implement the constructors and methods, and supply a test program.

■ E9.2 Implement a subclass of `BankAccount` called `BasicAccount` whose `withdraw` method will not withdraw more money than is currently in the account.

■ E9.3 Implement a subclass of `BankAccount` called `BasicAccount` whose `withdraw` method charges a penalty of $30 for each withdrawal that results in an overdraft.

■■ E9.4 Reimplement the `CheckingAccount` class from How To 9.1 so that the first overdraft in any given month incurs a $20 penalty, and any further overdrafts in the same month result in a $30 penalty.

■■ E9.5 Add a class `NumericQuestion` to the question hierarchy of Section 9.1. If the response and the expected answer differ by no more than 0.01, accept the response as correct.

■■ E9.6 Add a class `FillInQuestion` to the question hierarchy of Section 9.1. Such a question is constructed with a string that contains the answer, surrounded by _ _, for example, `"The inventor of Java was _James Gosling_"`. The question should be displayed as

```
The inventor of Java was _____
```

■ E9.7 Modify the `checkAnswer` method of the `Question` class so that it does not take into account different spaces or upper/lowercase characters. For example, the response `"JAMES gosling"` should match an answer of `"James Gosling"`.

■■ E9.8 Add a class `AnyCorrectChoiceQuestion` to the question hierarchy of Section 9.1 that allows multiple correct choices. The respondent should provide any one of the correct choices. The answer string should contain all of the correct choices, separated by spaces. Provide instructions in the question text.

■■ E9.9 Add a class `MultiChoiceQuestion` to the question hierarchy of Section 9.1 that allows multiple correct choices. The respondent should provide all correct choices, separated by spaces. Provide instructions in the question text.

■■ **E9.10** Add a method addText to the Question superclass and provide a different implementation of ChoiceQuestion that calls addText rather than storing an array list of choices.

■ **E9.11** Provide toString methods for the Question and ChoiceQuestion classes.

■■ **E9.12** Implement a superclass Person. Make two classes, Student and Instructor, that inherit from Person. A person has a name and a year of birth. A student has a major, and an instructor has a salary. Write the class declarations, the constructors, and the methods toString for all classes. Supply a test program for these classes and methods.

■■ **E9.13** Make a class Employee with a name and salary. Make a class Manager inherit from Employee. Add an instance variable, named department, of type String. Supply a method toString that prints the manager's name, department, and salary. Make a class Executive inherit from Manager. Supply appropriate toString methods for all classes. Supply a test program that tests these classes and methods.

■■ **E9.14** The java.awt.Rectangle class of the standard Java library does not supply a method to compute the area or perimeter of a rectangle. Provide a subclass BetterRectangle of the Rectangle class that has getPerimeter and getArea methods. *Do not add any instance variables.* In the constructor, call the setLocation and setSize methods of the Rectangle class. Provide a program that tests the methods that you supplied.

■■■ **E9.15** Repeat Exercise •• E9.14, but in the BetterRectangle constructor, invoke the superclass constructor.

■■ **E9.16** A labeled point has x- and y-coordinates and a string label. Provide a class LabeledPoint with a constructor LabeledPoint(int x, int y, String label) and a toString method that displays x, y, and the label.

■■ **E9.17** Reimplement the LabeledPoint class of Exercise •• E9.16 by storing the location in a java.awt.Point object. Your toString method should invoke the toString method of the Point class.

■■ **Business E9.18** Change the CheckingAccount class in How To 9.1 so that a $1 fee is levied for deposits or withdrawals in excess of three free monthly transactions. Place the code for computing the fee into a separate method that you call from the deposit and withdraw methods.

PROGRAMMING PROJECTS

■■ **P9.1** Implement a class ChessPiece with method setPosition(String coordinates). The coordinate string identifies the row and column in chess notation, such as "d8" for the initial position of the black queen. Also provide a method ArrayList<String> canMoveTo() that enumerates the valid moves from the current position. Provide subclasses Pawn, Knight, Bishop, Rook, Queen, and King.

■■ **P9.2** Implement a class Clock whose getHours and getMinutes methods return the current time at your location. (Call java.time.LocalTime.now().toString() and extract the time from that string.) Also provide a getTime method that returns a string with the hours and minutes by calling the getHours and getMinutes methods. Provide a subclass World-Clock whose constructor accepts a time offset. For example, if you live in California, a new WorldClock(3) should show the time in New York, three time zones ahead. Which methods did you override? (You should not override getTime.)

■■ **P9.3** Add an alarm feature to the Clock class of Exercise ●● P9.2. When setAlarm(hours, minutes) is called, the clock stores the alarm. When you call getTime, and the alarm time has been reached or exceeded, return the time followed by the string "Alarm" (or, if you prefer, the string "\u23F0") and clear the alarm. What do you need to do to make the setAlarm method work for WorldClock objects?

■■ **Business P9.4** Implement a superclass Appointment and sub-classes Onetime, Daily, and Monthly. An appointment has a description (for example, "see the dentist") and occurs on one or more dates. Write a method occursOn(int year, int month, int day) that checks whether the appointment occurs on that date. For example, for a monthly appointment, you must check whether the day of the month matches. Then fill an array of Appointment objects with a mixture of appointments. Have the user enter a date and print out all appointments that occur on that date.

© Pali Rao/iStockphoto.

■■ **Business P9.5** Improve the appointment book program of Exercise ●● Business P9.4. Give the user the option to add new appointments. The user must specify the type of the appointment, the description, and the date.

■■■ **Business P9.6** Improve the appointment book program of Exercises ●● Business P9.4 and ●● Business P9.5 by letting the user save the appointment data to a file and reload the data from a file. The saving part is straightforward: Make a method save. Save the type, description, and date to a file. The loading part is not so easy. First determine the type of the appointment to be loaded, create an object of that type, and then call a load method to load the data.

■■ **Science P9.7** Resonant circuits are used to select a signal (e.g., a radio station or TV channel) from among other competing signals. Resonant circuits are characterized by the frequency response shown in the figure below. The resonant frequency response is completely described by three parameters: the resonant frequency, ω_o, the band-width, B, and the gain at the resonant frequency, k.

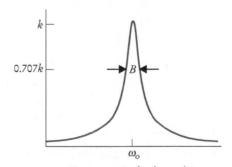

Frequency (rad/s, log scale)

Two simple resonant circuits are shown in the figure below. The circuit in (a) is called a *parallel resonant circuit*. The circuit in (b) is called a *series resonant circuit*.

Both resonant circuits consist of a resistor having resistance R, a capacitor having capacitance C, and an inductor having inductance L.

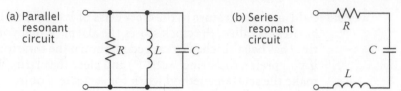

(a) Parallel resonant circuit

(b) Series resonant circuit

These circuits are designed by determining values of R, C, and L that cause the resonant frequency response to be described by specified values of ω_o, B, and k. The design equations for the parallel resonant circuit are:

$$R = k, \quad C = \frac{1}{BR}, \text{ and } L = \frac{1}{\omega_o^2 C}$$

Similarly, the design equations for the series resonant circuit are:

$$R = \frac{1}{k}, \quad L = \frac{R}{B}, \text{ and } C = \frac{1}{\omega_o^2 L}$$

Write a Java program that represents `ResonantCircuit` as a superclass and represents `SeriesResonantCircuit` and `ParallelResonantCircuit` as subclasses. Give the superclass three private instance variables representing the parameters ω_o, B, and k of the resonant frequency response. The superclass should provide public instance methods to get and set each of these variables. The superclass should also provide a `display` method that prints a description of the resonant frequency response.

Each subclass should provide a method that designs the corresponding resonant circuit. The subclasses should also override the `display` method of the superclass to print descriptions of both the frequency response (the values of ω_o, B, and k) and the circuit (the values of R, C, and L).

All classes should provide appropriate constructors.

Supply a class that demonstrates that the subclasses all work properly.

■■■ **Science P9.8** In this problem, you will model a circuit consisting of an arbitrary configuration of resistors. Provide a superclass `Circuit` with a instance method `getResistance`. Provide a subclass `Resistor` representing a single resistor. Provide subclasses `Serial` and `Parallel`, each of which contains an `ArrayList<Circuit>`. A `Serial` circuit models a series of circuits, each of which can be a single resistor or another circuit. Similarly, a `Parallel` circuit models a set of circuits in parallel. For example, the following circuit is a `Parallel` circuit containing a single resistor and one `Serial` circuit:

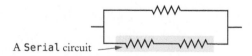

A `Serial` circuit

Use Ohm's law to compute the combined resistance.

■■ **Science P9.9** Part (a) of the figure below shows a symbolic representation of an electric circuit called an *amplifier*. The input to the amplifier is the voltage v_i and the output is the voltage v_o. The output of an amplifier is proportional to the input. The constant of proportionality is called the "gain" of the amplifier.

(a) Amplifier

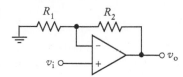

(b) Inverting
amplifier

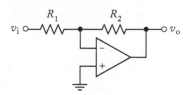

(c) Noninverting
amplifier

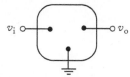

(d) Voltage
divider
amplifier

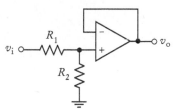

Parts (b), (c), and (d) show schematics of three specific types of amplifier: the *inverting amplifier*, *noninverting amplifier*, and *voltage divider amplifier*. Each of these three amplifiers consists of two resistors and an op amp. The value of the gain of each amplifier depends on the values of its resistances. In particular, the gain, g, of

the inverting amplifier is given by $g = -\dfrac{R_2}{R_1}$. Similarly the gains of the noninverting

amplifier and voltage divider amplifier are given by $g = 1 + \dfrac{R_2}{R_1}$ and $g = \dfrac{R_2}{R_1 + R_2}$, respectively.

Write a Java program that represents the amplifier as a superclass and represents the inverting, noninverting, and voltage divider amplifiers as subclasses. Give the superclass a getGain method and a getDescription method that returns a string identifying the amplifier. Each subclass should have a constructor with two arguments, the resistances of the amplifier. The subclasses need to override the getGain and getDescription methods of the superclass.

Supply a class that demonstrates that the subclasses all work properly for sample values of the resistances.

CHAPTER 10

INTERFACES

© supermimicry/iStockphoto.

CHAPTER GOALS

To be able to declare and use
interface types

To appreciate how interfaces can be
used to decouple classes

To learn how to implement helper
classes as inner classes

To implement event listeners in graphical applications

CHAPTER CONTENTS

A mixer rotates any tools that will attach to its motor's shaft. In other words, a single motor can be used with multiple tools. We want to be able to *reuse* software components in the same way. In this chapter, you will learn an important strategy for separating the reusable part of a computation from the parts that vary in each reuse scenario. The reusable part invokes methods of an *interface*, not caring how the methods are implemented—just as the mixer doesn't care about the shape of the attachment. In a program, the reusable code is combined with a class that implements the interface methods. To produce a different application, you plug in another class that implements the same interface.

10.1 Using Interfaces for Algorithm Reuse

When you provide a service, you want to make it available to the largest possible set of clients. A restaurant serves people, and in Java, one might model this with a method

```
public void serve(Person client)
```

But what if the restaurant is willing to serve other creatures too? Then it makes sense to define a new type with exactly the methods that need to be invoked as the service processes an object. Such a type is called an interface type.

For example, a `Customer` interface type might have methods eat and pay. We can then redeclare the service as

```
public void serve(Customer client)
```

© Oxana Oleynichenko/iStockphoto.

This restaurant is willing to serve anyone who conforms to the Customer *interface with* eat *and* pay *methods.*

If the `Person` and `Cat` classes conform to the interface, then you can pass objects of those classes to the serve method.

As a more practical example, you will study the `Comparable` interface type of the Java library. It has a method `compareTo` that determines which of two objects should come first in sorted order. It is then possible to implement a sorting service that accepts collections of many different classes. All that matters is that the classes conform to the `Comparable` interface. The sorting service doesn't care about anything other than the `compareTo` method, which it uses to arrange the objects in order.

In the following sections, you will learn how to discover when an interface type is useful, which methods it should require, how to define the interface, and how to define classes that conform to it.

10.1.1 Discovering an Interface Type

In this section, we will look at a service that computes averages, and we want to make it as general as possible. Let's start with one implementation of the service that computes the average balance of an array of bank accounts:

```
public static double average(BankAccount[] objects)
{
   double sum = 0;
   for (BankAccount obj : objects)
   {
      sum = sum + obj.getBalance();
   }
   if (objects.length > 0) { return sum / objects.length; }
   else { return 0; }
}
```

Now suppose we want to compute an average of other objects. We have to write that method again. Here it is for Country objects:

```
public static double average(Country[] objects)
{
   double sum = 0;
   for (Country obj : objects)
   {
      sum = sum + obj.getArea();
   }
   if (objects.length > 0) { return sum / objects.length; }
   else { return 0; }
}
```

Clearly, the algorithm for computing the average is the same in all cases, but the details of measurement differ. We would like to provide a *single* method that provides this service.

But there is a problem. Each class has a different name for the method that returns the value that is being averaged. In the BankAccount class, we call getBalance. In the Country class, we call getArea.

Suppose that the various classes agree on a method getMeasure that obtains the measure to be used in the data analysis. For bank accounts, getMeasure returns the balance. For countries, getMeasure returns the area, and so on.

Then we can implement a single method that computes

```
sum = sum + obj.getMeasure();
```

But agreeing on the name of the method is only half the solution. In Java, we also must declare the type of the variable obj. Of course, you can't write

```
BankAccount or Country or . . . obj; // No
```

We need to invent a new type that describes any class whose objects can be measured. You will see how to do that in the next section.

10.1.2 Declaring an Interface Type

A Java interface type declares the methods that can be applied to a variable of that type.

In Java, an **interface type** is used to specify required operations. The declaration is similar to the declaration of a class. You list the methods that the interface requires. However, you need not supply an implementation for the methods. For example, here is the declaration of an interface type that we call Measurable:

```
public interface Measurable
{
   double getMeasure();
}
```

The Measurable interface type requires a single method, getMeasure. In general, an interface type can require multiple methods.

Syntax 10.1 Declaring an Interface

Syntax   public interface *InterfaceName*
            {
                method headers
            }

```
                              public interface Measurable
                              {
The methods of an interface       double getMeasure();          No implementation is provided.
are automatically public.     }
```

An interface type is similar to a class, but there are several important differences:

- An interface type does not have instance variables.
- Methods in an interface must be *abstract* (that is, without an implementation) or static, default, or private methods (see Special Topic 10.2).
- All methods in an interface type are automatically public.
- An interface type has no constructor. Interfaces are not classes, and you cannot construct objects of an interface type.

Now that we have a type that denotes measurability, we can implement a reusable average method:

```java
public static double average(Measurable[] objects)
{
   double sum = 0;
   for (Measurable obj : objects)
   {
      sum = sum + obj.getMeasure();
   }
   if (objects.length > 0) { return sum / objects.length; }
   else { return 0; }
}
```

This method is useful for objects of any class that conforms to the Measurable type. In the next section, you will see what a class must do to make its objects measurable.

Note that the Measurable interface is not a type in the standard library—it was created specifically for this book, to provide a very simple example for studying the interface concept.

This standmixer provides the "rotation" service to any attachment that conforms to a common interface. Similarly, the average *method at the end of this section works with any class that implements a common interface.* © gregory horler/iStockphoto.

10.1.3 Implementing an Interface Type

Use the implements
reserved word to
indicate that a class
implements an
interface type.

The average method of the preceding section can process objects of any class that
implements the Measurable interface. A class **implements an interface** type if it
declares the interface in an implements clause, like this:

```
public class BankAccount implements Measurable
```

The class should then implement the abstract method or methods that the interface
requires:

```
public class BankAccount implements Measurable
{
    . . .
    public double getMeasure()
    {
        return balance;
    }
}
```

Note that the class must declare the method as public, whereas the interface need
not—all methods in an interface are public.

Once the BankAccount class implements the Measurable interface type, BankAccount
objects are instances of the Measurable type:

```
Measurable obj = new BankAccount(); // OK
```

A variable of type Measurable holds a reference to an object of some class that implements the Measurable interface.

Similarly, it is an easy matter to modify the Country class to implement the Measurable
interface:

```
public class Country implements Measurable
{
    . . .
    public double getMeasure()
    {
        return area;
    }
}
```

Syntax 10.2 Implementing an Interface

Syntax   public class *ClassName* implements *InterfaceName*, *InterfaceName*, . . .
{
    instance variables
    methods
}

```
                              public class BankAccount implements Measurable ⟍  List all interface types
                              {                                                  that this class implements.
         BankAccount            . . .
      instance variables      public double getMeasure() ⟍
                              {                              This method provides the
            Other                 return balance;           implementation for the abstract method
      BankAccount methods     }                             declared in the interface.
                                . . .
                              }
```

Figure 1
UML Diagram of the Data Class and the Classes that Implement the Measurable Interface

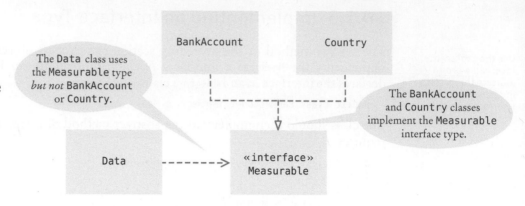

The program at the end of this section uses a single average method (placed in class Data) to compute the average of bank accounts and the average of countries.

This is a typical usage for interface types. By inventing the Measurable interface type, we have made the average method reusable.

Figure 1 shows the relationships between the Data class, the Measurable interface, and the classes that implement the interface. Note that the Data class depends only on the Measurable interface. It is decoupled from the BankAccount and Country classes.

In the UML notation, interfaces are tagged with an indicator «interface». A dotted arrow with a triangular tip (---▷) denotes the *implements* relationship between a class and an interface. You have to look carefully at the arrow tips—a dotted line with an open arrow tip (---≫) denotes the *uses* relationship or dependency.

Use interface types to make code more reusable.

sec01/MeasurableTester.java

```java
1   /**
2       This program demonstrates the measurable BankAccount and Country classes.
3   */
4   public class MeasurableTester
5   {
6      public static void main(String[] args)
7      {
8         // Calling the average method with an array of BankAccount objects
9         Measurable[] accounts = new Measurable[3];
10        accounts[0] = new BankAccount(0);
11        accounts[1] = new BankAccount(10000);
12        accounts[2] = new BankAccount(2000);
13
14        double averageBalance = Data.average(accounts);
15        System.out.println("Average balance: " + averageBalance);
16        System.out.println("Expected: 4000");
17
18        // Calling the average method with an array of Country objects
19        Measurable[] countries = new Measurable[3];
20        countries[0] = new Country("Uruguay", 176220);
21        countries[1] = new Country("Thailand", 513120);
22        countries[2] = new Country("Belgium", 30510);
23
24        double averageArea = Data.average(countries);
25        System.out.println("Average area: " + averageArea);
26        System.out.println("Expected: 239950");
27     }
28  }
```

sec01/Data.java

```
 1  public class Data
 2  {
 3     /**
 4         Computes the average of the measures of the given objects.
 5         @param objects an array of Measurable objects
 6         @return the average of the measures
 7     */
 8     public static double average(Measurable[] objects)
 9     {
10        double sum = 0;
11        for (Measurable obj : objects)
12        {
13           sum = sum + obj.getMeasure();
14        }
15        if (objects.length > 0) { return sum / objects.length;}
16        else { return 0; }
17     }
18  }
```

Program Run

```
Average balance: 4000
Expected: 4000
Average area: 239950
Expected: 239950
```

10.1.4 Comparing Interfaces and Inheritance

In Chapter 9, you saw how to use inheritance to model hierarchies of related classes, such as different kinds of quiz questions. Multiple-choice questions and fill-in questions are questions with specific characteristics.

Interfaces model a somewhat different relationship. Consider for example the BankAccount and Country classes in the preceding section. Both implement the Measurable interface type, but otherwise they have nothing in common. Being measurable is just one aspect of what it means to be a bank account or country. It is useful to model this common aspect, because it enables other programmers to write tools that exploit the commonality, such as the method for computing averages.

A class can implement more than one interface, for example

```
public class Country implements Measurable, Named
```

Here, Named is a different interface:

```
public interface Named
{
    String getName();
}
```

In contrast, a class can only extend (inherit from) a single superclass.

An interface describes the behavior that an implementation should supply. Prior to Java 8, an interface could not provide any implementation. Now, it is possible to supply a *default* implementation, and the distinction between interfaces and abstract classes (see Special Topic 9.3) has become more subtle. The significant difference that remains is that an interface type has *no state* (that is, no instance variables).

Generally, you will develop interfaces when you have code that processes objects of different classes in a common way. For example, a drawing program might have different objects that can be drawn, such as lines, images, text, and so on. In this situation, a `Drawable` interface with a `draw` method will be useful. Another example is a traffic simulation that models the movement of people, cars, dogs, balls, and so on. In this example, you might create a `Moveable` interface with methods `move` and `getPosition`.

Common Error 10.1

Forgetting to Declare Implementing Methods as Public

The methods in an interface are not declared as `public`, because they are public by default. However, the methods in a class are not public by default—their default access level is "package" access, which we discussed in Chapter 8. It is a common error to forget the `public` reserved word when declaring a method from an interface:

```
public class BankAccount implements Measurable
{
    . . .
    double getMeasure() // Oops—should be public
    {
        return balance;
    }
}
```

Then the compiler complains that the method has a weaker access level, namely package access instead of public access. The remedy is to declare the method as `public`.

Common Error 10.2

Trying to Instantiate an Interface

You can declare variables whose type is an interface, for example:

```
Measurable meas;
```

However, you can *never* construct an object of an interface type:

```
Measurable meas = new Measurable(); // Error
```

Interfaces aren't classes. There are no objects whose types are interfaces. If a variable of an interface type refers to an object, then the object must belong to some class—a class that implements the interface:

```
Measurable meas = new BankAccount(); // OK
```

Special Topic 10.1

Constants in Interfaces

Interfaces cannot have instance variables, but it is legal to specify **constants**. When declaring a constant in an interface, you can (and should) omit the reserved words `public static final`, because all variables in an interface are automatically `public static final`. For example,

```
public interface Named
{
    String NO_NAME = "(NONE)";
    . . .
}
```

Now the constant `Named.NO_NAME` can be used to denote the absence of a name.

It is not very common to have constants in interface types. In particular, you should avoid multiple related constants (such as `int NORTH = 1`, `int NORTHEAST = 2`, and so on). In that case, use an enumerated type instead (see Special Topic 5.4).

Special Topic 10.2
Nonabstract Interface Methods

Recent versions of Java allow methods with implementations in interfaces.

A *static* method of an interface does not operate on objects, and its purpose should relate to the interface that contains it. For example, it would be perfectly sensible to place the average method from Section 10.1.2 into the `Measurable` interface:

```
public interface Measurable
{
   double getMeasure();  // An abstract method
   static double average(Measurable[] objects) // A static method
   {
      . . . // Same implementation as in Section 10.1.2
   }
}
```

To call this method, provide the name of of the interface and the method name:

```
double meanArea = Measurable.average(countries);
```

EXAMPLE CODE   See special_topic_2 of your eText or companion code for an example of a static method in an interface.

A **default method** is a non-static method in an interface that has an implementation. A class that implements the method either inherits the default behavior or overrides it. By providing default methods in an interface, it is less work to define a class that implements an interface.

For example, the `Measurable` interface can declare `getMeasure` as a default method:

```
public interface Measurable
{
   default double getMeasure() { return 0; }
}
```

If a class implements the interface and doesn't provide a `getMeasure` method, then it inherits this default method.

This particular example isn't all that useful. One doesn't normally want each object to have measure zero. Here is a more interesting example, in which a default method calls another interface method:

```
public interface Measurable
{
   double getMeasure(); // An abstract method
   default boolean smallerThan(Measurable other)
   {
      return getMeasure() < other.getMeasure();
   }
}
```

The `smallerThan` method tests whether an object has a smaller measure than another, which is useful for arranging objects by increasing measure.

A class that implements the `Measurable` interface only needs to implement `getMeasure`, and it automatically inherits the `smallerThan` method. This can be a very useful mechanism. For example, the `Comparator` interface that is described in Special Topic 14.4 has one abstract method but more than a dozen default methods.

EXAMPLE CODE See your eText or companion code for an example of a default method in an interface.

Finally, an interface can have *private* methods. They can only be called from other methods of the interface.

10.2 Working with Interface Types

In the preceding section, you saw how to implement a simple service that accepted an interface. As you saw, you were able to pass objects of different classes to the service, and the service was able to invoke a method of the interface. In the following sections, you will learn the rules for working with interface types in Java.

10.2.1 Converting from Classes to Interfaces

Have a close look at the call

```
double averageBalance = Data.average(accounts);
```

from the program of the preceding section. Here, `accounts` is an array of `BankAccount` objects. However, the `average` method expects an array whose element type is `Measurable`:

```
public double average(Measurable[] objects)
```

It is legal to convert from the `BankAccount` type to the `Measurable` type. In general, you can convert from a class type to the type of any interface that the class implements. For example,

```
BankAccount account = new BankAccount(1000);
Measurable meas = account; // OK
```

Alternatively, a `Measurable` variable can refer to an object of the `Country` class of the preceding section because that class also implements the `Measurable` interface.

```
Country uruguay = new Country("Uruguay", 176220);
Measurable meas = uruguay; // Also OK
```

> You can convert from a class type to an interface type, provided the class implements the interface.

However, the `Rectangle` class from the standard library doesn't implement the `Measurable` interface. Therefore, the following assignment is an error:

```
Measurable meas = new Rectangle(5, 10, 20, 30); // Error
```

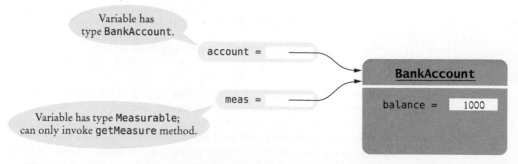

Figure 2 Variables of Class and Interface Types

10.2.2 Invoking Methods on Interface Variables

Now suppose that the variable meas has been initialized with a reference to an object of some class that implements the Measurable interface. You don't know to which class that object belongs. But you do know that the class implements the methods of the interface type, and you can invoke them:

```
double result = meas.getMeasure();
```

Now let's think through the call to the getMeasure method more carefully. Which get-Measure method is called? The BankAccount and Country classes provide two different implementations of that method. How does the correct method get called if the caller doesn't even know the exact class to which meas belongs?

This is again polymorphism in action. (See Section 9.4 for a discussion of polymorphism.) The Java virtual machine locates the correct method by first looking at the class of the actual object, and then calling the method with the given name in that class. That is, if meas refers to a BankAccount object, then the BankAccount.getMeasure method is called. If meas refers to a Country object, then the Country.getMeasure method is called.

> Method calls on an interface reference are polymorphic. The appropriate method is determined at run time.

Figure 3
An Interface Reference Can Refer to an Object of Any Class that Implements the Interface

10.2.3 Casting from Interfaces to Classes

Occasionally, it happens that you store an object in an interface reference and you need to convert its type back. Consider this method that returns the object with the larger measure:

```
public static Measurable larger(Measurable obj1, Measurable obj2)
{
   if (obj1.getMeasure() > obj2.getMeasure())
   {
      return obj1;
   }
   else
   {
      return obj2;
   }
}
```

The larger method returns the object with the larger measure, *as a* Measurable *reference*. It has no choice—it does not know the exact type of the object. Let's use the method:

```
Country uruguay = new Country("Uruguay", 176220);
Country thailand = new Country("Thailand", 513120);
Measurable max = larger(uruguay, thailand);
```

Now what can you do with the max reference? *You* know it refers to a Country object, but the compiler doesn't. For example, you cannot call the getName method:

```
String countryName = max.getName(); // Error
```

That call is an error, because the Measurable type has no getName method.

However, as long as you are absolutely sure that max refers to a Country object, you can use the **cast** notation to convert its type back:

```
Country maxCountry = (Country) max;
String name = maxCountry.getName();
```

If you are wrong, and the object doesn't actually refer to a country, a run-time exception will occur.

> You need a cast to convert from an interface type to a class type.

If a Person *object is actually a* Superhero, *you need a cast before you can apply any* Superhero *methods.*   © Andrew Rich/iStockphoto.

EXAMPLE CODE   See sec02 of your eText or companion code for a program that demonstrates conversions between class and interface types.

WORKED EXAMPLE 10.1
Investigating Number Sequences

Learn how to use a Sequence interface to investigate properties of arbitrary number sequences. See your eText or visit wiley.com/go/bjeo7.

© Norebbo/iStockphoto.

10.3 The Comparable Interface

> Implement the Comparable interface so that objects of your class can be compared, for example, in a sort method.

In the preceding sections, we defined the Measurable interface and provided an average method that works with any classes implementing that interface. In this section, you will learn about the Comparable interface of the standard Java library.

The Measurable interface is used for measuring a single object. The Comparable interface is more complex because comparisons involve two objects. The interface declares a compareTo method. The call

```
a.compareTo(b)
```

must return a negative number if a should come before b, zero if a and b are the same, and a positive number if b should come before a.

© Janis Dreosti/iStockphoto.

The compareTo *method checks whether another object is larger or smaller.*

The Comparable interface has a single method:

```java
public interface Comparable
{
    int compareTo(Object otherObject);
}
```

For example, the BankAccount class can implement Comparable like this:

```java
public class BankAccount implements Comparable
{
    . . .
    public int compareTo(Object otherObject)
    {
        BankAccount other = (BankAccount) otherObject;
        if (balance < other.balance) { return -1; }
        if (balance > other.balance) { return 1; }
        return 0;
    }
    . . .
}
```

This compareTo method compares bank accounts by their balance. Note that the compareTo method has a parameter variable of type Object. To turn it into a BankAccount reference, we use a cast:

```java
BankAccount other = (BankAccount) otherObject;
```

Once the BankAccount class implements the Comparable interface, you can sort an array of bank accounts with the Arrays.sort method:

```java
BankAccount[] accounts = new BankAccount[3];
accounts[0] = new BankAccount(10000);
accounts[1] = new BankAccount(0);
accounts[2] = new BankAccount(2000);
Arrays.sort(accounts);
```

The accounts array is now sorted by increasing balance.

EXAMPLE CODE   See sec03 of your eText or companion code for a program that demonstrates the Comparable interface with bank accounts.

Programming Tip 10.1

Comparing Integers and Floating-Point Numbers

When you implement a comparison method, you need to return a negative integer to indicate that the first object should come before the other, zero if they are equal, or a positive integer otherwise. You have seen how to implement this decision with three branches. When you compare *nonnegative* integers, there is a simpler way: subtract the integers:

```java
public class Person implements Comparable
{
    private int id; // Must be ≥ 0
    . . .
    public int compareTo(Object otherObject)
    {
        Person other = (Person) otherObject;
        return id - other.id;
    }
}
```

The difference is negative if id < other.id, zero if the values are the same, and positive otherwise.

This trick doesn't work if the integers can be negative because the difference can overflow (see Exercise •• R10.1). However, the Integer.compare method always works:

```
return Integer.compare(id, other.id); // Safe for negative integers
```

You cannot compare floating-point values by subtraction (see Exercise •• R10.2). Instead, use the Double.compare method:

```
public class BankAccount implements Comparable
{
   . . .
   public int compareTo(Object otherObject)
   {
      BankAccount other = (BankAccount) otherObject;
      return Double.compare(balance, other.balance);
   }
}
```

EXAMPLE CODE See programming_tip_1 of your eText or companion code for a program that uses compareTo with integers and floating-point numbers.

Special Topic 10.3

The clone Method and the Cloneable Interface

You know that copying an object reference simply gives you two references to the same object:

```
BankAccount account = new BankAccount(1000);
BankAccount account2 = account;
account2.deposit(500);
   // Now both account and account2 refer to a bank account with a balance of 1500
```

What can you do if you actually want to make a copy of an object? That is the purpose of the clone method. The clone method must return a *new* object that has an identical state to the existing object (see Figure 4).

Here is how to call it:

```
BankAccount clonedAccount = (BankAccount) account.clone();
```

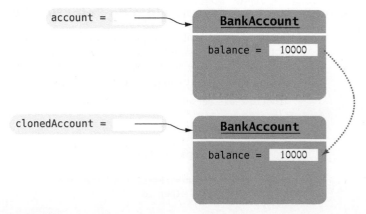

Figure 4 Cloning Objects

The return type of the clone method is the class Object. When you call the method, you must use a cast to inform the compiler that account.clone() really returns a BankAccount object.

The Object.clone method is the starting point for the clone methods in your own classes. It creates a new object of the same type as the original object. It also automatically copies the instance variables from the original object to the cloned object.

© Alex Gumerov/iStockphoto.

Here is a first attempt to implement the clone method for the BankAccount class:

```java
public class BankAccount
{
    . . .
    public Object clone()
    {
        // Not complete
        Object clonedAccount = super.clone();
        return clonedAccount;
    }
}
```

The clone *method makes an identical copy of an object.*

However, this Object.clone method must be used with care. It only shifts the problem of cloning by one level; it does not completely solve it. Specifically, if an object contains a reference to another object, then the Object.clone method makes a copy of that object reference, not a clone of that object. Figure 5 shows how the Object.clone method works with a Customer object that has references to a String object and a BankAccount object. As you can see, the Object.clone method copies the references to the cloned Customer object and does not clone the objects to which they refer. Such a copy is called a **shallow copy**.

There is a reason why the Object.clone method does not systematically clone all sub-objects. In some situations, it is unnecessary. For example, if an object contains a reference to a string, there is no harm in copying the string reference, because Java string objects can never change their contents. The Object.clone method does the right thing if an object contains only numbers, Boolean values, and strings. But it must be used with caution when an object contains references to mutable objects.

For that reason, there are two safeguards built into the Object.clone method to ensure that it is not used accidentally. First, the method is declared protected (see Special Topic 9.5). This prevents you from accidentally calling x.clone() if the class to which x belongs hasn't declared clone to be public.

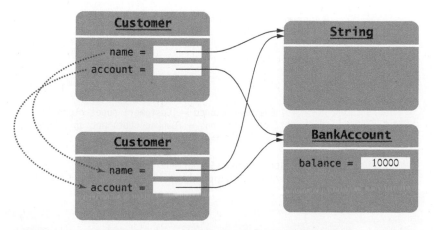

Figure 5 The Object.clone Method Makes a Shallow Copy

As a second precaution, Object.clone checks that the object being cloned implements the Cloneable interface. If not, it throws an exception. The Object.clone method looks like this:

```java
public class Object
{
   protected Object clone() throws CloneNotSupportedException
   {
      if (this instanceof Cloneable)
      {
         // Copy the instance variables
         . . .
       }
      else
      {
         throw new CloneNotSupportedException();
      }
   }
}
```

Unfortunately, all that safeguarding means that the legitimate callers of Object.clone() pay a price—they must catch that exception (see Chapter 11) *even if their class implements* Cloneable.

```java
public class BankAccount implements Cloneable
{
   . . .
   public Object clone()
   {
      try
      {
         return super.clone();
      }
      catch (CloneNotSupportedException e)
      {
         // Can't happen because we implement Cloneable but we still must catch it.
         return null;
      }
   }
}
```

If an object contains a reference to another mutable object, then you must call clone for that reference. For example, suppose the Customer class has an instance variable of class BankAccount. You can implement Customer.clone as follows:

```java
public class Customer implements Cloneable
{
   private String name;
   private BankAccount account;
   . . .
   public Object clone()
   {
      try
      {
         Customer cloned = (Customer) super.clone();
         cloned.account = (BankAccount) account.clone();
         return cloned;
      }
      catch(CloneNotSupportedException e)
      { // Can't happen because we implement Cloneable
         return null;
      }
   }
}
```

In general, implementing the clone method requires these steps:

- Make the class implement the Cloneable interface type.
- In the clone method, call super.clone(). Catch the CloneNotSupportedException if the superclass is Object.
- Clone any mutable instance variables.

10.4 Using Interfaces for Callbacks

In this section, we introduce the notion of a **callback**, show how it leads to a more flexible average method, and study how a callback can be implemented in Java by using interface types.

To understand why a further improvement to the average method is desirable, consider these limitations of the Measurable interface:

- You can add the Measurable interface only to classes under your control. If you want to process a set of Rectangle objects, you cannot make the Rectangle class implement another interface—it is a library class, which you cannot change.
- You can measure an object in only one way. If you want to analyze a set of cars both by speed and price, you are stuck.

Therefore, let's rethink the average method. The method measures objects, requiring them to be of type Measurable. The responsibility for measuring lies with the objects themselves. That is the cause for the limitations.

It would be better if we could give the average method the data to be averaged, and separately a method for measuring the objects. When collecting rectangles, we might give it a method for computing the area of a rectangle. When collecting cars, we might give it a method for getting the car's price.

> A callback is a mechanism for specifying code that is executed at a later time.

Such a method is called a **callback**. A callback is a mechanism for bundling up a block of code so that it can be invoked at a later time.

In some programming languages, it is possible to specify callbacks directly, as blocks of code or names of methods. But Java is an object-oriented programming language. Therefore, you turn callbacks into objects. This process starts by declaring an interface for the callback:

```java
public interface Measurer
{
    double measure(Object anObject);
}
```

The measure method measures an object and returns its measurement. Here we use the fact that all objects can be converted to the type Object.

A callback object waits to be called. The algorithm that has the callback object only calls it when it needs to have the information that the callback can provide.

© Dan Herrick/iStockphoto.

The code that makes the call to the callback receives an object of a class that implements this interface. In our case, the improved average method receives a Measurer object.

```java
public static double average(Object[] objects, Measurer meas)
{
    double sum = 0;
    for (Object obj : objects)
    {
        sum = sum + meas.measure(obj);
    }
    if (objects.length > 0) { return sum / objects.length; }
    else { return 0; }
}
```

The average method simply makes a callback to the measure method whenever it needs to measure any object.

Finally, a specific callback is obtained by implementing the Measurer interface. For example, here is how you can measure rectangles by area. Provide a class

```java
public class AreaMeasurer implements Measurer
{
    public double measure(Object anObject)
    {
        Rectangle aRectangle = (Rectangle) anObject;
        double area = aRectangle.getWidth() * aRectangle.getHeight();
        return area;
    }
}
```

Note that the measure method has a parameter variable of type Object, even though this particular measurer just wants to measure rectangles. The method parameter types must match those of the measure method in the Measurer interface. Therefore, the anObject parameter variable is cast to the Rectangle type:

```java
Rectangle aRectangle = (Rectangle) anObject;
```

What can you do with an AreaMeasurer? You need it to compute the average area of rectangles. Construct an object of the AreaMeasurer class and pass it to the average method:

```java
Measurer areaMeas = new AreaMeasurer();
Rectangle[] rects
    = { new Rectangle(5, 10, 20, 30), new Rectangle(10, 20, 30, 40) };
double averageArea = average(rects, areaMeas);
```

The average method will ask the AreaMeasurer object to measure the rectangles.

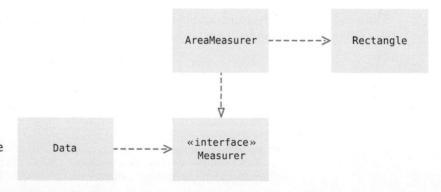

Figure 6
UML Diagram of the
Data Class and the
Measurer Interface

Figure 6 shows the UML diagram of the classes and interfaces of this solution. As in Figure 1, the Data class (which holds the average method) is decoupled from the class whose objects it processes (Rectangle). However, unlike in Figure 1, the Rectangle class is no longer coupled with another class. Instead, to process rectangles, you provide a small "helper" class AreaMeasurer. This helper class has only one purpose: to tell the average method how to measure its objects.

Here is the complete program.

sec04/Measurer.java

```java
1  /**
2      Describes any class whose objects can measure other objects.
3  */
4  public interface Measurer
5  {
6     /**
7         Computes the measure of an object.
8         @param anObject the object to be measured
9         @return the measure
10    */
11    double measure(Object anObject);
12 }
```

sec04/AreaMeasurer.java

```java
1  import java.awt.Rectangle;
2
3  /**
4      Objects of this class measure rectangles by area.
5  */
6  public class AreaMeasurer implements Measurer
7  {
8     public double measure(Object anObject)
9     {
10        Rectangle aRectangle = (Rectangle) anObject;
11        double area = aRectangle.getWidth() * aRectangle.getHeight();
12        return area;
13    }
14 }
```

sec04/Data.java

```java
1  public class Data
2  {
3     /**
4         Computes the average of the measures of the given objects.
5         @param objects an array of objects
6         @param meas the measurer for the objects
7         @return the average of the measures
8     */
9     public static double average(Object[] objects, Measurer meas)
10    {
11        double sum = 0;
12        for (Object obj : objects)
13        {
14           sum = sum + meas.measure(obj);
15        }
```

```
16        if (objects.length > 0) { return sum / objects.length; }
17        else { return 0; }
18     }
19  }
```

sec04/MeasurerTester.java

```
1   import java.awt.Rectangle;
2
3   /**
4      This program demonstrates the use of a Measurer.
5   */
6   public class MeasurerTester
7   {
8      public static void main(String[] args)
9      {
10        Measurer areaMeas = new AreaMeasurer();
11
12        Rectangle[] rects = new Rectangle[]
13           {
14              new Rectangle(5, 10, 20, 30),
15              new Rectangle(10, 20, 30, 40),
16              new Rectangle(20, 30, 5, 15)
17           };
18
19        double averageArea = Data.average(rects, areaMeas);
20        System.out.println("Average area: " + averageArea);
21        System.out.println("Expected: 625");
22     }
23  }
```

Program Run

```
Average area: 625
Expected: 625
```

Special Topic 10.4

Lambda Expressions

In the preceding section, you saw how to use interfaces for specifying variations in behavior. The average method needs to measure each object, and it does so by calling the measure method of the supplied Measurer object.

Unfortunately, the caller of the average method has to do a fair amount of work; namely, to define a class that implements the Measurer interface and to construct an object of that class. There is a convenient shortcut for these steps, provided that the interface has a *single abstract method*. Such an interface is called a **functional interface** because its purpose is to define a single function. The Measurer interface is an example of a functional interface.

To specify that single function, you can use a **lambda expression**, an expression that defines the parameters and return value of a method in a compact notation. Here is an example:

```
(Object obj) -> ((BankAccount) obj).getBalance()
```

This expression defines a function that, given an object, casts it to a BankAccount and returns the balance.

(The term "lambda expression" comes from a mathematical notation that uses the Greek letter lambda (λ) instead of the -> symbol. In other programming languages, such an expression is called a function expression.)

A lambda expression cannot stand alone. It needs to be assigned to a variable whose type is a functional interface:

```
Measurer accountMeas = (Object obj) -> ((BankAccount) obj).getBalance();
```

Now the following actions occur:

1. A class is defined that implements the functional interface. The single abstract method is defined by the lambda expression.
2. An object of that class is constructed.
3. The variable is assigned a reference to that object.

You can also pass a lambda expression to a method. Then the parameter variable of the method is initialized with the constructed object. For example, consider the call

```
double averageBalance = average(accounts,
    (Object obj) -> ((BankAccount) obj).getBalance());
```

In the same way as before, an object is constructed that belongs to a class implementing Measurer. The object is used to initialize the parameter variable meas of the average method. Recall that the parameter variable has type Measurer:

```
public static double average(Object[] objects, Measurer meas)
{
    . . .
    sum = sum + meas.measure(obj);
    . . .
}
```

The average method calls the measure method on meas, which in turn executes the body of the lambda expression.

In its simplest form, a lambda expression contains a list of parameters and the expression that is being computed from the parameters. If more work needs to be done, you can write a method body in the usual way, enclosed in braces and with a return statement:

```
Measurer areaMeas = (Object obj) ->
    {
        Rectangle r = (Rectangle) obj;
        return r.getWidth() * r.getHeight();
    };
```

Conceptually, lambda expressions are easiest to understand as a convenient notation for callbacks. Consider any method that needs to call some code that varies from one call to the next. This can be achieved as follows:

1. The implementor of the method defines an interface that describes the purpose of the code to be executed. That interface has a single method.
2. The method receives a parameter of that interface, and calls the single method of the interface whenever the code that can vary needs to be called.
3. The caller of the method provides a lambda expression whose body is the code that should be called in this invocation.

You will see additional examples of using lambda expressions for event handlers (Section 10.7) and comparators (Section 14.8). Chapter 19 uses lambda expressions extensively for processing complex data. In that chapter, we will study lambda expressions in greater depth.

EXAMPLE CODE   See special_topic_4 of your eText or companion code for a program that uses lambda expressions.

Special Topic 10.5
Generic Interface Types

In Section 10.3, you saw how to use the "raw" version of the Comparable interface type. In fact, the Comparable interface is a parameterized type, similar to the ArrayList type:

```java
public interface Comparable<T>
{
    int compareTo(T other)
}
```

The type parameter specifies the type of the objects that this class is willing to accept for comparison. Usually, this type is the same as the class type itself. For example, the BankAccount class would implement Comparable<BankAccount>, like this:

```java
public class BankAccount implements Comparable<BankAccount>
{
    . . .
    public int compareTo(BankAccount other)
    {
        return Double.compare(balance, other.balance);
    }
}
```

The type parameter has a significant advantage: You need not use a cast to convert an Object parameter variable into the desired type.

Similarly, the Measurer interface can be improved by making it into a generic type:

```java
public interface Measurer<T>
{
    double measure(T anObject);
}
```

The type parameter specifies the type of the parameter of the measure method. Again, you avoid the cast from Object when implementing the interface:

```java
public class AreaMeasurer implements Measurer<Rectangle>
{
    public double measure(Rectangle anObject)
    {
        double area = anObject.getWidth() * anObject.getHeight();
        return area;
    }
}
```

See Chapter 18 for an in-depth discussion of implementing and using generic classes.

10.5 Inner Classes

An inner class is declared inside another class.

The AreaMeasurer class of the preceding section is a very trivial class. We need this class only because the average method needs an object of some class that implements the Measurer interface. When you have a class that serves a very limited purpose, such as this one, you can declare the class inside the method that needs it:

```java
public class MeasurerTester
{
    public static void main(String[] args)
    {
```

© angelhell/iStockphoto.

An inner class is a class that is declared inside another class.

```
            class AreaMeasurer implements Measurer
            {
               . . .
            }
            . . .
            Measurer areaMeas = new AreaMeasurer();
            double averageArea = Data.average(rects, areaMeas);
            . . .
         }
      }
```

A class that is declared inside another class, such as the AreaMeasurer class in this example, is called an **inner class**. This arrangement signals to the reader of your program that the AreaMeasurer class is not interesting beyond the scope of this method. Because an inner class inside a method is not a publicly accessible feature, you don't need to document it as thoroughly.

You can also declare an inner class inside an enclosing class, but outside of its methods. Then the inner class is available to all methods of the enclosing class.

```
      public class MeasurerTester
      {
         class AreaMeasurer implements Measurer
         {
            . . .
         }

         public static void main(String[] args)
         {
            . . .
            Measurer areaMeas = new AreaMeasurer();
            double averageArea = Data.average(rects, areaMeas);
            . . .
         }
      }
```

Inner classes are commonly used for utility classes that should not be visible elsewhere in a program.

When you compile the source files for a program that uses inner classes, have a look at the class files in your program directory—you will find that the inner classes are stored in files with curious names, such as MeasurerTester$1AreaMeasurer.class. The exact names aren't important. The point is that the compiler turns an inner class into a regular class file.

EXAMPLE CODE   See sec05 of your eText or companion code for a sample program with an inner class.

10.6 Mock Objects

A mock object provides the same services as another object, but in a simplified manner.

When you work on a program that consists of multiple classes, you often want to test some of the classes before the entire program has been completed. A very effective technique for this purpose is the use of mock objects. A **mock object** provides the same services as another object, but in a simplified manner.

Consider a grade book application that manages quiz scores for students. This calls for a class GradeBook with methods such as

```
      public void addScore(int studentId, double score)
      public double getAverageScore(int studentId)
      public void save(String filename)
```

Now consider the class GradingProgram that manipulates a GradeBook object. That class calls the methods of the GradeBook class. We would like to test the GradingProgram class without having a fully functional GradeBook class.

To make this work, declare an interface type with the same methods that the Grade-Book class provides. A common convention is to use the letter I as the prefix for such an interface:

> Both the mock class and the actual class implement the same interface.

```java
public interface IGradeBook
{
    void addScore(int studentId, double score);
    double getAverageScore(int studentId);
    void save(String filename);
    . . .
}
```

The GradingProgram class should *only* use this interface, never the GradeBook class. Of course, the GradeBook class will implement this interface, but as already mentioned, it may not be ready for some time.

In the meantime, provide a mock implementation that makes some simplifying assumptions. Saving is not actually necessary for testing the user interface. We can also temporarily restrict it to the case of a single student.

```java
public class MockGradeBook implements IGradeBook
{
    private ArrayList<Double> scores;

    public MockGradeBook() { scores = new ArrayList<Double>(); }

    public void addScore(int studentId, double score)
    {
        // Ignore studentId
        scores.add(score);
    }
    public double getAverageScore(int studentId)
    {
        double total = 0;
        for (double x : scores) { total = total + x; }
        return total / scores.size();
    }
    public void save(String filename)
    {
        // Do nothing
    }
    . . .
}
```

Now construct an instance of MockGradeBook and use it in the GradingProgram class. You can immediately test the GradingProgram class. When you are ready to test the actual class, simply use a GradeBook instance instead. Don't erase the mock class—it will still come in handy for regression testing.

If you just want to practice arranging the Christmas decorations, you don't need a real tree. Similarly, you can use mock objects to test parts of your computer program.

© Don Nichols/iStockphoto.

EXAMPLE CODE See sec06 of your eText or companion code for a program that demonstrates the use of mock objects for testing.

10.7   Event Handling

This and the following sections continue the book's graphics track. You will learn how interfaces are used when programming graphical user interfaces.

In the applications that you have written so far, user input was under control of the *program*. The program asked the user for input in a specific order. For example, a program might ask the user to supply first a name, then a dollar amount. But the programs that you use every day on your computer don't work like that. In a program with a graphical user interface, the *user* is in control. The user can use both the mouse and the keyboard and can manipulate many parts of the user interface in any desired order. For example, the user can enter information into text fields, pull down menus, click buttons, and drag scroll bars in any order. The program must react to the user commands in whatever order they arrive. Having to deal with many possible inputs in random order is quite a bit harder than simply forcing the user to supply input in a fixed order.

> User-interface events include key presses, mouse moves, button clicks, menu selections, and so on.

In the following sections, you will learn how to write Java programs that can react to user-interface events, such as menu selections and mouse clicks. The Java windowing toolkit has a sophisticated mechanism that allows a program to specify the events in which it is interested and which objects to notify when one of these events occurs.

10.7.1   Listening to Events

Whenever the user of a graphical program types characters or uses the mouse anywhere inside one of the windows of the program, the Java windowing toolkit sends a notification to the program that an **event** has occurred. The windowing toolkit generates huge numbers of events. For example, whenever the mouse moves a tiny interval over a window, a "mouse move" event is generated. Whenever the mouse button is clicked, "mouse pressed" and "mouse released" events are generated. In addition, higher-level events are generated when a user selects a menu item or button.

© Seriy Tryapitsyn/iStockphoto.

In an event-driven user interface, the program receives an event whenever the user manipulates an input component.

Most programs don't want to be flooded by irrelevant events. For example, consider what happens when selecting a menu item with the mouse. The mouse moves over the menu item, then the mouse button is pressed, and finally the mouse button is released. Rather than receiving all these mouse events, a program can indicate that it only cares about menu selections, not about the underlying mouse events. However, if the mouse input is used for drawing shapes on a virtual canvas, it is necessary to closely track mouse events.

> An event listener belongs to a class that is provided by the application programmer. Its methods describe the actions to be taken when an event occurs.

Every program must indicate which events it needs to receive. It does that by installing **event listener** objects. An event listener object belongs to a class that you provide. The methods of your event listener classes contain the instructions that you want to have executed when the events occur.

To install a listener, you need to know the **event source**. The event source is the user-interface component that generates a particular event. You add an event listener object to the appropriate event sources. Whenever the event occurs, the event source calls the appropriate methods of all attached event listeners.

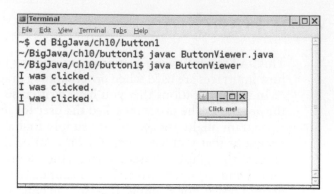

Figure 7 Implementing an Action Listener

Event sources report on events. When an event occurs, the event source notifies all event listeners.

This sounds somewhat abstract, so let's run through an extremely simple program that prints a message whenever a button is clicked (see Figure 7). Button listeners must belong to a class that implements the ActionListener interface:

```
public interface ActionListener
{
    void actionPerformed(ActionEvent event);
}
```

This particular interface has a single method, actionPerformed. It is your job to supply a class whose actionPerformed method contains the instructions that you want executed whenever the button is clicked.

Here is a very simple example of such a listener class.

sec07_01/ClickListener.java

```
1   import java.awt.event.ActionEvent;
2   import java.awt.event.ActionListener;
3
4   /**
5       An action listener that prints a message.
6   */
7   public class ClickListener implements ActionListener
8   {
9       public void actionPerformed(ActionEvent event)
10      {
11          System.out.println("I was clicked.");
12      }
13  }
```

We ignore the values of the event parameter variable of the actionPerformed method—it contains additional details about the event, such as the time at which it occurred.

Use JButton components for buttons. Attach an ActionListener to each button.

Once the listener class has been declared, we need to construct an object of the class and add it to the button:

```
ActionListener listener = new ClickListener();
button.addActionListener(listener);
```

Whenever the button is clicked, it calls

```
listener.actionPerformed(event);
```

As a result, the message is printed.

You can think of the actionPerformed method as another example of a callback, similar to the measure method of the Measurer class. The windowing toolkit calls the actionPerformed method whenever the button is pressed, whereas the Data class calls the measure method whenever it needs to measure an object.

The ButtonViewer class, shown below, constructs a frame with a button and adds a ClickListener to the button. You can test this program out by opening a console window, starting the ButtonViewer program from that console window, clicking the button, and watching the messages in the console window.

sec07_01/ButtonViewer.java

```java
1   import java.awt.event.ActionListener;
2   import javax.swing.JButton;
3   import javax.swing.JFrame;
4
5   /**
6      This program demonstrates how to install an action listener.
7   */
8   public class ButtonViewer
9   {
10     private static final int FRAME_WIDTH = 100;
11     private static final int FRAME_HEIGHT = 60;
12
13     public static void main(String[] args)
14     {
15        JFrame frame = new JFrame();
16        JButton button = new JButton("Click me!");
17        frame.add(button);
18
19        ActionListener listener = new ClickListener();
20        button.addActionListener(listener);
21
22        frame.setSize(FRAME_WIDTH, FRAME_HEIGHT);
23        frame.setDefaultCloseOperation(JFrame.EXIT_ON_CLOSE);
24        frame.setVisible(true);
25     }
26  }
```

10.7.2 Using Inner Classes for Listeners

In the preceding section, you saw how the code to be executed when a button is clicked is placed into a listener class. It is common to implement listener classes as inner classes like this:

```java
JButton button = new JButton(". . .");

// This inner class is declared in the same method as the button variable
class MyListener implements ActionListener
{
   . . .
};

ActionListener listener = new MyListener();
button.addActionListener(listener);
```

There are two advantages to making a listener class into an inner class. First, listener classes tend to be very short. You can put the inner class close to where it is needed, without cluttering up the remainder of the project. Moreover, inner classes have a very attractive feature: Their methods can access instance variables and methods of the surrounding class.

> Methods of an inner class can access variables from the surrounding class.

This feature is particularly useful when implementing event handlers. It allows the inner class to access variables without having to receive them as constructor or method arguments.

Let's look at an example. Suppose we want to add interest to a bank account whenever a button is clicked.

```java
JButton button = new JButton("Add Interest");
final BankAccount account = new BankAccount(INITIAL_BALANCE);

// This inner class is declared in the same method as the account and button variables.
class AddInterestListener implements ActionListener
{
   public void actionPerformed(ActionEvent event)
   {
      // The listener method accesses the account variable from the surrounding block
      double interest = account.getBalance() * INTEREST_RATE / 100;
      account.deposit(interest);
   }
};

ActionListener listener = new AddInterestListener();
button.addActionListener(listener);
```

> Local variables that are accessed by an inner class method must not change after they have been initialized.

There is a technical wrinkle. An inner class can access a surrounding local variable only if the variable is *effectively final*. Such a variable must behave like a final variable (that is, stay unchanged after it has been initialized), but it need not be declared with the final modifier. In our example, the account variable always refers to the same bank account, so it is legal to access it from the inner class.

An inner class can also access *instance* variables of the surrounding class, again with a restriction. The instance variable must belong to the object that constructed the inner class object. If the inner class object was created inside a static method, it can only access static variables.

Instead of declaring an inner class and adding an instance as a listener to a button, you can add a lambda expression as the listener (see Special Topic 10.4):

```java
button.addActionListener(event ->
   {
      double interest = account.getBalance() * INTEREST_RATE / 100;
      account.deposit(interest);
   });
```

This form is shorter, but we use inner classes in this book because they are more explicit.

Here is the source code for the program.

sec07_02/InvestmentViewer1.java

```java
1  import java.awt.event.ActionEvent;
2  import java.awt.event.ActionListener;
3  import javax.swing.JButton;
4  import javax.swing.JFrame;
5
6  /**
7     This program demonstrates how an action listener can access
8     a variable from a surrounding block.
```

```
 9  */
10  public class InvestmentViewer1
11  {
12     private static final int FRAME_WIDTH = 120;
13     private static final int FRAME_HEIGHT = 60;
14
15     private static final double INTEREST_RATE = 10;
16     private static final double INITIAL_BALANCE = 1000;
17
18     public static void main(String[] args)
19     {
20        JFrame frame = new JFrame();
21
22        // The button to trigger the calculation
23        JButton button = new JButton("Add Interest");
24        frame.add(button);
25
26        // The application adds interest to this bank account
27        BankAccount account = new BankAccount(INITIAL_BALANCE);
28
29        class AddInterestListener implements ActionListener
30        {
31           public void actionPerformed(ActionEvent event)
32           {
33              // The listener method accesses the account variable
34              // from the surrounding block
35              double interest = account.getBalance() * INTEREST_RATE / 100;
36              account.deposit(interest);
37              System.out.println("balance: " + account.getBalance());
38           }
39        }
40
41        ActionListener listener = new AddInterestListener();
42        button.addActionListener(listener);
43
44        frame.setSize(FRAME_WIDTH, FRAME_HEIGHT);
45        frame.setDefaultCloseOperation(JFrame.EXIT_ON_CLOSE);
46        frame.setVisible(true);
47     }
48  }
```

Program Run

```
balance: 1100.0
balance: 1210.0
balance: 1331.0
balance: 1464.1
```

Common Error 10.3
Modifying Parameter Types in the Implementing Method

When you implement an interface, you must declare each method *exactly* as it is specified in the interface. Accidentally making small changes to the parameter types is a common error. Here is the classic example:

```
class MyListener implements ActionListener
{
```

```
        public void actionPerformed() // Oops . . . forgot ActionEvent parameter variable
        {
            . . .
        }
    }
```

As far as the compiler is concerned, this class fails to provide the method

```
    public void actionPerformed(ActionEvent event)
```

You have to read the error message carefully and pay attention to the parameter and return types to find your error.

Common Error 10.4

Trying to Call Listener Methods

Some students try to call the listener methods themselves:

```
    ActionEvent event = new ActionEvent(. ..); // Don't do this
    listener.actionPerformed(event);
```

You should not call the listener. The Java user interface calls it when the program user has clicked a button.

10.8 Building Applications with Buttons

In this section, you will learn how to structure a graphical application that contains buttons. We will put a button to work in our simple investment viewer program. Whenever the button is clicked, interest is added to a bank account, and the new balance is displayed (see Figure 8).

First, we construct an object of the JButton class, passing the button label to the constructor, like this:

```
    JButton button = new JButton("Add Interest");
```

We also need a user-interface component that displays a message, namely the current bank balance. Such a component is called a *label*. You pass the initial message string to the JLabel constructor, like this:

```
    JLabel label = new JLabel("balance: " + account.getBalance());
```

> Use a JPanel container to group multiple user-interface components together.

The frame of our application contains both the button and the label. However, we cannot simply add both components directly to the frame—they would be placed on

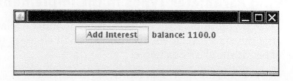

Figure 8   An Application with a Button

top of each other. The solution is to put them into a **panel**, a container for other user-interface components, and then add the panel to the frame:

```
JPanel panel = new JPanel();
panel.add(button);
panel.add(label);
frame.add(panel);
```

Now we are ready for the hard part—the event listener that handles button clicks. As in the preceding section, it is necessary to provide a class that implements the Action-Listener interface, and to place the button action into the actionPerformed method. Our listener class adds interest to the account and displays the new balance:

```
class AddInterestListener implements ActionListener
{
   public void actionPerformed(ActionEvent event)
   {
      double interest = account.getBalance() * INTEREST_RATE / 100;
      account.deposit(interest);
      label.setText("balance: " + account.getBalance());
   }
}
```

Let's put the pieces together:

```
public static void main(String[] args)
{
   . . .
   JButton button = new JButton("Add Interest");
   BankAccount account = new BankAccount(INITIAL_BALANCE);
   JLabel label = new JLabel("balance: " + account.getBalance());

   class AddInterestListener implements ActionListener
   {
      public void actionPerformed(ActionEvent event)
      {
         double interest = account.getBalance() * INTEREST_RATE / 100;
         account.deposit(interest);
         label.setText("balance: " + account.getBalance());
      }
   }

   ActionListener listener = new AddInterestListener();
   button.addActionListener(listener);
   . . .
}
```

With a bit of practice, you will learn to glance at this code and translate it into plain English: "When the button is clicked, add interest and set the label text."

*Whenever a button is pressed,
the* actionPerformed *method is called on all listeners.*   © Eduard Andras/iStockphoto.

Here is the complete program. It demonstrates how to add multiple components to a frame, by using a panel, and how to implement listeners as inner classes.

sec08/InvestmentViewer2.java

```java
1   import java.awt.event.ActionEvent;
2   import java.awt.event.ActionListener;
3   import javax.swing.JButton;
4   import javax.swing.JFrame;
5   import javax.swing.JLabel;
6   import javax.swing.JPanel;
7
8   /**
9      This program displays the growth of an investment.
10  */
11  public class InvestmentViewer2
12  {
13     private static final int FRAME_WIDTH = 400;
14     private static final int FRAME_HEIGHT = 100;
15
16     private static final double INTEREST_RATE = 10;
17     private static final double INITIAL_BALANCE = 1000;
18
19     public static void main(String[] args)
20     {
21        JFrame frame = new JFrame();
22
23        // The button to trigger the calculation
24        JButton button = new JButton("Add Interest");
25
26        // The application adds interest to this bank account
27        BankAccount account = new BankAccount(INITIAL_BALANCE);
28
29        // The label for displaying the results
30        JLabel label = new JLabel("balance: " + account.getBalance());
31
32        // The panel that holds the user-interface components
33        JPanel panel = new JPanel();
34        panel.add(button);
35        panel.add(label);
36        frame.add(panel);
37
38        class AddInterestListener implements ActionListener
39        {
40           public void actionPerformed(ActionEvent event)
41           {
42              double interest = account.getBalance() * INTEREST_RATE / 100;
43              account.deposit(interest);
44              label.setText("balance: " + account.getBalance());
45           }
46        }
47
48        ActionListener listener = new AddInterestListener();
49        button.addActionListener(listener);
50
51        frame.setSize(FRAME_WIDTH, FRAME_HEIGHT);
52        frame.setDefaultCloseOperation(JFrame.EXIT_ON_CLOSE);
53        frame.setVisible(true);
54     }
55  }
```

Common Error 10.5

Forgetting to Attach a Listener

If you run your program and find that your buttons seem to be dead, double-check that you attached the button listener. The same holds for other user-interface components. It is a surprisingly common error to program the listener class and the event handler action without actually attaching the listener to the event source.

10.9 Processing Timer Events

In this section we will study timer events and show how you can use them to implement simple animations.

The `Timer` class in the `javax.swing` package generates a sequence of action events, spaced at even time intervals. (You can think of a timer as an invisible button that is automatically clicked.) This is useful whenever you want to have an object updated at regular intervals. For example, in an animation, you may want to update a scene ten times per second and redisplay the image to give the illusion of movement.

© jeff giniewicz/iStockphoto.

A Swing timer notifies a listener with each "tick".

> A timer generates timer events at fixed intervals.

When you use a timer, you specify the frequency of the events and an object of a class that implements the `ActionListener` interface. Place whatever action you want to occur inside the `actionPerformed` method. Finally, start the timer.

```
class MyListener implements ActionListener
{
   public void actionPerformed(ActionEvent event)
   {
      Action that is executed at each timer event.
   }
}

MyListener listener = new MyListener();
Timer t = new Timer(interval, listener);
t.start();
```

Then the timer calls the `actionPerformed` method of the `listener` object every `interval` milliseconds.

Our sample program will display a moving rectangle. We first supply a `Rectangle-Component` class with a `moveRectangleBy` method that moves the rectangle by a given amount.

sec09/RectangleComponent.java

```
1  import java.awt.Graphics;
2  import java.awt.Graphics2D;
3  import java.awt.Rectangle;
4  import javax.swing.JComponent;
5
```

```
 6  /**
 7      This component displays a rectangle that can be moved.
 8  */
 9  public class RectangleComponent extends JComponent
10  {
11      private static final int BOX_X = 100;
12      private static final int BOX_Y = 100;
13      private static final int BOX_WIDTH = 20;
14      private static final int BOX_HEIGHT = 30;
15
16      private Rectangle box;
17
18      public RectangleComponent()
19      {
20          // The rectangle that the paintComponent method draws
21          box = new Rectangle(BOX_X, BOX_Y, BOX_WIDTH, BOX_HEIGHT);
22      }
23
24      public void paintComponent(Graphics g)
25      {
26          Graphics2D g2 = (Graphics2D) g;
27          g2.draw(box);
28      }
29
30      /**
31          Moves the rectangle by a given amount.
32          @param dx the amount to move in the x-direction
33          @param dy the amount to move in the y-direction
34      */
35      public void moveRectangleBy(int dx, int dy)
36      {
37          box.translate(dx, dy);
38          repaint();
39      }
40  }
```

The repaint method causes a component to repaint itself. Call repaint whenever you modify the shapes that the paintComponent method draws.

Note the call to repaint in the moveRectangleBy method. This call is necessary to ensure that the component is repainted after the state of the rectangle object has been changed. Keep in mind that the component object does not contain the pixels that show the drawing. The component merely contains a Rectangle object, which itself contains four coordinate values. Calling translate updates the rectangle coordinate values. The call to repaint forces a call to the paintComponent method. The paintComponent method redraws the component, causing the rectangle to appear at the updated location.

The actionPerformed method of the timer listener simply calls component.moveBy(1, 1). This moves the rectangle one pixel down and to the right. Because the actionPerformed method is called many times per second, the rectangle appears to move smoothly across the frame.

sec09/RectangleFrame.java

```
1  import java.awt.event.ActionEvent;
2  import java.awt.event.ActionListener;
3  import javax.swing.JFrame;
4  import javax.swing.Timer;
5
6  /**
```

```
 7       This frame contains a moving rectangle.
 8    */
 9    public class RectangleFrame extends JFrame
10    {
11       private static final int FRAME_WIDTH = 300;
12       private static final int FRAME_HEIGHT = 400;
13
14       private RectangleComponent scene;
15
16       class TimerListener implements ActionListener
17       {
18          public void actionPerformed(ActionEvent event)
19          {
20             scene.moveRectangleBy(1, 1);
21          }
22       }
23
24       public RectangleFrame()
25       {
26          scene = new RectangleComponent();
27          add(scene);
28
29          setSize(FRAME_WIDTH, FRAME_HEIGHT);
30
31          ActionListener listener = new TimerListener();
32
33          final int DELAY = 100; // Milliseconds between timer ticks
34          Timer t = new Timer(DELAY, listener);
35          t.start();
36       }
37    }
```

sec09/RectangleViewer.java

```
 1    import javax.swing.JFrame;
 2
 3    /**
 4       This program moves the rectangle.
 5    */
 6    public class RectangleViewer
 7    {
 8       public static void main(String[] args)
 9       {
10          JFrame frame = new RectangleFrame();
11          frame.setTitle("An animated rectangle");
12          frame.setDefaultCloseOperation(JFrame.EXIT_ON_CLOSE);
13          frame.setVisible(true);
14       }
15    }
```

Common Error 10.6

Forgetting to Repaint

You have to be careful when your event handlers change the data in a painted component.
When you make a change to the data, the component is not automatically painted with the
new data. You must call the repaint method of the component, either in the event handler or

in the component's mutator methods. Your component's paintComponent method will then be invoked with an appropriate Graphics object. Note that you should not call the paintComponent method directly.

This is a concern only for your own painted components. When you make a change to a standard Swing component such as a JLabel, the component is automatically repainted.

10.10 Mouse Events

Use a mouse listener to capture mouse events.

If you write programs that show drawings, and you want users to manipulate the drawings with a mouse, then you need to process mouse events. Mouse events are more complex than button clicks or timer ticks.

A mouse listener must implement the MouseListener interface, which contains the following five methods:

```
public interface MouseListener
{
    void mousePressed(MouseEvent event);
        // Called when a mouse button has been pressed on a component
    void mouseReleased(MouseEvent event);
        // Called when a mouse button has been released on a component
    void mouseClicked(MouseEvent event);
        // Called when the mouse has been clicked on a component
    void mouseEntered(MouseEvent event);
        // Called when the mouse enters a component
    void mouseExited(MouseEvent event);
        // Called when the mouse exits a component
}
```

The mousePressed and mouseReleased methods are called whenever a mouse button is pressed or released. If a button is pressed and released in quick succession, and the mouse has not moved, then the mouseClicked method is called as well. The mouseEntered and mouseExited methods can be used to paint a user-interface component in a special way whenever the mouse is pointing inside it.

The most commonly used method is mousePressed. Users generally expect that their actions are processed as soon as the mouse button is pressed.

You add a mouse listener to a component by calling the addMouseListener method:

```
public class MyMouseListener implements MouseListener
{
    // Implements five methods
}

MouseListener listener = new MyMouseListener();
component.addMouseListener(listener);
```

In Swing, a mouse event isn't a gathering of rodents; it's notification of a mouse click by the program user. © james Brey/iStockphoto.

In our sample program, a user clicks on a component containing a rectangle. Whenever the mouse button is pressed, the rectangle is moved to the mouse location. We first enhance the RectangleComponent class and add a moveRectangleTo method to move the rectangle to a new position.

sec10/RectangleComponent2.java

```
 1  import java.awt.Graphics;
 2  import java.awt.Graphics2D;
 3  import java.awt.Rectangle;
 4  import javax.swing.JComponent;
 5
 6  /**
 7     This component displays a rectangle that can be moved.
 8  */
 9  public class RectangleComponent2 extends JComponent
10  {
11     private static final int BOX_X = 100;
12     private static final int BOX_Y = 100;
13     private static final int BOX_WIDTH = 20;
14     private static final int BOX_HEIGHT = 30;
15
16     private Rectangle box;
17
18     public RectangleComponent2()
19     {
20        // The rectangle that the paintComponent method draws
21        box = new Rectangle(BOX_X, BOX_Y, BOX_WIDTH, BOX_HEIGHT);
22     }
23
24     public void paintComponent(Graphics g)
25     {
26        Graphics2D g2 = (Graphics2D) g;
27        g2.draw(box);
28     }
29
30     /**
31        Moves the rectangle to the given location.
32        @param x the x-position of the new location
33        @param y the y-position of the new location
34     */
35     public void moveRectangleTo(int x, int y)
36     {
37        box.setLocation(x, y);
38        repaint();
39     }
40  }
```

Note the call to repaint in the moveRectangleTo method. As explained in the preceding section, this call causes the component to repaint itself and show the rectangle in the new position.

Now, add a mouse listener to the component. Whenever the mouse is pressed, the listener moves the rectangle to the mouse location.

```
class MousePressListener implements MouseListener
{
   public void mousePressed(MouseEvent event)
   {
```

```
        int x = event.getX();
        int y = event.getY();
        component.moveRectangleTo(x, y);
    }

    // Do-nothing methods
    public void mouseReleased(MouseEvent event) {}
    public void mouseClicked(MouseEvent event) {}
    public void mouseEntered(MouseEvent event) {}
    public void mouseExited(MouseEvent event) {}
}
```

It often happens that a particular listener specifies actions only for one or two of the listener methods. Nevertheless, all five methods of the interface must be implemented. The unused methods are simply implemented as do-nothing methods.

Go ahead and run the `RectangleViewer2` program. Whenever you click the mouse inside the frame, the top-left corner of the rectangle moves to the mouse pointer (see Figure 9).

Figure 9
Clicking the Mouse
Moves the Rectangle

sec10/RectangleFrame2.java

```java
1  import java.awt.event.MouseListener;
2  import java.awt.event.MouseEvent;
3  import javax.swing.JFrame;
4
5  /**
6     This frame contains a moving rectangle.
7  */
8  public class RectangleFrame2 extends JFrame
9  {
10    private static final int FRAME_WIDTH = 300;
11    private static final int FRAME_HEIGHT = 400;
12
13    private RectangleComponent2 scene;
14
15    class MousePressListener implements MouseListener
16    {
17       public void mousePressed(MouseEvent event)
18       {
19          int x = event.getX();
20          int y = event.getY();
21          scene.moveRectangleTo(x, y);
22       }
23
24       // Do-nothing methods
25       public void mouseReleased(MouseEvent event) {}
26       public void mouseClicked(MouseEvent event) {}
27       public void mouseEntered(MouseEvent event) {}
28       public void mouseExited(MouseEvent event) {}
29    }
30
31    public RectangleFrame2()
32    {
33       scene = new RectangleComponent2();
34       add(scene);
35
```

```
36        MouseListener listener = new MousePressListener();
37        scene.addMouseListener(listener);
38
39        setSize(FRAME_WIDTH, FRAME_HEIGHT);
40     }
41 }
```

sec10/RectangleViewer2.java

```
1  import javax.swing.JFrame;
2
3  /**
4     This program displays a rectangle that can be moved with the mouse.
5  */
6  public class RectangleViewer2
7  {
8     public static void main(String[] args)
9     {
10        JFrame frame = new RectangleFrame2();
11        frame.setDefaultCloseOperation(JFrame.EXIT_ON_CLOSE);
12        frame.setVisible(true);
13     }
14 }
```

Special Topic 10.6
Keyboard Events

If you program a game, you may want to process keystrokes, such as the arrow keys. Add a key listener to the component on which you draw the game scene. The KeyListener interface has three methods. As with a mouse listener, you are most interested in key press events, and you can leave the other two methods empty. Your key listener class should look like this:

```
class MyKeyListener implements KeyListener
{
   public void keyPressed(KeyEvent event)
   {
      String key = KeyStroke.getKeyStrokeForEvent(event).toString();
      key = key.replace("pressed ", "");
      Process key.
   }

   // Do-nothing methods
   public void keyReleased(KeyEvent event) {}
   public void keyTyped(KeyEvent event) {}
}
```

Whenever the program user presses a key, a key event is generated.

© Shironosov/iStockphoto.com.

The call `KeyStroke.getKeyStrokeForEvent(event).toString()` turns the event object into a text description of the key, such as `"pressed LEFT"`. In the next line, we eliminate the `"pressed "` prefix. The remainder is a string such as `"LEFT"` or `"A"` that describes the key that was pressed. You can find a list of all key names in the API documentation of the `KeyStroke` class.

As always, remember to attach the listener to the event source:

```
KeyListener listener = new MyKeyListener();
scene.addKeyListener(listener);
```

In order to receive key events, your component must call

```
scene.setFocusable(true);
scene.requestFocus();
```

EXAMPLE CODE   See special_topic_6 of your eText or companion code for a program that uses the arrow keys to move a rectangle.

Special Topic 10.7

Event Adapters

In the preceding section you saw how to install a mouse listener into a mouse event source and how the listener methods are called when an event occurs. Usually, a program is not interested in all listener notifications. For example, a program may only be interested in mouse clicks and may not care that these mouse clicks are composed of "mouse pressed" and "mouse released" events. Of course, the program could supply a listener that implements all those methods in which it has no interest as "do-nothing" methods, for example:

```
class MouseClickListener implements MouseListener
{
   public void mouseClicked(MouseEvent event)
   {
      Mouse click action.
   }

   // Four do-nothing methods
   public void mouseEntered(MouseEvent event) {}
   public void mouseExited(MouseEvent event) {}
   public void mousePressed(MouseEvent event) {}
   public void mouseReleased(MouseEvent event) {}
}
```

To avoid this labor, some friendly soul has created a `MouseAdapter` class that implements the `MouseListener` interface such that all methods do nothing. You can *extend* that class, inheriting the do-nothing methods and overriding the methods that you care about, like this:

```
class MouseClickListener extends MouseAdapter
{
   public void mouseClicked(MouseEvent event)
   {
      Mouse click action.
   }
}
```

There is also a `KeyAdapter` class that implements the `KeyListener` interface with three do-nothing methods.

Computing & Society 10.1   Open Source and Free Software

Most companies that produce software regard the source code as a trade secret. After all, if customers or competitors had access to the source code, they could study it and create similar programs without paying the original vendor. For the same reason, customers dislike secret source code. If a company goes out of business or decides to discontinue support for a computer program, its users are left stranded. They are unable to fix bugs or adapt the program to a new operating system. Fortunately, many software packages are distributed as "open source software", giving its users the right to see, modify, and redistribute the source code of a program.

Having access to source code is not sufficient to ensure that software serves the needs of its users. Some companies have created software that spies on users or restricts access to previously purchased books, music, or videos. If that software runs on a server or in an embedded device, the user cannot change its behavior. In the article http://www.gnu.org/philosophy/free-software-even-more-important.en.html, Richard Stallman, a famous computer scientist and winner of a MacArthur "genius" grant, describes the "free software movement" that champions the right of users to control what their software does. This is an ethical position that goes beyond using open source for reasons of convenience or cost savings.

Stallman is the originator of the GNU project (http://gnu.org/gnu/the-gnu-project.html) that has produced an entirely free version of a UNIX-compatible operating system: the GNU operating system. All programs of the GNU project are licensed under the GNU General Public License (GNU GPL). The license allows you to make as many copies as you wish, make any modifications to the source, and redistribute the original and modified programs, charging nothing at all or whatever the market will bear. In return, you must agree that your modifications also fall under the license. You must give out the source code to any changes that you distribute, and anyone else can distribute them under the same conditions. The GNU GPL forms a social contract. Users of the software enjoy the freedom to use and modify the software, and in return they are obligated to share any improvements that they make available.

Some commercial software vendors have attacked the GPL as "viral" and "undermining the commercial software sector". Other companies have a more nuanced strategy, producing free or open source software, but charging for support or proprietary extensions. For example, the Java Development Kit is available under the GPL, but companies that need security updates for old versions or other support must pay Oracle.

Open source software sometimes lacks the polish of commercial software because many of the programmers are volunteers who are interested in solving their own problems, not in making a product that is easy to use by everyone. Open source software has been particularly successful in areas that are of interest to programmers, such as the Linux kernel, Web servers, and programming tools.

The open source software community can be very competitive and creative. It is quite common to see several competing projects that take ideas from each other, all rapidly becoming more capable. Having many programmers involved, all reading the source code, often means that bugs tend to get squashed quickly. Eric Raymond describes open source development in his famous article "The Cathedral and the Bazaar" (http://catb.org/~esr/writings/cathedral-bazaar/cathedral-bazaar/index.html). He writes "Given enough eyeballs, all bugs are shallow".

Courtesy of Richard Stallman published under a CC license.

Richard Stallman, a pioneer of the free software movement

CHAPTER SUMMARY

Use interfaces for making a service available to multiple classes.

- A Java interface type declares the methods that can be applied to a variable of that type.
- Use the implements reserved word to indicate that a class implements an interface type.
- Use interface types to make code more reusable.

Describe how to convert between class and interface types.

- You can convert from a class type to an interface type, provided the class implements the interface.
- Method calls on an interface reference are polymorphic. The appropriate method is determined at run time.
- You need a cast to convert from an interface type to a class type.

Use the `Comparable` interface from the Java library.

- Implement the `Comparable` interface so that objects of your class can be compared, for example, in a sort method.

Describe how to use interface types for providing callbacks.

- A callback is a mechanism for specifying code that is executed at a later time.

Use inner classes to limit the scope of a utility class.

- An inner class is declared inside another class.
- Inner classes are commonly used for utility classes that should not be visible elsewhere in a program.

Use mock objects for supplying test versions of classes.

- A mock object provides the same services as another object, but in a simplified manner.
- Both the mock class and the actual class implement the same interface.

Implement event listeners to react to events in user-interface programming.

- User-interface events include key presses, mouse moves, button clicks, menu selections, and so on.
- An event listener belongs to a class that is provided by the application programmer. Its methods describe the actions to be taken when an event occurs.
- Event sources report on events. When an event occurs, the event source notifies all event listeners.
- Use `JButton` components for buttons. Attach an `ActionListener` to each button.
- Methods of an inner class can access local and instance variables from the surrounding scope.
- Local variables that are accessed by an inner class method must not change after they have been initialized.

Build graphical applications that use buttons.

- Use a `JPanel` container to group multiple user-interface components together.
- Specify button click actions through classes that implement the `ActionListener` interface.

Use a timer for drawing animations.

- A timer generates timer events at fixed intervals.
- The repaint method causes a component to repaint itself. Call repaint whenever you modify the shapes that the paintComponent method draws.

Write programs that process mouse events.

- Use a mouse listener to capture mouse events.

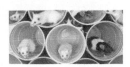

STANDARD LIBRARY ITEMS INTRODUCED IN THIS CHAPTER

java.awt.Component
  addKeyListener
  addMouseListener
  repaint
  setFocusable
java.awt.Container
  add
java.awt.Dimension
java.awt.Rectangle
  setLocation
java.awt.event.ActionListener
  actionPerformed
java.awt.event.KeyEvent
java.awt.event.KeyListener
  keyPressed
  keyReleased
  keyTyped
java.awt.event.MouseEvent
  getX
  getY

java.awt.event.MouseListener
  mouseClicked
  mouseEntered
  mouseExited
  mousePressed
  mouseReleased
java.lang.Comparable<T>
  compareTo
java.lang.Double
java.lang.Integer
  compare
javax.swing.AbstractButton
  addActionListener
javax.swing.JButton
javax.swing.JLabel
javax.swing.JPanel
javax.swing.KeyStroke
  getKeyStrokeForEvent
javax.swing.Timer
  start
  stop

REVIEW EXERCISES

■ ■ **R10.1** Suppose an `int` value a is two billion and b is -a. What is the result of a – b? Of b – a? What is the result of `Integer.compare(a, b)`? Of `Integer.compare(b – a)`?

■ ■ **R10.2** Suppose a `double` value a is 0.6 and b is 0.3. What is the result of `(int)(a - b)`? Of `(int)(b - a)`? What is the result of `Double.compare(a, b)`? Of `Double.compare(b - a)`?

■ **R10.3** Suppose C is a class that implements the interfaces I and J. Which of the following assignments require a cast?

```
C c = . . .;
I i = . . .;
J j = . . .;

a. c = i;
b. j = c;
c. i = j;
```

■ **R10.4** Suppose C is a class that implements the interfaces I and J, and suppose i is declared as: `I i = new C();`

Which of the following statements will throw an exception?

```
a. C c = (C) i;
b. J j = (J) i;
c. i = (I) null;
```

■ ■ **R10.5** What does this code fragment print? Why is this an example of polymorphism?

```
Measurable[] data = { new BankAccount(10000), new Country("Belgium", 30510) };
System.out.println(average(data));
```

■ **R10.6** Suppose the class `Sandwich` implements the `Edible` interface, and you are given the variable declarations

```
Sandwich sub = new Sandwich();
Rectangle cerealBox = new Rectangle(5, 10, 20, 30);
Edible e = null;
```

Which of the following assignment statements are legal?

```
a. e = sub;
b. sub = e;
c. sub = (Sandwich) e;
d. sub = (Sandwich) cerealBox;
e. e = cerealBox;
f. e = (Edible) cerealBox;
g. e = (Rectangle) cerealBox;
h. e = (Rectangle) null;
```

■ ■ **R10.7** The classes `Rectangle2D.Double`, `Ellipse2D.Double`, and `Line2D.Double` implement the `Shape` interface. The `Graphics2D` class depends on the `Shape` interface but not on the rectangle, ellipse, and line classes. Draw a UML diagram denoting these facts.

■■ **R10.8** Suppose r contains a reference to a new Rectangle(5, 10, 20, 30). Which of the following assignments is legal? (Look inside the API documentation to check which interfaces the Rectangle class implements.)

a. Rectangle a = r;
b. Shape b = r;
c. String c = r;
d. ActionListener d = r;
e. Measurable e = r;
f. Serializable f = r;
g. Object g = r;

■■ **R10.9** Classes such as Rectangle2D.Double, Ellipse2D.Double, and Line2D.Double implement the Shape interface. The Shape interface has a method

```
Rectangle getBounds()
```

that returns a rectangle completely enclosing the shape. Consider the method call:

```
Shape s = . . .;
Rectangle r = s.getBounds();
```

Explain why this is an example of polymorphism.

■■ **R10.10** Suppose you need to process an array of employees to find the average salary. Discuss what you need to do to use the Data.average method in Section 10.1.3 (which processes Measurable objects). What do you need to do to use the second implementation (in Section 10.4)? Which is easier?

■ **R10.11** What happens if you try to use an array of String objects with the Data.average method in Section 10.1.3?

■■ **R10.12** How can you use the Data.average method in Section 10.4 if you want to compute the average length of the strings?

■■ **R10.13** What happens if you pass an array of strings and an AreaMeasurer to the Data.average method of Section 10.4?

■■ **R10.14** Consider this top-level and inner class. Which variables can the f method access?

```
public class T
{
   private int t;

   public void m(final int x, int y)
   {
      int a;
      final int b;

      class C implements I
      {
         public void f()
         {
            . . .
         }
      }

      final int c;
      . . .
   }
}
```

■■ **R10.15** What happens when an inner class tries to access a local variable that assumes more than one value? Try it out and explain your findings.

■■■ **Graphics R10.16** How would you reorganize the InvestmentViewer1 program of Section 10.7.2 if you needed to make AddInterestListener into a top-level class (that is, not an inner class)?

■ **Graphics R10.17** What is an event object? An event source? An event listener?

■ **Graphics R10.18** From a programmer's perspective, what is the most important difference between the user interfaces of a console application and a graphical application?

■ **Graphics R10.19** What is the difference between an ActionEvent and a MouseEvent?

■■ **Graphics R10.20** Why does the ActionListener interface have only one method, whereas the Mouse-Listener has five methods?

■■ **Graphics R10.21** Can a class be an event source for multiple event types? If so, give an example.

■■ **Graphics R10.22** What information does an action event object carry? What additional information does a mouse event object carry?

■■■ **Graphics R10.23** Why are we using inner classes for event listeners? If Java did not have inner classes, could we still implement event listeners? How?

■■ **Graphics R10.24** What is the difference between the paintComponent and repaint methods?

■ **Graphics R10.25** What is the difference between a frame and a panel?

PRACTICE EXERCISES

■■ **E10.1** Add static methods largest and smallest to the Measurable interface. The methods should return the object with the largest or smallest measure from an array of Measurable objects.

■ **E10.2** Implement a class Quiz that implements the Measurable interface of Exercise ●● E10.1. A quiz has a score and a letter grade (such as B+). Modify the Data class from Section 10.1 to process an array of quizzes. Display the average score and the quiz with the highest score (both letter grade and score).

■ **E10.3** A person has a name and a height in centimeters. Use the Data class of Exercise ● E10.2 to process an array of Person objects. Display the average height and the name of the tallest person.

■■■ **E10.4** In the Sequence interface of Worked Example 10.1, add static methods that yield Sequence instances:

```
static Sequence multiplesOf(int n)
static Sequence powersOf(int n)
```

For example, Sequence.powersOf(2) should return the same sequence as the Square-Sequence class in the worked example.

■■ **E10.5** In Worked Example 10.1, add a default method

```
default int[] values(int n)
```

that yields an array of the first n values of the sequence.

■■ **E10.6** In Worked Example 10.1, make the process method a default method of the Sequence interface.

■■ **E10.7** Add a method to the Data class that returns the object with the largest measure, as measured by the supplied measurer:

```
public static Object largest(Object[] objects, Measurer m)
```

■ **E10.8** Using a different Measurer object, process a set of Rectangle objects to find the rectangle with the largest perimeter.

■ **E10.9** Modify the Coin class from Section 8.2.1 to have it implement the Comparable interface.

■ **E10.10** Repeat Exercise • E10.8, making the Measurer into an inner class inside the main method.

■ **E10.11** Repeat Exercise • E10.8, making the Measurer an inner class outside the main method.

■■ **E10.12** Implement a class Bag that stores items represented as strings. Items can be repeated. Supply methods for adding an item, and for counting how many times an item has been added:

```
public void add(String itemName)
public int count(String itemName)
```

Your Bag class should store the data in an ArrayList<Item>, where Item is an inner class with two instance variables: the name of the item and the quantity.

■■ **E10.13** Implement a class Grid that stores measurements in a rectangular grid. The grid has a given number of rows and columns, and a description string can be added for any grid location. Supply the following constructor and methods:

```
public Grid(int numRows, int numColumns)
public void add(int row, int column, String description)
public String getDescription(int row, int column)
public ArrayList<Location> getDescribedLocations()
```

Here, Location is an inner class that encapsulates the row and the column of a grid location.

■■■ **E10.14** Reimplement Exercise •• E10.13 where the grid is unbounded. The constructor has no arguments, and the row and column parameter variables of the add and getDescription methods can be arbitrary integers.

■■■ **Graphics E10.15** Write a method randomShape that randomly generates objects implementing the Shape interface in the Java library API: some mixture of rectangles, ellipses, and lines, with random positions. Call it ten times and draw all of them.

■ **Graphics E10.16** Enhance the ButtonViewer program in Section 10.7.1 so that it prints a message "I was clicked *n* times!" whenever the button is clicked. The value *n* should be incremented with each click.

■■ **Graphics E10.17** Enhance the ButtonViewer program so that it has two buttons, each of which prints a message "I was clicked *n* times!" whenever the button is clicked. Each button should have a separate click count.

■■ **Graphics E10.18** Enhance the ButtonViewer program so that it has two buttons labeled A and B, each of which prints a message "Button *x* was clicked!", where *x* is A or B.

■■ **Graphics E10.19** Implement a ButtonViewer program as in Exercise •• Graphics E10.18, using only a single listener class.

■ **Graphics E10.20** Enhance the ButtonViewer program so that it prints the time at which the button was clicked.

■■■ Graphics E10.21 Implement the AddInterestListener in the InvestmentViewer1 program as a regular class (that is, not an inner class). *Hint:* Store a reference to the bank account. Add a constructor to the listener class that sets the reference.

■■■ Graphics E10.22 Implement the AddInterestListener in the InvestmentViewer2 program as a regular class (that is, not an inner class). *Hint:* Store references to the bank account and the label in the listener. Add a constructor to the listener class that sets the references.

■■ Graphics E10.23 Reimplement the program in Section 10.7.2, specifying the listener with a lambda expression (as described at the end of Section 10.7.2).

■■ Graphics E10.24 Reimplement the program in Section 10.8, specifying the listener with a lambda expression (as described at the end of Section 10.7.2).

■■ Graphics E10.25 Reimplement the program in Section 10.9, specifying the listener with a lambda expression (as described at the end of Section 10.7.2).

■■ Graphics E10.26 Write a program that uses a timer to print the current time once a second. *Hint:* The following code prints the current time:

```
Date now = new Date();
System.out.println(now);
```

The Date class is in the java.util package.

■■■ Graphics E10.27 Change the RectangleComponent for the animation program in Section 10.9 so that the rectangle bounces off the edges of the component rather than moving outside.

■ Graphics E10.28 Change the RectangleComponent for the mouse listener program in Section 10.10 so that a new rectangle is added to the component whenever the mouse is clicked. *Hint:* Keep an ArrayList<Rectangle> and draw all rectangles in the paintComponent method.

■ E10.29 Supply a class Person that implements the Comparable interface. Compare persons by their names. Ask the user to input ten names and generate ten Person objects. Using the compareTo method, determine and print the first and last person among them.

PROGRAMMING PROJECTS

■■ P10.1 Suppose we have a string holding the text of an entire book. If we want to analyze segments of the text, it is inefficient to make substrings. Instead, we should just store a reference to the original text and the starting and ending positions. Design a class Segment that does this, and have it implement the CharSequence interface of the standard library.

Write a test program in which you demonstrate that you can pass your Segment objects to methods that accept CharSequence instances, such as String.join and PrintStream.append.

■■ P10.2 Modify the display method of the LastDigitDistribution class of Worked Example 10.1 so that it produces a histogram, like this:

```
0: *************
1: ******************
2: *************
```

Scale the bars so that widest one has length 40.

■■ P10.3 Write a class PrimeSequence that implements the Sequence interface of Worked Example 10.1, and produces the sequence of prime numbers.

■ **P10.4** Add a method hasNext to the Sequence interface of Worked Example 10.1 that returns false if the sequence has no more values. Implement a class MySequence producing a sequence of real data of your choice, such as populations of cities or countries, temperatures, or stock prices. Obtain the data from the Internet and reformat the values so that they are placed into an array. Return one value at a time in the next method, until you reach the end of the data. Your SequenceDemo class should display the distribution of the last digits of all sequence values.

■ **P10.5** Provide a class FirstDigitDistribution that works just like the LastDigitDistribution class of Worked Example 10.1, except that it counts the distribution of the first digit of each value. (It is a well-known fact that the first digits of random values are *not* uniformly distributed. This fact has been used to detect accounting fraud, when sequences of transaction amounts had an unnatural distribution of their first digits.)

■■ **P10.6** Declare an interface Filter as follows:

```
public interface Filter { boolean accept(Object x); }
```

Modify the implementation of the Data class in Section 10.4 to use both a Measurer and a Filter object. Only objects that the filter accepts should be processed. Demonstrate your modification by processing a collection of bank accounts, filtering out all accounts with balances less than $1,000.

■■ **P10.7** Solve Exercise •• P10.6, using a lambda expression for the filter.

■■ **P10.8** In Exercise •• P10.6, add a method to the Filter interface that counts how many objects are accepted by the filter:

```
static int count(Object[] values, Filter condition)
```

■■ **P10.9** In Exercise •• P10.6, add a method to the Filter interface that retains all objects accepted by the filter and removes the others:

```
static void retainAll(Object[] values, Filter condition)
```

■■ **P10.10** In Exercise •• P10.6, add a method default boolean reject(Object x) to the Filter interface that returns true for all objects that this filter doesn't accept.

■■ **P10.11** In Exercise •• P10.6, add a method default Filter invert() to the Filter interface that yields a filter accepting exactly the objects that this filter rejects.

■■ **P10.12** Consider an interface

```
public interface NumberFormatter
{
    String format(int n);
}
```

Provide four classes that implement this interface. A DefaultFormatter formats an integer in the usual way. A DecimalSeparatorFormatter formats an integer with decimal separators; for example, one million as 1,000,000. An AccountingFormatter formats negative numbers with parentheses; for example, –1 as (1). A BaseFormatter formats the number in base *n*, where *n* is any number between 2 and 36 that is provided in the constructor.

■■ **P10.13** Write a method that takes an array of integers and a NumberFormatter object (from Exercise •• P10.12) and prints each number on a separate line, formatted with the given formatter. The numbers should be right aligned.

■■ P10.14 The System.out.printf method has predefined formats for printing integers, floating-point numbers, and other data types. But it is also extensible. If you use the S format, you can print any class that implements the Formattable interface. That interface has a single method:

```
void formatTo(Formatter formatter, int flags, int width, int precision)
```

In this exercise, you should make the BankAccount class implement the Formattable interface. Ignore the flags and precision and simply format the bank balance, using the given width. In order to achieve this task, you need to get an Appendable reference like this:

```
Appendable a = formatter.out();
```

Appendable is another interface with a method

```
void append(CharSequence sequence)
```

CharSequence is yet another interface that is implemented by (among others) the String class. Construct a string by first converting the bank balance into a string and then padding it with spaces so that it has the desired width. Pass that string to the append method.

■■■ P10.15 Enhance the formatTo method of Exercise ■■ P10.14 by taking into account the precision.

■ P10.16 Your task is to design a general program for managing board games with two players. Your program should be flexible enough to handle games such as tic-tac-toe, chess, or the Game of Nim of Exercise P6.5.

Design an interface Game that describes a board game. Think about what your program needs to do. It asks the first player to input a move—a string in a game-specific format, such as Be3 in chess. Your program knows nothing about specific games, so the Game interface must have a method such as

```
boolean isValidMove(String move)
```

Once the move is found to be valid, it needs to be executed—the interface needs another method executeMove. Next, your program needs to check whether the game is over. If not, the other player's move is processed. You should also provide some mechanism for displaying the current state of the board.

Design the Game interface and provide two implementations of your choice—such as Nim and Chess (or TicTacToe if you are less ambitious). Your GamePlayer class should manage a Game reference without knowing which game is played, and process the moves from both players. Supply two programs that differ only in the initialization of the Game reference.

■■■ Graphics P10.17 Write a program that displays a scrolling message in a panel. Use a timer for the scrolling effect. In the timer's action listener, move the starting position of the message and repaint. When the message has left the window, reset the starting position to the other corner. Provide a user interface to customize the message text, font, foreground and background colors, and the scrolling speed and direction.

■■■ Graphics P10.18 Write a program that allows the user to specify a triangle with three mouse presses. After the first mouse press, draw a small dot. After the second mouse press, draw a line joining the first two points. After the third mouse press, draw the entire triangle. The fourth mouse press erases the old triangle and starts a new one.

∎∎∎ Graphics P10.19 Implement a program that allows two players to play tic-tac-toe. Draw the game grid and an indication of whose turn it is (X or O). Upon the next click, check that the mouse click falls into an empty location, fill the location with the mark of the current player, and give the other player a turn. If the game is won, indicate the winner. Also supply a button for starting over.

© KathyMuller/iStockphoto.

∎∎∎ Graphics P10.20 Write a program that lets users design bar charts with a mouse. When the user clicks inside a bar, the next mouse click extends the length of the bar to the x-coordinate of the mouse click. (If it is at or near 0, the bar is removed.) When the user clicks below the last bar, a new bar is added whose length is the x-coordinate of the mouse click.

∎ Testing P10.21 Consider the task of writing a program that plays tic-tac-toe against a human opponent. A user interface TicTacToeUI reads the user's moves and displays the computer's moves and the board. A class TicTacToeStrategy determines the next move that the computer makes. A class TicTacToeBoard represents the current state of the board. Complete all classes except for the strategy class. Instead, use a mock class that simply picks the first available empty square.

∎∎ Testing P10.22 Consider the task of translating a plain-text book from Project Gutenberg (http://gutenberg.org) to HTML. For example, here is the start of the first chapter of Tolstoy's *Anna Karenina*:

```
Chapter 1

Happy families are all alike; every unhappy family is unhappy in its own way.

Everything was in confusion in the Oblonskys' house. The wife had discovered
that the husband was carrying on an intrigue with a French girl, who had been
a governess in their family, and she had announced to her husband that she
could not go on living in the same house with him . . .
```

The equivalent HTML is:

```
<h1>Chapter 1</h1>
<p>Happy families are all alike; every unhappy family is unhappy in its
own way.</p>
<p>Everything was in confusion in the Oblonskys&rsquo; house. The wife had
discovered that the husband was carrying on an intrigue with a French girl,
who had been a governess in their family, and she had announced to her husband
that she could not go on living in the same house with him ...</p>
```

The HTML conversion can be carried out in two steps. First, the plain text is assembled into *segments*, blocks of text of the same kind (heading, paragraph, and so on). Then each segment is converted, by surrounding it with the HTML tags and converting special characters.

Fetching the text from the Internet and breaking it into segments is a challenging task. Provide an interface and a mock implementation. Combine it with a class that uses the mock implementation to finish the formatting task.

Plain Text	HTML
" "	“ (left) *or* ” (right)
' '	‘ (left) *or* ’ (right)
—	&emdash;
<	&lt;
>	&gt;
&	&amp;

■■ Graphics P10.23 Write a program that demonstrates the growth of a roach population. Start with two roaches and double the number of roaches with each button click.

■■ Graphics P10.24 Write a program that animates a car so that it moves across a frame.

■■■ Graphics P10.25 Write a program that animates two cars moving across a frame in opposite directions (but at different heights so that they don't collide.)

■■ Graphics P10.26 Write a program that prompts the user to enter the *x*- and *y*-positions of the center and a radius, using JOptionPane dialogs. When the user clicks a "Draw" button, prompt for the inputs and draw a circle with that center and radius in a component.

■■ Graphics P10.27 Write a program that allows the user to specify a circle by clicking on the center and then typing the radius in a JOptionPane. Note that you don't need a "Draw" button.

■■■ Graphics P10.28 Write a program that allows the user to specify a circle with two mouse presses, the first one on the center and the second on a point on the periphery. *Hint:* In the mouse press handler, you must keep track of whether you already received the center point in a previous mouse press.

■ Graphics P10.29 Design an interface MoveableShape that can be used as a generic mechanism for animating a shape. A moveable shape must have two methods: move and draw. Write a generic AnimationPanel that paints and moves any MoveableShape (or array list of MoveableShape objects). Supply moveable rectangle and car shapes.

CHAPTER **11**

INPUT/OUTPUT AND EXCEPTION HANDLING

James King-Holmes/Bletchley Park Trust/Photo Researchers, Inc.

CHAPTER GOALS

To read and write text files

To process command line arguments

To throw and catch exceptions

To implement programs that propagate checked exceptions

CHAPTER CONTENTS

In this chapter, you will learn how to read and write files—a very useful skill for processing real world data. As an application, you will learn how to encrypt data. (The Enigma machine shown at left is an encryption device used by Germany in World War II. Pioneering British computer scientists broke the code and were able to intercept encoded messages, which was a significant help in winning the war.) The remainder of this chapter tells you how your programs can report and recover from problems, such as missing files or malformed content, using the exception-handling mechanism of the Java language.

11.1 Reading and Writing Text Files

We begin this chapter by discussing the common task of reading and writing files that contain text. Examples of text files include not only files that are created with a simple text editor, such as Windows Notepad, but also Java source code and HTML files.

Use the Scanner class for reading text files.

In Java, the most convenient mechanism for reading text is to use the Scanner class. You already know how to use a Scanner for reading console input. To read input from a disk file, the Scanner class relies on another class, File, which describes disk files and directories. (The File class has many methods that we do not discuss in this book; for example, methods that delete or rename a file.)

To begin, construct a File object with the name of the input file:

```
File inputFile = new File("input.txt");
```

Then use the File object to construct a Scanner object:

```
Scanner in = new Scanner(inputFile);
```

This Scanner object reads text from the file input.txt. You can use the Scanner methods (such as nextInt, nextDouble, and next) to read data from the input file.

For example, you can use the following loop to process numbers in the input file:

```
while (in.hasNextDouble())
{
   double value = in.nextDouble();
   Process value.
}
```

When writing text files, use the PrintWriter class and the print/println/printf methods.

To write output to a file, you construct a PrintWriter object with the desired file name:

```
PrintWriter out = new PrintWriter("output.txt");
```

If the output file already exists, it is emptied before the new data are written into it. If the file doesn't exist, an empty file is created.

The PrintWriter class is an enhancement of the PrintStream class that you already know—System.out is a PrintStream object. You can use the familiar print, println, and printf methods with any PrintWriter object:

```
out.println("Hello, World!");
out.printf("Total: %8.2f%n", total);
```

When you are done processing a file, be sure to *close* the Scanner or PrintWriter:

```
in.close();
out.close();
```

Close all files
when you are done
processing them.

If your program exits without closing the `PrintWriter`, some of the output may not be written to the disk file.

The following program puts these concepts to work. It reads a file containing numbers and writes the numbers, lined up in a column and followed by their total, to another file.

For example, if the input file has the contents

```
32 54 67.5 29 35 80
115 44.5 100 65
```

then the output file is

```
        32.00
        54.00
        67.50
        29.00
        35.00
        80.00
       115.00
        44.50
       100.00
        65.00
Total:  622.00
```

There is one additional issue that we need to tackle. If the input file for a `Scanner` doesn't exist, a `FileNotFoundException` occurs when the `Scanner` object is constructed. The compiler insists that we specify what the program should do when that happens. Similarly, the `PrintWriter` constructor generates this exception if it cannot open the file for writing. (This can happen if the name is illegal or the user does not have the authority to create a file in the given location.) In our sample program, we want to terminate the `main` method if the exception occurs. To achieve this, we label the `main` method with a `throws` declaration:

```
public static void main(String[] args) throws FileNotFoundException
```

You will see in Section 11.4 how to deal with exceptions in a more professional way.

The `File`, `PrintWriter`, and `FileNotFoundException` classes are contained in the `java.io` package.

sec01/Total.java

```java
 1  import java.io.File;
 2  import java.io.FileNotFoundException;
 3  import java.io.PrintWriter;
 4  import java.util.Scanner;
 5
 6  /**
 7      This program reads a file with numbers, and writes the numbers to another
 8      file, lined up in a column and followed by their total.
 9  */
10  public class Total
11  {
12      public static void main(String[] args) throws FileNotFoundException
13      {
14          // Prompt for the input and output file names
15
16          Scanner console = new Scanner(System.in);
17          System.out.print("Input file: ");
18          String inputFileName = console.next();
```

```
19     System.out.print("Output file: ");
20     String outputFileName = console.next();
21
22     // Construct the Scanner and PrintWriter objects for reading and writing
23
24     File inputFile = new File(inputFileName);
25     Scanner in = new Scanner(inputFile);
26     PrintWriter out = new PrintWriter(outputFileName);
27
28     // Read the input and write the output
29
30     double total = 0;
31
32     while (in.hasNextDouble())
33     {
34        double value = in.nextDouble();
35        out.printf("%15.2f%n", value);
36        total = total + value;
37     }
38
39     out.printf("Total: %8.2f%n", total);
40
41     in.close();
42     out.close();
43   }
44 }
```

Common Error 11.1

Backslashes in File Names

When you specify a file name as a string literal, and the name contains backslash characters (as in a Windows file name), you must supply each backslash twice:

```
File inputFile = new File("c:\\homework\\input.dat");
```

A single backslash inside a quoted string is an **escape character** that is combined with the following character to form a special meaning, such as \n for a newline character. The \\ combination denotes a single backslash.

When a user supplies a file name to a program, however, the user should not type the backslash twice.

Common Error 11.2

Constructing a Scanner with a String

When you construct a PrintWriter with a string, it writes to a file:

```
PrintWriter out = new PrintWriter("output.txt");
```

However, this does *not* work for a Scanner. The statement

```
Scanner in = new Scanner("input.txt"); // Error?
```

does *not* open a file. Instead, it simply reads through the string: in.next() returns the string "input.txt". (This is occasionally useful—see Section 11.2.5.)

You must simply remember to use File objects in the Scanner constructor:

```
Scanner in = new Scanner(new File("input.txt")); // OK
```

Special Topic 11.1

Reading Web Pages

You can read the contents of a web page with this sequence of commands:

```
String address = "http://horstmann.com/index.html";
URL pageLocation = new URL(address);
Scanner in = new Scanner(pageLocation.openStream());
```

Now simply read the contents of the web page with the Scanner in the usual way. The URL constructor and the openStream method can throw an IOException, so you need to tag the main method with throws IOException. (See Section 11.4.3 for more information on the throws clause.)

The URL class is contained in the java.net package.

EXAMPLE CODE See special_topic 1 of your eText or companion code for a program that reads data from a web page.

Special Topic 11.2

File Dialog Boxes

In a program with a graphical user interface, you will want to use a file dialog box (such as the one shown in the figure below) whenever the users of your program need to pick a file. The JFileChooser class implements a file dialog box for the Swing user-interface toolkit.

The JFileChooser class has many options to fine-tune the display of the dialog box, but in its most basic form it is quite simple: Construct a file chooser object; then call the showOpenDialog or showSaveDialog method. Both methods show the same dialog box, but the button for selecting a file is labeled "Open" or "Save", depending on which method you call.

For better placement of the dialog box on the screen, you can specify the user-interface component over which to pop up the dialog box. If you don't care where the dialog box pops up, you can simply pass null. The showOpenDialog and showSaveDialog methods return either JFileChooser.APPROVE_OPTION, if the user has chosen a file, or JFileChooser.CANCEL_OPTION, if the

Call with showOpenDialog method

Button is "Save" when showSaveDialog method is called

A JFileChooser Dialog Box

user canceled the selection. If a file was chosen, then you call the getSelectedFile method to obtain a File object that describes the file.

Here is a complete example:

```
JFileChooser chooser = new JFileChooser();
Scanner in = null;
if (chooser.showOpenDialog(null) == JFileChooser.APPROVE_OPTION)
{
    File selectedFile = chooser.getSelectedFile();
    in = new Scanner(selectedFile);
    . . .
}
```

EXAMPLE CODE   See special_topic_2 of your eText or companion code for a program that demonstrates how to use a file chooser.

Special Topic 11.3

Character Encodings

A **character** (such as the letter A, the digit 0, the accented character é, the Greek letter π, the symbol $\int$, or the Chinese character 中) is encoded as a sequence of bytes. Each byte is a value between 0 and 255.

Unfortunately, the encoding is not uniform. In 1963, ASCII (the American Standard Code for Information Interchange) defined an encoding for 128 characters, which you can find in Appendix A. ASCII encodes all upper- and lowercase Latin letters and digits, as well as common symbols such as + * %, as values between 0 and 127. For example, the code for the letter A is 65.

As different populations felt the need to encode their own alphabets, they designed their own codes. Many of them built upon ASCII, using the values in the range from 128 to 255 for their own language. For example, in Spain, the letter é was encoded as 233. But in Greece, the code 233 denoted the letter ι (a lowercase iota). As you can imagine, if a Spanish tourist named José sent an e-mail to a Greek hotel, this created a problem.

To resolve this issue, the design of **Unicode** was begun in 1987. As described in Computing & Society 4.2, each character in the world is given a unique integer value. However, there are still multiple encodings of those integers in binary. The most popular encoding is called UTF-8. It encodes each character as a sequence of one to four bytes. For example, an A is still 65, as in ASCII, but an é is 195 169. The details of the encoding don't matter, as long as you specify that you want UTF-8 when you read and write a file.

As this book goes to print, the Windows and Macintosh operating systems have not yet made the switch to UTF-8. Java picks up the character encoding from the operating system. Unless you specifically request otherwise, the Scanner and PrintWriter classes will read and write files in that encoding. That's fine if your files contain only ASCII characters, or if the creator and the recipient use the same encoding. But if you need to process files with accented characters, Chinese characters, or special symbols, you should specifically request the UTF-8 encoding. Construct a scanner with

```
Scanner in = new Scanner(file, "UTF-8");
```

and a print writer with

```
PrintWriter out = new PrintWriter(file, "UTF-8");
```

You may wonder why Java can't just figure out the character encoding. However, consider the string José. In UTF-8, that's 74 111 115 195 169. The first three bytes, for Jos, are in the ASCII range and pose no problem. But the next two bytes, 195 169, could be é in UTF-8 or Ã¡ in the traditional Spanish encoding. The Scanner object doesn't understand Spanish, and it can't decide which encoding to choose.

Therefore, you should always specify the UTF-8 encoding when you exchange files with users from other parts of the world.

11.2 Text Input and Output

In the following sections, you will learn how to process text with complex contents, and you will learn how to cope with challenges that often occur with real data.

11.2.1 Reading Words

The next method of the Scanner class reads the next string. Consider the loop

```
while (in.hasNext())
{
   String input = in.next();
   System.out.println(input);
}
```

If the user provides the input:

```
Mary had a little lamb
```

this loop prints each word on a separate line:

```
Mary
had
a
little
lamb
```

> The next method reads a string that is delimited by white space.

However, the words can contain punctuation marks and other symbols. The next method returns any sequence of characters that is not white space. **White space** includes spaces, tab characters, and the newline characters that separate lines. For example, the following strings are considered "words" by the next method:

```
snow.
1729
C++
```

(Note the period after snow—it is considered a part of the word because it is not white space.)

Here is precisely what happens when the next method is executed. Input characters that are white space are *consumed*—that is, removed from the input. However, they do not become part of the word. The first character that is not white space becomes the first character of the word. More characters are added until either another white space character occurs, or the end of the input file has been reached. However, if the end of the input file is reached before any character was added to the word, a "no such element exception" occurs.

Sometimes, you want to read just the words and discard anything that isn't a letter. You achieve this task by calling the useDelimiter method on your Scanner object:

```
Scanner in = new Scanner(. . .);
in.useDelimiter("[^A-Za-z]+");
```

Here, we set the character pattern that separates words to "any sequence of characters other than letters". (See Special Topic 11.4.) With this setting, punctuation and numbers are not included in the words returned by the next method.

11.2.2 Reading Characters

Sometimes, you want to read a file one character at a time. You will see an example in Section 11.3 where we encrypt the characters of a file. You achieve this task by calling the useDelimiter method on your Scanner object with an empty string:

```
Scanner in = new Scanner(. . .);
in.useDelimiter("");
```

Now each call to next returns a string consisting of a single character. Here is how you can process the characters:

```
while (in.hasNext())
{
   char ch = in.next().charAt(0);
   Process ch.
}
```

11.2.3 Classifying Characters

The Character class has methods for classifying characters.

When you read a character, or when you analyze the characters in a word or line, you often want to know what kind of character it is. The Character class declares several useful methods for this purpose. Each of them has an argument of type char and returns a boolean value (see Table 1).

For example, the call

```
Character.isDigit(ch)
```

returns true if ch is a digit ('0' . . . '9' or a digit in another writing system—see Computing & Society 4.2), false otherwise.

Table 1 Character Testing Methods

Method	Examples of Accepted Characters
isDigit	0, 1, 2
isLetter	A, B, C, a, b, c
isUpperCase	A, B, C
isLowerCase	a, b, c
isWhitespace	space, newline, tab

11.2.4 Reading Lines

The nextLine method reads an entire line.

When each line of a file is a data record, it is often best to read entire lines with the nextLine method:

```
String line = in.nextLine();
```

The next input line (without the newline character) is placed into the string line. You can then take the line apart for further processing.

The hasNextLine method returns true if there is at least one more line in the input, false when all lines have been read. To ensure that there is another line to process, call the hasNextLine method before calling nextLine.

Here is a typical example of processing lines in a file. A file with population data from the CIA Fact Book site (https://www.cia.gov/library/publications/the-world-factbook/index.html) contains lines such as the following:

```
China  1330044605
India  1147995898
United States 303824646
. . .
```

Because some country names have more than one word, it would be tedious to read this file using the next method. For example, after reading United, how would your program know that it needs to read another word before reading the population count?

Instead, read each input line into a string:

```
while (in.hasNextLine())
{
    String line = in.nextLine();
    Process line.
}
```

Use the isDigit and isWhiteSpace methods in Table 1 to find out where the name ends and the number starts.

Locate the first digit:

```
int i = 0;
while (!Character.isDigit(line.charAt(i))) { i++; }
```

Then extract the country name and population:

```
String countryName = line.substring(0, i);
String population = line.substring(i);
```

However, the country name contains one or more spaces at the end. Use the trim method to remove them:

```
countryName = countryName.trim();
```

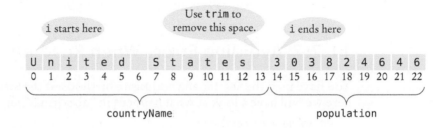

The trim method returns the string with all white space at the beginning and end removed.

There is one additional problem. The population is stored in a string, not a number. In Section 11.2.6, you will see how to convert the string to a number.

11.2.5 Scanning a String

In the preceding section, you saw how to break a string into parts by looking at individual characters. Another approach is occasionally easier. You can use a Scanner object to read the characters from a string:

```
Scanner lineScanner = new Scanner(line);
```

Then you can use lineScanner like any other Scanner object, reading words and numbers:

```
String countryName = lineScanner.next(); // Read first word
// Add more words to countryName until number encountered
while (!lineScanner.hasNextInt())
{
    countryName = countryName + " " + lineScanner.next();
}
int populationValue = lineScanner.nextInt();
```

11.2.6 Converting Strings to Numbers

Sometimes you have a string that contains a number, such as the population string in Section 11.2.4. For example, suppose that the string is the character sequence "303824646". To get the integer value 303824646, you use the Integer.parseInt method:

```
int populationValue = Integer.parseInt(population);
    // populationValue is the integer 303824646
```

To convert a string containing floating-point digits to its floating-point value, use the Double.parseDouble method. For example, suppose input is the string "3.95".

```
double price = Double.parseDouble(input);
    // price is the floating-point number 3.95
```

If a string contains the digits of a number, you use the Integer.parseInt or Double.parseDouble method to obtain the number value.

You need to be careful when calling the Integer.parseInt and Double.parseDouble methods. The argument must be a string containing the digits of an integer, without any additional characters. Not even spaces are allowed! In our situation, we happen to know that there won't be any spaces at the beginning of the string, but there might be some at the end. Therefore, we use the trim method:

```
int populationValue = Integer.parseInt(population.trim());
```

How To 11.1 on page 399 continues this example.

11.2.7 Avoiding Errors When Reading Numbers

You have used the nextInt and nextDouble methods of the Scanner class many times, but here we will have a look at what happens in "abnormal" situations. Suppose you call

```
int value = in.nextInt();
```

The nextInt method recognizes numbers such as 3 or -21. However, if the input is not a properly formatted number, an "input mismatch exception" occurs. For example, consider an input containing the characters

```
2 1 s t   c e n t u r y
```

White space is consumed and the word 21st is read. However, this word is not a properly formatted number, causing an input mismatch exception in the nextInt method.

If there is no input at all when you call nextInt or nextDouble, a "no such element exception" occurs. To avoid exceptions, use the hasNextInt method to screen the input when reading an integer. For example,

```
if (in.hasNextInt())
{
   int value = in.nextInt();
   . . .
}
```

Similarly, you should call the hasNextDouble method before calling nextDouble.

11.2.8 Mixing Number, Word, and Line Input

The nextInt, nextDouble, and next methods *do not* consume the white space that follows the number or word. This can be a problem if you alternate between calling nextInt/nextDouble/next and nextLine. Suppose a file contains country names and population values in this format:

```
China
1330044605
India
1147995898
United States
303824646
```

Now suppose you read the file with these instructions:

```
while (in.hasNextLine())
{
   String countryName = in.nextLine();
   int population = in.nextInt();
   Process the country name and population.
}
```

Initially, the input contains

C h i n a \n 1 3 3 0 0 4 4 6 0 5 \n I n d i a \n

After the first call to the nextLine method, the input contains

1 3 3 0 0 4 4 6 0 5 \n I n d i a \n

After the call to nextInt, the input contains

\n I n d i a \n

Note that the nextInt call did *not* consume the newline character. Therefore, the second call to nextLine reads an empty string!

The remedy is to add a call to nextLine after reading the population value:

```
String countryName = in.nextLine();
int population = in.nextInt();
in.nextLine(); // Consume the newline
```

The call to nextLine consumes any remaining white space *and* the newline character.

11.2.9 Formatting Output

When you write numbers or strings, you often want to control how they appear. For example, dollar amounts are usually formatted with two significant digits, such as

```
Cookies:     3.20
```

You know from Section 4.3.2 how to achieve this output with the `printf` method. In this section, we discuss additional options of the `printf` method.

Suppose you need to print a table of items and prices, each stored in an array, such as

```
Cookies:     3.20
Linguine:    2.95
Clams:      17.29
```

Note that the item strings line up to the left, whereas the numbers line up to the right. By default, the `printf` method lines up values to the right.

To specify left alignment, you add a hyphen (-) before the field width:

```
System.out.printf("%-10s%10.2f", items[i] + ":", prices[i]);
```

Here, we have two format specifiers.

- `%-10s` formats a left-justified string. The string `items[i] + ":"` is padded with spaces so it becomes ten characters wide. The - indicates that the string is placed on the left, followed by sufficient spaces to reach a width of 10.

- `%10.2f` formats a floating-point number, also in a field that is ten characters wide. However, the spaces appear to the left and the value to the right.

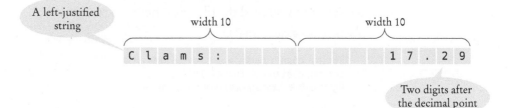

A construct such as `%-10s` or `%10.2f` is called a *format specifier:* it describes how a value should be formatted.

<table>
<tr><td colspan="3" align="center">Table 2 Format Flags</td></tr>
<tr><th>Flag</th><th>Meaning</th><th>Example</th></tr>
<tr><td>-</td><td>Left alignment</td><td>1.23 followed by spaces</td></tr>
<tr><td>0</td><td>Show leading zeroes</td><td>001.23</td></tr>
<tr><td>+</td><td>Show a plus sign for positive numbers</td><td>+1.23</td></tr>
<tr><td>(</td><td>Enclose negative numbers in parentheses</td><td>(1.23)</td></tr>
<tr><td>,</td><td>Show decimal separators</td><td>12,300</td></tr>
<tr><td>^</td><td>Convert letters to uppercase</td><td>1.23E+1</td></tr>
</table>

Table 3 Format Types

Code	Type	Example
d	Decimal integer	123
f	Fixed floating-point	12.30
e	Exponential floating-point	1.23e+1
g	General floating-point (exponential notation is used for very large or very small values)	12.3
s	String	Tax:

A format specifier has the following structure:

- The first character is a %.
- Next, there are optional "flags" that modify the format, such as - to indicate left alignment. See Table 2 for the most common format flags.
- Next is the field width, the total number of characters in the field (including the spaces used for padding), followed by an optional precision for floating-point numbers.
- The format specifier ends with the *format type*, such as f for floating-point values or s for strings. There are quite a few format types—Table 3 shows the most important ones.

EXAMPLE CODE   See sec02 of your eText or companion code for a program that processes a file containing a mixture of text and numbers.

Special Topic 11.4
Regular Expressions

A **regular expression** describes a character pattern. For example, numbers have a simple form. They contain one or more digits. The regular expression describing numbers is [0-9]+. The set [0-9] denotes any digit between 0 and 9, and the + means "one or more".

The search commands of professional programming editors understand regular expressions. Moreover, several utility programs use regular expressions to locate matching text. A commonly used program that uses regular expressions is **grep** (which stands for "global regular expression print"). You can run grep from a command line or from inside some compilation environments. Grep is part of the UNIX operating system, and versions are available for Windows. It needs a regular expression and one or more files to search. When grep runs, it displays a set of lines that match the regular expression.

Suppose you want to find all magic numbers (see Programming Tip 4.1) in a file.

```
grep [0-9]+ Homework.java
```

lists all lines in the file Homework.java that contain sequences of digits. That isn't terribly useful; lines with variable names x1 will be listed. OK, you want sequences of digits that do *not* immediately follow letters:

```
grep [^A-Za-z][0-9]+ Homework.java
```

The set [^A-Za-z] denotes any characters that are *not* in the ranges A to Z and a to z. This works much better, and it shows only lines that contain actual numbers.

The useDelimiter method of the Scanner class accepts a regular expression to describe delimiters—the blocks of text that separate words. As already mentioned, if you set the delimiter pattern to [^A-Za-z]+, a delimiter is a sequence of one or more characters that are not letters.

There are two useful methods of the String class that use regular expressions. The split method splits a string into an array of strings, with the delimiter specified as a regular expressions. For example,

```
String[] tokens = line.split("\\s+");
```

splits input along white space. The replaceAll method yields a string in which all matches of a regular expression are replaced with a string. For example, word.replaceAll("[aeiou]", "") is the word with all vowels removed.

For more information on regular expressions, consult one of the many tutorials on the Internet by pointing your search engine to "regular expression tutorial".

Special Topic 11.5

Reading an Entire File

In the preceding section, you saw how to read lines, words, and characters from a file. Alternatively, you can read the entire file into a list of lines, or into a single string. Use the Files and Paths classes, like this:

```
String filename = . . .;
List<String> lines = Files.readAllLines(Paths.get(filename));
String content = new String(Files.readAllBytes(Paths.get(filename)));
```

The Files class has many other uses—see Chapter 21.

11.3 Command Line Arguments

Depending on the operating system and Java development environment used, there are different methods of starting a program—for example, by selecting "Run" in the compilation environment, by clicking on an icon, or by typing the name of the program at the prompt in a command shell window. The latter method is called "invoking the program from the command line". When you use this method, you must of course type the name of the program, but you can also type in additional information that the program can use. These additional strings are called **command line arguments**. For example, if you start a program with the command line

```
java ProgramClass -v input.dat
```

then the program receives two command line arguments: the strings "-v" and "input. dat". It is entirely up to the program what to do with these strings. It is customary to interpret strings starting with a hyphen (-) as program options.

Should you support command line arguments for your programs, or should you prompt users, perhaps with a graphical user interface? For a casual and infrequent user, an interactive user interface is much better. The user interface guides the user along and makes it possible to navigate the application without much knowledge. But for a frequent user, a command line interface has a major advantage: it is easy to automate. If you need to process hundreds of files every day, you could spend all your time typing file names into file chooser dialog boxes. However, by using batch files or shell scripts (a feature of your computer's operating system), you can automatically call a program many times with different command line arguments.

Your program receives its command line arguments in the args parameter of the main method:

> Programs that start from the command line receive the command line arguments in the main method.

```
public static void main(String[] args)
```

In our example, args is an array of length 2, containing the strings

```
args[0]:   "-v"
args[1]:   "input.dat"
```

Let us write a program that *encrypts* a file—that is, scrambles it so that it is unreadable except to those who know the decryption method. Ignoring 2,000 years of progress in the field of encryption, we will use a method familiar to Julius Caesar, replacing A with a D, B with an E, and so on (see Figure 1).

The program takes the following command line arguments:

- An optional -d flag to indicate decryption instead of encryption
- The input file name
- The output file name

For example,

```
java CaesarCipher input.txt encrypt.txt
```

encrypts the file input.txt and places the result into encrypt.txt.

```
java CaesarCipher -d encrypt.txt output.txt
```

decrypts the file encrypt.txt and places the result into output.txt.

© xyno/iStockphoto.

The emperor Julius Caesar used a simple scheme to encrypt messages.

Plain text	M	e	e	t		m	e		a	t		t	h	e	
	↓	↓	↓	↓		↓	↓		↓	↓		↓	↓	↓	
Encrypted text	P	h	h	w		p	h		d	w		w	k	h	

Figure 1
Caesar Cipher

sec03/CaesarCipher.java

```java
1  import java.io.File;
2  import java.io.FileNotFoundException;
3  import java.io.PrintWriter;
4  import java.util.Scanner;
5
6  /**
7     This program encrypts a file using the Caesar cipher.
8  */
9  public class CaesarCipher
10 {
11    public static void main(String[] args) throws FileNotFoundException
12    {
13       final int DEFAULT_KEY = 3;
14       int key = DEFAULT_KEY;
15       String inFile = "";
16       String outFile = "";
17       int files = 0; // Number of command line arguments that are files
18
19       for (int i = 0; i < args.length; i++)
20       {
```

```
21            String arg = args[i];
22            if (arg.charAt(0) == '-')
23            {
24                // It is a command line option
25
26                char option = arg.charAt(1);
27                if (option == 'd') { key = -key; }
28                else { usage(); return; }
29            }
30            else
31            {
32                // It is a file name
33
34                files++;
35                if (files == 1) { inFile = arg; }
36                else if (files == 2) { outFile = arg; }
37            }
38        }
39        if (files != 2) { usage(); return; }
40
41        Scanner in = new Scanner(new File(inFile));
42        in.useDelimiter(""); // Process individual characters
43        PrintWriter out = new PrintWriter(outFile);
44
45        while (in.hasNext())
46        {
47            char from = in.next().charAt(0);
48            char to = encrypt(from, key);
49            out.print(to);
50        }
51        in.close();
52        out.close();
53    }
54
55    /**
56        Encrypts upper- and lowercase characters by shifting them
57        according to a key.
58        @param ch  the letter to be encrypted
59        @param key  the encryption key
60        @return  the encrypted letter
61    */
62    public static char encrypt(char ch, int key)
63    {
64        int base = 0;
65        if ('A' <= ch && ch <= 'Z') { base = 'A'; }
66        else if ('a' <= ch && ch <= 'z') { base = 'a'; }
67        else { return ch; } // Not a letter
68        int offset = ch - base + key;
69        final int LETTERS = 26; // Number of letters in the Roman alphabet
70        if (offset >= LETTERS) { offset = offset - LETTERS; }
71        else if (offset < 0) { offset = offset + LETTERS; }
72        return (char) (base + offset);
73    }
74
75    /**
76        Prints a message describing proper usage.
77    */
78    public static void usage()
79    {
```

```
80       System.out.println("Usage: java CaesarCipher [-d] infile outfile");
81    }
82 }
```

HOW TO 11.1

Processing Text Files

Processing text files that contain real data can be surprisingly challenging. This How To gives you step-by-step guidance using world population data.

Problem Statement Read two country data files, `worldpop.txt` and `worldarea.txt` (supplied with your companion code). Both files contain the same countries in the same order. Write a file `world_pop_density.txt` that contains country names and population densities (people per square km), with the country names aligned left and the numbers aligned right:

```
Afghanistan              50.56
Akrotiri                127.64
Albania                 125.91
Algeria                  14.18
American Samoa          288.92
. . .
```

© Oksana Perkins/iStockphoto.

Singapore is one of the most densely populated countries in the world.

Step 1 Understand the processing task.

As always, you need to have a clear understanding of the task before designing a solution. Can you carry out the task by hand (perhaps with smaller input files)? If not, get more information about the problem.

One important consideration is whether you can process the data as it becomes available, or whether you need to store it first. For example, if you are asked to write out sorted data, you first need to collect all input, perhaps by placing it in an array list. However, it is often possible to process the data "on the go", without storing it.

In our example, we can read each file one line at a time and compute the density for each line because our input files store the population and area data in the same order.

The following pseudocode describes our processing task.

> *While there are more lines to be read*
> *Read a line from each file.*
> *Extract the country name.*
> *population = number following the country name in the line from the first file*
> *area = number following the country name in the line from the second file*
> *If area != 0*
> *density = population / area*
> *Print country name and density.*

Step 2 Determine which files you need to read and write.

This should be clear from the problem. In our example, there are two input files, the population data and the area data, and one output file.

Step 3 Choose a mechanism for obtaining the file names.

There are three options:

- Hard-coding the file names (such as `"worldpop.txt"`).
- Asking the user:
  ```
  Scanner in = new Scanner(System.in);
  System.out.print("Enter filename: ");
  String inFile = in.nextLine();
  ```
- Using command-line arguments for the file names.

In our example, we use hard-coded file names for simplicity.

Step 4 Choose between line, word, and character-based input.

As a rule of thumb, read lines if the input data is grouped by lines. That is the case with tabular data, such as in our example, or when you need to report line numbers.

When gathering data that can be distributed over several lines, then it makes more sense to read words. Keep in mind that you lose all white space when you read words.

Reading characters is mostly useful for tasks that require access to individual characters. Examples include analyzing character frequencies, changing tabs to spaces, or encryption.

Step 5 With line-oriented input, extract the required data.

It is simple to read a line of input with the `nextLine` method. Then you need to get the data out of that line. You can extract substrings, as described in Section 11.2.4.

Typically, you will use methods such as `Character.isWhitespace` and `Character.isDigit` to find the boundaries of substrings.

If you need any of the substrings as numbers, you must convert them, using `Integer.parse-Int` or `Double.parseDouble`.

Step 6 Use classes and methods to factor out common tasks.

Processing input files usually has repetitive tasks, such as skipping over white space or extracting numbers from strings. It really pays off to isolate these tedious operations from the remainder of the code.

In our example, we have a task that occurs twice: splitting an input line into the country name and the value that follows. We implement a simple `CountryValue` class for this purpose, using the technique described in Section 11.2.4.

Here is the complete source code.

how_to_1/PopulationDensity.java

```
1  import java.io.File;
2  import java.io.FileNotFoundException;
3  import java.io.PrintWriter;
4  import java.util.Scanner;
5
6  public class PopulationDensity
7  {
8     public static void main(String[] args) throws FileNotFoundException
9     {
10        // Open input files
11        Scanner in1 = new Scanner(new File("worldpop.txt"));
12        Scanner in2 = new Scanner(new File("worldarea.txt"));
13
14        // Open output file
15        PrintWriter out = new PrintWriter("world_pop_density.txt");
16
17        // Read lines from each file
```

```
18        while (in1.hasNextLine() && in2.hasNextLine())
19        {
20           CountryValue population = new CountryValue(in1.nextLine());
21           CountryValue area = new CountryValue(in2.nextLine());
22
23           // Compute and print the population density
24           double density = 0;
25           if (area.getValue() != 0) // Protect against division by zero
26           {
27              density = population.getValue() / area.getValue();
28           }
29           out.printf("%-40s%15.2f%n", population.getCountry(), density);
30        }
31
32        in1.close();
33        in2.close();
34        out.close();
35     }
36 }
```

how_to_1/CountryValue.java

```
1  /**
2      Describes a value that is associated with a country.
3  */
4  public class CountryValue
5  {
6     private String country;
7     private double value;
8
9     /**
10        Constructs a CountryValue from an input line.
11        @param line a line containing a country name, followed by a value
12     */
13     public CountryValue(String line)
14     {
15        int i = 0; // Locate the start of the first digit
16        while (!Character.isDigit(line.charAt(i))) { i++; }
17        int j = i - 1; // Locate the end of the preceding word
18        while (Character.isWhitespace(line.charAt(j))) { j--; }
19        country = line.substring(0, j + 1); // Extract the country name
20        value = Double.parseDouble(line.substring(i).trim()); // Extract the value
21     }
22
23     /**
24        Gets the country name.
25        @return the country name
26     */
27     public String getCountry() { return country; }
28
29     /**
30        Gets the associated value.
31        @return the value associated with the country
32     */
33     public double getValue() { return value; }
34 }
```

Computing & Society 11.1   Encryption Algorithms

This chapter's exercise section gives a few algorithms for encrypting text. Don't actually use any of those methods to send secret messages to your lover. Any skilled cryptographer can *break* these schemes in a very short time—that is, reconstruct the original text without knowing the secret keyword.

In 1978, Ron Rivest, Adi Shamir, and Leonard Adleman introduced an encryption method that is much more powerful. The method is called *RSA encryption*, after the last names of its inventors. The exact scheme is too complicated to present here, but it is not actually difficult to follow. You can find the details in http://people.csail.mit.edu/rivest/Rsapaper.pdf.

RSA is a remarkable encryption method. There are two keys: a public key and a private key (see the figure). You can print the public key on your business card (or in your e-mail signature block) and give it to anyone. Then anyone can send you messages that only you can decrypt. Even though everyone else knows the public key, and even if they intercept all the messages coming to you, they cannot break the scheme and actually read the messages. With today's technology, the RSA algorithm is expected to be unbreakable provided that the keys are long enough. However, it is possible that "quantum computers" may be able to crack RSA in the future.

The inventors of the algorithm obtained a *patent* for it. A patent is a deal that society makes with an inventor. For a period of 20 years, the inventor has an exclusive right to its commercialization, may collect royalties from others wishing to manufacture the invention, and may even stop competitors from using it

altogether. In return, the inventor must publish the invention, so that others may learn from it, and must relinquish all claim to it after the monopoly period ends. The presumption is that in the absence of patent law, inventors would be reluctant to go through the trouble of inventing, or they would try to cloak their techniques to prevent others from copying their devices.

There has been some controversy about the RSA patent. Had there not been patent protection, would the inventors have published the method anyway, thereby giving the benefit to society without the cost of the 20-year monopoly? In this case, the answer is probably yes. The inventors were academic researchers who live on salaries rather than sales receipts and are usually rewarded for their discoveries by a boost in their reputation and careers. Would their followers have been as active in discovering (and patenting) improvements? There is no way of knowing, of course. Is an

algorithm even patentable, or is it a mathematical fact that belongs to nobody? The patent office did take the latter attitude for a long time. The RSA inventors and many others described their inventions in terms of imaginary electronic devices, rather than algorithms, to circumvent that restriction. Nowadays, the patent office will award software patents.

The existence of strong encryption methods bothers the United States government to no end. Criminals and foreign agents can send communications that the police and intelligence agencies cannot decipher. Devices such as cell phones use encryption so that thieves cannot read the information if the device is stolen. However, neither can government organizations. There have been serious proposals to make it illegal for private citizens to use these encryption methods, or to compel hardware and software makers to provide "back doors" that allow law enforcement access.

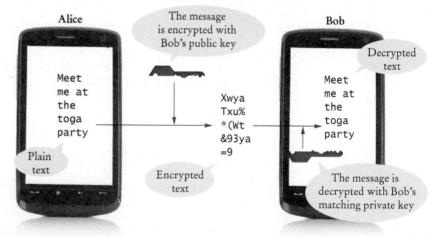

(mobile phone) © Anna Khomulo/iStockphoto.

Public-Key Encryption

WORKED EXAMPLE 11.1
Analyzing Baby Names

Learn how to use data from the Social Security Administration to analyze the most popular baby names. See your eText or visit wiley.com/go/bjeo7.

© Nancy Ross/iStockphoto.

11.4 Exception Handling

There are two aspects to dealing with program errors: *detection* and *handling*. For example, the Scanner constructor can detect an attempt to read from a non-existent file. However, it cannot handle that error. A satisfactory way of handling the error might be to terminate the program, or to ask the user for another file name. The Scanner class cannot choose between these alternatives. It needs to report the error to another part of the program.

In Java, *exception handling* provides a flexible mechanism for passing control from the point of error detection to a handler that can deal with the error. In the following sections, we will look into the details of this mechanism.

11.4.1 Throwing Exceptions

> To signal an exceptional condition, use the throw statement to throw an exception object.

When you detect an error condition, your job is really easy. You just *throw* an appropriate exception object, and you are done. For example, suppose someone tries to withdraw too much money from a bank account.

```
if (amount > balance)
{
    // Now what?
}
```

First look for an appropriate exception class. The Java library provides many classes to signal all sorts of exceptional conditions.

Syntax 11.1   Throwing an Exception

> *Syntax*   throw *exceptionObject*;

> Most exception objects can be constructed with an error message.

> A new exception object is constructed, then thrown.

```
if (amount > balance)
{
    throw new IllegalArgumentException("Amount exceeds balance");
}
balance = balance - amount;
```

> This line is not executed when the exception is thrown.

Figure 2 shows the most useful ones. (The classes are arranged as a tree-shaped inheritance hierarchy, with more specialized classes at the bottom of the tree.)

Look around for an exception type that might describe your situation. How about the ArithmeticException? Is it an arithmetic error to have a negative balance? No—Java can deal with negative numbers. Is the amount to be withdrawn illegal? Indeed it is. It is just too large. Therefore, let's throw an IllegalArgumentException.

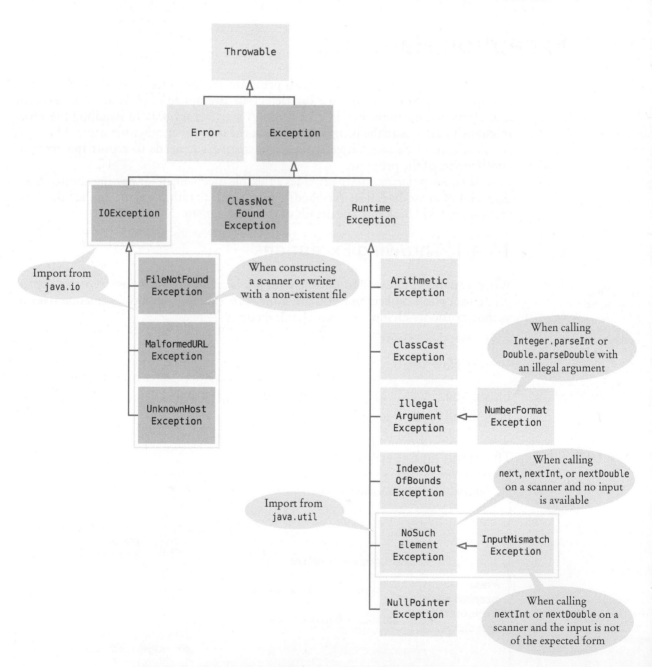

Figure 2 A Part of the Hierarchy of Exception Classes

```
if (amount > balance)
{
    throw new IllegalArgumentException("Amount exceeds balance");
}
```

When you throw
an exception,
processing
continues in an
exception handler.

When you **throw an exception**, execution does not continue with the next statement but with an **exception handler**. That is the topic of the next section.

When you throw an exception, the normal control flow is terminated. This is similar to a circuit breaker that cuts off the flow of electricity in a dangerous situation.

© Lisa F. Young/iStockphoto.

EXAMPLE CODE   See sec04_01 in your eText or companion code for a program that demonstrates throwing an exception.

11.4.2 Catching Exceptions

Place the statements
that can cause an
exception inside a
try block, and the
handler inside a
catch clause.

Every exception should be handled somewhere in your program. If an exception has no handler, an error message is printed, and your program terminates. Of course, such an unhandled exception is confusing to program users.

You handle exceptions with the try/catch statement. Place the statement into a location of your program that knows how to handle a particular exception. The **try statement** contains one or more statements that may cause an exception of the kind that you are willing to handle. Each catch clause contains the handler for an exception type. Here is an example:

```
try
{
    String filename = . . .;
    Scanner in = new Scanner(new File(filename));
    String input = in.next();
    int value = Integer.parseInt(input);
    . . .
}
catch (IOException exception)
{
    exception.printStackTrace();
}
catch (NumberFormatException exception)
{
    System.out.println(exception.getMessage());
}
```

Three exceptions may be thrown in this `try` block:

- The `Scanner` constructor can throw a `FileNotFound-Exception`.
- `Scanner.next` can throw a `NoSuchElementException`.
- `Integer.parseInt` can throw a `NumberFormatException`.

If any of these exceptions is actually thrown, then the rest of the instructions in the `try` block are skipped. Here is what happens for the various exception types:

© Andraz Cerar/iStockphoto.

You should only catch those exceptions that you can handle.

- If a `FileNotFoundException` is thrown, then the `catch` clause for the `IOException` is executed. (If you look at Figure 2, you will note that `FileNotFoundException` is a descendant of `IOException`.) If you want to show the user a different message for a `FileNotFoundException`, you must place the `catch` clause *before* the clause for an `IOException`.
- If a `NumberFormatException` occurs, then the second `catch` clause is executed.
- A `NoSuchElementException` is *not caught* by any of the `catch` clauses. The exception remains thrown until it is caught by another `try` statement.

Each `catch` clause contains a handler. When the `catch (IOException exception)` block is executed, then some method in the `try` block has failed with an `IOException` (or one of its descendants).

Syntax 11.2   Catching Exceptions

Syntax
```
try
{
    statement
    statement
    . . .
}
catch (ExceptionClass exceptionObject)
{
    statement
    statement
    . . .
}
```

This constructor can throw a FileNotFoundException.

```
try
{
    Scanner in = new Scanner(new File("input.txt"));
    String input = in.next();
    process(input);
}
catch (IOException exception)
{
    System.out.println("Could not open input file");
}
catch (Exception except)
{
    System.out.println(except.getMessage());
}
```

When an IOException is thrown, execution resumes here.

This is the exception that was thrown.

Additional catch clauses can appear here. Place more specific exceptions before more general ones.

A FileNotFoundException is a special case of an IOException.

In this handler, we produce a printout of the chain of method calls that led to the exception, by calling

```
exception.printStackTrace()
```

In the second exception handler, we call `exception.getMessage()` to retrieve the message associated with the exception. When the `parseInt` method throws a `NumberFormatException`, the message contains the string that it was unable to format. When you throw an exception, you can provide your own message string. For example, when you call

```
throw new IllegalArgumentException("Amount exceeds balance");
```

the message of the exception is the string provided in the constructor.

In these sample `catch` clauses, we merely inform the user of the source of the problem. Often, it is better to give the user another chance to provide a correct input—see Section 11.5 for a solution.

EXAMPLE CODE   See sec04_02 in your eText or companion code for a program that demonstrates catching exceptions.

11.4.3 Checked Exceptions

In Java, the exceptions that you can throw and catch fall into three categories.

- Internal errors are reported by descendants of the type `Error`. One example is the `OutOfMemoryError`, which is thrown when all available computer memory has been used up. These are fatal errors that happen rarely, and we will not consider them in this book.

- Descendants of `RuntimeException`, such as as `IndexOutOfBoundsException` or `IllegalArgumentException` indicate errors in your code. They are called **unchecked exceptions**.

- All other exceptions are **checked exceptions**. These exceptions indicate that something has gone wrong for some external reason beyond your control. In Figure 2, the checked exceptions are shaded in a darker color.

Checked exceptions are due to external circumstances that the programmer cannot prevent. The compiler checks that your program handles these exceptions.

Why have two kinds of exceptions? A checked exception describes a problem that can occur, no matter how careful you are. For example, an `IOException` can be caused by forces beyond your control, such as a disk error or a broken network connection. The compiler takes checked exceptions very seriously and ensures that they are handled. Your program will not compile if you don't indicate how to deal with a checked exception.

The unchecked exceptions, on the other hand, are your fault. The compiler does not check whether you handle an unchecked exception, such as an `IndexOutOfBoundsException`. After all, you should check your index values rather than install a handler for that exception.

If you have a handler for a checked exception in the same method that may throw it, then the compiler is satisfied. For example,

```
try
{
    File inFile = new File(filename);
    Scanner in = new Scanner(inFile); // Throws FileNotFoundException
    . . .
```

```
        }
        catch (FileNotFoundException exception) // Exception caught here
        {
            . . .
        }
```

However, it commonly happens that the current method *cannot handle* the exception. In that case, you need to tell the compiler that you are aware of this exception and that you want your method to be terminated when it occurs. You supply the method with a `throws` clause:

```
public void readData(String filename) throws FileNotFoundException
{
    File inFile = new File(filename);
    Scanner in = new Scanner(inFile);
    . . .
}
```

> Add a throws clause to a method that can throw a checked exception.

The **throws clause** signals to the caller of your method that it may encounter a File-NotFoundException. Then the caller needs to make the same decision—handle the exception, or declare that the exception may be thrown.

It sounds somehow irresponsible not to handle an exception when you know that it happened. Actually, the opposite is true. Java provides an exception handling facility so that an exception can be sent to the *appropriate* handler. Some methods detect errors, some methods handle them, and some methods just pass them along. The throws clause simply ensures that no exceptions get lost along the way.

© tillsonburg/iStockphoto.

Just as trucks with large or hazardous loads carry warning signs, the throws *clause warns the caller that an exception may occur.*

Syntax 11.3 The throws Clause

Syntax   *modifiers returnType methodName(parameterType parameterName, . . .)*
            throws *ExceptionClass, ExceptionClass, . . .*

```
public void readData(String filename)
    throws FileNotFoundException, NumberFormatException
```

You must specify all checked exceptions that this method may throw.

You may also list unchecked exceptions.

EXAMPLE CODE   See sec04_03 in your eText or companion code for a program that demonstrates throwing and catching checked exceptions.

11.4.4 Closing Resources

When you use a resource that must be closed, such as a PrintWriter, you need to be careful in the presence of exceptions. Consider this sequence of statements:

```
PrintWriter out = new PrintWriter(filename);
writeData(out);
out.close(); // May never get here
```

Now suppose that one of the methods before the last line throws an exception. Then the call to close is never executed! This is a problem—data that was written to the stream may never end up in the file.

The remedy is to use the **try-with-resources statement**. Declare the PrintWriter variable in a try statement, like this:

© archives/iStockphoto.

All visitors to a foreign country have to go through passport control, no matter what happened on their trip. Similarly, the try-with-resources *statement ensures that a resource is closed, even when an exception has occurred.*

```
try (PrintWriter out = new PrintWriter(filename))
{
    writeData(out);
} // out.close() is always called
```

> The try-with-resources statement ensures that a resource is closed when the statement ends normally or due to an exception.

When the try block is completed, the close method is called on the variable. If no exception has occurred, this happens when the writeData method returns. However, if an exception occurs, the close method is invoked before the exception is passed to its handler.

You can declare multiple variables in a try-with-resources statement, like this:

```
try (Scanner in = new Scanner(inFile); PrintWriter out = new PrintWriter(outFile))
{
    while (in.hasNextLine())
    {
        String input = in.nextLine();
        String result = process(input);
        out.println(result);
    }
} // Both in.close() and out.close() are called here
```

Syntax 11.4 The try-with-resources Statement

Syntax
```
try (Type1 variable1 = expression1; Type2 variable2 = expression2; . . .)
{
    . . .
}
```

This code may throw exceptions.

```
try (PrintWriter out = new PrintWriter(filename))
{
    writeData(out);
}
```

Implements the AutoCloseable *interface.*

At this point, out.close() *is called, even when an exception occurs.*

Use the try-with-resources statement whenever you work with a Scanner or Print-Writer to make sure that these resources are closed properly.

More generally, you can declare variables of any class that implements the Auto-Closeable interface in a try-with-resources statement. You will find other AutoCloseable classes in Chapters 21 and 24.

EXAMPLE CODE   See sec04_04 in your eText or companion code for a program that demonstrates closing resources.

11.4.5 Designing Your Own Exception Types

Sometimes none of the standard exception types describe your particular error condition well enough. In that case, you can design your own exception class. Consider a bank account. Let's report an InsufficientFundsException when an attempt is made to withdraw an amount from a bank account that exceeds the current balance.

```
if (amount > balance)
{
    throw new InsufficientFundsException(
        "withdrawal of " + amount + " exceeds balance of " + balance);
}
```

Now you need to provide the InsufficientFundsException class. Should it be a checked or an unchecked exception? Is it the fault of some external event, or is it the fault of the programmer? We take the position that the programmer could have prevented the exceptional condition—after all, it would have been an easy matter to check whether amount <= account.getBalance() before calling the withdraw method. Therefore, the exception should be an unchecked exception and extend the RuntimeException class or one of its subclasses.

It is a good idea to extend an appropriate class in the exception hierarchy. For example, we can consider an InsufficientFundsException a special case of an Illegal-ArgumentException. This enables other programmers to catch the exception as an IllegalArgumentException if they are not interested in the exact nature of the problem.

It is customary to provide two constructors for an exception class: a constructor with no arguments and a constructor that accepts a message string describing the reason for the exception.

Here is the declaration of the exception class:

```
public class InsufficientFundsException extends IllegalArgumentException
{
    public InsufficientFundsException() {}

    public InsufficientFundsException(String message)
    {
        super(message);
    }
}
```

When the exception is caught, its message string can be retrieved using the getMessage method of the Throwable class.

> To describe an error condition, provide a subclass of an existing exception class.

EXAMPLE CODE   See sec04_05 of your eText or companion code for a program that uses a custom exception type.

Programming Tip 11.1
Throw Early, Catch Late

When a method detects a problem that it cannot solve, it is better to throw an exception rather than try to come up with an imperfect fix. For example, suppose a method expects to read a number from a file, and the file doesn't contain a number. Simply using a zero value would be a poor choice because it hides the actual problem and perhaps causes a different problem elsewhere.

Conversely, a method should only catch an exception if it can really remedy the situation. Otherwise, the best remedy is simply to have the exception propagate to its caller, allowing it to be caught by a competent handler.

These principles can be summarized with the slogan "throw early, catch late".

> Throw an exception as soon as a problem is detected. Catch it only when the problem can be handled.

Programming Tip 11.2
Do Not Squelch Exceptions

When you call a method that throws a checked exception and you haven't specified a handler, the compiler complains. In your eagerness to continue your work, it is an understandable impulse to shut the compiler up by squelching the exception:

```
try
{
    Scanner in = new Scanner(new File(filename));
    // Compiler complained about FileNotFoundException
    . . .
}
catch (FileNotFoundException e) {} // So there!
```

The do-nothing exception handler fools the compiler into thinking that the exception has been handled. In the long run, this is clearly a bad idea. Exceptions were designed to transmit problem reports to a competent handler. Installing an incompetent handler simply hides an error condition that could be serious.

Programming Tip 11.3
Do Throw Specific Exceptions

When throwing an exception, you should choose an exception class that describes the situation as closely as possible. For example, it would be a bad idea to simply throw a Runtime-Exception object when a bank account has insufficient funds. This would make it far too difficult to catch the exception. After all, if you caught all exceptions of type RuntimeException, your catch clause would also be activated by exceptions of the type NullPointerException, ArrayIndexOutOfBoundsException, and so on. You would then need to carefully examine the exception object and attempt to deduce whether the exception was caused by insufficient funds.

If the standard library does not have an exception class that describes your particular error situation, simply provide a new exception class.

Special Topic 11.6
Assertions

An **assertion** is a condition that you believe to be true at all times in a particular program location. An assertion check tests whether an assertion is true.

Here is a typical assertion check:

```java
public double deposit (double amount)
{
    assert amount >= 0;
    balance = balance + amount;
}
```

In this method, the programmer expects that the quantity amount can never be negative. When the assertion is correct, no harm is done, and the program works in the normal way. If, for some reason, the assertion fails, and assertion checking is enabled, then the assert statement throws an exception of type AssertionError, causing the program to terminate.

However, if assertion checking is disabled, then the assertion is never checked, and the program runs at full speed. By default, assertion checking is disabled when you execute a program.

To execute a program with assertion checking turned on, use this command:

```
java -enableassertions MainClass
```

You can also use the shortcut -ea instead of -enableassertions. You should turn assertion checking on during program development and testing.

Special Topic 11.7

The try/finally Statement

You saw in Section 11.4.4 how to ensure that a resource is closed when an exception occurs. The try-with-resources statement calls the close methods of variables declared within the statement header. You should always use the try-with-resources statement when closing resources.

It can happen that you need to do some cleanup other than calling a close method. In that case, use the try/finally statement:

```java
public double deposit (double amount)
try
{
    . . .
}
finally
{
    Cleanup. // This code is executed whether or not an exception occurs
}
```

If the body of the try statement completes without an exception, the cleanup happens. If an exception is thrown, the cleanup happens and the exception is then propagated to its handler.

The try/finally statement is rarely required because most Java library classes that require cleanup implement the AutoCloseable interface. However, you will see a use of this statement in Chapter 22.

11.5 Application: Handling Input Errors

This section walks through a complete example of a program with exception handling. The program asks a user for the name of a file. The file is expected to contain data values. The first line of the file contains the total number of values, and the remaining lines contain the data. A typical input file looks like this:

```
3
1.45
-2.1
0.05
```

What can go wrong? There are two principal risks.

- The file might not exist.
- The file might have data in the wrong format.

When designing a program, ask yourself what kinds of exceptions can occur.

Who can detect these faults? The Scanner constructor will throw an exception when the file does not exist. The methods that process the input values need to throw an exception when they find an error in the data format.

What exceptions can be thrown? The Scanner constructor throws a FileNot-FoundException when the file does not exist, which is appropriate in our situation. When the file data is in the wrong format, we will throw a BadDataException, a custom checked exception class. We use a checked exception because corruption of a data file is beyond the control of the programmer.

For each exception, you need to decide which part of your program can competently handle it.

Who can remedy the faults that the exceptions report? Only the main method of the DataAnalyzer program interacts with the user. It catches the exceptions, prints appropriate error messages, and gives the user another chance to enter a correct file.

sec05/DataAnalyzer.java

```
1   import java.io.FileNotFoundException;
2   import java.io.IOException;
3   import java.util.Scanner;
4
5   /**
6      This program reads a file containing numbers and analyzes its contents.
7      If the file doesn't exist or contains strings that are not numbers, an
8      error message is displayed.
9   */
10  public class DataAnalyzer
11  {
12     public static void main(String[] args)
13     {
14        Scanner in = new Scanner(System.in);
15        DataSetReader reader = new DataSetReader();
16
17        boolean done = false;
18        while (!done)
19        {
20           try
21           {
22              System.out.println("Please enter the file name: ");
23              String filename = in.next();
24
25              double[] data = reader.readFile(filename);
26              double sum = 0;
27              for (double d : data) { sum = sum + d; }
28              System.out.println("The sum is " + sum);
29              done = true;
30           }
31           catch (FileNotFoundException exception)
32           {
33              System.out.println("File not found.");
34           }
35           catch (BadDataException exception)
36           {
37              System.out.println("Bad data: " + exception.getMessage());
38           }
```

```
39              catch (IOException exception)
40              {
41                  exception.printStackTrace();
42              }
43          }
44      }
45  }
```

The catch clauses in the main method give a human-readable error report if the file was not found or bad data was encountered.

The following readFile method of the DataSetReader class constructs the Scanner object and calls the readData method. It is unconcerned with any exceptions. If there is a problem with the input file, it simply passes the exception to its caller.

```java
public double[] readFile(String filename) throws IOException
{
    File inFile = new File(filename);
    try (Scanner in = new Scanner(inFile))
    {
        readData(in);
        return data;
    }
}
```

The method throws an IOException, the common superclass of FileNotFoundException (thrown by the Scanner constructor) and BadDataException (thrown by the readData method).

Next, here is the readData method of the DataSetReader class. It reads the number of values, constructs an array, and calls readValue for each data value.

```java
private void readData(Scanner in) throws BadDataException
{
    if (!in.hasNextInt())
    {
        throw new BadDataException("Length expected");
    }
    int numberOfValues = in.nextInt();
    data = new double[numberOfValues];

    for (int i = 0; i < numberOfValues; i++)
    {
        readValue(in, i);
    }

    if (in.hasNext())
    {
        throw new BadDataException("End of file expected");
    }
}
```

This method checks for two potential errors. The file might not start with an integer, or it might have additional data after reading all values.

However, this method makes no attempt to catch any exceptions. Plus, if the readValue method throws an exception—which it will if there aren't enough values in the file—the exception is simply passed on to the caller.

Here is the readValue method:

```java
private void readValue(Scanner in, int i) throws BadDataException
{
```

```
      if (!in.hasNextDouble())
      {
         throw new BadDataException("Data value expected");
      }
      data[i] = in.nextDouble();
   }
```

To see the exception handling at work, look at a specific error scenario:

1. `DataAnalyzer.main` calls `DataSetReader.readFile`.
2. `readFile` calls `readData`.
3. `readData` calls `readValue`.
4. `readValue` doesn't find the expected value and throws a `BadDataException`.
5. `readValue` has no handler for the exception and terminates immediately.
6. `readData` has no handler for the exception and terminates immediately.
7. `readFile` has no handler for the exception and terminates immediately after closing the `Scanner` object.
8. `DataAnalyzer.main` has a handler for a `BadDataException`. That handler prints a message to the user. Afterward, the user is given another chance to enter a file name. Note that the statements computing the sum of the values have been skipped.

This example shows the separation between error detection (in the `DataSetReader.readValue` method) and error handling (in the `DataAnalyzer.main` method). In between the two are the `readData` and `readFile` methods, which just pass exceptions along.

sec05/DataSetReader.java

```
1  import java.io.File;
2  import java.io.IOException;
3  import java.util.Scanner;
4
5  /**
6     Reads a data set from a file. The file must have the format
7     numberOfValues
8     value1
9     value2
10    . . .
11 */
12 public class DataSetReader
13 {
14    private double[] data;
15
16    /**
17       Reads a data set.
18       @param filename the name of the file holding the data
19       @return the data in the file
20    */
21    public double[] readFile(String filename) throws IOException
22    {
23       File inFile = new File(filename);
24       try (Scanner in = new Scanner(inFile))
25       {
26          readData(in);
27          return data;
28       }
```

```
29      }
30
31      /**
32         Reads all data.
33         @param in the scanner that scans the data
34      */
35      private void readData(Scanner in) throws BadDataException
36      {
37         if (!in.hasNextInt())
38         {
39            throw new BadDataException("Length expected");
40         }
41         int numberOfValues = in.nextInt();
42         data = new double[numberOfValues];
43
44         for (int i = 0; i < numberOfValues; i++)
45         {
46            readValue(in, i);
47         }
48
49         if (in.hasNext())
50         {
51            throw new BadDataException("End of file expected");
52         }
53      }
54
55      /**
56         Reads one data value.
57         @param in the scanner that scans the data
58         @param i the position of the value to read
59      */
60      private void readValue(Scanner in, int i) throws BadDataException
61      {
62         if (!in.hasNextDouble())
63         {
64            throw new BadDataException("Data value expected");
65         }
66         data[i] = in.nextDouble();
67      }
68   }
```

sec05/BadDataException.java

```
 1   import java.io.IOException;
 2
 3   /**
 4      This class reports bad input data.
 5   */
 6   public class BadDataException extends IOException
 7   {
 8      public BadDataException() {}
 9      public BadDataException(String message)
10      {
11         super(message);
12      }
13   }
```

Computing & Society 11.2   The Ariane Rocket Incident

The European Space Agency (ESA), Europe's counterpart to NASA, had developed a rocket model named Ariane that it had successfully used several times to launch satellites and scientific experiments into space. However, when a new version, the Ariane 5, was launched on June 4, 1996, from ESA's launch site in Kourou, French Guiana, the rocket veered off course about 40 seconds after liftoff. Flying at an angle of more than 20 degrees, rather than straight up, exerted such an aerodynamic force that the boosters separated, which triggered the automatic self-destruction mechanism. The rocket blew itself up.

The ultimate cause of this accident was an unhandled exception! The rocket contained two identical devices (called inertial reference systems) that processed flight data from measuring devices and turned the data into information about the rocket position. The onboard computer used the position information for controlling the boosters. The same inertial reference systems and computer software had worked fine on the Ariane 4.

However, due to design changes to the rocket, one of the sensors measured a larger

acceleration force than had been encountered in the Ariane 4. That value, expressed as a floating-point value, was stored in a 16-bit integer (like a short variable in Java). Unlike Java, the Ada language, used for the device software, generates an exception if a floating-point number is too large to be converted to an integer. Unfortunately, the programmers of the device had decided that this situation would never happen and didn't provide an exception handler.

When the overflow did happen, the exception was triggered and, because there was no handler, the device shut itself off. The onboard computer sensed the failure and switched over to the backup device. However, that device had shut itself off for exactly the same reason, something that the designers of the rocket had not expected. They figured that the devices might fail for mechanical

reasons, but the chance of them having the same mechanical failure was remote. At that point, the rocket was without reliable position information and went off course.

Perhaps it would have been better if the software hadn't been so thorough? If it had ignored the overflow, the device wouldn't have been shut off. It would have computed bad data. But then the device would have reported wrong position data, which could have been just as fatal. Instead, a correct implementation should have caught overflow exceptions and come up with some strategy to recompute the flight data. Clearly, giving up was not a reasonable option in this context.

The advantage of the exception-handling mechanism is that it makes these issues explicit to programmers—something to think about when you curse the Java compiler for complaining about uncaught exceptions.

© AP/Wide World Photos.

The Explosion of the Ariane Rocket

CHAPTER SUMMARY

Develop programs that read and write files.

- Use the Scanner class for reading text files.
- When writing text files, use the PrintWriter class and the print/println/printf methods.
- Close all files when you are done processing them.

Be able to process text in files.

- The next method reads a string that is delimited by white space.
- The Character class has methods for classifying characters.

- The nextLine method reads an entire line.
- If a string contains the digits of a number, you use the Integer.parseInt or Double.parseDouble method to obtain the number value.

Process the command line arguments of a program.

- Programs that start from the command line receive the command line arguments in the main method.

Use exception handling to transfer control from an error location to an error handler.

- To signal an exceptional condition, use the throw statement to throw an exception object.
- When you throw an exception, processing continues in an exception handler.
- Place the statements that can cause an exception inside a try block, and the handler inside a catch clause.
- Checked exceptions are due to external circumstances that the programmer cannot prevent. The compiler checks that your program handles these exceptions.
- Add a throws clause to a method that can throw a checked exception.
- The try-with-resources statement ensures that a resource is closed when the statement ends normally or due to an exception.
- To describe an error condition, provide a subclass of an existing exception class.
- Throw an exception as soon as a problem is detected. Catch it only when the problem can be handled.

Use exception handling in a program that processes input.

- When designing a program, ask yourself what kinds of exceptions can occur.
- For each exception, you need to decide which part of your program can competently handle it.

STANDARD LIBRARY ITEMS INTRODUCED IN THIS CHAPTER

java.io.File
java.io.FileNotFoundException
java.io.IOException
java.io.PrintWriter
   close
java.lang.AutoCloseable
java.lang.Character
   isDigit
   isLetter
   isLowerCase
   isUpperCase
   isWhiteSpace
java.lang.Double
   parseDouble

java.lang.Error
java.lang.Integer
   parseInt
java.lang.IllegalArgumentException
java.lang.NullPointerException
java.lang.NumberFormatException
java.lang.RuntimeException
java.lang.String
   replaceAll
   split
java.lang.Throwable
   getMessage
   printStackTrace

java.net.URL
   openStream
java.util.InputMismatchException
java.util.NoSuchElementException
java.util.Scanner
   close
   hasNextLine
   nextLine
   useDelimiter
javax.swing.JFileChooser
   getSelectedFile
   showOpenDialog
   showSaveDialog

REVIEW EXERCISES

- **R11.1** What happens when you supply the same name for the input and output files to the Total program of Section 11.1? Try it out if you are not sure.

- **R11.2** Suppose you wanted to add the total to an existing file instead of writing a new file. Exercise • R11.1 indicates that you cannot simply do this by specifying the same file for input and output. How can you achieve this task? Provide the pseudocode for the solution.

- **R11.3** What happens if you try to open a file for reading that doesn't exist? What happens if you try to open a file for writing that doesn't exist?

- **R11.4** What happens if you try to open a file for writing, but the file or device is write-protected (sometimes called read-only)? Try it out with a short test program.

- **R11.5** What happens when you write to a PrintWriter without closing it? Produce a test program that demonstrates how you can lose data.

- **R11.6** How do you open a file whose name contains a backslash, like c:temp\output.dat?

- **R11.7** Your input file contains a sequence of numbers, but sometimes a value is not available and is marked as N/A. How can you read the numbers and skip over the markers?

- **R11.8** If a program Woozle is started with the command

  ```
  java Woozle -Dname=piglet -I\eeyore -v heff.txt a.txt lump.txt
  ```

  what are the values of args[0], args[1], and so on?

- **R11.9** What is the difference between throwing an exception and catching an exception?

- **R11.10** What is a checked exception? What is an unchecked exception? Give an example for each. Which exceptions do you need to declare with the throws reserved word?

- **R11.11** Why don't you need to declare that your method might throw an IndexOutOfBounds-Exception?

- **R11.12** When your program executes a throw statement, which statement is executed next?

- **R11.13** What happens if an exception does not have a matching catch clause?

- **R11.14** What can your program do with the exception object that a catch clause receives?

- **R11.15** Is the type of the exception object always the same as the type declared in the catch clause that catches it? If not, why not?

- **R11.16** What is the purpose of the try-with-resources statement? Give an example of how it can be used.

- **R11.17** What happens when an exception is thrown, a try-with-resources statement calls close, and that call throws an exception of a different kind than the original one? Which one is caught by a surrounding catch clause? Write a sample program to try it out.

- **R11.18** Which exceptions can the next and nextInt methods of the Scanner class throw? Are they checked exceptions or unchecked exceptions?

■■ **R11.19** Suppose the program in Section 11.5 reads a file containing the following values:

```
1
2
3
4
```

What is the outcome? How could the program be improved to give a more accurate error report?

■■ **R11.20** Can the readFile method in Section 11.5 throw a NullPointerException? If so, how?

■■■ **R11.21** The following code tries to close the writer without using a try-with-resources statement:

```
PrintWriter out = new PrintWriter(filename);
try
{
    Write output.
    out.close();
}
catch (IOException exception)
{
    out.close();
}
```

What is the disadvantage of this approach? (*Hint:* What happens when the PrintWriter constructor or the close method throws an exception?)

PRACTICE EXERCISES

■ **E11.1** Write a program that carries out the following tasks:

Open a file with the name hello.txt.
Store the message "Hello, World!" in the file.
Close the file.
Open the same file again.
Read the message into a string variable and print it.

■ **E11.2** Write a program that reads a file, removes any blank lines, and writes the non-blank lines back to the same file.

■■ **E11.3** Write a program that reads a file, removes any blank lines at the beginning or end of the file, and writes the remaining lines back to the same file.

■ **E11.4** Write a program that reads a file containing text. Read each line and send it to the output file, preceded by *line numbers*. If the input file is

```
Mary had a little lamb
Whose fleece was white as snow.
And everywhere that Mary went,
The lamb was sure to go!
```

then the program produces the output file

```
/* 1 */ Mary had a little lamb
/* 2 */ Whose fleece was white as snow.
/* 3 */ And everywhere that Mary went,
/* 4 */ The lamb was sure to go!
```

© Chris Price/iStockphoto.

The line numbers are enclosed in /* */ delimiters so that the program can be used for numbering Java source files.

Prompt the user for the input and output file names.

■ **E11.5** Repeat Exercise • E11.4, but allow the user to specify the file name on the command-line. If the user doesn't specify any file name, then prompt the user for the name.

■ **E11.6** Write a program that reads a file containing two columns of floating-point numbers. Prompt the user for the file name. Print the average of each column.

■■ **E11.7** Write a program that reads a file containing rows of numbers. Each row may have a different length, and some may be blank. Print the average of each row, or zero if a row is blank.

■■ **E11.8** Write a program that asks the user for a file name and prints the number of characters, words, and lines in that file.

■■ **E11.9** Write a program Find that searches all files specified on the command line and prints out all lines containing a specified word. For example, if you call

```
java Find ring report.txt address.txt Homework.java
```

then the program might print

```
report.txt: has broken up an international ring of DVD bootleggers that
address.txt: Kris Kringle, North Pole
address.txt: Homer Simpson, Springfield
Homework.java: String filename;
```

The specified word is always the first command line argument.

■■ **E11.10** Write a program that checks the spelling of all words in a file. It should read each word of a file and check whether it is contained in a word list. A word list is available on Macintosh and Linux systems in the file /usr/share/dict/words. (If you don't have that file on your computer, use the file words.txt in the companion code for this book.) The program should print out all words that it cannot find in the word list.

■■ **E11.11** Write a program that replaces each line of a file with its reverse. For example, if you run

```
java Reverse HelloPrinter.java
```

then the contents of HelloPrinter.java are changed to

```
retnirPolleH ssalc cilbup
{
)sgra ][gnirtS(niam diov citats cilbup
{
wodniw elosnoc eht ni gniteerg a yalpsiD //

;)"!dlroW ,olleH"(nltnirp.tuo.metsyS
}
}
```

Of course, if you run Reverse twice on the same file, you get back the original file.

■■ **E11.12** Write a program that reads each line in a file, reverses its lines, and writes them to another file. For example, if the file input.txt contains the lines

```
Mary had a little lamb
Its fleece was white as snow
And everywhere that Mary went
The lamb was sure to go.
```

and you run

```
reverse input.txt output.txt
```

then output.txt contains

```
The lamb was sure to go.
And everywhere that Mary went
Its fleece was white as snow
Mary had a little lamb
```

•• E11.13 Get the data for names in prior decades from the Social Security Administration. Paste the table data in files named babynames80s.txt, etc. Modify the worked_example_1/ BabyNames.java program so that it prompts the user for a file name. The numbers in the files have comma separators, so modify the program to handle them. Can you spot a trend in the frequencies?

•• E11.14 Write a program that asks the user to input a set of floating-point values. When the user enters a value that is not a number, give the user a second chance to enter the value. After two chances, quit reading input. Add all correctly specified values and print the sum when the user is done entering data. Use exception handling to detect improper inputs.

• E11.15 Modify the BankAccount class to throw an IllegalArgumentException when the account is constructed with a negative balance, when a negative amount is deposited, or when an amount that is not between 0 and the current balance is withdrawn. Write a test program that causes all three exceptions to occur and that catches them all.

•• E11.16 Repeat Exercise • E11.15, but throw exceptions of three exception types that you provide.

•• E11.17 Modify the DataSetReader class so that you do not call hasNextInt or hasNextDouble. Simply have nextInt and nextDouble throw a NoSuchElementException and catch it in the main method.

PROGRAMMING PROJECTS

•• P11.1 Write a program that reads in worked_example_1/babynames.txt and produces two files, boynames.txt and girlnames.txt, separating the data for the boys and girls.

••• P11.2 Write a program that reads a file in the same format as worked_example_1/babynames.txt and prints all names that are both boy and girl names (such as Alexis or Morgan).

•• P11.3 Using the mechanism described in Special Topic 11.1, write a program that reads all data from a web page and writes them to a file. Prompt the user for the web page URL and the file.

••• P11.4 The CSV (or *comma-separated values*) format is commonly used for tabular data. Each table row is a line, with columns separated by commas. Items may be enclosed in quotation marks, and they must be if they contain commas or quotation marks. Quotation marks inside quoted fields are doubled. Here is a line with four fields:

```
1729, San Francisco, "Hello, World", "He asked: ""Quo vadis?"""
```

Implement a class `CSVReader` that reads a CSV file, and provide methods

```
int numberOfRows()
int numberOfFields(int row)
String field(int row, int column)
```

■■ **P11.5** Find an interesting data set in CSV format (or in spreadsheet format, then use a spreadsheet to save the data as CSV). Using the `CSVReader` class from Exercise ●●● P11.4, read the data and compute a summary, such as the maximum, minimum, or average of one of the columns.

■■ **P11.6** Download the file `airports.dat` from `https://openflights.org/data.html`. Write a program that prompts the user for the name of a city and then reads the airport data file, printing the names of all airports in the provided city.

■■ **P11.7** Using the mechanism described in Special Topic 11.1, write a program that reads all data from a web page and prints all hyperlinks of the form

```
<a href="link">link text</a>
```

Extra credit if your program can follow the links that it finds and find links in those web pages as well. (This is the method that search engines such as Google use to find web sites.)

■■ **P11.8** Write a program that reads in a set of coin descriptions from a file. The input file has the format

```
coinName1 coinValue1
coinName2 coinValue2
. . .
```

Add a method

```
void read(Scanner in) throws FileNotFoundException
```

to the `Coin` class of Section 8.2. Throw an exception if the current line is not properly formatted. Then implement a method

```
static ArrayList<Coin> readFile(String filename) throws FileNotFoundException
```

In the `main` method, call `readFile`. If an exception is thrown, give the user a chance to select another file. If you read all coins successfully, print the total value.

■■■ **P11.9** Design a class `Bank` that contains a number of bank accounts. Each account has an account number and a current balance. Add an `accountNumber` field to the `BankAccount` class. Store the bank accounts in an array list. Write a `readFile` method of the `Bank` class for reading a file with the format

```
accountNumber1   balance1
accountNumber2   balance2
. . .
```

Implement `read` methods for the `Bank` and `BankAccount` classes. Write a sample program to read in a file with bank accounts, then print the account with the highest balance. If the file is not properly formatted, give the user a chance to select another file.

■■ **Business P11.10** A hotel salesperson enters sales in a text file. Each line contains the following, separated by semicolons: The name of the client, the service sold (such as Dinner, Conference, Lodging, and so on), the amount of the sale, and the date of that event. Write a program that reads such a file and displays the total amount for each service category. Display an error if the file does not exist or the format is incorrect.

•• Business P11.11 Write a program that reads a text file as described in Exercise •• Business P11.10, and that writes a separate file for each service category, containing the entries for that category. Name the output files Dinner.txt, Conference.txt, and so on.

•• Business P11.12 A store owner keeps a record of daily cash transactions in a text file. Each line contains three items: The invoice number, the cash amount, and the letter P if the amount was paid or R if it was received. Items are separated by spaces. Write a program that prompts the store owner for the amount of cash at the beginning and end of the day, and the name of the file. Your program should check whether the actual amount of cash at the end of the day equals the expected value.

••• Science P11.13 After the switch in the figure below closes, the voltage (in volts) across the capacitor is represented by the equation

$$v(t) = B\left(1 - e^{-t/(RC)}\right)$$

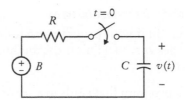

Suppose the parameters of the electric circuit are $B = 12$ volts, $R = 500 \, \Omega$, and $C = 0.25 \, \mu F$. Consequently

$$v(t) = 12\left(1 - e^{-0.008t}\right)$$

where t has units of μs. Read a file params.txt containing the values for B, R, C, and the starting and ending values for t. Write a file rc.txt of values for the time t and the corresponding capacitor voltage $v(t)$, where t goes from the given starting value to the given ending value in 100 steps. In our example, if t goes from 0 to 1,000 μs, the twelfth entry in the output file would be:

    110   7.02261

••• Science P11.14 The figure below shows a plot of the capacitor voltage from the circuit shown in Exercise ••• Science P11.13. The capacitor voltage increases from 0 volts to B volts. The "rise time" is defined as the time required for the capacitor voltage to change from $v_1 = 0.05 \times B$ to $v_2 = 0.95 \times B$.

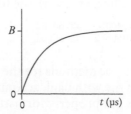

The file rc.txt contains a list of values of time t and the corresponding capacitor voltage $v(t)$. A time in μs and the corresponding voltage in volts are printed on the same line. For example, the line

    110   7.02261

indicates that the capacitor voltage is 7.02261 volts when the time is 110 μs. The time is increasing in the data file.

Write a program that reads the file rc.txt and uses the data to calculate the rise time. Approximate B by the voltage in the last line of the file, and find the data points that are closest to $0.05 \times B$ and $0.95 \times B$.

■■ **Science P11.15** Suppose a file contains bond energies and bond lengths for covalent bonds in the following format:

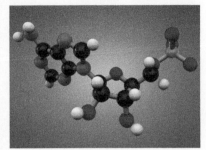

© Chris Dascher/iStockphoto.

Single, double, or triple bond	Bond energy (kJ/mol)	Bond length (nm)
C|C	370	0.154
C||C	680	0.13
C|||C	890	0.12
C|H	435	0.11
C|N	305	0.15
C|O	360	0.14
C|F	450	0.14
C|Cl	340	0.18
O|H	500	0.10
O|O	220	0.15
O|Si	375	0.16
N|H	430	0.10
N|O	250	0.12
F|F	160	0.14
H|H	435	0.074

Write a program that accepts data from one column and returns the corresponding data from the other columns in the stored file. If input data matches different rows, then return all matching row data. For example, a bond length input of 0.12 should return triple bond C\|\|\|C and bond energy 890 kJ/mol *and* single bond N\|O and bond energy 250 kJ/mol.

OBJECT-ORIENTED DESIGN

© Petrea Alexandru/iStockphoto.

CHAPTER GOALS

To learn how to discover new classes and methods

To use CRC cards for class discovery

To identify inheritance, aggregation, and dependency relationships between classes

To describe class relationships using UML class diagrams

To apply object-oriented design techniques to building complex programs

CHAPTER CONTENTS

Successfully implementing a software system—as simple as your next homework project or as complex as the next air traffic monitoring system—requires a great deal of planning and design. In fact, for larger projects, the amount of time spent on planning and design is much greater than the amount of time spent on programming and testing.

Do you find that most of your homework time is spent in front of the computer, keying in code and fixing bugs? If so, you can probably save time by focusing on a better design before you start coding. This chapter tells you how to approach the design of an object-oriented program in a systematic manner.

12.1 Classes and Their Responsibilities

When you design a program, you work from a *requirements specification*, a description of what your program should do. The designer's task is to discover structures that make it possible to implement the requirements in a computer program. In the following sections, we will examine the steps of the design process.

12.1.1 Discovering Classes

> To discover classes, look for nouns in the problem description.

When you solve a problem using objects and classes, you need to determine the classes required for the implementation. You may be able to reuse existing classes, or you may need to implement new ones.

One simple approach for discovering classes and methods is to look for the nouns and verbs in the requirements specification. Often, *nouns* correspond to classes, and *verbs* correspond to methods.

For example, suppose your job is to print an invoice such as the one in Figure 1.

INVOICE

Sam's Small Appliances
100 Main Street
Anytown, CA 98765

Item	Qty	Price	Total
Toaster	3	$29.95	$89.85
Hair Dryer	1	$24.95	$24.95
Car Vacuum	2	$19.99	$39.98

AMOUNT DUE: $154.78

Figure 1
An Invoice

Obvious classes that come to mind are `Invoice`, `LineItem`, and `Customer`. It is a good idea to keep a list of *candidate classes* on a whiteboard or a sheet of paper. As you brainstorm, simply put all ideas for classes onto the list. You can always cross out the ones that weren't useful after all.

In general, concepts from the problem domain, be it science, business, or a game, often make good classes. Examples are

> Concepts from the problem domain are good candidates for classes.

- `Cannonball`
- `CashRegister`
- `Monster`

The name for such a class should be a noun that describes the concept.

Not all classes can be discovered from the program requirements. Most complex programs need classes for tactical purposes, such as file or database access, user interfaces, control mechanisms, and so on.

Some of the classes that you need may already exist, either in the standard library or in a program that you developed previously. You also may be able to use inheritance to extend existing classes into classes that match your needs.

A common error is to overdo the class discovery process. For example, should an address be an object of an `Address` class, or should it simply be a string? There is no perfect answer—it depends on the task that you want to solve. If your software needs to analyze addresses (for example, to determine shipping costs), then an `Address` class is an appropriate design. However, if your software will never need such a capability, you should not waste time on an overly complex design. It is your job to find a balanced design; one that is neither too limiting nor excessively general.

12.1.2 The CRC Card Method

Once you have identified a set of classes, you define the behavior for each class. Find out what methods you need to provide for each class in order to solve the programming problem. A simple rule for finding these methods is to look for *verbs* in the task description, then match the verbs to the appropriate objects. For example, in the invoice program, a class needs to compute the amount due. Now you need to figure out *which class* is responsible for this method. Do customers compute what they owe? Do invoices total up the amount due? Do the items total themselves up? The best choice is to make "compute amount due" the responsibility of the `Invoice` class.

In a class scheduling system, potential classes from the problem domain include Class, LectureHall, Instructor, and Student. © Oleg Prikhodko/iStockphoto.

A CRC card describes a class, its responsibilities, and its collaborating classes.

An excellent way to carry out this task is the "**CRC card** method." *CRC* stands for "*classes*", "*responsibilities*", "*collaborators*", and in its simplest form, the method works as follows: Use an index card for each *class* (see Figure 2). As you think about verbs in the task description that indicate methods, you pick the card of the class that you think should be responsible, and write that *responsibility* on the card.

For each responsibility, you record which other classes are needed to fulfill it. Those classes are the **collaborators**.

For example, suppose you decide that an invoice should compute the amount due. Then you write "compute amount due" on the left-hand side of an index card with the title Invoice.

If a class can carry out that responsibility by itself, do nothing further. But if the class needs the help of other classes, write the names of these collaborators on the right-hand side of the card.

To compute the total, the invoice needs to ask each line item about its total price. Therefore, the LineItem class is a collaborator.

This is a good time to look up the index card for the LineItem class. Does it have a "get total price" method? If not, add one.

How do you know that you are on the right track? For each responsibility, ask yourself how it can actually be done, using the responsibilities written on the various cards. Many people find it helpful to group the cards on a table so that the collaborators are close to each other, and to simulate tasks by moving a token (such as a coin) from one card to the next to indicate which object is currently active.

Keep in mind that the responsibilities that you list on the CRC card are on a *high level*. Sometimes a single responsibility may need two or more Java methods for carrying it out. Some researchers say that a CRC card should have no more than three distinct responsibilities.

The CRC card method is informal on purpose, so that you can be creative and discover classes and their properties. Once you find that you have settled on a good set of classes, you will want to know how they are related to each other. Can you find classes with common properties, so that some responsibilities can be taken care of by a common superclass? Can you organize classes into clusters that are independent of each other? Finding class relationships and documenting them with diagrams is the topic of Section 12.2.

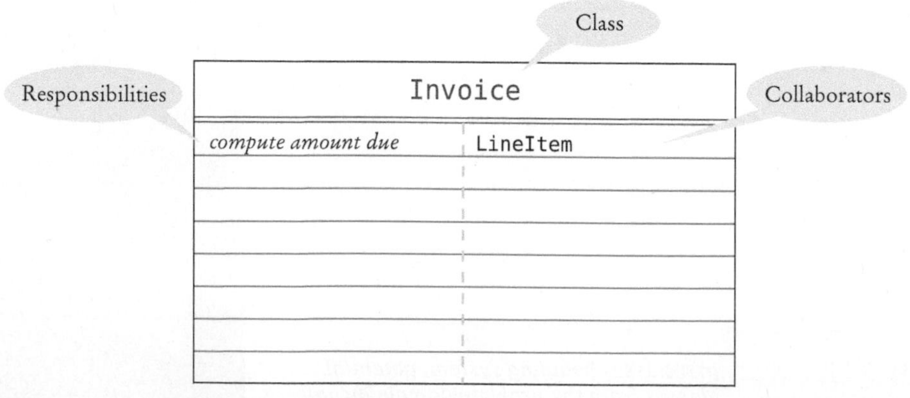

Figure 2   A CRC Card

12.2 Relationships Between Classes

When designing a program, it is useful to document the relationships between classes. This helps you in a number of ways. For example, if you find classes with common behavior, you can save effort by placing the common behavior into a superclass. If you know that some classes are *not* related to each other, you can assign different programmers to implement each of them, without worrying that one of them has to wait for the other.

In the following sections, we will describe the most common types of relationships.

12.2.1 Dependency

A class depends on another class if it uses objects of that class.

Many classes need other classes in order to do their jobs. For example, in Section 8.2.2, we described a design of a CashRegister class that depends on the Coin class to determine the value of the payment.

The dependency relationship is sometimes nicknamed the "knows about" relationship. The cash register knows that there are coin objects. In contrast, the Coin class does *not* depend on the CashRegister class. Coins have no idea that they are being collected in cash registers, and they can carry out their work without ever calling any method in the CashRegister class.

As you saw in Section 8.2, dependency is denoted by a dashed line with a ➤-shaped open arrow tip. The arrow tip points to the class on which the other class depends. Figure 3 shows a class diagram indicating that the CashRegister class depends on the Coin class.

© visual7/iStockphoto.

Too many dependencies make a system difficult to manage.

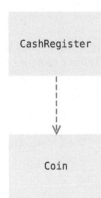

Figure 3
Dependency Relationship Between the CashRegister and Coin Classes

If many classes of a program depend on each other, then we say that the **coupling** between classes is high. Conversely, if there are few dependencies between classes, then we say that the coupling is low (see Figure 4).

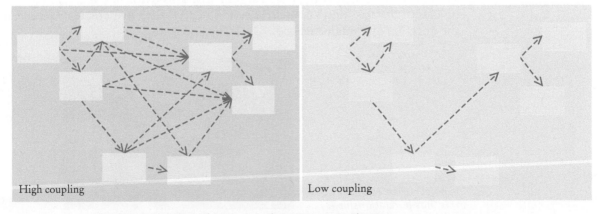

High coupling   Low coupling

Figure 4 High and Low Coupling Between Classes

Why does coupling matter? If the Coin class changes in the next release of the program, all the classes that depend on it may be affected. If the change is drastic, the coupled classes must all be updated. Furthermore, if we would like to use a class in another program, we have to take with it all the classes on which it depends. Thus, we want to remove unnecessary coupling between classes.

> It is a good practice to minimize the coupling (i.e., dependency) between classes.

12.2.2 Aggregation

Another fundamental relationship between classes is the "aggregation" relationship (which is informally known as the "has-a" relationship).

> A class aggregates another if its objects contain objects of the other class.

The **aggregation** relationship states that objects of one class contain objects of another class. Consider a quiz that is made up of questions. Because each quiz has one or more questions, we say that the class Quiz *aggregates* the class Question. In the UML notation, aggregation is denoted by a line with a diamond-shaped symbol attached to the aggregating class (see Figure 5).

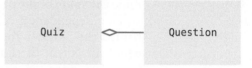

Figure 5
Class Diagram Showing Aggregation

Finding out about aggregation is very helpful for deciding how to implement classes. For example, when you implement the Quiz class, you will want to store the questions of a quiz as an instance variable.

Because a quiz can have any number of questions, an array or array list is a good choice for collecting them:

```
public class Quiz
{
    private ArrayList<Question> questions;
    . . .
}
```

Aggregation is a stronger form of dependency. If a class has objects of another class, it certainly knows about the other class. However, the converse is not true. For example, a class may use the Scanner class without ever declaring an instance variable of class Scanner. The class may simply construct a local variable of type Scanner, or its methods may receive Scanner objects as arguments. This use is not aggregation because the objects of the class don't contain Scanner objects—they just create or receive them for the duration of a single method.

A car has a motor and tires. In object-oriented design, this "has-a" relationship is called aggregation.

© bojan fatur/iStockphoto.

Generally, you need aggregation when an object needs to remember another object *between method calls.*

EXAMPLE CODE   See sec02 of your eText or companion code for a demonstration of the Quiz and Question classes.

12.2.3 Inheritance

Inheritance is a relationship between a more general class (the superclass) and a more specialized class (the subclass). This relationship is often described as the "is-a" relationship. Every truck *is a* vehicle. Every savings account *is a* bank account.

Inheritance is sometimes abused. For example, consider a Tire class that describes a car tire. Should the class Tire be a subclass of a class Circle? It sounds convenient. There are quite a few useful methods in the Circle class—for example, the Tire class may inherit methods that compute the radius, perimeter, and center point, which should come in handy when drawing tire shapes. Though it may be convenient for the programmer, this arrangement makes no sense conceptually. It isn't true that every tire is a circle. Tires are car parts, whereas circles are geometric objects. There is a relationship between tires and circles, though. A tire *has a* circle as its boundary. Use aggregation:

> Inheritance (the *is-a* relationship) is sometimes inappropriately used when the *has-a* relationship would be more appropriate.

```
public class Tire
{
    private String rating;
    private Circle boundary;
    . . .
}
```

Here is another example: Every car *is a* vehicle. Every car *has a* tire (in fact, it typically has four or, if you count the spare, five). Thus, you would use inheritance from Vehicle and use aggregation of Tire objects (see Figure 6 for the UML diagram):

> Aggregation (the *has-a* relationship) denotes that objects of one class contain references to objects of another class.

```
public class Car extends Vehicle
{
    private Tire[] tires;
    . . .
}
```

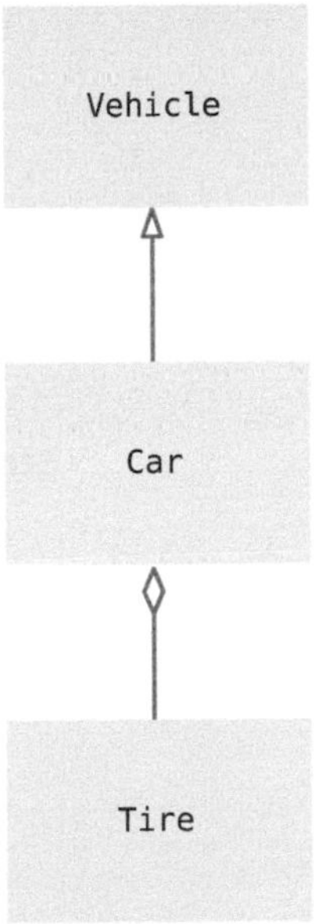

Figure 6
UML Notation for Inheritance and Aggregation

The arrows in the UML notation can get confusing. Table 1 shows a summary of the four UML relationship symbols that we use in this book.

> You need to be able to distinguish the UML notation for inheritance, interface implementation, aggregation, and dependency.

Table 1	UML Relationship Symbols		
Relationship	Symbol	Line Style	Arrow Tip
Inheritance	──────▷	Solid	Triangle
Interface Implementation	------▷	Dotted	Triangle
Aggregation	◇──────	Solid	Diamond
Dependency	------▷	Dotted	Open

HOW TO 12.1

Using CRC Cards and UML Diagrams in Program Design

Before writing code for a complex problem, you need to design a solution. The methodology introduced in this chapter suggests that you follow a design process that is composed of the following tasks:

- Discover classes.
- Determine the responsibilities of each class.
- Describe the relationships between the classes.

CRC cards and UML diagrams help you discover and record this information.

Step 1   Discover classes.

Highlight the nouns in the problem description. Make a list of the nouns. Cross out those that don't seem to be reasonable candidates for classes.

Step 2   Discover responsibilities.

Make a list of the major tasks that your system needs to fulfill. From those tasks, pick one that is not trivial and that is intuitive to you. Find a class that is responsible for carrying out that task. Make an index card and write the name and the task on it. Now ask yourself how an object of the class can carry out the task. It probably needs help from other objects. Then make CRC cards for the classes to which those objects belong and write the responsibilities on them.

Don't be afraid to cross out, move, split, or merge responsibilities. Rip up cards if they become too messy. This is an informal process.

You are done when you have walked through all major tasks and are satisfied that they can all be solved with the classes and responsibilities that you discovered.

Step 3   Describe relationships.

Make a class diagram that shows the relationships between all the classes that you discovered.

Start with inheritance—the *is-a* relationship between classes. Is any class a specialization of another? If so, draw inheritance arrows. Keep in mind that many designs, especially for simple programs, don't use inheritance extensively.

The "collaborators" column of the CRC card tells you which classes are used by that class. Draw dependency arrows for the collaborators on the CRC cards.

Some dependency relationships give rise to aggregations. For each of the dependency relationships, ask yourself: How does the object locate its collaborator? Does it navigate to it directly because it stores a reference? In that case, draw an aggregation arrow. Or is the collaborator a method parameter variable or return value? Then simply draw a dependency arrow.

Special Topic 12.1

Attributes and Methods in UML Diagrams

Sometimes it is useful to indicate class *attributes* and *methods* in a class diagram. An **attribute** is an externally observable property that objects of a class have. For example, name and price would be attributes of the Product class. Usually, attributes correspond to instance variables. But they don't have to—a class may have a different way of organizing its data. For example, a GregorianCalendar object from the Java library has attributes day, month, and year, and it would be appropriate to draw a UML diagram that shows these attributes. However, the class doesn't actually have instance variables that store these quantities. Instead, it internally represents all dates by counting the milliseconds from January 1, 1970—an implementation detail that a class user certainly doesn't need to know about.

You can indicate attributes and methods in a class diagram by dividing a class rectangle into three compartments, with the class name in the top, attributes in the middle, and methods in the bottom (see the figure below). You need not list *all* attributes and methods in a particular diagram. Just list the ones that are helpful for understanding whatever point you are making with a particular diagram.

Also, don't list as an attribute what you also draw as an aggregation. If you denote by aggregation the fact that a Car has Tire objects, don't add an attribute tires.

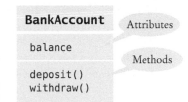

Attributes and Methods in a Class Diagram

Special Topic 12.2

Multiplicities

Some designers like to write *multiplicities* at the end(s) of an aggregation relationship to denote how many objects are aggregated. The notations for the most common multiplicities are:

- any number (zero or more): *
- one or more: 1..*
- zero or one: 0..1
- exactly one: 1

The figure below shows that a customer has one or more bank accounts.

An Aggregation Relationship with Multiplicities

Special Topic 12.3

Aggregation, Association, and Composition

Some designers find the aggregation or *has-a* terminology unsatisfactory. For example, consider customers of a bank. Does the bank "have" customers? Do the customers "have" bank accounts, or does the bank "have" them? Which of these "has" relationships should be modeled by aggregation? This line of thinking can lead us to premature implementation decisions.

Early in the design phase, it makes sense to use a more general relationship between classes called **association**. A class is associated with another if you can *navigate* from objects of one class to objects of the other class. For example, given a Bank object, you can navigate to Customer objects, perhaps by accessing an instance variable, or by making a database lookup.

The UML notation for an association relationship is a solid line, with optional arrows that show in which directions you can navigate the relationship. You can also add words to the line ends to further explain the nature of the relationship. The figure below shows that you can navigate from Bank objects to Customer objects, but you cannot navigate the other way around.

That is, in this particular design, the Customer class has no mechanism to determine in which banks it keeps its money.

An Association Relationship

The UML standard also recognizes a stronger form of the aggregation relationship called **composition**, where the aggregated objects do not have an existence independent of the containing object. For example, composition models the relationship between a bank and its accounts. If a bank closes, the account objects cease to exist as well. In the UML notation, composition looks like aggregation with a filled-in diamond.

A Composition Relationship

Frankly, the differences between aggregation, association, and composition can be confusing, even to experienced designers. If you find the distinction helpful, by all means use the relationship that you find most appropriate. But don't spend time pondering subtle differences between these concepts. From the practical point of view of a Java programmer, it is useful to know when objects of one class have references to objects of another class. The aggregation or *has-a* relationship accurately describes this phenomenon.

12.3 Application: Printing an Invoice

In this book, we discuss a five-part program development process that is particularly well suited for beginning programmers:

1. Gather requirements.
2. Use CRC cards to find classes, responsibilities, and collaborators.
3. Use UML diagrams to record class relationships.
4. Use javadoc to document method behavior.
5. Implement your program.

There isn't a lot of notation to learn. The class diagrams are simple to draw. The deliverables of the design phase are obviously useful for the implementation phase—you simply take the source files and start adding the method code. Of course, as your projects get more complex, you will want to learn more about formal design methods. There are many techniques to describe object scenarios, call sequencing, the large-scale structure of programs, and so on, that are very beneficial even for relatively simple projects. *The Unified Modeling Language User Guide* gives a good overview of these techniques.

In this section, we will walk through the object-oriented design technique with a very simple example. In this case, the methodology may feel overblown, but it is a good introduction to the mechanics of each step. You will then be better prepared for the more complex programs that you will encounter in the future.

12.3.1 Requirements

Before you begin designing a solution, you should gather all requirements for your program in plain English. Write down what your program should do. It is helpful to include typical scenarios in addition to a general description.

The task of our sample program is to print out an invoice. An invoice describes the charges for a set of products in certain quantities. (We omit complexities such as dates, taxes, and invoice and customer numbers.) The program simply prints the billing address, all line items, and the amount due. Each line item contains the description and unit price of a product, the quantity ordered, and the total price.

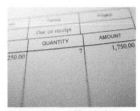

© Scott Cramer/iStockphoto.

An invoice lists the charges for each item and the amount due.

```
          I N V O I C E

Sam's Small Appliances
100 Main Street
Anytown, CA 98765

Description                Price  Qty  Total
Toaster                    29.95   3   89.85
Hair dryer                 24.95   1   24.95
Car vacuum                 19.99   2   39.98

AMOUNT DUE: $154.78
```

Also, in the interest of simplicity, we do not provide a user interface. We just supply a test program that adds line items to the invoice and then prints it.

12.3.2 CRC Cards

When designing an object-oriented program, you need to discover classes. Classes correspond to nouns in the requirements specification. In this problem, it is pretty obvious what the nouns are:

Invoice	Address	LineItem	Product	Description
Price	Quantity	Total	Amount due	

(Of course, Toaster doesn't count—it is the description of a LineItem object and therefore a data value, not the name of a class.)

Description and price are attributes of the Product class. What about the quantity? The quantity is not an attribute of a Product. Just as in the printed invoice, let's have a class LineItem that records the product and the quantity (such as "3 toasters").

The total and amount due are computed—not stored anywhere. Thus, they don't lead to classes.

After this process of elimination, we are left with four candidates for classes:

```
Invoice    Address    LineItem    Product
```

Each of them represents a useful concept, so let's make them all into classes.

The purpose of the program is to print an invoice. However, the Invoice class won't necessarily know whether to display the output in System.out, in a text area, or in a file. Therefore, let's relax the task slightly and make the invoice responsible for *formatting* the invoice. The result is a string (containing multiple lines) that can be printed out or displayed. Record that responsibility on a CRC card:

Invoice
format the invoice

How does an invoice format itself? It must format the billing address, format all line items, and then add the amount due. How can the invoice format an address? It can't— that really is the responsibility of the Address class. This leads to a second CRC card:

Address
format the address

Similarly, formatting of a line item is the responsibility of the LineItem class.

The format method of the Invoice class calls the format methods of the Address and LineItem classes. Whenever a method uses another class, you list that other class as a collaborator. In other words, Address and LineItem are collaborators of Invoice:

Invoice	
format the invoice	Address
	LineItem

When formatting the invoice, the invoice also needs to compute the total amount due. To obtain that amount, it must ask each line item about the total price of the item.

How does a line item obtain that total? It must ask the product for the unit price, and then multiply it by the quantity. That is, the Product class must reveal the unit price, and it is a collaborator of the LineItem class.

Product	
get description	
get unit price	

LineItem	
format the item	Product
get total price	

Finally, the invoice must be populated with products and quantities, so that it makes sense to format the result. That too is a responsibility of the Invoice class.

Invoice	
format the invoice	Address
add a product and quantity	LineItem
	Product

We now have a set of CRC cards that completes the CRC card process.

12.3.3 UML Diagrams

Use UML diagrams to record class relationships.

After you have discovered classes and their relationships with CRC cards, you should record your findings in a UML diagram. The dependency relationships come from the collaboration column on the CRC cards. Each class depends on the classes with which it collaborates. In our example, the Invoice class collaborates with the Address, LineItem, and Product classes. The LineItem class collaborates with the Product class.

Now ask yourself which of these dependencies are actually aggregations. How does an invoice know about the address, line item, and product objects with which it collaborates? An invoice object must hold references to the address and the line items when it formats the invoice. But an invoice object need not hold a reference to a product object when adding a product. The product is turned into a line item, and then it is the item's responsibility to hold a reference to it.

Therefore, the Invoice class aggregates the Address and LineItem classes. The LineItem class aggregates the Product class. However, there is no *has-a* relationship between an invoice and a product. An invoice doesn't store products directly — they are stored in the LineItem objects.

There is no inheritance in this example.

Figure 7 shows the class relationships that we discovered.

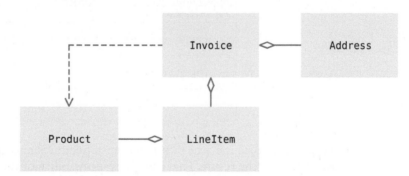

Figure 7
The Relationships Between the Invoice Classes

12.3.4 Method Documentation

Use javadoc comments (with the method bodies left blank) to record the behavior of classes.

The final step of the design phase is to write the documentation of the discovered classes and methods. Simply write a Java source file for each class, write the method comments for those methods that you have discovered, and leave the bodies of the methods blank.

```java
/**
    Describes an invoice for a set of purchased products.
*/
public class Invoice
{
    /**
        Adds a charge for a product to this invoice.
        @param aProduct the product that the customer ordered
        @param quantity the quantity of the product
    */
    public void add(Product aProduct, int quantity)
    {
```

```java
   }

   /**
      Formats the invoice.
      @return the formatted invoice
   */
   public String format()
   {
   }
}



/**
   Describes a quantity of an article to purchase.
*/
public class LineItem
{
   /**
      Computes the total cost of this line item.
      @return the total price
   */
   public double getTotalPrice()
   {
   }

   /**
      Formats this item.
      @return a formatted string of this item
   */
   public String format()
   {
   }
}



/**
   Describes a product with a description and a price.
*/
public class Product
{
   /**
      Gets the product description.
      @return the description
   */
   public String getDescription()
   {
   }

   /**
      Gets the product price.
      @return the unit price
   */
   public double getPrice()
   {
   }
}
```

```
/**
    Describes a mailing address.
*/
public class Address
{
    /**
        Formats the address.
        @return the address as a string with three lines
    */
    public String format()
    {
    }
}
```

Then run the `javadoc` program to obtain a neatly formatted version of your documentation in HTML format (see Figure 8).

This approach for documenting your classes has a number of advantages. You can share the HTML documentation with others if you work in a team. You use a format that is immediately useful—Java source files that you can carry into the implementation phase. And, most importantly, you supply the comments for the key methods—a task that less prepared programmers leave for later, and often neglect for lack of time.

12.3.5 Implementation

After completing the design, implement your classes.

After you have completed the object-oriented design, you are ready to implement the classes.

You already have the method parameter variables and comments from the previous step. Now look at the UML diagram to add instance variables. Aggregated classes

Figure 8
Class Documentation
in HTML Format

yield instance variables. Start with the Invoice class. An invoice aggregates Address and LineItem. Every invoice has one billing address, but it can have many line items. To store multiple LineItem objects, you can use an array list. Now you have the instance variables of the Invoice class:

```java
public class Invoice
{
    private Address billingAddress;
    private ArrayList<LineItem> items;
    . . .
}
```

A line item needs to store a Product object and the product quantity. That leads to the following instance variables:

```java
public class LineItem
{
    private int quantity;
    private Product theProduct;
    . . .
}
```

The methods themselves are now easy to implement. Here is a typical example. You already know what the getTotalPrice method of the LineItem class needs to do—get the unit price of the product and multiply it with the quantity:

```java
/**
    Computes the total cost of this line item.
    @return the total price
*/
public double getTotalPrice()
{
    return theProduct.getPrice() * quantity;
}
```

We will not discuss the other methods in detail—they are equally straightforward.

Finally, you need to supply constructors, another routine task.

The entire program is shown below. It is a good practice to go through it in detail and match up the classes and methods to the CRC cards and UML diagram.

Worked Example 12.1 (in your eText) demonstrates the design process with a more challenging problem, a simulated automatic teller machine. You should study that example as well.

In this chapter, you learned a systematic approach for building a relatively complex program. However, object-oriented design is definitely not a spectator sport. To really learn how to design and implement programs, you have to gain experience by repeating this process with your own projects. It is quite possible that you don't immediately home in on a good solution and that you need to go back and reorganize your classes and responsibilities. That is normal and only to be expected. The purpose of the object-oriented design process is to spot these problems in the design phase, when they are still easy to rectify, instead of in the implementation phase, when massive reorganization is more difficult and time consuming.

sec03/InvoicePrinter.java

```java
1  /**
2      This program demonstrates the invoice classes by printing
3      a sample invoice.
4  */
```

```
5  public class InvoicePrinter
6  {
7     public static void main(String[] args)
8     {
9        Address samsAddress
10           = new Address("Sam's Small Appliances",
11           "100 Main Street", "Anytown", "CA", "98765");
12
13        Invoice samsInvoice = new Invoice(samsAddress);
14        samsInvoice.add(new Product("Toaster", 29.95), 3);
15        samsInvoice.add(new Product("Hair dryer", 24.95), 1);
16        samsInvoice.add(new Product("Car vacuum", 19.99), 2);
17
18        System.out.println(samsInvoice.format());
19     }
20  }
```

sec03/Invoice.java

```
1  import java.util.ArrayList;
2
3  /**
4     Describes an invoice for a set of purchased products.
5  */
6  public class Invoice
7  {
8     private Address billingAddress;
9     private ArrayList<LineItem> items;
10
11     /**
12        Constructs an invoice.
13        @param anAddress the billing address
14     */
15     public Invoice(Address anAddress)
16     {
17        items = new ArrayList<LineItem>();
18        billingAddress = anAddress;
19     }
20
21     /**
22        Adds a charge for a product to this invoice.
23        @param aProduct the product that the customer ordered
24        @param quantity the quantity of the product
25     */
26     public void add(Product aProduct, int quantity)
27     {
28        LineItem anItem = new LineItem(aProduct, quantity);
29        items.add(anItem);
30     }
31
32     /**
33        Formats the invoice.
34        @return the formatted invoice
35     */
36     public String format()
37     {
38        String r =  String.format("%32s%n%n", "I N V O I C E")
39              + billingAddress.format()
40              + String.format("%n%n%-30s%8s%5s%8s%n",
41              "Description", "Price", "Qty", "Total");
```

```
42
43          for (LineItem item : items)
44          {
45             r = String.format("%s%s%n", r, item.format());
46          }
47
48          r = r + String.format("%nAMOUNT DUE: $%8.2f%n", getAmountDue());
49
50          return r;
51       }
52
53       /**
54          Computes the total amount due.
55          @return the amount due
56       */
57       private double getAmountDue()
58       {
59          double amountDue = 0;
60          for (LineItem item : items)
61          {
62             amountDue = amountDue + item.getTotalPrice();
63          }
64          return amountDue;
65       }
66    }
```

sec03/LineItem.java

```
1    /**
2       Describes a quantity of an article to purchase.
3    */
4    public class LineItem
5    {
6       private int quantity;
7       private Product theProduct;
8
9       /**
10          Constructs an item from the product and quantity.
11          @param aProduct the product
12          @param aQuantity the item quantity
13       */
14       public LineItem(Product aProduct, int aQuantity)
15       {
16          theProduct = aProduct;
17          quantity = aQuantity;
18       }
19
20       /**
21          Computes the total cost of this line item.
22          @return the total price
23       */
24       public double getTotalPrice()
25       {
26          return theProduct.getPrice() * quantity;
27       }
28
29       /**
30          Formats this item.
31          @return a formatted string of this line item
32       */
```

```
33   public String format()
34   {
35      return String.format("%-30s%8.2f%5d%8.2f",
36         theProduct.getDescription(), theProduct.getPrice(),
37         quantity, getTotalPrice());
38   }
39 }
```

sec03/Product.java

```
1  /**
2     Describes a product with a description and a price.
3  */
4  public class Product
5  {
6     private String description;
7     private double price;
8
9     /**
10        Constructs a product from a description and a price.
11        @param aDescription the product description
12        @param aPrice the product price
13     */
14     public Product(String aDescription, double aPrice)
15     {
16        description = aDescription;
17        price = aPrice;
18     }
19
20     /**
21        Gets the product description.
22        @return the description
23     */
24     public String getDescription()
25     {
26        return description;
27     }
28
29     /**
30        Gets the product price.
31        @return the unit price
32     */
33     public double getPrice()
34     {
35        return price;
36     }
37 }
```

sec03/Address.java

```
1  /**
2     Describes a mailing address.
3  */
4  public class Address
5  {
6     private String name;
7     private String street;
8     private String city;
9     private String state;
10    private String zip;
```

```
11
12      /**
13          Constructs a mailing address.
14          @param aName  the recipient name
15          @param aStreet  the street
16          @param aCity  the city
17          @param aState  the two-letter state code
18          @param aZip  the ZIP postal code
19      */
20      public Address(String aName, String aStreet,
21              String aCity, String aState, String aZip)
22      {
23          name = aName;
24          street = aStreet;
25          city = aCity;
26          state = aState;
27          zip = aZip;
28      }
29
30      /**
31          Formats the address.
32          @return the address as a string with three lines
33      */
34      public String format()
35      {
36          return String.format("%s%n%s%n%s, %s %s",
37              name, street, city, state, zip);
38      }
39 }
```

WORKED EXAMPLE 12.1

Simulating an Automatic Teller Machine

Learn to apply the object-oriented design methodology to the simulation of an automatic teller machine that works with both a console-based and graphical user interface. See your eText or visit wiley.com/go/bjeo7.

© Mark Evans/iStockphoto.

Computing & Society 12.1   Electronic Privacy

Most companies use computers to keep huge databases of customer records and other business information. Databases not only lower the cost of doing business, they improve the quality of service that companies can offer. Nowadays it is almost unimaginable how time-consuming it used to be to withdraw money from a bank branch or to make travel reservations.

As these databases became ubiquitous, they started creating problems for citizens. Consider the "no fly list" maintained by the U.S. government, which lists names used by suspected terrorists. On March 1, 2007, Professor Walter Murphy, a constitutional scholar of Princeton University and a decorated former Marine, was denied a boarding pass. The airline employee asked him, "Have you been in any

peace marches? We ban a lot of people from flying because of that." As Murphy tells it, "I explained that I had not so marched but had, in September 2006, given a lecture at Princeton, televised and put on the Web, highly critical of George Bush for his many violations of the constitution. 'That'll do it,' the man said."

We do not actually know if Professor Murphy's name was on the list because he was critical of the Bush administration or because some other potentially dangerous person had traveled under the same name. Travelers with similar misfortunes had serious difficulties trying to get themselves off the list.

Problems such as these have become commonplace. Companies and the government routinely merge multiple databases, derive information about us that may be quite inaccurate, and then use that information to make decisions. An insurance company may deny coverage, or charge a higher premium, if it finds that you have too many relatives with a certain disease. You may be denied a job because of a credit or medical report. You do not usually know what information about you is stored or how it is used. In cases where the information can be checked—such as credit reports—it is often difficult to correct errors.

Users of "free" social networks and other services voluntarily trade their privacy for convenience, and they are often surprised when they find out how their personal information is used. As judge Louis Brandeis wrote in 1928, "Privacy is the right to be alone—the most comprehensive of rights, and the right most valued by civilized man." When employers can see your old Facebook posts, divorce lawyers have access to toll road records, and Google mines your e-mails and searches to present you "targeted" advertising, you have little privacy left.

The 1948 "universal declaration of human rights" by the United Nations states, "No one shall be subjected to arbitrary interference with his privacy, family, home or correspondence, nor to attacks upon his honour and reputation. Everyone has the right to the protection of the law against such interference or attacks." The United States has surprisingly few legal protections against privacy invasion, apart from federal laws protecting student records and video rentals (the latter was passed after a Supreme Court

© Greg Nicholas/iStockphoto.

If you pay road or bridge tolls with an electronic pass, your records may not be private.

nominee's video rental records were published). Other industrialized countries have gone much further and recognize every citizen's right to control what information about them should be communicated to others and under what circumstances.

CHAPTER SUMMARY

Recognize how to discover classes and their responsibilities.

- To discover classes, look for nouns in the problem description.
- Concepts from the problem domain are good candidates for classes.
- A CRC card describes a class, its responsibilities, and its collaborating classes.

Categorize class relationships and produce UML diagrams that describe them.

- A class depends on another class if it uses objects of that class.
- It is a good practice to minimize the coupling (i.e., dependency) between classes.
- A class aggregates another if its objects contain objects of the other class.
- Inheritance (the *is-a* relationship) is sometimes inappropriately used when the *has-a* relationship would be more appropriate.
- Aggregation (the *has-a* relationship) denotes that objects of one class contain references to objects of another class.
- You need to be able to distinguish the UML notation for inheritance, interface implementation, aggregation, and dependency.

Apply an object-oriented development process to designing a program.

- Start the development process by gathering and documenting program requirements.
- Use CRC cards to find classes, responsibilities, and collaborators.
- Use UML diagrams to record class relationships.
- Use `javadoc` comments (with the method bodies left blank) to record the behavior of classes.
- After completing the design, implement your classes.

REVIEW EXERCISES

■■ **R12.1** List the steps in the process of object-oriented design that this chapter recommends for student use.

■ **R12.2** Give a rule of thumb for how to find classes when designing a program.

■ **R12.3** Suppose you are asked to implement a program that simulates your favorite social network. List the classes that you would implement.

■ **R12.4** Give a rule of thumb for how to find methods when designing a program.

■■ **R12.5** After discovering a method, why is it important to identify the object that is *responsible* for carrying out the action?

■■ **R12.6** Consider an enhancement of the quiz application from Chapter 9 such that a course has a number of quizzes and a number of students. Each student can log in (with a user name and password) and take a quiz. The scores are recorded. A teacher can log in, add students and quizzes, and see all scores. List responsibilities of the classes Teacher, Student, and Course.

■■ **R12.7** What relationship is appropriate between the following classes: aggregation, inheritance, or neither?
   a. University–Student
   b. Student–TeachingAssistant
   c. Student–Freshman
   d. Student–Professor
   e. Car–Door
   f. Truck–Vehicle
   g. Traffic–TrafficSign
   h. TrafficSign–Color

■■ **R12.8** Every BMW is a vehicle. Should a class BMW inherit from the class Vehicle? BMW is a vehicle manufacturer. Does that mean that the class BMW should inherit from the class VehicleManufacturer?

■■ **R12.9** Some books on object-oriented programming recommend using inheritance so that the class Circle extends the class java.awt.Point. Then the Circle class inherits the setLocation method from the Point superclass. Explain why the setLocation method need not be overridden in the subclass. Why is it nevertheless not a good idea to have Circle inherit from Point? Conversely, would inheriting Point from Circle fulfill the *is-a* rule? Would it be a good idea?

■ **R12.10** Write CRC cards for the Coin and CashRegister classes described in Section 8.2.

■ **R12.11** Write CRC cards for the Quiz and Question classes in Section 12.2.2.

■■ **R12.12** Draw a UML diagram for the Quiz, Question, and ChoiceQuestion classes. The Quiz class is described in Section 12.2.2.

■■■ **R12.13** A file contains a set of records describing countries. Each record consists of the name of the country, its population, and its area. Suppose your task is to write a program that reads in such a file and prints

- The country with the largest area.
- The country with the largest population.
- The country with the largest population density (people per square kilometer).

Think through the problems that you need to solve. What classes and methods will you need? Produce a set of CRC cards, a UML diagram, and a set of javadoc comments.

■■■ **R12.14** Discover classes and methods for generating a student report card that lists all classes, grades, and the grade point average for a semester. Produce a set of CRC cards, a UML diagram, and a set of javadoc comments.

■■ **R12.15** Consider the following problem description:

Users place coins in a vending machine and select a product by pushing a button. If the inserted coins are sufficient to cover the purchase price of the product, the product is dispensed and change is given. Otherwise, the inserted coins are returned to the user.

What classes should you use to implement a solution?

■■ **R12.16** Consider the following problem description:

Employees receive their biweekly paychecks. They are paid their hourly rates for each hour worked; however, if they worked more than 40 hours per week, they are paid overtime at 150 percent of their regular wage.

What classes should you use to implement a solution?

■■ **R12.17** Consider the following problem description:

Customers order products from a store. Invoices are generated to list the items and quantities ordered, payments received, and amounts still due. Products are shipped to the shipping address of the customer, and invoices are sent to the billing address.

Draw a UML diagram showing the aggregation relationships between the classes Invoice, Address, Customer, and Product.

PRACTICE EXERCISES

■■ **E12.1** Provide a user interface to the invoice program in Section 12.3 that allows a user to enter and print an arbitrary invoice. Do not modify any of the existing classes.

■ **E12.2** Enhance the invoice-printing program by providing for two kinds of line items: One kind describes products that are purchased in certain numerical quantities (such as "3 toasters"), another describes a fixed charge (such as "shipping: $5.00"). *Hint:* Use inheritance. Produce a UML diagram of your modified implementation.

■■ **E12.3** The invoice-printing program is somewhat unrealistic because the formatting of the LineItem objects won't lead to good visual results when the prices and quantities have varying numbers of digits. Enhance the format method in two ways: Accept an int[] array of column widths as an argument. Use the NumberFormat class to format the currency values.

•• **E12.4** The invoice-printing program has an unfortunate flaw—it mixes "application logic" (the computation of total charges) and "presentation" (the visual appearance of the invoice). To appreciate this flaw, imagine the changes that would be necessary to draw the invoice in HTML for presentation on the Web. Reimplement the program, using a separate InvoiceFormatter class to format the invoice. That is, the Invoice and LineItem methods are no longer responsible for formatting. However, they will acquire other responsibilities, because the InvoiceFormatter class needs to query them for the values that it requires.

••• **E12.5** Write a program that teaches arithmetic to a young child. The program tests addition and subtraction. In level 1, it tests only addition of numbers less than ten whose sum is less than ten. In level 2, it tests addition of arbitrary one-digit numbers. In level 3, it tests subtraction of one-digit numbers with a nonnegative difference.

Generate random problems and get the player's input. The player gets up to two tries per problem. Advance from one level to the next when the player has achieved a score of five points.

••• **E12.6** Implement a simple e-mail messaging system. A message has a recipient, a sender, and a message text. A mailbox can store messages. Supply a number of mailboxes for different users and a user interface for users to log in, send messages to other users, read their own messages, and log out. Follow the design process that was described in this chapter.

•• **E12.7** Modify the implementation of the classes in the ATM simulation in Worked Example 12.1 so that the bank manages a collection of bank accounts and a separate collection of customers. Allow joint accounts in which some accounts can have more than one customer.

PROGRAMMING PROJECTS

•• **P12.1** Write a program that simulates a vending machine. Products can be purchased by inserting coins with a value at least equal to the cost of the product. A user selects a product from a list of available products, adds coins, and either gets the product or gets the coins returned. The coins are returned if insufficient money was supplied or if the product is sold out. The machine does not give change if too much money was added. Products can be restocked and money removed by an operator. Follow the design process that was described in this chapter. Your solution should include a class VendingMachine that is not coupled with the Scanner or PrintStream classes.

••• **P12.2** Write a program to design an appointment calendar. An appointment includes the date, starting time, ending time, and a description; for example,

```
Dentist 2019/10/1 17:30 18:30
CS1 class 2019/10/2 08:30 10:00
```

Supply a user interface to add appointments, remove canceled appointments, and print out a list of appointments for a particular day. Follow the design process that was described in this chapter. Your solution should include a class Appointment-Calendar that is not coupled with the Scanner or PrintStream classes.

••• **P12.3** Write a program that administers and grades quizzes. A quiz consists of questions. There are four types of questions: text questions, number questions, choice questions with a single answer, and choice questions with multiple answers. When grading a text question, ignore leading or trailing spaces and letter case. When grading a numeric question, accept a response that is approximately the same as the answer.

A quiz is specified in a text file. Each question starts with a letter indicating the question type (T, N, S, M), followed by a line containing the question text. The next line of a non-choice question contains the answer. Choice questions have a list of choices that is terminated by a blank line. Each choice starts with + (correct) or - (incorrect). Here is a sample file:

```
T
Which Java reserved word is used to declare a subclass?
extends
S
What is the original name of the Java language?
- *7
- C--
+ Oak
- Gosling

M
Which of the following types are supertypes of Rectangle?
- PrintStream
+ Shape
+ RectangularShape
+ Object
- String

N
What is the square root of 2?
1.41421356
```

Your program should read in a quiz file, prompt the user for responses to all questions, and grade the responses. Follow the design process described in this chapter.

■■ **P12.4** Produce a requirements document for a program that allows a company to send out personalized mailings, either by e-mail or through the postal service. Template files contain the message text, together with variable fields (such as Dear [Title] [Last Name] . . .). A database (stored as a text file) contains the field values for each recipient. Use HTML as the output file format. Then design and implement the program.

■■■ **P12.5** Write a tic-tac-toe game that allows a human player to play against the computer. Your program will play many turns against a human opponent, and it will learn. When it is the computer's turn, the computer randomly selects an empty field, except that it won't ever choose a losing combination. For that purpose, your program must keep an array of losing combinations. Whenever the human wins, the immediately preceding combination is stored as losing. For example, suppose that X = computer and O = human.

Suppose the current combination is

O	X	X
	O	

Now it is the human's turn, who will of course choose

```
 O | X | X
---+---+---
   | O |
---+---+---
   |   | O
```

The computer should then remember the preceding combination

```
 O | X | X
---+---+---
   | O |
---+---+---
   |   |
```

as a losing combination. As a result, the computer will never again choose that combination from

```
 O | X |          O |   | X
---+---+---       ---+---+---
   | O |     or      | O |
---+---+---       ---+---+---
   |   |             |   |
```

Discover classes and supply a UML diagram before you begin to program.

■■■ **Business P12.6** *Airline seating.* Write a program that assigns seats on an airplane. Assume the airplane has 20 seats in first class (5 rows of 4 seats each, separated by an aisle) and 90 seats in economy class (15 rows of 6 seats each, separated by an aisle). Your program should take three commands: add passengers, show seating, and quit. When passengers are added, ask for the class (first or economy), the number of passengers traveling together (1 or 2 in first class; 1 to 3 in economy), and the seating preference (aisle or window in first class; aisle, center, or window in economy). Then try to find a match and assign the seats. If no match exists, print a message. Your solution should include a class Airplane that is not coupled with the Scanner or PrintStream classes. Follow the design process that was described in this chapter.

■■■ **Business P12.7** In an "instant runoff" election, voters mark their favorite candidate on the ballot as well as two alternate candidates (in case their first or second choice does not win). When the ballots are counted, the candidate with the least votes is eliminated, and the ballots for that candidate are redistributed to the next alternate. The process repeats until all but two candidates are eliminated. The one with the most votes wins. Write a program that implements this system, reading ballots from a file. Use classes Candidate, Ballot, and Election.

■■■ **Business P12.8** In an airplane, each passenger has a touch screen for ordering a drink and a snack. Some items are free and some are not. The system prepares two reports for speeding up service:

1. A list of all seats, ordered by row, showing the charges that must be collected.
2. A list of how many drinks and snacks of each type must be prepared for the front and the rear of the plane.

Follow the design process that was described in this chapter to identify classes, and implement a program that simulates the system.

•••Graphics P12.9 Implement a program to teach a young child to read the clock. In the game, present an analog clock, such as the one shown here.

An Analog Clock

Generate random times and display the clock. Accept guesses from the player. Reward the player for correct guesses. After two incorrect guesses, display the correct answer and make a new random time. Implement several levels of play. In level 1, only show full hours. In level 2, show quarter hours. In level 3, show five-minute multiples, and in level 4, show any number of minutes. After a player has achieved five correct guesses at one level, advance to the next level.

•••Graphics P12.10 Write a program that can be used to design a suburban scene, with houses, streets, and cars. Users can add houses and cars of various colors to a street. Write more specific requirements that include a detailed description of the user interface. Then, discover classes and methods, provide UML diagrams, and implement your program.

•••Graphics P12.11 Write a simple graphics editor that allows users to add a mixture of shapes (ellipses, rectangles, and lines in different colors) to a panel. Supply commands to load and save the picture. Discover classes, supply a UML diagram, and implement your program.

RECURSION

© Nicolae Popovici/iStockphoto.

CHAPTER GOALS

To learn to "think recursively"

To be able to use recursive helper methods

To understand the relationship between recursion and iteration

To understand when the use of recursion affects the efficiency of an algorithm

To analyze problems that are much easier to solve by recursion than by iteration

To process data with recursive structures using mutual recursion

CHAPTER CONTENTS

The method of recursion is a powerful technique for breaking up complex computational problems into simpler, often smaller, ones. The term "recursion" refers to the fact that the same computation recurs, or occurs repeatedly, as the problem is solved. Recursion is often the most natural way of thinking about a problem, and there are some computations that are very difficult to perform without recursion. This chapter shows you both simple and complex examples of recursion and teaches you how to "think recursively".

13.1 Triangle Numbers

We begin this chapter with a very simple example that demonstrates the power of thinking recursively. In this example, we will look at triangle shapes such as this one:

```
[]
[][]
[][][]
```

We'd like to compute the area of a triangle of width *n*, assuming that each [] square has area 1. The area of the triangle is sometimes called the nth *triangle number*. For example, as you can tell from looking at the triangle above, the third triangle number is 6.

© David Mantel/iStockphoto.

Using the same method as the one in this section, you can compute the volume of a Mayan pyramid.

You may know that there is a very simple formula to compute these numbers, but you should pretend for now that you don't know about it. The ultimate purpose of this section is not to compute triangle numbers, but to learn about the concept of **recursion** by working through a simple example.

Here is the outline of the class that we will develop:

```java
public class Triangle
{
    private int width;

    public Triangle(int aWidth)
    {
        width = aWidth;
    }

    public int getArea()
    {
        . . .
    }
}
```

If the width of the triangle is 1, then the triangle consists of a single square, and its area is 1. Let's take care of this case first:

```java
public int getArea()
{
    if (width == 1) { return 1; }
    . . .
}
```

To deal with the general case, consider this picture:

```
[]
[][]
[][][]
[][][][]
```

Suppose we knew the area of the smaller, colored triangle. Then we could easily compute the area of the larger triangle as

```
smallerArea + width
```

How can we get the smaller area? Let's make a smaller triangle and ask it!

```
Triangle smallerTriangle = new Triangle(width - 1);
int smallerArea = smallerTriangle.getArea();
```

Now we can complete the getArea method:

```
public int getArea()
{
   if (width == 1) { return 1; }
   else
   {
      Triangle smallerTriangle = new Triangle(width - 1);
      int smallerArea = smallerTriangle.getArea();
      return smallerArea + width;
   }
}
```

A recursive computation solves a problem by using the solution to the same problem with simpler inputs.

Here is an illustration of what happens when we compute the area of a triangle of width 4:

- The getArea method makes a smaller triangle of width 3.
- It calls getArea on that triangle.
  - That method makes a smaller triangle of width 2.
  - It calls getArea on that triangle.
    - That method makes a smaller triangle of width 1.
    - It calls getArea on that triangle.
      - That method returns 1.
    - The method returns smallerArea + width = 1 + 2 = 3.
  - The method returns smallerArea + width = 3 + 3 = 6.
- The method returns smallerArea + width = 6 + 4 = 10.

This solution has one remarkable aspect. To solve the area problem for a triangle of a given width, we use the fact that we can solve the same problem for a lesser width. This is called a *recursive* solution.

The call pattern of a **recursive method** looks complicated, and the key to the successful design of a recursive method is *not to think about it.* Instead, look at the getArea method one more time and notice how utterly reasonable it is. If the width is 1, then, of course, the area is 1. The next part is just as reasonable. Compute the area of the smaller triangle *and don't think about why that works.* Then the area of the larger triangle is clearly the sum of the smaller area and the width.

There are two key requirements to make sure that the recursion is successful:

- Every recursive call must simplify the computation in some way.
- There must be special cases to handle the simplest computations directly.

For a recursion to terminate, there must be special cases for the simplest values.

The getArea method calls itself again with smaller and smaller width values. Eventually the width must reach 1, and there is a special case for computing the area of a triangle with width 1. Thus, the getArea method always succeeds.

Actually, you have to be careful. What happens when you call the area of a triangle with width –1? It computes the area of a triangle with width –2, which computes the area of a triangle with width –3, and so on. To avoid this, the getArea method should return 0 if the width is ≤ 0.

Recursion is not really necessary to compute the triangle numbers. The area of a triangle equals the sum

```
1 + 2 + 3 + . . . + width
```

Of course, we can program a simple loop:

```
double area = 0;
for (int i = 1; i <= width; i++)
{
   area = area + i;
}
```

Many simple recursions can be computed as loops. However, loop equivalents for more complex recursions—such as the one in our next example—can be complex.

Actually, in this case, you don't even need a loop to compute the answer. The sum of the first n integers can be computed as

$$1 + 2 + \cdots + n = n \times (n + 1)/2$$

Thus, the area equals

```
width * (width + 1) / 2
```

Therefore, neither recursion nor a loop is required to solve this problem. The recursive solution is intended as a "warm-up" to introduce you to the concept of recursion.

sec01/Triangle.java

```
 1  /**
 2      A triangular shape composed of stacked unit squares like this:
 3      []
 4      [][]
 5      [][][]
 6      . . .
 7  */
 8  public class Triangle
 9  {
10     private int width;
11
12     /**
13         Constructs a triangular shape.
14         @param aWidth the width (and height) of the triangle
15     */
16     public Triangle(int aWidth)
17     {
18        width = aWidth;
19     }
20
21     /**
22         Computes the area of the triangle.
23         @return the area
24     */
```

```
25    public int getArea()
26    {
27       if (width <= 0) { return 0; }
28       else if (width == 1) { return 1; }
29       else
30       {
31          Triangle smallerTriangle = new Triangle(width - 1);
32          int smallerArea = smallerTriangle.getArea();
33          return smallerArea + width;
34       }
35    }
36 }
```

sec01/TriangleTester.java

```
 1 public class TriangleTester
 2 {
 3    public static void main(String[] args)
 4    {
 5       Triangle t = new Triangle(10);
 6       int area = t.getArea();
 7       System.out.println("Area: " + area);
 8       System.out.println("Expected: 55");
 9    }
10 }
```

Program Run

```
Area: 55
Expected: 55
```

Common Error 13.1

Infinite Recursion

A common programming error is an *infinite recursion:* a method calling itself over and over with no end in sight. The computer needs some amount of memory for bookkeeping for each call. After some number of calls, all memory that is available for this purpose is exhausted. Your program shuts down and reports a "stack overflow".

Infinite recursion happens either because the arguments don't get simpler or because a special terminating case is missing. For example, suppose the getArea method was allowed to compute the area of a triangle with width 0. If it weren't for the special test, the method would construct triangles with width –1, –2, –3, and so on.

Common Error 13.2

Tracing Through Recursive Methods

Debugging a recursive method can be somewhat challenging. When you set a **breakpoint** in a recursive method, the program stops as soon as that program line is encountered in *any call to the recursive method.* Suppose you want to debug the recursive getArea method of the Triangle class. Debug the TriangleTester program and run until the beginning of the getArea method. Inspect the width instance variable. It is 10.

Remove the breakpoint and now run until the statement return smallerArea + width; (see Figure 1). When you inspect width again, its value is 2! That makes no sense. There was no instruction that changed the value of width. Is that a bug with the debugger?

No. The program stopped in the first recursive call to getArea that reached the return statement. If you are confused, look at the **call stack** (top right in the figure). You will see that nine calls to getArea are pending.

You can debug recursive methods with the debugger. You just need to be particularly careful, and watch the call stack to understand which nested call you currently are in.

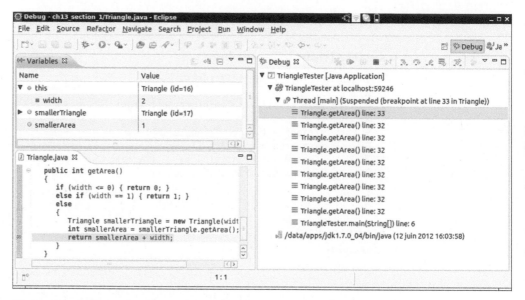

Figure 1   Debugging a Recursive Method

HOW TO 13.1

Thinking Recursively

Solving a problem recursively requires a different mindset than solving it by programming a loop. In fact, it helps if you pretend to be a bit lazy, asking others to do most of the work for you. If you need to solve a complex problem, pretend that "someone else" will do most of the heavy lifting and solve the problem for simpler inputs. Then you only need to figure out how you can turn the solutions with simpler inputs into a solution for the whole problem. To illustrate the technique of recursion, let us consider the following problem.

Problem Statement   Test whether a sentence is a *palindrome*—a string that is equal to itself when you reverse all characters.

Typical examples of palindromes are

- A man, a plan, a canal—Panama!

- Go hang a salami, I'm a lasagna hog

© Nikada/iStockphoto.

Thinking recursively is easy if you can recognize a subtask that is similar to the original task.

and, of course, the oldest palindrome of all:

- Madam, I'm Adam

When testing for a palindrome, we match upper- and lowercase letters, and ignore all spaces and punctuation marks.

We want to implement the isPalindrome method in the following class:

```java
public class Palindromes
{
    . . .
    /**
        Tests whether a text is a palindrome.
        @param text a string that is being checked
        @return true if text is a palindrome, false otherwise
    */
    public static boolean isPalindrome(String text)
    {
        . . .
    }
}
```

Step 1 Consider various ways to simplify inputs.

In your mind, focus on a particular input or set of inputs for the problem that you want to solve. Think how you can simplify the inputs in such a way that the same problem can be applied to the simpler input.

When you consider simpler inputs, you may want to remove just a little bit from the original input—maybe remove one or two characters from a string, or remove a small portion of a geometric shape. But sometimes it is more useful to cut the input in half and then see what it means to solve the problem for both halves.

In the palindrome test problem, the input is the string that we need to test. How can you simplify the input? Here are several possibilities:

- Remove the first character.
- Remove the last character.
- Remove both the first and last characters.
- Remove a character from the middle.
- Cut the string into two halves.

These simpler inputs are all potential inputs for the palindrome test.

Step 2 Combine solutions with simpler inputs into a solution of the original problem.

In your mind, consider the solutions of your problem for the simpler inputs that you discovered in Step 1. Don't worry *how* those solutions are obtained. Simply have faith that the solutions are readily available. Just say to yourself: These are simpler inputs, so someone else will solve the problem for me.

Now think how you can turn the solution for the simpler inputs into a solution for the input that you are currently thinking about. Maybe you need to add a small quantity, related to the quantity that you lopped off to arrive at the simpler input. Maybe you cut the original input in half and have solutions for each half. Then you may need to add both solutions to arrive at a solution for the whole.

Consider the methods for simplifying the inputs for the palindrome test. Cutting the string in half doesn't seem a good idea. If you cut

```
"Madam, I'm Adam"
```

in half, you get two strings:

```
"Madam, I"
```

and

```
"'m Adam"
```

Neither of them is a palindrome. Cutting the input in half and testing whether the halves are palindromes seems a dead end.

The most promising simplification is to remove the first *and* last characters. Removing the M at the front and the m at the back yields

```
"adam, I'm Ada"
```

Suppose you can verify that the shorter string is a palindrome. Then *of course* the original string is a palindrome—we put the same letter in the front and the back. That's extremely promising. A word is a palindrome if

- The first and last letters match (ignoring letter case)

and

- The word obtained by removing the first and last letters is a palindrome.

Again, don't worry how the test works for the shorter string. It just works.

There is one other case to consider. What if the first or last letter of the word is not a letter? For example, the string

```
"A man, a plan, a canal, Panama!"
```

ends in a ! character, which does not match the A in the front. But we should ignore non-letters when testing for palindromes. Thus, when the last character is not a letter but the first character is a letter, it doesn't make sense to remove both the first and the last characters. That's not a problem. Remove only the last character. If the shorter string is a palindrome, then it stays a palindrome when you attach a nonletter.

The same argument applies if the first character is not a letter. Now we have a complete set of cases.

- If the first and last characters are both letters, then check whether they match. If so, remove both and test the shorter string.
- Otherwise, if the last character isn't a letter, remove it and test the shorter string.
- Otherwise, the first character isn't a letter. Remove it and test the shorter string.

In all three cases, you can use the solution to the simpler problem to arrive at a solution to your problem.

Step 3 Find solutions to the simplest inputs.

A recursive computation keeps simplifying its inputs. Eventually it arrives at very simple inputs. To make sure that the recursion comes to a stop, you must deal with the simplest inputs separately. Come up with special solutions for them, which is usually very easy.

However, sometimes you get into philosophical questions dealing with *degenerate* inputs: empty strings, shapes with no area, and so on. Then you may want to investigate a slightly larger input that gets reduced to such a trivial input and see what value you should attach to the degenerate inputs so that the simpler value, when used according to the rules you discovered in Step 2, yields the correct answer.

Let's look at the simplest strings for the palindrome test:

- Strings with two characters
- Strings with a single character
- The empty string

We don't need a special solution for strings with two characters. Step 2 still applies to those strings—either or both of the characters are removed. But we do need to worry about strings of length 0 and 1. In those cases, Step 2 can't apply. There aren't two characters to remove.

The empty string is a palindrome—it's the same string when you read it backwards. If you find that too artificial, consider a string "mm". According to the rule discovered in Step 2, this string is a palindrome if the first and last characters of that string match and the remainder—that is, the empty string—is also a palindrome. Therefore, it makes sense to consider the empty string a palindrome.

A string with a single letter, such as "I", is a palindrome. How about the case in which the character is not a letter, such as "!"? Removing the ! yields the empty string, which is a palindrome. Thus, we conclude that all strings of length 0 or 1 are palindromes.

Step 4 Implement the solution by combining the simple cases and the reduction step.

Now you are ready to implement the solution. Make separate cases for the simple inputs that you considered in Step 3. If the input isn't one of the simplest cases, then implement the logic you discovered in Step 2.

Here is the isPalindrome method:

```java
public static boolean isPalindrome(String text)
{
    int length = text.length();

    // Separate case for shortest strings.
    if (length <= 1) { return true; }
    else
    {
        // Get first and last characters, converted to lowercase.
        char first = Character.toLowerCase(text.charAt(0));
        char last = Character.toLowerCase(text.charAt(length - 1));

        if (Character.isLetter(first) && Character.isLetter(last))
        {
            // Both are letters.
            if (first == last)
            {
                // Remove both first and last character.
                String shorter = text.substring(1, length - 1);
                return isPalindrome(shorter);
            }
            else
            {
                return false;
            }
        }
        else if (!Character.isLetter(last))
        {
            // Remove last character.
            String shorter = text.substring(0, length - 1);
            return isPalindrome(shorter);
        }
        else
        {
            // Remove first character.
            String shorter = text.substring(1);
            return isPalindrome(shorter);
        }
    }
}
```

EXAMPLE CODE See how_to_1 of your eText or companion code for the complete Palindromes class.

WORKED EXAMPLE 13.1

Finding Files

Learn how to use recursion to find all files with a given extension in a directory tree. See your eText or visit wiley.com/go/bjeo7.

13.2 Recursive Helper Methods

> Sometimes it is easier to find a recursive solution if you make a slight change to the original problem.

Sometimes it is easier to find a recursive solution if you change the original problem slightly. Then the original problem can be solved by calling a recursive helper method.

Here is a typical example: In the palindrome test of How To 13.1, it is a bit inefficient to construct new string objects in every step. Consider the following change in the problem: Instead of testing whether the entire sentence is a palindrome, let's check whether a substring is a palindrome:

© gerenme/iStockphoto.

Sometimes, a task can be solved by handing it off to a recursive helper method.

```
/**
    Tests whether a substring is a palindrome.
    @param text a string that is being checked
    @param start the index of the first character of the substring
    @param end the index of the last character of the substring
    @return true if the substring is a palindrome
*/
public static boolean isPalindrome(String text, int start, int end)
```

This method turns out to be even easier to implement than the original test. In the recursive calls, simply adjust the start and end parameter variables to skip over matching letter pairs and characters that are not letters. There is no need to construct new String objects to represent the shorter strings.

```
public static boolean isPalindrome(String text, int start, int end)
{
    // Separate case for substrings of length 0 and 1.
    if (start >= end) { return true; }
    else
    {
        // Get first and last characters, converted to lowercase.
        char first = Character.toLowerCase(text.charAt(start));
        char last = Character.toLowerCase(text.charAt(end));

        if (Character.isLetter(first) && Character.isLetter(last))
        {
            if (first == last)
            {
                // Test substring that doesn't contain the matching letters.
                return isPalindrome(text, start + 1, end - 1);
```

```
      }
      else
      {
         return false;
      }
   }
   else if (!Character.isLetter(last))
   {
      // Test substring that doesn't contain the last character.
      return isPalindrome(text, start, end - 1);
   }
   else
   {
      // Test substring that doesn't contain the first character.
      return isPalindrome(text, start + 1, end);
   }
   }
}
```

You should still supply a method to solve the whole problem—the user of your method shouldn't have to know about the trick with the substring positions. Simply call the helper method with positions that test the entire string:

```
public static boolean isPalindrome(String text)
{
   return isPalindrome(text, 0, text.length() - 1);
}
```

Note that this call is *not* a recursive method call. The isPalindrome(String) method calls the helper method isPalindrome(String, int, int). In this example, we use **overloading** to declare two methods with the same name. The isPalindrome method with just a String parameter variable is the method that we expect the public to use. The second method, with one String and two int parameter variables, is the recursive helper method. If you prefer, you can avoid overloaded methods by choosing a different name for the helper method, such as substringIsPalindrome.

Use the technique of recursive helper methods whenever it is easier to solve a recursive problem that is equivalent to the original problem—but more amenable to a recursive solution.

EXAMPLE CODE   See sec03 of your eText or companion code for the Palindromes class with a helper method.

13.3 The Efficiency of Recursion

As you have seen in this chapter, recursion can be a powerful tool for implementing complex algorithms. On the other hand, recursion can lead to algorithms that perform poorly. In this section, we will analyze the question of when recursion is beneficial and when it is inefficient.

In most cases, iterative and recursive approaches have comparable efficiency.   © pagadesign/iStockphoto.

Consider the Fibonacci sequence: a sequence of numbers defined by the equation

$$f_1 = 1$$
$$f_2 = 1$$
$$f_n = f_{n-1} + f_{n-2}$$

That is, each value of the sequence is the sum of the two preceding values. The first ten terms of the sequence are

$$1, 1, 2, 3, 5, 8, 13, 21, 34, 55$$

It is easy to extend this sequence indefinitely. Just keep appending the sum of the last two values of the sequence. For example, the next entry is $34 + 55 = 89$.

We would like to write a method that computes f_n for any value of n. Here we translate the definition directly into a recursive method.

sec03/RecursiveFib.java

```java
1  import java.util.Scanner;
2
3  /**
4     This program computes Fibonacci numbers using a recursive method.
5  */
6  public class RecursiveFib
7  {
8     public static void main(String[] args)
9     {
10        Scanner in = new Scanner(System.in);
11        System.out.print("Enter n: ");
12        int n = in.nextInt();
13
14        for (int i = 1; i <= n; i++)
15        {
16           long f = fib(i);
17           System.out.println("fib(" + i + ") = " + f);
18        }
19     }
20
21     /**
22        Computes a Fibonacci number.
23        @param n an integer
24        @return the nth Fibonacci number
25     */
26     public static long fib(int n)
27     {
28        if (n <= 2) { return 1; }
29        else { return fib(n - 1) + fib(n - 2); }
30     }
31  }
```

Program Run

```
Enter n: 50
fib(1) = 1
fib(2) = 1
fib(3) = 2
fib(4) = 3
fib(5) = 5
```

```
fib(6) = 8
fib(7) = 13
. . .
fib(50) = 12586269025
```

That is certainly simple, and the method will work correctly. But watch the output closely as you run the test program. The first few calls to the fib method are fast. For larger values, though, the program pauses an amazingly long time between outputs.

That makes no sense. Armed with pencil, paper, and a pocket calculator you could calculate these numbers pretty quickly, so it shouldn't take the computer anywhere near that long.

To find out the problem, let us insert **trace messages** into the method.

sec03/RecursiveFibTracer.java

```java
1   import java.util.Scanner;
2
3   /**
4      This program prints trace messages that show how often the
5      recursive method for computing Fibonacci numbers calls itself.
6   */
7   public class RecursiveFibTracer
8   {
9      public static void main(String[] args)
10     {
11        Scanner in = new Scanner(System.in);
12        System.out.print("Enter n: ");
13        int n = in.nextInt();
14
15        long f = fib(n);
16
17        System.out.println("fib(" + n + ") = " + f);
18     }
19
20     /**
21        Computes a Fibonacci number.
22        @param n an integer
23        @return the nth Fibonacci number
24     */
25     public static long fib(int n)
26     {
27        System.out.println("Entering fib: n = " + n);
28        long f;
29        if (n <= 2) { f = 1; }
30        else { f = fib(n - 1) + fib(n - 2); }
31        System.out.println("Exiting fib: n = " + n
32              + " return value = " + f);
33        return f;
34     }
35  }
```

Program Run

```
Enter n: 6
Entering fib: n = 6
Entering fib: n = 5
Entering fib: n = 4
Entering fib: n = 3
```

```
Entering fib: n = 2
Exiting fib: n = 2 return value = 1
Entering fib: n = 1
Exiting fib: n = 1 return value = 1
Exiting fib: n = 3 return value = 2
Entering fib: n = 2
Exiting fib: n = 2 return value = 1
Exiting fib: n = 4 return value = 3
Entering fib: n = 3
Entering fib: n = 2
Exiting fib: n = 2 return value = 1
Entering fib: n = 1
Exiting fib: n = 1 return value = 1
Exiting fib: n = 3 return value = 2
Exiting fib: n = 5 return value = 5
Entering fib: n = 4
Entering fib: n = 3
Entering fib: n = 2
Exiting fib: n = 2 return value = 1
Entering fib: n = 1
Exiting fib: n = 1 return value = 1
Exiting fib: n = 3 return value = 2
Entering fib: n = 2
Exiting fib: n = 2 return value = 1
Exiting fib: n = 4 return value = 3
Exiting fib: n = 6 return value = 8
fib(6) = 8
```

Figure 2 shows the pattern of recursive calls for computing fib(6). Now it is becoming apparent why the method takes so long. It is computing the same values over and over. For example, the computation of fib(6) calls fib(4) twice and fib(3) three times. That is very different from the computation we would do with pencil and paper. There we would just write down the values as they were computed and add up the last two to get the next one until we reached the desired entry; no sequence value would ever be computed twice.

If we imitate the pencil-and-paper process, then we get the following program:

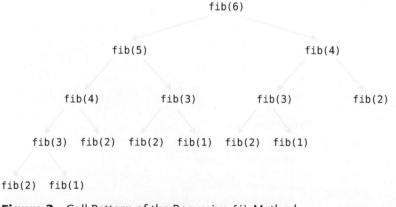

Figure 2   Call Pattern of the Recursive fib Method

sec03/LoopFib.java

```java
1  import java.util.Scanner;
2
3  /**
4     This program computes Fibonacci numbers using an iterative method.
5  */
6  public class LoopFib
7  {
8     public static void main(String[] args)
9     {
10        Scanner in = new Scanner(System.in);
11        System.out.print("Enter n: ");
12        int n = in.nextInt();
13
14        for (int i = 1; i <= n; i++)
15        {
16           long f = fib(i);
17           System.out.println("fib(" + i + ") = " + f);
18        }
19     }
20
21     /**
22        Computes a Fibonacci number.
23        @param n an integer
24        @return the nth Fibonacci number
25     */
26     public static long fib(int n)
27     {
28        if (n <= 2) { return 1; }
29        else
30        {
31           long olderValue = 1;
32           long oldValue = 1;
33           long newValue = 1;
34           for (int i = 3; i <= n; i++)
35           {
36              newValue = oldValue + olderValue;
37              olderValue = oldValue;
38              oldValue = newValue;
39           }
40           return newValue;
41        }
42     }
43  }
```

Program Run

```
Enter n: 50
fib(1) = 1
fib(2) = 1
fib(3) = 2
fib(4) = 3
fib(5) = 5
fib(6) = 8
fib(7) = 13
. . .
fib(50) = 12586269025
```

This method runs *much* faster than the recursive version.

In this example of the `fib` method, the recursive solution was easy to program because it followed the mathematical definition, but it ran far more slowly than the iterative solution, because it computed many intermediate results multiple times.

Can you always speed up a recursive solution by changing it into a loop? Frequently, the iterative and recursive solution have essentially the same performance. For example, here is an iterative solution for the palindrome test:

> Occasionally, a recursive solution is much slower than its iterative counterpart. However, in most cases, the recursive solution is only slightly slower.

```java
public static boolean isPalindrome(String text)
{
   int start = 0;
   int end = text.length() - 1;
   while (start < end)
   {
      char first = Character.toLowerCase(text.charAt(start));
      char last = Character.toLowerCase(text.charAt(end));

      if (Character.isLetter(first) && Character.isLetter(last))
      {
         // Both are letters.
         if (first == last)
         {
            start++;
            end--;
         }
         else { return false; }
      }
      if (!Character.isLetter(last)) { end--; }
      if (!Character.isLetter(first)) { start++; }
   }
   return true;
}
```

This solution keeps two index variables: `start` and `end`. The first index starts at the beginning of the string and is advanced whenever a letter has been matched or a non-letter has been ignored. The second index starts at the end of the string and moves toward the beginning. When the two index variables meet, the iteration stops.

Both the iteration and the recursion run at about the same speed. If a palindrome has n characters, the iteration executes the loop between $n/2$ and n times, depending on how many of the characters are letters, because one or both index variables are moved in each step. Similarly, the recursive solution calls itself between $n/2$ and n times, because one or two characters are removed in each step.

In such a situation, the iterative solution tends to be a bit faster, because each recursive method call takes a certain amount of processor time. In principle, it is possible for a smart compiler to avoid recursive method calls if they follow simple patterns, but most Java compilers don't do that. From that point of view, an iterative solution is preferable.

> In many cases, a recursive solution is easier to understand and implement correctly than an iterative solution.

However, many problems have recursive solutions that are easier to understand and implement correctly than their iterative counterparts. Sometimes there is no obvious iterative solution at all—see the example in the next section. There is a certain elegance and economy of thought to recursive solutions that makes them more appealing. As the computer scientist (and creator of the GhostScript interpreter for the PostScript graphics description language) L. Peter Deutsch put it: "To iterate is human, to recurse divine."

EXAMPLE CODE   See sec03 of your eText or companion code for the LoopPalindromes class.

13.4 Permutations

In this section, we will study a more complex example of recursion that would be difficult to program with a simple loop. (As Exercise ••• P13.6 shows, it is possible to avoid the recursion, but the resulting solution is quite complex, and no faster).

We will design a method that lists all permutations of a string. A permutation is simply a rearrangement of the letters in the string. For example, the string "eat" has six permutations (including the original string itself):

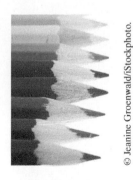

Using recursion, you can find all arrangements of a set of objects.

```
"eat"     "ate"
"eta"     "tea"
"aet"     "tae"
```

Now we need a way to generate the permutations recursively. Consider the string "eat". Let's simplify the problem. First, we'll generate all permutations that start with the letter 'e', then those that start with 'a', and finally those that start with 't'. How do we generate the permutations that start with 'e'? We need to know the permutations of the substring "at". But that's the same problem—to generate all permutations—with a simpler input, namely the shorter string "at". Thus, we can use recursion. Generate the permutations of the substring "at". They are

```
"at"
"ta"
```

For each permutation of that substring, prepend the letter 'e' to get the permutations of "eat" that start with 'e', namely

```
"eat"
"eta"
```

Now let's turn our attention to the permutations of "eat" that start with 'a'. We need to produce the permutations of the remaining letters, "et". They are:

```
"et"
"te"
```

We add the letter 'a' to the front of the strings and obtain

```
"aet"
"ate"
```

We generate the permutations that start with 't' in the same way.

That's the idea. The implementation is fairly straightforward. In the permutations method, we loop through all positions in the word to be permuted. For each of them, we compute the shorter word that is obtained by removing the ith letter:

```
String shorter = word.substring(0, i) + word.substring(i + 1);
```

We compute the permutations of the shorter word:

```
ArrayList<String> shorterPermutations = permutations(shorter);
```

Finally, we add the removed letter to the front of all permutations of the shorter word.

```
for (String s : shorterPermutations)
{
    result.add(word.charAt(i) + s);
}
```

As always, we have to provide a special case for the simplest strings. The simplest possible string is the empty string, which has a single permutation—itself.

Here is the complete Permutations class.

sec04/Permutations.java

```java
 1  import java.util.ArrayList;
 2
 3  /**
 4     This class computes permutations of a string.
 5  */
 6  public class Permutations
 7  {
 8     public static void main(String[] args)
 9     {
10        for (String s : permutations("eat"))
11        {
12           System.out.println(s);
13        }
14     }
15
16     /**
17        Gets all permutations of a given word.
18        @param word the string to permute
19        @return a list of all permutations
20     */
21     public static ArrayList<String> permutations(String word)
22     {
23        ArrayList<String> result = new ArrayList<String>();
24
25        // The empty string has a single permutation: itself
26        if (word.length() == 0)
27        {
28           result.add(word);
29           return result;
30        }
31        else
32        {
33           // Loop through all character positions
34           for (int i = 0; i < word.length(); i++)
35           {
36              // Form a shorter word by removing the ith character
37              String shorter = word.substring(0, i) + word.substring(i + 1);
38
39              // Generate all permutations of the simpler word
40              ArrayList<String> shorterPermutations = permutations(shorter)
41
42              // Add the removed character to the front of
43              // each permutation of the simpler word
44              for (String s : shorterPermutations)
45              {
46                 result.add(word.charAt(i) + s);
47              }
48           }
49           // Return all permutations
50           return result;
51        }
52     }
53  }
```

Program Run

```
eat
eta
aet
ate
tea
tae
```

Compare the Permutations and Triangle classes. Both of them work on the same principle. When they work on a more complex input, they first solve the problem for a simpler input. Then they combine the result for the simpler input with additional work to deliver the results for the more complex input. There really is no particular complexity behind that process as long as you think about the solution on that level only. However, behind the scenes, the simpler input creates even simpler input, which creates yet another simplification, and so on, until one input is so simple that the result can be obtained without further help. It is interesting to think about this process, but it can also be confusing. What's important is that you can focus on the one level that matters—putting a solution together from the slightly simpler problem, ignoring the fact that the simpler problem also uses recursion to get its results.

Computing & Society 13.1 **The Limits of Computation**

Have you ever wondered how your instructor or grader makes sure your programming homework is correct? In all likelihood, they look at your solution and perhaps run it with some test inputs. But usually they have a correct solution available. That suggests that there might be an easier way. Perhaps they could feed your program and their correct program into a "program comparator", a computer program that analyzes both programs and determines whether they both compute the same results. Of course, your solution and the program that is known to be correct need not be identical—what matters is that they produce the same output when given the same input.

How could such a program comparator work? Well, the Java compiler knows how to read a program and make sense of the classes, methods, and statements. So it seems plausible that someone could, with some effort, write a program that reads two Java programs, analyzes what they do, and determines whether they solve the same task. Of course, such a program would be very attractive to instructors, because it could automate the grading process. Thus, even though no such program exists today, it might be tempting to try to develop one and sell it to universities around the world.

However, before you start raising venture capital for such an effort, you should know that theoretical computer scientists have proven that it is impossible to develop such a program, *no matter how hard you try.*

There are quite a few of these unsolvable problems. The first one, called the *halting problem,* was discovered by the British researcher Alan Turing in 1936. Because his research occurred before the first actual computer was constructed, Turing had to devise a theoretical device, the **Turing machine**, to explain how computers could work. The Turing machine consists of a long magnetic tape, a read/write head, and a program that has numbered instructions of the form: "If the current symbol under the head is *x*, then replace it with *y*, move the head one unit left or right, and continue with instruction *n*" (see the figure). Interestingly enough, with only these instructions, you can program just as much as with Java, even though it is incredibly tedious to do

so. Theoretical computer scientists like Turing machines because they can be described using nothing more than the laws of mathematics.

Expressed in terms of Java, the halting problem states: "It is impossible to write a program with two inputs, namely the source code of an arbitrary Java program *P* and a string *I*, that decides whether the program *P*, when executed with the input *I*, will

Alan Turing

Science Photo Library/Photo Researchers.

halt—that is, the program will not get into an infinite loop with the given input". Of course, for some kinds of programs and inputs, it is possible to decide whether the program halts with the given input. The halting problem asserts that it is impossible to come up with a single decision-making algorithm that works with all programs and inputs. Note that you can't simply run the program *P* on the input *I* to settle this question. If the program runs for 1,000 days, you don't know that the program is in an infinite loop. Maybe you just have to wait another day for it to stop.

Such a "halt checker", if it could be written, might also be useful for grading homework. An instructor could use it to screen student submissions to see if they get into an infinite loop with a particular input, and then stop checking them. However, as Turing demonstrated, such a program cannot be written. His argument is ingenious and quite simple.

Suppose a "halt checker" program existed. Let's call it *H*. From *H*, we will develop another program, the "killer" program *K*. *K* does the following computation. Its input is a string containing the source code for a program *R*. It then applies the halt checker on the input program *R* and the input string *R*. That is, it checks whether the program *R* halts if its input is its own source code. It sounds bizarre to feed a program to itself, but it isn't impossible.

For example, the Java compiler is written in Java, and you can use it to compile itself. Or, as a simpler example, a word counting program can count the words in its own source code.

When *K* gets the answer from *H* that *R* halts when applied to itself, it is programmed to enter an infinite loop. Otherwise *K* exits. In Java, the program might look like this:

```java
public class Killer
{
    public static void main(
        String[] args)
    {
        String r = read program input;
        HaltChecker checker =
            new HaltChecker();
```

```java
        if (checker.check(r, r))
        {
            while (true)
            { // Infinite loop
            }
        }
        else
        {
            return;
        }
    }
}
```

Now ask yourself: What does the halt checker answer when asked whether *K* halts when given *K* as the input? Maybe it finds out that *K* gets into an infinite loop with such an input. But wait, that can't be right. That would mean that `checker.check(r, r)` returns false when r is the program code of *K*. As you can plainly see, in that case, the killer method returns, so K didn't get into an infinite loop. That shows that *K* must halt when analyzing itself, so `checker.check(r, r)` should return true. But then the killer method doesn't terminate—it goes into an infi-

nite loop. That shows that it is logically impossible to implement a program that can check whether *every* program halts on a particular input.

It is sobering to know that there are *limits* to computing. There are problems that no computer program, no matter how ingenious, can answer.

Theoretical computer scientists are working on other research involving the nature of computation. One important question that remains unsettled to this day deals with problems that in practice are very time-consuming to solve. It may be that these problems are intrinsically hard, in which case it would be pointless to try to look for better algorithms. Such theoretical research can have important practical applications. For example, right now, nobody knows whether the most common encryption schemes used today could be broken by discovering a new algorithm. Knowing that no fast algorithms exist for breaking a particular code could make us feel more comfortable about the security of encryption.

Program

Instruction number	If tape symbol is	Replace with	Then move head	Then go to instruction
1	0	2	right	2
	1	1	left	4
2	0	0	right	2
	1	1	right	2
	2	0	left	3
3	0	0	left	3
	1	1	left	3
	2	2	right	1
4	1	1	right	5
	2	0	left	4

Control unit

Read/write head

Tape

The Turing Machine

13.5 Mutual Recursion

In a mutual recursion, a set of cooperating methods calls each other repeatedly.

In the preceding examples, a method called itself to solve a simpler problem. Sometimes, a set of cooperating methods calls each other in a recursive fashion. In this section, we will explore such a **mutual recursion**. This technique is significantly more advanced than the simple recursion that we discussed in the preceding sections.

We will develop a program that can compute the values of arithmetic expressions such as

```
3+4*5
(3+4)*5
1-(2-(3-(4-5)))
```

Computing such an expression is complicated by the fact that * and / bind more strongly than + and -, and that parentheses can be used to group subexpressions.

Figure 3 shows a set of **syntax diagrams** that describes the syntax of these expressions. To see how the syntax diagrams work, consider the expression 3+4*5:

- Enter the *expression* syntax diagram. The arrow points directly to *term*, giving you no alternative.
- Enter the *term* syntax diagram. The arrow points to *factor*, again giving you no choice.
- Enter the *factor* diagram. You have two choices: to follow the top branch or the bottom branch. Because the first input token is the number 3 and not a (, follow the bottom branch.
- Accept the input token because it matches the number. The unprocessed input is now +4*5.
- Follow the arrow out of *number* to the end of *factor*. As in a method call, you now back up, returning to the end of the *factor* element of the *term* diagram.
- Now you have another choice—to loop back in the *term* diagram, or to exit. The next input token is a +, and it matches neither the * or the / that would be required to loop back. So you exit, returning to *expression*.

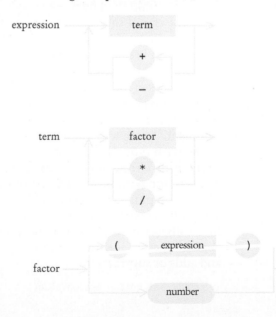

Figure 3
Syntax Diagrams for
Evaluating an Expression

- Again, you have a choice, to loop back or to exit. Now the + matches one of the choices in the loop. Accept the + in the input and move back to the *term* element. The remaining input is 4*5.

In this fashion, an expression is broken down into a sequence of terms, separated by + or -, each term is broken down into a sequence of factors, each separated by * or /, and each factor is either a parenthesized expression or a number. You can draw this breakdown as a tree. Figure 4 shows how the expressions 3+4*5 and (3+4)*5 are derived from the syntax diagram.

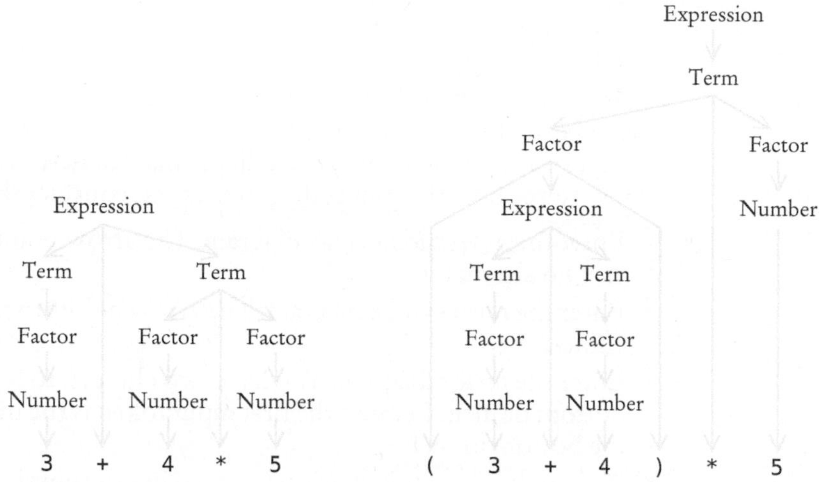

Figure 4 Syntax Trees for Two Expressions

Why do the syntax diagrams help us compute the value of the tree? If you look at the syntax trees, you will see that they accurately represent which operations should be carried out first. In the first tree, 4 and 5 should be multiplied, and then the result should be added to 3. In the second tree, 3 and 4 should be added, and the result should be multiplied by 5.

At the end of this section, you will find the implementation of the Evaluator class, which evaluates these expressions. The Evaluator makes use of an ExpressionTokenizer class, which breaks up an input string into **tokens**—numbers, operators, and parentheses. (For simplicity, we only accept positive integers as numbers, and we don't allow spaces in the input.)

When you call nextToken, the next input token is returned as a string. We also supply another method, peekToken, which allows you to see the next token without consuming it. To see why the peekToken method is necessary, consider the syntax diagram of the term type. If the next token is a "*" or "/", you want to continue adding and subtracting terms. But if the next token is another character, such as a "+" or "-", you want to stop without actually consuming it, so that the token can be considered later.

To compute the value of an expression, we implement three methods: getExpressionValue, getTermValue, and getFactorValue. The getExpressionValue method first calls getTermValue to get the value of the first term of the expression. Then it checks whether the next input token is one of + or -. If so, it calls getTermValue again and adds or subtracts it.

```
public int getExpressionValue()
{
```

```
      int value = getTermValue();
      boolean done = false;
      while (!done)
      {
         String next = tokenizer.peekToken();
         if ("+".equals(next) || "-".equals(next))
         {
            tokenizer.nextToken(); // Discard "+" or "-"
            int value2 = getTermValue();
            if ("+".equals(next)) { value = value + value2; }
            else { value = value - value2; }
         }
         else
         {
            done = true;
         }
      }
      return value;
   }
```

The getTermValue method calls getFactorValue in the same way, multiplying or dividing the factor values.

Finally, the getFactorValue method checks whether the next input is a number, or whether it begins with a (token. In the first case, the value is simply the value of the number. However, in the second case, the getFactorValue method makes a recursive call to getExpressionValue. Thus, the three methods are mutually recursive.

```
public int getFactorValue()
{
   int value;
   String next = tokenizer.peekToken();
   if ("(".equals(next))
   {
      tokenizer.nextToken(); // Discard "("
      value = getExpressionValue();
      tokenizer.nextToken(); // Discard ")"
   }
   else
   {
      value = Integer.parseInt(tokenizer.nextToken());
   }
   return value;
}
```

To see the mutual recursion clearly, trace through the expression (3+4)*5:

- getExpressionValue calls getTermValue
  - getTermValue calls getFactorValue
    - getFactorValue consumes the (input
    - getFactorValue calls getExpressionValue
      - getExpressionValue returns eventually with the value of 7, having consumed 3 + 4. This is the recursive call.
    - getFactorValue consumes the) input
    - getFactorValue returns 7
  - getTermValue consumes the inputs * and 5 and returns 35
- getExpressionValue returns 35

As always with a recursive solution, you need to ensure that the recursion terminates. In this situation, that is easy to see when you consider the situation in which
getExpressionValue calls itself. The second call works on a shorter subexpression than
the original expression. At each recursive call, at least some of the tokens of the input
string are consumed, so eventually the recursion must come to an end.

sec05/Evaluator.java

```java
1   /**
2       A class that can compute the value of an arithmetic expression.
3   */
4   public class Evaluator
5   {
6       private ExpressionTokenizer tokenizer;
7
8       /**
9           Constructs an evaluator.
10          @param anExpression a string containing the expression
11          to be evaluated
12      */
13      public Evaluator(String anExpression)
14      {
15          tokenizer = new ExpressionTokenizer(anExpression);
16      }
17
18      /**
19          Evaluates the expression.
20          @return the value of the expression
21      */
22      public int getExpressionValue()
23      {
24          int value = getTermValue();
25          boolean done = false;
26          while (!done)
27          {
28              String next = tokenizer.peekToken();
29              if ("+".equals(next) || "-".equals(next))
30              {
31                  tokenizer.nextToken(); // Discard "+" or "-"
32                  int value2 = getTermValue();
33                  if ("+".equals(next)) { value = value + value2; }
34                  else { value = value - value2; }
35              }
36              else
37              {
38                  done = true;
39              }
40          }
41          return value;
42      }
43
44      /**
45          Evaluates the next term found in the expression.
46          @return the value of the term
47      */
48      public int getTermValue()
49      {
50          int value = getFactorValue();
51          boolean done = false;
```

```
52          while (!done)
53          {
54             String next = tokenizer.peekToken();
55             if ("*".equals(next) || "/".equals(next))
56             {
57                tokenizer.nextToken();
58                int value2 = getFactorValue();
59                if ("*".equals(next)) { value = value * value2; }
60                else { value = value / value2; }
61             }
62             else
63             {
64                done = true;
65             }
66          }
67          return value;
68       }
69
70       /**
71          Evaluates the next factor found in the expression.
72          @return the value of the factor
73       */
74       public int getFactorValue()
75       {
76          int value;
77          String next = tokenizer.peekToken();
78          if ("(".equals(next))
79          {
80             tokenizer.nextToken(); // Discard "("
81             value = getExpressionValue();
82             tokenizer.nextToken(); // Discard ")"
83          }
84          else
85          {
86             value = Integer.parseInt(tokenizer.nextToken());
87          }
88          return value;
89       }
90    }
```

sec05/ExpressionTokenizer.java

```
1   /**
2      This class breaks up a string describing an expression
3      into tokens: numbers, parentheses, and operators.
4   */
5   public class ExpressionTokenizer
6   {
7      private String input;
8      private int start; // The start of the current token
9      private int end; // The position after the end of the current token
10
11     /**
12        Constructs a tokenizer.
13        @param anInput the string to tokenize
14     */
15     public ExpressionTokenizer(String anInput)
16     {
17        input = anInput;
18        start = 0;
```

```
19        end = 0;
20        nextToken(); // Find the first token
21     }
22
23     /**
24        Peeks at the next token without consuming it.
25        @return the next token or null if there are no more tokens
26     */
27     public String peekToken()
28     {
29        if (start >= input.length()) { return null; }
30        else { return input.substring(start, end); }
31     }
32
33     /**
34        Gets the next token and moves the tokenizer to the following token.
35        @return the next token or null if there are no more tokens
36     */
37     public String nextToken()
38     {
39        String r = peekToken();
40        start = end;
41        if (start >= input.length()) { return r; }
42        if (Character.isDigit(input.charAt(start)))
43        {
44           end = start + 1;
45           while (end < input.length()
46                 && Character.isDigit(input.charAt(end)))
47           {
48              end++;
49           }
50        }
51        else
52        {
53           end = start + 1;
54        }
55        return r;
56     }
57  }
```

sec05/ExpressionCalculator.java

```
1   import java.util.Scanner;
2
3   /**
4      This program calculates the value of an expression
5      consisting of numbers, arithmetic operators, and parentheses.
6   */
7   public class ExpressionCalculator
8   {
9      public static void main(String[] args)
10     {
11        Scanner in = new Scanner(System.in);
12        System.out.print("Enter an expression: ");
13        String input = in.nextLine();
14        Evaluator e = new Evaluator(input);
15        int value = e.getExpressionValue();
16        System.out.println(input + "=" + value);
17     }
18  }
```

Program Run

```
Enter an expression: 3+4*5
3+4*5=23
```

13.6 Backtracking

Backtracking examines partial solutions, abandoning unsuitable ones and returning to consider other candidates.

Backtracking is a problem solving technique that builds up partial solutions that get increasingly closer to the goal. If a partial solution cannot be completed, one abandons it and returns to examining the other candidates.

Backtracking can be used to solve crossword puzzles, escape from mazes, or find solutions to systems that are constrained by rules. In order to employ backtracking for a particular problem, we need two characteristic properties:

1. A procedure to examine a partial solution and determine whether to
   - Accept it as an actual solution.
   - Abandon it (either because it violates some rules or because it is clear that it can never lead to a valid solution).
   - Continue extending it.
2. A procedure to extend a partial solution, generating one or more solutions that come closer to the goal.

Backtracking can then be expressed with the following recursive algorithm:

Solve(partialSolution)
> *Examine(partialSolution).*
> *If accepted*
>> *Add partialSolution to the list of solutions.*
> *Else if continuing*
>> *For each p in extend(partialSolution)*
>>> *Solve(p).*

Of course, the processes of examining and extending a partial solution depend on the nature of the problem.

As an example, we will develop a program that finds all solutions to the eight queens problem: the task of positioning eight queens on a chess board so that none of

In a backtracking algorithm, one explores all paths toward a solution. When one path is a dead end, one needs to backtrack and try another choice.

© Lanica Klein/iStockphoto.

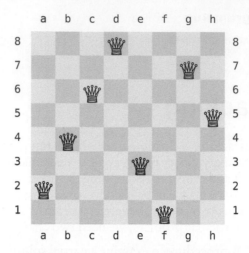

Figure 5 A Solution to the Eight Queens Problem

them attacks another according to the rules of chess. In other words, there are no two queens on the same row, column, or diagonal. Figure 5 shows a solution.

In this problem, it is easy to examine a partial solution. If two queens attack another, reject it. Otherwise, if it has eight queens, accept it. Otherwise, continue.

It is also easy to extend a partial solution. Simply add another queen on an empty square.

However, in the interest of efficiency, we will be a bit more systematic about the extension process. We will place the first queen in row 1, the next queen in row 2, and so on.

We provide a class `PartialSolution` that collects the queens in a partial solution, and that has methods to examine and extend the solution:

```
public class PartialSolution
{
   private Queen[] queens;

   public int examine() { . . . }
   public PartialSolution[] extend() { . . . }
}
```

The examine method simply checks whether two queens attack each other:

```
public int examine()
{
   for (int i = 0; i < queens.length; i++)
   {
      for (int j = i + 1; j < queens.length; j++)
      {
         if (queens[i].attacks(queens[j])) { return ABANDON; }
      }
   }
   if (queens.length == NQUEENS) { return ACCEPT; }
   else { return CONTINUE; }
}
```

The extend method takes a given solution and makes eight copies of it. Each copy gets a new queen in a different column.

```
public PartialSolution[] extend()
{
   // Generate a new solution for each column
   PartialSolution[] result = new PartialSolution[NQUEENS];
   for (int i = 0; i < result.length; i++)
   {
      int size = queens.length;

      // The new solution has one more row than this one
      result[i] = new PartialSolution(size + 1);

      // Copy this solution into the new one
      for (int j = 0; j < size; j++)
      {
         result[i].queens[j] = queens[j];
      }

      // Append the new queen into the ith column
      result[i].queens[size] = new Queen(size, i);
   }
   return result;
}
```

You will find the Queen class at the end of the section. The only challenge is to determine when two queens attack each other diagonally. Here is an easy way of checking that. Compute the slope and check whether it is ±1. This condition can be simplified as follows:

$$(\text{row}_2 - \text{row}_1)/(\text{column}_2 - \text{column}_1) = \pm 1$$

$$\text{row}_2 - \text{row}_1 = \pm(\text{column}_2 - \text{column}_1)$$

$$|\text{row}_2 - \text{row}_1| = |\text{column}_2 - \text{column}_1|$$

Have a close look at the solve method in the EightQueens class on page 474. The method is a straightforward translation of the pseudocode for backtracking. Note how there

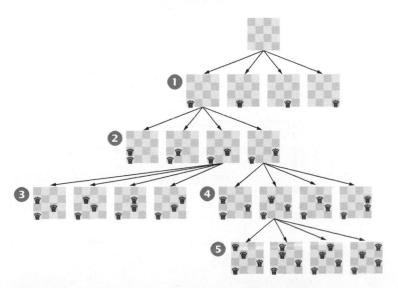

Figure 6 Backtracking in the Four Queens Problem

is nothing specific about the eight queens problem in this method—it works for any partial solution with an examine and extend method (see Exercise •• E13.23).

Figure 6 shows the solve method in action for a four queens problem. Starting from a blank board, there are four partial solutions with a queen in row 1 ❶. When the queen is in column 1, there are four partial solutions with a queen in row 2 ❷. Two of them are abandoned immediately. The other two lead to partial solutions with three queens ❸ and ❹, all but one of which are abandoned. One partial solution is extended to four queens, but all of those are abandoned as well ❺. Then the algorithm backtracks, giving up on a queen in position a1, instead extending the solution with the queen in position b1 (not shown).

When you run the program, it lists 92 solutions, including the one in Figure 5. Exercise ••• E13.24 asks you to remove those that are rotations or reflections of another.

sec06/PartialSolution.java

```java
import java.util.Arrays;

/**
    A partial solution to the eight queens puzzle.
*/
public class PartialSolution
{
    private Queen[] queens;
    private static final int NQUEENS = 8;

    public static final int ACCEPT = 1;
    public static final int ABANDON = 2;
    public static final int CONTINUE = 3;

    /**
        Constructs a partial solution of a given size.
        @param size the size
    */
    public PartialSolution(int size)
    {
        queens = new Queen[size];
    }

    /**
        Examines a partial solution.
        @return one of ACCEPT, ABANDON, CONTINUE
    */
    public int examine()
    {
        for (int i = 0; i < queens.length; i++)
        {
            for (int j = i + 1; j < queens.length; j++)
            {
                if (queens[i].attacks(queens[j])) { return ABANDON; }
            }
        }
        if (queens.length == NQUEENS) { return ACCEPT; }
        else { return CONTINUE; }
    }
```

```
41     /**
42         Yields all extensions of this partial solution.
43         @return an array of partial solutions that extend this solution.
44     */
45     public PartialSolution[] extend()
46     {
47         // Generate a new solution for each column
48         PartialSolution[] result = new PartialSolution[NQUEENS];
49         for (int i = 0; i < result.length; i++)
50         {
51             int size = queens.length;
52
53             // The new solution has one more row than this one
54             result[i] = new PartialSolution(size + 1);
55
56             // Copy this solution into the new one
57             for (int j = 0; j < size; j++)
58             {
59                 result[i].queens[j] = queens[j];
60             }
61
62             // Append the new queen into the ith column
63             result[i].queens[size] = new Queen(size, i);
64         }
65         return result;
66     }
67
68     public String toString() { return Arrays.toString(queens); }
69 }
```

sec06/Queen.java

```
1  /**
2      A queen in the eight queens problem.
3  */
4  public class Queen
5  {
6      private int row;
7      private int column;
8
9      /**
10         Constructs a queen at a given position.
11         @param r the row
12         @param c the column
13     */
14     public Queen(int r, int c)
15     {
16         row = r;
17         column = c;
18     }
19
20     /**
21         Checks whether this queen attacks another.
22         @param other the other queen
23         @return true if this and the other queen are in the same
24         row, column, or diagonal
25     */
26     public boolean attacks(Queen other)
27     {
```

```
28         return row == other.row
29            || column == other.column
30            || Math.abs(row - other.row) == Math.abs(column - other.column);
31      }
32
33      public String toString()
34      {
35         return "" + "abcdefgh".charAt(column) + (row + 1) ;
36      }
37 }
```

sec06/EightQueens.java

```
1  /**
2      This class solves the eight queens problem using backtracking.
3  */
4  public class EightQueens
5  {
6      public static void main(String[] args)
7      {
8         solve(new PartialSolution(0));
9      }
10
11      /**
12         Prints all solutions to the problem that can be extended from
13         a given partial solution.
14         @param sol the partial solution
15      */
16      public static void solve(PartialSolution sol)
17      {
18         int exam = sol.examine();
19         if (exam == PartialSolution.ACCEPT)
20         {
21            System.out.println(sol);
22         }
23         else if (exam == PartialSolution.CONTINUE)
24         {
25            for (PartialSolution p : sol.extend())
26            {
27               solve(p);
28            }
29         }
30      }
31 }
```

Program Run

```
 [a1, e2, h3, f4, c5, g6, b7, d8]
 [a1, f2, h3, c4, g5, d6, b7, e8]
 [a1, g2, d3, f4, h5, b6, e7, c8]
  . . .
 [f1, a2, e3, b4, h5, c6, g7, d8]
  . . .
 [h1, c2, a3, f4, b5, e6, g7, d8]
 [h1, d2, a3, c4, f5, b6, g7, e8]
```
(92 solutions)

WORKED EXAMPLE 13.2

Towers of Hanoi

No discussion of recursion would be complete without the "Towers of Hanoi". Learn how to solve this classic puzzle with an elegant recursive solution. See your eText or visit wiley.com/go/bjeo7.

CHAPTER SUMMARY

Understand the control flow in a recursive computation.

- A recursive computation solves a problem by using the solution to the same problem with simpler inputs.
- For a recursion to terminate, there must be special cases for the simplest values.

Identify recursive helper methods for solving a problem.

- Sometimes it is easier to find a recursive solution if you make a slight change to the original problem.

Contrast the efficiency of recursive and non-recursive algorithms.

- Occasionally, a recursive solution is much slower than its iterative counterpart. However, in most cases, the recursive solution is only slightly slower.
- In many cases, a recursive solution is easier to understand and implement correctly than an iterative solution.

Review a complex recursion example that cannot be solved with a simple loop.

- The permutations of a string can be obtained more naturally through recursion than with a loop.

Recognize the phenomenon of mutual recursion in an expression evaluator.

- In a mutual recursion, a set of cooperating methods calls each other repeatedly.

Use backtracking to solve problems that require trying out multiple paths.

- Backtracking examines partial solutions, abandoning unsuitable ones and returning to consider other candidates.

REVIEW EXERCISES

- **R13.1** Define the terms
  - **a.** Recursion
  - **b.** Iteration
  - **c.** Infinite recursion
  - **d.** Recursive helper method

- **R13.2** To compute the sum of the values in an array, add the first value to the sum of the remaining values, computing recursively. Design a recursive helper method to solve this problem.

- **R13.3** How can you write a recursive method `public static void sum(int[] a)` without needing a helper function? Why is this less efficient?

- **R13.4** Outline, but do not implement, a recursive solution for finding the smallest value in an array.

- **R13.5** Outline, but do not implement, a recursive solution for finding the kth smallest element in an array. *Hint:* Look at the elements that are less than the initial element. Suppose there are m of them. How should you proceed if $k \leq m$? If $k > m$?

- **R13.6** Outline, but do not implement, a recursive solution for sorting an array of numbers. *Hint:* First find the smallest value in the array.

- **R13.7** Outline, but do not implement, a recursive solution for sorting an array of numbers. *Hint:* First sort the subarray without the initial element.

- **R13.8** Write a recursive definition of x^n, where $n \geq 0$, similar to the recursive definition of the Fibonacci numbers. *Hint:* How do you compute x^n from x^{n-1}? How does the recursion terminate?

- **R13.9** Improve upon Exercise • R13.8 by computing x^n as $(x^{n/2})^2$ if n is even. Why is this approach significantly faster? *Hint:* Compute x^{1023} and x^{1024} both ways.

- **R13.10** Write a recursive definition of $n! = 1 \times 2 \times \cdots \times n$, similar to the recursive definition of the Fibonacci numbers.

- **R13.11** Find out how often the recursive version of `fib` calls itself. Keep a static variable `fibCount` and increment it once in every call to `fib`. What is the relationship between `fib(n)` and `fibCount`?

- **R13.12** Let moves(n) be the number of moves required to solve the Towers of Hanoi problem (see Worked Example 13.2). Find a formula that expresses moves(n) in terms of moves($n-1$). Then show that moves(n) = $2^n - 1$.

- **R13.13** Outline, but do not implement, a recursive solution for generating all subsets of the set $\{1, 2, \ldots, n\}$.

- **R13.14** Exercise ••• P13.6 shows an iterative way of generating all permutations of the sequence $(0, 1, \ldots, n-1)$. Explain why the algorithm produces the correct result.

- **R13.15** Trace the expression evaluator program from Section 13.5 with inputs 3 − 4 + 5, 3 − (4 + 5), (3 − 4) * 5, and 3 * 4 + 5 * 6.

PRACTICE EXERCISES

■ **E13.1** Given a class Rectangle with instance variables width and height, provide a recursive getArea method. Construct a rectangle whose width is one less than the original and call its getArea method.

■■ **E13.2** Given a class Square with an instance variable width, provide a recursive getArea method. Construct a square whose width is one less than the original and call its getArea method.

■ **E13.3** In some cultures, numbers containing the digit 8 are lucky numbers. What is wrong with the following method that tries to test whether a number is lucky?

```
public static boolean isLucky(int number)
{
    int lastDigit = number % 10;
    if (lastDigit == 8) { return true; }
    else
    {
        return isLucky(number / 10); // Test the number without the last digit
    }
}
```

■ **E13.4** Write a recursive method for factoring an integer n. First, find a factor f, then recursively factor n/f.

■ **E13.5** Write a recursive method for computing a string with the binary digits of a number. If n is even, then the last digit is 0. If n is odd, then the last digit is 1. Recursively obtain the remaining digits.

■ **E13.6** Write a recursive method String reverse(String text) that reverses a string. For example, reverse("Hello!") returns the string "!olleH". Implement a recursive solution by removing the first character, reversing the remaining text, and combining the two.

■■ **E13.7** Redo Exercise • E13.6 with a recursive helper method that reverses a substring of the message text.

■ **E13.8** Implement the reverse method of Exercise • E13.6 as an iteration.

■■ **E13.9** Use recursion to implement a method

```
public static boolean find(String text, String str)
```

that tests whether a given text contains a string. For example, find("Mississippi", "sip") returns true.

Hint: If the text starts with the string you want to match, then you are done. If not, consider the text that you obtain by removing the first character.

■■ **E13.10** Use recursion to implement a method

```
public static int indexOf(String text, String str)
```

that returns the starting position of the first substring of the text that matches str. Return −1 if str is not a substring of the text.

For example, s.indexOf("Mississippi", "sip") returns 6.

Hint: This is a bit trickier than Exercise •• E13.9, because you must keep track of how far the match is from the beginning of the text. Make that value a parameter variable of a helper method.

- **E13.11** Using recursion, find the largest element in an array.

  Hint: Find the largest element in the subset containing all but the last element. Then compare that maximum to the value of the last element.

- **E13.12** Using recursion, compute the sum of all values in an array.

- ■■ **E13.13** Using recursion, compute the area of a polygon. Cut off a triangle and use the fact that a triangle with corners (x_1, y_1), (x_2, y_2), (x_3, y_3) has area

  $$\frac{\left| x_1 y_2 + x_2 y_3 + x_3 y_1 - y_1 x_2 - y_2 x_3 - y_3 x_1 \right|}{2}$$

- ■■ **E13.14** The following method was known to the ancient Greeks for computing square roots. Given a value $x > 0$ and a guess g for the square root, a better guess is $(g + x/g) / 2$. Write a recursive helper method `public static squareRootGuess(double x, double g)`. If g^2 is approximately equal to x, return g, otherwise, return `squareRootGuess` with the better guess. Then write a method `public static squareRoot(double x)` that uses the helper method.

- ■■■ **E13.15** Implement a `SubstringGenerator` that generates all substrings of a string. For example, the substrings of the string `"rum"` are the seven strings

  `"r"`, `"ru"`, `"rum"`, `"u"`, `"um"`, `"m"`, `""`

  Hint: First enumerate all substrings that start with the first character. There are n of them if the string has length n. Then enumerate the substrings of the string that you obtain by removing the first character.

- ■■■ **E13.16** Implement a `SubsetGenerator` that generates all subsets of the characters of a string. For example, the subsets of the characters of the string `"rum"` are the eight strings

  `"rum"`, `"ru"`, `"rm"`, `"r"`, `"um"`, `"u"`, `"m"`, `""`

  Note that the subsets don't have to be substrings—for example, `"rm"` isn't a substring of `"rum"`.

- ■■■ **E13.17** Recursively generate all ways in which an array list can be split up into a sequence of nonempty sublists. For example, if you are given the array list [1, 7, 2, 9], return the following lists of lists:

  ```
  [[1], [7], [2], [9]], [[1, 7], [2], [9]], [[1], [7, 2], [9]], [[1, 7, 2], [9]],
  [[1], [7], [2, 9]], [[1, 7], [2, 9]], [[1], [7, 2, 9]], [[1, 7, 2, 9]]
  ```

  Hint: First generate all sublists of the list with the last element removed. The last element can either be a subsequence of length 1, or it can be added to the last subsequence.

- ■■ **E13.18** Given an array list a of integers, recursively find all lists of elements of a whose sum is a given integer n.

- ■■ **E13.19** Suppose you want to climb a staircase with n steps and you can take either one or two steps at a time. Recursively enumerate all paths. For example, if n is 5, the possible paths are:

  ```
  [1, 2, 3, 4, 5], [1, 3, 4, 5], [1, 2, 4, 5], [1, 2, 3, 5], [1, 4, 5]
  ```

- ■■■ **E13.20** Repeat Exercise •• E13.19, where the climber can take up to k steps at a time.

- - **E13.21** Given an integer price, list all possible ways of paying for it with $100, $20, $5, and $1 bills, using recursion. Don't list duplicates.

- - **E13.22** Extend the expression evaluator in Section 13.5 so that it can handle the % operator as well as a "raise to a power" operator ^. For example, 2 ^ 3 should evaluate to 8. As in mathematics, raising to a power should bind more strongly than multiplication: 5 * 2 ^ 3 is 40.

- - **E13.23** The backtracking algorithm will work for any problem whose partial solutions can be examined and extended. Provide a PartialSolution interface type with methods examine and extend, a solve method that works with this interface type, and a class EightQueensPartialSolution that implements the interface.

- - - **E13.24** Refine the program for solving the eight queens problem so that rotations and reflections of previously displayed solutions are not shown. Your program should display twelve unique solutions.

- - - **E13.25** Refine the program for solving the eight queens problem so that the solutions are written to an HTML file, using tables with black and white background for the board and the Unicode character ♕ '\u2655' for the white queen.

- - **E13.26** Generalize the program for solving the eight queens problem to the n queens problem. Your program should prompt for the value of n and display the solutions.

- - **E13.27** Using backtracking, write a program that solves summation puzzles in which each letter should be replaced by a digit, such as

      send + more = money

   Your program should find the solution 9567 + 1085 = 10652. Other examples are base + ball = games and kyoto + osaka = tokyo.

   Hint: In a partial solution, some of the letters have been replaced with digits. In the third example, you would consider all partial solutions where k is replaced by 0, 1, ... 9: 0yoto + osa0a = to0yo, 1yoto + osa1a = to1yo, and so on. To extend a partial solution, find the first letter and replace all instances with a digit that doesn't yet occur in the partial solution. If a partial solution has no more letters, check whether the sum is correct.

- - **E13.28** The recursive computation of Fibonacci numbers can be speeded up significantly by keeping track of the values that have already been computed. Provide an implementation of the fib method that uses this strategy. Whenever you return a new value, also store it in an auxiliary array. However, before embarking on a computation, consult the array to find whether the result has already been computed. Compare the running time of your improved implementation with that of the original recursive implementation and the loop implementation.

PROGRAMMING PROJECTS

- - **P13.1** Using the isPalindrome method from Section 13.2 and a recursive reverse method from Exercise • E13.6, write a program to address the following mathematical hypothesis.

   It is believed (but not proven) that, given any decimal number, adding the number and its reversal, will eventually reach a palindrome. For example,

$$89 + 98 = 187$$
$$187 + 781 = 968$$
$$968 + 869 = 1837$$

. . .

$$1801200002107 + 7012000021081 = 8813200023188$$

Write a program that follows this process, starting with a random big integer

```
new BigInteger(16, new java.util.Random())
```

■■ **P13.2** Phone numbers and PIN codes can be easier to remember when you find words that spell out the number on a standard phone pad. For example, instead of remembering the combination 5282, you can just think of JAVA.

Write a recursive method that, given a number, yields all possible spellings (which may or may not be real words).

■■ **P13.3** Continue Exercise •• P13.2, checking the words against the /usr/share/dict/words file on your computer, or the words.txt file in the companion code for this book. For a given number, return only actual words.

■■■ **P13.4** With a longer number, you may need more than one word to remember it on a phone pad. For example, 263-346-5282 is CODE IN JAVA. Using your work from Exercise •• P13.3, write a program that, given any number, lists all word sequences that spell the number on a phone pad.

■■■ **P13.5** Change the permutations method of Section 13.4 (which computed all permutations at once) to a PermutationIterator (which computes them one at a time).

```
public class PermutationIterator
{
    public PermutationIterator(String s) { . . . }
    public String nextPermutation() { . . . }
    public boolean hasMorePermutations() { . . . }
}
```

Here is how you would print out all permutations of the string "eat":

```
PermutationIterator iter = new PermutationIterator("eat");
while (iter.hasMorePermutations())
{
    System.out.println(iter.nextPermutation());
}
```

Now we need a way to iterate through the permutations recursively. Consider the string "eat". As before, we'll generate all permutations that start with the letter 'e', then those that start with 'a', and finally those that start with 't'. How do we generate the permutations that start with 'e'? Make another PermutationIterator object (called tailIterator) that iterates through the permutations of the substring "at". In the nextPermutation method, simply ask tailIterator what *its* next permutation is, and then add the 'e' at the front. However, there is one special case. When the tail generator runs out of permutations, all permutations that start with the current letter have been enumerated. Then

- Increment the current position.
- Compute the tail string that contains all letters except for the current one.
- Make a new permutation iterator for the tail string.

You are done when the current position has reached the end of the string.

■■■ **P13.6** The following class generates all permutations of the numbers 0, 1, 2, ..., $n-1$, without using recursion.

```java
public class NumberPermutationIterator
{
   private int[] a;

   public NumberPermutationIterator(int n)
   {
      a = new int[n];
      done = false;
      for (int i = 0; i < n; i++) { a[i] = i; }
   }

   public int[] nextPermutation()
   {
      if (a.length <= 1) { return a; }

      for (int i = a.length - 1; i > 0; i--)
      {
         if (a[i - 1] < a[i])
         {
            int j = a.length - 1;
            while (a[i - 1] > a[j]) { j--; }
            swap(i - 1, j);
            reverse(i, a.length - 1);
            return a;
         }
      }
      return a;
   }

   public boolean hasMorePermutations()
   {
      if (a.length <= 1) { return false; }
      for (int i = a.length - 1; i > 0; i--)
      {
         if (a[i - 1] < a[i]) { return true; }
      }
      return false;
   }

   public void swap(int i, int j)
   {
      int temp = a[i];
      a[i] = a[j];
      a[j] = temp;
   }

   public void reverse(int i, int j)
   {
      while (i < j) { swap(i, j); i++; j--; }
   }
}
```

The algorithm uses the fact that the set to be permuted consists of distinct numbers. Thus, you cannot use the same algorithm to compute the permutations of the characters in a string. You can, however, use this class to get all permutations of the character positions and then compute a string whose ith character is `word.charAt(a[i])`. Use this approach to reimplement the `PermutationIterator` of Exercise ●●● P13.5 without recursion.

■■■ P13.7 Implement an iterator that produces the moves for the Towers of Hanoi puzzle described in Worked Example 13.2. Provide methods hasMoreMoves and nextMove. The nextMove method should yield a string describing the next move. For example, the following code prints all moves needed to move five disks from peg 1 to peg 3:

```
DiskMover mover = new DiskMover(5, 1, 3);
while (mover.hasMoreMoves())
{
    System.out.println(mover.nextMove());
}
```

Hint: A disk mover that moves a single disk from one peg to another simply has a nextMove method that returns a string

```
Move disk from peg source to target
```

A disk mover with more than one disk to move must work harder. It needs another DiskMover to help it move the first $d - 1$ disks. Then nextMove asks that disk mover for its next move until it is done. Then the nextMove method issues a command to move the dth disk. Finally, it constructs another disk mover that generates the remaining moves.

It helps to keep track of the state of the disk mover:

- BEFORE_LARGEST: A helper mover moves the smaller pile to the other peg.
- LARGEST: Move the largest disk from the source to the destination.
- AFTER_LARGEST: The helper mover moves the smaller pile from the other peg to the target.
- DONE: All moves are done.

■■■ P13.8 *Escaping a Maze.* You are currently located inside a maze. The walls of the maze are indicated by asterisks (*).

```
* *******
*     * *
* ***** *
* * *   *
* * *** *
*   *   *
*** * * *
*     * *
******* *
```

Use the following recursive approach to check whether you can escape from the maze: If you are at an exit, return true. Recursively check whether you can escape from one of the empty neighboring locations without visiting the current location. This method merely tests whether there is a path out of the maze. Extra credit if you can print out a path that leads to an exit.

■■ P13.9 Using backtracking, write a program to find whether a given word can be spelled with symbols for the chemical elements. For example, brother can be spelled as Br O Th Er, the symbols for bromium, oxygen, thorium, and erbium.

■■ P13.10 Using the PartialSolution interface and solve method from Exercise ■■ E13.23, provide a class MazePartialSolution for solving the maze escape problem of Exercise ■■■ P13.8.

■■■ P13.11 The expression evaluator in Section 13.5 returns the value of an expression. Modify the evaluator so that it returns an instance of the Expression interface with five implementing classes, Constant, Sum, Difference, Product, and Quotient. The Expression interface has a method int value(). The Constant class stores a number, which is returned by the value method. The other four classes store two arguments of type Expression, and their value method returns the sum, difference, product, and quotient of the values of the arguments. Write a test program that reads an expression string, translates it into an Expression object, and prints the result of calling value.

■■■ P13.12   Refine the expression evaluator of Exercise ••• P13.11 so that expressions can contain the variable x. For example, 3*x*x+4*x+5 is a valid expression. Change the Expression interface so that its value method has as parameter the value that x should take. Add a class Variable that denotes an x. Write a program that reads an expression string and a value for x, translates the expression string into an Expression object, and prints the result of calling value(x).

■■ P13.13   Add a toString method to the Expression class (as described in Exercise ••• P13.11 and Exercise ••• P13.12) that returns a string representation of the expression. It is ok to use more parentheses than required in mathematical notation. For example, for the expression 3*x*x+5, you can print (((3*x)*x)+5).

■■■ P13.14   Write a program that reads an expression involving integers and the variable x into an Expression object, and then computes the derivative. Add a method Expression derivative() to the Expression interface. Use the rules from calculus for computing the derivative of a sum, difference, product, quotient, constant, or variable. Don't simplify the result. Print the resulting expression. For example, when reading x * x, you should print ((1*x)+(x*1)).

■■■ Graphics P13.15   *The Koch Snowflake.* A snowflake-like shape is recursively defined as follows. Start with an equilateral triangle:

Next, increase the size by a factor of three and replace each straight line with four line segments:

Repeat the process:

Write a program that draws the iterations of the snowflake shape. Supply a button that, when clicked, produces the next iteration.

SORTING AND SEARCHING

© Volkan Ersoy/iStockphoto.

CHAPTER GOALS

To study several sorting and searching algorithms

To appreciate that algorithms for the same task can differ widely in performance

To understand the big-Oh notation

To estimate and compare the performance of algorithms

To write code to measure the running time of a program

CHAPTER CONTENTS

One of the most common tasks in data processing is sorting. For example, an array of employees often needs to be displayed in alphabetical order or sorted by salary. In this chapter, you will learn several sorting methods as well as techniques for comparing their performance. These techniques are useful not just for sorting algorithms, but also for analyzing other algorithms.

Once an array of elements is sorted, one can rapidly locate individual elements. You will study the *binary search* algorithm that carries out this fast lookup.

14.1 Selection Sort

In this section, we show you the first of several sorting algorithms. A *sorting algorithm* rearranges the elements of a collection so that they are stored in sorted order. To keep the examples simple, we will discuss how to sort an array of integers before going on to sorting strings or more complex data. Consider the following array a:

```
    [0] [1] [2] [3] [4]
    11   9  17   5  12
```

An obvious first step is to find the smallest element. In this case the smallest element is 5, stored in a[3]. We should move the 5 to the beginning of the array. Of course, there is already an element stored in a[0], namely 11. Therefore we cannot simply move a[3] into a[0] without moving the 11 somewhere else. We don't yet know where the 11 should end up, but we know for certain that it should not be in a[0]. We simply get it out of the way by *swapping* it with a[3]:

```
    [0] [1] [2] [3] [4]
     5   9  17  11  12
```

Now the first element is in the correct place. The darker color in the figure indicates the portion of the array that is already sorted.

In selection sort, pick the smallest element and swap it with the first one. Pick the smallest element of the remaining ones and swap it with the next one, and so on.

© Zone Creative/iStockphoto.

Next we take the minimum of the remaining entries a[1] . . . a[4]. That minimum value, 9, is already in the correct place. We don't need to do anything in this case and can simply extend the sorted area by one to the right:

Repeat the process. The minimum value of the unsorted region is 11, which needs to be swapped with the first value of the unsorted region, 17:

Now the unsorted region is only two elements long, but we keep to the same successful strategy. The minimum value is 12, and we swap it with the first value, 17:

That leaves us with an unprocessed region of length 1, but of course a region of length 1 is always sorted. We are done.

Let's program this algorithm, called **selection sort**. For this program, as well as the other programs in this chapter, we will use a utility method to generate an array with random entries. We place it into a class ArrayUtil so that we don't have to repeat the code in every example. To show the array, we call the static toString method of the Arrays class in the Java library and print the resulting string (see Section 7.3.4). We also add a method for swapping elements to the ArrayUtil class. (See Section 7.3.8 for details about swapping array elements.)

This algorithm will sort any array of integers. If speed were not an issue, or if there were no better sorting method available, we could stop the discussion of sorting right here. As the next section shows, however, this algorithm, while entirely correct, shows disappointing performance when run on a large data set.

Special Topic 14.2 discusses insertion sort, another simple sorting algorithm.

sec01/SelectionSorter.java

```java
1  /**
2     The sort method of this class sorts an array, using the selection
3     sort algorithm.
4  */
5  public class SelectionSorter
6  {
7     /**
8        Sorts an array, using selection sort.
9        @param a the array to sort
10    */
11    public static void sort(int[] a)
12    {
13       for (int i = 0; i < a.length - 1; i++)
14       {
15          int minPos = minimumPosition(a, i);
16          ArrayUtil.swap(a, minPos, i);
17       }
18    }
```

```
19
20      /**
21          Finds the smallest element in a tail range of the array.
22          @param a the array to sort
23          @param from the first position in a to compare
24          @return the position of the smallest element in the
25          range a[from] . . . a[a.length - 1]
26      */
27      private static int minimumPosition(int[] a, int from)
28      {
29          int minPos = from;
30          for (int i = from + 1; i < a.length; i++)
31          {
32              if (a[i] < a[minPos]) { minPos = i; }
33          }
34          return minPos;
35      }
36 }
```

sec01/SelectionSortDemo.java

```
 1  import java.util.Arrays;
 2
 3  /**
 4      This program demonstrates the selection sort algorithm by
 5      sorting an array that is filled with random numbers.
 6  */
 7  public class SelectionSortDemo
 8  {
 9      public static void main(String[] args)
10      {
11          int[] a = ArrayUtil.randomIntArray(20, 100);
12          System.out.println(Arrays.toString(a));
13
14          SelectionSorter.sort(a);
15
16          System.out.println(Arrays.toString(a));
17      }
18  }
```

sec01/ArrayUtil.java

```
 1  import java.util.Random;
 2
 3  /**
 4      This class contains utility methods for array manipulation.
 5  */
 6  public class ArrayUtil
 7  {
 8      private static Random generator = new Random();
 9
10      /**
11          Creates an array filled with random values.
12          @param length the length of the array
13          @param n the number of possible random values
14          @return an array filled with length numbers between
15          0 and n - 1
16      */
17      public static int[] randomIntArray(int length, int n)
18      {
```

```
19          int[] a = new int[length];
20          for (int i = 0; i < a.length; i++)
21          {
22              a[i] = generator.nextInt(n);
23          }
24
25          return a;
26      }
27
28      /**
29          Swaps two entries of an array.
30          @param a the array
31          @param i the first position to swap
32          @param j the second position to swap
33      */
34      public static void swap(int[] a, int i, int j)
35      {
36          int temp = a[i];
37          a[i] = a[j];
38          a[j] = temp;
39      }
40  }
```

Program Run

```
[65, 46, 14, 52, 38, 2, 96, 39, 14, 33, 13, 4, 24, 99, 89, 77, 73, 87, 36, 81]
[2, 4, 13, 14, 14, 24, 33, 36, 38, 39, 46, 52, 65, 73, 77, 81, 87, 89, 96, 99]
```

14.2 Profiling the Selection Sort Algorithm

To measure the performance of a program, you could simply run it and use a stopwatch to measure how long it takes. However, most of our programs run very quickly, and it is not easy to time them accurately in this way. Furthermore, when a program takes a noticeable time to run, a certain amount of that time may simply be used for loading the program from disk into memory and displaying the result (for which we should not penalize it).

In order to measure the running time of an algorithm more accurately, we will create a StopWatch class. This class works like a real stopwatch. You can start it, stop it, and read out the elapsed time. The class uses the System.currentTimeMillis method, which returns the milliseconds that have elapsed since midnight at the start of January 1, 1970. Of course, you don't care about the absolute number of seconds since this historical moment, but the *difference* of two such counts gives us the number of milliseconds in a given time interval.

Here is the code for the StopWatch class.

sec02/StopWatch.java

```
1  /**
2      A stopwatch accumulates time when it is running. You can
3      repeatedly start and stop the stopwatch. You can use a
4      stopwatch to measure the running time of a program.
5  */
6  public class StopWatch
7  {
8      private long elapsedTime;
```

```java
 9      private long startTime;
10      private boolean isRunning;
11
12      /**
13          Constructs a stopwatch that is in the stopped state
14          and has no time accumulated.
15      */
16      public StopWatch()
17      {
18          reset();
19      }
20
21      /**
22          Starts the stopwatch. Time starts accumulating now.
23      */
24      public void start()
25      {
26          if (isRunning) { return; }
27          isRunning = true;
28          startTime = System.currentTimeMillis();
29      }
30
31      /**
32          Stops the stopwatch. Time stops accumulating and is
33          is added to the elapsed time.
34      */
35      public void stop()
36      {
37          if (!isRunning) { return; }
38          isRunning = false;
39          long endTime = System.currentTimeMillis();
40          elapsedTime = elapsedTime + endTime - startTime;
41      }
42
43      /**
44          Returns the total elapsed time.
45          @return the total elapsed time
46      */
47      public long getElapsedTime()
48      {
49          if (isRunning)
50          {
51              long endTime = System.currentTimeMillis();
52              return elapsedTime + endTime - startTime;
53          }
54          else
55          {
56              return elapsedTime;
57          }
58      }
59
60      /**
61          Stops the watch and resets the elapsed time to 0.
62      */
63      public void reset()
64      {
65          elapsedTime = 0;
66          isRunning = false;
67      }
68  }
```

Here is how to use the stopwatch to measure the sorting algorithm's performance.

sec02/SelectionSortTimer.java

```java
 1  import java.util.Scanner;
 2
 3  /**
 4      This program measures how long it takes to sort an
 5      array of a user-specified size with the selection
 6      sort algorithm.
 7  */
 8  public class SelectionSortTimer
 9  {
10      public static void main(String[] args)
11      {
12          Scanner in = new Scanner(System.in);
13          System.out.print("First array length: ");
14          int firstLength = in.nextInt();
15          System.out.print("Number of arrays: ");
16          int numberOfArrays = in.nextInt();
17
18          StopWatch timer = new StopWatch();
19
20          for (int k = 1; k <= numberOfArrays; k++)
21          {
22              int n = k * firstLength;
23
24              // Construct random array
25
26              int[] a = ArrayUtil.randomIntArray(n, 100);
27
28              // Use stopwatch to time selection sort
29
30              timer.start();
31              SelectionSorter.sort(a);
32              timer.stop();
33
34              System.out.printf("Length:%8d Elapsed milliseconds:%8d%n",
35                  n, timer.getElapsedTime());
36              timer.reset();
37          }
38      }
39  }
```

Program Run

```
First array length: 10000
Number of arrays: 6
Length:   10000 Elapsed milliseconds:      786
Length:   20000 Elapsed milliseconds:     2148
Length:   30000 Elapsed milliseconds:     4796
Length:   40000 Elapsed milliseconds:     9192
Length:   50000 Elapsed milliseconds:    13321
Length:   60000 Elapsed milliseconds:    19299
```

By starting to measure the time just before sorting, and stopping the stopwatch just after, you get the time required for the sorting process, without counting the time for input and output.

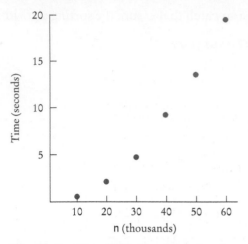

n	Milliseconds
10,000	786
20,000	2,148
30,000	4,796
40,000	9,192
50,000	13,321
60,000	19,299

Figure 1 Time Taken by Selection Sort

To measure the running time of a method, get the current time immediately before and after the method call.

The table in Figure 1 shows the results of some sample runs. These measurements were obtained with an Intel processor with a clock speed of 2 GHz, running Java 6 on the Linux operating system. On another computer the actual numbers will look different, but the relationship between the numbers will be the same.

The graph in Figure 1 shows a plot of the measurements. As you can see, when you double the size of the data set, it takes about four times as long to sort it.

14.3 Analyzing the Performance of the Selection Sort Algorithm

Let us count the number of operations that the program must carry out to sort an array with the selection sort algorithm. We don't actually know how many machine operations are generated for each Java instruction, or which of those instructions are more time-consuming than others, but we can make a simplification. We will simply count how often an array element is *visited*. Each visit requires about the same amount of work by other operations, such as incrementing subscripts and comparing values.

Let n be the size of the array. First, we must find the smallest of n numbers. To achieve that, we must visit n array elements. Then we swap the elements, which takes two visits. (You may argue that there is a certain probability that we don't need to swap the values. That is true, and one can refine the computation to reflect that observation. As we will soon see, doing so would not affect the overall conclusion.) In the next step, we need to visit only $n - 1$ elements to find the minimum. In the following step, $n - 2$ elements are visited to find the minimum. The last step visits two elements to find the minimum. Each step requires two visits to swap the elements. Therefore, the total number of visits is

$$n + 2 + (n - 1) + 2 + \cdots + 2 + 2 = \left(n + (n - 1) + \cdots + 2 \right) + (n - 1) \cdot 2$$

$$= \left(2 + \cdots + (n - 1) + n \right) + (n - 1) \cdot 2$$

$$= \frac{n(n + 1)}{2} - 1 + (n - 1) \cdot 2$$

because

$$1 + 2 + \cdots + (n - 1) + n = \frac{n(n + 1)}{2}$$

After multiplying out and collecting terms of n, we find that the number of visits is

$$\tfrac{1}{2}n^2 + \tfrac{5}{2}n - 3$$

We obtain a quadratic equation in n. That explains why the graph of Figure 1 looks approximately like a parabola.

Now simplify the analysis further. When you plug in a large value for n (for example, 1,000 or 2,000), then $\tfrac{1}{2}n^2$ is 500,000 or 2,000,000. The lower term, $\tfrac{5}{2}n - 3$, doesn't contribute much at all; it is only 2,497 or 4,997, a drop in the bucket compared to the hundreds of thousands or even millions of comparisons specified by the $\tfrac{1}{2}n^2$ term. We will just ignore these lower-level terms. Next, we will ignore the constant factor $\tfrac{1}{2}$. We are not interested in the actual count of visits for a single n. We want to compare the ratios of counts for different values of n. For example, we can say that sorting an array of 2,000 numbers requires four times as many visits as sorting an array of 1,000 numbers:

$$\frac{\left(\tfrac{1}{2} \cdot 2000^2\right)}{\left(\tfrac{1}{2} \cdot 1000^2\right)} = 4$$

The factor $\tfrac{1}{2}$ cancels out in comparisons of this kind. We will simply say, "The number of visits is of order n^2." That way, we can easily see that the number of comparisons increases fourfold when the size of the array doubles: $(2n)^2 = 4n^2$.

To indicate that the number of visits is of order n^2, computer scientists often use **big-Oh notation**: The number of visits is $O(n^2)$. This is a convenient shorthand. (See Special Topic 14.1 for a formal definition.)

To turn a polynomial expression such as

$$\tfrac{1}{2}n^2 + \tfrac{5}{2}n - 3$$

into big-Oh notation, simply locate the fastest-growing term, n^2, and ignore its constant coefficient, no matter how large or small it may be.

We observed before that the actual number of machine operations, and the actual amount of time that the computer spends on them, is approximately proportional to the number of element visits. Maybe there are about 10 machine operations (increments, comparisons, memory loads, and stores) for every element visit. The number of machine operations is then approximately $10 \times \tfrac{1}{2}n^2$. As before, we aren't interested in the coefficient, so we can say that the number of machine operations, and hence the time spent on the sorting, is of the order n^2 or $O(n^2)$.

The sad fact remains that doubling the size of the array causes a fourfold increase in the time required for sorting it with selection sort. When the size of the array increases by a factor of 100, the sorting time increases by a factor of 10,000. To sort an array of a million entries (for example, to create a telephone directory), takes 10,000 times as long as sorting 10,000 entries. If 10,000 entries can be sorted in about 3/4 of a second (as in our example), then sorting one million entries requires well over two hours. We will see in the next section how one can dramatically improve the performance of the sorting process by choosing a more sophisticated algorithm.

Computer scientists use the big-Oh notation to describe the growth rate of a function.

Selection sort is an $O(n^2)$ algorithm. Doubling the data set means a fourfold increase in processing time.

Special Topic 14.1

Oh, Omega, and Theta

We have used the big-Oh notation somewhat casually in this chapter to describe the growth behavior of a function. Here is the formal definition of the big-Oh notation: Suppose we have a function $T(n)$. Usually, it represents the processing time of an algorithm for a given input of size n. But it could be any function. Also, suppose that we have another function $f(n)$. It is usually chosen to be a simple function, such as $f(n) = n^k$ or $f(n) = \log(n)$, but it too can be any function. We write

$$T(n) = O(f(n))$$

if $T(n)$ grows at a rate that is bounded by $f(n)$. More formally, we require that for all n larger than some threshold, the ratio $T(n) / f(n) \leq C$ for some constant value C.

If $T(n)$ is a polynomial of degree k in n, then one can show that $T(n) = O(n^k)$. Later in this chapter, we will encounter functions that are $O(\log(n))$ or $O(n \log(n))$. Some algorithms take much more time. For example, one way of sorting a sequence is to compute all of its permutations, until you find one that is in increasing order. Such an algorithm takes $O(n!)$ time, which is very bad indeed.

Table 1 shows common big-Oh expressions, sorted by increasing growth.

Strictly speaking, $T(n) = O(f(n))$ means that T grows no faster than f. But it is permissible for T to grow much more slowly. Thus, it is technically correct to state that $T(n) = n^2 + 5n - 3$ is $O(n^3)$ or even $O(n^{10})$.

Computer scientists have invented additional notation to describe the growth behavior of functions more accurately. The expression

$$T(n) = \Omega(f(n))$$

means that T grows at least as fast as f, or, formally, that for all n larger than some threshold, the ratio $T(n) / f(n) \geq C$ for some constant value C. (The Ω symbol is the capital Greek letter omega.) For example, $T(n) = n^2 + 5n - 3$ is $\Omega(n^2)$ or even $\Omega(n)$.

The expression

$$T(n) = \Theta(f(n))$$

means that T and f grow at the same rate—that is, both $T(n) = O(f(n))$ and $T(n) = \Omega(f(n))$ hold. (The Θ symbol is the capital Greek letter theta.)

Table 1 Common Big-Oh Growth Rates	
Big-Oh Expression	Name
$O(1)$	Constant
$O(\log(n))$	Logarithmic
$O(n)$	Linear
$O(n \log(n))$	Log-linear
$O(n^2)$	Quadratic
$O(n^3)$	Cubic
$O(2^n)$	Exponential
$O(n!)$	Factorial

The Θ notation gives the most precise description of growth behavior. For example, $T(n) = n^2 + 5n - 3$ is $\Theta(n^2)$ but not $\Theta(n)$ or $\Theta(n^3)$.

The notations are very important for the precise analysis of algorithms. However, in casual conversation it is common to stick with big-Oh, while still giving an estimate as good as one can make.

Special Topic 14.2

Insertion Sort

Insertion sort is another simple sorting algorithm. In this algorithm, we assume that the initial sequence

```
a[0] a[1] ... a[k]
```

of an array is already sorted. (When the algorithm starts, we set k to 0.) We enlarge the initial sequence by inserting the next array element, a[k + 1], at the proper location. When we reach the end of the array, the sorting process is complete.

For example, suppose we start with the array

| 11 | 9 | 16 | 5 | 7 |

Of course, the initial sequence of length 1 is already sorted. We now add a[1], which has the value 9. The element needs to be inserted before the element 11. The result is

| 9 | 11 | 16 | 5 | 7 |

Next, we add a[2], which has the value 16. This element does not have to be moved.

| 9 | 11 | 16 | 5 | 7 |

We repeat the process, inserting a[3] or 5 at the very beginning of the initial sequence.

| 5 | 9 | 11 | 16 | 7 |

Finally, a[4] or 7 is inserted in its correct position, and the sorting is completed.

The following class implements the insertion sort algorithm:

```java
public class InsertionSorter
{
   /**
      Sorts an array, using insertion sort.
      @param a the array to sort
   */
   public static void sort(int[] a)
   {
      for (int i = 1; i < a.length; i++)
      {
         int next = a[i];
         // Move all larger elements up
         int j = i;
         while (j > 0 && a[j - 1] > next)
         {
            a[j] = a[j - 1];
            j--;
         }
         // Insert the element
         a[j] = next;
      }
   }
}
```

How efficient is this algorithm? Let n denote the size of the array. We carry out $n - 1$ iterations. In the kth iteration, we have a sequence of k elements that is already sorted, and we need to insert a new element into the sequence. For each insertion, we need to visit the elements of the initial sequence until we have found the location in which the new element can be inserted. Then we need to move up the remaining elements of the sequence. Thus, $k + 1$ array elements are visited. Therefore, the total number of visits is

$$2 + 3 + \cdots + n = \frac{n(n+1)}{2} - 1$$

Insertion sort is an $O(n^2)$ algorithm.

We conclude that insertion sort is an $O(n^2)$ algorithm, on the same order of efficiency as selection sort.

Insertion sort has a desirable property: Its performance is $O(n)$ if the array is already sorted—see Exercise ••• R14.23. This is a useful property in practical applications, in which data sets are often partially sorted.

Insertion sort is the method that many people use to sort playing cards. Pick up one card at a time and insert it so that the cards stay sorted.

© Kirby Hamilton/iStockphoto.

EXAMPLE CODE   See your eText or companion code for a program that illustrates sorting with insertion sort.

14.4 Merge Sort

In this section, you will learn about the **merge sort** algorithm, a much more efficient algorithm than selection sort. The basic idea behind merge sort is very simple.

Suppose we have an array of 10 integers. Let us engage in a bit of wishful thinking and hope that the first half of the array is already perfectly sorted, and the second half is too, like this:

5	9	10	12	17	1	8	11	20	32

Now it is simple to *merge* the two sorted arrays into one sorted array, by taking a new element from either the first or the second subarray, and choosing the smaller of the elements each time:

5	9	10	12	17	1	8	11	20	32		1									
5	9	10	12	17	1	8	11	20	32		1	5								
9	10	12	17	11	20	32		1	5	8										

1 5 8 9
1 5 8 9 10
1 5 8 9 10 11
1 5 8 9 10 11 12
1 5 8 9 10 11 12 17
1 5 8 9 10 11 12 17 20
1 5 8 9 10 11 12 17 20 32

In fact, you may have performed this merging before if you and a friend had to sort a pile of papers. You and the friend split the pile in half, each of you sorted your half, and then you merged the results together.

That is all well and good, but it doesn't seem to solve the problem for the computer. It still must sort the first and second halves of the array, because it can't very well ask a few buddies to pitch in. As it turns out, though, if the computer keeps dividing the array into smaller and smaller subarrays, sorting each half and merging them back together, it carries out dramatically fewer steps than the selection sort requires.

Let's write a `MergeSorter` class that implements this idea. When the `MergeSorter` sorts an array, it makes two arrays, each half the size of the original, and sorts them recursively. Then it merges the two sorted arrays together:

© Rich Legg/iStockphoto.

In merge sort, one sorts each half, then merges the sorted halves.

The merge sort algorithm sorts an array by cutting the array in half, recursively sorting each half, and then merging the sorted halves.

```java
public static void sort(int[] a)
{
    if (a.length <= 1) { return; }
    int[] first = new int[a.length / 2];
    int[] second = new int[a.length - first.length];
    // Copy the first half of a into first, the second half into second
    . . .
    sort(first);
    sort(second);
    merge(first, second, a);
}
```

The `merge` method is tedious but quite straightforward. You will find it in the code that follows.

sec04/MergeSorter.java

```java
1   /**
2       The sort method of this class sorts an array, using the merge
3       sort algorithm.
4   */
5   public class MergeSorter
6   {
7       /**
8           Sorts an array, using merge sort.
9           @param a the array to sort
10      */
11      public static void sort(int[] a)
12      {
13          if (a.length <= 1) { return; }
14          int[] first = new int[a.length / 2];
15          int[] second = new int[a.length - first.length];
16          // Copy the first half of a into first, the second half into second
17          for (int i = 0; i < first.length; i++)
18          {
19              first[i] = a[i];
20          }
21          for (int i = 0; i < second.length; i++)
22          {
23              second[i] = a[first.length + i];
24          }
25          sort(first);
26          sort(second);
```

```
27        merge(first, second, a);
28     }
29
30     /**
31        Merges two sorted arrays into an array.
32        @param first the first sorted array
33        @param second the second sorted array
34        @param a the array into which to merge first and second
35     */
36     private static void merge(int[] first, int[] second, int[] a)
37     {
38        int iFirst = 0;  // Next element to consider in the first array
39        int iSecond = 0;  // Next element to consider in the second array
40        int j = 0;  // Next open position in a
41
42        // As long as neither iFirst nor iSecond past the end, move
43        // the smaller element into a
44        while (iFirst < first.length && iSecond < second.length)
45        {
46           if (first[iFirst] < second[iSecond])
47           {
48              a[j] = first[iFirst];
49              iFirst++;
50           }
51           else
52           {
53              a[j] = second[iSecond];
54              iSecond++;
55           }
56           j++;
57        }
58
59        // Note that only one of the two loops below copies entries
60        // Copy any remaining entries of the first array
61        while (iFirst < first.length)
62        {
63           a[j] = first[iFirst];
64           iFirst++; j++;
65        }
66        // Copy any remaining entries of the second half
67        while (iSecond < second.length)
68        {
69           a[j] = second[iSecond];
70           iSecond++; j++;
71        }
72     }
73 }
```

sec04/MergeSortDemo.java

```
1  import java.util.Arrays;
2
3  /**
4     This program demonstrates the merge sort algorithm by
5     sorting an array that is filled with random numbers.
6  */
7  public class MergeSortDemo
8  {
9     public static void main(String[] args)
10    {
```

```
11        int[] a = ArrayUtil.randomIntArray(20, 100);
12        System.out.println(Arrays.toString(a));
13
14        MergeSorter.sort(a);
15
16        System.out.println(Arrays.toString(a));
17    }
18 }
```

Program Run

```
[8, 81, 48, 53, 46, 70, 98, 42, 27, 76, 33, 24, 2, 76, 62, 89, 90, 5, 13, 21]
[2, 5, 8, 13, 21, 24, 27, 33, 42, 46, 48, 53, 62, 70, 76, 76, 81, 89, 90, 98]
```

14.5 Analyzing the Merge Sort Algorithm

The merge sort algorithm looks a lot more complicated than the selection sort algorithm, and it appears that it may well take much longer to carry out these repeated subdivisions. However, the timing results for merge sort look much better than those for selection sort.

Figure 2 shows a table and a graph comparing both sets of performance data. As you can see, merge sort is a tremendous improvement. To understand why, let us estimate the number of array element visits that are required to sort an array with the merge sort algorithm. First, let us tackle the merge process that happens after the first and second halves have been sorted.

Each step in the merge process adds one more element to a. That element may come from first or second, and in most cases the elements from the two halves must be compared to see which one to take. We'll count that as 3 visits (one for a and one each for first and second) per element, or $3n$ visits total, where n denotes the length of a. Moreover, at the beginning, we had to copy from a to first and second, yielding another $2n$ visits, for a total of $5n$.

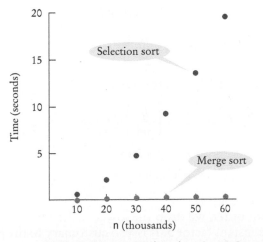

n	Merge Sort (milliseconds)	Selection Sort (milliseconds)
10,000	40	786
20,000	73	2,148
30,000	134	4,796
40,000	170	9,192
50,000	192	13,321
60,000	205	19,299

Figure 2   Time Taken by Merge Sort and Selection Sort

If we let $T(n)$ denote the number of visits required to sort a range of n elements through the merge sort process, then we obtain

$$T(n) = T\left(\frac{n}{2}\right) + T\left(\frac{n}{2}\right) + 5n$$

because sorting each half takes $T(n/2)$ visits. Actually, if n is not even, then we have one subarray of size $(n-1)/2$ and one of size $(n+1)/2$. Although it turns out that this detail does not affect the outcome of the computation, we will nevertheless assume for now that n is a power of 2, say $n = 2^m$. That way, all subarrays can be evenly divided into two parts.

Unfortunately, the formula

$$T(n) = 2T\left(\frac{n}{2}\right) + 5n$$

does not clearly tell us the relationship between n and $T(n)$. To understand the relationship, let us evaluate $T(n/2)$, using the same formula:

$$T\left(\frac{n}{2}\right) = 2T\left(\frac{n}{4}\right) + 5\frac{n}{2}$$

Therefore

$$T(n) = 2 \times 2T\left(\frac{n}{4}\right) + 5n + 5n$$

Let us do that again:

$$T\left(\frac{n}{4}\right) = 2T\left(\frac{n}{8}\right) + 5\frac{n}{4}$$

hence

$$T(n) = 2 \times 2 \times 2T\left(\frac{n}{8}\right) + 5n + 5n + 5n$$

This generalizes from 2, 4, 8, to arbitrary powers of 2:

$$T(n) = 2^k T\left(\frac{n}{2^k}\right) + 5nk$$

Recall that we assume that $n = 2^m$; hence, for $k = m$,

$$T(n) = 2^m T\left(\frac{n}{2^m}\right) + 5nm$$
$$= nT(1) + 5nm$$
$$= n + 5n\log_2(n)$$

Because $n = 2^m$, we have $m = \log_2(n)$.

To establish the growth order, we drop the lower-order term n and are left with $5n\log_2(n)$. We drop the constant factor 5. It is also customary to drop the base of the logarithm, because all logarithms are related by a constant factor.

For example,

$$\log_2(x) = \log_{10}(x) / \log_{10}(2) \approx \log_{10}(x) \times 3.32193$$

Hence we say that merge sort is an $O(n \log(n))$ algorithm.

Is the $O(n \log(n))$ merge sort algorithm better than the $O(n^2)$ selection sort algorithm? You bet it is. Recall that it took $100^2 = 10,000$ times as long to sort a million records as it took to sort 10,000 records with the $O(n^2)$ algorithm. With the $O(n \log(n))$ algorithm, the ratio is

Merge sort is an $O(n \log(n))$ algorithm. The $n \log(n)$ function grows much more slowly than n^2.

$$\frac{1,000,000 \log(1,000,000)}{10,000 \log(10,000)} = 100\left(\frac{6}{4}\right) = 150$$

Suppose for the moment that merge sort takes the same time as selection sort to sort an array of 10,000 integers, that is, 3/4 of a second on the test machine. (Actually, it is much faster than that.) Then it would take about 0.75×150 seconds, or under two minutes, to sort a million integers. Contrast that with selection sort, which would take over two hours for the same task. As you can see, even if it takes you several hours to learn about a better algorithm, that can be time well spent.

In this chapter we have barely begun to scratch the surface of this interesting topic. There are many sorting algorithms, some with even better performance than merge sort, and the analysis of these algorithms can be quite challenging. These important issues are often revisited in later computer science courses.

EXAMPLE CODE   See your eText or companion code for a program for timing the merge sort algorithm.

Special Topic 14.3
The Quicksort Algorithm

Quicksort is a commonly used algorithm that has the advantage over merge sort that no temporary arrays are required to sort and merge the partial results.

The quicksort algorithm, like merge sort, is based on the strategy of divide and conquer. To sort a range a[from] ... a[to] of the array a, first rearrange the elements in the range so that no element in the range a[from] ... a[p] is larger than any element in the range a[p + 1] ... a[to]. This step is called *partitioning* the range.

For example, suppose we start with a range

| 5 | 3 | 2 | 6 | 4 | 1 | 3 | 7 |

Here is a partitioning of the range. Note that the partitions aren't yet sorted.

| 3 | 3 | 2 | 1 | 4 | | 6 | 5 | 7 |

You'll see later how to obtain such a partition. In the next step, sort each partition, by recursively applying the same algorithm to the two partitions. That sorts the entire range, because the largest element in the first partition is at most as large as the smallest element in the second partition.

| 1 | 2 | 3 | 3 | 4 | | 5 | 6 | 7 |

Quicksort is implemented recursively as follows:

```java
public static void sort(int[] a, int from, int to)
{
   if (from >= to) { return; }
   int p = partition(a, from, to);
   sort(a, from, p);
   sort(a, p + 1, to);
}
```

Let us return to the problem of partitioning a range. Pick an element from the range and call it the *pivot*. There are several variations of the quicksort algorithm. In the simplest one, we'll pick the first element of the range, a[from], as the pivot.

Now form two regions a[from] ... a[i], consisting of values at most as large as the pivot and a[j] ... a[to], consisting of values at least as large as the pivot. The region a[i + 1] ... a[j - 1] consists of values that haven't been analyzed yet. (See the figure below.) At the beginning, both the left and right areas are empty; that is, i = from - 1 and j = to + 1.

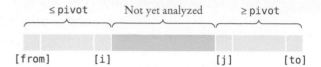

Partitioning a Range

Then keep incrementing i while a[i] < pivot and keep decrementing j while a[j] > pivot. The figure below shows i and j when that process stops.

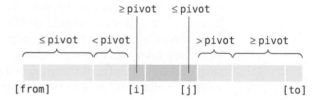

Extending the Partitions

Now swap the values in positions i and j, increasing both areas once more. Keep going while i < j. Here is the code for the partition method:

```
private static int partition(int[] a, int from, int to)
{
   int pivot = a[from];
   int i = from - 1;
   int j = to + 1;
   while (i < j)
   {
      i++; while (a[i] < pivot) { i++; }
      j--; while (a[j] > pivot) { j--; }
      if (i < j) { ArrayUtil.swap(a, i, j); }
   }
   return j;
}
```

On average, the quicksort algorithm is an $O(n \log(n))$ algorithm. There is just one unfortunate aspect to the quicksort algorithm. Its *worst-case* run-time behavior is $O(n^2)$. Moreover, if the pivot element is chosen as the first element of the region, that worst-case behavior occurs

In quicksort, one partitions the elements into two groups, holding the smaller and larger elements. Then one sorts each group.

© Christopher Futcher/iStockphoto.

when the input set is already sorted—a common situation in practice. By selecting the pivot element more cleverly, we can make it extremely unlikely for the worst-case behavior to occur. Such "tuned" quicksort algorithms are commonly used because their performance is generally excellent. For example, the sort method in the Arrays class uses a quicksort algorithm.

Another improvement that is commonly made in practice is to switch to insertion sort when the array is short, because the total number of operations using insertion sort is lower for short arrays. The Java library makes that switch if the array length is less than seven.

EXAMPLE CODE See your eText or companion code for a program that demonstrates the quicksort algorithm.

14.6 Searching

Searching for an element in an array is an extremely common task. As with sorting, the right choice of algorithms can make a big difference.

14.6.1 Linear Search

Suppose you need to find your friend's telephone number. You look up the friend's name in the telephone book, and naturally you can find it quickly, because the telephone book is sorted alphabetically. Now suppose you have a telephone number and you must know to what party it belongs. You could of course call that number, but suppose nobody picks up on the other end. You could look through the telephone book, a number at a time, until you find the number. That would obviously be a tremendous amount of work, and you would have to be desperate to attempt it.

This thought experiment shows the difference between a search through an unsorted data set and a search through a sorted data set. The following two sections will analyze the difference formally.

> A linear search examines all values in an array until it finds a match or reaches the end.

If you want to find a number in a sequence of values that occur in arbitrary order, there is nothing you can do to speed up the search. You must simply look through all elements until you have found a match or until you reach the end. This is called a **linear** or **sequential search**.

How long does a linear search take? If we assume that the element v is present in the array a, then the average search visits $n/2$ elements, where n is the length of the array. If it is not present, then all n elements must be inspected to verify the absence. Either way, a linear search is an $O(n)$ algorithm.

> A linear search locates a value in an array in $O(n)$ steps.

Here is a class that performs linear searches through an array a of integers. When searching for a value, the search method returns the first index of the match, or -1 if the value does not occur in a.

sec06_01/LinearSearcher.java

```
1   /**
2       A class for executing linear searches in an array.
3   */
4   public class LinearSearcher
5   {
6       /**
7           Finds a value in an array, using the linear search
8           algorithm.
```

```
 9              @param a the array to search
10              @param value the value to find
11              @return the index at which the value occurs, or -1
12              if it does not occur in the array
13         */
14         public static int search(int[] a, int value)
15         {
16            for (int i = 0; i < a.length; i++)
17            {
18               if (a[i] == value) { return i; }
19            }
20            return -1;
21         }
22      }
```

sec06_01/LinearSearchDemo.java

```
 1   import java.util.Arrays;
 2   import java.util.Scanner;
 3
 4   /**
 5      This program demonstrates the linear search algorithm.
 6   */
 7   public class LinearSearchDemo
 8   {
 9      public static void main(String[] args)
10      {
11         int[] a = ArrayUtil.randomIntArray(20, 100);
12         System.out.println(Arrays.toString(a));
13         Scanner in = new Scanner(System.in);
14
15         boolean done = false;
16         while (!done)
17         {
18            System.out.print("Enter number to search for, -1 to quit: ");
19            int n = in.nextInt();
20            if (n == -1)
21            {
22               done = true;
23            }
24            else
25            {
26               int pos = LinearSearcher.search(a, n);
27               System.out.println("Found in position " + pos);
28            }
29         }
30      }
31   }
```

Program Run

```
[46, 99, 45, 57, 64, 95, 81, 69, 11, 97, 6, 85, 61, 88, 29, 65, 83, 88, 45, 88]
Enter number to search for, -1 to quit: 12
Found in position -1
Enter number to search for, -1 to quit: -1
```

14.6.2 Binary Search

Now let us search for an item in a data sequence that has been previously sorted. Of course, we could still do a linear search, but it turns out we can do much better than that.

Consider the following sorted array a. The data set is:

```
[0] [1] [2] [3] [4] [5] [6] [7] [8] [9]
 1   4   5   8   9  12  17  20  24  32
```

We would like to see whether the value 15 is in the data set. Let's narrow our search by finding whether the value is in the first or second half of the array. The last value in the first half of the data set, a[4], is 9, which is smaller than the value we are looking for. Hence, we should look in the second half of the array for a match, that is, in the sequence:

```
[0] [1] [2] [3] [4] [5] [6] [7] [8] [9]
 1   4   5   8   9  12  17  20  24  32
```

The middle element of this sequence is 20; hence, the value must be located in the sequence:

```
[0] [1] [2] [3] [4] [5] [6] [7] [8] [9]
 1   4   5   8   9  12  17  20  24  32
```

The last value of the first half of this very short sequence is 12, which is smaller than the value that we are searching, so we must look in the second half:

```
[0] [1] [2] [3] [4] [5] [6] [7] [8] [9]
 1   4   5   8   9  12  17  20  24  32
```

It is trivial to see that we don't have a match, because 15 ≠ 17. If we wanted to insert 15 into the sequence, we would need to insert it just before a[6].

This search process is called a **binary search**, because we cut the size of the search in half in each step. That cutting in half works only because we know that the sequence of values is sorted.

The following class implements binary searches in a sorted array of integers. The search method returns the position of the match if the search succeeds, or –1 if the value is not found in a. Here, we show a recursive version of the binary search algorithm.

> A binary search locates a value in a sorted array by determining whether the value occurs in the first or second half, then repeating the search in one of the halves.

sec06_02/BinarySearcher.java

```java
1  /**
2      A class for executing binary searches in an array.
3  */
4  public class BinarySearcher
5  {
6      /**
7          Finds a value in a range of a sorted array, using the binary
8          search algorithm.
9          @param a the array in which to search
10         @param low the low index of the range
11         @param high the high index of the range
12         @param value the value to find
13         @return the index at which the value occurs, or -1
14         if it does not occur in the array
15     */
```

```
16    public int search(int[] a, int low, int high, int value)
17    {
18       if (low <= high)
19       {
20          int mid = (low + high) / 2;
21
22          if (a[mid] == value)
23          {
24             return mid;
25          }
26          else if (a[mid] < value )
27          {
28             return search(a, mid + 1, high, value);
29          }
30          else
31          {
32             return search(a, low, mid - 1, value);
33          }
34       }
35       else
36       {
37          return -1;
38       }
39    }
40 }
```

EXAMPLE CODE   See your eText or companion code for a program that demonstrates binary search.

Now let's determine the number of visits to array elements required to carry out a binary search. We can use the same technique as in the analysis of merge sort. Because we look at the middle element, which counts as one visit, and then search either the left or the right subarray, we have

$$T(n) = T\left(\frac{n}{2}\right) + 1$$

Using the same equation,

$$T\left(\frac{n}{2}\right) = T\left(\frac{n}{4}\right) + 1$$

By plugging this result into the original equation, we get

$$T(n) = T\left(\frac{n}{4}\right) + 2$$

That generalizes to

$$T(n) = T\left(\frac{n}{2^k}\right) + k$$

As in the analysis of merge sort, we make the simplifying assumption that n is a power of 2, $n = 2^m$, where $m = \log_2(n)$. Then we obtain

$$T(n) = 1 + \log_2(n)$$

Therefore, binary search is an $O(\log(n))$ algorithm.

<table>
<tr><td>A binary search locates a value in a sorted array in $O(\log(n))$ steps.</td><td></td></tr>
</table>

That result makes intuitive sense. Suppose that n is 100. Then after each search, the size of the search range is cut in half, to 50, 25, 12, 6, 3, and 1. After seven comparisons we are done. This agrees with our formula, because $\log_2(100) \approx 6.64386$, and indeed the next larger power of 2 is $2^7 = 128$.

Because a binary search is so much faster than a linear search, is it worthwhile to sort an array first and then use a binary search? It depends. If you search the array only once, then it is more efficient to pay for an $O(n)$ linear search than for an $O(n \log(n))$ sort and an $O(\log(n))$ binary search. But if you will be making many searches in the same array, then sorting it is definitely worthwhile.

Computing & Society 14.1 The First Programmer

Before pocket calculators and personal computers existed, navigators and engineers used mechanical adding machines, slide rules, and tables of logarithms and trigonometric functions to speed up computations. Unfortunately, the tables—for which values had to be computed by hand—were notoriously inaccurate. The mathematician Charles Babbage (1791–1871) had the insight that if a machine could be constructed that produced printed tables automatically, both calculation and typesetting errors could be avoided. Babbage set out to develop a machine for this purpose, which he called a *Difference Engine* because it used successive differences to compute polynomials. For example, consider the function $f(x) = x^3$. Write down the values for $f(1)$, $f(2)$, $f(3)$, and so on. Then take the *differences* between successive values:

```
1
      7
8
      19
27
      37
64
      61
125
      91
216
```

Repeat the process, taking the difference of successive values in the second column, and then repeat once again:

```
1
      7
8           12
      19          6
27          18
      37          6
64          24
      61          6
125         30
      91
216
```

Now the differences are all the same. You can retrieve the function values by a pattern of additions—you need to know the values at the fringe of the pattern and the constant difference. You can try it out yourself: Write the highlighted numbers on a sheet of paper and fill in the others by adding the numbers that are in the north and northwest positions.

This method was very attractive, because mechanical addition machines had been known for some time. They consisted of cog wheels, with 10 cogs per wheel, to represent digits, and mechanisms to handle the carry from one digit to the next. Mechanical multiplication machines, on the other hand, were fragile and unreliable. Babbage built a successful prototype of the Difference Engine and, with his own money and government grants, proceeded to build the table-printing machine. However, because of funding problems and the difficulty of building the machine to the required precision, it was never completed.

While working on the Difference Engine, Babbage conceived of a much grander vision that he called the *Analytical Engine*. The Difference Engine was designed to carry out a limited set of computations—it was no smarter than a pocket calculator is today. But Babbage realized that such a machine could be made *programmable* by storing programs as well as data. The internal storage of the Analytical Engine was to consist of 1,000 registers of 50 decimal digits each. Programs and constants were to be stored on punched cards—a technique that was, at that time, commonly used on looms for weaving patterned fabrics.

Ada Augusta, Countess of Lovelace (1815–1852), the only child of Lord Byron, was a friend and sponsor of Charles Babbage. Ada Lovelace was one of the first people to realize the potential of such a machine, not just for computing mathematical tables but for processing data that were not numbers. She is considered by many to be the world's first programmer.

Topham/The Image Works.

Replica of Babbage's Difference Engine

14.7 Problem Solving: Estimating the Running Time of an Algorithm

In this chapter, you have learned how to estimate the running time of sorting algorithms. As you have seen, being able to differentiate between $O(n \log(n))$ and $O(n^2)$ running times has great practical implications. Being able to estimate the running times of other algorithms is an important skill. In this section, we will practice estimating the running time of array algorithms.

14.7.1 Linear Time

Let us start with a simple example, an algorithm that counts how many elements have a particular value:

```
int count = 0;
for (int i = 0; i < a.length; i++)
{
   if (a[i] == value) { count++; }
}
```

What is the running time in terms of n, the length of the array?

Start with looking at the pattern of array element visits. Here, we visit each element once. It helps to visualize this pattern. Imagine the array as a sequence of light bulbs. As the ith element gets visited, imagine the ith bulb lighting up.

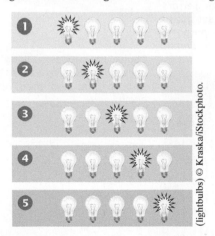

(lightbulbs) © Kraska/iStockphoto.

Now look at the work per visit. Does each visit involve a fixed number of actions, independent of n? In this case, it does. There are just a few actions—read the element, compare it, maybe increment a counter.

Therefore, the running time is n times a constant, or $O(n)$.

What if we don't always run to the end of the array? For example, suppose we want to check whether the value occurs in the array, without counting it:

```
boolean found = false;
for (int i = 0; !found && i < a.length; i++)
{
   if (a[i] == value) { found = true; }
}
```

A loop with n iterations has $O(n)$ running time if each step consists of a fixed number of actions.

Then the loop can stop in the middle:

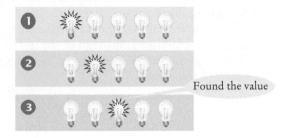

Found the value

Is this still $O(n)$? It is, because in some cases the match may be at the very end of the array. Also, if there is no match, one must traverse the entire array.

14.7.2 Quadratic Time

Now let's turn to a more interesting case. What if we do a lot of work with each visit? Here is an example: We want to find the most frequent element in an array.
 Suppose the array is

8	7	5	7	7	5	4

It's obvious by looking at the values that 7 is the most frequent one. But now imagine an array with a few thousand values.

8	7	5	7	7	5	4	1	2	3	3	4	9	12	3	2	5	···	11	9	2	3	7	8

We can count how often the value 8 occurs, then move on to count how often 7 occurs, and so on. For example, in the first array, 8 occurs once, and 7 occurs three times. Where do we put the counts? Let's put them into a second array of the same length.

a:

8	7	5	7	7	5	4

counts:

1	3	2	3	3	2	1

Then we take the maximum of the counts. It is 3. We look up where the 3 occurs in the counts, and find the corresponding value. Thus, the most common value is 7.
 Let us first estimate how long it takes to compute the counts.

```
for (int i = 0; i < a.length; i++)
{
    counts[i] = Count how often a[i] occurs in a
}
```

A loop with n iterations has $O(n^2)$ running time if each step takes $O(n)$ time.

We still visit each array element once, but now the work per visit is much larger. As you have seen in the previous section, each counting action is $O(n)$. When we do $O(n)$ work in each step, the total running time is $O(n^2)$.
 This algorithm has three phases:

1. Compute all counts.
2. Compute the maximum.
3. Find the maximum in the counts.

We have just seen that the first phase is $O(n^2)$. Computing the maximum is $O(n)$—look at the algorithm in Section 7.3.3 and note that each step involves a fixed amount of work. Finally, we just saw that finding a value is $O(n)$.

How can we estimate the total running time from the estimates of each phase? Of course, the total time is the sum of the individual times, but for big-Oh estimates, we take the *maximum* of the estimates. To see why, imagine that we had actual equations for each of the times:

> The big-Oh running time for doing several steps in a row is the largest of the big-Oh times for each step.

$$T_1(n) = an^2 + bn + c$$

$$T_2(n) = dn + e$$

$$T_3(n) = fn + g$$

Then the sum is

$$T(n) = T_1(n) + T_2(n) + T_3(n) = an^2 + (b + d + f)n + c + e + g$$

But only the largest term matters, so $T(n)$ is $O(n^2)$.

Thus, we have found that our algorithm for finding the most frequent element is $O(n^2)$.

14.7.3 The Triangle Pattern

Let us see if we can speed up the algorithm from the preceding section. It seems wasteful to count elements again if we have already counted them.

Can we save time by eliminating repeated counting of the same element? That is, before counting a[i], should we first check that it didn't occur in a[0] ... a[i - 1]?

Let us estimate the cost of these additional checks. In the *i*th step, the amount of work is proportional to *i*. That's not quite the same as in the preceding section, where you saw that a loop with *n* iterations, each of which takes $O(n)$ time, is $O(n^2)$. Now each step just takes $O(i)$ time.

To get an intuitive feel for this situation, look at the light bulbs again. In the second iteration, we visit a[0] again. In the third iteration, we visit a[0] and a[1] again, and so on. The light bulb pattern is

> A loop with *n* iterations has $O(n^2)$ running time if the *i*th step takes $O(i)$ time.

If there are *n* light bulbs, about half of the square above, or $n^2/2$ of them, light up. That's unfortunately still $O(n^2)$.

Here is another idea for time saving. When we count a[i], there is no need to do the counting in a[0] ... a[i - 1]. If a[i] never occurred before, we get an accurate count by just looking at a[i] ... a[n - 1]. And if it did, we already have an accurate count. Does that help us? Not really—it's the triangle pattern again, but this time in the other direction.

That doesn't mean that these improvements aren't worthwhile. If an $O(n^2)$ algorithm is the best one can do for a particular problem, you still want to make it as fast as possible. However, we will not pursue this plan further because it turns out that we can do much better.

14.7.4 Logarithmic Time

Logarithmic time estimates arise from algorithms that cut work in half in each step. You have seen this in the algorithms for binary search and merge sort.

In particular, when you use sorting or binary search in a phase of an algorithm, you will encounter logarithmic time in the big-Oh estimates.

Consider this idea for improving our algorithm for finding the most frequent element. Suppose we first *sort* the array:

8	7	5	7	7	5	4	⟶	4	5	5	7	7	7	8

> An algorithm that cuts the size of work in half in each step runs in $O(\log(n))$ time.

That cost us $O(n \log(n))$ time. If we can complete the algorithm in $O(n)$ time, we will have found a better algorithm than the $O(n^2)$ algorithm of the preceding sections.

To see why this is possible, imagine traversing the sorted array. As long as you find a value that was equal to its predecessor, you increment a counter. When you find a different value, save the counter and start counting anew:

a:	4	5	5	7	7	7	8
counts:	1	1	2	1	2	3	1

Or in code,

```
int count = 0;
for (int i = 0; i < a.length; i++)
{
   count++;
   if (i == a.length - 1 || a[i] != a[i + 1])
   {
```

```
            counts[i] = count;
            count = 0;
        }
    }
```

That's a constant amount of work per iteration, even though it visits two elements:

$2n$ is still $O(n)$. Thus, we can compute the counts in $O(n)$ time from a sorted array. The entire algorithm is now $O(n \log(n))$.

Note that we don't actually need to keep all counts, only the highest one that we encountered so far (see Exercise •• E14.14). That is a worthwhile improvement, but it does not change the big-Oh estimate of the running time.

EXAMPLE CODE   See your eText or companion code for a program for comparing the speed of algorithms that find the most frequent element.

14.8 Sorting and Searching in the Java Library

When you write Java programs, you don't have to implement your own sorting algorithms. The Arrays and Collections classes provide sorting and searching methods that we will introduce in the following sections.

14.8.1 Sorting

> The Arrays class implements a sorting method that you should use for your Java programs.

The Arrays class contains static sort methods to sort arrays of integers and floating-point numbers. For example, you can sort an array of integers simply as

```
int[] a = . . .;
Arrays.sort(a);
```

That sort method uses the quicksort algorithm—see Special Topic 14.3 for more information about that algorithm.

> The Collections class contains a sort method that can sort array lists.

If your data are contained in an ArrayList, use the Collections.sort method instead; it uses the merge sort algorithm:

```
ArrayList<String> names = . . .;
Collections.sort(names);
```

14.8.2 Binary Search

The `Arrays` and `Collections` classes contain static `binarySearch` methods that implement the binary search algorithm, but with a useful enhancement. If a value is not found in the array, then the returned value is not −1, but −k − 1, where k is the position before which the element should be inserted. For example,

```
int[] a = { 1, 4, 9 };
int v = 7;
int pos = Arrays.binarySearch(a, v);
// Returns −3; v should be inserted before position 2
```

14.8.3 Comparing Objects

The sort method of the Arrays class sorts objects of classes that implement the Comparable interface.

In application programs, you often need to sort or search through collections of objects. Therefore, the `Arrays` and `Collections` classes also supply `sort` and `binarySearch` methods for objects. However, these methods cannot know how to compare arbitrary objects. Suppose, for example, that you have an array of `Country` objects. It is not obvious how the countries should be sorted. Should they be sorted by their names or by their areas? The `sort` and `binarySearch` methods cannot make that decision for you. Instead, they require that the objects belong to classes that implement the `Comparable` interface type that was introduced in Section 10.3. That interface has a single method:

```
public interface Comparable<T>
{
    int compareTo(T other);
}
```

The call

```
a.compareTo(b)
```

must return a negative number if a should come before b, 0 if a and b are the same, and a positive number otherwise.

Note that `Comparable` is a generic type, similar to the `ArrayList` type. With an `ArrayList`, the type parameter denotes the type of the elements. With `Comparable`, the type parameter is the type of the parameter of the `compareTo` method. Therefore, a class that implements `Comparable` will want to be "comparable to itself". For example, the `Country` class implements `Comparable<Country>`.

Many classes in the standard Java library, including the `String` class, number wrappers, dates, and file paths, implement the `Comparable` interface.

You can implement the `Comparable` interface for your own classes as well. For example, to sort a collection of countries by area, the `Country` class would implement the `Comparable<Country>` interface and provide a `compareTo` method like this:

```
public class Country implements Comparable<Country>
{
    public int compareTo(Country other)
    {
        return Double.compare(area, other.area);
    }
}
```

The `compareTo` method compares countries by their area. Note the use of the helper method `Double.compare` (see Programming Tip 10.1) that returns a negative integer, 0, or a positive integer. This is easier than programming a three-way branch.

Now you can pass an array of countries to the `Arrays.sort` method:

```
Country[] countries = new Country[n];
// Add countries
Arrays.sort(countries); // Sorts by increasing area
```

Whenever you need to carry out sorting or searching, use the methods in the `Arrays` and `Collections` classes and not those that you write yourself. The library algorithms have been fully debugged and optimized. Thus, the primary purpose of this chapter was not to teach you how to implement practical sorting and searching algorithms. Instead, you have learned something more important, namely that different algorithms can vary widely in performance, and that it is worthwhile to learn more about the design and analysis of algorithms.

EXAMPLE CODE   See your eText or companion code for a program that demonstrates the Java library methods for sorting and searching.

Common Error 14.1

The compareTo Method Can Return Any Integer, Not Just –1, 0, and 1

The call `a.compareTo(b)` is allowed to return *any* negative integer to denote that a should come before b, not necessarily the value –1. That is, the test

```
if (a.compareTo(b) == -1) // Error!
```

is generally wrong. Instead, you should test

```
if (a.compareTo(b) < 0) // OK
```

Why would a `compareTo` method ever want to return a number other than –1, 0, or 1? Sometimes, it is convenient to just return the difference of two integers. For example, the `compareTo` method of the `String` class compares characters in matching positions:

```
char c1 = charAt(i);
char c2 = other.charAt(i);
```

If the characters are different, then the method simply returns their difference:

```
if (c1 != c2) { return c1 - c2; }
```

This difference is a negative number if c1 is less than c2, but it is not necessarily the number –1.

Note that returning a difference only works if it doesn't overflow (see Programming Tip 10.1).

Special Topic 14.4

The Comparator Interface

Sometimes you want to sort an array or array list of objects, but the objects don't belong to a class that implements the `Comparable` interface. Or, perhaps, you want to sort the array in a different order. For example, you may want to sort countries by name rather than by value.

You wouldn't want to change the implementation of a class simply to call `Arrays.sort`. Fortunately, there is an alternative. One version of the `Arrays.sort` method does not require that the objects belong to classes that implement the `Comparable` interface. Instead, you can supply arbitrary objects. However, you must also provide a *comparator* object whose job is to compare objects. The comparator object must belong to a class that implements the `Comparator` interface. That interface has a single method, `compare`, which compares two objects.

Just like `Comparable`, the `Comparator` interface is a parameterized type. The type parameter specifies the type of the `compare` parameter variables.

For example, `Comparator<Country>` looks like this:

```
public interface Comparator<Country>
{
    int compare(Country a, Country b);
}
```

The call

```
comp.compare(a, b)
```

must return a negative number if a should come before b, 0 if a and b are the same, and a positive number otherwise. (Here, `comp` is an object of a class that implements `Comparator<Country>`.)

For example, here is a `Comparator` class for country:

```
public class CountryComparator implements Comparator<Country>
{
    public int compare(Country a, Country b)
    {
        return Double.compare(a.getArea(), b.getArea());
    }
}
```

To sort an array of countries by area, call

```
Arrays.sort(countries, new CountryComparator());
```

Special Topic 14.5

Comparators with Lambda Expressions

It is cumbersome to specify a comparator by defining a class that implements the `Comparator` interface. You must implement the `compare` method and construct an object of that class.

With lambda expressions, it is easier to specify a comparator (see Special Topic 10.4). For example, to sort an array of words by increasing lengths, call

```
Arrays.sort(words, (v, w) -> v.length() - w.length());
```

There is a convenient shortcut for this case. Note that the comparison depends on a function that maps each string to a numeric value, namely its length. The static method `Comparator.comparing` constructs a comparator from a lambda expression. For example, you can call

```
Arrays.sort(words, Comparator.comparing(w -> w.length()));
```

A comparator is constructed that calls the supplied function on both objects that are to be compared, and then compares the function results.

The `Comparator.comparing` method takes care of many common cases. For example, to sort countries by area, call

```
Arrays.sort(countries, Comparator.comparing(c -> c.getArea()));
```

EXAMPLE CODE   See your eText or companion code for a program that uses a comparator with a lambda expressions.

WORKED EXAMPLE 14.1

Enhancing the Insertion Sort Algorithm

Learn how to implement an improvement of the insertion sort algorithm shown in Special Topic 14.2. The enhanced algorithm is called *Shell sort* after its inventor, Donald Shell. See your eText or visit wiley.com/go/bjeo7.

CHAPTER SUMMARY

Describe the selection sort algorithm.

- The selection sort algorithm sorts an array by repeatedly finding the smallest element of the unsorted tail region and moving it to the front.

Measure the running time of a method.

- To measure the running time of a method, get the current time immediately before and after the method call.

Use the big-Oh notation to describe the running time of an algorithm.

- Computer scientists use the big-Oh notation to describe the growth rate of a function.
- Selection sort is an $O(n^2)$ algorithm. Doubling the data set means a fourfold increase in processing time.
- Insertion sort is an $O(n^2)$ algorithm.

Describe the merge sort algorithm.

- The merge sort algorithm sorts an array by cutting the array in half, recursively sorting each half, and then merging the sorted halves.

Contrast the running times of the merge sort and selection sort algorithms.

- Merge sort is an $O(n \log(n))$ algorithm. The $n \log(n)$ function grows much more slowly than n^2.

Describe the running times of the linear search algorithm and the binary search algorithm.

- A linear search examines all values in an array until it finds a match or reaches the end.
- A linear search locates a value in an array in $O(n)$ steps.
- A binary search locates a value in a sorted array by determining whether the value occurs in the first or second half, then repeating the search in one of the halves.
- A binary search locates a value in a sorted array in $O(\log(n))$ steps.

Practice developing big-Oh estimates of algorithms.

- A loop with n iterations has $O(n)$ running time if each step consists of a fixed number of actions.
- A loop with n iterations has $O(n^2)$ running time if each step takes $O(n)$ time.
- The big-Oh running time for doing several steps in a row is the largest of the big-Oh times for each step.

- A loop with n iterations has $O(n^2)$ running time if the ith step takes $O(i)$ time.
- An algorithm that cuts the size of work in half in each step runs in $O(\log(n))$ time.

Use the Java library methods for sorting and searching data.

- The Arrays class implements a sorting method that you should use for your Java programs.
- The Collections class contains a sort method that can sort array lists.
- The sort method of the Arrays class sorts objects of classes that implement the Comparable interface.

STANDARD LIBRARY ITEMS INTRODUCED IN THIS CHAPTER

```
java.lang.System                 java.util.Collections
    currentTimeMillis                binarySearch
java.util.Arrays                     sort
    binarySearch                 java.util.Comparator<T>
    sort                             compare
                                     comparing
```

REVIEW EXERCISES

▪ R14.1   What is the difference between searching and sorting?

▪ R14.2   How can you change the selection sort algorithm so that it sorts the elements in descending order (that is, with the largest element at the beginning of the array)?

▪ R14.3   Suppose we modified the selection sort algorithm to start at the end of the array, working toward the beginning. In each step, the current position is swapped with the minimum. What is the result of this modification?

▪▪ R14.4   *Checking against off-by-one errors.* When writing the selection sort algorithm of Section 14.1, a programmer must make the usual choices of < versus <=, a.length versus a.length - 1, and from versus from + 1. This is fertile ground for off-by-one errors. Conduct code walkthroughs of the algorithm with arrays of length 0, 1, 2, and 3 and check carefully that all index values are correct.

▪▪ R14.5   For the following expressions, what is the order of the growth of each?

   a. $n^2 + 2n + 1$
   b. $n^{10} + 9n^9 + 20n^8 + 145n^7$
   c. $(n + 1)^4$
   d. $(n^2 + n)^2$
   e. $n + 0.001n^3$
   f. $n^3 - 1000n^2 + 10^9$
   g. $n + \log(n)$
   h. $n^2 + n \log(n)$
   i. $2^n + n^2$
   j. $\dfrac{n^3 + 2n}{n^2 + 0.75}$

▪ R14.6   We determined that the actual number of visits in the selection sort algorithm is

$$T(n) = \tfrac{1}{2}n^2 + \tfrac{5}{2}n - 3$$

We characterized this method as having $O(n^2)$ growth. Compute the actual ratios

$$T(2,000)/T(1,000)$$
$$T(5,000)/T(1,000)$$
$$T(10,000)/T(1,000)$$

and compare them with

$$f(2,000)/f(1,000)$$
$$f(5,000)/f(1,000)$$
$$f(10,000)/f(1,000)$$

where $f(n) = n^2$.

- **R14.7** Suppose algorithm A takes five seconds to handle a data set of 1,000 records. If the algorithm A is an $O(n)$ algorithm, approximately how long will it take to handle a data set of 2,000 records? Of 10,000 records?

- **R14.8** Suppose an algorithm takes five seconds to handle a data set of 1,000 records. Fill in the following table, which shows the approximate growth of the execution times depending on the complexity of the algorithm.

	$O(n)$	$O(n^2)$	$O(n^3)$	$O(n \log(n))$	$O(2^n)$
1,000	5	5	5	5	5
2,000					
3,000		45			
10,000					

  For example, because $3000^2/1000^2 = 9$, the algorithm would take nine times as long, or 45 seconds, to handle a data set of 3,000 records.

- **R14.9** Sort the following growth rates from slowest to fastest growth.

$O(n)$	$O(\log(n))$	$O(2^n)$	$O(n\sqrt{n})$
$O(n^3)$	$O(n^2 \log(n))$	$O(\sqrt{n})$	$O(n^{\log(n)})$
$O(n^n)$	$O(n \log(n))$		

- **R14.10** What is the growth rate of the standard algorithm to find the minimum value of an array? Of finding both the minimum and the maximum?

- **R14.11** What is the big-Oh time estimate of the following method in terms of n, the length of a? Use the "light bulb pattern" method of Section 14.7 to visualize your result.

  ```java
  public static void swap(int[] a)
  {
     int i = 0;
     int j = a.length - 1;
     while (i < j)
     {
        int temp = a[i];
        a[i] = a[j];
        a[j] = temp;
        i++;
        j--;
     }
  }
  ```

- **R14.12** Consider this algorithm for sorting an array. Set k to the length of the array. Find the maximum of the first k elements. Remove it, using the second algorithm of Section 7.3.6. Decrement k and place the removed element into the kth position. Stop if k is 1. What is the algorithm's running time in big-Oh notation?

- **R14.13** Why does only one of the two while loops at the end of the merge method in Section 14.4 do any work?

■ **R14.14** A *run* is a sequence of adjacent repeated values (see Exercise R7.21). Describe an $O(n)$ algorithm to find the length of the longest run in an array.

■■ **R14.15** Consider the task of finding the most frequent element in an array of length n. Here are three approaches:

    a. Sort the array, then find the longest run.

    b. Allocate an array of counters of the same size as the original array. For each element, traverse the array and count how many other elements are equal to it, updating its counter. Then find the maximum count.

    c. Keep variables for the most frequent element that you have seen so far and its frequency. For each index i, check whether a[i] occurs in a[0] ... a[i - 1]. If not, count how often it occurs in a[i + 1] ... a[n - 1]. If a[i] is more frequent than the most frequent element so far, update the variables.

Describe the big-Oh efficiency of each approach.

■ **R14.16** Trace a walkthrough of selection sort with these sets:

    a. 4 7 11 4 9 5 11 7 3 5

    b. –7 6 8 7 5 9 0 11 10 5 8

■ **R14.17** Trace a walkthrough of merge sort with these sets:

    a. 5 11 7 3 5 4 7 11 4 9

    b. 9 0 11 10 5 8 –7 6 8 7 5

■ **R14.18** Trace a walkthrough of:

    a. Linear search for 7 in   –7 1 3 3 4 7 11 13

    b. Binary search for 8 in   –7 2 2 3 4 7 8 11 13

    c. Binary search for 8 in   –7 1 2 3 5 7 10 13

■■ **R14.19** Your task is to remove all duplicates from an array. For example, if the array has the values

                    4 7 11 4 9 5 11 7 3 5

then the array should be changed to

                    4 7 11 9 5 3

Here is a simple algorithm: Look at a[i]. Count how many times it occurs in a. If the count is larger than 1, remove it. What is the growth rate of the time required for this algorithm?

■■■ **R14.20** Modify the merge sort algorithm to remove duplicates in the merging step to obtain an algorithm that removes duplicates from an array. Note that the resulting array does not have the same ordering as the original one. What is the efficiency of this algorithm?

■■ **R14.21** Consider the following algorithm to remove all duplicates from an array: Sort the array. For each element in the array, look at its next neighbor to decide whether it is present more than once. If so, remove it. Is this a faster algorithm than the one in Exercise ●● R14.19?

■■■ **R14.22** Develop an $O(n \log(n))$ algorithm for removing duplicates from an array if the resulting array must have the same ordering as the original array. When a value occurs multiple times, all but its first occurrence should be removed.

▪▪▪ R14.23 Why does insertion sort perform significantly better than selection sort if an array is already sorted?

▪▪▪ R14.24 Consider the following speedup of the insertion sort algorithm of Special Topic 14.2. For each element, use the enhanced binary search algorithm that yields the insertion position for missing elements. Does this speedup have a significant impact on the efficiency of the algorithm?

▪▪ R14.25 Consider the following algorithm known as *bubble sort*:

> *While the array is not sorted*
> * For each adjacent pair of elements*
> *   If the pair is not sorted*
> *   Swap its elements.*

What is the big-Oh efficiency of this algorithm?

▪▪ R14.26 The *radix sort* algorithm sorts an array of n integers with d digits, using ten auxiliary arrays. First place each value v into the auxiliary array whose index corresponds to the last digit of v. Then move all values back into the original array, preserving their order. Repeat the process, now using the next-to-last (tens) digit, then the hundreds digit, and so on. What is the big-Oh time of this algorithm in terms of n and d? When is this algorithm preferable to merge sort?

▪▪ R14.27 A *stable sort* does not change the order of elements with the same value. This is a desirable feature in many applications. Consider a sequence of e-mail messages. If you sort by date and then by sender, you'd like the second sort to preserve the relative order of the first, so that you can see all messages from the same sender in date order. Is selection sort stable? Insertion sort? Why or why not?

▪▪ R14.28 Give an $O(n)$ algorithm to sort an array of n bytes (numbers between −128 and 127). *Hint:* Use an array of counters.

▪▪ R14.29 You are given a sequence of arrays of words, representing the pages of a book. Your task is to build an index (a sorted array of words), each element of which has an array of sorted numbers representing the pages on which the word appears. Describe an algorithm for building the index and give its big-Oh running time in terms of the total number of words.

▪▪ R14.30 Given two arrays of n integers each, describe an $O(n \log(n))$ algorithm for determining whether they have an element in common.

▪▪▪ R14.31 Given an array of n integers and a value v, describe an $O(n \log(n))$ algorithm to find whether there are two values x and y in the array with sum v.

▪▪ R14.32 Given two arrays of n integers each, describe an $O(n \log(n))$ algorithm for finding all elements that they have in common.

▪▪ R14.33 Suppose we modify the quicksort algorithm from Special Topic 14.3, selecting the middle element instead of the first one as pivot. What is the running time on an array that is already sorted?

▪▪ R14.34 Suppose we modify the quicksort algorithm from Special Topic 14.3, selecting the middle element instead of the first one as pivot. Find a sequence of values for which this algorithm has an $O(n^2)$ running time.

PRACTICE EXERCISES

■ **E14.1** Modify the selection sort algorithm to sort an array of integers in descending order.

■ **E14.2** Modify the selection sort algorithm to sort an array of coins by their value.

■■ **E14.3** Write a program that automatically generates the table of sample run times for the selection sort algorithm. The program should ask for the smallest and largest value of n and the number of measurements and then make all sample runs.

■ **E14.4** Modify the merge sort algorithm to sort an array of strings in lexicographic order.

■■ **E14.5** Modify the selection sort algorithm to sort an array of objects that implement the Measurable interface from Chapter 10.

■■ **E14.6** Modify the selection sort algorithm to sort an array of objects that implement the Comparable interface (without a type parameter).

■■ **E14.7** Modify the selection sort algorithm to sort an array of objects, given a parameter of type Comparator (without a type parameter).

■■■ **E14.8** Write a telephone lookup program. Read a data set of 1,000 names and telephone numbers from a file that contains the numbers in random order. Handle lookups by name and also reverse lookups by phone number. Use a binary search for both lookups.

■■ **E14.9** Implement a program that measures the performance of the insertion sort algorithm described in Special Topic 14.2.

■■ **E14.10** Implement a general merge method that can merge any number of sorted subsequences. The method gets an ArrayList<int[]> with the sorted sequences that should be merged.

■■ **E14.11** Use the general merge method of the preceding exercise to implement the following sort algorithm. Find all non-descending subsequences of an array (that is, sequences such that $a[i] \leq a[i + 1] \leq ... \leq a[i + k]$). Some of these sequences might have length 1. Then merge all these sequences.

■■ **E14.12** Reimplement Exercise ●● E14.11 so that you don't generate new arrays with the subsequences, but instead collect the starting index values. Then implement the generalized merge method so that it receives the array of values to be sorted, and an array list of the starting index values.

■ **E14.13** Implement the bubble sort algorithm described in Exercise ●● R14.25.

■■ **E14.14** Implement the algorithm described in Section 14.7.4, but only remember the value with the highest frequency so far:

```
int mostFrequent = 0;
int highestFrequency = -1;
for (int i = 0; i < a.length; i++)
    Count how often a[i] occurs in a[i + 1] ... a[a.length - 1]
    If it occurs more often than highestFrequency
        highestFrequency = that count
        mostFrequent = a[i]
```

■■■ **E14.15** Write a program that sorts an ArrayList<Country> in decreasing order so that the largest country is at the beginning of the array. Use a Comparator.

■■ **E14.16** Consider the binary search algorithm in Section 14.6.2. If no match is found, the search method returns −1. Modify the method so that if a is not found, the method returns −k − 1, where k is the position before which the element should be inserted. (This is the same behavior as Arrays.binarySearch.)

■■ **E14.17** Implement the sort method of the merge sort algorithm without recursion, where the length of the array is a power of 2. First merge adjacent regions of size 1, then adjacent regions of size 2, then adjacent regions of size 4, and so on.

■■■ **E14.18** Use insertion sort and the binary search from Exercise ■■ E14.16 to sort an array as described in Exercise ■■■ R14.24. Implement this algorithm and measure its performance.

■ **E14.19** Supply a class Person that implements the Comparable interface. Compare persons by their names. Ask the user to input ten names and generate ten Person objects. Using the compareTo method, determine the first and last person among them and print them.

■■ **E14.20** Sort an array list of strings by increasing *length*. *Hint:* Supply a Comparator.

■■■ **E14.21** Sort an array list of strings by increasing length, and so that strings of the same length are sorted lexicographically. *Hint:* Supply a Comparator.

PROGRAMMING PROJECTS

■■ **P14.1** It is common for people to name directories as dir1, dir2, and so on. When there are ten or more directories, the operating system displays them in dictionary order, as dir1, dir10, dir11, dir12, dir2, dir3, and so on. That is irritating, and it is easy to fix. Provide a comparator that compares strings that end in digit sequences in a way that makes sense to a human. First compare the part before the digits as strings, and then compare the numeric values of the digits.

■■■ **P14.2** Sometimes, directory or file names have numbers in the middle, and there may be more than one number, for example, sec3_14.txt or sec10_1.txt. Provide a comparator that can compare such strings in a way that makes sense to humans. Break each string into strings not containing digits and digit groups. Then compare two strings by comparing the first non-digit groups as strings, the first digit groups as integers, and so on.

■■ **P14.3** Implement the following sorting algorithm. First split the given array a into non-decreasing and decreasing segments (that is, segments such that a[i] ≤ a[i + 1] ≤ ... ≤ a[i + k] or a[j] > a[j + 1] > ... > a[j + m]). Reverse all decreasing segments. Now the array is partitioned into non-decreasing segments. Merge the first two segments, then the next two, and so on, each into a non-decreasing segment. Repeat this process until all segments are merged.

■■ **P14.4** The median m of a sequence of n elements is the element that would fall in the middle if the sequence was sorted. That is, $e \leq m$ for half the elements, and $m \leq e$ for the others. Clearly, one can obtain the median by sorting the sequence, but one can do quite a bit better with the following algorithm that finds the kth element of a sequence between a (inclusive) and b (exclusive). (For the median, use $k = n/2$, $a = 0$, and $b = n$.)

select(k, a, b):
Pick a pivot p in the subsequence between a and b.
Partition the subsequence elements into three subsequences: the elements <p, =p, >p
Let n1, n2, n3 be the sizes of each of these subsequences.
if k < n1
    return select(k, 0, n1).
else if (k > n1 + n2)
    return select(k, n1 + n2, n).
else
    return p.

Implement this algorithm and measure how much faster it is for computing the median of a random large sequence, when compared to sorting the sequence and taking the middle element.

■■ **P14.5** Implement the following modification of the quicksort algorithm, due to Bentley and McIlroy. Instead of using the first element as the pivot, use an approximation of the median.

If $n \leq 7$, use the middle element. If $n \leq 40$, use the median of the first, middle, and last element. Otherwise compute the "pseudomedian" of the nine elements a[i * (n - 1) / 8], where i ranges from 0 to 8. The pseudomedian of nine values is med(med(v_0, v_1, v_2), med(v_3, v_4, v_5), med(v_6, v_7, v_8)).

Compare the running time of this modification with that of the original algorithm on sequences that are nearly sorted or reverse sorted, and on sequences with many identical elements. What do you observe?

■■■ **P14.6** Bentley and McIlroy suggest the following modification to the quicksort algorithm when dealing with data sets that contain many repeated elements.

Instead of partitioning as

≤ ≥

(where ≤ denotes the elements that are ≤ the pivot), it is better to partition as

< = >

However, that is tedious to achieve directly. They recommend to partition as

= < > =

and then swap the two = regions into the middle. Implement this modification and check whether it improves performance on data sets with many repeated elements.

■ **P14.7** Implement the radix sort algorithm described in Exercise ●● R14.26 to sort arrays of numbers between 0 and 999.

■ **P14.8** Implement the radix sort algorithm described in Exercise ●● R14.26 to sort arrays of numbers between 0 and 999. However, use a single auxiliary array, not ten.

■■ **P14.9** Implement the radix sort algorithm described in Exercise ●● R14.26 to sort arbitrary int values (positive or negative).

■■■ **P14.10** Implement the sort method of the merge sort algorithm without recursion, where the length of the array is an arbitrary number. Keep merging adjacent regions whose size is a power of 2, and pay special attention to the last area whose size is less.

■■ **P14.11** Modify the binary search algorithm so that it returns an array of length 2 with the lowest index and highest index of those element(s) that equal the searched value. For example, when searching for 3, if the array contains the values 1 1 3 3 3 4 5 5, the algorithm should return [2, 4].

If the value is not found, return an array of length 1 containing the index at which the value should be inserted.

Your implementation should have $O(\log n)$ running time even if most elements of the array have the same value.

CHAPTER 15

THE JAVA COLLECTIONS FRAMEWORK

© nicholas belton/iStockphoto.

CHAPTER GOALS

To learn how to use the collection
classes supplied in the Java library

To use iterators to traverse collections

To choose appropriate collections for solving programming problems

To study applications of stacks and queues

CHAPTER CONTENTS

If you want to write a program that collects objects (such as the stamps to the left), you have a number of choices. Of course, you can use an array list, but computer scientists have invented other mechanisms that may be better suited for the task. In this chapter, we introduce the collection classes and interfaces that the Java library offers. You will learn how to use the Java collection classes, and how to choose the most appropriate collection type for a problem.

15.1 An Overview of the Collections Framework

A collection groups together elements and allows them to be retrieved later.

When you need to organize multiple objects in your program, you can place them into a **collection**. The ArrayList class that was introduced in Chapter 7 is one of many collection classes that the standard Java library supplies. In this chapter, you will learn about the Java *collections framework*, a hierarchy of interface types and classes for collecting objects. Each interface type is implemented by one or more classes (see Figure 1).

At the root of the hierarchy is the Collection interface. That interface has methods for adding and removing elements, and so on. Table 1 on page 514 shows all the methods. Because all collections implement this interface, its methods are available for all collection classes. For example, the size method reports the number of elements in *any* collection.

The List interface describes an important category of collections. In Java, a *list* is a collection that remembers the order of its elements (see Figure 2). The ArrayList class implements the List interface. An ArrayList is simply a class containing an array that is expanded as needed. If you are not concerned about efficiency, you can use the Array-List class whenever you need to collect objects. However, several common operations are inefficient with array lists. In particular, if an element is added or removed, the elements at larger positions must be moved.

The Java library supplies another class, LinkedList, that also implements the List interface. Unlike an array list, a linked list allows efficient insertion and removal of elements in the middle of the list. We will discuss that class in the next section.

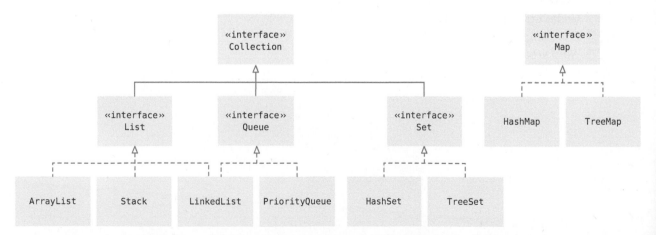

Figure 1 Interfaces and Classes in the Java Collections Framework

© Filip Fuxa/iStockphoto.

Figure 2   A List of Books

© parema/iStockphoto.

Figure 3   A Set of Books

© Vladimir Trenin/iStockphoto.

Figure 4   A Stack of Books

A list is a collection that remembers the order of its elements.

You use a list whenever you want to retain the order that you established. For example, on your bookshelf, you may order books by topic. A list is an appropriate data structure for such a collection because the ordering matters to you.

However, in many applications, you don't really care about the order of the elements in a collection. Consider a mail-order dealer of books. Without customers browsing the shelves, there is no need to order books by topic. Such a collection without an intrinsic order is called a **set**—see Figure 3.

A set is an unordered collection of unique elements.

Because a set does not track the order of the elements, it can arrange the elements so that the operations of finding, adding, and removing elements become more efficient. Computer scientists have invented mechanisms for this purpose. The Java library provides classes that are based on two such mechanisms (called *hash tables* and *binary search trees*). You will learn in this chapter how to choose between them.

Another way of gaining efficiency in a collection is to reduce the number of operations. A **stack** remembers the order of its elements, but it does not allow you to insert elements in every position. You can add and remove elements only at the top—see Figure 4.

In a **queue**, you add items to one end (the tail) and remove them from the other end (the head). For example, you could keep a queue of books, adding required reading at the tail and taking a book from the head whenever you have time to read another one. A **priority queue** is an unordered collection that has an efficient operation for removing the element with the highest priority. You might use a priority queue for organizing your reading assignments. Whenever you have some time, remove the book with the highest priority and read it. We will discuss stacks, queues, and priority queues in Section 15.5.

A map keeps associations between key and value objects.

Finally, a **map** manages associations between *keys* and *values*. Every key in the map has an associated value (see Figure 5). The map stores the keys, values, and the associations between them.

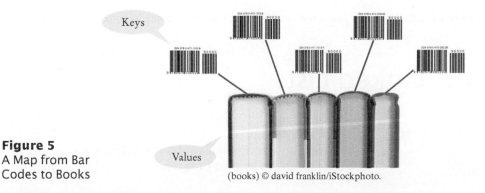

Figure 5
A Map from Bar Codes to Books

(books) © david franklin/iStockphoto.

For an example, consider a library that puts a bar code on each book. The program used to check books in and out needs to look up the book associated with each bar code. A map associating bar codes with books can solve this problem. We will discuss maps in Section 15.4.

Starting with this chapter, we will use the "diamond syntax" for constructing instances of generic classes (see Special Topic 7.5). For example, when constructing an array list of strings, we will use

```
ArrayList<String> coll = new ArrayList<>();
```

Note that there is an empty pair of brackets <> after new ArrayList on the right-hand side. The compiler infers from the left-hand side that an array list of strings is constructed.

Table 1   The Methods of the Collection Interface

`Collection<String> coll = new ArrayList<>();`	The ArrayList class implements the Collection interface.
`coll = new TreeSet<>();`	The TreeSet class (Section 15.3) also implements the Collection interface.
`int n = coll.size();`	Gets the size of the collection. n is now 0.
`coll.add("Harry");` `coll.add("Sally");`	Adds elements to the collection.
`String s = coll.toString();`	Returns a string with all elements in the collection. s is now [Harry, Sally].
`System.out.println(coll);`	Invokes the toString method and prints [Harry, Sally].
`coll.remove("Harry");` `boolean b = coll.remove("Tom");`	Removes an element from the collection, returning false if the element is not present. b is false.
`b = coll.contains("Sally");`	Checks whether this collection contains a given element. b is now true.

`for (String s : coll)`
`{`
`    System.out.println(s);`
`}`
	You can use the "for each" loop with any collection. This loop prints the elements on separate lines.

`Iterator<String> iter = coll.iterator();`	You use an iterator for visiting the elements in the collection (see Section 15.2.3).

EXAMPLE CODE   See your eText or companion code for a sample program that demonstrates several collection classes.

15.2 Linked Lists

A **linked list** is a data structure used for collecting a sequence of objects that allows efficient addition and removal of elements in the middle of the sequence. In the following sections, you will learn how a linked list manages its elements and how you can use linked lists in your programs.

15.2.1 The Structure of Linked Lists

To understand the inefficiency of arrays and the need for a more efficient data structure, imagine a program that maintains a sequence of employee names. If an employee leaves the company, the name must be removed. In an array, the hole in the sequence needs to be closed up by moving all objects that come after it. Conversely, suppose an employee is added in the middle of the sequence. Then all names following the new hire must be moved toward the end. Moving a large number of elements can involve a substantial amount of processing time. A linked list structure avoids this movement.

© andrea laurita/iStockphoto.

Each node in a linked list is connected to the neighboring nodes.

A linked list uses a sequence of *nodes*. A node is an object that stores an element and references to the neighboring nodes in the sequence (see Figure 6).

> A linked list consists of a number of nodes, each of which has a reference to the next node.

Figure 6
A Linked List

When you insert a new node into a linked list, only the neighboring node references need to be updated (see Figure 7).

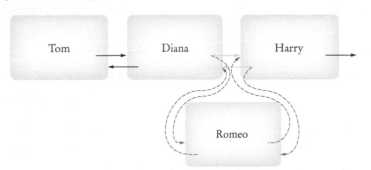

Figure 7 Inserting a Node into a Linked List

The same is true when you remove a node (see Figure 8). What's the catch? Linked lists allow efficient insertion and removal, but element access can be inefficient.

Figure 8 Removing a Node from a Linked List

Adding and removing elements at a given location in a linked list is efficient.

Visiting the elements of a linked list in sequential order is efficient, but random access is not.

For example, suppose you want to locate the fifth element. You must first traverse the first four. This is a problem if you need to access the elements in arbitrary order. The term "random access" is used in computer science to describe an access pattern in which elements are accessed in arbitrary (not necessarily random) order. In contrast, sequential access visits the elements in sequence.

Of course, if you mostly visit all elements in sequence (for example, to display or print the elements), the inefficiency of random access is not a problem. You use linked lists when you are concerned about the efficiency of inserting or removing elements and you rarely need element access in random order.

15.2.2 The LinkedList Class of the Java Collections Framework

The Java library provides a LinkedList class in the java.util package. It is a **generic class,** just like the ArrayList class. That is, you specify the type of the list elements in angle brackets, such as LinkedList<String> or LinkedList<Employee>.

Table 2 shows important methods of the LinkedList class. (Remember that the LinkedList class also inherits the methods of the Collection interface shown in Table 1.)

As you can see from Table 2, there are methods for accessing the beginning and the end of the list directly. However, to visit the other elements, you need a list **iterator.** We discuss iterators next.

Table 2 Working with Linked Lists

`LinkedList<String> list = new LinkedList<>();`	An empty list.
`list.addLast("Harry");`	Adds an element to the end of the list. Same as add.
`list.addFirst("Sally");`	Adds an element to the beginning of the list. list is now [Sally, Harry].
`list.getFirst();`	Gets the element stored at the beginning of the list; here "Sally".
`list.getLast();`	Gets the element stored at the end of the list; here "Harry".
`String removed = list.removeFirst();`	Removes the first element of the list and returns it. removed is "Sally" and list is [Harry]. Use removeLast to remove the last element.
`ListIterator<String> iter = list.listIterator()`	Provides an iterator for visiting all list elements (see Table 3 on page 518).

15.2.3 List Iterators

You use a list iterator to access elements inside a linked list.

An iterator encapsulates a position anywhere inside the linked list. Conceptually, you should think of the iterator as pointing between two elements, just as the cursor in a word processor points between two characters (see Figure 9). In the conceptual view, think of each element as being like a letter in a word processor, and think of the iterator as being like the blinking cursor between letters.

Figure 9 A Conceptual View of the List Iterator

You obtain a list iterator with the `listIterator` method of the `LinkedList` class:

```
LinkedList<String> employeeNames = . . .;
ListIterator<String> iterator = employeeNames.listIterator();
```

Note that the iterator class is also a generic type. A `ListIterator<String>` iterates through a list of strings; a `ListIterator<Book>` visits the elements in a `LinkedList<Book>`.

Initially, the iterator points before the first element. You can move the iterator position with the `next` method:

```
iterator.next();
```

The `next` method throws a `NoSuchElementException` if you are already past the end of the list. You should always call the iterator's `hasNext` method before calling `next`—it returns `true` if there is a next element.

```
if (iterator.hasNext())
{
    iterator.next();
}
```

The `next` method returns the element that the iterator is passing. When you use a `ListIterator<String>`, the return type of the `next` method is `String`. In general, the return type of the `next` method matches the list iterator's type parameter (which reflects the type of the elements in the list).

You traverse all elements in a linked list of strings with the following loop:

```
while (iterator.hasNext())
{
    String name = iterator.next();
    Do something with name.
}
```

As a shorthand, if your loop simply visits all elements of the linked list, you can use the "for each" loop:

```
for (String name : employeeNames)
{
    Do something with name.
}
```

Then you don't have to worry about iterators at all. Behind the scenes, the `for` loop uses an iterator to visit all list elements.

The nodes of the `LinkedList` class store two links: one to the next element and one to the previous one. Such a list is called a **doubly-linked list**. You can use the `previous` and `hasPrevious` methods of the `ListIterator` interface to move the iterator position backward.

Table 3 Methods of the `Iterator` and `ListIterator` Interfaces

`String s = iter.next();`	Assume that `iter` points to the beginning of the list `[Sally]` before calling `next`. After the call, `s` is `"Sally"` and the iterator points to the end.
`iter.previous();` `iter.set("Juliet");`	The `set` method updates the last element returned by `next` or `previous`. The list is now `[Juliet]`.
`iter.hasNext()`	Returns `false` because the iterator is at the end of the collection.

`if (iter.hasPrevious())`
`{`
`    s = iter.previous();`
`}`
	`hasPrevious` returns `true` because the iterator is not at the beginning of the list. `previous` and `hasPrevious` are `ListIterator` methods.

`iter.add("Diana");`	Adds an element before the iterator position (`ListIterator` only). The list is now `[Diana, Juliet]`.
`iter.next();` `iter.remove();`	`remove` removes the last element returned by `next` or `previous`. The list is now `[Diana]`.

The `add` method adds an object before the iterator position.

```
iterator.add("Juliet");
```

You can visualize insertion to be like typing text in a word processor. Each character is inserted after the cursor, then the cursor moves past the inserted character (see Figure 9). Most people never pay much attention to this—you may want to try it out and watch carefully how your word processor inserts characters.

The `remove` method removes the object that was returned by the last call to `next` or `previous`. For example, this loop removes all names that fulfill a certain condition:

```
while (iterator.hasNext())
{
    String name = iterator.next();
    if (condition is fulfilled for name)
    {
        iterator.remove();
    }
}
```

You have to be careful when calling `remove`. It can be called only *once* after calling `next` or `previous`, and you cannot call it immediately after a call to `add`. If you call the method improperly, it throws an `IllegalStateException`.

Table 3 summarizes the methods of the `ListIterator` interface. The `ListIterator` interface extends a more general `Iterator` interface that is suitable for arbitrary collections, not just lists. The table indicates which methods are specific to list iterators.

Following is a sample program that inserts strings into a list and then iterates through the list, adding and removing elements. Finally, the entire list is printed. The comments indicate the iterator position.

sec02/ListDemo.java

```
1   import java.util.LinkedList;
2   import java.util.ListIterator;
3
```

```
4   /**
5       This program demonstrates the LinkedList class.
6   */
7   public class ListDemo
8   {
9      public static void main(String[] args)
10     {
11        LinkedList<String> staff = new LinkedList<>();
12        staff.addLast("Diana");
13        staff.addLast("Harry");
14        staff.addLast("Romeo");
15        staff.addLast("Tom");
16
17        // | in the comments indicates the iterator position
18
19        ListIterator<String> iterator = staff.listIterator(); // |DHRT
20        iterator.next(); // D|HRT
21        iterator.next(); // DH|RT
22
23        // Add more elements after second element
24
25        iterator.add("Juliet"); // DHJ|RT
26        iterator.add("Nina"); // DHJN|RT
27
28        iterator.next(); // DHJNR|T
29
30        // Remove last traversed element
31
32        iterator.remove(); // DHJN|T
33
34        // Print all elements
35
36        System.out.println(staff);
37        System.out.println("Expected: [Diana, Harry, Juliet, Nina, Tom]");
38     }
39  }
```

Program Run

```
[Diana, Harry, Juliet, Nina, Tom]
Expected: [Diana, Harry, Juliet, Nina, Tom]
```

Computing & Society 15.1 **Standardization**

You encounter the benefits of standardization every day. When you buy a light bulb, you can be assured that it fits the socket without having to measure the socket at home and the light bulb in the store. In fact, you may have experienced how painful the lack of standards can be if you have ever purchased a flashlight with nonstandard bulbs. Replacement bulbs for such a flashlight can be difficult and expensive to obtain.

Programmers have a similar desire for standardization. Consider the important goal of platform independence for Java programs. After you compile a Java program into class files, you can execute the class files on any computer that has a Java virtual machine. For this to work, the behavior of the virtual machine has to be strictly defined. If all virtual machines don't behave exactly the same way, then the slogan of "write once, run anywhere" turns into "write once,

© Denis Vorob'yev/iStockphoto.

debug everywhere". In order for multiple implementors to create compatible virtual machines, the virtual machine needed to be *standardized*. That is, someone needed to create a definition of the virtual machine and its expected behavior.

Who creates standards? Some of the most successful standards have been created by volunteer groups such as the Internet Engineering Task Force (IETF) and the World Wide Web Consortium (W3C). The IETF standardizes protocols used in the Internet, such as the protocol for exchanging e-mail messages. The W3C standardizes the Hypertext Markup Language (HTML), the format for web pages. These standards have been instrumental in the creation of the World Wide Web as an open platform that is not controlled by any one company.

Many programming languages, such as C++ and Scheme, have been standardized by independent standards organizations, such as the American National Standards Institute (ANSI) and the International Organization for Standardization—called ISO for short (not an acronym; see https://www.iso.org/about-us.html). ANSI and ISO are associations of industry professionals who develop standards for everything from car tires to credit card shapes to programming languages.

Many standards are developed by dedicated experts from a multitude of vendors and users, with the objective of creating a set of rules that codifies best practices. But sometimes, standards are very contentious. By 2005, Microsoft started losing government contracts when its customers became concerned that many of their documents were stored in proprietary, undocumented formats. Instead of supporting existing standard formats, or working with an industry group to improve those standards, Microsoft wrote its own standard that simply codified what its product was currently doing, even though that format is widely regarded as being inconsistent and very complex. (The description of the format spans over 6,000 pages.) The company first proposed its standard to the European Computer Manufacturers Association (ECMA), which approved it with minimal discussion. Then ISO "fast-tracked" it as an existing standard, bypassing the normal technical review mechanism.

For similar reasons, Sun Microsystems, the inventor of Java, never agreed to have a third-party organization standardize the Java language. Instead, they put in place their own standardization process, involving

other companies but refusing to relinquish control.

Of course, many important pieces of technology aren't standardized at all. Consider the Windows operating system. Although Windows is often called a de-facto standard, it really is no standard at all. Nobody has ever attempted to define formally what the Windows operating system should do. The behavior changes at the whim of its vendor. That suits Microsoft just fine, because it makes it impossible for a third party to create its own version of Windows.

As a computer professional, there will be many times in your career when you need to make a decision whether to support a particular standard. Consider a simple example. In this chapter, you learn about the collection classes from the standard Java library. However, many computer scientists dislike these classes because of their numerous design issues. Should you use the Java collections in your own code, or should you implement a better set of collections? If you do the former, you have to deal with a design that is less than optimal. If you do the latter, other programmers may have a hard time understanding your code because they aren't familiar with your classes.

15.3 Sets

As you learned in Section 15.1, a **set** organizes its values in an order that is optimized for efficiency, which may not be the order in which you add elements. Inserting and removing elements is more efficient with a set than with a list.

In the following sections, you will learn how to choose a set implementation and how to work with sets.

15.3.1 Choosing a Set Implementation

The Set interface in the standard Java library has the same methods as the Collection interface, shown in Table 1. However, there is an essential difference between arbitrary collections and sets. A set does not admit duplicates. If you add an element to a set that is already present, the insertion is ignored.

The HashSet and TreeSet classes both implement the Set interface.

The HashSet and TreeSet classes implement the Set interface. These two classes provide set implementations based on two different mechanisms, called **hash tables** and **binary search trees**. Both implementations arrange the set elements so that finding, adding, and removing elements is efficient, but they use different strategies.

The basic idea of a hash table is simple. Set elements are grouped into smaller collections of elements that share the same characteristic. You can imagine a hash set of books as having a group for each color, so that books of the same color are in the same group. To find whether a book is already present, you just need to check it against the books in the same color group. Actually, hash tables don't use colors, but integer values (called hash codes) that can be computed from the elements.

In order to use a hash table, the elements must have a method to compute those integer values. This method is called hashCode. The elements must also belong to a class with a properly defined equals method (see Section 9.5.2).

© Alfredo Ragazzoni/iStockphoto.

On this shelf, books of the same color are grouped together. Similarly, in a hash table, objects with the same hash code are placed in the same group.

Many classes in the standard library implement these methods, for example String, Integer, Double, Point, Rectangle, Color, and all the collection classes. Therefore, you can form a HashSet<String>, HashSet<Rectangle>, or even a HashSet<HashSet<Integer>>.

Suppose you want to form a set of elements belonging to a class that you declared, such as a HashSet<Book>. Then you need to provide hashCode and equals methods for the class Book. There is one exception to this rule. If all elements are distinct (for example, if your program never has two Book objects with the same author and title), then you can simply inherit the hashCode and equals methods of the Object class.

The TreeSet class uses a different strategy for arranging its elements. Elements are kept in sorted order. For example, a set of books might be arranged by height, or alphabetically by author and title. The elements are not stored in an array—that would make adding and removing elements too inefficient. Instead, they are stored in nodes, as in a linked list. However, the nodes are not arranged in a linear sequence but in a tree shape.

In order to use a TreeSet, it must be possible to compare the elements and determine which one is "larger". You can use a TreeSet for classes such as String and Integer that implement the Comparable interface, which we discussed in Section 10.3. (That section also shows you how you can implement comparison methods for your own classes.)

As a rule of thumb, you should choose a TreeSet if you want to visit the set's elements in sorted order. Otherwise choose a HashSet—as long as the hash function is well chosen, it is a bit more efficient.

A tree set keeps its elements in sorted order. © Volkan Ersoy/iStockphoto.

When you construct a HashSet or TreeSet, store the reference in a Set variable. For example,

```
Set<String> names = new HashSet<>();
```

or

```
Set<String> names = new TreeSet<>();
```

After you construct the collection object, the implementation no longer matters; only the interface is important.

15.3.2 Working with Sets

You add and remove set elements with the add and remove methods:

```
names.add("Romeo");
names.remove("Juliet");
```

Sets don't have duplicates. Adding a duplicate of an element that is already present is ignored.

As in mathematics, a set collection in Java rejects duplicates. Adding an element has no effect if the element is already in the set. Similarly, attempting to remove an element that isn't in the set is ignored.

The contains method tests whether an element is contained in the set:

```
if (names.contains("Juliet")) . . .
```

The contains method uses the equals method of the element type. If your set collects String or Integer objects, you don't have to worry. Those classes provide an equals method. However, if you implemented the element type yourself, then you need to define the equals method—see Section 9.5.2.

Finally, to list all elements in the set, get an iterator. As with list iterators, you use the next and hasNext methods to step through the set.

```
Iterator<String> iter = names.iterator();
while (iter.hasNext())
{
    String name = iter.next();
    Do something with name.
}
```

You can also use the "for each" loop instead of explicitly using an iterator:

```
for (String name : names)
{
    Do something with name.
}
```

A set iterator visits the elements in the order in which the set implementation keeps them.

A set iterator visits the elements in the order in which the set implementation keeps them. This is not necessarily the order in which you inserted them. The order of elements in a hash set seems quite random because the hash code spreads the elements into different groups. When you visit elements of a tree set, they always appear in sorted order, even if you inserted them in a different order.

There is an important difference between the Iterator that you obtain from a set and the ListIterator that a list yields. The ListIterator has an add method to add an element at the list iterator position. The Iterator interface has no such method. It makes no sense to add an element at a particular position in a set, because the set can order the elements any way it likes. Thus, you always add elements directly to a set, never to an iterator of the set.

You cannot add an element to a set at an iterator position.

However, you can remove a set element at an iterator position, just as you do with list iterators.

Table 4 Working with Sets

`Set<String> names;`	Use the interface type for variable declarations.
`names = new HashSet<>();`	Use a `TreeSet` if you need to visit the elements in sorted order.
`names.add("Romeo");`	Now `names.size()` is 1.
`names.add("Fred");`	Now `names.size()` is 2.
`names.add("Romeo");`	`names.size()` is still 2. You can't add duplicates.
`if (names.contains("Fred"))`	The `contains` method checks whether a value is contained in the set. In this case, the method returns `true`.
`System.out.println(names);`	Prints the set in the format `[Fred, Romeo]`. The elements need not be shown in the order in which they were inserted.

`for (String name : names)`
`{`
` . . .`
`}`
	Use this loop to visit all elements of a set.

`names.remove("Romeo");`	Now `names.size()` is 1.
`names.remove("Juliet");`	It is not an error to remove an element that is not present. The method call has no effect.

Also, the `Iterator` interface has no previous method to go backward through the elements. Because the elements are not ordered, it is not meaningful to distinguish between "going forward" and "going backward".

The following program shows a practical application of sets. It reads in all words from a dictionary file that contains correctly spelled words and places them in a set. It then reads all words from a document—here, the book *Alice in Wonderland*—into a second set. Finally, it prints all words from that set that are not in the dictionary set. These are the potential misspellings. (As you can see from the output, we used an American dictionary, and words with British spelling, such as *honour*, are flagged as potential errors. Moreover, the preamble contains words such as *etext* and *ascii* that are not in the dictionary.)

sec03/SpellCheck.java

```java
1  import java.util.HashSet;
2  import java.util.Scanner;
3  import java.util.Set;
4  import java.io.File;
5  import java.io.FileNotFoundException;
6
7  /**
8     This program checks which words in a file are not present in a dictionary.
9  */
10 public class SpellCheck
11 {
```

```
12      public static void main(String[] args)
13         throws FileNotFoundException
14      {
15         // Read the dictionary and the document
16
17         Set<String> dictionaryWords = readWords("words");
18         Set<String> documentWords = readWords("alice30.txt");
19
20         // Print all words that are in the document but not the dictionary
21
22         for (String word : documentWords)
23         {
24            if (!dictionaryWords.contains(word))
25            {
26               System.out.println(word);
27            }
28         }
29      }
30
31      /**
32         Reads all words from a file.
33         @param filename the name of the file
34         @return a set with all lowercased words in the file. Here, a
35         word is a sequence of upper- and lowercase letters.
36      */
37      public static Set<String> readWords(String filename)
38         throws FileNotFoundException
39      {
40         Set<String> words = new HashSet<>();
41         Scanner in = new Scanner(new File(filename));
42         // Use any characters other than a-z or A-Z as delimiters
43         in.useDelimiter("[^a-zA-Z]+");
44         while (in.hasNext())
45         {
46            words.add(in.next().toLowerCase());
47         }
48         return words;
49      }
50   }
```

Program Run

```
...
favourite
hearthrug
gryphon
righthand
dutchess
honour
...
```

Programming Tip 15.1

Use Interface References to Manipulate Data Structures

It is considered good style to store a reference to a HashSet or TreeSet in a variable of type Set:

```
Set<String> words = new HashSet<>();
```

This way, you have to change only one line if you decide to use a TreeSet instead.

If a method can operate on arbitrary collections, use the Collection interface type for the parameter variable:

```
public static void removeLongWords(Collection<String> words)
```

In theory, we should make the same recommendation for the List interface, namely to save ArrayList and LinkedList references in variables of type List. However, the List interface has get and set methods for random access, even though these methods are very inefficient for linked lists. You can't write efficient code if you don't know whether the methods that you are calling are efficient or not. This is plainly a serious design error in the standard library, and it makes the List interface somewhat unattractive.

15.4 Maps

A **map** allows you to associate elements from a *key set* with elements from a *value collection*. You use a map when you want to look up objects by using a key. For example, Figure 10 shows a map from the names of people to their favorite colors.

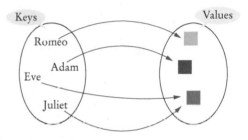

Figure 10 A Map

The HashMap and TreeMap classes both implement the Map interface.

Just as there are two kinds of set implementations, the Java library has two implementations for the Map interface: HashMap and TreeMap.

After constructing a HashMap or TreeMap, you can store the reference to the map object in a Map reference:

```
Map<String, Color> favoriteColors = new HashMap<>();
```

Use the put method to add an association:

```
favoriteColors.put("Juliet", Color.RED);
```

You can change the value of an existing association, simply by calling put again:

```
favoriteColors.put("Juliet", Color.BLUE);
```

The get method returns the value associated with a key.

```
Color julietsFavoriteColor = favoriteColors.get("Juliet");
```

If you ask for a key that isn't associated with any values, the get method returns null.

To remove an association, call the remove method with the key:

```
favoriteColors.remove("Juliet");
```

To find all keys and values in a map, iterate through the key set and find the values that correspond to the keys.

Sometimes you want to enumerate all keys in a map. The keySet method yields the set of keys. You can then ask the key set for an iterator and get all keys. From each key, you can find the associated value with the get method. Thus, the following instructions print all key/value pairs in a map m whose keys have type String:

```
Set<String> keySet = m.keySet();
for (String key : keySet)
{
    Color value = m.get(key);
    System.out.println(key + "->" + value);
}
```

Table 5 Working with Maps

`Map<String, Integer> scores;`	Keys are strings, values are `Integer` wrappers. Use the interface type for variable declarations.
`scores = new TreeMap<>();`	Use a `HashMap` if you don't need to visit the keys in sorted order.
`scores.put("Harry", 90);` `scores.put("Sally", 95);`	Adds keys and values to the map.
`scores.put("Sally", 100);`	Modifies the value of an existing key.
`int n = scores.get("Sally");` `Integer n2 = scores.get("Diana");`	Gets the value associated with a key, or `null` if the key is not present. `n` is 100, `n2` is `null`.
`System.out.println(scores);`	Prints `scores.toString()`, a string of the form `{Harry=90, Sally=100}`

`for (String key : scores.keySet())`
`{`
`   Integer value = scores.get(key);`
`   . . .`
`}`
	Iterates through all map keys and values.

`scores.remove("Sally");`	Removes the key and value.

This sample program shows a map in action.

sec04/MapDemo.java

```java
1  import java.awt.Color;
2  import java.util.HashMap;
3  import java.util.Map;
4  import java.util.Set;
5
6  /**
7     This program demonstrates a map that maps names to colors.
8  */
9  public class MapDemo
10 {
11    public static void main(String[] args)
12    {
13       Map<String, Color> favoriteColors = new HashMap<>();
14       favoriteColors.put("Juliet", Color.BLUE);
15       favoriteColors.put("Romeo", Color.GREEN);
16       favoriteColors.put("Adam", Color.RED);
17       favoriteColors.put("Eve", Color.BLUE);
18
19       // Print all keys and values in the map
20
21       Set<String> keySet = favoriteColors.keySet();
22       for (String key : keySet)
23       {
24          Color value = favoriteColors.get(key);
25          System.out.println(key + " : " + value);
26       }
27    }
28 }
```

Program Run

```
Juliet : java.awt.Color[r=0,g=0,b=255]
Adam : java.awt.Color[r=255,g=0,b=0]
Eve : java.awt.Color[r=0,g=0,b=255]
Romeo : java.awt.Color[r=0,g=255,b=0]
```

Special Topic 15.1
Updating Map Entries

Maps are commonly used for counting how often an item occurs. For example, Worked Example 15.1 uses a Map<String, Integer> to track how many times a word occurs in a file.

It is a bit tedious to deal with the special case of inserting the first value. Consider the following code from Worked Example 15.1:

```
Integer count = frequencies.get(word); // Get the old frequency count
// If there was none, put 1; otherwise, increment the count
if (count == null) { count = 1; }
else { count = count + 1; }
frequencies.put(word, count);
```

This task can be simplified with the merge method of the Map interface. You specify

- A key.
- A value to be used if the key is not yet present.
- A function to compute the updated value if the key is present.

The function is specified as a lambda expression (see Special Topic 10.4). For example,

```
frequencies.merge(word, 1, (oldValue, notPresentValue) -> oldValue + notPresentValue);
```

does the same as the four lines of code above. If word is not present, the value is set to 1. Otherwise, the old value is incremented.

The merge method is also useful if the map values are sets or comma-separated strings—see Exercises •• E15.6 and •• E15.7.

HOW TO 15.1
Choosing a Collection

Suppose you need to store objects in a collection. You have now seen a number of different data structures. This How To reviews how to pick an appropriate collection for your application.

© Tom Hahn/iStockphoto.

Step 1 Determine how you access the values.

You store values in a collection so that you can later retrieve them. How do you want to access individual values? You have several choices:

- Values are accessed by an integer position. Use an ArrayList.
- Values are accessed by a key that is not a part of the object. Use a map.
- Values are accessed only at one of the ends. Use a queue (for first-in, first-out access) or a stack (for last-in, first-out access).
- You don't need to access individual values by position. Refine your choice in Steps 3 and 4.

Step 2   Determine the element types or key/value types.

For a list or set, determine the type of the elements that you want to store. For example, if you collect a set of books, then the element type is Book.

Similarly, for a map, determine the types of the keys and the associated values. If you want to look up books by ID, you can use a Map<Integer, Book> or Map<String, Book>, depending on your ID type.

Step 3   Determine whether element or key order matters.

When you visit elements from a collection or keys from a map, do you care about the order in which they are visited? You have several choices:

- Elements or keys must be sorted. Use a TreeSet or TreeMap. Go to Step 6.
- Elements must be in the same order in which they were inserted. Your choice is now narrowed down to a LinkedList or an ArrayList.
- It doesn't matter. As long as you get to visit all elements, you don't care in which order. If you chose a map in Step 1, use a HashMap and go to Step 5.

Step 4   For a collection, determine which operations must be efficient.

You have several choices:

- Finding elements must be efficient. Use a HashSet.
- It must be efficient to add or remove elements at the beginning, or, provided that you are already inspecting an element there, another position. Use a LinkedList.
- You only insert or remove at the end, or you collect so few elements that you aren't concerned about speed. Use an ArrayList.

Step 5   For hash sets and maps, decide whether you need to implement the hashCode and equals methods.

- If your elements or keys belong to a class that someone else implemented, check whether the class has its own hashCode and equals methods. If so, you are all set. This is the case for most classes in the standard Java library, such as String, Integer, Rectangle, and so on.
- If not, decide whether you can compare the elements by identity. This is the case if you never construct two distinct elements with the same contents. In that case, you need not do anything—the hashCode and equals methods of the Object class are appropriate.
- Otherwise, you need to implement your own equals and hashCode methods—see Section 9.5.2 and Special Topic 15.2.

Step 6   If you use a tree, decide whether to supply a comparator.

Look at the class of the set elements or map keys. Does that class implement the Comparable interface? If so, is the sort order given by the compareTo method the one you want? If yes, then you don't need to do anything further. This is the case for many classes in the standard library, in particular for String and Integer.

If not, then your element class must implement the Comparable interface (Section 10.3), or you must declare a class that implements the Comparator interface (see Special Topic 14.4).

WORKED EXAMPLE 15.1

Word Frequency

Learn how to create a program that reads a text file and prints a list of all words in the file in alphabetical order, together with a count that indicates how often each word occurred in the file. See your eText or visit wiley.com/go/bjeo7.

© Ermin Gutenberger/iStockphoto.

Special Topic 15.2

Hash Functions

If you use a hash set or hash map with your own classes, you may need to implement a hash function. A **hash function** is a function that computes an integer value, the **hash code**, from an object in such a way that different objects are likely to yield different hash codes. Because hashing is so important, the Object class has a hashCode method. The call

```
int h = x.hashCode();
```

computes the hash code of any object x. If you want to put objects of a given class into a HashSet or use the objects as keys in a HashMap, the class should override this method. The method should be implemented so that different objects are likely to have different hash codes.

A hash function computes an integer value from an object.

For example, the String class declares a hash function for strings that does a good job of producing different integer values for different strings. Table 6 shows some examples of strings and their hash codes.

Table 6 Sample Strings and Their Hash Codes

String	Hash Code
"eat"	100184
"tea"	114704
"Juliet"	−2065036585
"Ugh"	84982
"VII"	84982

A good hash function minimizes *collisions*—identical hash codes for different objects.

It is possible for two or more distinct objects to have the same hash code; this is called a *collision*. For example, the strings "Ugh" and "VII" happen to have the same hash code, but these collisions are very rare for strings (see Exercise •• P15.5).

The hashCode method of the String class combines the characters of a string into a numerical code. The code isn't simply the sum of the character values—that would not scramble the

A good hash function produces different hash values for each object so that they are scattered about in a hash table.

© one clear vision/iStockphoto.

character values enough. Strings that are permutations of another (such as "eat" and "tea") would all have the same hash code.

Here is the method the standard library uses to compute the hash code for a string:

```
final int HASH_MULTIPLIER = 31;
int h = 0;
for (int i = 0; i < s.length(); i++)
{
    h = HASH_MULTIPLIER * h + s.charAt(i);
}
```

For example, the hash code of "eat" is

```
31 * (31 * 'e' + 'a') + 't' = 100184
```

The hash code of "tea" is quite different, namely

```
31 * (31 * 't' + 'e') + 'a' = 114704
```

(Use the Unicode table from Appendix A to look up the character values: 'a' is 97, 'e' is 101, and 't' is 116.)

> Override hashCode methods in your own classes by combining the hash codes for the instance variables.

For your own classes, you should make up a hash code that combines the hash codes of the instance variables in a similar way. For example, let us declare a hashCode method for the Country class from Section 10.1. There are two instance variables: the country name and the area. First, compute their hash codes. You know how to compute the hash code of a string. To compute the hash code of a floating-point number, first wrap the floating-point number into a Double object, and then compute its hash code.

```
public class Country
{
    . . .
    public int hashCode()
    {
        int h1 = name.hashCode();
        int h2 = new Double(area).hashCode();
        . . .
    }
}
```

Then combine the two hash codes:

```
final int HASH_MULTIPLIER = 31;
int h = HASH_MULTIPLIER * h1 + h2;
return h;
```

However, it is easier to use the Objects.hash method which takes the hash codes of all arguments and combines them with a multiplier.

```
public int hashCode()
{
    return Objects.hash(name, area);
}
```

When you supply your own hashCode method for a class, you must also provide a compatible equals method. The equals method is used to differentiate between two objects that happen to have the same hash code.

> A class's hashCode method must be compatible with its equals method.

The equals and hashCode methods must be *compatible* with each other. Two objects that are equal must yield the same hash code.

You get into trouble if your class declares an equals method but not a hashCode method. Suppose the Country class declares an equals method (checking that the name and area are the same), but no hashCode method. Then the hashCode method is inherited from the Object superclass. That method computes a hash code from the *memory location* of the object. Then it is very likely that two objects with the same contents will have different hash codes, in which case a hash set will store them as two distinct objects.

However, if you declare *neither* equals *nor* hashCode, then there is no problem. The equals method of the Object class considers two objects equal only if their memory location is the same. That is, the Object class has compatible equals and hashCode methods. Of course, then the notion of equality is very restricted: Only identical objects are considered equal. That can be a perfectly valid notion of equality, depending on your application.

EXAMPLE CODE   See your eText or companion code for a program that demonstrates a hash set with objects of the Country class.

15.5 Stacks, Queues, and Priority Queues

In the following sections, we cover stacks, queues, and priority queues. These data structures each have a different policy for data removal. Removing an element yields the most recently added element, the least recently added, or the element with the highest priority.

15.5.1 Stacks

A stack is a collection of elements with "last-in, first-out" retrieval.

A **stack** lets you insert and remove elements only at one end, traditionally called the *top* of the stack. New items can be added to the top of the stack. Items are removed from the top of the stack as well. Therefore, they are removed in the order that is opposite from the order in which they have been added, called *last-in, first-out* or *LIFO* order.

For example, if you add items A, B, and C and then remove them, you obtain C, B, and A. With stacks, the addition and removal operations are called push and pop.

© John Madden/iStockphoto.

The last pancake that has been added to this stack will be the first one that is consumed.

```
Stack<String> s = new Stack<>();
s.push("A"); s.push("B"); s.push("C");
while (s.size() > 0)
{
    System.out.print(s.pop() + " "); // Prints C B A
}
```

There are many applications for stacks in computer science. Consider the undo feature of a word processor. It keeps the issued commands in a stack. When you select "Undo", the *last* command is undone, then the next-to-last, and so on.

The Undo key pops commands off a stack so that the last command is the first to be undone.   © budgetstockphoto/iStockphoto.

Another important example is the **run-time stack** that a processor or virtual machine keeps to store the values of variables in nested methods. Whenever a new method is called, its parameter variables and local variables are pushed onto a stack. When the method exits, they are popped off again.

You will see other applications in Section 15.6.

The Java library provides a simple Stack class with methods push, pop, and peek—the latter gets the top element of the stack but does not remove it (see Table 7).

Table 7 Working with Stacks

`Stack<Integer> s = new Stack<>();`	Constructs an empty stack.

`s.push(1);`
`s.push(2);`
`s.push(3);`
	Adds to the top of the stack; s is now [1, 2, 3]. (Following the toString method of the Stack class, we show the top of the stack at the end.)

`int top = s.pop();`	Removes the top of the stack; top is set to 3 and s is now [1, 2].
`head = s.peek();`	Gets the top of the stack without removing it; head is set to 2.

EXAMPLE CODE   See your eText or companion code for a program that simulates an undo stack.

15.5.2 Queues

A **queue** lets you add items to one end of the queue (the *tail*) and remove them from the other end of the queue (the *head*). Queues yield items in a *first-in, first-out* or *FIFO* fashion. Items are removed in the same order in which they were added.

A typical application is a print queue. A printer may be accessed by several applications, perhaps running on different computers. If each of the applications tried to access the printer at the same time, the printout would be garbled. Instead, each application places its print data into a file and adds that file to the print queue. When the printer is done printing one file, it retrieves the next one from the queue. Therefore, print jobs are printed using the "first-in, first-out" rule, which is a fair arrangement for users of the shared printer.

The Queue interface in the standard Java library has methods add to add an element to the tail of the queue, remove to remove the head of the queue, and peek to get the head element of the queue without removing it (see Table 8).

To visualize a queue, think of people lining up.   Jack Hollingsworth/Photodisc/Getty Images.

Table 8 Working with Queues

`Queue<Integer> q = new LinkedList<>();`	The `LinkedList` class implements the `Queue` interface.

`q.add(1);`
`q.add(2);`
`q.add(3);`
	Adds to the tail of the queue; q is now [1, 2, 3].

`int head = q.remove();`	Removes the head of the queue; head is set to 1 and q is [2, 3].
`head = q.peek();`	Gets the head of the queue without removing it; head is set to 2.

The `LinkedList` class implements the `Queue` interface. Whenever you need a queue, simply initialize a `Queue` variable with a `LinkedList` object:

```
Queue<String> q = new LinkedList<>();
q.add("A"); q.add("B"); q.add("C");
while (q.size() > 0) { System.out.print(q.remove() + " "); } // Prints A B C
```

The standard library provides several queue classes that we do not discuss in this book. Those classes are intended for work sharing when multiple activities (called threads) run in parallel.

EXAMPLE CODE See your eText or companion code for a program that simulates a print queue.

15.5.3 Priority Queues

> When removing an element from a priority queue, the element with the most urgent priority is retrieved.

A **priority queue** collects elements, each of which has a *priority*. A typical example of a priority queue is a collection of work requests, some of which may be more urgent than others. Unlike a regular queue, the priority queue does not maintain a first-in, first-out discipline. Instead, elements are retrieved according to their priority. In other words, new items can be inserted in any order. But whenever an item is removed, it is the item with the most urgent priority.

It is customary to give low values to urgent priorities, with priority 1 denoting the most urgent priority. Thus, each removal operation extracts the *minimum* element from the queue.

For example, consider this code in which we add objects of a class `WorkOrder` into a priority queue. Each work order has a priority and a description.

```
PriorityQueue<WorkOrder> q = new PriorityQueue<>();
q.add(new WorkOrder(3, "Shampoo carpets"));
q.add(new WorkOrder(1, "Fix broken sink"));
q.add(new WorkOrder(2, "Order cleaning supplies"));
```

When you retrieve an item from a priority queue, you always get the most urgent one. © paul kline/iStockphoto.

When calling q.remove() for the first time, the work order with priority 1 is removed. The next call to q.remove() removes the work order whose priority is highest among those remaining in the queue—in our example, the work order with priority 2. If there happen to be two elements with the same priority, the priority queue will break ties arbitrarily.

Because the priority queue needs to be able to tell which element is the smallest, the added elements should belong to a class that implements the Comparable interface. (See Section 10.3 for a description of that interface type.)

Table 9 shows the methods of the PriorityQueue class in the standard Java library.

Table 9 Working with Priority Queues

`PriorityQueue<Integer> q =` `   new PriorityQueue<>();`	This priority queue holds Integer objects. In practice, you would use objects that describe tasks.
`q.add(3); q.add(1); q.add(2);`	Adds values to the priority queue.
`int first = q.remove();` `int second = q.remove();`	Each call to remove removes the most urgent item: first is set to 1, second to 2.
`int next = q.peek();`	Gets the smallest value in the priority queue without removing it.

EXAMPLE CODE   See your eText or companion code for a program that demonstrates a priority queue of work orders.

15.6 Stack and Queue Applications

Stacks and queues are, despite their simplicity, very versatile data structures. In the following sections, you will see some of their most useful applications.

15.6.1 Balancing Parentheses

A stack can be used to check whether parentheses in an expression are balanced.

In Common Error 4.2, you saw a simple trick for detecting unbalanced parentheses in an expression such as

```
-(b * b - (4 * a * c ) ) / (2 * a)
 1         2         1 0   1     0
```

Increment a counter when you see a (and decrement it when you see a). The counter should never be negative, and it should be zero at the end of the expression.

That works for expressions in Java, but in mathematical notation, one can have more than one kind of parentheses, such as

$$-\{[b \cdot b - (4 \cdot a \cdot c)]/(2 \cdot a)\}$$

To see whether such an expression is correctly formed, place the parentheses on a stack:

When you see an opening parenthesis, push it on the stack.
When you see a closing parenthesis, pop the stack.
If the opening and closing parentheses don't match
    The parentheses are unbalanced. Exit.
If at the end the stack is empty
    The parentheses are balanced.
Else
    The parentheses are not balanced.

Here is a walkthrough of the sample expression:

Stack	Unread expression	Comments
Empty	-{ [b * b - (4 * a * c)] / (2 * a) }	
{	[b * b - (4 * a * c)] / (2 * a) }	
{ [	b * b - (4 * a * c)] / (2 * a) }	
{ [(	4 * a * c)] / (2 * a) }	
{ [	] / (2 * a) }	(matches)
{	/ (2 * a) }	[matches]
{ (	2 * a) }	
{	}	(matches)
Empty	No more input	{ matches }
		The parentheses are balanced

EXAMPLE CODE   See your eText or companion code for a program for checking balanced parentheses.

15.6.2 Evaluating Reverse Polish Expressions

Use a stack to evaluate expressions in reverse Polish notation.

Consider how you write arithmetic expressions, such as $(3 + 4) \times 5$. The parentheses are needed so that 3 and 4 are added before multiplying the result by 5.

However, you can eliminate the parentheses if you write the operators *after* the numbers, like this: $3\ 4 + 5 \times$ (see Special Topic 15.3). To evaluate this expression, apply + to 3 and 4, yielding 7, and then simplify $7\ 5 \times$ to 35. It gets trickier for complex expressions. For example, $3\ 4\ 5 + \times$ means to compute $4\ 5 +$ (that is, 9), and then evaluate $3\ 9 \times$. If we evaluate this expression left-to-right, we need to leave the 3 somewhere while we work on $4\ 5 +$. Where? We put it on a stack. The algorithm for evaluating reverse Polish expressions is simple:

If you read a number
    Push it on the stack.
Else if you read an operand
    Pop two values off the stack.
    Combine the values with the operand.
    Push the result back onto the stack.
Else if there is no more input
    Pop and display the result.

Here is a walkthrough of evaluating the expression 3 4 5 + x:

Stack	Unread expression	Comments
Empty	3 4 5 + x	
3	4 5 + x	Numbers are pushed on the stack
3 4	5 + x	
3 4 5	+ x	
3 9	x	Pop 4 and 5, push 4 5 +
27	No more input	Pop 3 and 9, push 3 9 x
Empty		Pop and display the result, 27

The following program simulates a reverse Polish calculator.

sec06_02/Calculator.java

```java
1   import java.util.Scanner;
2   import java.util.Stack;
3
4   /**
5      This calculator uses the reverse Polish notation.
6   */
7   public class Calculator
8   {
9      public static void main(String[] args)
10     {
11        Scanner in = new Scanner(System.in);
12        Stack<Integer> results = new Stack<>();
13        System.out.println("Enter one number or operator per line, Q to quit. ");
14        boolean done = false;
15        while (!done)
16        {
17           String input = in.nextLine();
18
19           // If the command is an operator, pop the arguments and push the result
20
21           if (input.equals("+"))
22           {
23              results.push(results.pop() + results.pop());
24           }
25           else if (input.equals("-"))
26           {
27              Integer arg2 = results.pop();
28              results.push(results.pop() - arg2);
29           }
30           else if (input.equals("*") || input.equals("x"))
31           {
32              results.push(results.pop() * results.pop());
33           }
34           else if (input.equals("/"))
35           {
36              Integer arg2 = results.pop();
37              results.push(results.pop() / arg2);
38           }
39           else if (input.equals("Q") || input.equals("q"))
40           {
```

```
41              done = true;
42          }
43          else
44          {
45              // Not an operator--push the input value
46
47              results.push(Integer.parseInt(input));
48          }
49          System.out.println(results);
50      }
51    }
52 }
```

15.6.3 Evaluating Algebraic Expressions

Using two stacks, you can evaluate expressions in standard algebraic notation.

In the preceding section, you saw how to evaluate expressions in reverse Polish notation, using a single stack. If you haven't found that notation attractive, you will be glad to know that one can evaluate an expression in the standard algebraic notation using two stacks—one for numbers and one for operators.

First, consider a simple example, the expression 3 + 4. We push the numbers on the number stack and the operators on the operator stack. Then we pop both numbers and the operator, combine the numbers with the operator, and push the result.

	Number stack	Operator stack	Unprocessed input	Comments
	Empty	Empty	3 + 4	
❶	3		+ 4	
❷	3	+	4	
❸	4		No more input	Evaluate the top.
	3	+		
❹	7			The result is 7.

This operation is fundamental to the algorithm. We call it "evaluating the top".

In algebraic notation, each operator has a *precedence*. The + and - operators have the lowest precedence, * and / have a higher (and equal) precedence.

Use two stacks to evaluate algebraic expressions.   © Jorge Delgado/iStockphoto.

Consider the expression 3 × 4 + 5. Here are the first processing steps:

	Number stack Empty	Operator stack Empty	Unprocessed input 3 × 4 + 5	Comments
❶	3		× 4 + 5	
❷	3	×	4 + 5	
❸	4 3	×	+ 5	Evaluate × before +.

Because × has a higher precedence than +, we are ready to evaluate the top:

	Number stack	Operator stack		Comments
❹	12	+	5	
❺	5 12	+	No more input	Evaluate the top.
❻	17			That is the result.

With the expression, 3 + 4 × 5, we add × to the operator stack because we must first read the next number; then we can evaluate × and then the +:

	Number stack Empty	Operator stack Empty	Unprocessed input 3 + 4 × 5	Comments
❶	3		+ 4 × 5	
❷	3	+	4 × 5	
❸	4 3	+	× 5	Don't evaluate + yet.
❹	4 3	× +	5	

In other words, we keep operators on the stack until they are ready to be evaluated. Here is the remainder of the computation:

	Number stack	Operator stack		Comments
❺	5 4 3	× +	No more input	Evaluate the top.
❻	20 3	+		Evaluate top again.
❼	23			That is the result.

To see how parentheses are handled, consider the expression $3 \times (4 + 5)$. A (is pushed on the operator stack. The + is pushed as well. When we encounter the), we know that we are ready to evaluate the top until the matching (reappears:

	Number stack	Operator stack	Unprocessed input	Comments
	Empty	Empty	$3 \times (4 + 5)$	
1	3		$\times (4 + 5)$	
2	3	$\times$	$(4 + 5)$	
3	3	($\times$	$4 + 5)$	Don't evaluate $\times$ yet.
4	4 3	($\times$	$+ 5)$	
5	4 3	+ ($\times$	5)	
6	5 4 3	+ ($\times$	)	Evaluate the top.
7	9 3	($\times$	No more input	Pop (.
8	9 3	$\times$		Evaluate top again.
9	27			That is the result.

Here is the algorithm:

> *If you read a number*
> *   Push it on the number stack.*
> *Else if you read a (*
> *   Push it on the operator stack.*
> *Else if you read an operator op*
> *   While the top of the stack has a higher precedence than op*
> *   Evaluate the top.*
> *   Push op on the operator stack.*
> *Else if you read a)*
> *   While the top of the stack is not a (*
> *   Evaluate the top.*
> *   Pop the (.*
> *Else if there is no more input*
> *   While the operator stack is not empty*
> *   Evaluate the top.*

At the end, the remaining value on the number stack is the value of the expression.

The algorithm makes use of this helper method that evaluates the topmost operator with the topmost numbers:

Evaluate the top:
Pop two numbers off the number stack.
Pop an operator off the operator stack.
Combine the numbers with that operator.
Push the result on the number stack.

EXAMPLE CODE See your eText or companion code for the complete code for the expression calculator.

15.6.4 Backtracking

Use a stack to remember choices you haven't yet made so that you can backtrack to them.

Suppose you are inside a maze. You need to find the exit. What should you do when you come to an intersection? You can continue exploring one of the paths, but you will want to remember the other ones. If your chosen path didn't work, you can go back to one of the other choices and try again.

Of course, as you go along one path, you may reach further intersections, and you need to remember your choice again. Simply use a stack to remember the paths that still need to be tried. The process of returning to a choice point and trying another choice is called *back-tracking.* By using a stack, you return to your more recent choices before you explore the earlier ones.

© Skip ODonnell/iStockphoto.

A stack can be used to track positions in a maze.

Figure 11 shows an example. We start at a point in the maze, at position (3, 4). There are four possible paths. We push them all on a stack ❶. We pop off the topmost one, traveling north from (3, 4). Following this path leads to position (1, 4). We now push two choices on the stack, going west or east ❷. Both of them lead to dead ends ❸ ❹

Now we pop off the path from (3, 4) going east. That too is a dead end ❺. Next is the path from (3, 4) going south. At (5, 4), it comes to an intersection. Both choices are pushed on the stack ❻. They both lead to dead ends ❼ ❽.

Finally, the path from (3, 4) going west leads to an exit ❾.

Using a stack, we have found a path out of the maze. Here is the pseudocode for our maze-finding algorithm:

Push all paths from the point on which you are standing on a stack.
While the stack is not empty
  Pop a path from the stack.
  Follow the path until you reach an exit, intersection, or dead end.
  If you found an exit
    Congratulations!
  Else if you found an intersection
    Push all paths meeting at the intersection, except the current one, onto the stack.

This algorithm will find an exit from the maze, provided that the maze has no *cycles.* If it is possible that you can make a circle and return to a previously visited intersection along a different sequence of paths, then you need to work harder—see Exercise • E15.21.

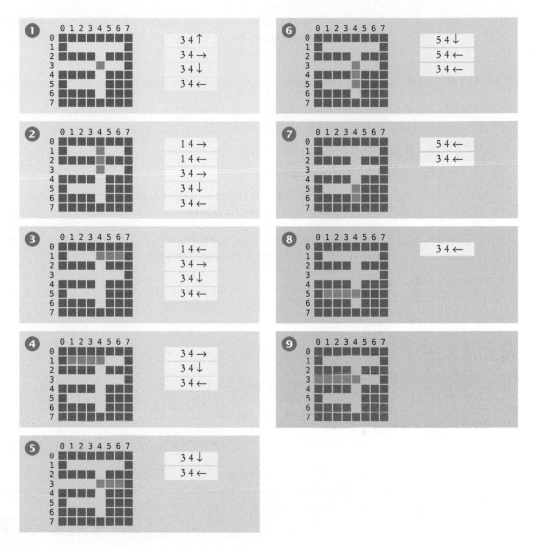

Figure 11 Backtracking Through a Maze

How you implement this algorithm depends on the description of the maze. In the example code, we use a two-dimensional array of characters, with spaces for corridors and asterisks for walls, like this:

In the example code, a Path object is constructed with a starting position and a direction (North, East, South, or West). The Maze class has a method that extends a path until it reaches an intersection or exit, or until it is blocked by a wall, and a method that computes all paths from an intersection point.

Note that you can use a queue instead of a stack in this algorithm. Then you explore the earlier alternatives before the later ones. This can work just as well for finding an answer, but it isn't very intuitive in the context of exploring a maze—you would have to imagine being teleported back to the initial intersections rather than just walking back to the last one.

EXAMPLE CODE   See your eText or companion code for the complete program demonstrating backtracking.

Special Topic 15.3
Reverse Polish Notation

In the 1920s, the Polish mathematician Jan Łukasiewicz realized that it is possible to dispense with parentheses in arithmetic expressions, provided that you write the operators *before* their arguments, for example, + 3 4 instead of 3 + 4. Thirty years later, Australian computer scientist Charles Hamblin noted that an even better scheme would be to have the operators *follow* the operands. This was termed **reverse Polish notation** or RPN.

Standard Notation	Reverse Polish Notation
3 + 4	3 4 +
3 + 4 × 5	3 4 5 × +
3 × (4 + 5)	3 4 5 + ×
(3 + 4) × (5 + 6)	3 4 + 5 6 + ×
3 + 4 + 5	3 4 + 5 +

Reverse Polish notation might look strange to you, but that is just an accident of history. Had earlier mathematicians realized its advantages, today's schoolchildren might be using it and not worrying about precedence rules and parentheses.

In 1972, Hewlett-Packard introduced the HP 35 calculator that used reverse Polish notation. The calculator had no keys labeled with parentheses or an equals symbol. There is just a key labeled ENTER to push a number onto a stack. For that reason, Hewlett-Packard's marketing department used to refer to their product as "the calculators that have no equal".

Over time, calculator vendors have adapted to the standard algebraic notation rather than forcing its users to learn a new notation. However, those users who have made the effort to learn reverse Polish notation tend to be fanatic proponents, and to this day, some Hewlett-Packard calculator models still support it.

The Calculator with No Equal   Courtesy of Nigel Tout.

WORKED EXAMPLE 15.2

Simulating a Queue of Waiting Customers

Learn how to use a queue to simulate an actual queue of waiting customers. See your eText or visit wiley.com/go/bjeo7.

CHAPTER SUMMARY

Understand the architecture of the Java collections framework.

- A collection groups together elements and allows them to be retrieved later.
- A list is a collection that remembers the order of its elements.
- A set is an unordered collection of unique elements.
- A map keeps associations between key and value objects.

Understand and use linked lists.

- A linked list consists of a number of nodes, each of which has a reference to the next node.
- Adding and removing elements at a given position in a linked list is efficient.
- Visiting the elements of a linked list in sequential order is efficient, but random access is not.
- You use a list iterator to access elements inside a linked list.

Choose a set implementation and use it to manage sets of values.

- The HashSet and TreeSet classes both implement the Set interface.
- Set implementations arrange the elements so that they can locate them quickly.
- You can form hash sets holding objects of type String, Integer, Double, Point, Rectangle, or Color.
- You can form tree sets for any class that implements the Comparable interface, such as String or Integer.

- Sets don't have duplicates. Adding a duplicate of an element that is already present is ignored.
- A set iterator visits the elements in the order in which the set implementation keeps them.
- You cannot add an element to a set at an iterator position.

Use maps to model associations between keys and values.

- The HashMap and TreeMap classes both implement the Map interface.
- To find all keys and values in a map, iterate through the key set and find the values that correspond to the keys.

- A hash function computes an integer value from an object.
- A good hash function minimizes *collisions*—identical hash codes for different objects.
- Override hashCode methods in your own classes by combining the hash codes for the instance variables.
- A class's hashCode method must be compatible with its equals method.

Use the Java classes for stacks, queues, and priority queues.

- A stack is a collection of elements with "last-in, first-out" retrieval.
- A queue is a collection of elements with "first-in, first-out" retrieval.
- When removing an element from a priority queue, the element with the most urgent priority is retrieved.

Solve programming problems using stacks and queues.

- A stack can be used to check whether parentheses in an expression are balanced.
- Use a stack to evaluate expressions in reverse Polish notation.
- Using two stacks, you can evaluate expressions in standard algebraic notation.
- Use a stack to remember choices you haven't yet made so that you can backtrack to them.

STANDARD LIBRARY ITEMS INTRODUCED IN THIS CHAPTER

java.util.Collection<E>
  add
  contains
  iterator
  remove
  size
java.util.HashMap<K, V>
java.util.HashSet<E>
java.util.Iterator<E>
  hasNext
  next
  remove
java.util.LinkedList<E>
  addFirst
  addLast
  getFirst
  getLast
  removeFirst
  removeLast
java.util.List<E>
  listIterator
java.util.ListIterator<E>
  add
  hasPrevious
  previous
  set

java.util.Map<K, V>
  get
  keySet
  put
  remove
java.util.Objects
  hash
java.util.PriorityQueue<E>
  remove
java.util.Queue<E>
  peek
java.util.Set<E>
java.util.Stack<E>
  peek
  pop
  push
java.util.TreeMap<K, V>
java.util.TreeSet<E>

REVIEW EXERCISES

■■ R15.1 An invoice contains a collection of purchased items. Should that collection be implemented as a list or set? Explain your answer.

■■ R15.2 Consider a program that manages an appointment calendar. Should it place the appointments into a list, stack, queue, or priority queue? Explain your answer.

■■■ R15.3 One way of implementing a calendar is as a map from date objects to event objects. However, that only works if there is a single event for a given date. How can you use another collection type to allow for multiple events on a given date?

■■ R15.4 Look up the descriptions of the methods addAll, removeAll, retainAll, and containsAll in the Collection interface. Describe how these methods can be used to implement common operations on sets (union, intersection, difference, subset).

■ R15.5 Explain what the following code prints. Draw a picture of the linked list after each step.

```
LinkedList<String> staff = new LinkedList<>();
staff.addFirst("Harry");
staff.addFirst("Diana");
staff.addFirst("Tom");
System.out.println(staff.removeFirst());
System.out.println(staff.removeFirst());
System.out.println(staff.removeFirst());
```

■ R15.6 Explain what the following code prints. Draw a picture of the linked list after each step.

```
LinkedList<String> staff = new LinkedList<>();
staff.addFirst("Harry");
staff.addFirst("Diana");
staff.addFirst("Tom");
System.out.println(staff.removeLast());
System.out.println(staff.removeFirst());
System.out.println(staff.removeLast());
```

■ R15.7 Explain what the following code prints. Draw a picture of the linked list after each step.

```
LinkedList<String> staff = new LinkedList<>();
staff.addFirst("Harry");
staff.addLast("Diana");
staff.addFirst("Tom");
System.out.println(staff.removeLast());
System.out.println(staff.removeFirst());
System.out.println(staff.removeLast());
```

■ R15.8 Explain what the following code prints. Draw a picture of the linked list and the iterator position after each step.

```
LinkedList<String> staff = new LinkedList<>();
ListIterator<String> iterator = staff.listIterator();
iterator.add("Tom");
iterator.add("Diana");
iterator.add("Harry");
iterator = staff.listIterator();
if (iterator.next().equals("Tom")) { iterator.remove(); }
while (iterator.hasNext()) { System.out.println(iterator.next()); }
```

- **R15.9** Explain what the following code prints. Draw a picture of the linked list and the iterator position after each step.

```
LinkedList<String> staff = new LinkedList<>();
ListIterator<String> iterator = staff.listIterator();
iterator.add("Tom");
iterator.add("Diana");
iterator.add("Harry");
iterator = staff.listIterator();
iterator.next();
iterator.next();
iterator.add("Romeo");
iterator.next();
iterator.add("Juliet");
iterator = staff.listIterator();
iterator.next();
iterator.remove();
while (iterator.hasNext()) { System.out.println(iterator.next()); }
```

- **R15.10** You are given a linked list of strings. How do you remove all elements with length less than or equal to three?

- **R15.11** Repeat Exercise •• R15.10, using the removeIf method. (Read the description in the API of the Collection interface.) Use a lambda expression (see Special Topic 10.4).

- **R15.12** What advantages do linked lists have over arrays? What disadvantages do they have?

- **R15.13** Suppose you need to organize a collection of telephone numbers for a company division. There are currently about 6,000 employees, and you know that the phone switch can handle at most 10,000 phone numbers. You expect several hundred look-ups against the collection every day. Would you use an array list or a linked list to store the information?

- **R15.14** Suppose you need to keep a collection of appointments. Would you use a linked list or an array list of Appointment objects?

- **R15.15** Suppose you write a program that models a card deck. Cards are taken from the top of the deck and given out to players. As cards are returned to the deck, they are placed on the bottom of the deck. Would you store the cards in a stack or a queue?

- **R15.16** Suppose the strings "A" ... "Z" are pushed onto a stack. Then they are popped off the stack and pushed onto a second stack. Finally, they are all popped off the second stack and printed. In which order are the strings printed?

- **R15.17** Arrays and lists remember the order in which you added elements; sets do not. Why would you want to use a set instead of an array or list?

- **R15.18** Why are set iterators different from list iterators?

- **R15.19** What is the difference between a set and a map?

- **R15.20** Why is the collection of the keys of a map a set and not a list?

- **R15.21** Why is the collection of the values of a map not a set?

- **R15.22** The union of two sets A and B is the set of all elements that are contained in A, B, or both. The intersection is the set of all elements that are contained in A and B. How can you compute the union and intersection of two sets, using the add and contains methods, together with an iterator?

R15.23 How can you compute the union and intersection of two sets, using some of the methods that the java.util.Set interface provides, but without using an iterator? (Look up the interface in the API documentation.)

R15.24 Can a map have two keys with the same value? Two values with the same key?

R15.25 A map can be implemented as a set of (*key*, *value*) pairs. Explain.

R15.26 How can you print all key/value pairs of a map, using the keySet method? The entrySet method? The forEach method with a lambda expression? (See Special Topic 10.4 on lambda expressions.)

R15.27 Verify the hash code of the string "Juliet" in Table 6.

R15.28 Verify that the strings "VII" and "Ugh" have the same hash code.

R15.29 Consider the algorithm for traversing a maze from Section 15.6.4 Assume that we start at position A and push in the order West, South, East, and North. In which order will the lettered locations of the sample maze be visited?

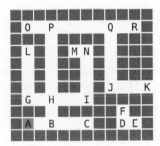

R15.30 Repeat Exercise • R15.29, using a queue instead of a stack.

PRACTICE EXERCISES

E15.1 Write a method

```
public static void downsize(LinkedList<String> employeeNames, int n)
```

that removes every nth employee from a linked list.

E15.2 Write a method

```
public static void reverse(LinkedList<String> strings)
```

that reverses the entries in a linked list.

E15.3 Implement the *sieve of Eratosthenes:* a method for computing prime numbers, known to the ancient Greeks. This method will compute all prime numbers up to n. Choose an n. First insert all numbers from 2 to n into a set. Then erase all multiples of 2 (except 2); that is, 4, 6, 8, 10, 12, ... Erase all multiples of 3; that is, 6, 9, 12, 15, ... Go up to $\sqrt{n}$. Then print the set.

© martin mcelligott/iStockphoto.

E15.4 Write a program that keeps a map in which both keys and values are strings—the names of students and their course grades. Prompt the user of the program to add or remove students, to modify grades, or to print all grades. The printout should be sorted by name and formatted like this:

```
Carl: B+
Joe: C
Sarah: A
```

■■■ **E15.5** Write a program that reads a Java source file and produces an index of all identifiers in the file. For each identifier, print all lines in which it occurs. For simplicity, we will consider each string consisting only of letters, numbers, and underscores an identifier. Declare a `Scanner in` for reading from the source file and call `in.useDelimiter("[^A-Za-z0-9_]+")`. Then each call to `next` returns an identifier.

■■ **E15.6** Read all words from a file and add them to a map whose keys are the first letters of the words and whose values are sets of words that start with that same letter. Then print out the word sets in alphabetical order.

Provide two versions of your solution, one that uses the `merge` method (see Special Topic 15.1) and one that updates the map as in Worked Example 15.1.

■■ **E15.7** Read all words from a file and add them to a map whose keys are word lengths and whose values are comma-separated strings of words of the same length. Then print out those strings, in increasing order by the length of their entries.

Provide two versions of your solution, one that uses the `merge` method (see Special Topic 15.1) and one that updates the map as in Worked Example 15.1.

■■ **E15.8** Use a stack to reverse the words of a sentence. Keep reading words until you have a word that ends in a period, adding them onto a stack. When you have a word with a period, pop the words off and print them. Stop when there are no more words in the input. For example, you should turn the input

```
Mary had a little lamb. Its fleece was white as snow.
```

into

```
Lamb little a had mary. Snow as white was fleece its.
```

Pay attention to capitalization and the placement of the period.

■ **E15.9** Your task is to break a number into its individual digits, for example, to turn 1729 into 1, 7, 2, and 9. It is easy to get the last digit of a number n as $n \% 10$. But that gets the numbers in reverse order. Solve this problem with a stack. Your program should ask the user for an integer, then print its digits separated by spaces.

■■ **E15.10** A homeowner rents out parking spaces in a driveway during special events. The driveway is a "last-in, first-out" stack. Of course, when a car owner retrieves a vehicle that wasn't the last one in, the cars blocking it must temporarily move to the street so that the requested vehicle can leave. Write a program that models this behavior, using one stack for the driveway and one stack for the street. Use integers as license plate numbers. Positive numbers add a car, negative numbers remove a car, zero stops the simulation. Print out the stack after each operation is complete.

■ **E15.11** Implement a to do list. Tasks have a priority between 1 and 9, and a description. When the user enters the command `add` *priority description,* the program adds a new task. When the user enters `next`, the program removes and prints the most urgent task. The `quit` command quits the program. Use a priority queue in your solution.

■ **E15.12** Write a program that reads text from a file and breaks it up into individual words. Insert the words into a tree set. At the end of the input file, print all words, followed by the size of the resulting set. This program determines how many unique words a text file has.

- **E15.13** Insert all words from a large file (such as the novel "War and Peace", which is available on the Internet) into a hash set and a tree set. Time the results. Which data structure is more efficient?

- **E15.14** Supply compatible hashCode and equals methods to the BankAccount class of Chapter 3. Test the hashCode method by printing out hash codes and by adding BankAccount objects to a hash set.

- **E15.15** A labeled point has x- and y-coordinates and a string label. Provide a class Labeled-Point with a constructor LabeledPoint(int x, int y, String label) and hashCode and equals methods. Two labeled points are considered the same when they have the same location and label.

- **E15.16** Reimplement the LabeledPoint class of Exercise •• E15.15 by storing the location in a java.awt.Point object. Your hashCode and equals methods should call the hashCode and equals methods of the Point class.

- **E15.17** Modify the LabeledPoint class of Exercise •• E15.15 so that it implements the Comparable interface. Sort points first by their x-coordinates. If two points have the same x-coordinate, sort them by their y-coordinates. If two points have the same x- and y-coordinates, sort them by their label. Write a tester program that checks all cases by inserting points into a TreeSet.

- **E15.18** Add a % (remainder) operator to the expression calculator of Section 15.6.3.

- **E15.19** Add a ^ (power) operator to the expression calculator of Section 15.6.3. For example, 2 ^ 3 evaluates to 8. As in mathematics, your power operator should be evaluated from the right. That is, 2 ^ 3 ^ 2 is 2 ^ (3 ^ 2), not (2 ^ 3) ^ 2. (That's more useful because you could get the latter as 2 ^ (3 × 2).)

- **E15.20** Write a program that checks whether a sequence of HTML tags is properly nested. For each opening tag, such as <p>, there must be a closing tag </p>. A tag such as <p> may have other tags inside, for example

      <p> <ul> <li> </li> </ul> <a> </a> </p>

  The inner tags must be closed before the outer ones. Your program should process a file containing tags. For simplicity, assume that the tags are separated by spaces, and that there is no text inside the tags.

- **E15.21** Modify the maze solver program of Section 15.6.4 to handle mazes with cycles. Keep a set of visited intersections. When you have previously seen an intersection, treat it as a dead end and do not add paths to the stack.

- **E15.22** In a paint program, a "flood fill" fills all empty pixels of a drawing with a given color, stopping when it reaches occupied pixels. In this exercise, you will implement a simple variation of this algorithm, flood-filling a 10 × 10 array of integers that are initially 0.

  Prompt for the starting row and column.
  Push the (row, column) pair onto a stack.

  You will need to provide a simple Pair class.

  Repeat the following operations until the stack is empty.

Pop off the (row, column) pair from the top of the stack.
If it has not yet been filled, fill the corresponding array location with a number 1, 2, 3,
    and so on (to show the order in which the square is filled).
Push the coordinates of any unfilled neighbors in the north, east, south, or west direction
    on the stack.

When you are done, print the entire array.

PROGRAMMING PROJECTS

■■ P15.1 Read all words from a list of words and add them to a map
whose keys are the phone keypad spellings of the word, and
whose values are sets of words with the same code. For example,
26337 is mapped to the set { "Andes", "coder", "codes", . . .}.
Then keep prompting the user for numbers and print out all
words in the dictionary that can be spelled with that number. In
your solution, use a map that maps letters to digits.

© klenger/iStockphoto.

■■■ P15.2 Reimplement Exercise •• E15.4 so that the keys of the map are objects of class
Student. A student should have a first name, a last name, and a unique integer ID. For
grade changes and removals, lookup should be by ID. The printout should be sorted
by last name. If two students have the same last name, then use the first name as a
tie breaker. If the first names are also identical, then use the integer ID. *Hint:* Use
two maps.

■■■ P15.3 Write a class Polynomial that stores a polynomial such as

$$p(x) = 5x^{10} + 9x^7 - x - 10$$

as a linked list of terms. A term contains the coefficient and the power of x. For
example, you would store $p(x)$ as

$$(5,10),(9,7),(-1,1),(-10,0)$$

Supply methods to add, multiply, and print polynomials. Supply a constructor that
makes a polynomial from a single term. For example, the polynomial p can be
constructed as

```
Polynomial p = new Polynomial(new Term(-10, 0));
p.add(new Polynomial(new Term(-1, 1)));
p.add(new Polynomial(new Term(9, 7)));
p.add(new Polynomial(new Term(5, 10)));
```

Then compute $p(x) \times p(x)$.

```
Polynomial q = p.multiply(p);
q.print();
```

■■■ P15.4 Repeat Exercise ••• P15.3, but use a Map<Integer, Double> for the coefficients.

■■ P15.5 Try to find two words with the same hash code in a large file. Keep a Map<Integer,
HashSet<String>>. When you read in a word, compute its hash code h and put the
word in the set whose key is h. Then iterate through all keys and print the sets whose
size is greater than one.

■■ **P15.6**   Supply compatible hashCode and equals methods to the Student class described in Exercise ••• P15.2. Test the hash code by adding Student objects to a hash set.

■■■ **P15.7**   Modify the expression calculator of Section 15.6.3 to convert an expression into reverse Polish notation. *Hint:* Instead of evaluating the top and pushing the result, append the instructions to a string.

■ **P15.8**   Repeat Exercise ••• E15.22, but use a queue instead.

■■ **P15.9**   Use a stack to enumerate all permutations of a string. Suppose you want to find all permutations of the string meat.

> Push the string +meat on the stack.
> While the stack is not empty
>   Pop off the top of the stack.
>   If that string ends in a + (such as tame+)
>   Remove the + and add the string to the list of permutations.
>   Else
>   Remove each letter in turn from the right of the +.
>   Insert it just before the +.
>   Push the resulting string on the stack.

For example, after popping e+mta, you push em+ta, et+ma, and ea+mt.

■■ **P15.10**   Repeat Excrcise •• P15.9, but use a queue instead.

■■ **Business P15.11**   An airport has only one runway. When it is busy, planes wishing to take off or land have to wait. Implement a simulation, using two queues, one each for the planes waiting to take off and land. Landing planes get priority. The user enters commands takeoff *flightSymbol*, land *flightSymbol*, next, and quit. The first two commands place the flight in the appropriate queue. The next command finishes the current takeoff or landing and enables the next one, printing the action (takeoff or land) and the flight symbol.

■■ **Business P15.12**   Suppose you buy 100 shares of a stock at $12 per share, then another 100 at $10 per share, and then sell 150 shares at $15. You have to pay taxes on the gain, but exactly what is the gain? In the United States, the FIFO rule holds: You first sell all shares of the first batch for a profit of $300, then 50 of the shares from the second batch, for a profit of $250, yielding a total profit of $550. Write a program that can make these calculations for arbitrary purchases and sales of shares in a single company. The user enters commands buy *quantity price*, sell *quantity price* (which causes the gain to be displayed), and quit. *Hint:* Keep a queue of objects of a class Block that contains the quantity and price of a block of shares.

■■■ **Business P15.13**   Extend Exercise •• Business P15.12 to a program that can handle shares of multiple companies. The user enters commands buy *symbol quantity price* and sell *symbol quantity price*. *Hint:* Keep a Map<String, Queue<Block>> that manages a separate queue for each stock symbol.

■■■ **Business P15.14**   Consider the problem of finding the least expensive routes to all cities in a network from a given starting point. For example, in the network shown on the mapbelow, the least expensive route from Pendleton to Peoria has cost 8 (going through Pierre and Pueblo).

The following helper class expresses the distance to another city:

```java
public class DistanceTo implements Comparable<DistanceTo>
{
   private String target;
   private int distance;

   public DistanceTo(String city, int dist) { target = city; distance = dist; }
   public String getTarget() { return target; }
   public int getDistance() { return distance; }
   public int compareTo(DistanceTo other) { return distance - other.distance; }
}
```

All direct connections between cities are stored in a `Map<String, HashSet<DistanceTo>>`.
The algorithm now proceeds as follows:

> *Let from be the starting point.*
> *Add DistanceTo(from, 0) to a priority queue.*
> *Construct a map shortestKnownDistance from city names to distances.*
> *While the priority queue is not empty*
>   *Get its smallest element.*
>   *If its target is not a key in shortestKnownDistance*
>   *Let d be the distance to that target.*
>   *Put (target, d) into shortestKnownDistance.*
>   *For all cities c that have a direct connection from target*
>   *Add DistanceTo(c, d + distance from target to c) to the priority queue.*

When the algorithm has finished, *shortestKnownDistance* contains the shortest distance
from the starting point to all reachable targets.

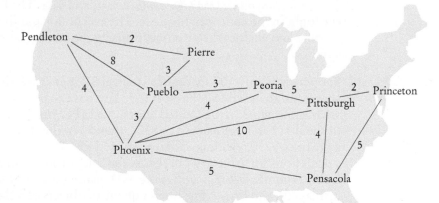

Your task is to write a program that implements this algorithm. Your program
should read in lines of the form *city$_1$ city$_2$ distance*. The starting point is the first city in
the first line. Print the shortest distances to all other cities.

CHAPTER 16

BASIC DATA STRUCTURES

© andrea laurita/iStockphoto.

CHAPTER GOALS

To understand the implementation of linked lists and array lists

To analyze the efficiency of fundamental operations of lists and arrays

To implement the stack and queue data types

To implement a hash table and understand the efficiency of its operations

CHAPTER CONTENTS

In the preceding chapter, you learned how to use the collection classes in the Java library. In this and the next chapter, we will study how these classes are implemented. This chapter deals with simple data structures in which elements are arranged in a linear sequence. By investigating how these data structures add, remove, and locate elements, you will gain valuable experience in designing algorithms and estimating their efficiency.

16.1 Implementing Linked Lists

In Chapter 15 you saw how to use the linked list class supplied by the Java library. Now we will look at the implementation of a simplified version of this class. This will show you how the list operations manipulate the links as the list is modified.

To keep this sample code simple, we will not implement all methods of the linked list class. We will implement only a singly-linked list, and the list class will supply direct access only to the first list element, not the last one. (A worked example and several exercises explore additional implementation options.) Our list will not use a type parameter. We will simply store raw Object values and insert casts when retrieving them. (You will see how to use type parameters in Chapter 18.) The result will be a fully functional list class that shows how the links are updated when elements are added or removed, and how the iterator traverses the list.

16.1.1 The Node Class

A linked list stores elements in a sequence of nodes. We need a class to represent the nodes. In a singly-linked list, a Node object stores an element and a reference to the next node.

Because the methods of both the linked list class and the iterator class have frequent access to the Node instance variables, we do not make the instance variables of the Node class private. Instead, we make Node an **inner class** inside the LinkedList class. The methods of the outer class can access the public features of the inner class. (We could even declare the inner class as private, so that it cannot be accessed anywhere other than from the outer class. For simplicity, we do not do that in this book.)

```
public class LinkedList
{
   . . .
   class Node
   {
      public Object data;
      public Node next;
   }
}
```

A linked list object holds a reference to the first node, and each node object holds a reference to the next node.

Our LinkedList class holds a reference first to the first node (or null, if the list is completely empty):

```
public class LinkedList
{
   private Node first;
```

```java
public LinkedList() { first = null; }

public Object getFirst()
{
   if (first == null) { throw new NoSuchElementException(); }
   return first.data;
}
}
```

16.1.2 Adding and Removing the First Element

When adding or removing the first element, the reference to the first node must be updated.

Figure 1 shows the addFirst method in action. When a new node is added, it becomes the head of the list, and the node that was the old list head becomes its next node:

```java
public class LinkedList
{
   . . .
   public void addFirst(Object element)
   {
      Node newNode = new Node(); ❶
      newNode.data = element;
      newNode.next = first; ❷
      first = newNode; ❸
   }
   . . .
}
```

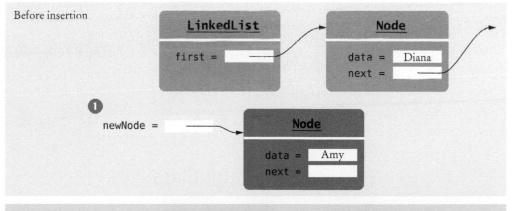

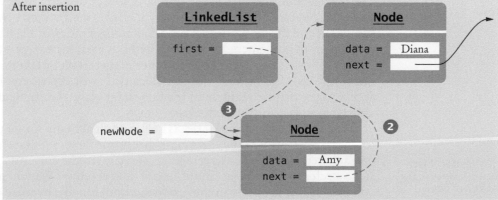

Figure 1
Adding a Node
to the Head of a
Linked List

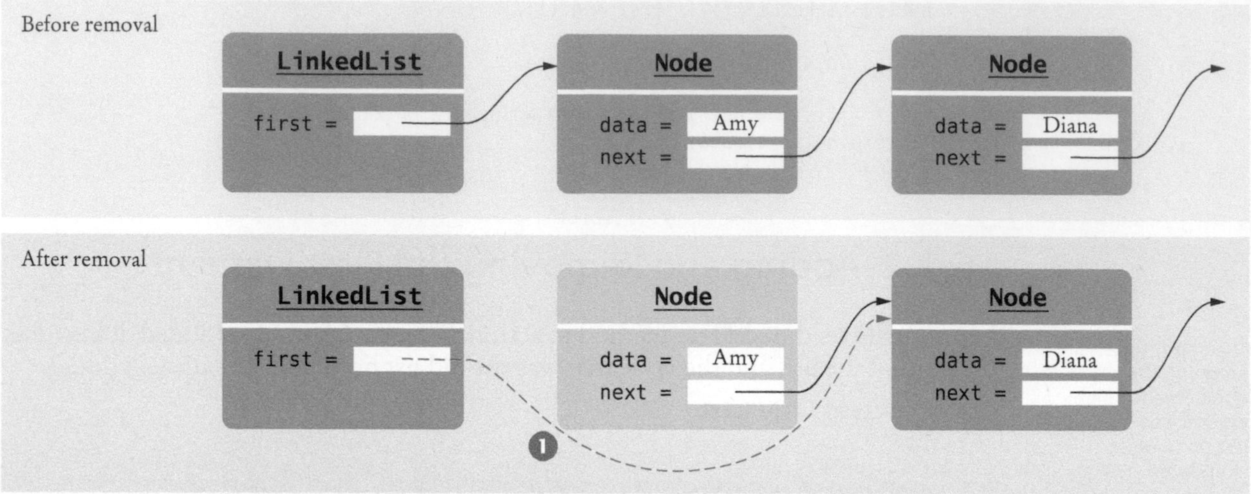

Before removal

After removal

Figure 2 Removing the First Node from a Linked List

Removing the first element of the list works as follows. The data of the first node are saved and later returned as the method result. The successor of the first node becomes the first node of the shorter list (see Figure 2). Then there are no further references to the old node, and the garbage collector will eventually recycle it.

```java
public class LinkedList
{
   . . .
   public Object removeFirst()
   {
      if (first == null) { throw new NoSuchElementException(); }
      Object element = first.data;
      first = first.next; ❶
      return element;
   }
   . . .
}
```

16.1.3 The Iterator Class

The ListIterator interface in the standard library declares nine methods. Our simplified ListIterator interface omits four of them (the methods that move the iterator backward and the methods that report an integer index of the iterator). Our interface requires us to implement list iterator methods next, hasNext, remove, add, and set.

Our LinkedList class declares an inner class LinkedListIterator, which implements our simplified ListIterator interface. Because LinkedListIterator is an inner class, it has access to the private features of the LinkedList class—in particular, the instance variable first and the private Node class.

Note that clients of the LinkedList class don't actually know the name of the iterator class. They only know it is a class that implements the ListIterator interface.

Each iterator object has a reference, position, to the currently visited node. We also store a reference to the last node before that, previous. We will need that reference to adjust the links properly in the remove method. Finally, because calls to remove and set

A list iterator object has a reference to the last visited node.

are only valid after a call to next, we use the isAfterNext flag to track when the next method has been called.

```
public class LinkedList
{
    . . .
    public ListIterator listIterator()
    {
        return new LinkedListIterator();
    }

    class LinkedListIterator implements ListIterator
    {
        private Node position;
        private Node previous;
        private boolean isAfterNext;

        public LinkedListIterator()
        {
            position = null;
            previous = null;
            isAfterNext = false;
        }
        . . .
    }
}
```

16.1.4 Advancing an Iterator

To advance an iterator, update the position and remember the old position for the remove method.

When advancing an iterator with the next method, the position reference is updated to position.next, and the old position is remembered in previous. The previous position is used for just one purpose: to remove the element if the remove method is called after the next method.

There is a special case, however—if the iterator points before the first element of the list, then the old position is null, and position must be set to first:

```
class LinkedListIterator implements ListIterator
{
    . . .
    public Object next()
    {
        if (!hasNext()) { throw new NoSuchElementException(); }
        previous = position; // Remember for remove
        isAfterNext = true;

        if (position == null)
        {
            position = first;
        }
        else
        {
            position = position.next;
        }

        return position.data;
    }
    . . .
}
```

The next method is supposed to be called only when the iterator is not yet at the end of the list, so we declare the hasNext method accordingly. The iterator is at the end if the list is empty (that is, first == null) or if there is no element after the current position (position.next == null):

```java
class LinkedListIterator implements ListIterator
{
    . . .
    public boolean hasNext()
    {
        if (position == null)
        {
            return first != null;
        }
        else
        {
            return position.next != null;
        }
    }
    . . .
}
```

16.1.5 Removing an Element

Next, we implement the remove method of the list iterator. Recall that, in order to remove an element, one must first call next and then call remove on the iterator.

If the element to be removed is the first element, we just call removeFirst. Otherwise, an element in the middle of the list must be removed, and the node preceding it needs to have its next reference updated to skip the removed element (see Figure 3).

We also need to update the position reference so that a subsequent call to the next method skips over the element after the removed one.

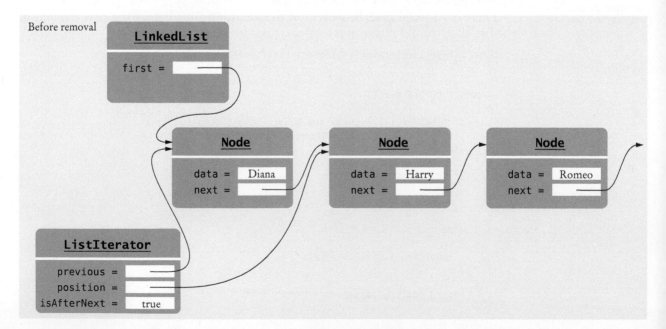

Figure 3 Removing a Node from the Middle of a Linked List

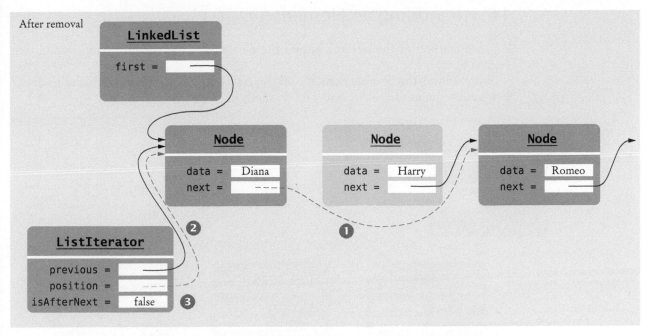

Figure 3 (continued)   Removing a Node from the Middle of a Linked List

According to the specification of the remove method, it is illegal to call remove twice in a row. Our implementation handles this situation correctly. After completion of the remove method, the isAfterNext flag is set to false. An exception occurs if remove is called again without another call to next.

```
class LinkedListIterator implements ListIterator
{
   . . .
   public void remove()
   {
      if (!isAfterNext) { throw new IllegalStateException(); }

      if (position == first)
      {
         removeFirst();
      }
      else
      {
         previous.next = position.next;  ❶
      }
      position = previous;  ❷

      isAfterNext = false;  ❸
   }
   . . .
}
```

There is a good reason for disallowing remove twice in a row. After the first call to remove, the current position reverts to the predecessor of the removed element. Its predecessor is no longer known, which makes it impossible to efficiently remove the current element.

16.1.6 Adding an Element

The add method of the iterator inserts the new node after the last visited node (see Figure 4).

After adding the new element, we set the isAfterNext flag to false, in order to disallow a subsequent call to the remove or set method.

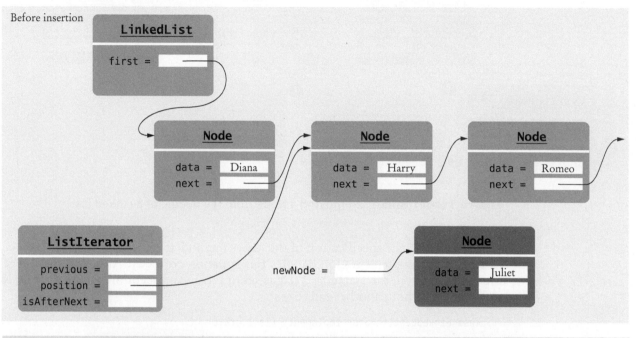

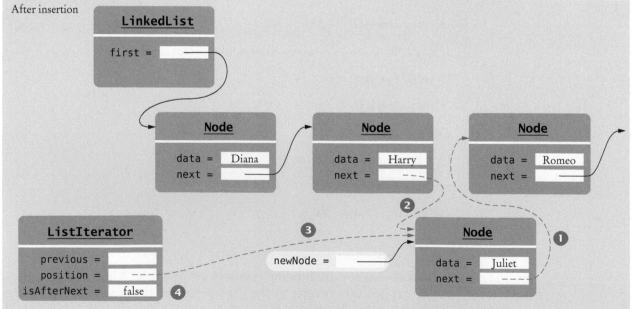

Figure 4 Adding a Node to the Middle of a Linked List

```
class LinkedListIterator implements ListIterator
{
   . . .
   public void add(Object element)
   {
      if (position == null)
      {
         addFirst(element);
         position = first;
      }
      else
      {
         Node newNode = new Node();
         newNode.data = element;
         newNode.next = position.next;  ❶
         position.next = newNode;        ❷
         position = newNode;             ❸
      }
      isAfterNext = false;  ❹
   }
   . . .
}
```

16.1.7 Setting an Element to a Different Value

The set method changes the data stored in the previously visited element:

```
public void set(Object element)
{
   if (!isAfterNext) { throw new IllegalStateException(); }
   position.data = element;
}
```

As with the remove method, a call to set is only valid if it was preceded by a call to the next method. We throw an exception if we find that there was a call to add or remove immediately before calling set.

You will find the complete implementation of our LinkedList class after the next section.

16.1.8 Efficiency of Linked List Operations

In a doubly-linked list, accessing an element is an $O(n)$ operation; adding and removing an element is $O(1)$.

Now that you have seen how linked list operations are implemented, we can determine their efficiency.

Consider first the cost of accessing an element. To get the kth element of a linked list, you start at the beginning of the list and advance the iterator k times. Suppose it takes an amount of time T to advance the iterator once. This quantity is independent of the iterator position—advancing an iterator does some checking and then it follows the next reference of the current node (see Section 16.1.4).

Therefore, advancing the iterator to the kth element consumes kT time. If the linked list has n elements and k is chosen at random, then k will average out to be $n/2$, and kT is on average $nT/2$. Because $T/2$ is a constant, this is an $O(n)$ expression. We have determined that accessing an element in a linked list of length n is an $O(n)$ operation.

Now consider the cost of adding an element at a given position, assuming that we already have an iterator to the position. Look at the implementation of the add

© Kris Hanke/iStockphoto.

To get to the kth node of a linked list, one must skip over the preceding nodes.

method in Section 16.1.6. To add an element, one updates a couple of references in the neighboring nodes and the iterator. This operation requires a constant number of steps, independent of the size of the linked list.

Using the big-Oh notation, an operation that requires a bounded amount of time, regardless of the total number of elements in the structure, is denoted as $O(1)$. Adding an element to a linked list takes $O(1)$ time.

Similar reasoning shows that removing an element at a given position is an $O(1)$ operation.

Now consider the task of adding an element at the end of the list. We first need to get to the end, at a cost of $O(n)$. Then it takes $O(1)$ time to add the element. However, we can improve on this performance if we add a reference to the last node to the LinkedList class:

```java
public class LinkedList
{
    private Node first;
    private Node last;
    . . .
}
```

Of course, this reference must be updated when the last node changes, as elements are added or removed. In order to keep the code as simple as possible, our implementation does not have a reference to the last node. However, we will always assume that a linked list implementation can access the last element in constant time. This is the case for the LinkedList class in the standard Java library, and it is an easy enhancement to our implementation. Worked Example 16.1 shows how to add the last reference, update it as necessary, and provide an addLast method for adding an element at the end.

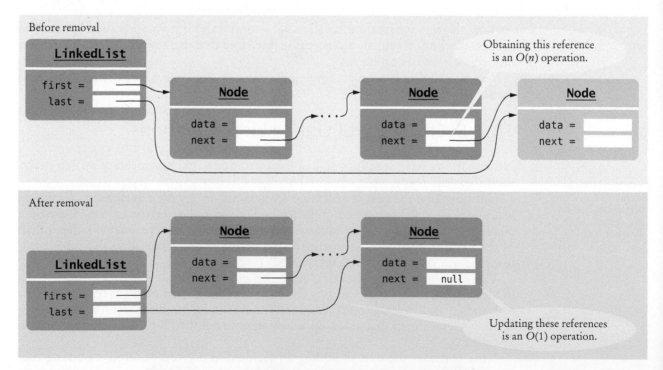

Figure 5   Removing the Last Element of a Singly-Linked List

The code for the addLast method is very similar to the addFirst method in Section 16.1.2. It too requires constant time, independent of the length of the list. We conclude that, with an appropriate implementation, adding an element at the end of a linked list is an $O(1)$ operation.

How about removing the last element? We need a reference to the next-to-last element, so that we can set its next reference to null. (See Figure 5.)

We also need to update the last reference and set it to the next-to-last reference. But how can we get that next-to-last reference? It takes $n - 1$ iterations to obtain it, starting at the beginning of the list. Thus, removing an element from the back of a singly-linked list is an $O(n)$ operation.

We can do better in a doubly-linked list, such as the one in the standard Java library. In a doubly-linked list, each node has a reference to the previous node in addition to the next one (see Figure 6).

```java
public class LinkedList
{
    . . .
    class Node
    {
        public Object data;
        public Node next;
        public Node previous;
    }
}
```

In that case, removal of the last element takes a constant number of steps:

```java
last = last.previous; ❶
last.next = null; ❷
```

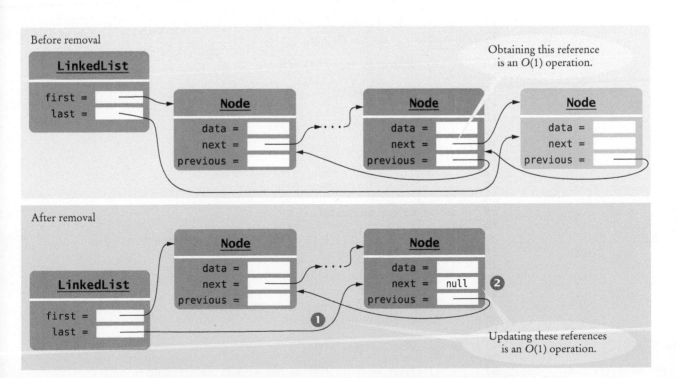

Figure 6   Removing the Last Element of a Doubly-Linked List

Table 1 Efficiency of Linked List Operations		
Operation	Singly-Linked List	Doubly-Linked List
Access an element.	$O(n)$	$O(n)$
Add/remove at an iterator position.	$O(1)$	$O(1)$
Add/remove first element.	$O(1)$	$O(1)$
Add last element.	$O(1)$	$O(1)$
Remove last element.	$O(n)$	$O(1)$

Therefore, removing an element from the end of a doubly-linked list is also an $O(1)$ operation. Worked Example 16.1 contains a full implementation.

Table 1 summarizes the efficiency of linked list operations.

sec01/LinkedList.java

```java
1   import java.util.NoSuchElementException;
2
3   /**
4      A linked list is a sequence of nodes with efficient
5      element insertion and removal. This class
6      contains a subset of the methods of the standard
7      java.util.LinkedList class.
8   */
9   public class LinkedList
10  {
11     private Node first;
12
13     /**
14        Constructs an empty linked list.
15     */
16     public LinkedList()
17     {
18        first = null;
19     }
20
21     /**
22        Returns the first element in the linked list.
23        @return the first element in the linked list
24     */
25     public Object getFirst()
26     {
27        if (first == null) { throw new NoSuchElementException(); }
28        return first.data;
29     }
30
31     /**
32        Removes the first element in the linked list.
33        @return the removed element
34     */
35     public Object removeFirst()
36     {
37        if (first == null) { throw new NoSuchElementException(); }
38        Object element = first.data;
```

```
39       first = first.next;
40       return element;
41    }
42
43    /**
44        Adds an element to the front of the linked list.
45        @param element the element to add
46    */
47    public void addFirst(Object element)
48    {
49       Node newNode = new Node();
50       newNode.data = element;
51       newNode.next = first;
52       first = newNode;
53    }
54
55    /**
56        Returns an iterator for iterating through this list.
57        @return an iterator for iterating through this list
58    */
59    public ListIterator listIterator()
60    {
61       return new LinkedListIterator();
62    }
63
64    class Node
65    {
66       public Object data;
67       public Node next;
68    }
69
70    class LinkedListIterator implements ListIterator
71    {
72       private Node position;
73       private Node previous;
74       private boolean isAfterNext;
75
76       /**
77           Constructs an iterator that points to the front
78           of the linked list.
79       */
80       public LinkedListIterator()
81       {
82          position = null;
83          previous = null;
84          isAfterNext = false;
85       }
86
87       /**
88           Moves the iterator past the next element.
89           @return the traversed element
90       */
91       public Object next()
92       {
93          if (!hasNext()) { throw new NoSuchElementException(); )
94          previous = position; // Remember for remove
95          isAfterNext = true;
96
97          if (position == null)
98          {
```

```
 99                    position = first;
100                }
101                else
102                {
103                    position = position.next;
104                }
105
106                return position.data;
107            }
108
109            /**
110                Tests if there is an element after the iterator position.
111                @return true if there is an element after the iterator position
112            */
113            public boolean hasNext()
114            {
115                if (position == null)
116                {
117                    return first != null;
118                }
119                else
120                {
121                    return position.next != null;
122                }
123            }
124
125            /**
126                Adds an element before the iterator position
127                and moves the iterator past the inserted element.
128                @param element the element to add
129            */
130            public void add(Object element)
131            {
132                if (position == null)
133                {
134                    addFirst(element);
135                    position = first;
136                }
137                else
138                {
139                    Node newNode = new Node();
140                    newNode.data = element;
141                    newNode.next = position.next;
142                    position.next = newNode;
143                    position = newNode;
144                }
145
146                isAfterNext = false;
147            }
148
149            /**
150                Removes the last traversed element. This method may
151                only be called after a call to the next method.
152            */
153            public void remove()
154            {
155                if (!isAfterNext) { throw new IllegalStateException(); }
156
157                if (position == first)
158                {
```

```
159                     removeFirst();
160                 }
161                 else
162                 {
163                     previous.next = position.next;
164                 }
165                 position = previous;
166                 isAfterNext = false;
167             }
168
169             /**
170                 Sets the last traversed element to a different value.
171                 @param element the element to set
172             */
173             public void set(Object element)
174             {
175                 if (!isAfterNext) { throw new IllegalStateException(); }
176                 position.data = element;
177             }
178         }
179 }
```

sec01/ListIterator.java

```
1   /**
2       A list iterator allows access to a position in a linked list.
3       This interface contains a subset of the methods of the
4       standard java.util.ListIterator interface. The methods for
5       backward traversal are not included.
6   */
7   public interface ListIterator
8   {
9       /**
10          Moves the iterator past the next element.
11          @return the traversed element
12      */
13      Object next();
14
15      /**
16          Tests if there is an element after the iterator position.
17          @return true if there is an element after the iterator position
18      */
19      boolean hasNext();
20
21      /**
22          Adds an element before the iterator position
23          and moves the iterator past the inserted element.
24          @param element the element to add
25      */
26      void add(Object element);
27
28      /**
29          Removes the last traversed element. This method may
30          only be called after a call to the next method.
31      */
32      void remove();
33
34      /**
35          Sets the last traversed element to a different value.
36          @param element the element to set
```

```
37    */
38    void set(Object element);
39 }
```

EXAMPLE CODE   See your eText or companion code for a program that demonstrates linked list operations.

Special Topic 16.1

Static Classes

You first saw the use of inner classes for event handlers in Section 10.7.2. Inner classes are useful in that context, because their methods have the privilege of accessing private instance variables of outer-class objects. The same is true for the LinkedListIterator inner class in the sample code for this section. The iterator needs to access the first instance variable of its linked list.

However, there is a cost for this feature. Every object of the inner class has a reference to the object of the enclosing class that constructed it. If an inner class has no need to access the enclosing class, you can declare the class as static and eliminate the reference to the enclosing class. This is the case with the Node class.

You can declare it as follows:

```
public class LinkedList
{
   . . .
   static class Node
   {
      . . .
   }
}
```

However, the LinkedListIterator class cannot be a static class. Its methods must access the first element of the enclosing LinkedList.

WORKED EXAMPLE 16.1

Implementing a Doubly-Linked List

Learn how to modify a singly-linked list to implement a doubly-linked list. See your eText or visit wiley.com/go/bjeo7.

16.2 Implementing Array Lists

Array lists were introduced in Chapter 7. They are conceptually similar to linked lists, allowing you to add and remove elements at any position. In the following sections, we will develop an implementation of an array list, study the efficiency of operations on array lists, and compare them with the equivalent operations on linked lists.

16.2.1 Getting and Setting Elements

An array list maintains a reference to an array of elements. The array is large enough to hold all elements in the collection—in fact, it is usually larger to allow for adding

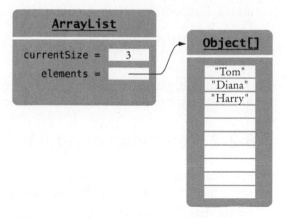

Figure 7 An Array List Stores Its Elements in an Array

additional elements. When the array gets full, it is replaced by a larger one. We discuss that process in Section 16.2.3.

In addition to the internal array of elements, an array list has an instance field that stores the current number of elements (see Figure 7).

For simplicity, our ArrayList implementation does not work with arbitrary element types, but it simply manages elements of type Object. (Chapter 18 shows how to implement classes with type parameters.)

```java
public class ArrayList
{
    private Object[] elements;
    private int currentSize;

    public ArrayList()
    {
        final int INITIAL_SIZE = 10;
        elements = new Object[INITIAL_SIZE];
        currentSize = 0;
    }

    public int size() { return currentSize; }
    . . .
}
```

To access array list elements, we provide get and set methods. These methods simply check for valid positions and access the internal array at the given position:

```java
private void checkBounds(int n)
{
    if (n < 0 || n >= currentSize)
    {
        throw new IndexOutOfBoundsException();
    }
}

public Object get(int pos)
{
    checkBounds(pos);
    return element[pos];
}
```

```
public void set(int pos, Object element)
{
   checkBounds(pos);
   elements[pos] = element;
}
```

Getting or setting an array list element is an O(1) operation.

As you can see, getting and setting an element can be carried out with a bounded set of instructions, independent of the size of the array list. These are $O(1)$ operations.

16.2.2 Removing or Adding Elements

When removing an element at position k, the elements with higher index values need to move (see Figure 8). Here is the implementation, following Section 7.3.6:

```
public Object remove(int pos)
{
   checkBounds(pos);

   Object removed = elements[pos];

   for (int i = pos + 1; i < currentSize; i++)
   {
      elements[i - 1] = elements[i];
   }

   currentSize--;
   return removed;
}
```

How many elements are affected? If we assume that removal happens at random locations, then on average, each removal moves $n/2$ elements, where n is the size of the array list.

The same argument holds for inserting an element. On average, $n/2$ elements need to be moved. Therefore, we say that adding and removing elements are $O(n)$ operations.

Inserting or removing an array list element is an O(n) operation.

There is one situation where adding an element to an array list isn't so costly: when the insertion happens *after* the last element. If the current size is less than the length of the array, the size is incremented and the new element is simply stored in the array. This is an $O(1)$ operation.

```
public boolean addLast(Object newElement)
{
   growIfNecessary();
   currentSize++;

   elements[currentSize - 1] = newElement;
   return true;
}
```

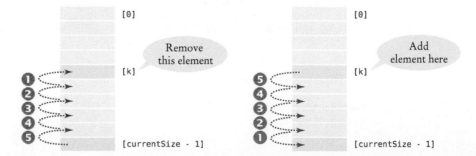

Figure 8
Removing and Adding Elements

One issue remains: If there is no more room in the internal array, then we need to grow it. That is the topic of the next section.

16.2.3 Growing the Internal Array

Before inserting an element into an internal array that is completely full, we must replace the array with a bigger one. This new array is typically twice the size of the current array. (See Figure 9.) The existing elements are then copied into the new array. Reallocation is an $O(n)$ operation because all elements need to be copied to the new array.

When an array list is completely full, we must move the contents to a larger array.

```
private void growIfNecessary()
{
   if (currentSize == elements.length)
   {
      Object[] newElements =
         new Object[2 * elements.length]; ❶
      for (int i = 0; i < elements.length; i++)
      {
         newElements[i] = elements[i]; ❷
      }
      elements = newElements; ❸
   }
}
```

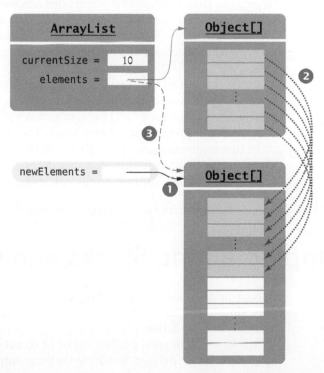

Figure 9
Reallocating the
Internal Array

Table 2 Efficiency of Array List and Linked List Operations

Operation	Array List	Doubly-Linked List
Add/remove element at end.	$O(1)+$	$O(1)$
Add/remove element in the middle.	$O(n)$	$O(1)$
Get kth element.	$O(1)$	$O(k)$

If we carefully analyze the total cost of a sequence of addLast operations, it turns out that these reallocations are not as expensive as they first appear. The key observation is that array growth does not happen very often. Suppose we start with an array list of capacity 10 and double the size with each reallocation. We must reallocate the array of elements when it reaches sizes 10, 20, 40, 80, 160, 320, 640, 1280, and so on.

Let us assume that one insertion without reallocation takes time T_1 and that reallocation of k elements takes time kT_2. What is the cost of 1280 addLast operations?

Of course, we pay $1280 \cdot T_1$ for the insertions. The reallocation cost is

$$10T_2 + 20T_2 + 40T_2 + \cdots + 1280T_2 = (1 + 2 + 4 + \cdots + 128) \cdot 10 \cdot T_2$$
$$= 255 \cdot 10 \cdot T_2$$
$$< 256 \cdot 10 \cdot T_2$$
$$= 1280 \cdot 2 \cdot T_2$$

Therefore, the total cost is a bit less than

$$1280 \cdot (T_1 + 2T_2)$$

In general, the total cost of n addLast operations is less than $n \cdot (T_1 + 2T_2)$. Because the second factor is a constant, we conclude that n addLast operations take $O(n)$ time.

We know that it isn't quite true that an individual addLast operation takes $O(1)$ time. After all, occasionally a call to addLast is unlucky and must reallocate the elements array.

But if the cost of that reallocation is distributed over the preceding addLast operations, then the surcharge for each of them is still a constant amount. We say that addLast takes *amortized* $O(1)$ time, which is written as $O(1)+$. (Accountants say that a cost is amortized when it is distributed over multiple periods.)

In our implementation, we do not shrink the array when elements are removed. However, it turns out that you can (occasionally) shrink the array and still have $O(1)+$ performance for removing the last element (see Exercise • E16.10).

> Adding or removing the last element in an array list takes amortized $O(1)$ time.

EXAMPLE CODE   See your companion code to see a program that demonstrates this array list implementation.

16.3 Implementing Stacks and Queues

In Section 15.5, we introduced the stack and queue data types. Stacks and queues are very simple. Elements are added and retrieved, either in *last-in, first-out* order or in *first-in, first-out* order.

Stacks and queues are examples of **abstract data types**. We only specify how the operations must behave, not how they are implemented. In the following sections, we will study several implementations of stacks and queues and determine how efficient they are.

16.3.1 Stacks as Linked Lists

A stack can be implemented as a linked list, adding and removing elements at the front.

Let us first implement a stack as a sequence of nodes. New elements are added (or "pushed") to an end of the sequence, and they are removed (or "popped") from the same end.

Which end? It is up to us to choose, and we will make the least expensive choice: to add and remove elements at the front (see Figure 10).

The push and pop operations are identical to the addFirst and removeFirst operations from Section 16.1.2. They are both $O(1)$ operations.

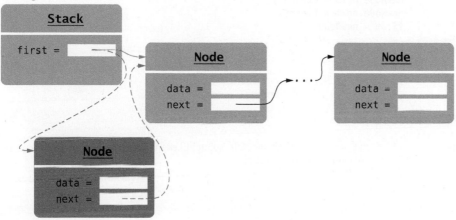

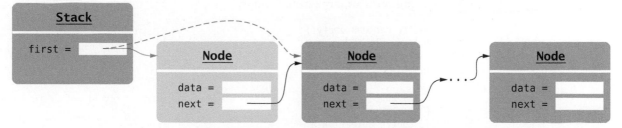

Figure 10 Push and Pop for a Stack Implemented as a Linked List

Here is the complete implementation:

sec03_01/LinkedListStack.java

```java
1  import java.util.NoSuchElementException;
2
3  /**
4     An implementation of a stack as a sequence of nodes.
5  */
6  public class LinkedListStack
7  {
```

```
 8     private Node first;
 9
10     /**
11        Constructs an empty stack.
12     */
13     public LinkedListStack()
14     {
15        first = null;
16     }
17
18     /**
19        Adds an element to the top of the stack.
20        @param element the element to add
21     */
22     public void push(Object element)
23     {
24        Node newNode = new Node();
25        newNode.data = element;
26        newNode.next = first;
27        first = newNode;
28     }
29
30     /**
31        Removes the element from the top of the stack.
32        @return the removed element
33     */
34     public Object pop()
35     {
36        if (first == null) { throw new NoSuchElementException(); }
37        Object element = first.data;
38        first = first.next;
39        return element;
40     }
41
42     /**
43        Checks whether this stack is empty.
44        @return true if the stack is empty
45     */
46     public boolean empty()
47     {
48        return first == null;
49     }
50
51     class Node
52     {
53        public Object data;
54        public Node next;
55     }
56  }
```

16.3.2 Stacks as Arrays

When implementing a stack as an array, add and remove elements at the back.

In the preceding section, you saw how a stack was implemented as a sequence of nodes. In this section, we will instead store the values in an array, thus saving the storage of the node references.

Again, it is up to us at which end of the array we place new elements. This time, it is better to add and remove elements at the back of the array (see Figure 11).

Of course, an array may eventually fill up as more elements are pushed on the stack. As with the ArrayList implementation of Section 16.2, the array must grow when it gets full.

The push and pop operations are identical to the addLast and removeLast operations of an array list. They are both $O(1)+$ operations.

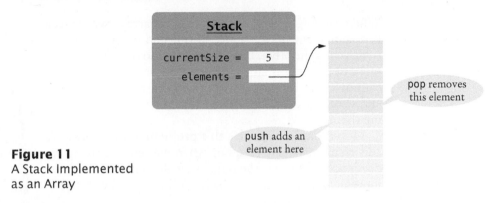

Figure 11
A Stack Implemented
as an Array

16.3.3 Queues as Linked Lists

A queue can be implemented as a linked list, adding elements at the back and removing them at the front.

We now turn to the implementation of a queue. When implementing a queue as a sequence of nodes, we add nodes at one end and remove them at the other. As we discussed in Section 16.1.8, a singly-linked node sequence is not able to remove the last node in $O(1)$ time. Therefore, it is best to remove elements at the front and add them at the back (see Figure 12).

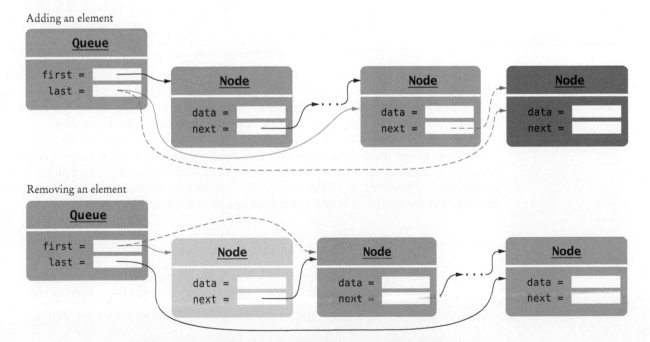

Figure 12 A Queue Implemented as a Linked List

The add and remove operations of a queue are $O(1)$ operations because they are the same as the addLast and removeFirst operations of a doubly-linked list. Note that we need a reference to the last node so that we can efficiently add elements.

16.3.4 Queues as Circular Arrays

When storing queue elements in an array, we have a problem: elements get added at one end of the array and removed at the other. But adding or removing the first element of an array is an $O(n)$ operation, so it seems that we cannot avoid this expensive operation, no matter which end we choose for adding elements and which for removing them.

© ihsanyildizli/iStockphoto.

However, we can solve this problem with a trick. We add elements at the end, but when we remove them, we don't actually move the remaining elements. Instead, we increment the index at which the head of the queue is located (see Figure 13).

In a circular array, we wrap around to the beginning after the last element.

In a circular array implementation of a queue, element locations wrap from the end of the array to the beginning.

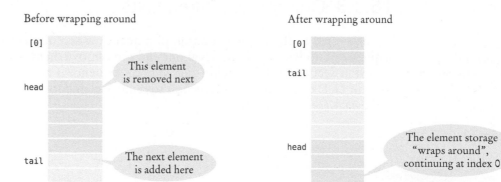

Figure 13
Queue Elements
in a Circular Array

After adding sufficiently many elements, the last element of the array will be filled. However, if there were also a few calls to remove, then there is additional room in the front of the array. Then we "wrap around" and start storing elements again at index 0 — see part 2 of Figure 13. For that reason, the array is called "circular".

Eventually, of course, the tail reaches the head, and a larger array must be allocated.

As you can see from the source code that follows, adding or removing an element requires a bounded set of operations, independent of the queue size, except for array reallocation. However, as discussed in Section 16.2.3, reallocation happens rarely enough that the total cost is still amortized constant time, $O(1)+$.

Table 3 **Efficiency of Stack and Queue Operations**				
	Stack as Linked List	Stack as Array	Queue as Linked List	Queue as Circular Array
Add an element.	$O(1)$	$O(1)+$	$O(1)$	$O(1)+$
Remove an element.	$O(1)$	$O(1)+$	$O(1)$	$O(1)+$

sec03_04/CircularArrayQueue.java

```java
1  import java.util.NoSuchElementException;
2
3  /**
4     An implementation of a queue as a circular array.
5  */
6  public class CircularArrayQueue
7  {
8     private Object[] elements;
9     private int currentSize;
10    private int head;
11    private int tail;
12
13    /**
14       Constructs an empty queue.
15    */
16    public CircularArrayQueue()
17    {
18       final int INITIAL_SIZE = 10;
19       elements = new Object[INITIAL_SIZE];
20       currentSize = 0;
21       head = 0;
22       tail = 0;
23    }
24
25    /**
26       Checks whether this queue is empty.
27       @return true if this queue is empty
28    */
29    public boolean empty() { return currentSize == 0; }
30
31    /**
32       Adds an element to the tail of this queue.
33       @param newElement the element to add
34    */
35    public void add(Object newElement)
36    {
37       growIfNecessary();
38       currentSize++;
39       elements[tail] = newElement;
40       tail = (tail + 1) % elements.length;
41    }
42
43    /**
44       Removes an element from the head of this queue.
45       @return the removed element
46    */
47    public Object remove()
48    {
49       if (currentSize == 0) { throw new NoSuchElementException(); }
50       Object removed = elements[head];
51       head = (head + 1) % elements.length;
52       currentSize--;
53       return removed;
54    }
55
56    /**
57       Grows the element array if the current size equals the capacity.
58    */
59    private void growIfNecessary()
60    {
```

```
61        if (currentSize == elements.length)
62        {
63           Object[] newElements = new Object[2 * elements.length];
64           for (int i = 0; i < elements.length; i++)
65           {
66              newElements[i] = elements[(head + i) % elements.length];
67           }
68           elements = newElements;
69           head = 0;
70           tail = currentSize;
71        }
72     }
73 }
```

16.4 Implementing a Hash Table

In Section 15.3, you were introduced to the set data structure and its two implementations in the Java collections framework, hash sets and tree sets. In these sections, you will see how hash sets are implemented and how efficient their operations are.

16.4.1 Hash Codes

A good hash function minimizes *collisions*—identical hash codes for different objects.

The basic idea behind hashing is to place objects into an array, at a location that can be determined from the object itself. Each object has a **hash code**, an integer value that is computed from an object in such a way that different objects are likely to yield different hash codes.

Table 4 shows some examples of strings and their hash codes. Special Topic 15.2 shows how these values are computed.

It is possible for two or more distinct objects to have the same hash code; this is called a *collision*. For example, the strings "VII" and "Ugh" happen to have the same hash code.

Table 4 Sample Strings and Their Hash Codes			
String	Hash Code	String	Hash Code
"Adam"	2035631	"Juliet"	−2065036585
"Eve"	70068	"Katherine"	2079199209
"Harry"	69496448	"Sue"	83491
"Jim"	74478	"Ugh"	84982
"Joe"	74656	"VII"	84982

16.4.2 Hash Tables

A hash code is used as an array index into a **hash table**, an array that stores the set elements. In the simplest implementation of a hash table, you could make a very long array and insert each object at the location of its hash code (see Figure 14).

Figure 14
A Simplistic Implementation of a Hash Table

> A hash table uses the hash code to determine where to store each element.

If there are no collisions, it is a very simple matter to find out whether an object is already present in the set or not. Compute its hash code and check whether the array position with that hash code is already occupied. This doesn't require a search through the entire array!

Of course, it is not feasible to allocate an array that is large enough to hold all possible integer index positions. Therefore, we must pick an array of some reasonable size and then "compress" the hash code to become a valid array index. Compression can be easily achieved by using the remainder operation:

```
int h = x.hashCode();
position = h % arrayLength;
if (h < 0) { h = -h; }
```

See Exercise • E16.20 for an alternative compression technique.

> A hash table can be implemented as an array of *buckets*—sequences of nodes that hold elements with the same hash code.

After compressing the hash code, it becomes more likely that several objects will collide. There are several techniques for handling collisions. The most common one is called *separate chaining*. All colliding elements are collected in a linked list of elements with the same position value (see Figure 15). Such a list is called a "bucket". Special Topic 16.2 discusses *open addressing*, in which colliding elements are placed in empty locations of the hash table.

In the following, we will use the first technique. Each entry of the hash table points to a sequence of nodes containing elements with the same (compressed) hash code.

© Neil Kurtzman/iStockphoto.

Elements with the same hash code are placed in the same bucket.

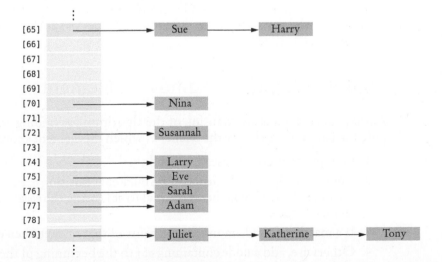

Figure 15 A Hash Table with Buckets to Store Elements with the Same Hash Code

16.4.3 Finding an Element

Let's assume that our hash table has been filled with a number of elements. Now we want to find out whether a given element is already present.

Here is the algorithm for finding an object obj in a hash table:

1. Compute the hash code and compress it. This gives an index h into the hash table.

2. Iterate through the elements of the bucket at position h. For each element of the bucket, check whether it is equal to obj.

3. If a match is found among the elements of that bucket, then obj is in the set. Otherwise, it is not.

> If there are no or only a few collisions, then adding, locating, and removing hash table elements takes constant or $O(1)$ time.

How efficient is this operation? It depends on the hash code computation. In the best case, in which there are no collisions, all buckets either are empty or have a single element.

But in practice, some collisions will occur. We need to make some assumptions that are reasonable in practice.

First, we assume that the hash code does a good job scattering the elements into different buckets. In practice, the hash functions described in Special Topic 15.2 work well.

Next, we assume that the table is large enough. This is measured by the *load factor* $F = n/L$, where n is the number of elements and L the table length. For example, if the table is an array of length 1,000, and it has 700 elements, then the load factor is 0.7.

If the load factor gets too large, the elements should be moved into a larger table. The hash table in the standard Java library reallocates the table when the load factor exceeds 0.75.

Under these assumptions, each bucket can be expected to have, on average, F elements.

Finally, we assume that the hash code, its compression, and the equals method can be computed in bounded time, independent of the size of the set.

Now let us compute the cost of finding an element. Computing the array index takes constant time, due to our last assumption. Now we traverse a chain of buckets, which on average has a bounded length F. Finally, we invoke the equals method on each bucket element, which we also assume to be $O(1)$. The entire operation takes constant or $O(1)$ time.

16.4.4 Adding and Removing Elements

Adding an element is an extension of the algorithm for finding an object. First compute the hash code to locate the bucket in which the element should be inserted:

1. Compute the compressed hash code h.

2. Iterate through the elements of the bucket at position h. For each element of the bucket, check whether it is equal to obj (using the equals method of the element type).

3. If a match is found among the elements of that bucket, then exit.

4. Otherwise, add a node containing obj to the beginning of the node sequence.

5. If the load factor exceeds a fixed threshold, reallocate the table.

As described in the preceding section, the first three steps are $O(1)$. Inserting at the beginning of a node sequence is also $O(1)$. As with array lists, we can choose the new table to be twice the size of the old table, and amortize the cost of reallocation over the preceding insertions. That is, adding an element to a hash table is $O(1)+$.

Removing an element is equally simple. First compute the hash code to locate the bucket in which the element should be inserted. Try finding the object in that bucket. If it is present, remove it. Otherwise, do nothing. Again, this is a constant time operation. If we shrink a table that becomes too sparse, the cost is $O(1)+$.

16.4.5 Iterating over a Hash Table

An iterator for a linked list points to the current node in a list. A hash table has multiple node chains. When we are at the end of one chain, we need to move to the start of the next one. Therefore, the iterator also needs to store the bucket number (see Figure 16).

When the iterator points into the middle of a node chain, then it is easy to advance it to the next element. However, when the iterator points to the last node in a chain, then we must skip past all empty buckets. When we find a non-empty bucket, we advance the iterator to its first node:

```
if (current != null && current.next != null)
{
    current = current.next; // Move to next element in bucket
}
else // Move to next bucket
{
    do
    {
        bucketIndex++;
        if (bucketIndex == buckets.length)
        {
            throw new NoSuchElementException();
        }
        current = buckets[bucketIndex];
    }
    while (current == null);
}
```

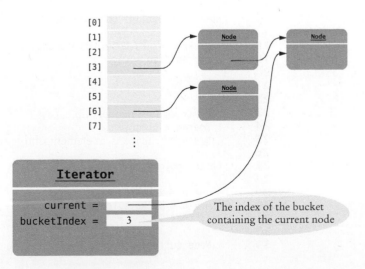

Figure 16
An Iterator to
a Hash Table

As you can see, the cost of iterating over all elements of a hash table is proportional to the table length. Note that the table length could be in excess of $O(n)$ if the table is sparsely filled. This can be avoided if we shrink the table when the load factor gets too small. In that case, iterating over the entire table is $O(n)$, and each iteration step is $O(1)$.

Table 5 summarizes the efficiency of the operations on a hash table.

Table 5 Hash Table Efficiency

Operation	Hash Table
Find an element.	$O(1)$
Add/remove an element.	$O(1)+$
Iterate through all elements.	$O(n)$

Here is an implementation of a hash set. For simplicity, we do not reallocate the table when it grows or shrinks, and we do not support the remove operation on iterators. Exercise •• E16.18 and Exercise ••• E16.19 ask you to provide these enhancements.

sec04/HashSet.java

```java
1   import java.util.Iterator;
2   import java.util.NoSuchElementException;
3
4   /**
5      This class implements a hash set using separate chaining.
6   */
7   public class HashSet
8   {
9      private Node[] buckets;
10     private int currentSize;
11
12     /**
13        Constructs a hash table.
14        @param bucketsLength the length of the buckets array
15     */
16     public HashSet(int bucketsLength)
17     {
18        buckets = new Node[bucketsLength];
19        currentSize = 0;
20     }
21
22     /**
23        Tests for set membership.
24        @param x an object
25        @return true if x is an element of this set
26     */
27     public boolean contains(Object x)
28     {
29        int h = x.hashCode();
30        h = h % buckets.length;
31        if (h < 0) { h = -h; }
32
33        Node current = buckets[h];
```

```
34        while (current != null)
35        {
36           if (current.data.equals(x)) { return true; }
37           current = current.next;
38        }
39        return false;
40     }
41
42     /**
43        Adds an element to this set.
44        @param x an object
45        @return true if x is a new object, false if x was
46        already in the set
47     */
48     public boolean add(Object x)
49     {
50        int h = x.hashCode();
51        h = h % buckets.length;
52        if (h < 0) { h = -h; }
53
54        Node current = buckets[h];
55        while (current != null)
56        {
57           if (current.data.equals(x)) { return false; }
58              // Already in the set
59           current = current.next;
60        }
61        Node newNode = new Node();
62        newNode.data = x;
63        newNode.ncxt = buckets[h];
64        buckets[h] = newNode;
65        currentSize++;
66        return true;
67     }
68
69     /**
70        Removes an object from this set.
71        @param x an object
72        @return true if x was removed from this set, false
73        if x was not an element of this set
74     */
75     public boolean remove(Object x)
76     {
77        int h = x.hashCode();
78        h = h % buckets.length;
79        if (h < 0) { h = -h; }
80
81        Node current = buckets[h];
82        Node previous = null;
83        while (current != null)
84        {
85           if (current.data.equals(x))
86           {
87              if (previous == null) { buckets[h] = current.next; }
88              else { previous.next = current.next; }
89              currentSize--;
90              return true;
91           }
92           previous = current;
93           current = current.next;
```

```
 94          }
 95          return false;
 96      }
 97
 98      /**
 99          Returns an iterator that traverses the elements of this set.
100          @return a hash set iterator
101      */
102      public Iterator iterator()
103      {
104          return new HashSetIterator();
105      }
106
107      /**
108          Gets the number of elements in this set.
109          @return the number of elements
110      */
111      public int size()
112      {
113          return currentSize;
114      }
115
116      class Node
117      {
118          public Object data;
119          public Node next;
120      }
121
122      class HashSetIterator implements Iterator
123      {
124          private int bucketIndex;
125          private Node current;
126
127          /**
128              Constructs a hash set iterator that points to the
129              first element of the hash set.
130          */
131          public HashSetIterator()
132          {
133              current = null;
134              bucketIndex = -1;
135          }
136
137          public boolean hasNext()
138          {
139              if (current != null && current.next != null) { return true; }
140              for (int b = bucketIndex + 1; b < buckets.length; b++)
141              {
142                  if (buckets[b] != null) { return true; }
143              }
144              return false;
145          }
146
147          public Object next()
148          {
149              if (current != null && current.next != null)
150              {
151                  current = current.next; // Move to next element in bucket
```

```
152            }
153            else // Move to next bucket
154            {
155               do
156               {
157                  bucketIndex++;
158                  if (bucketIndex == buckets.length)
159                  {
160                     throw new NoSuchElementException();
161                  }
162                  current = buckets[bucketIndex];
163               }
164               while (current == null);
165            }
166            return current.data;
167         }
168
169         public void remove()
170         {
171            throw new UnsupportedOperationException();
172         }
173      }
174 }
```

sec04/HashSetDemo.java

```java
1  import java.util.Iterator;
2
3  /**
4     This program demonstrates the hash set class.
5  */
6  public class HashSetDemo
7  {
8     public static void main(String[] args)
9     {
10        HashSet names = new HashSet(101);
11
12        names.add("Harry");
13        names.add("Sue");
14        names.add("Nina");
15        names.add("Susannah");
16        names.add("Larry");
17        names.add("Eve");
18        names.add("Sarah");
19        names.add("Adam");
20        names.add("Tony");
21        names.add("Katherine");
22        names.add("Juliet");
23        names.add("Romeo");
24        names.remove("Romeo");
25        names.remove("George");
26
27        Iterator iter = names.iterator();
28        while (iter.hasNext())
29        {
30           System.out.println(iter.next());
31        }
32     }
33 }
```

Program Run

```
Sue
Harry
Nina
Susannah
Larry
Eve
Sarah
Adam
Juliet
Katherine
Tony
```

Special Topic 16.2

Open Addressing

In the preceding sections, you studied a hash table implementation that uses separate chaining for collision handling, placing all elements with the same hash code in a bucket. This implementation is fast and easy to understand, but it requires storage for the links to the nodes. If one places the elements directly into the hash table, then one doesn't need to store any links. This alternative technique is called *open addressing*. It can be beneficial if one must minimize the memory usage of a hash table.

Of course, open addressing makes collision handling more complicated. If you have two elements with (compressed) hash code h, and the first one is placed at index h, then the second must be placed in another location.

There are different techniques for placing colliding elements. The simplest is *linear probing*. If possible, place the colliding element at index $h + 1$. If that slot is occupied, try $h + 2$, $h + 3$, and so on, wrapping around to 0, 1, 2, and so on, if necessary. This sequence of index values is called the *probing sequence*. (You can see other probing sequences in Exercise ••• P16.15 and Exercise ••• P16.16.) If the probing sequence contains no empty slots, one must reallocate to a larger table.

How do we find an element in such a hash table? We compute the hash code and traverse the probing sequence until we either find a match or an empty slot. As long as the hash table is not too full, this is still an $O(1)$ operation, but it may require more comparisons than with separate chaining. With separate chaining, we only compare objects with the same hash code. With open addressing, there may be some objects with different hash codes that happen to lie on the probing sequence.

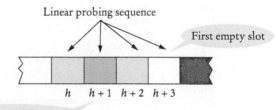

Adding an element is similar. Try finding the element first. If it is not present, add it in the first empty slot in the probing sequence.

Removing an element is trickier. You cannot simply empty the slot at which you find the element. Instead, you must traverse the probing sequence, look for the last element with the same hash code, and move that element into the slot of the removed element. Then rehash all elements that follow until you reach an empty slot (Exercise ••• P16.14).

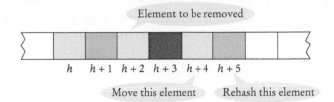

Element to be removed

h $h+1$ $h+2$ $h+3$ $h+4$ $h+5$

Move this element   Rehash this element

Alternatively, you can replace the removed element with a special "inactive" marker that, unlike an empty slot, does not indicate the end of a probing sequence. When adding another element, you can overwrite an inactive slot (Exercise ••• P16.17).

CHAPTER SUMMARY

Describe the implementation and efficiency of linked list operations.

- A linked list object holds a reference to the first node object, and each node holds a reference to the next node.
- When adding or removing the first element, the reference to the first node must be updated.
- A list iterator object has a reference to the last visited node.
- To advance an iterator, update the position and remember the old position for the remove method.
- In a doubly-linked list, accessing an element is an $O(n)$ operation; adding and removing an element is $O(1)$.

Understand the implementation and efficiency of array list operations.

- Getting or setting an array list element is an $O(1)$ operation.
- Inserting or removing an array list element is an $O(n)$ operation.
- Adding or removing the last element in an array list takes amortized $O(1)$ time.

Compare different implementations of stacks and queues.

- A stack can be implemented as a linked list, adding and removing elements at the front.
- When implementing a stack as an array, add and remove elements at the back.
- A queue can be implemented as a linked list, adding elements at the back and removing them at the front.
- In a circular array implementation of a queue, element locations wrap from the end of the array to the beginning.

Understand the implementation of hash tables and the efficiencies of its operations.

- A good hash function minimizes *collisions*—identical hash codes for different objects.
- A hash table uses the hash code to determine where to store each element.
- A hash table can be implemented as an array of *buckets*—sequences of nodes that hold elements with the same hash code.
- If there are no or only a few collisions, then adding, locating, and removing hash table elements takes constant or $O(1)$ time.

REVIEW EXERCISES

▪ R16.1 The linked list class in the Java library supports operations addLast and removeLast. To carry out these operations efficiently, the LinkedList class has an added reference last to the last node in the linked list. Draw a "before/after" diagram of the changes to the links in a linked list when the addLast method is executed.

▪▪ R16.2 The linked list class in the Java library supports bidirectional iterators. To go backward efficiently, each Node has an added reference, previous, to the predecessor node in the linked list. Draw a "before/after" diagram of the changes to the links in a linked list when the addFirst and removeFirst methods execute. The diagram should show how the previous references need to be updated.

▪ R16.3 What is the big-Oh efficiency of replacing all negative values in a linked list of Integer objects with zeroes? Of removing all negative values?

▪ R16.4 What is the big-Oh efficiency of replacing all negative values in an array list of Integer objects with zeroes? Of removing all negative values?

▪▪ R16.5 In the LinkedList implementation of Section 16.1, we use a flag isAfterNext to ensure that calls to the remove and set methods occur only when they are allowed. It is not actually necessary to introduce a new instance variable for this check. Instead, one can set the previous instance variable to a special value at the end of every call to add or remove. With that change, how should the remove and set methods check whether they are allowed?

▪ R16.6 What is the big-Oh efficiency of the size method of Exercise • E16.4?

▪ R16.7 Show that the introduction of the size method in Exercise • E16.6 does not affect the big-Oh efficiency of the other list operations.

▪▪ R16.8 Given the size method of Exercise • E16.6 and the get method of Exercise • P16.1, what is the big-Oh efficiency of this loop?

```
for (int i = 0; i < myList.size(); i++) { System.out.println(myList.get(i)); }
```

▪▪ R16.9 Given the size method of Exercise • E16.6 and the get method of Exercise ••• P16.3, what is the big-Oh efficiency of this loop?

```
for (int i = 0; i < myList.size(); i++) { System.out.println(myList.get(i)); }
```

▪▪ R16.10 It is not safe to remove the first element of a linked list with the removeFirst method when an iterator has just traversed the first element. Explain the problem by tracing the code and drawing a diagram.

▪▪ R16.11 Continue Exercise •• R16.10 by providing a code example demonstrating the problem.

▪▪▪ R16.12 It is not safe to simultaneously modify a linked list using two iterators. Find a situation where two iterators refer to the same linked list, and when you add an element with one iterator and remove an element with the other, the result is incorrect. Explain the problem by tracing the code and drawing a diagram.

▪▪▪ R16.13 Continue Exercise ••• R16.12 by providing a code example demonstrating the problem.

■■■ **R16.14** In the implementation of the `LinkedList` class of the standard Java library, the problem described in Exercise •• R16.10 and Exercise ••• R16.12 results in a `ConcurrentModificationException`. Describe how the `LinkedList` class and the iterator classes can discover that a list was modified through multiple sources. *Hint:* Count mutating operations. Where are the counts stored? Where are they updated? Where are they checked?

■ **R16.15** Consider the efficiency of locating the kth element in a doubly-linked list of length n. If $k > n/2$, it is more efficient to start at the end of the list and move the iterator to the previous element. Why doesn't this increase in efficiency improve the big-Oh estimate of element access in a doubly-linked list?

■ **R16.16** A linked list implementor, hoping to improve the speed of accessing elements, provides an array of `Node` references, pointing to every tenth node. Then the operation `get(n)` looks up the reference at index `n / 10` and follows `n % 10` links.

   a. With this implementation, what is the efficiency of the `get` operation?

   b. What is the disadvantage of this implementation?

■ **R16.17** Suppose an array list implementation were to add ten elements at each reallocation instead of doubling the capacity. Show that the `addLast` operation no longer has amortized constant time.

■ **R16.18** Consider an array list implementation with a `removeLast` method that shrinks the internal array to half of its size when it is at most half full. Give a sequence of `addLast` and `removeLast` calls that does not have amortized $O(1)$ efficiency.

■■■ **R16.19** Suppose the `ArrayList` implementation of Section 16.2 had a `removeLast` method that shrinks the internal array by 50 percent when it is less than 25 percent full. Show that any sequence of `addLast` and `removeLast` calls has amortized $O(1)$ efficiency.

■ **R16.20** Given a queue with $O(1)$ methods `add`, `remove`, and `size`, what is the big-Oh efficiency of moving the element at the head of the queue to the tail? Of moving the element at the tail of the queue to the head? (The order of the other queue elements should be unchanged.)

■ **R16.21** A deque (double-ended queue) is a data structure with operations `addFirst`, `removeFirst`, `addLast`, and `removeLast`. What is the $O(1)$ efficiency of these operations if the deque is implemented as

   a. a singly-linked list?

   b. a doubly-linked list?

   c. a circular array?

■■ **R16.22** In our circular array implementation of a queue, can you compute the value of the `currentSize` from the values of the `head` and `tail` fields? Why or why not?

■ **R16.23** Draw the contents of a circular array implementation of a queue q, with an initial array size of 10, after each of the following loops:

```
a. for (int i = 1; i <= 5; i++) { q.add(i); }
b. for (int i = 1; i <= 3; i++) { q.remove(); }
c. for (int i = 1; i <= 10; i++) { q.add(i); }
d. for (int i = 1; i <= 8; i++) { q.remove(); }
```

■■ R16.24 Suppose you are stranded on a desert island on which stacks are plentiful, but you need a queue. How can you implement a queue using two stacks? What is the big-Oh running time of the queue operations?

■■ R16.25 Suppose you are stranded on a desert island on which queues are plentiful, but you need a stack. How can you implement a stack using two queues? What is the big-Oh running time of the stack operations?

© Philip Dyer/iStockphoto.

■■ R16.26 Craig Coder doesn't like the fact that he has to implement a hash function for the objects that he wants to collect in a hash table. "Why not assign a unique ID to each object?" he asks. What is wrong with his idea?

PRACTICE EXERCISES

■■■ E16.1 Add a method reverse to our LinkedList implementation that reverses the links in a list. Implement this method by directly rerouting the links, not by using an iterator.

■■ E16.2 Consider a version of the LinkedList class of Section 16.1.8 in which the addFirst method has been replaced with the following faulty version:

```java
public void addFirst(Object element)
{
    Node newNode = new Node();
    first = newNode;
    newNode.data = element;
    newNode.next = first;
}
```

Develop a program ListTest with a test case that shows the error. That is, the program should print a failure message with this implementation but not with the correct implementation.

■■ E16.3 Consider a version of the LinkedList class of Section 16.1.8 in which the iterator's hasNext method has been replaced with the following faulty version:

```java
public boolean hasNext() { return position != null; }
```

Develop a program ListTest with a test case that shows the error. The program should print a failure message with this implementation but not with the correct one.

■ E16.4 Add a method size to our implementation of the LinkedList class that computes the number of elements in the list by following links and counting the elements until the end of the list is reached.

■■ E16.5 Solve Exercise • E16.4 recursively by calling a recursive helper method

```java
private static int size(Node start)
```

Hint: If start is null, then the size is 0. Otherwise, it is one larger than the size of start.next.

■ E16.6 Add an instance variable currentSize to our implementation of the LinkedList class. Modify the add, addLast, and remove methods of both the linked list and the list iterator to update the currentSize variable so that it always contains the correct size. Change the size method of Exercise • E16.4 so that it simply returns the value of currentSize.

■■■ **E16.7** Reimplement the LinkedList class of Section 16.1.8 so that the Node and LinkedList-Iterator classes are not inner classes.

■■■ **E16.8** Reimplement the LinkedList class of Section 16.1.8 so that it implements the java.util.List interface. *Hint:* Extend the java.util.AbstractSequentialList class.

■■■ **E16.9** Provide a listIterator method for the ArrayList implementation in Section 16.2.3. Your method should return an object of a class implementing java.util.ListIterator. Also have the ArrayList class implement the Iterable interface type and provide a test program that demonstrates that your array list can be used in an enhanced for loop.

■ **E16.10** Provide a removeLast method for the ArrayList implementation in Section 16.2.3 that shrinks the internal array by 50 percent when it is less than 25 percent full.

■ **E16.11** Complete the implementation of a stack in Section 16.3.2, using an array for storing the elements.

■ **E16.12** Complete the implementation of a queue in Section 16.3.3, using a sequence of nodes for storing the elements.

■ **E16.13** Add a method firstToLast to the implementation of a queue in Exercise • E16.12. The method moves the element at the head of the queue to the tail of the queue. The element that was second in line will now be at the head.

■ **E16.14** Add a method lastToFirst to the implementation of a queue in Exercise • E16.12. The method moves the element at the tail of the queue to the head.

■ **E16.15** Add a method firstToLast, as described in Exercise • E16.13, to the circular array implementation of a queue.

■ **E16.16** Add a method lastToFirst, as described in Exercise • E16.14, to the circular array implementation of a queue.

■ **E16.17** The hasNext method of the hash set implementation in Section 16.4.5 finds the location of the next element, but when next is called, the same search happens again. Improve the efficiency of these methods so that next (or a repeated call to hasNext) uses the position located by a preceding call to hasNext.

■■ **E16.18** Reallocate the buckets of the hash set implementation in Section 16.4.5 when the load factor is greater than 1.0 or less than 0.5, doubling or halving its size. Note that you need to recompute the hash values of all elements.

■■■ **E16.19** Implement the remove operation for iterators on the hash set in Section 16.4.5.

■ **E16.20** Implement the hash set in Section 16.4.5, using the "MAD (multiply-add-divide) method" for hash code compression. For that method, you choose a prime number p larger than the length L of the hash table and two values a and b between 1 and $p - 1$. Then reduce h to $|((a\,h + b)\,\%\,p)\,\%\,L|$.

■ **E16.21** Add methods to count collisions to the hash set in Section 16.4.5 and the one in Exercise • E16.20. Insert all words from a dictionary (in /usr/share/dict/words or in words.txt in your companion code) into both hash set implementations. Does the MAD method reduce collisions? (Use a table size that equals the number of words in the file. Choose p to be the next prime greater than L, $a = 3$, and $b = 5$.)

PROGRAMMING PROJECTS

- **P16.1** Add methods `Object get(int n)` and `void set(int n, Object newElement)` to the `LinkedList` class. Use a helper method that starts at `first` and follows n links:

  ```
  private Node getNode(int n)
  ```

- **P16.2** Solve Exercise • P16.1 by using a recursive helper method

  ```
  private static Node getNode(Node start, int distance)
  ```

- **P16.3** Improve the efficiency of the `get` and `set` methods of Exercise • P16.1 by storing (or "caching") the last known (node, index) pair. If n is larger than the last known index, start from the corresponding node instead of the front of the list. Be sure to discard the last known pair when it is no longer accurate. (This can happen when another method edits the list).

- **P16.4** Add a method `boolean contains(Object obj)` that checks whether our `LinkedList` implementation contains a given object. Implement this method by directly traversing the links, not by using an iterator.

  Use the `equals` method to determine whether `obj` equals `node.data` for a given node.

- **P16.5** Solve Exercise •• P16.4 recursively, by calling a recursive helper method

  ```
  private static boolean contains(Node start, Object obj)
  ```

  Hint: If start is `null`, then it can't contain the object. Otherwise, check `start.data` before recursively moving on to `start.next`.

- **P16.6** A linked list class with an $O(1)$ `addLast` method needs an efficient mechanism to get to the end of the list, for example by setting an instance variable to the last element. It is then possible to remove the reference to the first node if one makes the `next` reference of the last node point to the first node, so that all nodes form a cycle. Such an implementation is called a circular linked list. Turn the linked list implementation of Section 16.1.8 into a circular singly-linked list.

- **P16.7** In a circular doubly-linked list, the `previous` reference of the first node points to the last node, and the `next` reference of the last node points to the first node. Change the doubly-linked list implementation of Worked Example 16.1 into a circular list. You should remove the `last` instance variable because you can reach the last element as `first.previous`.

- **P16.8** Modify the insertion sort algorithm of Special Topic 14.2 to sort a linked list.

- **P16.9** The LISP language, created in 1960, implements linked lists in a very elegant way. You will explore a Java analog in this set of exercises. Conceptually, the *tail* of a list— that is, the list with its head node removed—is also a list. The tail of that list is again a list, and so on, until you reach the empty list. Here is a Java interface for such a list:

  ```java
  public interface LispList
  {
     boolean empty();
     Object head();
     LispList tail();
     . . .
  }
  ```

There are two kinds of lists, empty lists and nonempty lists:

```
public class EmptyList implements LispList { ... }
public class NonEmptyList implements LispList { ... }
```

These classes are quite trivial. The EmptyList class has no instance variables. Its head and tail methods simply throw an UnsupportedOperationException, and its empty method returns true. The NonEmptyList class has instance variables for the head and tail.

Here is one way of making a LISP list with three elements:

```
LispList list = new NonEmptyList("A", new NonEmptyList("B",
    new NonEmptyList("C", new EmptyList())));
```

This is a bit tedious, and it is a good idea to supply a convenience method cons that calls the constructor, as well as a static variable NIL that is an instance of an empty list. Then our list construction becomes

```
LispList list = LispList.NIL.cons("C").cons("B").cons("A");
```

Note that you need to build up the list starting from the (empty) tail.

To see the elegance of this approach, consider the implementation of a toString method that produces a string containing all list elements. The method must be implemented by both classes:

```
public class EmptyList implements LispList
{
    . . .
    public String toString() { return ""; }
}

public class NonEmptyList implements LispList
{
    . . .
    public String toString() { return head() + " " + tail().toString(); }
}
```

Note that no if statement is required. A list is either empty or nonempty, and the correct toString method is invoked due to polymorphism.

In this exercise, complete the LispList interface and the EmptyList and NonEmptyList classes. Write a test program that constructs a list and prints it.

■ **P16.10** Add a method length to the LispList interface of Exercise •• P16.9 that returns the length of the list. Implement the method in the EmptyList and NonEmptyList classes.

■■ **P16.11** Add a method

```
LispList merge(LispList other)
```

to the LispList interface of Exercise •• P16.9. Implement the method in the EmptyList and NonEmptyList classes. When merging two lists, alternate between the elements, then add the remainder of the longer list. For example, merging the lists with elements 1 2 3 4 and 5 6 yields 1 5 2 6 3 4.

■■ **P16.12** Add a method

```
boolean contains(Object obj)
```

to the LispList interface of Exercise •• P16.9 that returns true if the list contains an element that equals obj.

■■ **P16.13** A deque (double-ended queue) is a data structure with operations addFirst, remove-First, addLast, removeLast, and size. Implement a deque as a circular array, so that these operations have amortized constant time.

■■■ **P16.14** Implement a hash table with open addressing. When removing an element that is followed by other elements with the same hash code, replace it with the last such element and rehash the remaining elements of the probing sequence.

■■■ **P16.15** Modify Exercise ●●● P16.14 to use *quadratic probing*. The ith index in the probing sequence is computed as $(h + i^2)$ % L.

■■■ **P16.16** Modify Exercise ●●● P16.14 to use *double hashing*. The ith index in the probing sequence is computed as $(h + i\,h_2(k))$ % L, where k is the original hash key before compression and h_2 is a function mapping integers to non-zero values. A common choice is $h_2(k) = 1 + k$ % q for a prime q less than L.

■■■ **P16.17** Modify Exercise ●●● P16.14 so that you mark removed elements with an "inactive" element. You can't use null—that is already used for empty elements. Instead, declare a static variable

```
private static final Object INACTIVE = new Object();
```

Use the test if (table[i] == INACTIVE) to check whether a table entry is inactive.

CHAPTER 17

TREE STRUCTURES

CHAPTER GOALS

To study trees and binary trees

To understand how binary search trees can implement sets

To learn how red-black trees provide performance guarantees for set operations

To choose appropriate methods for tree traversal

To become familiar with the heap data structure

To use heaps for implementing priority queues and for sorting

CHAPTER CONTENTS

In this chapter, we study data structures that organize elements hierarchically, creating arrangements that resemble trees. These data structures offer better performance for adding, removing, and finding elements than the linear structures you have seen so far. You will learn about commonly used tree-shaped structures and study their implementation and performance.

17.1 Basic Tree Concepts

A tree is composed of nodes, each of which can have child nodes.

In computer science, a **tree** is a hierarchical data structure composed of *nodes*. Each node has a sequence of *child nodes*, and one of the nodes is the *root node*.

Like a linked list, a tree is composed of nodes, but with a key difference. In a linked list, a node can have only one child node, so the data structure is a linear chain of nodes. In a tree, a node can have more than one child. The resulting shape resembles an actual tree with branches. However, in computer science, it is customary to draw trees upside-down, with the root on top (see Figure 1).

The root is the node with no parent. A leaf is a node with no children.

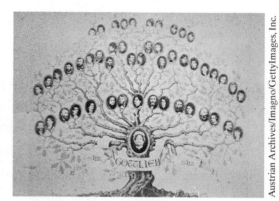

A family tree shows the descendants of a common ancestor.

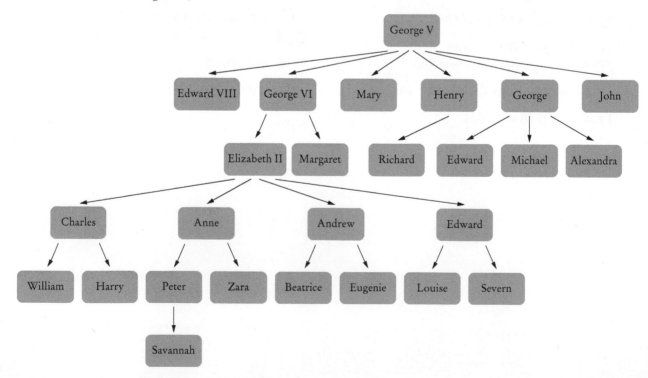

Figure 1 A Family Tree

Trees are commonly used to represent hierarchical relationships. When we talk about nodes in a tree, it is customary to use intuitive words such as roots and leaves, but also parents, children, and siblings—see Table 1 for commonly used terms.

Table 1 Tree Terminology

Term	Definition	Example (using Figure 1)
Node	The building block of a tree: A tree is composed of linked nodes.	This tree has 26 nodes: George V, Edward VIII, ..., Savannah.
Child	Each node has, by definition, a sequence of links to other nodes called its child nodes.	The children of Elizabeth II are Charles, Anne, Andrew, and Edward.
Leaf	A node with no child nodes.	This tree has 16 leaves, including William, Harry, and Savannah.
Interior node	A node that is not a leaf.	George V or George VI, but not Mary.
Parent	If the node c is a child of the node p, then p is a parent of c.	Elizabeth II is the parent of Charles.
Sibling	If the node p has children c and d, then these nodes are siblings.	Charles and Anne are siblings.
Root	The node with no parent. By definition, each tree has one root node.	George V.
Path	A sequence of nodes $c_1, c_2, ..., c_k$ where c_{i+1} is a child of c_i.	Elizabeth II, Anne, Peter, Savannah is a path of length 4.
Descendant	d is a descendant of c if there is a path from c to d.	Peter is a descendant of Elizabeth II but not of Henry.
Ancestor	c is an ancestor of d if d is a descendant of c.	Elizabeth II is an ancestor of Peter, but Henry is not.
Subtree	The subtree rooted at node n is the tree formed by taking n as the root node and including all its descendants.	The subtree with root Anne is
Height	The number of nodes in the longest path from the root to a leaf. (Some authors define the height to be the number of edges in the longest path, which is one less than the height used in this book.)	This tree has height 6. The longest path is George V, George VI, Elizabeth II, Anne, Peter, Savannah.

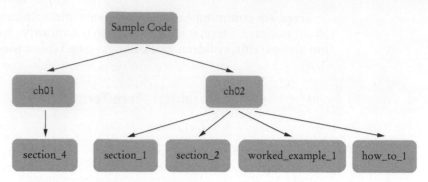

Figure 2 A Directory Tree

Trees have many applications in computer science; see for example Figures 2 and 3.

There are multiple ways of implementing a tree. Here we present an outline of a simple implementation that is further explored in Exercises ••• P17.1 and ••• P17.2. A node holds a data item and a list of references to the child nodes. A tree holds a reference to the root node.

> A tree class uses a node class to represent nodes and has an instance variable for the root node.

```
public class Tree
{
   private Node root;

   class Node
   {
      public Object data;
      public List<Node> children;
   }

   public Tree(Object rootData)
   {
      root = new Node();
      root.data = rootData;
      root.children = new ArrayList<>();
   }

   public void addSubtree(Tree subtree)
   {
      root.children.add(subtree.root);
   }
   . . .
}
```

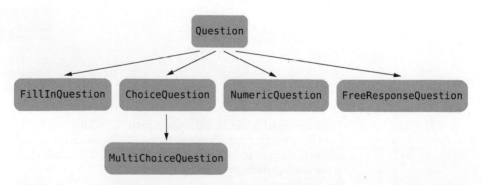

Figure 3 An Inheritance Tree

Note that, as with linked lists, the Node class is nested inside the Tree class. It is considered an implementation detail. Users of the class only work with Tree objects.

When computing properties of trees, it is often convenient to use recursion. For example, consider the task of computing the tree size, that is, the number of nodes in the tree. Compute the sizes of its subtrees, add them up, and add one for the root.

For example, in Figure 1, the tree with root node Elizabeth II has four subtrees, with node counts 3, 4, 3, and 3, yielding a count of $1 + 3 + 4 + 3 + 3 = 14$ for that tree.

Formally, if r is the root node of a tree, then

$$size(r) = 1 + size(c_1) + \cdots + size(c_k),$$
$$\text{where } c_1 \ldots c_k \text{ are the children of } r$$

© Yvette Harris/iStockphoto.

When computing tree properties, it is common to recursively visit smaller and smaller subtrees.

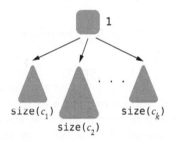

To implement this size method, first provide a recursive helper:

Many tree properties are computed with recursive methods.

```
class Node
{
   . . .
   public int size()
   {
      int sum = 0;
      for (Node child : children) { sum = sum + child.size(); }
      return 1 + sum;
   }
}
```

Then call this helper method from a method of the Tree class:

```
public class Tree
{
   . . .
   public int size() { return root.size(); }
}
```

It is useful to allow an *empty tree*; a tree whose root node is null. This is analogous to an empty list—a list with no elements. Because we can't invoke the helper method on a null reference, we need to refine the Tree class's size method:

```
public int size()
{
   if (root == null) { return 0; }
   else { return root.size(); }
}
```

EXAMPLE CODE   See your eText or companion code to see the Tree class and recursive size method.

17.2 Binary Trees

A binary tree consists of nodes, each of which has at most two child nodes.

In the following sections, we discuss **binary trees**, trees in which each node has at most two children. As you will see throughout this chapter, binary trees have many very important applications.

© kali9/iStockphoto.

In a binary tree, each node has a left and a right child node.

17.2.1 Binary Tree Examples

In this section, you will see several typical examples of binary trees. Figure 4 shows a *decision tree* for guessing an animal from one of several choices. Each non-leaf node contains a question. The left subtree corresponds to a "yes" answer, and the right subtree to a "no" answer.

A decision tree contains questions used to decide among a number of options.

© AlbanyPictures/iStockphoto.

This is a binary tree because every node has either two children (if it is a decision) or no children (if it is a conclusion). Exercises •• E17.4 and ••• P17.7 show you how you can build decision trees that ask good questions for a particular data set.

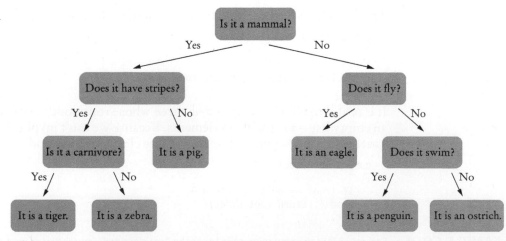

Figure 4   A Decision Tree for an Animal Guessing Game

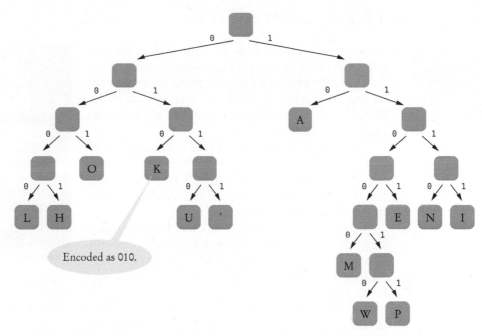

Figure 5   A Huffman Tree for Encoding the Thirteen Characters of Hawaiian Text

Another example of a binary tree is a *Huffman tree*. In a Huffman tree, the leaves contain symbols that we want to encode. To encode a particular symbol, walk along the path from the root to the leaf containing the symbol, and produce a zero for every left turn and a one for every right turn. For example, in the Huffman tree of Figure 5, an H is encoded as 0001 and an A as 10. Worked Example 17.1 shows how to build a Huffman tree that gives the shortest codes for the most frequent symbols.

Binary trees are also used to show the evaluation order in arithmetic expressions. For example, Figure 6 shows the trees for the expressions

```
(3 + 4) * 5
3 + 4 * 5
```

The leaves of the expression trees contain numbers, and the interior nodes contain the operators. Because each operator has two operands, the tree is binary.

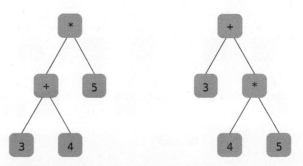

Figure 6   Expression Trees

17.2.2 Balanced Trees

In a balanced tree, all paths from the root to the leaves have approximately the same length.

When we use binary trees to store data, as we will in Section 17.3, we would like to have trees that are *balanced*. In a balanced tree, all paths from the root to one of the leaf nodes have approximately the same length. Figure 7 shows examples of a balanced and an unbalanced tree.

Recall that the height of a tree is the number of nodes in the longest path from the root to a leaf. The trees in Figure 7 have height 5. As you can see, for a given height, a balanced tree can hold more nodes than an unbalanced tree.

We care about the height of a tree because many tree operations proceed along a path from the root to a leaf, and their efficiency is better expressed by the height of the tree than the number of elements in the tree.

© Emrah Turudu/iStockphoto.

In a balanced binary tree, each subtree has approximately the same number of nodes.

A binary tree of height h can have up to $n = 2^h - 1$ nodes. For example, a completely filled binary tree of height 4 has $1 + 2 + 4 + 8 = 15 = 2^4 - 1$ nodes (see Figure 8).

In other words, $h = \log_2(n + 1)$ for a completely filled binary tree. For a balanced tree, we still have $h \approx \log_2 n$. For example, the height of a balanced binary tree with 1,000 nodes is approximately 10 (because $1000 \approx 1024 = 2^{10}$). A balanced binary tree with 1,000,000 nodes has a height of approximately 20 (because $10^6 \approx 2^{20}$). As you will see in Section 17.3, you can find any element in such a tree in about 20 steps. That is a lot faster than traversing the 1,000,000 elements of a list.

Balanced

Unbalanced

Figure 7 Balanced and Unbalanced Trees

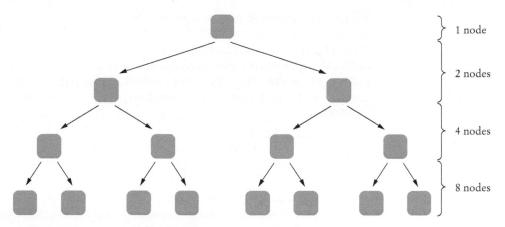

Figure 8 A Completely Filled Binary Tree of Height 4

17.2.3 A Binary Tree Implementation

Every node in a binary tree has references to two children, a left child and a right child. Either one may be null. A node in which both children are null is a leaf.

A binary tree can be implemented in Java as follows:

```java
public class BinaryTree
{
   private Node root;

   public BinaryTree() { root = null; } // An empty tree

   public BinaryTree(Object rootData, BinaryTree left, BinaryTree right)
   {
      root = new Node();
      root.data = rootData;
      root.left = left.root;
      root.right = right.root;
   }

   class Node
   {
      public Object data;
      public Node left;
      public Node right;
   }

   . . .
}
```

As with general trees, we often use recursion to define operations on binary trees. Consider computing the height of a tree; that is, the number of nodes in the longest path from the root to a leaf.

To get the height of the tree t, take the larger of the heights of the children and add one, to account for the root.

$$\text{height}(t) = 1 + \max(\text{height}(l), \text{height}(r))$$

where l and r are the left and right subtrees.

When we implement this method, we could add a height method to the Node class. However, nodes can be null and you can't call a method on a null reference. It is easier to make the recursive helper method a static method of the Tree class, like this:

```java
public class BinaryTree
{
    . . .
    private static int height(Node n)
    {
        if (n == null) { return 0; }
        else { return 1 + Math.max(height(n.left), height(n.right)); }
    }
    . . .
}
```

To get the height of the tree, we provide this public method:

```java
public class BinaryTree
{
    . . .
    public int height() { return height(root); }
}
```

Note that there are two height methods: a public method with no arguments, returning the height of the tree, and a private recursive helper method, returning the height of a subtree with a given node as its root.

EXAMPLE CODE   See your eText or companion code for a program that implements the animal guessing game in Figure 4.

WORKED EXAMPLE 17.1

Building a Huffman Tree

Learn how to build a Huffman tree for compressing the color data of an image. See your eText or visit wiley.com/go/bjeo7.

Charlotte and Emily

17.3 Binary Search Trees

A set implementation is allowed to rearrange its elements in any way it chooses so that it can find elements quickly. Suppose a set implementation *sorts* its entries. Then it can use **binary search** to locate elements quickly. Binary search takes $O(\log(n))$ steps, where n is the size of the set. For example, binary search in an array of 1,000 elements is able to locate an element in at most 10 steps by cutting the size of the search interval in half in each step.

If we use an array to store the elements of a set, inserting or removing an element is an $O(n)$ operation. In the following sections, you will see how tree-shaped data structures can keep elements in sorted order with more efficient insertion and removal.

17.3.1 The Binary Search Property

A **binary search tree** is a binary tree in which *all nodes* fulfill the following property:

- The data values of *all* descendants to the left are less than the data value stored in the node, and *all* descendants to the right have greater data values.

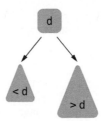

The tree in Figure 9 is a binary search tree.

We can verify the binary search property for each node in Figure 9. Consider the node "Juliet". All descendants to the left have data before "Juliet". All descendants to the right have data after "Juliet". Move on to "Eve". There is a single descendant to the left, with data "Adam" before "Eve", and a single descendant to the right, with data "Harry" after "Eve". Check the remaining nodes in the same way.

All nodes in a binary search tree fulfill the property that the descendants to the left have smaller data values than the node data value, and the descendants to the right have larger data values.

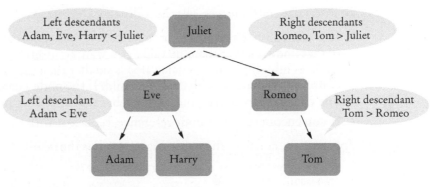

Figure 9   A Binary Search Tree

Figure 10 shows a binary tree that is not a binary search tree. Look carefully—the root node passes the test, but its two children do not.

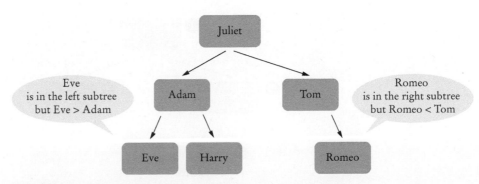

Figure 10   A Binary Tree That Is Not a Binary Search Tree

When you implement binary search tree classes, the data variable should have type Comparable, not Object. After all, you must be able to compare the values in a binary search tree in order to place them into the correct position.

```
public class BinarySearchTree
{
   private Node root;

   public BinarySearchTree() { . . . }
   public void add(Comparable obj) { . . . }
   . . .
   class Node
   {
      public Comparable data;
      public Node left;
      public Node right;

      public void addNode(Node newNode) { . . . }
      . . .
   }
}
```

17.3.2 Insertion

To insert data into the tree, use the following algorithm:

• If you encounter a non-null node reference, look at its data value. If the data value of that node is larger than the value you want to insert, continue the process with the left child. If the node's data value is smaller than the one you want to insert, continue the process with the right child. If the node's data value is the same as the one you want to insert, you are done, because a set does not store duplicate values.

• If you encounter a null node reference, replace it with the new node.

For example, consider the tree in Figure 11. It is the result of the following statements:

```
BinarySearchTree tree = new BinarySearchTree();
tree.add("Juliet");   ❶
tree.add("Tom");      ❷
tree.add("Diana");    ❸
tree.add("Harry");    ❹
```

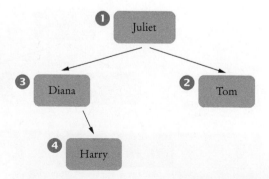

Figure 11 Binary Search Tree After Four Insertions

> To insert a value into a binary search tree, keep comparing the value with the node data and follow the nodes to the left or right, until reaching a null node.

We want to insert a new element Romeo into it:

```
tree.add("Romeo");
```

Start with the root node, Juliet. Romeo comes after Juliet, so you move to the right subtree. You encounter the node Tom. Romeo comes before Tom, so you move to the left subtree. But there is no left subtree. Hence, you insert a new Romeo node as the left child of Tom (see Figure 12).

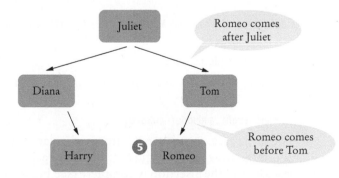

Figure 12   Binary Search Tree After Five Insertions

You should convince yourself that the resulting tree is still a binary search tree. When Romeo is inserted, it must end up as a right descendant of Juliet — that is what the binary search tree condition means for the root node Juliet. The root node doesn't care where in the right subtree the new node ends up. Moving along to Tom, the right child of Juliet, all it cares about is that the new node Romeo ends up somewhere on its left. There is nothing to its left, so Romeo becomes the new left child, and the resulting tree is again a binary search tree.

Here is the code for the add method of the BinarySearchTree class:

```
public void add(Comparable obj)
{
   Node newNode = new Node();
   newNode.data = obj;
   newNode.left = null;
   newNode.right = null;
   if (root == null) { root = newNode; }
   else { root.addNode(newNode); }
}
```

If the tree is empty, simply set its root to the new node. Otherwise, you know that the new node must be inserted somewhere within the nodes, and you can ask the root node to perform the insertion. That node object calls the addNode method of the Node class, which checks whether the new object is less than the object stored in the node. If so, the element is inserted in the left subtree; if not, it is inserted in the right subtree:

```
class Node
{
   . . .
   public void addNode(Node newNode)
   {
      int comp = newNode.data.compareTo(data);
      if (comp < 0)
      {
         if (left == null) { left = newNode; }
         else { left.addNode(newNode); }
```

```
      }
      else if (comp > 0)
      {
         if (right == null) { right = newNode; }
         else { right.addNode(newNode); }
      }
   }
   . . .
}
```

Let's trace the calls to addNode when inserting Romeo into the tree in Figure 11. The first call to addNode is

```
root.addNode(newNode)
```

Because root points to Juliet, you compare Juliet with Romeo and find that you must call

```
root.right.addNode(newNode)
```

The node root.right is Tom. Compare the data values again (Tom vs. Romeo) and find that you must now move to the left. Because root.right.left is null, set root.right.left to newNode, and the insertion is complete (see Figure 12).

Unlike a linked list or an array, and like a hash table, a binary tree has no *insert positions.* You cannot select the position where you would like to insert an element into a binary search tree. The data structure is *self-organizing;* that is, each element finds its own place.

17.3.3 Removal

We will now discuss the removal algorithm. Our task is to remove a node from the tree. Of course, we must first *find* the node to be removed. That is a simple matter, due to the characteristic property of a binary search tree. Compare the data value to be removed with the data value that is stored in the root node. If it is smaller, keep looking in the left subtree. Otherwise, keep looking in the right subtree.

Let us now assume that we have located the node that needs to be removed. First, let us consider the easiest case. If the node to be removed has no children at all, then the parent link is simply set to null (Figure 13).

When the node to be removed has only one child, the situation is still simple (see Figure 14).

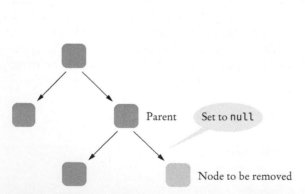

Figure 13   Removing a Node with No Children

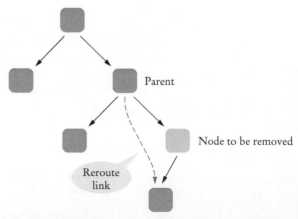

Figure 14   Removing a Node with One Child

To remove the node, simply modify the parent link that points to the node so that it points to the child instead.

The case in which the node to be removed has two children is more challenging. Rather than removing the node, it is easier to replace its data value with the next larger value in the tree. That replacement preserves the binary search tree property. (Alternatively, you could use the largest element of the left subtree—see Exercise ••• P17.5).

To locate the next larger value, go to the right subtree and find its smallest data value. Keep following the left child links. Once you reach a node that has no left child, you have found the node containing the smallest data value of the subtree. Now remove that node—it is easily removed because it has at most one child to the right. Then store its data value in the original node that was slated for removal. Figure 15 shows the details.

At the end of this section, you will find the source code for the BinarySearchTree class. It contains the add and remove methods that we just described, a find method that tests whether a value is present in a binary search tree, and a print method that we will analyze in Section 17.4.

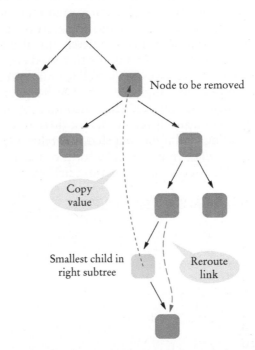

Figure 15 Removing a Node with Two Children

17.3.4 Efficiency of the Operations

Now that you have seen the implementation of this data structure, you may well wonder whether it is any good. Like nodes in a list, the nodes are allocated one at a time. No existing elements need to be moved when a new element is inserted or removed; that is an advantage. How fast insertion and removal are, however, depends on the shape of the tree. These operations are fast if the tree is balanced.

Table 2 Efficiency of Binary Search Tree Operations		
Operation	Balanced Binary Search Tree	Unbalanced Binary Search Tree
Find an element.	$O(\log(n))$	$O(n)$
Add an element.	$O(\log(n))$	$O(n)$
Remove an element.	$O(\log(n))$	$O(n)$

Because the operations of finding, adding, and removing an element process the nodes along a path from the root to a leaf, their execution time is proportional to the height of the tree, and not to the total number of nodes in the tree.

For a balanced tree, we have $h \approx O(\log(n))$. Therefore, inserting, finding, or removing an element is an $O(\log(n))$ operation. On the other hand, if the tree happens to be *unbalanced*, then binary tree operations can be slow—in the worst case, as slow as insertion into a linked list. Table 2 summarizes these observations.

> If a binary search tree is balanced, then adding, locating, or removing an element takes $O(\log(n))$ time.

If elements are added in fairly random order, the resulting tree is likely to be well balanced. However, if the incoming elements happen to be in sorted order already, then the resulting tree is completely unbalanced. Each new element is inserted at the end, and the entire tree must be traversed every time to find that end!

Binary search trees work well for random data, but if you suspect that the data in your application might be sorted or have long runs of sorted data, you should not use a binary search tree. There are more sophisticated tree structures whose methods keep trees balanced at all times. In these tree structures, one can guarantee that finding, adding, and removing elements takes $O(\log(n))$ time. The standard Java library uses *red-black trees*, a special form of balanced binary trees, to implement sets and maps. We discuss these structures in Section 17.5.

sec03/BinarySearchTree.java

```
1  /**
2      This class implements a binary search tree whose
3      nodes hold objects that implement the Comparable
4      interface.
5  */
6  public class BinarySearchTree
7  {
8      private Node root;
9
10     /**
11         Constructs an empty tree.
12     */
13     public BinarySearchTree()
14     {
15         root = null;
16     }
17
18     /**
19         Inserts a new node into the tree.
20         @param obj the object to insert
21     */
22     public void add(Comparable obj)
```

```
23      {
24         Node newNode = new Node();
25         newNode.data = obj;
26         newNode.left = null;
27         newNode.right = null;
28         if (root == null) { root = newNode; }
29         else { root.addNode(newNode); }
30      }
31
32      /**
33         Tries to find an object in the tree.
34         @param obj the object to find
35         @return true if the object is contained in the tree
36      */
37      public boolean find(Comparable obj)
38      {
39         Node current = root;
40         while (current != null)
41         {
42            int d = current.data.compareTo(obj);
43            if (d == 0) { return true; }
44            else if (d > 0) { current = current.left; }
45            else { current = current.right; }
46         }
47         return false;
48      }
49
50      /**
51         Tries to remove an object from the tree. Does nothing
52         if the object is not contained in the tree.
53         @param obj the object to remove
54      */
55      public void remove(Comparable obj)
56      {
57         // Find node to be removed
58
59         Node toBeRemoved = root;
60         Node parent = null;
61         boolean found = false;
62         while (!found && toBeRemoved != null)
63         {
64            int d = toBeRemoved.data.compareTo(obj);
65            if (d == 0) { found = true; }
66            else
67            {
68               parent = toBeRemoved;
69               if (d > 0) { toBeRemoved = toBeRemoved.left; }
70               else { toBeRemoved = toBeRemoved.right; }
71            }
72         }
73
74         if (!found) { return; }
75
76         // toBeRemoved contains obj
77
78         // If one of the children is empty, use the other
79
80         if (toBeRemoved.left == null || toBeRemoved.right == null)
81         {
82            Node newChild;
```

```
83            if (toBeRemoved.left == null)
84            {
85                newChild = toBeRemoved.right;
86            }
87            else
88            {
89                newChild = toBeRemoved.left;
90            }
91
92            if (parent == null) // Found in root
93            {
94                root = newChild;
95            }
96            else if (parent.left == toBeRemoved)
97            {
98                parent.left = newChild;
99            }
100           else
101           {
102               parent.right = newChild;
103           }
104           return;
105        }
106
107        // Neither subtree is empty
108
109        // Find smallest element of the right subtree
110
111        Node smallestParent = toBeRemoved;
112        Node smallest = toBeRemoved.right;
113        while (smallest.left != null)
114        {
115            smallestParent = smallest;
116            smallest = smallest.left;
117        }
118
119        // smallest  contains smallest child in right subtree
120
121        // Move contents, unlink child
122
123        toBeRemoved.data = smallest.data;
124        if (smallestParent == toBeRemoved)
125        {
126            smallestParent.right = smallest.right;
127        }
128        else
129        {
130            smallestParent.left = smallest.right;
131        }
132    }
133
134    /**
135       Prints the contents of the tree in sorted order.
136    */
137    public void print()
138    {
139        print(root);
140        System.out.println();
141    }
142
```

```
143    /**
144        Prints a node and all of its descendants in sorted order.
145        @param parent the root of the subtree to print
146    */
147    private static void print(Node parent)
148    {
149        if (parent == null) { return; }
150        print(parent.left);
151        System.out.print(parent.data + " ");
152        print(parent.right);
153    }
154
155    /**
156        A node of a tree stores a data item and references
157        to the left and right child nodes.
158    */
159    class Node
160    {
161        public Comparable data;
162        public Node left;
163        public Node right;
164
165        /**
166            Inserts a new node as a descendant of this node.
167            @param newNode the node to insert
168        */
169        public void addNode(Node newNode)
170        {
171            int comp = newNode.data.compareTo(data);
172            if (comp < 0)
173            {
174                if (left == null) { left = newNode; }
175                else { left.addNode(newNode); }
176            }
177            else if (comp > 0)
178            {
179                if (right == null) { right = newNode; }
180                else { right.addNode(newNode); }
181            }
182        }
183    }
184 }
```

17.4 Tree Traversal

We often want to visit all elements in a tree. There are many different orderings in which one can visit, or *traverse*, the tree elements. The following sections introduce the most common ones.

17.4.1 Inorder Traversal

Suppose you inserted a number of data values into a binary search tree. What can you do with them? It turns out to be surprisingly simple to print all elements in sorted order. You *know* that all data in the left subtree of any node must come before the root node and before all data in the right subtree. That is, the following algorithm will print the elements in sorted order:

Print the left subtree.
Print the root data.
Print the right subtree.

Let's try this out with the tree in Figure 12 on page 593. The algorithm tells us to

1. Print the left subtree of Juliet; that is, Diana and descendants.
2. Print Juliet.
3. Print the right subtree of Juliet; that is, Tom and descendants.

How do you print the subtree starting at Diana?

1. Print the left subtree of Diana. There is nothing to print.
2. Print Diana.
3. Print the right subtree of Diana, that is, Harry.

That is, the left subtree of Juliet is printed as

Diana Harry

The right subtree of Juliet is the subtree starting at Tom. How is it printed? Again, using the same algorithm:

1. Print the left subtree of Tom, that is, Romeo.
2. Print Tom.
3. Print the right subtree of Tom. There is nothing to print.

Thus, the right subtree of Juliet is printed as

Romeo Tom

Now put it all together: the left subtree, Juliet, and the right subtree:

Diana Harry Juliet Romeo Tom

The tree is printed in sorted order.

It is very easy to implement this print method. We start with a recursive helper method:

```
private static void print(Node parent)
{
   if (parent == null) { return; }
   print(parent.left);
   System.out.print(parent.data + " ");
   print(parent.right);
}
```

To print the entire tree, start this recursive printing process at the root:

```
public void print()
{
   print(root);
}
```

This visitation scheme is called *inorder traversal* (visit the left subtree, the root, the right subtree). There are two related traversal schemes, called *preorder traversal* and *postorder traversal*, which we discuss in the next section.

To visit all elements in a tree, visit the root and recursively visit the subtrees.

17.4.2 Preorder and Postorder Traversals

We distinguish between preorder, inorder, and postorder traversal.

In Section 17.4.1, we visited a binary tree in order: first the left subtree, then the root, then the right subtree. By modifying the visitation rules, we obtain other traversals.

In preorder traversal, we visit the root *before* visiting the subtrees, and in postorder traversal, we visit the root *after* the subtrees.

© Pawel Gaul/iStockphoto.

When visiting all nodes of a tree, one needs to choose a traversal order.

Preorder(n)
Visit n.
For each child c of n
    Preorder(c).

Postorder(n)
For each child c of n
    Postorder(c).
Visit n.

These two visitation schemes will not print a binary search tree in sorted order. However, they are important in other applications. Here is an example.

In Section 17.2, you saw trees for arithmetic expressions. Their leaves store numbers, and their interior nodes store operators. The expression trees describe the order in which the operators are applied.

Let's apply postorder traversal to the expression trees in Figure 6 on page 587. The first tree yields

    3 4 + 5 *

whereas the second tree yields

    3 4 5 * +

Postorder traversal of an expression tree yields the instructions for evaluating the expression on a stack-based calculator.

You can interpret the traversal result as an expression in "reverse Polish notation" (see Special Topic 15.3), or equivalently, instructions for a stack-based calculator (see Section 15.6.2).

Here is another example of the importance of traversal order. Consider a directory tree such as the following:

This directory is removed last.

Sample Code

ch01   ch02

These directories are removed first.

section_4   section_1   section_2   worked_example_1   how_to_1

Consider the task of removing all directories from such a tree, with the restriction that you can only remove a directory when it contains no other directories. In this case, you use a postorder traversal.

Conversely, if you want to copy the directory tree, you start copying the root, because you need a target directory into which to place the children. This calls for preorder traversal.

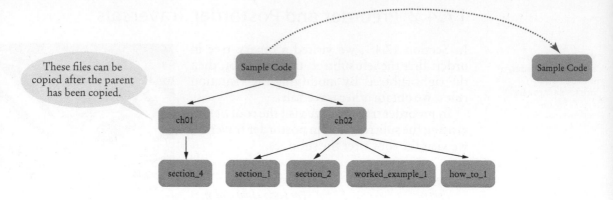

These files can be copied after the parent has been copied.

Note that pre- and postorder traversal can be defined for *any* trees, not just binary trees (see the sample code for this section). However, inorder traversal makes sense only for binary trees.

17.4.3 The Visitor Pattern

In the preceding sections, we simply printed each tree node that we visited. Often, we want to process the nodes in some other way. To make visitation more generic, we define an interface type

```java
public interface Visitor
{
   void visit(Object data);
}
```

The preorder method receives an object of some class that implements this interface type, and calls its visit method:

```java
private static void preorder(Node n, Visitor v)
{
   if (n == null) { return; }
   v.visit(n.data);
   for (Node c : n.children) { preorder(c, v); }
}

public void preorder(Visitor v) { preorder(root, v); }
```

Methods for postorder and, for a binary tree, inorder traversals can be implemented in the same way.

Let's say we want to count short names (with at most five letters). The following visitor will do the job. We'll make it into an inner class of the method that uses it.

```java
public static void main(String[] args)
{
   BinarySearchTree bst = . . .;

   class ShortNameCounter implements Visitor
   {
      public int counter = 0;
      public void visit(Object data)
      {
         if (data.toString().length() <= 5) { counter++; }
      }
   }
```

```
        ShortNameCounter v = new ShortNameCounter();
        bst.inorder(v);
        System.out.println("Short names: " + v.counter);
    }
```

Here, the visitor object accumulates the count. After the visit is complete, we can obtain the result. Because the class is an inner class, we don't worry about making the counter private.

17.4.4 Depth-First and Breadth-First Search

The traversals in the preceding sections are expressed using recursion. If you want to process the nodes of a tree, you supply a visitor, which is applied to all nodes. Sometimes, it is useful to use an iterative approach instead. Then you can stop processing nodes when a goal has been met.

To visit the nodes of a tree iteratively, we replace the recursive calls with a stack that keeps track of the children that need to be visited. Here is the algorithm:

© David Jones/iStockphoto.

In a depth-first search, one moves as quickly as possible to the deepest nodes of the tree.

> *Push the root node on a stack.*
> *While the stack is not empty*
>   *Pop the stack; let n be the popped node.*
>   *Process n.*
>   *Push the children of n on the stack, starting with the last one.*

> **Depth-first search uses a stack to track the nodes that it still needs to visit.**

This algorithm is called *depth-first search* because it goes deeply into the tree and then backtracks when it reaches the leaves (see Figure 16). Note that the tree can be an arbitrary tree—it need not be binary.

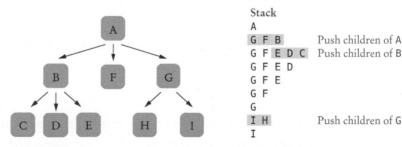

Figure 16 Depth-First Search

We push the children on the stack in right-to-left order so that the visit starts with the leftmost path. In this way, the nodes are visited in preorder. If the leftmost child had been pushed first, we would still have a depth-first search, just in a less intuitive order.

If we replace the stack with a queue, the visitation order changes. Instead of going deeply into the tree, we first visit all nodes at the same level before going on to the next level. This is called *breadth-first search* (Figure 17).

Figure 17
Breadth-First
Search

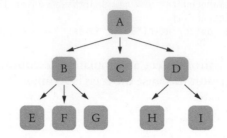

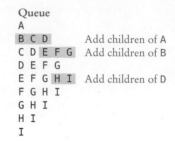

Queue	
A	
B C D	Add children of A
C D E F G	Add children of B
D E F G	
E F G H I	Add children of D
F G H I	
G H I	
H I	
I	

Breadth-first search first visits all nodes on the same level before visiting the children.

For this algorithm, we modify the Visitor interface of Section 17.4.3. The visit method now returns a flag indicating whether the traversal should continue. For example, if you want to visit the first ten nodes, you should provide an implementation of the Visitor interface whose visit method returns false when it has visited the tenth node.

Here is an implementation of the breadth-first algorithm:

```java
public interface Visitor
{
   boolean visit(Object data);
}

public void breadthFirst(Visitor v)
{
   if (root == null) { return; }
   Queue<Node> q = new LinkedList<>();
   q.add(root);
   boolean more = true;
   while (more && q.size() > 0)
   {
      Node n = q.remove();
      more = v.visit(n.data);
      if (more)
      {
         for (Node c : n.children) { q.add(c); }
      }
   }
}
```

For depth-first search, replace the queue with a stack (Exercise • E17.9).

17.4.5 Tree Iterators

The Java collection library uses iterators to process elements of a tree, like this:

```java
TreeSet<String> t = . . .
Iterator<String> iter = t.iterator();
String first = iter.next();
String second = iter.next();
```

It is easy to implement such an iterator with depth-first or breadth-first search. Make the stack or queue into an instance variable of the iterator object. The next method executes one iteration of the loop that you saw in the last section.

```java
class BreadthFirstIterator
{
   private Queue<Node> q;
```

```
      public BreadthFirstIterator(Node root)
      {
         q = new LinkedList<>();
         if (root != null) { q.add(root); }
      }
      public boolean hasNext() { return q.size() > 0; }
      public Object next()
      {
         Node n = q.remove();
         for (Node c : n.children) { q.add(c); }
         return n.data;
      }
   }
```

Note that there is no visit method. The user of the iterator receives the node data, processes it, and decides whether to call next again.

This iterator produces the nodes in breadth-first order. For a binary search tree, one would want the nodes in sorted order instead. Exercise ••• P17.9 shows how to implement such an iterator.

EXAMPLE CODE   See your eText or companion code to see preorder and breadth-first traversal in a tree.

17.5 Red-Black Trees

As you saw in Section 17.3, insertion and removal in a binary search tree are $O(\log(n))$ operations *provided that the tree is balanced*. In this section, you will learn about **red-black trees**, a special kind of binary search tree that rebalances itself after each insertion or removal. With red-black trees, we can guarantee efficiency of these operations. In fact, the Java Collections framework uses red-black trees to implement tree sets and tree maps.

17.5.1 Basic Properties of Red-Black Trees

A red-black tree is a binary search tree with the following additional properties:

In a red-black tree, node coloring rules ensure that the tree is balanced.

- Every node is colored red or black.
- The root is black.
- A red node cannot have a red child (the "no double reds" rule).
- All paths from the root to a null have the same number of black nodes (the "equal exit cost" rule).

© Virginia N/iStockphoto.

Think of each node of a red-black tree as a toll booth. The total toll to each exit is the same.

Of course, the nodes aren't actually colored. Each node simply has a flag to indicate whether it is considered red or black. (The choice of these colors is traditional; one could have equally well used some other attributes. Perhaps, in an alternate universe, students learn about chocolate-vanilla trees.)

Instead of thinking of the colors, imagine each node to be a toll booth. As you travel from the root to one of the null references (an exit), you have to pay $1 at each black toll booth, but the red toll booths are free. The "equal exit cost" rule says that the cost of the trip is the same, no matter which exit you choose.

Figure 18
A Red-Black Tree

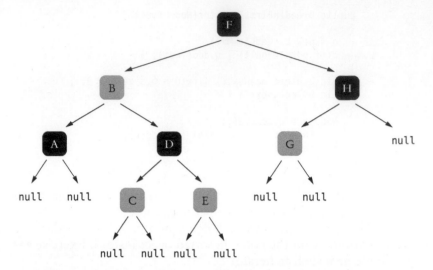

Figure 18 shows an example of a red-black tree. Figures 19 and 20 show examples of trees that violate the "equal exit cost" and "no double reds" rules.

Note that the "equal exit cost" rule does not just apply to paths that end in a leaf, but to any path from the root to a node with one or two empty children. For example, in Figure 19, the path F–B violates the equal exit cost, yet B is not a leaf.

The "equal exit cost" rule eliminates highly unbalanced trees. You can't have null references high up in the tree. In other words, the nodes that aren't near the leaves need to have two children.

The "no double reds" rule gives some flexibility to add nodes without having to restructure the tree all the time. Some paths can be a bit longer than others—by alternating red and black nodes—but none can be longer than twice the black height.

The cost of traveling on a path from a given node to a null (that is, the number of black nodes on the path), is called the *black height* of the node. The cost of traveling from the root to a null is called the black height of the tree.

A tree with given black height bh can't be too sparse—it must have at least $2^{bh} - 1$ nodes (see Exercise ●● R17.18). Or, if we turn this relationship around,

$$2^{bh} - 1 \leq n$$

$$2^{bh} \leq n + 1$$

$$bh \leq \log_2(n + 1)$$

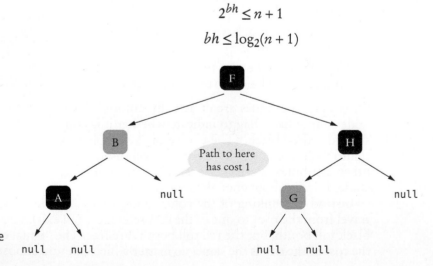

Figure 19
A Tree that Violates the "Equal Exit Cost" Rule

Figure 20
A Tree that Violates the
"No Double Red" Rule

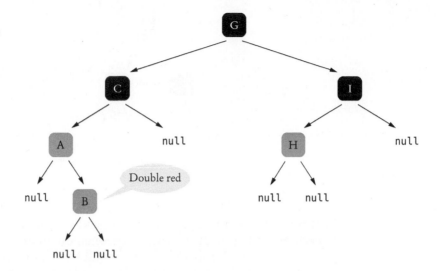

The "no double reds" rule says that the total height h of a tree is at most twice the black height:

$$h \leq 2 \cdot bh \leq 2 \cdot \log_2(n+1)$$

Therefore, traveling from the root to a null is $O(\log(n))$.

17.5.2 Insertion

To insert a new node into a red-black tree, first insert it as you would into a regular binary search tree (see Section 17.3.2). Note that the new node is a leaf.

If it is the first node of the tree, it must be black. Otherwise, color it red. If its parent is black, we still have a red-black tree, and we are done.

However, if the parent is also red, we have a "double red" and need to fix it. Because the rest of the tree is a proper red-black tree, we know that the grandparent is black.

There are four possible configurations of a "double red", shown in Figure 21.

> To rebalance a red-black tree after inserting an element, fix all double-red violations.

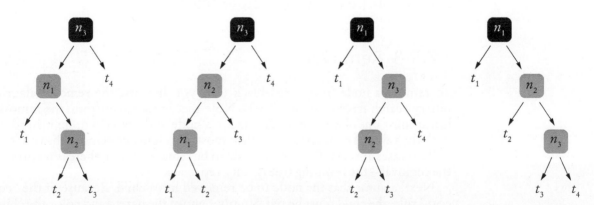

Figure 21   The Four Possible Configurations of a "Double Red"

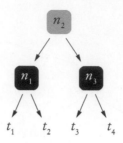

Figure 22   Fixing the "Double Red" Violation

Of course, our tree is a binary search tree, and we will now take advantage of that fact. In each tree of Figure 21, we labeled the smallest, middle, and largest of the three nodes as n_1, n_2, and n_3. We also labeled their children in sorted order, starting with t_1. To fix the "double red", rearrange the three nodes as shown in Figure 22, keeping their data values, but updating their left and right references.

Because the fix preserves the sort order, the result is a binary search tree. The fix does not change the number of black nodes on a path. Therefore, it preserves the "equal exit cost" rule.

If the parent of n_2 is black, we get a red-black tree, and we are done. If that parent is red, we have another "double red", but it is one level closer to the root. In that case, fix the double-red violation of n_2 and its parent. You may have to continue fixing double-red violations, moving closer to the root each time. If the red parent is the root, simply turn it black. This increments all path costs, preserving the "equal exit cost" rule.

Worked Example 17.2 has an implementation of this algorithm.

We can determine the efficiency with more precision than we were able to in Section 17.5.1. To find the insertion location requires at most h steps, where h is the height of the tree. To fix the "double red" violations takes at most $h/2$ steps. (Look carefully at Figure 21 and Figure 22 to see that each fix pushes the violation up *two* nodes. If the top node of each subtree in Figure 21 has height t, then the nodes of the double-red violation have heights $t + 1$ and $t + 2$. In Figure 22, the top node also has height t. If there is a double-red violation, it is between that node and its parent at height $t - 1$.) We know from Section 17.5.1 that $h = O(\log(n))$. Therefore, insertion into a red-black tree is guaranteed to be $O(\log(n))$.

17.5.3 Removal

To remove a node from a red-black tree, you first use the removal algorithm for binary search trees (Section 17.3.3). Note that in that algorithm, the removed node has at most one child. We never remove a node with two children; instead, we fill it with the value of another node with at most one child and remove that node.

Two cases are easy. First, if the node to be removed is red, there is no problem with the removal—the resulting tree is still a red-black tree.

Next, assume that the node to be removed has a child. Because of the "equal exit cost" rule, the child must be red. Simply remove the parent and color the child black.

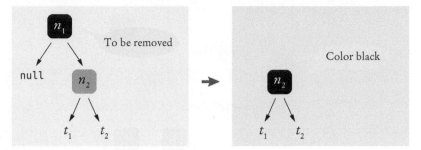

The troublesome case is the removal of a black leaf. We can't just remove it because the exit cost to the `null` replacing it would be too low. Instead, we'll first turn it into a red node.

To turn a black node into a red one, we will temporarily "bubble up" the costs, raising the cost of the parent by 1 and lowering the cost of the children by 1.

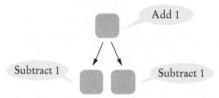

This process leaves all path costs unchanged, and it turns the black leaf into a red one which we can safely remove.

Now consider a black leaf that is to be removed. Because of the equal-exit rule, it must have a sibling. The sibling and the parent can be black or red, but they can't both be red. The leaf to be removed can be to the left or to the right. The figure below shows all possible cases.

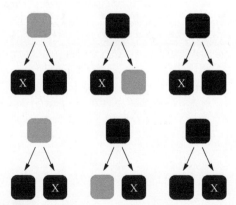

In the first column, bubbling up will work perfectly—it simply turns the red node into a black one and the black ones into red ones. One of the red ones is removed. The other may cause a double-red violation with one of its children, which we fix if necessary.

But in the other cases, a new problem arises. Adding 1 to a black parent yields a price of 2, which we call *double-black*. Subtracting 1 from a red child yields a *negative-red* node with a price of −1. These are not valid nodes in a red-black tree, and we need to eliminate them.

Before removing a node in a red-black tree, turn it red and fix any double-black and double-red violations.

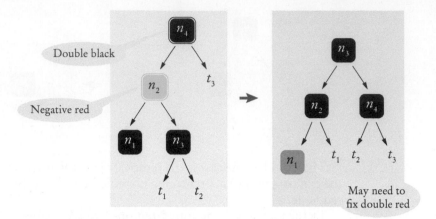

Figure 23   Eliminating a Negative-Red Node with a Double-Black Parent

A negative-red node is always below a double-black one, and the pair can be elimi-nated by the transformation shown in Figure 23.

Sometimes, the creation of a double-black node also causes a double-red violation below. We can fix the double-red violation as in the preceding section, but now we color the middle node black instead of red—see Figure 24.

To see that this transformation is valid, imagine a trip through one of the node sequences in Figure 24 from the top node to one of the trees below. The price of that portion of the trip is 2 for each tree, both before and after the transformation.

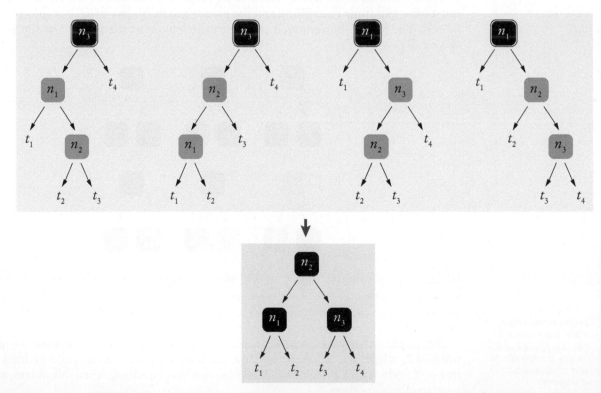

Figure 24   Fixing a Double-Red Violation Also Fixes a Double-Black Grandparent

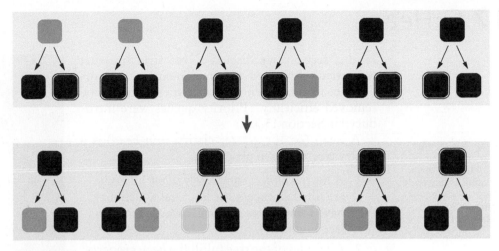

Figure 25 Bubbling Up a Double-Black Node

Sometimes, neither of the two transformations applies, and then we need to "bubble up" again, which pushes the double-black node closer to the root. Figure 25 shows the possible cases.

If the double-black node reaches the root, we can replace it with a regular black node. This reduces the cost of all paths by 1 and preserves the "equal exit cost" rule.

See Worked Example 17.2 for an implementation of node removal.

Let us now determine the efficiency of this process. Removing a node from a binary search tree requires $O(h)$ steps, where h is the height of the tree. The double-black node may bubble up, perhaps all the way to the root. Bubbling up will happen at most h times, and its cost is constant—it only involves changing the costs of three nodes. If we generate a negative red, we remove it (as shown in Figure 23), and the bubbling stops. We may have to fix one double-red violation, which takes $O(h)$ steps. It is also possible that bubbling creates a double-red violation, but its fix will absorb the double-black node, and bubbling also stops. The entire process takes $O(h)$ steps. Because $h = O(\log(n))$, removal from a red-black tree is also guaranteed to be $O(\log(n))$.

> Adding or removing an element in a red-black tree is an $O(\log(n))$ operation.

Table 3 Efficiency of Red-Black Tree Operations

Find an element.	$O(\log(n))$
Add an element.	$O(\log(n))$
Remove an element.	$O(\log(n))$

WORKED EXAMPLE 17.2

Implementing a Red-Black Tree

Learn how to implement a red-black tree as described in Section 17.5. See your eText or visit wiley.com/go/bjeo7.

17.6 Heaps

In this section, we discuss a tree structure that is particularly suited for implementing a priority queue from which the smallest element can be removed efficiently. (Priority queues were introduced in Section 15.5.3.)

A **heap** (or, for greater clarity, *min-heap*) is a binary tree with two properties:

> A heap is an almost completely filled binary tree in which the value of any node is less than or equal to the values of its descendants.

1. A heap is *almost completely filled:* all nodes are filled in, except the last level which may have some nodes missing toward the right (see Figure 26).

2. All nodes of the tree fulfill the *heap property:* the node value is at most as large as the values of all descendants (see Figure 27).

© Lisa Marzano/iStockphoto.

In an almost complete tree, all layers but one are completely filled.

In particular, because the root fulfills the heap property, its value is the minimum of all values in the tree.

A heap is superficially similar to a binary search tree, but there are two important differences:

1. The shape of a heap is very regular. Binary search trees can have arbitrary shapes.

2. In a heap, the left and right subtrees both store elements that are larger than the root element. In contrast, in a binary search tree, smaller elements are stored in the left subtree and larger elements are stored in the right subtree.

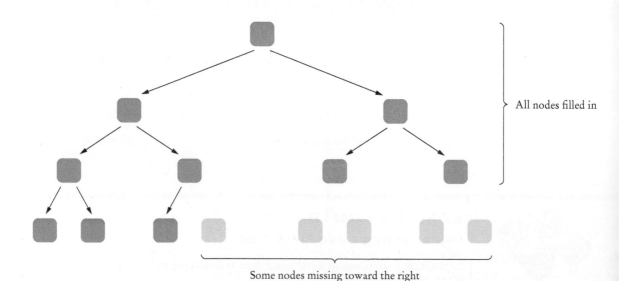

All nodes filled in

Some nodes missing toward the right

Figure 26 An Almost Completely Filled Tree

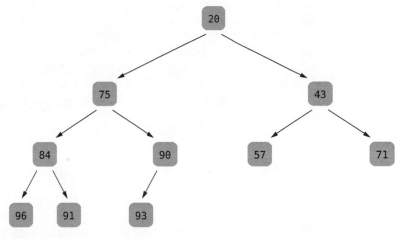

Figure 27 A Heap

Suppose you have a heap and want to insert a new element. After insertion, the heap property should again be fulfilled. The following algorithm carries out the insertion (see Figure 28).

1. First, add a vacant slot to the end of the tree.

2. Next, demote the parent of the empty slot if it is larger than the element to be inserted. That is, move the parent value into the vacant slot, and move the vacant slot up. Repeat this demotion as long as the parent of the vacant slot is larger than the element to be inserted.

3. At this point, either the vacant slot is at the root, or the parent of the vacant slot is smaller than the element to be inserted. Insert the element into the vacant slot.

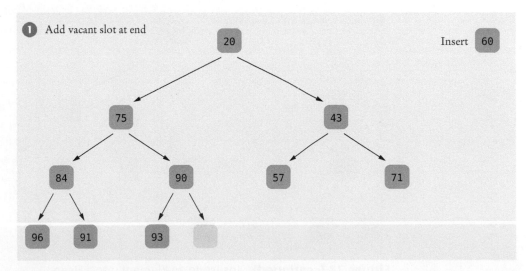

Figure 28 Inserting an Element into a Heap

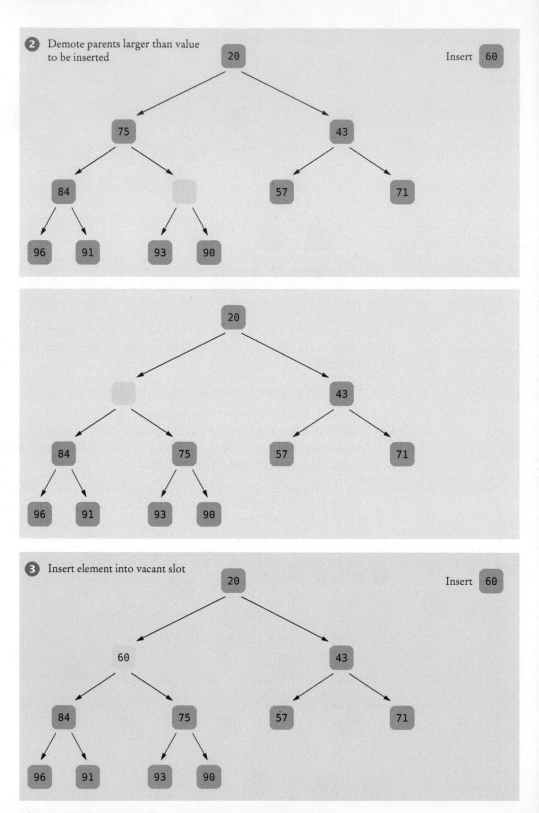

Figure 28 (continued)   Inserting an Element into a Heap

We will not consider an algorithm for removing an arbitrary node from a heap. The only node that we will remove is the root node, which contains the minimum of all of the values in the heap. Figure 29 shows the algorithm in action.

1. Extract the root node value.

2. Move the value of the last node of the heap into the root node, and remove the last node. Now the heap property may be violated for the root node, because one or both of its children may be smaller.

3. Promote the smaller child of the root node. Now the root node again fulfills the heap property. Repeat this process with the demoted child. That is, promote the smaller of its children. Continue until the demoted child has no smaller children. The heap property is now fulfilled again. This process is called "fixing the heap".

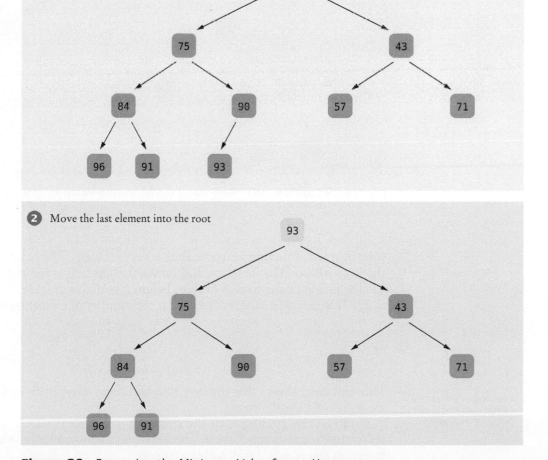

Figure 29 Removing the Minimum Value from a Heap

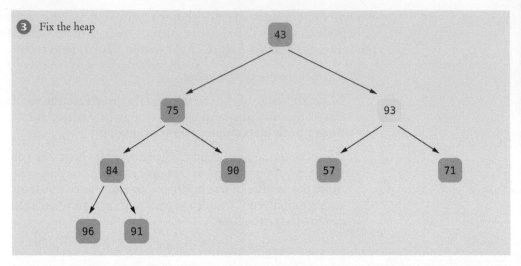

③ Fix the heap

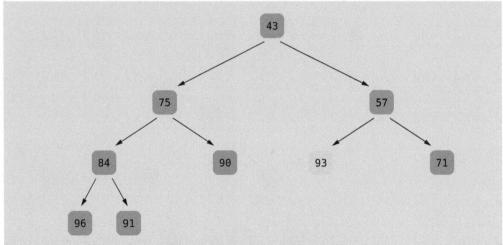

Figure 29 (continued)   Removing the Minimum Value from a Heap

Inserting and removing heap elements is very efficient. The reason lies in the balanced shape of a heap. The insertion and removal operations visit at most h nodes, where h is the height of the tree. A heap of height h contains at least 2^{h-1} elements, but less than 2^h elements. In other words, if n is the number of elements, then

$$2^{h-1} \leq n < 2^h$$

or

$$h - 1 \leq \log_2(n) < h$$

Inserting or removing a heap element is an $O(\log(n))$ operation.

This argument shows that the insertion and removal operations in a heap with n elements take $O(\log(n))$ steps.

Contrast this finding with the situation of a binary search tree. When a binary search tree is unbalanced, it can degenerate into a linked list, so that in the worst case insertion and removal are $O(n)$ operations.

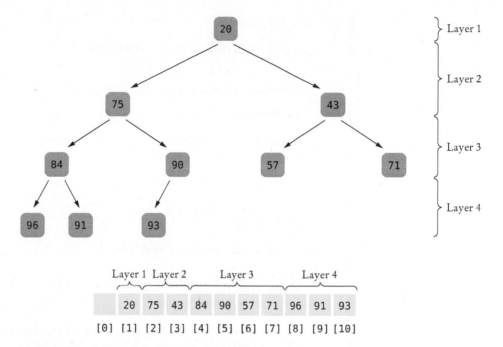

Figure 30 Storing a Heap in an Array

The regular layout of a heap makes it possible to store heap nodes efficiently in an array.

Heaps have another major advantage. Because of the regular layout of the heap nodes, it is easy to store the node values in an array or array list. First store the first layer, then the second, and so on (see Figure 30). For convenience, we leave the 0 element of the array empty. Then the child nodes of the node with index i have index $2 \cdot i$ and $2 \cdot i + 1$, and the parent node of the node with index i has index $i/2$. For example, as you can see in Figure 30, the children of the node with index 4 are the nodes with index values 8 and 9, and the parent is the node with index 2.

Storing the heap values in an array may not be intuitive, but it is very efficient. There is no need to allocate individual nodes or to store the links to the child nodes. Instead, child and parent positions can be determined by very simple computations.

The program at the end of this section contains an implementation of a heap. For greater clarity, the computation of the parent and child index positions is carried out in methods getParentIndex, getLeftChildIndex, and getRightChildIndex. For greater efficiency, the method calls could be avoided by using expressions index / 2, 2 * index, and 2 * index + 1 directly.

In this section, we have organized our heaps such that the smallest element is stored in the root. It is also possible to store the largest element in the root, simply by reversing all comparisons in the heap-building algorithm. If there is a possibility of misunderstanding, it is best to refer to the data structures as min-heap or max-heap.

The test program demonstrates how to use a min-heap as a priority queue.

sec06/MinHeap.java

```
1  import java.util.*;
2
3  /**
4     This class implements a heap.
5  */
```

```
6  public class MinHeap
7  {
8     private ArrayList<Comparable> elements;
9
10    /**
11       Constructs an empty heap.
12    */
13    public MinHeap()
14    {
15       elements = new ArrayList<>();
16       elements.add(null);
17    }
18
19    /**
20       Adds a new element to this heap.
21       @param newElement the element to add
22    */
23    public void add(Comparable newElement)
24    {
25       // Add a new leaf
26       elements.add(null);
27       int index = elements.size() - 1;
28
29       // Demote parents that are larger than the new element
30       while (index > 1
31             && getParent(index).compareTo(newElement) > 0)
32       {
33          elements.set(index, getParent(index));
34          index = getParentIndex(index);
35       }
36
37       // Store the new element in the vacant slot
38       elements.set(index, newElement);
39    }
40
41    /**
42       Gets the minimum element stored in this heap.
43       @return the minimum element
44    */
45    public Comparable peek()
46    {
47       return elements.get(1);
48    }
49
50    /**
51       Removes the minimum element from this heap.
52       @return the minimum element
53    */
54    public Comparable remove()
55    {
56       Comparable minimum = elements.get(1);
57
58       // Remove last element
59       int lastIndex = elements.size() - 1;
60       Comparable last = elements.remove(lastIndex);
61
62       if (lastIndex > 1)
63       {
64          elements.set(1, last);
65          fixHeap();
```

```
66          }
67
68          return minimum;
69      }
70
71      /**
72          Turns the tree back into a heap, provided only the root
73          node violates the heap condition.
74      */
75      private void fixHeap()
76      {
77          Comparable root = elements.get(1);
78
79          int lastIndex = elements.size() - 1;
80          // Promote children of removed root while they are smaller than root
81
82          int index = 1;
83          boolean more = true;
84          while (more)
85          {
86              int childIndex = getLeftChildIndex(index);
87              if (childIndex <= lastIndex)
88              {
89                  // Get smaller child
90
91                  // Get left child first
92                  Comparable child = getLeftChild(index);
93
94                  // Use right child instead if it is smaller
95                  if (getRightChildIndex(index) <= lastIndex
96                          && getRightChild(index).compareTo(child) < 0)
97                  {
98                      childIndex = getRightChildIndex(index);
99                      child = getRightChild(index);
100                 }
101
102                 // Check if smaller child is smaller than root
103                 if (child.compareTo(root) < 0)
104                 {
105                     // Promote child
106                     elements.set(index, child);
107                     index = childIndex;
108                 }
109                 else
110                 {
111                     // Root is smaller than both children
112                     more = false;
113                 }
114             }
115             else
116             {
117                 // No children
118                 more = false;
119             }
120         }
121
122         // Store root element in vacant slot
123         elements.set(index, root);
124     }
125
```

```
126     /**
127         Checks whether this heap is empty.
128     */
129     public boolean empty()
130     {
131         return elements.size() == 1;
132     }
133
134     /**
135         Returns the index of the left child.
136         @param index the index of a node in this heap
137         @return the index of the left child of the given node
138     */
139     private static int getLeftChildIndex(int index)
140     {
141         return 2 * index;
142     }
143
144     /**
145         Returns the index of the right child.
146         @param index the index of a node in this heap
147         @return the index of the right child of the given node
148     */
149     private static int getRightChildIndex(int index)
150     {
151         return 2 * index + 1;
152     }
153
154     /**
155         Returns the index of the parent.
156         @param index the index of a node in this heap
157         @return the index of the parent of the given node
158     */
159     private static int getParentIndex(int index)
160     {
161         return index / 2;
162     }
163
164     /**
165         Returns the value of the left child.
166         @param index the index of a node in this heap
167         @return the value of the left child of the given node
168     */
169     private Comparable getLeftChild(int index)
170     {
171         return elements.get(2 * index);
172     }
173
174     /**
175         Returns the value of the right child.
176         @param index the index of a node in this heap
177         @return the value of the right child of the given node
178     */
179     private Comparable getRightChild(int index)
180     {
181         return elements.get(2 * index + 1);
182     }
183
184     /**
185         Returns the value of the parent.
```

```
186          @param index the index of a node in this heap
187          @return the value of the parent of the given node
188       */
189       private Comparable getParent(int index)
190       {
191          return elements.get(index / 2);
192       }
193    }
```

sec06/WorkOrder.java

```
1    /**
2        This class encapsulates a work order with a priority.
3    */
4    public class WorkOrder implements Comparable
5    {
6       private int priority;
7       private String description;
8
9       /**
10          Constructs a work order with a given priority and description.
11          @param aPriority the priority of this work order
12          @param aDescription the description of this work order
13       */
14       public WorkOrder(int aPriority, String aDescription)
15       {
16          priority = aPriority;
17          description = aDescription;
18       }
19
20       public String toString()
21       {
22          return "priority=" + priority + ", description=" + description;
23       }
24
25       public int compareTo(Object otherObject)
26       {
27          WorkOrder other = (WorkOrder) otherObject;
28          if (priority < other.priority) { return -1; }
29          if (priority > other.priority) { return 1; }
30          return 0;
31       }
32    }
```

sec06/HeapDemo.java

```
1    /**
2        This program demonstrates the use of a heap as a priority queue.
3    */
4    public class HeapDemo
5    {
6       public static void main(String[] args)
7       {
8          MinHeap q = new MinHeap();
9          q.add(new WorkOrder(3, "Shampoo carpets"));
10         q.add(new WorkOrder(7, "Empty trash"));
11         q.add(new WorkOrder(8, "Water plants"));
12         q.add(new WorkOrder(10, "Remove pencil sharpener shavings"));
13         q.add(new WorkOrder(6, "Replace light bulb"));
14         q.add(new WorkOrder(1, "Fix broken sink"));
```

```
15        q.add(new WorkOrder(9, "Clean coffee maker"));
16        q.add(new WorkOrder(2, "Order cleaning supplies"));
17
18        while (!q.empty())
19        {
20           System.out.println(q.remove());
21        }
22     }
23  }
```

Program Run

```
priority=1, description=Fix broken sink
priority=2, description=Order cleaning supplies
priority=3, description=Shampoo carpets
priority=6, description=Replace light bulb
priority=7, description=Empty trash
priority=8, description=Water plants
priority=9, description=Clean coffee maker
priority=10, description=Remove pencil sharpener shavings
```

17.7 The Heapsort Algorithm

The heapsort algorithm is based on inserting elements into a heap and removing them in sorted order.

Heaps are not only useful for implementing priority queues, they also give rise to an efficient sorting algorithm, heapsort. In its simplest form, the **heapsort algorithm** works as follows. First insert all elements to be sorted into the heap, then keep extracting the minimum.

This algorithm is an $O(n \log(n))$ algorithm: each insertion and removal is $O(\log(n))$, and these steps are repeated n times, once for each element in the sequence that is to be sorted.

Heapsort is an $O(n \log(n))$ algorithm.

The algorithm can be made a bit more efficient. Rather than inserting the elements one at a time, we will start with a sequence of values in an array. Of course, that array does not represent a heap. We will use the procedure of "fixing the heap" that you encountered in the preceding section as part of the element removal algorithm. "Fixing the heap" operates on a binary tree whose child trees are heaps but whose root value may not be smaller than the descendants. The procedure turns the tree into a heap, by repeatedly promoting the smallest child value, moving the root value to its proper location.

Of course, we cannot simply apply this procedure to the initial sequence of unsorted values—the child trees of the root are not likely to be heaps. But we can first fix small subtrees into heaps, then fix larger trees. Because trees of size 1 are automatically heaps, we can begin the fixing procedure with the subtrees whose roots are located in the next-to-last level of the tree.

The sorting algorithm uses a generalized fixHeap method that fixes a subtree:

```
public static void fixHeap(int[] a, int rootIndex, int lastIndex)
```

The subtree is specified by the index of its root and of its last node.

The fixHeap method needs to be invoked on all subtrees whose roots are in the next-to-last level. Then the subtrees whose roots are in the next level above are fixed, and so on. Finally, the fixup is applied to the root node, and the tree is turned into a heap (see Figure 31).

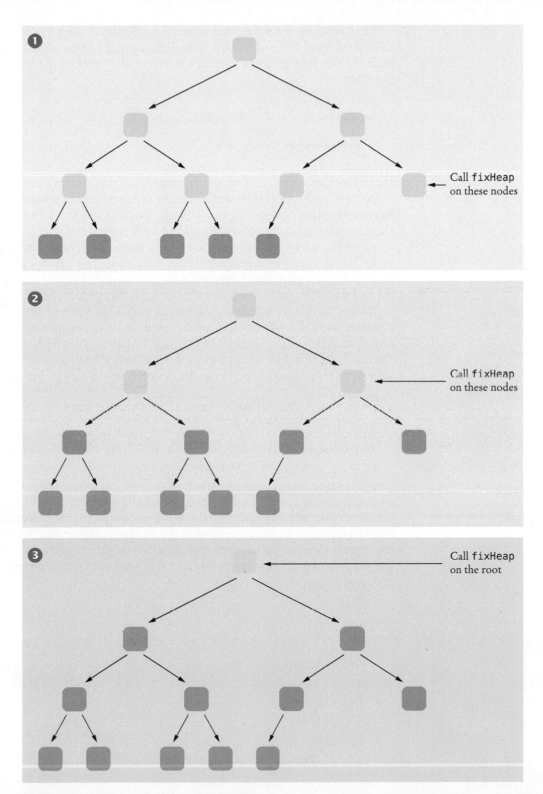

Figure 31 Turning a Tree into a Heap

That repetition can be programmed easily. Start with the *last* node on the next-to-lowest level and work toward the left. Then go to the next higher level. The node index values then simply run backward from the index of the last node to the index of the root.

```
int n = a.length - 1;
for (int i = (n - 1) / 2; i >= 0; i--)
{
    fixHeap(a, i, n);
}
```

It can be shown that this procedure turns an arbitrary array into a heap in $O(n)$ steps.

Note that the loop ends with index 0. When working with a given array, we don't have the luxury of skipping the 0 entry. We consider the 0 entry the root and adjust the formulas for computing the child and parent index values.

After the array has been turned into a heap, we repeatedly remove the root element. Recall from the preceding section that removing the root element is achieved by placing the last element of the tree in the root and calling the fixHeap method. Because we call the $O(\log(n))$ fixHeap method n times, this process requires $O(n \log(n))$ steps.

Rather than moving the root element into a separate array, we can *swap* the root element with the last element of the tree and then reduce the tree size. Thus, the removed root ends up in the last position of the array, which is no longer needed by the heap. In this way, we can use the same array both to hold the heap (which gets shorter with each step) and the sorted sequence (which gets longer with each step).

```
while (n > 0)
{
    ArrayUtil.swap(a, 0, n);
    n--;
    fixHeap(a, 0, n);
}
```

There is just a minor inconvenience. When we use a min-heap, the sorted sequence is accumulated in reverse order, with the smallest element at the end of the array. We could reverse the sequence after sorting is complete. However, it is easier to use a max-heap rather than a min-heap in the heapsort algorithm. With this modification, the largest value is placed at the end of the array after the first step. After the next step, the next-largest value is swapped from the heap root to the second position from the end, and so on (see Figure 32).

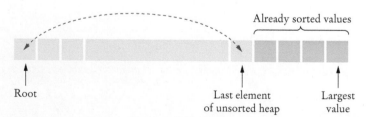

Figure 32 Using Heapsort to Sort an Array

The following Heapsorter class implements the heapsort algorithm.

sec07/HeapSorter.java

```java
1   /**
2      The sort method of this class sorts an array, using the heap
3      sort algorithm.
4   */
5   public class HeapSorter
6   {
7      /**
8         Sorts an array, using heap sort.
9         @param a the array to sort
10     */
11     public static void sort(int[] a)
12     {
13        int n = a.length - 1;
14        for (int i = (n - 1) / 2; i >= 0; i--)
15        {
16           fixHeap(a, i, n);
17        }
18        while (n > 0)
19        {
20           ArrayUtil.swap(a, 0, n);
21           n--;
22           fixHeap(a, 0, n);
23        }
24     }
25
26     /**
27        Ensures the heap property for a subtree, provided its
28        children already fulfill the heap property.
29        @param a the array to sort
30        @param rootIndex the index of the subtree to be fixed
31        @param lastIndex the last valid index of the tree that
32        contains the subtree to be fixed
33     */
34     private static void fixHeap(int[] a, int rootIndex, int lastIndex)
35     {
36        // Remove root
37        int rootValue = a[rootIndex];
38
39        // Promote children while they are larger than the root
40
41        int index = rootIndex;
42        boolean more = true;
43        while (more)
44        {
45           int childIndex = getLeftChildIndex(index);
46           if (childIndex <= lastIndex)
47           {
48              // Use right child instead if it is larger
49              int rightChildIndex = getRightChildIndex(index);
50              if (rightChildIndex <= lastIndex
51                  && a[rightChildIndex] > a[childIndex])
52              {
53                 childIndex = rightChildIndex;
54              }
55
56              if (a[childIndex] > rootValue)
57              {
```

```
58                        // Promote child
59                        a[index] = a[childIndex];
60                        index = childIndex;
61                    }
62                    else
63                    {
64                        // Root value is larger than both children
65                        more = false;
66                    }
67                }
68                else
69                {
70                    // No children
71                    more = false;
72                }
73            }
74
75            // Store root value in vacant slot
76            a[index] = rootValue;
77        }
78
79        /**
80            Returns the index of the left child.
81            @param index  the index of a node in this heap
82            @return  the index of the left child of the given node
83        */
84        private static int getLeftChildIndex(int index)
85        {
86            return 2 * index + 1;
87        }
88
89        /**
90            Returns the index of the right child.
91            @param index  the index of a node in this heap
92            @return  the index of the right child of the given node
93        */
94        private static int getRightChildIndex(int index)
95        {
96            return 2 * index + 2;
97        }
98  }
```

CHAPTER SUMMARY

Describe and implement general trees.

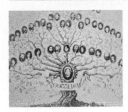

- A tree is composed of nodes, each of which can have child nodes.
- The root is the node with no parent. A leaf is a node with no children.
- A tree class uses a node class to represent nodes and has an instance variable for the root node.
- Many tree properties are computed with recursive methods.

Describe binary trees and their applications.

- A binary tree consists of nodes, each of which has at most two child nodes.
- In a Huffman tree, the left and right turns on the paths to the leaves describe binary encodings.
- An expression tree shows the order of evaluation in an arithmetic expression.
- In a balanced tree, all paths from the root to the leaves have approximately the same length.

Explain the implementation of a binary search tree and its performance characteristics.

- All nodes in a binary search tree fulfill the property that the descendants to the left have smaller data values than the node data value, and the descendants to the right have larger data values.
- To insert a value into a binary search tree, keep comparing the value with the node data and follow the nodes to the left or right, until reaching a null node.
- When removing a node with only one child from a binary search tree, the child replaces the node to be removed.
- When removing a node with two children from a binary search tree, replace it with the smallest node of the right subtree.
- In a balanced tree, all paths from the root to the leaves have about the same length.
- If a binary search tree is balanced, then adding, locating, or removing an element takes $O(\log(n))$ time.

Describe preorder, inorder, and postorder tree traversal.

- To visit all elements in a tree, visit the root and recursively visit the subtrees.
- We distinguish between preorder, inorder, and postorder traversal.
- Postorder traversal of an expression tree yields the instructions for evaluating the expression on a stack-based calculator.
- Depth-first search uses a stack to track the nodes that it still needs to visit.
- Breadth-first search first visits all nodes on the same level before visiting the children.

Describe how red-black trees provide guaranteed $O(\log(n))$ operations.

- In a red-black tree, node coloring rules ensure that the tree is balanced.
- To rebalance a red-black tree after inserting an element, fix all double-red violations.
- Before removing a node in a red-black tree, turn it red and fix any double-black and double-red violations.
- Adding or removing an element in a red-black tree is an $O(\log(n))$ operation.

Describe the heap data structure and the efficiency of its operations.

- A heap is an almost completely filled tree in which the value of any node is less than or equal to the values of its descendants.
- Inserting or removing a heap element is an $O(\log(n))$ operation.
- The regular layout of a heap makes it possible to store heap nodes efficiently in an array.

Describe the heapsort algorithm and its run-time performance.

- The heapsort algorithm is based on inserting elements into a heap and removing them in sorted order.
- Heapsort is an $O(n \log(n))$ algorithm.

REVIEW EXERCISES

■ R17.1 What are all possible shapes of trees of height *h* with one leaf? Of height 2 with *k* leaves?

■■ R17.2 Describe a recursive algorithm for finding the maximum number of siblings in a tree.

■■■ R17.3 Describe a recursive algorithm for finding the total path length of a tree. The total path length is the sum of the lengths of all paths from the root to the leaves. (The length of a path is the number of nodes on the path.) What is the efficiency of your algorithm?

■■ R17.4 Show that a binary tree with *l* leaves has at least *l* – 1 interior nodes, and exactly *l* – 1 interior nodes if all of them have two children.

■ R17.5 What is the difference between a binary tree and a binary search tree? Give examples of each.

■ R17.6 What is the difference between a balanced tree and an unbalanced tree? Give examples of each.

■ R17.7 The following elements are inserted into a binary search tree. Make a drawing that shows the resulting tree after each insertion.

```
Adam
Eve
Romeo
Juliet
Tom
Diana
Harry
```

■■ R17.8 Insert the elements of Exercise • R17.7 in opposite order. Then determine how the BinarySearchTree.print method from Section 17.4.1 prints out both the tree from Exercise • R17.7 and this tree. Explain how the printouts are related.

■■ R17.9 Consider the following tree. In which order are the nodes printed by the Binary-SearchTree.print method? The numbers identify the nodes. The data stored in the nodes is not shown.

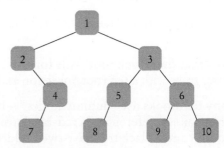

■■ R17.10 Design an algorithm for finding the *k*th element (in sort order) of a binary search tree. How efficient is your algorithm?

■■ R17.11 Design an $O(\log(n))$ algorithm for finding the *k*th element in a binary search tree, provided that each node has an instance variable containing the size of the subtree. Also describe how these instance variables can be maintained by the insertion and removal operations without affecting their big-Oh efficiency.

■■ **R17.12** Design an algorithm for deciding whether two binary trees have the same shape. What is the running time of your algorithm?

■ **R17.13** Insert the following eleven words into a binary search tree:

> Mary had a little lamb. Its fleece was white as snow.

Draw the resulting tree.

■ **R17.14** What is the result of printing the tree from Exercise • R17.13 using preorder, inorder, and postorder traversal?

■■ **R17.15** Locate nodes with no children, one child, and two children in the tree of Exercise • R17.13. For each of them, show the tree of size 10 that is obtained after removing the node.

■■ **R17.16** Repeat Exercise • R17.13 for a red-black tree.

■■■ **R17.17** Repeat Exercise •• R17.15 for a red-black tree.

■■ **R17.18** Show that a red-black tree with black height bh has at least $2^{bh} - 1$ nodes. *Hint:* Look at the root. A black child has black height $bh - 1$. A red child must have two black children of black height $bh - 1$.

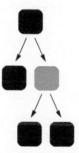

■■ **R17.19** Let $rbts(bh)$ be the number of red-black trees with black height bh. Give a recursive formula for $rbts(bh)$ in terms of $rbts(bh - 1)$. How many red-black trees have heights 1, 2, and 3? *Hint:* Look at the hint for Exercise •• R17.18.

■■ **R17.20** What is the maximum number of nodes in a red-black tree with black height bh?

■■ **R17.21** Show that any red-black tree must have fewer interior red nodes than it has black nodes.

■■■ **R17.22** Show that the "black root" rule for red-black trees is not essential. That is, if one allows trees with a red root, insertion and deletion still occur in $O(\log(n))$ time.

■■ **R17.23** Many textbooks use "dummy nodes"—black nodes with two null children—instead of regular null references in red-black trees. In this representation, all non-dummy nodes of a red-black tree have two children. How does this simplify the description of the removal algorithm?

■■ **R17.24** Why does Figure 21 show all possible configurations of a double-red violation?

■■ **R17.25** Could a priority queue be implemented efficiently as a binary search tree? Give a detailed argument for your answer.

■■■ **R17.26** Will preorder, inorder, or postorder traversal print a heap in sorted order? Why or why not?

■■■ **R17.27** Prove that a heap of height h contains at least 2^{h-1} elements but less than 2^h elements.

■■■ **R17.28** Suppose the heap nodes are stored in an array, starting with index 1. Prove that the child nodes of the heap node with index i have index $2 \cdot i$ and $2 \cdot i + 1$, and the parent node of the heap node with index i has index $i/2$.

■■ **R17.29** Simulate the heapsort algorithm manually to sort the array

```
11 27 8 14 45 6 24 81 29 33
```

Show all steps.

PRACTICE EXERCISES

■ **E17.1** Write a method that counts the number of all leaves in a tree.

■ **E17.2** Add a method `countNodesWithOneChild` to the `BinaryTree` class.

■ **E17.3** Add a method `swapChildren` that swaps all left and right children to the `BinaryTree` class.

■■ **E17.4** Implement the animal guessing game described in Section 17.2.1. Start with the tree in Figure 4, but present the leaves as "Is it a(n) X?" If it wasn't, ask the user what the animal was, and ask for a question that is true for that animal but false for X. For example,

```
Is it a mammal? Y
Does it have stripes? N
Is it a pig? N
I give up. What is it? A hamster
Please give me a question that is true for a hamster and false for a pig.
Is it small and cuddly?
```

In this way, the program learns additional facts.

■■ **E17.5** Reimplement the `addNode` method of the `Node` class in `BinarySearchTree` as a static method of the `BinarySearchTree` class:

```
private static Node addNode(Node parent, Node newNode)
```

If `parent` is `null`, return `newNode`. Otherwise, recursively add `newNode` to `parent` and return `parent`. Your implementation should replace the three `null` checks in the `add` and original `addNode` methods with just one `null` check.

■ **E17.6** Write a method of the `BinarySearchTree` class

```
Comparable smallest()
```

that returns the smallest element of a tree. You will also need to add a method to the `Node` class.

■ **E17.7** Add methods

```
void preorder(Visitor v)
void inorder(Visitor v)
void postorder(Visitor v)
```

to the `BinaryTree` class of Section 17.2.3.

■■ **E17.8** Using a visitor, compute the average value of the elements in a binary tree filled with `Integer` objects.

- **E17.9** Add a method void depthFirst(Visitor v) to the Tree class of Section 17.4. Keep visiting until the visit method returns false.

- **E17.10** Implement an inorder method for the BinaryTree class of Section 17.2 so that it stops visiting when the visit method returns false. (*Hint:* Have inorder return false when visit returns false.)

- **E17.11** Write a method for the RedBlackTree class of Worked Example 17.2 that checks that the tree fulfills the rules for a red-black tree.

- **E17.12** Modify the implementation of the MinHeap class so that the parent and child index positions and elements are computed directly, without calling helper methods.

- **E17.13** Time the results of heapsort and merge sort. Which algorithm behaves better in practice?

PROGRAMMING PROJECTS

- **P17.1** A general tree (in which each node can have arbitrarily many children) can be implemented as a binary tree in this way: For each node with *n* children, use a chain of *n* binary nodes. Each left reference points to a child and each right reference points to the next node in the chain. Using the binary tree implementation of Section 17.2, implement a tree class with the same interface as the one in Section 17.1.

- **P17.2** A general tree in which all non-leaf nodes have null data can be implemented as a list of lists. For example, the tree

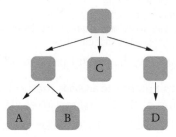

is the list [[A, B], C, [D]].

  Using the list implementation from Section 16.1.8, implement a tree class with the same interface as the one in Section 17.1. *Hint:* Use n instanceof List to check whether a list element n is a subtree or a leaf.

- **P17.3** Continue Exercise •• E17.4 and write the tree to a file when the program exits. Load the file when the program starts again.

- **P17.4** Change the BinarySearchTree.print method of Section 17.3.4 to print the tree as a tree shape. You can print the tree sideways. Extra credit if you instead display the tree with the root node centered on the top.

- **P17.5** In the BinarySearchTree class of Section 17.3.4, modify the remove method so that a node with two children is replaced by the largest child of the left subtree.

- **P17.6** Reimplement the remove method in the RedBlackTree class of Worked Example 17.2 so that the node is first removed using the binary search tree removal algorithm, and the tree is rebalanced after removal.

••• **P17.7** The ID3 algorithm describes how to build a decision tree for a given a set of sample facts. The tree asks the most important questions first. We have a set of criteria (such as "Is it a mammal?") and an objective that we want to decide (such as "Can it swim?"). Each fact has a value for each criterion and the objective. Here is a set of five facts about animals. (Each row is a fact.) There are four criteria and one objective (the columns of the table). For simplicity, we assume that the values of the criteria and objective are binary (Y or N).

Is it a mammal?	Does it have fur?	Does it have a tail?	Does it lay eggs?	Can it swim?
N	N	Y	Y	N
N	N	N	Y	Y
N	N	Y	Y	Y
Y	N	Y	N	Y
Y	Y	Y	N	N

We now need several definitions. Given any probability value p between 0 and 1, its uncertainty is

$$U(p) = -p \log_2(p) - (1-p)\log_2(1-p)$$

If p is 0 or 1, the outcome is certain, and the uncertainty $U(p)$ is 0. If $p = 1/2$, then the outcome is completely uncertain and $U(p) = 1$.

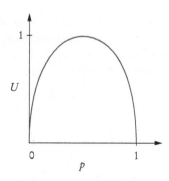

Let n be the number of facts and $n(c = \text{Y})$ be the number of facts for which the criterion c has the value Y. Then the uncertainty $U(c, o)$ that c contributes to the outcome o is the weighted average of two uncertainties:

$$U(c,o) = \frac{n(c = \text{Y})}{n} \cdot U\left(\frac{n(c = \text{Y}, o = \text{Y})}{n(c = \text{Y})}\right) + \frac{n(c = \text{N})}{n} \cdot U\left(\frac{n(c = \text{N}, o = \text{Y})}{n(c = \text{N})}\right)$$

Find the criterion c that minimizes the uncertainty $U(c, o)$. That question becomes the root of your tree. Recursively, repeat for the subsets of the facts for which c is Y (in the left subtree) and N (in the right subtree). If it happens that the objective is constant, then you have a leaf with an answer, and the recursion stops.

In our example, we have

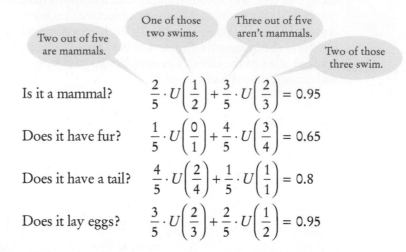

Is it a mammal? $\dfrac{2}{5} \cdot U\!\left(\dfrac{1}{2}\right) + \dfrac{3}{5} \cdot U\!\left(\dfrac{2}{3}\right) = 0.95$

Does it have fur? $\dfrac{1}{5} \cdot U\!\left(\dfrac{0}{1}\right) + \dfrac{4}{5} \cdot U\!\left(\dfrac{3}{4}\right) = 0.65$

Does it have a tail? $\dfrac{4}{5} \cdot U\!\left(\dfrac{2}{4}\right) + \dfrac{1}{5} \cdot U\!\left(\dfrac{1}{1}\right) = 0.8$

Does it lay eggs? $\dfrac{3}{5} \cdot U\!\left(\dfrac{2}{3}\right) + \dfrac{2}{5} \cdot U\!\left(\dfrac{1}{2}\right) = 0.95$

Therefore, we choose "Does it have fur?" as our first criterion.

In the left subtree, look at the animals with fur. There is only one, a non-swimmer, so you can declare "It doesn't swim." For the right subtree, you now have four facts (the animals without fur) and three criteria. Repeat the process.

■■■ **P17.8** Modify the expression evaluator from Section 13.5 to produce an expression tree. (Note that the resulting tree is a binary tree but not a binary search tree.) Then use postorder traversal to evaluate the expression, using a stack for the intermediate results.

■■■ **P17.9** Implement an iterator for the BinarySearchTree class that visits the nodes in sorted order. *Hint:* In the constructor, keep pushing left nodes on a stack until you reach null. In each call to next, deliver the top of the stack as the visited node, but first push the left nodes in its right subtree.

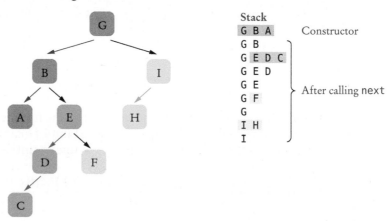

■■■ **P17.10** Implement an iterator for the RedBlackTree class in Worked Example 17.2 that visits the nodes in sorted order. *Hint:* Take advantage of the parent links.

■■■ **P17.11** Modify the implementation of the MinHeap class in Section 17.6 so that the 0 element of the array is not wasted.

GENERIC CLASSES

© Don Bayley/iStockphoto.

CHAPTER GOALS

To understand the objective of generic programming

To implement generic classes and methods

To explain the execution of generic methods in the virtual machine

To describe the limitations of generic programming in Java

CHAPTER CONTENTS

In the supermarket, a generic product can be sourced from multiple suppliers. In computer science, generic programming involves the design and implementation of data structures and algorithms that work for multiple types. You have already seen the generic ArrayList class that can be used to collect elements of arbitrary types. In this chapter, you will learn how to implement your own generic classes and methods.

18.1 Generic Classes and Type Parameters

Generic programming is the creation of programming constructs that can be used with many different types. For example, the Java library programmers who implemented the ArrayList class used the technique of generic programming. As a result, you can form array lists that collect elements of different types, such as Array-List<String>, ArrayList<BankAccount>, and so on.

The LinkedList class that we implemented in Section 16.1 is also an example of generic programming—you can store objects of any class inside a LinkedList. That LinkedList class achieves genericity by using *inheritance.* It uses references of type Object and is therefore capable of storing objects of any class. For example, you can add elements of type String because the String class extends Object. In contrast, the ArrayList and LinkedList classes from the standard Java library are **generic classes**. Each of these classes has a **type parameter** for specifying the type of its elements. For example, an ArrayList<String> stores String elements.

> In Java, generic programming can be achieved with inheritance or with type parameters.

When declaring a generic class, you supply a variable for each type parameter. For example, the standard library declares the class ArrayList<E>, where E is the **type variable** that denotes the element type. You use the same variable in the declaration of the methods, whenever you need to refer to that type. For example, the ArrayList<E> class declares methods

> A generic class has one or more type parameters.

```
public void add(E element)
public E get(int index)
```

You could use another name, such as ElementType, instead of E. However, it is customary to use short, uppercase names for type variables.

In order to use a generic class, you need to *instantiate* the type parameter, that is, supply an actual type. You can supply any class or interface type, for example

```
ArrayList<BankAccount>
ArrayList<Measurable>
```

However, you cannot substitute any of the eight primitive types for a type parameter. It would be an error to declare an ArrayList<double>. Use the corresponding wrapper class instead, such as ArrayList<Double>.

> Type parameters can be instantiated with class or interface types.

When you instantiate a generic class, the type that you supply replaces all occurrences of the type variable in the declaration of the class. For example, the add method for ArrayList<BankAccount> has the type variable E replaced with the type BankAccount:

```
public void add(BankAccount element)
```

Contrast that with the add method of the LinkedList class in Chapter 16:

```
public void add(Object element)
```

The add method of the generic ArrayList class is safer. It is impossible to add a String object into an ArrayList<BankAccount>, but you can accidentally add a String into a LinkedList that is intended to hold bank accounts:

```
ArrayList<BankAccount> accounts1 = new ArrayList<>();
LinkedList accounts2 = new LinkedList(); // Should hold BankAccount objects
accounts1.add("my savings"); // Compile-time error
accounts2.addFirst("my savings"); // Not detected at compile time
```

The latter will result in a class cast exception when some other part of the code retrieves the string, believing it to be a bank account:

```
BankAccount account = (BankAccount) accounts2.getFirst(); // Run-time error
```

Code that uses the generic ArrayList class is also easier to read. When you spot an ArrayList<BankAccount>, you know right away that it must contain bank accounts. When you see a LinkedList, you have to study the code to find out what it contains.

In Chapters 16 and 17, we used inheritance to implement generic linked lists, hash tables, and binary trees, because you were already familiar with the concept of inheritance. Using type parameters requires new syntax and additional techniques—those are the topic of this chapter.

Type parameters make generic code safer and easier to read.

EXAMPLE CODE See your eText or companion code to see programs that demonstrate safety problems when using collections without type parameters.

18.2 Implementing Generic Types

In this section, you will learn how to implement your own generic classes. We will write a very simple generic class that stores *pairs* of objects, each of which can have an arbitrary type. For example,

```
Pair<String, Integer> result = new Pair<>("Harry Morgan", 1729);
```

The getFirst and getSecond methods retrieve the first and second values of the pair:

```
String name = result.getFirst();
Integer number = result.getSecond();
```

This class can be useful when you implement a method that computes two values at the same time. A method cannot simultaneously return a String and an Integer, but it can return a single object of type Pair<String, Integer>.

The generic Pair class requires two type parameters, one for the type of the first element and one for the type of the second element.

We need to choose variables for the type parameters. It is considered good form to use short uppercase names for type variables, such as those in the following table:

Type Variable	Meaning
E	Element type in a collection
K	Key type in a map
V	Value type in a map
T	General type
S, U	Additional general types

Syntax 18.1   Declaring a Generic Class

Syntax   *modifier* class *GenericClassName*<*TypeVariable₁*, *TypeVariable₂*, . . .>
{
    instance variables
    constructors
    methods
}

Supply a variable for each type parameter.

```
public class Pair<T, S>
{
    private T first;
    private S second;
    . . .
    public T getFirst() { return first; }
    . . .
}
```

Instance variables with a variable data type

A method with a variable return type

Type variables of a generic class follow the class name and are enclosed in angle brackets.

You place the type variables for a generic class after the class name, enclosed in angle brackets (< and >):

```
public class Pair<T, S>
```

When you declare the instance variables and methods of the Pair class, use the variable T for the first element type and S for the second element type:

```
public class Pair<T, S>
{
    private T first;
    private S second;

    public Pair(T firstElement, S secondElement)
    {
        first = firstElement;
        second = secondElement;
    }
    public T getFirst() { return first; }
    public S getSecond() { return second; }
}
```

Some people find it simpler to start out with a regular class, choosing some actual types instead of the type parameters. For example,

```
public class Pair // Here we start out with a pair of String and Integer values
{
    private String first;
    private Integer second;

    public Pair(String firstElement, Integer secondElement)
    {
        first = firstElement;
        second = secondElement;
    }

    public String getFirst() { return first; }
    public Integer getSecond() { return second; }
}
```

Use type parameters for the types of generic instance variables, method parameter variables, and return values.

Now it is an easy matter to replace all String types with the type variable T and all Integer types with the type variable S.

This completes the declaration of the generic Pair class. It is ready to use whenever you need to form a pair of two objects of arbitrary types.

The following sample program shows how to make use of a Pair for returning two values from a method.

sec02/Pair.java

```java
1  /**
2      This class collects a pair of elements of different types.
3  */
4  public class Pair<T, S>
5  {
6     private T first;
7     private S second;
8
9     /**
10        Constructs a pair containing two given elements.
11        @param firstElement the first element
12        @param secondElement the second element
13     */
14     public Pair(T firstElement, S secondElement)
15     {
16        first = firstElement;
17        second = secondElement;
18     }
19
20     /**
21        Gets the first element of this pair.
22        @return the first element
23     */
24     public T getFirst() { return first; }
25
26     /**
27        Gets the second element of this pair.
28        @return the second element
29     */
30     public S getSecond() { return second; }
31
32     public String toString() { return "(" + first + ", " + second + ")"; }
33  }
```

sec02/PairDemo.java

```java
1  public class PairDemo
2  {
3     public static void main(String[] args)
4     {
5        String[] names = { "Tom", "Diana", "Harry" };
6        Pair<String, Integer> result = firstContaining(names, "a");
7        System.out.println(result.getFirst());
8        System.out.println("Expected: Diana");
9        System.out.println(result.getSecond());
10       System.out.println("Expected: 1");
11    }
12
```

```
13    /**
14        Gets the first String containing a given string, together
15        with its index.
16        @param strings an array of strings
17        @param sub a string
18        @return a pair (strings[i], i) where strings[i] is the first
19        string containing sub, or a pair (null, -1) if there is no
20        match
21    */
22    public static Pair<String, Integer> firstContaining(
23        String[] strings, String sub)
24    {
25        for (int i = 0; i < strings.length; i++)
26        {
27            if (strings[i].contains(sub))
28            {
29                return new Pair<>(strings[i], i);
30            }
31        }
32        return new Pair<>(null, -1);
33    }
34 }
```

Program Run

```
Diana
Expected: Diana
1
Expected: 1
```

18.3 Generic Methods

A generic method is a method with a type parameter.

A **generic method** is a method with a type parameter. Such a method can occur in a class that in itself is not generic. You can think of it as a template for a set of methods that differ only by one or more types. For example, we may want to declare a method that can print an array of any type:

```
public class ArrayUtil
{
    /**
        Prints all elements in an array.
        @param a the array to print
    */
    public static <T> void print(T[] a)
    {
        . . .
    }
    . . .
}
```

As described in the previous section, it is often easier to see how to implement a generic method by starting with a concrete example. This method prints the elements in an array of *strings:*

```
public class ArrayUtil
{
```

```java
public static void print(String[] a)
{
    for (String e : a)
    {
        System.out.print(e + " ");
    }
    System.out.println();
}
. . .
}
```

In order to make the method into a generic method, replace String with a type variable, say E, to denote the element type of the array. Add a type parameter list, enclosed in angle brackets, between the modifiers (public static) and the return type (void):

```java
public static <E> void print(E[] a)
{
    for (E e : a)
    {
        System.out.print(e + " ");
    }
    System.out.println();
}
```

When you call the generic method, you need not specify which type to use for the type parameter. (In this regard, generic methods differ from generic classes.) Simply call the method with appropriate arguments, and the compiler will match up the type parameters with the argument types. For example, consider this method call:

```java
Rectangle[] rectangles = . . .;
ArrayUtil.print(rectangles);
```

The type of the rectangles argument is Rectangle[], and the type of the parameter variable is E[]. The compiler deduces that E is Rectangle.

This particular generic method is a static method in an ordinary class. You can also declare generic methods that are not static. You can even have generic methods in generic classes.

Syntax 18.2   Declaring a Generic Method

Syntax   *modifiers* <*TypeVariable₁*, *TypeVariable₂*, . . .> *returnType methodName*(*parameters*)
              {
                  body
              }

Supply the type variable before the return type.

```java
public static <E> String toString(ArrayList<E> a)
{
    String result = "";
    for (E e : a)
    {
        result = result + e + " ";
    }
    return result;
}
```

Local variable with a variable data type

As with generic classes, you cannot replace type parameters with primitive types. The generic `print` method can print arrays of any type *except* the eight primitive types. For example, you cannot use the generic `print` method to print an array of type `int[]`. That is not a major problem. Simply implement a `print(int[] a)` method in addition to the generic `print` method.

EXAMPLE CODE   See your eText or companion code for a program with a generic method for printing an array of objects and a non-generic method for printing an array of integers.

18.4 Constraining Type Parameters

Type parameters can be constrained with bounds.

It is often necessary to specify what types can be used in a generic class or method. Consider a generic method that finds the average of the values in an array list of objects. How can you compute averages when you know nothing about the element type? You need to have a mechanism for measuring the elements. In Chapter 10, we designed an interface for that purpose:

© Mike Clark/iStockphoto.

You can place restrictions on the type parameters of generic classes and methods.

```
public interface Measurable
{
    double getMeasure();
}
```

We can constrain the type of the elements, requiring that the type implement the `Measurable` type. In Java, this is achieved by adding the clause `extends Measurable` after the type parameter:

```
public static <E extends Measurable> double average(ArrayList<E> objects)
```

This means, "E or one of its superclasses extends or implements `Measurable`". In this situation, we say that E is a subtype of the `Measurable` type.

Here is the complete average method:

```
public static <E extends Measurable> double average(ArrayList<E> objects)
{
    if (objects.size() == 0) { return 0; }
    double sum = 0;
    for (E obj : objects)
    {
        sum = sum + obj.getMeasure();
    }
    return sum / objects.size();
}
```

Note the call `obj.getMeasure()`. The variable `obj` has type E, and E is a subtype of `Measurable`. Therefore, we know that it is legal to apply the `getMeasure` method to `obj`.

If the `BankAccount` class implements the `Measurable` interface, then you can call the average method with an array list of `BankAccount` objects. But you cannot compute the average of an array list of strings because the `String` class does not implement the `Measurable` interface.

Now consider the task of finding the minimum in an array list. We can return the element with the smallest measure. However, the `Measurable` interface was created for this book and is not widely used. Instead, we will use the `Comparable` interface type that many classes implement. The Comparable interface is itself a generic type. The type parameter specifies the type of the parameter variable of the compareTo method:

```java
public interface Comparable<T>
{
    int compareTo(T other);
}
```

For example, String implements Comparable<String>. You can compare strings with other strings, but not with objects of different classes.

If the array list has elements of type E, then we want to require that E implements Comparable<E>. Here is the method:

```java
public static <E extends Comparable<E>> E min(ArrayList<E> objects)
{
    E smallest = objects.get(0);
    for (int i = 1; i < objects.size(); i++)
    {
        E obj = objects.get(i);
        if (obj.compareTo(smallest) < 0)
        {
            smallest = obj;
        }
    }
    return smallest;
}
```

Because of the type constraint, we know that obj has a method

```java
int compareTo(E other)
```

Therefore, the call

```java
obj.compareTo(smallest)
```

is valid.

Very occasionally, you need to supply two or more type bounds. Then you separate them with the & character, for example

```java
<E extends Comparable<E> & Measurable>
```

The extends reserved word, when applied to type parameters, actually means "extends or implements". The bounds can be either classes or interfaces, and the type parameter can be replaced with a class or interface type.

EXAMPLE CODE   See your eText or companion code for a program that demonstrates a constraint on a type parameter.

Common Error 18.1
Genericity and Inheritance

If SavingsAccount is a subclass of BankAccount, is ArrayList<SavingsAccount> a subclass of Array-List<BankAccount>? Perhaps surprisingly, it is not. Inheritance of type parameters does not lead to inheritance of generic classes. There is no relationship between ArrayList<SavingsAccount> and ArrayList<BankAccount>.

This restriction is necessary for type checking. Without the restriction, it would be possible to add objects of unrelated types to a collection.

Suppose it was possible to assign an `ArrayList<SavingsAccount>` object to a variable of type `ArrayList<BankAccount>`:

```
ArrayList<SavingsAccount> savingsAccounts = new ArrayList<>();
ArrayList<BankAccount> bankAccounts = savingsAccounts;
    // Not legal, but suppose it was
BankAccount harrysChecking = new CheckingAccount();
    // CheckingAccount is another subclass of BankAccount
bankAccounts.add(harrysChecking); // OK—can add BankAccount object
```

But `bankAccounts` and `savingsAccounts` refer to the same array list! If the assignment was legal, we would be able to add a `CheckingAccount` into an `ArrayList<SavingsAccount>`.

In many situations, this limitation can be overcome by using wildcards—see Special Topic 18.1.

Common Error 18.2

The Array Store Exception

In Common Error 18.1, you saw that one cannot assign a subclass list to a superclass list. For example, an `ArrayList<SavingsAccount>` cannot be used where an `ArrayList<BankAccount>` is expected.

This is surprising, because you *can* perform the equivalent assignment with arrays. For example,

```
SavingsAccount[] savingsAccounts = new SavingsAccount[10];
BankAccount[] bankAccounts = savingsAccounts; // Legal
```

But there was a reason the assignment wasn't legal for array lists—it would have allowed storing a `CheckingAccount` into `savingsAccounts`.

Let's try that with arrays:

```
BankAccount harrysChecking = new CheckingAccount();
bankAccounts[0] = harrysChecking; // Throws ArrayStoreException
```

This code compiles. The object `harrysChecking` is a `CheckingAccount` and hence a `BankAccount`. But `bankAccounts` and `savingsAccounts` are references to the same array—an array of type `SavingsAccount[]`. When the program runs, that array refuses to store a `CheckingAccount`, and throws an `ArrayStoreException`.

Both `ArrayList` and arrays avoid the type error, but they do it in different ways. The `ArrayList` class avoids it at compile time, and arrays avoid it at run time. Generally, we prefer a compile-time error notification, but the cost is steep, as you can see from Special Topic 18.1. It is a lot of work to tell the compiler precisely which conversions should be permitted.

Special Topic 18.1

Wildcard Types

It is often necessary to formulate subtle constraints on type parameters. Wildcard types were invented for this purpose. There are three kinds of wildcard types:

Name	Syntax	Meaning
Wildcard with upper bound	`? extends B`	Any subtype of B
Wildcard with lower bound	`? super B`	Any supertype of B
Unbounded wildcard	`?`	Any type

A wildcard type is a type that can remain unknown. For example, we can declare the following method in the `LinkedList<E>` class:

```java
public void addAll(LinkedList<? extends E> other)
{
   ListIterator<E> iter = other.listIterator();
   while (iter.hasNext())
   {
      add(iter.next());
   }
}
```

The method adds all elements of `other` to the end of the linked list.

The `addAll` method doesn't require a specific type for the element type of `other`. Instead, it allows you to use any type that is a subtype of `E`. For example, you can use `addAll` to add a `LinkedList<SavingsAccount>` to a `LinkedList<BankAccount>`.

To see a wildcard with a super bound, have another look at the `min` method:

```java
public static <E extends Comparable<E>> E min(ArrayList<E> objects)
```

However, this bound is too restrictive. Suppose the `BankAccount` class implements `Comparable<BankAccount>`. Then the subclass `SavingsAccount` also implements `Comparable<BankAccount>` and *not* `Comparable<SavingsAccount>`. If you want to use the `min` method with a `Savings-Account` array list, then the type parameter of the `Comparable` interface should be *any supertype* of the array list's element type:

```java
public static <E extends Comparable<? super E>> E min(ArrayList<E> objects)
```

Here is an example of an unbounded wildcard. The `Collections` class declares a method

```java
public static void reverse(List<?> list)
```

You can think of that declaration as a shorthand for

```java
public static <T> void reverse(List<T> list)
```

Common Error 18.2 compares this limitation with the seemingly more permissive behavior of arrays in Java.

EXAMPLE CODE   See your eText or companion code for a program that demonstrates the need for wildcards.

18.5 Type Erasure

The virtual machine erases type parameters, replacing them with their bounds or Objects.

Because generic types are a fairly recent addition to the Java language, the virtual machine that executes Java programs does not work with generic classes or methods. Instead, type parameters are "erased", that is, they are replaced with ordinary Java types. Each type parameter is replaced with its bound, or with `Object` if it is not bounded.

In the Java virtual machine, generic types are erased.   © VikramRaghuvanshi/iStockphoto.

For example, the generic class Pair<T, S> turns into the following raw class:

```
public class Pair
{
   private Object first;
   private Object second;

   public Pair(Object firstElement, Object secondElement)
   {
      first = firstElement;
      second = secondElement;
   }
   public Object getFirst() { return first; }
   public Object getSecond() { return second; }
}
```

As you can see, the type parameters T and S have been replaced by Object. The result is an ordinary class.

The same process is applied to generic methods. Consider this method:

```
public static <E extends Measurable> E min(E[] objects)
{
   E smallest = objects[0];
   for (int i = 1; i < objects.length; i++)
   {
      E obj = objects[i];
      if (obj.getMeasure() < smallest.getMeasure())
      {
         smallest = obj;
      }
   }
   return smallest;
}
```

When erasing the type parameter, it is replaced with its bound, the Measurable interface:

```
public static Measurable min(Measurable[] objects)
{
   Measurable smallest = objects[0];
   for (int i = 1; i < objects.length; i++)
   {
      Measurable obj = objects[i];
      if (obj.getMeasure() < smallest.getMeasure())
      {
         smallest = obj;
      }
   }
   return smallest;
}
```

You cannot construct objects or arrays of a generic type.

Knowing about type erasure helps you understand the limitations of Java generics. For example, you cannot construct new objects of a generic type. The following method, which tries to fill an array with copies of default objects, would be wrong:

```
public static <E> void fillWithDefaults(E[] a)
{
   for (int i = 0; i < a.length; i++)
   {
      a[i] = new E(); // Error
   }
}
```

To see why this is a problem, carry out the type erasure process, as if you were the compiler:

```
public static void fillWithDefaults(Object[] a)
{
    for (int i = 0; i < a.length; i++)
    {
        a[i] = new Object(); // Not useful
    }
}
```

Of course, if you start out with a Rectangle[] array, you don't want it to be filled with Object instances. But that's what the code would do after erasing types.

In situations such as this one, the compiler will report an error. You then need to come up with another mechanism for solving your problem. In this particular example, you can supply a default object:

```
public static <E> void fill(E[] a, E defaultValue)
{
    for (int i = 0; i < a.length; i++)
    {
        a[i] = defaultValue;
    }
}
```

Similarly, you cannot construct an array of a generic type:

```
public class Stack<E>
{
    private E[] elements;
    . . .
    public Stack()
    {
        elements = new E[MAX_SIZE]; // Error
    }
}
```

Because the array construction expression new E[] would be erased to new Object[], the compiler disallows it. A remedy is to use an array list instead:

```
public class Stack<E>
{
    private ArrayList<E> elements;
    . . .
    public Stack()
    {
        elements = new ArrayList<>(); // OK
    }
    . . .
}
```

Another solution is to use an array of objects and provide a cast when reading elements from the array:

```
public class Stack<E>
{
    private Object[] elements;
    private int currentSize;
    . . .
    public Stack()
    {
        elements = new Object[MAX_SIZE]; // OK
```

```
        }
        . . .
        public E pop()
        {
            size--;
            return (E) elements[currentSize];
        }
    }
```

The cast (E) generates a warning because it cannot be checked at run time.

These limitations are frankly awkward. It is hoped that a future version of Java will no longer erase types so that the current restrictions due to erasure can be lifted.

EXAMPLE CODE   See your eText or companion code to see a program that shows how to implement a generic stack as an array of objects.

Common Error 18.3

Using Generic Types in a Static Context

You cannot use type parameters to declare static variables, static methods, or static inner classes. For example, the following would be illegal:

```
public class LinkedList<E>
{
    private static E defaultValue; // Error
    . . .
    public static List<E> replicate(E value, int n) { . . . } // Error
    static class Node { public E data; public Node next; } // Error
}
```

In the case of static variables, this restriction is very sensible. After the generic types are erased, there is only a single variable LinkedList.defaultValue, whereas the static variable declaration gives the false impression that there is a separate variable for each LinkedList<E>.

For static methods and inner classes, there is an easy workaround; simply add a type parameter:

```
public class LinkedList<E>
{
    . . .
    public static <T> List<T> replicate(T value, int n) { . . . } // OK
    static class Node<T> { public T data; public Node<T> next; } // OK
}
```

Special Topic 18.2

Reflection

As you have seen, type erasure makes it impossible for a generic method to construct a generic array. There is an advanced technique called *reflection* that you can sometimes use to overcome this limitation. Reflection lets you work with classes in a running program.

In Java, the virtual machine keeps a Class object for each class that has been loaded. That object has information about each class, as well as methods to construct new objects of the class.

Given an object, you can get its class object by calling getClass:

```
Class objsClass = obj.getClass();
```

You can then make a new instance of that class by calling the newInstance method:

```
Object newObj = objsClass.newInstance();
```

This method throws an exception if it cannot access a constructor with no arguments.
Given an array, you can get the type of the elements this way:

```
Class arrayClass = array.getClass();
Class elementClass = arrayClass.getComponentType();
```

If you want to create a new array, use the Array.newInstance method:

```
Object[] newArray = Array.newInstance(elementClass, length);
```

Using these methods, you can implement the fillWithDefaults method:

```
public static <E> void fillWithDefaults(E[] a)
{
   Class arrayClass = a.getClass();
   Class elementClass = arrayClass.getComponentType();
   try
   {
      for (int i = 0; i < a.length; i++)
      {
         a[i] = elementClass.newInstance();
      }
   }
   catch (. . .) { . . . }
}
```

Note that we must ask for the element type of a. It does no good asking for a[0].getClass. The array might have length 0, or a[0] might be null, or a[0] might be an instance of a subclass of E.
Here is another example. The Arrays class implements a method

```
static <T> T[] copyOf(T[] original, int newLength)
```

That method can't simply call

```
T[] result = new T[newLength]; // Error
```

Instead, it must construct a new array with the same element type as the original:

```
Class arrayClass = original.getClass();
Class elementClass = arrayClass.getComponentType();
T[] newArray = (T[]) Array.newInstance(elementClass, newLength);
```

For this technique to work, you must have an element or array of the desired type. You couldn't use it to build a Stack<E> that uses an E[] array because the stack starts out empty.

WORKED EXAMPLE 18.1

Making a Generic Binary Search Tree Class

Learn how to turn the binary search tree class from Chapter 17 into a generic BinarySearchTree<E> class that stores elements of type E. See your eText or visit wiley.com/go/bjeo7.

CHAPTER SUMMARY

Describe generic classes and type parameters.

- In Java, generic programming can be achieved with inheritance or with type parameters.
- A generic class has one or more type parameters.
- Type parameters can be instantiated with class or interface types.
- Type parameters make generic code safer and easier to read.

Implement generic classes and interfaces.

- Type variables of a generic class follow the class name and are enclosed in angle brackets.
- Use type parameters for the types of generic instance variables, method parameter variables, and return values.

Implement generic methods.

- A generic method is a method with a type parameter.
- Supply the type parameters of a generic method between the modifiers and the method return type.
- When calling a generic method, you need not instantiate the type parameters.

Specify constraints on type parameters.

- Type parameters can be constrained with bounds.

Recognize how erasure of type parameters places limitations on generic programming in Java.

- The virtual machine erases type parameters, replacing them with their bounds or Objects.
- You cannot construct objects or arrays of a generic type.

- **R18.1** What is a type parameter?

- **R18.2** What is the difference between a generic class and an ordinary class?

- **R18.3** What is the difference between a generic class and a generic method?

- **R18.4** Why is it necessary to provide type arguments when instantiating a generic class, but not when invoking an instantiation of a generic method?

- **R18.5** Find an example of a non-static generic method in the standard Java library.

- **R18.6** Find four examples of a generic class with two type parameters in the standard Java library.

- **R18.7** Find an example of a generic class in the standard library that is not a collection class.

- **R18.8** Why is a bound required for the type parameter T in the following method?

      <T extends Comparable> int binarySearch(T[] a, T key)

- **R18.9** Why is a bound not required for the type parameter E in the HashSet<E> class?

- **R18.10** What is an ArrayList<Pair<T, T>>?

- **R18.11** Explain the type bounds of the following method of the Collections class.

      public static <T extends Comparable<? super T>> void sort(List<T> a)

  Why doesn't T extends Comparable or T extends Comparable<T> suffice?

- **R18.12** What happens when you pass an ArrayList<String> to a method with an ArrayList parameter variable? Try it out and explain.

- **R18.13** What happens when you pass an ArrayList<String> to a method with an ArrayList parameter variable, and the method stores an object of type BankAccount into the array list? Try it out and explain.

- **R18.14** What is the result of the following test?

      ArrayList<BankAccount> accounts = new ArrayList<>();
      if (accounts instanceof ArrayList<String>) . . .

  Try it out and explain.

- **R18.15** The ArrayList<E> class in the standard Java library must manage an array of objects of type E, yet it is not legal to construct a generic array of type E[] in Java. Locate the implementation of the ArrayList class in the library source code that is a part of the JDK. Explain how this problem is overcome.

- **E18.1** Modify the generic Pair class so that both values have the same type.

- **E18.2** Add a method swap to the Pair class of Exercise • E18.1 that swaps the first and second elements of the pair.

- **E18.3** Implement a static generic method PairUtil.swap whose argument is a Pair object, using the generic class declared in Section 18.2. The method should return a new pair, with the first and second element swapped.

▪ **E18.4**   Implement a static generic method that, given a `Map<K, V>`, yields a `List<Pair<K, V>>` of the key/value pairs in the map.

▪▪ **E18.5**   Implement a generic version of the binary search algorithm.

▪▪ **E18.6**   Implement a generic version of the selection sort algorithm.

▪▪▪ **E18.7**   Implement a generic version of the merge sort algorithm. Your program should compile without warnings.

▪ **E18.8**   Implement a generic version of the `LinkedList` class of Section 16.1.

▪▪ **E18.9**   Turn the `HashSet` implementation of Section 16.4 into a generic class. Use an array list instead of an array to store the buckets.

▪▪ **E18.10**   Provide suitable `hashCode` and `equals` methods for the `Pair` class of Section 18.2 and implement a HashMap class, using a `HashSet<Pair<K, V>>`.

▪▪▪ **E18.11**   Implement a generic version of the permutation generator in Section 13.4. Generate all permutations of a `List<E>`.

▪▪ **E18.12**   Write a generic static method `print` that prints the elements of any object that implements the `Iterable<E>` interface. The elements should be separated by commas. Place your method into an appropriate utility class.

▪▪ **E18.13**   Turn the `MinHeap` class of Section 17.6 into a generic class. As with the `TreeSet` class of the standard library, allow a `Comparator` to compare elements. If no comparator is supplied, assume that the element type implements the `Comparable` interface.

▪▪ **E18.14**   Make the `Measurer` interface from Section 10.4 into a generic interface. Provide a static method `T max(T[] values, Measurer<T> meas)`.

▪ **E18.15**   Provide a static method `void append(ArrayList<T> a, ArrayList<T> b)` that appends the elements of `b` to `a`.

▪▪ **E18.16**   Modify the method of Exercise • E18.15 so that the second array list can contain elements of a subclass. For example, if `people` is an `ArrayList<Person>` and `students` is an `ArrayList<Student>`, then `append(people, students)` should compile but `append(students, people)` should not.

▪▪ **E18.17**   Modify the method of Exercise • E18.15 so that it leaves the first array list unchanged and returns a new array list containing the elements of both array lists.

▪▪ **E18.18**   Modify the method of Exercise •• E18.17 so that it receives and returns arrays, not array lists. *Hint:* `Arrays.copyOf`.

▪ **E18.19**   Provide a static method that reverses the elements of a generic array list.

▪ **E18.20**   Provide a static method that returns the reverse of a generic array list, without modifying the original list.

▪▪ **E18.21**   Provide a static method that checks whether a generic array list is a palindrome; that is, whether the values at index `i` and `n - 1 - i` are equal to each other, where `n` is the size of the array list.

▪▪ **E18.22**   Provide a static method that checks whether the elements of a generic array list are in increasing order. The elements must be comparable.

PROGRAMMING PROJECTS

•• P18.1 Write a static generic method `PairUtil.minmax` that computes the minimum and maximum elements of an array of type T and returns a pair containing the minimum and maximum value. Require that the array elements implement the `Measurable` interface of Section 10.1.2.

•• P18.2 Repeat Exercise •• P18.1, but require that the array elements implement the `Comparable` interface.

••• P18.3 Repeat Exercise •• P18.2, but refine the bound of the type parameter to extend the generic `Comparable` type.

•• P18.4 Make the `Measurable` interface from Section 10.1.2 into a generic interface. Provide a static method that returns the largest element of an `ArrayList<T>`, provided that the elements are instances of `Measurable<T>`. Be sure to return a value of type T.

••• P18.5 Enhance Exercise •• P18.4 so that the elements of the `ArrayList<T>` can implement `Measurable<U>` for appropriate types U.

•• P18.6 Using the `java.util.function.Predicate` interface, write a static generic method

```
List<T> filter(List<T> values, Predicate<? super T> p)
```

that returns a list of all values for which the predicate returns `true`. Demonstrate how to use this method by getting a list of all strings with length greater than ten from a given list of strings. Use a lambda expression (see Special Topic 10.4).

•• P18.7 Write a static generic method

```
List<R> map(List<T> values, Function<T, R> f)
```

that returns a list of the values returned by the function when called with arguments in the `values` list.

••• P18.8 Write a static generic method

```
List<Pair<T, R>> map(List<T> values, Function<T, R> f)
```

that returns a list of pairs (v, f.apply(v)), where v ranges over the given values.

STREAM PROCESSING

© adventtr/iStockphoto.

Streams let you process data by specifying what you want to have done, leaving the details to the stream library. The library can execute operations lazily, skipping those that are not needed for computing the result, or distribute work over multiple processors. This is particularly useful when working with very large data sets. Moreover, stream computations are often easier to understand because they express the intent of the programmer more clearly than explicit loops. In this chapter, you will learn how to use Java streams for solving common "big data" processing problems.

19.1 The Stream Concept

When analyzing data, you often write a loop that examines each item and collects the results. For example, suppose you have a list of words and want to know how many words have more than ten letters. You could use the "counting matches" algorithm from Section 6.7.2, like this:

```
List<String> wordList = . . .;
long count = 0;
for (String w : wordList)
{
    if (w.length() > 10) { count++; }
}
```

The stream library uses a different approach. With a **stream** of words, you can use the filter method to pick out the words that you want, then the count method to count them, like this:

```
Stream<String> words = . . .;
long count = words
    .filter(w -> w.length() > 10)
    .count();
```

As you can see, you tell a stream *what* you want to achieve, not how to achieve it. That can lead to code that is easier to understand. It also allows the library to optimize the execution. For example, it can take advantage of multiple processors in a computer and have each of them work on a part of the data.

© pullia/iStockphoto.

A filter removes undesired elements from a stream.

The stream library makes heavy use of **lambda expressions** such as w -> w.length() > 10 that denote small snippets of computation that a method should execute. For example, the filter method subjects each stream element to the test "Is this string longer than ten characters?" Lambda expressions were briefly introduced in Special Topic 10.4, and we will discuss them in detail in Section 19.5. For now, you should simply have an intuitive idea what they mean. To the left of the -> symbol, you have parameters, and to the right, the result of a computation. In this case, each stream element w is tested with the expression w.length() > 10.

Streams are similar to the collections that you have seen in Chapter 15, but there are significant differences.

Unlike a collection, a stream does not store its data. The data comes from elsewhere—perhaps a collection, a file, a database, or a data source on the Internet.

Unlike a collection, a stream is immutable. You cannot insert, remove, or modify elements. However, you can create a new stream from a given one. For example, `words.filter(w -> w.length() > 10)` is a new stream, containing the long words from the original stream. The original stream has not changed. In general, you work with streams by transforming them into new streams, which contain a subset of the elements or transformations of the elements.

> **A stream is an immutable sequence of values that are processed lazily.**

Stream processing is *lazy*. Transformations are done as late as possible, and only when necessary. For example, suppose you ask for five long words:

```
Stream<String> fiveLongWords = words
    .filter(w -> w.length() > 10)
    .limit(5);
```

> **Lazy processing means to defer operations until they are needed, and to skip those that are not needed.**

Then the intermediate stream of long words is not actually computed in its entirety. The computation flows backwards. Because only five words are requested in the end, the filtering stops when the fifth match has been found. How does that work? It's not your problem, but that of the implementors of the stream library. Remember, you specify what you want, not how it should be done.

In this chapter, you will learn how to work with streams: how to create and transform them, and how to harvest results. In particular, you will learn in detail how to specify functionality with lambda expressions, such as

© beetle8/iStockphoto.

Lazy processing means not to do work until it is absolutely necessary.

```
w -> w.length() > 10
```

for expressing "w is a long word".

As computer scientists work with ever bigger data sets and have machines with multiple processors at their disposal, the "what, not how" principle becomes very important. The Java stream library is a good introduction to "big data" thinking.

The following program contrasts the traditional approach of counting matches with the use of a stream.

sec01/StreamDemo.java

```java
1  import java.io.File;
2  import java.io.IOException;
3  import java.util.ArrayList;
4  import java.util.List;
5  import java.util.Scanner;
6
7  public class StreamDemo
8  {
9     public static void main(String[] args) throws IOException
10    {
11       Scanner in = new Scanner(new File("../countries.txt"));
12          // This file contains one country name per line
13       List<String> wordList = new ArrayList<>();
14       while (in.hasNextLine()) { wordList.add(in.nextLine()); }
15          // Now wordList is a list of country names
```

```
16
17      // Traditional loop for counting the long words
18      long count = 0;
19      for (String w : wordList)
20      {
21          if (w.length() > 10) { count++; }
22      }
23
24      System.out.println("Long words: " + count);
25
26      // The same computation with streams
27      count = wordList.stream()
28          .filter(w -> w.length() > 10)
29          .count();
30
31      System.out.println("Long words: " + count);
32      }
33 }
```

Program Run

```
Long words: 63
Long words: 63
```

19.2 Producing Streams

The Stream.of static
method and the
stream methods of
collection classes
yield streams.

To do stream processing, you need a stream. The simplest way of getting one is with the static Stream.of method. You specify the elements, like this:

```
Stream<String> words = Stream.of("Mary", "had", "a", "little", "lamb");
Stream<Integer> digits = Stream.of(3, 1, 4, 1, 5, 9);
```

With the same method, you can turn an array of objects into a stream:

```
Integer[] digitArray = { 3, 1, 4, 1, 5, 9 };
Stream<Integer> digitStream = Stream.of(digitArray);
```

Note, by the way, that Stream is a generic type, just like the collection types. A Stream<String> yields strings, and a Stream<Integer> yields wrapper objects for integers. (As with all generic types, the type parameter cannot be a primitive type, so you must use wrappers for int, double, and so on.)

If you have a list, set, or other collection in the Java collections framework, call the stream method to obtain a stream that looks up the elements in the collection.

```
List<String> wordList = new ArrayList<>();
// Populate wordList
Stream<String> words = wordList.stream();
```

You can turn any collection into a stream.   © microgen/iStockphoto.

Several utility methods of the Java library yield streams. You can get a stream of the lines in a file with the `Files.lines` method. That method requires a `Path` object to describe a file. We will introduce the `Path` interface in Chapter 21, but for now all you need to know is how to make a path from a file name, as shown in the following code fragment:

```
String filename = . . .;
try (Stream<String> lineStream = Files.lines(Paths.get(filename)))
{
    . . .
} // The file is closed here; see Section 11.4.4
```

You can even make an **infinite stream**—see Special Topic 19.1.

Moreover, you can make a **parallel stream**, which causes stream operations to be distributed over the available processors. Today, most computers have multiple processors, and programs run faster if they can take advantage of them. The `parallel` method turns any stream into a parallel stream. Because distributing the work over multiple processors involves some housekeeping, you should only do that with streams that have many elements (see Exercise •• P19.1).

Table 1 Producing Streams

Example	Result
`Stream.of(1, 2, 3)`	A stream containing the given elements. You can also pass an array.
`Collection<String> coll = . . .;` `coll.stream()`	A stream containing the elements of a collection.
`Files.lines(path)`	A stream of the lines in the file with the given path. Use a try-with-resources statement to ensure that the underlying file is closed.
`Stream<String> stream = . . .;` `stream.parallel()`	Turns a stream into a parallel stream.
`Stream.generate(() -> 1)`	An infinite stream of ones (see Special Topic 19.1).
`Stream.iterate(0, n -> n + 1)`	An infinite stream of Integer values (see Special Topic 19.1).
`IntStream.range(0, 100)`	An IntStream of int values between 0 (inclusive) and 100 (exclusive)—see Section 19.8.
`Random generator = new Random();` `generator.ints(0, 100)`	An infinite stream of random int values drawn from a random generator—see Section 19.8.
`"Hello".codePoints()`	An IntStream of code points of a string—see Section 19.8.

EXAMPLE CODE See your eText or companion code to see a program that shows different ways of creating a stream.

19.3 Collecting Results

Once you have a stream, you transform it into other streams, as will be shown in detail in the following sections. Eventually, you will want to harvest a result. If the result is a number (such as a count, sum, maximum, minimum, or average), there are methods for computing it—see Section 19.8. But often, you want to put the final stream values back into an array or collection. Here is how to do the former:

```
String[] result = stream.toArray(String[]::new);
```

The call looks rather mysterious—see Special Topic 19.2 for an explanation. Of course, if your stream contains elements of a type other than strings, you need to use that type instead of String.

If you want to save the stream values in a collection, use the collect method. That method requires a "**collector**", an object that is responsible for placing stream values into a result object. The Collectors class has static methods that produce collectors for various result types. Here is how to obtain the stream values as a list or set:

```
List<String> result = stream.collect(Collectors.toList());
Set<String> result = stream.collect(Collectors.toSet());
```

> To turn a stream into an array or collection, use the toArray or collect methods.

When you have a stream of strings, you can use a collector to combine them into one large string. You call the Collectors.joining method and supply a string that is used to separate the values. For example, here we join the values of the words stream, separating the words with commas:

```
String result = words.collect(Collectors.joining(", "));
   // A string such as "a, am, an, ant, ..."
   // with comma separators
```

Finally, you will see in Section 19.9 how to collect stream values into maps.

After processing a stream, you can collect its elements in an array or collection. © Jamesmcq24/iStockphoto.

Table 2 Collecting Results from a Stream<T>

Example	Comments
`stream.toArray(T[]::new)`	Yields a T[] array.
`stream.collect(Collectors.toList())` `stream.collect(Collectors.toSet())`	Yields a List<T> or Set<T>.
`stream.collect(Collectors.joining(", ")`	Yields a string, joining the elements by the given separator. Only for Stream<String>.
`stream.collect(Collectors.groupingBy(` *keyFunction, collector*)	Yields a map that associates group keys with collected group values—see Section 19.9.

EXAMPLE CODE   See your eText or companion code to see a program that shows different ways of collecting stream results.

Now you know how to turn a collection into a stream, and a stream back into a collection. In between, you will want to transform the streams, turning the initial values into those that you want to compute. You will see how to do that in the next section.

Programming Tip 19.1
One Stream Operation Per Line

Stream operations are very powerful, and you can achieve a lot of work with a small number of method calls. Your code will be much easier to understand if you put each stream operation in a separate line. Then you can mentally track each step.

```
List<String> result = list.stream()          Create the stream.
   .filter(w -> w.length() > 10)      Keep long strings.
   .limit(50)        Keep only the first fifty.
   .collect(Collectors.toList());       Turn into a list.
```

In contrast, if you cram as much as possible in one line, it is tedious to figure out the steps.

```
List<String> result = list.stream().filter(w -> w.length() > 10).limit(50).collect(
   Collectors.toList()); // Don't use this formatting style
```

Special Topic 19.1
Infinite Streams

You can make an **infinite stream** with the generate method. Provide a lambda expression with no arguments, and it is applied for each stream element. For example,

```
Stream<Integer> ones = Stream.generate(() -> 1);
```

is an infinite stream of ones, and

```
Stream<Integer> dieTosses = Stream.generate(() -> 1 + (int)(6 * Math.random()));
```

is an infinite stream of random integers between 1 and 6.

If you want to have more interesting infinite streams, use the iterate method. You provide an initial value and an iteration function that is applied to each preceding value. For example,

```
Stream<Integer> integers = Stream.iterate(0, n -> n + 1);
```

is an infinite stream with elements 0, 1, 2, 3, and so on.

By filtering, you can get more interesting streams. For example, if isPrime is a static method that checks whether an integer is prime, then

```
Stream<Integer> primes = integers.filter(n -> isPrime(n));
```

is a stream of prime numbers.

Of course, you cannot generate all elements for such a stream. At some point, you need to limit the results. If you want to find the first 500 primes, call

```
List<Integer> firstPrimes = primes
   .limit(500)
   .collect(Collectors.toList());
```

What is the advantage of using an infinite stream even though it eventually gets truncated to a finite one? You don't need to know in advance how many integers to use to end up with the desired number of primes.

EXAMPLE CODE   See your eText or companion code for a program that demonstrates an infinite stream.

19.4 Transforming Streams

© DragonImages/iStockphoto.

The map *method yields a new stream with the transformed elements.*

Suppose you have a stream of words, some uppercase, some lowercase, and you want them all lowercase. In such a situation, you take the stream that you are given and transform it, by applying a function to all elements and collecting the results in a new stream. That is what the map method does.

```
Stream<String> words = Stream.of("A", "Tale", "of", "Two", "Cities");
Stream<String> lowerCaseWords = words.map(w -> w.toLowerCase());
    // "a", "tale", "of", "two", "cities"
```

Perhaps you aren't interested in vowels. Then you can remove them:

```
Stream<String> consonantsOnly = lowerCaseWords.map(
    w -> w.replaceAll("[aeiou]", ""));
    // "", "tl", "f", "tw", "cts"
```

Maybe you just wanted to know how many consonants each had:

```
Stream<Integer> consonantCount = consonantsOnly.map(w -> w.length());
    // 0, 2, 1, 2, 3
```

The map method applies a function to all elements of a stream, yielding another stream.

As you can see, the map method takes a function and applies it to each element of the stream, yielding a new stream with the results. The function syntax is pretty self-explanatory: to the left of the -> is the parameter variable, and to the right the returned value. We will go over the syntax in detail in Section 19.5.

You have already seen the filter transformation. It takes a function with a boolean result. (Such a function is called a *predicate*.) The resulting stream retains all elements that "pass the test"; that is, for which the function returns true.

The filter method yields a stream of all elements fulfilling a condition.

For example, suppose we have a stream of words and only want to look at those starting with the letter a. You get them as

```
Stream<String> aWords = words.filter(w -> w.substring(0, 1).equals("a"));
```

Note that the expression to the right of the -> has a boolean value. Either the first letter is an a, or it is not.

The map and filter methods are the "bread and butter" of stream transformations. Usually, you get a stream, filter away what you don't need, and transform the desired elements to the desired form.

Table 3 Stream Transformations

Example	Comments
stream.filter(*condition*)	A stream with the elements matching the condition.
stream.map(*function*)	A stream with the results of applying the function to each element.
stream.mapToInt(*function*) stream.mapToDouble(*function*) stream.mapToLong(*function*)	A primitive-type stream with the results of applying a function with a return value of a primitive type—see Section 19.8.
stream.limit(n) stream.skip(n)	A stream consisting of the first n, or all but the first n elements.
stream.distinct() stream.sorted() stream.sorted(*comparator*)	A stream of the distinct or sorted elements from the original stream.

Sometimes, you first need to transform the elements so you can apply a filter. You can string together as many map and filter operations as you like. They are evaluated lazily, without creating unnecessary intermediate results.

Here are several more useful stream transformations.

1. You have already seen the limit method. The call

   ```
   stream.limit(n)
   ```

   yields a new stream containing the first n elements of the original stream (or the entire original stream if it had fewer than n elements).

2. The call stream.skip(n) does the opposite, returning the stream obtained by dropping the first n elements. This operation lets you drop initial elements that don't contribute to the end result.

3. The distinct method drops replicated elements:

   ```
   Stream<String> words = Stream.of(
       "how much wood could a wood chuck chuck".split(" "));
   Stream<String> distinctWords = words.distinct();
       // "how", "much", "wood", "could", "a", "chuck"
   ```

4. The sorted method yields a new stream with the elements of the original stream in sorted order.

   ```
   Stream<String> sortedWords = distinctWords.sorted();
       // "a", "chuck", "could", "how", "much", "wood"
   ```

   For this method to work, the stream elements must belong to a class that implements the Comparable interface. In the next section, you will see how to specify a different comparator.

The following sample program puts several stream transformations to use, producing a list of abbreviated country names.

sec04/StreamDemo.java

```java
1  import java.io.IOException;
2  import java.nio.file.Files;
3  import java.nio.file.Paths;
4  import java.util.List;
5  import java.util.stream.Collectors;
6  import java.util.stream.Stream;
7
8  public class StreamDemo
9  {
10     public static void main(String[] args) throws IOException
11     {
12        try (Stream<String> lines = Files.lines(Paths.get("countries.txt")))
13        { // Read the lines
14           List<String> result = lines
15              .filter(w -> w.length() > 10) // Keep only long words
16              .map(w -> w.substring(0, 7)) // Truncate to seven characters
17              .map(w -> w + "...") // Add ellipses
18              .distinct() // Remove duplicates
19              .limit(20) // Keep only the first twenty
20              .collect(Collectors.toList()); // Collect into a list
21           System.out.println(result);
22        }
23     }
24  }
```

Program Run

```
[Afghani..., America..., Antigua..., Bahamas..., Bosnia ...,
British..., Burkina..., Cayman ..., Central..., Christm...,
Cocos (..., Congo, ..., Cook Is..., Cote d'..., Czech R...,
Dominic..., El Salv..., Equator..., Falklan..., Faroe I...]
```

Common Error 19.1

Don't Use a Terminated Stream

Once you obtain a result from a stream, by calling a method such as as toArray or collect, the stream is "used up", and you can no longer apply other operations to it. For example, you cannot put the first fifty elements in one list and then take the next fifty:

```
Stream<String> stream = list.stream();
List<String> result1 = stream.limit(50).collect(Collectors.toList());
stream = stream.skip(50); // Error—the stream can no longer be used
```

If you want to collect two sets of fifty elements, you need to recreate the stream.

```
List<String> result1 = list.stream()
   .limit(50)
   .collect(Collectors.toList()); // This stream can no longer be used
List<String> result2 = list.stream() // Create another stream
   .skip(50)
   .limit(50)
   .collect(Collectors.toList());
```

To avoid this error, it is a good idea to write stream operations as a "pipeline" that starts with stream creation, is followed by transformations, and ends with collecting a result. Format the pipeline as described in Programming Tip 19.1.

19.5 Lambda Expressions

A lambda expression consists of one or more parameter variables, an arrow ->, and an expression or block yielding the result.

In the arguments to the filter and map methods, you have seen lambda expressions such as

```
w -> w.length() > 10
```

This is a function, in the mathematical sense, like a static method in Java. It has a parameter variable (w in this example) that is mapped to a result. To the right of the -> is the result, namely the value of the expression w.length() > 10, which is true for long strings and false for short ones.

When you use this function with a Stream<String>, then the Java compiler can figure out that w must be a String. When the compiler cannot figure out the parameter type from the context, you need to specify it. Then the syntax is

```
(String w) -> w.length() > 10
```

In other situations, you need a function with two parameters. Then you specify both parameters, enclosed in parentheses, like this:

```
(v, w) -> v.length() - w.length()
```

This function takes two strings and returns the difference of their lengths.

Syntax 19.1 Lambda Expressions

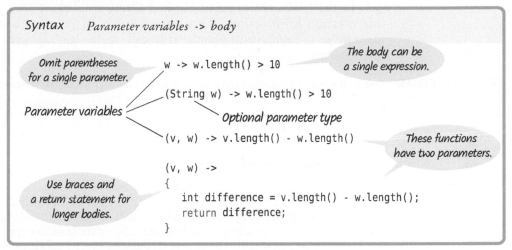

As an application of such a function, consider the task of sorting a sequence of objects. In order to sort, you need to compare elements. You can use the `Comparable` interface for this purpose, but there is another way (shown in Special Topic 14.4). You provide a function that compares two elements and returns an integer. If the result is negative, the first argument comes before the second. If the result is zero, the arguments can come in either order. Otherwise, the first argument comes after the second.

The function that computes the difference between the lengths of two strings is such a comparison function. It compares strings by length.

You can pass this function to the `sorted` method of the `Stream` class, and it yields a stream whose elements are sorted by increasing length. For example,

```
Stream<String> byLength = Stream.of("A", "Tale", "of", "Two", "Cities")
    .sorted((v, w) -> v.length() - w.length());
    // "A", "of", "Two", "Tale", "Cities"
```

A functional interface is an interface with a single abstract method.

The preceding example showed a typical use of a lambda expression. The `sorted` method has a parameter of type `Comparator`, an interface with a single abstract method or **functional interface**. You can pass a lambda expression, and it is converted to an instance of the interface.

A lambda expression can be converted to an instance of a functional interface.

In all these examples, the result of the function was so simple that the computation happened in a single expression. You can also distribute the code over multiple statements, enclosed in braces. Then use a `return` statement for the result, as you do with methods:

```
(v, w) ->
{
    int first = v.length();
    int second = w.length();
    return first - second;
}
```

That is all that you have to know about lambda expressions in order to use stream methods such as `filter`, `map`, and `sorted`. When the result expression is just a method call, you can optionally use an even shorter syntax—see Special Topic 19.2.

By the way, the term lambda expression comes from the history of mathematics. In the 1930s, the logician Haskell Curry used the Greek letter lambda (λ) in his notation for functions, λ*parameter. result*. In Java one uses an arrow instead: *parameter -> result*, but people still call them lambda expressions, not arrow expressions.

EXAMPLE CODE   See your eText or companion code for a program that demonstrates lambda expressions.

Programming Tip 19.2

Keep Lambda Expressions Short

Lambda expressions are passed to methods such as `map`, `filter`, and `sorted`, which themselves can occur in sequences of stream operations. If the lambda expression is too long, or if its purpose is not immediately apparent, then it becomes difficult to focus on the sequence of operations. In that case, make a helper method and call it in the lambda expression.

For example, suppose you want to sort countries first by continent and then alphabetically. It is syntactically correct to use a complex expression:

```
List<Country> result = stream.sorted((c, d) ->
    {
        int difference = c.getContinent().compareTo(d.getContinent());
        if (difference != 0) { return difference; }
        else { return c.getName().compareTo(d.getName); }
    })
    .collect(Collectors.toList());
```

You can make the code easier to read by calling a helper method:

```
List<Country> result = stream.sorted((c, d) -> byContinentThenByName(c, d))
    .collect(Collectors.toList());
```

If you don't want to declare a separate method, use a separate variable whose type is the appropriate functional interface:

```
Comparator<Country> byContinentThenByName =
    (c, d) ->
    {
        int difference = c.getContinent().compareTo(d.getContinent());
        if (difference != 0) { return 0; }
        else { return c.getName().compareTo(d.getName); }
    };

List<Country> result = stream.sorted(byContinentThenByName)
    .collect(Collectors.toList());
```

Also note that it is customary to use single-letter parameter variables in lambda expressions to keep them short.

Check out Special Topic 19.2 and Special Topic 19.4 for additional ways of making lambda expressions more compact.

Special Topic 19.2

Method and Constructor References

When a lambda expression consists of just one method call, you can use a very concise syntax, called a **method reference**. A class name followed by a `::` symbol and method name is equivalent to a lambda expression with parameters "at the right places".

For example, the method reference

```
String::toUpperCase
```

is a shorthand for the lambda expression

```
(String w) -> w.toUpperCase()
```

There are several forms of method references. You have just seen the case of an instance method of a class with no parameters. If the method has parameters, they are parameters of the equivalent lambda expression. For example, the method reference

```
String::compareTo
```

is the same as the lambda expression

```
(String s, String t) -> s.compareTo(t)
```

If the method is a static method, then there is no implicit parameter. The expression

```
Double::compare
```

is the same as `(double x, double y) -> Double.compare(x, y)`

Finally, you can have an object to the left of the :: symbol, for example

```
System.out::println
```

That is the same as `x -> System.out.println(x)`, where the type of x is inferred from context.

To invoke a constructor, use the keyword new after the :: symbol. For example,

```
BankAccount::new
```

is the same as `() -> new BankAccount()` or `b -> new BankAccount(b)`, depending on where it is used.

One constructor reference that you will see frequently is for creating an array:

```
String[]::new
```

is the same as `n -> new String[n]`, creating a string array of a given length. When the expression is invoked, one must pass an integer, namely the desired length of the array.

Such a constructor reference is used as the argument of the toArray method of streams. When you call

```
String[] array = words.toArray(String[]::new)
```

then the toArray method calls the array constructor with the number of elements of the stream. This sounds more complicated than it should be, but unfortunately, it is not possible in Java to construct an array of a generic type without providing the constructor—see Section 18.5.

You don't have to use method or constructor references, but many programmers prefer them because they find them clearer and more concise than the equivalent lambda expressions.

EXAMPLE CODE   See your eText or companion code for a program that demonstrates method references.

Special Topic 19.3

Higher-Order Functions

Methods such as map and filter consume functions. There is no real difference between a method and a function—a method is just a function where one of the parameters is in a special position. Thus, map and filter are often called **higher-order functions** because they are functions that consume functions.

To implement a higher-order function in Java, you need to use a **functional interface**, an interface with exactly one abstract method. The Comparator interface is one such interface, with a single method compare. Another one is the Predicate<T> interface. It has an abstract method

```
boolean test(T t)
```

The filter method has a parameter of type Predicate<T>, where T is the same type as the element type of the stream.

Here is how you would implement such a method. For simplicity, the method works on lists, not streams.

```java
public static <T> List<T> filter(List<T> values, Predicate<T> p)
{
   List<T> result = new ArrayList<>();
   for (T value : values)
   {
      if (p.test(value)) { result.add(value); }
   }
   return result;
}
```

Note how the filter method invokes the test method on the function parameter p.

When you call

```java
List<String> filtered = filter(wordList, w -> w.length() > 10);
```

then the filter method receives as its parameter p an object of some class that implements Predicate<String>. The test method of that object returns the boolean value w.length() > 10.

A higher-order function can also return a function. Consider this example:

```java
public static Predicate<String> contains(String target)
{
   return s -> s.indexOf(target) >= 0;
}
```

The call contains("and") yields a predicate that tests whether a string contains the substring "and". You can pass that function to a method that expects a predicate, such as filter:

```java
List<String> filtered = filter(wordList, contains("and"));
```

EXAMPLE CODE   See your eText or companion code for a program that demonstrates higher-order functions.

Special Topic 19.4

Higher-Order Functions and Comparators

A useful higher-order function that receives and returns a function is Comparator.comparing. You give it an *extractor* function that extracts a value from an element. The result is a comparison function that compares the extracted values. For example, consider

```java
Comparator<String> comp = Comparator.comparing(t -> t.length())
```

That is the same function as

```java
Comparator<String> comp = (v, w) -> v.length() - w.length();
```

You can write it even more succinctly with a method reference:

```java
Comparator.comparing(String::length)
```

This reads quite nicely—the comparator that compares strings by their length.

You can add a secondary comparison with the thenComparing method:

```java
Collections.sort(countries,
   Comparator.comparing(Country::getContinent)
      .thenComparing(Country::getName));
```

The countries are compared first by continent. If the continents are the same, they are compared by name.

EXAMPLE CODE   See your eText or companion code for a program that demonstrates such a comparator.

19.6 The Optional Type

In Java, it has been common to use the value null to indicate that a method has no result. However, that's a bit dangerous. If a caller doesn't expect the "no answer" case and uses the result, a NullPointerException occurs, which can terminate the program.

```
String result = oldFashionedMethod(searchParameters);
    // Returns null if no match
int length = result.length();
    // Throws a NullPointerException when result is null
```

The stream library takes a different approach. Whenever a query might not yield any answer, it returns a result of the type Optional<T>.

Here is a good example. Suppose you want to find the first long string in a stream of strings. Use the findFirst method and call

> **The Optional class is a wrapper for objects that may or may not be present.**

```
words.filter(w -> w.length() > 10).findFirst()
```

But what if words has no elements with more than ten characters? Then there can't be a first element in the filtered stream.

For that reason, the findFirst method returns an Optional<String>, not a String:

```
Optional<String> optResult = words
    .filter(w -> w.length() > 10)
    .findFirst();
```

An Optional object is a wrapper that holds a value or an indication that no value is present.

Use the orElse method to extract the value, or the provided alternative:

```
int length = optResult.orElse("").length();
```

> **Use the orElse method to obtain the value of an Optional or, if no value is present, an alternative.**

If there is a result, then its length is computed. Otherwise, the orElse method returns an alternative, "", on which it is safe to invoke the length method.

Another alternative is to call the ifPresent method and give it a function that consumes the value. For example,

```
optResult.ifPresent(v -> results.add(v));
```

If a value v is present, it is added to the results collection. If not, nothing happens.

The isPresent method tests whether there really was a result:

```
if (!optResult.isPresent())
{
    System.out.println("No element has more than ten characters");
}
```

If you know there is a result, you can use the get method to retrieve it. But if you were wrong and there was no value, a NoSuchElementException is thrown.

Now you have learned how to use the Optional type. If you write a method that returns an Optional value, return either Optional.of(result), if there is a result, or Optional.empty() if there is none.

An Optional *value may or may not be present.*   © Tomwang112/iStockphoto.

Table 4 Working with Optional Values

Example	Comments
`result = optional.orElse("");`	Extracts the wrapped value or the specified default if no value is present.
`optional.ifPresent(v -> Process v);`	Processes the wrapped value if present or does nothing if no value is present.

`if (optional.isPresent())`
`{`
   `Process optional.get()`
`}`
`else`
`{`
   `Handle the absence of a value.`
`}`
	Processes the wrapped value if present, or deals with the situation when it is not present.

`double average = pstream.average()` `.getAsDouble();`	Gets the wrapped value from a primitive-type stream—see Section 19.8.

`if (there is a result)`
`{`
   `return Optional.of(result);`
`}`
`else`
`{`
   `return Optional.empty();`
`}`
	Returns an Optional value from a method.

EXAMPLE CODE   See your eText or companion code for a program that shows how to work with Optional values.

Common Error 19.2

Optional **Results Without Values**

Methods such as findFirst and max return an Optional result for a good reason—there might not be any result. If you ignore that possibility and just call get to retrieve the wrapped value, you run the risk of a NoSuchElementException.

It is best to avoid the get method and use orElse or ifPresent if at all possible.

Of course, you can call isPresent followed by get, but the resulting code is usually more complex.

Consider the example of finding a long word. Don't just call

```
String result = stream
   .filter(w -> w.length() > 10)
   .findFirst()
   .get(); // Throws an exception if no value is present
```

What do you want to do if there is no long word? If you want to print either the word or a message, you can use orElse:

```
String result = stream
   .filter(w -> w.length() > 10)
   .findFirst()
   .orElse("None");
System.out.println("Long word: " + result);
```

If you want to only process the result when it exists and otherwise do nothing, use ifPresent:

```
List<String> results = . . .;
stream
   .filter(w -> w.length() > 10)
   .findFirst()
   .ifPresent(w -> results.add(w));
```

Reserve the use of isPresent and get for complex situations where you carry out entirely different actions depending on the outcome:

```
Optional<String> result = stream
   .filter(w -> w.length() > 10)
   .findFirst();
if (result.isPresent())
{
   results.add(result.get()); // Safe to call get
}
else
{
   System.out.println("No long words");
}
```

19.7 Other Terminal Operations

A terminal operation triggers the lazy operations on a stream and yields a non-stream value.

Methods such as count and findFirst are **terminal operations**. A terminal operation forces the execution of all pending lazy operations and yields a value that is not a stream. Afterward, the stream is no longer usable.

Another terminal operation is findAny. It works like findFirst, but it returns any match, not necessarily the first one. That is faster on parallel streams. Suppose you want to find a long word that ends with y, and you don't care which word is chosen if there is more than one. Then call

```
result = words
   .parallel()
   .filter(w -> w.length() > 10)
   .filter(w -> w.endsWith("y"))
   .findAny()
   .orElse("");
```

When a bus reaches the terminal, the journey comes to an end, just as a stream does when you apply a terminal operation to it.

© Veronica Garbutt/Getty Images.

Other terminal operations are `max` and `min`. You need to supply a comparator when calling these methods. For example, to get the longest string (or, if there are multiple strings of maximum length, one of them), call

```
Optional<String> result = words.max((v, w) -> v.length() - w.length());
```

Because it is possible that the stream is empty, `max` and `min` return `Optional` values.

The `toArray` and `collect` methods from Section 19.3 are also terminal operations. Another one is `forEach`, which doesn't yield a result but instead applies a function to all elements. For example,

```
words.forEach(w -> System.out.println(w))
```

prints all words in the stream. You need to be cautious with the `forEach` method on a parallel stream. For example, printing all words in a parallel stream can result in a garbled output.

Finally, there are three terminal operations that return a `boolean` value, to test whether all, any, or no stream elements match a condition: `allMatch`, `anyMatch`, and `noneMatch`.

```
boolean result = words.allMatch(w -> w.contains("e"));
    // result is true if all words contain the letter e
    // Use anyMatch or noneMatch to check for some or no matches
```

EXAMPLE CODE   See your eText or companion code for a program that illustrates the terminal operations in this section.

Common Error 19.3

Don't Apply Mutations in Parallel Stream Operations

Often, you can speed up stream operations by making the stream parallel. Then the work is distributed over multiple processors. However, that only works when the operations don't interfere with each other. If you print output, it may appear interleaved. If you store values in a data structure, it can get corrupted. Here is an example of something that will not work:

```
List<String> longWords = new ArrayList<>();
wordList.stream()
    .parallel()
    .forEach(w ->
      {
          if (w.length() > 10)
          {
              longWords.add(w); // Error—don't mutate in a parallel stream
          }
      });
```

If you try this with a sufficiently long list of words on a computer with more than one processor, chances are great that your program will crash when the array list is corrupted. And if your program happens not to crash, the list will probably not contain all results. Chapter 21 has much more to say about the dangers of accessing shared data at the same time.

In this example, you should just use `filter` and `collect` to safely return the result. In general, it is safe to use parallel streams when none of the stream operations mutate shared objects.

EXAMPLE CODE   See your eText or companion code for a program that demonstrates the effect of mutations on parallel stream operations.

19.8 Primitive-Type Streams

It is inefficient to have streams of wrappers to primitive types, such as Stream<Integer>, because each individual int element needs a separate wrapper. There are three specialized stream interfaces, IntStream, LongStream, and DoubleStream, that store elements of type int, long, and double. (The remaining five primitive types (float, byte, char, short, and boolean) don't occur often enough in streams to warrant special cases.)

© the_guitar_mann/iStockphoto.

An IntStream *stores* int *values, not* Integer *wrappers.*

19.8.1 Creating Primitive-Type Streams

You can create an IntStream from individual integers, or from an array:

```
IntStream stream = IntStream.of(3, 1, 4, 1, 5, 9);
int[] values = . . .;
stream = IntStream.of(values);
```

> The IntStream.range method yields a stream of consecutive integers.

To get a stream consisting of the integers a, a + 1, a + 2, up to, but not including b, call

```
IntStream stream = IntStream.range(a, b);
```

The doubles method of the Random class yields a DoubleStream of random values between 0 and 1. The ints method yields random numbers between an inclusive lower bound and an exclusive upper bound:

```
Random generator = new Random();
IntStream dieTosses = generator.ints(1, 7);
```

You can turn a String object str into an IntStream of its Unicode code points with

```
IntStream codePoints = str.codePoints();
```

> The mapToInt method applies an int-valued function to stream elements and yields an IntStream.

Often, you will create an IntStream from another stream by applying a function with int results to the elements, using the mapToInt method. For example, if you want to process word lengths, you get a stream of them with

```
IntStream lengths = words.mapToInt(w -> w.length());
```

Similarly, there are methods mapToDouble and mapToLong that yield a DoubleStream and a LongStream.

19.8.2 Mapping a Primitive-Type Stream

The map method of an IntStream yields another IntStream. For example,

```
IntStream stream = IntStream.range(0, 20)
    .map(n -> Math.min(n, 10));
```

yields a stream with twenty elements 0, 1, 2, ..., 9, 10, 10, ..., 10.

If you want to convert an IntStream to a stream of objects, call mapToObj. This is often useful to imitate a loop over a range of integers. Here, we generate a stream of strings of increasing length:

```
String river = "Mississippi";
int n = river.length();
```

```
Stream<String> prefixes = IntStream.range(0, n)
    .mapToObj(i -> river.substring(0, i));
// "", "M", "Mi", "Mis", "Miss", "Missi", ...
```

The IntStream class also has methods mapToDouble and mapToLong. The DoubleStream and LongStream classes have similar methods.

19.8.3 Processing Primitive-Type Streams

An IntStream has all the methods for streams that you have seen in the preceding sections. Some of them are adjusted for the fact that the stream contains int values and not objects. For example, the toArray method yields an int[] array.

In addition to the count method, primitive-type streams have four additional methods that yield a numeric result: sum, average, max, and min. For example,

Primitive-type streams have methods sum, average, max, and min.

```
int sumOfLengths = words
    .mapToInt(w -> w.length())
    .sum();
```

yields the sum of all word lengths. Unlike the max and min methods for arbitrary streams, the max and min methods for primitive streams do not require a comparator.

The average method returns an OptionalDouble, because the stream might be empty. That type is just like an Optional<Double>, except that it holds a double value, not a Double wrapper. As with all Optional values, it is best to use orElse to obtain the wrapped value or an alternative.

```
double average = words
    .mapToInt(w -> w.length())
    .average()
    .orElse(0);
```

Table 5 Computing Results from a Stream<T>

Example	Comments
stream.count()	Yields the number of elements as a long value.
stream.findFirst() stream.findAny()	Yields the first, or an arbitrary element as an Optional<T>—see Section 19.6.
stream.max(*comparator*) stream.min(*comparator*)	Yields the largest or smallest element as an Optional<T>—see Section 19.7.
pstream.sum() pstream.average() pstream.max() pstream.min()	The sum, average, maximum, or minimum of a primitive-type stream—see Section 19.8.
stream.allMatch(*condition*) stream.anyMatch(*condition*) stream.noneMatch(*condition*)	Yields a boolean variable indicating whether all, any, or no elements match the condition—see Section 19.7.
stream.forEach(*action*)	Carries out the action on all stream elements—see Section 19.7.

Similarly, the max and min methods of the IntStream class return an OptionalInt because they might be invoked on an empty stream.

The DoubleStream and LongStream classes have equivalent methods, with return types that match the element type.

EXAMPLE CODE See your eText or companion code for a program that shows how to work with primitive-type streams.

19.9 Grouping Results

So far, you have seen how to put data into a stream, transform it, and obtain a result. Sometimes, you would like to split a stream into *groups* and then get a result for each group.

To form a group, call

© pong6400/iStockphoto.

A grouping collector gathers groups of related elements.

```
stream.collect(Collectors.groupingBy(function))
```

The function determines a "key" for each element in the stream. Elements with the same key form a group.

Like all calls to collect, this is a terminal operation, yielding a non-stream result. The result is a map that associates each key with its group.

Let's try this with a stream of words and a key function w -> w.substring(0, 1). That is, the key for each element is the first letter.

```
Map<String, List<String>> groups = Stream.of(words)
    .collect(Collectors.groupingBy(
        w -> w.substring(0, 1))); // The function for extracting the keys
```

The result is a map, where groups.get("a") is a list of all words starting with the letter a, groups.get("b") has all words starting with b, and so on.

It is nice to be able to split a stream into groups, but you can do even more. You can process each group with a *collector*. In Section 19.3, you saw the methods Collectors.toSet and Collectors.joining that yield collectors.

For example, if you prefer to have sets of strings instead of lists, use

```
Map<String, Set<String>> groupOfSets = Stream.of(words)
    .collect(Collectors.groupingBy(
        w -> w.substring(0, 1), // The function for extracting the keys
        Collectors.toSet())); // The group collector
```

There are two collectors. The groupingBy collector collects the stream into a map. The toSet collector collects each group into a set.

There are several collectors for computing a count, sum, average, maximum, or minimum in each group. (You can't use the stream methods that you have already seen because the groups are lists, not streams.)

To count each group, pass Collectors.counting():

```
Map<String, Long> groupCounts = Stream.of(words)
    .collect(Collectors.groupingBy(
        w -> w.substring(0, 1),
        Collectors.counting()));
```

This is a pretty interesting result. You get to find out how many words start with each letter.

The summingInt, summingDouble, and summingLong collectors apply a function to each element in a group. The sum is associated with the group key.

As an example, here is how to compute the total population of each continent from a stream of countries:

```
Map<String, Long> groupSum = countries.collect(
    Collectors.groupingBy(
        c -> c.getContinent(), // The function for extracting the keys
        Collectors.summingLong(
            c -> c.getPopulation()))); // The function for getting the summands
```

Note that there are two functions: one for extracting the key, and one for getting the values that are being summed.

The averagingInt, averagingDouble, and averagingLong collectors work just like the summing collectors, but they collect the averages for each group.

To get the largest or smallest element in each group, use maxBy or minBy, with a comparison function. Here is a map of the longest strings for each letter:

```
Map<String, Optional<String>> groupLongest = Stream.of(words)
    .collect(
        Collectors.groupingBy(
            w -> w.substring(0, 1), // The function for extracting the keys
            Collectors.maxBy(
                (v, w) -> v.length() - w.length()))); // The comparator function
```

The following program shows the grouping operations in action. See Worked Example 19.1 and Worked Example 19.2 for examples of forming groups with real-world data.

sec09/GroupDemo.java

```
 1  import java.util.List;
 2  import java.util.Map;
 3  import java.util.Optional;
 4  import java.util.Set;
 5  import java.util.stream.Stream;
 6  import java.util.stream.Collectors;
 7
 8  public class GroupDemo
 9  {
10     public static void main(String[] args)
11     {
12        String[] words = ("how much wood would a woodchuck chuck "
13           + "if a woodchuck could chuck wood").split(" ");
14
15        Map<String, List<String>> groups = Stream.of(words)
16           .collect(Collectors.groupingBy(
17              w -> w.substring(0, 1)));
18        System.out.println("Lists by first letter: " + groups);
19
20        Map<String, Set<String>> groupOfSets = Stream.of(words)
21           .collect(Collectors.groupingBy(
22              w -> w.substring(0, 1), // The function for extracting the keys
23              Collectors.toSet())); // The group collector
24        System.out.println("Sets by first letter: "
25           + groupOfSets);
26
27        Map<String, Long> groupCounts = Stream.of(words)
28           .collect(Collectors.groupingBy(
```

```
29              w -> w.substring(0, 1),
30              Collectors.counting()));
31       System.out.println("Counts by first letter: "
32          + groupCounts);
33
34       Map<String, Optional<String>> groupLongest = Stream.of(words)
35          .collect(
36             Collectors.groupingBy(
37                w -> w.substring(0, 1), // The function for extracting the keys
38                Collectors.maxBy(
39                   (v, w) -> v.length() - w.length())));
40                   // The comparator function
41       System.out.println("Longest word by first letter: "
42          + groupLongest);
43    }
44 }
```

Program Run

```
Lists by first letter: {a=[a, a], c=[chuck, could, chuck],
w=[wood, would, woodchuck, woodchuck, wood], h=[how], i=[if], m=[much]}
Sets by first letter: {a=[a], c=[could, chuck], w=[would, woodchuck, wood],
h=[how], i=[if], m=[much]}
Counts by first letter: {a=2, c=3, w=5, h=1, i=1, m=1}
Longest word by first letter: {a=Optional[a], c=Optional[chuck],
w=Optional[woodchuck], h=Optional[how], i=Optional[if], m=Optional[much]}
```

EXAMPLE CODE   See your eText or companion code for a second demonstration program.

19.10 Common Algorithms Revisited

Many common processing tasks that involve sequences of values can be carried out easily with streams.

In Sections 6.7 and 7.3, you saw a number of common algorithms for sequences of values. Many of them are quite a bit easier with streams. Let's revisit them and see how using streams simplifies them.

19.10.1 Filling

To fill an array with squares (0, 1, 4, 9, 16, ...), you can use a loop

```
int[] squares = new int[n];
for (int i = 0; i < squares.length; i++)
{
   squares[i] = i * i;
}
```

With streams, you start out with a range and map it to the desired form.

```
int[] squares = IntStream.range(0, n)
   .map(i -> i * i)
   .toArray();
```

The stream form is shorter and, with a bit of practice, easier to understand.

19.10.2 Sum, Average, Maximum, and Minimum

© CEFutcher/iStockphoto.

Chapter 7 had explicit loops for what are simply method calls with streams.

```
double[] values = . . .;
double total = DoubleStream.of(values).sum();
double average = DoubleStream.of(values).average().orElse(0);
double largest = DoubleStream.of(values).max().orElse(Double.MIN_VALUE);
double smallest = DoubleStream.of(values).min().orElse(Double.MAX_VALUE);
```

The elegance of streams becomes even more convincing when you process objects, not numbers. Here is the loop for computing the average area from a list of countries:

```
double total = 0;
for (Country country : countries)
{
    total = total + country.getArea();
}
double average = 0;
if (values.length > 0) { average = total / countries.size(); }
```

With streams, that computation is much simpler:

```
double average = countries.stream()
    .mapToDouble(c -> c.getArea())
    .average()
    .orElse(0);
```

19.10.3 Counting Matches

In Chapter 6, you saw how to count the number of spaces in a string.

```
int spaces = 0;
for (int i = 0; i < str.length(); i++)
{
    char ch = str.charAt(i);
    if (ch == ' ')
    {
        spaces++;
    }
}
```

© Hiob/iStockphoto.

In a loop that counts matches, a counter is incremented whenever a match is found.

In general, it is easy to count matches in a stream by filtering and counting. To express this example with streams, turn the string into a stream instead of looping over the positions.

```
long spaces = str.codePoints()
    .filter(ch -> ch == ' ')
    .count();
```

19.10.4 Element Separators

You need one fewer separator than elements to separate values with commas or vertical lines, such as

32 | 54 | 67.5 | 29 | 35

In Chapter 7, this was solved like this:

```
double[] values = . . .;
String result = "";
for (int i = 0; i < values.length; i++)
{
   if (i > 0)
   {
      result = result + " | ";
   }
   result = result + values[i];
}
```

© trutenka/iStockphoto.

To print five elements, you need four separators.

With streams, this is easily done with the `joining` collector, but you first have to convert the values to strings:

```
String result = DoubleStream.of(values)
   .mapToObj(v -> "" + v)
   .collect(Collectors.joining(" | "));
```

19.10.5 Linear Search

© yekorzh/Getty Images.

To search for a specific element, visit the elements and stop when you encounter the match.

With streams, it is very easy to search for a match. Suppose you are asked for the first value larger than 100 in an array. That is

```
OptionalDouble result = DoubleStream.of(values)
   .filter(v -> v > 100)
   .findFirst();
```

But the example in Chapter 7 asked for the first element that is *equal* to 100. When you call `filter(v -> v == 100).findFirst()`, you either get 100 or no match, whereas in Chapter 7, you also got the position of the match. If you want that with streams, use a stream of positions:

```
int n = values.length;
int pos = IntStream.range(0, n)
   .filter(i -> values[i] == 100)
   .findFirst()
   .orElse(-1);
```

19.10.6 Comparing Adjacent Values

Section 6.7.6 has an algorithm for finding adjacent values in a sequence of inputs:

```
double input = in.nextDouble();
while (in.hasNextDouble())
{
   double previous = input;
   input = in.nextDouble();
   if (input == previous) { System.out.println("Duplicate input"); }
}
```

Streams are not easily applicable to algorithms that compare adjacent elements of a sequence.

This is an example of an algorithm that cannot easily be adapted to Java streams. Stream operations such as `map`, `filter`, and `findFirst` process their elements in isolation, without looking at their neighbors. It is possible to overcome this by storing the previous value (see Exercise ••• E19.20). But that solution doesn't work for parallel streams.

Streams are not a solution for all data processing problems, but as you have seen, in many common cases they offer a solution that is clearer than a loop.

EXAMPLE CODE   See your eText or companion code for a program demonstrating algorithms adapted to use streams.

HOW TO 19.1

Working with Streams

Streams are particularly useful for extracting information from large real-world data sets. This How To tells you how to process a data set by transforming the data and extracting the features of interest.

© FONG_KWONG_CHO/iStockphoto.

Step 1   Get the data.

Generally, when you are asked to process a data set, you need to work at getting it into a form that a Java program can handle. A stream is a sequence of objects of a particular class that describes the data, so you need to design that class first. Suppose you process information about movies. Then you need a class Movie, with the information that is in your data set, such as the title, director, actors, and so on. (See Worked Example 19.2 for more on this particular example.) Similarly, if you process data about countries, you will want a Country class.

Next, you need to read the data. If you are lucky, the data is in a text file in a format that you can easily process, using the principles that you learned in Chapter 11. But sometimes, data is in a spreadsheet. Then you should export the data into a text format called CSV (comma-separated values). A row in such a file might look like

```
United States,North America,318892103
```

You can easily read such a row, split it into fields, and build a Country object.

If the fields can contain commas, choose a different field separator (such as the | character) before exporting your data.

You can now read the data into a list, such as an ArrayList<Country> if you are processing Country objects.

Step 2   Make a stream.

If you read your data into an array list, just call the stream method and you have your stream.

```
List<Country> countryList = new ArrayList<>();
// Fill countryList
Stream<Country> countries = countryList.stream();
```

Alternatively, if it happens that your input file has one line per item, then you can use a more efficient approach. First read in a stream of lines and then transform each line into an object. For example,

```
try (Stream<String> lines = Files.lines(path))
{
    Stream<Country> countries = lines.map(line -> Country.parse(line));
    . . .
}
```

The parse method is a static helper method that breaks an input line into fields and constructs a Country object.

Step 3   Transform the stream.

Often, you will want to analyze just a part of the provided data; perhaps only the movies since 1990 or only countries in Africa. Then you use filter to pick the desired items.

```
Stream<Country> africanCountries = countries
    .filter(c -> c.getContinent().equals("Africa"));
```

At times, you may only be interested in a part of the data, or you want the data in a different form. Then you use the map method to transform the items. For example, if you only care about the continents,

```
Stream<String> continents = countries.map(c -> c.getContinent());
```

When you map to a numeric type, you should use the methods mapToInt, mapToLong, or mapToDouble. The resulting primitive-type streams store their values more efficiently than object streams, and you can compute their sums and averages.

The sorted method sorts the elements of the stream.

Another useful transformation is the distinct method that drops duplicates from the stream.

Of course, you can combine these operations. Here are the continents that have countries with at least a hundred million inhabitants:

```
Stream<String> continentsWithPopulousCountries = countries
    .filter(c -> c.getPopulation() >= 100000000)
    .map(c -> c.getContinent())
    .distinct();
```

Sometimes, it is not so obvious what you want to do with the stream elements. You may want to skip ahead to the next step and figure out what the stream should look like so that you can easily collect the desired result, then figure out how to transform it.

Step 4   Collect the results.

There are four kinds of result that you can harvest from a stream, and we'll look at each in turn:

1. A single element from the stream
2. A collection of values
3. A count, sum, or average
4. A map that associates groups with group properties

A single element can be one of the following:

- The largest or smallest, by some ordering: max, min
- The first, or any, element fulfilling a condition: filter followed by findFirst or findAny

For example, in a stream of countries, you may want to find the one with the largest population, or any country with a population of at least a hundred million:

```
Optional<Country> aPopulousCountry = countries
    .filter(country -> country.getPopulation() > 100_000_000)
    .findAny();
```

Now suppose you want to collect multiple values. If you like, you can restrict the number of values with the limit method before you collect the result. For example, adding limit(10) to the processing pipeline returns at most ten elements.

You need to decide where you want your answer:

- In an array: toArray(*ElementType*::new)
- In a list: collect(Collectors.toList())
- In a set: collect(Collectors.toSet())
- In a string: collect(Collectors.joining(", "))

For example, suppose you want the ten most populous countries in a list. This requires a little cleverness. Because limit(10) yields the *first* ten values, you want to sort so that the most populous elements are at the beginning of the stream. You can flip the comparison like this:

```
List<Country> mostPopulous = countries
    .sorted((c, d) -> Double.compare(d.getPopulation(), c.getPopulation()))
    .limit(10)
    .collect(Collectors.toList());
```

In the preceding cases, the result consisted of one or more stream values. Sometimes, you want a summary value instead. You have these choices:

- The count of the elements: count
- The sum, average, maximum, or minimum of a numeric stream: sum, average, max, min
- A boolean indicating whether all, some, or none of the stream elements fulfill a condition: allMatch, anyMatch, noneMatch

For example, to get the average population, first transform countries to populations, and then get the average:

```
double average = countries
    .mapToInt(country -> country.getPopulation())
    .average()
    .orElse(0);
```

The call to orElse is necessary because average returns an OptionalDouble.

Finally, let's look at the most complex case, where each element belongs to a group, and you want to collect results for each group. First, you need to come up with a function that yields the group of an element. If you want to group countries by continent, that function is c -> c.getContinent(). If you want to group them by the first letter of the name, use the function c -> c.getName().substring(0, 1).

You pass that function to the groupingBy method. The result is a map. If you do nothing else, each group key is associated with a list of the group's elements. The call

```
Map<String, List<Country>> countriesByContinent = countries
    .collect(
        Collectors.groupingBy(c -> c.getContinent()));
```

yields a map, where, for example, countriesByContinent.get("Africa") is a list of all countries in Africa.

You can apply another collector to each group, computing

- The number of group elements: counting
- The sum of a numeric attribute: summingInt, summingDouble, summingLong
- The average of a numeric attribute: averagingInt, averagingDouble, averagingLong
- The largest or smallest element, as determined by a comparator: maxBy, minBy

Here is how you can get the average population per continent:

```
Map<String, Double> averagePopulationByContinent = countries
    .collect(
        Collectors.groupingBy(
            c -> c.getContinent(),
            Collectors.averagingInt(c -> c.getPopulation())));
```

EXAMPLE CODE   See your eText or companion code for the example code from this How To.

WORKED EXAMPLE 19.1

Word Properties

Learn how to use streams to find words with interesting properties. See your eText or visit wiley.com/go/bjeo7.

© iStock.com/tigermad.

WORKED EXAMPLE 19.2

A Movie Database

Learn how to analyze a large database of movies and use streams to obtain interesting statistics from the data. See your eText or visit wiley.com/go/bjeo7.

© Ivan Cholakov/iStockphoto.

CHAPTER SUMMARY

Understand the concept of streams.

- A stream is an immutable sequence of values that are processed lazily.
- Lazy processing means to defer operations until they are needed, and to skip those that are not needed.

Be able to create streams.

- The Stream.of static method and the stream methods of collection classes yield streams.

Collect results from streams.

- To turn a stream into an array or collection, use the toArray or collect methods.

Determine how to transform streams into a form from which you can collect results.

- The map method applies a function to all elements of a stream, yielding another stream.
- The filter method yields a stream of all elements fulfilling a condition.

Master the syntax of lambda expressions.

- A lambda expression consists of one or more parameter variables, an arrow ->, and an expression or block yielding the result.
- A functional interface is an interface with a single abstract method.
- A lambda expression can be converted to an instance of a functional interface.

Work with values of the Optional type.

- The Optional class is a wrapper for objects that may or may not be present.
- Use the orElse method to obtain the value of an Optional or, if no value is present, an alternative.

Know the terminal stream operations.

- A terminal operation triggers the lazy operations on a stream and yields a non-stream value.

Work with streams that contain values of primitive types.

- The `IntStream.range` method yields a stream of consecutive integers.
- The `mapToInt` method applies an `int`-valued function to stream elements and yields an `IntStream`.
- Primitive-type streams have methods `sum`, `average`, `max`, and `min`.

Group stream results with common characteristics.

- Using grouping collectors, you can group together elements with the same key.
- A grouping collector can apply another collector to each group.

Express common algorithms with stream operations.

- Many common processing tasks that involve sequences of values can be carried out easily with streams.
- Streams are not easily applicable to algorithms that compare adjacent elements of a sequence.

STANDARD LIBRARY ITEMS INTRODUCED IN THIS CHAPTER

java.util.Collection<T>
  stream
java.util.Comparator<T>
  comparing
  thenComparing
java.util.stream.Collectors
  averagingDouble, averagingInt,
    averagingLong
  counting
  groupingBy
  joining
  maxBy
  minBy
  summingDouble, summingInt,
    summingLong
  toList
  toSet
java.util.stream.DoubleStream
java.util.stream.IntStream
java.util.stream.LongStream
  mapToObj
  of
  range (use with IntStream only)

java.nio.file.Files
  lines
java.util.Optional<T>
java.util.OptionalDouble
java.util.OptionalInt
java.util.OptionalLong
  empty
  get
  getAsDouble, getAsInt,
    getAsLong
  ifPresent
  isPresent
  of
  orElse
java.util.function.Predicate<T>
  test
java.util.stream.Stream<T>
  allMatch
  anyMatch
  collect
  count
  distinct
  filter

findAny
findFirst
forEach
generate
iterate
limit
map
mapToDouble, mapToInt,
  mapToLong
noneMatch
of
parallel
skip
sorted
toArray
java.lang.String
  codePoints

■ **R19.1** Provide expressions that compute the following information about a Stream<String>.

   a. How many elements start with the letter a?

   b. How many elements of length greater than ten start with the letter a?

   c. Are there at least 100 elements that start with the letter a? (Don't count them all if there are more.)

■■ **R19.2** How can you collect five long words (that is, with more than ten letters) from an ArrayList<String> without using streams? Compare your solution with the code fragment in Section 19.1. Which is easier to understand? Why?

■ **R19.3** What is the difference between these two expressions?

```
words.filter(w -> w.length() > 10).limit(100).count()
words.limit(100).filter(w -> w.length() > 10).count()
```

■■ **R19.4** Give three ways of making a Stream<String> (or five, including the ones described in Special Topic 19.1).

■ **R19.5** How can you place all elements from a Stream<Integer> into

   a. a List<Integer>?

   b. an Integer[] array?

   c. an int[] array?

■ **R19.6** How do you turn a Stream<Double> into a Stream<String>, with each number turned into the equivalent string? How do you turn it back into a Stream<Double>?

■■ **R19.7** Give three ways of making a lambda expression that applies the length method to a String (or four if you read Special Topic 19.2).

■■ **R19.8** Given an Optional<String>, what are three different ways of printing it when it is present and not printing anything when it isn't? Which of these can be adapted to print the string "None" if no string is present?

■ **R19.9** Describe five different ways of producing an IntStream. Which of them can be adapted to producing a DoubleStream?

■■ **R19.10** Suppose you want to find the length of the longest string in a stream. Describe two approaches: using mapToInt followed by the max method of the IntStream class, and calling the max method of Stream<String>. What are the advantages and disadvantages of each approach?

■ **R19.11** List all terminal operations on object streams and primitive-type streams that have been discussed in this chapter.

■ **R19.12** List all collectors that were introduced in this chapter.

■■ **R19.13** Explain the values used in the orElse clauses in Section 19.10.2.

PRACTICE EXERCISES

■ **E19.1**   Write a program that reads all lines from a file and, using a Stream<String>, prints how many of them contain the word "the".

■ **E19.2**   Write a program that reads all words from a file and, using a Stream<String>, prints how many of them are the word "the".

■ **E19.3**   Write a program that reads all lines from a file and, using a Stream<String>, prints all lines containing the word "the".

■■ **E19.4**   Write a program that reads all words from a file and, using a Stream<String>, prints all distinct words with at most four letters (in some order).

■■■ **E19.5**   Write a method

```
public static <T> String toString(Stream<T> stream, int n)
```

that turns a Stream<T> into a comma-separated list of its first n elements.

■■ **E19.6**   The static getAvailableCurrencies method of the java.util.Currency class yields a set of Currency objects. Turn it into a stream and transform it into a stream of the currency display names. Print them in sorted order.

© Jaap2/iStockphoto.

■■ **E19.7**   Write a lambda expression for a function that turns a string into a string made of the first letter, three periods, and the last letter, such as "W...d". (Assume the string has at least two letters.) Then write a program that reads words into a stream, applies the lambda expression to each element, and prints the result. Filter out any words with fewer than two letters.

■ **E19.8**   Write a program that sorts an array of bank accounts by increasing balance. Pass an appropriate lambda expression to Arrays.sort.

■ **E19.9**   Write a program that reads in words from a file and prompts the user for another word. Print the longest word from the file that contains the given word, or "No match" if the word does not occur in the file. Use the max method of Stream<String>.

■■ **E19.10**   Write a method

```
public static Optional<Integer> smallestProperDivisor(int n)
```

that returns the smallest proper divisor of n or, if n is a prime number, a value indicating that no result is present.

■■ **E19.11**   Write a program that reads an integer n and then prints all squares of the integers from 1 to n that are palindromes (that is, their decimal representation equals its reverse). Use IntStream.range, map, and filter.

■■ **E19.12**   Write a method

```
public static Stream<String> characters(String str)
```

that yields a stream of strings of length 1 that contains the characters of the string str. Use the codePoints method and skip code points greater than 65535. Extra credit if you don't skip them and instead produce strings of length 2.

■■ **E19.13** Read all words from a file and print the one with the maximum number of vowels. Use a Stream<String> and the max method. Extra credit if you define the comparator with the Comparator.comparing method described in Special Topic 19.4.

■■ **E19.14** Read all words from a file into an ArrayList<String>, then turn it into a parallel stream. Use the dictionary file words.txt provided with the book's companion code. Use filters and the findAny method to find any palindrome that has at least five letters, then print the word. What happens when you run the program multiple times?

■■ **E19.15** Read all words in a file and group them by length. Print out how many words of each length are in the file. Use collect and Collectors.groupingBy.

■■ **E19.16** Read all words in a file and group them by the first letter (in lowercase). Print the average word length for each initial letter. Use collect and Collectors.groupingBy.

■■ **E19.17** Assume that a BankAccount class has methods for yielding the account owner's name and the current balance. Write a function that, given a list of bank accounts, produces a map that associates owner names with the total balance in all their accounts. Use collect and Collectors.groupingBy.

■■ **E19.18** Write a program that reads a Stream<Country> from a file that contains country names and numbers for the population and area. Print the most densely populated country.

© Oksana Perkins/iStockphoto.

■■ **E19.19** Write a function that returns a list of all positions of a given character in a string. Produce two versions—one with streams and one without. Which one is easier to implement?

■■■ **E19.20** Find all adjacent duplicates of a Stream<String>, by using a predicate that compares each element against the previous one (stashed away in an array of length 1), updates the array, and returns the result of the comparison. You have to be careful with the first element.

© tingberg/iStockphoto.

PROGRAMMING PROJECTS

■■ **P19.1** In a stream of random integers, filter out the even ones, call limit(n), and count the result. Set n to 10, 100, 1000, and so on. Measure the amount of time these operations take with a regular stream and a parallel stream. How big does n have to be for parallel streams to be faster on your computer?

■■ **P19.2** Write a program that generates an infinite stream of integers that are perfect squares and then displays the first *n* of them that are palindromes (that is, their decimal representation equals its reverse). Extra credit if you use BigInteger so that you can find solutions of arbitrary length.

■■■ **P19.3** Repeat Exercise •• P19.2 with prime numbers instead of perfect squares.

■■■ **P19.4** Produce an infinite stream that contains the factorials 1!, 2!, 3!, and so on. *Hint:* First produce a stream containing arrays [1, 1!], [2, 2!], [3, 3!], and so on. Use BigInteger values for the factorials.

▪▪ **P19.5** Worked Example 19.1 showed you how to find all words with five distinct vowels (which might occur more than once). Using a similar approach, find all words in which each vowel occurs exactly once.

▪▪ **P19.6** Using an approach similar to that in Worked Example 19.1, find all words with length of at least ten in which no letter is repeated. What is the longest one? How many such words exist for each length?

▪▪ **P19.7** Using an approach similar to that in Worked Example 19.1, find all words with exactly one vowel (which might be repeated). What is the longest one? How many such words exist for each length?

▪▪ **P19.8** Perhaps the reason that so many movie titles start with the letter A is that their first word is "A" or "An"? Count how many movies in the data set of Worked Example 19.2 start with these words.

▪▪ **P19.9** What are the 100 most common initial words in movie titles contained in the data set in Worked Example 19.2?

▪▪▪ **P19.10** Write a program to determine how many actors there are in the data set in Worked Example 19.2. Note that many actors are in multiple movies. The challenge in this assignment is that each movie has a list of actors, not a single actor, and there is no ready-made collector to form the union of these lists. However, there is another `collect` method that has three parameters:

- A function to generate an instance of the target
- A function to add an element to a target
- A function to merge two targets into one

For example,

```
stream.collect(
    () -> 0,
    (t, e) -> t + e,
    (t, u) -> t + u)
```

computes the sum of elements in a `Stream<Integer>`. Note that the last function is only needed for parallel streams.

Define methods for generating a set, adding a list of actors into one, and for combining two sets.

▪▪▪ **P19.11** Write a program to determine the 100 actors with the most movies, and the number of movies in which they appear. For each movie, produce a map whose keys are the actors, all with value 1. Merge those maps as in Exercise ●●● P19.10. Then extract the top 100 actors from a stream of actors.

▪▪▪ **P19.12** Find an online database with a large number of cities and their locations. Write a program that prints all cities within a given distance from a location. (You will need to find a formula for computing the distance between two points on Earth.)

CHAPTER 20

GRAPHICAL USER INTERFACES

© Carlos Santa Maria/iStockphoto.

CHAPTER GOALS

To use layout managers to arrange user-interface components in a container

To use text components to capture and display text in a graphical application

To become familiar with common user-interface components, such as radio buttons, check boxes, and menus

To browse the Java documentation effectively

CHAPTER CONTENTS

The graphical applications with which you are familiar have many visual gadgets for information entry: text fields, buttons, scroll bars, menus, and so on. In this chapter, you will learn how to create programs that use the most common user-interface components in the Java Swing toolkit. We also show you how to effectively use the documentation for Swing components, so you can make use of additional components in your applications.

20.1 Layout Management

Up to now, you have had limited control over the layout of user-interface components. You learned how to add components to a panel, and the panel arranged the components from left to right. In this section, you will see how to achieve more sophisticated arrangements.

20.1.1 Using Layout Managers

User-interface components are arranged by placing them inside containers. Containers can be placed inside larger containers.

Each container has a layout manager that directs the arrangement of its components.

Three useful layout managers are the border layout, flow layout, and grid layout.

In Java, you build up user interfaces by adding components into containers such as **panels**. Each container has its own **layout manager**, which determines how components are laid out.

By default, a JPanel uses a **flow layout**. A flow layout simply arranges its components from left to right and starts a new row when there is no more room in the current row.

Another commonly used layout manager is the **border layout**. The border layout groups components into five areas: center, north, south, west, and east (see Figure 1). Each area can hold a single component, or it can be empty.

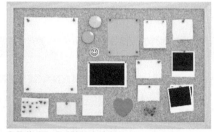

© Felix Mockel/iStockphoto.

A layout manager arranges user-interface components.

The border layout is the default layout manager for a frame (or, more technically, the frame's content pane). But you can also use the border layout in a panel:

```
panel.setLayout(new BorderLayout());
```

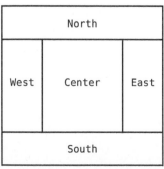

Figure 1
Components Expand to Fill
Space in the Border Layout

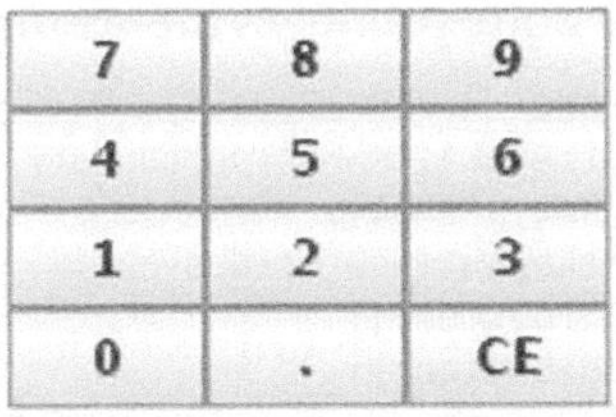

Figure 2
The Grid Layout

When adding a component to a container with the border layout, specify the NORTH, SOUTH, WEST, EAST, or CENTER position.

Now the panel is controlled by a border layout, not the flow layout. When adding a component, you specify the position, like this:

```
panel.add(component, BorderLayout.NORTH);
```

The content pane of a frame has a border layout by default. A panel has a flow layout by default.

The **grid layout** manager arranges components in a grid with a fixed number of rows and columns. All components are resized so that they all have the same width and height. Like the border layout, it also expands each component to fill the entire allotted area. (If that is not desirable, you need to place each component inside a panel.) Figure 2 shows a number pad panel that uses a grid layout. To create a grid layout, you supply the number of rows and columns in the constructor, then add the components, row by row, left to right:

```
JPanel buttonPanel = new JPanel();
buttonPanel.setLayout(new GridLayout(4, 3));
buttonPanel.add(button7);
buttonPanel.add(button8);
buttonPanel.add(button9);
buttonPanel.add(button4);
. . .
```

20.1.2 Achieving Complex Layouts

Sometimes you want to have a tabular arrangement of components where columns have different sizes or one component spans multiple columns. A more complex layout manager called the *grid bag layout* can handle these situations. The grid bag layout is quite complex to use, however, and we do not cover it in this book. Another manager, the *group layout*, is designed for use by interactive tools—see Programming Tip 20.1.

Fortunately, you can create acceptable-looking layouts in nearly all situations by nesting panels. You give each panel an appropriate layout manager. Panels don't have visible borders, so you can use as many panels as you need to organize your components. Figure 3 shows an example. The keypad buttons are contained in a panel with grid layout. That panel is itself contained in a larger panel with border layout. The label is in the northern position of the larger panel.

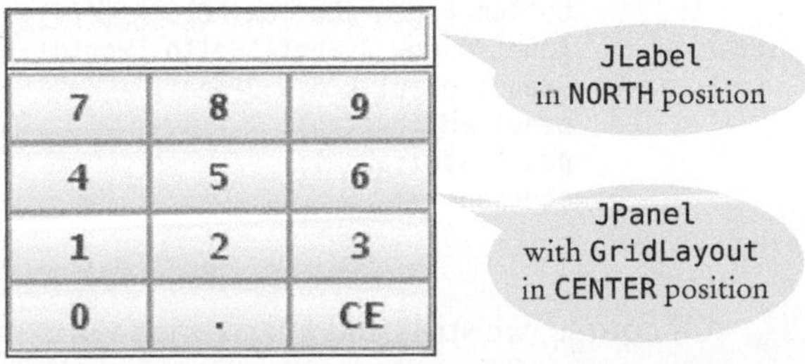

Figure 3
Nesting Panels

The following code produces the arrangement in Figure 3:

```
JPanel keypadPanel = new JPanel();
keypadPanel.setLayout(new BorderLayout());
buttonPanel = new JPanel();
buttonPanel.setLayout(new GridLayout(4, 3));
buttonPanel.add(button7);
buttonPanel.add(button8);
// . . .
keypadPanel.add(buttonPanel, BorderLayout.CENTER);
JLabel display = new JLabel("0");
keypadPanel.add(display, BorderLayout.NORTH);
```

EXAMPLE CODE   See your eText or companion code for the code for a calculator's user interface.

20.1.3 Using Inheritance to Customize Frames

As you add more user-interface components to a frame, the frame can get quite complex. Your programs will become easier to understand when you use inheritance for complex frames.

To do so, design a subclass of JFrame. Store the components as instance variables. Initialize them in the constructor of your subclass. This approach makes it easy to add helper methods for organizing your code.

It is also a good idea to set the frame size in the frame constructor. The frame usually has a better idea of the preferred size than the program displaying it.

For example,

```
public class FilledFrame extends JFrame
{
    // Use instance variables for components
    private JButton button;
    private JLabel label;

    private static final int FRAME_WIDTH = 300;
    private static final int FRAME_HEIGHT = 100;

    public FilledFrame()
    {
        // Now we can use a helper method
        createComponents();

        // It is a good idea to set the size in the frame constructor
        setSize(FRAME_WIDTH, FRAME_HEIGHT);
    }

    private void createComponents()
    {
        button = new JButton("Click me!");
        label = new JLabel("Hello, World!");
        JPanel panel = new JPanel();
        panel.add(button);
        panel.add(label);
        add(panel);
    }
}
```

Of course, we still need a class with a main method:

```
public class FilledFrameViewer2
{
   public static void main(String[] args)
   {
      JFrame frame = new FilledFrame();
      frame.setTitle("A frame with two components");
      frame.setDefaultCloseOperation(JFrame.EXIT_ON_CLOSE);
      frame.setVisible(true);
   }
}
```

EXAMPLE CODE   See your eText or companion code for the complete FilledFrame program.

Common Error 20.1

By Default, Components Have Zero Width and Height

You must be careful when you add a painted component, such as a component displaying a car, to a panel. You add the component in the same way as a button or label:

```
panel.add(button);
panel.add(label);
panel.add(carComponent);
```

However, the default size for a component is 0 by 0 pixels, and the car component will not be visible. The remedy is to call the setPreferredSize method, like this:

```
carComponent.setPreferredSize(new Dimension(CAR_COMPONENT_WIDTH, CAR_COMPONENT_HEIGHT));
```

This is an issue only for painted components. Buttons, labels, and so on know how to compute their preferred size.

Special Topic 20.1

Adding the main Method to the Frame Class

Have another look at the FilledFrame and FilledFrameViewer2 classes. Some programmers prefer to combine these two classes, by adding the main method to the frame class:

```
public class FilledFrame extends JFrame
{
   . . .
   public static void main(String[] args)
   {
      JFrame frame = new FilledFrame();
      frame.setTitle("A frame with two components");
      frame.setDefaultCloseOperation(JFrame.EXIT_ON_CLOSE);
      frame.setVisible(true);
   }

   public FilledFrame()
   {
      createComponents();
      setSize(FRAME_WIDTH, FRAME_HEIGHT);
   }
   . . .
}
```

This is a convenient shortcut that you will find in many programs, but it does not separate the responsibilities between the frame class and the program.

20.2 Processing Text Input

We continue our discussion with graphical user interfaces that accept text input. Of course, a graphical application can receive text input by calling the showInputDialog method of the JOptionPane class, but popping up a separate dialog box for each input is not a natural user interface. Most graphical programs collect text input through *text components* (see Figure 4 and Figure 6). In the following two sections, you will learn how to add text components to a graphical application, and how to read what the user types into them.

20.2.1 Text Fields

Use a JTextField component for reading a single line of input. Place a JLabel next to each text field.

The JTextField class provides a **text field** for reading a single line of text. When you construct a text field, you need to supply the width—the approximate number of characters that you expect the user to type:

```
final int FIELD_WIDTH = 10;
rateField = new JTextField(FIELD_WIDTH);
```

Users can type additional characters, but then a part of the contents of the field becomes invisible.

You will want to label each text field so that the user knows what to type into it. Construct a JLabel object for each label:

```
JLabel rateLabel = new JLabel("Interest Rate: ");
```

You want to give the user an opportunity to enter all information into the text field before processing it. Therefore, you should supply a button that the user can press to indicate that the input is ready for processing.

When that button is clicked, its actionPerformed method should read the user input from each text field, using the getText method of the JTextField class. The getText method returns a String object. In our sample program, we turn the string into a number, using the Double.parseDouble method. After updating the account, we show the balance in another label.

```
class AddInterestListener implements ActionListener
{
    public void actionPerformed(ActionEvent event)
    {
        double rate = Double.parseDouble(rateField.getText());
        double interest = balance * rate / 100;
        balance = balance + interest;
        resultLabel.setText("Balance: " + balance);
    }
}
```

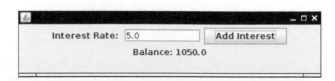

Figure 4 An Application with a Text Field

The following application is a useful prototype for a graphical user-interface front end for arbitrary calculations. You can easily modify it for your own needs. Place input components into the frame. In the actionPerformed method, carry out the needed calculations. Display the result in a label.

sec02_01/InvestmentFrame2.java

```java
1  import java.awt.event.ActionEvent;
2  import java.awt.event.ActionListener;
3  import javax.swing.JButton;
4  import javax.swing.JFrame;
5  import javax.swing.JLabel;
6  import javax.swing.JPanel;
7  import javax.swing.JTextField;
8
9  /**
10    A frame that shows the growth of an investment with variable interest.
11  */
12 public class InvestmentFrame2 extends JFrame
13 {
14    private static final int FRAME_WIDTH = 450;
15    private static final int FRAME_HEIGHT = 100;
16
17    private static final double DEFAULT_RATE = 5;
18    private static final double INITIAL_BALANCE = 1000;
19
20    private JLabel rateLabel;
21    private JTextField rateField;
22    private JButton button;
23    private JLabel resultLabel;
24    private double balance;
25
26    public InvestmentFrame2()
27    {
28       balance = INITIAL_BALANCE;
29
30       resultLabel = new JLabel("Balance: " + balance);
31
32       createTextField();
33       createButton();
34       createPanel();
35
36       setSize(FRAME_WIDTH, FRAME_HEIGHT);
37    }
38
39    private void createTextField()
40    {
41       rateLabel = new JLabel("Interest Rate: ");
42
43       final int FIELD_WIDTH = 10;
44       rateField = new JTextField(FIELD_WIDTH);
45       rateField.setText("" + DEFAULT_RATE);
46    }
47
48    /**
49       Adds interest to the balance and updates the display.
50    */
51    class AddInterestListener implements ActionListener
52    {
```

```
53       public void actionPerformed(ActionEvent event)
54       {
55          double rate = Double.parseDouble(rateField.getText());
56          double interest = balance * rate / 100;
57          balance = balance + interest;
58          resultLabel.setText("Balance: " + balance);
59       }
60    }
61
62    private void createButton()
63    {
64       button = new JButton("Add Interest");
65
66       ActionListener listener = new AddInterestListener();
67       button.addActionListener(listener);
68    }
69
70    private void createPanel()
71    {
72       JPanel panel = new JPanel();
73       panel.add(rateLabel);
74       panel.add(rateField);
75       panel.add(button);
76       panel.add(resultLabel);
77       add(panel);
78    }
79 }
```

20.2.2 Text Areas

Use a JTextArea to show multiple lines of text.

In the preceding section, you saw how to construct text fields. A text field holds a single line of text. To display multiple lines of text, use the JTextArea class.

When constructing a text area, you can specify the number of rows and columns:

```
final int ROWS = 10; // Lines of text
final int COLUMNS = 30; // Characters in each row
JTextArea textArea = new JTextArea(ROWS, COL-
UMNS);
```

Use the setText method to set the text of a text field or text area. The append method adds text to the end of a text area. Use newline characters to separate lines, like this:

```
textArea.append(balance + "\n");
```

If you want to use a text field or text area for display purposes only, call the set-Editable method like this

```
textArea.setEditable(false);
```

Now the user can no longer edit the contents of the field, but your program can still call setText and append to change it.

As shown in Figure 5, the JTextField and JTextArea classes are subclasses of the class JTextComponent. The methods setText and setEditable are declared in the JTextComponent

© Kyoungil Jeon/iStockphoto.

You can use a text area for reading or displaying multi-line text.

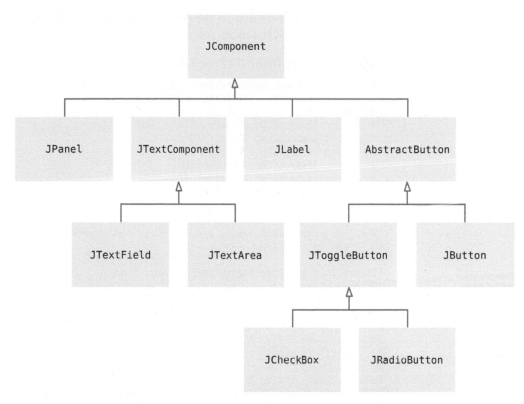

Figure 5   A Part of the Hierarchy of Swing User-Interface Components

class and inherited by JTextField and JTextArea. However, the append method is declared in the JTextArea class.

To add scroll bars to a text area, use a JScrollPane, like this:

```
JTextArea textArea = new JTextArea(ROWS, COLUMNS);
JScrollPane scrollPane = new JScrollPane(textArea);
```

Then add the scroll pane to the panel. Figure 6 shows the result.

The following sample program puts these concepts together. A user can enter numbers into the interest rate text field and then click on the "Add Interest" button. The interest rate is applied, and the updated balance is appended to the text area. The text area has scroll bars and is not editable.

You can add scroll bars to any component with a JScrollPane.

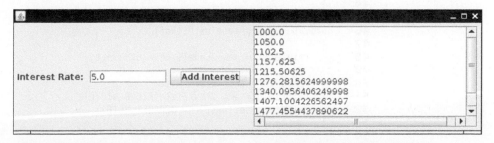

Figure 6   The Investment Application with a Text Area Inside Scroll Bars

This program is similar to the previous investment viewer program, but it keeps track of all the bank balances, not just the last one.

sec02_02/InvestmentFrame3.java

```java
1  import java.awt.event.ActionEvent;
2  import java.awt.event.ActionListener;
3  import javax.swing.JButton;
4  import javax.swing.JFrame;
5  import javax.swing.JLabel;
6  import javax.swing.JPanel;
7  import javax.swing.JScrollPane;
8  import javax.swing.JTextArea;
9  import javax.swing.JTextField;
10
11 /**
12    A frame that shows the growth of an investment with variable interest,
13    using a text area.
14 */
15 public class InvestmentFrame3 extends JFrame
16 {
17    private static final int FRAME_WIDTH = 400;
18    private static final int FRAME_HEIGHT = 250;
19
20    private static final int AREA_ROWS = 10;
21    private static final int AREA_COLUMNS = 30;
22
23    private static final double DEFAULT_RATE = 5;
24    private static final double INITIAL_BALANCE = 1000;
25
26    private JLabel rateLabel;
27    private JTextField rateField;
28    private JButton button;
29    private JTextArea resultArea;
30    private double balance;
31
32    public InvestmentFrame3()
33    {
34       balance = INITIAL_BALANCE;
35       resultArea = new JTextArea(AREA_ROWS, AREA_COLUMNS);
36       resultArea.setText(balance + "\n");
37       resultArea.setEditable(false);
38
39       createTextField();
40       createButton();
41       createPanel();
42
43       setSize(FRAME_WIDTH, FRAME_HEIGHT);
44    }
45
46    private void createTextField()
47    {
48       rateLabel = new JLabel("Interest Rate: ");
49
50       final int FIELD_WIDTH = 10;
51       rateField = new JTextField(FIELD_WIDTH);
52       rateField.setText("" + DEFAULT_RATE);
53    }
54
```

```
55      class AddInterestListener implements ActionListener
56      {
57         public void actionPerformed(ActionEvent event)
58         {
59            double rate = Double.parseDouble(rateField.getText());
60            double interest = balance * rate / 100;
61            balance = balance + interest;
62            resultArea.append(balance + "\n");
63         }
64      }
65
66      private void createButton()
67      {
68         button = new JButton("Add Interest");
69
70         ActionListener listener = new AddInterestListener();
71         button.addActionListener(listener);
72      }
73
74      private void createPanel()
75      {
76         JPanel panel = new JPanel();
77         panel.add(rateLabel);
78         panel.add(rateField);
79         panel.add(button);
80         JScrollPane scrollPane = new JScrollPane(resultArea);
81         panel.add(scrollPane);
82         add(panel);
83      }
84   }
```

20.3 Choices

In the following sections, you will see how to present a finite set of choices to the user. Which Swing component you use depends on whether the choices are mutually exclusive or not, and on the amount of space you have for displaying the choices.

20.3.1 Radio Buttons

For a small set of mutually exclusive choices, use a group of radio buttons or a combo box.

If the choices are mutually exclusive, use a set of **radio buttons**. In a radio button set, only one button can be selected at a time. When the user selects another button in the same set, the previously selected button is automatically turned off. (These buttons are called radio buttons because they work like the station selector buttons on a car radio: If you select a new station, the old station is automatically deselected.) For example, in Figure 7, the font sizes are mutually exclusive. You can select small, medium, or large, but not a combination of them.

© Michele Cornelius/iStockphoto.

In an old fashioned radio, pushing down one station button released the others.

Figure 7 A Combo Box, Check Boxes, and Radio Buttons

To create a set of radio buttons, first create each button individually, then add all buttons in the set to a ButtonGroup object:

```
JRadioButton smallButton = new JRadioButton("Small");
JRadioButton mediumButton = new JRadioButton("Medium");
JRadioButton largeButton = new JRadioButton("Large");

ButtonGroup group = new ButtonGroup();
group.add(smallButton);
group.add(mediumButton);
group.add(largeButton);
```

> Add radio buttons to a ButtonGroup so that only one button in the group is selected at any time.

Note that the button group does *not* place the buttons close to each other in the container. The purpose of the button group is simply to find out which buttons to turn off when one of them is turned on. It is still your job to arrange the buttons on the screen.

The isSelected method is called to find out whether a button is currently selected or not. For example,

```
if (largeButton.isSelected()) { size = LARGE_SIZE; }
```

Unfortunately, there is no convenient way of finding out which button in a group is currently selected. You have to call isSelected on each button. Because users will expect one radio button in a radio button group to be selected, call setSelected(true) on the default radio button before making the enclosing frame visible.

> You can place a border around a panel to group its contents visually.

If you have multiple button groups, it is a good idea to group them together visually. It is a good idea to use a panel for each set of radio buttons, but the panels themselves are invisible. You can add a *border* to a panel to make it visible. In Figure 7, for example, the panels containing the Size radio buttons and Style check boxes have borders.

There are a large number of border types. We will show only a couple of variations and leave it to the border enthusiasts to look up the others in the Swing documentation.

The EtchedBorder class yields a border with a three-dimensional, etched effect. You can add a border to any component, but most commonly you apply it to a panel:

```
JPanel panel = new JPanel();
panel.setBorder(new EtchedBorder());
```

If you want to add a title to the border (as in Figure 7), you need to construct a Titled-Border. You make a titled border by supplying a basic border and then the title you want. Here is a typical example:

```
panel.setBorder(new TitledBorder(new EtchedBorder(), "Size"));
```

20.3.2 Check Boxes

For a binary choice, use a check box.

A **check box** is a user-interface component with two states: checked and unchecked. You use a group of check boxes when one selection does not exclude another. For example, the choices for "Bold" and "Italic" in Figure 7 are not exclusive. You can choose either, both, or neither. Therefore, they are implemented as a set of separate check boxes. Radio buttons and check boxes have different visual appearances. Radio buttons are round and have a black dot when selected. Check boxes are square and have a check mark when selected.

You construct a check box by providing the name in the constructor:

```
JCheckBox italicCheckBox = new JCheckBox("Italic");
```

Because check box settings do not exclude each other, you do not place a set of check boxes inside a button group.

As with radio buttons, you use the isSelected method to find out whether a check box is currently checked or not.

20.3.3 Combo Boxes

For a large set of choices, use a combo box.

If you have a large number of choices, you don't want to make a set of radio buttons because that would take up a lot of space. Instead, you can use a **combo box**. This component is called a combo box because it is a combination of a list and a text field. The text field displays the name of the current selection. When you click on the arrow to the right of the text field of a combo box, a list of selections drops down, and you can choose one of the items in the list (see Figure 8).

If the combo box is *editable*, you can also type in your own selection. To make a combo box editable, call the setEditable method.

You add strings to a combo box with the addItem method.

```
JComboBox facenameCombo = new JComboBox();
facenameCombo.addItem("Serif");
facenameCombo.addItem("SansSerif");
. . .
```

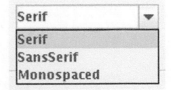

Figure 8
An Open Combo Box

You get the item that the user has selected by calling the getSelectedItem method. However, because combo boxes can store other objects in addition to strings, the get-SelectedItem method has return type Object. Hence, in our example, you must cast the returned value back to String:

```
String selectedString = (String) facenameCombo.getSelectedItem();
```

You can select an item for the user with the setSelectedItem method.

Radio buttons, check boxes, and combo boxes generate action events, just as buttons do.

Radio buttons, check boxes, and combo boxes generate an ActionEvent whenever the user selects an item. In the following program, we don't care which component was clicked—all components notify the same listener object. Whenever the user clicks on any one of them, we simply ask each component for its current content, using the isSelected and getSelectedItem methods. We then redraw the label with the new font.

Figure 9 shows how the components are arranged in the frame.

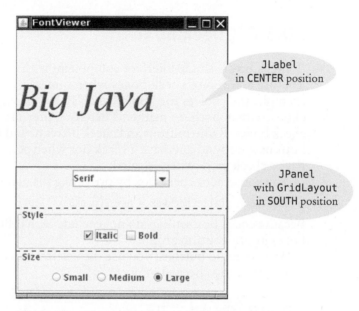

Figure 9 The Components of the Font Frame

sec03/FontViewer.java

```
1  import javax.swing.JFrame;
2
3  /**
4     This program allows the user to view font effects.
5  */
6  public class FontViewer
7  {
8     public static void main(String[] args)
9     {
10        JFrame frame = new FontFrame();
11        frame.setDefaultCloseOperation(JFrame.EXIT_ON_CLOSE);
12        frame.setTitle("FontViewer");
13        frame.setVisible(true);
14     }
15  }
```

sec03/FontFrame.java

```
1  import java.awt.BorderLayout;
2  import java.awt.Font;
3  import java.awt.GridLayout;
4  import java.awt.event.ActionEvent;
```

```java
 5  import java.awt.event.ActionListener;
 6  import javax.swing.ButtonGroup;
 7  import javax.swing.JButton;
 8  import javax.swing.JCheckBox;
 9  import javax.swing.JComboBox;
10  import javax.swing.JFrame;
11  import javax.swing.JLabel;
12  import javax.swing.JPanel;
13  import javax.swing.JRadioButton;
14  import javax.swing.border.EtchedBorder;
15  import javax.swing.border.TitledBorder;
16
17  /**
18      This frame contains a text sample and a control panel
19      to change the font of the text.
20  */
21  public class FontFrame extends JFrame
22  {
23      private static final int FRAME_WIDTH = 300;
24      private static final int FRAME_HEIGHT = 400;
25
26      private JLabel label;
27      private JCheckBox italicCheckBox;
28      private JCheckBox boldCheckBox;
29      private JRadioButton smallButton;
30      private JRadioButton mediumButton;
31      private JRadioButton largeButton;
32      private JComboBox facenameCombo;
33      private ActionListener listener;
34
35      /**
36          Constructs the frame.
37      */
38      public FontFrame()
39      {
40          // Construct text sample
41          label = new JLabel("Big Java");
42          add(label, BorderLayout.CENTER);
43
44          // This listener is shared among all components
45          listener = new ChoiceListener();
46
47          createControlPanel();
48          setLabelFont();
49          setSize(FRAME_WIDTH, FRAME_HEIGHT);
50      }
51
52      class ChoiceListener implements ActionListener
53      {
54          public void actionPerformed(ActionEvent event)
55          {
56              setLabelFont();
57          }
58      }
59
60      /**
61          Creates the control panel to change the font.
62      */
63      public void createControlPanel()
64      {
```

```java
65      JPanel facenamePanel = createComboBox();
66      JPanel sizeGroupPanel = createCheckBoxes();
67      JPanel styleGroupPanel = createRadioButtons();
68
69      // Line up component panels
70
71      JPanel controlPanel = new JPanel();
72      controlPanel.setLayout(new GridLayout(3, 1));
73      controlPanel.add(facenamePanel);
74      controlPanel.add(sizeGroupPanel);
75      controlPanel.add(styleGroupPanel);
76
77      // Add panels to content pane
78
79      add(controlPanel, BorderLayout.SOUTH);
80   }
81
82   /**
83      Creates the combo box with the font style choices.
84      @return the panel containing the combo box
85   */
86   public JPanel createComboBox()
87   {
88      facenameCombo = new JComboBox();
89      facenameCombo.addItem("Serif");
90      facenameCombo.addItem("SansSerif");
91      facenameCombo.addItem("Monospaced");
92      facenameCombo.setEditable(true);
93      facenameCombo.addActionListener(listener);
94
95      JPanel panel = new JPanel();
96      panel.add(facenameCombo);
97      return panel;
98   }
99
100  /**
101     Creates the check boxes for selecting bold and italic styles.
102     @return the panel containing the check boxes
103  */
104  public JPanel createCheckBoxes()
105  {
106     italicCheckBox = new JCheckBox("Italic");
107     italicCheckBox.addActionListener(listener);
108
109     boldCheckBox = new JCheckBox("Bold");
110     boldCheckBox.addActionListener(listener);
111
112     JPanel panel = new JPanel();
113     panel.add(italicCheckBox);
114     panel.add(boldCheckBox);
115     panel.setBorder(new TitledBorder(new EtchedBorder(), "Style"));
116
117     return panel;
118  }
119
120  /**
121     Creates the radio buttons to select the font size.
122     @return the panel containing the radio buttons
123  */
```

```java
124    public JPanel createRadioButtons()
125    {
126       smallButton = new JRadioButton("Small");
127       smallButton.addActionListener(listener);
128
129       mediumButton = new JRadioButton("Medium");
130       mediumButton.addActionListener(listener);
131
132       largeButton = new JRadioButton("Large");
133       largeButton.addActionListener(listener);
134       largeButton.setSelected(true);
135
136       // Add radio buttons to button group
137
138       ButtonGroup group = new ButtonGroup();
139       group.add(smallButton);
140       group.add(mediumButton);
141       group.add(largeButton);
142
143       JPanel panel = new JPanel();
144       panel.add(smallButton);
145       panel.add(mediumButton);
146       panel.add(largeButton);
147       panel.setBorder(new TitledBorder(new EtchedBorder(), "Size"));
148
149       return panel;
150    }
151
152    /**
153       Gets user choice for font name, style, and size
154       and sets the font of the text sample.
155    */
156    public void setLabelFont()
157    {
158       // Get font name
159       String facename = (String) facenameCombo.getSelectedItem();
160
161       // Get font style
162
163       int style = 0;
164       if (italicCheckBox.isSelected())
165       {
166          style = style + Font.ITALIC;
167       }
168       if (boldCheckBox.isSelected())
169       {
170          style = style + Font.BOLD;
171       }
172
173       // Get font size
174
175       int size = 0;
176
177       final int SMALL_SIZE = 24;
178       final int MEDIUM_SIZE = 36;
179       final int LARGE_SIZE = 48;
180
181       if (smallButton.isSelected()) { size = SMALL_SIZE; }
182       else if (mediumButton.isSelected()) { size = MEDIUM_SIZE; }
```

```
183          else if (largeButton.isSelected()) { size = LARGE_SIZE; }
184
185          // Set font of text field
186
187          label.setFont(new Font(facename, style, size));
188          label.repaint();
189      }
190 }
```

HOW TO 20.1

Laying Out a User Interface

A graphical user interface is made up of components such as buttons and text fields. The Swing library uses containers and layout managers to arrange these components. This How To explains how to group components into containers and how to pick the right layout managers.

Step 1   Make a sketch of your desired component layout.

Draw all the buttons, labels, text fields, and borders on a sheet of paper. Graph paper works best.

Here is an example—a user interface for ordering pizza. The user interface contains

- Three radio buttons
- Two check boxes
- A label: "Your Price:"
- A text field
- A border

Step 2   Find groupings of adjacent components with the same layout.

Usually, the component arrangement is complex enough that you need to use several panels, each with its own layout manager. Start by looking at adjacent components that are arranged top to bottom or left to right. If several components are surrounded by a border, they should be grouped together.

Here are the groupings from the pizza user interface:

Step 3   Identify layouts for each group.

When components are arranged horizontally, choose a flow layout. When components are arranged vertically, use a grid layout with one column.

In the pizza user interface example, you would choose

- A (3, 1) grid layout for the radio buttons
- A (2, 1) grid layout for the check boxes
- A flow layout for the label and text field

Step 4   Group the groups together.

Look at each group as one blob, and group the blobs together into larger groups, just as you grouped the components in the preceding step. If you note one large blob surrounded by smaller blobs, you can group them together in a border layout.

You may have to repeat the grouping again if you have a very complex user interface. You are done if you have arranged all groups in a single container.

For example, the three component groups of the pizza user interface can be arranged as:

- A group containing the first two component groups, placed in the center of a container with a border layout.
- The third component group, in the southern area of that container.

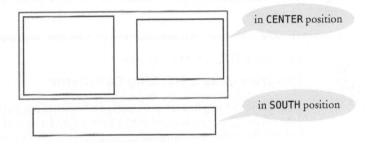

In this step, you may run into a couple of complications. The group "blobs" tend to vary in size more than the individual components. If you place them inside a grid layout, the grid layout forces them all to be the same size. Also, you occasionally would like a component from one group to line up with a component from another group, but there is no way for you to communicate that intent to the layout managers.

These problems can be overcome by using more sophisticated layout managers or implementing a custom layout manager. However, those techniques are beyond the scope of this book. Sometimes, you may want to start over with Step 1, using a component layout that is easier to manage. Or you can decide to live with minor imperfections of the layout. Don't worry about achieving the perfect layout—after all, you are learning programming, not user-interface design.

Step 5   Write the code to generate the layout.

This step is straightforward but potentially tedious, especially if you have a large number of components.

Start by constructing the components. Then construct a panel for each component group and set its layout manager if it is not a flow layout (the default for panels). Add a border to the panel if required. Finally, add the components to their panels. Continue in this fashion until you reach the outermost containers, which you add to the frame.

Here is an outline of the code required for the pizza ordering user interface:

```
JPanel radioButtonPanel = new JPanel();
radioButtonPanel.setLayout(new GridLayout(3, 1));
radioButtonPanel.setBorder(new TitledBorder(new EtchedBorder(), "Size"));
radioButtonPanel.add(smallButton);
```

```
radioButtonPanel.add(mediumButton);
radioButtonPanel.add(largeButton);

JPanel checkBoxPanel = new JPanel();
checkBoxPanel.setLayout(new GridLayout(2, 1));
checkBoxPanel.add(pepperoniButton);
checkBoxPanel.add(anchoviesButton);

JPanel pricePanel = new JPanel(); // Uses FlowLayout by default
pricePanel.add(new JLabel("Your Price: "));
pricePanel.add(priceTextField);

JPanel centerPanel = new JPanel(); // Uses FlowLayout
centerPanel.add(radioButtonPanel);
centerPanel.add(checkBoxPanel);

// Frame uses BorderLayout by default
add(centerPanel, BorderLayout.CENTER);
add(pricePanel, BorderLayout.SOUTH);
```

WORKED EXAMPLE 20.1

Programming a Working Calculator

Learn how to implement arithmetic and scientific operations for a calculator. The sample program in Section 20.1 showed how to lay out the buttons for a simple calculator, and we use that program as a starting point. See your eText or visit wiley.com/go/bjeo7.

Programming Tip 20.1

Use a GUI Builder

As you have seen, implementing even a simple graphical user interface in Java is quite tedious. You have to write a lot of code for constructing components, using layout managers, and providing event handlers. Most of the code is repetitive.

A GUI builder takes away much of the tedium. Most GUI builders help you in three ways:

- You drag and drop components onto a panel. The GUI builder writes the layout management code for you.

- You customize components with a dialog box, setting properties such as fonts, colors, text, and so on. The GUI builder writes the customization code for you.

- You provide event handlers by picking the event to process and providing just the code snippet for the listener method. The GUI builder writes the boilerplate code for attaching a listener object.

GroupLayout is a powerful layout manager that was specifically designed to be used by GUI builders. The free NetBeans development environment, available from http://netbeans.org, makes use of this layout manager—see Figure 10.

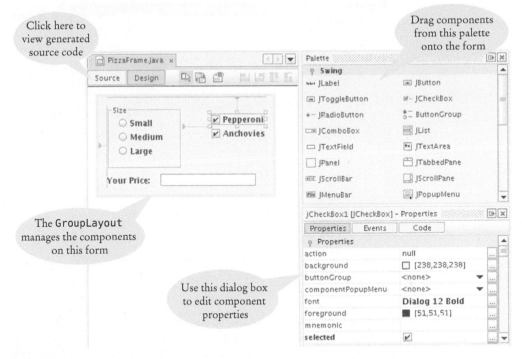

Figure 10   A GUI Builder

If you need to build a complex user interface, you will find that learning to use a GUI builder is a very worthwhile investment. You will spend less time writing boring code, and you will have more fun designing your user interface and focusing on the functionality of your program.

20.4 Menus

A frame contains a menu bar. The menu bar contains menus. A menu contains submenus and menu items.

Anyone who has ever used a graphical user interface is familiar with pull-down menus (see Figure 11). At the top of the frame is a *menu bar* that contains the top-level menus. Each menu is a collection of *menu items* and *submenus*.

A menu provides a list of available choices.   © lillisphotography/iStockphoto.

Figure 11
Pull-Down Menus

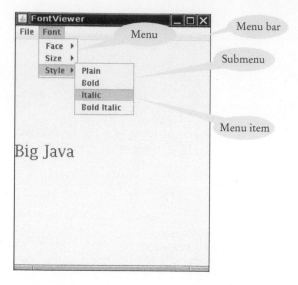

The sample program for this section builds up a small but typical menu and traps the action events from the menu items. The program allows the user to specify the font for a label by selecting a face name, font size, and font style. In Java it is easy to create these menus.

You add the menu bar to the frame:

```
public class MyFrame extends JFrame
{
    public MyFrame()
    {
        JMenuBar menuBar = new JMenuBar();
        setJMenuBar(menuBar);
        . . .
    }
    . . .
}
```

Menus are then added to the menu bar:

```
JMenu fileMenu = new JMenu("File");
JMenu fontMenu = new JMenu("Font");
menuBar.add(fileMenu);
menuBar.add(fontMenu);
```

You add menu items and submenus with the add method:

```
JMenuItem exitItem = new JMenuItem("Exit");
fileMenu.add(exitItem);

JMenu styleMenu = new JMenu("Style");
fontMenu.add(styleMenu); // A submenu
```

Menu items generate action events.

A menu item has no further submenus. When the user selects a menu item, the menu item sends an action event. Therefore, you want to add a listener to each menu item:

```
ActionListener listener = new ExitItemListener();
exitItem.addActionListener(listener);
```

You add action listeners only to menu items, not to menus or the menu bar. When the user clicks on a menu name and a submenu opens, no action event is sent.

To keep the program readable, it is a good idea to use a separate method for each menu or set of related menus. For example,

```
public JMenu createFaceMenu()
{
    JMenu menu = new JMenu("Face");
    menu.add(createFaceItem("Serif"));
    menu.add(createFaceItem("SansSerif"));
    menu.add(createFaceItem("Monospaced"));
    return menu;
}
```

Now consider the createFaceItem method. It has a string parameter variable for the name of the font face. When the item is selected, its action listener needs to

1. Set the current face name to the menu item text.

2. Make a new font from the current face, size, and style, and apply it to the label.

We have three menu items, one for each supported face name. Each of them needs to set a different name in the first step. Of course, we can make three listener classes SerifListener, SansSerifListener, and MonospacedListener, but that is not very elegant. After all, the actions only vary by a single string. We can store that string inside the listener class and then make three objects of the same listener class:

```
class FaceItemListener implements ActionListener
{
    private String name;

    public FaceItemListener(String newName) { name = newName; }

    public void actionPerformed(ActionEvent event)
    {
        faceName = name; // Sets an instance variable of the frame class
        setLabelFont();
    }
}
```

Now we can install a listener object with the appropriate name:

```
public JMenuItem createFaceItem(String name)
{
    JMenuItem item = new JMenuItem(name);
    ActionListener listener = new FaceItemListener(name);
    item.addActionListener(listener);
    return item;
}
```

This approach is still a bit tedious. We can do better by using a local inner class inside the createFaceItem method (see Section 10.5). Then the actionPerformed method can access the name parameter variable directly (because it is essentially final).

```
public JMenuItem createFaceItem(String name)
// Essentially final variables can be accessed from an inner class method
{
    class FaceItemListener implements ActionListener // A local inner class
    {
        public void actionPerformed(ActionEvent event)
        {
```

```
         facename = name; // Accesses the local variable name
         setLabelFont();
      }
   }

   JMenuItem item = new JMenuItem(name);
   ActionListener listener = new FaceItemListener();
   item.addActionListener(listener);
   return item;
}
```

The same strategy is used for the createSizeItem and createStyleItem methods.

sec04/FontViewer2.java

```java
1   import javax.swing.JFrame;
2
3   /**
4       This program uses a menu to display font effects.
5   */
6   public class FontViewer2
7   {
8      public static void main(String[] args)
9      {
10         JFrame frame = new FontFrame2();
11         frame.setDefaultCloseOperation(JFrame.EXIT_ON_CLOSE);
12         frame.setTitle("FontViewer");
13         frame.setVisible(true);
14      }
15   }
```

sec04/FontFrame2.java

```java
1   import java.awt.BorderLayout;
2   import java.awt.Font;
3   import java.awt.event.ActionEvent;
4   import java.awt.event.ActionListener;
5   import javax.swing.JFrame;
6   import javax.swing.JLabel;
7   import javax.swing.JMenu;
8   import javax.swing.JMenuBar;
9   import javax.swing.JMenuItem;
10
11   /**
12       This frame has a menu with commands to change the font
13       of a text sample.
14   */
15   public class FontFrame2 extends JFrame
16   {
17      private static final int FRAME_WIDTH = 300;
18      private static final int FRAME_HEIGHT = 400;
19
20      private JLabel label;
21      private String facename;
22      private int fontstyle;
23      private int fontsize;
24
25      /**
26          Constructs the frame.
27      */
```

```java
28    public FontFrame2()
29    {
30       // Construct text sample
31       label = new JLabel("Big Java");
32       add(label, BorderLayout.CENTER);
33
34       // Construct menu
35       JMenuBar menuBar = new JMenuBar();
36       setJMenuBar(menuBar);
37       menuBar.add(createFileMenu());
38       menuBar.add(createFontMenu());
39
40       facename = "Serif";
41       fontsize = 24;
42       fontstyle = Font.PLAIN;
43
44       setLabelFont();
45       setSize(FRAME_WIDTH, FRAME_HEIGHT);
46    }
47
48    class ExitItemListener implements ActionListener
49    {
50       public void actionPerformed(ActionEvent event)
51       {
52          System.exit(0);
53       }
54    }
55
56    /**
57       Creates the File menu.
58       @return the menu
59    */
60    public JMenu createFileMenu()
61    {
62       JMenu menu = new JMenu("File");
63       JMenuItem exitItem = new JMenuItem("Exit");
64       ActionListener listener = new ExitItemListener();
65       exitItem.addActionListener(listener);
66       menu.add(exitItem);
67       return menu;
68    }
69
70    /**
71       Creates the Font submenu.
72       @return the menu
73    */
74    public JMenu createFontMenu()
75    {
76       JMenu menu = new JMenu("Font");
77       menu.add(createFaceMenu());
78       menu.add(createSizeMenu());
79       menu.add(createStyleMenu());
80       return menu;
81    }
82
83    /**
84       Creates the Face submenu.
85       @return the menu
86    */
```

```
87    public JMenu createFaceMenu()
88    {
89       JMenu menu = new JMenu("Face");
90       menu.add(createFaceItem("Serif"));
91       menu.add(createFaceItem("SansSerif"));
92       menu.add(createFaceItem("Monospaced"));
93       return menu;
94    }
95
96    /**
97       Creates the Size submenu.
98       @return the menu
99    */
100   public JMenu createSizeMenu()
101   {
102      JMenu menu = new JMenu("Size");
103      menu.add(createSizeItem("Smaller", -1));
104      menu.add(createSizeItem("Larger", 1));
105      return menu;
106   }
107
108   /**
109      Creates the Style submenu.
110      @return the menu
111   */
112   public JMenu createStyleMenu()
113   {
114      JMenu menu = new JMenu("Style");
115      menu.add(createStyleItem("Plain", Font.PLAIN));
116      menu.add(createStyleItem("Bold", Font.BOLD));
117      menu.add(createStyleItem("Italic", Font.ITALIC));
118      menu.add(createStyleItem("Bold Italic", Font.BOLD
119            + Font.ITALIC));
120      return menu;
121   }
122
123   /**
124      Creates a menu item to change the font face and set its action listener.
125      @param name the name of the font face
126      @return the menu item
127   */
128   public JMenuItem createFaceItem(String name)
129   {
130      class FaceItemListener implements ActionListener
131      {
132         public void actionPerformed(ActionEvent event)
133         {
134            facename = name;
135            setLabelFont();
136         }
137      }
138
139      JMenuItem item = new JMenuItem(name);
140      ActionListener listener = new FaceItemListener();
141      item.addActionListener(listener);
142      return item;
143   }
144
```

```
145    /**
146       Creates a menu item to change the font size
147       and set its action listener.
148       @param name the name of the menu item
149       @param increment the amount by which to change the size
150       @return the menu item
151    */
152    public JMenuItem createSizeItem(String name, int increment)
153    {
154       class SizeItemListener implements ActionListener
155       {
156          public void actionPerformed(ActionEvent event)
157          {
158             fontsize = fontsize + increment;
159             setLabelFont();
160          }
161       }
162
163       JMenuItem item = new JMenuItem(name);
164       ActionListener listener = new SizeItemListener();
165       item.addActionListener(listener);
166       return item;
167    }
168
169    /**
170       Creates a menu item to change the font style
171       and set its action listener.
172       @param name the name of the menu item
173       @param style the new font style
174       @return the menu item
175    */
176    public JMenuItem createStyleItem(String name, int style)
177    {
178       class StyleItemListener implements ActionListener
179       {
180          public void actionPerformed(ActionEvent event)
181          {
182             fontstyle = style;
183             setLabelFont();
184          }
185       }
186
187       JMenuItem item = new JMenuItem(name);
188       ActionListener listener = new StyleItemListener();
189       item.addActionListener(listener);
190       return item;
191    }
192
193    /**
194       Sets the font of the text sample.
195    */
196    public void setLabelFont()
197    {
198       Font f = new Font(facename, fontstyle, fontsize);
199       label.setFont(f);
200    }
201 }
```

20.5 Exploring the Swing Documentation

You should learn to navigate the API documentation to find out more about user-interface components.

In the preceding sections, you saw the basic properties of the most common user-interface components. We purposefully omitted many options and variations to simplify the discussion. You can go a long way by using only the simplest properties of these components. If you want to implement a more sophisticated effect, you can look inside the Swing documentation. You may find the documentation intimidating at first glance, though. The purpose of this section is to show you how you can use the documentation to your advantage without being overwhelmed.

© René Mansi/iStockphoto.

In order to use the Swing library effectively, you need to study the API documentation.

As an example, consider a program for mixing colors by specifying the red, green, and blue values. How can you specify the colors? Of course, you could supply three text fields, but sliders would be more convenient for users of your program (see Figure 12).

The Swing user-interface toolkit has a large set of user-interface components. How do you know if there is a slider? You can buy a book that illustrates all Swing components. Or you can run the sample application included in the Java Development Kit that shows off all Swing components (see Figure 13). Or you can look at the names of all of the classes that start with J and decide that JSlider may be a good candidate.

Next, you need to ask yourself a few questions:

- How do I construct a JSlider?
- How can I get notified when the user has moved it?
- How can I tell to which value the user has set it?

Figure 12 A Color Viewer with Sliders

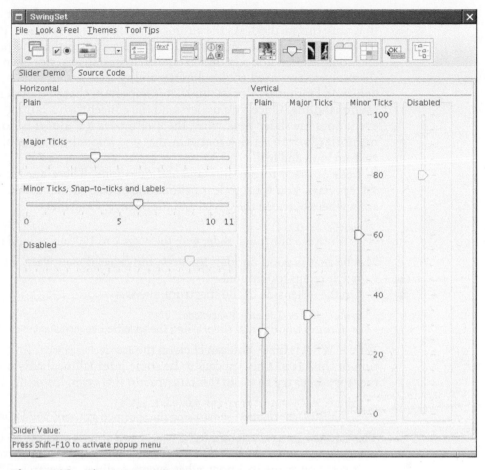

Figure 13 The SwingSet Demo

When you look at the documentation of the JSlider class, you will probably not be happy. There are over 50 methods in the JSlider class and over 250 inherited methods, and some of the method descriptions look downright scary, such as the one in Figure 14. Apparently some folks out there are concerned about the valueIsAdjusting property, whatever that may be, and the designers of this class felt it necessary to

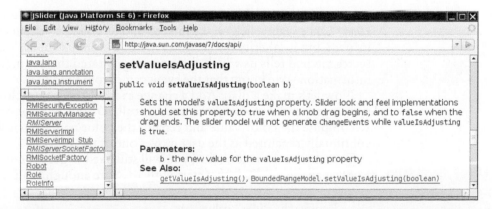

Figure 14 A Mysterious Method Description from the API Documentation

supply a method to tweak that property. Until you too feel that need, your best bet is to ignore this method. As the author of an introductory book, it pains me to tell you to ignore certain facts. But the truth of the matter is that the Java library is so large and complex that nobody understands it in its entirety, not even the designers of Java themselves. You need to develop the ability to separate fundamental concepts from ephemeral minutiae. For example, it is important that you understand the concept of event handling. Once you understand the concept, you can ask the question, "What event does the slider send when the user moves it?" But it is not important that you memorize how to set tick marks or that you know how to implement a slider with a custom look and feel.

Let's go back to our fundamental questions. There are six constructors for the `JSlider` class. You want to learn about one or two of them. You must strike a balance somewhere between the trivial and the bizarre. Consider

```
public JSlider()
```
Creates a horizontal slider with the range 0 to 100 and an initial value of 50.

Maybe that is good enough for now, but what if you want another range or initial value? It seems too limited.

On the other side of the spectrum, there is

```
public JSlider(BoundedRangeModel brm)
```
Creates a horizontal slider using the specified `BoundedRangeModel`.

Whoa! What is that? You can click on the `BoundedRangeModel` link to get a long explanation of this class. This appears to be some internal mechanism for the Swing implementors. Let's try to avoid this constructor if we can. Looking further, we find

```
public JSlider(int min, int max, int value)
```
Creates a horizontal slider using the specified `min`, `max`, and `value`.

This sounds general enough to be useful and simple enough to be usable. You might want to stash away the fact that you can have vertical sliders as well.

Next, you want to know what events a slider generates. There is no `addAction-Listener` method. That makes sense. Adjusting a slider seems different from clicking a button, and Swing uses a different event type for these events. There is a method

```
public void addChangeListener(ChangeListener l)
```

Click on the `ChangeListener` link to find out more about this interface. It has a single method

```
void stateChanged(ChangeEvent e)
```

Apparently, that method is called whenever the user moves the slider. What is a `Change-Event`? Once again, click on the link, to find out that this event class has *no* methods of its own, but it inherits the `getSource` method from its superclass `EventObject`. The `get-Source` method tells us which component generated this event, but we don't need that information—we know that the event came from the slider.

Now let's make a plan: Add a change event listener to each slider. When the slider is changed, the `stateChanged` method is called. Find out the new value of the slider. Recompute the color value and repaint the color panel. That way, the color panel is continually repainted as the user moves one of the sliders.

To compute the color value, you will still need to get the current value of the slider. Look at all the methods that start with `get`. Sure enough, you find

```
public int getValue()
```
Returns the slider's value.

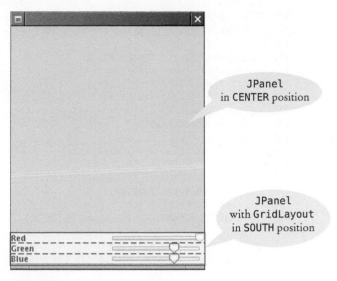

Figure 15 The Components of the Color Viewer Frame

Now you know everything you need to write the program. The program uses one new Swing component and one event listener of a new type. After having mastered the basics, you may want to explore the capabilities of the component further, for example by adding tick marks — see Exercise •• E20.12.

Figure 15 shows how the components are arranged in the frame.

sec05/ColorViewer.Java

```
 1  import javax.swing.JFrame;
 2
 3  public class ColorViewer
 4  {
 5     public static void main(String[] args)
 6     {
 7        JFrame frame = new ColorFrame();
 8        frame.setDefaultCloseOperation(JFrame.EXIT_ON_CLOSE);
 9        frame.setVisible(true);
10     }
11  }
```

sec05/ColorFrame.java

```
 1  import java.awt.BorderLayout;
 2  import java.awt.Color;
 3  import java.awt.GridLayout;
 4  import javax.swing.JFrame;
 5  import javax.swing.JLabel;
 6  import javax.swing.JPanel;
 7  import javax.swing.JSlider;
 8  import javax.swing.event.ChangeListener;
 9  import javax.swing.event.ChangeEvent;
10
11  public class ColorFrame extends JFrame
12  {
```

```
13    private static final int FRAME_WIDTH = 300;
14    private static final int FRAME_HEIGHT = 400;
15
16    private JPanel colorPanel;
17    private JSlider redSlider;
18    private JSlider greenSlider;
19    private JSlider blueSlider;
20
21    public ColorFrame()
22    {
23       colorPanel = new JPanel();
24
25       add(colorPanel, BorderLayout.CENTER);
26       createControlPanel();
27       setSampleColor();
28       setSize(FRAME_WIDTH, FRAME_HEIGHT);
29    }
30
31    class ColorListener implements ChangeListener
32    {
33       public void stateChanged(ChangeEvent event)
34       {
35          setSampleColor();
36       }
37    }
38
39    public void createControlPanel()
40    {
41       ChangeListener listener = new ColorListener();
42
43       redSlider = new JSlider(0, 255, 255);
44       redSlider.addChangeListener(listener);
45
46       greenSlider = new JSlider(0, 255, 175);
47       greenSlider.addChangeListener(listener);
48
49       blueSlider = new JSlider(0, 255, 175);
50       blueSlider.addChangeListener(listener);
51
52       JPanel controlPanel = new JPanel();
53       controlPanel.setLayout(new GridLayout(3, 2));
54
55       controlPanel.add(new JLabel("Red"));
56       controlPanel.add(redSlider);
57
58       controlPanel.add(new JLabel("Green"));
59       controlPanel.add(greenSlider);
60
61       controlPanel.add(new JLabel("Blue"));
62       controlPanel.add(blueSlider);
63
64       add(controlPanel, BorderLayout.SOUTH);
65    }
66
67    /**
68       Reads the slider values and sets the panel to
69       the selected color.
70    */
71    public void setSampleColor()
72    {
```

```
73        // Read slider values
74
75        int red = redSlider.getValue();
76        int green = greenSlider.getValue();
77        int blue = blueSlider.getValue();
78
79        // Set panel background to selected color
80
81        colorPanel.setBackground(new Color(red, green, blue));
82        colorPanel.repaint();
83      }
84 }
```

CHAPTER SUMMARY

Learn how to arrange multiple components in a container.

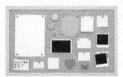

- User-interface components are arranged by placing them inside containers. Containers can be placed inside larger containers.
- Each container has a layout manager that directs the arrangement of its components.
- Three useful layout managers are the border layout, flow layout, and grid layout.
- When adding a component to a container with the border layout, specify the NORTH, SOUTH, WEST, EAST, or CENTER position.
- The content pane of a frame has a border layout by default. A panel has a flow layout by default.

Use text components for reading text input.

- Use a JTextField component for reading a single line of input. Place a JLabel next to each text field.
- Use a JTextArea to show multiple lines of text.
- You can add scroll bars to any component with a JScrollPane.

Select among the Swing components for presenting choices to the user.

- For a small set of mutually exclusive choices, use a group of radio buttons or a combo box.
- Add radio buttons to a ButtonGroup so that only one button in the group is selected at any time.
- You can place a border around a panel to group its contents visually.
- For a binary choice, use a check box.
- For a large set of choices, use a combo box.
- Radio buttons, check boxes, and combo boxes generate action events, just as buttons do.

Implement menus in a Swing program.

- A frame contains a menu bar. The menu bar contains menus. A menu contains submenus and menu items.
- Menu items generate action events.

Use the Swing documentation.

- You should learn to navigate the API documentation to find out more about user-interface components.

STANDARD LIBRARY ITEMS INTRODUCED IN THIS CHAPTER

```
java.awt.BorderLayout
  CENTER
  EAST
  NORTH
  SOUTH
  WEST
java.awt.Component
  setPreferredSize
java.awt.Container
  setLayout
java.awt.FlowLayout
java.awt.Font
  BOLD
  ITALIC
java.awt.GridLayout
javax.swing.AbstractButton
  isSelected
  setSelected
javax.swing.ButtonGroup
  add
javax.swing.JCheckBox
javax.swing.JComboBox
  addItem
  getSelectedItem
  isEditable
  setEditable
  setSelectedItem
```

```
javax.swing.JComponent
  setBorder
  setFocusable
  setFont
javax.swing.JFrame
  setJMenuBar
javax.swing.JMenu
  add
javax.swing.JMenuBar
  add
javax.swing.JMenuItem
javax.swing.JRadioButton
javax.swing.JSlider
  addChangeListener
  getValue
javax.swing.JTextArea
  append
javax.swing.JTextField
javax.swing.text.JTextComponent
  getText
  isEditable
  setEditable
  setText
javax.swing.border.EtchedBorder
javax.swing.border.TitledBorder
javax.swing.event.ChangeEvent
javax.swing.event.ChangeListener
  stateChanged
```

REVIEW EXERCISES

- **R20.1** Can you use a flow layout for the components in a frame? If yes, how?

- **R20.2** What is the advantage of a layout manager over telling the container "place this component at position (x, y)"?

- **R20.3** What happens when you place a single button into the CENTER area of a container that uses a border layout? Try it out by writing a small sample program if you aren't sure of the answer.

- **R20.4** What happens if you place multiple buttons directly into the SOUTH area, without using a panel? Try it out by writing a small sample program if you aren't sure of the answer.

- **R20.5** What happens when you add a button to a container that uses a border layout and omit the position? Try it out and explain.

- **R20.6** What happens when you try to add a button to another button? Try it out and explain.

- **R20.7** The ColorFrame in Section 20.5 uses a grid layout manager. Explain a drawback of the grid that is apparent from Figure 15. What could you do to overcome this drawback?

- **R20.8** What is the difference between the grid layout and the grid bag layout?

- **R20.9** Can you add icons to check boxes, radio buttons, and combo boxes? Browse the Java documentation to find out. Then write a small test program to verify your findings.

- **R20.10** What is the difference between radio buttons and check boxes?

- **R20.11** Why do you need a button group for radio buttons but not for check boxes?

- **R20.12** What is the difference between a menu bar, a menu, and a menu item?

- **R20.13** When browsing through the Java documentation for more information about sliders, we ignored the JSlider constructor with no arguments. Why? Would it have worked in our sample program?

- **R20.14** How do you construct a vertical slider? Consult the Swing documentation for an answer.

- **R20.15** Why doesn't a JComboBox send out change events?

- **R20.16** What component would you use to show a set of choices, as in a combo box, but so that several items are visible at the same time? Run the Swing demo application or look at a book with Swing example programs to find the answer.

- **R20.17** How many Swing user-interface components are there? Look at the Java documentation to get an approximate answer.

- **R20.18** How many methods does the JProgressBar component have? Be sure to count inherited methods. Look at the Java documentation.

- **R20.19** Is it a requirement to use inheritance for frames, as described in Section 20.1.3? (*Hint:* Consider Special Topic 20.1.)

- **R20.20** What is the difference between a label, a text field, and a text area?

■■ **R20.21** Name a method that is declared in JTextArea, a method that JTextArea inherits from JTextComponent, and a method that JTextArea inherits from JComponent.

■■ **R20.22** Why did the program in Section 20.2.2 use a text area and not a label to show how the interest accumulates? How could you have achieved a similar effect with an array of labels?

PRACTICE EXERCISES

■ **E20.1** Write an application with three buttons labeled "Red", "Green", and "Blue" that changes the background color of a panel in the center of the frame to red, green, or blue.

■■ **E20.2** Add icons to the buttons of Exercise • E20.1. Use a JButton constructor with an Icon argument and supply an ImageIcon.

■ **E20.3** Write an application with three radio buttons labeled "Red", "Green", and "Blue" that changes the background color of a panel in the center of the frame to red, green, or blue.

■ **E20.4** Write an application with three check boxes labeled "Red", "Green", and "Blue" that adds a red, green, or blue component to the background color of a panel in the center of the frame. This application can display a total of eight color combinations.

■ **E20.5** Write an application with a combo box containing three items labeled "Red", "Green", and "Blue" that change the background color of a panel in the center of the frame to red, green, or blue.

■ **E20.6** Write an application with a Color menu and menu items labeled "Red", "Green", and "Blue" that change the background color of a panel in the center of the frame to red, green, or blue.

■ **E20.7** Write a program that displays a number of rectangles at random positions. Supply menu items "Fewer" and "More" that generate fewer or more random rectangles. Each time the user selects "Fewer", the count should be halved. Each time the user clicks on "More", the count should be doubled.

■■■ **E20.8** Enhance the font viewer program to allow the user to select different font faces. Research the API documentation to find out how to find the available fonts on the user's system.

■■■ **E20.9** Write a program that lets users design charts such as the following:

Golden Gate

Brooklyn

Delaware Memorial

Mackinac

Use appropriate components to ask for the length, label, and color, then apply them when the user clicks an "Add Item" button.

■ **E20.10** Write a graphical application simulating a bank account. Supply text fields and buttons for depositing and withdrawing money, and for displaying the current balance in a label.

- **E20.11** Write a graphical application describing an earthquake, as in Section 5.3. Supply a text field and button for entering the strength of the earthquake. Display the earthquake description in a label.

- ■ **E20.12** Modify the slider test program in Section 20.5 to add a set of tick marks to each slider that show the exact slider position.

PROGRAMMING PROJECTS

- ■ **P20.1** Modify the program of Exercise • E20.7 to replace the buttons with a slider to generate more or fewer random rectangles.

- **P20.2** Write a graphical application for computing statistics of a data set. Supply a text field and button for adding floating-point values, and display the current minimum, maximum, and average in a label.

- **P20.3** Write an application with three labeled text fields, one each for the initial amount of a savings account, the annual interest rate, and the number of years. Add a button "Calculate" and a read-only text area to display the balance of the savings account after the end of each year.

- ■ **P20.4** In the application from Exercise • P20.3, replace the text area with a bar chart that shows the balance after the end of each year.

- ■ **Business P20.5** Write a program with a graphical interface that allows the user to convert an amount of money between U.S. dollars (USD), euros (EUR), and British pounds (GBP). The user interface should have the following elements: a text box to enter the amount to be converted, two combo boxes to allow the user to select the currencies, a button to make the conversion, and a label to show the result. Display a warning if the user does not choose different currencies. Use the following conversion rates:

  1 EUR is equal to 1.42 USD.

  1 GBP is equal to 1.64 USD.

  1 GBP is equal to 1.13 EUR.

- ■ **Business P20.6** Write a program with a graphical interface that implements a login window with text fields for the user name and password. When the login is successful, hide the login window and open a new window with a welcome message. Follow these rules for validating the password:

  1. The user name is not case sensitive.

  2. The password is case sensitive.

  3. The user has three opportunities to enter valid credentials.

  Otherwise, display an error message and terminate the program. When the program starts, read the file users.txt. Each line in that file contains a user name and password, separated by a space. You should make a users.txt file for testing your program.

- **Science P20.7** In Exercise •• Business P20.6, the password is shown as it is typed. Browse the Swing documentation to find an appropriate component for entering a password. Improve the solution of Exercise •• Business P20.6 by using this component instead of a text field. Each time the user types a letter, show a ■ character.

**A**

THE BASIC LATIN AND LATIN-1 SUBSETS OF UNICODE

This appendix lists the Unicode characters that are most commonly used for processing Western European languages. A complete listing of Unicode characters can be found at http://unicode.org.

Table 1 Selected Control Characters			
Character	Code	Decimal	Escape Sequence
Tab	'\u0009'	9	'\t'
Newline	'\u000A'	10	'\n'
Return	'\u000D'	13	'\r'
Space	'\u0020'	32	

Table 2 The Basic Latin (ASCII) Subset of Unicode

Char.	Code	Dec.	Char.	Code	Dec.	Char.	Code	Dec.
			@	'\u0040'	64	`	'\u0060'	96
!	'\u0021'	33	A	'\u0041'	65	a	'\u0061'	97
"	'\u0022'	34	B	'\u0042'	66	b	'\u0062'	98
#	'\u0023'	35	C	'\u0043'	67	c	'\u0063'	99
$	'\u0024'	36	D	'\u0044'	68	d	'\u0064'	100
%	'\u0025'	37	E	'\u0045'	69	e	'\u0065'	101
&	'\u0026'	38	F	'\u0046'	70	f	'\u0066'	102
'	'\u0027'	39	G	'\u0047'	71	g	'\u0067'	103
(	'\u0028'	40	H	'\u0048'	72	h	'\u0068'	104
)	'\u0029'	41	I	'\u0049'	73	i	'\u0069'	105
*	'\u002A'	42	J	'\u004A'	74	j	'\u006A'	106
+	'\u002B'	43	K	'\u004B'	75	k	'\u006B'	107
,	'\u002C'	44	L	'\u004C'	76	l	'\u006C'	108
-	'\u002D'	45	M	'\u004D'	77	m	'\u006D'	109
.	'\u002E'	46	N	'\u004E'	78	n	'\u006E'	110
/	'\u002F'	47	O	'\u004F'	79	o	'\u006F'	111
0	'\u0030'	48	P	'\u0050'	80	p	'\u0070'	112
1	'\u0031'	49	Q	'\u0051'	81	q	'\u0071'	113
2	'\u0032'	50	R	'\u0052'	82	r	'\u0072'	114
3	'\u0033'	51	S	'\u0053'	83	s	'\u0073'	115
4	'\u0034'	52	T	'\u0054'	84	t	'\u0074'	116
5	'\u0035'	53	U	'\u0055'	85	u	'\u0075'	117
6	'\u0036'	54	V	'\u0056'	86	v	'\u0076'	118
7	'\u0037'	55	W	'\u0057'	87	w	'\u0077'	119
8	'\u0038'	56	X	'\u0058'	88	x	'\u0078'	120
9	'\u0039'	57	Y	'\u0059'	89	y	'\u0079'	121
:	'\u003A'	58	Z	'\u005A'	90	z	'\u007A'	122
;	'\u003B'	59	[	'\u005B'	91	{	'\u007B'	123
<	'\u003C'	60	\	'\u005C'	92	|	'\u007C'	124
=	'\u003D'	61	]	'\u005D'	93	}	'\u007D'	125
>	'\u003E'	62	^	'\u005E'	94	~	'\u007E'	126
?	'\u003F'	63	_	'\u005F'	95			

Table 3   The Latin-1 Subset of Unicode

Char.	Code	Dec.	Char.	Code	Dec.	Char.	Code	Dec.
			À	'\u00C0'	192	à	'\u00E0'	224
¡	'\u00A1'	161	Á	'\u00C1'	193	á	'\u00E1'	225
¢	'\u00A2'	162	Â	'\u00C2'	194	â	'\u00E2'	226
£	'\u00A3'	163	Ã	'\u00C3'	195	ã	'\u00E3'	227
¤	'\u00A4'	164	Ä	'\u00C4'	196	ä	'\u00E4'	228
¥	'\u00A5'	165	Å	'\u00C5'	197	å	'\u00E5'	229
¦	'\u00A6'	166	Æ	'\u00C6'	198	æ	'\u00E6'	230
§	'\u00A7'	167	Ç	'\u00C7'	199	ç	'\u00E7'	231
¨	'\u00A8'	168	È	'\u00C8'	200	è	'\u00E8'	232
©	'\u00A9'	169	É	'\u00C9'	201	é	'\u00E9'	233
ª	'\u00AA'	170	Ê	'\u00CA'	202	ê	'\u00EA'	234
«	'\u00AB'	171	Ë	'\u00CB'	203	ë	'\u00EB'	235
¬	'\u00AC'	172	Ì	'\u00CC'	204	ì	'\u00EC'	236
-	'\u00AD'	173	Í	'\u00CD'	205	í	'\u00ED'	237
®	'\u00AE'	174	Î	'\u00CE'	206	î	'\u00EE'	238
¯	'\u00AF'	175	Ï	'\u00CF'	207	ï	'\u00EF'	239
°	'\u00B0'	176	Ð	'\u00D0'	208	ð	'\u00F0'	240
±	'\u00B1'	177	Ñ	'\u00D1'	209	ñ	'\u00F1'	241
²	'\u00B2'	178	Ò	'\u00D2'	210	ò	'\u00F2'	242
³	'\u00B3'	179	Ó	'\u00D3'	211	ó	'\u00F3'	243
´	'\u00B4'	180	Ô	'\u00D4'	212	ô	'\u00F4'	244
µ	'\u00B5'	181	Õ	'\u00D5'	213	õ	'\u00F5'	245
¶	'\u00B6'	182	Ö	'\u00D6'	214	ö	'\u00F6'	246
·	'\u00B7'	183	×	'\u00D7'	215	÷	'\u00F7'	247
¸	'\u00B8'	184	Ø	'\u00D8'	216	ø	'\u00F8'	248
¹	'\u00B9'	185	Ù	'\u00D9'	217	ù	'\u00F9'	249
º	'\u00BA'	186	Ú	'\u00DA'	218	ú	'\u00FA'	250
»	'\u00BB'	187	Û	'\u00DB'	219	û	'\u00FB'	251
¼	'\u00BC'	188	Ü	'\u00DC'	220	ü	'\u00FC'	252
½	'\u00BD'	189	Ý	'\u00DD'	221	ý	'\u00FD'	253
¾	'\u00BE'	190	Þ	'\u00DE'	222	þ	'\u00FE'	254
¿	'\u00BF'	191	ß	'\u00DF'	223	ÿ	'\u00FF'	255

JAVA OPERATOR SUMMARY

The Java operators are listed in groups of decreasing *precedence* in the table below. The horizontal lines in the table indicate a change in operator precedence. Operators with higher precedence bind more strongly than those with lower precedence. For example, x + y * z means x + (y * z) because the * operator has higher precedence than the + operator. Looking at the table below, you can tell that x && y || z means (x && y) || z because the || operator has lower precedence.

The *associativity* of an operator indicates whether it groups left to right, or right to left. For example, the - operator binds left to right. Therefore, x - y - z means (x - y) - z. But the = operator binds right to left, and x = y = z means x = (y = z).

Operator	Description	Associativity
.	Access class feature	
[ ]	Array subscript	Left to right
( )	Function call	
++	Increment	
--	Decrement	
!	Boolean *not*	
~	Bitwise *not*	
+ *(unary)*	(Has no effect)	Right to left
- *(unary)*	Negative	
(*TypeName*)	Cast	
new	Object allocation	
*	Multiplication	
/	Division or integer division	Left to right
%	Integer remainder	
+	Addition, string concatenation	Left to right
-	Subtraction	
<<	Shift left	
>>	Right shift with sign extension	Left to right
>>>	Right shift with zero extension	

Operator	Description	Associativity
<	Less than	Left to right
<=	Less than or equal	
>	Greater than	
>=	Greater than or equal	
instanceof	Tests whether an object's type is a given type or a subtype thereof	
==	Equal	Left to right
!=	Not equal	
&	Bitwise *and*	Left to right
^	Bitwise exclusive *or*	Left to right
|	Bitwise *or*	Left to right
&&	Boolean "short circuit" *and*	Left to right
||	Boolean "short circuit" *or*	Left to right
? :	Conditional	Right to left
=	Assignment	Right to left
op=	Assignment with binary operator (*op* is one of +, -, *, /, &, |, ^, <<, >>, >>>)	

JAVA RESERVED WORD SUMMARY

Reserved Word	Description
abstract	An abstract class or method
assert	An assertion that a condition is fulfilled
boolean	The Boolean type
break	Breaks out of the current loop or labeled statement
byte	The 8-bit signed integer type
case	A label in a switch statement
catch	The handler for an exception in a try block
char	The 16-bit Unicode character type
class	Defines a class
const	Not used
continue	Skips the remainder of a loop body
default	The default label in a switch statement
do	A loop whose body is executed at least once
double	The 64-bit double-precision floating-point type
else	The alternative clause in an if statement
enum	An enumeration type
extends	Indicates that a class is a subclass of another class
final	A value that cannot be changed after it has been initialized, a method that cannot be overridden, or a class that cannot be extended
finally	A clause of a try block that is always executed
float	The 32-bit single-precision floating-point type
for	A loop with initialization, condition, and update expressions
goto	Not used
if	A conditional branch statement
implements	Indicates that a class realizes an interface

Reserved Word	Description
import	Allows the use of class names without the package name
instanceof	Tests whether an object's type is a given type or a subtype thereof
int	The 32-bit integer type
interface	An abstract type with only abstract or default methods and constants
long	The 64-bit integer type
native	A method implemented in non-Java code
new	Allocates an object
package	A collection of related classes
private	A feature that is accessible only by methods of the same class
protected	A feature that is accessible only by methods of the same class, a subclass, or another class in the same package
public	A feature that is accessible by all methods
return	Returns from a method
short	The 16-bit integer type
static	A feature that is defined for a class, not for individual instances
strictfp	Uses strict rules for floating-point computations
super	Invokes the superclass constructor or a superclass method
switch	A selection statement
synchronized	A block of code that is accessible to only one thread at a time
this	The implicit parameter of a method; or invocation of another constructor of the same class
throw	Throws an exception
throws	Indicates the exceptions that a method may throw
transient	Instance variables that should not be serialized
try	A block of code with exception handlers or a finally handler
var	Declares a local variable and infers its type
void	Tags a method that doesn't return a value
volatile	A variable that may be accessed by multiple threads without synchronization
while	A loop statement

Java 9 adds "restricted keywords" exports, module, open, opens, requires, transitive, to, uses, provides, and with, which have special meanings only in module declarations, which this book does not cover.

THE JAVA LIBRARY

This appendix lists all classes and methods from the standard Java library that are used in this book. Classes are sorted first by package, then alphabetically within a package.

In the following inheritance hierarchy, superclasses that are not used in this book are shown in gray type. Some classes implement interfaces not covered in this book; they are omitted.

```
java.awt.Shape
java.io.Serializable
java.lang.AutoCloseable
java.lang.Cloneable
java.lang.Object
    java.awt.BorderLayout implements Serializable
    java.awt.Color implements Serializable
    java.awt.Component implements Serializable
        java.awt.Container
            javax.swing.JComponent
                javax.swing.AbstractButton
                    javax.swing.JButton
                    javax.swing.JMenuItem
                        javax.swing.JMenu
                    javax.swing.JToggleButton
                        javax.swing.JCheckBox
                        javax.swing.JRadioButton
                javax.swing.JComboBox
                javax.swing.JFileChooser
                javax.swing.JLabel
                javax.swing.JMenuBar
                javax.swing.JPanel
                javax.swing.JOptionPane
                javax.swing.JScrollPane
                javax.swing.JSlider
                javax.swing.text.JTextComponent
                    javax.swing.JTextArea
                    javax.swing.JTextField
            java.awt.Window
                java.awt.Frame
                    javax.swing.JFrame
    java.awt.Dimension2D
        java.awt.Dimension implements Cloneable, Serializable
    java.awt.FlowLayout implements Serializable
    java.awt.Font implements Serializable
    java.awt.Graphics
        java.awt.Graphics2D;
    java.awt.GridLayout implements Serializable
    java.awt.event.MouseAdapter implements MouseListener
    java.awt.geom.Line2D implements Cloneable, Shape
        java.awt.geom.Line2D.Double implements Serializable
    java.awt.geom.Point2D implements Cloneable
        java.awt.geom.Point2D.Double implements Serializable
    java.awt.geom.RectangularShape implements Cloneable, Shape
        java.awt.geom.Rectangle2D
            java.awt.Rectangle implements Serializable
        java.awt.geom.Ellipse2D
            java.awt.geom.Ellipse2D.Double implements Serializable
```

```
java.io.File implements Comparable<File>, Serializable
java.io.InputStream
   java.io.FileInputStream
   java.io.ObjectInputStream
java.io.OutputStream
   java.io.FileOutputStream
   java.io.FilterOutputStream
      java.io.PrintStream
   java.io.ObjectOutputStream
java.io.RandomAccessFile
java.io.Writer
   java.io.PrintWriter
java.lang.Boolean implements Comparable<Boolean>, Serializable
java.lang.Character implements Comparable<Character>, Serializable
java.lang.Class implements Serializable
java.lang.Math
java.lang.Number implements Serializable
   java.math.BigDecimal implements Comparable<BigDecimal>
   java.math.BigInteger implements Comparable<BigInteger>
   java.lang.Double implements Comparable<Double>
   java.lang.Integer implements Comparable<Integer>
java.lang.String implements Comparable<String>, Serializable
java.lang.System
java.lang.Thread implements Runnable
java.lang.Throwable
   java.lang.Error
   java.lang.Exception
      java.lang.CloneNotSupportedException
      java.lang.InterruptedException
      java.io.IOException
         java.io.EOFException
         java.io.FileNotFoundException
      java.lang.RuntimeException
         java.lang.IllegalArgumentException
            java.lang.NumberFormatException
         java.lang.IllegalStateException
         java.util.NoSuchElementException
            java.util.InputMismatchException
         java.lang.NullPointerException
      java.sql.SQLException
      javax.xml.xpath.XPathException
         javax.xml.xpath.XPathExpressionException
      org.xml.sax.SAXException
java.net.ServerSocket
java.net.Socket
java.net.URL implements Serializable
java.net.URLConnection
   java.net.HttpURLConnection
java.nio.file.Files
java.nio.file.Paths
java.sql.DriverManager
java.text.Format implements Serializable
   java.text.DateFormat
java.util.AbstractCollection<E>
   java.util.AbstractList<E>
      java.util.AbstractSequentialList<E>
         java.util.LinkedList<E> implements List<E>, Queue<E>, Serializable
      java.util.ArrayList<E> implements List<E>, Serializable
   java.util.AbstractQueue<E>
      java.util.PriorityQueue<E> implements Serializable
   java.util.AbstractSet<E>
      java.util.HashSet<E> implements Serializable, Set<E>
      java.util.TreeSet<E> implements Serializable, SortedSet<E>
java.util.AbstractMap<K, V>
   java.util.HashMap<K, V> implements Map<K, V>, Serializable
      java.util.LinkedHashMap<K, V>
   java.util.TreeMap<K, V> implements Serializable, Map<K, V>
```

```
java.util.Arrays
java.util.Collections
java.util.Calendar
    java.util.GregorianCalendar
java.util.Date implements Serializable
java.util.Dictionary<K, V>
    java.util.Hashtable<K, V>
        java.util.Properties implements Serializable
java.util.EventObject implements Serializable
    java.awt.AWTEvent
        java.awt.event.ActionEvent
        java.awt.event.ComponentEvent
            java.awt.event.InputEvent
                java.awt.event.KeyEvent
                java.awt.event.MouseEvent
    javax.swing.event.ChangeEvent
java.util.Objects
java.util.Optional<T>
java.util.OptionalDouble
java.util.OptionalInt
java.util.OptionalLong
java.util.Random implements Serializable
java.util.Scanner
java.util.TimeZone implements Serializable
java.util.concurrent.locks.ReentrantLock implements Lock, Serializable
java.util.logging.Level implements Serializable
java.util.logging.Logger
java.util.stream.Collectors
javax.swing.ButtonGroup implements Serializable
javax.swing.ImageIcon implements Serializable
javax.swing.Keystroke implements Serializable
javax.swing.Timer implements Serializable
javax.swing.border.AbstractBorder implements Serializable
    javax.swing.border.EtchedBorder
    javax.swing.border.TitledBorder
javax.xml.parsers.DocumentBuilder
javax.xml.parsers.DocumentBuilderFactory
javax.xml.xpath.XPathFactory
java.lang.Comparable<T>
java.lang.Runnable
java.nio.file.Path
java.sql.Connection
java.sql.ResultSet
java.sql.ResultSetMetaData
java.sql.Statement
    java.sql.PreparedStatement
java.util.Collection<E>
    java.util.List<E>
    java.util.Set<E>
        java.util.SortedSet<E>
java.util.Comparator<T>
java.util.EventListener
    java.awt.event.ActionListener
    java.awt.event.KeyListener
    java.awt.event.MouseListener
    javax.swing.event.ChangeListener
java.util.Iterator<E>
    java.util.ListIterator<E>
java.util.Map<K, V>
java.util.Queue<E> extends Collection<E>
java.util.concurrent.locks.Condition
java.util.concurrent.locks.Lock
java.util.function.Predicate<T>
java.util.stream.DoubleStream
java.util.stream.IntStream
java.util.stream.LongStream
java.util.stream.Stream<T>
```

```
javax.sql.DataSource
javax.xml.xpath.XPath
org.w3c.dom.DOMConfiguration
org.w3c.dom.DOMImplementaton
org.w3c.dom.Node
    org.w3c.dom.CharacterData
        org.w3c.dom.Text
    org.w3c.dom.Document
    org.w3c.dom.Element
org.w3c.dom.ls.DOMImplementationLS
org.w3c.dom.ls.LSSerializer
```

In the following descriptions, the phrase "this object" ("this component", "this container", and so forth) means the object (component, container, and so forth) on which the method is invoked (the implicit parameter, this).

Package java.awt

Class java.awt.BorderLayout

- **BorderLayout**()
  This constructs a border layout. A border layout has five regions for adding components, called "North", "East", "South", "West", and "Center".

- static final int **CENTER**
  This value identifies the center position of a border layout.

- static final int **EAST**
  This value identifies the east position of a border layout.

- static final int **NORTH**
  This value identifies the north position of a border layout.

- static final int **SOUTH**
  This value identifies the south position of a border layout.

- static final int **WEST**
  This value identifies the west position of a border layout.

Class java.awt.Color

- **Color**(int red, int green, int blue)
  This creates a color with the specified red, green, and blue values between 0 and 255.

  Parameters: red The red component
  green The green component
  blue The blue component

Class java.awt.Component

- void **addKeyListener**(KeyListener listener)
  This method adds a key listener to the component.
  Parameters: listener The key listener to be added

- void **addMouseListener**(MouseListener listener)
  This method adds a mouse listener to the component.
  Parameters: listener The mouse listener to be added

- int **getHeight**()
  This method gets the height of this component.
  Returns: The height in pixels

- int **getWidth**()
  This method gets the width of this component.
  Returns: The width in pixels

- void **repaint**()
  This method repaints this component by scheduling a call to the paint method.

- void **setFocusable**(boolean focusable)
  This method controls whether or not the component can receive input focus.
  Parameters: focusable true to have focus, or false to lose focus

- void **setPreferredSize**(Dimension preferredSize)
  This method sets the preferred size of this component.

- void **setSize**(int width, int height)
  This method sets the size of this component.
  Parameters: width the component width
  height   the component height

- void **setVisible**(boolean visible)
  This method shows or hides the component.
  Parameters: visible true to show the component, or false to hide it

Class java.awt.`Container`

- void **add**(Component c)
- void **add**(Component c, Object position)

  These methods add a component to the end of this container. If a position is given, the layout manager is called to position the component.

  Parameters: c The component to be added
  position An object expressing position information for the layout manager

- void **setLayout**(LayoutManager manager)

  This method sets the layout manager for this container.

  Parameters: manager A layout manager

Class java.awt.`Dimension`

- **Dimension**(int width, int height)

  This constructs a `Dimension` object with the given width and height.

  Parameters: width The width
  height The height

Class java.awt.`FlowLayout`

- **FlowLayout**()

  This constructs a new flow layout. A flow layout places as many components as possible in a row, without changing their size, and starts new rows as needed.

Class java.awt.`Font`

- **Font**(String name, int style, int size)

  This constructs a font object from the specified name, style, and point size.

  Parameters: name The font name, either a font face name or a logical font name, which must be one of "Dialog", "DialogInput", "Monospaced", "Serif", or "SansSerif"
  style One of Font.PLAIN, Font.ITALIC, Font.BOLD, or Font.ITALIC+Font.BOLD
  size The point size of the font

Class java.awt.`Frame`

- void **setTitle**(String title)

  This method sets the frame title.

  Parameters: title The title to be displayed in the border of the frame

Class java.awt.`Graphics`

- void **drawLine**(int x1, int y1, int x2, int y2)

  Draws a line between two points.

  Parameters: x1, y1 The starting point
  x2, y2 The endpoint

- void **setColor**(Color c)

  This method sets the current color. After the method call, all graphics operations use this color.

  Parameters: c The new drawing color

Class java.awt.`Graphics2D`

- void **draw**(Shape s)

  This method draws the outline of the given shape. Many classes—among them Rectangle and Line2D.Double—implement the Shape interface.

  Parameters: s The shape to be drawn

- void **drawString**(String s, int x, int y)
- void **drawString**(String s, float x, float y)

  These methods draw a string in the current font.

  Parameters: s The string to draw
  x,y The basepoint of the first character in the string

- void **fill**(Shape s)

  This method draws the given shape and fills it with the current color.

  Parameters: s The shape to be filled

Class java.awt.`GridLayout`

- **GridLayout**(int rows, int cols)

  This constructor creates a grid layout with the specified number of rows and columns. The components in a grid layout are arranged in a grid with equal widths and heights. One, but not both, of rows and cols can be zero, in which case any number of objects can be placed in a row or in a column, respectively.

  Parameters: rows The number of rows in the grid
  cols The number of columns in the grid

Class java.awt.`Rectangle`

- **Rectangle**()

  This constructs a rectangle with a top-left corner at (0, 0) and width and height set to 0.

- **Rectangle**(int x, int y, int width, int height)

  This constructs a rectangle with given top-left corner and size.

  Parameters: x, y The top-left corner
  width The width
  height The height

- double **getHeight**()
- double **getWidth**()

  These methods get the height and width of the rectangle.

- double **getX**()
- double **getY**()

These methods get the x- and y-coordinates of the top-left corner of the rectangle.

- void **grow**(int dw, int dh)

This method adjusts the width and height of this rectangle.

Parameters: dw The amount to add to the width (can be negative)
dh The amount to add to the height (can be negative)

- Rectangle **intersection**(Rectangle other)

This method computes the intersection of this rectangle with the specified rectangle.

Parameters: other A rectangle
Returns: The largest rectangle contained in both this and other

- void **setLocation**(int x, int y)

This method moves this rectangle to a new location.

Parameters: x, y The new top-left corner

- void **setSize**(int width, int height)

This method sets the width and height of this rectangle to new values.

Parameters: width The new width
height The new height

- void **translate**(int dx, int dy)

This method moves this rectangle.

Parameters: dx The distance to move along the x-axis
dy The distance to move along the y-axis

- Rectangle **union**(Rectangle other)

This method computes the union of this rectangle with the specified rectangle. This is not the set-theoretic union but the smallest rectangle that contains both this and other.

Parameters: other A rectangle
Returns: The smallest rectangle containing both this and other

Interface java.awt.Shape

The Shape interface describes shapes that can be drawn and filled by a Graphics2D object.

Package java.awt.event

Interface java.awt.event.ActionListener

- void **actionPerformed**(ActionEvent e)

The event source calls this method when an action occurs.

Class java.awt.event.KeyEvent

This event is passed to the KeyListener methods. Use the KeyStroke class to obtain the key information from the key event.

Interface java.awt.event.KeyListener

- void **keyPressed**(KeyEvent e)
- void **keyReleased**(KeyEvent e)

These methods are called when a key has been pressed or released.

- void **keyTyped**(KeyEvent e)

This method is called when a keystroke has been composed by pressing and releasing one or more keys.

Class java.awt.event.MouseEvent

- int **getX**()

This method returns the horizontal position of the mouse as of the time the event occurred.

Returns: The x-position of the mouse

- int **getY**()

This method returns the vertical position of the mouse as of the time the event occurred.

Returns: The y-position of the mouse

Interface java.awt.event.MouseListener

- void **mouseClicked**(MouseEvent e)

This method is called when the mouse has been clicked (that is, pressed and released in quick succession).

- void **mouseEntered**(MouseEvent e)

This method is called when the mouse has entered the component to which this listener was added.

- void **mouseExited**(MouseEvent e)

This method is called when the mouse has exited the component to which this listener was added.

- void **mousePressed**(MouseEvent e)

This method is called when a mouse button has been pressed.

- void **mouseReleased**(MouseEvent e)

This method is called when a mouse button has been released.

Package java.awt.geom

Class java.awt.geom.Ellipse2D.Double

- **Ellipse2D.Double**(double x, double y, double w, double h)

  This constructs an ellipse from the specified coordinates.

  Parameters: x, y The top-left corner of the bounding rectangle
  w The width of the bounding rectangle
  h The height of the bounding rectangle

Class java.awt.geom.Line2D

- double **getX1**()
- double **getX2**()
- double **getY1**()
- double **getY2**()

  These methods get the requested coordinate of an endpoint of this line.

  Returns: The *x*- or *y*-coordinate of the first or second endpoint

- void **setLine**(double x1, double y1, double x2, double y2)

  This methods sets the endpoints of this line.

  Parameters: x1, y1 A new endpoint of this line
  x2, y2 The other new endpoint

Class java.awt.geom.Line2D.Double

- **Line2D.Double**(double x1, double y1, double x2, double y2)

  This constructs a line from the specified coordinates.

  Parameters: x1, y1 One endpoint of the line
  x2, y2 The other endpoint

- **Line2D.Double**(Point2D p1, Point2D p2)

  This constructs a line from the two endpoints.

  Parameters: p1, p2 The endpoints of the line

Class java.awt.geom.Point2D

- double **getX**()
- double **getY**()

  These methods get the requested coordinates of this point.

  Returns: The *x*- or *y*-coordinate of this point

- void **setLocation**(double x, double y)

  This method sets the *x*- and *y*-coordinates of this point.

  Parameters: x, y The new location of this point

Class java.awt.geom.Point2D.Double

- **Point2D.Double**(double x, double y)

  This constructs a point with the specified coordinates.

  Parameters: x, y The coordinates of the point

Class java.awt.geom.RectangularShape

- int **getHeight**()
- int **getWidth**()

  These methods get the height or width of the bounding rectangle of this rectangular shape.

  Returns: The height or width, respectively

- double **getCenterX**()
- double **getCenterY**()
- double **getMaxX**()
- double **getMaxY**()
- double **getMinX**()
- double **getMinY**()

  These methods get the requested coordinate value of the corners or center of the bounding rectangle of this shape.

  Returns: The center, maximum, or minimum *x*- and *y*-coordinates

Package java.io

Class java.io.EOFException

- **EOFException**(String message)

  This constructs an "end of file" exception object.

  Parameters: message The detail message

Class java.io.File

- **File**(String name)

  This constructs a File object that describes a file (which may or may not exist) with the given name.

  Parameters: name The name of the file

- boolean **exists**()

  This method checks whether there is a file in the local file system that matches this File object.

  Returns: true if there is a matching file, false otherwise

- static final String pathSeparator

  The sytem-dependent separator between path names. A colon (:) in Linux or Mac OS X; a semicolon (;) in Windows.

Class java.io.FileInputStream

- **FileInputStream**(File f)
  This constructs a file input stream and opens the chosen file. If the file cannot be opened for reading, a FileNotFoundException is thrown.
  Parameters: f The file to be opened for reading

- **FileInputStream**(String name)
  This constructs a file input stream and opens the named file. If the file cannot be opened for reading, a FileNotFoundException is thrown.
  Parameters: name The name of the file to be opened for reading

Class java.io.FileNotFoundException

This exception is thrown when a file could not be opened.

Class java.io.FileOutputStream

- **FileOutputStream**(File f)
  This constructs a file output stream and opens the chosen file. If the file cannot be opened for writing, a FileNotFoundException is thrown.
  Parameters: f The file to be opened for writing

- **FileOutputStream**(String name)
  This constructs a file output stream and opens the named file. If the file cannot be opened for writing, a FileNotFoundException is thrown.
  Parameters: name The name of the file to be opened for writing

Class java.io.InputStream

- void **close**()
  This method closes this input stream (such as a FileInputStream) and releases any system resources associated with the stream.

- int **read**()
  This method reads the next byte of data from this input stream.
  Returns: The next byte of data, or −1 if the end of the stream is reached

Class java.io.InputStreamReader

- **InputStreamReader**(InputStream in)
  This constructs a reader from a specified input stream.
  Parameters: in The stream to read from

Class java.io.IOException

This type of exception is thrown when an input/output error is encountered.

Class java.io.ObjectInputStream

- **ObjectInputStream**(InputStream in)
  This constructs an object input stream.
  Parameters: in The input stream to read from

- Object **readObject**()
  This method reads the next object from this object input stream.
  Returns: The next object

Class java.io.ObjectOutputStream

- **ObjectOutputStream**(OutputStream out)
  This constructs an object output stream.
  Parameters: out The output stream to write to

- Object **writeObject**(Object obj)
  This method writes the next object to this object output stream.
  Parameters: obj The object to write

Class java.io.OutputStream

- void **close**()
  This method closes this output stream (such as a FileOutputStream) and releases any system resources associated with this stream. A closed stream cannot perform output operations and cannot be reopened.

- void **write**(int b)
  This method writes the lowest byte of b to this output stream.
  Parameters: b The integer whose lowest byte is written

Class java.io.PrintStream / Class java.io.PrintWriter

- **PrintStream**(String name)
- **PrintWriter**(String name)
  This constructs a PrintStream or PrintWriter and opens the named file. If the file cannot be opened for writing, a FileNotFoundException is thrown.
  Parameters: name The name of the file to be opened for writing

- void **close**()
  This method closes this stream or writer and releases any associated system resources.

- void **print**(int x)
- void **print**(double x)
- void **print**(Object x)
- void **print**(String x)
- void **println**()
- void **println**(int x)
- void **println**(double x)

- void **println**(Object x)
- void **println**(String x)

  These methods print a value to this PrintStream or PrintWriter. The println methods print a newline after the value. Objects are printed by converting them to strings with their toString methods.

  Parameters: x The value to be printed

- PrintStream **printf**(String format, Object... values)
- Printwriter **printf**(String format, Object... values)

  These methods print the format string to this PrintStream or PrintWriter, substituting the given values for placeholders that start with %.

  Parameters: format The format string
  values The values to be printed. You can supply any number of values

  Returns: The implicit parameter

Class java.io.RandomAccessFile

- **RandomAccessFile**(String name, String mode)

  This method opens a named random access file for reading or read/write access.

  Parameters: name The file name
  mode "r" for reading or "rw" for read/write access

- long **getFilePointer**()

  This method gets the current position in this file.

  Returns: The current position for reading and writing

- long **length**()

  This method gets the length of this file.

  Returns: The file length

- char **readChar**()
- double **readDouble**()
- int **readInt**()

  These methods read a value from the current position in this file.

  Returns: The value that was read from the file

- void **seek**(long position)

  This method sets the position for reading and writing in this file.

  Parameters: position The new position

- void **writeChar**(int x)
- void **writeChars**(String x)
- void **writeDouble**(double x)
- void **writeInt**(int x)

  These methods write a value to the current position in this file.

  Parameters: x The value to be written

Interface java.io.Serializable

A class should implement this interface in order to enable serialization of objects.

Package java.lang

Interface java.lang.AutoCloseable

- void **close**()

  This method is called automatically at the end of a try-with-resources statement.

Class java.lang.Boolean

- **Boolean**(boolean value)

  This constructs a wrapper object for a boolean value.

  Parameters: value The value to store in this object

- boolean **booleanValue**()

  This method returns the value stored in this boolean object.

  Returns: The Boolean value of this object

Class java.lang.Character

- static boolean **isDigit**(ch)

  This method tests whether a given character is a Unicode digit.

  Parameters: ch The character to test
  Returns: true if the character is a digit

- static boolean **isLetter**(ch)

  This method tests whether a given character is a Unicode letter.

  Parameters: ch The character to test
  Returns: true if the character is a letter

- static boolean **isLowerCase**(ch)

  This method tests whether a given character is a lowercase Unicode letter.

  Parameters: ch The character to test
  Returns: true if the character is a lowercase letter

- static boolean **isUpperCase**(ch)

  This method tests whether a given character is an uppercase Unicode letter.

  Parameters: ch The character to test
  Returns: true if the character is an uppercase letter

Class java.lang.Class

- static Class **forName**(String className)

  This method loads a class with a given name. Loading a class initializes its static variables.

  Parameters: className The name of the class to load
  Returns: The type descriptor of the class

Interface java.lang.Cloneable

A class implements this interface to indicate that the Object.clone method is allowed to make a shallow copy of its instance variables.

Class java.lang.CloneNotSupportedException

This exception is thrown when a program tries to use Object.clone to make a shallow copy of an object of a class that does not implement the Cloneable interface.

Interface java.lang.Comparable<T>

- int **compareTo**(T other)

  This method compares this object with the other object.

  Parameters: other The object to be compared

  Returns: A negative integer if this object is less than the other, zero if they are equal, or a positive integer otherwise

Class java.lang.Double

- **Double**(double value)

  This constructs a wrapper object for a double-precision floating-point number.

  Parameters: value The value to store in this object

- static int **compare**(double x, double y)

  This method compares two numbers.

  Parameters: x, y Two floating-point values

  Returns: A negative integer if x is less than y, zero if they are equal, or a positive integer otherwise

- double **doubleValue**()

  This method returns the floating-point value stored in this Double wrapper object.

  Returns: The value stored in the object

- static double **parseDouble**(String s)

  This method returns the floating-point number that the string represents. If the string cannot be interpreted as a number, a NumberFormatException is thrown.

  Parameters: s The string to be parsed

  Returns: The value represented by the string argument

Class java.lang.Error

This is the superclass for all unchecked system errors.

Class java.lang.IllegalArgumentException

- **IllegalArgumentException**()

  This constructs an IllegalArgumentException with no detail message.

Class java.lang.IllegalStateException

This exception is thrown if the state of an object indicates that a method cannot currently be applied.

Class java.lang.Integer

- **Integer**(int value)

  This constructs a wrapper object for an integer.

  Parameters: value The value to store in this object

- static int **compare**(int x, int y)

  This method compares two numbers.

  Parameters: x, y Two integer values

  Returns: A negative integer if x is less than y, zero if they are equal, or a positive integer otherwise

- int **intValue**()

  This method returns the integer value stored in this wrapper object.

  Returns: The value stored in the object

- static int **parseInt**(String s)

  This method returns the integer that the string represents. If the string cannot be interpreted as an integer, a NumberFormatException is thrown.

  Parameters: s The string to be parsed

  Returns: The value represented by the string argument

- static Integer **parseInt**(String s, int base)

  This method returns the integer value that the string represents in a given number system. If the string cannot be interpreted as an integer, a NumberFormatException is thrown.

  Parameters: s The string to be parsed
  base The base of the number system (such as 2 or 16)

  Returns: The value represented by the string argument

- static String **toString**(int i)
- static String **toString**(int i, int base)

  This method creates a string representation of an integer in a given number system. If no base is given, a decimal representation is created.

  Parameters: i An integer number
  base The base of the number system (such as 2 or 16)

  Returns: A string representation of the argument in the number system

- static final int MAX_VALUE
  This constant is the largest value of type int.
- static final int MIN_VALUE
  This constant is the smallest (negative) value of type int.

Class java.lang.InterruptedException

This exception is thrown to interrupt a thread, usually with the intention of terminating it.

Class java.lang.Math

- static double **abs**(double x)
  This method returns the absolute value $|x|$.
  Parameters: x A floating-point value
  Returns: The absolute value of the argument
- static double **acos**(double x)
  This method returns the angle with the given cosine, $\cos^{-1} x \in [0, \pi]$.
  Parameters: x A floating-point value between −1 and 1
  Returns: The arc cosine of the argument, in radians
- static double **asin**(double x)
  This method returns the angle with the given sine, $\sin^{-1} x \in [-\pi/2, \pi/2]$.
  Parameters: x A floating-point value between −1 and 1
  Returns: The arc sine of the argument, in radians
- static double **atan**(double x)
  This method returns the angle with the given tangent, $\tan^{-1} x$ $(-\pi/2, \pi/2)$.
  Parameters: x A floating-point value
  Returns: The arc tangent of the argument, in radians
- static double **atan2**(double y, double x)
  This method returns the arc tangent, $\tan^{-1} (y/x) \in (-\pi, \pi)$. If x can equal zero, or if it is necessary to distinguish "northwest" from "southeast" and "northeast" from "southwest", use this method instead of atan(y/x).
  Parameters: y, x Two floating-point values
  Returns: The angle, in radians, between the points (0,0) and (x,y)
- static double **ceil**(double x)
  This method returns the smallest integer $\geq x$ (as a double).
  Parameters: x A floating-point value
  Returns: The smallest integer greater than or equal to the argument

- static double **cos**(double radians)
  This method returns the cosine of an angle given in radians.
  Parameters: radians An angle, in radians
  Returns: The cosine of the argument
- static double **exp**(double x)
  This method returns the value e^x, where e is the base of the natural logarithms.
  Parameters: x A floating-point value
  Returns: e^x
- static double **floor**(double x)
  This method returns the largest integer $\leq x$ (as a double).
  Parameters: x A floating-point value
  Returns: The largest integer less than or equal to the argument
- static int **floorMod**(int x, int y)
  This method returns the "floor modulus" remainder of the integer division of x by y. If y is positive, the result is the (nonnegative) mathematical remainder.
  Parameters: x, y Two integers
  Returns: For positive y, the smallest nonnegative number r such that $x = qy + r$ for some r. For negative y, -Math.floorMod(x, -y).
- static double **log**(double x)
- static double **log10**(double x)
  This method returns the natural (base e) or decimal (base 10) logarithm of x, $\ln x$.
  Parameters: x A number greater than 0.0
  Returns: The natural logarithm of the argument
- static int **max**(int x, int y)
- static double **max**(double x, double y)
  These methods return the larger of the given arguments.
  Parameters: x, y Two integers or floating-point values
  Returns: The maximum of the arguments
- static int **min**(int x, int y)
- static double **min**(double x, double y)
  These methods return the smaller of the given arguments.
  Parameters: x, y Two integers or floating-point values
  Returns: The minimum of the arguments
- static double **pow**(double x, double y)
  This method returns the value x^y ($x > 0$, or $x = 0$ and $y > 0$, or $x < 0$ and y is an integer).
  Parameters: x, y Two floating-point values
  Returns: The value of the first argument raised to the power of the second argument

- static long **round**(double x)

  This method returns the closest long integer to the argument.

  Parameters: x   A floating-point value

  Returns: The argument rounded to the nearest long value

- static double **sin**(double radians)

  This method returns the sine of an angle given in radians.

  Parameters: radians   An angle, in radians

  Returns: The sine of the argument

- static double **sqrt**(double x)

  This method returns the square root of x, $\sqrt{x}$.

  Parameters: x   A nonnegative floating-point value

  Returns: The square root of the argument

- static double **tan**(double radians)

  This method returns the tangent of an angle given in radians.

  Parameters: radians   An angle, in radians

  Returns: The tangent of the argument

- static double **toDegrees**(double radians)

  This method converts radians to degrees.

  Parameters: radians   An angle, in radians

  Returns: The angle in degrees

- static double **toRadians**(double degrees)

  This methods converts degrees to radians.

  Parameters: degrees   An angle, in degrees

  Returns: The angle in radians

- static final double E

  This constant is the value of e, the base of the natural logarithms.

- static final double PI

  This constant is the value of π.

Class java.lang.NullPointerException

This exception is thrown when a program tries to use an object through a null reference.

Class java.lang.NumberFormatException

This exception is thrown when a program tries to parse the numerical value of a string that is not a number.

Class java.lang.Object

- protected Object **clone**()

  This constructs and returns a shallow copy of this object whose instance variables are copies of the instance variables of this object. If an instance variable of the object is an object reference itself, only the reference is copied, not the object itself. However, if the class does not implement the Cloneable interface, a CloneNotSupportedException is thrown. Subclasses should redefine this method to make a deep copy.

  Returns: A copy of this object

- boolean **equals**(Object other)

  This method tests whether this and the other object are equal. This method tests only whether the object references are to the same object. Subclasses should redefine this method to compare the instance variables.

  Parameters: other   The object with which to compare

  Returns: true if the objects are equal, false otherwise

- void **notify**()

  This method notifies one of the threads that is currently on the wait list for the lock of this object.

- void **notifyAll**()

  This method notifies all of the threads that are currently on the wait list for the lock of this object.

- String **toString**()

  This method returns a string representation of this object. This method produces only the class name and locations of the objects. Subclasses should redefine this method to print the instance variables.

  Returns: A string describing this object

- void **wait**()

  This method blocks the currently executing thread and puts it on the wait list for the lock of this object.

Interface java.lang.Runnable

- void **run**()

  This method should be overridden to define the tasks to be carried out when this runnable is executed.

Class java.lang.RuntimeException

This is the superclass for all unchecked exceptions.

Class java.lang.String

- int **compareTo**(String other)

  This method compares this string and the other string lexicographically.

  Parameters: other   The other string to be compared

  Returns: A value less than 0 if this string is lexicographically less than the other, 0 if the strings are equal, and a value greater than 0 otherwise

- `IntStream codePoints()`
This method yields a stream of all code points in this string.

- `boolean equals(String other)`
- `boolean equalsIgnoreCase(String other)`
These methods test whether two strings are equal, or whether they are equal when letter case is ignored.
Parameters: other The other string to be compared
Returns: true if the strings are equal

- `static String format(String format, Object... values)`
This method formats the given string by substituting placeholders beginning with % with the given values.
Parameters: format The string with the placeholders
values The values to be substituted for the placeholders
Returns: The formatted string, with the placeholders replaced by the given values

- `int length()`
This method returns the length of this string.
Returns: The count of characters in this string

- `String replace(String match, String replacement)`
This method replaces matching substrings with a given replacement.
Parameters: match The string whose matches are to be replaced
replacement The string with which matching substrings are replaced
Returns: A string that is identical to this string, with all matching substrings replaced by the given replacement

- `String replaceAll(String regex, String replacement)`
This method replaces occurrences of a regular expression.
Parameters: regex A regular expression
replacement The replacement string
Returns: A string in which all substrings matching regex are replaced with a replacement string

- `String[] split(String regex)`
This method splits a string around delimiters that match a regular expression.
Parameters: regex a regular expression
Returns: An array of strings that results from breaking this string along matches of regex. For example, "a,b;c".split("[,;]") yields an array of strings "a", "b", and "c".

- `String substring(int begin)`
- `String substring(int begin, int pastEnd)`
These methods return a new string that is a substring of this string, made up of all characters starting at position begin and up to either position pastEnd - 1, if it is given, or the end of the string.
Parameters: begin The beginning index, inclusive
pastEnd The ending index, exclusive
Returns: The specified substring

- `String toLowerCase()`
This method returns a new string that consists of all characters in this string converted to lowercase.
Returns: A string with all characters in this string converted to lowercase

- `String toUpperCase()`
This method returns a new string that consists of all characters in this string converted to uppercase.
Returns: A string with all characters in this string converted to uppercase

Class java.lang.System

- `static long currentTimeMillis()`
This method returns the difference, measured in milliseconds, between the current time and midnight, Universal Time, January 1, 1970.
Returns: The current time in milliseconds since January 1, 1970.

- `static void exit(int status)`
This method terminates the program.
Parameters: status Exit status. A nonzero status code indicates abnormal termination

- `static final InputStream in`
This object is the "standard input" stream. Reading from this stream typically reads keyboard input.

- `static final PrintStream out`
This object is the "standard output" stream. Printing to this stream typically sends output to the console window.

Class java.lang.Thread

- `boolean interrupted()`
This method tests whether another thread has called the interrupt method on the current thread.
Returns: true if the thread has been interrupted

- `static void sleep(int millis)`
This method puts the calling thread to sleep.
Parameters: millis The number of milliseconds to sleep

- void **start**()
  This method starts the thread and executes its run method.

Class java.lang.Throwable

This is the superclass of exceptions and errors.

- **Throwable**()
  This constructs a Throwable with no detail message.

- String **getMessage**()
  This method gets the message that describes the exception or error.
  Returns: The message

- void **printStackTrace**()
  This method prints a stack trace to the "standard error" stream. The stack trace lists this object and all calls that were pending when it was created.

Package java.math

Class java.math.BigDecimal

- **BigDecimal**(String value)
  This constructs an arbitrary-precision floating-point number from the digits in the given string.
  Parameters: value A string representing the floating-point number

- BigDecimal **add**(BigDecimal other)
- BigDecimal **multiply**(BigDecimal other)
- BigDecimal **subtract**(BigDecimal other)
  These methods return a BigDecimal whose value is the sum, difference, product, or quotient of this number and the other.
  Parameters: other The other number
  Returns: The result of the arithmetic operation

Class java.math.BigInteger

- **BigInteger**(String value)
  This constructs an arbitrary-precision integer from the digits in the given string.
  Parameters: value A string representing an arbitrary-precision integer

- BigInteger **add**(BigInteger other)
- BigInteger **divide**(BigInteger other)
- BigInteger **mod**(BigInteger other)
- BigInteger **multiply**(BigInteger other)
- BigInteger **subtract**(BigInteger other)
  These methods return a BigInteger whose value is the sum, quotient, remainder, product, or difference of this number and the other.

Parameters: other The other number
Returns: The result of the arithmetic operation

Package java.net

Class java.net.HttpURLConnection

- int **getResponseCode**()
  This method gets the response status code from this connection. A value of HTTP_OK indicates success.
  Returns: The HTTP response code

- String **getResponseMessage**()
  This method gets the response message of this connection's HTTP request.
  Returns: The message, such as "OK" or "File not found"

- static int **HTTP_OK**
  This response code indicates a successful fulfillment of the request.

Class java.net.ServerSocket

- **ServerSocket**(int port)
  This constructs a server socket that listens to the given port.
  Parameters: port The port number to listen to

- Socket **accept**()
  This method waits for a client to connect to the port to which this server socket listens. When a connection occurs, the method returns a socket through which the server can communicate with the client.
  Returns: The socket through which the server can communicate with the client

- void **close**()
  This method closes the server socket. Clients can no longer connect.

Class java.net.Socket

- **Socket**(String host, int port)
  This constructs a socket that connects to a server.
  Parameters: host The host name
  port The port number to connect to

- void **close**()
  This method closes the connection with the server.

- InputStream **getInputStream**()
  This method gets the input stream through which the client can read the information that the server sends.
  Returns: The input stream associated with this socket

- OutputStream **getOutputStream**()
  This method gets the output stream through which
  the client can send information to the server.
  Returns: The output stream associated with this
  socket

Class java.net.URL

- URL(String s)
  This constructs a URL object from a string containing
  the URL.
  Parameters: s The URL string, such as "http://
  horstmann.com/index.html"

- InputStream **openStream**()
  This method gets the input stream through
  which the client can read the information that the
  server sends.
  Returns: The input stream associated with this
  URL

Class java.net.URLConnection

- URLConnection(URL u)
  This constructs a URLConnection object from a URL
  object.
  Parameters: u The resource to which you intend to
  connect

- int **getContentLength**()
  This method gets the value of the content-length
  header of this URL connection.
  Returns: The number of bytes in the content
  that the server is sending

- String **getContentType**()
  This method gets the value of the content-type header
  of this URL connection.
  Returns: The MIME type of the content that the
  server is sending, such as "text/plain" or
  "image/gif"

- InputStream **getInputStream**()
  This method gets the input stream through
  which the client can read the information that the
  server sends.
  Returns: The input stream associated with this
  URL

- void **setIfModifiedSince**(Date d)
  This method instructs the connection to request
  that the server send data only if the content has been
  modified since a given date.
  Parameters: d The modification date

Package java.nio.file

Class java.nio.file.Files

- static Path **copy**(Path source, Path target)
- static Path **move**(Path source, Path target)
  These methods copy or move a file to another. The
  target must not exist.
  Parameters: source The path to the source file
                  target The path to the target file
  Returns: target

- static Path **createFile**(Path path)
- static Path **createDirectory**(Path path)
  This method creates a file or directory. The parent
  directory must exist.
  Parameters: path The path to the file or directory to
                  be created
  Returns: path

- static void **delete**(Path file)
  This method deletes a file. The file must exist.
  Parameters: file The path to the file

- static boolean **exists**(Path path)
- static boolean **isDirectory**(Path path)
- static boolean **isRegularFile**(Path path)
  These methods check whether the given path exists,
  is a directory, or a regular file.
  Parameters: path The path to check

- static Stream<Path> **list**(Path dir)
- static Stream<Path> **walk**(Path dir)
  These methods yield streams to all children or
  descendants of a directory.
  Parameters: dir The path to the directory

- static byte[] **readAllBytes**(Path file)
- static List<String> **readAllLines**(Path file)
- static Stream<String> **lines**(Path file)
  These methods read all bytes or lines in a file.
  Parameters: file The path to the file

Interface java.nio.file.Path

- Path **getFileName**()
- Path **getParent**()
  These methods yield the last part, or all but the last
  part, of this path.

- Path **resolve**(Path other)
  This method yields a path that is obtained by first
  following this path, then the other if the other path
  is relative. If other is absolute, then it is returned.
  Parameters: other The path to follow relative to this
                  path

Class java.nio.file.Paths

- static Path get(String... components)

  This method constructs a path with the given components.

Package java.sql

Interface java.sql.Connection

- void close()

  This method closes the connection with the database.

- void commit()

  This method commits all database changes since the last call to commit or rollback.

- Statement createStatement()

  This method creates a statement object, which can be used to issue database commands.

  Returns: A statement object

- PreparedStatement prepareStatement(String command)

  This method creates a prepared statement for a SQL command that is issued repeatedly.

  Parameters: command The SQL command

  Returns: The statement object for setting parameters and executing the call

- void rollback()

  This method abandons all database changes since the last call to commit or rollback.

- void setAutoCommit(boolean b)

  This method sets the auto commit mode. By default, it is true. If it is set to false, then transactions are indicated with calls to commit or rollback.

  Parameters: b The desired auto commit mode

Class java.sql.DriverManager

- static Connection getConnection(String url, String username, String password)

  This method obtains a connection to the database specified in the database URL.

  Parameters: url The database URL

  username The database user name

  password The password for the database user

  Returns: A connection to the database

Interface java.sql.PreparedStatement

- boolean execute()

  This method executes this prepared statement.

  Returns: true if the execution yielded a result set

- ResultSet executeQuery()

  This method executes this prepared query.

  Returns: The query result

- int executeUpdate()

  This method executes this prepared update command.

  Returns: The number of records affected by the update

- void setDouble(int index, double value)

  This method sets a floating-point parameter for a call of this prepared statement.

  Parameters: index The parameter index (starting with 1)

  value The parameter value

- void setInt(int index, int value)

  This method sets an integer parameter for a call of this prepared statement.

  Parameters: index The parameter index (starting with 1)

  value The parameter value

- void setString(int index, String value)

  This method sets a string parameter for a call of this prepared statement.

  Parameters: index The parameter index (starting with 1)

  value The parameter value

Interface java.sql.ResultSet

- void close()

  This method closes the result set.

- double getDouble(int column)

  This method returns the floating-point value at the cursor row and the given column.

  Parameters: column The column index (starting with 1)

  Returns: The data value

- double getDouble(String columnName)

  This method returns the floating-point value at the cursor row and the given column name.

  Parameters: columnName The column name

  Returns: The data value

- int getInt(int column)

  This method returns the integer value at the cursor row and the given column.

  Parameters: column The column index (starting with 1)

  Returns: The data value

- int **getInt**(String columnName)
This method returns the integer value at the cursor row and the given column name.
Parameters: columnName The column name
Returns: The data value

- ResultSetMetaData **getMetaData**()
This method returns the metadata associated with this result set.
Returns: The metadata

- String **getString**(int column)
This method returns the value at the cursor row and the given column.
Parameters: column The column index (starting with 1)
Returns: The data value, as a string

- String **getString**(String columnName)
This method returns the value at the cursor row and the given column name.
Parameters: columnName The column name
Returns: The data value, as a string

- boolean **next**()
This method positions the cursor to the next row. You must call next once to move the cursor to the first row before calling any of the get methods.
Returns: true if the cursor has been positioned on a row, false at the end of the result set

Interface java.sql.ResultSetMetaData

- int **getColumnCount**()
This method returns the number of columns of this result set.
Returns: The number of columns

- int **getColumnDisplaySize**(int column)
This method returns the number of characters that should be used to display the specified column in this result set.
Parameters: column The column index (starting with 1)
Returns: The number of characters that should be used to display this column

- String **getColumnLabel**(int column)
This method returns the label for a column in this result set.
Parameters: column The column index (starting with 1)
Returns: The column label

Class java.sql.SQLException
This exception is thrown when a database error occurs.

Interface java.sql.Statement

- void **close**()
This method closes this statement.

- boolean **execute**(String command)
This method executes a SQL command.
Parameters: command The command to execute
Returns: true if the execution yielded a result set

- ResultSet **executeQuery**(String command)
This method executes a SQL query.
Parameters: command The query command to execute
Returns: The query result

- int **executeUpdate**(String command)
This method executes a SQL update command.
Parameters: command The update command to execute
Returns: The number of records affected by the update

- ResultSet **getResultSet**()
This method gets the result of the last command.
Returns: The query result from the last command

- int **getUpdateCount**()
This method gets the update count of the last command.
Returns: The number of records affected by the last command

Package java.text

Class java.text.DateFormat

- String **format**(Date aDate)
This method formats a date.
Parameters: aDate The date to format
Returns: A string containing the formatted date

- static DateFormat **getTimeInstance**()
This method returns a formatter that formats only the time portion of a date.
Returns: The formatter object

- void **setTimeZone**(TimeZone zone)
This method sets the time zone to be used when formatting dates.
Parameters: zone The time zone to use

Package java.util

Class java.util.ArrayList<E>

- ArrayList()

  This constructs an empty array list.

- boolean add(E element)

  This method appends an element to the end of this array list.

  Parameters: element The element to add

  Returns: true (This method returns a value because it overrides a method in the List interface.)

- void add(int index, E element)

  This method inserts an element into this array list at the given position.

  Parameters: index Insert position
                element The element to insert

- E get(int index)

  This method gets the element at the specified position in this array list.

  Parameters: index Position of the element to return

  Returns: The requested element

- E remove(int index)

  This method removes the element at the specified position in this array list and returns it.

  Parameters: index Position of the element to remove

  Returns: The removed element

- E set(int index, E element)

  This method replaces the element at a specified position in this array list.

  Parameters: index Position of element to replace
                element Element to be stored at the specified position

  Returns: The element previously at the specified position

- int size()

  This method returns the number of elements in this array list.

  Returns: The number of elements in this array list

Class java.util.Arrays

- static int binarySearch(Object[] a, Object key)

  This method searches the specified array for the specified object using the binary search algorithm. The array elements must implement the Comparable interface. The array must be sorted in ascending order.

  Parameters: a The array to be searched
                key The value to be searched for

  Returns: The position of the search key, if it is contained in the array; otherwise, $-index - 1$, where $index$ is the position where the element may be inserted

- static T[] copyOf(T[] a, int newLength)

  This method copies the elements of the array a, or the first newLength elements if a.length > newLength, into an array of length newLength and returns that array. T can be a primitive type, class, or interface type.

  Parameters: a The array to be copied
                key The value to be searched for

  Returns: The position of the search key, if it is contained in the array; otherwise, $-index - 1$, where $index$ is the position where the element may be inserted

- static void sort(Object[] a)

  This method sorts the specified array of objects into ascending order. Its elements must implement the Comparable interface.

  Parameters: a The array to be sorted

- static String toString(T[] a)

  This method creates and returns a string containing the array elements. T can be a primitive type, class, or interface type.

  Parameters: a An array

  Returns: A string containing a comma-separated list of string representations of the array elements, surrounded by brackets.

Class java.util.Calendar

- int get(int field)

  This method returns the value of the given field.

  Parameters: field   One of Calendar.YEAR, Calendar.MONTH, Calendar.DAY_OF_MONTH, Calendar.HOUR, Calendar.MINUTE, Calendar.SECOND, or Calendar.MILLISECOND

Interface java.util.Collection<E>

- boolean add(E element)

  This method adds an element to this collection.

  Parameters: element The element to add

  Returns: true if adding the element changes the collection

- boolean **contains**(E element)
  This method tests whether an element is present in this collection.
  Parameters: element The element to find
  Returns: true if the element is contained in the collection

- Iterator **iterator**()
  This method returns an iterator that can be used to traverse the elements of this collection.
  Returns: An object of a class implementing the Iterator interface

- boolean **remove**(E element)
  This method removes an element from this collection.
  Parameters: element The element to remove
  Returns: true if removing the element changes the collection

- int **size**()
  This method returns the number of elements in this collection.
  Returns: The number of elements in this collection

- default Stream<E> **stream**()
  This method yields a stream of the elements in this collection.

Class java.util.Collections

- static <T> int **binarySearch**(List<T> a, T key)
  This method searches the specified list for the specified object using the binary search algorithm. The list elements must implement the Comparable interface. The list must be sorted in ascending order.
  Parameters: a The list to be searched
  key The value to be searched for
  Returns: The position of the search key, if it is contained in the list; otherwise, *–index – 1*, where *index* is the position where the element may be inserted

- static <T> void **sort**(List<T> a)
  This method sorts the specified list of objects into ascending order. Its elements must implement the Comparable interface.
  Parameters: a The list to be sorted

Interface java.util.Comparator<T>

- int **compare**(T first, T second)
  This method compares the given objects.
  Parameters: first, second The objects to be compared

  Returns: A negative integer if the first object is less than the second, zero if they are equal, or a positive integer otherwise

- static <T, U extends Comparable<? super U>> Comparator<T> **comparing**(
  Function<? super T, ? extends U> keyFunction)
  This method makes a comparator from a function that maps objects of type T to objects of a type U that implements the Comparable interface.
  Parameters: keyFunction A function that derives a comparable key
  Returns: A comparator that compares the results of applying the key function. For example, Comparator.comparing(account -> account.getBalance()) compares bank accounts by their balance.

- default <U extends Comparable<? super U>> Comparator<T> **thenComparing**(
  Function<? super T, ? extends U> keyExtractor)
  This method makes a comparator from this comparator and a function that maps objects of type T to objects of a type U that implements the Comparable interface.
  Parameters: keyFunction A function that derives a comparable key
  Returns: A comparator that first applies this comparator, using the key function to break ties. For example, Comparator.comparing(person -> person.getLastName()).thenComparing(person -> person.getFirstName()) compares people by their last name, then by their first name if the last names are the same.

Class java.util.Date

- **Date**()
  This constructs an object that represents the current date and time.

Class java.util.EventObject

- Object **getSource**()
  This method returns a reference to the object on which this event initially occurred.
  Returns: The source of this event

Class java.util.GregorianCalendar

- **GregorianCalendar**()
  This constructs a calendar object that represents the current date and time.

- **GregorianCalendar**(int year, int month, int day)
  This constructs a calendar object that represents the start of the given date.
  Parameters: year, month, day The given date

Class java.util.HashMap<K, V>

- **HashMap**<K, V>()
  This constructs an empty hash map.

Class java.util.HashSet<E>

- **HashSet**<E>()
  This constructs an empty hash set.

Class java.util.InputMismatchException

This exception is thrown if the next available input item does not match the type of the requested item.

Interface java.util.Iterator<E>

- boolean **hasNext**()
  This method checks whether the iterator is past the end of the list.
  Returns: true if the iterator is not yet past the end of the list

- E **next**()
  This method moves the iterator over the next element in the linked list. This method throws an exception if the iterator is past the end of the list.
  Returns: The object that was just skipped over

- void **remove**()
  This method removes the element that was returned by the last call to next or previous. This method throws an exception if there was an add or remove operation after the last call to next or previous.

Class java.util.LinkedHashMap<K, V>

- **LinkedHashMap**<K, V>()
  This constructs an empty linked hash map. The iterator of a linked hash map visits the entries in the order in which they were added to the map.

Class java.util.LinkedList<E>

- void **addFirst**(E element)
- void **addLast**(E element)
  These methods add an element before the first or after the last element in this list.
  Parameters: element The element to be added

- E **getFirst**()
- E **getLast**()
  These methods return a reference to the specified element from this list.
  Returns: The first or last element

- E **removeFirst**()
- E **removeLast**()
  These methods remove the specified element from this list.
  Returns: A reference to the removed element

Interface java.util.List<E>

- ListIterator<E> **listIterator**()
  This method gets an iterator to visit the elements in this list.
  Returns: An iterator that points before the first element in this list

Interface java.util.ListIterator<E>

Objects implementing this interface are created by the listIterator methods of list classes.

- void **add**(E element)
  This method adds an element after the iterator position and moves the iterator after the new element.
  Parameters: element The element to be added

- boolean **hasPrevious**()
  This method checks whether the iterator is before the first element of the list.
  Returns: true if the iterator is not before the first element of the list

- E **previous**()
  This method moves the iterator over the previous element in the linked list. This method throws an exception if the iterator is before the first element of the list.
  Returns: The object that was just skipped over

- void **set**(E element)
  This method replaces the element that was returned by the last call to next or previous. This method throws an exception if there was an add or remove operation after the last call to next or previous.
  Parameters: element The element that replaces the old list element

Interface java.util.Map<K, V>

- V **get**(K key)
  Gets the value associated with a key in this map.
  Parameters: key The key for which to find the associated value
  Returns: The value associated with the key, or null if the key is not present in the map

- Set<K> **keySet**()
  This method returns all keys this map.
  Returns: A set of all keys in this map

- V **put**(K key, V value)

  This method associates a value with a key in this map.

  Parameters: key The lookup key
  value The value to associate with the key

  Returns: The value previously associated with the key, or null if the key was not present in the map

- V **remove**(K key)

  This method removes a key and its associated value from this map.

  Parameters: key The lookup key

  Returns: The value previously associated with the key, or null if the key was not present in the map

Class java.util.NoSuchElementException

This exception is thrown if an attempt is made to retrieve a value that does not exist.

Class java.util.Objects

- static int **hashCode**(Object... values)

  This method computes a hash code from a sequence of values.

  Parameters: values A sequence of values

  Returns: A hash code that combines the hash codes of the given values

Class java.util.Optional<T>

- static <T> Optional<T> **empty**()
- static <T> Optional<T> **of**(T value)

  These methods yield an Optional object representing no value, or the given value.

- T **get**()
- T **orElse**(T other)

  These methods yield the value represented by this Optional. If it represents no value, the first method throws a NoSuchElementException, and the second method returns the value other.

- void **ifPresent**(Consumer<? super T> f)

  This method applies the function f to the value represented by this Optional, or does nothing if it represents no value.

  Parameters: f A function accepting a value of type T

- boolean **isPresent**()

  This method returns true if this Optional represents a value.

Class java.util.OptionalDouble
Class java.util.OptionalInt
Class java.util.OptionalLong

These classes represent an optional value of type double, int, or long. They have the same methods as Optional<T>, with T replaced with double, int, or long, except for the methods to yield the represented value.

- double **getAsDouble**()
- int **getAsInt**()
- long **getAsLong**()

  These methods yield the value represented by this Optional, throwing a NoSuchElementException if no value is present.

Class java.util.PriorityQueue<E>

- **PriorityQueue**<E>()

  This constructs an empty priority queue. The element type E must implement the Comparable interface.

- E **remove**()

  This method removes the smallest element in the priority queue.

  Returns: The removed value

Class java.util.Properties

- String **getProperty**(String key)

  This method gets the value associated with a key in this properties map.

  Parameters: key The key for which to find the associated value

  Returns: The value, or null if the key is not present in the map

- void **load**(InputStream in)

  This method loads a set of key/value pairs into this properties map from an input stream.

  Parameters: in The input stream from which to read the key/value pairs (it must be a sequence of lines of the form key=value)

Interface java.util.Queue<E>

- E **peek**()

  Gets the element at the head of the queue without removing it.

  Returns: The head element or null if the queue is empty

Class java.util.Random

- **Random**()

  This constructs a new random number generator.

- double **nextDouble**()

This method returns the next pseudorandom, uniformly distributed floating-point number between 0.0 (inclusive) and 1.0 (exclusive) from this random number generator's sequence.

Returns: The next pseudorandom floating-point number

- int **nextInt**(int n)

This method returns the next pseudorandom, uniformly distributed integer between 0 (inclusive) and the specified value (exclusive) drawn from this random number generator's sequence.

Parameters: n Number of values to draw from

Returns: The next pseudorandom integer

Class java.util.Scanner

- **Scanner**(File in)
- **Scanner**(InputStream in)
- **Scanner**(Reader in)

These construct a scanner that reads from the given file, input stream, or reader.

Parameters: in The file, input stream, or reader from which to read

- void **close**()

This method closes this scanner and releases any associated system resources.

- boolean **hasNext**()
- boolean **hasNextDouble**()
- boolean **hasNextInt**()
- boolean **hasNextLine**()

These methods test whether it is possible to read any non-empty string, a floating-point value, an integer, or a line, as the next item.

Returns: true if it is possible to read an item of the requested type, false otherwise (either because the end of the file has been reached, or because a number type was tested and the next item is not the desired number type)

- String **next**()
- double **nextDouble**()
- int **nextInt**()
- String **nextLine**()

These methods read the next whitespace-delimited string, floating-point value, integer, or line.

Returns: The value that was read

- Scanner **useDelimiter**(String pattern)

Sets the pattern for the delimiters between input tokens.

Parameters: pattern A regular expression for the delimiter pattern

Returns: This scanner

Interface java.util.Set<E>

This interface describes a collection that contains no duplicate elements.

Class java.util.TimeZone

- static String[] **getAvailableIDs**()

This method gets the supported time zone IDs.

Returns: An array of ID strings

- static TimeZone **getTimeZone**(String id)

This method gets the time zone for a time zone ID.

Parameters: id The time zone ID, such as "America/Los_Angeles"

Returns: The time zone object associated with the ID, or null if the ID is not supported

Class java.util.TreeMap<K, V>

- TreeMap<K, V>()

This constructs an empty tree map. The iterator of a TreeMap visits the entries in sorted order.

Class java.util.TreeSet<E>

- TreeSet<E>()

This constructs an empty tree set.

Package java.util.concurrent. locks

Interface java.util.concurrent.locks. Condition

- void **await**()

This method blocks the current thread until it is signalled or interrupted.

- void **signal**()

This method unblocks one thread that is waiting on this condition.

- void **signalAll**()

This method unblocks all threads that are waiting on this condition.

Interface java.util.concurrent.locks.Lock

- void **lock**()

This method causes the current thread to acquire this lock. The thread blocks if the lock is not available.

- Condition **newCondition**()
  This method creates a new condition object for this lock.
  Returns: The condition object

- void **unlock**()
  This method causes the current thread to relinquish this lock.

Class java.util.concurrent.locks. ReentrantLock

- **ReentrantLock**()
  This constructs a new reentrant lock.

Package java.util.function

Interface java.util.function.Predicate<T>

- boolean **test**(T t)
  This method tests whether a value fulfills this predicate.
  Parameters: t The value to test

Package java.util.logging

Class java.util.logging.Level

- static final int **INFO**
  This value indicates informational logging.

- static final int **OFF**
  This value indicates logging of no messages.

Class java.util.logging.Logger

- static Logger **getGlobal**()
  This method gets the global logger.
  Returns: The global logger that, by default, displays messages with level INFO or a higher severity on the console.

- void **info**(String message)
  This method logs an informational message.
  Parameters: message The message to log

- void **setLevel**(Level aLevel)
  This method sets the logging level. Logging messages with a lesser severity than the current level are ignored.
  Parameters: aLevel The minimum level for logging messages

Package java.util.stream

Class java.util.stream.Collectors

The static methods of this class yield Collector objects that you use with the collect method of the java.util.stream.Stream interface.

- static <T> Collector<T, ?, Double> **averagingDouble** (ToDoubleFunction<? super T> f)

- static <T> Collector<T, ?, Double> **averagingInt**(ToIntFunction<? super T> f)

- static <T> Collector<T, ?, Double> **averagingLong**(ToLongFunction<? super T> mapper)

- static <T> Collector<T, ?, Double> **summingDouble**(ToDoubleFunction<? super T> f)

- static <T> Collector<T, ?, Integer> **summingInt**(ToIntFunction<? super T> f)

- static <T> Collector<T, ?, Long> **summingDouble**(ToLongFunction<? super T> f)
  These methods yield a collector that produces the average or sum of the results of applying f to its input elements.
  Parameters: f A function mapping values of type T to double, int, or long

- static <T> Collector<T, ?, Long> **counting**()
  This method yields a collector that counts the number of input elements.

- static <T, K> Collector<T, ?, Map<K, List<T>>> **groupingBy**(Function<? super T, ? extends K> f)
  This method yields a collector that produces a map associating f(x) with x for all inputs x.
  Parameters: f A function mapping values of type T to a key type K

- static Collector<String, ?, String> **joining**()
  This method yields a collector that concatenates all input strings.

- static <T> Collector<T, ?, Optional<T>> **maxBy**(Comparator<? super T> comparator)

- static <T> Collector<T, ?, Optional<T>> **minBy**(Comparator<? super T> comparator)
  These methods yield a collector that produces the largest or smallest of its inputs.
  Parameters: comparator The comparator to use for comparing inputs

- static <T> Collector<T, ?, List<T>> **toList**()

- static <T> Collector<T, ?, Set<T>> **toSet**()
  These methods yield a collector that produces a list or set of its inputs.

Interface java.util.stream.DoubleStream

This interface has the methods of `java.util.stream.Stream<T>`, with T replaced by `double`, as well as the following method:

- `<U> Stream<U> mapToObj(`
  `DoubleFunction<? extends U> f)`
  This method yields a stream of objects containing `f(x)` for all elements x in this stream.
  Parameters: f A function mapping `double` values to a type U

Interface java.util.stream.IntStream

This interface has the methods of `java.util.stream.Stream<T>`, with T replaced by `int`, as well as the following methods:

- `<U> Stream<U> mapToObj(IntFunction<? extends U> f)`
  This method yields a stream of objects containing `f(x)` for all elements x in this stream.
  Parameters: f A function mapping `int` values to a type U

- `static IntStream range(int from, int to)`
  This method yields an `IntStream` containing the integers between `from` (inclusive) and `to` (exclusive).

Interface java.util.stream.LongStream

This interface has the methods of `java.util.stream.Stream<T>`, with T replaced by `long`, as well as the following method:

- `<U> Stream<U> mapToObj(LongFunction<? extends U> f)`
  This method yields a stream of objects containing `f(x)` for all elements x in this stream.
  Parameters: f A function mapping `long` values to a type U

Interface java.util.stream.Stream<T>

- `boolean allMatch(Predicate<? super T> p)`
- `boolean anyMatch(Predicate<? super T> p)`
- `boolean noneMatch(Predicate<? super T> p)`
  These terminal operations check whether all, any, or no elements of this stream fulfill the predicate.
  Parameters: p A function mapping values of the type T to `boolean`

- `<R, A> R collect(`
  `Collector<? super T, A, R> collector)`
  This terminal operation passes all elements of this stream to a collector.
  Parameters: collector A collector, usually produced by one of the static methods in `java.util.stream.Collectors`

- `long count()`
  This terminal operation counts the number of elements of this stream.

- `Stream<T> distinct()`
  This operation yields a stream of the elements of this stream, with duplicates removed.

- `Stream<T> filter(Predicate<? super T> p)`
  This operation yields a stream of the elements of this stream that fulfill the predicate.
  Parameters: p A function mapping values of the type T to `boolean`

- `Optional<T> findAny()`
- `Optional<T> findFirst()`
  These terminal operations yield any element, or the first element, of this stream (which usually was the result from a filter operation).

- `void forEach(Consumer<? super T> f)`
  This terminal operation applies a function to each stream element.
  Parameters: f A function accepting values of type T

- `static <T> Stream<T> generate(Supplier<T> f)`
  This method yields an infinite stream consisting of values returned by f.
  Parameters: f A function with no parameters yielding values of type T

- `static <T> Stream<T> iterate(T seed,`
  `UnaryOperator<T> f)`
  This method yields an infinite stream consisting of `seed, f(seed), f(f(seed))`, and so on.
  Parameters: seed A value of type T
  f A function that accepts and returns values of type T

- `Stream<T> limit(long n)`
  This operation yields a stream consisting of up to n elements of this stream.
  Parameters: n The maximum length of the resulting stream

- `<R> Stream<R> map(`
  `Function<? super T, ? extends R> f)`
- `DoubleStream mapToDouble(`
  `ToDoubleFunction<? super T> f)`
- `IntStream mapToInt(ToIntFunction<? super T> f)`
- `LongStream mapToLong(ToLongFunction<? super T> f)`
  These operations yield a stream consisting of the results of applying f to the elements of this stream.
  Parameters: f A function mapping values of type T to values of type R, `double`, `int`, or `long`

- `static <T> Stream<T> of(T... values)`
  This operation yields a stream consisting of the given values.
  Parameters: `values` A sequence of values of type `T`

- `Stream<T> parallel()`
  This operation yields a stream with the same elements as this stream, whose operations are parallelized when possible.

- `Stream<T> skip(n)`
  This operation yields a stream with the same elements as this stream after discarding the first `n` elements.
  Parameters: `n` The number of elements to be discarded

- `Stream<T> sorted()`
  This operation yields a stream with the same elements as this stream in sorted order.

- `<A> A[] toArray(IntFunction<A[]> arrayConstructor)`
  This terminal operation yields an array containing the elements of this stream.
  Parameters: `arrayConstructor` The constructor for the resulting array, usually a constructor expression `A[]::new`

Package `javax.sql`

Interface `javax.sql.DataSource`

- `Connection getConnection()`
  This method returns a connection to the data source represented by this object.

Package `javax.swing`

Class `javax.swing.AbstractButton`

- `void addActionListener(ActionListener listener)`
  This method adds an action listener to the button.
  Parameters: `listener` The action listener to be added

- `boolean isSelected()`
  This method returns the selection state of the button.
  Returns: `true` if the button is selected

- `void setSelected(boolean state)`
  This method sets the selection state of the button. This method updates the button but does not trigger an action event.
  Parameters: `state` `true` to select, `false` to deselect

Class `javax.swing.ButtonGroup`

- `void add(AbstractButton button)`
  This method adds the button to the group.
  Parameters: `button` The button to add

Class `javax.swing.ImageIcon`

- `ImageIcon(String filename)`
  This constructs an image icon from the specified graphics file.
  Parameters: `filename` A string specifying a file name

Class `javax.swing.JButton`

- `JButton(String label)`
  This constructs a button with the given label.
  Parameters: `label` The button label

Class `javax.swing.JCheckBox`

- `JCheckBox(String text)`
  This constructs a check box with the given text, which is initially deselected. (Use the `setSelected` method to make the box selected; see the `javax.swing.AbstractButton` class.)
  Parameters: `text` The text displayed next to the check box

Class `javax.swing.JComboBox`

- `JComboBox()`
  This constructs a combo box with no items.

- `void addItem(Object item)`
  This method adds an item to the item list of this combo box.
  Parameters: `item` The item to add

- `Object getSelectedItem()`
  This method gets the currently selected item of this combo box.
  Returns: The currently selected item

- `boolean isEditable()`
  This method checks whether the combo box is editable. An editable combo box allows the user to type into the text field of the combo box.
  Returns: `true` if the combo box is editable

- `void setEditable(boolean state)`
  This method is used to make the combo box editable or not.
  Parameters: `state` `true` to make editable, `false` to disable editing

- void **setSelectedItem**(Object item)
  This method sets the item that is shown in the display area of the combo box as selected.
  Parameters: item   The item to be displayed as selected

Class javax.swing.JComponent

- protected void **paintComponent**(Graphics g)
  Override this method to paint the surface of a component. Your method needs to call super.paintComponent(g).
  Parameters: g The graphics context used for drawing

- void **setBorder**(Border b)
  This method sets the border of this component.
  Parameters: b The border to surround this component

- void **setFont**(Font f)
  Sets the font used for the text in this component.
  Parameters: f A font

Class javax.swing.JFileChooser

- **JFileChooser**()
  This constructs a file chooser.

- File **getSelectedFile**()
  This method gets the selected file from this file chooser.
  Returns: The selected file

- int **showOpenDialog**(Component parent)
  This method displays an "Open File" file chooser dialog box.
  Parameters: parent The parent component or null
  Returns: The return state of this file chooser after it has been closed by the user: either APPROVE_OPTION or CANCEL_OPTION. If APPROVE_OPTION is returned, call get-SelectedFile() on this file chooser to get the file

- int **showSaveDialog**(Component parent)
  This method displays a "Save File" file chooser dialog box.
  Parameters: parent The parent component or null
  Returns: The return state of the file chooser after it has been closed by the user: either APPROVE_OPTION or CANCEL_OPTION

Class javax.swing.JFrame

- void **setDefaultCloseOperation**(int operation)
  This method sets the default action for closing the frame.
  Parameters: operation The desired close operation. Choose among DO_NOTHING_ON_CLOSE, HIDE_ON_CLOSE (the default), DISPOSE_ON_CLOSE, or EXIT_ON_CLOSE

- void **setJMenuBar**(JMenuBar mb)
  This method sets the menu bar for this frame.
  Parameters: mb The menu bar. If mb is null, then the current menu bar is removed

- static final int EXIT_ON_CLOSE
  This value indicates that when the user closes this frame, the application is to exit.

Class javax.swing.JLabel

- **JLabel**(String text)
- **JLabel**(String text, int alignment)
  These containers create a JLabel instance with the specified text and horizontal alignment.
  Parameters: text The label text to be displayed by the label
  alignment One of SwingConstants.LEFT, SwingConstants.CENTER, or SwingConstants.RIGHT

Class javax.swing.JMenu

- **JMenu**()
  This constructs a menu with no items.

- JMenuItem **add**(JMenuItem menuItem)
  This method appends a menu item to the end of this menu.
  Parameters: menuItem The menu item to be added
  Returns: The menu item that was added

Class javax.swing.JMenuBar

- **JMenuBar**()
  This constructs a menu bar with no menus.

- JMenu **add**(JMenu menu)
  This method appends a menu to the end of this menu bar.
  Parameters: menu The menu to be added
  Returns: The menu that was added

Class javax.swing.JMenuItem

- **JMenuItem**(String text)
  This constructs a menu item.
  Parameters: text The text to appear in the menu item

Class javax.swing.JOptionPane

- static String **showInputDialog**(Object prompt)

This method brings up a modal input dialog box, which displays a prompt and waits for the user to enter an input in a text field, preventing the user from doing anything else in this program.
Parameters: prompt The prompt to display
Returns: The string that the user typed

- static void **showMessageDialog**(Component parent, Object message)

This method brings up a confirmation dialog box that displays a message and waits for the user to confirm it.
Parameters: parent The parent component or null
message The message to display

Class javax.swing.JPanel

This class is a component without decorations. It can be used as an invisible container for other components.

Class javax.swing.JRadioButton

- **JRadioButton**(String text)

This constructs a radio button having the given text that is initially deselected. (Use the setSelected method to select it; see the javax.swing.AbstractButton class.)
Parameters: text The string displayed next to the radio button

Class javax.swing.JScrollPane

- **JScrollPane**(Component c)

This constructs a scroll pane around the given component.
Parameters: c The component that is decorated with scroll bars

Class javax.swing.JSlider

- **JSlider**(int min, int max, int value)

This constructor creates a horizontal slider using the specified minimum, maximum, and value.
Parameters: min The smallest possible slider value
max The largest possible slider value
value The initial value of the slider

- void **addChangeListener**(ChangeListener listener)

This method adds a change listener to the slider.
Parameters: listener The change listener to add

- int **getValue**()

This method returns the slider's value.
Returns: The current value of the slider

Class javax.swing.JTextArea

- **JTextArea**()

This constructs an empty text area.

- **JTextArea**(int rows, int columns)

This constructs an empty text area with the specified number of rows and columns.
Parameters: rows The number of rows
columns The number of columns

- void **append**(String text)

This method appends text to this text area.
Parameters: text The text to append

Class javax.swing.JTextField

- **JTextField**()

This constructs an empty text field.

- **JTextField**(int columns)

This constructs an empty text field with the specified number of columns.
Parameters: columns The number of columns

Class javax.swing.KeyStroke

- static KeyStroke **getKeyStrokeForEvent**(KeyEvent event)

Gets a KeyStroke object describing the key stroke that caused the event.
Parameters: event   The key event to be analyzed
Returns: A KeyStroke object. Call toString on this object to get a string representation such as "pressed LEFT"

Class javax.swing.Timer

- **Timer**(int millis, ActionListener listener)

This constructs a timer that notifies an action listener whenever a time interval has elapsed.
Parameters: millis The number of milliseconds between timer notifications
listener The object to be notified when the time interval has elapsed

- void **start**()

This method starts the timer. Once the timer has started, it begins notifying its listener.

- void **stop**()

This method stops the timer. Once the timer has stopped, it no longer notifies its listener.

Package javax.swing.border

Class javax.swing.border.EtchedBorder

- `EtchedBorder()`
  This constructor creates a lowered etched border.

Class javax.swing.border.TitledBorder

- `TitledBorder(Border b, String title)`
  This constructor creates a titled border that adds a title to a given border.
  Parameters: b The border to which the title is added
  title The title the border should display

Package javax.swing.event

Class javax.swing.event.ChangeEvent

Components such as sliders emit change events when they are manipulated by the user.

Interface javax.swing.event.ChangeListener

- `void stateChanged(ChangeEvent e)`
  This event is called when the event source has changed its state.
  Parameters: e A change event

Package javax.swing.text

Class javax.swing.text.JTextComponent

- `String getText()`
  This method returns the text contained in this text component.
  Returns: The text

- `boolean isEditable()`
  This method checks whether this text component is editable.
  Returns: true if the component is editable

- `void setEditable(boolean state)`
  This method is used to make this text component editable or not.
  Parameters: state true to make editable, false to disable editing

- `void setText(String text)`
  This method sets the text of this text component to the specified text. If the argument is the empty string, the old text is deleted.
  Parameters: text The new text to be set

Package javax.xml.parsers

Class javax.xml.parsers.DocumentBuilder

- `Document newDocument()`
  This constructs a new document object.
  Returns: An empty document

- `Document parse(File in)`
  This method parses an XML document in a file.
  Parameters: in The file containing the document
  Returns: The parsed document

- `Document parse(InputStream in)`
  This method parses an XML document in a stream.
  Parameters: in The input stream containing the document
  Returns: The parsed document

Class javax.xml.parsers.DocumentBuilderFactory

- `DocumentBuilder newDocumentBuilder()`
  This method creates a new document builder object.
  Returns: The document builder

- `static DocumentBuilderFactory newInstance()`
  This method creates a new document builder factory object.
  Returns: The document builder factory object

- `void setIgnoringElementContentWhitespace(boolean b)`
  This method sets the parsing mode for ignoring white space in element content for all document builders that are generated from this factory.
  Parameters: b true if white space should be ignored

- `void setValidating(boolean b)`
  This method sets the validation mode for all document builders that are generated from this factory.
  Parameters: b true if documents should be validated during parsing

Package javax.xml.xpath

Interface javax.xml.xpath.XPath

- `String evaluate(String path, Object context)`
  This method evaluates the given path expression in the given context.
  Parameters: path An XPath expression
  context The starting context for the evaluation, such as a document, node, or node list
  Returns: The result of the evaluation

Class javax.xml.xpath.
  XPathExpressionException

This exception is thrown when an XPath expression cannot be evaluated.

Class javax.xml.xpath.XPathFactory

- static XPathFactory **newInstance**()

  This method returns a factory instance that can be used to construct XPath objects.
  Returns: An XPathFactory instance

- XPath **newXPath**()

  This method returns an XPath object that can be used to evaluate XPath expressions.
  Returns: An XPath object

Package org.w3c.dom

Interface org.w3c.dom.Document

- Element **createElement**(String tagName)

  This method creates a new document element with a given tag.
  Parameters: tagName The name of the XML tag
  Returns: The created element

- Text **createTextNode**(String text)

  This method creates a text node with the given text.
  Parameters: text The text for the text node
  Returns: The created text node

- DOMImplementation **getImplementation**()

  This method returns the DOMImplementation object associated with this document.

Interface org.w3c.dom.DOMConfiguration

- void **setParameter**(String name, Object value)

  This method sets the value of a configuration parameter.
  Parameters: name The name of the parameter to set
              value The new value or null to unset the parameter

Interface org.w3c.dom.DOMImplementation

- Object **getFeature**(String feature, String version)

  This method gets an object that implements a specialized API (such as loading and saving of DOM trees).
  Parameters: feature The feature version (such as "LS")
              version The version number (such as "3.0")
  Returns: The feature object

Interface org.w3c.dom.Element

- String **getAttribute**(String attributeName)

  This method returns the value of a given attribute.
  Parameters: attributeName The name of the XML attribute
  Returns: The attribute value, or the empty string "" if that attribute does not exist for this element

- void **setAttribute**(String name, String value)

  This method sets the value of a given attribute.
  Parameters: name The name of the XML attribute
              value The desired value of the XML attribute

Interface org.w3c.dom.Text

This interface describes a node that contains the textual content of an XML element.

Package org.w3c.dom.ls

Interface org.w3c.dom.ls.DOMImplementationLS

- LSSerializer **createLSSerializer**()

  This method creates a serializer object that can be used to convert a DOM tree to a string or stream.
  Returns: The serializer object

Interface org.w3c.dom.ls.LSSerializer

- DOMConfiguration **getDomConfig**()

  This method gets the configuration object that allows customization of the serializer behavior.

- String **writeToString**(Node root)

  This method converts the DOM tree starting at the given node to a string.
  Parameters: node The root node of the tree
  Returns: The string representation of the tree

JAVA LANGUAGE CODING GUIDELINES

Introduction

This coding style guide is a simplified version of one that has been used with good success both in industrial practice and for college courses.

A style guide is a set of mandatory requirements for layout and formatting. Uniform style makes it easier for you to read code from your instructor and classmates. You will really appreciate that if you do a team project. It is also easier for your instructor and your grader to grasp the essence of your programs quickly.

A style guide makes you a more productive programmer because it *reduces gratuitous choice.* If you don't have to make choices about trivial matters, you can spend your energy on the solution of real problems.

In these guidelines, several constructs are plainly outlawed. That doesn't mean that programmers using them are evil or incompetent. It does mean that the constructs are not essential and can be expressed just as well or even better with other language constructs.

If you already have programming experience, in Java or another language, you may be initially uncomfortable at giving up some fond habits. However, it is a sign of professionalism to set aside personal preferences in minor matters and to compromise for the benefit of your group.

These guidelines are necessarily somewhat dull. They also mention features that you may not yet have seen in class. Here are the most important highlights:

- Tabs are set every three spaces.
- Variable and method names are lowercase, with occasional upperCase characters in the middle.
- Class names start with an Uppercase letter.
- Constant names are UPPERCASE, with an occasional UNDER_SCORE.
- There are spaces after reserved words and surrounding binary operators.
- Braces must line up horizontally or vertically.
- No magic numbers may be used.
- Every method, except for main and overridden methods, must have a comment.
- At most 30 lines of code may be used per method.
- No continue or break is allowed.
- All non-final variables must be private.

Note to the instructor: Of course, many programmers and organizations have strong feelings about coding style. If this style guide is incompatible with your own preferences or with local custom, please feel free to modify it.

Source Files

Each Java program is a collection of one or more source files. The executable program is obtained by compiling these files. Organize the material in each file as follows:

- `package` statement, if appropriate
- `import` statements
- A comment explaining the purpose of this file
- A `public` class
- Other classes, if appropriate

The comment explaining the purpose of this file should be in the format recognized by the `javadoc` utility. Start with a `/**`, and use the `@author` and `@version` tags:

```
/**
    Classes to manipulate widgets.
    Solves CS101 homework assignment #3
    COPYRIGHT (C) 2019 Harry Morgan. All Rights Reserved.
    @author  Harry Morgan
    @version  1.01 2019-02-15
*/
```

Classes

Each class should be preceded by a class comment explaining the purpose of the class.
First list all public features, then all private features.
Within the public and private sections, use the following order:

1. Instance variables
2. Static variables
3. Constructors
4. Instance methods
5. Static methods
6. Inner classes

Leave a blank line after every method.

All non-`final` variables must be private. (However, instance variables of an inner class may be public.) Methods and final variables can be either public or private, as appropriate.

All features must be tagged `public` or `private`. Do not use the default visibility (that is, package visibility) or the `protected` attribute.

Avoid static variables (except `final` ones) whenever possible. In the rare instance that you need static variables, you are permitted one static variable per class.

Methods

Every method (except for `main`) starts with a comment in `javadoc` format.

```
/**
    Convert calendar date into Julian day.
    Note: This algorithm is from Press et al., Numerical Recipes
    in C, 2nd ed., Cambridge University Press, 1992.
    @param day  day of the date to be converted
    @param month  month of the date to be converted
    @param year  year of the date to be converted
    @return  the Julian day number that begins at noon of the
    given calendar date.
*/
public static int getJulianDayNumber(int day, int month, int year)
{
    . . .
}
```

Parameter variable names must be explicit, especially if they are integers or Boolean:

```
public Employee remove(int d, double s)
    // Huh?
public Employee remove(int department, double severancePay)
    // OK
```

Methods must have at most 30 lines of code. The method signature, comments, blank lines, and lines containing only braces are not included in this count. This rule forces you to break up complex computations into separate methods.

Variables and Constants

Do not define all variables at the beginning of a block:

```
{
    double xold; // Don't
    double xnew;
    boolean done;
    . . .
}
```

Define each variable just before it is used for the first time:

```
{
    . . .
    double xold = Integer.parseInt(input);
    boolean done = false;
    while (!done)
    {
        double xnew = (xold + a / xold) / 2;
        . . .
    }
    . . .
}
```

Do not define two variables on the same line:

```
int dimes = 0, nickels = 0; // Don't
```

Instead, use two separate definitions:

```
int dimes = 0; // OK
int nickels = 0;
```

In Java, constants must be defined with the reserved word `final`. If the constant is used by multiple methods, declare it as `static final`. It is a good idea to define static final variables as `private` if no other class has an interest in them.

Do not use *magic numbers!* A magic number is a numeric constant embedded in code, without a constant definition. Any number except −1, 0, 1, and 2 is considered magic:

```
if (p.getX() < 300) // Don't
```

Use `final` variables instead:

```
final double WINDOW_WIDTH = 300;
. . .
if (p.getX() < WINDOW_WIDTH) // OK
```

Even the most reasonable cosmic constant is going to change one day. You think there are 365 days per year? Your customers on Mars are going to be pretty unhappy about your silly prejudice. Make a constant

```
public static final int DAYS_PER_YEAR = 365;
```

so that you can easily produce a Martian version without trying to find all the 365s, 364s, 366s, 367s, and so on, in your code.

When declaring array variables, group the [] with the type, not the variable.

```
int[] values; // OK
int values[]; // Ugh—this is an ugly holdover from C
```

When using collections, use type parameters and not "raw" types.

```
ArrayList<String> names = new ArrayList<>(); // OK
ArrayList names = new ArrayList(); // Not OK
```

Control Flow

Statement Bodies

Use braces to enclose the bodies of branch and loop statements, even if they contain only a single statement. For example,

```
if (x < 0)
{
   x++;
}
```

and not

```
if (x < 0)
   x++; // Not OK--no braces
```

The for Statement

Use `for` loops only when a variable runs from somewhere to somewhere with some constant increment/decrement:

```
for (int i = 0; i < a.length; i++)
{
```

```
    System.out.println(a[i]);
}
```

Or, even better, use the enhanced for loop:

```
for (int e : a)
{
    System.out.println(e);
}
```

Do not use the for loop for weird constructs such as

```
for (a = a / 2; count < ITERATIONS; System.out.println(xnew))    // Don't
```

Make such a loop into a while loop. That way, the sequence of instructions is much clearer:

```
a = a / 2;
while (count < ITERATIONS) // OK
{
    . . .
    System.out.println(xnew);
}
```

Nonlinear Control Flow

Avoid the switch statement, because it is easy to fall through accidentally to an unwanted case. Use if/else instead.

Avoid the break or continue statements. Use another boolean variable to control the execution flow.

Exceptions

Do not tag a method with an overly general exception specification:

```
Widget readWidget(Reader in) throws Exception // Bad
```

Instead, specifically declare any checked exceptions that your method may throw:

```
Widget readWidget(Reader in)
        throws IOException, MalformedWidgetException // Good
```

Do not "squelch" exceptions:

```
try
{
    double price = in.readDouble();
}
catch (Exception e)
{ } // Bad
```

Beginners often make this mistake "to keep the compiler happy". If the current method is not appropriate for handling the exception, simply use a throws specification and let one of its callers handle it.

Always use the try-with-resources statement to ensure that resources are closed even when an exception occurs. For example,

```
try (Scanner in = new Scanner(. . .); PrintWriter out = new PrintWriter(. . .))
{
    while (in.hasNextLine())
    {
        out.println(in.nextLine);
    }
}
```

Lexical Issues

Naming Conventions

The following rules specify when to use upper- and lowercase letters in identifier names:

- All variable and method names are in lowercase (maybe with an occasional upperCase in the middle); for example, `firstPlayer`.
- All constants are in uppercase (maybe with an occasional UNDER_SCORE); for example, `CLOCK_RADIUS`.
- All class and interface names start with uppercase and are followed by lowercase letters (maybe with an occasional UpperCase letter); for example, `BankTeller`.
- Generic type variables are in uppercase, usually a single letter.

Names must be reasonably long and descriptive. Use `firstPlayer` instead of `fp`. No drppng f vwls. Local variables that are fairly routine can be short (`ch`, `i`) as long as they are really just boring holders for an input character, a loop counter, and so on. Also, do not use `ctr`, `c`, `cntr`, `cnt`, `c2` for variables in your method. Surely these variables all have specific purposes and can be named to remind the reader of them (for example, `current`, `next`, `previous`, `result`, ...). However, it is customary to use single-letter names, such as `T` or `E` for generic types.

Indentation and White Space

Use tab stops every three columns. That means you will need to change the tab stop setting in your editor!

Use blank lines freely to separate parts of a method that are logically distinct.

Use a blank space around every binary operator:

```
x1 = (-b - Math.sqrt(b * b - 4 * a * c)) / (2 * a);
// Good

x1=(-b-Math.sqrt(b*b-4*a*c))/(2*a);
// Bad
```

Leave a blank space after (and not before) each comma or semicolon. Do not leave a space before or after a parenthesis or bracket in an expression. Leave spaces around the (. . .) part of an `if`, `while`, `for`, or `catch` statement.

```
if (x == 0) { y = 0; }

f(a, b[i]);
```

Every line must fit in 80 columns. If you must break a statement, add an indentation level for the continuation:

```
a[n] = .................................................
       + .................;
```

Start the indented line with an operator (if possible).

Braces

Opening and closing braces must line up, either horizontally or vertically:

```
while (i < n) { System.out.println(a[i]); i++; }
```

```
while (i < n)
{
    System.out.println(a[i]);
    i++;
}
```

Some programmers don't line up vertical braces but place the { behind the reserved word:

```
while (i < n) { // DON'T
    System.out.println(a[i]);
    i++;
}
```

Doing so makes it hard to check that the braces match.

Unstable Layout

Some programmers take great pride in lining up certain columns in their code:

```
firstRecord = other.firstRecord;
lastRecord  = other.lastRecord;
cutoff      = other.cutoff;
```

This is undeniably neat, but the layout is not stable under change. A new variable name that is longer than the preallotted number of columns requires that you move all entries around:

```
firstRecord = other.firstRecord;
lastRecord  = other.lastRecord;
cutoff      = other.cutoff;
marginalFudgeFactor = other.marginalFudgeFactor;
```

This is just the kind of trap that makes you decide to use a short variable name like mff instead. Use a simple layout that is easy to maintain as your programs change.

GLOSSARY

Abstract class   A class that cannot be instantiated.

Abstract data type   A specification of the fundamental operations that characterize a data type, without supplying an implementation.

Abstract method   A method with a name, parameter variable types, and return type but without an implementation.

Access specifier   A reserved word that indicates the accessibility of a feature, such as private or public.

Accessor method   A method that accesses an object but does not change it.

Aggregation   The *has-a* relationship between classes.

Algorithm   An unambiguous, executable, and terminating specification of a way to solve a problem.

Anonymous class   A class that does not have a name.

Anonymous object   An object that is not stored in a named variable.

API (Application Programming Interface)   A code library for building programs.

API Documentation   Information about each class in the Java library.

Applet   A graphical Java program that executes inside a web browser or applet viewer.

Argument   A value supplied in a method call, or one of the values combined by an operator.

Array   A collection of values of the same type stored in contiguous memory locations, each of which can be accessed by an integer index.

Array list   A Java class that implements a dynamically-growable array of objects.

Assertion   A claim that a certain condition holds in a particular program location.

Assignment   Placing a new value into a variable.

Association   A relationship between classes in which one can navigate from objects of one class to objects of the other class, usually by following object references.

Asymmetric bounds   Bounds that include the starting index but not the ending index.

Attribute   A named property that an object is responsible for maintaining.

Auto-boxing   Automatically converting a primitive type value into a wrapper type object.

Balanced tree   A tree in which each subtree has the property that the number of descendants to the left is approximately the same as the number of descendants to the right.

Big-Oh notation   The notation $g(n) = O(f(n))$, which denotes that the function g grows at a rate that is bounded by the growth rate of the function f with respect to n. For example, $10n^2 + 100n - 1000 = O(n^2)$.

Binary file   A file in which values are stored in their binary representation and cannot be read as text.

Binary operator   An operator that takes two arguments, for example + in $x + y$.

Binary search   A fast algorithm for finding a value in a sorted array. It narrows the search down to half of the array in every step.

Binary search tree   A binary tree in which *each* subtree has the property that all left descendants are smaller than the value stored in the root, and all right descendants are larger.

Binary tree   A tree in which each node has at most two child nodes.

Bit   Binary digit; the smallest unit of information, having two possible values: 0 and 1. A data element consisting of n bits has 2^n possible values.

Black-box testing   Testing a method without knowing its implementation.

Block   A group of statements bracketed by {}.

Body   All statements of a method or block.

Boolean operator   An operator that can be applied to Boolean values. Java has three Boolean operators: &&, ||, and !.

Boolean type   A type with two possible values: true and false.

Border layout   A layout management scheme in which components are placed into the center or one of the four borders of their container.

Boundary test case   A test case involving values that are at the outer boundary of the set of legal values. For example, if a method is expected to work for all nonnegative integers, then 0 is a boundary test case.

Bounds error   Trying to access an array element that is outside the legal range.

break statement   A statement that terminates a loop or switch statement.

Breakpoint   A point in a program, specified in a debugger, at which the debugger stops executing the program and lets the user inspect the program state.

Buffer   A temporary storage location for holding values that have been produced (for example, characters typed by the user) and are waiting to be consumed (for example, read a line at a time).

Bug   A programming error.

Byte   A number made up of eight bits. Essentially all currently manufactured computers use a byte as the smallest unit of storage in memory.

Bytecode   Instructions for the Java virtual machine.

Call stack   The ordered set of all methods that currently have been called but not yet terminated, starting with the current method and ending with main.

Callback   A mechanism for specifying a block of code so it can be executed at a later time.

Case sensitive   Distinguishing upper- and lowercase characters.

Cast   Explicitly converting a value from one type to a different type. For example, the cast from a floating-point number x to an integer is expressed in Java by the cast notation (int) x.

catch clause   A part of a try block that is executed when a matching exception is thrown by any statement in the try block.

Central processing unit (CPU)   The part of a computer that executes the machine instructions.

Character   A single letter, digit, or symbol.

Check box   A user-interface component that can be used for a binary selection.

Checked exception   An exception that the compiler checks. All checked exceptions must be declared or caught.

Class   A programmer-defined data type.

Client   A computer program or system that issues requests to a server and processes the server responses.

Code coverage   A measure of the amount of source code that has been executed during testing.

Cohesive   A class is cohesive if its features support a single abstraction.

Collaborator   A class on which another class depends.

Collection   A data structure that provides a mechanism for adding, removing, and locating elements.

Collector   An object that collects elements, usually from a stream, combining them into a result.

Combo box   A user-interface component that combines a text field with a drop-down list of selections.

Command line   The line the user types to start a program in DOS or UNIX or a command window in Windows. It consists of the program name followed by any necessary arguments.

Comment   An explanation to help the human reader understand a section of a program; ignored by the compiler.

Compiler   A program that translates code in a high-level language (such as Java) to machine instructions (such as bytecode for the Java virtual machine).

Compile-time error   An error that is detected when a program is compiled.

Component   See **User-interface component**.

Composition   An aggregation relationship where the aggregated objects do not have an existence independent of the containing object.

Computer program   A sequence of instructions that is executed by a computer.

Concatenation   Placing one string after another to form a new string.

Concrete class   A class that can be instantiated.

Condition object   An object that manages threads that currently cannot proceed.

Console program   A Java program that does not have a graphical window. A console program reads input from the keyboard and writes output to the terminal screen.

Constant   A value that cannot be changed by a program. In Java, constants are defined with the reserved word final.

Construction   Setting a newly allocated object to an initial state.

Constructor   A sequence of statements for initializing a newly instantiated object.

Constructor reference   An expression of the form `Class::new` or `Class[]::new` that, like a lambda expression, can be converted into an instance of a functional interface.

Container   A user-interface component that can hold other components and present them together to the user. Also, a data structure, such as a list, that can hold a collection of objects and present them individually to a program.

Content pane   The part of a Swing frame that holds the user-interface components of the frame.

Coupling   The degree to which classes are related to each other by dependency.

CRC card   An index card representing a class that lists its responsibilities and collaborating classes.

De Morgan's Law   A law about logical operations that describes how to negate expressions formed with *and* and *or* operations.

Deadlock   A state in which no thread can proceed because each thread is waiting for another to do some work first.

Deadly embrace   A set of blocked threads, each of which could only be unblocked by the action of other threads in the set.

Debugger   A program that lets a user run another program one or a few steps at a time, stop execution, and inspect the variables in order to analyze it for bugs.

Default method   A non-static method that has an implementation in an interface.

Dependency   The *uses* relationship between classes, in which one class needs services provided by another class.

Directory   A structure on a disk that can hold files or other directories; also called a folder.

Documentation comment   A comment in a source file that can be automatically extracted into the program documentation by a program such as `javadoc`.

Dot notation   The notation *object.method(arguments)* or *object.variable* used to invoke a method or access a variable.

Doubly-linked list   A linked list in which each link has a reference to both its predecessor and successor links.

DTD (Document Type Definition)   A sequence of rules that describes the legal child elements and attributes for each element type in an SGML or XML document.

Dynamic method lookup   Selecting a method to be invoked at run time. In Java, dynamic method lookup considers the class of the implicit parameter object to select the appropriate method.

Editor   A program for writing and modifying text files.

Embedded system   The processor, software, and supporting circuitry that is included in a device other than a computer.

Encapsulation   The hiding of implementation details.

Enumeration type   A type with a finite number of values, each of which has its own symbolic name.

Escape character   A character in text that is not taken literally but has a special meaning when combined with the character or characters that follow it. The \ character is an escape character in Java strings.

Escape sequence   A sequence of characters that starts with an escape character, such as \n or \".

Event   See **User-interface event**.

Event class   A class that contains information about an event, such as its source.

Event adapter   A class that implements an event listener interface by defining all methods to do nothing.

Event handler   A method that is executed when an event occurs.

Event listener   An object that is notified by an event source when an event occurs.

Event source   An object that can notify other classes of events.

Exception   A class that signals a condition that prevents the program from continuing normally. When such a condition occurs, an object of the exception class is thrown.

Exception handler   A sequence of statements that is given control when an exception of a particular type has been thrown and caught.

Explicit parameter   A parameter of a method other than the object on which the method is invoked.

Expression   A syntactical construct that is made up of constants, variables, method calls, and the operators combining them.

Extension   The last part of a file name, which specifies the file type. For example, the extension `.java` denotes a Java file.

Fibonacci numbers   The sequence of numbers 1, 1, 2, 3, 5, 8, 13, . . . , in which every term is the sum of its two predecessors.

File   A sequence of bytes that is stored on disk.

File pointer   The position within a random-access file of the next byte to be read or written. It can be moved so as to access any byte in the file.

finally clause   A part of a try block that is executed no matter how the try block is exited.

Flag   See **Boolean type**.

Floating-point number   A number that can have a fractional part.

Flow layout   A layout management scheme in which components are laid out left to right.

Flushing an output stream   Sending all characters that are still held in a buffer to their destination.

Folder   See **Directory**.

Font   A set of character shapes in a particular style and size.

Foreign key   A reference to a primary key in a linked table.

Frame   A window with a border and a title bar.

Function   A function, in the mathematical sense, yields a result for any assignment of values to its parameters. In Java, functions can be implemented as lambda expressions or instances of functional interfaces.

Functional interface   An interface with a single abstract method whose purpose is to define a single function.

Garbage collection   Automatic reclamation of memory occupied by objects that are no longer referenced.

Generic class   A class with one or more type parameters.

Generic method   A method with one or more type parameters.

Generic programming   Providing program components that can be reused in a wide variety of situations.

Grammar   A set of rules that specifies which sequences of tokens are legal for a particular document set.

Graphics context   A class through which a programmer can cause shapes to appear on a window or off-screen bitmap.

grep   The "global regular expression print" search program, useful for finding all strings matching a pattern in a set of files.

Grid layout   A layout management scheme in which components are placed into a two-dimensional grid.

GUI (Graphical User Interface)   A user interface in which the user supplies inputs through graphical components such as buttons, menus, and text fields.

Hard disk   A device that stores information on rotating platters with magnetic coating.

Hardware   The physical equipment for a computer or another device.

Hash code   A value that is computed by a hash function.

Hash collision   Two different objects for which a hash function computes identical values.

Hash function   A function that computes an integer value from an object in such a way that different objects are likely to yield different values.

Hash table   A data structure in which elements are mapped to array positions according to their hash function values.

Hashing   Applying a hash function to a set of objects.

Heap   A balanced binary tree that is used for implementing sorting algorithms and priority queues.

Heapsort algorithm   A sorting algorithm that inserts the values to be sorted into a heap.

High-level programming language   A programming language that provides an abstract view of a computer and allows programmers to focus on their problem domain.

Higher-order function   A function that has another function as a parameter, or that yields another function.

HTML (Hypertext Markup Language)   The language in which web pages are described.

HTTP (Hypertext Transfer Protocol)   The protocol that defines communication between web browsers and web servers.

IDE (Integrated Development Environment)   A programming environment that includes an editor, compiler, and debugger.

Immutable class   A class without a mutator method.

Implementing an interface   Implementing a class that defines all methods specified in the interface.

Implicit parameter The object on which a method is invoked. For example, in the call x.f(y), the object x is the implicit parameter of the method f.

Importing a class or package Indicating the intention of referring to a class, or all classes in a package, by the simple name rather than the qualified name.

Infinite stream A stream with an infinite number of elements.

Inheritance The *is-a* relationship between a more general superclass and a more specialized subclass.

Initialize Set a variable to a well-defined value when it is created.

Inner class A class that is defined inside another class.

Input stream See **Stream (input/output)**.

Instance method A method with an implicit parameter; that is, a method that is invoked on an instance of a class.

Instance of a class An object whose type is that class.

Instance variable A variable defined in a class for which every object of the class has its own value.

Instantiation of a class Construction of an object of that class.

Integer A number that cannot have a fractional part.

Integer division Taking the quotient of two integers and discarding the remainder. In Java the / symbol denotes integer division if both arguments are integers. For example, 11/4 is 2, not 2.75.

Interface type A type with no instance variables, only abstract or default methods and constants.

Internet A worldwide collection of networks, routing equipment, and computers using a common set of protocols that define how participants interact with each other.

Iterator An object that can inspect all elements in a container such as a linked list.

JavaBean A class with a no-argument constructor that exposes properties through its get and set methods.

javadoc The documentation generator in the Java SDK. It extracts documentation comments from Java source files and produces a set of linked HTML files.

JavaServer Faces (JSF) A framework for developing web applications that aids in the separation of user interface and program logic.

JDBC (Java Database Connectivity) The technology that enables a Java program to interact with relational databases.

JDK The Java software development kit that contains the Java compiler and related development tools.

Join A database query that involves multiple tables.

JSF container A program that executes JSF applications.

Lambda expression An expression that defines the parameters and return value of a method in a compact notation.

Layout manager A class that arranges user-interface components inside a container.

Lexicographic ordering Ordering strings in the same order as in a dictionary, by skipping all matching characters and comparing the first non-matching characters of both strings. For example, "orbit" comes before "orchid" in lexicographic ordering. Note that in Java, unlike a dictionary, the ordering is case sensitive: Z comes before a.

Library A set of precompiled classes that can be included in programs.

Linear search Searching a container (such as an array or list) for an object by inspecting each element in turn.

Linked list A data structure that can hold an arbitrary number of objects, each of which is stored in a link object, which contains a pointer to the next link.

Literal A notation for a fixed value in a program, such as –2, 3.14, 6.02214115E23, "Harry", or 'H'.

Local variable A variable whose scope is a block.

Lock A data structure to regulate the scheduling of multiple threads. Once a thread has acquired a lock, other threads that also wish to acquire it must wait until the first thread relinquishes it.

Lock object An object that allows a single thread to execute a section of a program.

Logging Sending messages that trace the progress of a program to a file or window.

Logical operator See **Boolean operator**.

Logic error An error in a syntactically correct program that causes it to act differently from its specification. (A form of run-time error.)

Loop A sequence of instructions that is executed repeatedly.

Loop and a half   A loop whose termination decision is neither at the beginning nor at the end.

Machine code   Instructions that can be executed directly by the CPU.

Magic number   A number that appears in a program without explanation.

main method   The method that is first called when a Java application executes.

Managed bean   A JavaBean that is managed by a JSF container.

Map   A data structure that keeps associations between key and value objects.

Markup   Information about data that is added as humanly readable instructions. An example is the tagging of HTML documents with elements such as <h1> or <b>.

Memory location   A value that specifies the location of data in computer memory.

Merge sort   A sorting algorithm that first sorts two halves of a data structure and then merges the sorted subarrays together.

Metadata   Data that describe properties of a data set.

Method   A sequence of statements that has a name, may have parameter variables, and may return a value. A method can be invoked any number of times, with different values for its parameter variables.

Method expression   In JSF, an expression describing a bean and a method that is to be applied to the bean at a later time.

Method reference   An expression of the form Class::method or object::method that, like a lambda expression, can be converted into an instance of a functional interface.

Mixed content   In XML, a markup element that contains both text and other elements.

Modifier   A reserved word that indicates the accessibility of a feature, such as private or public.

Modulus   The % operator that computes the remainder of an integer division.

Mock object   An object that is used during program testing, replacing another object and providing similar behavior. Usually, the mock object is simpler to implement or provides better support for testing.

Mutator method   A method that changes the state of an object.

Mutual recursion   Cooperating methods that call each other.

Name clash   Accidentally using the same name to denote two program features in a way that cannot be resolved by the compiler.

Navigation rule   In JSF, a rule that describes when to move from one web page to another.

Nested loop   A loop that is contained in another loop.

Networks   An interconnected system of computers and other devices.

new operator   An operator that allocates new objects.

Newline   The '\n' character, which indicates the end of a line.

No-argument constructor   A constructor that takes no arguments.

Null reference   A reference that does not refer to any object.

Number literal   A fixed value in a program this is explicitly written as a number, such as –2 or 6.02214115E23.

Object   A value of a class type.

Object-oriented programming   Designing a program by discovering objects, their properties, and their relationships.

Object reference   A value that denotes the location of an object in memory. In Java, a variable whose type is a class contains a reference to an object of that class.

Off-by-one error   A common programming error in which a value is one larger or smaller than it should be.

Opening a file   Preparing a file for reading or writing.

Operating system   The software that launches application programs and provides services (such as a file system) for those programs.

Operator   A symbol denoting a mathematical or logical operation, such as + or &&.

Operator associativity   The rule that governs in which order operators of the same precedence are executed. For example, in Java the - operator is left-associative because a - b - c is interpreted as (a - b) - c, and = is right-associative because a = b = c is interpreted as a = (b = c).

Operator precedence   The rule that governs which operator is evaluated first. For example, in Java the && operator has a higher precedence than the || operator.

Hence a || b && c is interpreted as a || (b && c). (See Appendix B.)

Optional value   An instance of the Optional<T> class, representing either a value of type T or the absence of such a value.

Output stream   See **Stream (input/output)**.

Overloading   Giving more than one meaning to a method name.

Overriding   Redefining a method in a subclass.

Package   A collection of related classes. The import statement is used to access one or more classes in a package.

Panel   A user-interface component with no visual appearance. It can be used to group other components.

Parallel arrays   Arrays of the same length, in which corresponding elements are logically related.

Parallel stream   A stream that attempts to apply operations in parallel.

Parameter passing   Specifying expressions to be arguments for a method when it is called.

Parameter variable   A variable of a method that is initialized with a value when the method is called.

Parse tree   A tree structure that shows how a string conforms to the rules of a grammar.

Parser   A program that reads a document, checks whether it is syntactically correct, and takes some action as it processes the document.

Partially filled array   An array that is not filled to capacity, together with a companion variable that indicates the number of elements actually stored.

Path (to a file or directory)   The sequence of directory names and, for a file, a file name at the end, that describes how to reach the file or directory from a given starting point.

Permutation   A rearrangement of a set of values.

Polymorphism   Selecting a method among several methods that have the same name on the basis of the actual types of the implicit parameters.

Postfix operator   A unary operator that is written after its argument.

Prefix operator   A unary operator that is written before its argument.

Prepared statement   A SQL statement with a precomputed query strategy.

Primary key   A column (or combination of columns) whose value uniquely specifies a table record.

Primitive type   In Java, a number type or boolean.

Priority queue   An abstract data type that enables efficient insertion of elements and efficient removal of the smallest element.

Programming   The act of designing and implementing computer programs.

Project   A collection of source files and their dependencies.

Prompt   A string that tells the user to provide input.

Property   A named value that is managed by a component.

Pseudocode   A high-level description of the actions of a program or algorithm, using a mixture of English and informal programming language syntax.

Pseudorandom number   A number that appears to be random but is generated by a mathematical formula.

Public interface   The features (methods, variables, and nested types) of a class that are accessible to all clients.

Queue   A collection of items with "first in, first out" retrieval.

Quicksort   A generally fast sorting algorithm that picks an element, called the pivot, partitions the sequence into the elements smaller than the pivot and those larger than the pivot, and then recursively sorts the subsequences.

Race condition   A condition in which the effect of multiple threads on shared data depends on the order in which the threads are scheduled.

Radio button   A user-interface component that can be used for selecting one of several options.

Random access   The ability to access any value directly without having to read the values preceding it.

Reader   In the Java input/output library, a class from which to read characters.

Recursion   A method for computing a result by decomposing the inputs into simpler values and applying the same method to them.

Recursive method   A method that can call itself with simpler values. It must handle the simplest values without calling itself.

Red-black tree A kind of binary search tree that rebalances itself after each insertion and removal.

Redirection Linking the input or output of a program to a file instead of the keyboard or display.

Reference See **Object reference**.

Regression testing Keeping old test cases and testing every revision of a program against them.

Regular expression A string that defines a set of matching strings according to their content. Each part of a regular expression can be a specific required character; one of a set of permitted characters such as [abc], which can be a range such as [a-z]; any character not in a set of forbidden characters, such as [^0-9]; a repetition of one or more matches, such as [0-9]+, or zero or more, such as [ACGT]; one of a set of alternatives, such as and|et|und; or various other possibilities. For example, "[A-Za-z][0-9]+" matches "Cloud9" or "007" but not "Jack".

Relational database A data repository that stores information in tables and retrieves data as the result of queries that are formulated in terms of table relationships.

Relational operator An operator that compares two values, yielding a Boolean result.

Reserved word A word that has a special meaning in a programming language and therefore cannot be used as a name by the programmer.

Return value The value returned by a method through a return statement.

Reverse Polish notation A style of writing expressions in which the operators are written following the operands, such as 2 3 4 * + for 2 + 3 * 4.

Roundoff error An error introduced by the fact that the computer can store only a finite number of digits of a floating-point number.

Runnable thread A thread that can proceed provided it is given a time slice to do work.

Run-time error An error in a syntactically correct program that causes it to act differently from its specification.

Run-time stack The data structure that stores the local variables of all called methods as a program runs.

Scope The part of a program in which a variable is defined.

Secondary storage Storage that persists without electricity, e.g., a hard disk.

Selection sort A sorting algorithm in which the smallest element is repeatedly found and removed until no elements remain.

Sentinel A value in input that is not to be used as an actual input value but to signal the end of input.

Sequential access Accessing values one after another without skipping over any of them.

Sequential search See **Linear search**.

Serialization The process of saving an object, and all the objects that it references, to a stream.

Set An unordered collection that allows efficient addition, location, and removal of elements.

Shadowing Hiding a variable by defining another one with the same name.

Shallow copy Copying only the reference to an object.

Shell script A file that contains commands for running programs and manipulating files. Typing the name of the shell script file on the command line causes those commands to be executed.

Shell window A window for interacting with an operating system through textual commands.

Short-circuit evaluation Evaluating only a part of an expression if the remainder cannot change the result.

Side effect An effect of a method other than returning a value.

Sign bit The bit of a binary number that indicates whether the number is positive or negative.

Socket An object that encapsulates a TCP/IP connection. To communicate with the other endpoint of the connection, you use the input and output streams attached to the socket.

Software The intangible instructions and data that are necessary for operating a computer or another device.

Source code Instructions in a programming language that need to be translated before execution on a computer.

Source file A file containing instructions in a programming language such as Java.

SQL (Structured Query Language) A command language for interacting with a database.

Stack A data structure with "last-in, first-out" retrieval. Elements can be added and removed only at one position, called the top of the stack.

Stack trace   A printout of the call stack, listing all currently pending method calls.

State   The current value of an object, which is determined by the cumulative action of all methods that were invoked on it.

State diagram   A diagram that depicts state transitions and their causes.

Statement   A syntactical unit in a program. In Java a statement is either a simple statement, a compound statement, or a block.

Static method   A method with no implicit parameter.

Static variable   A variable defined in a class that has only one value for the whole class, and which can be accessed and changed by any method of that class.

Stored procedure   A database procedure that is executed in the database kernel.

Stream   A data structure representing a sequence of elements, each of which is visited at most once, that enables operations to be applied in an efficient way (for example, lazily, or in parallel).

Stream (input/output)   An abstraction for a sequence of bytes from which data can be read or to which data can be written.

String   A sequence of characters.

Subclass   A class that inherits variables and methods from a superclass but may also add instance variables, add methods, or redefine methods.

Substitution principle   The principle that a subclass object can be used in place of any superclass object.

Superclass   A general class from which a more specialized class (a subclass) inherits.

Swing   A Java toolkit for implementing graphical user interfaces.

Symmetric bounds   Bounds that include the starting index and the ending index.

Synchronized block   A block of code that is controlled by a lock. To start execution, a thread must acquire the lock. Upon completion, it relinquishes the lock.

Synchronized method   A method that is controlled by a lock. In order to execute the method, the calling thread must acquire the lock.

Syntax   Rules that define how to form instructions in a particular programming language.

Syntax diagram   A graphical representation of grammar rules.

Syntax error   An instruction that does not follow the programming language rules and is rejected by the compiler. (A form of compile-time error.)

Tab character   The '\t' character, which advances the next character on the line to the next one of a set of fixed positions known as tab stops.

TCP/IP (Transmission Control Protocol/Internet Protocol)   The pair of communication protocols that is used to establish reliable transmission of data between two computers on the Internet.

Terminal operation   An operation on a stream that yields a value, causing any required pending stream operations to be executed.

Ternary operator   An operator with three arguments. Java has one ternary operator, a ? b : c.

Test suite   A set of test cases for a program.

Text field   A user-interface component that allows a user to provide text input.

Text file   A file in which values are stored in their text representation.

Thread   A program unit that is executed independently of other parts of the program.

Three-tier application   An application that is composed of separate tiers for presentation logic, business logic, and data storage.

Throw an exception   Indicate an abnormal condition by terminating the normal control flow of a program and transferring control to a matching catch clause.

throws clause   Indicates the types of the checked exceptions that a method may throw.

Time slice   A small amount of time used when scheduling threads. Each thread is given a small amount of time (a slice) in which to do its work, then control is given to another thread.

Token   A sequence of consecutive characters from an input source that belongs together for the purpose of analyzing the input. For example, a token can be a sequence of characters other than white space.

Trace message   A message that is printed during a program run for debugging purposes.

Transaction   A set of database operations that should either succeed in their entirety, or not happen at all.

Tree   A data structure consisting of nodes, each of which has a list of child nodes, and one of which is distinguished as the root node.

try statement   A statement with a body containing one or more statements that are executed until the end of the body is reached or an exception occurs, together with clauses that are invoked when exceptions of a particular type occur.

try-with-resources   A version of the try statement whose header initializes a variable of a class that implements the AutoCloseable interface. The close method is invoked on that variable when the try statement terminates, either normally or through an exception.

Turing machine   A very simple model of computation that is used in theoretical computer science to explore computability of problems.

Two-dimensional array   A tabular arrangement of elements in which an element is specified by a row and a column index.

Type   A named set of values and the operations that can be carried out with them.

Type parameter   A parameter in a generic class or method that can be replaced with an actual type.

Type variable   A variable in the declaration of a generic type that can be instantiated with a type.

Unary operator   An operator with one argument.

Unchecked exception   An exception that the compiler doesn't check.

Unicode   A standard code that assigns code values consisting of two bytes to characters used in scripts around the world. Java stores all characters as their Unicode values.

Unified Modeling Language (UML)   A notation for specifying, visualizing, constructing, and documenting the artifacts of software systems.

Uninitialized variable   A variable that has not been set to a particular value. In Java, using an uninitialized local variable is a syntax error.

Unit testing   Testing a method by itself, isolated from the remainder of the program.

URL (Uniform Resource Locator)   A pointer to an information resource (such as a web page or an image) on the World Wide Web.

User-interface component   A building block for a graphical user interface, such as a button or a text field. User-interface components are used to present information to the user and allow the user to enter information to the program.

User-interface event   A notification to a program that a user action such as a key press, mouse move, or menu selection has occurred.

Value expression   In JSF, an expression describing a bean and a property that is to be accessed at a later time.

Variable   A symbol in a program that identifies a storage location that can hold different values.

Virtual machine   A program that simulates a CPU that can be implemented efficiently on a variety of actual machines. A given program in Java bytecode can be executed by any Java virtual machine, regardless of which CPU is used to run the virtual machine itself.

void   A reserved word indicating no type or an unknown type.

Walkthrough   A step-by-step manual simulation of a computer program.

Web application   An application that executes on a web server and whose user interface is displayed in a web browser.

White-box testing   Testing methods by taking their implementations into account, in contrast to black-box testing; for example, by selecting boundary test cases and ensuring that all branches of the code are covered by some test case.

White space   Any sequence of only space, tab, and newline characters.

Wrapper class   A class that contains a primitive type value, such as Integer.

Writer   In the Java input/output library, a class to which characters are to be sent.

XML (Extensible Markup Language)   A simple format for structured data in which the structure is indicated by markup instructions.

INDEX

Page references followed by t indicate tables; those preceded by A indicate Appendices.

ILLUSTRATION CREDITS

Icons

Common Error icon (spider): © John Bell/iStockphoto.
Computing & Society icon (rhinoceros): Media Bakery.
How To icon (compass): © Steve Simzer/iStockphoto.
Paperclips: © Yvan Dube/iStockphoto.
Programming Tip icon (toucan): Eric Isselé/iStockphoto.
Self Check icon (stopwatch): © Nicholas Homrich/
    iStockphoto.
Special Topic icon (tiger): © Eric Isselé/iStockphoto.
Worked Example icon (binoculars): Tom Horyn/
    iStockphoto.

Chapter 8

Page 291–294, EX8-8 (left to right, top to bottom):
Gogh, Vincent van *The Olive Orchard:* Chester Dale
    Collection 1963.10.152/National Gallery of Art.
Degas, Edgar *The Dance Lesson:* Collection of Mr. and Mrs.
    Paul Mellon 1995.47.6/National Gallery of Art.
Fragonard, Jean-Honoré *Young Girl Reading:* Gift of Mrs.
    Mellon Bruce in memory of her father, Andrew W.
    Mellon 1961.16.1/National Gallery of Art.
Gauguin, Paul *Self-Portrait:* Chester Dale Collection
    1963.10.150/National Gallery of Art.
Gauguin, Paul *Breton Girls Dancing, Pont-Aven:* Collection
    of Mr. and Mrs. Paul Mellon 1983.1.19/National Gallery
    of Art.
Guigou, Paul *Washerwomen on the Banks of the Durance:*
    Chester Dale Fund 2007.73.1/National Gallery of Art.
Guillaumin, Jean-Baptiste-Armand *The Bridge of Louis
    Philippe:* Chester Dale Collection 1963.10.155/National
    Gallery of Art.
Manet, Edouard *The Railway:* Gift of Horace Havemeyer
    in memory of his mother, Louisine W. Havemeyer
    1956.10.1/National Gallery of Art.
Manet, Edouard *Masked Ball at the Opera:* Gift of Mrs.
    Horace Havemeyer in memory of her mother-in-law,
    Louisine W. Havemeyer 1982.75.1/National Gallery
    of Art.

Manet, Edouard *The Old Musician:* Chester Dale
    Collection 1963.10.162/National Gallery of Art.
Monet, Claude *The Japanese Footbridge:* Gift of Victoria
    Nebeker Coberly, in memory of her son John W. Mudd,
    and Walter H. and Leonore Annenberg 1992.9.1/
    National Gallery of Art.
Monet, Claude *Woman with a Parasol— Madame Monet
    and Her Son:* Collection of Mr. and Mrs. Paul Mellon
    1983.1.29/National Gallery of Art.
Monet, Claude *The Bridge at Argenteuil:* Collection of Mr.
    and Mrs. Paul Mellon 1983.1.24/National Gallery of Art.
Monet, Claude *The Artist's Garden in Argenteuil (A Corner
    of the Garden with Dahlias):* Gift of Janice H. Levin, in
    Honor of the 50th Anniversary of the National Gallery
    of Art 1991.27.1/National Gallery of Art.

Page EX8-8, continued:
Pissarro, Camille *Peasant Girl with a Straw Hat:* Ailsa
    Mellon Bruce Collection/National Gallery of Art.
Monet, Claude *Sainte-Adresse:* Gift of Catherine Gamble
    Curran and Family, in Honor of the 50th Anniversary of
    the National Gallery of Art 1990.59.1/National Gallery
    of Art.
Renoir, Auguste *Oarsmen at Chatou:* Gift of Sam A.
    Lewisohn 1951.5.2/National Gallery of Art.
Seurat, Georges *Seascape at Port-en-Bessin, Normandy:* Gift
    of the W. Averell Harriman Foundation in memory of
    Marie N. Harriman 1972.9.21/National Gallery of Art.
Renoir, Auguste *A Girl with a Watering Can:* Chester Dale
    Collection 1963.10.206/National Gallery of Art.
Renoir, Auguste *Pont Neuf, Paris;* Ailsa Mellon Bruce
    Collection 1970.17.58/National Gallery of Art.

Variable and Constant Declarations

```
 Type      Name      Initial value
    /        /         /
t cansPerPack = 6;

nal double CAN_VOLUME = 0.335;
```

Method Declaration

```
                              Parameter
  Modifiers    Return type    type and name
  /    \        /             /        /
blic static double cubeVolume(double sideLength)

 double volume = sideLength * sideLength * sideLength;
 return volume;
```

Exits method and returns result.

Mathematical Operations

th.pow(x, y)	Raising to a power x^y
th.sqrt(x)	Square root $\sqrt{x}$
th.log10(x)	Decimal log $\log_{10}(x)$
th.abs(x)	Absolute value $\|x\|$
th.sin(x)	
th.cos(x)	Sine, cosine, tangent of x (x in radians)
th.tan(x)	

elected Operators and Their Precedence

e Appendix B for the complete list.)

	Array element access
-- !	Increment, decrement, Boolean *not*
/ %	Multiplication, division, remainder
-	Addition, subtraction
<= > >=	Comparisons
!=	Equal, not equal
	Boolean *and*
	Boolean *or*
	Assignment

String Operations

```
String s = "Hello";
int n = s.length(); // 5
char ch = s.charAt(1); // 'e'
String t = s.substring(1, 4); // "ell"
String u = s.toUpperCase(); // "HELLO"
if (u.equals("HELLO")) ... // Use equals, not ==
for (int i = 0; i < s.length(); i++)
{
    char ch = s.charAt(i);
    Process ch
}
```

Conditional Statement

```
if (floor >= 13)          Condition
{
    actualFloor = floor - 1;          Executed when condition is true
}
else if (floor >= 0)      Second condition (optional)
{
    actualFloor = floor;
}
else
{                                     Executed when
    System.out.println("Floor negative");   all conditions are
}                                            false (optional)
```

Class Declaration

```
public class BankAccount
{
    private double balance;          Instance variables
    private int transactions;

    public BankAccount(double initialBalance)
    {
        balance = initialBalance;          Constructor
        transactions = 1;
    }

    public void deposit(double amount)
    {
        balanace = balance + amount;       Method
        transactions++;
    }
    . . .
}
```

oop Statements

```
          Condition
             /
ile (balance < TARGET)

 year++;                           Executed while
 balance = balance * (1 + rate / 100);   condition is true
```

```
do                    Loop body executed
{                     at least once
    System.out.print("Enter a positive integer: ");
    input = in.nextInt();
}
while (input <= 0);
```

```
  Initialization  Condition  Update
        /            /        /
r (int i = 0; i < 10; i++)

 System.out.println(i);
```

```
            Set to a new element in each iteration        An array or collection
                                                              /
for (double value : values)
{
    sum = sum + value;       Executed for each element
}
```

Input

```java
Scanner in = new Scanner(System.in);
  // Can also use new Scanner(new File("input.txt"));

int n = in.nextInt();
double x = in.nextDouble();
String word = in.next();
String line = in.nextLine();

while (in.hasNextDouble())
{
    double x = in.nextDouble();
    Process x
}
```

Output

Does not advance to new line.

```java
System.out.print("Enter a value: ");
```

Use + to concatenate values.

```java
System.out.println("Volume: " + volume);
```

Field width   Precision

```java
System.out.printf("%-10s %10d %10.2f", name, qty, price);
```

Left-justified string   Integer   Floating-point number

```java
try (PrintWriter out = new PrintWriter("output.txt"))
{
    Write to out
}
```

Use the print/println/printf methods.

The output is closed at the end of the try-with-resources statement.

Arrays

Element type   Element type   Length

All elements are zero.

```java
int[] numbers = new int[5];
int[] squares = { 0, 1, 4, 9, 16 };
int[][] magicSquare =
    {
        { 16,  3,  2, 13},
        {  5, 10, 11,  8},
        {  9,  6,  7, 12},
        {  4, 15, 14,  1}
    };

for (int i = 0; i < numbers.length; i++)
{
    numbers[i] = i * i;
}

for (int element : numbers)
{
    Process element
}

System.out.println(Arrays.toString(numbers));
    // Prints [0, 1, 4, 9, 16]
```

Array Lists

Use wrapper type, Integer, Double, etc., for primitive types.   *Initially empty*

Element (optional)

```java
ArrayList<String> names = new ArrayList<String>();
```

Add elements to the end

```java
names.add("Ann");
names.add("Cindy"); // [Ann, Cindy], names.size() is now

names.add(1, "Bob"); // [Ann, Bob, Cindy]
names.remove(2); // [Ann, Bob]
names.set(1, "Bill"); // [Ann, Bill]

String name = names.get(0); // Gets "Ann"
System.out.println(names); // Prints [Ann, Bill]
```

Linked Lists, Sets, and Iterators

```java
LinkedList<String> names = new LinkedList<>();
names.add("Bob"); // Adds at end

ListIterator<String> iter = names.listIterator();
iter.add("Ann"); // Adds before current position

String name = iter.next(); // Returns "Ann"
iter.remove(); // Removes "Ann"

Set<String> names = new HashSet<>();
names.add("Ann"); // Adds to set if not present
names.remove("Bob"); // Removes if present

Iterator<String> iter = names.iterator();
while (iter.hasNext())
{
    Process iter.next()
}
```

Maps

Key type   Value type

```java
Map<String, Integer> scores = new HashMap<>();

scores.put("Bob", 10);
Integer score = scores.get("Bob");

for (String key : scores.keySet())
{
    Process key and scores.get(key)
}
```

Returns null if key not pres

Interfaces

```java
public interface Measurable
{
    double getMeasure();
}
```

No implementation is provided

The methods of an interface are automatically public.